FIRST CANADIAN EDITION

SOCIOLOGY

A Brief Introduction

Sociology around the world

The countries that are identified on this map are cited in the book, either in the context of research studies or in relevant statistical data. Refer to the subject index for specific page references.

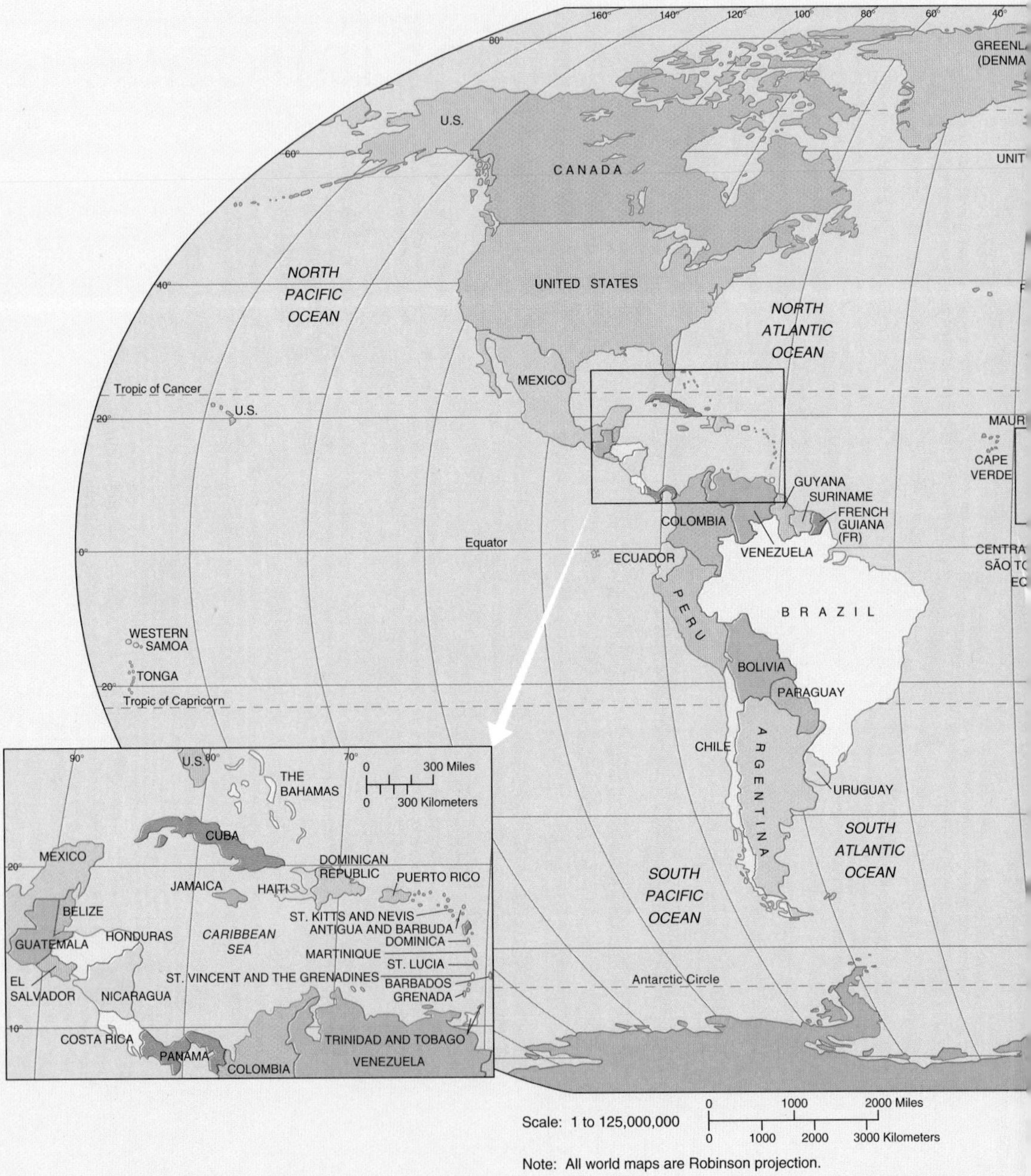

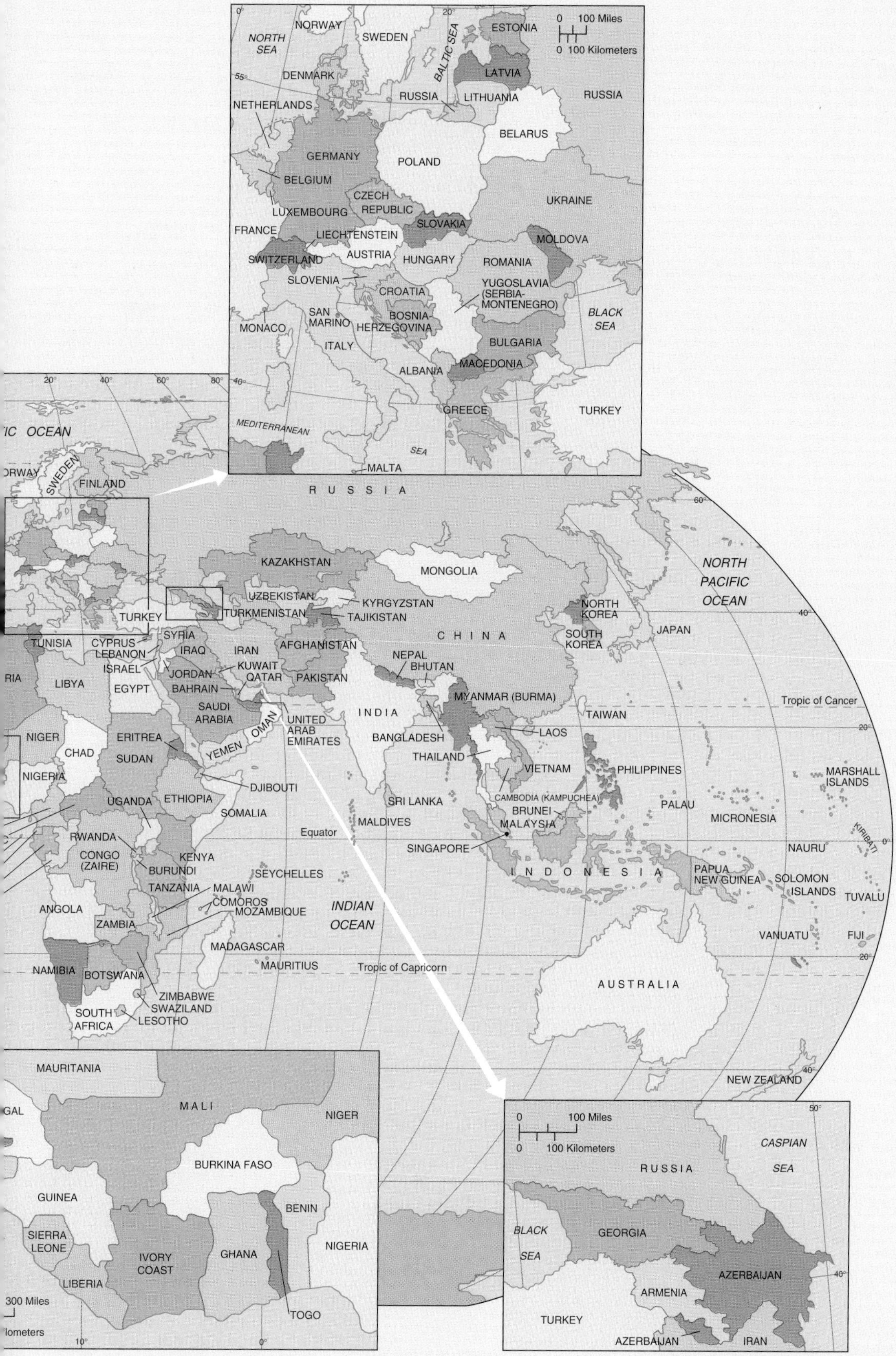

NORWAY
NORTH SEA
SWEDEN
BALTIC SEA
ESTONIA
0 100 Miles
0 100 Kilometers
LATVIA
DENMARK
RUSSIA
LITHUANIA
RUSSIA
NETHERLANDS
BELARUS
GERMANY
POLAND
BELGIUM
CZECH REPUBLIC
UKRAINE
LUXEMBOURG
SLOVAKIA
FRANCE
LIECHTENSTEIN
MOLDOVA
AUSTRIA
SWITZERLAND
HUNGARY
ROMANIA
SLOVENIA
CROATIA
YUGOSLAVIA (SERBIA-MONTENEGRO)
BLACK SEA
SAN MARINO
BOSNIA-HERZEGOVINA
MONACO
ITALY
BULGARIA
ALBANIA
MACEDONIA
GREECE
TURKEY
MEDITERRANEAN SEA
MALTA
TIC OCEAN
ORWAY
SWEDEN
FINLAND
RUSSIA
KAZAKHSTAN
MONGOLIA
NORTH PACIFIC OCEAN
UZBEKISTAN
KYRGYZSTAN
NORTH KOREA
TURKEY
TURKMENISTAN
TAJIKISTAN
SOUTH KOREA
JAPAN
CHINA
TUNISIA
CYPRUS
SYRIA
LEBANON
IRAQ
IRAN
AFGHANISTAN
ISRAEL
KUWAIT
NEPAL
RIA
LIBYA
JORDAN
QATAR
BHUTAN
EGYPT
BAHRAIN
PAKISTAN
Tropic of Cancer
MYANMAR (BURMA)
SAUDI ARABIA
UNITED ARAB EMIRATES
INDIA
TAIWAN
OMAN
NIGER
ERITREA
BANGLADESH
LAOS
CHAD
SUDAN
YEMEN
THAILAND
VIETNAM
PHILIPPINES
MARSHALL ISLANDS
NIGERIA
DJIBOUTI
ETHIOPIA
CAMBODIA (KAMPUCHEA)
UGANDA
SRI LANKA
BRUNEI
PALAU
SOMALIA
MALDIVES
MALAYSIA
MICRONESIA
KIRIBATI
RWANDA
Equator
SINGAPORE
NAURU
CONGO (ZAIRE)
KENYA
INDONESIA
BURUNDI
SEYCHELLES
PAPUA NEW GUINEA
SOLOMON ISLANDS
TUVALU
TANZANIA
MALAWI
COMOROS
INDIAN OCEAN
ANGOLA
MOZAMBIQUE
ZAMBIA
VANUATU
FIJI
MADAGASCAR
NAMIBIA
BOTSWANA
MAURITIUS
Tropic of Capricorn
AUSTRALIA
ZIMBABWE
SWAZILAND
SOUTH AFRICA
LESOTHO
NEW ZEALAND
MAURITANIA
MALI
GAL
NIGER
BURKINA FASO
GUINEA
BENIN
SIERRA LEONE
IVORY COAST
GHANA
NIGERIA
LIBERIA
300 Miles
lometers
TOGO
0 100 Miles
0 100 Kilometers
RUSSIA
CASPIAN SEA
BLACK SEA
GEORGIA
AZERBAIJAN
ARMENIA
TURKEY
AZERBAIJAN
IRAN

FIRST CANADIAN EDITION

SOCIOLOGY

A Brief Introduction

Richard T. Schaefer
DePaul University

Richard Floyd
Kwantlen University College

Bonnie Haaland
Kwantlen University College

McGraw-Hill Ryerson

Toronto Montréal Boston Burr Ridge, IL Dubuque, IA Madison, WI New York
San Francisco St. Louis Bangkok Bogotá Caracas Kuala Lumpur Lisbon London
Madrid Mexico City Milan New Delhi Santiago Seoul Singapore Sydney Taipei

McGraw-Hill
Ryerson Limited

A Subsidiary of The ***McGraw-Hill*** *Companies*

Sociology: A Brief Introduction
First Canadian Edition

ISBN: 0-07-094853-4

1 2 3 4 5 6 7 8 9 10 VH 0 9 8 7 6 5 4

Printed and bound in Canada

Vice President and Editorial Director: Pat Ferrier
Senior Sponsoring Editor: James Buchanan
Senior Developmental Editor: Jennifer DiDomenico
Marketing Manager: Sharon Loeb
Supervising Editor: Anne Macdonald
Copy Editor: Dawn du Quesnay
Production Coordinator: Madeleine Harrington
Composition: Bookman Typesetting Co. Inc./Chris Hudson
Cover Design: Dianna Little
Cover Image Credits: Copyright © Private Collection/Diana Ong/SuperStock
Printer: Von Hoffman Press

National Library of Canada Cataloguing in Publication Data

Schaefer, Richard T.
Sociology: a brief introduction/Richard T. Schaefer, Richard Floyd, Bonnie Haaland.—
1st Canadian ed.

Includes bibliographical references and index.
ISBN 0-07-094853-4

1. Sociology. I. Haaland, Bonnie II. Floyd, Richard, 1946-
III. Title.

HM586.S32 2002 301 C2002-901988-5

Dedication

To my mother-in-law,
Violet Erlandson, and to the
memory of my father-in-law,
Stanley B. Erlandson.
Richard T. Schaefer

Thank you to my wife, Verian,
for her ear, her mind, and most
of all, for her patience.
Richard Floyd

To Jay and Jordie, I express heartfelt
gratitude for their patience,
understanding, and trust that
daily life, eventually, would regain
some semblance of order.
Bonnie Haaland

About the Authors

Taking Sociology to Work

RICHARD T. SCHAEFER:
Professor, DePaul University

Growing up in Chicago at a time when neighbourhoods were going through transitions in ethnic and racial composition, Richard T. Schaefer found himself increasingly intrigued by what was happening, how people were reacting, and how these changes were affecting neighbourhoods and people's jobs. His interest in social issues caused him to gravitate to sociology courses at Northwestern University, where he eventually received a BA in sociology.

"Originally as an undergraduate I thought I would go on to law school and become a lawyer. But after taking a few sociology courses, I found myself wanting to learn more about what sociologists studied, and fascinated by the kinds of questions they raised." This fascination led him to obtain his MA and PhD in sociology from the University of Chicago. Richard's continuing interest in race relations led him to write his master's thesis on the membership of the Ku Klux Klan and his doctoral thesis on racial prejudice and race relations in Great Britain.

Richard went on to become a professor of sociology. He has taught introductory sociology for 31 years to students in colleges, adult education programs, nursing programs, and even a maximum-security prison. Richard's love of teaching is apparent in his interaction with his students. "I find myself constantly learning from the students who are in my classes and from reading what they write. Their insights into the material we read or current events that we discuss often become part of future course material and sometimes even find their way into my writing."

Richard is author of the seventh edition of *Sociology* (McGraw-Hill, 2001). He is also the author of *Racial and Ethnic Groups*, now in its ninth edition (Prentice Hall, 2002), and *Race and Ethnicity in the United States*, second edition (Prentice Hall, 2001). His articles and book reviews have appeared in many journals, including *American Journal of Sociology; Phylon: A Review of Race and Culture; Contemporary Sociology; Sociology and Social Research; Sociological Quarterly;* and *Teaching Sociology*. He served as president of the Midwest Sociological Society in 1994–1995.

Richard's advice to students is to "look at the material and make connections to your own life and experiences. Sociology will make you a more attentive observer of how people in groups interact and function. It will also make you more aware of people's different needs and interests—and perhaps more ready to work for the common good, while still recognizing people's individuality."

RICHARD FLOYD:
Full-Time Faculty Member and former Chair, Department of Sociology and Anthropology, Kwantlen University College

After graduating from high school, Richard Floyd pursued a writing career. Then, at the advanced age of 38, he decided it was time to finish his education, and enrolled as a first-year student at the University of British Columbia. Six years later, he had earned a double major in sociology and psychology, and an MA in sociology. In 1989, he began teaching at Kwantlen College—now Kwantlen University College. In his 13 years at Kwantlen, Richard has served as department chair twice, as well as working on an assortment of academic and administrative committees.

Richard is the author of *Success in the Social Sciences*, a how-to book dealing with the process of researching and writing undergraduate papers (Harcourt Brace, 1995). He has also been involved in more than a dozen research projects focusing primarily on issues of marginalization as it affects Canadian seniors and street youth.

Richard is the proud dad of four grown children, Sarah and Katie from a previous marriage, and Jennifer and Jessica, daughters of his wife, Verian. He and Verian live in the cozy community of Crescent Beach, south of Vancouver, British Columbia.

BONNIE HAALAND:
Full-Time Faculty Member, Department of Sociology and Anthropology, Kwantlen University College

Bonnie Haaland completed her BA, with distinction, at the University of Saskatchewan and her MA in sociology at The University of Western Ontario. In 1992, she earned a PhD from the Ontario Institute for Studies in Education, University of Toronto, specializing in feminist theory. Bonnie has taught sociology for over 15 years, teaching first at the University of Western Ontario, then the University of Regina and now at Kwantlen University College. She is the author of *Emma Goldman: Sexuality and the*

Impurity of the State (Black Rose Books, 1993), as well as articles published in Canadian and American journals. She is also the recipient of the Canadian Association for University Continuing Education's Award of Excellence for her article "In Pursuit of Self: The Values of the Post-War Baby Boom Generation and the Implications for Continuing Education." Bonnie lives in South Surrey/White Rock, British Columbia, with her family—Jay, Jordie, and various four-legged companions.

Contents in Brief

Contents

15 COMMUNITIES AND THE ENVIRONMENT 386

16 SOCIAL MOVEMENTS, SOCIAL CHANGE, AND TECHNOLOGY 416

List of Boxes

Sociology in the Global Community

Research in Action

Eye on the Media

Taking Sociology to Work

Social Policy Sections

Preface

"What has sociology got to do with my life?" Any student might well ask this question before signing up for a sociology course. Here are some things for that student to consider: Are you influenced by what you see on television? Do you know someone with hockey hair? Did you neglect to vote in the last election? Are you familiar with safety provisions on campus? Do you use alternative medicine? These are just of few of the everyday life situations described in this book that sociology can shed light on, revealing patterns and meanings.

Sociology also looks at large social issues. It seeks to explore the factors behind the changing nature of the workforce in Canada and worldwide. It assesses the ways in which the availability of computer technology and the Internet may increase or reduce inequality. Sociology investigates the social forces that promote prejudice, the issues surrounding multiculturalism, the social networks established by women, the process of growing old in different cultures, and the factors that lead someone to join a social movement and work for social change. These issues, along with many others, are of great interest to us, but it is the sociological explanations for them that we find especially compelling. The introductory sociology class provides students with an opportunity to see the social world, whether their own neighbourhood or a country on the other side of the globe, from a new perspective. Our hope is that, through their reading of this book, students will begin to use their sociological imagination and employ sociological theories and concepts to make sense of the social interactions they encounter each day.

Beginning with the introduction of the concept of sociological imagination in Chapter 1, the First Canadian Edition of *Sociology: A Brief Introduction* stresses the distinctive way in which sociologists examine and question even the most familiar patterns of social behaviour.

Sociology: A Brief Introduction, First Canadian Edition provides the tools Canadian students need to sharpen their sociological imagination and become sociological thinkers:

- **Strong Canadian content in the form of examples, data, statistics, sociological research, and visuals.** The First Canadian Edition offers content that is relevant and meaningful to Canadian students. Canada's multiculturalism is represented with continual attention to the varied regions, and ethnic groups—including First Nations, francophones, and immigrants—that make up Canada. Canadian data and visuals provide snapshots of life in Canadian society, while end-of-chapter Social Policy sections describe Canada's solutions to contemporary social problems. In each chapter, Canadian research is complemented by research from the United States and elsewhere. Furthermore, the experiences and achievements of Canadian individuals are highlighted in the Taking Sociology to Work boxes. For a detailed list of issues, topics, and features new to this edition, please see "Enhancements Made for the First Canadian Edition" on page xxiii.
- **Comprehensive and balanced coverage of the four major theoretical perspectives—functionalist, conflict, interactionist, and feminist—throughout the text.** Chapter 1 introduces, defines, and contrasts the functionalist, conflict, interactionist, and feminist perspectives, attending to the diversity of feminist viewpoints. Rather than treating feminism as a subset of conflict theory, the text explores four distinct views of such topics as culture (Chapter 3), social institutions (Chapter 5), deviance (Chapter 7), racial and ethnic inequality (Chapter 9), the family (Chapter 11), education (Chapter 12), health, illness, and aging (Chapter 14), and social change (Chapter 16).
- **Strong coverage of issues pertaining to gender, race, ethnicity, and class throughout the text.** Examples of this coverage include sections on John Porter's "vertical mosaic" (Chapter 9), the relationship between social class and gender role socialization (Chapter 10), and the environment (Chapter 15); Social Policy sections on multiculturalism (Chapter 3), day care (Chapter 4), illicit drug use (Chapter 7), and abortion and sex selection (Chapter 10); and boxes on women in public places (Chapter 1), domestic violence (Chapter 11), and violence in schools (Chapter 12).
- **Use of cross-cultural material throughout the text.** A major part of Chapter 8 treats the topic of stratification from a global perspective. The chapter introduces world systems analysis, dependency theory, and modernization theory and examines multinational corporations and the global economy. Every chapter presents global material and makes use of cross-cultural examples. Among the topics examined are:

  The global "McDonaldization" of society (Chapter 3)

  Neglect of children in Eastern European orphanages (Chapter 4)

Global immigration patterns (Chapter 9)
The status of women around the world (Chapter 10)
Transmission of cultural values (Chapter 12)
Population policy in China (Chapter 14)
Homelessness worldwide (Chapter 15)
The global disconnect in technology (Chapter 16)

- **A focus on applying sociological thought.** The distinctive emphasis on social policy in the text shows students how to use sociology to examine such issues as sexual harassment, the AIDS crisis, and privacy and censorship. The Taking Sociology to Work boxes and Chapter 1 Appendix on careers provide examples of the various career paths open to Canadian students of sociology, and motivate students to engage with the material. Internet Connection exercises prompt students to apply the concepts they have learned while using a variety of resources on the World Wide Web.

The Plan for this Book

Sociology: A Brief Introduction, First Canadian Edition is divided into 16 chapters that study human behaviour concisely from the perspective of sociologists. The opening chapter ("Understanding Sociology") presents a brief history of the discipline and introduces the four basic theories and perspectives used in sociology. Chapter 2 ("Sociological Research") describes the major quantitative and qualitative research methods.

The next five chapters focus on key sociological concepts. Chapter 3 ("Culture") illustrates how sociologists study the behaviour we have learned and share. Chapter 4 ("Socialization") reveals how humans are most distinctively social animals who learn the attitudes and behaviour viewed as appropriate in their particular cultures. We examine "Social Interaction and Social Structure" in Chapter 5 and the workings of "Groups and Organizations" in Chapter 6. Chapter 7 ("Deviance and Social Control") reviews how we conform to and deviate from established norms.

The next three chapters consider the social hierarchies present in societies. Chapter 8 ("Stratification in Canada and Worldwide") introduces us to the presence of social inequality, while Chapter 9 ("Racial and Ethnic Inequality") and Chapter 10 ("Gender Relations") analyze specific types of inequality.

The following chapters examine the major social institutions of human society. Marriage, family diversity, and divorce are some of the topics discussed in Chapter 11 ("The Family and Intimate Relationships"). Other social institutions are considered in Chapter 12 ("Religion and Education") and Chapter 13 ("Government and the Economy").

The final chapters of the text introduce major themes in our changing world. Chapter 14 ("Population, Aging, and Health") helps us understand the impact of these issues on Canadian society and around the world. In Chapter 15 we examine the importance of "Communities and the Environment" in our lives. Chapter 16 ("Social Movements, Social Change, and Technology") presents sociological analysis of the process of change and has a special focus on technology and the future.

Pedagogy to Hone the Sociological Imagination

The First Canadian Edition of *Sociology: A Brief Introduction* offers a complete and integrated pedagogical system to help students to think sociologically.

Chapter Openers

Each chapter opens with graphic art that illustrates a key theme or concept of the chapter and a lively excerpt from writings of sociologists and others who explore sociological topics. For example, Chapter 3 begins with Horace Miner's classic take on Nacirema culture. Chapter 5 opens with a description of Zimbardo's mock prison study. John Ralston Saul's musings on the power of the modern media and marketing in *Voltaire's Bastards* introduce Chapter 6, and an excerpt from Thomas Homer-Dixon's *The Ingenuity Gap* sets the stage for Chapter 8's discussion of global stratification. Later, in Chapter 15, Kai Erikson reflects on the value of sociology in understanding the connection between the population and the environment.

Each excerpt is followed by a chapter overview that links it to key themes and describes the content of the chapter in narrative form.

Boxes

The First Canadian Edition of *Sociology: A Brief Introduction* contains four types of themed boxes, each of which contains a set of "Let's Discuss" questions to foster student involvement.

- **Research in Action** boxes present timely and relevant sociological findings on topics such as minority women and federal candidacy in Canada and impression management by students after exams.
- **Sociology in the Global Community** boxes provide a global perspective on topics such as disability as a master status, domestic violence, and population policy.

- **Eye on the Media** boxes illustrate how the media affect, and are affected by, social trends and events. Topics include the social construction of rock music as a social problem, coalition building in *Survivor*, and the Doukhobors and the Canadian media.

- **Taking Sociology to Work** boxes profile Canadian individuals who majored in sociology and use its principles in their work. These people work in a variety of occupations and professions, and all share the conviction that their background in sociology has been valuable in their careers.

Social Policy Sections

The Social Policy sections that close Chapters 2 to 16 play a critical role in helping students to think like sociologists. They apply sociological principles and theories to important social and political issues debated by policymakers and the general public. These include multiculturalism (Chapter 3), reproductive technology (Chapter 11), religion in the schools (Chapter 12), and financing health care (Chapter 14). Each Social Policy section provides Canadian content while retaining a global perspective.

Illustrations

The photographs, cartoons, figures, and tables are closely linked to the themes of the chapters. The maps, titled "Mapping Life Nationwide" and "Mapping Life Worldwide" show the prevalence of a variety of social trends. A world map highlighting those countries used as examples in the text appears at the beginning of the book.

Cross-Reference Icons

When the text discussion refers to a concept introduced earlier in the book, an icon in the margin points the reader to the exact page, facilitating student comprehension and encouraging good study habits.

p. 156

Chapter Summaries

Each chapter includes a brief numbered summary to aid students in reviewing important concepts.

Critical Thinking Questions

After the summary, each chapter includes critical thinking questions that will help students analyze the social world in which they participate. Critical thinking is an essential element of the sociological imagination.

Additional Readings

An annotated list of books concludes each chapter; these works have been selected as additional readings because of their sociological soundness and their accessibility for introductory students.

Internet Connection Exercises

An Internet exercise appears at the end of each chapter to take students online to analyze social issues relevant to chapter topics. Additional Internet Connection exercises are available at the Schaefer Online Learning Centre at **http://www.mcgrawhill.ca/college/schaefer.**

CBC Videos

At the end of Chapters 1, 9, 10, 12, and 14, an icon leads students to the Online Learning Centre, where they can view CBC video clips related to chapter content. Each clip is accompanied by a series of discussion questions.

Enhancements Made for the First Canadian Edition

As described above, the First Canadian Edition of *Sociology: A Brief Introduction* is fully adapted for a Canadian audience. All chapters and pedagogical features have been updated with Canadian data and examples and coverage of issues, concepts, and theories important to Canadian students and instructors. Below is a chapter-by-chapter summary of just some of the content changes in this adaptation.

CHAPTER 1 Understanding Sociology

- New opening excerpt by Doug Saunders on the "mullet" hairstyle
- Data on food banks in Edmonton is included
- Coverage of the Montreal Massacre and the Firearms Act
- Introduction of Canadian sociologists Harold A. Innis, S.D. Clark, John Porter, and Patricia Marchak
- Addition of feminist perspectives to "Major Theoretical Perspectives"
- Revised appendix focuses on sociology and careers in Canada

CHAPTER 2 Sociological Research

- New opening extract from *Generation on Hold* by J.E. Côté and A.L. Allahar, about contemporary youth and consumerism
- More material on qualitative research is included
- Canadian studies on home-leaving serve as examples to illustrate the sociological research process

- New Research in Action box on Framing Survey Questions for Marginal Populations
- Discussion of the Target Inclusion Model for impacting survey data
- Discussion of Dr. Martha Foschi and social psychological research
- Explanation of the CSAA Statement of Professional Ethics
- Russel Ogden's study of suicide and euthanasia among individuals with AIDS illustrates the concepts of confidentiality and politics in research
- Discussion of Eurocentrism and androcentrism in sociological research
- New Taking Sociology to Work box on Marylee Stephenson, founder and president of CS/RESORS Consulting Limited
- Incorporation of Canadian data and policies into Social Policy box on studying human sexuality

CHAPTER 3 Culture

- New Figure 3-1: "What is Canadian?" illustrates Canadian content law
- New Taking Sociology to Work box on Angus Reid
- Discussion of Canadian values, including Figure 3-3 on "Valued Means of Teenagers and Adults"
- Data on Canadian public opinion about poverty is included
- Discussion of the FLQ as a subculture
- New section on cultural diversity in Canada focusing on the goals of the Multiculturalism Program of 1997
- Discussion of the American influence and Canadian uniqueness, including Figure 3-5, "Applicability of Traits to Canadians and Americans"
- New Social Policy section on multiculturalism

CHAPTER 4 Socialization

- Discussion of the media's undermining of the contributions of minorities in Canadian society
- New sub-section on family and gender socialization
- Canadian data on gender bias in the classroom and bullying is included
- New sub-section on peer group and gender socialization
- Canadian data on television viewing habits is included
- New Table 4-1 "Distorted Viewing: The Mass Media's Treatment of Women"
- Coverage of day care in Canada added to the Social Policy section

CHAPTER 5 Social Interaction and Social Structure

- Incorporation of feminist perspectives
- New youth-focused examples
- New Taking Sociology to Work box on Cathy MacDonald, Dean, College Resources, Kwantlen University College
- Coverage of the Campbell River Access Awareness Committee, which identifies and procures resources for people with physical challenges
- New information on cyberspace communication's effect on the influence potential of status characteristics
- Canadian data on Internet use
- New Research in Action box on Teens at Work
- Genocide and the Beothuk nation
- Canadian data on AIDS

CHAPTER 6 Groups and Organizations

- New opening excerpt from John Ralston Saul's *Voltaire's Bastards: The Dictatorship of Reason in the West*
- Globalization from the Canadian perspective
- Coverage of the September 11, 2001 terrorist attacks to illustrate the differential standards of in-groups
- New Taking Sociology to Work box on János John Maté, Representative to the United Nations, Greenpeace International
- Local community response to Toronto's bid for the 2008 summer Olympics is addressed
- Expanded discussion of bureaucracies and bureaucratization
- Discussion of Canada as a multicultural society
- Data on Canadian e-mail use is included
- Social Policy Box on sexual harassment fully updated with Canadian legislation, data, and policy initiatives

CHAPTER 7 Deviance and Social Control

- New Research in Action box, on "Street Kids"
- Discussion of feminist perspectives added
- Canadian data on physical punishment of children is included
- Canadian data on prison sentencing is included
- New table Table 7-2 "Selected Cosmetic Procedures Performed by Members of the American Society of Plastic and Reconstruction Surgeons in Canada and the United States"
- New data on Internet addiction is included
- Coverage of legalized gambling in Canada

- Canadian data on crime rates, with attention to regional differences, including new figure "Crime Rates by Province and Territory, 2000"
- New Taking Sociology to Work box on Holly Johnson, Chief of Research, Canadian Centre for Justice Statistics, Statistics Canada
- Coverage of safety on Canadian campuses
- New Social Policy section on illicit drug use in Canada

CHAPTER 8 Stratification in Canada and Worldwide

- New opening extract from Thomas Homer-Dixon's *The Ingenuity Gap*
- Full incorporation of feminist perspectives
- Coverage of the history of slavery in Canada
- Extensive Canadian income data and discussion of income quintiles
- Measuring poverty in Canada, with particular focus on women and children
- Responses to poverty by different Canadian regions
- Expanded discussion of status consistency and social mobility
- New Table 8-2 "Low Income Rates in Canada"
- New Research in Action box on poverty in Canada
- Discussion of health care and class issues in Canada
- Canadian labour force participation data is included
- New Canadian data and policy initiatives in the Social Policy Section section on "Rethinking Welfare in North America and Europe"

CHAPTER 9 Racial and Ethnic Inequality

- New opening excerpt from *Web of Hate: Inside Canada's Far Right Network* by Warren Kinsella
- Focus on the social construction of racial and ethnic categories
- New tables and figures illustrate immigration patterns of different groups to Canada
- Discussion of the Metis people as an example of amalgamation in Canadian society
- Discussion of John Porter's concept of Canada as a "vertical mosaic"
- Coverage of the United States and Canadian governments' responses to racially motivated attacks as a result of the events of September 11, 2001
- New Research in Action box, on "Minority Women and Federal Candidacy in Canada"
- Full discussion of implications of the Canadian Citizenship Act of 1967
- Information on institutional discrimination in the Canadian housing market
- Integration of feminist perspectives
- Discussion of self-segregation
- Expanded treatment of institutional completeness
- Coverage of the Canadian Charter of Rights and Freedoms and the Multiculturalism Act of 1988
- Discussion of racial groups in Canada includes First Nations people and Asian Canadians
- Discussion of ethnic groups in Canada focuses on French Canadians and Europeans
- New Eye on the Media box on the Doukhobors and the Canadian Media
- Social Policy box on global immigration covers Canadian immigration policy initiatives

CHAPTER 10 Gender Relations

- Section on impact of social class location on gender role socialization
- Further discussion of varied feminist perspectives set out in Chapter 1: liberal, Marxist, socialist, radical, and standpoint
- Discussion of the 2000 United Nations report on world population from a gender perspective
- Data on women in Canada's government
- New table comparing salaries of visible minority men and women versus non–visible minority men and women in Canada
- Data on Canadian women and poverty and women's participation in the Canadian labour force, including figures and tables on "Employment by Family Status," "Canadian Women in Selected Occupations as a Percentage of Total Employed in Occupations," and "Gender Differences in Daily Hours of Paid and Unpaid Labour in Canada"
- Discussion of compounded effects of discrimination experienced by First Nations women in Canada
- Coverage of the role complexity and time stress experienced by Canadian women
- Discussion of the history of the feminist movement in Canada, including the first and second waves of feminism, the "Famous Five," and the "Persons Case"
- New Taking Sociology to Work box on Prudence Hannis, Researcher and Community Activist, Quebec Native Women
- Social Policy section on abortion and sex selection in Canada and worldwide

CHAPTER 11 The Family and Intimate Relationships

- Data on the portrayal of women on Canadian television is included
- Feminist views on the family are incorporated

- New figure included, on "Types of Family Households in Canada"
- Data on marriage and divorce in Canada is included
- Discussion of intermarriage among ethnic groups in Canada
- Data on First Nations families and black families in Canada is included
- New Taking Sociology to Work box on Karla Jessen Williamson, Executive Director, The Arctic Institute of North America
- Data on Canadian lone-parent families and discussion of global trends in lone-parent families
- Discussion of regional variation relating to rates of marriage and cohabitation in Canada
- New section on family violence in Canada
- Extensive attention to family diversity in Canada, including coverage of the status of same-sex partnerships in Canada
- Discussion of the potential changes to the definitions of motherhood and fatherhood due to new reproductive technologies

CHAPTER 12 Religion and Education

- New opening extract, "Grandfather was a Knowing Christian" by Noah Augustine, examines the conflict in religious identity among different generations of First Nations people
- Canadian data on women in positions of spiritual leadership is included
- Discussion of Canadian trends in religious membership, noting regional variations
- New Taking Sociology to Work box on Pat Duffy Hutcheon, Secular Humanist
- Coverage of residential schools for First Nations children in Canada
- Data on Canadian levels of educational attainment and socioeconomic status
- Feminist perspectives on education are incorporated
- Discussion of Canadian school violence
- Canadian data on adult education and "informal" learning is included
- Discussion of private schools and home schooling in Canada
- Social Policy box focuses on Canadian debates about religion in the public schools

CHAPTER 13 Government and the Economy

- New opening excerpt from *Chips and Pop: Decoding the Nexus Generation* by Barnard, Cosgrave, and Welsh examines the forces that are impacting on post-adolescents in contemporary Canadian society
- Discussion of crown corporations
- Discussion of social democracy and its applicability to Canada
- Discussion of political parties in Canada
- Coverage of Canadian interest groups
- Data on Canadian voter turnout is included
- Data on women in Canadian government is included
- New material on Canadian protest movements of the 1960s
- Coverage of multiculturalism
- Discussion of the changing nature of the Canadian workforce and employment patterns of Canadians
- New Social Policy box section on gender inequality and the progress of women's rights in Canada

CHAPTER 14 Population, Aging, and Health

- Expansion of chapter to include the topic of aging
- New chapter opening excerpt on smoking as an addiction by Peter Gzowski
- Information on the Canadian census and its history
- New population structure figure comparing Kenya and Canada
- Feminist theories on aging and health and illness are incorporated
- New Section on the aging Canadian population
- Coverage of Health Canada's 12 determinants of health
- Discussion of health and illness in First Nations groups
- Canadian life expectancy data is included
- The relationship between gender, culture, and health in Canada is explored
- New section on sexual orientation and health and illness
- Historical overview of Canada's medicare program and the role the government plays in its administration
- New Taking Sociology to Work box on Kelsie Lenor Wilson-Dorsett, Deputy Director, Department of Statistics, Government of Bahamas
- Social Policy section on financing health care worldwide is centred on Canadian policy initiatives

CHAPTER 15 Communities and the Environment

- Discussion of Statistics Canada's population categories—Metropolitan Influence Zones, Census Areas, Census Metropolitan Areas, and Census Area Influence Zones
- Discussion of city–suburb migration patterns and gentrification in Canada

- New Research in Action box on protecting Canada's endangered species
- Discussion of the problem of public transportation in Canada
- Discussion of diversity in the suburbs of Canada
- Statistics on rural Canadians are included
- Coverage of pollution in Canada
- Discussion of water contamination in Walkerton, Ontario
- Social Policy section on "Seeking Shelter Worldwide" includes Canadian policy initiatives on homelessness

CHAPTER 16 Social Movements, Social Change, and Technology

- Feminist approaches to social change are incorporated
- Discussion of vested interests using example of Canadian Medical Association
- Discussion of DNA evidence in Canada
- Discussion of computer use in Canada
- Coverage of Canadian society and social change
- Canadian data added to the Social Policy section on "Privacy and Censorship in a Global Village"

Support for Instructors

i-Learning Sales Specialist

Your *Integrated Learning Sales Specialist* is a McGraw-Hill Ryerson representative who has the experience, product knowledge, training, and support to help you assess and integrate any of the below-noted products, technology, and services into your course for optimum teaching and learning performance. Whether it's how to use our test bank software, helping your students improve their grades, or how to put your entire course on-line, your *i*-Learning Sales Specialist is there to help. Contact your local *i*-Learning Sales Specialist today to learn how to maximize all McGraw-Hill Ryerson resources!

*i*Learning Services Program

McGraw-Hill Ryerson offers a unique *i*Services package designed for Canadian faculty. Our mission is to equip providers of higher education with superior tools and resources required for excellence in teaching. For additional information, visit **www.mcgrawhill.ca/highereducation/eservices/**.

Instructor's Resource Manual

This manual, adapted for Canada by authors Richard Floyd and Bonnie Haaland, provides sociology instructors with additional lecture ideas, class discussion topics, essay questions, and CBC video cases.

Test Bank and Computerized Test Bank

The test bank features short-answer questions, multiple-choice questions, and essay questions.

The test bank is also available electronically in a Brownstone format that allows instructors to select, edit, and/or write their own questions, print exams, and more.

Online Learning Centre

Visit the Schaefer Online Learning Centre at **www.mcgrawhill.ca/college/schaefer** to download the **Instructor's Resource Manual** and a complete set of **PowerPoint slides** to accompany the text. The site also features six **CBC video clips**, as well as associated discussion questions and suggested answers.

PowerWeb

Add the Internet to your course. PowerWeb includes current articles, curriculum-based materials, weekly updates with assessment, informative and timely world news, refereed Web links, research tools, student study tools, interactive exercises, and much more. To learn more, visit **www.dushkin.com/powerweb**.

E-STAT

E-STAT is an educational resource designed by Statistics Canada and made available to Canadian educational institutions. Using 450 000 current CANSIM (Canadian Socio-economic Information Management System) Time Series and the most recent—as well as historical—census data, E-STAT lets you bring data to life in colourful graphs and maps. You can access such data as population, income, language, ethnic groups, federal debt, imports and exports, and more. Easy-to-use, thorough, and dynamic, E-STAT is a stimulating teaching and learning resource that spurs students on to discover Canada, past and present.

Data Liberation Initiative

The Data Liberation Initiative (DLI) is a cost-effective method for improving data resources for Canadian post-secondary institutions. Prior to the start of the DLI program, Canadian universities and colleges had to purchase Statistics Canada data, file by file. With the advent of the DLI, participating post-secondary institutions pay an annual subscription fee that allows their faculty and students unlimited access to numerous Statistics Canada public-use microdata files, databases, and geographic files.

PageOut: The Course Web Site Development Centre

PageOut was designed for the professor just beginning to explore Web options. In less than an hour, even the novice computer user can create a course Web site with a template provided by McGraw-Hill (no programming knowledge required).

To find out more about PageOut: The Course Web site Development Centre, contact your *i*-Learning Sales Specialist.

Support for Students

Reel Society Interactive Movie CD-ROM

Exercise your sociological imagination and step into the world of Reel Society, an interactive movie that brings key sociological concepts to life. You become part of the story of several university students during three challenging days on campus. You take part by making decisions for them. You see the consequences of your choices. Through it all, a wide variety of issues and perspectives are shown for the purpose of relating sociological thought to real life. To learn more about Reel Society, visit **www.mhhe.com/reelsociety**.

Study to Go: A Mobile Learning Application for Palm and PocketPC

Do you use a handheld Personal Digital Assistant (PDA)? McGraw-Hill Ryerson's Study to Go application gives you the opportunity to study any time, anywhere. And it's free for students using *Sociology: A Brief Introduction*! To download quizzes, key terms, and flashcards, visit the Online Learning Centre at **www.mcgrawhill.ca/college/schaefer**.

Study Guide

The study guide includes a variety of resources for each chapter to help students review and succeed in the course.

Online Learning Centre

Visit the Schaefer Online Learning Centre at **www.mcgrawhill.ca/college/schaefer** to take multiple-choice chapter quizzes, view CBC video clips and answer related questions, search the book glossary, engage with additional Internet Connections for each chapter, and more.

Acknowledgments from Richard T. Schaefer

Virginia Joyner collaborated with me on the fourth edition, bringing fresh insight into presenting the sociological imagination. Robert P. Lamm had been part of several previous brief and comprehensive editions of *Sociology*, and his contributions are still apparent.

I deeply appreciate the contributions to this book made by my editors. Rhona Robbin, a senior development editor at McGraw-Hill, has continually and successfully challenged me to make each edition better than its predecessor.

I have received strong support and encouragement from Phillip Butcher, editorial director, and Sally Constable, sponsoring editor. Additional guidance and support were provided by Alyson DeMonte, editorial assistant; Kimberly Hooker, project manager; Laurie Entringer, designer; Elyse Rieder, photo editor; and Diane Kraut, permissions editor. I would also like to express appreciation to Melissa Haeffner and Todd Fuist for their research assistance.

I would also like to acknowledge the contributions of the following individuals: Mark Kassop of Bergen Community College in New Jersey for his work on the instructor's resource manual, as well as the annotations that appear in the annotated instructor's edition; Kenrick Thompson of Arkansas State University for preparing the test items for the Interactive e-Source CD-ROM and John Tenuto of the College of Lake County in Illinois for developing the Internet exercises in the text and for his contributions to the annotated instructor's edition.

Academic Reviewers

I would like to express my thanks to the following people who have reviewed all or various portions of the manuscript:

Sally Caldwell
Southwest Texas State University

Mirelle Cohen
Green River Community College

Kelly A. Dagan
Kent State University

Lee F. Hamilton
New Mexico State University

Jeanne Humble
Lexington Community College

Janet Hund
Long Beach City College

William L. Smith
Georgia Southern University

Tracy Faye Tolbert
California State University, Long Beach

James E. Trela
University of Maryland, Baltimore County

Jacquelyn Troup
Cerritos College

As is evident from these acknowledgements, the preparation of a textbook is truly a team effort. The most valuable member of this effort continues to be my wife, Sandy. She provides the support so necessary in my creative and scholarly activities.

I have had the good fortune to be able to introduce students to sociology for many years. These students have been enormously helpful in spurring on my own sociological imagination. In ways I can fully appreciate but cannot fully acknowledge, their questions in class and queries in the hallway have found their way into this textbook.

Richard T. Schaefer
schaeferrt@aol.com

Acknowledgments from Richard Floyd and Bonnie Haaland

We are deeply indebted to a number of individuals at McGraw-Hill Ryerson who provided support, encouragement, and technical expertise throughout the development of this project. We express our sincere thanks and appreciation to Veronica Visentin, Senior Sponsoring Editor; James Buchanan, Sponsoring Editor; Lesley Mann and Jennifer DiDomenico, Developmental Editors; Anne Macdonald, Supervising Editor; Madeleine Harrington, Production Coordinator; Dawn du Quesnay, Copy Editor; and Dianna Little and Greg Devitt, Designers.

We would also like to extend our thanks to those instructors whose thoughtful reviews helped to inform this text:

Merle Amodeo
Durham College

Jean Ballard
University College of Fraser Valley

Tami Bereska
Grant MacEwan College

Stephen Dooley
Kwantlen University College

David Dwyer
Fanshawe College

James M. Jackson
Humber College

Raymond Liew
John Abbott College

Bev Matthews
Mount Royal College

Jim Richardson
University of New Brunswick

We are also indebted to department colleagues in Sociology at Kwantlen University College for their patience, generosity, and support. To Roger Elmes, Dean of Social Science and Music, Kwantlen University College, we also wish to extend our thanks for his unwavering support and encouragement.

Our students, over the course of many years, have provided the basis for our professional commitment and inspiration. To them, we offer our sincere thanks with the hope that in some way—great or small—this book may contribute to a deepened understanding of their own lives and a sustained curiosity in their social world.

Richard Floyd
Bonnie Haaland

McGraw-Hill Ryerson
Online Learning Centre

McGraw-Hill Ryerson offers you an online resource that combines the best content with the flexibility and power of the Internet. Organized by chapter, the SCHAEFER Online Learning Centre (OLC) offers the following features to enhance your learning and understanding of sociology:

- Online Quizzes
- Web Links
- CBC Video Clips
- Additional Internet Connection Exercises

By connecting to the "real world" through the OLC, you will enjoy a dynamic and rich source of current information that will help you get more from your course and improve your chances for success, both in sociology and in the future.

For the Instructor

Downloadable Supplements

The complete Instructor's Manual and PowerPoint® slides to accompany each chapter are available, password-protected, for instant access!

PageOut

Create your own course Web page for free, quickly and easily. Your professionally designed Web site links directly to OLC material, allows you to post a class syllabus, offers an online gradebook, and much more! Visit www.pageout.net

Primis Online

Primis Online gives you access to our resources in the best medium for your students: printed textbooks or electronic ebooks. There are over 350,000 pages of content available from which you can create customized learning tools from our online database at www.mhhe.com/primis

Knowledge Gateway

Knowledge Gateway is a Web site–based service and resource for instructors teaching online. It provides instructional design services, and information and technical support for course management systems. It is located at http://mhhe.eduprise.com/

Higher Learning. Forward Thinking.™ **McGraw-Hill Ryerson**

ning Centre

For the Student

Online Quizzes

Do you understand the material? You'll know after taking an Online Quiz! Try the Multiple Choice and True/False questions for each chapter. They're auto-graded with feedback and the option to send results directly to faculty.

Web Links

This section references useful and relevant Web sites by text chapter.

CBC Video Clips

View CBC video clips linked to chapter content in **Sociology: A Brief Introduction** and answer related questions.

Additional Internet Connection Exercises

Explore sociological topics while enhancing your web research skills with additional Internet Connection Exercises for each chapter.

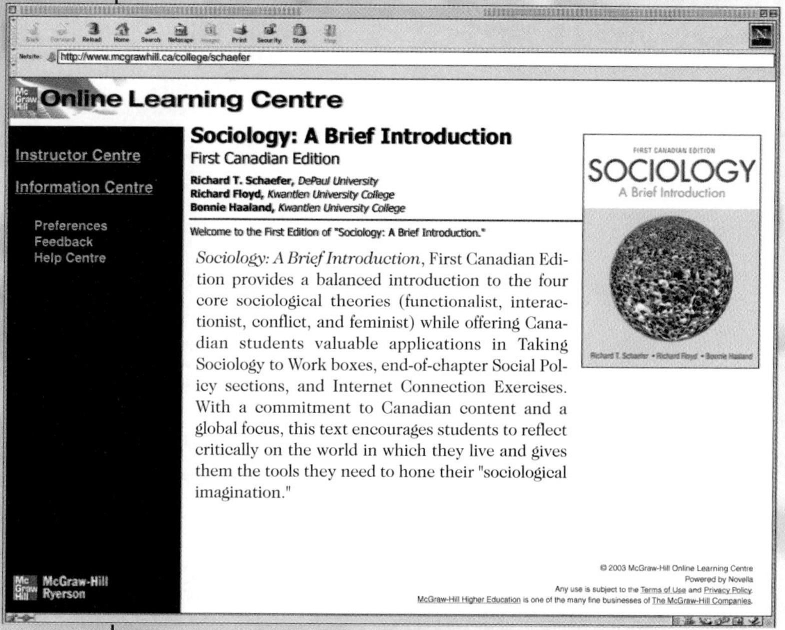

Your Internet companion to the most exciting educational tools on the Web!

The Online Learning Centre can be found at:

www.mcgrawhill.ca/college/schaefer

CHAPTER

1 UNDERSTANDING SOCIOLOGY

Sociology places us in the context of groups, cultures, and societies. People interact in all three of these settings in the Olympic games. This poster promotes the bid of Osaka, Japan, for the 2008 Summer Olympics.

If you wanted one in Michigan, you'd ask your barber to give you a Canadian. In many parts of Canada, you'd ask for a Hockey Cut. Or you could call it the Bi-level, the Camaro Cut, the SFLB (Short in Front, Long in Back), the Beaver Paddle, the Two-in-One, the Kentucky Waterfall or the Neck Blanket.

The mullet, as this cut is properly and notoriously known, is perhaps the most derided hairdo on earth, at least among chic urbanites. It is the haircut preferred by the sort of people for whom coffee comes with doughnuts, not lemon twists—country singers, high-school bullies, farm kids, hockey players, wrestlers, truck drivers, recent husbands of Elizabeth Taylor.

It has been the spawn of more than 60 Web sites devoted to its ridicule (try **http://www.mulletsgalore.com** or **http://www.mulletmadness.com**), and of a punch-buggy sort of sidewalk game: Spot a mullet, score a point.

The mullet has entered the lowest circle of fashion hell, that infernal place occupied by narrow neckties and pleated trousers in the 1990s.

And you know where that sentence must inevitably lead: Yes indeed, mullets have begun to sprout on the pointy pates of the most sophisticated sort of downtown folks.

"I've had mine for three weeks, and I think it's just the best!" So says Andy Le Compte, who is decidedly not a Billy Ray Cyrus fan or a hockey player. In fact, he is a hairdresser at Salon Privé, one of the fanciest hair salons on L.A.'s Melrose Place (the street, not the show).

In recent weeks, Le Compte says he's given mullets to dozens of people, all of them from the oh-so-right side of the tracks.

"It's a look that's become so white trash, so trailer trash, and you know, trash is always just so cool," he enthuses between haircuts that begin at $150 (Cdn). "It's just so much more practical than all that big hair."

Inevitably, Hollywood's attention has been captured by this unkindest of cuts. This month, two mullet-themed feature films went into development, and major stars are jockeying for a piece of the mullet.

"The 'mullets' are sort of the nerds of the 21st century, and in this movie they become the good guys and they fight back," Rob Ritger, writer of *American Mullet*, said from his Santa Monica home. "Of course, we have a lot of fun with them, too."

His film will be a full-blown studio flick, financed by Gaylord Films, a division of the Nashville company that owns the mullet-friendly Grand Ole Opry.

On the other side of the tracks is *The Mullet Chronicles*, a feature-length documentary being produced by a group of Hollywood rebels who travelled across the United States seeking the truth behind the locks.

"I'd noticed that there are five groups of people in society who have mullets, and I wanted to go discover the missing link that unites them," says director Jennifer Arnold. In her view, those five groups are country fans; athletes; Native Americans; Mexican-Americans; and lesbians.

Arnold got hip to the cut through the latter group, which she encountered en masse at a women's music gathering in California. "Everyone except me had a mullet, and no clothes," she remembers. "So I decided to get on the bandwagon before mullet saturation hits."

Entire schools of theory have developed around the mullet, which probably had its sole moment of official acceptance in 19th-century North America. Although theorizing about a mullet cut seems about as useful as basting a hot dog, observers do believe the cut's sudden resurgence is somehow reflective of our culture's larger direction.

"Not to get philosophical," says Ritger, "but it's both short on top, which indicates conformity, and long in the back, which indicates rebellion. It's as if it's saying you can be conservative, but still not part of mainstream society." *(Saunders 2001)* ■

What makes a hair style an appropriate subject for study in sociology? Uniting all sociological studies is their focus on *patterns* of human behaviour. Doug Saunders' article on the mullet haircut discusses how this cut suddenly became a badge of social status, rather than a symbol of poor fashion sense, among urban trendsetters. Worn by such groups as hockey players, country singers, farm kids, wrestlers, and truckers, the mullet had long been the subject of mockery on the part of young, "fashionable" urbanites. However, the cut, also known as the "Canadian" in parts of the U.S. and as the "hockey cut" in parts of Canada, has recently become trendy in cutting-edge hair salons in cities such as Los Angeles.

Sociologists are not concerned with what one individual does or does not do, but with what people do as members of a group or while interacting with one another, and what that means for the individuals and for society as a whole. Hairstyles are, in fact, a subject that sociologists can study in any number of ways. They might examine their history or their use in different groups, regions, and cultures. (Synott 1987; Craig 1997).

As a field of study, then, sociology is extremely broad in scope. You will see throughout this book the range of topics sociologists investigate—from suicide to TV viewing habits, from Amish society to global economic patterns, from peer pressure to pickpocketing techniques. Sociology looks at how others influence our behaviour as well as how major social institutions like the government, religion, and the economy affect us.

This chapter will explore the nature of sociology as a field of inquiry and an exercise of the "sociological imagination." We'll look at the discipline as a science and consider its relationship to other social sciences. We will evaluate the contributions of three pioneering thinkers—Émile Durkheim, Max Weber, and Karl Marx—to the development of sociology. Next we will discuss a number of important theoretical perspectives used by sociologists. Finally, we will consider the ways sociology helps us to develop our sociological imagination. ■

What Is Sociology?

Sociology is the systematic study of social behaviour and human groups. It focuses primarily on the influence of social relationships on people's attitudes and behaviour and on how societies are established and change. This textbook deals with such varied topics as families, the workplace, street gangs, business firms, political parties, genetic engineering, schools, religions, and labour unions. It is concerned with love, poverty, conformity, discrimination, illness, technology, and community.

The Sociological Imagination

In attempting to understand social behaviour, sociologists rely on an unusual type of creative thinking. C. Wright Mills (1959) described such thinking as the ***sociological imagination***—an awareness of the relationship between an individual and the wider society. This awareness allows all of us (not just sociologists) to comprehend the links between our immediate, personal social settings and the remote, impersonal social world that surrounds us and helps to shape us.

A key element in the sociological imagination is the ability to view one's own society as an outsider would, rather than only from the perspective of personal experiences and cultural biases. Consider something as simple as the practice of eating while walking. In Canada we think nothing of seeing people consuming coffee or chocolate bars as they walk along. Sociologists would see this as a pattern of acceptable behaviour because others regard it as acceptable. Yet sociologists need to go beyond one culture to place the practice in perspective. This "normal" behaviour is quite unacceptable elsewhere. For example, in Japan people do not eat while walking. Streetside sellers and vending machines dispense food everywhere, but the Japanese will stop to eat or drink whatever they buy before they continue on their way. In their eyes, to engage in another activity while eating shows disrespect for the food preparation, even if the food comes out of a vending machine.

The sociological imagination allows us to go beyond personal experiences and observations to understand broader public issues. Unemployment, for example, is unquestionably a personal hardship for a man or woman without a job. However, C. Wright Mills pointed out that when unemployment is a social problem shared by millions of people, it is appropriate to question the way that a society is structured or organized. Similarly, Mills advocated using the sociological imagination to view divorce not simply as the personal problem of a particular man or woman, but rather as a societal problem, since it is the

Do you consider talking on a cell phone while driving "normal" behaviour? Some cultural practices are so new that their acceptability in a society is still being determined.

outcome of many marriages. And he was writing this in the 1950s, when the divorce rate was but a fraction of what it is today (I. Horowitz 1983).

Sociological imagination can bring new understanding to daily life around us. For example, in Canada, families are turning to food banks in growing numbers to provide them with daily necessities. A 1999 report on hunger, homelessness, and food bank use published by Edmonton's Food Bank and the Edmonton Social Planning Council found that 54 percent of Edmonton families using food banks live on less than $1000 per month. The majority of these families (71 percent) reported that they turn to food banks because of ongoing money shortages. Most of the families utilizing food banks (55 percent) were led by female single parents with children under 12.

Many observers would uncritically applaud the distribution of food to the needy. But let's look deeper. While supportive of and personally involved in such efforts, Miller and Schaefer (1993) have drawn on the sociological imagination to offer a more probing view of these activities. They note that powerful forces in American society—such as the federal government, major food retailers, and other large corporations—have joined in charitable food distribution arrangements. Perhaps as a result, the focus of such relief programs is too restricted. The homeless are to be fed, not housed; the unemployed are to be given meals, not jobs. Relief efforts assist hungry individuals and families without challenging the existing social order (for example, by demanding a redistribution of wealth). Of course, without these limited successes in distributing food, starving people might assault patrons of restaurants, loot grocery stores, or literally die of starvation on the steps of city halls. Such critical thinking is typical of sociologists, as they draw on the sociological imagination to study a social issue—in this case, hunger in North America (Vladimiroff 1998).

Sociology and the Social Sciences

Is sociology a science? The term ***science*** refers to the body of knowledge obtained by methods based on systematic observation. Just like other scientific disciplines, sociology engages in organized, systematic study of phenomena (in this case, human behaviour) in order to enhance understanding. All scientists, whether studying mushrooms or murderers, attempt to collect precise information through methods of study that are as objective as possible. They rely on careful recording of observations and accumulation of data.

Of course, there is a great difference between sociology and physics, between psychology and astronomy. For this reason, the sciences are commonly divided into natural and social sciences. ***Natural science*** is the study of the physical features of nature and the ways in which they interact and change. Astronomy, biology, chemistry, geology, and physics are all natural sciences. ***Social science*** is the study of various aspects of human society. The social sciences include sociology, anthropology, economics, history, psychology, and political science.

These academic disciplines have a common focus on the social behaviour of people, yet each has a particular orientation. Anthropologists usually study past cultures and preindustrial societies that continue today, as well as the origins of men and women; this knowledge is used to examine contemporary societies, including even industrial societies. Economists explore the ways in which people produce and exchange goods and services, along with money and other resources. Historians are concerned with the peoples and events of the past and their significance for us today. Political scientists study international relations, the workings of government, and the exercise of power and authority. Psychologists investigate personality and individual behaviour. So what does sociology focus on? It emphasizes the influence that society has on people's attitudes and behaviour and the ways in which people shape society. Humans are social animals; therefore, sociologists scientifically examine our social relationships with people.

Let's consider how the different social sciences might approach the issue of gun control. This issue received increased public attention in Canada after December 6, 1987, when Marc Lepine systematically shot and killed 14 women, engineering students at l'École Polytechnique in Montreal. The event became known as the "Montreal Massacre" and eventually led to stricter gun control laws in Canada in the form of registration requirements under the Firearms Act. Political scientists would look at the impact of political action groups, such as the National Firearms Association, on lawmakers. Historians would examine how guns were used over time in our country and elsewhere. Anthropologists would focus on the use of weapons in a variety of cultures as means of protection as well as symbols of power. Psychologists would look at individual cases and assess the impact guns have on their owners as well as on individual victims of gunfire. Economists would be interested in how firearm manufacture and sales affect communities. Sociologists would gather data to inform policymakers. For example, they would examine data from different regions to evaluate the effect of gun restrictions on the incidence of firearm accidents or violent crimes involving firearms. They would ask: What explanations can be offered for the gender, racial, age, rural/urban, and geographic differences in gun ownership? How would these differences affect the formulation of a government policy? Sociologists might also look at data that show how Canada compares to other nations, particularly the United States, in gun ownership and use.

Sociologists put their imagination to work in a variety of areas—including aging, criminal justice, the family, human ecology, and religion. Throughout this textbook, the sociological imagination will be used to examine Canada (and other societies) from the viewpoint of respectful but questioning outsiders.

Do disasters produce panic or an organized, structured response? Common sense might tell us the former, but, in fact, disasters bring out a great deal of structure and organization to deal with their aftermath. Prime Minister Jean Chrétien thanks rescue workers for their effort at the World Trade Center at Ground Zero, September 29, 2001.

Sociology and Common Sense

Sociology focuses on the study of human behaviour. Yet we all have experience with human behaviour and at least some knowledge of it. All of us might well have theories about why people get tattoos, for example, or why people become homeless. Our theories and opinions typically come from "common sense"—that is, from our experiences and conversations, from what we read, from what we see on television, and so forth.

In our daily lives, we rely on common sense to get us through many unfamiliar situations. However, this commonsense knowledge, while sometimes accurate, is not always reliable, because it rests on commonly held beliefs rather than on systematic analysis of facts. It was once considered "common sense" to accept that the earth was flat—a view rightly questioned by Pythagoras and Aristotle. Incorrect commonsense notions are not just a part of the distant past; they remain with us today.

"Common sense," for example, tells us that people panic when faced with natural disasters, such as floods, earthquakes, or ice storms. However, these particular "commonsense" notions—like the notion that the earth is flat—are untrue; they are not supported by sociological research. Disasters do not generally produce panic. In the aftermath of disasters and even explosions, greater social organization and structure emerge to deal with a community's problems. In Canada, for example, emergency response teams often coordinate public services and even certain services normally performed by the private sector, such as food distribution. Decision making becomes more centralized in times of disaster.

Like other social scientists, sociologists do not accept something as a fact because "everyone knows it." Instead, each piece of information must be tested and recorded, then analyzed in relationship to other data. Sociology relies on scientific studies in order to describe and understand a social environment. At times, the findings of sociologists may seem like common sense because they deal with facets of everyday life. The difference is that such findings have been *tested* by researchers. Common sense now tells us that the earth is round. But this particular commonsense notion is based on centuries of scientific work upholding the breakthrough made by Pythagoras and Aristotle.

What Is Sociological Theory?

Why do people commit suicide? One traditional commonsense answer is that people inherit the desire to kill themselves. Another view is that sunspots drive people to take their own lives. These explanations may not seem especially convincing to contemporary researchers, but they represent beliefs widely held as recently as 1900.

Sociologists are not particularly interested in why any one individual commits suicide; they are more concerned with the social forces that systematically cause some people to take their own lives. In order to undertake this research, sociologists develop a theory that offers a general explanation of suicidal behaviour.

We can think of theories as attempts to explain events, forces, materials, ideas, or behaviour in a comprehensive manner. Within sociology, a ***theory*** is a set of statements that seeks to explain problems, actions, or behaviour. An effective theory may have both explanatory and predictive power. That is, it can help us to see the relationships among seemingly isolated phenomena as well as to understand how one type of change in an environment leads to others.

Émile Durkheim (1951, original edition 1897) looked into suicide data in great detail and developed a highly original theory about the relationship between suicide and social factors. He was primarily concerned not with the personalities of individual suicide victims, but rather with suicide *rates* and how they varied from country to country. As a result, when he looked at the number of reported suicides in France, England, and Denmark in 1869, he also examined the populations of these nations to determine their rates of suicide. He found that whereas England had only 67 reported suicides per million inhabitants, France had 135 per million and Denmark had 277 per million. The question then became: "Why did Denmark have a comparatively high rate of reported suicides?"

Durkheim went much deeper into his investigation of suicide rates, and the result was his landmark work *Suicide,* published in 1897. Durkheim refused to automatically accept unproven explanations regarding suicide, including the beliefs that cosmic forces or inherited tendencies caused such deaths. Instead, he focused on such problems as the cohesiveness or lack of cohesiveness of religious, social, and occupational groups.

Durkheim's research suggested that suicide, while a solitary act, is related to group life. Protestants had much higher suicide rates than Catholics did; the unmarried had much higher rates than married people did; soldiers were more likely to take their lives than civilians were. In addition, it appeared that there were higher rates of suicide in times of peace than in times of war and revolution, and in times of economic instability and recession rather than in times of prosperity. Durkheim concluded that the suicide rates of a society reflected the extent to which people were or were not integrated into the group life of the society.

Émile Durkheim, like many other social scientists, developed a theory to explain how individual behaviour can be understood within a social context. He pointed out the influence of groups and societal forces on what had always been viewed as a highly personal act. Clearly, Durkheim offered a more *scientific* explanation for the causes of suicide than that of sunspots or inherited tendencies. His theory has predictive power, since it suggests that suicide rates will rise or fall in conjunction with certain social and economic changes.

Of course, a theory—even the best of theories—is not a final statement about human behaviour. Durkheim's theory of suicide is no exception; sociologists continue to examine factors that contribute to differences in suicide rates around the world and to a particular society's rate of suicide. For example, although the overall rate of suicide in New Zealand is only marginally higher than in the United States, the suicide rate among young people is 41 percent higher in New Zealand. Sociologists and psychiatrists from that country suggest that their remote, sparsely populated society maintains exaggerated standards of masculinity that are especially difficult for young males. Gay adolescents who fail to conform to their peers' preference for sports are particularly vulnerable to suicide (Shenon 1995; for a critique of Durkheim's work, see Douglas 1967).

The Development of Sociology

People have always been curious about sociological matters—such as how we get along, what we do, and whom we select as our leaders. Philosophers and religious authorities of ancient and medieval societies made countless observations about human behaviour. They did not test or verify these observations scientifically; nevertheless, these observations often became the foundation for moral codes. Several of the early social philosophers predicted that a systematic study of human behaviour would one day emerge. Beginning in the 19th century, European theorists made pioneering contributions to the development of a science of human behaviour.

Early Thinkers: Comte, Martineau, and Spencer

The 19th century was an unsettling time in France. The French monarchy had been deposed earlier in the revolution of 1789, and Napoleon had subsequently suffered defeat in his effort to conquer Europe. Amidst this chaos, philosophers considered how society might be improved. Auguste Comte (1798–1857), credited with being the most influential of these philosophers of the early 1800s, believed that a theoretical science of society and systematic investigation of behaviour were needed to improve

Harriet Martineau was an early pioneer of sociology who studied social behaviour both in her native England and in the United States.

society. He coined the term *sociology* to apply to the science of human behaviour.

Writing in the 1800s, Comte feared that the excesses of the French Revolution had permanently impaired France's stability. Yet he hoped that the study of social behaviour in a systematic way would eventually lead to more rational human interactions. In Comte's hierarchy of sciences, sociology was at the top. He called it the "queen" and its practitioners "scientist-priests." This French theorist did not simply give sociology its name; he also presented a rather ambitious challenge to the fledgling discipline.

Scholars were able to learn of Comte's works largely through translations by the English sociologist Harriet Martineau (1802–1876). But Martineau was a pathbreaker in her own right as a sociologist. She offered insightful observations of the customs and social practices of both her native Britain and the United States. Martineau's book *Society in America* (1962, original edition 1837) examines religion, politics, child rearing, and immigration in the young nation. Martineau gives special attention to social class distinctions and to such factors as gender and race.

Martineau's writings emphasized the impact that the economy, law, trade, and population could have on the social problems of contemporary society. She spoke out in favour of the rights of women, the emancipation of slaves, and religious tolerance. In Martineau's (1896) view, intellectuals and scholars should not simply offer observations of social conditions; they should act upon their convictions in a manner that will benefit society. In line with this view, Martineau conducted research on the nature of female employment and pointed to the need for further investigation of this important issue (Lengermann and Niebrugge-Brantley 1998).

Another important contributor to the discipline of sociology was Herbert Spencer (1820–1903). A relatively prosperous Victorian Englishman, Spencer (unlike Martineau) did not feel compelled to correct or improve society; instead, he merely hoped to understand it better. Drawing on Charles Darwin's study *On the Origin of Species,* Spencer applied the concept of evolution of the species to societies in order to explain how they change, or evolve, over time. Similarly, he adapted Darwin's evolutionary view of the "survival of the fittest" by arguing that it is "natural" that some people are rich while others are poor.

Spencer's approach to societal change was extremely popular in his own lifetime. Unlike Comte, Spencer suggested that societies are bound to change eventually; therefore, one need not be highly critical of present social arrangements or work actively for social change. This position appealed to many influential people in England and the United States who had a vested interest in the status quo and were suspicious of social thinkers who endorsed change.

Émile Durkheim

Émile Durkheim made many pioneering contributions to sociology, including his important theoretical work on suicide. The son of a rabbi, Durkheim (1858–1917) was educated in both France and Germany. He established an impressive academic reputation and was appointed as one of the first professors of sociology in France. Above all, Durkheim will be remembered for his insistence that behaviour must be understood within a larger social context, not just in individualistic terms.

As one example of this emphasis, Durkheim (1947, original edition 1912) developed a fundamental thesis to help understand all forms of society through intensive study of the Arunta, an Australian tribe. He focused on the functions that religion performed for the Arunta and underscored the role that group life plays in defining that which we consider religious. Durkheim concluded that, like other forms of group behaviour, religion reinforces a group's solidarity.

Another of Durkheim's main interests was the consequences of work in modern societies. In his view, the growing division of labour found in industrial societies as workers became much more specialized in their tasks led to what he called *anomie.* ***Anomie*** refers to the loss of direction that a society feels when social control of individual behaviour has become ineffective. The state of anomie occurs when people have lost their sense of purpose or direction, often during a time of profound social change. In a period of anomie, people are so confused and unable to cope with the new social environment that they may resort to taking their own lives.

Durkheim was concerned about the dangers that alienation, loneliness, and isolation might pose for modern industrial societies. He shared Comte's belief that sociology should provide direction for social change. As a result, he advocated the creation of new social groups—between the individual's family and the state—which would ideally provide a sense of belonging for members of huge, impersonal societies. Unions would be an example of such a group.

Like many other sociologists, Durkheim did not limit his interests to one aspect of social behaviour. Later in this book, we will consider his thinking on crime and punishment, religion, and the workplace. Few sociologists have had such a dramatic impact on so many different areas within the discipline.

Max Weber

Another important early theorist was Max Weber (pronounced "VAY-ber"). Born in Germany in 1864, Weber took his early academic training in legal and economic history, but he gradually developed an interest in sociology. Eventually, he became a professor at various German universities. Weber taught his students that they should employ ***Verstehen,*** the German word for "understanding" or "insight," in their intellectual work. He pointed out that we cannot analyze much of our social behaviour by the kinds of objective criteria we use to measure weight or temperature. To fully comprehend behaviour, we must learn the subjective meanings people attach to their actions—how they themselves view and explain their behaviour.

For example, suppose that a sociologist was studying the social ranking of students at a high school. Weber would expect the researcher to employ *Verstehen* to determine the significance of the school's social hierarchy for its members. The researcher might examine the effects of athleticism or grades or social skills or physical appearance in the school. He or she would seek to learn how the students relate to other students of higher or lower status. While investigating these questions, the researcher would take into account people's emotions, thoughts, beliefs, and attitudes (L. Coser 1977).

We also owe credit to Weber for a key conceptual tool: the ideal type. An ***ideal type*** is a construct, a made-up model that serves as a measuring rod against which actual cases can be evaluated. In his own works, Weber identified various characteristics of bureaucracy as an ideal type (discussed in detail in Chapter 6). In presenting this model of bureaucracy, Weber was not describing any particular business, nor was he using the term *ideal* in a way that suggested a positive evaluation. Instead, his purpose was to provide a useful standard for measuring just how bureaucratic an actual organization is (Gerth and Mills 1958). Later in this textbook, we use the concept of ideal type to study the family, religion, authority, and economic systems and to analyze bureaucracy.

Although their professional careers coincided, Émile Durkheim and Max Weber never met and probably were unaware of each other's existence, let alone ideas. This was certainly not true of the work of Karl Marx. Durkheim's thinking about the impact of the division of labour in industrial societies was related to Marx's writings, while Weber's concern for a value-free, objective sociology was a direct response to Marx's deeply held convictions. Thus, it is not surprising that Karl Marx is viewed as a major figure in the development of sociology as well as several other social sciences (see Figure 1-1).

Karl Marx

Karl Marx (1818–1883) shared with Durkheim and Weber a dual interest in abstract philosophical issues and the concrete reality of everyday life. Unlike the others, Marx was so critical of existing institutions that a conventional academic career was impossible, and although he was born and educated in Germany, he spent most of his life in exile.

Marx's personal life was a difficult struggle. When a paper that he had written was suppressed, he fled his native land for France. In Paris, he met Friedrich Engels (1820–1895), with whom he formed a lifelong friendship. They lived at a time when European and North American economic life was increasingly being dominated by the factory rather than the farm.

In 1847, Marx and Engels attended secret meetings in London of an illegal coalition of labour unions, known as the Communist League. The following year, they prepared a platform called *The Communist Manifesto,* in which they argued that the masses of people who have no resources other than their labour (whom they referred to as the *proletariat*) should unite to fight for the overthrow of capitalist societies. In the words of Marx and Engels:

> The history of all hitherto existing society is the history of class struggles. . . . The proletarians have nothing to lose but their chains. They have a world to win. WORKING MEN OF ALL COUNTRIES UNITE! (Feuer 1959:7, 41).

After completing *The Communist Manifesto,* Marx returned to Germany, only to be expelled. He then moved

FIGURE 1-1

Early Social Thinkers

	Émile Durkheim 1858–1917	**Max Weber 1864–1920**	**Karl Marx 1818–1883**
Academic training	Philosophy	Law, economics, history, philosophy	Philosophy, law
Key works	1893—*The Division of Labor in Society* 1897—*Suicide: A Study in Sociology* 1912—*Elementary Forms of Religious Life*	1904–1905—*The Protestant Ethic and the Spirit of Capitalism* 1922—*Wirtschaft und Gesellschaft*	1848—*The Communist Manifesto* 1867—*Das Kapital*

to England, where he continued to write books and essays. Marx lived there in extreme poverty. He pawned most of his possessions, and several of his children died of malnutrition and disease. Marx clearly was an outsider in British society, a fact that may well have affected his view of Western cultures.

In Marx's analysis, society was fundamentally divided between classes that clash in pursuit of their own class interests. When he examined the industrial societies of his time, such as Germany, England, and the United States, he saw the factory as the centre of conflict between the exploiters (the owners of the means of production) and the exploited (the workers). Marx viewed these relationships in systematic terms; that is, he believed that an entire system of economic, social, and political relationships maintained the power and dominance of the owners over the workers. Consequently, Marx and Engels argued that the working class needed to overthrow the existing class system. Marx's influence on contemporary thinking has been dramatic. Marx's writings inspired those who were later to lead communist revolutions in Russia, China, Cuba, Vietnam, and elsewhere.

Even apart from the political revolutions that his work fostered, Marx's influence on contemporary thinking has been dramatic. Marx emphasized the *group* identifications and associations that influence an individual's place in society. This area of study is the major focus of contemporary sociology. Throughout this textbook, we will consider how membership in a particular gender classification, age group, racial group, or economic class affects a person's attitudes and behaviour. In an important sense, we can trace this way of understanding society back to the pioneering work of Karl Marx.

Modern Developments

Sociology today builds on the firm foundation developed by Émile Durkheim, Max Weber, and Karl Marx. However, the discipline of sociology has certainly not remained stagnant over the last century. While Europeans have continued to make contributions to the discipline, sociologists from throughout the world have advanced sociological theory and research. Their new insights have helped them to better understand the workings of society.

Charles Horton Cooley (1864–1929) was typical of the sociologists who came to prominence in the early 1900s. Cooley received his graduate training in economics but later became a sociology professor at the University of Michigan. Like other early sociologists, he had become interested in this "new" discipline while pursuing a related area of study.

Cooley shared the desire of Durkheim, Weber, and Marx to learn more about society. But to do so effectively, Cooley preferred to use the sociological perspective to look first at smaller units—intimate, face-to-face groups such as families, gangs, and friendship networks. He saw these groups as the seedbeds of society in the sense that they shape people's ideals, beliefs, values, and social nature. Cooley's work increased our understanding of groups of relatively small size.

Sociologist Robert Merton (1968) made an important contribution to the discipline by successfully combining theory and research. Born in 1910 of Slavic immigrant parents in Philadelphia, Merton's teaching career has been based at Columbia University in New York.

Merton produced a theory that is one of the most frequently cited explanations of deviant behaviour. He noted different ways in which people attempt to achieve success in life. In his view, some may not share the socially agreed-upon goal of accumulating material goods or the accepted means of achieving this goal. For example, in Merton's classification scheme, "innovators" are people who accept the goal of pursuing material wealth but use illegal means to do so, including robbery, burglary, and extortion. Merton bases his explanation of crime on individual behaviour—influenced by society's approved goals and means—yet it has wider applications. It helps to account for the high crime rates among the nation's poor, who may see no hope of advancing themselves through traditional roads to success. Chapter 7 discusses Merton's theory in greater detail.

Merton also emphasized that sociology should strive to bring together the "macro-level" and "micro-level" approaches to the study of society. ***Macrosociology*** concentrates on large-scale phenomena or entire civilizations. Thus, Émile Durkheim's cross-cultural study of suicide is an example of macro-level research. More recently, macrosociologists have examined international crime rates (see Chapter 7), the stereotype of Asians as a "model minority" (see Chapter 9), and the population patterns of Islamic countries (see Chapter 14). By contrast, ***microsociology*** stresses study of small groups and often uses experimental study in laboratories. Sociological research on the microlevel has included studies of how divorced men and women, for example, disengage from significant social roles (see Chapter 5); of how conformity can influence the expression of prejudiced attitudes (see Chapter 7); and of how a teacher's expectations can affect a student's academic performance (see Chapter 12).

In Canada, the work of sociologists Harold A. Innis (1894–1952) and S.D. Clark (1910–) established a strong foundation for the examination of Canada from a political economy perspective. Innis rejected existing interpretations of Canadian society and theorized about the relationship between the extraction of products such as fish, timber, wheat, and hydroelectric power and the development of the Canadian state. Clark's body of work helped to win increasing respect for sociology as a discipline in Canada, and he is credited with establishing the Department of Sociology at the University of Toronto in 1963.

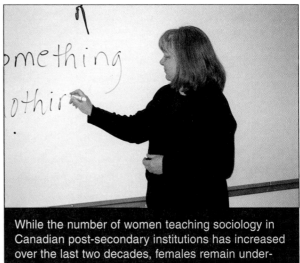

While the number of women teaching sociology in Canadian post-secondary institutions has increased over the last two decades, females remain under-represented in the profession.

Later, John Porter's *Vertical Mosaic* (1965) provided a formative examination of social inequality as it relates to race, ethnicity, social class, and gender in Canada. Porter's depiction of Canadian society as a "mosaic" continues to be used in contrast to the American metaphor of the "melting pot." (These concepts will be discussed in more detail in Chapter 3).

In 1975, Patricia Marchak contributed to the foundation of Canadian sociology through the publication of *Ideological Perspectives in Canada*. In this work, Marchak examines the way in which Canadians perceive and make sense of their social world.

Contemporary sociology reflects the diverse contributions of earlier theorists. As sociologists approach such topics as divorce, drug addiction, and religious cults, they can draw on the theoretical insights of the discipline's pioneers. A careful reader can hear Comte, Durkheim, Weber, Marx, Cooley, and many others speaking through the pages of current research. Sociology has also broadened beyond the intellectual confines of North America and Europe. Contributions to the discipline now come from sociologists studying and researching human behaviour in other parts of the world. In describing the work of today's sociologists, it is helpful to examine a number of influential theoretical approaches (also known as *perspectives*).

Major Theoretical Perspectives

Sociologists view society in different ways. Some see the world basically as a stable and ongoing entity. They are impressed with the endurance of the family, organized religion, and other social institutions. Some sociologists see society as composed of many groups in conflict, competing for scarce resources. To other sociologists, the most fascinating aspects of the social world are the everyday, routine interactions among individuals that we sometimes take for granted. Others see the world in terms of how gender is socially constructed. These four views, the ones most widely used by sociologists, are the functionalist, conflict, feminist, and interactionist perspectives. They will provide an introductory look at the discipline.

Functionalist Perspective

Think of society as a living organism in which each part of the organism contributes to its survival. This view is the ***functionalist perspective***, which emphasizes the way that parts of a society are structured to maintain its stability.

Talcott Parsons (1902–1979), a Harvard University sociologist, was a key figure in the development of functionalist theory. Parsons had been greatly influenced by the work of Émile Durkheim, Max Weber, and other European sociologists. For over four decades, Parsons dominated sociology in the United States with his advocacy of functionalism. He saw any society as a vast network of connected parts, each of which helps to maintain the system as a whole. The functionalist approach holds that if an aspect of social life does not contribute to a society's stability or survival—if it does not serve some identifiably useful function or promote value consensus among members of a society—it will not be passed on from one generation to the next.

Let's examine prostitution as an example of the functionalist perspective. Why is it that a practice so widely condemned continues to display such persistence and vitality? Functionalists suggest that prostitution satisfies needs of patrons that may not be readily met through more socially acceptable forms such as courtship or marriage. The "buyer" receives sex without any responsibility for procreation or sentimental attachment; at the same time, the "seller" makes a living through this exchange.

Such an examination leads us to conclude that prostitution does perform certain functions that society seems to need. However, this is not to suggest that prostitution is a desirable or legitimate form of social behaviour. Functionalists do not make such judgments. Rather, advocates of the functionalist perspective hope to explain how an aspect of society that is so frequently attacked can nevertheless manage to survive (K. Davis 1937).

Manifest and Latent Functions

Your college or university calendar typically states various functions of the institution. It may inform you, for example, that the university intends to "offer each student a broad education in classical and contemporary thought, in the humanities, in the sciences, and in the arts." However, it would be quite a surprise to find a calendar that declared "This university was founded in 1895 to keep people between the ages of 18 and 22 out of the job market, thus reducing unemployment." No post-secondary institution would declare that this is the purpose of post-secondary education. Yet societal institutions serve many functions, some of them quite subtle. Post-secondary education, in fact, *does* delay people's entry into the job market.

Robert Merton (1968) made an important distinction between manifest and latent functions. ***Manifest functions*** of institutions are open, stated, conscious functions. They involve the intended, recognized consequences of an aspect of society, such as the college or university's role in certifying academic competence and excellence. By contrast, ***latent functions*** are unconscious or unintended functions and may reflect hidden purposes of an institution. One latent function of colleges and universities is to hold down unemployment. Another is to serve as a meeting ground for people seeking marital partners.

Dysfunctions

Functionalists acknowledge that not all parts of a society contribute to its stability all the time. A ***dysfunction*** refers to an element or a process of society that may actually disrupt a social system or lead to a decrease in stability.

We consider many dysfunctional behaviour patterns, such as homicide, as undesirable. Yet we should not automatically interpret dysfunctions as negative. The evaluation of a dysfunction depends on one's own values or, as the saying goes, on "where you sit." For example, the official view in prisons in the United States is that inmates' gangs should be eradicated because they are dysfunctional to smooth operations. Yet some guards have actually come to view the presence of prison gangs as functional for

Canadian soldiers fill a function by providing peacekeeping in countries around the world. Two members of the Royal Canadian Regiment take a break while on patrol outside Coralici, Bosnia, in April 1999.

their jobs. The danger posed by gangs creates a "threat to security," requiring increased surveillance and more overtime work for guards (Hunt et al. 1993:400).

Conflict Perspective

In contrast to functionalists' emphasis on stability and consensus, conflict sociologists see the social world in continual struggle. The ***conflict perspective*** assumes that social behaviour is best understood in terms of conflict or tension between competing groups. Such conflict need not be violent; it can take the form of labour negotiations, gender relations, party politics, competition between religious groups for members, or disputes over the federal budget.

Throughout most of the 1900s, the functionalist perspective had the upper hand in sociology in North America. However, the conflict approach has become increasingly persuasive since the late 1960s. The rise of the feminist and gay rights movements, First Nations land claims, and confrontations at abortion clinics offered support for the conflict approach—the view that our social world is characterized by continual struggle between competing groups. Currently, the discipline of sociology accepts conflict theory as one valid way to gain insight into a society.

The Marxist View

As we saw earlier, Karl Marx viewed struggle between social classes as inevitable, given the exploitation of workers under capitalism. Expanding on Marx's work, sociologists and other social scientists have come to see conflict not merely as a class phenomenon but as a part of everyday life in all societies. Thus, in studying any culture, organization, or social group, sociologists want to know who benefits, who suffers, and who dominates at the expense of others. They are concerned with the conflicts between women and men, parents and children, and urban and rural areas, to name only a few. Conflict theorists are interested in how society's institutions—including the family, government, religion, education, and the media—may help to maintain the privileges of some groups and keep others in a subservient position. Their emphasis on social change and redistribution of resources makes conflict theorists more "radical" and "activist" than functionalists (Dahrendorf 1958).

Feminist Perspectives

Feminist perspectives attempt to explain, understand, and change the ways in which gender socially organizes our public and private lives in such a way as to produce inequality between men and women.

There are as many feminist perspectives as there are social and political philosophies; they run the gamut from liberal feminism to Marxist feminism and from anarchist feminism to eco-feminism. There is no *one* feminist perspective. Feminist perspectives have been a major contributor to contemporary sociological theory, providing frameworks within which gender inequality can be examined, understood, and changed. While these perspectives differ in terms of their views of the causes of and solutions to gender inequality, they share a common starting point—that is, they begin from the standpoint *of* women and advocate solutions *for* women (Lengermann and Niebrugge-Brantley 1996).

Despite their differences, feminist theories often share four elements (Jagger and Rothenberg 1984). They are:

1. A desire to understand how gender is part of all aspects of social life
2. A belief that gender, as well as class, race, and sexuality, is socially constructed, producing inequality in the workplace, at home, in leisure activities, and in society at large
3. A belief that gender relations are not "natural," but are products of history and culture
4. An advocacy for social change

Dorothy Smith (1926–) is a Canadian sociologist whose contributions to sociology in general and feminist sociology in particular have been influential worldwide.

In 1987, Canadian sociologist Dorothy E. Smith produced *The Everyday World as Problematic,* which has become a landmark in feminist sociology.

Smith argues for a sociology that is built on the everyday experiences of women, pointing out how sociology has previously ignored these experiences. Smith's groundbreaking work, *The Everyday World as Problematic* (1987), has been influential in helping students of sociology see the everyday world from the standpoint of women.

Margrit Eichler (1942–), also a Canadian sociologist, was among the first sociologists in this country to examine the ways in which sexism can influence research in social science (Nelson and Robinson 1999). She examined sexist language, sexist concepts, the androcentric perspective, sexist methodology, and sexist interpretation of results (Eichler 1984:20).

The work of sociologists such as Smith and Eichler addresses the long-standing exclusion of women's standpoint in sociology, as well as sexist biases in the way in which sociological research has been conducted.

Interactionist Perspective

Workers interacting on the job, encounters in public places like bus stops and parks, behaviour in small groups—these are all aspects of microsociology that catch the attention of interactionists. Whereas functionalist and conflict theorists both analyze large-scale societywide patterns of behaviour, the ***interactionist perspective*** generalizes about everyday forms of social interaction in order to understand society as a whole. In the 1990s, for example, the workings of juries became a subject of public scrutiny. High-profile trials ended in verdicts that left some people shaking their heads. Long before jury members were being interviewed on their front lawns following trials, interactionists tried to better understand behaviour in the small-group setting of a jury deliberation room.

Interactionism is a sociological framework for viewing human beings as living in a world of meaningful objects. These "objects" may include material things, actions, other people, relationships, and even symbols.

While functionalist and conflict approaches were initiated in Europe, interactionism developed first in the United States. George Herbert Mead (1863–1931) is widely regarded as the founder of the interactionist perspective. Mead taught at the University of Chicago from 1893 until his death. His sociological analysis, like that of Charles Horton Cooley, often focused on human interactions within one-to-one situations and small groups. Mead was interested in observing the most minute forms of communication—smiles, frowns, nodding of one's head—and in understanding how such individual behaviour was influenced by the larger context of a group or society. Despite his innovative views, Mead only occasionally wrote articles, and never a book. He was an extremely popular teacher, and most of his insights have come to us through edited volumes of lectures that his students published after his death.

The interactionist perspective is sometimes referred to as the *symbolic interactionist perspective,* because interactionists see symbols as an especially important part of human communication. Members of a society share the social meanings of symbols. In Canada, for example, a handshake symbolizes congeniality, while a middle-finger salute signifies disrespect. However, another culture might use different gestures to convey a feeling of congeniality or disrespect.

Consider the different ways various societies portray suicide without the use of words. People in Canada point a finger at the head (shooting); urban Japanese bring a fist against the stomach (stabbing); and the South Fore of Papua, New Guinea, clench a hand at the throat (hanging). These types of symbolic interaction are classified as forms of ***nonverbal communication,*** which can include many other gestures, facial expressions, and postures.

Since Mead's teachings have become well known, sociologists have expressed greater interest in the interactionist perspective. Many have moved away from what may have been an excessive preoccupation with the large-scale (macro) level of social behaviour and have redirected their attention toward behaviour that occurs in small groups (microlevel).

Erving Goffman (1922–1982) popularized a particular type of interactionist method known as the ***dramaturgical approach.*** The dramaturgist compares everyday life to the setting of the theatre and stage. Just as actors project certain images, all of us seek to present particular features of our personalities while we hide other qualities. Thus, in a class, we may feel the need to project a serious image; at a party, we want to look relaxed and friendly.

The Sociological Approach

Which perspective should a sociologist use in studying human behaviour? Functionalist? Conflict? Interactionist? Feminist?

Sociology makes use of all four perspectives (see Table 1-1), since each offers unique insights into the same issue. Box 1-1 shows how television might look from the functionalist, conflict, interactionist, and feminist points of view.

No one approach to a particular issue is "correct." This textbook assumes that we can gain the broadest understanding of our society by drawing on all four perspectives in the study of human behaviour and institutions. These perspectives overlap as their interests coincide but can diverge according to the dictates of each approach and of the issue being studied. A sociologist's theoretical orientation influences his or her approach to a research problem in important ways.

Table 1-1 Comparing Major Theoretical Perspectives

	Functionalist	Conflict	Interactionist	Feminist
View of society	Stable, well integrated	Characterized by tension and struggle between groups	Active in influencing and affecting everyday social interaction	Characterized by gender and inequality; causes and solutions vary
Level of analysis emphasized	Macro	Macro	Micro analysis as a way of understanding the larger macro phenomena	Both macro and micro levels of analysis
Key concepts	Manifest functions Latent functions Dysfunction	Inequality Capitalism Stratification	Symbols Nonverbal communication Face-to-face	Standpoint of women Political action Gender inequality Oppression
View of the individual	People are socialized to perform societal functions	People are shaped by power, coercion, and authority	People manipulate symbols and create their social worlds through interaction	Differs according to social class, race, ethnicity, age, sexual orientation and physical ability
View of the social order	Maintained through cooperation and consensus	Maintained through force and coercion	Maintained by shared understanding of everyday behaviour	Maintained through standpoints that do not include those of women
View of social change	Predictable, reinforcing	Change takes place all the time and may have positive consequences	Reflected in people's social positions and their communications with others	Essential in order to bring about equality
Example	Public punishments reinforce the social order	Laws reinforce the positions of those in power	People respect laws or disobey them based on their own past experience	Spousal violence, date rape, and economic inequality need to be eliminated
Proponents	Émile Durkheim Talcott Parsons Robert Merton	Karl Marx C. Wright Mills	George Herbert Mead Charles Horton Cooley Erving Goffman	Dorothy Smith Margrit Eichler

Developing the Sociological Imagination

In this book, we will be illustrating the sociological imagination in several different ways—by showing theory in practice and research in action; by speaking across race, gender, class, and national boundaries; and by highlighting social policy throughout the world.

Theory in Practice

We will illustrate how the four sociological perspectives—functionalist, conflict, interactionist, and feminist—are helpful in understanding today's issues. Sociologists do not necessarily declare "here I am using functionalism," but their research and approaches do tend to draw on one or more theoretical frameworks, as will become clear in the pages to follow.

Research in Action

Sociologists actively investigate a variety of issues and social behaviour. We have already seen that such research might involve the meaning of television programs and decision making in the jury box. Often the research has direct applications for improving people's lives, as in the case of increasing the participation of blacks in Canada and the United States in diabetes testing. Throughout the rest of the book,

Eye on the Media

1-1 Looking at Television from Four Perspectives

Television to most of us is that box sitting on the shelf or table that diverts us, occasionally entertains us, and sometimes puts us to sleep. But sociologists would look much more deeply at the medium. Here is what they would find using the four sociological perspectives.

FUNCTIONALIST VIEW

In examining any aspect of society, including television, functionalists emphasize the contribution it makes to overall social stability. Functionalists regard television as a powerful force in communicating the common values of our society and in promoting an overall feeling of unity and social solidarity:

- Television vividly presents important national and international news. On a local level, television communicates vital information on everything from storm warnings and school closings to locations of emergency shelters.
- Television programs transmit valuable learning skills (*Sesame Street*) and factual information (CBC's *The National*).
- Television "brings together" members of a community or even a nation by broadcasting important events and ceremonies (press conferences, parades, and state funerals) and through coverage of disasters such as the September 11, 2001, terrorist attacks on the United States.
- Television contributes to economic stability and prosperity by promoting and advertising services and (through shopping channels) serving as a direct marketplace for products.

CONFLICT VIEW

Conflict theorists argue that the social order is based on coercion and exploitation. They emphasize that television reflects and even exacerbates many of the divisions of our society and world, including those based on gender, race, ethnicity, and social class:

- Television is a form of big business in which profits are more important than the quality of the product (programming).
- Television's decision makers are overwhelmingly white, male, and prosperous; by contrast, television programs tend to ignore the lives and ambitions of subordinate groups, among them working-class people, visible minorities, First Nations people, gays and lesbians, people with disabilities, and older people.
- Television distorts the political process, as candidates with the most money (often backed by powerful lobbying groups) buy exposure to voters and saturate the air with attack commercials.

On a local level, television communicates vital information on everything from storm warnings and school closings to locations of emergency shelters.

- By exporting *Survivor, Baywatch*, and other programs around the world, U.S. television undermines the distinctive traditions and art forms of other societies and encourages their cultural and economic dependence on the United States.

INTERACTIONIST VIEW

In studying the social order, interactionists are especially interested in shared understandings of everyday behaviour. Consequently, interactionists examine television on the microlevel by focusing on how day-to-day social behaviour is shaped by television:

- Television literally serves as a babysitter or a "playmate" for many children for long periods of their lives.
- Friendship networks can emerge from shared viewing habits or from recollections of a cherished series from the past. Family members and friends often gather for parties centred on the broadcasting of popular events such as a Stanley Cup game, the Academy Awards, or even series like *Survivor.*
- The frequent appearance of violence in news and entertainment programming creates feelings of fear and may actually make interpersonal relations more aggressive.
- The power of television encourages political leaders and even entertainment figures to carefully manipulate symbols (through public appearances) and to attempt to convey self-serving definitions of social reality.

FEMINIST VIEWS

Feminist theorists believe that gender is constructed by society; thus, television plays a major role not only in reflecting society's ideas about gender, but also in constructing its own images:

- Television reinforces gender inequality through its portrayal of women as subordinate and powerless and men as dominant and powerful.
- Television objectifies women through its portrayal of women as objects to be admired for their physical appearance and sexual attractiveness.
- Television creates the false impression that all women are the same—young, white, middle-class, slim, and heterosexual.

Despite their differences, feminist theorists functionalists, conflict theorists, and interactionists would agree that there is much more to television than simply "entertainment." They would also agree that television and other popular forms of culture are worthy subjects for serious study by sociologists.

Let's Discuss

1. What functions does television serve? What might be some "dysfunctions"?
2. If you were a television network executive, which perspective would influence your choice of programs? Why?

Sociology in the Global Community

1-2 Women in Public Places Worldwide

By definition, a public place, such as a sidewalk or a park, is open to all persons. Even some private establishments, such as restaurants, are intended to belong to people as a whole. Yet sociologists and other social scientists have found that societies define access to these places differently for women and men.

In many Middle Eastern societies, women are prohibited from public places and are restricted to certain places in the house. In such societies, the coffeehouse and the market are considered male domains. Under Taliban rule, women in Afghanistan were not allowed to go out into public places without being accompanied by a male member of the family. When women were permitted to leave their homes, they were required to wear a burka, a garment that covers the body from head to toe, allowing vision only through a narrow mesh strip across the eyes. Some other societies, such as Malagasy, strictly limit the presence of women in "public places" yet allow women to conduct the haggling that is a part of shopping in open-air markets. In some West African societies, women actually control the marketplace. In various eastern European countries and Turkey, women appear to be free to move about in public places, but the coffeehouse remains the exclusive preserve of males. Similarly in Taiwan today, wine houses are the exclusive domains of businessmen; even female managers are unwelcome. Contrast this with coffeehouses and taverns in North America, where women and men mingle freely and even engage each other in conversation as total strangers.

While casual observers may view both private and public space in North America as gender-neutral, private all-male clubs do persist, and even in public spaces women experience some inequality. Erving Goffman, an interactionist, conducted classic studies of public spaces, which he found to be innocuous settings for routine interactions, such as "helping" encounters when a person is lost and asks for directions. But sociologist Carol Brooks Gardner has offered a feminist critique of Goffman's work: "Rarely does Goffman emphasize the habitual disproportionate fear that women can come to feel in public toward men, much less the routine trepidation that ethnic and racial minorities and the disabled can experience" (1989:45). Women are well aware that a casual helping encounter with a man in a public place can too easily lead to undesired sexual queries or advances.

Women are well aware that a casual helping encounter with a man in a public place can too easily lead to undesired sexual queries or advances.

Whereas Goffman suggests that street remarks about women occur rarely—and that they generally hold no unpleasant or threatening implications—Gardner (1989:49) counters that "for young women especially, . . . appearing in public places carries with it the constant possibility of evaluation, compliments that are not really so complimentary after all, and harsh or vulgar insults if the woman is found wanting." She adds that these remarks are sometimes accompanied by tweaks, pinches, or even blows, unmasking the latent hostility of many male-to-female street remarks.

According to Gardner, many women have a well-founded fear of the sexual harassment, assault, and rape that can occur in public places. She concludes that "public places are arenas for the enactment of inequality in everyday life for women and for many others" (1989:56).

Let's Discuss

1. How would a coffeehouse in Turkey differ from one in Vancouver, British Columbia? What might account for these differences?
2. Do you know a woman who has encountered sexual harassment in a public place? How did she react? How has her social behaviour been changed by the experience?

Sources: Cheng and Liao 1994; Gardner 1989, 1990, 1995; Goffman 1963b, 1971; Rosman and Rubel 1994; D. Spain 1992.

the research performed by sociologists and other social scientists will shed light on group behaviour of all types.

Speaking across Race, Gender, Class, and National Boundaries

Sociologists include both men and women, people from a variety of socioeconomic backgrounds (some privileged and many not), and individuals from a wealth of ethnic, national, and religious origins. In their work, sociologists seek to draw conclusions that speak to all people—not just the affluent or powerful. This is not always easy. Insights into how a corporation can increase its profits tend to attract more attention and financial support than do, say, the merits of a needle exchange program for low-income, urban residents. Yet sociology today, more than ever, seeks to better understand the experiences of *all* people. In Box 1-2, we take a look at how a woman's role in public places is defined differently from that of a man in different parts of the world.

Social Policy throughout the World

One important way we can use the sociological imagination is to enhance our understanding of current social issues throughout the world. Beginning with Chapter 2, which focuses on research, each chapter will conclude with a discussion of a contemporary social policy issue. In some cases, we will examine a specific issue facing national governments. For example, government funding of child care centres will be discussed in Chapter 4, Socialization; sexual harassment in Chapter 6, Groups and Organizations; and the search for shelters in Chapter 15, Communities and the Environment. These social policy sections will demonstrate how fundamental sociological concepts can enhance our critical thinking skills and help us to better understand current public policy debates taking place around the world.

Sociologists expect the next quarter-century to be perhaps the most exciting and critical period in the history of the discipline. This is because of a growing recognition—both in Canada and around the world—that current social problems *must* be addressed before their magnitude overwhelms human societies. We can expect sociologists to play an increasing role in the government sector by researching and developing public policy alternatives. It seems only natural for this textbook to focus on the connection between the work of sociologists and the difficult questions confronting the policymakers and people of Canada.

Chapter Resources

Summary

Sociology is the systematic study of social behaviour and human groups. In this chapter, we examine the nature of sociological theory, the founders of the discipline, theoretical perspectives of contemporary sociology, and ways to exercise the "sociological imagination."

1. An important element in the ***sociological imagination***—which is an awareness of the relationship between an individual and the wider society—is the ability to view our own society as an outsider might, rather than from the perspective of our limited experiences and cultural biases.
2. Knowledge that relies on "common sense" is not always reliable. Sociologists must test and analyze each piece of information that they use.
3. In contrast to other ***social sciences,*** sociology emphasizes the influence that groups can have on people's behaviour and attitudes and the ways in which people shape society.
4. Sociologists employ ***theories*** to examine the relationships between observations or data that may seem completely unrelated.
5. Nineteenth-century thinkers who contributed sociological insights included Auguste Comte, a French philosopher; Harriet Martineau, an English sociologist; and Herbert Spencer, an English scholar.
6. Other important figures in the development of sociology were Émile Durkheim, who pioneered work on suicide; Max Weber, who taught the need for "insight" in intellectual work; and Karl Marx, who emphasized the importance of the economy and of conflict in society.
7. In the 20th century, the discipline of sociology is indebted to sociologists such as Charles Horton Cooley, Robert Merton, Harold A. Innis, S.D. Clark, John Porter, and Patricia Marchak.
8. ***Macrosociology*** concentrates on large-scale phenomena or entire civilizations, whereas ***microsociology*** stresses study of small groups.
9. The ***functionalist perspective*** of sociology emphasizes the way that parts of a society are structured to maintain its stability. Social change should be slow and evolutionary.
10. The ***conflict perspective*** assumes that social behaviour is best understood in terms of conflict or tension between competing groups. Social change, spurred by conflict and competition, should be swift and revolutionary.
11. The ***interactionist perspective*** is primarily concerned with fundamental or everyday forms of interaction, including symbols and other types of nonverbal communication. Social change is ongoing, as individuals get shaped by society and in turn shape it.
12. ***Feminist perspectives*** are varied and diverse; however, they argue that women's inequality is constructed by our society. Feminist perspectives include both micro- and macrolevels of analysis.

13. Sociologists make use of all four perspectives, since each offers unique insights into the same issue.
14. This textbook makes use of the sociological imagination by showing theory in practice and research in action; by speaking across race, gender, class, and national boundaries; and by highlighting social policy around the world.

Critical Thinking Questions

1. What aspects of the social and work environment in a fast-food restaurant would be of particular interest to a sociologist because of his or her "sociological imagination"?
2. What are the manifest and latent functions of a health club?
3. How might the interactionist perspective be applied to a place where you have been employed or to an organization you joined?

Key Terms

Anomie The loss of direction felt in a society when social control of individual behaviour has become ineffective. (page 10)

Conflict perspective A sociological approach that assumes that social behaviour is best understood in terms of conflict or tension between competing groups. (14)

Dramaturgical approach A view of social interaction that examines people as if they were theatrical performers. (15)

Dysfunction An element or a process of society that may disrupt a social system or lead to a decrease in stability. (13)

Feminist perspectives Sociological approaches that attempt to explain, understand, and change the ways in which gender socially organizes our public and private lives in such a way as to produce inequality between men and women. (14)

Functionalist perspective A sociological approach that emphasizes the way that parts of a society are structured to maintain its stability. (13)

Ideal type A construct or model that serves as a measuring rod against which actual cases can be evaluated. (10)

Interactionist perspective A sociological approach that generalizes about fundamental or everyday forms of social interaction. (15)

Latent functions Unconscious or unintended functions; hidden purposes. (13)

Macrosociology Sociological investigation that concentrates on large-scale phenomena or entire civilizations. (12)

Manifest functions Open, stated, and conscious functions. (13)

Microsociology Sociological investigation that stresses study of small groups and often uses laboratory experimental studies. (12)

Natural science The study of the physical features of nature and the ways in which they interact and change. (6)

Nonverbal communication The sending of messages through the use of posture, facial expressions, and gestures. (15)

Science The body of knowledge obtained by methods based upon systematic observation. (6)

Social science The study of various aspects of human society. (6)

Sociological imagination An awareness of the relationship between an individual and the wider society. (5)

Sociology The systematic study of social behaviour and human groups. (5)

Theory In sociology, a set of statements that seeks to explain problems, actions, or behaviour. (8)

Verstehen The German word for "understanding" or "insight"; used to stress the need for sociologists to take into account people's emotions, thoughts, beliefs, and attitudes. (10)

Additional Readings

Glassner, Barry. 1999. *The Culture of Fear.* New York: Basic Books. Glassner looks at how people's fears of crime, drug use, and other social problems are growing, even though the social reality often does not match the public perceptions.

Levin, Jack. 1999. *Sociological Snapshots 3: Seeing Social Structure and Change in Everyday Life.* Thousand Oaks, CA: Pine Forge Press. The sociological imagination is employed to look at everything from elevator culture and television soap operas to religious cults and the death penalty.

McDonald, Lynn. 1994. *Women Founders of the Social Sciences.* Ottawa: Carlton University Press. The author examines the important but often overlooked contributions of such pioneers as Mary Wollstonecraft, Harriet Martineau, Beatrice Webb, Jane Addams, and many more.

Internet Connection

www.mcgrawhill.ca/college/schaefer

For additional Internet exercises relating to sociological theory and sociological fields of inquiry, visit the Schaefer Online Learning Centre at ***http://www.mcgrawhill.ca/college/schaefer****. Please note that while the URLs listed were current at the time of printing, these sites often change—check the Online Learning Centre for updates.*

Sociologists use four main theoretical perspectives when analyzing the social world, including events both historical and current. Log onto Yahoo!Canada (**http://www.yahoo.ca**) and choose one of the breaking stories from the "In the News" section. Follow the links given, reading articles and viewing pictures from online newspapers and networks on your chosen story. Next, apply functionalist, conflict, interactionist, and feminist perspectives to the story (Table 1-1 in your text will be especially helpful).

(a) How would Karl Marx and conflict thinkers view such an event? Is there tension and struggle between groups? Which groups?

(b) How would Émile Durkheim and functionalist thinkers examine the story? Can you apply concepts such as manifest functions, latent functions, and dysfunctions?

(c) What would be the perspective of George Herbert Mead and other interactionists? What symbols are being used to describe the story by the media? Can you apply dramaturgy to the events? Are players in the story trying to project a certain image using symbols?

(d) How might a feminist theorist interpret this event? How much significance would be placed on patriarchy in this analysis?

(e) Which perspective did you find to be the most interesting? Is one perspective better suited than the others to analyze the story? Why or why not?

CBC Video

Visit the Schaefer Online Learning Centre at **http://www.mcgrawhill.ca/college/schaefer** to view the CBC video segment "A Community in Despair: The Case of Port Hardy" and answer related questions.

Appendix CAREERS IN SOCIOLOGY

An undergraduate degree in sociology doesn't just serve as excellent preparation for future graduate work in sociology. It also provides a strong liberal arts background for entry-level positions in business, social services, foundations, community organizations, not-for-profit groups, law enforcement, and governmental jobs. Many fields—among them marketing, public relations, and broadcasting—now require investigative skills and an understanding of diverse groups found in today's multiethnic and multinational environment. Moreover, a sociology degree requires accomplishment in oral and written communication, interpersonal skills, problem solving, and critical thinking—all job-related skills that may give sociology graduates an advantage over those who pursue more technical degrees (Benner and Hitchcock 1986; Billson and Huber 1993).

Consequently, while few occupations specifically require an undergraduate degree in sociology, such academic training can be an important asset in entering a wide range of occupations. Just to bring this home, a number of chapters highlight a real-life professional who describes how the study of sociology has helped in his or her career. Look for the "Taking Sociology to Work" boxes.

The accompanying figure summarizes sources of employment for those with BA degrees in sociology. It shows that the areas of social work, counselling, social service work, clergy, probation and administrative service management offer career opportunities for sociology graduates. Undergraduates who know where their career interests lie are well advised to enroll in sociology courses and specialties best suited for those interests. For example, students hoping to become health planners would take a class in medical sociology; students seeking employment as social science research assistants would focus on courses in statistics and methods. Internships, such as placements at city planning agencies and survey research organizations, afford another way for sociology students to prepare for careers. Studies show that students who choose an internship placement have less trouble finding jobs, obtain better jobs, and enjoy greater job satisfaction than students without internship placements (Salem and Grabarek 1986).

Many post-secondary students view social work as the field most closely associated with sociology. Traditionally, social workers received their undergraduate training in sociology and allied fields such as psychology and counselling. After some practical experience, social workers would generally seek a master's degree in social work (MSW) to be considered for supervisory or administrative positions. Today, however, some students choose (where it is available) to pursue an undergraduate degree in social work (BSW). This degree prepares graduates for direct service positions such as caseworker or group worker.

Many students continue their sociological training beyond the bachelor's degree. More than 25 universities in Canada have graduate programs in sociology that offer PhD and/or master's degrees. These programs differ greatly in their areas of specialization, course requirements, costs, and research and teaching opportunities available to graduate students (Association of Universities and Colleges of Canada 2001).

Higher education is an important source of employment for sociologists with graduate degrees. About 80

Occupations for 1995 Sociology Graduates in Canada, 1997

	% of Bachelor's Degree Graduates
Psychologists, Social Workers, Counsellors, Clergy and Probation Officers	12.8
Library, Correspondence and Related Information Clerks	9.8
Administrative Service Managers	9.1
Paralegal, Social Services Workers and Occupations in Education and Religion	7.5
Security Guards and Related Occupations	5.1
Self Employed	1.4

Note: Percentages do not add up to 100 because these statistics include only bachelor's degree graduates who entered the labour force, and those not pursuing their education on a full-time basis six to nine months after graduation.

Source: Human Resources Development Canada 2000

SOCIOLOGY
GRADUATE?
OH YEAH, THAT HAS FUTURE
CEO WRITTEN ALL OVER IT.
Many people believe a sociology degree doesn't prepare you for the job market (let alone the CEO's office). The truth is more than 90% of liberal arts students start their careers within six months of graduation. But university isn't job training. It's broader. It's mind training. So a sociology grad can jump into the high-tech field of telecommunications. And, in some cases, end up running the company. Just like Carol Stephenson, President and CEO of Lucent Technologies Canada.
UNIVERSITY OF TORONTO
Faculty of Arts and Science
STEPHENSON
CAROL
UNIVERSITY OF TORONTO. GREAT MINDS FOR A GREAT FUTURE.

The skills acquired through studying sociology can be applied to a number of positions in government, business, and community organizations. University of Toronto sociology graduate Carol Stephenson became the CEO of Lucent Technologies Canada.

percent of recent PhD recipients in sociology sought employment in post-secondary institutions. These sociologists teach not only majors committed to the discipline but also students hoping to become doctors, nurses, lawyers, police officers, and so forth.

For sociology graduates interested in academic careers, the road to a PhD degree (or doctorate) can be long and difficult. This degree symbolizes competence in original research; each candidate must prepare a book-length study known as a *dissertation.* Typically, a doctoral student in sociology will engage in four to seven years of intensive work, including the time required to complete the dissertation. Yet even this effort is no guarantee of a job as a sociology professor.

The good news is that over the next 10 years, the demand for instructors is expected to increase because of high rates of retirement among faculty from the baby-boom generation, as well as the anticipated slow but steady growth in the post-secondary student population in Canada. Nonetheless, anyone who launches an academic career must be prepared for considerable uncertainty and competition in the post-secondary job market.

Of course, not all people working as sociologists teach or hold doctoral degrees. Take government, for example. Statistics Canada relies on people with sociological training to interpret data for other government departments and the general public. Virtually every department depends on survey research—a field in which sociology students can specialize—in order to assess everything from community needs to the morale of the department's own workers. In addition, people with sociological training can put their academic knowledge to effective use in corrections, health sciences, community development, and recreational services. Some people working in government or private industry have a master's degree (MA) in sociology; others have a bachelor's degree (BA).

A 1996 survey of 11 sociology departments in Canada showed that approximately 20 percent of PhD graduates use their sociological skills outside the academic world, either in government or the private sector (Davies and Denton 1996). A renewed interest in applied sociology has led to the hiring of an increasing number of sociologists with graduate degrees by businesses, industry, hospitals, and nonprofit organizations. Indeed, studies show that many sociology graduates are making career changes from social service areas to business and commerce. As an undergraduate major, sociology is excellent preparation for employment in many parts of the business world (Billson 1994).

Whether you take a few courses in sociology or actually complete a degree, you will benefit from the critical thinking skills developed in this discipline. Sociologists emphasize the value of being able to analyze, interpret, and function within a variety of working situations; this is an asset in virtually any career. Moreover, given the rapid technological change evident in the last decade and the expanding global economy, all of us will need to adapt to substantial social change, even in our own careers. Sociology provides a rich conceptual framework that can serve as a foundation for flexible career development and can assist us in taking advantage of new employment opportunities.

CHAPTER

2 SOCIOLOGICAL RESEARCH

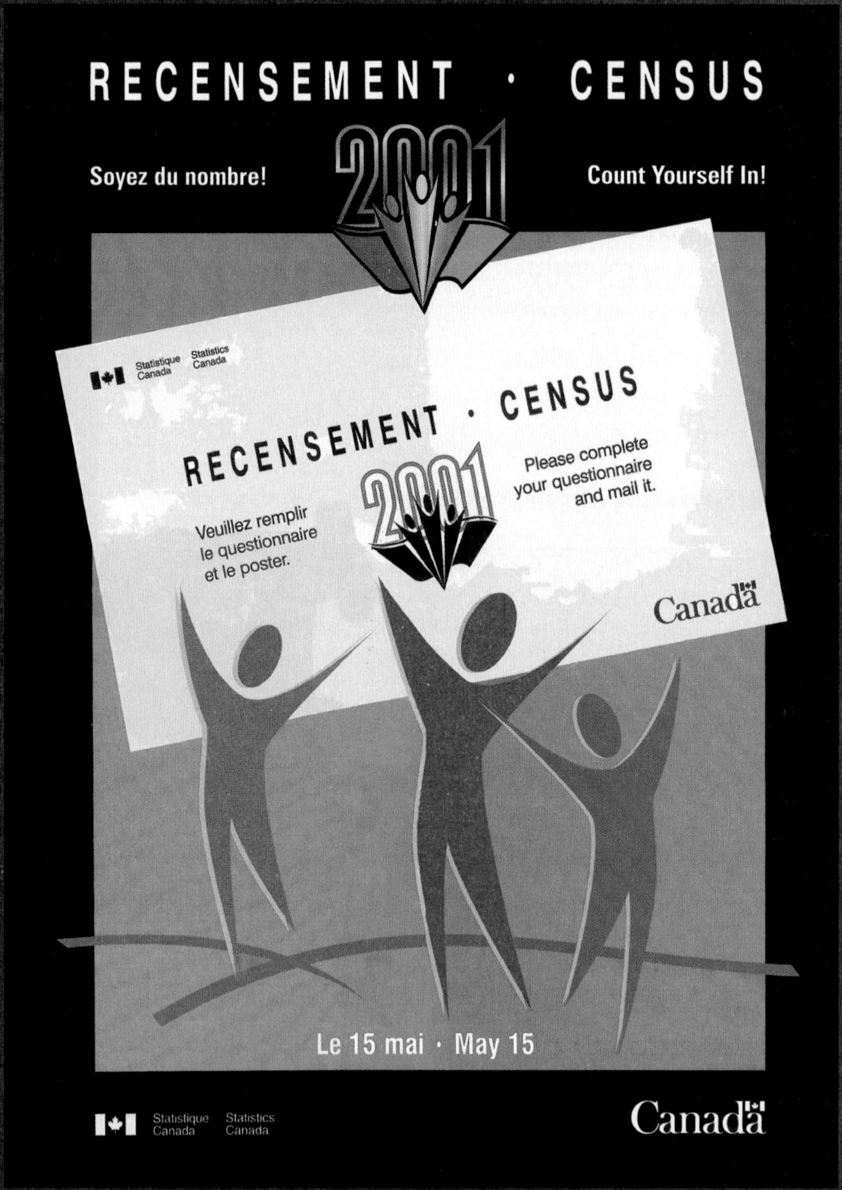

Canada's first census was carried out in 1666, when the population of the French colony was counted at just over 3000. In 1871, the initial national count was performed in accordance with an act of Parliament. Beginning in 1918, the Dominion Bureau of Statistics, later Statistics Canada, took on the task of counting the Canadian people every five years. Since then, on the '1' years (1921, 1931, etc.) a major survey has been performed, and on the '6' years (1926, 1936, etc.) a smaller scale count has been done.

The dissent we are now witnessing is a manifestation of the frustration and alienation felt by a disenfranchised and economically manipulated group. The rioting in major Western cities, the growing necessity for armed guards in violence-prone high schools where students carry weapons, the formation of violent gangs, even in small towns, high levels of un- and underemployment, epidemic levels of suicide, and mindless consumerism are all part of the same problem that leaves many young people aimlessly groping to come of age in the 1990s. . .

[T]he changing circumstances confronting young people as they grow up and try to come of age in advanced industrial societies . . . include the long wait adolescents must face between the time when they become physically mature and when they are considered to be socially mature, or "adult." The delay is characterized by economic and social marginality; sequestration into age-segregated groups, and extended financial and emotional dependence on parents. The young are also subject to manipulation and control by a variety of groups formed by adults who are out to protect their own interests.

. . . we propose that as we moved into the most recent phase of industrial capitalism, which began in the 1950s, the coming-of-age process has become even longer, primarily because the labor of adolescents and youth is no longer needed, except in service industries. Consequently, young people have lost a "franchise." Now they participate less in the labor force, and when they do, it is in a more subservient manner. Accordingly, fewer young people have the full rights and privileges of citizenship, and they must wait longer before they are fully recognized as adults. In addition to not being able to make a meaningful contribution to the economy, young people have been forced to remain in school longer, where they are under the watchful eye of massive educational bureaucracies.

. . . young people have been targeted as consumers rather than as producers by the service, leisure, information, and high-technology sectors of the advanced industrial economy. In other words, young people have increasingly been targeted as consumers of "leisure industries" (e.g., media and music) and "identity industries" (e.g., fashion and education).

. . . these leisure and identity industries have merged to create a culture in which coming of age involves allying oneself with one of these forces—for example, adopting one of the images manufactured by the leisure industries, or predicating an identity on the credentials conferred by the educational system.

. . . young people today face a situation where conflict, chaos, and confusion underlie a superficial harmony. Developing a viable adult identity has become an increasingly tenuous process for those coming of age because many of the identities they are sold by adult profiteers are illusory and fleeting. *(Côté and Allahar 1994: xiv–xvii)* ■

This excerpt comes from the book *Generation on Hold*, by Côté and Allahar. It is an attempt to examine adolescence from a variety of multidisciplinary and sociological perspectives. Even though the authors looked at adolescence from different angles, their studies have one thing in common: all of the research cited in the book was done using the scientific method outlined in this chapter.

For instance, in *Teen Trends: A Nation in Motion*, Reginald Bibby and Donald Posterski use qualitative instruments to capture the attitudes of Canadian students about violence in high schools, concluding that the phenomenon is considered to be very serious (Côté et al. 1994:141). The authors of this research gathered their data directly from the youth population using surveys.

By contrast, Lucie Norbert, in her study of underemployment among university graduates in Canada, used existing data files to conclude that 43 percent of the graduates whose employment outcomes were tracked reported being in a job that did not require a degree (Côté et al. 1994:126). This kind of archival research is a cost-effective way to produce a profile of a demographic group selected from the larger population.

For his study of the socioeconomic environment and life course of First Nations youth in Canada, David Ross (Côté et al. 1994:77) used a combination of first person interviews and archival records to conclude that these young people are marginalized to an even greater extent than are mainstream youth. Ross' examination of education outcomes shows that over three quarters of reserve First Nations persons have not finished high school. Interviews reveal that the situation is even worse for those living in the far North, where a lack of access to services and facilities leads many to crime as a way of escaping the deprivation that is so prevalent.

Sociologists and other social scientists face new and complex challenges every time they venture to confirm an hypothesis through original research. While methods are well defined under the "scientific" paradigm, the *choice* of method often involves applying a little creativity.

Effective sociological research can be quite thought-provoking. It may suggest many new questions about social interactions that require further study, such as why we make assumptions about people's intentions based merely on their gender or age or race. In some cases, rather than raising additional questions, a study will simply confirm previous beliefs and findings.

This chapter will examine the research process used in conducting sociological studies. We will first look at the steps that make up the scientific method in doing research. Then we will take a look at various techniques commonly used in sociological research, such as experiments, observations, and surveys. We will pay particular attention to the ethical challenges sociologists face in studying human behaviour and to the debate raised by Max Weber's call for "value neutrality" in social science research. We will also examine the role that technology plays in research today. The social policy section considers the difficulties in researching human sexuality.

Whatever the area of sociological inquiry and whatever the perspective of the sociologist—whether functionalist, conflict, interactionist, feminist, or any other—there is one crucial requirement: imaginative, responsible research that meets the highest scientific and ethical standards. ■

What Is the Scientific Method?

Like all of us, sociologists are interested in the central questions of our time. Is the family falling apart? Is there too much crime in Canada? Are we lagging behind in our ability to feed the world population? Such issues concern most people, whether or not they have academic training. However, unlike the typical citizen, the sociologist has a commitment to the use of the scientific method in studying society. The ***scientific method*** is a systematic, organized series of steps that ensures maximum objectivity and consistency in researching a problem.

The scientific method can be applied to either quantitative or qualitative research. ***Quantitative research*** (think "quantity") looks at data that can easily be expressed in numbers. It answers questions such as "At what age did you leave home?" or "How many times per week do you go to the mall?" ***Qualitative research*** (think "quality") looks at data that is difficult to express in numbers—for example, observations about consumer behaviour or transcripts from a focus group.

Many of us will never actually conduct scientific research. Why, then, is it important that we understand the scientific method? Because it plays a major role in the workings of our society.

The scientific method requires precise preparation in developing useful research. Otherwise, the research data collected may not prove useful. Sociologists and other researchers follow eight basic steps in the scientific method: (1) defining the problem, (2) reviewing the

FIGURE 2-1

The Scientific Method

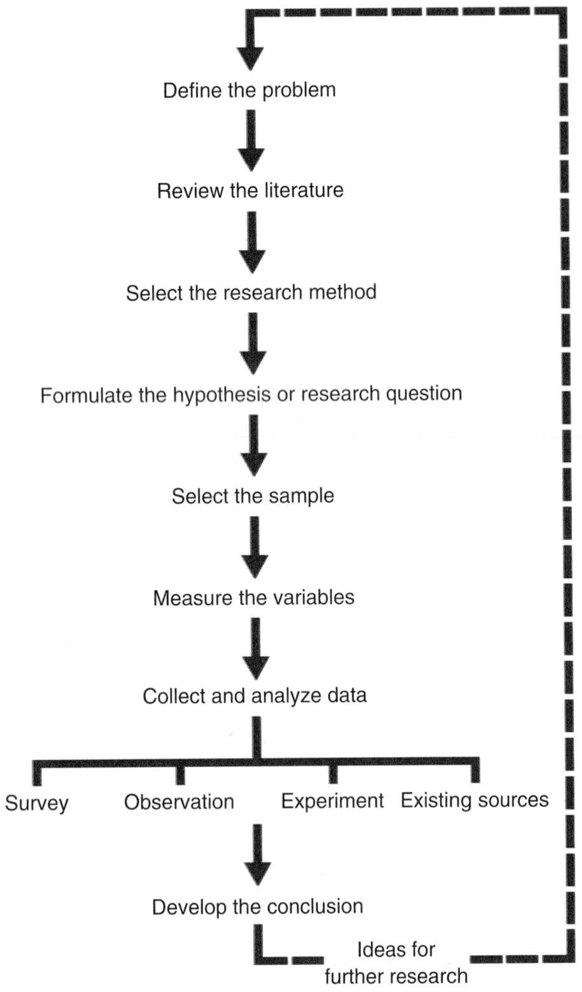

The scientific method allows sociologists to objectively and logically evaluate the facts collected. This can lead to further ideas for sociological research.

literature, (3) selecting the research method, (4) formulating the hypothesis, (5) selecting the sample, (6) measuring the variables, (7) collecting and analyzing the data, and (8) developing the conclusion (see Figure 2-1). We'll use an actual example to illustrate the workings of the scientific method.

Defining the Problem

During the latter part of the 1990s, the stereotypical image of young people desperate to escape the parental home faded somewhat from the popular imagination. During this time, there was plenty of anecdotal evidence pointing to the trend for youth to remain living at home several years longer than their parents' generation had done. Despite the pervasiveness of this anecdotal evidence, we need proper research employing the scientific method to confirm the existence of and to pinpoint the causes associated with such social change. In other words, we need to know "the facts." This is where social scientists have a role to play.

Two studies were undertaken to address this challenge. The first, by Zhao, Rajulton, and Ravanera (1995), looked at the influence of family structure, gender, and culture on the timing of children's home-leaving. The second, by Gee, Mitchell, and Wister (1995), examined the increase in co-residence between young adults and their parents. This study sought to confirm that this increase is a result of the fact that adult children stay under the parental roof longer than similar age cohorts did traditionally, and that they are more likely to return home after leaving.

The first step in any research project is to state, as clearly as possible, what you hope to investigate—that is, *define the problem.* In the examples cited above, the researchers were interested in two facets of the same issue. The Zhao study focused exclusively on the variables

As the Zhao (1995) study shows, Canadian youth leave home for a variety of reasons. Many, like the Montreal students below, move out as part of the transition from high school to university.

which influenced home-leaving, while the Gee research looked at this event in terms of its influence on a secondary life-choice—returning to the parental home.

Early on, any social science researcher must develop an operational definition of each concept being studied. An ***operational definition*** is an explanation of an abstract concept that is specific enough to allow the research team to measure the concept. While many concepts may not appear to be abstract—"happiness," or "threat," for example—they cannot be measured without using some sort of marker or indicator. If you wanted to determine someone's level of happiness, you would have to select a marker, such as smiling or laughter, to gauge its presence.

In the Gee study, the researchers wanted to examine the effects of the "child's main activity" on the probability of returning to the parental home. Activity, as a concept, is abstract, and requires an operational definition in order for the findings to have any value. For the purposes of the study, "activity" was defined as "going to school" or "going to work."

In the Zhao study, "stability in the home" was identified as one of the key variables influencing children's leaving their parental home. Since "stability" is abstract in the sense that it cannot be measured in and of itself, the researchers were required to find a concrete indicator. They did this by using marital status of the parents, adopting categories such as "Married," "Common Law," and "Single Parent," as defined by Statistics Canada in the 1990 General Social Survey.

Reviewing the Literature

By conducting a *review of the literature*—the relevant scholarly studies and information—researchers refine the problem under study, clarify possible techniques to be used in collecting data, and eliminate or reduce avoidable mistakes. The phenomenon of young adult children remaining longer in or returning to the parental home—coined "the cluttered nest" (Zhao 1995:122)—is a relatively new one, but there is no lack of relevant research. Prior to the 1960s, the age at which children left the home had fallen continuously since the beginning of the 20th century. The dramatic shift in this trend has made the study of intergenerational living a burgeoning area of research.

Both the Zhao and the Gee studies required a review of this existing research. They would have read the studies that have been done throughout North America (Boyd and Pryor 1989; Boyd and Norris 1994; Glick and Lin, 1986; Grigsby and McGowan 1986) and in Europe (Aquilino 1990). Zhao et al. relied on research done in a number of areas to inform their study: Cherlin (1992) is cited for examining the effect of cohabitation on individualism, and Kiernan (1992) offered the authors insight into the relationship between step-parents and a child's decision to leave home.

Selecting the Research Method

Once you have defined the problem and reviewed the literature, the next step is to decide which data-gathering format to use. There are four methods: archival research, survey research, observation, and experiment. While these will be discussed in more detail later in the chapter, the following brief explanations provide an introduction to the basic idea behind each method.

Archival research involves the use of—not surprisingly—archives, the most common of which are libraries. This method of research involves looking at existing data and/or studies with an eye to reinterpreting them from a fresh angle, or viewing them as part of the big picture with other studies of the same research problem.

Experiment, the measure of cause and effect in a controlled environment, is seldom used in sociology because of the difficulties in reproducing realistic social conditions in a laboratory.

Observation is the recording of events and impressions in a real-life social situation. Observation can be used in either quantitative or qualitative studies. For instance, researchers looking into youth consumerism might record the number of bags each adolescent has as he or she leaves the mall. This would be a quantitative study. Or, the research team might record their impressions of youths' satisfaction in a store: Do they look happy as they leave? This type of study would be qualitative.

Survey research is the gathering of data by directly questioning members of the population being studied. Survey research is the most commonly used methodology in social research primarily because it enables the collection of large amounts of data while minimizing cost. While most surveys are designed to collect quantitative information, open-ended questions—those that ask an opinion—can be used to examine qualitative issues.

In recent years, social research has increasingly used a combination of surveys and observation to gather more comprehensive data. Focus groups are a good example of this method. In these settings, group facilitators guide the discussion with specific questions to which they record the answers. At the same time, they can be making notes about the qualitative aspects of the process, like body language and tone of voice.

Formulating the Hypothesis or Research Question

After reviewing earlier research, drawing on the contributions of sociological theorists, and selecting a methodology, researchers now need to formulate the focus of their project. This is done either by setting a *research question*, in the case of a qualitative study, or by *creating a hypothesis*, in the case of a quantitative study. Finding the answer to the research question is the goal of the qualitative study. Whereas qualitative research begins with a question, quantitative research begins with an answer, the hypothesis. A ***hypothesis*** is a speculative statement about the relationship between two or more factors known as *variables.* Income, religion, occupation, and gender can all serve as variables in a study. We can define a ***variable*** as a measurable trait or characteristic that is subject to change under different conditions.

Researchers who formulate a hypothesis generally must suggest how one aspect of human behaviour influences or affects another. The variable hypothesized to cause or influence another is called the ***independent variable.*** The second variable is termed the ***dependent variable*** because its action "depends" on the influence of the independent variable.

FIGURE 2-2

Causal Logic

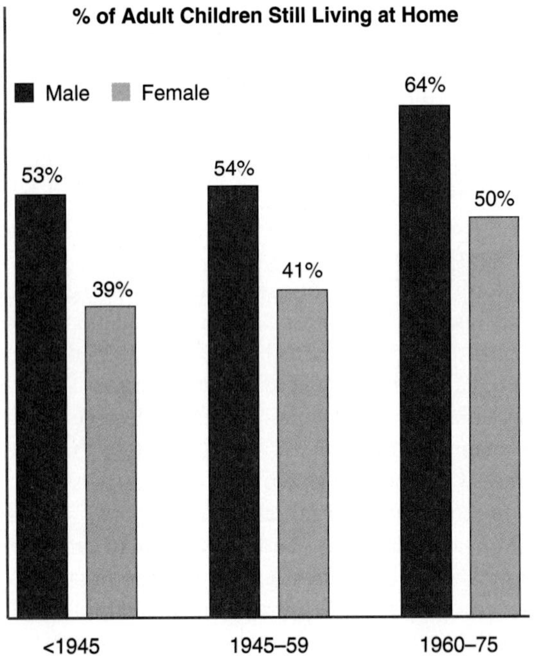

In *causal logic* an independent variable (often designated by the symbol *x*) influences a dependent variable (generally designated as *y*); thus, *x* leads to *y*. For example, in the graph above, gender is the independent variable (*x*) and "probability of still living at home" is the dependent variable (*y*). Notice that the first two pairs of variables are taken from studies already described in this textbook.

Source: Gee et al. 1995.

Zhao hypothesized that the timing of children's home-leaving (the dependent variable) would be influenced by the number of children in the family, whether the parents were the child's natural or step-parents, and by the ethnic affiliation of the household (all independent variables). Specifically, it was suggested that children with more than two siblings would leave home earlier than others, that stepfamilies result in earlier home-leaving, and that children whose parents are immigrants, especially non-European, are likely to take up separate residence at a younger age.

The Gee study focused on the phenomenon of young adult children returning to live in the parental home. The researchers developed a number of hypotheses, including that higher parental socioeconomic status (independent variable) would influence the likelihood of children returning home, and that the marital status (independent variable) would affect the child's decision whether or not to return to the parental home (dependent variable). Gee determined that homes where the parents' socioeconomic status was higher were less often "cluttered nests." Also, as intuition would suggest, children who have spouses of their own are not as inclined to return home.

Identifying independent and dependent variables—in this case, what causes home-leaving—is a critical step in clarifying cause-and-effect relationships in society. As shown in Figure 2-2, ***causal logic***, or *causality*, involves the relationship between a condition or variable and a particular consequence, with one event leading to the other. To claim a causal relationship between two variables, three criteria must be met (Lazarsfeld 1959):

1. The independent variable must be present before the dependent variable.
2. There must be empirical evidence of a cause-and-effect link between the variables.
3. The cause-and-effect link cannot be explained by a third factor.

Consider, for example, the September 11, 2001, attacks on the Pentagon and the World Trade Center. To support their claim that Osama bin Laden (the independent variable) caused the disasters (the dependent variable), the Americans had to meet Lazarfeld's criteria: that bin Laden had contact with the terrorists prior to September 11; that bin Laden had motivation and means for such an act; and that the contact between the al-Qaeda leader and the terrorists could not be reasonably attributed to another factor.

A ***correlation*** exists when a change in one variable coincides with a change in the other. Correlations are an indication that causality *may* be present; they do not necessarily indicate causation. Sociologists seek to identify the *causal* link between variables; this causal link is generally advanced by researchers in their hypotheses.

Whether it is the census or any other type of research, sampling methods have a direct impact on the accuracy of the results.

Selecting the Sample

In most studies, social scientists must carefully select what is known as a *sample.* A ***representative sample*** is a selection from a larger population that is statistically typical of that population. There are many kinds of samples, but the one social scientists most frequently use is the random sample. In a ***random sample,*** every member of an entire population being studied has the same chance of being selected. Thus, if researchers want to examine the opinions of people listed in a city directory (a book that, unlike the telephone directory, lists all households), they might call every 10th or 50th or 100th name listed. This would constitute a random sample. The advantage of using specialized sampling techniques is that sociologists do not need to question everyone in a population.

Sampling is a complex aspect of research design. In Box 2-1, we consider the approach some researchers took when trying to create an appropriate sample of people in the world's most populous nation—China. We'll also see how they made use of data from the sample.

Measuring the Variables

There are four types of measures used in sociology: nominal, ordinal, interval, and ratio. A *nominal* measure is one that only identifies membership in a category. For instance, a young person is either of driving age or not. An *ordinal* measure is one that allows for the various states of the variable to be ranked but not necessarily compared. For instance, classifying Driver A as having driven longer than Driver B indicates that A has more experience than B, but not how much. It could be one month or 20 years.

An *interval* measure is used when there are predictable intervals between the various states of the variable, allowing them to be compared. In a study of young drivers, this could be the number of months they have been driving, enabling the researcher to say that A has been at the wheel six months longer than B. Just a slight change in the sample, from "young drivers" to "adolescents," would transform the interval measurement into a *ratio* measure—one that allows for precise comparisons, and in which there is a zero value. For instance, if two drivers have 15 and 5 years behind the wheel, respectively, then the first driver has three times the experience of the second. Also, some adolescents will not have their driver's licence yet, and so will have no driving experience.

Analyzing the Data

Once data have been gathered, they need to be interpreted. Sociologists use many complex interpretive tools in assessing the meaning of their data. Only a few of the most basic measures are presented below.

One way to determine the significance of data is to calculate proportions. The fact that 400 survey respondents left their parents' home at the age of 14 does not tell us very much. The raw numbers must be analyzed for meaning. If we know that the sample size is 500, though, the "400" might tell us something significant about the population being studied—80 percent left home at an early age. If the sample is 50 000, however, we know that 400 is too small a proportion (0.8 percent of the total) to be meaningful.

Finding the *measure of central tendency* is another way to determine the significance of data. There are three of these measures—mean, median, and mode. The *mean* is the average. In our example, this would be the average

Sociology in the Global Community 2-1 "Sent-down" in China

Imagine arriving at school and learning that the entire college was being closed and that, in fact, the government was closing *all* universities. Furthermore, since there was no school for you to attend, you were now being taken to the countryside to work on farms so the country could increase agricultural production.

This is basically what happened to students in China from 1967 to 1978, a period historians refer to as the Cultural Revolution, when China was trying to rid itself of outside influences. During this time, 17 million young urban people—about a third of the youth entering the labour force—were the victims of the government's "send-down" policy. They were forced to live and work in rural areas rather than attend school or work at government jobs they may have held.

Sociologists Xueguang Zhou and Liren Hou of Duke University were interested in what impact these state policies had on the people's lives. To learn more, the researchers decided to interview those who were "sent-down" as well as comparable people who were not sent to rural areas. They did their representative sampling in several stages: first selecting cities from different geographical areas, then systematically selecting blocks within those cities, and finally randomly selecting and interviewing adults within the blocks. They accumulated a sample of 2793 people, of whom 855 had been sent-down.

17 million young urban people were the victims of the government's "send-down" policy.

Zhou and Hou found that those who stayed in rural areas more than six years were likely to marry later, have fewer children, and hold poorer jobs than those who spent less time or those who stayed in urban areas. While these differences may be expected, some findings were surprising. For example, those who were sent-down for only a few years were more likely to graduate from college than those young people who were never sent-down. The researchers argue that many of the youths who left "early" from rural areas were well-connected politically and therefore probably came from more prosperous backgrounds. Also, these young people may have resolved to quickly overcome the adverse effects of the state policy.

Let's Discuss

1. How did the researchers make sure their sample was representative? Do you think selecting names from a phone book would produce the same results? How would you go about selecting a sample population?
2. Describe the independent and dependent variables in this study. (Refer to page 30 if you need to.)

Source: Zhou and Hou 1999.

age at which the respondents left their parental home. The *median* is the number at which 50 percent of respondents fall below and 50 percent above. In the Zhao study, analysis showed that the median age at which men left home in 1945 was 21.25. This indicates that half of all men moved out of their parental home by the time they were this age. The *mode* is the most frequent answer to a question. More men left the parental home at this age than any other.

When the research question is as straightforward as "At what age did you leave home?" answers inevitably come out as numbers: "I left home at 18." This is *quantitative data*—data that is numerical and self-explanatory; "18" needs no interpretation. Often, however, questions elicit responses that are not so clear-cut. This is referred to as *qualitative data*, which requires interpretation. A young woman who says she left home because her parents were too strict simply gives us an opinion. There is no right or wrong answer, and the one she has provided can only inform the research if we understand what "strict" means. The answer needs to be interpreted within the context of the study.

Ensuring Validity and Reliability

The scientific method requires that research results be both valid and reliable. ***Validity*** refers to the degree to which a measure or scale truly reflects the phenomenon under study. For Zhao, a valid measure of the reasons why young adults leave home depended on gathering accurate data. One of the considerations for this study was settling on a specific definition of "leaving home." The researchers had to decide if a temporary absence such as living away for school or a summer job represented departure. To deal with this problem, the Zhao team was careful to look only at those children who had left home permanently.

Reliability refers to consistency of results. In a research project, reliability is achieved if a particular measure repeatedly provides substantially similar findings. For example, to be reliable, the question, "Why did you return home?" would have to produce the same findings for the Gee research team each time it was asked of a different sample group for the same population.

Developing the Conclusion

Scientific studies, including those conducted by sociologists, do not aim to answer all the questions that can be raised about a particular subject. Therefore, the conclusion of a research study represents both an end and a beginning. It terminates a specific phase of the investigation, but it should also generate ideas for future study. Both Zhao and Gee recognize a need for ongoing research in their areas.

Supporting Hypotheses

Sociological studies do not always generate data that support the original hypothesis. In many instances, a hypothesis is refuted, and researchers must reformulate their conclusions. Unexpected results may also lead sociologists to reexamine their methodology and make changes in the research design.

Using the existing literature, Zhao was able to identify several independent variables influencing the age of home-leaving for young adults. For instance, the Zhao team hypothesized that children living in homes where the parental relationship was cohabitational, rather than formalized through marriage, would leave home earlier. The same outcome was predicted for single-parent families—that children would strike out on their own at a younger age. The team also hypothesized that the presence of a stepfamily would encourage early exit from the parental nest. As to the effects of ethnicity, Zhao et al. were looking for confirmation that the parents' cultural affiliation is a critical causal factor in home-leaving. It was hypothesized that children coming from homes where the cultural norms emphasized strong familial relations, such as those in Asia and Eastern Europe, would remain living with their parents for a longer period.

However, while Zhao's hypotheses were supported, it is important to recognize that evidence refuting one or more of these would have been just as valuable. For instance, if the research team had discovered that stability in the parental home had no effect on leaving, this would be an important finding.

Controlling for Other Factors

A ***control variable*** is a factor held constant to test the relative impact of the independent variable. For example, if researchers wanted to know how adults feel about restrictions on smoking in public places, they would probably attempt to use a respondent's smoking behaviour as a control variable. That is, how do smokers versus nonsmokers feel about smoking in public places? Consequently, the researchers would compile separate statistics on how smokers and nonsmokers feel about antismoking regulations.

In Summary: The Scientific Method

Let us briefly summarize the process of the scientific method through a review of the example. Both Zhao and Gee *defined the problem,* identifying the issue to be focused on—either home-leaving or return to the parental home. They *reviewed the literature,* examining what other researchers had already done in the area of interest, which helped them *formulate hypotheses* about the connection between various environmental factors and children leaving the parental home. They *selected a research method,* choosing a format for data collection, and *selected a sample* identifying their population and method of respondent selection. Finally, they *collected and analyzed the data,* using statistics to extract the meaning from the raw numbers.

Major Research Designs

Because the selection of a methodology is so critical to the success of a piece of research, it is important to understand this aspect of the scientific process more fully. For this reason, the following section expands on the brief definitions of the various types of research design provided earlier. p. 29

Surveys

Almost all of us have responded to surveys of one kind or another. We may have been asked what kind of detergent we use, which political candidate we intend to vote for, or what our favourite television program is. A ***survey*** is a study, generally in the form of an interview or questionnaire, that provides sociologists with information concerning how people think and act. Among Canada's best-known surveys of opinion are the Ipsos-Reid and Decima polls. As anyone who watches the news during political campaigns knows, polls have become a staple of political life.

When you think of surveys, you may recall seeing many "person on the street" interviews on local television news shows. While such interviews can be highly entertaining, they are not necessarily an accurate indication of public opinion. First, they reflect the opinions of only those people who happen to be at a certain location. Such a sample can be biased in favour of commuters, middle-class shoppers, or factory workers, depending on which street or area the newspeople select. Second, television interviews tend to attract outgoing people who are willing to appear on the air, while they frighten away others who

Research in Action 2-2 Framing Survey Questions for Marginal Populations

The most difficult populations to study are those which exist at the margins of society. Groups as disparate as the elderly and street youth share a common social status: they operate outside the mainstream.

Both groups, as you might expect, are suspicious of the world around them. The elderly fear exploitation and being physically or financially harmed. Street youth, most of whom, research has shown, come from dysfunctional backgrounds, fear those in positions of authority. This creates challenges for the researcher, particularly in the area of communication.

For instance, when creating a questionnaire for seniors, one of the basic rules is not to ask direct questions about financial status. Nothing will put an elderly respondent on his or her guard more quickly than to ask, "How much money do you have in the bank?" But what do you do in these circumstances if it is critical to your study to determine socioeconomic status?

One strategy is to ask questions that will indirectly give you the information you need. In this instance, you might be able to ask the respondents what make and model of car they own, or whether they own their own home. Questions like these will provide a solid indication of their financial situation.

In approaching the street youth population, the research team is not only faced with skepticism, but also with a language barrier created by the jargon of the street. If you were to ask a street youth whether his or her mother was living, the question might be misconstrued, either deliberately or unin-

One strategy is to ask questions that will indirectly give you the information you need.

tentionally. Young people who live on the street frequently adopt street parents to replace those they have left behind, an understandable practice when you consider that the majority of them come from abusive home environments. Here the question would have to include the phrase "birth mother" to be clear.

In building questions for a survey, the researcher must take into account the characteristics of the population to be studied. Not all questions mean the same thing to all people.

Students in sociology classes often find hands-on exercises, such as practising interview skills, enhance technical descriptions of the process.

Let's Discuss

1. Think of a marginal population other than street youth or seniors. How do they qualify as "marginal"?
2. What difficulty might you encounter in creating questions to ask this group?
3. Compose a question that overcomes this difficulty.

may feel intimidated by a camera. As we've seen, a survey must be based on precise, representative sampling if it is to genuinely reflect a broad range of the population.

In preparing to conduct a survey, sociologists must not only develop representative samples; they must exercise great care in the wording of questions. An effective survey question must be simple and clear enough for people to understand it. It must also be specific enough so that there are no problems in interpreting the results. Even questions that are less structured ("What do you think of programming on educational television?") must be carefully phrased to solicit the type of information desired. Box 2-2 illustrates some of the challenges researchers face in phrasing survey questions for marginal populations. Surveys can be indispensable sources of information, but only if the sampling is done properly and the questions are worded accurately.

There are two main forms of surveys: the ***interview*** and the ***questionnaire.*** Each of these has its own advantages. An interviewer can obtain a high response rate because people find it more difficult to turn down a personal request for an interview than to throw away a written questionnaire. In addition, a skillful interviewer can go beyond written questions and "probe" for a subject's underlying feelings and reasons. On the other hand, questionnaires have the advantage of being cheaper, especially when large samples are used.

Studies have shown that characteristics of the interviewer have an impact on survey data. To get around this problem, Canadian sociologists Richard Floyd and Stephen

Dooley (Floyd and Dooley 1998) developed the Target Inclusion Model (TIM). Researchers using the TIM recruit members of the target population as part of the research team, both during the development of the survey and in the field as interviewers. Being interviewed by their peers puts street youth, for example, at ease during the data-gathering process.

Observation

Investigators who collect information through direct participation and/or observation of a group, tribe, or community under study are engaged in ***observation***. This method allows sociologists to examine certain behaviours and communities that could not be investigated through other research techniques.

As we mentioned earlier, observation research is the most common form of *qualitative research,* relying on what is seen in field or naturalistic settings more than on statistical data. Generally, such studies focus on small groups or communities rather than large groups or whole nations. An increasingly popular form of qualitative research in sociology today is ethnography. ***Ethnography*** refers to efforts to describe an entire social setting through extended, systematic observation. William Whyte's study, described below, involved understanding behaviour of not just the people on one street corner, but all facets of life in an urban neighbourhood. Anthropologists rely heavily on ethnography. Much as an anthropologist seeks to understand the people of some Polynesian island, the sociologist as an ethnographer seeks to understand and present to us an entire way of life in some setting.

Quantitative research collects and reports data primarily in numerical form. Most of the survey research discussed so far in this book has been this type of research. While quantitative research can make use of larger samples than qualitative research, it can't look at a topic in the same depth. Neither type of research is necessarily better; indeed we are usually best informed when we rely on studies using a variety of research designs that look at both qualitative and quantitative aspects of the same subject.

In some cases, the sociologist actually "joins" a group for a period of time to get an accurate sense of how it operates. This is called *participant observation.*

During the late 1930s, in the classic example of participant-observation research we referred to a moment ago, William F. Whyte moved into a low-income Italian neighbourhood in Boston. For nearly four years, he was a member of the social circle of "corner boys" that he describes in *Street Corner Society.* Whyte revealed his identity to these men and joined in their conversations, bowling, and other leisure-time activities. His goal was to gain greater insight into the community that these men had established. As Whyte (1981:303) listened to Doc, the leader of the group, he "learned the answers to questions I would not even have had the sense to ask if I had been getting my information solely on an interviewing basis." Whyte's work was especially valuable, since, at the time, the academic world had little direct knowledge of the poor and tended to rely for information on the records of social service agencies, hospitals, and courts (Adler and Johnson 1992).

The initial challenge that Whyte faced—and that every participant observer encounters—was to gain acceptance into an unfamiliar group. It is no simple matter for a university-trained sociologist to win the trust of a religious cult, a youth gang, a poor rural community, or a First Nations group. It requires a great deal of patience and an accepting, nonthreatening type of person.

Observation research poses other complex challenges for the investigator. Sociologists must be able to fully understand what they are observing. In a sense, then, researchers such as William F. Whyte must learn to see the world as the group sees it in order to fully comprehend the events taking place around them.

This African city in the Ivory Coast provides a rich setting for observation research. An ethnographer would take note of the interaction of Western and African cultures in the everyday life.

This raises a delicate issue. If the research is to be successful, the observer cannot allow the close associations or even friendships that inevitably develop to influence the subjects' behaviour or the conclusions of the study. Anson Shupe and David Bromley (1980), two sociologists who have used participant observation, have likened this challenge to that of "walking a tightrope." Even while working hard to gain acceptance from the group being studied, the participant observer *must* maintain some degree of detachment.

Managers may rely on observation research to improve working conditions or productivity. For example, when Norway's shipping industry was faced with severe cutbacks, a team of researchers worked aboard a merchant ship as part of an effort to improve the social organization and efficiency of Norway's fleet. Similarly, when faced with growing competition in the photocopying industry, Xerox Corporation employed a research team to propose cost-cutting measures to managers and union leaders. In each case, the methodology of participant observation proved useful in solving practical problems (W. Whyte 1989).

Experiments

When sociologists want to study a possible cause-and-effect relationship, they may conduct experiments. An ***experiment*** is an artificially created situation that allows the researcher to manipulate variables.

In the classic method of conducting an experiment, two groups of people are selected and matched for similar characteristics such as age or education. The researchers then assign the subjects to one of two groups—the experimental or the control group. The ***experimental group*** is exposed to an independent variable; the ***control group*** is not. Thus, if scientists were testing a new type of antibiotic drug, they would administer that drug to an experimental group but not to a control group.

Sociologists don't often rely on this classic form of experiment because it generally involves manipulating human behaviour in an inappropriate manner, especially in a laboratory setting. However, there are sociologists whose area of research falls into the social psychological domain, and they may use experiments as a means of research. Canadian sociologist Martha Foschi has conducted a series of experiments over the past 30 years, focusing on diffuse status characteristics (those characteristics that provide status across situations, e.g., age, gender, ethnicity, etc.) and expectation states (the expectations, created by status characteristics, that someone brings to a social interaction).

In one such experiment, subjects are paired with someone of the opposite gender, and their willingness to accept influence from that other person is measured. In this experiment, the subjects perform a task that they are told will test their visual perception by having them gauge the amount of white on a slide containing black and white blocks. The subjects perform this task once, and are given information about their performance. Then, they are asked to do a second set of evaluations using the same sensory skill, only this time they are given access to second opinions. After making their initial determination of whether the slide has more black or white, they are shown the other individual's choice, and asked if they want to change their selection.

The experiment looks at how often subjects change their mind when the other person is a woman compared to how often they change it when the other person is a man. The findings indicate that people are more willing to be influenced by someone who is male than someone who is female. Over the course of many years, Dr. Foschi's experiments have provided valuable information about the interplay of status characteristics and influence.

How do people respond to being observed? Evidently these employees at the Hawthorne plant enjoyed the attention paid them when researchers observed them at work. No matter what variables were changed, the workers increased their productivity every time, including when the level of lighting was *reduced.*

In some experiments, as in observation research, the presence of a social scientist or other observer may affect the behaviour of people being studied. The recognition of this phenomenon grew out of an experiment conducted during the 1920s and 1930s at the Hawthorne plant of the Western Electric Company. A group of researchers set out to determine how to improve the productivity of workers at the plant. The investigators manipulated such variables as the lighting and working hours to see what impact changes in them had on productivity. To their surprise, they found that *every* step they took seemed to increase productivity. Even measures that seemed likely to have the opposite effect, such as reducing the amount of lighting in the plant, led to higher productivity.

Why did the plant's employees work harder even under less favourable conditions? Their behaviour apparently was influenced by the greater attention being paid to them in the course of the research and by the novelty of being subjects in an experiment. Since that time, sociologists have used the term ***Hawthorne effect*** to refer to subjects of research who deviate from their typical behaviour because they realize that they are under observation (S. Jones 1992; Lang 1992; Pelton 1994).

Archival Research

Sociologists do not necessarily have to collect new data in order to conduct research and test hypotheses. The term ***secondary analysis*** refers to a variety of research techniques that make use of publicly accessible information and data. In the case study of the effect of family type on children leaving home, the researchers made use of existing data. Generally, in conducting secondary analysis, researchers utilize data in ways unintended by the initial collectors of information. For example, census data are compiled for specific uses by the government but are valuable for marketing specialists in locating everything from bicycle stores to nursing homes.

Sociologists consider secondary analysis to be *nonreactive,* since it does not influence people's behaviour. As an example, Émile Durkheim's statistical analysis of suicide neither increased nor decreased human self-destruction. Subjects of an experiment or observation research are often aware that they are being watched—an awareness that can influence their behaviour—but this is not the case with secondary analysis. Researchers, then, can avoid the Hawthorne effect by using secondary analysis.

There is one inherent problem, however: the researcher who relies on data collected by someone else may not find exactly what is needed. Social scientists studying family violence can use statistics from police and social service agencies on *reported* cases of spouse abuse and child abuse. Yet such government bodies have no precise data on *all* cases of abuse.

Table 2-1 Existing Sources Used in Sociological Research

Most Frequently Used Sources
Statistics Canada
Crime statistics
Birth, death, marriage, and divorce statistics
Other Sources
Newspapers and periodicals
Personal journals, diaries, e-mail, and letters
Records and archival material of religious organizations, corporations, and other organizations
Transcripts of radio programs
Videotapes of motion pictures and television programs
Webpages
Song lyrics
Scientific records (such as patent applications)
Speeches of public figures (such as politicians)
Votes cast in elections or by elected officials on specific legislative proposals
Attendance records for public events
Videotapes of social protests and rallies
Literature, including folklore

Many social scientists find it useful to study cultural, economic, and political documents, including newspapers, periodicals, radio and television tapes, the Internet, scripts, diaries, songs, folklore, and legal papers, to name some examples (see Table 2-1). In examining these sources, researchers employ a technique known as ***content analysis,*** which is the systematic coding and objective recording of data, guided by some rationale.

Using content analysis, Erving Goffman conducted a pioneering exploration of how advertisements in 1979 portrayed women as inferior to men. Women typically were shown being subordinate to or dependent on others or being instructed by men. They used caressing and touching gestures more than men. Even when presented in leadership-type roles, women were likely to be shown in seductive poses or gazing out into space. Similarly, researchers today are analyzing films to look at the increase in smoking in motion pictures, despite increased public health concerns. This type of content analysis can have clear social policy implications if it draws the attention of the motion picture industry to the message it may be delivering (especially to young people) that smoking is acceptable, even desirable. For example, a 1999 content analysis found that tobacco use appeared in 89 percent of the 200 most popular movie rentals in the United States (Goffman 1979; Kang 1997; and Roberts et al. 1999).

These examples underscore the value of using existing sources in studying contemporary material. Researchers have learned, in addition, that such analysis can be essential in helping us to understand social behaviour from the distant past. For example, sociologist Karen Barkey (1991) examined village court records from the 17th-century Ottoman Empire (centred in modern-day Turkey) to assess the extent of peasant rebellions against the empire and, more specifically, its tax policies. Barkey could hardly have relied on surveys, observations, or experiments to study the Ottoman Empire; like other scholars studying earlier civilizations, she turned to secondary analysis.

Ethics of Research

A biochemist cannot inject a serum into a human being unless the serum has been thoroughly tested and the subject agrees to the shot. To do otherwise would be both unethical and illegal. Sociologists must also abide by certain specific standards in conducting research—a ***code of ethics.*** The professional society of the discipline, the Canadian Sociology and Anthropology Association (CSAA), published a code of ethics in 1994. Below is a short excerpt from the CSAA's *Statement of Professional Ethics*. The complete statement is available online at **http://alcor.concordia.ca/~csaa1/eng/englcode.htm**.

Organizing and initiating research

1. Codes of professional ethics arise from the need to protect vulnerable or subordinate populations from harm incurred, knowingly or unknowingly, by the intervention of researchers into their lives and cultures. Sociologists and anthropologists have a responsibility to respect the rights, and be concerned with the welfare, of all the vulnerable and subordinate populations affected by their work. . .

Protecting people in the research environment

9. Researchers must respect the rights of citizens to privacy, confidentiality and anonymity, and not to be studied. Researchers should make every effort to determine whether those providing information wish to remain anonymous or to receive recognition and then respect their wishes. . .

Informed consent

12. Researchers must not expose respondents to risk of personal harm. Informed consent must be obtained when the risks of research are greater than the risks of everyday life. . .

Covert research and deception

17. Subjects should not be deceived if there is any reasonably anticipated risk to the subjects or if the harm cannot be offset or the extent of the harm be reasonably predicted.

On the surface, these and the rest of the basic principles of the CSAA's *Statement of Professional Ethics* probably seem clear-cut. How could they lead to any disagreement or controversy? However, many delicate ethical questions cannot be resolved simply by reading the *Statement*. For example, should a sociologist engaged in participant-observation research *always* protect the confidentiality of subjects? What if the subjects are members of a religious cult allegedly engaged in unethical and possibly illegal activities? What if the sociologist is interviewing political activists and is questioned by police about his or her research?

Most sociological research uses *people* as sources of information—as respondents to survey questions, subjects of observation, or participants in experiments. In all cases, sociologists need to be certain that they are not invading the privacy of their subjects. Generally, this is handled by assuring those involved of anonymity and by guaranteeing that personal information disclosed will remain confidential. However, a study by William Zellner raised important questions about the extent to which sociologists can threaten people's right to privacy.

Accident or Suicide?

An ethical issue—with the right to know posed against the right to privacy—became apparent in research on automobile accidents in which fatalities occur. Sociologist William Zellner (1978) wanted to learn if fatal car crashes are sometimes suicides that have been disguised as accidents in order to protect family and friends (and perhaps to collect otherwise unredeemable insurance benefits). These acts of "autocide" are by nature covert.

In his efforts to assess the frequency of such suicides, Zellner sought to interview the friends, coworkers, and family members of the deceased. He hoped to obtain information that would allow him to ascertain whether the deaths were accidental or purposeful. Zellner told the people approached for interviews that his goal was to con-

Are some people who die in single-occupant car crashes actually suicides? One sociological study of possible "autocides" concluded that at least 12 percent of such accident victims have in fact committed suicide. But the study also raised some ethical questions concerning the right to know and the right to privacy.

tribute to a reduction of future accidents by learning about the emotional characteristics of accident victims. He made no mention of his suspicions of autocide, out of fear that potential respondents would refuse to meet with him.

Zellner eventually concluded that at least 12 percent of all fatal single-occupant crashes are suicides. This information could be valuable for society, particularly since some of the probable suicides actually killed or critically injured innocent bystanders in the process of taking their own lives. Yet the ethical questions still must be faced. Was Zellner's research unethical because he misrepresented the motives of his study and failed to obtain his subjects' informed consent? Or was his deception justified by the social value of his findings?

The answers to these questions are not immediately apparent. Zellner appeared to have admirable motives and took great care in protecting confidentiality. He did not reveal names of suspected suicides to insurance companies, though Zellner did recommend that the insurance industry drop double indemnity (payment of twice the person's life insurance benefits in the event of accidental death) in the future.

Zellner's study raised an additional ethical issue: the possibility of harm to those who were interviewed. Subjects were asked if the deceased had "talked about suicide" and if they had spoken of how "bad or useless" they were. Could these questions have led people to guess the true intentions of the researcher? Perhaps, but according to Zellner, none of the informants voiced such suspicions. More seriously, might the study have caused the bereaved to *suspect* suicide—when before the survey they had accepted the deaths as accidental? Again, there is no evidence to suggest this, but we cannot be sure.

Given our uncertainty about this last question, was the research justified? Was Zellner taking too big a risk in asking the friends and families if the deceased victims had spoken of suicide before their death? Does the right to know outweigh the right to privacy in this type of situation? And who has the right to make such a judgment? In practice, as in Zellner's study, it is the *researcher,* not the subjects of inquiry, who makes the critical ethical decisions. Therefore, sociologists and other investigators bear the responsibility for establishing clear and sensitive boundaries for ethical scientific investigation.

Preserving Confidentiality

Like journalists, sociologists occasionally find themselves subject to questions from law enforcement authorities or to legal threats because of knowledge they have gained in conducting research and maintaining confidentiality. This situation raises profound ethical questions.

In 1994, Russel Ogden was a graduate student at Simon Fraser University (SFU). In his research, Ogden conducted interviews with people involved in assisted suicide or euthanasia among persons with AIDS. A newspaper report about the study came to the attention of the Vancouver coroner, who was already holding an inquest into the death of an "unknown female." Ogden's thesis reported that two research participants had knowledge about her death. The coroner subpoenaed Ogden to identify his sources, but he cited a promise of "absolute confidentiality" and refused to name them. This promise had been authorized by SFU's Research Ethics Board.

The coroner initially found Ogden to be in contempt of court but later accepted a common law argument that the communications between Ogden and his participants were privileged. In doing so, the coroner released Ogden from "any stain or suggestion of contempt." Ogden's battle in coroner's court was fought without the support of his university. He sued SFU, unsuccessfully, to recover his legal costs. However, the judge condemned SFU for failing to protect academic freedom and urged the university to remedy the situation. SFU's president responded with a written apology to Ogden, compensation for legal costs and lost wages, and a guarantee that the university would assist "any researchers who find themselves in the position of having to challenge a subpoena" (Lowman and Palys 2000).

This case points to the delicate balance researchers and sponsoring institutions must maintain among the value of research, the confidentiality of the subjects, and the threat of litigation.

Neutrality and Politics in Research

The ethical considerations of sociologists lie not only in the methods they use but also in the way they interpret results. Max Weber (1949, original edition 1904) recognized that personal values would influence the questions that sociologists select for research. In his view, that was perfectly acceptable, but under no conditions could a researcher allow his or her personal feelings to influence the *interpretation* of data. In Weber's phrase, sociologists must practise ***value neutrality*** in their research.

As part of this neutrality, investigators have an ethical obligation to accept research findings even when the data run counter to their own personal views, to theoretically based explanations, or to widely accepted beliefs. For example, Émile Durkheim challenged popular conceptions when he reported that social (rather than supernatural) forces were an important factor in suicide.

p. 8

Some sociologists believe that it is impossible for scholars to prevent their personal values from influencing their work. If that is true, then Weber's insistence on value-free sociology may lead the public to accept sociological conclusions without exploring the biases of the researchers. Furthermore, drawing on the conflict perspective, Alvin Gouldner (1970), among others, has suggested that sociologists may use objectivity as a sacred justification for remaining uncritical of existing institutions and centres of power. These arguments are attacks not so much on Weber himself as on how his goals have been incorrectly interpreted. As we have seen, Weber was quite clear that sociologists may bring values to their subject matter. In his view, however, they must not confuse their own values with the social reality under study (Bendix 1968).

Let's consider what might happen when researchers bring their own biases to the investigation. A person investigating the impact of intercollegiate sports on alumni contributions, for example, may focus only on the highly visible, revenue-generating sports of football and basketball and neglect the so-called "minor sports" such as tennis or soccer that are more likely to involve women athletes. Despite the early work of Dorothy Smith and others, sociologists still need to be reminded that the discipline often fails to adequately consider *all* people's social behaviour.

One of the frequent criticisms levelled against all of the social sciences, but at sociology in particular because of its cultural focus, is that the concepts and theories are not broadly representative. The charge of ***Eurocentrism*** refers to the fact that the sociological knowledge base has essentially been built to reflect the European standards of its authors.

Sociology has also been accused of ***androcentrism***, a tendency to represent the world from a male perspective. Recently, feminist sociologist Shulamit Reinharz (1992) has argued that sociological research should not only be inclusive but should also be open to bringing about social change and drawing on relevant research by non-sociologists. Reinharz maintains that research should always analyze whether women's unequal social status has affected the study in any way.

To avoid Eurocentrism in the study of children leaving home, which we have been using as an example throughout this chapter, one might broaden it to include a cross-cultural perspective. It is possible that, due to tradition, young people growing up in first-generation, immigrant homes in Canada may leave home much later than others in their age cohort. The issue of value neutrality does not mean you can't have opinions, but it does mean you must work to overcome any biases, however unintentional, that you may bring to the research.

These homeless youth in a Toronto tent city represent one of the most difficult populations for researchers to access. The lack of a permanent address hinders most sampling procedures.

Even the most experienced researchers, however, face situations in which their professional resolve is put to the test. In the study of street youth mentioned earlier in this chapter, the field research team encountered tragedy, literally, on every street corner.

One case involved a girl whom the team met on their first night of doing interviews. The 14-year-old had arrived in the large Canadian city only hours earlier, and was already high. Concerned about her vulnerability in this situation, researchers questioned their police liaison officer about possible interventions. The experienced officer told them that there was nothing he could legally do, despite his belief that the girl was now caught in a subculture that would inevitably result in her rapid deterioration. Confirming the researchers' worst fears, the officer was brutal in his assessment of the girl's prospects, suggesting that she would probably be quickly caught up in the drug and sex trade.

The patrolman's insight was borne out in the subsequent months of the study. Encountering the girl time and again, the research team watched as she went from being a typical (though stoned) teenager on that first night, to a hardened, street-wise, and battered shell of her former self when the data-gathering ended just three months later.

The dilemma for the researchers was to fight their instincts to be "good Samaritans" and help the girl. The debriefings after that first night and many subsequent nights included discussions of options, which ranged from having one of the researchers take her home, to finding her a job, to pressuring the government to step in, to going to the media with the story. The consensus was that *something* had to be done. Yet in the end, nothing was. The team concluded, to their professional credit, that if neutrality was to be maintained they could not attempt to assist the girl.

There are two good reasons for their decision. First, and perhaps most important, there is always the potential that intervention by outsiders would put the girl's well-being at risk by marginalizing her within her own social network. Street youth are very distrustful of those who do not belong to their group. Second, if word of the team's intervention had spread among the street youth population, there may have been negative consequences for the validity of the project sample.

Technology and Sociological Research

Advances in technology have affected all aspects of life, and sociological research is no exception. The increased speed and capacity of computers have enabled sociologists to handle much larger sets of data. In the recent past, only people with large grants or major institutional support could easily work with census data. Now anyone with a desktop computer and modem can access information to learn more about social behaviour. Moreover, data from foreign countries concerning crime statistics and health care are just as available as information from our own country.

Researchers usually rely on computers to deal with quantitative data—that is, numerical measures—but electronic technology is also assisting us with qualitative data, such as information obtained in observation research. Numerous software programs such as *Ethnograph* and *NUD*IST* allow the researcher not only to record his or her observations, like a word-processing program, but also to identify common behavioural patterns or similar concerns expressed in interviews. For example, after observing students in a college cafeteria over several weeks and putting your observations into the computer, you could then group all your observations related to certain variables, such as "sorority" or "study group."

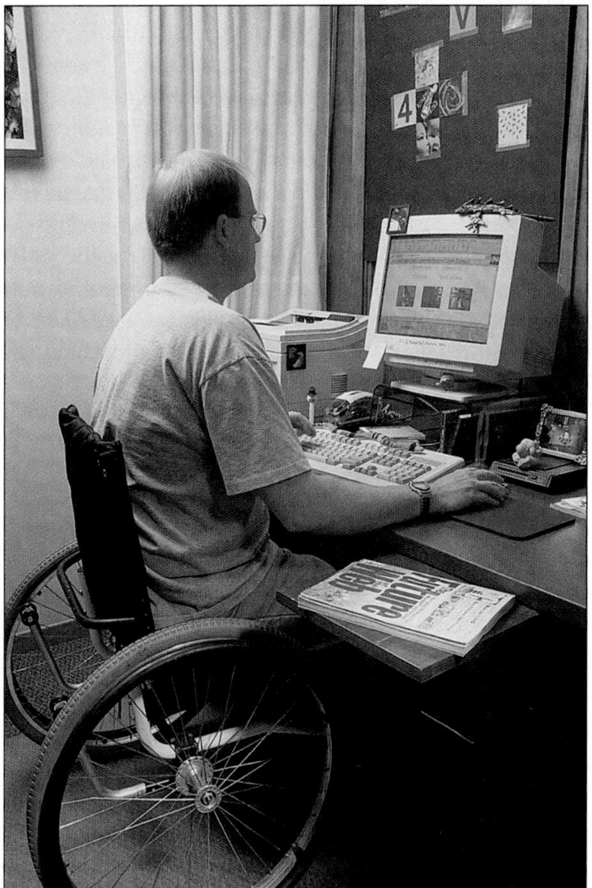

Computers have tremendously extended the range and capability of sociological research, from allowing large amounts of data to be stored and analyzed to facilitating communication with other researchers via websites, newsgroups, and e-mail.

Taking Sociology to Work

MARYLEE STEPHENSON: Founder and President, CS/RESORS Consulting

Marylee Stephenson holds ultimate responsibility for the organization, management, and quality of all work undertaken in her socioeconomic research company, CS/RESORS Consulting. Stephenson manages the company, collaborating with senior associates in Ottawa, Montreal, and Vancouver, as well as with those research associates who are brought onto the team for projects in other parts of Canada.

Stephenson brings a strong academic background to her research work. Her education includes an MA in sociology from the University of Essex in the United Kingdom, and a PhD from the University of British Columbia. She has five years' experience as Senior Research Officer and then Director of Research with the Canadian Advisory Council on the Status of Women, in Ottawa. It was the latter experience that developed her skills in planning and managing projects that are national in scope.

Among the substantive areas that CS/RESORS Consulting addresses, those in which Stephenson specializes are justice issues, especially as they relate to vulnerable groups, women's issues, employment issues, and tourism and recreation. From a methodological standpoint, she is particularly well versed in the use of qualitative methodologies.

Stephenson has written several books, including the only visitor's guide to all of the national parks of Canada, and a guidebook to the Galapagos Islands. She also was the editor of the first interdisciplinary textbook in women's studies in Canada.

This combination of academic, governmental, and private sector experience gives Stephenson a very broad background in social policy issues. She has a clear understanding of the research and policy environment within which government agencies, non-governmental organizations, and the private sector operate. Her extensive experience in project management is a key to CS/RESORS Consulting's ability to complete the highest quality work within the time and budgetary framework allotted.

Interestingly, Stephenson has recently developed a distinctive application of her combined analytical and presentational skills—as a very busy stand-up comic. She delivers comedy and commentary at conferences and workshops, and in clubs and cafés across Canada (see www.sociocomic.com).

Let's Discuss

1. Identify a non-profit organization that might benefit from Stephenson's expertise, and explain how sociological research would help that group.
2. How might Stephenson's sociology background come into play in her study of environmental issues?

Source: Based on Stephenson 2000. See also http://www.csresors.com and www.sociocomic.com.

The Internet affords an excellent opportunity to communicate with fellow researchers as well as to locate useful information on social issues posted on websites. It would be impossible to calculate all the sociological postings on Internet mailing lists or World Wide Web sites. Of course, you need to apply the same critical scrutiny to Internet material that you would use on any printed resource.

How useful is the Internet for conducting survey research? That's unclear as yet. It is relatively easy to send out or post on an electronic bulletin board a questionnaire and solicit responses. It is an inexpensive way to reach large numbers of potential respondents and get a quick return of responses. However, there are some obvious dilemmas. How do you protect a respondent's anonymity? Second, how do you define the potential audience? Even if you know to whom you sent the questionnaire, the respondents may forward it on to others.

While web-based surveys are still in their early stages, the initial results are promising. For example, InterSurvey has created a pool of Internet respondents, initially selected by telephone to be a diverse and representative sample. Using similar methods to locate 50 000 adult respondents in 33 nations, the National Geographic Society conducted an online survey that focused on migration and regional culture. Social scientists are closely monitoring these new approaches to gauge how they might revolutionize one type of research design (W. Bainbridge 1999; R. Morin 2000).

SOCIAL POLICY AND SOCIOLOGICAL RESEARCH

Studying Human Sexuality

The Issue

Historically, the subject of human sexuality has been viewed as a private issue in Canadian society. It was a topic to be discussed awkwardly by parents and their children, or in hushed tones among friends. But as Canadian culture in particular and the social standards of Western societies in general have undergone a transformation in recent decades, the formerly taboo topic has become public fare. Sex education is a regular part of high-school education, with topics such as birth control being discussed in the classroom. In the media, television has established new, and previously unimaginable boundaries. *Sex and the City* has weekly plot lines focusing on the sexual attitudes and exploits of its young female characters. *Seinfeld*, during its successful run as one of television's most popular shows, frequently explored the sex lives of Jerry and his friends.

You can find similar plots in dozens of TV shows today. Human sexuality is a topic of drama and comedy as well as life. Certainly, it is an important aspect of human behaviour. As we will see, however, it is a difficult topic to research because of all the preconceptions, myths, and beliefs we bring to the topic of sexuality. Yet, in this age of devastating sexually transmitted diseases, there is no better time to increase our scientific understanding of human sexuality.

The Setting

We have few reliable national data on patterns of sexual behaviour. Until recently, the only comprehensive study of sexual behaviour was the famous two-volume Kinsey Report prepared in the 1940s (Kinsey et al. 1948, 1953). While the Kinsey Report is still widely quoted, the volunteers interviewed for the report were not representative of the adult population. Since then, social scientific studies of sexual behaviour have typically been rather limited in scope but still useful.

In part, we have few reliable data on patterns of sexual behaviour because it is difficult for researchers to obtain accurate information about this sensitive subject. Moreover, until AIDS emerged in the 1980s, there was little scientific demand for data on sexual behaviour, except in specific areas such as contraception. Finally, even though the AIDS crisis has reached dramatic proportions (as will be discussed in the social policy section of Chapter 5), government funding for studies of sexual behaviour is controversial. Ironically, perhaps, given Canadians' history of dwelling in the shadow of their more flamboyant neighbours to the south, the government in Ottawa has never been as reluctant about funding research on sexual issues as has Washington. A good example of such government-funded research is found in the General Social Survey data in Figure 2-3.

Sociological Insights

The controversy surrounding research on human sexual behaviour raises the issue of value neutrality. And this becomes especially delicate when one considers the relationship of sociology to the government. The government

Research into sexual behaviour in Canada is complicated by the sensitivity of the subject.

FIGURE 2-3

Women Whose First Conjugal Union Was Common-Law Were Nearly Twice as Likely to Separate

	Age in 1995			
	60–69	50–59	40–49	30–39
	Born in			
Proportion of women separating if	1926–1935	1936–1945	1946–1955	1956–1965
Married first	25	30	36	33
Common-law first (including those separated after marrying their partner)	—	77	60	63

— Sample too small to produce reliable estimate.
Source: Statistics Canada 2000e.

has become the major source of funding for sociological research. Yet Max Weber urged that sociology remain an autonomous discipline and not become unduly influenced by any one segment of society. According to his ideal of value neutrality, sociologists must remain free to reveal information that is embarrassing to government or, for that matter, is supportive of government institutions. Thus, researchers investigating a prison riot must be ready to examine objectively not only the behaviour of inmates but also the conduct of prison officials before and during the outbreak.

Conflict theorists and feminists, among others, are critical of some research that claims to be objective. In turn, their research is occasionally criticized for not sufficiently addressing Weber's concern for value neutrality. In any case, maintaining objectivity may be difficult if sociologists fear that findings critical of government or business institutions will jeopardize their chances of obtaining support for new research projects.

The issue of bias associated with research funding is approached differently by the Canadian Sociology and Anthropology Association (in its *Statement of Professional Ethics*) from the way it is handled by the American Sociological Association. American researchers are required to reveal funding sources. The American code of ethics, however, does not address whether a sociologist who accepts funding from a particular agency may also accept its perspective on what needs to be studied.

The Canadian code focuses more on the implications of funding affiliations. The Canadian Sociology and Anthropology Association's *Statement of Professional Ethics* says:

> Researchers must guard against the uncritical promotion of research, which in design, execution, or results, furthers the power of states, corporations, churches, or other institutions, over the lives and cultures of research subjects. . . .

and

> Researchers should be sensitive to the possible exploitation of individuals and groups. . . .

The Canadian code warns that it is inappropriate for studies to be designed to fit marketing plans or the agenda of some government agency. The implications for research on human sexuality are significant.

Lewis Coser (1956:27) has argued that as sociologists in the United States have increasingly turned from basic sociological research to applied research for government agencies and the private sector, "they have relinquished to a large extent the freedom to choose their own problems, substituting the problems of their clients for those which might have interested them on purely theoretical grounds." Viewed in this light, the importance of government and corporate funding for sociological studies raises troubling questions for those who cherish Weber's ideal of value neutrality in research. As we'll see in the next section, applied sociological research on human sexuality has run into barriers.

Policy Initiatives

Research on sexual behaviours and/or attitudes toward sex have always been met with some skepticism by funding agencies. Governments, perhaps concerned about political fallout, have resisted proposals that address issues in this area. This has been particularly true in the United States. While Canada's reputation as a more conservative society would seem to suggest that the government in Ottawa would be less willing than that in Washington to sponsor studies of sexuality, the reverse appears to be the case.

The federal government, through its socioeconomic research arm, Statistics Canada, has funded a number of studies of Canadians' sexual activities, including a recent examination of these behaviours in young people and an ongoing series of reports on the age at which Canadians first experience intercourse.

This openness can be taken as an indication of the ability of funding agencies in Canada to remain objective when determining the value of a research proposal. This neutrality provides scientists, particularly social scientists such as sociologists, with the ability to examine trends and phenomena in Canadian society without being constrained by a political agenda.

It is quite a different story in the United States, where researchers have been forced to rely on private, corporate funding for projects such as the one undertaken by sociologists Laumann, Gagnon, Michaels, and Michael, described below. Whether such an alliance could be formed in Canada without contravening the CSAA's standards, which warn against research resulting in the increased power of corporations, is open to debate. In 1991, the United States Senate voted 66–34 to forbid funding any survey on adult sexual practices.

Despite the vote, sociologists Edward Laumann, John Gagnon, Stuart Michaels, and Robert Michael developed the National Health and Social Life Survey (NHSLS) to better understand the sexual practices of adults in the United States. The researchers raised US$1.6 million of *private* funding to make their study possible.

The researchers made great efforts to ensure privacy during the NHSLS interviews, as well as confidentiality of responses and security in maintaining data files. Perhaps because of this careful effort, the interviewers did not typically experience problems even though they were asking people about their sexual behaviour. All interviews were conducted in person, although there was also a confidential form that included questions about such sensitive subjects as family income and masturbation. The researchers used several techniques to test the accuracy of subjects' responses, such as asking redundant questions at different times in different ways during the 90-minute interview. These careful procedures helped establish the validity of the NHSLS findings.

Let's Discuss

1. Why is human sexuality a difficult subject to research? Would you feel comfortable answering questions about your own sex life?
2. How does value neutrality become an important issue in research sponsored by the government?
3. If you were to conduct a survey in your community of people who engage in premarital sex, how would you set it up?

Chapter Resources

Summary

Sociologists are committed to the use of the scientific method in their research efforts. In this chapter, we examine the basic principles of the scientific method and study various techniques used by sociologists in conducting research.

1. There are eight basic steps in the ***scientific method***: defining the problem, reviewing the literature, selecting the research method, formulating the hypothesis or research question, selecting the sample, measuring the variables, analyzing the data, and developing the conclusion.
2. Whenever researchers wish to study abstract concepts, such as intelligence or prejudice, they must develop workable ***operational definitions***.
3. A ***hypothesis*** usually states a possible relationship between two or more variables.
4. By using sampling techniques, sociologists avoid having to test everyone in a population.

5. According to the scientific method, research results must possess both ***validity*** and ***reliability.***
6. The two principal forms of ***survey*** research are the ***interview*** and the ***questionnaire.***
7. ***Observation*** allows sociologists to study certain behaviours and communities that cannot be investigated through other research methods.
8. When sociologists wish to study a cause-and-effect relationship, they may conduct an ***experiment.***
9. Sociologists also make use of archives as in ***secondary analysis*** and ***content analysis.***
10. The Canadian Sociology and Anthropology Association's *Statement of Professional Ethics* calls for objectivity and integrity in research, respect for the subject's privacy, and confidentiality.
11. Max Weber urged sociologists to practise ***value neutrality*** in their research by ensuring that their personal feelings do not influence the interpretation of data.
12. Technology today plays an important role in sociological research, whether it be a computer database or information from the Internet.
13. The increased involvement of corporations in funding university-based research has made it more difficult to maintain objectivity.

Critical Thinking Questions

1. Suppose that your sociology instructor has asked you to do a study of homelessness. Which research technique (survey, observation, experiment, existing sources) would you find most useful? How would you use that technique to complete your assignment?
2. How can a sociologist genuinely maintain value neutrality while studying a group that he or she finds repugnant (for example, a white supremacist organization, a satanic cult, or a group of prison inmates convicted of rape)?
3. Why is it important for sociologists to have a code of ethics?

Key Terms

Androcentrism A world view that favours the male perspective. (page 40)

Causal logic The relationship between a condition or variable and a particular consequence, with one event leading to the other. (30)

Code of ethics The standards of acceptable behaviour developed by and for members of a profession. (38)

Content analysis The systematic coding and objective recording of data, guided by some rationale. (37)

Control group Subjects in an experiment who are not introduced to the independent variable by the researcher. (36)

Control variable A factor held constant to test the relative impact of an independent variable. (33)

Correlation A relationship between two variables whereby a change in one coincides with a change in the other. (30)

Dependent variable The variable in a causal relationship that is subject to the influence of another variable. (30)

Ethnography The study of an entire social setting through extended systematic observation. (35)

Eurocentrism A world view that assumes European values are the desired standard. (40)

Experiment An artificially created situation that allows the researcher to manipulate variables and introduce control variables. (36)

Experimental group Subjects in an experiment who are exposed to an independent variable introduced by a researcher. (36)

Hawthorne effect The unintended influence that observers or experiments can have on their subjects. (37)

Hypothesis A speculative statement about the relationship between two or more variables. (30)

Independent variable The variable in a causal relationship that, when altered, causes or influences a change in a second variable. (30)

Interview A face-to-face or telephone questioning of a respondent to obtain desired information. (34)

Observation A research technique in which an investigator collects information through direct involvement with and observation of a group, tribe, or community. (35)

Operational definition An explanation of an abstract concept that is specific enough to allow a researcher to measure the concept. (29)

Qualitative research Research that relies on what is seen in field or naturalistic settings more than on statistical data. (27)

Quantitative research Research that collects and reports data primarily in numerical form. (27)

Questionnaire A research instrument employed to obtain desired information from a respondent. (34)

Random sample A sample for which every member of the entire population has the same chance of being selected. (31)

Reliability The extent to which a measure provides consistent results. (32)

Representative sample A selection from a larger population that is statistically typical of that population. (31)

Scientific method A systematic, organized series of steps that ensures maximum objectivity and consistency in researching a problem. (27)

Secondary analysis A variety of research techniques that make use of publicly accessible information and data. (37)

Survey A study, generally in the form of interviews or questionnaires, that provides sociologists and other researchers with information concerning how people think and act. (33)

Validity The degree to which a scale or measure truly reflects the phenomenon under study. (32)

Value neutrality Objectivity of sociologists in the interpretation of data. (40)

Variable A measurable trait or characteristic that is subject to change under different conditions. (30)

Additional Readings

Canadian Sociology and Anthropology Association. *Canadian Review of Sociology and Anthropology*. Montreal: CSAA. Since its inception in 1964, the *Review* has provided peer-reviewed articles and critiques on topics of sociology and anthropology. This journal provides an excellent scholarly source for research about social issues in Canada.

Denzin, Norman K., and Yvonna S. Lincoln, eds. 2000. *Handbook of Qualitative Research*. 2d ed. Thousand Oaks, CA: Sage. The 40 articles in this anthology cover newer techniques used in conducting observation and biographical research, as well as ethical issues facing researchers.

Ericksen, Julia A. 1999. *Kiss and Tell: Surveying Sex in the Twentieth Century*. Cambridge, MA: Harvard University Press. Evaluates the methodology of the hundreds of surveys of human sexuality conducted by sociologists and other social scientists.

Internet Connection

www.mcgrawhill.ca/college/schaefer

For additional Internet exercises relating to content analysis and codes of ethics, visit the Schaefer Online Learning Centre at **http://www.mcgrawhill.ca/college/schaefer**. *Please note that while the URLs listed were current at the time of printing, these sites often change—check the Online Learning Centre for updates.*

A variety of web sites offer compilations of Canadian research sources available on the Internet. One of the best can be found at **http://www.canadiansocialresearch.net**. This site provides access to hundreds of data sources including those from both government and non-government organizations, as well as the corporate world. By looking for answers to the following questions on any particular site you find linked there, you can gain a working familiarity with the site's potential. All of the following information can be found through the site's links.

(a) Find the official site for your home province. Which ministry is responsible for post-secondary education?

(b) What programs assist disabled persons in Manitoba to achieve independent living?

(c) Find an electronic meeting place designed specifically to meet the needs of Aboriginal youth. How is this site being used? What issues are being raised by the contributors?

(d) The Canadian Council on Social Development claims that the 2001 Federal budget fell short of achieving its goal to "help Canadians through difficult times." What argument is presented to support that claim?

(e) See if your community has an official website. Does it have information about social programs?

(f) What is the mandate of the International Council of Canadian Studies?

CHAPTER 3

CULTURE

One of many comic book stalls that line the streets near a railroad station in Bombay, India. At first glance, the comic books may look different from those in North America, but closer inspection reveals some common themes—adventure, romance, beauty, and crime.

Nacirema culture is characterized by a highly developed market economy which has evolved in a rich natural habitat. While much of the people's time is devoted to economic pursuits, a large part of the fruits of these labors and a considerable portion of the day are spent in ritual activity. The focus of this activity is the human body, the appearance and health of which loom as a dominant concern in the ethos of the people. While such concern is certainly not unusual, its ceremonial aspects and associated philosophy are unique.

The fundamental belief underlying the whole system appears to be that the human body is ugly and that its natural tendency is to debility and disease. Incarcerated in such a body, man's only hope is to avert these characteristics through the use of the powerful influences of ritual and ceremony. Every household has one or more shrines devoted to this purpose. The more powerful individuals in this society have several shrines in their houses, and, in fact, the opulence of a house is often referred to in terms of the number of such ritual centers it possesses. . . .

While each family has at least one such shrine, the rituals associated with it are not family ceremonies but are private and secret. The rites are normally only discussed with children, and then only during the period when they are being initiated into these mysteries. I was able, however, to establish sufficient rapport with the natives to examine these shrines and to have the rituals described to me.

The focal point of the shrine is a box or chest which is built into the wall. In this chest are kept the many charms and magical potions without which no native believes he could live. These preparations are secured from a variety of specialized practitioners. The most powerful of these are the medicine men, whose assistance must be rewarded with substantial gifts. However, the medicine men do not provide the curative potions for their clients, but decide what the ingredients should be and then write them down in an ancient and secret language. This writing is understood only by the medicine men and by the herbalists who, for another gift, provide the required charm. *(Miner 1956)* ■

Anthropologist Horace Miner cast his observant eyes on the intriguing behaviour of the Nacirema. If we look a bit closer, however, some aspects of this culture may seem familiar, for what Miner is describing is actually the culture of the United States ("Nacirema" is "American" spelled backward). The "shrine" is the bathroom, and we are correctly informed that in this culture a measure of wealth is often how many bathrooms are in one's house. The bathroom rituals make use of charms and magical potions (beauty products and prescription drugs) obtained from specialized practitioners (such as hair stylists), herbalists (pharmacists), and medicine men (physicians). Using our sociological imagination we could update the Nacirema "shrine" by describing blow-dryers, mint-flavoured dental floss, Water Piks, and hair gel.

We begin to appreciate how to understand behaviour when we step back and examine it thoughtfully, objectively—whether it is "Nacirema" culture or another one. Take the case of Fiji, an island in the Pacific. A recent study showed that for the first time eating disorders were showing up among the young people there. This was a society where, traditionally, "you've gained weight" was a compliment and "your legs are skinny" was a major insult. Having a robust, nicely rounded body was the expectation for both men and women. What happened to change this cultural ideal? With the introduction of cable television in 1995, many Fiji islanders, especially girls, have come to want to look like the thin-waisted stars of *Ally McBeal* and *Friends*, not their full-bodied mothers and aunts. By understanding life in Fiji, we can also come to understand our own society much better (Becker 1995; Becker and Burwell 1999).

The study of culture is basic to sociology. In this chapter we will examine the meaning of culture and society as well as the development of culture from its roots in the prehistoric human experience to the technological advances of today. The major aspects of culture—including language, norms, sanctions, and values—will be defined and explored. We will see how cultures develop a dominant ideology, and how functionalist and conflict theorists view culture. The discussion will focus both on general cultural practices found in all societies and on the wide variations that can distinguish one society from another. The social policy section will look at the conflicts in cultural values that underlie current debates about multiculturalism. ■

Culture and Society

Culture is the totality of learned, socially transmitted customs, knowledge, material objects, and behaviour. It includes the ideas, values, customs, and artifacts (for example, CDs, comic books, and birth control devices) of groups of people. Patriotic attachment to the game of hockey in Canada is an aspect of culture, as is national addiction to the tango in Argentina.

Sometimes people refer to a particular person as "very cultured" or to a city as having "lots of culture." That use of the term *culture* is different from our use in this textbook. In sociological terms, *culture* does not refer solely to the fine arts and refined intellectual taste. It consists of all objects and ideas within a society, including ice cream cones, rock music, and slang words. Sociologists consider both a portrait by Rembrandt and a portrait by a billboard painter to be aspects of a culture. A tribe that cultivates soil by hand has just as much of a culture as a people that relies on computer-operated machinery. Each people has a distinctive culture with its own characteristic ways of gathering and preparing food, constructing homes, structuring the family, and promoting standards of right and wrong.

Sharing a similar culture helps to define the group or society to which we belong. A fairly large number of people are said to constitute a ***society*** when they live in the same territory, are relatively independent of people outside their area, and participate in a common culture. Mexico City is more populous than many nations of the world, yet sociologists do not consider it a society in its own right. Rather, it is seen as part of—and dependent on—the larger society of Mexico.

A society is the largest form of human group. It consists of people who share a common heritage and culture. Members of the society learn this culture and transmit it from one generation to the next. They even preserve their distinctive culture through literature, art, video recordings, and other means of expression. If it were not for the social transmission of culture, each generation would have to reinvent television, not to mention the wheel.

Having a common culture also simplifies many day-to-day interactions. For example, when you buy an airline ticket, you know you don't have to bring along hundreds of dollars in cash. You can pay with a credit card. When you are part of a society, there are many small (as well as more important) cultural patterns that you take for granted. You assume that theatres will provide seats for the audience, that physicians will not disclose confidential information, and that parents will be careful when crossing the street with young children. All these assumptions reflect the basic values, beliefs, and customs of the culture of Canada.

Language is a critical element of culture that sets humans apart from other species. Members of a society generally share a common language, which facilitates day-to-day exchanges with others. When you ask a hardware store clerk for a flashlight, you don't need to draw a picture of the instrument. You share the same cultural term for a small, battery-operated, portable light. However, if you were in England and needed this item, you would have to ask for an "electric torch." Of course, even within the same society, a term can have a number of different meanings. In Canada, *grass* signifies both a plant eaten by grazing animals and an intoxicating drug.

Development of Culture around the World

We've come a long way from our prehistoric heritage. As we begin a new millennium, we can transmit an entire book around the world via the Internet, we can clone cells, and we can prolong lives through organ transplants. The human species has produced such achievements as the ragtime compositions of Scott Joplin, the poetry of Emily Dickinson, the paintings of Vincent Van Gogh, the novels of Jane Austen, and the films of Akira Kurosawa. We can peer into the outermost reaches of the universe, and we can analyze our innermost feelings. In all these ways, we are remarkably different from other species of the animal kingdom.

The process of expanding culture has been under way for thousands of years. The first archaeological evidence of humanlike primates places our ancestors back many millions of years. About 700 000 years ago, people built hearths to harness fire. Archaeologists have uncovered tools that date back about 100 000 years. From 35 000 years ago we have evidence of paintings, jewellery, and statues. By that time, marriages, births, and deaths had already developed elaborate ceremonies (Harris 1997; Haviland 1999).

Tracing the development of culture is not easy. Archaeologists cannot "dig up" weddings, laws, or governments, but they are able to locate items that point to the emergence of cultural traditions. Our early ancestors were primates that had characteristics of human beings. These curious and communicative creatures made important advances in the use of tools. Recent studies of chimpanzees in the wild have revealed that they frequently use sticks and other natural objects in ways learned from other members of the group. However, unlike chimpanzees, our ancestors gradually made tools from increasingly durable materials. As a result, the items could be reused and refined into more effective implements.

Cultural Universals

Despite their differences, all societies have developed certain common practices and beliefs, known as ***cultural universals***. Many cultural universals are, in fact, adaptations to meet essential human needs, such as people's need for food, shelter, and clothing. Anthropologist George Murdock (1945:124) compiled a list of cultural universals. Some of these include athletic sports, cooking, funeral ceremonies, medicine, and sexual restrictions.

The cultural practices listed by Murdock may be universal, but the manner in which they are expressed varies from culture to culture. For example, one society may let its members choose their own marriage partners. Another may encourage marriages arranged by the parents.

Not only does the expression of cultural universals vary from one society to another, it also may change dra-

Sports are a cultural universal, but the variety of expression is endless. Shown here: traditional Japanese archery and camel racing in Saudi Arabia.

matically over time within a society. Thus, the most popular styles of dancing in North America today are sure to be different from the styles dominant in the 1950s or the 1970s. Each generation, and each year for that matter, most human cultures change and expand through the processes of innovation and diffusion.

Innovation

The process of introducing an idea or object that is new to a culture is known as ***innovation***. Innovation interests sociologists because of the social consequences that introducing something new can have in any society. There are two forms of innovation: discovery and invention. A ***discovery*** involves making known or sharing the existence of an aspect of reality. The finding of the DNA molecule and the identification of a new moon of Saturn are both acts of discovery. A significant factor in the process of discovery is the sharing of newfound knowledge with others. By contrast, an ***invention*** results when existing cultural items are combined into a form that did not exist before. The bow and arrow, the automobile, and the television are all examples of inventions, as are Protestantism and democracy.

Diffusion and Technology

You don't have to sample gourmet food to eat "foreign" foods. Breakfast cereal comes originally from Germany, candy from the Netherlands, and chewing gum from Mexico. The United States has also "exported" foods to other lands. Residents of many nations enjoy pizza, which was popularized in the United States. However, in Japan they add squid, in Australia it is eaten with pineapple, and in England people like kernels of corn with the cheese.

Just as a culture does not always discover or invent its foods, it may also adopt ideas, technology, and customs from other cultures. Sociologists use the term ***diffusion*** to refer to the process by which a cultural item is spread from group to group or society to society. Diffusion can occur through a variety of means, among them exploration, military conquest, missionary work, the influence of the mass media, tourism, and the Internet.

Early in human history, culture changed rather slowly through discovery. Then, as the number of discoveries in a culture increased, inventions became possible. The more inventions there were, the more rapidly additional inventions could be created. In addition, as diverse cultures came into contact with one another, they could each take advantage of the other's innovations. Thus, when people in Canada read a newspaper, we look at characters invented by the ancient Semites, printed by a process invented in Germany, on a material invented in China (Linton 1936).

Nations tend to feel a loss of identity when they accept culture from outside. Countries throughout the world decry American exports, from films to language to Bart Simpson. Movies produced in the United States account for 65 percent of the global box office. Magazines as diverse as *Cosmopolitan* and *Reader's Digest* sell two issues abroad for every one they sell in the United States. *The X-Files* airs in 60 countries. These examples of canned culture all facilitate the diffusion of cultural practices (Farhi and Rosenfeld 1998).

Many societies try to protect themselves from the invasion of too much culture from other countries, especially the economically dominant United States. The Canadian government, for example, requires that 35 percent of a station's daytime radio programming be Canadian songs or artists (see Figure 3-1). In Brazil, a toy manufacturer has eclipsed Barbie's popularity by designing a doll named Susi that looks more like Brazilian girls. Susi has a slightly smaller chest, much wider thighs, and darker skin than Barbie. Her wardrobe includes the skimpy bikinis favoured on Brazilian beaches as well as a soccer shirt honouring the Brazilian team. According to the toy company's marketing director, "we wanted Susi to be more Latin, more voluptuous. We Latins appreciate those attributes." Brazilians seem to agree: Before Christmas in 1999, five Susi dolls were sold for every two Barbies (DePalma 1999; Downie 2000).

Technology in its many forms has now increased the speed by which aspects of culture are shared and has broadened the distribution of cultural elements. Sociologist Gerhard Lenski has defined ***technology*** as "information about how to use the material resources of the environment to satisfy human needs and desires" (Nolan and Lenski 1999:41). Today's technological developments no longer have to await publication in journals with limited circulation. Press conferences, often simultaneously carried on the Internet, now trumpet new developments.

Technology not only accelerates the diffusion of scientific innovations but also transmits culture. Later, in Chapter 16, we will discuss the concern in many parts of the world that the English language and North American culture dominate the Internet and World Wide Web. Control, or at least dominance, of technology influences the direction of diffusion of culture. Websites abound with the most superficial aspects of Canadian and American culture but little information about the pressing issues faced by citizens of other nations. People all over the world find it easier to visit electronic chat rooms about daytime television soaps like *All My Children* than to learn about their own government's policies on day care or infant nutrition programs.

Sociologist William F. Ogburn (1922) made a useful distinction between the elements of material and nonmaterial culture. ***Material culture*** refers to the physical or

FIGURE 3-1

What Is Canadian?

Canadians try to ward off American influence by controlling what is played on the radio. The government requires that 35 percent of a station's programming in the daytime be Canadian. But what is Canadian? A complicated set of rules gives points based on whether the artist, the composer, the lyricist, or the production is Canadian. A song that earns two points meets the government requirements. Canadian Celine Dion singing "My Heart Will Go On" would not be classified as Canadian.

Celine Dion		Lenny Kravitz
Canadian	**Nationality**	Not Canadian
"My Heart Will Go On"	**Song**	"American Woman"
Not Canadian	**Lyricist**	**Canadian**
Not Canadian	**Composer**	**Canadian**
1 point*		2 points*

**At least two points are required for music to be considered Canadian.*

Source: DePalma 1999.

technological aspects of our daily lives, including food items, houses, factories, and raw materials. ***Nonmaterial culture*** refers to ways of using material objects and to customs, beliefs, philosophies, governments, and patterns of communication. Generally, the nonmaterial culture is more resistant to change than the material culture. Consequently, Ogburn introduced the term ***culture lag*** to refer to the period of maladjustment when the nonmaterial culture is still adapting to new material conditions. For example, the ethics of using the Internet, particularly privacy and censorship issues, have not yet caught up with the explosion in Internet use and technology. Technology has a globalizing effect as diverse cultures become interconnected through the material and nonmaterial elements of its use. Technological applications such as the Internet provide a shared element of material culture, while the behaviours employed and attitudes acquired while participating in an online chat room contribute to shared nonmaterial culture.

Diffusion can involve a single word like "cyber" or an entirely new orientation toward living, which may be transmitted through advances in electronic communication. Sociologist George Ritzer (1995b) coined the term "McDonaldization of society" to describe how the principles of fast-food restaurants developed in the United States have come to dominate more and more sectors of societies throughout the world. For example, hair salons and medical clinics now take walk-in appointments. In Hong Kong, sex selection clinics offer a menu of items—from fertility enhancement to methods of increasing the likelihood of producing a child of the desired sex. Religious groups—from evangelical preachers on local stations or websites to priests at the Vatican Television Center—use marketing techniques similar to those that sell "happy meals."

McDonaldization is associated with the melding of cultures, so that we see more and more similarities in cultural expression. In Japan, for example, African entrepreneurs have found a thriving market for hip-hop fashions popularized by teens in the United States. In Austria, the McDonald's organization itself has drawn on the Austrians' love of coffee, cake, and conversation to create the McCafe as part of its fast-food chain. Many observers believe that McDonaldization and the use of technology to spread elements of culture through diffusion both serve to dilute the distinctive aspects of a society's culture (Alfino et al. 1998; T. Clark 1994; Ritzer 1995b; Rocks 1999). (Cultural diffusion via the media is discussed in more detail in Chapter 4.)

Elements of Culture

Each culture considers its own distinctive ways of handling basic societal tasks as "natural." But, in fact, methods of education, marital ceremonies, religious doctrines, and other aspects of culture are learned and transmitted through human interactions within specific societies. Parents in India are accustomed to arranging marriages for their children, whereas most parents in Canada leave marital decisions up to their offspring. Lifelong residents of Naples consider it natural to speak Italian, whereas lifelong residents of Buenos Aires feel the same way about Spanish. We'll now take a look at the major aspects of culture that shape the way the members of a society live—language, norms, sanctions, and values.

Language

The English language makes extensive use of words dealing with war. We speak of "conquering" space, "fighting" the "battle" of the budget, "waging a war" on drugs, making a "killing" on the stock market, and "bombing" an examination; something monumental or great is "the bomb." An observer from an entirely different and warless culture could gauge the importance that war and the military have had on our lives simply by recognizing the prominence that militaristic terms have in our language. In the old West, words such as *gelding, stallion, mare, piebald,* and *sorrel* were all used to describe one animal—the horse. Even if we knew little of this period of history, we could conclude from the list of terms that horses were quite important in this culture. The Slave First Nations people, who live in the Northwest Territories, have 14 terms to describe ice, including eight for different kinds of "solid ice" and others for "seamed ice," "cracked ice," and "floating ice." Clearly, language reflects the priorities of a culture (Basso 1972; Haviland 1999).

Language is, in fact, the foundation of every culture. ***Language*** is an abstract system of word meanings and symbols for all aspects of culture. It includes speech, written characters, numerals, symbols, and gestures and expressions of nonverbal communication. Figure 3-2 shows where the major languages of the world are spoken.

Language is not an exclusively human attribute. Although they are incapable of human speech, primates such as chimpanzees have been able to use symbols to communicate. However, even at their most advanced level, animals operate with essentially a fixed set of signs with fixed meanings. By contrast, humans can manipulate symbols in order to express abstract concepts and rules and to expand human cultures.

Unlike some other elements of culture, language permeates all parts of society. Certain cultural skills, such as cooking or carpentry, can be learned without the use of language through the process of imitation. However, is it possible to transmit complex legal and religious systems to the next generation simply by observing how they are performed? You could put on a black robe and sit behind a bench as a judge does, but would you ever be able to understand legal reasoning without language? People invariably depend on language for the use and transmission of the rest of a culture.

While language is a cultural universal, striking differences in the use of language are evident around the world. This is the case even when two countries use the same spoken language. For example, an English-speaking person from Canada who is visiting London may be puzzled the first time an English friend says "I'll ring you up." The friend means "I'll call you on the telephone." Similarly, the meanings of nonverbal gestures vary from one culture to another. Whereas residents of North America attach positive meanings to the commonly used "thumbs up" gesture, this gesture has only vulgar connotations in Greece (Ekman et al. 1984).

Sapir-Whorf Hypothesis

Language does more than simply describe reality; it also serves to *shape* the reality of a culture. For example, most people in the southern parts of Canada cannot easily make the verbal distinctions about ice that are possible in the Slave First Nations culture. As a result, they are less likely to notice such differences.

The ***Sapir-Whorf hypothesis,*** named for two linguists, describes the role of language in interpreting our world. According to Sapir and Whorf, since people can conceptualize the world only through language, language *precedes* thought. Thus, the word symbols and grammar of a language organize the world for us. The Sapir-Whorf hypothesis also holds that language is not a "given." Rather, it is culturally determined and leads to different interpretations of reality by focusing our attention on certain phenomena.

In a literal sense, language may colour how we see the world. Berlin and Kay (1991) have noted that humans possess the physical ability to make millions of colour distinctions, yet languages differ in the number of colours that are recognized. The English language distinguishes between yellow and orange, but some other languages do not. In the Dugum Dani language of New Guinea's West Highlands, there are only two basic colour terms—*modla* for "white" and *mili* for "black." By contrast, there are 11 basic terms in English. Russian and Hungarian, though, have 12 colour terms. Russians have terms for light blue and dark blue, while Hungarians have terms for two different shades of red.

Gender-related language can reflect—although in itself it will not determine—the traditional acceptance of men and women in certain occupations. Each time we use a term such as *mailman, policeman,* or *fireman,* we are implying (especially to young children) that these occupations can be filled only by males. Yet many women work as *letter carriers, police officers,* and *firefighters*—a fact that is being increasingly recognized and legitimized through the use of such nonsexist language (Henley et al. 1985; Martyna 1983).

Language can also transmit stereotypes related to race. Look up the meanings of the adjective *black* in dictionaries published in the United States. You will find

FIGURE 3-2

Languages of the World

Mapping Life WORLDWIDE

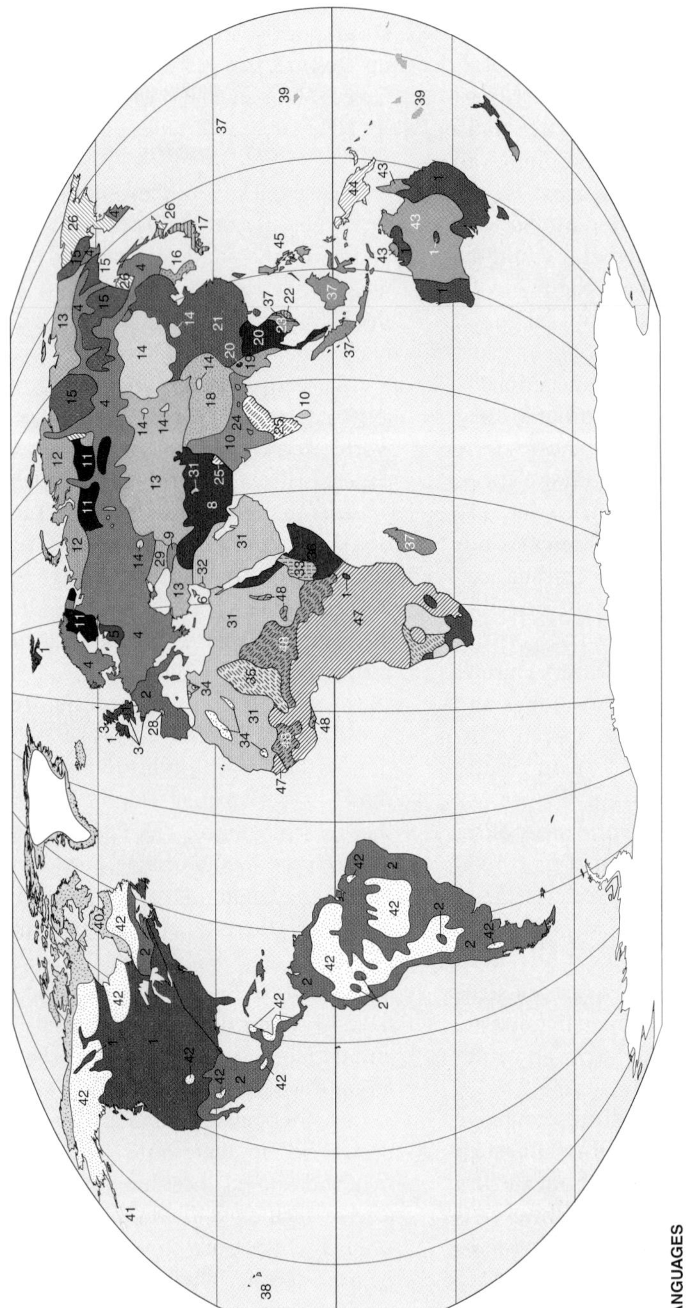

LANGUAGES

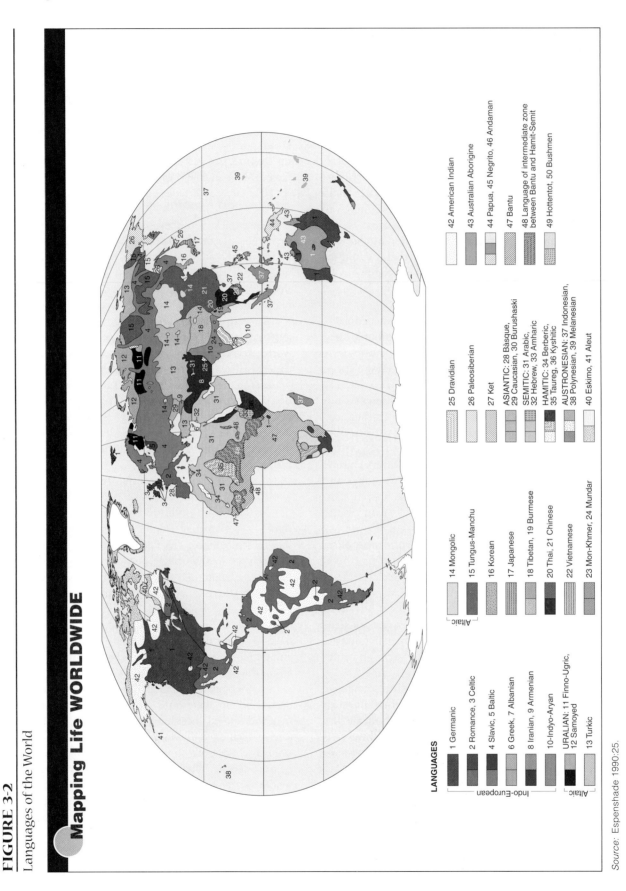

Indo-European
- 1 Germanic
- 2 Romance, 3 Celtic
- 4 Slavic, 5 Baltic
- 6 Greek, 7 Albanian
- 8 Iranian, 9 Armenian
- 10-Indyo-Aryan

URALIAN: 11 Finno-Ugric, 12 Samoyed

Altaic
- 13 Turkic
- 14 Mongolic
- 15 Tungus-Manchu

- 16 Korean
- 17 Japanese
- 18 Tibetan, 19 Burmese
- 20 Thai, 21 Chinese
- 22 Vietnamese
- 23 Mon-Khmer, 24 Mundar
- 25 Dravidian
- 26 Paleosiberian
- 27 Ket
- ASIANTIC: 28 Básque, 29 Caucasian, 30 Burushaski
- SEMITIC: 31 Arabic, 32 Hebrew, 33 Amharic
- HAMITIC: 34 Berberic, 35 Taureg, 36 Kyshitic
- AUSTRONESIAN: 37 Indonesian, 38 Polynesian, 39 Melanesian
- 40 Eskimo, 41 Aleut
- 42 American Indian
- 43 Australian Aborigine
- 44 Papua, 45 Negrito, 46 Andaman
- 47 Bantu
- 48 Language of intermediate zone between Bantu and Hamit-Semit
- 49 Hottentot, 50 Bushmen

Source: Espenshade 1990:25.

dismal, gloomy or *forbidding, destitute of moral light or goodness, atrocious, evil, threatening, clouded with anger.* By contrast, dictionaries list *pure* and *innocent* among the meanings of the adjective *white.* Through such patterns of language, our culture reinforces positive associations with the term (and skin colour) *white* and a negative association with *black.* Is it surprising, then, that a list preventing people from working in a profession is called a *blacklist,* while a lie that we think of as somewhat acceptable is called a *white lie?*

Language can shape how we see, taste, smell, feel, and hear. It also influences the way we think about the people, ideas, and objects around us. Language communicates a culture's most important norms, values, and sanctions to people. That's why the introduction of a new language into a society is such a sensitive issue in many parts of the world.

Nonverbal Communication

You know the appropriate distance to stand from someone when you talk informally. You know the circumstances under which it is appropriate to touch others, with a pat on the back or by taking someone's hand. If you are in the midst of a friendly meeting and one member suddenly sits back, folds his arms, and turns down the corners of his mouth, you know at once that trouble has arrived. These are all examples of *nonverbal communication,* the use of gestures, facial expressions, and other visual images to communicate.

Non-verbal communication can take many forms. The Canadian flag at half mast in Niagara after September 11, 2001, symbolizes respect and grief for those who lost their lives in the terrorist attacks.

We are not born with these expressions. We learn them, just as we learn other forms of language, from people who share our same culture. This is as true for the basic expressions of smiling, laughter, and crying as it is for more complex emotions such as shame or distress (Fridlund et al. 1987).

Like other forms of language, nonverbal communication is not the same in all cultures. For example, sociological research at the microlevel documents that people from various cultures differ in the degree to which they touch others during the course of normal social interaction.

Norms

"Wash your hands before dinner." "Thou shalt not kill." "Respect your elders." All societies have ways of encouraging and enforcing what they view as appropriate behaviour while discouraging and punishing what they consider to be improper behaviour. ***Norms*** are established standards of behaviour maintained by a society.

In order for a norm to become significant, it must be widely shared and understood. For example, in movie theatres in Canada, we typically expect that people will be quiet while the film is shown. Because of this norm, an usher can tell a member of the audience to stop talking so loudly. Of course, the application of this norm can vary, depending on the particular film and type of audience. People attending a serious artistic film will be more likely to insist on the norm of silence than those attending a slapstick comedy or horror movie.

Types of Norms

Sociologists distinguish between norms in two ways. First, norms are classified as either formal or informal. ***Formal norms*** generally have been written down and specify strict rules for punishment of violators. In North America, we often formalize norms into laws, which must be very precise in defining proper and improper behaviour. Sociologist Donald Black (1995) has termed ***law*** to be "governmental social control," establishing laws as formal norms enforced by the state. Laws are just one example of formal norms. The requirements for a college major and the rules of a card game are also considered formal norms.

By contrast, ***informal norms*** are generally understood but they are not precisely recorded. Standards of proper dress are a common example of informal norms. Our society has no specific punishment or sanction for a person who comes to school, say, wearing a monkey suit. Making fun of the nonconforming student is usually the most likely response.

Norms are also classified by their relative importance to society. When classified in this way, they are known as *mores* and *folkways.*

Taking Sociology to Work

ANGUS REID: Senior Fellow, Liu Centre for the Study of Global Issues

Angus Reid is a Senior Fellow at the Liu Centre for the Study of Global Issues at the University of British Columbia. The name "Angus Reid," however, is most often associated with public opinion and market research. After completing his PhD in sociology from Carleton University and teaching at the University of Manitoba, he founded Angus Reid Group Inc. in 1979. In 2000, his Vancouver-based company merged with the French company Ipsos Group to become one of North America's largest market research companies, with regional offices in cities such as New York, Toronto, San Francisco, Ottawa, Montreal, Calgary, Winnipeg, and St. Louis.

The company conducts research for governments, media organizations, corporations, and public affairs organizations. Some of the company's research includes a global poll on the Palestinian–Israeli conflict, a study of the time youth in Europe and America spend online, a poll about music file-sharing on the Internet, and Canadians' views on capital punishment. Reid stated that the company "provides clients with a broad sociological context, not just data" (Canadian Press Newswire 2000).

As of 2002, Reid began applying his experience in public opinion research around the world in his new position at a university centre dedicated to global issues.

Let's Discuss

1. What topics in this text would be of particular interest to someone who wanted to become a market researcher?
2. What issues affecting Canadians today would you like to see researched by someone like Angus Reid?

Mores (pronounced "MOR-ays") are norms deemed highly necessary to the welfare of a society, often because they embody the most cherished principles of a people. Each society demands obedience to its mores; violation can lead to severe penalties. Thus, Canada has strong mores against murder and child abuse, which have been institutionalized into formal norms.

Folkways are norms governing everyday behaviour. Folkways play an important role in shaping the daily behaviour of members of a culture. Consider, for example, something as simple as footwear. In Japan it is a folkway for youngsters to wear flip-flop sandals while learning to walk. A study of Japanese adults has found that, even barefoot, they walk as if wearing flip-flops—braking their thigh muscles and leaning forward as they step. This folkway may even explain why Japan produces so few competitive runners (Stedman 1998).

Society is less likely to formalize folkways than mores, and their violation raises comparatively little concern. For example, walking up a "down" escalator in a department store challenges our standards of appropriate behaviour, but it will not result in a fine or a jail sentence.

While the behaviour of students during "Frosh Week" may appear to violate society's norms, the behaviour may actually represent adherence to the norms of a student group.

In many societies around the world, folkways exist to reinforce patterns of male dominance. Various folkways reveal men's hierarchical position above women within the traditional Buddhist areas of southeast Asia. In the sleeping cars of trains, women do not sleep in upper berths above men. Hospitals that house men on the first floor do not place women patients on the second floor. Even on clotheslines, folkways dictate male dominance: women's attire is hung lower than that of men (Bulle 1987).

Acceptance of Norms

People do not follow norms, whether mores or folkways, in all situations. In some cases, they can evade a norm because they know it is weakly enforced. It is illegal for young Canadian teenagers to drink alcoholic beverages, yet drinking by minors is common throughout the nation.

In some instances, behaviour that appears to violate society's norms may actually represent adherence to the norms of a particular group. Teenage drinkers conform to the standards of a peer group. Conformity to group norms also governed the behaviour of the members of a religious cult associated with the Branch Davidians. In 1993, after a deadly gun battle with United States federal officials, nearly 100 members of the cult defied government orders to abandon their compound near Waco, Texas. After a 51-day standoff, the United States Department of Justice ordered an assault on the compound and 86 cult members died.

Norms are violated in some instances because one norm conflicts with another. For example, suppose that you live in an apartment building and one night hear the screams of the woman next door, who is being beaten by her husband. If you decide to intervene by ringing their doorbell or calling the police, you are violating the norm of "minding your own business" while, at the same time, following the norm of assisting a victim of violence.

Even when norms do not conflict, there are always exceptions to any norm. The same action, under different circumstances, can cause one to be viewed either as a hero or as a villain. Secretly taping telephone conversations is normally considered illegal and abhorrent. However, it can be done with a court order to obtain valid evidence for a criminal trial.

Acceptance of norms is subject to change as the political, economic, and social conditions of a culture are transformed. For example, under traditional norms in Canada, a woman was expected to marry, rear children, and remain at home if her husband could support the family without her assistance. However, these norms have been changing in recent decades, in part as a result of the contemporary feminist movement (see Chapter 10). As support for traditional norms weakens, people feel free to violate them more frequently and openly and are less likely to be punished for doing so.

Sanctions

Suppose that a football coach sends a 13th player onto the field. Or imagine a business school graduate showing up in shorts for a job interview at a large bank. Or consider a driver who neglects to put any money into a parking meter. These people have violated widely shared and understood norms. So what happens? In each of these situations, the person will receive sanctions if his or her behaviour is detected.

Sanctions are penalties and rewards for conduct concerning a social norm. Note that the concept of *reward* is included in this definition. Conformity to a norm can lead to positive sanctions such as a pay raise, a medal, a word of gratitude, or a pat on the back. Negative sanctions include fines, threats, imprisonment, and stares of contempt.

Table 3-1 summarizes the relationship between norms and sanctions. As you can see, the sanctions that are associated with formal norms (those written down and codified) tend to be formalized as well. If a football coach sends too many players onto the field, the team will be penalized 15 yards. The driver who fails to put money in the parking meter will be given a ticket and expected to pay a fine. But sanctions for violations of informal norms can vary. The business school graduate who comes to the bank interview in shorts will probably lose any chance of getting the job; on the other hand, he or she might be so brilliant the bank officials will overlook the unconventional attire.

Applying sanctions entails first *detecting* violations of norms or obedience to norms. A person cannot be penalized or rewarded unless someone with the power to provide sanctions is aware of the person's actions. Therefore, if none of the officials in the football game realizes that there is an extra player on the field, there will be no penalty. If the police do not check the parking meter, there will be no fine or ticket. Furthermore, there can be *improper* application of sanctions in certain situations. The referee may make an error in counting the number of football players and levy an undeserved penalty on one team for "too many players on the field."

Table 3-1 Norms and Sanctions

Norms	*Sanctions*	
	Positive	**Negative**
Formal	Salary bonus	Demotion
	Testimonial dinner	Firing from a job
	Medal	Jail sentence
	Diploma	Expulsion
Informal	Smile	Frown
	Compliment	Humiliation
	Cheers	Belittling

The entire fabric of norms and sanctions in a culture reflects that culture's values and priorities. The most cherished values will be most heavily sanctioned; matters regarded as less critical, on the other hand, will carry light and informal sanctions.

Values

We each have our own personal set of standards—which may include such things as caring or fitness or success in business—but we also share a general set of objectives as members of a society. Cultural ***values*** are these collective conceptions of what is considered good, desirable, and proper—or bad, undesirable, and improper—in a culture. They indicate what people in a given culture prefer as well as what they find important and morally right (or wrong). Values may be specific, such as honouring one's parents and owning a home, or they may be more general, such as health, love, and democracy. Of course, the members of a society do not uniformly share its values. Angry political debates and billboards promoting conflicting causes tell us that much. In Box 3-1 we explore how rock music reflects people's values. Those whose values conflict with the music tend to regard the music as a social problem.

Values influence people's behaviour and serve as criteria for evaluating the actions of others. There is often a direct relationship among the values, norms, and sanctions of a culture. For example, if a culture highly values the institution of marriage, it may have norms (and strict sanctions) that prohibit the act of adultery. If a culture views private property as a basic value, it will probably have stiff laws against theft and vandalism.

In a study by the federal government, "Citizens' Forum on Canada's Future," conducted between November, 1990, and July, 1991, 400 000 Canadians were asked which values they thought of as "Canadian" values (1991: 35–45).

The values that emerged included:

1. *Equality and fairness in a democratic society.*
2. *Consultation and dialogue.* Canadians believe that, as citizens, we value our ability to resolve problems and differences peacefully, through discussion, debate and negotiation.
3. *Accommodation and tolerance.* Accommodation of the differences in Canadian society—ethnic, linguistic, and regional—is considered to be a value of Canadian culture.
4. *Support for diversity.* Canadians value diversity and support it as a part of what makes us Canadian.
5. *Compassion and generosity.* Caring about others, particularly those who are less fortunate, and our willingness to act to make our society more humane, are values Canadians espouse.
6. *Respect for Canada's national beauty.* Preserving Canada's natural environment for future generations is a highly prized value of its citizens.
7. *Commitment to freedom, peace and non-violent change.* Canadians want to see their country as a leader in peacemaking and resolution of international conflicts.

People's values may differ according to factors such as their age, gender, region, ethnic background and language. For example, in a major study by Bibby and Posterski, Canadian teens were found to value what many Canadians have valued for some time. These values include relationships, freedom, success, and comfortable living (1992:18). However, the means through which to achieve these goals were valued differently by the teens compared to the adult group. The values of hard work, honesty, politeness, and forgiveness are considered increasingly less important to Canadian teens.

Figure 3-3 shows the decline in the importance of these values between 1984 and 1992 for Canadian teens, as well as how they compare to the level of importance attributed to them by adults.

Culture and the Dominant Ideology

Both functionalist and conflict theorists agree that culture and society are in harmony with each other, but for different reasons. Functionalists maintain that stability requires a consensus and the support of society's mem-

FIGURE 3-3

Valued means of Teenagers and Adults

% Viewing as "Very Important"

	YOUTH		ADULTS	
	1984	1992	1985	1990
Cleanliness	79	72	75	69
Honesty	85	70	96	89
Humour	—	69	—	—
Forgiveness	66	59	75	55
Intelligence	63	56	61	58
Politeness	64	53	70	62
Working hard	69	49	67	58
Creativity	—	45	—	38
Imagination	42	—	41	41
Generosity	—	40	—	52

Source: Bibby and Posterski 1992:19.

Eye on the Media

3-1 Knockin' Rock—Making Music a Social Problem

In 1990 rock artist Judas Priest was sued by the parents of two boys who carried out a suicide pact. The parents claimed that the lyrics of Priest's song "Beyond the Realms of Death" encouraged the boys to opt out of life. That case was dismissed, but it symbolizes the antagonism that rock music has aroused in society, creating a cultural divide between generations.

In fact, rock music has come under attack for decades as the source of all sorts of evils—sexual promiscuity, teen pregnancy, drug use, satanism, suicide, abuse of women, and communism, to name just a few. Critics, who generally come from the religious and political right, point to the obscene lyrics of heavy metal, the anger of rap songs, the decadent lifestyles of rock artists, and the explicit movements and gestures of the performers as causes of deviant behaviour in the youth generation.

The criticisms have had an impact. The United States Senate held hearings about obscene music, and record companies instigated voluntary labelling, to alert buyers to explicit lyrics. Cities and towns have cancelled public performances of controversial rock musicians (Marilyn Manson was even paid US$40 000 *not* to play in South Carolina). In the 1950s Ed Sullivan instructed his TV camera crew to show Elvis Presley only from the waist up while he was performing. Anxious parents today attempt to monitor the music their kids buy and the music videos they watch. In a word, rock music has been made into a social problem.

But is rock truly a social problem in that it causes undesirable behaviour? Sociologist Deena Weinstein thinks not. In her research she found "no sociologically credible evidence that rock caused sexual promiscuity, rape, drug abuse, satanism, and suicide. Indeed, there is clear evidence that it is not the cause of such behaviours" (1999). That is not to say that rock music has no part to play in these problems. According to Weinstein, rock music functions as a symbolic rebellion. It reflects the values of those who cherish the music, and these may be values that other groups in society want to inhibit. Rock music legitimizes the "disapproved" behaviours by giving them a symbolic form and making them public. Weinstein acknowledges, however, that symbols can have "complex and varied relations to behaviour."

Rock music has come under attack for decades as the source of all sorts of evils—sexual promiscuity, teen pregnancy, drug use, satanism, suicide, abuse of women, and communism, to name just a few.

Weinstein shows how the symbolic function of rock has changed over succeeding generations, matching the concerns and values of each youth generation. In the 1950s early "rock'n'roll" expressed the rebellion of teenagers against a society conforming to respectable middle-class codes. In the 1960s rock provided an outlet for feelings of political rebellion and a desire for consciousness expansion. The 1970s and 1980s gave rise to a number of distinct styles catering to special audiences. For example, the defiance of rap music and the satanic appeals of heavy metal symbolized the alienation of marginalized youth.

In every decade, rock's detractors have tended to be the older generation—generally white, middle class, politically conservative, and religious. They are intent on preserving the cultural values they hold dear and passing these on intact and unchanged to the generations to follow. Bewildered by rapid social changes and a youth culture resisting adult authority, the older generation makes rock into a convenient scapegoat for all their own fears and failures. The result is that they are more concerned with "killing the messenger" than paying attention to the message embedded in rock's symbolic rebellion. But, as Weinstein (1999) points out, "what could be more gratifying for a young symbolic rebel than to be thought of by the adult world as really important, as really dangerous?"

Let's Discuss

1. Does rock music today reflect your values? Why or why not? What kind of effect (if any) does the music have on the behaviour of those you know?
2. How would a conflict theorist and a functionalist look at the interplay of rock music and its supporters and detractors?

Sources: Weinstein 1999, 2000.

bers; consequently, there are strong central values and common norms. This view of culture became popular in sociology beginning in the 1950s. It was borrowed from British anthropologists who saw cultural traits as all working toward stabilizing a culture. From a functionalist perspective, a cultural trait or practice will persist if it performs functions that society seems to need or contributes to overall social stability and consensus. This view helps explain why widely condemned social practices such as prostitution continue to survive.

p. 13

Research in Action 3-2 Dominant Ideology and Poverty

Why do we think people are poor? *Individualistic* explanations emphasize personal responsibility: Poor people lack the proper work ethic, lack ability, or are unsuited to the workplace because of problems like drinking or drug abuse. *Structural* explanations, on the other hand, lay the blame for poverty on such external factors as inferior educational opportunities, prejudice, and low wages in some industries. Research documents that people in Canada and the United States generally go along with the individualistic explanation. The dominant ideology in Canada and the United States holds that people are poor largely because of their own shortcomings.

In a world survey assessing the causes of poverty, Canadians were asked "Why are there people in this country who live in need?" (Institute for Social Research 1994). Canadians responded that personal laziness and societal injustice caused poverty with equal frequency (31.8 percent for each reason). Countries such as Sweden, where individualistic beliefs are not as strong as in North America, responded that societal injustice far outweighed personal laziness as being the cause of poverty.

How pervasive is this individualistic view? Do the poor and rich alike subscribe to it? In seeking answers, sociologists have conducted studies of how various groups of people view poverty. The research has shown that people with lower incomes are more likely than the wealthy to see the larger socioeconomic system as the cause of poverty. In part this structural view, focusing on the larger job market, relieves them of some personal responsibility for their plight, but it also reflects the social reality that they are close to. On the other hand, the wealthy tend to embrace the dominant individualistic view because continuation of the socioeconomic status quo is in their best interest. They also prefer to regard their own success as the result of their own accomplishments, with little or no help from external factors.

. . . the dominant ideology holds that people are poor largely because of their own shortcomings.

Is the dominant ideology on poverty widespread? Yes, but it appears that the individualist ideology is dominant in Canadian society not because of a lack of alternatives, but because those who see things differently lack the political influence and status needed to get the ear of the mainstream culture.

Let's Discuss

1. Does support for the dominant ideology about poverty divide along income lines among racial and ethnic minorities? Why or why not?
2. Does your school administration have a "dominant ideology"? How is it manifested? Are there any groups that challenge it? On what basis?

Sources: Bobo 1991; Institute for Social Research 1994.

Conflict theorists agree that a common culture may exist, but they argue that it serves to maintain the privileges of certain groups. Moreover, while protecting their own self-interests, powerful groups may keep others in a subservient position. The term ***dominant ideology*** describes the set of cultural beliefs and practices that helps to maintain powerful social, economic, and political interests. This concept was first used by Hungarian Marxist Georg Lukacs (1923) and Italian Marxist Antonio Gramsci (1929). In Karl Marx's view, a capitalist society has a dominant ideology that serves the interests of the ruling class. Box 3-2 illustrates that there is a dominant ideology about poverty that derives its strength from the more powerful segments of society.

From a conflict perspective, the dominant ideology has major social significance. Not only do a society's most powerful groups and institutions control wealth and property; even more important, they control the means of producing beliefs about reality through religion, education, and the media. For example, if all of a society's most important institutions tell women that they should be subservient to men, this dominant ideology will help to control women and keep them in a subordinate position (Abercrombie et al. 1980, 1990; R. Robertson 1988).

Neither the functionalist nor the conflict perspective can alone explain all aspects of a culture. For example, we can trace the custom of tossing rice at a bride and groom back to the wish to have children and to the view of rice as a symbol of fertility, rather than to the powerlessness of the proletariat. Nevertheless, certain cultural practices in our society and others clearly benefit some to the detriment of many. These practices may indeed promote social stability and consensus—but at whose expense?

Cultural Diversity

Each culture has a unique character. The Inuit people of this country have little in common with farmers in Southeast Asia. Cultures adapt to meet specific sets of circumstances, such as climate, level of technology, population, and geography. This adaptation to different conditions shows up in differences in all elements of culture, including norms, sanctions, values, and language. Thus, despite the presence of cultural universals such as courtship and religion, there is still great diversity among the world's many cultures. Moreover, even within a single nation, certain segments of the populace develop cultural patterns that differ from the patterns of the dominant society.

FIGURE 3-4

The Argot of Pickpockets

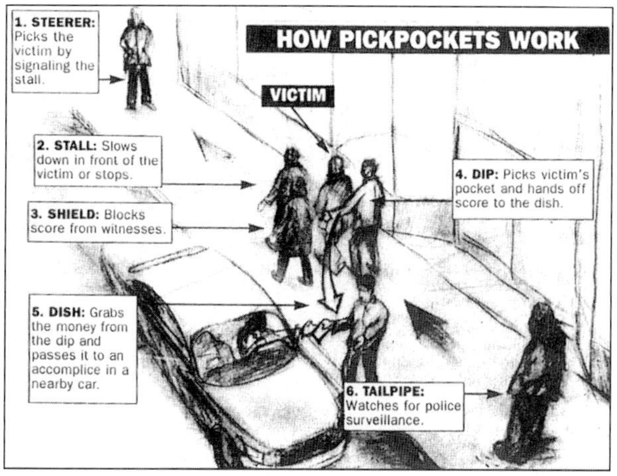

Source: Gearty 1996.

Aspects of Cultural Diversity

Subcultures

Residents of a retirement community, workers on an offshore oil rig, rodeo cowboys, street gangs, goth music fans—all are examples of what sociologists refer to as *subcultures.* A ***subculture*** is a segment of society that shares a distinctive pattern of mores, folkways, and values that differs from the pattern of the larger society. In a sense, a subculture can be thought of as a culture existing within a larger, dominant culture. The existence of many subcultures is characteristic of complex and diverse societies such as Canada.

You can get an idea of the impact of subcultures within Canada by considering the variety of seasonal traditions in December. The religious and commercial celebration of the Christmas holiday is an event well entrenched in the dominant culture of our society. However, the Jewish subculture observes Hanukkah, Muslims observe Ramadan (which falls at different times during the year, but at present is occurring during the winter months), and some people join in rituals celebrating the winter solstice.

Members of a subculture participate in the dominant culture, while at the same time engaging in unique and distinctive forms of behaviour. Frequently, a subculture will develop an ***argot,*** or specialized language, that distinguishes it from the wider society. For example, if you were to join a band of pickpockets you would need to learn what the dip, dish, and tailpipe are expected to do (see Figure 3-4).

An argot allows "insiders," the members of the subculture, to understand words with special meanings. It also establishes patterns of communication that "outsiders" can't understand. Sociologists associated with the interactionist perspective emphasize that language and symbols offer a powerful way for a subculture to feel cohesive and maintain its identity.

Subcultures develop in a number of ways. Often a subculture emerges because a segment of society faces problems or even privileges unique to its position. Subcultures may be based on common age (teenagers or old

Cultures vary because they need to adapt to the special conditions of their environment. Peruvians who live in the high Andes near the equator must adapt to a climate that can range from hot to cold within a single day. These women in Cuzco wear layers of clothing and cover their heads both for warmth and for protection from the high-altitude sun.

people), region (Newfoundlanders), ethnic heritage (Indo-Canadians), occupation (firefighters), or beliefs (environmentalists). Certain subcultures, such as computer "hackers," develop because of a shared interest or hobby. In still other subcultures, such as that of prison inmates, members have been excluded from conventional society and are forced to develop alternative ways of living.

Functionalist and conflict theorists agree that variation exists within a culture. Functionalists view subcultures as variations of particular social environments and as evidence that differences can exist within a common culture. However, conflict theorists suggest that variation often reflects the inequality of social arrangements within a society. A conflict perspective would view the challenge to dominant social norms by Quebec separatists, the feminist movement, and disabled groups as a reflection of inequity based on ethnicity, gender, and disability status. Conflict theorists also argue that subcultures sometimes emerge when the dominant society unsuccessfully tries to suppress a practice, such as the use of illegal drugs.

Countercultures

By the end of the 1960s, an extensive subculture had emerged in North America composed of young people turned off by a society they believed was too materialistic and technological. This group primarily included political radicals and "hippies" who had "dropped out" of mainstream social institutions. These young men and women rejected the pressure to accumulate more and more cars, larger and larger homes, and an endless array of material goods. Instead, they expressed a desire to live in a culture based on more humanistic values, such as sharing, love, and coexistence with the environment.

When a subculture conspicuously and deliberately *opposes* certain aspects of the larger culture, it is known as a ***counterculture.*** Countercultures typically thrive among the young, who have the least investment in the existing culture. In most cases, a 20-year-old can adjust to new cultural standards more easily than someone who has spent 60 years following the patterns of the dominant culture (Zellner 1995).

An example of a counterculture in Canadian history is the *Front du libération du Québec* (FLQ). In 1970, the FLQ opposed the social, economic, political, and educational institutions of the dominant culture of Quebec. Its activities included the murder of a prominent Quebec politician and the kidnapping of a British Trade Commissioner posted in Quebec. The FLQ produced a manifesto containing all of its demands, which was broadcast through public media.

"IT'S ENDLESS. WE JOIN A COUNTER-CULTURE; IT BECOMES THE CULTURE. WE JOIN ANOTHER COUNTER-CULTURE; IT BECOMES THE CULTURE..."

Cultures change. Aspects we once regarded as unacceptable—such as men wearing earrings and people wearing jeans in the workplace—and associated with fringe groups are now widely accepted. Countercultural practices are sometimes absorbed by the mainstream culture.

Culture Shock

Anyone who feels disoriented, uncertain, out of place, or even fearful when immersed in an unfamiliar culture may be experiencing ***culture shock.*** For example, a resident of Canada who visits certain areas in China and wants a local dinner may be stunned to learn that the specialty is scorpian. Similarly, someone from a strict Islamic culture may be shocked upon first seeing the comparatively provocative dress styles and open displays of affection that are common in North American and various European cultures. Culture shock can also occur within the larger confines of one's own culture. For example, a 14-year-old boy from a small town in northern Saskatchewan might feel the effects of culture shock while visiting Toronto for the first time. The speed of the traffic, the level of the street noise and the intensity and variation of external stimuli may cause him to feel disoriented and uncomfortable with his surroundings.

All of us, to some extent, take for granted the cultural practices of our society. As a result, it can be surprising and even disturbing to realize that other cultures do not follow our "way of life." The fact is that customs that seem strange to us are considered normal and proper in other cultures, which may see *our* mores and folkways as odd.

Cultural Diversity in Canada

If a tourist were to travel across Canada for the first time, he or she would most certainly be struck by this country's diversity—diversity of region, ethnicity, race, and language. Cultural diversity, as the traveller would observe, is greatest in Canada's metropolitan areas, where the greatest number of cultural minorities and particularly visible minorities reside. On the basis of his or her observations of cultural diversity, the traveller might conclude that Canada is a "multicultural" society. But what does multiculturalism really mean? Does it simply describe (numerically) the variety of cultures represented in Canada?

Multiculturalism is not only a description of the reality of Canada's cultural makeup—"what is" (Fleras and Kunz 2001)—but, in Canada, it is an explicit policy set out by the government. ***Multiculturalism*** is a policy that promotes cultural and racial diversity and full and equal participation of individuals and communities of all origins as a fundamental characteristic of Canadian identity. The federal Multiculturalism Program of 1997 has three main goals (Communications Canada 2001):

1. *Identity*—fostering a society where people of all backgrounds feel a sense of attachment and belonging to Canada.
2. *Civic participation*—developing citizens who are actively involved in their communities and country.
3. *Social justice*—building a country that ensures fair and equitable treatment of people of all origins.

Multiculturalism can also take the form of an ideology—a set of beliefs, goals, ideals, and attitudes about what multiculturalism *should be.* In embracing multiculturalism as an ideology, Canadians often compare their society's way of expressing cultural diversity to the way it is expressed in the United States (Fleras and Kunz 2001). The analogy of the "mosaic" is commonly used to describe Canada's cultural diversity, where various tiles represent distinct cultural groups that collectively form the whole. In the United States, the "melting pot" analogy represents the model of assimilation, in which Americans become more like one another, rather than distinct from one another.

Support for the "mosaic" version of Canada has been declining and shifting toward the "melting pot." Across region, age, and education levels, in 1985, 56 percent of Canadians said they preferred the "mosaic" and 28 percent the "melting pot." In 1995, only 44 percent preferred the mosaic, while 40 percent preferred the melting pot (Bibby 1995).

The ideal of multiculturalism in Canada has two desirable outcomes—the survival of ethnic groups and their cultures, and tolerance of this diversity as reflected by an absence of prejudice towards ethnic minorities (Weinfeld 1994). Multiculturalism, however, is not without its critics. Some argue that it is a divisive rather than unifying force in Canada, while others claim that it is only "window dressing," diverting attention from the real problems of ethnic and racial prejudice and discrimination (Nelson and Fleras 1998).

The American Influence One of the original purposes of multiculturalism was to establish a national uniqueness that would make Canadians distinct from Americans (Bibby 1990). In 1972, Prime Minister Pierre Trudeau stated, if we implement this policy, "We become less like others; we become less susceptible to cultural, social, or political envelopment by others" (Bibby 1990:49). Despite the significant Americanization of Canadian life, the view that Americans have "too much power in our nation's affairs" has not increased since the 1970s (Bibby 1995).

Even though Canadians generally hold the view that Americans do not have "too much power" in our society, Canadians frequently consider Americans to be their favourite authors, TV personalities, and screen stars (Bibby 1995). Given Canadians' reliance on American culture (particularly outside Quebec) our "heroes" may be those that are defined by America (Bibby 1995). In 1995, when Canadians were asked to name the greatest living

Women in certain areas of Thailand traditionally elongated their necks by wearing layers of coils. The custom began dying out until the Thai people discovered that tourists would pay money to be "shocked" by the practice. These girls are members of the "Long Neck" tribe.

Canadian, 73 percent said "no one came to mind" (Bibby 1995:47). Furthermore, when asked what characteristics describe Americans and Canadians, Canadians felt that the traits of confidence, patriotism, and risk-taking had greater applicability to Americans, while generosity was a trait more applicable to Canadians. As Figure 3-5 illustrates, Canadian teenagers view the description "world's best at what they do" as applicable to Americans almost 50 percent more often than they view it applying to Canadians (Bibby 1995). If Canadian broadcasting and publishing regulations promoting Canadian cultural content were not in place, one might wonder how much more "Americanized" our cultural preferences might be. In 1995, 64 percent of Canadians believed that "CBC television continues to play a unique role in enhancing Canadian culture" (Bibby 1995:1210).

Attitudes toward Cultural Diversity

Ethnocentrism

Many everyday statements reflect our attitude that our culture is best. We use terms such as *underdeveloped*, *backward*, and *primitive* to refer to other societies. What "we" believe is a religion; what "they" believe is superstition and mythology (Spradley and McCurdy 1980).

It is tempting to evaluate the practices of other cultures on the basis of our own perspectives. Sociologist William Graham Sumner (1906) coined the term ***ethnocentrism*** to refer to the tendency to assume that one's culture and way of life constitute the norm or are superior to all others. The ethnocentric person sees his or her own group as the centre or defining point of culture and views all other cultures as deviations from what is "normal."

FIGURE 3-5

Applicability of Traits to Canadians and Americans

Traits Describe "Very Well" or "Fairly Well"

	ADULTS		TEENAGERS	
	Canadians	Americans	Canadians	Americans
Confident	61%	87	66%	91
Patriotic	58	92	47	89
Generous	84	53	**	**
Risk-takers	33	82	43	84
World's best	56	48	40	62

Source: Bibby 1995:49.

Those westerners who are contemptuous of India's Hindu religion and culture because of its view of cattle as sacred are engaged in ethnocentrism. As another manifestation of ethnocentrism, people in one culture may dismiss as unthinkable the mate-selection or child-rearing practices of another culture. We might, in fact, be tempted to view the Nacirema culture from an ethnocentric point of view—until we learn it is a culture similar to our own that Miner describes (see the chapter opening).

Conflict theorists point out that ethnocentric value judgments serve to devalue diversity and to deny equal opportunities. The treatment of First Nations children in Christian-based residential schools during the mid-point of the last century is an example of ethnocentrism that conflict theorists might point to in Canadian history. Church authorities were so convinced of the cultural superiority of their own beliefs that they set out to deny First Nations children the expression of theirs.

Functionalists note that ethnocentrism serves to maintain a sense of solidarity by promoting group pride. Canadians' view of our country as peaceful, safe, and relatively free from violence may create a feeling of national solidarity when comparing ourselves to our American neighbours.

Cultural Relativism

While ethnocentrism evaluates foreign cultures using the familiar culture of the observer as a standard of correct behaviour, ***cultural relativism*** views people's behaviour from the perspective of their own culture. It places a priority on understanding other cultures, rather than dismissing them as "strange" or "exotic." Unlike ethnocentrism, cultural relativism employs the kind of value neutrality in scientific study that Max Weber saw as so important.

p. 40

Cultural relativism stresses that different social contexts give rise to different norms and values. Thus, we must examine practices such as polygamy, bullfighting, and monarchy within the particular contexts of the cultures in which they are found. While cultural relativism does not suggest that we must unquestionably *accept* every cultural variation, it does require a serious and unbiased effort to evaluate norms, values, and customs in light of their distinctive culture.

There is an interesting extension of cultural relativism, referred to as *xenocentrism*. ***Xenocentrism*** is the belief that the products, styles, or ideas of one's society are *inferior* to those that originate elsewhere (W. Wilson et al. 1976). In a sense, it is a reverse ethnocentrism. For example, people in Canada often assume that French wine or Japanese electronic devices are superior to our own. Are they? Or are people unduly charmed by the lure of goods from exotic places? Such fascination with overseas products can be damaging to competitors in Canada. Conflict theorists are most likely to consider the economic impact of xenocentrism in the developing world. Consumers in developing nations frequently turn their backs on locally produced goods and instead purchase items imported from Europe or North America.

How one views one's culture—whether from an ethnocentric point of view or through the lens of cultural relativism—has important consequences in the area of social policy concerned with multiculturalism. We'll take a close look at this issue in the next section.

SOCIAL POLICY AND CULTURE

Multiculturalism

The Issue

In 1971, multiculturalism became official government policy in Canada. It was a policy established to promote tolerance for cultural minorities, or in the words of then Prime Minister Pierre Elliott Trudeau, to "explore the delights of many cultures." Although the Canadian policy on multiculturalism provides an alternative to the American melting pot approach to cultural diversity, it has generated a great deal of conflict and faced a great deal of opposition (Nelson and Fleras 1998).

A great deal of the conflict surrounding multiculturalism stems from the variety of meanings or definitions Canadians have for the concept. The term *multiculturalism* can be used to refer to a) the fact (what *is*, i.e., the existing complexion of Canadian society); b) an ideology (what should be); c) policy (what is proposed); d) a process (what really happens); e) a critical discussion (what is being challenged) and f) a social movement (collective resistance) (Fleras and Elliott 1999). In general, multiculturalism can be defined as a process through which Canadians come to be engaged in their society as different from one another, yet equal to one another (Fleras and Kunz 2001).

The Setting

According to Citizenship and Immigration Canada, Canada accepts more immigrants, proportional to the size of its population, than any other country in the world. One in every six residents in this country was born outside Canada. The top five sources for immigration since 1998 have been countries in Asia (Citizenship and Immigration Canada 2001). According to the 2001 census, 38 percent of Canadians declared their ethnicity to be that of "multiple origins"; that is, they declared two or more ethnic origins. Overall, multicultural minorities tend to live in Canada's large urban centres, making Vancouver, Montreal, and Toronto the most culturally diverse regions of the country. Approximately three quarters of all immigrants who arrived in Canada between 1991 and 1996 settled in one of these three centres (Fleras and Kunz 2001).

From the standpoint of the two major sociological perspectives—conflict theory and structural-functional theory—the implementation of multiculturalism as a social policy has two distinct interpretations. Conflict sociologists

Policies on multiculturalism attempt to preserve, protect, and nurture different cultural traditions in the midst of domination of one cultural group.

view multiculturalism as an attempt to "empower minorities to pursue the dual goals of ethnicity and equality" (Nelson and Fleras 1998:259). It is seen as an attempt to nurture, preserve, and protect different cultural traditions in the midst of domination by one cultural group. Multiculturalism policies also aim to make diversity, and the inevitable struggles that result, an accepted and welcome element of the cultural fabric of Canadian life.

Functional sociologists view culture as something that all Canadians share. It is the common values that unite and integrate us, resulting in a shared sense of identity. Therefore, according to functional thinkers, the more we diversify Canadian culture, the less we share in common; the more we hyphenate our identities (e.g., Indo-Canadian, Chinese-Canadian, Italian-Canadian, etc.) the less "Canadian" we actually become. However, both functionalist and conflict theorists have criticized multiculturalism for a number of reasons. Sociologists Fleras and Elliott (1999) argue that criticisms regarding multiculturalism can be classified into four categories. They are:

- Those that claim that multiculturalism is "divisive" and serves to weaken Canadian society
- Those that see multicultural programs and policies as "regressive," as a tool to pacify the needs and legitimate claims of the minority cultural groups
- Those that consider the efforts of multiculturalism to be "ornamental" or superficial, with much form and little substance
- Those that consider multiculturalism as a policy "impractical" in a capitalist society such as Canada, where the principles of individualism, private property, profit, and consumerism prevail (Fleras and Elliott 1999).

Policy Initiatives

Official multiculturalism in Canada currently comes under the portfolio of Citizenship and Canadian Identity, which is in turn under the ministry of Canadian Heritage. According to Fleras and Kunz (2001), policies on multiculturalism have evolved from those in the 1970s, which celebrated Canadians' differences (e.g., cultural sensitivity training programs); to those in the 1980s, which "managed" diversity through policies on employment equity and race relations; to those of the 1990s, with the objectives of inclusion and integration of cultural minorities. The current policies on multiculturalism encourage the full participation of all cultural groups, based on the goals of social justice. As Fleras and Kunz (2001:16) state, "Emphasis is on what we have in common as rights-bearing and equality-seeking individuals rather than on what separates or divides us." Special activities such as Black History Month and the "Racism: Stop It!" campaign, which focus on the promotion of social justice, have been created by the federal government's multicultural programs.

Fleras and Elliott (1999) state that multiculturalism is not what divides Canada, but is rather what unites us, separating us and making us distinct from Americans. They claim that multiculturalism policies focus on institutional barriers for minority groups and therefore attempt to break down the "vertical mosaic."

Let's Discuss

1. What functions do you think the policy of multiculturalism serves? Do you think these functions are real or simply serve as "window-dressing"?
2. How does the ideology of multiculturalism differ from the reality of living in a multicultural country?

Chapter Resources

Summary

Culture is the totality of learned, socially transmitted customs, knowledge, material objects, and behaviour. This chapter examines the basic elements that make up a culture, social practices common to all cultures, and variations that distinguish one culture from another.

1. Sharing a similar culture helps to define the group or society to which we belong.
2. Anthropologist George Murdock has compiled a list of ***cultural universals,*** general practices found in every culture, including courtship, family, games, language, medicine, religion, and sexual restrictions.
3. Human culture is constantly expanding through ***innovation,*** including both ***discovery*** and ***invention.***
4. ***Diffusion***—the spread of cultural items from one place to another—also changes cultures. But societies resist ideas that seem too foreign as well as those that are perceived as threatening to their own values and beliefs.
5. ***Language,*** an important element of culture, includes speech, written characters, numerals,

symbols, and gestures and other forms of nonverbal communication. Language both describes culture and shapes it for us.

6. Sociologists distinguish between ***norms*** in two ways. They are classified as either ***formal*** or ***informal*** norms and as ***mores*** or ***folkways.***
7. The more cherished ***values*** of a culture will receive the heaviest sanctions; matters that are regarded as less critical, on the other hand, will carry light and informal sanctions.
8. The ***dominant ideology*** of a culture describes the set of cultural beliefs and practices that help to maintain powerful social, economic, and political interests.
9. In a sense, a ***subculture*** can be thought of as a culture existing within a larger, dominant culture. ***Countercultures*** are subcultures that deliberately oppose aspects of the larger culture.
10. People who measure other cultures by the standard of their own engage in ***ethnocentrism.*** Using ***cultural relativism*** allows us to view people from the perspective of their own culture.
11. ***Multiculturalism*** is a process through which citizens come to be engaged in their society as different from one another, yet equal to one another.

Critical Thinking Questions

1. Select three cultural universals from George Murdock's list (see p. 52) and analyze them from a functionalist perspective. Why are these practices found in every culture? What functions do they serve?
2. Drawing on the theories and concepts presented in the chapter, apply sociological analysis to one subculture with which you are familiar. Describe the norms, values, argot, and sanctions evident in that subculture.
3. In what ways is the dominant ideology of Canada evident in the nation's literature, music, movies, theatre, television programs, and sporting events?

Key Terms

Argot Specialized language used by members of a group or subculture. (page 63)

Counterculture A subculture that deliberately opposes certain aspects of the larger culture. (64)

Cultural relativism The viewing of people's behaviour from the perspective of their own culture. (66)

Cultural universals General practices found in every culture. (52)

Culture The totality of learned, socially transmitted customs, knowledge, material objects, and behaviour. (51)

Culture lag Ogburn's term for a period of maladjustment during which the nonmaterial culture is still adapting to new material conditions. (54)

Culture shock The feeling of surprise and disorientation that is experienced when people witness cultural practices different from their own. (64)

Diffusion The process by which a cultural item is spread from group to group or society to society. (53)

Discovery The process of making known or sharing the existence of an aspect of reality. (53)

Dominant ideology A set of cultural beliefs and practices that helps to maintain powerful social, economic, and political interests. (62)

Ethnocentrism The tendency to assume that one's own culture and way of life represent the norm or are superior to all others. (66)

Folkways Norms governing everyday social behaviour whose violation raises comparatively little concern. (58)

Formal norms Norms that generally have been written down and that specify strict rules for punishment of violators. (57)

Informal norms Norms that generally are understood but are not precisely recorded. (57)

Innovation The process of introducing new elements into a culture through either discovery or invention. (53)

Invention The combination of existing cultural items into a form that did not previously exist. (53)

Language An abstract system of word meanings and symbols for all aspects of culture. It also includes gestures and other nonverbal communication. (55)

Law Governmental social control. (57)

Material culture The physical or technological aspects of our daily lives. (53)

Mores Norms deemed highly necessary to the welfare of a society. (58)

Multiculturalism A policy that promotes cultural and racial diversity and full and equal participation of individuals and communities of all origins as a fundamental characteristic of Canadian identity. (65)

Nonmaterial culture Cultural adjustments to material conditions, such as customs, beliefs, patterns of communication, and ways of using material objects. (54)

Norms Established standards of behaviour maintained by a society. (57)

Sanctions Penalties and rewards for conduct concerning a social norm. (59)

Sapir-Whorf hypothesis A hypothesis concerning the role of language in shaping cultures. It holds that language is culturally determined and serves to influence our mode of thought. (55)

Society A fairly large number of people who live in the same territory, are relatively independent of people outside it, and participate in a common culture. (51)

Subculture A segment of society that shares a distinctive pattern of mores, folkways, and values that differs from the pattern of the larger society. (63)

Technology Information about how to use the material resources of the environment to satisfy human needs and desires. (53)

Values Collective conceptions of what is considered good, desirable, and proper—or bad, undesirable, and improper—in a culture. (60)

Xenocentrism The belief that the products, styles, or ideas of one's society are inferior to those that originate elsewhere. (66)

Additional Readings

Bibby, Reginald. 1995. *The Bibby Report: Social Trends Canadian Style.* Toronto: Stoddart. Based on national surveys of 1975, 1980, 1985, 1990, and 1995, this book examines Canadians' values on such issues as multiculturalism, Americanization, bilingualism, and spirituality.

Fleras, Augie, and Jean Lock Kunz. 2001. *Media and Minorities: Representing Diversity in Multicultural Canada.* Toronto: Thompson Educational Publishing. Fleras and Kunz analyze and assess the representation of minority groups in the mass media against a backdrop of Canada's commitment to multiculturalism.

Kraybill, Donald B., and Steven M. Nott. 1995. *Amish Enterprises: From Plows to Profits.* Baltimore: Johns Hopkins University Press. An examination of how the Amish have adapted to capitalism in the United States while maintaining their distinctive values and subculture.

Weinstein, Deena. 2000. *Heavy Metal: The Music and Its Culture.* Cambridge, MA: Da Capo. A sociologist examines the subculture associated with "heavy metal" music and efforts to curtail this subculture.

Zellner, William M. 1995. *Countercultures: A Sociological Analysis.* New York: St. Martin's. An overview of six countercultures found in the United States: the Unification Church, the Church of Scientology, satanists, skinheads, survivalists, and the Ku Klux Klan.

Internet Connection

www.mcgrawhill.ca/college/schaefer

*For additional Internet exercises relating to culture and nonverbal communication, visit the Schaefer Online Learning Centre at **http://www.mcgrawhill.ca/college/schaefer**. Please note that while the URLs listed were current at the time of printing, these sites often change—check the Online Learning Centre for updates.*

Your text offers a contrast of subcultures and countercultures. In general, both groups are segments of society that share distinctive features, such as argots, beliefs, and particular dress codes. However, a counterculture conspicuously and deliberately opposes certain aspects of the larger culture in a way that a subculture does not. To see this difference in action, compare the Amish described through the links found at **http://dir.yahoo.com/ Society_and_Culture/ Religion_and_Spirituality/Faiths_and_Practices/ Christianity/ Denominations_and_Sects/ Amish** to street gangs described through the links found at **http://dir. yahoo.com/Society_and_ Culture/Cultures_and_Groups/Gangs**. For each of the two groups, explore the following:

(a) Identify the argot of the group. Describe some specific examples of special forms of verbal, written, and gestural communication. How are those gestures and words used to communicate? What kinds of messages are sent through the argot? In what ways can a subculture or counterculture make use of an argot to build solidarity among its members, while at the same time keeping outsiders at a distance?

(b) What special clothing or dress codes are used? What symbols and messages do members communicate through clothing? What purpose does specialized dress serve for the group?

(c) What are some of the special practices or beliefs of the group? Do these beliefs or practices put the group at odds with the larger culture? How so?

(d) What purpose or meaning can being a member of the group have for those who belong?

(e) Draw some comparisons and contrasts between the two groups. What do the Amish and street gangs have in common? In what ways are they different? Why would the Amish be labelled a subculture, but street gangs a counterculture? Do you agree with these labels? Why or why not?

CHAPTER 4

SOCIALIZATION

Schools can sometimes be stressful arenas of socialization. This poster informs schoolchildren in Japan that they can call a hotline and receive advice concerning stress, bullying by classmates, and corporal punishment from their teachers.

In sixth grade, the popular girls' clique split into two subgroups, whose leaders were Tiffany and Emily. The girls from the two groups liked each other, but the leaders did not. Tiffany was jealous of the attention Emily got from her followers and from the popular boys, wanting center stage all to herself. Emily resented Tiffany's intrusions and manipulations. They polarized their groups against each other.

By spring, Tiffany could no longer control her hatred. She persuaded one of the less popular boys to steal Emily's backpack, empty it, and take it into the rest room and smear it with excrement. Emily discovered her backpack missing, searched for it, and alerted her teacher. The backpack was finally found in the boys' rest room (where it could not be traced back to Tiffany), clogging up a toilet, soaking in urine and feces. Although the school administrators interviewed numerous people to try to uncover the truth, they were never able to solve the crime.

Tiffany used Emily's anguish to ridicule her, portray her as weak, and turn the bulk of the popular people (boys and girls) against her. The following year Emily's parents sent her to boarding school.

* * *

One day Larry, Brad, and Trevor were at Rick's house. Larry had just turned twelve and had a lot of birthday money in his wallet. Brad noticed Larry's wallet lying on Rick's bed and climbed on top of it. He motioned Trevor to join him. From his perch, Brad asked Larry where his wallet was, and when Larry could not find it, Brad accused Rick of stealing it. Despite Rick's fervent denials, Brad eventually convinced Larry of Rick's guilt, whipping him into a frenzy of anger and outrage. Larry tore Rick's room apart looking for his wallet. Brad slyly showed Trevor the wallet he was sitting on, inviting him to join him in conspiratorial silence.

Brad's accusations, Larry's fear for his money and anger at Rick, and Rick's pathetic denials escalated to the point where Larry began threatening to break Rick's things if he did not turn over the wallet. Helplessly, Rick professed innocence and ignorance. Larry broke Rick's lamp. Then he smashed the telephone in Rick's room (a birthday gift) to the floor, shattering it. He stomped on video games. Rick wailed and cried. Larry ran out of the room, moving to the kitchen to find more things to destroy, his anger out of control. Rick followed him, screaming, terrified. As Larry was about to throw down a blender, Rick's mother came home and stopped him. Assessing the situation, she sent the three boys home. Searching the house, she found the wallet on the bed and called Larry's mother.

The next day in school, Brad and Trevor bragged exultantly to everybody about their caper. Rick was out of the group. *(Adler and Adler 1998: 2–3)* ■

Patricia and Peter Adler's intensive research into preadolescent culture began with their own children, when they were five and nine. As participant observers, the parents jumped into the lives of their children, their children's friends, and children of their own friends as well as other children in their community over a period of eight years. They uncovered a dynamic peer culture—one in which the preadolescents' interactions help determine such things as status, popularity, friendships, and activities. In their book *Peer Power,* the Adlers show that children are active agents in creating their social world and getting socialized into it; they are not just the passive objects of socialization by parents, teachers, and other authority figures in their lives. These researchers found that while each child has his or her own special issues and experiences, the influence of the peer culture forms lifelong patterns.

Sociologists, in general, are interested in the patterns of behaviour and attitudes that emerge *throughout* the life course, from infancy to old age. These patterns are part of the process of ***socialization,*** whereby people learn the attitudes, values, and behaviours appropriate for members of a particular culture. Socialization occurs through human interactions. We learn a great deal from those people most important in our lives—immediate family members, best friends, and teachers. But we also learn from people we see on the street, on television, on the Internet, and in films and magazines. From a microsociological perspective, socialization helps us to discover how to behave "properly" and what to expect from others if we follow (or challenge) society's norms and values. From a macrosociological perspective, socialization provides for the transmission of a culture from one generation to the next and thereby for the long-term continuance of a society.

Socialization affects the overall cultural practices of a society, and it also shapes our self-images. For example, in North America, a person who is viewed as "too heavy" or "too short" does not conform to the ideal cultural standard of physical attractiveness. This kind of unfavourable evaluation can significantly influence the person's self-esteem. In this sense, socialization experiences can help shape our personalities. In everyday speech, the term ***personality*** is used to refer to a person's typical patterns of attitudes, needs, characteristics, and behaviour.

This chapter will examine the role of socialization in human development. It begins by analyzing the interaction of heredity and environmental factors. We pay particular attention to how people develop perceptions, feelings, and beliefs about themselves. The chapter will also explore the lifelong nature of the socialization process, as well as important agents of socialization, among them the family, schools, peers, and the media. Finally, the social policy section will focus on the socialization experience of group child care for young children. ■

The Role of Socialization

What makes us who we are? Is it the genes we are born with? Or the environment in which we grow up? Researchers have traditionally clashed over the relative importance of biological inheritance and environmental factors in human development—a conflict called the *nature versus nurture* (or *heredity versus environment*) debate. Today, most social scientists have moved beyond this debate, acknowledging instead the *interaction* of these variables in shaping human development. However, we can better appreciate how heredity and environmental factors interact and influence the socialization process if we first examine situations in which one factor operates almost entirely without the other (Homans 1979).

Environment: The Impact of Isolation

In the 1994 movie *Nell,* Jodie Foster played a young woman hidden from birth by her mother in a backwoods cabin. Raised without normal human contact, Nell crouches like an animal, screams wildly, and speaks or sings in a language all her own. This movie was drawn from the actual account of an emaciated 16-year-old boy who mysteriously appeared in 1828 in the town square of Nuremberg, Germany (Lipson 1994).

The Case of Isabelle

Some viewers may have found the story of Nell difficult to believe, but the painful childhood of Isabelle was all too real. For the first six years of her life, Isabelle lived in almost total seclusion in a darkened room. She had little contact with other people, with the exception of her mother, who could neither speak nor hear. Isabelle's mother's parents had been so deeply ashamed of Isabelle's illegitimate birth that they kept her hidden away from the world. Ohio authorities finally discovered the child in 1938, when Isabelle's mother escaped from her parents' home, taking her daughter with her.

When she was discovered at age six, Isabelle could not speak. She could merely make various croaking sounds. Her only communications with her mother were simple gestures. Isabelle had been largely deprived of the typical interactions and socialization experiences of childhood. Since she had actually seen few people, she initially showed a strong fear of strangers and reacted almost like a wild animal when confronted with an unfamiliar person. As she became accustomed to seeing certain individuals, her reaction changed to one of extreme apathy. At first, it was believed that Isabelle was deaf, but she soon began to react to nearby sounds. On tests of maturity, she scored at the level of an infant rather than a six-year-old.

Specialists developed a systematic training program to help Isabelle adapt to human relationships and socialization. After a few days of training, she made her first attempt to verbalize. Although she started slowly, Isabelle quickly passed through six years of development. In a little over two months, she was speaking in complete sentences. Nine months later, she could identify both words and sentences. Before Isabelle reached the age of nine, she was ready to attend school with other children. By her 14th year, she was in sixth grade, doing well in school, and emotionally well-adjusted.

Yet, without an opportunity to experience socialization in her first six years, Isabelle had been hardly human in the social sense when she was first discovered. Her inability to communicate at the time of her discovery—despite her physical and cognitive potential to learn—and her remarkable progress over the next few years underscore the impact of socialization on human development (K. Davis 1940, 1947).

Isabelle's experience is important for researchers because it is one of few cases of children reared in total isolation. Unfortunately, however, there are many cases of children raised in extremely neglectful social circumstances. Recently, attention has focused on infants and young children in orphanages in the formerly communist countries of Eastern Europe. For example, in Romanian orphanages, babies lie in their cribs for 18 or 20 hours a day, curled against their feeding bottles and receiving little adult care. Such minimal attention continues for the first five years of their lives. Many of them are fearful of human contact and prone to unpredictable antisocial behaviour. This situation came to light as families in North America and Europe began adopting thousands of these children. The adjustment problems for about 20 percent of them were often so dramatic that the adopting families suffered guilty fears of being ill-fit adoptive parents. Many of them have asked for assistance in dealing with the children. Slowly, efforts are being made to introduce the deprived youngsters to feelings of attachment that they never had experienced before (V. Groza et al. 1999; M. Talbot 1998).

Increasingly, researchers are emphasizing the importance of early socialization experiences for children who grow up in more normal environments. We now know that it is not enough to care for an infant's physical needs; parents must also concern themselves with children's social development. If, for example, children are discouraged from having friends, they will miss out on social interactions with peers that are critical for emotional growth.

Primate Studies

Studies of animals raised in isolation also support the importance of socialization in development. Harry Harlow (1971), a researcher at the primate laboratory of the University of Wisconsin, conducted tests with rhesus monkeys that had been raised away from their mothers and away from contact with other monkeys. As was the case with Isabelle, the rhesus monkeys raised in isolation were fearful and easily frightened. They did not mate, and the females who were artificially inseminated became abusive mothers. Apparently, isolation had had a damaging effect on the monkeys.

These children in a Romanian orphanage enjoy little adult contact and spend much of their time confined to cribs. This neglect can result in adjustment problems later in life.

A creative aspect of Harlow's experimentation was his use of "artificial mothers." In one such experiment, Harlow presented monkeys raised in isolation with two substitute mothers—one cloth-covered replica and one covered with wire that had the ability to offer milk. Monkey after monkey went to the wire mother for the life-giving milk, yet spent much more time clinging to the more motherlike cloth model. In this study, the monkeys valued the artificial mothers that provided a comforting physical sensation (conveyed by the terry cloth) more highly than those that provided food. It appears that the infant monkeys developed greater social attachments from their need for warmth, comfort, and intimacy than from their need for milk.

While the isolation studies discussed above may seem to suggest that inheritance can be dismissed as a factor in the social development of humans and animals, studies of twins provide insight into a fascinating interplay between hereditary and environmental factors.

The Influence of Heredity

Oskar Stohr and Jack Yufe are identical twins who were separated soon after their birth and raised on different continents in very different cultural settings. Oskar was reared as a strict Catholic by his maternal grandmother in the Sudetenland of Czechoslovakia. As a member of the Hitler Youth movement in Nazi Germany, he learned to hate Jews. By contrast, his brother Jack was reared in Trinidad by the twins' Jewish father. Jack joined an Israeli kibbutz (a collective settlement) at age 17 and later served in the Israeli army. But when they were reunited in middle age, some startling similarities emerged:

> Both were wearing wire-rimmed glasses and mustaches, both sported two pocket shirts with epaulets. They share idiosyncrasies galore: they like spicy foods and sweet liqueurs, are absent-minded, have a habit of falling asleep in front of the television, think it's funny to sneeze in a crowd of strangers, flush the toilet before using it, store rubber bands on their wrists, read magazines from back to front, dip buttered toast in their coffee (Holden 1980).

The twins also were found to differ in many important respects: Jack is a workaholic; Oskar enjoys leisure-time activities. Whereas Oskar is a traditionalist who is domineering toward women, Jack is a political liberal who is much more accepting of feminism. Finally, Jack is extremely proud of being Jewish, while Oskar never mentions his Jewish heritage (Holden 1987).

Oskar and Jack are prime examples of the interplay of heredity and environment. For a number of years, researchers at the Minnesota Center for Twin and Adoption Research have been studying pairs of identical twins reared apart to determine what similarities, if any, they show in personality traits, behaviour, and intelligence. Thus far, the preliminary results from the available twin studies indicate that both genetic factors and socialization experiences are influential in human development. Certain characteristics, such as temperaments, voice patterns, and nervous habits, appear to be strikingly similar even in twins reared apart, suggesting that these qualities may be linked to hereditary causes. However, identical twins reared apart differ far more in their attitudes, values, types of mates chosen, and even drinking habits; these qualities, it would seem, are influenced by environmental patterns. In examining clusters of personality traits among such twins, the Minnesota studies have found marked similarities in their tendency toward leadership or dominance, but significant differences in their need for intimacy, comfort, and assistance.

Researchers have also been impressed with the similar scores on intelligence tests of twins reared apart in *roughly similar* social settings. Most of the identical twins register scores even closer than those that would be expected if the same person took a test twice. At the same time, however, identical twins brought up in *dramatically different* social environments score quite differently on intelligence tests—a finding that supports the impact of socialization on human development (McGue and Bouchard 1998).

We need to be cautious when reviewing the studies of twin pairs and other relevant research. Widely broadcast findings have often been based on extremely small samples and preliminary analysis. For example, one study (not involving twin pairs) was frequently cited as confirming genetic links with behaviour. Yet the researchers had to retract their conclusions after they increased the sample from 81 to 91 cases and reclassified two of the original 81 cases. After these change, the initial findings were no longer valid. Critics add that the studies on twin pairs have not provided satisfactory information concerning the extent to which these separated identical twins may have had contact with each other, even though they were "raised apart." Such interactions—especially if they were extensive—could call into question the validity of the twin studies (Kelsoe et al. 1989).

Psychologist Leon Kamin fears that overgeneralizing from the Minnesota twin results—and granting too much importance to the impact of heredity—may lead to blaming the poor and downtrodden for their unfortunate condition. As this debate continues, we can certainly anticipate numerous efforts to replicate the research and clarify the interplay between hereditary and environmental factors in human development (Horgan 1993; Leo 1987; Plomin 1989; Wallis 1987).

Sociobiology

Do the *social* traits that human groups display have biological origins? As part of the continuing debate on the relative influences of heredity and the environment, there has been renewed interest in sociobiology in recent years. ***Sociobiology*** is the systematic study of the biological bases of social behaviour. Sociobiologists basically apply naturalist Charles Darwin's principles of natural selection to the study of social behaviour. They assume that particular forms of behaviour become genetically linked to a species if they contribute to its fitness to survive (van den Berghe 1978). In its extreme form, sociobiology suggests that *all* behaviour is the result of genetic or biological factors and that social interactions play no role in shaping people's conduct.

Sociobiology does not seek to describe individual behaviour on the level of "Why is Fred more aggressive than Jim?" Rather, sociobiologists focus on how human nature is affected by the genetic composition of a *group* of people who share certain characteristics (such as men or women, or members of isolated tribal bands). Many sociologists are highly critical of sociobiologists' tendency to explain, or seemingly justify, human behaviour on the basis of nature, and ignore its cultural and social basis.

Some researchers insist that intellectual interest in sociobiology will only deflect serious study of the more significant factor influencing human behaviour—socialization. Yet Lois Wladis Hoffman (1985), in her presidential address to the Society for the Psychological Study of Social Issues, argued that sociobiology poses a valuable challenge to social scientists to better document their own research. Interactionists, for example, could show how social behaviour is not programmed by human biology but instead adjusts continually to the attitudes and responses of others.

Conflict theorists (like functionalists and interactionists) believe that people's behaviour rather than their genetic structure defines social reality. Conflict theorists fear that the sociobiological approach could be used as an argument against efforts to assist disadvantaged people, such as schoolchildren who are not competing successfully (M. Harris 1997).

Edward O. Wilson, a zoologist at Harvard University, has argued that there should be parallel studies of human behaviour with a focus on both genetic and social causes. Certainly most social scientists would agree that there is a biological basis for social behaviour. But there is less support for the most extreme positions taken by certain advocates of sociobiology (S. Begley 1998; Gove 1987; Wilson 1975, 1978; see also Guterman 2000; Segerstråle 2000).

The Self and Socialization

We all have various perceptions, feelings, and beliefs about who we are and what we are like. How do we come to develop these? Do they change as we age?

We were not born with these understandings. Building on the work of George Herbert Mead (1964b), sociologists recognize that we create our own designation: the self. The ***self*** is a distinct identity that sets us apart from others. It is not a static phenomenon but continues to develop and change throughout our lives.

Sociologists and psychologists alike have expressed interest in how the individual develops and modifies the sense of self as a result of social interaction. The work of sociologists Charles Horton Cooley and George Herbert Mead, pioneers of the interactionist approach, has been especially useful in furthering our understanding of these important issues (Gecas 1982).

p. 15

Sociological Approaches to the Self

Cooley: Looking-Glass Self

In the early 1900s, Charles Horton Cooley advanced the belief that we learn who we are by interacting with others. Our view of ourselves, then, comes not only from direct contemplation of our personal qualities but also from our impressions of how others perceive us. Cooley used the phrase ***looking-glass self*** to emphasize that the self is the product of our social interactions with other people.

The process of developing a self-identity or self-concept has three phases. First, we imagine how we present ourselves to others—to relatives, friends, even strangers on the street. Then we imagine how others evaluate us (attractive, intelligent, shy, or strange). Finally, we develop some sort of feeling about ourselves, such as respect or shame, as a result of these impressions (Cooley 1902; Howard 1989).

A subtle but critical aspect of Cooley's looking-glass self is that the self results from an individual's "imagination" of how others view him or her. As a result, we can develop self-identities based on *incorrect* perceptions of how others see us. A student may react strongly to a teacher's criticism and decide (wrongly) that the instructor views the student as stupid. This misperception can easily be converted into a negative self-identity through the following process: (1) the teacher criticized me, (2) the teacher must think that I'm stupid, (3) I *am* stupid. Yet self-identities are also subject to change. If the student receives an "A" at the end of the course, he or she will probably no longer feel stupid.

Mead: Stages of the Self

George Herbert Mead continued Cooley's exploration of interactionist theory. Mead (1934, 1964a) developed a useful model of the process by which the self emerges, defined by three distinct stages: the preparatory stage, the play stage, and the game stage.

During the *preparatory stage*, children merely imitate the people around them, especially family members with whom they continually interact. Thus, a small child will bang on a piece of wood while a parent is engaged in carpentry work or will try to throw a ball if an older sibling is doing so nearby.

"Say cheese!" Children imitate the people around them, especially family members they continually interact with, during the *preparatory stage* described by George Herbert Mead.

As they grow older, children become more adept at using symbols to communicate with others. ***Symbols*** are the gestures, objects, and language that form the basis of human communication. By interacting with relatives and friends, as well as by watching cartoons on television and looking at picture books, children in the preparatory stage begin to understand the use of symbols. Like spoken languages, symbols vary from culture to culture and even between subcultures. Raising one's eyebrows may mean astonishment in North America, but in Peru it means "money" or "pay me," while in the Pacific island nation of Tonga it means "yes" or "I agree" (R. Axtell 1990).

Mead was among the first to analyze the relationship of symbols to socialization. As children develop skill in communicating through symbols, they gradually become more aware of social relationships. As a result, during the *play stage,* the child becomes able to pretend to be other people. Just as an actor "becomes" a character, a child becomes a doctor, parent, superhero, or ship captain.

Mead, in fact, noted that an important aspect of the play stage is role playing. ***Role taking*** is the process of mentally assuming the perspective of another, thereby enabling one to respond from that imagined viewpoint. For example, through this process, a young child will gradually learn when it is best to ask a parent for favours. If the parent usually comes home from work in a bad mood, the child will wait until after dinner when the parent is more relaxed and approachable.

In Mead's third stage, the *game stage,* the child of about eight or nine years old no longer just plays roles but begins to consider several actual tasks and relationships simultaneously. At this point in development, children grasp not only their own social positions, but also those of others around them—just as in a football game the players must understand their own and everyone else's positions. Consider a girl or boy who is part of a scout troop out on a weekend hike in the mountains. The child must understand what he or she is expected to do, but also must recognize the responsibilities of other scouts as well as the leaders. This is the final stage of development under Mead's model; the child can now respond to numerous members of the social environment.

Mead uses the term ***generalized others*** to refer to the attitudes, viewpoints, and expectations of society as a whole that a child takes into account. Simply put, this concept suggests that when an individual acts, he or she takes into account an entire group of people. For example, a child will not act courteously merely to please a particular parent. Rather, the child comes to understand that courtesy is a widespread social value endorsed by parents, teachers, and religious leaders.

At the game stage, children can take a more sophisticated view of people and the social environment. They now understand what specific occupations and social positions are and no longer equate Mr. Sahota only with the role of "librarian" or Ms. La Haigue only with "principal." It has become clear to the child that Mr. Sahota can be a librarian, a parent, and a marathon runner at the same time and that Ms. La Haigue is one of many principals in our society. Thus, the child has reached a new level of sophistication in his or her observations of individuals and institutions.

Mead: Theory of the Self

Mead is best known for his theory of the self. According to Mead (1964b), the self begins as a privileged, central position in a person's world. Young children picture themselves as the focus of everything around them and find it difficult to consider the perspectives of others. For example, when shown a mountain scene and asked to describe what an observer on the opposite side of the mountain sees (such as a lake or hikers), young children describe only objects visible from their own vantage point. This childhood tendency to place ourselves at the centre of events never entirely disappears. Many people with a fear of flying automatically assume that if any plane goes down, it will be the one they are on. And who

A young gymnast is receiving guidance from her coach. Individuals such as coaches, teachers, friends, and parents often play a major role in shaping a person's self.

reads the horoscope section in the paper without looking at their own horoscope first? And why else do we buy lottery tickets if we do not imagine ourselves winning?

As people mature, the self changes and begins to reflect greater concern about the reactions of others. Parents, friends, coworkers, coaches, and teachers are often among those who play a major role in shaping a person's self. Mead used the term ***significant others*** to refer to those individuals who are most important in the development of the self. Many young people, for example, find themselves drawn to the same kind of work their parents engage in (Schlenker 1985).

Goffman: Presentation of the Self

How do we manage our "self"? How do we display to others who we are? Erving Goffman, a sociologist associated with the interactionist perspective, suggested that many of our daily activities involve attempts to convey impressions of who we are.

Early in life, the individual learns to slant his or her presentation of the self in order to create distinctive appearances and satisfy particular audiences. Goffman (1959) refers to this altering of the presentation of the self as ***impression management.*** Box 4-1 provides an everyday example of this concept by describing how students engage in impression management after getting their examination grades.

In examining such everyday social interactions, Goffman makes so many explicit parallels to the theatre that his view has been termed the ***dramaturgical approach.*** According to this perspective, people resemble performers in action. For example, a clerk may try to appear busier than he or she actually is if a supervisor happens to be watching. A customer in a singles' bar may try to look as if he or she is waiting for a particular person to arrive.

Goffman (1959) has also drawn attention to another aspect of the self—***face-work.*** How often do you initiate some kind of face-saving behaviour when you feel embarrassed or rejected? In response to a rejection at the singles' bar, a person may engage in face-work by saying, "There really isn't an interesting person in this entire crowd." We feel the need to maintain a proper image of the self if we are to continue social interaction.

Goffman's approach is generally regarded as an insightful perspective on everyday life, but it is not without its critics. Writing from a conflict perspective, sociologist Alvin Gouldner (1970) sees Goffman's work as implicitly reaffirming the status quo, including social class inequalities. Using Gouldner's critique, one might ask if women and minorities are expected to deceive both themselves and others while paying homage to those with power. In considering impression management and other concepts developed by Goffman, sociologists must remember that by describing social reality, one is not necessarily endorsing its harsh impact on many individuals and groups (S. Williams 1986).

Goffman's work represents a logical progression of the sociological efforts begun by Cooley and Mead on how personality is acquired through socialization and how we manage the presentation of our self to others. Cooley stressed the process by which we come to create a self; Mead focused on how the self develops as we learn to interact with others; Goffman emphasized the ways in which we consciously create images of ourselves for others.

Psychological Approaches to the Self

Psychologists have shared the interest of Cooley, Mead, and other sociologists in the development of the self. Early work in psychology, such as that of Sigmund Freud (1856–1939), stressed the role of inborn drives—among them the drive for sexual gratification—in channelling

Research in Action 4-1 Impression Management by Students after Exams

When you get an exam back, you probably react differently with fellow classmates, depending on the grades that you and they earned. This is all part of impression management, as sociologists Daniel Albas and Cheryl Albas (1988) demonstrated. They explored the strategies that post-secondary students use to create desired appearances after receiving their grades on exams. Albas and Albas divide these encounters into three categories: those between students who have all received high grades (Ace–Ace encounters), those between students who have received high grades and those who have received low or even failing grades (Ace–Bomber encounters), and those between students who have all received low grades (Bomber–Bomber encounters).

Ace–Ace encounters occur in a rather open atmosphere because there is comfort in sharing a high mark with another high achiever. It is even acceptable to violate the norm of modesty and brag when among other Aces since, as one student admitted, "It's much easier to admit a high mark to someone who has done better than you, or at least as well."

Ace–Bomber encounters are often sensitive. Bombers generally attempt to avoid such exchanges because "you . . . emerge looking like the dumb one" or "feel like you are lazy or unreliable." When forced into interactions with Aces, Bombers work to appear gracious and congratulatory. For their part, Aces offer sympathy and support for the dissatisfied Bombers and even rationalize their own "lucky" high scores. To help Bombers save face, Aces may emphasize the difficulty and unfairness of the examination.

When forced into interactions with Aces, Bombers work to appear gracious and congratulatory.

Bomber–Bomber encounters tend to be closed, reflecting the group effort to wall off the feared disdain of others. Yet, within the safety of these encounters, Bombers openly share their disappointment and engage in expressions of mutual self-pity that they themselves call "pity parties." They devise face-saving excuses for their poor performances, such as "I wasn't feeling well all week" or "I had four exams and two papers due that week." If the grade distribution in a class included particularly low scores, Bombers may blame the professor, who will be attacked as a sadist, a slave driver, or simply an incompetent.

As is evident from these descriptions, students' impression management strategies conform to society's informal norms regarding modesty and consideration for less successful peers. In classroom settings, as in the workplace and in other types of human interactions, efforts at impression management are most intense when status differentials are more pronounced as in encounters between the high-scoring Aces and the low-scoring Bombers.

Let's Discuss

1. What social norms govern the students' impression management strategies?
2. How do you react with those who have received higher or lower grades than you? Do you engage in impression management? How would you like others to react to your grade?

Source: Albas and Albas 1988.

human behaviour. More recently, psychologists such as Jean Piaget have emphasized the stages through which human beings progress as the self develops.

Like Charles Horton Cooley and George Herbert Mead, Freud believed that the self is a social product and that aspects of one's personality are influenced by other people (especially one's parents). However, unlike Cooley and Mead, he suggested that the self has components that are always fighting with each other. According to Freud, our natural impulsive instincts are in constant conflict with societal constraints. Part of us seeks limitless pleasure, while another part seeks out rational behaviour. By interacting with others, we learn the expectations of society and then select behaviour most appropriate to our own culture. (Of course, as Freud was well aware, we sometimes distort reality and behave irrationally.)

Research on newborn babies by the Swiss child psychologist Jean Piaget (1896–1980) has underscored the importance of social interactions in developing a sense of self. Piaget found that newborns have no self in the sense of a looking-glass image. Ironically, though, they are quite self-centred; they demand that all attention be directed toward them. Newborns have not yet separated themselves from the universe of which they are a part. For these babies, the phrase "you and me" has no meaning; they understand only "me." However, as they mature, children are gradually socialized into social relationships even within their rather self-centred world.

In his well-known ***cognitive theory of development***, Piaget (1954) identifies four stages in the development of children's thought processes. In the first, or *sensorimotor*, stage, young children use their senses to make discoveries. For example, through touching they discover that their hands are actually a part of themselves. During the second, or *preoperational*, stage, children begin to use words and symbols to distinguish objects and ideas. The milestone in the third, or *concrete operational*, stage is that children engage in more logical thinking. They learn that even when a formless lump of clay is shaped into a snake, it is still the same clay. Finally, in the fourth, or *formal operational*, stage, adolescents are capable of sophisticated abstract thought and can deal with ideas and values in a logical manner.

Piaget has suggested that moral development becomes an important part of socialization as children develop the ability to think more abstractly. When children learn the rules of a game such as checkers or jacks, they are learning to obey societal norms. Those under eight years old display a rather basic level of morality: rules are rules, and there is no concept of "extenuating circumstances." However, as they mature, children become capable of greater autonomy and begin to experience moral dilemmas as to what constitutes proper behaviour.

According to Jean Piaget, social interaction is the key to development. As they grow older, children give increasing attention to how other people think and why they act in particular ways. In order to develop a distinct personality, each of us needs opportunities to interact with others. As we saw earlier, Isabelle was deprived of the chance for normal social interactions, and the consequences were severe (Kitchener 1991).

Body painting is a ritual marking the passage to puberty among young people in Liberia in northern Africa.

Socialization and the Life Course

The Life Course

Adolescents among the Kota people of the Congo in Africa paint themselves blue, Mexican American girls go on a daylong religious retreat before dancing the night away, Egyptian mothers step over their newborn infants seven times, and graduating North American students may throw hats in the air. These are all ways of celebrating ***rites of passage,*** a means of dramatizing and validating changes in a person's status. The Kota rite marks the passage to adulthood. The colour blue, viewed as the colour of death, symbolizes the death of childhood. Hispanic girls in the United States celebrate reaching womanhood with a *quinceañera* ceremony at age 15. In Miami, Florida, the popularity of the *quinceañera* supports a network of party planners, caterers, dress designers, and the Miss Quinceañera Latina pageant. For thousands of years, Egyptian mothers have welcomed their newborns to the world in the Soboa ceremony by stepping over the seven-day-old infant seven times. North American graduates may celebrate their graduation from college or university by hurling their hats skyward (D. Cohen 1991; Garza 1993; McLane 1995; Quadagno 1999).

These specific ceremonies mark stages of development in the life course. They indicate that the socialization process continues throughout all stages of the human life cycle. Sociologists and other social scientists use the life-course approach in recognition that biological changes mould but do not dictate human behaviour from birth until death.

Within the cultural diversity of Canada, each individual has a "personal biography" that is influenced by events both in the family and in the larger society. While the completion of religious confirmations, school graduations, marriage, and parenthood can all be regarded as rites of passage in our society, people do not necessarily experience them at the same time. The timing of these events depends on such factors as one's gender, economic background, region (urban or rural area), and even when one was born.

Sociologists and other social scientists have moved away from identifying specific life stages that we are all expected to pass through at some point. Indeed, people today are much less likely to follow an "orderly" progression of life events (leaving school, then obtaining their first job, then getting married) than they were in the past. For example, an increasing number of women in Canada are beginning or returning to post-secondary education after marrying and having children. With such changes in mind, researchers are increasingly reluctant to offer sweeping generalizations about stages in the life course.

We encounter some of the most difficult socialization challenges (and rites of passage) in the later years of life. Assessing one's accomplishments, coping with declining physical abilities, experiencing retirement, and facing the inevitability of death may lead to painful adjustments. Old age is further complicated by the negative way that many societies view and treat the elderly. The common stereotypes of the elderly as helpless and dependent may well weaken an older person's self-image. However, as we will explore more fully in Chapter 14, many older people continue to lead active, productive, fulfilled lives—whether within the paid labour force or as retirees.

Anticipatory Socialization and Resocialization

The development of a social self is literally a lifelong transformation that begins in the crib and continues as one prepares for death. Two types of socialization occur at many points throughout the life course: anticipatory socialization and resocialization.

Anticipatory socialization refers to the processes of socialization in which a person "rehearses" for future positions, occupations, and social relationships. A culture can function more efficiently and smoothly if members become acquainted with the norms, values, and behaviour associated with a social position before actually assuming that status. Preparation for many aspects of adult life begins with anticipatory socialization during childhood and adolescence and continues throughout our lives as we prepare for new responsibilities.

You can see the process of anticipatory socialization take place when high school students start to consider which post-secondary institutions they may attend. Traditionally, this meant looking at publications received in the mail or making campus visits. However, with new technology, more and more students are using the Web to begin their educational experience. Institutions are investing more time and money in developing attractive websites where students can take "virtual" campus walks and hear audio clips of everything from the campus cheer to a sample zoology lecture.

Occasionally, assuming new social and occupational positions requires us to *unlearn* a previous orientation. ***Resocialization*** refers to the process of discarding former behaviour patterns and accepting new ones as part of a transition in one's life. Often resocialization occurs when there is an explicit effort to transform an individual, as happens in therapy groups, prisons, religious conversion settings, and political indoctrination camps. The process of resocialization typically involves considerable stress for the individual, much more so than socialization in general or even anticipatory socialization (Gecas 1992).

Resocialization is particularly effective when it occurs within a total institution. Erving Goffman (1961) coined the term ***total institutions*** to refer to institutions, such as prisons, the military, mental hospitals, and convents, that regulate all aspects of a person's life under a single authority. Because the total institution is generally cut off from the rest of society, it provides for all the needs of its members. Quite literally, the crew of a merchant vessel at sea becomes part of a total institution. So elaborate are its requirements, and so all-encompassing are its activities, a total institution often represents a miniature society.

Goffman (1961) has identified four common traits of total institutions:

- All aspects of life are conducted in the same place and are under the control of a single authority.
- Any activities within the institution are conducted in the company of others in the same circumstances—for example, novices in a convent or army recruits.
- The authorities devise rules and schedule activities without consulting the participants.
- All aspects of life within a total institution are designed to fulfill the purpose of the organization. Thus, all activities in a monastery might be centred on prayer and communion with God (Davies 1989; P. Rose et al. 1979).

People often lose their individuality within total institutions. For example, a person entering prison may experience the humiliation of a ***degradation ceremony*** as he or she is stripped of clothing, jewellery, and other personal possessions. Even the person's self is taken away to some extent; the prison inmate loses a name and becomes known to authorities as a number. From this point on, scheduled daily routines allow for little or no personal initiative. The individual becomes secondary and rather invisible in the overbearing social environment (Garfinkel 1956).

Back in 1934, the world was gripped by the birth of quintuplets to Olivia and Elzire Dionne in Ontario. In the midst of the Depression, people wanted to hear and see all they could about these five girls, born generations before fertility drugs made multiple births more common. What seemed like a heartwarming story turned out to be a tragic case of Goffman's total institutionalization. The government of Ontario soon took the quintuplets from their home and set them up in a facility complete with an observation gallery overlooking their playground. Each month, 10 000 tourists paid an entry fee to view the five little "Cinderellas." When the girls left the nine-room compound, it was always to raise money for some worthwhile cause or to merchandise some product. Within their compound, even their parents and their older siblings had to make appointments to see them. A child psychiatrist responsible for their child rearing ordered they never be spanked—or hugged (to prevent the chance of infection).

After nine years, the quintuplets were reunited with their family. But the legacy of total institutionalization persisted. Sharp divisions and jealousies had developed between the five girls and other siblings. The parents were caught up in charges of doing too much or too little for all their children. In 1997 the three surviving quintuplets made public a poignant letter to the parents of recently born septuplets in Iowa:

> We three would like you to know we feel a natural affinity and tenderness for your children. We hope your children receive more respect than we did. Their fate should be no different from that of other children. Multiple births should not be confused with entertainment, nor should they be an opportunity to sell products. . . .
>
> Our lives have been ruined by the exploitation we suffered at the hands of the government of Ontario, our place of birth. We were displayed as a curiosity three times a day for millions of tourists. . . .
>
> We sincerely hope a lesson will be learned from examining how our lives were forever altered by our childhood experiences. If this letter changes the course of events for these newborns, then perhaps our lives will have served a higher purpose (Dionne et al. 1997:39).

It is to be hoped that the Iowa septuplets won't find themselves in the position of the Dionne women in 1998, waging a lawsuit against the government for the way they were raised in an institutional environment.

How would you like to be "on view" for thousands of tourists? That was the fate of the Dionne quintuplets during the 1930s near the village of Corbeil in Ontario. The five little girls were removed from their parents and kept under sharp watch in a nine-room compound called "Quintland"—a form of a *total institution.*

Agents of Socialization

As we have seen, the continuing and lifelong socialization process involves many different social forces that influence our lives and alter our self-images.

The family is the most important agent of socialization in Canada, especially for children. We'll also give particular attention in this chapter to five other agents of socialization: the school, the peer group, the mass media, the workplace, and the state. The role of religion in socializing young people into society's norms and values will be explored in Chapter 12.

Family

Children in Amish communities are raised in a highly structured and disciplined manner. But they are not immune to the temptations posed by their peers in the non-Amish world—"rebellious" acts such as dancing, drinking, and riding in cars. Still, Amish families don't get too concerned; they know the strong influence they ultimately exert over their offspring (see Box 4-2). The same is true for the family in general. It is tempting to say that the "peer group" or even the "media" really raise kids these days, especially when the spotlight falls on young people involved in shooting sprees and hate crimes. Almost all available research, however, shows that the role of the family in socializing a child cannot be under-

Sociology in the Global Community

4-2 Raising Amish Children

Jacob is a typical teenager in his Amish community in Lancaster County, Pennsylvania. At 14 he is in his final year of schooling. Over the next few years he will become a full-time worker on the family farm, taking breaks only for a three-hour religious service each morning. When he is a bit older, Jacob may bring a date in his family's horse-drawn buggy to a community "singing." But he will be forbidden to date outside his own community and can marry only with the deacon's consent. Jacob is well aware of the rather different way of life of the "English" (the Amish term for non-Amish people). One summer he and his friends hitchhiked late at night to a nearby town to see a movie, breaking several Amish taboos. His parents learned of his adventure, but like most Amish they are confident that their son will choose the Amish way of life. What is this way of life and how can the parents be so sure of its appeal?

Jacob and his family live in a manner very similar to their ancestors, members of the conservative Mennonite church who migrated to North America from Europe in the 18th and 19th centuries. Schisms in the church after 1850 led to a division between those who wanted to preserve the "old order" and those who favoured a "new order" with more progressive methods and organization. Today the old order Amish live in about 50 communities in the United States and Canada. Estimates put their number at about 80 000 with approximately 75 percent living in three American states—Ohio, Pennsylvania, and Indiana.

The old order Amish live a "simple" life and reject most aspects of modernization and contemporary technology. That's why they spurn such conveniences as electricity, automobiles, radio, and television. The Amish maintain their own schools and traditions, and they do not want their children socialized into many norms and values of the dominant cultures of the United States and Canada. Those who stray too far from Amish mores may be excommunicated and shunned by all other members of the community—a practice of social control called *Meiding*. Sociologists sometimes use the term "secessionist minorities" to refer to groups like the Amish who reject assimilation and coexist with the rest of society primarily on their own terms.

The old order Amish live a "simple" life and reject most aspects of modernization and contemporary technology.

Life for Amish youth attracts particular attention since their socialization pushes them to forgo movies, radio, television, cosmetics, jewellery, musical instruments of any kind, and motorized vehicles. Yet, like Jacob did, Amish youth often test their subculture's boundaries during a period of discovery called *rumspringe*, a term that literally means "running around." Amish young people attend barn dances where taboos like drinking, smoking, and driving cars are commonly broken. Parents often react by looking the other way, sometimes literally. For example, when they hear radio sounds from a barn or a motorcycle entering the property in the middle of the night, they don't immediately investigate and punish their offspring. Instead, they will pretend not to notice, secure in the comfort that their children almost always return to the traditions of the Amish lifestyle. Occasionally, young people go too far. For example, in 1997 a motorcycle gang of ten Amish youth were caught selling drugs, including cocaine, in suburban Philadelphia. But cases like this are so rare that they make headlines when they happen. Research shows that only about 20 percent of Amish youth leave the fold, generally to join a more liberal Mennonite group, and rarely does a baptized adult ever leave. The socialization of Amish youth moves them gently but firmly into becoming Amish adults.

Let's Discuss

1. What makes Amish parents so sure that their children will choose to remain in the Amish community?
2. If you lived in an Amish community, how would your life differ from the way it is now? In your opinion, what advantages and disadvantages would that lifestyle have?

Sources: Zellner 2001; Meyers 1992; Remnick 1998.

estimated (W. Williams 1998; for a different view see J. Harris 1998).

The lifelong process of learning begins shortly after birth. Since newborns can hear, see, smell, taste, and feel heat, cold, and pain, they are constantly orienting themselves to the surrounding world. Human beings, especially family members, constitute an important part of their social environment. People minister to the baby's needs by feeding, cleansing, carrying, and comforting the baby.

The caretakers of a newborn are not concerned with teaching social skills per se. Nevertheless, babies are hardly asocial. An infant enters an organized society, becomes part of a generation, and typically joins a family.

Depending on how they are treated, infants can develop strong social attachments and dependency on others.

Most infants go through a relatively formal period of socialization generally called *habit training.* Caregivers impose schedules for eating and sleeping, for terminating breast- or bottle-feeding, and for introducing new foods. In these and other ways, infants can be viewed as objects of socialization. Yet they also function as socializers. Even as the behaviour of a baby is being modified by interactions with people and the environment, the baby is causing others to change their behaviour patterns. He or she converts adults into mothers and fathers, who, in turn, assist the baby in progressing into childhood (Rheingold 1969).

As both Charles Horton Cooley and George Herbert Mead noted, the development of the self is a critical aspect of the early years of one's life. However, how children develop this sense of self can vary from one society to another. For example, parents in Canada would never think of sending six-year-olds to school unsupervised. But this is the norm in Japan, where parents push their children to commute to school on their own from an early age. In cities like Tokyo, first-graders must learn to negotiate buses, subways, and long walks. To ensure their safety, parents carefully lay out rules: never talk to strangers; check with a station attendant if you get off at the wrong stop; if you miss your stop stay on to the end of the line, then call; take stairs, not escalators; don't fall asleep. Some parents equip the children with cell phones or pagers. One parent acknowledges that she worries, "but after they are 6, children are supposed to start being independent from the mother. If you're still taking your child to school after the first month, everyone looks at you funny" (Tolbert 2000:17).

In Canada, social development includes exposure to cultural assumptions regarding gender, class, and race. Fleras and Kunz (2001) argue that the news media tend to undermine the contributions of minorities in Canadian society, emphasizing "their status as athletes, entertainers, or criminals, while the occasional fawning reference to minorities in position of political or economic power represents an exception that simply proves the rule" (Fleras and Kunz 2001:83). Since children are watching television at an increasingly younger age, they are increasingly susceptible to absorbing the images packaged for and by the dominant culture.

Family and Gender Socialization

Have you ever noticed when parents mention their newborn babies they may describe their daughters as "pretty," "sweet," or "angelic" and their sons as "tough," "rugged," or "strong"? Although newborn babies look much the same regardless of sex, with one noticeable exception, parents often apply cultural and social assumptions about femininity and masculinity to their children from the moment of birth. Now, with the development of technologies such as ultrasound and amniocentesis, which can reveal the sex of the fetus, parents may well begin to apply these assumptions before birth. This pattern begins a lifelong process of ***gender socialization***—an aspect of socialization through which we learn the attitudes, behaviours, and practices associated with being male or female (called ***gender roles***) according to our society and social groups within it. Our society (and various social groups such as social classes and ethnic groups) produces ideals and expectations about gender roles, reinforcing these ideals and expectations at each stage of the life course. As we will see in Chapter 10, other cultures do not necessarily assign these qualities to each gender in the way that our culture does.

As the primary agents of childhood socialization, parents play a critical role in guiding children into those gender roles deemed appropriate in a society. Other adults, older siblings, the mass media, and religious and educational institutions also have noticeable impact on a child's socialization into feminine and masculine norms. A culture or subculture may require that one sex or the other take primary responsibility for socialization of children, economic support of the family, or religious or intellectual leadership.

Social class may also play a role in gender socialization. Members of certain social classes may be more or less likely to engage in socialization patterns geared to traditional gender roles. Tuck et al. (1994), for example, studied gender socialization in middle-class homes with career-oriented mothers. They found these homes to be less stereotypic in terms of behaviour expectations than working-class homes. Other studies have found that working-class homes are more likely to conform to traditional or stereotypical notions of masculinity and femininity and socialize their children accordingly (Nelson and Robinson 2002). Daughters in a working-class family might, for example, be called on more often to help with domestic chores such as cooking or attending to the needs of younger siblings. Sons, on the other hand, might not be expected to help out with chores or younger children and instead might be encouraged to pursue independent activities outside the home.

The differential gender roles absorbed in early childhood often help define a child's popularity later on. In the extract that opened this chapter, the Adlers give a picture of the dynamics of "in" and "out" groups among both girls and boys. Patricia Adler has found that boys typically achieve high status on the basis of their athletic ability, "coolness," toughness, social skills, and success in relationships with girls. By contrast, girls owe their popularity to their parents' status and their own physical appearance, social skills, and academic success (Adler and Adler 1998; P. Adler et al. 1992).

Like other elements of culture, socialization patterns are not fixed. The last 30 years, for example, have witnessed a sustained challenge to traditional gender-role socialization in North America, due in good part to the efforts of the feminist movement (see Chapter 10). Nevertheless, despite such changes, children growing up today are hardly free of traditional gender roles.

Interactionists remind us that socialization concerning not only masculinity and femininity, but also marriage and parenthood, begins in childhood as a part of family life. Children observe their parents as they express affection, deal with finances, quarrel, complain about in-laws, and so forth. This represents an informal process of anticipatory socialization. The child develops a tentative model of what being married and being a parent are like. (We will explore socialization for marriage and parenthood more fully in Chapter 11.)

School

Where did you learn the national anthem? Who taught you about the early Canadian explorers? Where were you first tested on your knowledge of your culture? Like the family, schools have an explicit mandate to socialize people in Canada—and especially children—into the norms and values of the dominant culture.

As conflict theorists Samuel Bowles and Herbert Gintis (1976) have observed, schools foster competition through built-in systems of reward and punishment, such as grades and evaluations by teachers. Consequently, a child who is working intently to learn a new skill can sometimes come to feel stupid and unsuccessful. However, as the self matures, children become capable of increasingly realistic assessments of their intellectual, physical, and social abilities.

Functionalists point out that, as agents of socialization, schools fulfill the function of teaching children the values and customs of the larger society. Conflict theorists agree but add that schools can reinforce the divisive aspects of society, especially those of social class. For example, higher education in Canada is quite costly despite the existence of student aid programs. Students from affluent backgrounds have an advantage in gaining access to universities and professional training. At the same time, less affluent young people may never receive the preparation that would qualify them for the best-paying and most prestigious jobs. The contrast between the functionalist and conflict views of education will be discussed in more detail in Chapter 12.

In other cultures as well, schools serve socialization functions. During the 1980s, for example, Japanese parents and educators were distressed to realize that children were gradually losing the knack of eating with chopsticks. This became a national issue in 1997 when school lunch programs introduced plastic "sporks" (combined fork and spoon). National leaders, responding to the public outcry, banished sporks in favour of *hashi* (chopsticks). On a more serious note, Japanese schools have come under increasing pressure in recent years as working parents have abdicated more and more responsibility to educational institutions. To rectify the imbalance, the Japanese government in 1998 promoted a guide to better parenting, calling on parents to read more with their children, allow for more playtime, limit TV watching, and plan family activities, among other things (Gauette 1998).

This Japanese school maintains the Japanese cultural practice of eating with chopsticks. When school lunch programs introduced the "spork" (combined plastic spoon and fork) in the late 1990s, Japanese parents raised a fuss and forced a return to the traditional chopsticks.

School and Gender Socialization

In teaching students the values and customs of the larger society, schools in Canada have traditionally socialized children into conventional gender roles. Professors of education Myra Sadker and David Sadker (1985:54; 1995) note that "although many believe that classroom sexism disappeared in the early '70s, it hasn't."

Sadker and Sadker's research points to a gender bias in terms of the time, effort, and attention that is given to boys in the classroom, as opposed to that given to girls. For example, boys were called on more frequently by teachers to answer questions and, even when they were not directly asked to participate, boys tended to call out in class (Sadker and Sadker 1994). A study carried out in a Toronto high school classroom showed that males spoke out 75 to 80 percent of the time (Gaskell et al. 1995).

Despite the apparent gender bias that exists in classroom participation, educators in Canada are becoming concerned that boys are lagging behind girls in academic achievement as demonstrated by girls' overrepresentation on the high school honour rolls in Ontario and British Columbia (Galt 1998). Patricia Clarke, former president of the B.C. Teacher's Federation, suggests that boys are immersed in a gender-specific culture that undervalues academic achievement and that greater attention needs to be paid to dispelling the myth that "the coolest thing to do is be stupid" (Holmes 2000:11). Similar gender gaps in academic performance are being experienced in other countries, such as Britain, where girls are also academically outperforming their male classmates (Galt 1998).

Peer Group

Ask 13-year-olds who matters most in their lives and they are likely to answer "friends." As a child grows older, the family becomes somewhat less important in social development. Instead, peer groups increasingly assume the role of Mead's significant others. Within the peer group, young people associate with others who are approximately their own age and who often enjoy a similar social status.

Peer groups can ease the transition to adult responsibilities. At home, parents tend to dominate; at school, the teenager must contend with teachers and administrators. But within the peer group, each member can assert himself or herself in a way that may not be possible elsewhere. Nevertheless, almost all adolescents in our culture remain economically dependent on their parents, and most are emotionally dependent as well.

Teenagers imitate their friends in part because the peer group maintains a meaningful system of rewards and punishments. The group may encourage a young person to follow pursuits that society considers admirable, as in a school club engaged in volunteer work in hospitals and nursing homes. On the other hand, the group may encourage someone to violate the culture's norms and values by driving recklessly, shoplifting, engaging in acts of vandalism, taking drugs, and the like.

Peers can be the source of harassment as well as support, as the chapter opening extract showed. This problem has received considerable attention in Japan, where bullying in school is a constant fact of life. Groups of students act together to humiliate, disgrace, or torment a specific student, a practice known in Japan as *ijime.* Most students go along with the bullying out of fear that they might be the target some time. In some cases the *ijime* has led to a child's suicide. In 1998 the situation became so desperate that a volunteer association set up a 24-hour telephone hotline in Tokyo just for children (see the chapter opening poster). The success of this effort convinced the government to sponsor a nationwide hotline system (Matsushita 1999; Sugimoto 1997).

Peer Group and Gender Socialization

A study done in British Columbia schools points to the prevalence of bullying and some of the gender-related patterns of the activity. Approximately 10 to 15 percent of British Columbia students are bullies, while approximately 8 to 10 percent are victims (*The Vancouver Sun* 2000). Researchers Debra Pepler of York University and Wendy Craig of Queen's University found that girls do more of the verbal and social bullying while boys' bullying behaviour tends to be more physical. Girls bullied boys approximately half of the time, while boys primarily bullied other boys. Bullies of both sexes tended to be perceived as popular and powerful by their peer group while victims are perceived as lacking humour, having a tendency to cry easily, and deserving to be picked on. Pepler and Craig's research also showed that families of bullies tend to be permissive and display more positive attitudes toward aggression, and that other students who have not yet been victimized may want to align with bullies to avoid possible bullying in the future.

Gender differences are noteworthy in the social world of adolescents. Males are more likely to spend time in *groups* of males, while females are more likely to interact with a *single* other female. This pattern reflects differences in levels of emotional intimacy; teenage males are less likely to develop strong emotional ties than are females. Instead, males are more inclined to share in group activities. These patterns are evident among adolescents in many societies around the world (Dornbusch 1989).

Mass Media and Technology

In the last 75 years, media innovations—radio, motion pictures, recorded music, television, and the Internet—have become important agents of socialization. Television, in particular, is a critical force in the socialization of children in North America. In Canada, for example, 99 percent of households own at least one television set (Withers and Brown 2001). In addition, a 1999 survey estimated that 86 percent of Canadians live in households containing a VCR and 75 percent live in households with cable TV service (Withers and Brown 2001).

This research of viewing habits revealed that, on a per capita basis, Canadians watched an average of 21.6 hours per week during the fall of 1999, the survey period.

Women who were 18 years and older were the heaviest viewers (25.5 hours per week), while children (2 to 11) and teens (12 to 17) each viewed 15.5 hours per week. A Canadian feminist organization known as MediaWatch was established in 1981 to identify and monitor trends in the mass media (particularly in advertising) as they relate to the portrayal of women. Table 4-1 shows some of the ways the mass media presents a distorted view of women.

Television has certain characteristics that distinguish it from other agents of socialization. It permits imitation and role playing but does not encourage more complex forms of learning. Watching television is, above all, a passive experience; one sits back and waits to be entertained. Critics of television are further alarmed by the programming that children view as they sit for hours in front of a television set. It is generally agreed that children (as well as adults) are exposed to a great deal of violence on television. Despite recent attention to the issue, a 1998 study showed that the situation had not changed over the last two years. Of particular concern is that 40 percent of violent incidents on television are initiated by "good" characters, who are likely to be perceived as positive role models (J. Federman 1998; L. Mifflin 1999).

While we have focused on television as an agent of socialization, it is important to note that similar issues have been raised regarding the content of popular music (especially rock music and "rap"), music videos, motion pictures, video games, and Internet websites. These forms of entertainment, like television, p. 61 serve as powerful agents of socialization for many young people around the globe. Continuing controversy about the content of music, music videos, and films has sometimes led to celebrated court battles, as certain parents' organizations and religious groups challenge the intrusion of these media into the lives of children and adolescents. In recent years, people have expressed concern about the type of material that children can access on the Internet, especially pornography.

Finally, sociologists and other social scientists have begun to consider the impact of technology on socialization, especially as it applies to family life. The Silicon Valley Cultures Project studied families in California's Silicon Valley (a technological corridor) for ten years beginning in 1991. While these families may not be typical, they probably represent a lifestyle that more and more households will approximate. This study has found that technology in the form of e-mail, webpages, cellular phones, voice mail, digital organizers, and pagers is allowing householders to let outsiders do everything from grocery shopping to soccer pools. The researchers are also finding that families are socialized into multitasking (doing more than one task at a time) as the social norm; devoting one's full attention to one task—even eating or driving—is less and less common on a typical day (Silicon Valley Cultures Project 1999).

Table 4-1 Distorted Viewing: The Mass Media's Treatment of Women

• **Objectification**	Portraying women as objects that can be manipulated, bought, and sold.
• **Irrelevant sexualization**	Portraying women's bodies in a sexual way in order to attract attention and perpetuate the attitude that women's primary role is to attract male attention.
• **Infanticization**	Presenting women as childlike, coy, silly, and powerless.
• **Domestication**	Defining women in relation to their children, husbands, and family in a domestic environment.
• **Victimization**	Portraying women as victims of male brutality, inside and outside their own homes.

Source: Based on Graydon 2001.

Workplace

Learning to behave appropriately within an occupation is a fundamental aspect of human socialization. In North America, working full-time confirms adult status; it is an indication to all that one has passed out of adolescence. In a sense, socialization into an occupation can represent both a harsh reality ("I have to work in order to buy food and pay the rent") and the realization of an ambition ("I've always wanted to be an airline pilot") (W. Moore 1968:862).

Some observers feel that the increasing number of teenagers who are working earlier in life and for longer hours are now finding the workplace almost as important an agent of socialization as school. In fact, a number of educators complain that student time at work is adversely affecting schoolwork. Will Boyce, a professor of education at Queen's University, found that the number of working high school students in Ontario is increasing (Philip 2001). Boyce discovered that 46.3 percent of high school students in Ontario were working, while in 1996 the number was 31 percent. Researchers are trying to gauge the impact on students' lives, and have found that those students who work less than 20 hours per week often do

This boy's day doesn't end when school lets out. So many teenagers now work after school, the workplace has become another important agent of socialization for that age group.

better academically and are more involved in hobbies and sports than those students without jobs (Philip 2001).

Socialization in the workplace changes when it involves a more permanent shift from an afterschool job to full-time employment. Wilbert Moore (1968:871–80) has divided occupational socialization into four phases. The first phase is *career choice,* which involves selection of academic or vocational training appropriate for the desired job. The second phase, *anticipatory socialization,* may last only a few months or may extend for a period of years. In a sense, young people experience anticipatory socialization throughout childhood and adolescence as they observe their parents at work.

The third phase of occupational socialization—*conditioning and commitment*—occurs in the work-related role. *Conditioning* consists of reluctantly adjusting to the more unpleasant aspects of one's job. Most people find that the novelty of a new daily schedule quickly wears off and then realize that parts of the work experience are rather tedious. *Commitment* refers to the enthusiastic acceptance of pleasurable duties that comes with recognition of the positive tasks of an occupation.

In Moore's view, if a job proves to be satisfactory, the person will enter a fourth stage of socialization, which he calls *continuous commitment.* At this point, the job becomes an indistinguishable part of the person's self-identity. Violation of proper conduct becomes unthinkable. A person may choose to join professional associations, unions, or other groups that represent the occupation in the larger society.

Occupational socialization can be most intense during the transition from school to job, but it continues through one's work history. Technological advances may alter the requirements of the position and necessitate some degree of resocialization. Many men and women today change occupations, employers, or places of work many times during their adult years. Therefore, occupational socialization continues throughout a person's years in the labour market.

The State

Social scientists have increasingly recognized the importance of the state as an agent of socialization because of its growing impact on the life course. Traditionally, family members have served as the primary caregivers in our culture, but in the 20th century, the family's protective function has steadily been transferred to outside agencies such as hospitals, mental health clinics, and insurance companies. The state runs many of these agencies or licenses and regulates them (Ogburn and Tibbits 1934).

In the past, heads of households and local groups such as religious organizations influenced the life course most significantly. However, today national interests are increasingly influencing the individual as a citizen and an economic actor. For example, labour unions and political parties serve as intermediaries between the individual and the state.

The state has had a noteworthy impact on the life course by reinstituting the rites of passage that had disappeared in agricultural societies and in periods of early industrialization. For example, government regulations stipulate the ages at which a person may drive a car, drink alcohol, vote in elections, marry without parental permission, work overtime, and retire. These regulations do not constitute strict rites of passage: most 18-year-olds choose not to vote, and most people choose their age of retirement without reference to government dictates. Still, the state shapes the socialization process by regulating the life course to some degree and by influencing our views of appropriate behaviour at particular ages (Mayer and Schoepflin 1989).

In the social policy section that follows, we will see that the state is under pressure to become a provider of child care, which would give it a new and direct role in the socialization of infants and young children.

SOCIAL POLICY AND SOCIALIZATION

Day Care around the World

The Issue

The rise in single-parent families, increased job opportunities for women, and the need for additional family income have all propelled an increasing number of mothers of young children into Canada's paid labour force. In 1998, 62 percent of all mothers with children under the age of six were part of the labour force. Who, then, takes care of the children of these women during work hours?

Day care centres have become the functional equivalent of the nuclear family, performing some of the nurturing and socialization functions previously handled only by family members (Abelson 1997). But how does group day care compare to care in the home? And what is the state's responsibility to assure quality care?

The Setting

In 1997, the United States was transfixed by the murder trial in Massachusetts of British au pair Louise Woodward for the death of an eight-month-old boy in her care. Eventually convicted but given a suspended sentence, Woodward brought attention to the complex problem of child care. Many were critical of the behaviour of the 19-year-old au pair; others questioned the mother's (but rarely the father's) desire to work outside the home. Yet few people in the United States, Canada, Great Britain, or elsewhere can afford the luxury of having a parent stay at home or pay for high-quality live-in child care. For millions of mothers and fathers, finding the right kind of child care is a challenge to parenting and to the pocketbook.

Researchers have found that high-quality child care centres do not adversely affect the socialization of children; in fact, good day care benefits children. The value of preschool programs was documented in a series of studies conducted by the National Institute of Child Health and Human Development in the United States and the University of North London in England. They found no significant differences in infants who had received extensive nonmaternal care as compared with those who had been cared for solely by their mothers.

Sociological Insights

Studies assessing the quality of child care outside of the home reflect the microlevel of analysis and the interest that interactionists have in the impact of face-to-face interaction. They also explore macro-level implications for the functioning of social institutions like the family. But some of the issues surrounding day care have also been of interest from the conflict perspective.

Quality day care in most industrialized countries is not equally available to all families. Parents in wealthy neighbourhoods have an easier time finding day care than those in poor or working-class communities. And their chances of finding quality care are much better as well. In a study done in the United States covering 36 states, Harvard researchers Bruce Fuller and Xiaoyan Liang (1993) found wide disparities in the availability of child care. In the richest communities, there is one preschool teacher for every 45 children ages three to five; in the poorest communities, there is one teacher for every 77 children. *Affordable* child care is also a problem. Viewed from a conflict perspective, child care costs are an especially serious burden for lower-class families. Indeed, the poorest families spend 25 percent of their income for preschool child care, while families who are *not* poor pay only 6 percent or less of their income for day care.

Feminists echo the concern of conflict theorists that high-quality child care receives little governmental support because it is regarded as "merely a way to let women work." Nearly all child care workers (95 percent) are women; many find themselves in low-status, minimum-wage jobs. The average salary of a child care worker in Canada is among the lowest of all occupational groups, and there are few fringe benefits. Although parents may complain of child care costs, the staff, in effect, subsidizes children's care by working for low wages.

Policy Initiatives

Policies regarding child care outside the home vary throughout the world. Most developing nations do not have the economic base to provide subsidized child care. Working mothers largely rely on relatives or take their children to work. Even those industrial countries with elaborate programs of subsidized child care occasionally fall short of the ideal for quality supervised child care.

When policymakers decide that publicly funded child care is desirable, they must determine the degree to which taxpayers should subsidize it. A number of European nations, including the Netherlands and Sweden,

People in Sweden pay higher taxes than do Canadian citizens, but they have access to excellent preschool day care at little or no cost.

impose higher taxes than the United States and Canada while providing excellent preschool care at little or no cost. In 1991, about half of all Danish children ages three to six attended public child care programs. Parents pay a maximum of 30 percent of the costs. In France, where child care providers enjoy status and good wages, virtually all children ages three to five attend free schooling, and free after-school care is widely available. By contrast, in Canada, the total cost of child care typically falls on the individual family, and while the costs and options vary from urban to rural communities, informal care by friends, neighbours, relatives, and paid sitters is the most prevalent among parents who work for pay and whose children are under six years old (Baker 2001). According to the Childcare Resource and Research Unit at the University of Toronto, licensed or regulated family day care accounted for less than 14 percent of all regulated spaces in Canada in 1998 (Childcare Resource and Research Unit 2000).

There is a long way to go in making quality child care more affordable and more accessible, not just in Canada, but throughout the world. Government day care facilities in Mexico have lengthy waiting lists. In an attempt to reduce government spending, France is considering cutting back the budgets of subsidized nurseries, even though waiting lists already exist and the French public heartily disapproves of any cutbacks (L. King 1998; Simons 1997; Women's International Network 1995).

Margrit Eichler, Canadian feminist and sociologist, proposes a "social responsibility model" for family life, endorsing the establishment and support of public day care centres (Eichler 1997). Eichler argues that the establishment and support of such centres would make good economic sense, generating jobs for day care workers and enabling mothers to work for pay. In addition, children would benefit from the social setting of the day care as well as the more individualized setting of the home. Eichler states:

> Financing does not have to come from the federal government alone. Part of it can come from municipalities, from employers, and from parents according to the ability to pay (Eicher 1997:159–160).

Given the upward trend of labour-force participation of mothers with children under six years of age, the demand for quality day care and the debates over government funding are bound to continue.

Let's Discuss

1. Do you think it is desirable to expose young children to the socializing influence of day care? Were you ever in a day care program? Do you recall the experience as positive or negative?
2. In the view of conflict theorists, why does child care receive little government support?
3. Should the costs of day care programs be paid by government, by the private sector, or entirely by parents?

Chapter Resources

Summary

Socialization is the process whereby people learn the attitudes, values, and actions appropriate for members of a particular culture. This chapter examined the role of socialization in human development; the way in which people develop perceptions, feelings, and beliefs about themselves; the lifelong nature of the socialization process; and the important agents of socialization.

1. Socialization affects the overall cultural practices of a society, and it also shapes the images that we hold of ourselves.
2. Heredity and environmental factors interact in influencing the socialization process. ***Sociobiology*** is the systematic study of the biological bases of social behaviour.
3. In the early 1900s, Charles Horton Cooley advanced the belief that we learn who we are by interacting with others, a phenomenon he called the ***looking-glass self.***
4. George Herbert Mead, best known for his theory of the ***self,*** proposed that as people mature, their selves begin to reflect their concern about reactions from others—both ***generalized others*** and ***significant others.***
5. Erving Goffman has shown that many of our daily activities involve attempts to convey distinct impressions of who we are, a process called ***impression management.***
6. Socialization proceeds throughout the life course. Some societies mark stages of development with formal ***rites of passage.*** In Canadian culture, significant events such as marriage and parenthood serve to change a person's status.
7. As the primary agents of socialization, parents play a critical role in guiding children into those ***gender roles*** deemed appropriate in a society.
8. Like the family, schools in Canada have an explicit mandate to socialize people—and especially children—into the norms and values of our culture.
9. Peer groups and the mass media, especially television, are important agents of socialization for adolescents.
10. We are most fully exposed to occupational roles through observing the work of our parents, of people whom we meet while they are performing their duties, and of people portrayed in the media.
11. The state shapes the socialization process by regulating the life course and by influencing our views of appropriate behaviour at particular ages.
12. As more and more mothers of young children have entered Canada's labour market, the demand for child care has increased dramatically, posing policy questions for nations around the world.

Critical Thinking Questions

1. Should social research in areas such as sociobiology be conducted even though many investigators believe that this analysis is potentially detrimental to large numbers of people?
2. Drawing on Erving Goffman's dramaturgical approach, discuss how the following groups engage in impression management: athletes, college instructors, parents, physicians, politicians.
3. How would functionalists and conflict theorists differ in their analyses of socialization by the mass media?

Key Terms

Anticipatory socialization Processes of socialization in which a person "rehearses" for future positions, occupations, and social relationships. (page 83)

Cognitive theory of development Jean Piaget's theory explaining how children's thought progresses through four stages. (82)

Degradation ceremony An aspect of the socialization process within total institutions, in which people are subjected to humiliating rituals. (83)

Dramaturgical approach A view of social interaction that examines people as if they were theatrical performers. (80)

Face-work The efforts of people to maintain the proper image and avoid embarrassment in public. (80)

Gender roles Expectations regarding the proper behaviour, attitudes, and activities of males and females. (86)

Gender socialization An aspect of socialization through which we learn the attitudes, behaviours, and practices associated with being male and female according to our society and social groups within it. (86)

Generalized others The attitudes, viewpoints, and expectations of society as a whole that a child takes into account in his or her behaviour. (79)

Impression management The altering of the presentation of the self in order to create distinctive appearances and satisfy particular audiences. (80)

Looking-glass self A concept that emphasizes the self as the product of our social interactions with others. (78)

Personality In everyday speech, a person's typical patterns of attitudes, needs, characteristics, and behaviour. (75)

Resocialization The process of discarding former behaviour patterns and accepting new ones as part of a transition in one's life. (83)

Rites of passage Rituals marking the symbolic transition from one social position to another. (82)

Role taking The process of mentally assuming the perspective of another, thereby enabling one to respond from that imagined viewpoint. (79)

Self A distinct identity that sets us apart from others. (78)

Significant others Those individuals who are most important in the development of the self, such as parents, friends, and teachers. (80)

Socialization The process whereby people learn the attitudes, values, and behaviours appropriate for members of a particular culture. (75)

Sociobiology The systematic study of biological bases of social behaviour. (77)

Symbols The gestures, objects, and language that form the basis of human communication. (79)

Total institutions Institutions that regulate all aspects of a person's life under a single authority, such as prisons, the military, mental hospitals, and convents. (83)

Additional Readings

Adler, Patricia A., and Peter Adler. 1998. *Peer Power: Preadolescent Culture and Identity.* New Brunswick, NJ: Rutgers University Press. Using eight years of observation research, sociologists discuss the role of peer groups and family as they relate to popularity, social isolation, bullying, and boy–girl relationships.

Goffman, Erving. 1959. *The Presentation of Self in Everyday Life.* New York: Doubleday. Goffman demonstrates his interactionist theory that the self is managed in everyday situations in much the same way that a theatrical performer carries out a stage role.

Graydon, Shari. 2001. "The Portrayal of Women in Media: The Good, the Bad and the Beautiful." Pp. 179–195 in *Communications in Canadian Society*, 5th ed., edited by Craig McKie and Benjamin D. Singer. Toronto: Thomson. Graydon outlines the mass media's role (with special attention to advertising) in constructing images and ideals of women in our society.

Pollack, William. 1998. *Real Boys: Rescuing Our Sons from the Myths of Boyhood.* New York: Henry Holt. A clinical psychologist looks at the disenchantment experienced by so many boys because their true emotions are kept hidden.

Sadker, Myra, and David Sadker. 1994. *Failing at Fairness: How America's Schools Cheat Girls.* New York: Scribner. A gender-based examination of the treatment of girls in the United States' school system.

Internet Connection

www.mcgrawhill.ca/college/schaefer

For additional Internet exercises relating to day care around the world and MediaWatch, a Canadian non-profit feminist organization working to eliminate sexism in the mass media, visit the Schaefer Online Learning Centre at ***http://www.mcgrawhill.ca/college/schaefer****. Please note that while the URLs listed were current at the time of printing, these sites often change—check the Online Learning Centre for updates.*

Erving Goffman's exploration of total institutions offers a sociological perspective of daily life inside prisons, the military, mental hospitals, and convents. Review the list of four common traits shared by all total institutions on page 83 of your text. Then, log onto the Cybrary of the Holocaust (**http://remember.org**). Spend time learning about the Holocaust in general, and life in concentration camps in particular, utilizing the video, photographs, stories, and research links on the site.

(a) What story or image had the greatest impact on you? Why? What new facts did you learn through your online visit?
(b) Reflecting on Goffman's ideas, identify how Nazi-run concentration camps qualify as total institutions. What occurred during the degradation ceremony that prisoners were exposed to upon entering the camps?
(c) What/who was the authority in the camps under which all aspects of life were conducted?
(d) In what specific ways were the activities of prisoners monitored by others?
(e) What was the daily routine of prisoners? What control, if any, did they have over their own lives?
(f) What were the main purposes of these camps, and how were prisoners forced to fulfill those purposes?
(g) Has looking at the Holocaust through a sociological lens changed the way you view this time in history? How so?

CHAPTER 5

SOCIAL INTERACTION AND SOCIAL STRUCTURE

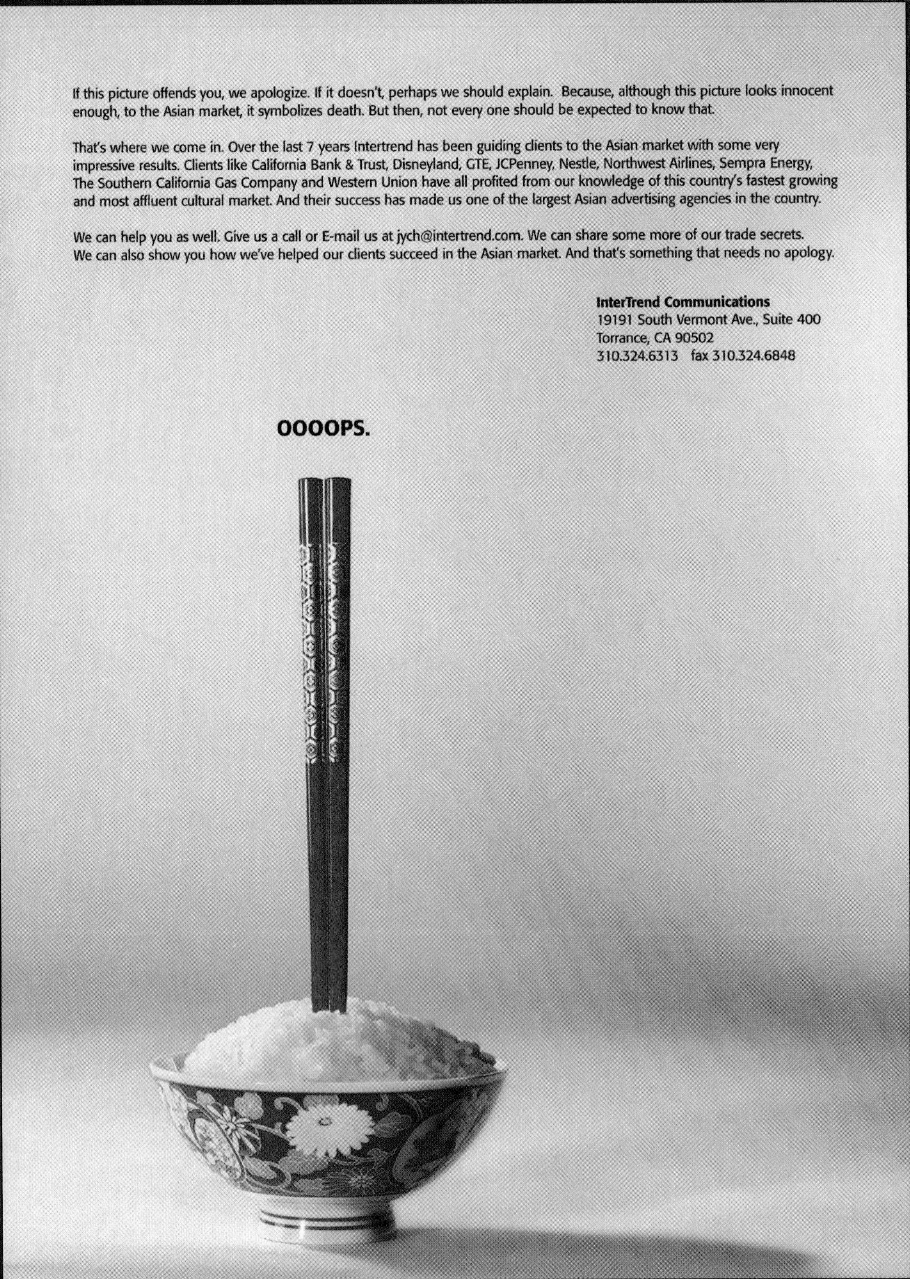
If this picture offends you, we apologize. If it doesn't, perhaps we should explain. Because, although this picture looks innocent enough, to the Asian market, it symbolizes death. But then, not every one should be expected to know that.
That's where we come in. Over the last 7 years Intertrend has been guiding clients to the Asian market with some very impressive results. Clients like California Bank & Trust, Disneyland, GTE, JCPenney, Nestle, Northwest Airlines, Sempra Energy, The Southern California Gas Company and Western Union have all profited from our knowledge of this country's fastest growing and most affluent cultural market. And their success has made us one of the largest Asian advertising agencies in the country.
We can help you as well. Give us a call or E-mail us at jych@intertrend.com. We can share some more of our trade secrets. We can also show you how we've helped our clients succeed in the Asian market. And that's something that needs no apology.
InterTrend Communications
19191 South Vermont Ave., Suite 400
Torrance, CA 90502
310.324.6313 fax 310.324.6848
OOOOPS.

Social Interaction and Reality

Defining and Reconstructing Reality

Negotiated Order

Elements of Social Structure

Statuses

Social Roles

Groups

Social Networks and Technology

Social Institutions

Social Structure in Global Perspective

Tönnies's *Gemeinschaft* and *Gesellschaft*

Lenski's Sociocultural Evolution Approach

Social Policy and Social Structure: The AIDS Crisis

The Issue

The Setting

Sociological Insights

Policy Initiatives

Boxes

SOCIOLOGY IN THE GLOBAL COMMUNITY: Disability as a Master Status

RESEARCH IN ACTION: Teens at Work

TAKING SOCIOLOGY TO WORK: Cathy MacDonald, Dean, College Resources, Kwantlen University College

In our social interaction with other cultures it is important to know what social rules apply. In Japan, for example, it is impolite to have your chopsticks sticking up in the rice bowl—a symbol of death for the Japanese and an insult to their ancestors. This poster was created by an advertising agency that promises to steer its North American clients clear of such gaffes in the Asian market.

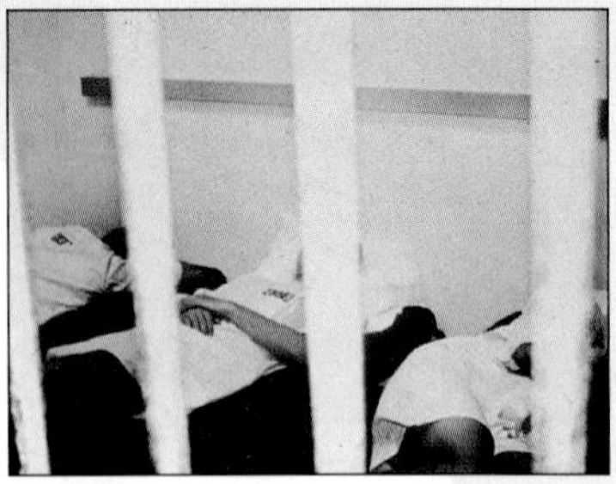

The quiet of a summer Sunday morning in Palo Alto, California was shattered by a screeching squad car siren as police swept through the city picking up college students in a surprise mass arrest. Each suspect was charged with a felony, warned of his constitutional rights, spread-eagled against the car, searched, handcuffed and carted off in the back seat of the squad car to the police station for booking.

After being fingerprinted and having identification forms prepared for his "jacket" (central information file), each prisoner was left isolated in a detention cell to wonder what he had done to get himself into this mess. After a while, he was blindfolded and transported to the "Stanford County Prison." Here he began the induction process of becoming a prisoner—stripped naked, skin searched, deloused, and issued a uniform, bedding, soap and towel. By late afternoon when nine such arrests had been completed, these youthful "first offenders" sat in dazed silence on the cots in their barren cells.

These men were part of a very unusual kind of prison, an experimental or mock prison, created by social psychologists for the purpose of intensively studying the effects of imprisonment upon volunteer research subjects. When we planned our two-week long simulation of prison life, we were primarily concerned about understanding the process by which people adapt to the novel and alien environment in which those called "prisoners" lose their liberty, civil rights, independence and privacy, while those called "guards" gain social power by accepting the responsibility for controlling and managing the lives of their dependent charges. . . .

Our final sample of participants (10 prisoners and 11 guards) were selected from over 75 volunteers recruited through ads in the city and campus newspapers. . . . Half were randomly assigned to role-play being guards, the others to be prisoners. Thus, there were no measurable differences between the guards and the prisoners at the start of this experiment. . . .

At the end of only six days we had to close down our mock prison because what we saw was frightening. It was no longer apparent to most of the subjects (or to us) where reality ended and their roles began. The majority had indeed become prisoners or guards, no longer able to clearly differentiate between role playing and self. There were dramatic changes in virtually every aspect of their behavior, thinking and feeling. In less than a week the experience of imprisonment undid (temporarily) a lifetime of learning; human values were suspended, self-concepts were challenged and the ugliest, most base, pathological side of human nature surfaced. We were horrified because we saw some boys (guards) treat others as if they were despicable animals, taking pleasure in cruelty, while other boys (prisoners) became servile, dehumanized robots who thought only of escape, of their own individual survival and of their mounting hatred for the guards. *(Zimbardo et al. 1974:61, 62, 63; Zimbardo 1972:4)* ■

The Zimbardo study effectively demonstrates how social interactions are determined by the social institutions in which they take place. While the student guards quickly assumed the abusive characteristics associated with their roles within the prison environment, they would have been unlikely to behave the same way if, for instance, they had been asked to watch over (guard) children in a schoolyard. Institutionally specific expectations informed their actions.

Sociologists use the term ***social interaction*** to refer to the ways in which people respond to one another, whether face to face or over the telephone or computer. In the mock prison, social interactions between guards and prisoners were highly impersonal. The guards addressed the prisoners by number rather than name, and wore reflector sunglasses that made eye contact with them impossible.

As in many real-life prisons, the simulated prison at Stanford University had a social structure in which guards held virtually total control over prisoners. The term ***social structure*** refers to the way in which a society is organized into predictable relationships. The social structure of Zimbardo's mock prison influenced the interactions between the guards and prisoners. Zimbardo (1992:576) notes that it was a real prison "in the minds of the jailers and their captives." His simulated prison experiment, first conducted more than 25 years ago, has subsequently been repeated (with similar findings) in many other countries.

The concepts of social interaction and social structure, which are closely linked to each other, are central to sociological study. Sociologists observe patterns of behaviour closely to understand and accurately describe the social interactions of a community or society and the social structure in which they take place.

This chapter begins by considering how social interaction shapes the way we view the world around us. We will then focus on five basic elements of social structure: statuses, social roles, groups, social networks, and social institutions. Groups are important because much of our social interaction occurs in them. Social institutions such as the family, religion, and government are a fundamental aspect of social structure. We will contrast the functionalist, conflict, feminist, and interactionist approaches to the study of social institutions. We will also examine the typologies developed by Ferdinand Tönnies and Gerhard Lenski for comparing modern societies with simpler forms of social structure. The social policy section will consider the AIDS crisis and its implications for social institutions throughout the world. ■

Social Interaction and Reality

According to sociologist Herbert Blumer (1969:79), the distinctive characteristic of social interaction among people is that "human beings interpret or 'define' each other's actions instead of merely reacting to each other's actions." In other words, our response to someone's behaviour is based on the *meaning* we attach to his or her actions. Reality is shaped by our perceptions, evaluations, and definitions.

These meanings typically reflect the norms and values of the dominant culture and our socialization experiences within that culture. As interactionists emphasize, the meanings that we attach to people's behaviour are shaped by our interactions with them and with the larger society. Consequently, social reality is literally constructed from our social interactions (Berger and Luckmann 1966).

Defining and Reconstructing Reality

How do we define our social reality? As an example, let us consider something as simple as how we regard tattoos. Even as recently as a few years ago, many of us in Canada considered tattoos as something "weird" or "kooky." We associated them with fringe countercultural groups, such as punk rockers, bike gangs, and skinheads. A tattoo elicited an automatic negative response among many people. Now, however, there are so many people tattooed, including society's trendsetters, and the ritual of getting a tattoo has become so legitimized, the mainstream culture regards tattoos differently. At this point, as a result of increased social interactions with tattooed people, tattoos look perfectly normal to us in a number of settings.

The ability to define social reality reflects a group's power within a society. Indeed, one of the most crucial aspects of the relationship between dominant and subordinate groups is the ability of the dominant or majority group to define a society's values. Sociologist William I. Thomas (1923), an early critic of theories of racial and gender differences, recognized that the "definition of the situation" could mould the thinking and personality of the individual. Writing from an interactionist perspective, Thomas observed that people respond not only to the objective features of a person or situation but also to the *meaning* that the person or situation has for them. For example, in Philip Zimbardo's mock prison experiment, student "guards" and "prisoners" accepted the definition of the situation (including the traditional roles and behaviour associated with being a guard or prisoner) and acted accordingly.

As we have seen throughout the last 40 years, groups that have historically been marginalized in Canadian society—such as French Canadians, women, visible minorities, the elderly, gays and lesbians, and people with physical or mental challenges—have fought to redefine their place in society. An important aspect of the process of social change involves *re*constructing social reality. Members of subordinate groups challenge traditional definitions and begin to perceive and experience reality in a new way. Feminists have struggled to highlight the importance of the construction of reality in limiting women's participation in society. At the macrolevel, male-dominated institutions have established a reality that legitimizes the power imbalance between men and women. If our culture teaches us to see women in junior roles in business, for example, then it becomes difficult to recognize exploitation.

The world champion boxer Muhammad Ali reconstructed his own social reality. He insisted on his own political views (including refusing to serve in the Vietnam War), his own religion (Black Muslim), and his own name (which he changed from Cassius Clay to Muhammad Ali). Not only did Ali change the world of sports, he also had a hand in altering the world of race relations in the United States (Remnick 1998).

Viewed from a sociological perspective, Ali was redefining social reality by looking much more critically at the racist thinking and terminology that restricted him.

Negotiated Order

As we have just seen, people can reconstruct social reality through a process of internal change, taking a different view of everyday behaviour. Yet people also reshape reality by *negotiating* changes in patterns of social interaction. The term ***negotiation*** refers to the attempt to reach agreement with others concerning some objective. Negotiation does not involve coercion; it goes by many names, including *bargaining, compromising, trading off, mediating, exchanging, "wheeling and dealing,"* and *collusion.* It is through negotiation as a form of social interaction that society creates its social structure (Strauss 1977; see also G. Fine 1984).

Negotiation occurs in many ways. As interactionists point out, some social situations, such as buying groceries, involve no mediation, while other situations require significant amounts of negotiation. For example, we may negotiate with others regarding time ("When should we arrive?"), space ("Can we have a meeting at your house?"), or even assignment of places while waiting for concert tickets. In traditional societies, impending marriage often leads to negotiations between the families of the future husband and wife. For example, anthropologist Ray Abrahams (1968) has described how the Labwor people of Africa arrange for an amount of property to go from the groom's to the bride's family at the time of marriage. In the view of the Labwor, such bargaining over an exchange of cows and sheep culminates not only in a marriage but, more importantly, in the linking of two clans or families.

Boxing champion Muhammad Ali has been helping to redefine stereotypes throughout his public life. As an athlete, he helped to create a new social reality for American blacks; now, as a person with Parkinson's disease, he is establishing a public presence for those with degenerative conditions.

While such family-to-family bargaining is common in traditional cultures, negotiation can take much more elaborate forms in modern industrial societies. Consider Canada's tax laws. From a sociological perspective, such laws are formal norms (reflected in federal and provincial codes). The entire tax code undergoes revision through negotiated outcomes involving many competing interests, including big business, foreign nations, and political action

Taking Sociology to Work

CATHY MACDONALD: Dean, College Resources, Kwantlen University College

As a dean of a diverse set of services—from library stacks to day care—at the largest university college in Canada, Cathy MacDonald faces logistical challenges that require a clear understanding of systems, the most important of which are those involving the coordination of human activities. MacDonald, whose undergraduate major was sociology, was drawn to her academic specialty by a keen interest in group dynamics and social organization.

As an administrator responsible for library and communication resources, she believes her foundation in sociology has played an important role throughout her working life. "My professional work, first as a librarian and later as an administrator, has always involved dealing with people. The theoretical course background received in university has been a key factor in my career success," MacDonald says.

The implication is clear: sociology offers a broad-based foundation in people and human systems management skills that can be a valuable asset in a variety of career settings.

Let's Discuss

1. Why is an understanding of social interaction and social structure especially important for people in administrative positions?
2. Let's say you have been hired as a manager in a large company. How would an understanding of the interactional and structural aspects of the corporation's culture help you do a better job?

committees (see Chapter 13). On an individual level, taxpayers, if audited, will mediate with agents of Canada Custom and Revenue Agency. Changes in the taxpayers' individual situations will occur through such negotiations. Canada's tax structure can hardly be viewed as fixed; rather, it reflects the sum of negotiations for change at any time.

Negotiations underlie much of our social behaviour. Because most elements of social structure are not static, they are subject to change through bargaining and exchanging. Sociologists use the term *negotiated order* to underscore the fact that the social order is continually being constructed and altered through negotiation. ***Negotiated order*** refers to a social structure that derives its existence from the social interactions through which people define and redefine its character. At a microlevel, feminist theory views these negotiations as skewed by a socialization process that teaches one gender that the other is superior. If women are taught to be deferential to men, any negotiated order will inevitably favour those with power—in this case, men.

We can add negotiation to our list of cultural universals because all societies provide guidelines or norms within which negotiations take place. The recurring role of negotiation in social interaction and social structure will be apparent as we examine statuses, social roles, groups, networks, and institutions (Strauss 1977).

pp. 52–53

Elements of Social Structure

We can examine predictable social relationships in terms of five elements: statuses, social roles, groups, social networks, and social institutions. These elements make up social structure just as a foundation, walls, and ceilings make up a building's structure. The elements of social structure are developed through the lifelong process of socialization, described in Chapter 4.

Statuses

We normally think of a person's "status" as having to do with influence, wealth, and/or fame. However, sociologists use ***status*** to refer to any of the full range of socially defined positions within a large group or society—from the lowest to the highest position. Within our society, a person can occupy the status of Prime Minister of Canada, fruit picker, son or daughter, violinist, teenager, resident of Halifax, dental technician, or neighbour. Clearly, a person holds more than one status simultaneously.

Ascribed and Achieved Status

Sociologists view some statuses as *ascribed,* while they categorize others as *achieved* (see Figure 5-1). An ***ascribed status*** is "assigned" to a person by society without regard for the person's unique talents or characteristics. Generally, this assignment takes place at birth; thus, a person's racial background, gender, and age are all considered ascribed statuses. These characteristics are biological in origin but are significant mainly because of the social meanings they have in our culture.

In most cases, there is little that people can do to change an ascribed status. But we can attempt to change the traditional constraints associated with such statuses. As

FIGURE 5-1

Social Statuses

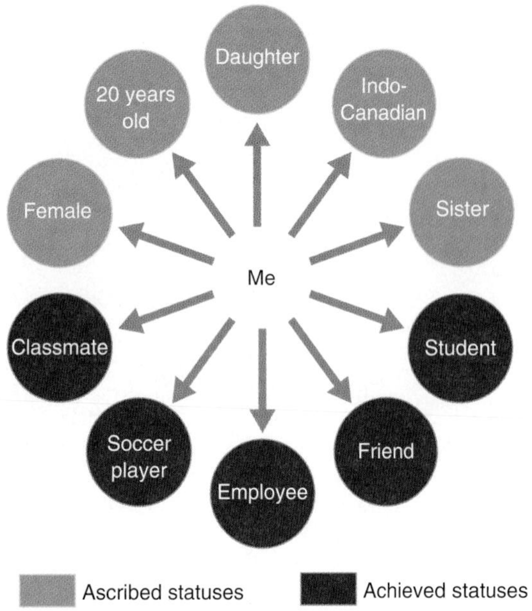

The person in this figure—"me"—occupies many positions in society, each of which involves distinct statuses. How would you define your statuses?

an example, the Canadian Association of Retired Persons (CARP)—an activist political group founded in 1984 to work for the rights of older people—has tried to modify society's negative and confining stereotypes of the elderly. As a result of its work and that of other groups supporting older citizens, the ascribed status of "senior citizen" is no longer as difficult for millions of older people.

An ascribed status does not necessarily have the same social meaning in every society. In a cross-cultural study, sociologist Gary Huang (1988) confirmed the long-held view that respect for the elderly is an important cultural norm in China. In many cases, the prefix "old" is used respectfully: calling someone "old teacher" or "old person" is like calling a judge in North America "Your Honour." Huang points out that positive age-seniority distinctions in language are absent in North America; consequently, we view the term *old man* as more of an insult than a celebration of seniority and wisdom.

Unlike ascribed statuses, an ***achieved status*** comes to us largely through our own efforts. Both "bank president" and "prison guard" are achieved statuses, as are "lawyer," "student," "advertising executive," and "skateboarder." You must do something to acquire an achieved status—go to school, learn a skill, establish a friendship, or invent a new product. As we see in the next section, our achieved status is heavily influenced by our ascribed status. Being male, for example, will decrease the likelihood that a person would consider being a child care worker.

One of the interesting effects of increased cyberspace communication has been to limit the influence of status characteristics. It is impossible to tell someone's race or exact age over the Internet, and therefore the stereotypes that might alter one person's treatment of another in real life are simply not present. Although they are perhaps more evident, even achieved status characteristics may be difficult to discern in this medium. While disguising one's level of education may prove impossible, it is easy for the unemployed labourer to claim to be a self-made construction millionaire.

Master Status

Each person holds many different statuses; some may indicate higher social positions, and some, lower positions. How is one's overall social position viewed by others in light of these conflicting statuses? According to sociologist Everett Hughes (1945), societies deal with such inconsistencies by agreeing that certain statuses are more important than others. A ***master status*** is a status that dominates one's other statuses and thereby determines a person's general position within society. For example, Arthur Ashe,

Ron Nicolaye, Chair of the Campbell River Access Awareness Committee, represents a new, proactive attitude among Canadians dealing with restricted mobility. Mr. Nicolaye and those like him are committed to making government and the public aware that interest in outdoor activities is not limited by physical challenges.

Sociology in the Global Community

5-1 Disability as a Master Status

At first, the Campbell River Access Committee had a difficult time convincing Vancouver Island officials that there was a need for wheelchair access to wilderness sites. However, after a demonstration of their abilities to traverse rough ground, climb into and out of canoes, and deal with the tasks required to set up a camp, the outdoor enthusiasts were afforded the access they were seeking. Accommodations for those in wheelchairs included ramps and wider trails, while individuals with reduced vision benefited from handrails and easily read markings. Stereotypes about the disabled are gradually falling away as a result of such feats. But the status of *disabled* still carries a stigma, as it has for ages.

Throughout history and around the world, people with disabilities have often been subjected to cruel and inhuman treatment. For example, in the early 20th century, the disabled were frequently viewed as subhuman creatures who were a menace to society. In fact, many state legislatures in the United States passed compulsory sterilization laws aimed at "handicapped people." In Japan more than 16 000 women with disabilities were involuntarily sterilized with government approval from 1945 to 1995. Sweden recently apologized for the same action taken against 62 000 of its citizens in the 1970s.

Such blatantly hostile treatment of people with disabilities generally gave way to a *medical model,* which views the disabled as chronic patients. Increasingly, however, people concerned with the rights of the disabled have criticized this model as well. In their view, it is the unnecessary and discriminatory barriers present in the environment—both physical and attitudinal—that stand in the way of people with disabilities more than any biological limitations do. Applying a *civil rights model,* activists emphasize that those with disabilities face widespread prejudice, discrimination, and segregation. For example, most voting places are inaccessible to wheelchair users and fail to provide ballots that can be used by those unable to read print.

Drawing on the earlier work of Erving Goffman, contemporary sociologists have suggested that society has attached a stigma to many forms of disability and that this stigma leads to prejudicial treatment. Indeed, people with disabilities frequently observe that the nondisabled see them only as blind, wheelchair users, and so forth, rather than as complex human beings with individual strengths and weaknesses, whose blindness or use of a wheelchair is merely one aspect of their lives. A review of studies of people with disabilities disclosed that most academic research on the subject does not differentiate gender—thereby perpetuating the view that a disability overrides other personal characteristics. Consequently, disability serves as a master status.

In Japan more than 16 000 women with disabilities were involuntarily sterilized with government approval from 1945 to 1995.

Without question, people with disabilities occupy a subordinate position in Canada and the United States. By 1970, a strong political movement for disability rights had emerged in both countries. Since then, women and men involved in this movement have been working to challenge negative views of disabled people and to modify the social structure by reshaping laws, institutions, and environments so that people with disabilities can be fully integrated into mainstream society.

The effort to overcome the master status is global in nature. The African nation of Botswana has plans to assist its disabled, most of whom live in rural areas and are in need of special services relating to mobility and economic development. Kenya, however, fails to outlaw discrimination against people with disabilities, even though its constitution outlaws discrimination on the basis of other characteristics, including sex, tribe, race, place of origin, creed, or religion. In many countries, disability rights activists are targeting issues essential to overcoming master status and to being a full citizen, such as employment, housing, and access to public buildings.

Let's Discuss

1. Does your campus present barriers to disabled students? If so, what kind of barriers—physical, attitudinal, or both? Describe some of them.
2. Why do you think nondisabled people see disability as the most important characteristic of a disabled person? What can be done to help people see beyond the wheelchair and the seeing-eye dog?

Sources: Albrecht et al. 2000; Goffman 1963a; Gove 1980; D. Murphy 1997; Newsday 1997; Ponczek 1998; Shapiro 1993; Willet and Deegan 2000.

who died of AIDS in 1993, had a remarkable career as a tennis star; but at the end of his life, his status as a well-known personality with AIDS may have outweighed his statuses as a retired athlete, an author, and a political activist. Throughout the world many people with disabilities find that their status as "disabled" is given undue weight and overshadows their actual ability to perform successfully in meaningful employment (See Box 5-1).

Society places such importance on external characteristics that they often come to dominate our lives.

Indeed, such ascribed statuses often influence achieved status. Ron Nicholaye's life has been influenced by a number of these characteristics. Nicholaye is a member of the Nuu Cha Nulth nation from the northeast coast of Vancouver Island. Complicating his status in society, he also requires a wheelchair. Within the traditional society where Nicholaye grew up, either of these characteristics could have become his master status. However, this has not been the case. A great advocate of the environment and a keen participant in outdoor activities, Nicholaye has devoted his energies to identifying and procuring opportunities for the disabled. Nicholaye is Chairman of the Campbell River Access Awareness Committee, an advocate group that advises the local mayor and city council.

Social Roles

What Are Social Roles?

Throughout our lives, we acquire what sociologists call *social roles.* A ***social role*** is a set of expectations for people who occupy a given social position or status. Thus, in Canada, we expect that taxi drivers will know how to get around a city, that receptionists will be reliable in handling phone messages, and that police officers will take action if they see a citizen being threatened. With each distinctive social status—whether ascribed or achieved—come particular role expectations. However, actual performance varies from individual to individual. One secretary may assume extensive administrative responsibilities, while another may focus on clerical duties. Similarly, in Philip Zimbardo's mock prison experiment, some students were brutal and sadistic as guards, but others were not.

Roles are a significant component of social structure. Viewed from a functionalist perspective, roles contribute to a society's stability by enabling members to anticipate the behaviour of others and to pattern their own actions accordingly. Yet social roles can also be dysfunctional by restricting people's interactions and relationships. If we view a person *only* as a "computer geek" or a "teacher," it will be difficult to relate to this person as a friend or neighbour.

Role Conflict

Imagine the delicate situation of a woman who has worked for a decade as a police constable and has recently been promoted to sergeant. How is this woman expected to relate to her longtime friends and coworkers? Should she still go out for drinks with them after work on Friday, as she has done for years? Is it her responsibility to recommend the firing of an old friend who cannot keep up with the demands of the job?

Role conflict occurs when incompatible expectations arise from two or more social positions held by the same person. Fulfillment of the roles associated with one status may directly violate the roles linked to a second status. In the example above, the newly promoted sergeant will experience a serious conflict between certain social and occupational roles.

Role conflicts call for important ethical choices. In the example just given, the new sergeant has to make a difficult decision about how much allegiance she owes her friend whose job performance is unsatisfactory. Our culture tells us that success is more important than friendship. If friends are holding us back, we should leave them and pursue our ambitions. Yet, at the same time, we are told that abandoning our friends is contemptible. The sergeant must decide whether she will risk her pro-

Imagine you are a journalist walking down this alley as you witness the mugging going on here. What do you do? Try to stop the crime? Or take a picture for your magazine? This was the role conflict that Sarah Leen, a professional photographer, experienced when she stopped to change a lens and take a picture of this scene. At the same time, Leen felt fear for her own safety. People in certain professions—among them, journalism—commonly experience role conflict during disasters, crimes, and other distressing situations.

motion out of concern for her friend. This type of role conflict involves the restructuring of in-group and out-group affiliations. It has been one of the major obstacles faced by women who try to break free of traditional gender assignments. Some feminist theorists have cited the elimination of such institutionalized roles as critical to the full integration of women into modern Canadian society.

Another type of role conflict occurs when individuals move into occupations that are not common among people with their ascribed status. The female police officer in the last paragraph is a good example. Traditionally in Canadian society police officers were male and society's expectations reflected that reality. But those expectations have meant that female officers have had to strive to reconcile their workplace role in law enforcement with the societal view of women. The result is a contradictory set of standards that require these women to be stoic and nurturing, physically strong and feminine, and deferential and forceful all at the same time.

Role Strain

Role conflict describes the situation of a person dealing with the challenge of occupying two social positions simultaneously. However, even a single position can cause problems. Sociologists use the term ***role strain*** to describe difficulties that result from the differing demands and expectations associated with the same social position. The role strain endured by Canadian women in recent years has been a focus of feminist theory. The concept of "Superwoman" is the best example of this strain, describing women who try to meet the expectations of several demanding roles—mother, wife, full-time employee—at the same time.

In the opening example, social psychologist Philip Zimbardo unexpectedly experienced role strain. He initially saw himself merely as a university professor directing an imaginative experiment in which students played the roles of either guard or inmate. However, he soon found that as a professor, he was also expected to look after the welfare of the students or at least not to endanger them. Eventually he resolved the role strain by making the difficult decision to terminate the experiment.

Parks Canada employees also experience role strain. For generations their primary role has been to help visitors enjoy the beauty that the park system offers. However, increasingly, the social problems of the larger society, ranging from traffic jams to crime, have intruded, as more and more people seek to "escape" the routine workday world. Employees now find themselves torn between encouraging tourists to explore certain activities and curtailing other activities that might interfere with the enjoyment of others, or even worse, actually harm the park. Park employees in parts of Africa face similar role strain. Photo safaris generate huge revenues for countries such as Kenya, but national wildlife refuges also are a target for people who traffic in illegal animal skins or ivory. Park employees have to carry out two very different tasks at the same time—to be welcoming ambassadors to visitors and government enforcers of park regulations.

Role Exit

Often, when we think of assuming a social role, we focus on the preparation and anticipatory socialization that a person undergoes for that role. Even though *leaving* a role can be just as demanding, social scientists have only recently given more attention to the adjustments involved in leaving social roles.

Sociologist Helen Rose Fuchs Ebaugh (1988) developed the term ***role exit*** to describe the process of disengagement from a role that is central to one's self-identity and reestablishment of an identity in a new role. Drawing on interviews with 185 people—among them ex-convicts, divorced men and women, recovering alcoholics, ex-nuns, former doctors, retirees, and transsexuals—Ebaugh (herself a former nun) studied the process of voluntarily exiting from significant social roles.

The pictures in this student's dorm room in India may signify his attempt to create a new identity, the final stage in role exit.

Ebaugh has offered a four-stage model of role exit. The first stage begins with *doubt*—as the person experiences frustration, burnout, or simply unhappiness with an accustomed status and the tasks associated with this social position. The second stage involves a *search for alternatives.* A person unhappy with his or her career may take a leave of absence; an unhappily married couple may begin what they see as a temporary separation.

The third stage of role exit is the *action stage* or *departure.* Ebaugh found that the vast majority of her respondents could identify a clear turning point that made them feel it was essential to take final action and leave their job, end their marriage, or engage in another type of role exit. However, 20 percent of respondents saw their role exit as a gradual, evolutionary process that had no single turning point. The last stage of role exit involves the *creation of a new identity.*

Many of you participated in a role exit when you made the transition from high school to college or university. At the same time, you may have declared your independence by exiting from the role of living with your parents. By moving out and setting up your own residence, you establish a different status for yourself in society. Sociologist Ira Silver (1996) has made a study of the central role that material objects play in this type of transition. The objects that students choose to leave home (like stuffed animals and dolls) are associated with their prior identities. They may remain deeply attached to these objects but do not want them to be seen as part of their new independent identity. The objects they bring with them symbolize how they now see themselves and how they wish to be perceived. CDs, tapes, and wall posters, for example, all are calculated to say, "This is me."

Groups

In sociological terms, a ***group*** is any number of people with similar norms, values, and expectations who interact with one another on a regular basis. The members of a women's hockey team, of a hospital's business office, or of a garage band constitute a group. However, the entire staff of a large hospital would not be considered a group, since the staff members rarely interact with one another at one time. Perhaps the only point at which they all come together is an annual party.

Every society is composed of many groups in which daily social interaction takes place. We seek out groups to establish friendships, to accomplish certain goals, and to fulfill social roles that we have acquired. We'll explore the various types of groups in which people interact in detail in Chapter 6, where sociological investigations of group behaviour will also be examined.

Groups play a vital part in a society's social structure. Much of our social interaction takes place within groups and is influenced by their norms and sanctions. Being a teenager or a retired person takes on special meaning when you interact within groups designed for people with that particular status. The expectations associated with many social roles, including those accompanying the statuses of brother, sister, and student, become more clearly defined in the context of a group.

Social Networks and Technology

New technology has broadened the definition of groups to include those who interact electronically—a significant number of Canadians. A 2001 Canadian Social Trends article revealed that over half of the young Canadians surveyed used chat rooms, with males (61 percent) outnumbering females (56 percent) (Statistics Canada, Winter 2001).

For the human participant, online exchanges offer a new opportunity to alter one's image—what Goffman (1959) refers to as impression management. How might you present yourself to an online discussion group?

Groups do not merely serve to define other elements of the social structure, such as roles and statuses; they also are an intermediate link between the individual and the larger society. We are all members of a number of different groups and through our acquaintances make connections with people in different social circles. This connection is known as a ***social network***—that is, a series of social relationships that links a person directly to others and therefore indirectly to still more people. Social networks may constrain people by limiting the range of their interactions, yet these networks may also empower people by making available vast resources (N. Lin 1999).

Involvement in social networks—commonly known as *networking*—is especially valuable in finding employment. For example, while looking for a job one year after finishing school, Albert Einstein was successful only when a classmate's father put him in touch with his future employer. These kinds of contacts, even if they are weak and distant, can be crucial in establishing social networks and facilitating transmission of information.

With advances in technology, we can now maintain social networks electronically. We don't need face-to-face contacts for knowledge sharing anymore. It is not uncommon for those looking for employment or for a means of identifying someone with common interests to first turn to the Internet. First impressions now begin on the web. A survey of college and university students found that 79 percent consider the quality of an employer's website important in deciding whether or not to apply for a job there (Jobtrak.com 2000b).

Sociologist Manuel Castells (1996, 1997, 1998) views the emerging electronic social networks as fundamental to new organizations and the growth of existing businesses and associations. One emerging electronic network, in particular, is changing the way people interact. "Texting" began first in Asia in 2000 and has now taken off in North America and Europe. It refers to wireless e-mails exchanged over cell phones in the small screens featured in newer models. Initially, texting was popular among young users, who sent shorthand messages such as "WRU" (where are you?) and "CU2NYT" (see you tonight). But now the business world has seen the advantages of transmitting updated business or financial e-mails via cell phones or handheld Palm Pilots. Sociologists, however, caution that such devices create a workday that never ends and that increasingly people are busy checking their digital devices rather than holding conversations with those around them (W. Arnold 2000; K. Hafner 2000).

A study released in 2000 documented a rise in the amount of time people are spending online in their homes. The increase suggests that face-to-face interactions may well be declining, since there are only so many hours in anyone's day. Indeed, a third of the respondents said they spent more than five hours a week online while at home. Of those heavy users, 8 percent reported attending fewer social events as a result of their surfing, and 13 percent said they were spending less time with family and friends. Of course, the Internet can also promote social contacts, especially among those who have few opportunities, such as the disabled and the geographically isolated. Significantly, the number of retired people who frequent chatrooms created for older users has increased sharply. Participants at websites such as ThirdAge report that they have formed new online friendships to replace old ones formed at the workplace (Galant 2000; Nie and Erbring 2000). In Chapter 16, we will examine further the ways in which computer technology has assisted the formation of larger and even international social networks.

In the workplace, networking pays off more for men than for women because of the traditional presence of men in leadership positions. A 1997 survey of executives found that 63 percent of men use networking to find new jobs compared to 41 percent of women. Thirty-one percent of the women use classified advertisements to find jobs, compared to only 13 percent of the men. Still, women at all levels of the paid labour force are beginning to make effective use of social networks. A study of women who were leaving the welfare rolls in the United States to enter the paid workforce found that networking was an effective tool in their search for employment. Informal networking also helped them to locate child care and better housing—both of which are key to successful employment (Carey and McLean 1997; Henly 1999).

Historically, Canadian youth have used networking to help them find work during the school year and summer to supplement parental support. This employment also serves as a means of becoming enculturated to the adult workplace. As we can see in Box 5-2, this has changed in recent years.

In a recent study of informal networks among middle-aged managers at four Fortune 500 firms, Herminia Ibarra (1995) of the Harvard Business School noted the impact of race on networking. Whereas white managers often participate in all-white social networks, black managers are more likely to be part of racially integrated networks—in part because there are comparatively fewer blacks with whom to network. Race and gender clearly play a role in face-to-face networking, but electronic networking allows one to assume different or, at least, ambiguous social identities (Moskos 1991; S. Turkle 1995; L. Williams 1995).

Even though you may not be totally sure whom you are "talking" to online, the Internet has added a massive new dimension to social interaction.

Social Institutions

The mass media, the government, the economy, the family, and the health care system are all examples of social institutions found in our society. ***Social institutions*** are

Research in Action 5-2 Teens at Work

There has been a long-standing tradition in Canadian society that young people participate in the workforce from an early age. For generations, that tradition has included newspaper routes and babysitting as youngsters, evolving to part-time work on weekends and during the summers in the teenage years. However, the place of Canadian youth in the negotiated order of the economy has changed in recent years as teens and young adults have become entrenched as regular and significant participants in the workplace.

At a macrolevel, the changes in participation of young people in the paid labour force has altered their place in the Canadian social structure. At the interpersonal level, because of the hours spent working each week, the types of interactions young people engage in today are different from those someone of a similar age might have had only a couple of decades ago.

Despite the long-term trend indicating that teens are working more today than ever, the numbers from the 1990s reveal that during the first three quarters of that decade, the participation rate fell from 51.6 percent in 1989 to 37.1 percent in 1997. This overall number reflects a reduction in both part-time school-year employment (from 43.6 percent down to 30.2 percent) and in summer employment (from 65.5 percent down to 44.2 percent). In their study, *Still Struggling: An Update on Teenagers at Work*, authors Andrew Jackson and Sylvain Schetagne (2001) conclude that the employment rate of teenagers "fell sharply from 1989 to 1997." There are in fact more teenage workers now than there were a decade ago, but this is primarily because there are more teenagers now than there were a decade ago. So, while the number working has increased, the employment rate, particularly in economically disadvantaged regions like the Maritimes, has declined.

There are in fact more teenage workers now than there were a decade ago, but this is primarily because there are more teenagers now than there were a decade ago.

The data documented a shift in participation patterns. The authors concluded that while there was only a slight drop in the particpation rate of those teens no longer in school (from 69.3 percent in 1989 to 67.2 percent in 1999), the ratio of full-time to part-time work had deteriorated from 5 to 1 (five full-time workers for every part-timer) in 1989 to 3 to 1 in 1999.

Another important finding involves the distribution of work according to gender. Over the decade of the 1990s, girls virtually eliminated the long-standing employment gap. By 1999, girls made up a greater proportion of students who held jobs during the school year (36.3 percent versus 32.3 percent), and were less than 1 percent behind the boys when it came to summer employment. While 49.8 percent of boys had summer jobs, 49.3 percent of girls also did.

As youth work patterns change from being substantially a socialization experience to being an economic one, the associated social networks are marginalized. Instead of preparing for the real world of work, youth find themselves ghettoized in a sector of the labour market designed especially for them.

Let's Discuss

1. Did you have a summer job while in high school? Have you found it easier or more difficult to get a job in recent years?
2. How have you and your friends been impacted by the diminished opportunities for youth? How long has it taken you to find a part-time or summer job?

Source: Jackson and Schetagne 2001.

organized patterns of beliefs and behaviour centred on basic social needs, such as replacing personnel (the family) and preserving order (the government).

By studying social institutions, sociologists gain insight into the structure of a society. For example, the institution of religion adapts to the segment of society that it serves. Church work has very different meanings for ministers who serve a skid row area, a remote northern community, or a suburban middle-class community. Religious leaders assigned to a skid row mission will focus on tending to the ill and providing food and shelter. By contrast, clergy in affluent suburbs will be occupied with counselling those considering marriage and divorce, arranging youth activities, and overseeing cultural events.

Functionalist View

One way to understand social institutions is to see how they fulfill essential functions. Anthropologist David F. Aberle and his colleagues (1950) and sociologists Raymond Mack and Calvin Bradford (1979) have identified five major tasks, or functional prerequisites, that a society or relatively permanent group must accomplish if it is to survive (see Table 5-1):

1. *Replacing personnel.* Any group or society must replace personnel when they die, leave, or become incapacitated. This is accomplished through such means as immigration, annexation of neighbouring groups of people, acquisition of slaves, or

Table 5-1 Functions and Institutions

Functional Prerequisite	Social Institutions
Replacing personnel	Family Government (immigration)
Teaching new recruits	Family (basic skills) Economy (occupations) Education (schools) Religion (sacred teachings)
Producing and distributing goods and services	Family (food preparation) Economy Government Health care system
Preserving order	Family (child rearing, regulation of sexuality) Government Religion (morals)
Providing and maintaining a sense of purpose	Government (social democracy) Religion

normal sexual reproduction of members. The Shakers, a religious sect that emigrated to the United States in 1774, are a conspicuous example of a group that has *failed* to replace personnel. Their religious beliefs commit the Shakers to celibacy; to survive, the group must recruit new members. At first, the Shakers proved quite successful in attracting members and reached a peak of about 6000 members during the 1840s. However, as of 1999, the only Shaker community left was a farm in Maine with seven members (Swanson 1999).

2. *Teaching new recruits.* No group can survive if many of its members reject the established behaviour and responsibilities of the group. Thus, finding or producing new members is not sufficient. The group must encourage recruits to learn and accept its values and customs. This learning can take place formally within schools (where learning is a manifest function) or informally through interaction and negotiation in peer groups (where instruction is a latent function).
3. *Producing and distributing goods and services.* Any relatively permanent group or society must provide and distribute desired goods and services for its members. Each society establishes a set of rules for the allocation of financial and other resources. The group must satisfy the needs of most members at least to some extent, or it will risk the possibility of discontent and, ultimately, disorder.
4. *Preserving order.* Every society must have a means for maintaining order if it is to survive. This means having institutions and standards that organize the members of the society and their activities in a way that supports the existing structure.

   The Beothuk people of Newfoundland, Canada's newest province, survived the initial European contact, but were ultimately destroyed by people who believed them less than human. The last member of the Beothuk nation, a woman who spent her final years in servitude to the white community, died in 1829. During the preceding 200 years, Beothuk numbers had been decimated as the result of indifferent treatment and exploitation at the hands of newcomers. Victims of abuse and marginalization, and exposed to previously unknown diseases such as smallpox and measles, against which they had no immunity, the Beothuk eventually succumbed. Their culture had been overwhelmed by the dominant influence of the colonizers.
5. *Providing and maintaining a sense of purpose.* People must be motivated to continue as members of a group in order for it to remain viable; there must be a clear purpose for belonging. Political leaders often use the spectre of an outside enemy to reaffirm the commitment of citizens to their country or their cause. This process can be found in the arsenals of both sides in the ongoing battle between terrorist groups and the West. The president of the United States, George W. Bush, has told Americans that patriotism is one of their country's most potent weapons against "the evildoers." On the other side of the conflict, Osama bin Laden and other al-Qaeda leaders have called on Muslims to engage in a *jihad*—a holy war—to protect themselves from being overrun by the American imperialists. The purpose of the appeals is the same for these two groups—to defend their way of life.

   Many aspects of a society can assist people in developing and maintaining a sense of purpose. For some people, religious values or personal moral codes are most crucial; for others, national or tribal identities are especially meaningful. Whatever these differences, in any society there

Pro–Falun Gong advocates protest the treatment of members of their group by the Chinese government and show their appreciation of Canadian support for their cause.

remains one common and critical reality. If an individual does not have a sense of purpose, he or she has little reason to contribute to a society's survival.

This list of functional prerequisites does not specify *how* a society and its corresponding social institutions will perform each task. For example, the United States protects itself from external attack by amassing a frightening arsenal of weaponry, while Canada makes determined efforts to remain neutral in world politics and to promote cooperative relationships with its neighbours. No matter what its particular strategy, any society or relatively permanent group must attempt to satisfy all these functional prerequisites for survival. If it fails on even one condition, as the Beothuks did, the society runs the risk of extinction.

Conflict View

Conflict theorists do not concur with the functionalist approach to social institutions. While both perspectives agree that institutions are organized to meet basic social needs, conflict theorists object to the implication that the outcome is necessarily efficient and desirable.

From a conflict perspective, the present organization of social institutions is no accident. Major institutions, such as education, help to maintain the privileges of the most powerful individuals and groups within a society, while contributing to the powerlessness of others. As one example, public schools in Canada are financed largely through income taxes. This allows more affluent areas to provide their children with better-equipped schools and better-paid teachers than low-income areas can afford. As a result, children from prosperous communities are better prepared to compete academically than children from impoverished communities. The structure of our country's educational system permits and even promotes such unequal treatment of school children.

Conflict theorists argue that social institutions such as education have an inherently conservative nature. Without question, it has been difficult to implement educational reforms that promote equal opportunity—whether in the area of ESL (English as a Second Language) education, or mainstreaming students with disabilities. From a functionalist perspective, social change can be dysfunctional, since it often leads to instability. However, from a conflict view, why should we preserve the existing social structure if it is unfair and discriminatory?

Social institutions also operate in gendered and racist environments, as conflict theorists, as well as feminists and interactionists, have pointed out. In schools, offices, and governmental institutions, assumptions about what people can do reflect the sexism and racism of the larger society. For instance, many people assume that women cannot make tough decisions—even those in the top echelons of corporate management. Others assume that all black students at elite universities represent affirmative action admissions. Inequality based on gender, economic status, race, and ethnicity thrives in such an environment—to which we might add discrimination based on age, physical disability, and sexual orientation. The truth of this assertion can be seen in routine decisions to advertise jobs and provide or withhold fringe benefits like child care and parental leave.

Feminist Views

As we pointed out in Chapter 1, feminist theory, rather than being a single perspective, analyzes the social world at a number of different levels. Whether they focus on the family, the business world, or the political arena, however, all of these theorists share the view that institutionalized discrimination is at the core of women's exclusion from a broader level of participation in society. While the plight of women in Canada may seem mild, especially when compared to that of, say, women under the former Taliban regime in Afghanistan, it cannot be discounted as the real and significant barrier that it was, and in many cases, continues to be.

In the family, women have traditionally been socialized to submissive roles within the household, deferring to the culturally established authority of husbands and fathers. This reality is the main cause of "Superwoman" role strain, which we discussed earlier. While Canadian women have made inroads into the paid labour force, the addition of this set of responsibilities has not been offset by a similar reduction in their traditional duties. The result is that women continue to do most of the cleaning, cooking, and child care in Canadian homes, despite the expectation that they make a full financial contribution to the two-income household.

To describe the interlocking models of oppression that are built into most institutions, feminist sociologist Patricia Hill Collins (1990) coined the phrase *matrix of domination*. There is an implicit interconnectedness among the various institutions in society that results in the standards of one spilling over to influence the standards of others. Thus, the paternalistic patterns of authority that are found in a single institution can be expected to have parallels in others—male dominance in the family supports male dominance in business, politics, education, and so on.

Much more than other theorists, feminists are concerned with the proactive potential of their analysis. Their view of institutions as perpetuators of female marginalization is not an academic exercise; rather, their research is directed at urging policymakers to change decision-making processes, so that the less advantaged will not remain mired at the bottom of Canadian society's power hierarchy.

Interactionist View

Social institutions affect our everyday behaviour, whether we are driving down the street or waiting in a long shopping line. Sociologist Mitchell Duneier (1994a, 1994b) studied the social behaviour of the data entry clerks, all women, who work in the service centre of a large Chicago law firm. Duneier was interested in the informal social norms that emerge in this work environment and the rich social network that these female employees had created.

The Network Center, as it is called, is merely a single, windowless room in a large office building where the firm occupies seven floors. This centre is staffed by two shifts of data entry clerks, who work either from 4:00 P.M. to midnight or midnight to 8:00 A.M. Each clerk works in a cubicle with just enough room for her keyboard, terminal, printer, and telephone. Work assignments for the clerks are placed in a central basket and then completed according to precise procedures.

At first glance, we might think that these women labour with little social contact, apart from limited work breaks and occasional conversations with their supervisor. However, drawing on the interactionist perspective, Duneier learned that despite working in a large office, these women find private moments to talk (often in the halls or outside the washroom) and share a critical view of the law firm's attorneys and day-shift secretaries. Indeed, the data entry clerks routinely suggest that their assignments represent work that the "lazy" secretaries should have completed during the normal workday. Duneier (1994b) tells of one clerk who resented the lawyers' superior attitude and pointedly refused to recognize or speak with any attorney who would not address her by name.

Interactionist theory analyzes exchanges that occur during social contact. These rafters must communicate quickly and clearly to ensure that their trip through treacherous water is a safe one.

Interactionist theorists emphasize that our social behaviour is conditioned by the roles and statuses that we accept, the groups to which we belong, and the institutions within which we function. For example, the social roles associated with being a judge occur within the larger context of the criminal justice system. The status of "judge" stands in relation to other statuses, such as attorney, plaintiff, defendant, and witness, as well as to the social institution of government. While the symbolic aspects of courts and jails are awesome, the judicial system derives its continued significance from the roles people carry out in social interactions (Berger and Luckmann 1966).

Social Structure in Global Perspective

Modern societies are complex, especially when compared with earlier social arrangements. Sociologists Ferdinand Tönnies and Gerhard Lenski have offered important typologies for contrasting modern societies with simpler forms of social structure.

For Tönnies, the emergence of industrial society represented a loss of community. He saw the transformation as a dehumanizing one, forcing people to interact as machines rather than as neighbours. Lenski, on the other hand, viewed the process of technological advancement as evolutionary. From his perspective, humans could only benefit from the efficiencies of the machine age.

Tönnies's *Gemeinschaft* and *Gesellschaft*

Ferdinand Tönnies (1855–1936) was appalled by the rise of an industrial city in his native Germany during the late 1800s. In his view, this city marked a dramatic change from the ideal type of a close-knit community, which Tönnies (1988, original edition 1887) termed *Gemeinschaft,* to that of an impersonal mass society known as *Gesellschaft.*

The ***Gemeinschaft*** (pronounced guh-MINE-shoft) community is typical of rural life. It is a small community in which people have similar backgrounds and life experiences. Virtually everyone knows one another, and social interactions are intimate and familiar, almost as one might find among kinfolk. There is a commitment to the larger social group and a sense of togetherness among community members. People relate to others in a personal way, not just as "clerk" or "manager." With this more personal interaction comes less privacy: we know more about everyone.

Do you think many of the people at this party know each other? Strangers who congregate together can be part of a *Gesellschaft.*

"I'd like to think of you as a person, David, but it's my job to think of you as personnel."

In a *Gesellschaft,* people are likely to relate to one another in terms of their roles rather than their individual backgrounds.

Social control in the *Gemeinschaft* community is maintained through informal means such as moral persuasion, gossip, and even gestures. These techniques work effectively because people are genuinely concerned about how others feel toward them. Social change is relatively limited in the *Gemeinschaft;* the lives of members of one generation may be quite similar to those of their grandparents.

By contrast, the ***Gesellschaft*** (pronounced guh-ZELL-shoft) is an ideal type characteristic of modern urban life. Most people are strangers and feel little in common with other community residents. Relationships are governed by social roles that grow out of immediate tasks, such as purchasing a product or arranging a business meeting. Self-interests dominate, and there is generally little consensus concerning values or commitment to the group. As a result, social control must rely on more formal techniques, such as laws and legally defined punishments.

Social change is an important aspect of life in the *Gesellschaft;* it can be strikingly evident even within a single generation.

Table 5-2 summarizes the differences between the *Gemeinschaft* and the *Gesellschaft* as described by Tönnies. Sociologists have used these terms to compare social structures stressing close relationships with those that emphasize less personal ties. It is easy to view *Gemeinschaft* with nostalgia as a far better way of life than the "rat race" of contemporary existence. However, the more intimate relationships of the *Gemeinschaft* come with a price. The prejudice and discrimination found within *Gemeinschaft* can be quite confining; more emphasis is placed on such ascribed statuses as family background than on people's unique talents and achievements. In addition, *Gemeinschaft* tends to be distrustful of the individual who seeks to be creative or just to be different.

Lenski's Sociocultural Evolution Approach

Sociologist Gerhard Lenski takes a very different view of society and social structure. Rather than distinguishing between two opposite types of societies, as Tönnies had, Lenski sees human societies as undergoing change according to a dominant pattern, known as ***sociocultural evolution.*** This term refers to the "process of change and development in human societies that results from cumulative growth in their stores of cultural information" (Lenski et al. 1995:75). In the sections that follow, we will examine the consequences of sociocultural evolution for the social structure of a society.

In Lenski's view, a society's level of technology is critical to the way it is organized. He defines ***technology*** as "information about the ways in which the material resources of the environment may be used to satisfy human needs and desires" (Nolan and Lenski 1999:414). The available technology does not completely define the form that a particular society and its social structure take. Nevertheless, a low level of technology may limit the degree to which it can depend on such things as irrigation or complex machinery.

Preindustrial Societies

How does a preindustrial society organize its economy? If we know that, it is possible to categorize the society. The first type of preindustrial society to emerge in human history was the ***hunting-and-gathering society***, in which people simply relied on whatever foods and fibres were readily available. Technology in such societies is minimal.

Table 5-2 Comparison of *Gemeinschaft* and *Gesellschaft*

Gemeinschaft	*Gesellschaft*
Rural life typifies this form.	Urban life typifies this form.
People share a feeling of community that results from their similar backgrounds and life experiences.	People perceive little sense of commonality. Their differences in background appear more striking than their similarities.
Social interactions, including negotiations, are intimate and familiar.	Social interactions, including negotiations, are more likely to be task-specific.
There is a spirit of cooperation and unity of will.	Self-interests dominate.
Tasks and personal relationships cannot be separated.	The task being performed is paramount; relationships are subordinate.
There is little emphasis on individual privacy.	Privacy is valued.
Informal social control predominates.	Formal social control is evident.
There is less tolerance of deviance.	There is greater tolerance of deviance.
Emphasis is on ascribed statuses.	There is more emphasis on achieved statuses.
Social change is relatively limited.	Social change is very evident—even within a generation.

People are organized in groups and are constantly on the move in search of food. There is little division of labour into specialized tasks.

Hunting-and-gathering societies are composed of small, widely dispersed groups. Each group consists almost entirely of people related to one another. As a result, kinship ties are the source of authority and influence, and the social institution of the family takes on a particularly important role. Tönnies would certainly view such societies as examples of *Gemeinschaft*.

Since resources are scarce, there is relatively little inequality in terms of material goods. Social differentiation within the hunting-and-gathering society is based on such ascribed statuses as gender, age, and family background. The last hunting-and-gathering societies were located in the southern tip of South America and in the Kalahari Desert of southwest Africa; they had virtually disappeared by the close of the 20th century (Nolan and Lenski 1999).

Horticultural societies, in which people plant seeds and crops rather than subsist merely on available foods, emerged about 10 000 to 12 000 years ago. Members of horticultural societies are much less nomadic than hunters and gatherers. They place greater emphasis on the production of tools and household objects. Yet technology within horticultural societies remains rather limited. They cultivate crops with the aid of digging sticks or hoes (J. Wilford 1997).

The last stage of preindustrial development is the ***agrarian society***, which emerged about 5000 years ago. As in horticultural societies, members of agrarian societies are primarily engaged in the production of food. However, the introduction of new technological innovations such as the plow allows farmers to dramatically increase their crop yield. They can cultivate the same fields over generations, thereby allowing the emergence of still larger settlements.

The social structure of the agrarian society continues to rely on the physical power of humans and animals (as opposed to mechanical power). Nevertheless, the social structure has more carefully defined roles than in horticultural societies. Individuals focus on specialized tasks, such as repair of fishing nets or work as a blacksmith. As human settlements become more established and stable, social institutions become more elaborate and property rights take on greater importance. The comparative permanence and greater surpluses of the agrarian society make it more feasible to create artifacts such as statues, public monuments, and art objects and to pass them on from one generation to the next.

Industrial Societies

Although the Industrial Revolution did not topple monarchs, it produced changes every bit as significant as those resulting from political revolutions. The Industrial Revolution, which began in England during the period 1760 to 1830, was a scientific revolution focused on the application of nonanimal (mechanical) sources of power to labour-intensive tasks. It involved changes in the social organization of the workplace, as people left the homestead and began working in central locations such as factories.

As the Industrial Revolution proceeded, a new form of social structure emerged. An ***industrial society*** is a society that depends on mechanization to produce its goods and services. Industrial societies relied on new inventions that facilitated agricultural and industrial production and on new sources of energy such as steam. Many societies underwent an irrevocable shift from an agrarian-oriented economy to an industrial base. No longer did an individual or a family typically make an entire product. Instead, specialization of tasks and manufacturing of goods became increasingly common. Workers, generally men but also women and even children, left the home to labour in central factories.

The process of industrialization had distinctive social consequences. Families and communities could not continue to function as self-sufficient units. Individuals, villages, and regions began to exchange goods and services and become interdependent. As people came to rely on the labour of members of other communities, the family lost its unique position as the source of power and authority. The need for specialized knowledge led to more formalized education, and education emerged as a social institution distinct from the family.

Postindustrial and Postmodern Societies

When the sociocultural evolutionary approach first appeared in the 1960s, it paid relatively little attention to how maturing industrialized societies may change with the emergence of even more advanced forms of technology. More recently, in evaluating the increasingly rapid pace of technological and social change, Gerhard Lenski and his collaborators have observed,

> The only things that might conceivably slow the rate of technological innovation in the next several decades are nuclear war, collapse of the world economy, or an environmental catastrophe. Fortunately, none of these appears likely in that time frame. (Lenski et al. 1995:441)

Lenski and other sociologists have studied the significant changes in the occupational structure of industrial societies as they shift from manufacturing to service economies. Social scientists call these technologically advanced nations *postindustrial societies*. Sociologist Daniel Bell (1999) defines ***postindustrial society*** as a society whose economic system is engaged primarily in the processing and control of information. The main output of a postindustrial society is services rather than manufactured goods. Large numbers of people become involved in occupations devoted to the teaching, generation, or dissemination of ideas.

Taking a functionalist perspective, Bell views this transition from industrial to postindustrial society as a positive development. He sees a general decline in organized working-class groups and a rise in interest groups concerned with such national issues as health, education, and the environment. Bell's outlook is functionalist because he portrays postindustrial society as basically consensual. Organizations and interest groups will engage in an open and competitive process of decision making. The level of conflict between diverse groups will diminish, and there will be much greater social stability.

Conflict theorists take issue with Bell's analysis of postindustrial society. For example, Michael Harrington (1980), who alerted the nation to the problems of the poor in his book *The Other America,* was critical of the significance that Bell attached to the growing class of white-collar workers. Harrington conceded that scientists, engineers, and economists are involved in important political and economic decisions, but he disagreed with Bell's claim that they have a free hand in decision making, independent of the interests of the rich. Harrington followed in the tradition of Marx by arguing that conflict between social classes will continue in postindustrial society.

More recently, sociologists have gone beyond discussing postindustrial societies to the ideal type of postmodern society. A ***postmodern society*** is a technologically sophisticated society that is preoccupied with consumer goods and media images (Brannigan 1992). Such societies consume goods and information on a mass scale. Postmodern theorists take a global perspective and note the ways that aspects of culture cross national boundaries (Lyotard 1993). For example, residents of Manitoba may listen to reggae music from Jamaica, eat sushi and other types of Japanese food, and wear clogs from Sweden.

Postmodern theorists point to this diversity in their rejection of the notion that the social world can be explained by a single paradigm. The intermingling of cultures and ideologies that characterizes the modern, electronically connected planet has led to a relativist approach. Postmodernists reject science as a panacea, arguing that no single explanation can accurately explain the causes and consequences of postmodern global society.

The emphasis of postmodern theorists is on describing emerging cultural forms and patterns of social interaction. Within sociology, the postmodern view offers support for integrating the insights of various theoretical perspectives—functionalism, conflict theory, interactionism, and labelling theory—while also incorporating feminist theories and other contemporary approaches. Feminist sociologists argue optimistically that, with its indifference to hierarchies and distinctions, postmodernism will discard traditional values of male dominance in favour of gender equality. Yet others contend that despite new technology, postindustrial and postmodern societies can be expected to experience the problems of inequality that have plagued industrial societies (Ritzer 1995a; Sale 1996; Smart 1990; B. Turner 1990; van Vucht Tijssen 1990).

Ferdinand Tönnies and Gerhard Lenski present two visions of society's social structure. While different, both approaches are useful, and this textbook will draw on both. The sociocultural evolutionary approach emphasizes a historical perspective. It does not picture different types of social structures coexisting within the same society. Consequently, according to this approach, one would not expect a single society to include hunters and gatherers along with a postmodern culture. By contrast, sociologists frequently observe that a *Gemeinschaft* and a *Gesellschaft* can be found in the same society. For example, a rural Ontario community less than 100 kilometres from Toronto is linked to the metropolitan area by the technology of the modern information age.

The work of Tönnies and Lenski reminds us that a major focus of sociology has been to identify changes in social structure and the consequences for human behaviour. At the macrolevel, we see society shifting to more advanced forms of technology. The social structure becomes increasingly complex, and new social institutions assume functions previously performed by the family. On the microlevel, these changes affect the nature of social interactions between people. Each individual takes on multiple social roles, and people come to rely more on social networks rather than solely on kinship ties. As the social structure becomes more complex, people's relationships tend to become more impersonal, transient, and fragmented.

In the social policy section we will examine the impact of the AIDS crisis on the social structure and social interaction.

SOCIAL POLICY AND SOCIAL STRUCTURE

The AIDS Crisis

The Issue

In his novel *The Plague,* Albert Camus (1948:34) wrote, "There have been as many plagues as wars in history, yet always plagues and wars take people equally by surprise." Regarded by many as the distinctive plague of the modern era, AIDS certainly caught major social institutions—particularly the government, the health care system, and the economy—by surprise when it was initially noticed by medical practitioners in the 1970s. It has since spread around the world. While there are encouraging new therapies, there is currently no way to eradicate AIDS by medical means. Therefore, it is essential to protect people by reducing the transmission of the fatal virus. But how is this to be done? And whose responsibility is it? What roles do social institutions have?

The Setting

AIDS is the acronym for *acquired immune deficiency syndrome.* Rather than being a distinct disease, AIDS is actually a predisposition to disease caused by a virus, the human immunodeficiency virus (HIV). This virus gradually destroys the body's immune system, leaving the carrier vulnerable to infections, such as pneumonia, that those with healthy immune systems can generally resist. Transmission of the virus from one person to another appears to require either intimate sexual contact or exchange of blood or bodily fluids (whether from contaminated hypodermic needles or syringes, transfusions of infected blood, or transmission from an infected mother to her child before or during birth). Health practitioners pay particular attention to methods of transmitting HIV because there is no cure or vaccine for AIDS at this time.

The first cases of AIDS in Canada were reported in 1980. While the numbers of new cases have recently declined, from 2989 in 1995 to 2233 in 1999, there had been 17 165 diagnosed cases in Canada up to June 30, 2000. Overall, women account for approximately 20 percent of diagnosed cases. However, that proportion has been increasing in recent years, from 19.8 percent of new cases in 1997 to 24.3 percent in 1999. Worldwide, AIDS is on the increase, with an estimated 34.2 million people infected and 2.8 million dying annually (see Figure 5-2). AIDS is not evenly distributed, and those areas least equipped to deal with it—the developing nations of Africa and South Asia—face the greatest challenge (Kaiser Family Foundation 2000; UNAIDS 2000).

Sociological Insights

Dramatic crises like the AIDS epidemic are likely to bring about certain transformations in a society's social structure. From a functionalist perspective, if established social institutions cannot meet a crucial need, new social networks are likely to emerge to fill that function. In the case of AIDS, self-help groups—especially in the gay communities of major cities—have organized to care for the sick, educate the healthy, and lobby for more responsive public policies. The government has restructured Heath Canada, moving its Bureau of AIDS/HIV to the newly created Centre for Infectious Disease Prevention and Control. In addition, every major community across the nation has organizations such as YouthCo, which helps young people with AIDS, the Positive Women's Network, and Healing Our Spirit, created to meet the special challenges faced by First Nations people with AIDS.

The label of "person with AIDS" or "HIV-positive" often functions as a master status. Indeed, people with AIDS or infected with the virus face a powerful dual stigma. Not only are they associated with a lethal and contagious disease, but they have a disease that disproportionately afflicts already stigmatized groups, such as gay males and intravenous drug users. This linkage with stigmatized groups delayed recognition of the severity of the AIDS epidemic; the media took little interest in the disease until it seemed to be spreading beyond the gay community. Viewed from a conflict perspective, policymakers were slow to respond to the AIDS crisis because those in high-risk groups—gay men and IV drug users—were comparatively powerless. However, studies have shown that people with the virus and with AIDS who receive appropriate medical treatment are living longer than before. This may put additional pressure on policymakers to address the issues raised by the spread of AIDS (Epstein 1997; Shilts 1987).

On the microlevel of social interaction, observers widely forecast that AIDS would lead to a more conservative sexual climate—among both homosexuals and heterosexuals—in which people would be much more cautious about involvement with new partners. Yet it

FIGURE 5-2

The Geography of HIV

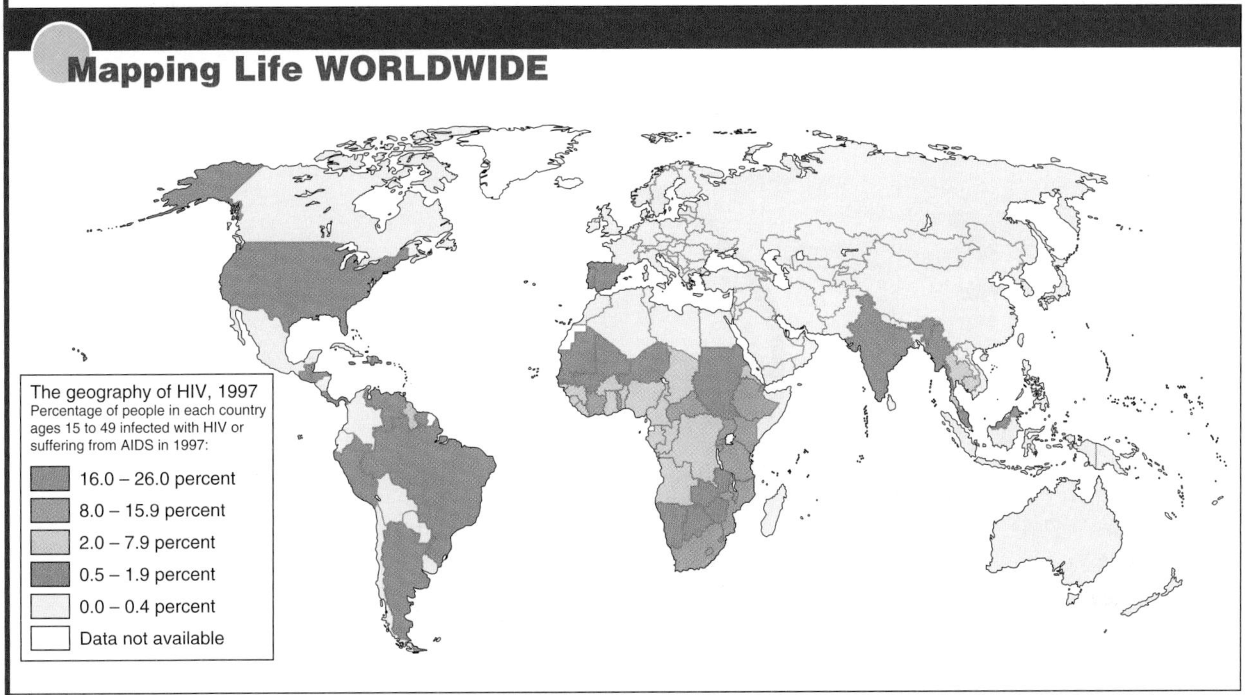

Source: United Nations data reproduced by L. Altman 1998:A1.

appears that many sexually active people have not heeded precautions about "safe sex." Data from studies conducted in the 1990s indicated that there is growing complacency about AIDS, even among those most vulnerable (*AIDS Alert* 1999).

Another interactionist concern is the tremendous impact that taking the appropriate medication has on one's daily routine. Tens of thousands of AIDS patients are having to reorder their lives around their medical regimens. Even patients without the symptoms of HIV find the concentrated effort that is needed to fight the disease—taking 95 doses of 16 different medications every 24 hours—extremely taxing. Think for a moment about the effect such a regimen would have on your own life, from eating and sleeping to work, study, child care, and recreation (see Figure 5-3).

Policy Initiatives

Given the absence of a medical cure or vaccine, policy initiatives emphasize the need for more information about how AIDS is contracted and spread. In an address before the American Sociological Association, Canadian sociologist Barry Adam (1992) argued that sociologists can make an important contribution to AIDS-related research. He outlined four directions for such sociological research:

- How is information about AIDS produced and distributed? Is the distribution of information about how to have "safer sex" being limited or even censored?
- How does an AIDS "folklore"—false information about remedies and cures—emerge and become integrated into a community? Why do certain communities and individuals resist or ignore scientific information about the dangers of AIDS?
- How are medical and social services made available to people with AIDS? Why are these services often denied to the poorest patients?
- How is ***homophobia*** (fear of and prejudice against homosexuality) related to fears concerning AIDS? In what ways does homophobia correlate with other forms of bias?

Adam's questions underscore the impact of the AIDS crisis on social interaction and social structure. Addressing these questions will allow policymakers to better assess such initiatives as sex education programs

FIGURE 5-3

Daily Dosing for AIDS

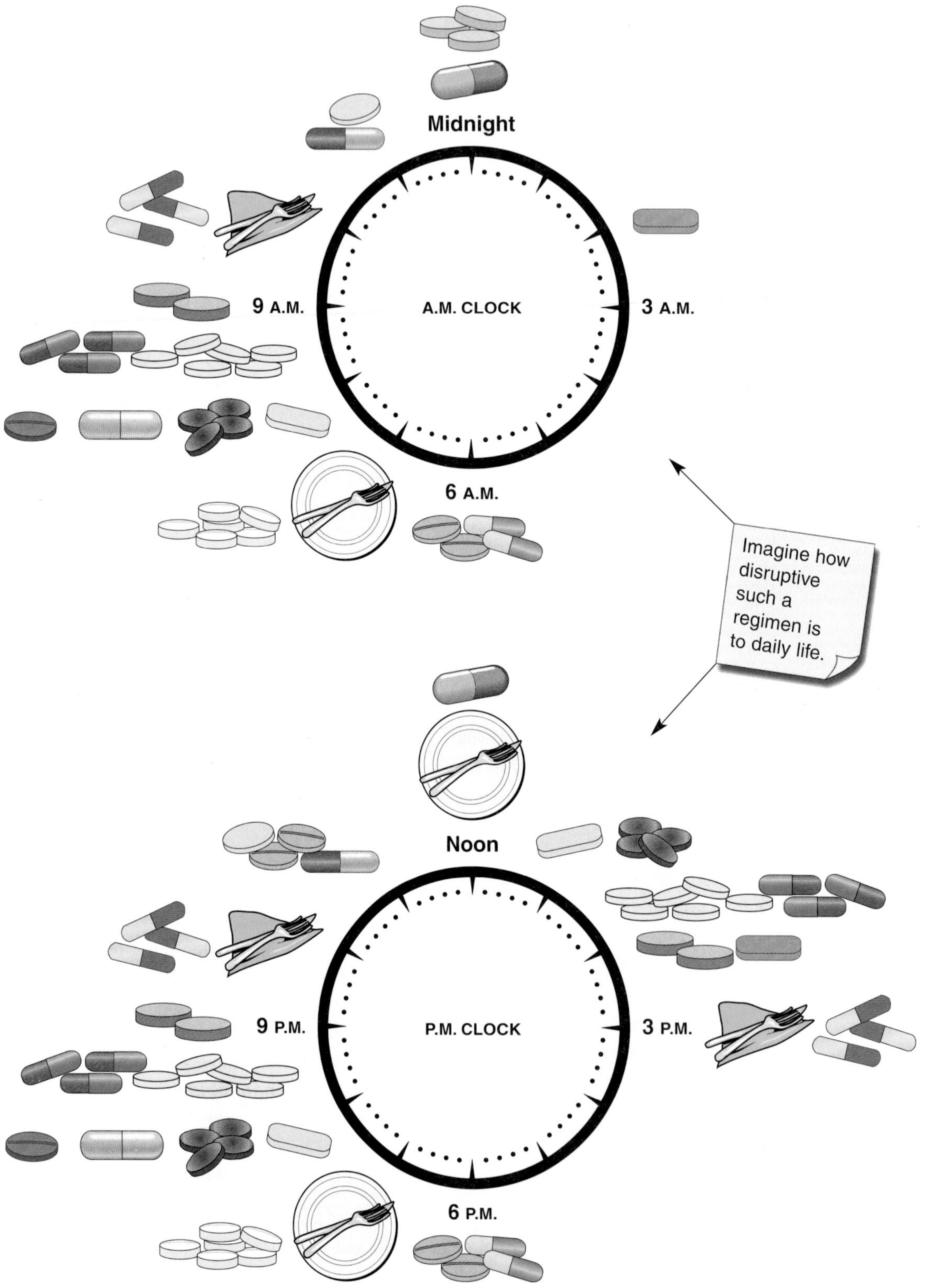

Note: Regimen may vary due to individual reactions to medications taken together. Shapes and colours of the 16 different prescriptive drugs are symbolic rather than realistic.

Source: Schaefer in consultation with Roxane Laboratories 2000.

in schools, needle exchange programs, and policies regarding AIDS testing.

AIDS has struck all societies, but not all nations can respond in the same manner. In some nations, cultural practices may prevent people from dealing with the AIDS epidemic realistically. They are less likely to take the necessary preventive measures, including more open discussion of sexuality, homosexuality, and drug use. Prevention has shown signs of working among target groups, such as drug users, pregnant women, and gay men and lesbians, but these initiatives are few and far between in developing nations. The prescribed treatment for a pregnant woman to reduce mother-to-baby transmission of AIDS costs about US$1000—many times the average annual income in Africa, which accounts for 90 percent of the world's AIDS deaths. Even more costly is the medication for adult patients with HIV, which can cost over US$71 000 per year (Pear 1997a; Sawyer 2000; Specter 1998b; Sternberg 1999).

The issues that divide rich and poor nations also manifest themselves within industrial nations. Canadians with AIDS or HIV have had to struggle to gain comprehensive medical coverage for the cost of new drugs. Making the challenge even greater is the fact that drug coverage policy is a provincial jurisdiction. Although significant progress has been made in most provinces, for instance in British Columbia where 100 percent of treatment cost is covered, others have yet to develop a comprehensive strategy. Access to drugs also varies, accounting for per patient costs ranging from $8 000 to $12 000 across the country. Acting for the federal government, Health Canada has focused on tracking and analyzing the spread of AIDS and HIV in Canada.

Let's Discuss

1. Has information on how to avoid getting AIDS been made available to you? Do you personally know of a case in which such information was withheld from someone or censored? If so, why and by whom?
2. Have you come across AIDS "folklore" (misinformation) on your campus or in your neighbourhood? If so, how widespread do you think it is?
3. If you were a sociologist who wanted to understand why some people knowingly ignore the dangers of AIDS, how would you go about studying the problem?

Chapter Resources

Summary

Social interaction refers to the ways in which people respond to one another. ***Social structure*** refers to the way in which a society is organized into predictable relationships. This chapter examines the basic elements of social structure—statuses, social roles, groups, networks, and institutions.

1. We shape our social reality based on what we learn through our social interactions. Social change comes from redefining or reconstructing social reality. Sometimes change is *negotiated.*
2. An ***ascribed status*** is generally assigned to a person at birth, whereas an ***achieved status*** is attained largely through one's own effort.
3. In Canada, ascribed statuses, such as race and gender, can function as ***master statuses***, which have an important impact on one's potential to achieve a desired professional and social status.
4. With each distinctive status—whether ascribed or achieved—come particular ***social roles,*** the set of expectations for people who occupy that status.
5. ***Role strain*** refers to the difficulties that result when a role is too demanding on the individual trying to fulfill it. ***Role conflict*** occurs when meeting the requirements of one role contravenes the requirements of another.
6. Much of our patterned behaviour takes place within ***groups*** and is influenced by the norms and sanctions established by groups. Groups serve as links to ***social networks*** and their vast resources.
7. The mass media, the government, the economy, the family, and the health care system are all examples of ***social institutions.***
8. One way to understand social institutions is to see how they fulfill essential functions, such as replacing personnel, training new recruits, and preserving order.
9. The conflict perspective argues that social institutions help to maintain the privileges of the powerful while contributing to the powerlessness of others.

10. Interactionist theorists emphasize that our social behaviour is conditioned by the roles and statuses that we accept, the groups to which we belong, and the institutions within which we function.
11. Feminist perspectives try to draw our attention to the fact that social structure can make stratification seem normal. The challenge for Canadian society is to recognize that the historical power imbalance between men and women is sustained by social structures, and without systemic solutions, it cannot be displaced.
12. Ferdinand Tönnies distinguished the close-knit community of ***Gemeinschaft*** from the impersonal mass society known as ***Gesellschaft.***
13. Gerhard Lenski views human societies as changing historically along one dominant pattern, which he calls ***sociocultural evolution.***
14. The AIDS crisis affects every social institution, including the family, the schools, the health care system, the economy, and the government.

Critical Thinking Questions

1. People in certain professions seem particularly susceptible to role conflict. For example, journalists commonly experience role conflict during disasters, crimes, and other distressing situations. Should they offer assistance to the needy or cover breaking news as reporters? Select two other professions and discuss the types of role conflict they might experience.
2. All of the theoretical perspectives discussed in this text can be used to understand the structure and processes of social institutions. Choose an institution and identify the potential strengths or weaknesses of each perspective's analysis.
3. In what ways does HIV serve to underscore issues of race, class, and gender in Canada today?

Key Terms

Achieved status A social position attained by a person largely through his or her own efforts. (page 102)

Agrarian society The most technologically advanced form of preindustrial society. Members are primarily engaged in the production of food but increase their crop yield through such innovations as the plow. (114)

Ascribed status A social position "assigned" to a person by society without regard for the person's unique talents or characteristics. (101)

Gemeinschaft Close-knit communities, often found in rural areas, in which strong personal bonds unite members. (112)

Gesellschaft Communities, often urban, that are large and impersonal, with little commitment to the group or consensus on values. (112)

Group Any number of people with similar norms, values, and expectations who interact meaningfully with one another on a regular basis. (106)

Homophobia Fear of and prejudice against homosexuality. (117)

Horticultural societies Preindustrial societies in which people plant seeds and crops rather than subsist merely on available foods. (114)

Hunting-and-gathering society A preindustrial society in which people rely on whatever foods and fibres are readily available in order to live. (113)

Industrial society A society that depends on mechanization to produce its goods and services. (114)

Master status A status that dominates one's other statuses and thereby determines a person's general position within society. (102)

Negotiated order A social structure that derives its existence from the social interactions through which people define and redefine its character. (101)

Negotiation The attempt to reach agreement with others concerning some objective. (100)

Postindustrial society A society whose economic system is primarily engaged in the processing and control of information. (114)

Postmodern society A technologically sophisticated society that is preoccupied with consumer goods and media images. (115)

Role conflict Difficulties that occur when incompatible expectations arise from two or more social positions held by the same person. (104)

Role exit The process of disengagement from a role that is central to one's self-identity and reestablishment of an identity in a new role. (105)

Role strain Difficulties that result from the differing demands and expectations associated with the same social position. (105)

Social institutions Organized patterns of beliefs and behaviour centred on basic social needs. (107)

Social interaction The ways in which people respond to one another. (99)

Social network A series of social relationships that links a person directly to others and therefore indirectly to still more people. (106)

Social role A set of expectations for people who occupy a given social position or status. (104)

Social structure The way in which a society is organized into predictable relationships. (99)

Sociocultural evolution The process of change and development in human societies that results from cumulative growth in their stores of cultural information. (113)

Status A term used by sociologists to refer to any of the full range of socially defined positions within a large group or society. (101)

Technology Information about the ways in which the material resources of the environment may be used to satisfy human needs and desires. (113)

Additional Readings

Epstein, Steven. 1996. *Impure Science: AIDS, Activism, and the Politics of Knowledge.* Berkeley, CA: University of California Press. A sociologist examines AIDS research from the perspective of how it has been influenced by social and political forces.

Ignatieff, Michael. 2000. *The Rights Revolution.* Toronto: House of Anansi Press. Ignatieff looks at Canada as a liberal society heading into the 21st century, and argues that the proliferation of individual and special interest group rights that has occurred in recent decades does not pose a threat to the stability of our society.

Kephart, William M., and William M. Zellner. 1998. *Extraordinary Groups: An Examination of Unconventional Life-Styles.* 6th ed. New York: St. Martin's. Among the groups described in this very readable book are the Amish, the Oneida community, the Mormons, Hasidic Jews, Jehovah's Witnesses, and the Romani (commonly known as Gypsies).

Internet Connection

www.mcgrawhill.ca/college/schaefer

For additional Internet exercises relating to the Zimbardo prison experiment and Gemeinschaft *and* Gesellschaft, *visit the Schaefer Online Learning Centre at* ***http://www.mcgrawhill.ca/college/schaefer****. Please note that while the URLs listed were current at the time of printing, these sites often change—check the Online Learning Centre for updates.*

Visit the website **http://www.prisonexp.org**. This web site deals with Phillip Zimbardo's ill-fated 1971 experiment dealing with human relations in an artificial prison setting. Explore the site and see if you can find answers to these questions:

(a) Why do you think there is still a fascination with this study even 30 years after it apparently failed?
(b) What insights about this experiment has Zimbardo had over time?
(c) Can you explain how the environment the researchers created developed social networks?
(d) Can you think of a parallel situation from your own life experience, in which social circumstances influenced you to become a member of a group very quickly? What were the consequences of that involvement?
(e) Would you participate in a similar experiment today? Why or why not?

CHAPTER

6 GROUPS AND ORGANIZATIONS

Groups come in all sizes and cover a broad array of interests. The group shown here is the Flying Seven, the first women's aviator club in Canada. From left to right: Miss Jean Pike, Miss Tosca Trasolini, Mrs. E. Flaherty, Mrs. F. Gilbert, President Elainne Roberge, Miss Margaret Fane, and Miss Rolie Moore.

For decades there has been an all-out war between two soft drinks of almost identical taste—Coca-Cola and Pepsi-Cola. Hundreds of millions have been sunk into financing this war. More important, billions have been spent by the public on one or the other of the products. Both drinks lay claim to the same properties—youth, freedom, physical exploits, having fun and getting girls or, conversely, getting boys. In many parts of the Third World, they also possess the properties necessary to help political freedom defeat dictatorship. Coke, in particular, has become a minor idol which promises freedom, money and escape to bigtime individualism in the West.

Clearly we are not talking about soft drinks. We are dealing here with what people want to believe about themselves. After all, you can scarcely claim to possess freedom of spirit and existential individualism on the grounds that you consume the same soft drink as three billion other people. This is conformism, not nonconformism.

The same could be said about the millions of McDonald's hamburgers eaten daily around the world. Clearly, this modern success story has nothing to do with selling the best hamburger. One look at the thin, grayish patties is enough to eliminate that possibility. One taste confirms that the meat is almost indistinguishable from the soft, innocuous bun and gooey ketchup. Sweetness seems to run each of these elements together. This is not a good hamburger. For that matter, McDonald's isn't even about people choosing the hamburger they like best. The corporation's approach has never seemed to involve winning the public through the mechanism of choice. Mac McDonald himself made it clear that he was removing freedom of choice: "if you gave people a choice there would be chaos."

And yet at some level, conscious or unconscious, people are convinced that by going to McDonald's they are demonstrating a sort of individualism—an individualism which turns its back on the middle-class social convention by going out and eating a Big Mac. They don't have to dress up or eat decent, let alone good food or, indeed, eat off plates or clear the table or wash dishes or deal with some snooty waiter or make conversation or sit up straight or sit still. They don't even have to sit down. Eating a McDonald's and drinking a Coke is an act of nonconformity and tens of millions of people are doing exactly that every day. *(Ralston Saul 1993)* ■

In this excerpt from *Voltaire's Bastards: The Dictatorship of Reason in the West,* John Ralston Saul refers to the power of modern media and marketing to influence our perceptions of which groups we belong to. McDonald's and other major transnational corporations spend billions of dollars a year to make sure that the groups we see as desirable, and subsequently join, are defined for us. Consumers have been convinced that the drive-thru lane is the route to independence and self-expression, even though it is simply a path from one group in society—the "old" generation, with its tradition of family dinners around the dining table—to another—the "new" generation of movers and shakers who don't have time for such things. In his book *The McDonaldization of Society,* sociologist George Ritzer contemplates the enormous influence of this corporation on modern-day culture and social life. Ritzer defines ***McDonaldization*** as "the process by which the principles of the fast food restaurant are coming to dominate more and more sectors of American society as well as the rest of the world" (Ritzer 2000:1). In other words, corporate marketing is now able to set standards that become part of the culture in Canada and many other societies.

Despite the runaway success of McDonald's and its imitators, and the widely applauded economic benefits attributed to them, Saul sees such organizations as having effects on people's lives that may be far from constructive. On top of the propagandizing that leads a gullible public into joining client-base groups unwittingly, there is the waste and environmental degradation created by billions of disposable containers and the dehumanized work routines of fast-food crews. We must ask the question: Would people choose to become members of a group devoted to eating tasteless hamburgers were it not for the influence of mass marketing?

This chapter considers the impact of groups, group membership, and organizations on social interaction. It will begin by noting the distinctions between various types of groups, with particular attention given to the dynamics of small groups. We will examine how and why formal organizations came into existence and describe Max Weber's model of the modern bureaucracy. We'll also look at technology's impact on the organization of the workplace. The social policy section will focus on the issue of sexual harassment, which has become a major concern of both governmental and private-sector organizations. ■

Understanding Groups

In everyday speech, people use the term *group* to describe any collection of individuals, whether three strangers sharing an elevator or hundreds attending a rock concert. p. 106 However, in sociological terms a group is any number of people with similar norms, values, and expectations who interact with one another on a regular basis. People that gather together regularly to have their morning coffee at the local McDonald's, the Canadian Olympic Team, and the Ontario Minor Hockey Association are all considered examples of groups. The important point is that members of a group share some sense of belonging. This characteristic distinguishes groups from mere *aggregates* of people, such as passengers who happen to be together on an airplane flight, or from *categories* who share a common feature (such as being retired) but otherwise do not act together.

Consider the case of an *a cappella* singing group. It has agreed-upon values and social norms. All members want to improve their singing skills and schedule lots of performances. In addition, like many groups, the singing ensemble has both a formal and an informal structure. The members meet regularly to rehearse; they choose leaders to run the rehearsals and manage their affairs. At the same time, some group members may take on unofficial leadership roles by coaching new members in singing techniques and performing skills.

The study of groups has become an important part of sociological expression and investigation because they play such a key role in the transmission of culture. As we interact with others, we pass on our ways of thinking and acting—from language and values to ways of dressing and leisure activities.

Types of Groups

Sociologists have made a number of useful distinctions between types of groups—primary and secondary groups, in-groups and out-groups, and reference groups.

Primary and Secondary Groups

Charles Horton Cooley (1902:2357) coined the term ***primary group*** to refer to a small group characterized by intimate, face-to-face association and cooperation. The members of a family constitute a primary group. Members of a work crew can also be part of a primary group. Perhaps ironically, given Saul's introduction to McDonald's at the beginning of this chapter, one of the goals of the company's training program is to create a team atmosphere in the workplace so employees feel a sense of connection similar to that in the family. Primary groups play a pivotal role both in the socialization process (see Chapter 4) and in the development of roles and statuses (see Chapter 5).

When we find ourselves identifying closely with a group, it is probably a primary group. However, people in Canada participate in many groups that are not characterized by close bonds of friendship, such as large college or university classes and fan clubs. The term ***secondary group*** refers to a formal, impersonal group in which there is little social intimacy or mutual understanding (see Table 6-1). As in the McDonald's example above, the distinction between primary and secondary groups is not always clear-cut.

In-Groups and Out-Groups

A group can hold special meaning for members because of its relationship to other groups. People in one group sometimes feel antagonistic to or threatened by another group, especially if the group is perceived as being different culturally or racially. Sociologists identify these "we" and "they" feelings by using two terms first employed by William Graham Sumner (1906:1213): *in-group* and *out-group.*

An ***in-group*** can be defined as any group or category to which people feel they belong. Simply put, it comprises everyone who is regarded as "we" or "us." The in-group may be as narrow as one's family or as broad as an entire society. The very existence of an in-group implies that there is an out-group viewed as "they" or "them." More formally, an ***out-group*** is a group or category to which people feel they do not belong.

One typical consequence of in-group membership is a feeling of distinctiveness and superiority among members, who see themselves as better than people in the out-group. A double standard held by members of the in-group can enhance this sense of superiority. Proper behaviour for the in-group is simultaneously viewed as unacceptable behaviour for the out-group. Sociologist Robert Merton (1968:480-88) describes this process as the conversion of "in-group virtues" into "out-group vices." Since the September 11, 2001, attacks on the United States, this differential standard has been apparent in the rhetoric of the American government and the supporters of the terrorist's actions. On the one hand, many Americans see nothing wrong with bombing villages and killing civilians as a cost of eliminating terrorism. On the other hand, supporters of the terrorists see nothing wrong with flying an airplane into a skyscraper to make a statement about their beliefs. Supporters of both sides—members of their in-groups—have no trouble applauding the actions of those with whom they identify, and condemning the actions of the other group.

Conflict between in-groups and out-groups can turn violent on a personal as well as a political level. In 1999 two disaffected students at Columbine High School in Littleton, Colorado, launched an attack on the school that

Table 6-1 Comparison of Primary and Secondary Groups

Primary Group	Secondary Group
Generally small	Usually large
Relatively long period of interaction	Short duration, temporary
Intimate, face-to-face association	Little social intimacy or mutual understanding
Some emotional depth in relationships	Relationships generally superficial
Cooperative, friendly	More formal and impersonal

"So long, Bill. This is my club. You can't come in."

An exclusive social club is an in-group whose members consider themselves superior to others.

Taking Sociology to Work

JÁNOS JOHN MATÉ: Representative to the United Nations, Greenpeace International

János John Maté graduated from Simon Fraser University in 1972 with a master's degree in sociology. Since that time, his understanding of the social world has served him in a variety of careers ranging from producing gala concerts to counselling couples to reporting on human rights for the National Film Board of Canada. But from the time he joined Greenpeace in 1989, his passion has been environmental issues. Maté began as director of the organization's Canada Nuclear Disarmament Campaign before coordinating the first anti-nuclear delegation to Israel. In 1995, he sailed to Moruroa from Tahiti to protest nuclear testing in the South Pacific. In the early 1990s, Maté began to focus his attentions on the depletion of the ozone layer, becoming Director of Greenpeace Canada's campaign to raise public awareness of the thinning of the planet's atmosphere. He has moved on to similar duties with Greenpeace International, coordinating the promotion and adoption of Greenfreeze, an environmentally friendly alternative to the ozone-destroying chemical used in refrigerators and car air conditioners for decades. Today, Maté is the organization's representative to the United Nations' Meeting of Parties to the Montreal Protocol, a group dedicated to stopping and reversing damage to the ozone in the earth's atmosphere. Throughout his career, Maté has benefited from the insight into the structures and processes of social life provided to him by his sociological background.

Let's Discuss

1. What kinds of sociological issues would be relevant to someone working in an environmental group such as Greenpeace?
2. Would you consider working or volunteering for an environmental organization? If so, what issues would you consider to be of top priority?

left 15 students and teachers dead, including themselves. One week later, a 16-year-old former student walked into W.R. Myers High School in the small town of Taber, Alberta, and shot two students, killing one and seriously wounding the other. In both of these cases and others similar to them, the individuals involved claimed to have been victims of harassment for being different. Not being able to fit into one of their school's cliques may have prompted them to strike out against more popular classmates, with dire consequences.

Reference Groups

Both in-groups and primary groups can dramatically influence the way an individual thinks and behaves. Sociologists use the term ***reference group*** when speaking of any group that individuals use as a standard for evaluating themselves and their own behaviour. For example, a high school student who aspires to join a social circle will begin dressing like these peers, listening to the same music, and hanging out at the same stores and clubs.

Reference groups have two basic purposes. They serve a normative function by setting and enforcing standards. The high school student who wants the approval of the in-group will have to follow the group's dictates at least to some extent. Reference groups also perform a comparison function by serving as a standard against which people can measure themselves and others (Merton and Kitt 1950). For example, a snowboarder who can "tweak a Canadian Bacon" or "slam a Crippler" may be reluctant to include someone whose best half-pipe manoeuvre is a straight 180 as part of her in-group.

In many cases, people model their behaviour after groups to which they do not yet belong but aspire to belong to in the future. For example, a university student majoring in finance may read the financial pages of *The Globe and Mail* and seek out social events attended by successful businesspeople. The student is engaging in the process of anticipatory socialization by using the Bay Street corporate elite as a reference group to which he or she aspires.

p. 83

Often, two or more reference groups influence us at the same time. Our family members, peers, and coworkers all shape different aspects of our self-evaluation. In addition, certain reference group attachments change during the life cycle. This is dramatically demonstrated as young people go through adolescence, often finding that their group of friends from Grade 9 no longer appeal to them in Grade 10. We shift reference groups as we take on different statuses during our lives.

Studying Small Groups

Studying small groups is an important aspect of sociological research. The term ***small group*** is used to refer to a group small enough for all members to interact simultaneously, that is, to talk with one another or at least be well acquainted. Certain primary groups, such as families, may also be classified as small groups. However, many small groups are secondary in nature, and may be formed spontaneously. On the morning of September 11, 2001, for example, in the skies over rural Pennsylvania, a group of strangers created a small group when they joined together to prevent terrorists from crashing a fourth plane into a pre-selected target.

Groups come in all sizes. This group of puppeteers, a secondary group, has 120 members.

We may think of small groups as being informal and unpatterned; yet, interactionist researchers have revealed that there are distinct and predictable processes at work in the functioning of small groups. Airlines and hospitals have developed sophisticated training programs in recent years to deal with the communication challenges found in cockpits and operating rooms. Studies had shown that the skewed distribution of power among flight crews, for example, led to situations in which the pilot—the authority figure in the group—failed to communicate with or be receptive to communication from the rest of his small group. The result was predictable dysfunction at times when the need for clear communication was the greatest (Sexton and Helmreich 2000; Waitzkin and Stoeckle 1976).

Size of a Group

At what point does a collection of people become too large to be called a small group? That is not clear. If there are more than 20 members, it is difficult for individuals to interact regularly in a direct and intimate manner. But even within a range of 2 to 20 people, group size can substantially alter the quality of social relationships. For example, as the number of group participants increases, the most active communicators become even more active relative to others. Therefore, a person who dominates a group of 3 or 4 members will be relatively more dominant in a 15-person group.

Group size also has noticeable social implications for members who do not assume leadership roles. In a larger group, each member has less time to speak, more points of view to absorb, and a more elaborate structure to function in. At the same time, an individual has greater freedom to ignore certain members or viewpoints than he or she would in a smaller group. Clearly, it is harder to disregard someone in a 4-person workforce than in an office with 30 employees, or someone in a string quartet than in a high school band with 50 members.

German sociologist Georg Simmel (1858–1918) is credited as the first sociologist to emphasize the importance of interaction processes within groups. Reflecting on group size, Simmel (1950, original edition 1917) suggested that smaller groups have distinctive qualities and patterns of interaction that inevitably disappear as they expand in size. Larger groups, in Simmel's view, develop particular forms of interaction that are unnecessary in small groups.

The simplest of all social groups or relationships is the ***dyad,*** or two-member group. A boyfriend and a girlfriend constitute a dyad, as does a business partnership or a singing duo. In a dyad, one is able to achieve a special level of intimacy that cannot be duplicated in larger groups. However, as Simmel (1950) noted, a dyad, unlike any other group, can be destroyed by the loss of a single member. Therefore, the threat of termination hangs over a dyadic relationship perhaps more than over any other type.

Obviously, the introduction of one additional person to a dyad dramatically transforms the character of the small group. The dyad now becomes a three-member group, or ***triad.*** The new member has at least three basic ways of interacting with and influencing the dynamics of the group. The new person may play a *unifying* role within a triad. When a married couple has its first child, the baby may serve to bind the group closer together. A newcomer may also play a *mediating* role within a three-person group. If two roommates in an apartment are perpetually sniping at each other, the third roommate may attempt to remain

Eye on the Media

6-1 Surviving *Survivor*—A Sociological View

Richard, Kelly, Rudy, and Susan all want to get ahead of other members of their group. So they agree to form a coalition aimed at keeping the other members from advancing or from receiving precious resources. Sometimes the coalition breaks down, but in the end they prevail. Along the way they give out disinformation, deny their collusion, and even appear to be friendly to those they scheme against.

Sound like office politics? It well could be, but you probably recognize the four coalition members as the final four castaways in the first *Survivor,* the hit TV show in the summer of 2000. This four-person coalition, calling itself the "Tagi Alliance," turned on fellow members of the Tagi tribe, voting them off the island one by one at tribal councils, and eventually banded against the remaining contestants in the merged tribe the last six weeks of the 12-episode contest. Coalitions like theirs occur in all organizations from schools to corporate board rooms.

The *Survivor* castaways knew that after the 39 days of filming, they would have nothing to do with one another beyond publicity appearances.

But what would sociologists have to say about the *Survivor* coalition? They would be quick to point out that this coalition does not truly represent everyday coalition-building. Coalitions can be temporary, but usually the members have to weigh the long-term social consequences of what they do against others. The *Survivor* castaways knew that after the 39 days of filming, they would have nothing to do with one another beyond publicity appearances. While the stakes were high (US$1 million to the final survivor) and emotions were high, there were virtually no long-term social implications. For example, Susan expressed her strong dislike of Kelly in an emotional speech at the final tribal council, but what did it matter? They were not coworkers or classmates or family members.

The "Tagi Alliance": Kelly, Rudy, Susan, and Richard (left to right).

Many observers have billed this type of show as "reality TV" and use the term to describe such offshoots as *Big Brother* and *Chains of Love.* Sociologists, however, would note there is nothing real about taking 16 middle-class (or better) individuals and placing them on the island of Pulau Tiga to compete for a million dollar windfall. That island is a part of Malaysia, a nation representative of much of the world's people who would welcome just one of the *Survivor* castaways' pre-island paycheques. Malaysians have a per capita annual income that is just a fraction of that of Canadians. Now that is reality!

Let's Discuss

1. Put yourself in the place of one of the TV show's castaways. Would you have joined a coalition? What would have been the advantages and disadvantages of such an action?
2. Did you watch the 2000 *Survivor* show? If so, why do you think the ringleader of the coalition won the contest? Would you have voted for him against Kelly to be the winner? Why or why not?

Source: For GNP data, Haub and Cornelius 2000.

on good terms with each and arrange compromise solutions to problems. Finally, a member of a triad can choose to employ a *divide-and-rule* strategy. This is the case, for example, with a coach who hopes to gain greater control over two assistants by making them rivals (Nixon 1979).

Coalitions

As groups grow to the size of triads or larger, we can expect coalitions to develop. A ***coalition*** is a temporary or permanent alliance geared toward a common goal. Coalitions can be broad-based or narrow, and can take on many different objectives. Sociologist William Julius Wilson (1999b) has described community-based organizations that include whites and visible minorities, working-class and affluent, who have banded together to work for improved sidewalks, better drainage systems, and comprehensive street paving. Out of this type of coalition building, Wilson hopes, will emerge better interracial understanding.

Some coalitions are intentionally short-lived. When Toronto announced its intention to submit a bid for the 2008 Summer Olympics, local community groups expressed their concerns by banding together to create a group called "Bread not Circuses" (BnC). This coalition of over 30 disparate community organizations, including the Toronto Disaster Relief Committee, a group fighting for the homeless, and the St. Lawrence Neighbourhood Association, a group defending the rights of condominium and house owners, combined their resources to oppose the bid. Their efforts may have been a factor when, on July 13, 2001, the Games were awarded to Beijing. The popular TV show *Survivor* demonstrated the power of the coalition, however short-term it might be (see Box 6-1 on the previous page).

The effects of group size and coalition on group dynamics are but two of the many aspects of the small group that sociologists have studied. Another area, conformity and deviance, is examined in Chapter 7. While it is clear that small-group encounters have a considerable influence on our lives, we are also deeply affected by much larger groupings of people, as we'll see in the next section.

Understanding Organizations

Formal Organizations and Bureaucracies

As contemporary societies have shifted to more advanced forms of technology and their social structures have become more complex, our lives have become increasingly dominated by large secondary groups referred to as *formal organizations* and designed for a specific purpose. A ***formal organization*** is a special-purpose group designed and structured for maximum efficiency. The Nova Scotia Symphony, the McDonald's fast-food industry, Canadian Association of Snowboard Instructors, and the school you attend are all examples of formal organizations. Organizations vary in their size, specificity of goals, and degree of efficiency, but they all are structured in such a way as to facilitate the management of large-scale operations. They also have a bureaucratic form of organization (described in the next section of the chapter).

In our society, formal organizations fulfill an enormous variety of personal and societal needs and shape the lives of every one of us. In fact, formal organizations have become such a dominant force that we must create organizations to supervise other organizations, such as the Ontario Securities Commission to regulate the brokerage companies. It sounds much more exciting to say that we live in the "computer age" than in the "age of formal organization"; however, the latter is probably a more accurate description of our times (Azumi and Hage 1972; Etzioni 1964).

Ascribed statuses such as gender, race, and ethnicity influence how we see ourselves within formal organizations. For example, a study of women lawyers in the largest law firms in the United States found significant differences in these women's self-images. In firms in which fewer than 15 percent of partners were women, the female lawyers were likely to believe that "feminine" traits were strongly devalued and that masculinity was equated with success. As one female attorney put it, "Let's face it: this is a man's environment, and it's sort of Jock City, especially at my firm." Women in firms where female lawyers were well represented in positions of power (where more than 15 percent of partners were women) had a stronger desire for and higher expectations of promotion (Ely 1995:619). (The impact of race, ethnicity, and gender on people's experiences and career prospects will be examined more fully in Chapters 9 and 10.)

Characteristics of a Bureaucracy

A ***bureaucracy*** is a component of formal organization in which rules and hierarchical ranking are used to achieve efficiency. Rows of desks staffed by seemingly faceless people, endless lines and forms, impossibly complex language, and frustrating encounters with red tape—all these unpleasant images have combined to make *bureaucracy* a dirty word and an easy target in political campaigns. As a result, few people want to identify their occupation as "bureaucrat" despite the fact that all of us perform various bureaucratic tasks. Elements of bureaucracy enter into almost every occupation in a post-industrial society such as Canada.

Complaints about bureaucracy are not limited to developed countries. In 1993, the bureaucratic nature of the United Nations' humanitarian efforts in Somalia came under attack. The five international agencies designated to run relief efforts in Somalia had more than 12 000 employees, of whom only 116 were serving in the impoverished, war-torn African nation. Moreover, like many bureaucracies, the relief apparatus was slow in dealing with a drastic problem. In the words of a former United Nations worker in Somalia, "The average UN person takes 15 days to reply to a fax. . . . 3000 people can die in 15 days" (Longworth 1993:9).

Max Weber (1947, original edition 1922), first directed researchers to the significance of bureaucratic structure. In an important sociological advance, Weber emphasized the basic similarity of structure and process found in the otherwise dissimilar enterprises of religion, government, education, and business. Weber saw bureaucracy as a form of organization quite different from the family-run business. For analytical purposes, he developed an *ideal type* of bureaucracy that would reflect the most characteristic aspects of all human organizations. By *ideal type* Weber meant a construct or model that could serve as a point of reference against which specific cases could be evaluated. In actu-

p. 10

ality, perfect bureaucracies do not exist; no real-world organization corresponds exactly to Weber's ideal type.

Weber proposed that whether the purpose is to run a church, a corporation, or an army, the ideal bureaucracy displays five basic characteristics. A discussion of those characteristics, as well as the *dysfunctions* (or potential negative consequences) of a bureaucracy, follows. (Table 6-2 summarizes the discussion.)

p. 13

1. Division of Labour. Specialized experts are employed in each position to perform specific tasks. In a university's bureaucracy, the admissions officer does not do the job of registrar; the educational advisors don't see to the maintenance of buildings. Yet, the performance of each of these individual workers is dependent in some greater or lesser way on the performance of the others. By working at a specific task, people are more likely to become highly skilled and carry out a job with maximum efficiency. This emphasis on specialization is so basic a part of our lives that we may not realize that it is a fairly recent development in Western culture. The fragmentation of tasks at a McDonald's franchise is a perfect example of this specialization.

Unfortunately, the fragmentation of work into smaller and smaller tasks can divide workers and remove any connection they might feel to the overall objective of the bureaucracy. In *The Communist Manifesto* (written in 1848), Karl Marx and Friedrich Engels charged that the capitalist system reduces workers to a mere "appendage of the machine" (Feuer 1959). Such a work arrangement, they wrote, produces extreme ***alienation***—a condition of estrangement or dissociation from the surrounding

Table 6-2 Characteristics of a Bureaucracy

		Negative Consequence	
Characteristic	**Positive Consequence**	**For the Individual**	**For the Organization**
Division of labour	Produces efficiency in large-scale corporation	Produces trained incapacity	Produces a narrow perspective
Hierarchy of authority	Clarifies who is in command	Deprives employees of a voice in decision making	Permits concealment of mistakes
Written rules and regulations	Let workers know what is expected of them	Stifle initiative and imagination	Lead to goal displacement
Impersonality	Reduces bias	Contributes to feelings of alienation	Discourages loyalty to company
Employment based on technical qualifications	Discourages favouritism and reduces petty rivalries	Discourages ambition to improve oneself elsewhere	Allows Peter Principle to operate

society. For example, at McDonald's, the people who make the french fries cannot take credit for someone's dining experience because they contributed but a small part of the overall meal. (Alienation will be discussed in greater detail in Chapter 13.) According to both Marx and conflict theorists, restricting workers to very small tasks also weakens their job security, since new employees can be easily trained to replace them.

Although division of labour has certainly enhanced the performance of many complex bureaucracies, in some cases it can lead to ***trained incapacity;*** that is, workers become so specialized that they develop blind spots and fail to notice obvious problems. Even worse, they may not *care* about what is happening in the next department. For example, when a baggage conveyor at Pearson International Airport in Toronto failed during the 2001 Christmas season, all of the other systems at Air Canada continued to function as usual. The result: several thousand travellers waited for hours to claim their bags. This is evidence that huge bureaucracies have caused workers in Canada and other developed nations to become less productive on the job.

The explosion of the United States space shuttle *Challenger* in 1986, in which seven astronauts died, is one of the most dramatic examples of the negative consequences of a bureaucratic division of labour. While the *Challenger* disaster is remembered primarily as a technical failure, its roots lay in the social organization of the National Aeronautics and Space Administration (NASA), whose officials decided to proceed with the launch despite a potentially serious problem. According to sociologist Diane Vaughan (1996, 1999), the defect that caused the accident was discovered as early as 1977; in 1985 it was labelled a "launch constraint" (reason not to launch). On the day the *Challenger* was scheduled to take off, engineers from a company that manufactured a critical part recommended that NASA cancel the launch, but the 34 people who participated in the final prelaunch teleconference ignored their warning. Ultimately, no one was held responsible for the catastrophe. At its worst, a narrow division of labour can allow everyone to avoid responsibility for a critical decision.

The 1986 *Challenger* disaster was not just a technical failure, but an example of the negative consequences of the bureaucratic division of labour.

2. Hierarchy of Authority. Bureaucracies follow the principle of hierarchy; that is, each position is under the supervision of a higher authority. A president heads a university bureaucracy; he or she selects members of the administration, who in turn hire their own staff. In Parliament, it is the prime minister who has the authority to name cabinet ministers, and to hire senior bureaucrats in the federal system. In the Roman Catholic church, the pope is the supreme authority; under him are cardinals, bishops, and so forth. In some social hierarchies, the ultimate authority may be obscure. In the Canadian confederation, for example, the prime minister is seen as holding the highest-ranking position in the country (within a democracy, however, it is the voters who have the final word). Even at McDonald's, there is a shift supervisor, crew chief, trainers, and managers, all of whom have authority that is defined within the company's employee handbook.

3. Written Rules and Regulations. What if the financial awards officer gave you a scholarship for having such a friendly smile? It would certainly be a pleasant surprise, but it would also be "against the rules."

Rules and regulations, as our frustrating interactions with phone companies and financial services have demonstrated, are an important characteristic of bureaucracies. Ideally, through such procedures, a bureaucracy ensures uniform performance of every task. This prohibits you from receiving a scholarship for a nice smile, but it also guarantees that no one else will, either.

On the other hand, the written rules and regulations of bureaucracies generally offer employees clear standards as to what is considered an adequate (or exceptional) performance. In addition, procedures provide a valuable sense of continuity in a bureaucracy. Individual workers will come and go, but the structure and past records give the organization a life of its own that outlives the services of any one bureaucrat.

Of course, rules and regulations can overshadow the larger goals of an organization and become dysfunctional. If blindly applied, they will no longer serve as a means to achieving an objective but instead will become important (and perhaps too important) in their own right. This would certainly be the case if a hospital emergency room physician failed to treat a seriously injured person because he or she had no valid proof that she or he was a member of a provincial medical plan. Robert

Merton (1968) has used the term ***goal displacement*** to refer to overzealous conformity to official regulations.

4. Impersonality. Max Weber wrote that in a bureaucracy, work is carried out *sine ira et studio,* "without hatred or passion." Bureaucratic norms dictate that officials perform their duties without the personal consideration of people as individuals. This is intended to guarantee equal treatment for each person; however, it also contributes to the often cold and uncaring feeling associated with modern organizations. We typically think of big government and big business when we think of impersonal bureaucracies. But today even small companies have telephone systems greeting callers with an electronic menu. While McDonald's may try to achieve a sense of in-group amongst a shift team, dealing with customers is proscribed so that there is little or no room for personal initiative.

5. Employment Based on Technical Qualifications. Within a bureaucracy, hiring is based on technical qualifications rather than on favouritism, and performance is measured against specific standards. At a McDonald's franchise, written personnel policies dictate who gets promoted. However, in all provinces with a labour-standards branch of government, people often have a right to appeal if they believe that particular rules have been violated. Such procedures protect bureaucrats against arbitrary dismissal, provide a measure of security, and encourage loyalty to the organization.

In this sense, the "impersonal" bureaucracy can be an improvement over nonbureaucratic organizations. University faculty members, for example, are ideally hired and promoted according to their professional qualifications, including degrees earned and research published, and not because of favours they do the dean. Once they are granted tenure, their jobs are protected against the whims of individuals in positions of authority.

Although any bureaucracy ideally will value technical and professional competence, personnel decisions do not always follow this ideal pattern. Dysfunctions within bureaucracy have become well publicized, particularly because of the work of Laurence J. Peter. According to the ***Peter Principle,*** every employee within a hierarchy tends to rise to his or her level of incompetence (Peter and Hull 1969). The Principle states that workers are promoted every time they do their job well, and it is only after they move into a position in which they are incompetent that they will stop advancing up the hierarchy. This hypothesis, which has not been directly or systematically tested, reflects a possible dysfunctional outcome of structuring advancement on the basis of merit. Talented people receive promotion after promotion until, sadly, they finally achieve positions that they cannot handle with their usual competence (Blau and Meyer 1987).

The five characteristics of bureaucracy, developed by Max Weber more than 75 years ago, describe an ideal type rather than offer a precise definition of an actual bureaucracy. Not every formal organization will possess all of Weber's characteristics. In fact, there can be wide variation among actual bureaucratic organizations. In Box 6-2, we consider how some bureaucracies actually function in different cultural settings, including Weber's native country of Germany.

These members of the Toronto Symphony Orchestra must be technically proficient and professionally trained, or they will never make beautiful music together. Technical qualification is one of the characteristics of a well-structured bureaucracy.

Bureaucratization as a Process

Sociologists have used the term ***bureaucratization*** to refer to the process by which a group, organization, or social movement becomes increasingly bureaucratic. Normally, we think of bureaucratization in terms of large organizations. In a typical citizen's nightmare, one may have to speak to 10 or 12 individuals in a corporation or government agency to find out which official has jurisdiction over a particular problem. Callers can get transferred from one department to another until they

Sociology in the Global Community

6-2 The Varying Cultures of Formal Organizations

The Canadian negotiator in a business deal with a German company is running late for an appointment in Berlin. He rushes into his German counterpart's office, drops his briefcase on the woman's desk while apologizing, "I'm terribly sorry for keeping you waiting, Elsa," and proceeds to regale Elsa with an amusing story about his taxi ride to the office. Unwittingly, he has violated four rules of polite behaviour in German organizations: punctuality, personal space, privacy, and proper greetings. In German formal organizations, meetings take place on time, business is not mixed with pleasure or joking, greetings are formal, and the casual use of first names is frowned on.

Now picture a formal business meeting that takes place in a corporation in France. A Japanese negotiating team enters the conference room, but is dismayed to find a round table. The Japanese do not use round tables in business settings. They prefer to sit facing the opposite side and have a prescribed seating order, with the power position in the middle, flanked by interpreters, key advisers, note takers, and finally the most junior personnel at the ends. The French negotiators get down to business and make direct offers, for which they expect quick answers from the Japanese team. But the protocol in Japanese organizations is to nurture business relationships first and conduct indirect negotiations until the real decision making can take place later in private.

What these examples show is that national cultures influence formal organizations. They reflect the ways we all have been socialized. Geert Hofstede, an international management scholar based in the Netherlands, calls these ingrained patterns of thinking, feeling, and acting *mental programs* (or "software of the mind"). If business is to be successful, the participants have to have some understanding of the customs, values, and procedures of other cultures. In the examples above, this holds true equally for the Germans *and* the Canadians, for the French *and* the Japanese.

The Japanese do not use round tables in business settings.

Hofstede explored some of the cross-cultural differences in formal organizations by means of a study of IBM employees in 50 different countries. Since the respondents to his survey were matched in almost every respect *except for nationality,* he felt the national differences in their answers would show up clearly. He found four dimensions in which the countries differed:

1. *Power distance.* This refers to the degree to which a culture thinks it is appropriate to distribute power unequally and to accept the decisions of power holders. At one extreme on this dimension are the Arab countries, Guatemala, Malaysia, and the Philippines, each of which tolerates hierarchy and inequality and believes the actions of authorities should not be challenged. At the opposite end of this scale are Austria, Denmark, Israel, and New Zealand. The North American business model—both in Canada and the

Sources: Frazee 1997; Hofstede 1997; Lustig and Koester 1999.

finally hang up in disgust. One of the ironies of this situation is that the inefficiency of this process may serve the goals of the organization by discouraging some callers, such as those wishing to lodge complaints, who might otherwise put a strain on resources.

Bureaucratization also takes place within small-group settings. American sociologist Jennifer Bickman Mendez (1998) studied domestic houseworkers employed in central California by a nationwide franchise. She found that housekeeping tasks were minutely defined, to the point that employees had to follow 22 written steps for cleaning a bathroom. Complaints and special requests went not to the workers, but to an office-based manager. The impersonality and efficiency of this bureaucratic system is yet another example of the McDonaldization of the workplace.

Oligarchy: Rule by a Few

Conflict theorists have examined the bureaucratizing influence on social movements. German sociologist Robert Michels (1915) studied socialist parties and labour unions in Europe before World War I, and found that such organizations were becoming increasingly bureaucratic. The emerging leaders of these organizations—even some of the most radical—had a vested interest in clinging to power. If they lost their leadership posts, they would have to return to full-time work as manual labourers.

United States—leans toward the hierarchical model.

2. *Uncertainty avoidance.* Cultures differ in how much they can tolerate uncertainty and adapt to change. Those that feel threatened by uncertainty will establish more structure; examples include Greece, Portugal, and Uruguay. At the other extreme are countries that minimize rules and rituals, accept dissent, and take risks in trying new things: Denmark, Ireland, Jamaica, and Singapore can be found among these nations. Canadian society is one that encourages open debate and critical thinking of both ideas and systems.
3. *Individualism/collectivism.* This dimension refers to how cultures vary in encouraging people to be unique and independent versus conforming and interdependent. In other words, what is the balance between allegiance to the self or to the group? Canadian culture, in part because of its commitment to multiculturalism, tends to be neutral in its expectations between these two styles. Other cultures, however, have more directive guidelines. Guatemala, Indonesia, Pakistan, and West Africa all take a collectivist orientation: absolute loyalty to the group and an emphasis on belonging. On the other hand, Australia, Belgium, the Netherlands, and the United States are highly individualistic societies, valuing the autonomy of the individual.
4. *Masculinity/femininity.* To what extent do cultures prefer achievement, assertiveness, and acquisition of wealth (masculinity) to nurturance, social support, and quality of life (femininity)? Countries high in the masculinity index include Austria, Italy, Japan, and Mexico. High-scoring feminine cultures include Chile, Portugal, Sweden, and Thailand. While Canada tends to follow the American consumer-based model, there is a greater emphasis on non-material quality of life factors here.

Hofstede's data come with some baggage attached. His respondents were for the most part males working in one large multinational corporation. Their point of view may be unique to their gender and level of education. Moreover, he collected his data in 1974; since then economic and political changes are sure to have affected cultural patterns. Still, his work is valuable for showing the cultural differences within the range of his respondents and for alerting all of us, and especially those in the business community, of the need to understand the cultural settings of formal organizations.

Let's Discuss

1. Which of the four business negotiating styles (Canadian, German, Japanese, French) would you feel most comfortable with in a business setting? Do your classmates' answers differ based on their nationality or cultural background?
2. Analyze your campus culture. How much power distance is there between students, professors, and administrators? How much individualism is tolerated on your campus? How much pressure is there to conform?

Through his research, Michels originated the idea of the ***iron law of oligarchy,*** which describes how even a democratic organization will develop into a bureaucracy ruled by a few (the oligarchy). Almost everyone who has ever had to do group work as part of a class project has, at one time or another, watched as a few individuals took over the group and ran it as their own. Why do these oligarchies emerge? People who achieve leadership roles usually have the skills, knowledge, or charismatic appeal (as Weber noted) to direct, if not control, others. Michels argues that the rank and file of a movement or organization look to leaders for direction and thereby reinforce the process of rule by a few. In addition, members of an oligarchy are strongly motivated to maintain their leadership roles, privileges, and power.

Michels's insights continue to be relevant today. Contemporary labour unions in Canada and elsewhere bear little resemblance to those organized after spontaneous activity by exploited workers. Conflict theorists have pointed to the longevity of union leaders, who are not always responsive to the needs and demands of membership and seem more concerned with maintaining their own positions and power. Feminist theorists have pointed to the bureaucratization process as a tool used by a patriarchal society to sustain male dominance.

At least one study, however, raises questions about Michels's views. Based on her research on "pro-choice" organizations, which endorse the right to legal abortions, sociologist Suzanne Staggenborg (1988) disputes the assertion that formal organizations with professional leaders inevitably become conservative and oligarchical. Indeed, she notes that many formal organizations in the pro-choice movement appear to be more democratic than informal groups; the routinized procedures that they follow make it more difficult for leaders to grab excessive power (see also E. Scott 1993).

While the "iron law" may sometimes help us to understand the concentration of formal authority within organizations, sociologists recognize that there are a number of checks on leadership. Groups often compete for power within a formal organization. For example, in an automotive corporation, divisions manufacturing heavy machinery and passenger cars compete against each other for limited research and development funds. Moreover, informal channels of communication and control can undercut the power of top officials of an organization.

Bureaucracy and Organizational Culture

How does bureaucratization affect the average individual who works in an organization? The early theorists of formal organizations tended to neglect this question. Max Weber, for example, focused on management personnel within bureaucracies, but he had little to say about workers in industry or clerks in government agencies.

According to the ***classical theory*** of formal organizations, also known as the ***scientific management approach,*** workers are motivated almost entirely by economic rewards. This theory stresses that productivity is limited only by the physical constraints of workers. Therefore, workers are treated as a resource, much like the machines that began to replace them in the 20th century. Management attempts to achieve maximum work efficiency through scientific planning, established performance standards, and careful supervision of workers and production. Planning under the scientific management approach involves efficiency studies but not studies of workers' attitudes or feelings of job satisfaction. Minimum-wage policies adopted by franchises like McDonald's appear to reject the idea that workers are motivated only by wages as opposed to job satisfaction. However, their adoption of scientific management processes serves to ensure that the system will provide a predictable outcome regardless of employee motivation.

It was not until workers certified union membership (a process that had failed at several other McDonald's franchises in Canada)—and forced management to recognize that they were not objects—that theorists of formal organizations began to revise the classical approach. Along with management and administrators, social scientists became aware that informal groups of workers have an important impact on organizations (Perrow 1986). An alternative way of considering bureaucratic dynamics, the ***human relations approach,*** emphasizes the role of people, communication, and participation within a bureaucracy. This type of analysis reflects the interest of interactionist theorists in small-group behaviour. Unlike planning under the scientific management approach, planning based on the human relations perspective focuses on workers' feelings, frustrations, and emotional need for job satisfaction. In Box 6-2, we saw how understanding human relations in the corporate structure can enhance doing business abroad. McDonald's, to its credit, does provide opportunities for employee feedback via suggestion boxes and meetings.

The gradual move away from a sole focus on physical aspects of getting the job done—and toward the concerns and needs of workers—led advocates of the human relations approach to stress the less formal aspects of bureaucratic structure. Informal structures and social networks within organizations develop partly as a result of people's ability to create more direct forms of communication than under the formal structure. Charles Page (1946) has used the term *bureaucracy's other face* to refer to the unofficial activities and interactions that are such a basic part of daily organizational life.

A series of classic studies illustrates the value of the human relations approach. The Hawthorne studies alerted sociologists to the fact that research subjects may alter their behaviour to match the experimenter's expectations. p. 37 The major focus of the Hawthorne studies, however, was the role of social factors in workers' productivity. One aspect of the research investigated the switchboard-bank wiring room, where 14 men were making parts of switches for telephone equipment. The researchers discovered that these men were producing far below their physical capabilities. This was especially surprising because they would earn more money if they produced more parts.

Why was there such an unexpected restriction of output? The men feared that if they produced switch parts at a faster rate, their pay rate might be reduced or some might lose their jobs. As a result, this group of workers established their own (unofficial) norm for a proper day's work. They created informal rules and sanctions to enforce it. Yet management was unaware of such practices and actually believed that the men were working as hard as they could (Roethlisberger and Dickson 1939; for a different perspective, see S. Vallas 1999).

Recent research has underscored the impact of informal structures within organizations. Sociologist James Tucker (1993) studied everyday forms of resistance by temporary employees working in short-term positions. Tucker points out that informal social networks can offer advice to a temporary employee on how to pursue a grievance. For example, a female receptionist working for an automobile dealer was being sexually harassed both physically and verbally by a male supervisor. Other female employees, who were aware of the supervisor's behaviour, suggested that she complain to the manager of the dealership. Although the manager said there was little that he could do, he apparently spoke with the supervisor and the harassment stopped. We will examine sexual harassment within organizations in the social policy section.

Technology's Impact on the Workplace

In 1968, Stanley Kubrick's motion picture *2001: A Space Odyssey* dazzled audiences with its futuristic depiction of travel to Jupiter. With 2001 behind us, it is clear that we have not lived up to this target of outer space exploration. However, what about the portrayal of computers? In *2001* a mellow-voiced computer named HAL is very efficient and helpful to the crew, only to try to take over the entire operation and destroy the crew in the process. While computers may now successfully compete against chess champions, they are as far short of achieving the artificial intelligence of HAL as earthlings are of accomplishing manned travel to Jupiter.

Still, the computer today is a commanding presence in our lives, and in the workplace in particular. It is not just that the computer makes tedious, routine tasks easier, such as checking spelling in a term paper. It has affected the workplace in far more dramatic ways (Liker et al. 1999).

Automation

Jeremy Rifkin (1996)—the president of the Foundation on Economic Trends—noted that computer-generated automation has completely transformed the nature of manufacturing. Every year, the proportion of the Canadian workforce engaged in physical tasks, such as those found in manufacturing, shrinks. By 2020, less than 2 percent of the global workforce will be performing factory work. Moreover, automation is reshaping the service sector of the economy in a similar way, leading to substantial reductions in employees ("downsizing") and the increasing use of temporary or contingent workers (see Chapter 13).

Telecommuting

Increasingly, the workforce is turning into *telecommuters* in many industrial countries. ***Telecommuters*** are employees of business firms or government agencies who work full-time or part-time at home rather than in an outside office and who are linked to their supervisors and colleagues through computer terminals, phones, and fax machines (see Chapter 13). A 2001 study by Ottawa-based Ekos Research found that the idea of working from home was either "Appealing" or "Very Appealing" to 52 percent of the Canadian population (Ekos Research 2001). According to Statistics Canada, 15 percent of working Canadians now telecommute at least part of the time (Galt, 2003).

What are the social implications of this shift toward the virtual office? From an interactionist perspective, the workplace is a major source of friendships; restricting face-to-face social opportunities could destroy the trust that is created by face-to-face "handshake agreements." Thus, telecommuting may move society further along the continuum from *Gemeinschaft* to *Gesellschaft.* On a more positive note, telecommuting may be the first social change that pulls fathers and mothers back into the home rather than pushing them out. The trend, if it continues, should also increase autonomy and job satisfaction for many employees (Nie 1999).

Telecommuters are linked to their supervisors and colleagues through computer terminals, phones, and fax machines.

Electronic Communication

Electronic communication in the workplace has generated some heat lately. On the one hand, e-mailing is a convenient way to push messages around, especially with the CC (carbon copy) button. It's democratic too—lower-status employees are more likely to participate in e-mail discussion than in face-to-face communications, which gives organizations the benefit of the experiences and views of more of their workforce. But e-mailing is almost too easy to use. According to

Statistics Canada, 96.6 percent of public organizations and 52.2 percent of private businesses in Canada use e-mail (Statistics Canada 1999g). Students can get a sense of the massive volume of correspondence that moves through this medium by looking at their own inboxes. Not only are there messages from friends and business contacts, there is a steady flow of unsolicited material. At Computer Associates, a software company, managers were receiving 300 e-mails a day each and people were e-mailing colleagues in the next cubicle. To deal with the electronic chaos, the company's CEO took the unusual step of banning all e-mails from 9:30 to 12 and 1:30 to 4. Other companies have limited the number of CCs that can be sent and banned systemwide messages (Gwynne and Dickerson 1997; Sproull and Kiesler 1991). Some post-secondary institutions in Canada have faced similar problems, and have responded by banning system-wide messages.

There are other problems with e-mail. It doesn't convey body language, which in face-to-face communication can soften insensitive phrasing and make unpleasant messages (such as a reprimand) easier to take. It also leaves a permanent record, and that can be a problem if messages are written thoughtlessly. Finally, as will be discussed in detail in Chapter 16, companies can monitor e-mail as a means of "watching" their employees. Dartmouth College professor Paul Argenti advises those who use e-mail, "Think before you write. The most important thing to know is what not to write" (Gwynne and Dickerson 1997:90).

SOCIAL POLICY AND ORGANIZATIONS

Sexual Harassment

The Issue

In 1999, Canadian space researcher Judith Lapierre took part in a Russian simulation that involved living in a replica of a Mir space station for 110 days. The 32-year-old former nurse shared the cramped quarters with three men, an Austrian, a Japanese, and a Russian, as well as another four-man Russian crew. When she emerged from the isolation study, Lapierre accused one of the Russians of sexual harassment. According to Lapierre, the colleague had attempted to forcibly kiss her on New Year's Day. The cosmonaut's behaviour was condemned by the Russian space agency, and he subsequently apologized.

In 1994, 29 female employees from the Mitsubishi Corporation's auto plant at Normal, Illinois, filed a private lawsuit, accusing the company of fostering a climate of sexual harassment. Three years later, the company settled the lawsuit with 27 of the women for US$9.5 million, and then with 350 other women for another US$34 million.

The Canadian Labour Code was amended in 1984 to include *sexual harassment*. In that legislation, the federal government set labour standards that made employers responsible for responding to complaints about sexual harassment. Then, in 1987, the Supreme Court of Canada ruled on a case involving a federal employee and the Treasury Board, which expanded that responsibility. The Court held that employers should also be expected to establish and maintain a workplace that is free from sexual harassment.

In the Canada Labour Code, ***sexual harassment*** is defined as:

> Any conduct, comment, gesture or contact of a sexual nature (a) that is likely to cause offense or humiliation to any employee; or (b) that might, on reasonable grounds, be perceived by that employee as placing a condition of a sexual nature on employment or on any opportunity for training or promotion (Section 247.1).

The Setting

Sexual harassment is not new, but it has received increased attention in many parts of the world as growing numbers of women enter the paid labour force and growing numbers of people in positions of influence pay attention to victims' stories. Feminist analysis has gone a long way toward raising consciousness of the potential for victimization in a paternalistic setting. In a recent 10-year period, the proportion of women participating in the labour force has grown by at least 12 percent in Ireland, the Netherlands, South Korea, the United States, and Canada. In 2000, almost half of Canada's working population (47 percent) was female. However, a comparison of male and female labour-force participation rates shows that 90.1 percent of men aged 25 to 44 worked in 2000, compared to only 80 percent of the female population in the same age range.

Women of all ages and racial and ethnic groups—and men as well—have been the victims of sexual

Sexual harassment can be as subtle as an unwanted hand on the shoulder. Repeated actions of this kind can lead to a "hostile environment."

harassment. Such harassment may occur as a single encounter or as a repeated pattern of behaviour. Surveys typically show that 20 to 50 percent of women feel victimized by sexual harassment. Even higher proportions can be found if nonverbal forms of harassment, such as the posting of pornography in the workplace, are included (S. Welsh 1999:170-171).

Sociological Insights

In Canada, actions in the workplace are deemed to be sexual harassment when they can reasonably be perceived as such, and result in restricting someone's access to or participation in employment. Whether it occurs in the government, in the corporate world, or in universities, in Canada, sexual harassment generally takes place in organizations in which the hierarchy of authority finds white males at the top and women's work is valued less than men's. One survey in the private sector in the United States found that black women were three times more likely than white women to experience sexual harassment. From a conflict perspective, it is not surprising that women—and especially women of colour—are most likely to become victims of sexual harassment. These groups are typically an organization's most vulnerable employees in terms of job security (J. Jones 1988).

Many bureaucracies have traditionally given little attention to the pervasive sexual harassment in their midst; the emotional costs of this discrimination suffered largely by female employees have not been a major concern. However, more regulations prohibiting sexual harassment have been issued as managers and executives confront the costs of sexual harassment *for the organization.* Given Mitsubishi's experience (noted at the beginning of the section), many formal organizations are developing zero tolerance for sexual harassment. Nine out of 10 companies now have rules and regulations dealing with the issue. However, many of these are weak and constitute only a single paragraph in the company handbook (Cloud 1998).

Policy Initiatives

As indicated earlier, sexual harassment has been defined by the Canadian Labour Code. Beyond requiring employers to be vigilant in dealing with incidents of sexual harassment, the Code also makes it mandatory for organizations, whether they be corporate or not-for-profit, to be proactive in creating and distributing a formal statement of policy that outlines their guidelines for defining and responding to sexual harassment. Although we have been focusing on sexual harassment in the workplace, there are similar issues on university and college campuses. See Table 6-3, a quiz designed to raise students' awareness of sexual harassment.

The policy for dealing with sexual harassment in Canada is still evolving as courts at all levels hear cases and reach conclusions that are not necessarily consistent. The confusion will continue, but the old patriarchal system in which male bosses behaved as they pleased with female subordinates is ending. Organizations are developing their own formal regulations in anticipation of the problems they may face, in an effort to create a climate that is nonhostile for all workers. And most large formal organizations have initiated sensitivity and diversity training, to facilitate employees' awareness of situations that might lead to complaints of harassment or intolerance. To be effective, such training must be ongoing and an integral part of an organization's behavioural norms. Occasional antibigotry lectures and one-shot sessions on the theme of "Let's avoid harassment" are unlikely to accomplish the desired results (Fernandez 1999).

Table 6-3 When Does a Joke or Flirtation Become Sexual Harassment?

True or False?	Answers
1. Anyone who is offended by a dirty joke has a poor sense of humour.	1. False. Some jokes offend because the point of the joke is to make someone feel worthless or humiliated. If someone feels less valuable than others when they hear a joke, then it's no joking matter.
2. It's okay to tell somebody you think they look really nice.	2. True. Compliments about a person such as "You look really cool" are usually appreciated. Sexual comments about the body are less likely to be received as compliments.
3. Staring at somebody's body shows that you really like them.	3. False. Although eye contact usually happens without making anyone uncomfortable, it can cross the line. A quick glance or a smile is usually considered flirting; constant staring at your body's sexual places is not.
4. It's not a big deal for students and teachers to flirt with one another.	4. False. Flirting happens between peers—it is not appropriate between people in authority and somebody over whom they have control.
5. Patting somebody on the bottom is a way of flirting with them.	5. False. Flirting is not patting, grabbing, pinching or groping.
6. If nobody complains when you wear a T-shirt with a sexual message, it means you haven't offended anybody.	6. False. Just because nobody complains doesn't mean it's okay. There are lots of reasons why people don't tell about sexual harassment. They may not want to attract attention or be called a "prude" or a "rat."
7. It shouldn't bother you to be teased about your body and appearance.	7. False. Although teasing and good-natured joking are part of life, constant teasing is hurtful. Boys, girls, women, and men are all affected by harassment.
8. A teacher who continually makes students uneasy should be told to stop.	8. True. If students worry that a teacher will purposefully say things that embarrass them, it is not just a form of teasing. What the teacher is doing should be reported to parents or school authorities and the teacher should be told to stop.

Source: Public Legal and Education Service of New Brunswick 2001.

The battle against sexual harassment is being fought not only in Canada but around the world. In 1991, the European Economic Community established a code of conduct that holds employers ultimately responsible for combatting sexual harassment. In 1992, France joined many European countries in banning such behaviour. That same year, in an important victory for Japan's feminist movement, a district court ruled that a small publishing company and one of its male employees had violated the rights of a female employee because of crude remarks that led her to quit her job. The complainant had charged that her male supervisor had spread rumours about her, telling others that she was promiscuous. When she attempted to get him to stop making such comments, she was advised to quit her job. In the view of the complainant's lawyer, "Sexual harassment is a big problem in Japan, and we hope this will send a signal to men that they have to be more careful" (Kanagae 1993; Perlez 1996; Pollack 1996; Weisman 1992:A3).

Let's Discuss

1. Have you ever been sexually harassed, either at work or at school? If so, did you complain about it? What was the outcome?
2. In the instances of sexual harassment you are personally familiar with, was there a difference in power between the victim and the person being harassed? If so, was the difference in power based on gender, age, status, or race?
3. Use the quiz in Table 6-3 to explore the attitudes of your classmates. What did you find? Based on these findings, do you think there is a need for a sexual harassment awareness program at your school?

Chapter Resources

Summary

Social interaction among human beings is necessary to the transmission of culture and the survival of every society. This chapter examines the social behaviour of groups and formal organizations.

1. When we find ourselves identifying closely with a group, it is probably a ***primary group.*** A ***secondary group*** is more formal and impersonal.
2. People tend to see the world in terms of ***in-groups*** and ***out-groups,*** a perception often fostered by the very groups to which they belong.
3. ***Reference groups*** set and enforce standards of conduct and perform a comparison function for people's evaluations of themselves and others.
4. Interactionist researchers have revealed that there are distinct and predictable processes at work in the functioning of ***small groups.*** The simplest group is a ***dyad,*** composed of two members. ***Triads*** and larger groups increase ways of interacting and allow for ***coalitions*** to form.
5. As societies have become more complex, large ***formal organizations*** have become more powerful and pervasive.
6. Max Weber argued that, in its ideal form, every ***bureaucracy*** will share these five basic characteristics: division of labour, hierarchical authority, written rules and regulations, impersonality, and employment based on technical qualifications.
7. Bureaucracy can be understood as a process and as a matter of degree; thus, an organization is more or less bureaucratic than other organizations.
8. When leaders of an organization build up their power, it can lead to oligarchy (rule by a few).
9. The informal structure of an organization can undermine and redefine official bureaucratic policies.
10. Technology has transformed the workplace through automation, telecommuting, and electronic communication.
11. ***Sexual harassment*** has been reported not only in government workplaces and in private-sector organizations but also in schools.

Critical Thinking Questions

1. Think about how behaviour is shaped by reference groups. Drawing on your own experience, what different reference groups at different periods have shaped your outlook and your goals? In what ways have they done so?
2. Within a formal organization, are you likely to find primary groups, secondary groups, in-groups, out-groups, and reference groups? What functions do these groups serve for the formal organization? What dysfunctions might occur as a result of their presence?
3. Max Weber identified five basic characteristics of bureaucracy. Select an actual organization with which you are familiar (for example, your college, a business at which you work, a religious institution or civic association to which you belong) and apply Weber's analysis to that organization. To what degree does it correspond to Weber's ideal type of bureaucracy?

Key Terms

Alienation A condition of estrangement or dissociation from the surrounding society. (page 131)

Bureaucracy A component of formal organization in which rules and hierarchical ranking are used to achieve efficiency. (130)

Bureaucratization The process by which a group, organization, or social movement becomes increasingly bureaucratic. (133)

Classical theory An approach to the study of formal organizations that views workers as being motivated almost entirely by economic rewards. (136)

Coalition A temporary or permanent alliance geared toward a common goal. (129)

Dyad A two-member group. (128)

Formal organization A special-purpose group designed and structured for maximum efficiency. (130)

Goal displacement Overzealous conformity to official regulations within a bureaucracy. (133)

Human relations approach An approach to the study of formal organizations that emphasizes the role of people, communication, and participation within a bureaucracy and tends to focus on the informal structure of the organization. (136)

In-group Any group or category to which people feel they belong. (126)

Iron law of oligarchy A principle of organizational life under which even democratic organizations will become bureaucracies ruled by a few individuals. (135)

McDonaldization The process by which the principles of the fast-food restaurant have come to dominate certain sectors of society, both in Canada and throughout the world. (125)

Out-group A group or category to which people feel they do not belong. (126)

Peter Principle A principle of organizational life according to which each individual within a hierarchy tends to rise to his or her level of incompetence. (133)

Primary group A small group characterized by intimate, face-to-face association and cooperation. (125)

Reference group Any group that individuals use as a standard in evaluating themselves and their own behaviour. (127)

Scientific management approach Another name for the *classical theory* of formal organizations. (136)

Secondary group A formal, impersonal group in which there is little social intimacy or mutual understanding. (126)

Sexual harassment Any conduct, comment, gesture or contact of a sexual nature that is likely to cause offense or humiliation to any employee or that might, on reasonable grounds, be perceived by that employee as placing a condition of a sexual nature on employment or on any opportunity for training or promotion. (138)

Small group A group small enough for all members to interact simultaneously, that is, to talk with one another or at least be acquainted. (127)

Telecommuters Employees of business firms or government agencies who work full-time or part-time at home rather than in an outside office and who are linked to their supervisors and colleagues through computer terminals, phone lines, and fax machines. (137)

Trained incapacity The tendency of workers in a bureaucracy to become so specialized that they develop blind spots and fail to notice obvious problems. (132)

Triad A three-member group. (128)

Additional Readings

Alfino, Mark, John S. Caputo, and Robin Wynyard. 1998. *McDonaldization Revisited: Critical Essays on Consumer Culture.* Westport, CT: Praeger. A multidisciplinary look at George Ritzer's approach to Max Weber's theory of rationalization and how it has been applied first to McDonald's restaurants and now to institutions worldwide.

Fagenson, Ellen A. 1993. *Women in Management: Trends, Issues, and Challenges in Managerial Diversity.* Newbury Park, CA: Sage. This anthology focuses on the continued underrepresentation of women in managerial positions within formal organizations.

Nishiguchi, Toshihiro. 1994. *Strategic Industrial Sourcing: The Japanese Advantage.* New York: Oxford University Press. Drawing on eight years of research and more than 1000 interviews, Nishiguchi offers insight into how very large industrial corporations have developed in Japan and have come to dominate that nation's economy.

Vaughan, Diane. 1996. *The Challenger Launch Decision: Risky Technology, Culture, and Deviance at NASA.* Chicago: University of Chicago Press. A detailed look at the work culture of the National Aeronautics and Space Administration (NASA) and its suppliers—and the impact of that work culture on the fatal launch of the United States space shuttle *Challenger* in 1986.

Internet Connection

www.mcgrawhill.ca/college/schaefer

*For additional Internet exercises relating to Max Weber's examination of bureaucracies and technology's impact on the workplace, visit the Schaefer Online Learning Centre at **http://www.mcgrawhill.ca/college/schaefer**. Please note that while the URLs listed were current at the time of printing, these sites often change—check the Online Learning Centre for updates.*

The construction of fair, clear, and workable social policy regarding sexual harassment has become a challenge for modern organizations and institutions. Review your text's discussion of sexual harassment at the end of this chapter. Then, direct your web browser to a search engine such as alltheweb (**http://www.alltheweb.com**) or Lycos (**http://www.lycos.com**). Search for your college or university's homepage and find the sexual harassment policy. If this policy is not online, try the name of another school in your area. After reflecting on your text's discussion and on the website, answer the following:

(a) How does the college or university define sexual harassment? How does it compare to the definition offered in your book?
(b) Who is included in this definition? Do you feel any groups or persons have been left out of the definition who should be included?
(c) What examples are given of sexual harassment?
(d) What are the consequences for those who engage in such behaviour?
(e) If you were to draft the next version of this policy, what changes would you make? Why?

CHAPTER 7 DEVIANCE AND SOCIAL CONTROL

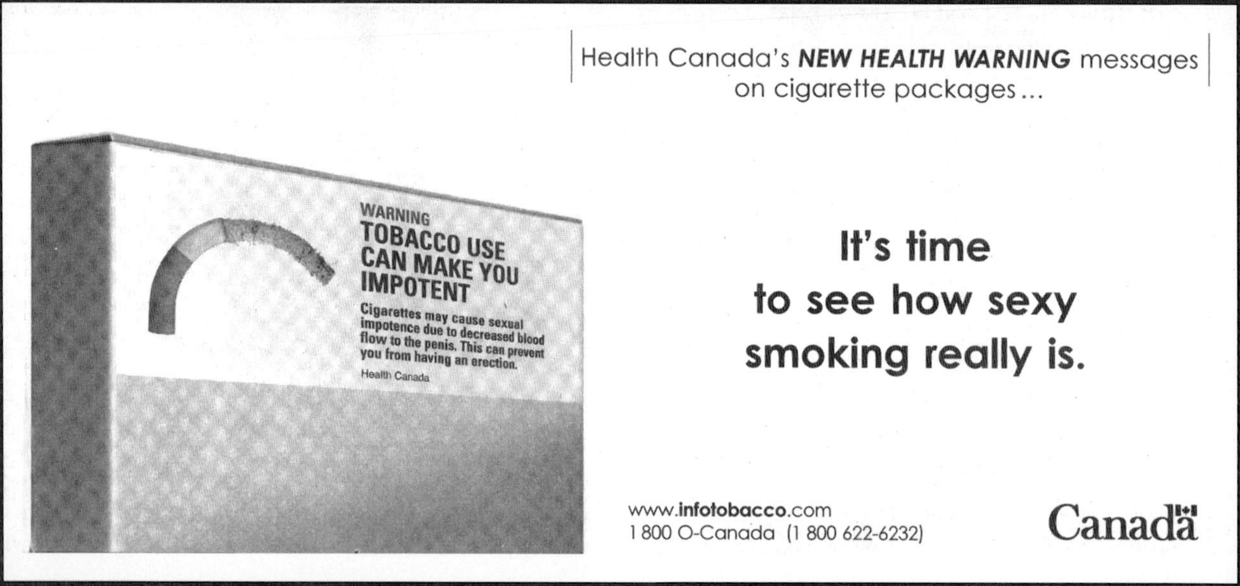

Cigarette smoking has become stigmatized in Canada. This newspaper advertisement, sponsored by Health Canada, reverses the typical advertising strategy of equating smoking with sexiness.

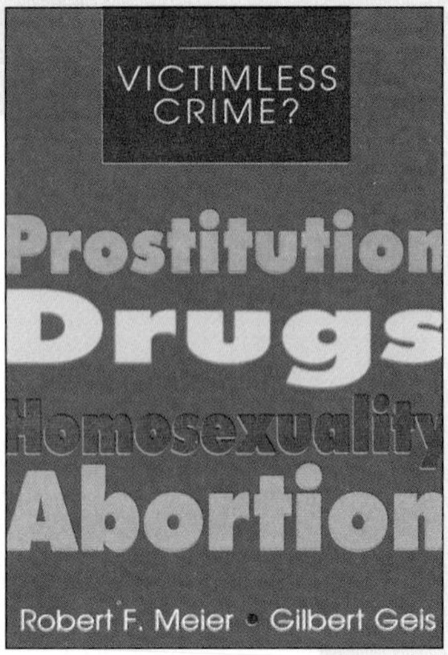

Heidi Fleiss was in her late twenties when she was arrested for operating a call girl service. At the time, her pediatrician father had reacted flippantly, "I guess I didn't do such a good job on Heidi after all." Later, he would be convicted of conspiring to hide profits from his daughter's call girl ring. Fleiss had dropped out of school when she was sixteen and established a liaison with a playboy-financier who gave her a Rolls-Royce for her twenty-first birthday. In her early twenties, Fleiss interned in the world of prostitution by working for Madame Alex (Elizabeth Adams), Hollywood's reigning call girl entrepreneur until her death in 1995. In 1990, backed by television director and pornography filmmaker Ivan Nagy, 24-year-old Fleiss opened her own business. She now refers to her call girl operation as nothing more than a sensible adjunct to many other Hollywood enterprises. One telling anecdote was how she was paid $40,000 a night by a customer to do little more than play Scheherazade, the Sultan's wife in *Arabian Nights*.

On her income tax return, Fleiss reported that her earnings were generated by "personal counseling." SONY officials paid her thousands of dollars for one such counseling session for executives of an overseas branch; SONY's tax report listed the outlay as a "development deal." Government officials estimate that Fleiss earned several hundred thousand dollars during a period in which she reported income of only $33,000 on her tax return.

At Fleiss' trial, business executive Manuel Santos testified that he sent his private jet to pick up some of Fleiss' call girls. One of them alleged that she flew to Paris, Athens, and Las Vegas to have sex with clients, and that she gave 40 percent of what she earned to Fleiss. Fleiss was sentenced to three years in prison and a $1,000 fine after a jury found her guilty of three counts of pandering. She was also convicted in federal court of eight counts of conspiracy, income tax evasion, and laundering money.

In January, 1997, Fleiss received a 37-month prison sentence for the federal crimes. She also was fined $400, ordered to participate in a substance-abuse program and to perform 300 hours of community service.

Earlier, the California District Court of Appeal had thrown out the previous state verdict and ordered a new trial on the grounds that jury members had been confused about their decision: They had opted for guilt on the pandering charge because they believed that it would result in a lesser sentence than a narcotics conviction, not understanding that pandering carried an automatic three-year term of imprisonment. The appellate court decision further determined that jury members had "traded" votes on the different charges in order to avoid a deadlock, an impermissible procedure. . . .

For some, Fleiss' situation aroused passions that have remained persistently prominent in the feminist debate over prostitution. In an op-ed piece, attorneys Gloria Allred and Lisa Bloom asked rhetorically: "Why is it immoral to be paid for an act that is perfectly legal if done for free?" *(Meier and Geis 1997:36–37)* ■

In this excerpt from their book *Victimless Crime? Prostitution, Drugs, Homosexuality, Abortion*, sociologists Robert F. Meier and Gilbert Geis explore the role of law and social control in four areas commonly thought of as "victimless crimes." In the case of prostitution, as exemplified by Heidi Fleiss, some people argue that laws on the books create a social problem rather than solving one. Because there is so much disagreement about whether prostitution is wrong or to what extent it is deviant, the law is limited in its scope and effectiveness.

As these authors point out, what behaviours should be considered deviant is not always obvious. Take the issue of binge drinking on campus. On the one hand, we can view it as *deviant*, violating a school's standards of conduct, but on the other hand it can be seen as *conforming*, complying with a peer culture. In Canada, people are socialized to have mixed feelings about both conforming and nonconforming behaviour. The term *conformity* can conjure up images of mindless imitation of one's peer group—whether a group of teenagers with pierced tongues or a group of business executives dressed in similar gray suits. Yet the same term can also suggest that an individual is cooperative or a "team player." What about those who do not conform? They may be respected as individualists, leaders, or creative thinkers who break new ground. Or they may be labelled as "troublemakers" and "weirdos" (Aronson 1999).

This chapter examines the relationship between conformity, deviance, and social control. It begins by distinguishing between conformity and obedience and then looks at two experiments regarding conforming behaviour and obedience to authority. The informal and formal mechanisms used by societies to encourage conformity and discourage deviance are analyzed. We give particular attention to the legal order and how it reflects underlying social values.

The second part of the chapter focuses on theoretical explanations for deviance, including the functionalist approach employed by Émile Durkheim and Robert Merton; the interactionist-based theories; labelling theory, which draws upon both the interactionist and the conflict perspectives; conflict theory; and feminist theories.

The third part of the chapter focuses on crime, a specific type of deviant behaviour. As a form of deviance subject to official, written norms, crime has been a special concern of policymakers and the public in general. We will take a look at various types of crime found in Canada, the ways crime is measured, and international crime rates. Finally, the social policy section considers the use of illicit drugs in Canada and in the rest of the world. ■

Social Control

As we saw in Chapter 3, each culture, subculture, and group has distinctive norms governing what it deems appropriate behaviour. Laws, dress codes, bylaws of organizations, course requirements, and rules of sports and games all express social norms.

How does a society bring about acceptance of basic norms? The term ***social control*** refers to the techniques and strategies for preventing deviant human behaviour in any society. Social control occurs on all levels of society. In the family, we are socialized to obey our parents simply because they are our parents. Peer groups introduce us to informal norms, such as dress codes, that govern the behaviour of members. Colleges establish standards they expect of their students. In bureaucratic organizations, workers encounter a formal system of rules and regulations. Finally, the government of every society legislates and enforces social norms.

Most of us respect and accept basic social norms and assume that others will do the same. Even without thinking, we obey the instructions of police officers, follow the day-to-day rules at our jobs, and move to the rear of elevators when people enter. Such behaviour reflects an effective process of socialization to the dominant standards of a culture. At the same time, we are well aware that individuals, groups, and institutions *expect* us to act "properly." If we fail to do so, we may face punishment through informal *sanctions* such as fear and ridicule, or formal sanctions such as jail sentences or fines. The challenge to effective social control is that people often receive competing messages about how to behave. While the state or government may clearly define acceptable behaviour, friends or fellow employees may encourage quite different behaviour patterns. Box 7-1 presents the latest research on a behaviour that is officially frowned upon, but nevertheless engaged in by many young people—living in the streets.

p. 59

Functionalists contend that people must respect social norms if any group or society is to survive. In their view, societies literally could not function if massive numbers of people defied standards of appropriate conduct. By contrast, conflict theorists maintain that "successful functioning" of a society will consistently benefit

Research in Action 7-1 Street Kids

Fiona was a fairly typical 16-year-old, living in Barrie, Ontario. She was struggling to complete high school and to learning how to get along with her mother's new common-law partner. Often she and her mother's partner would argue over Fiona's contribution to the running of their household or whether she should be able to stay over night at her boyfriend's apartment. He often would resort to verbal and physical abuse in attempting to make Fiona comply with his wishes. Although Fiona felt her mother loved her, she felt betrayed by her mother's silence when it came to protecting her from the abuse.

Fiona decided she couldn't endure the strain and sense of betrayal at home and convinced her boyfriend, Michael, to leave Ontario. They drove across Canada, ending up at the west coast—in Vancouver. Shortly after Fiona and Michael arrived in Vancouver, Michael's money supply ran out and he decided to return to Ontario. Fiona, also facing a shortage of cash, resorted to panhandling on Robson Street in downtown Vancouver and began "living on the streets."

Fiona's case is reflective of a general pattern of street kids in British Columbia. That is, nearly 61 percent of street kids in Vancouver are from provinces other than British Columbia. A major report released in 2001 by the McCreary Centre Society, entitled "No Place to Call Home," noted that most street youth have experienced sexual or physical abuse and most have either run away or been kicked out of home. Many engage in behaviours that are considered "high risk," such as involvement in the sex trade and addiction to drugs. The study revealed that most street youth in the cities are not literally homeless, but live in shelters or abandoned buildings or "squats."

Although it is common to view the phenomenon of youth living on the street as a big city problem, the study revealed that, while many troubled young people migrate to the larger cities, smaller communities, such as Prince Rupert, also experience the phenomenon.

> **Fiona decided she couldn't endure the strain and sense of betrayal at home and convinced her boyfriend, Michael, to leave Ontario.**

Other major findings of the study revealed:

- Over one quarter of street youth have attempted suicide in the past year.
- Over half of street youth have been in government care, including foster care or group homes.
- Street youth reported that they began risky behaviour young, many when they were thirteen. Some of these risky behaviours include involvement in the sex trade, having unprotected sex, and addiction to alcohol and drugs.
- Street kids had an average age of 16 in the smaller centres, while the average age was 18 for those in Vancouver.
- Over a third planned to attend some form of post-secondary education.

When the researchers asked the over 500 youth, aged 12 to 19, why they were living on the street, the responses included:

- Friends hang out on street (34 percent)
- Don't get along with parents (37 percent)
- Feel accepted there, kicked out of home (38 percent)
- Travelling (35 percent)
- Ran away from home (30 percent)
- Can't find a job (24 percent)
- Addiction problems (22 percent)
- Violence or abuse at home (20 percent)
- Can't find affordable housing (18 percent)
- Conflict at home because of sexual orientation (4 percent)

Let's Discuss

1. What behaviours that society considers deviant are associated with kids living on the street?
2. Evaluate the factors that contribute to children becoming "street kids."

Source: The McCreary Centre Society 2001; Steffenhagen 2001.

the powerful and work to the disadvantage of other groups. They point out, for example, that widespread resistance to social norms was necessary to overturn the institution of slavery in the United States.

Conformity and Obedience

Techniques for social control operate on both the group level and the societal level. People whom we regard as our peers or as our equals influence us to act in particular ways; the same is true of people who hold authority over us or occupy awe-inspiring positions. Stanley Milgram (1975) made a useful distinction between these two important levels of social control.

Milgram defined ***conformity*** as going along with peers—individuals of our own status, who have no special right to direct our behaviour. By contrast, ***obedience*** is defined as compliance with higher authorities in a hierarchical structure. Thus, a recruit entering military service will typically *conform* to the habits and language of other recruits and will obey the orders of superior officers. Students will *conform* to the drinking behaviour of their peers and will *obey* the requests of campus security officers.

Conformity to Prejudice

We often think of conformity in terms of rather harmless situations, such as members of an expensive health club who all work out in elaborate and costly sportswear. But researchers have found that people may conform to the attitudes and behaviour of their peers even when such conformity means expressing intolerance toward others.

Fletcher Blanchard, Teri Lilly, and Leigh Ann Vaughn (1991) conducted an experiment at an American university and found that statements people overhear others make influence their own expressions of opinion on the issue of racism. A student employed by the researchers approached 72 white students as each was walking across the campus to get responses for an opinion poll she said she was conducting for a class. At the same time, a second white student—actually another working with the researchers—was stopped and asked to participate in the survey. Both students were then asked how their university should respond to anonymous racist notes actually sent to four black students in 1989. The student employed by the researchers always answered first. In some cases, she condemned the notes; in others, she justified them.

Blanchard and his colleagues (1991:102–103) conclude that "hearing at least one other person express strongly antiracist opinions produced dramatically more strongly antiracist public reactions to racism than hearing others express equivocal opinions or opinions more accepting of racism." A second experiment demonstrated that when the student working on behalf of the researchers expressed sentiments justifying racism, subjects were much *less* likely to express antiracist opinions than were those who heard no one else offer opinions. In these experiments, social control (through the process of conformity) influenced people's attitudes, or at least the expression of those attitudes. In the next section, we will see that social control (through the process of obedience) can alter people's behaviour.

Obedience to Authority

If ordered to do so, would you comply with an experimenter's instruction to give people increasingly painful electric shocks? Most people would say no; yet, the research of social psychologist Stanley Milgram (1963, 1975) suggests that most of us *will* obey such orders. In Milgram's words (1975:xi), "Behaviour that is unthinkable in an individual . . . acting on his own may be executed without hesitation when carried out under orders."

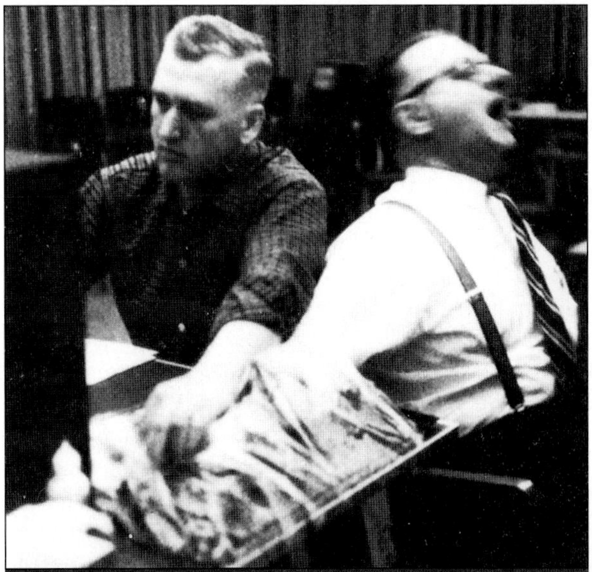

In one of Stanley Milgram's experiments, a supposed "victim" received an electric shock when his hand rested on a shock plate. At the 150-volt level, the "victim" would demand to be released, and would refuse to place his hand on the shock plate. The experimenter would then order the actual subject to force the "victim's" hand onto the plate, as shown in the photo. Though 40 percent of the true subjects stopped complying with Milgram at this point, 30 percent did force the "victim's" hand onto the shock plate, despite his pretended agony.

Milgram placed advertisements in New Haven, Connecticut, newspapers to recruit subjects for what was announced as a learning experiment at Yale University. Participants included postal clerks, engineers, high school teachers, and labourers. They were told that the purpose of the research was to investigate the effects of punishment on learning. The experimenter, dressed in a gray technician's coat, explained that in each testing, one subject would be randomly selected as the "learner" while another would function as the "teacher." However, this lottery was rigged so that the "real" subject would always be the teacher while an associate of Milgram's served as the learner.

At this point, the learner's hand was strapped to an electric apparatus. The teacher was taken to an electronic "shock generator" with 30 lever switches. Each switch was labelled with graduated voltage designations from 15 to 450 volts. Before beginning the experiment, subjects were given sample shocks of 45 volts to convince them of the authenticity of the experiment.

The experimenter instructed the teacher to apply shocks of increasing voltage each time the learner gave an incorrect answer on a memory test. Teachers were told that "although the shocks can be extremely painful, they cause no permanent tissue damage." In reality, the learner did not receive any shocks.

The learner deliberately gave incorrect answers and acted out a prearranged script. For example, at 150 volts, the learner would cry out, "Experimenter, get me out of here! I won't be in the experiment any more!" At 270 volts, the learner would scream in agony. When the shock reached 350 volts, the learner would fall silent. If the teacher wanted to stop the experiment, the experimenter would insist that the teacher continue, using such statements as "The experiment requires that you continue" and "You have no other choice; you *must* go on" (Milgram 1975:19–23).

The results of this unusual experiment stunned and dismayed Milgram and other social scientists. A sample of psychiatrists had predicted that virtually all subjects would refuse to shock innocent victims. In their view, only a "pathological fringe" of less than 2 percent would continue administering shocks up to the maximum level. Yet almost *two thirds* of participants fell into the category of "obedient subjects."

Why did these subjects obey? Why were they willing to inflict seemingly painful shocks on innocent victims who had never done them any harm? There is no evidence that these subjects were unusually sadistic; few seemed to enjoy administering the shocks. Instead, in Milgram's view, the key to obedience was the experimenter's social role as a "scientist" and "seeker of knowledge."

Milgram pointed out that in the modern industrial world, we are accustomed to submitting to impersonal authority figures whose status is indicated by a title (professor, lieutenant, doctor) or by a uniform (the technician's coat). The authority is viewed as larger and more important than the individual; consequently, the obedient individual shifts responsibility for his or her behaviour to the authority figure. Milgram's subjects frequently stated, "If it were up to me, I would not have administered shocks." They saw themselves as merely doing their duty (Milgram 1975).

From an interactionist perspective, one important aspect of Milgram's findings is the fact that subjects in follow-up studies were less likely to inflict the supposed shocks as they were moved physically closer to their victims. Moreover, interactionists emphasize the effect of *incrementally* administering additional dosages of 15 volts. In effect, the experimenter negotiated with the teacher and convinced the teacher to continue inflicting higher levels of punishment. It is doubtful that anywhere near the two-thirds rate of obedience would have been reached had the experimenter told the teachers to administer 450 volts immediately to the learners (B. Allen 1978; Katovich 1987).

Milgram launched his experimental study of obedience to better understand the involvement of Germans in the annihilation of six million Jews and millions of other people during World War II. In an interview conducted long after the publication of his study, he suggested that "if a system of death camps were set up in the United States of the sort we had seen in Nazi Germany, one would be able to find sufficient personnel for those camps in any medium-sized American town" (CBS News 1979:7–8).

Informal and Formal Social Control

The sanctions used to encourage conformity and obedience—and to discourage violation of social norms—are carried out through informal and formal social control. As the term implies, people use ***informal social control*** casually to enforce norms. Examples of informal social control include smiles, laughter, raising an eyebrow, and ridicule.

p. 59

In Canada, the United States, and many other cultures, one common and yet controversial example of informal social control is parental use of corporal punishment. Adults often view spanking, slapping, or kicking children as a proper and necessary means of maintaining authority. Child development specialists counter that corporal punishment is inappropriate because it teaches children to solve problems through violence. They warn that slapping and spanking can escalate into more serious forms of abuse. Yet, despite the fact that pediatric experts now believe that physical forms of discipline are undesirable and encourage their patients to use non-physical means of discipline (Tidmarsh 2000), approximately 70 percent of Canadian parents have used physical punishment (Durrant and Rose-Krasnor 1995). In 1999, the Canadian Foundation for Youth and the Law challenged the constitutionality of section 43 of the Criminal Code of Canada, which allows parents to use reasonable force in disciplining their children.

Sometimes informal methods of social control are not adequate to enforce conforming or obedient behaviour. In those cases, ***formal social control*** is carried out by authorized agents, such as police officers, physicians, school administrators, employers, military officers, and managers of movie theatres. It can serve as a last resort when socialization and informal sanctions do not bring about desired behaviour. In Canada, for every 43 offences that occur, one person is sentenced to a penitentiary or prison. Of those who end up in a penitentiary or prison, a disproportionately high number are First Nations people, who account for between 8 and 10 percent of federal correctional institutions' population, and even a greater percentage of the population in provincial and territorial institutions (Nelson and Fleras 1995).

Societies vary in deciding which behaviours will be subjected to formal social control and how severe the sanctions will be. In the nation of Singapore, chewing of

Sociology in the Global Community

7-2 Singapore: A Nation of Campaigns

"Males with Long Hair Will Be Attended to Last!" "Throwing Litter from Apartments Can Kill!" "No Spitting!" These are some of the posters sponsored by the Singapore government in its effort to enforce social norms in this small nation of some four million people living in a totally urbanized area in southeast Asia.

While Singapore is governed by a democratically elected parliament, one party has dominated the government since its independence in 1965. And it has not hesitated to use its authority to launch a number of campaigns to shape the social behaviour of its citizens. In most cases these campaigns are directed against "disagreeable" behaviour—littering, spitting, chewing gum, failing to flush public toilets, teenage smoking, and the like. Courtesy is a major concern, with elaborate "Courtesy Month" celebrations scheduled to both entertain and educate the populace.

Some campaigns take on serious issues and are backed by legislation. For example, in the 1970s the government asked its citizens to "Please Stop at Two" in family planning; tax and schooling benefits rewarded those who complied. However, this campaign was so successful that in the 1980s the government began a "Have Three or More If You Can Afford to" campaign. In this case it provided school benefits for larger families. In another attempt at social control, the government has launched a "Speak Mandarin" campaign to encourage the multiethnic, multilingual population to accept Mandarin as the dialect of choice.

Courtesy is a major concern, with elaborate "Courtesy Month" celebrations scheduled to both entertain and educate the populace.

For the most part, Singaporeans cheerfully accept their government's admonitions and encouragement. They see the results of being clean and courteous: Singapore is a better place to live. Corporations also go along with the government and even help to sponsor some of the campaigns. As one corporate sponsor noted: "If (people) see Singapore as a clean country, they will view companies here as clean." Political scientist Michael Haas refers to this compliance as "the Singapore puzzle": citizens of Singapore accept strict social control dictates in exchange for continuing prosperity and technological leadership in the world.

Let's Discuss

1. How would you react to an administration-sponsored campaign at your educational institution against drinking? What would be some positive aspects of such a campaign? What would be some negative aspects?
2. Why do you think these social control campaigns work in Singapore? If there was a strong two-party system there, do you think the campaigns would be as prevalent and as effective? Why or why not?

Sources: Dorai 1998; Haas 1999; Haub and Cornelius 2000; Instituto del Tercer Mundo 1999.

gum is prohibited, feeding birds can lead to fines of up to US$640, and there is even a US$95 fine for failing to flush the toilet (see Box 7-2). Singapore deals with serious crimes especially severely. The death penalty is mandatory for murder, drug trafficking, and crimes committed with firearms. Japan has created a special prison for reckless drivers. While some are imprisoned for vehicular homicide, others serve prison time for drunken driving and fleeing the scene of an accident (Elliott 1994).

Another controversial example of formal social control is the use of surveillance techniques. In 1992, police in Great Britain began to install closed-circuit television systems on "high streets" (the primary shopping and business areas of local communities) in an effort to reduce street crime. Within two years, 300 British towns had installed or made plans to install such surveillance cameras, and the use of public surveillance had spread to North America. Supporters of surveillance believe that it will make the public feel more secure. Moreover, it can be cheaper to install and maintain cameras than to put more police officers on street patrol. For critics, however, the use of surveillance cameras brings to mind the grim, futuristic world presented by Britain's own George Orwell (1949) in his famous novel *1984*. In the world of *1984,* an all-seeing "Big Brother" represented an authoritarian government that watched people's every move and took immediate action against anyone who questioned the oppressive regime (Halbfinger 1998; Uttley 1993).

Law and Society

Some norms are so important to a society they are formalized into laws controlling people's behaviour. *Law* may be defined as governmental social control (Black 1995). Some laws, such as the prohibition against murder, are directed at all members of society. Others, such as fishing and hunting regulations, primarily affect particular categories of people. Still others govern

p. 57

"Big Brother" is watching you! In an attempt to reduce street crime, the city of Baltimore, Maryland, installed a video surveillance camera in its business district. Some residents are comforted by the camera's presence, but critics charge that it is inappropriate in a free society.

the behaviour of social institutions (corporate law and laws regarding the taxing of nonprofit enterprises).

Sociologists have become increasingly interested in the creation of laws as a social process. Laws are created in response to perceived needs for formal social control. Sociologists have sought to explain how and why such perceptions arise. In their view, law is not merely a static body of rules handed down from generation to generation. Rather, it reflects continually changing standards of what is right and wrong, of how violations are to be determined, and of what sanctions are to be applied (Schur 1968).

Sociologists representing varying theoretical perspectives agree that the legal order reflects underlying social values. Therefore, the creation of criminal law can be a most controversial matter. Should it be against the law to employ illegal immigrants in a factory (see Chapter 9), to have an abortion (see Chapter 10), or to smoke on an airplane? Such issues have been bitterly debated because they require a choice among competing values. Not surprisingly, laws that are unpopular—such as the Canadian law requiring the registration of firearms—become difficult to enforce owing to lack of consensus supporting the norms.

Socialization is actually the primary source of conforming and obedient behaviour, including obedience to law. Generally, it is not external pressure from a peer group or authority figure that makes us go along with social norms. Rather, we have internalized such norms as valid and desirable and are committed to observing them. In a profound sense, we want to see ourselves (and to be seen) as loyal, cooperative, responsible, and respectful of others. In Canada and other societies around the world, people are socialized both to want to belong and to fear being viewed as different or deviant.

Control theory suggests that our connection to members of society leads us to systematically conform to society's norms. According to sociologist Travis Hirschi and other control theorists, we are bonded to our family members, friends, and peers in a way that leads us to follow the mores and folkways of our society, while giving little conscious thought to whether we will be sanctioned if we fail to conform. Socialization develops our self-control so well that we don't need further pressure to obey social norms. While control theory does not effectively explain the rationale for every conforming act, it nevertheless reminds us that while the media may focus on crime and disorder, most members of most societies conform to and obey basic norms (Gottfredson and Hirschi 1990; Hirschi 1969).

Deviance

What Is Deviance?

For sociologists, the term *deviance* does not mean perversion or depravity. ***Deviance*** is behaviour that violates the standards of conduct or expectations of a group or society (Wickman 1991:85). In Canada, alcoholics, compulsive gamblers, and the mentally ill would all be classified as deviants. Being late for class is categorized as a deviant act; the same is true of dressing too casually for a formal wedding. On the basis of the sociological definition, we are all deviant from time to time. Each of us violates common social norms in certain situations.

Is being overweight an example of deviance? In North America and many other cultures, unrealistic standards of appearance and body image place a huge strain on people—especially on women and girls—based on how they look. Journalist Naomi Wolf (1992) has used the term *the beauty myth* to refer to an exaggerated ideal of beauty, beyond the reach of all but a few females, which has unfortunate consequences. In order to shed their

The current ideal of feminine beauty in North America is the wafer-thin physique of a fashion model, epitomized by actress Calista Flockhart. In an effort to live up to the ideal, many young girls develop eating disorders.

"deviant" image and conform to (unrealistic) societal norms, many women and girls become consumed with adjusting their appearances. For example, in a *People* magazine "health" feature, a young actress stated that she knows it is time to eat when she passes out on the set. When females carry adherence to "the beauty myth" to an extreme, they may develop eating disorders or undertake costly and unnecessary cosmetic surgery procedures. Yet what is deviant in our culture may be celebrated in another. In Nigeria, for example, being fat is a mark of beauty. Part of the coming-of-age ritual calls for young girls to spend months in a "fattening room." Among the Nigerians, being thin at this point in the life course is deviant (Simmons 1998).

Deviance involves the violation of group norms, which may or may not be formalized into law. It is a comprehensive concept that includes not only criminal behaviour but also many actions not subject to prosecution. The public official who takes a bribe has defied social norms, but so has the high school student who refuses to sit in an assigned seat or cuts class. Of course, deviation from norms is not always negative, let alone criminal. A member of an exclusive social club who speaks out against its traditional policy of excluding women and Jews from admittance is deviating from the club's norms. So is a police officer who "blows the whistle" on corruption or brutality within the department.

Standards of deviance vary from one group (or subculture) to another. In Canada, it is generally considered acceptable to sing along at a folk or rock concert, but not at the opera. Just as deviance is defined by place, so too is it relative to time. For instance, drinking alcohol at 6:00 P.M. is a common practice in our society, but engaging in the same behaviour at breakfast is viewed as a deviant act and as symptomatic of a drinking problem. Table 7-1 offers additional examples of untimely acts that we regard as deviant in North America.

From a sociological perspective, deviance is hardly objective. Rather, it is subject to social definitions within a particular society; in most instances, those individuals and groups with the greatest status and power define what is acceptable and what is deviant. For example, despite serious medical warnings about the dangers of tobacco as far back as 30 years ago, cigarette smoking continued to be accepted—in good part because of the power of tobacco farmers and cigarette manufacturers. It was only after a long campaign led by public health and anti-cancer activists that cigarette smoking became more of a deviant activity. Today many local laws limit where people can smoke.

While deviance can include relatively minor day-to-day decisions about our personal behaviour, in some

Table 7-1 Untimely Acts

Ringing a doorbell at 2 A.M.
Working on New Year's Eve
Having sex on a first date
Playing a stereo loudly in early morning hours
Having an alcoholic drink with breakfast
An instructor's ending a college class after 15 minutes
Getting married after having been engaged for only a few days

Source: Reese and Katovich 1989.

cases it can become part of a person's identity. This process is called *stigmatization,* as we will now see.

Deviance and Social Stigma

There are many ways a person can acquire a deviant identity. Because of physical or behavioural characteristics, some people are unwillingly cast in negative social roles. Once they have been assigned a deviant role, they have trouble presenting a positive image to others, and may even experience lowered self-esteem. Whole groups of people—for instance, "short people" or "redheads"—may be labelled in this way (Heckert and Best 1997). The interactionist Erving Goffman (see Chapters 1 and 4) coined the term ***stigma*** to describe the labels society uses to devalue members of certain social groups (Goffman 1963a).

Prevailing expectations about beauty and body shape may prevent people who are regarded as ugly or obese from advancing as rapidly as their abilities permit. Both overweight and anorexic people are assumed to be weak in character, slaves to their appetites or to media images. Because they do not conform to the beauty myth, they may be viewed as "disfigured" or "strange" in appearance, bearers of what Goffman calls a "spoiled identity." However, what constitutes disfigurement is a matter of interpretation. Of the over one million cosmetic procedures done every year in Canada and the United States, many are performed on women who would be objectively defined as having a normal appearance. And while feminist sociologists have accurately noted that the beauty myth makes many women feel uncomfortable with themselves, men too lack confidence in their appearance. The number of males who choose to undergo cosmetic procedures has risen sharply in recent years; men now account for 9 percent of such surgeries, including liposuction (C. Kalb 1999; P. Saukko 1999).

The American Board of Plastic Surgery, made up of doctors from Canada and the United States, released a report in 1999 that documented the increase in the number of cosmetic surgeries performed in both countries. Since 1992, the number has tripled (to 1 045 000 as of 1998), as Table 7-2 illustrates.

Often people are stigmatized for deviant behaviours they may no longer engage in. The labels "compulsive gambler," "ex-convict," "recovering alcoholic," and "ex-mental patient" can stick to a person for life. Goffman draws a useful distinction between a prestige symbol that draws attention to a positive aspect of one's identity, such as a wedding band or a badge, and a stigma symbol that discredits or debases one's identity, such as a conviction for child molestation. While stigma symbols may not always be obvious, they can become a matter of public knowledge. Some communities, for instance, publish the names and addresses, and in some instances even the pictures, of convicted sex offenders on the web.

A person need not be guilty of a crime to be stigmatized. Homeless people often have trouble getting a job, because employers are wary of applicants who cannot give a home address. Moreover, hiding one's homelessness is difficult, since agencies generally use the telephone to contact applicants about job openings. If a homeless person has access to a telephone at a shelter, the staff generally answer the phone by announcing the name of the institution—a sure way to discourage prospective employers. Even if a homeless person surmounts these obstacles and manages to get a job, she or he is often fired when the employer learns of the situation.

> Kim had been working as a receptionist in a doctor's office for several weeks when the doctor learned she was living in a shelter and fired her. "If I had known you lived in a shelter," Kim said the doctor told her, "I would never have hired you. Shelters are places of disease." "No," said Kim. "Doctors' offices are places of disease." (Liebow 1993:64–54)

Table 7-2 Selected Cosmetic Procedures Performed by Members of the American Society of Plastic and Reconstruction Surgeons in Canada and the United States

	1992	1998
Liposuction	47 212	172 079
Breast Augmentation	32 607	132 378
Facelift	40 077	70 947
Nose Surgery (rhinoplasty)	50 175	55 953
Tummy Tuck (abdominoplasty)	16 810	46 597
Breast Lift	7 963	31 525
Male breast reduction	4 997	9 023
Buttock lift	291	1 246

Source: Adapted from American Society of Plastic Surgeons 2002.

Regardless of a person's positive attributes, employers regard the spoiled identity of homelessness as sufficient reason to dismiss an employee.

While some types of deviance will stigmatize a person, other types do not carry a significant penalty. Some good examples of socially tolerated forms of deviance can be found in the world of high technology.

Deviance and Technology

Technological innovations like pagers and voice mail can redefine social interactions and the standards of behaviour related to them. When the Internet was first made available to the general public, no norms or regulations governed its use. Because online communication offers a high degree of anonymity, uncivil behaviour—speaking harshly of others or monopolizing chat room "space"—quickly became common. Today, online bulletin boards designed to carry items of community interest must be policed to prevent users from posting commercial advertisements. Such deviant acts are beginning to provoke calls for the establishment of formal rules for online behaviour. For example, policymakers have debated the wisdom of regulating the content of websites featuring hate speech and pornography.

The sheer length of time people spend using the Internet may soon be an indication of deviance. Some psychiatrists and psychologists are now debating whether or not Internet "addiction" may eventually be labelled a new disorder and, thus, a new form of deviant behaviour. Dr. Kimberly Young, of the University of Pittsburgh, has studied Internet addiction in the United States, placing it in the same category as pathological gambling and compulsive shopping. She found "addicted" users spent an average of 38 hours per week online, compared with 8 hours per week for "non-addicts." (Dalfen 2000). Canadians, according to a January 2000 Media Matrix study, use the Internet 27 percent more than Americans (Dalfen 2000).

Some deviant uses of technology are criminal, though not all participants see it that way. The pirating of software, motion pictures, and CDs has become a big business (see Figure 7-1). At conventions and swap meets, pirated copies of movies and CDs are sold openly. Some of the products are obviously counterfeit, but many come

FIGURE 7-1

A New Form of Deviance Digital Piracy

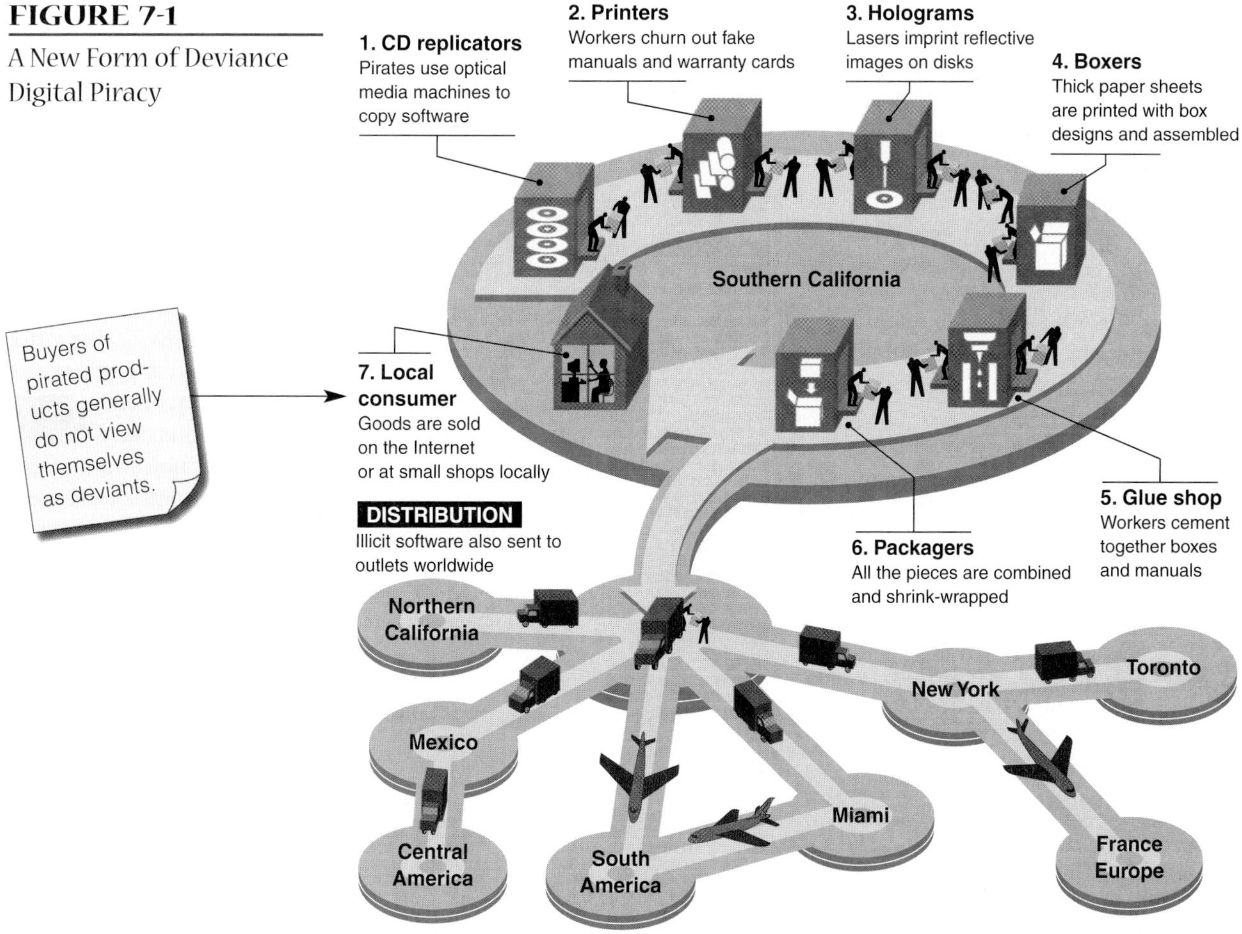

Source: Huffstutter et al. 1999:A29.

in sophisticated packaging, complete with warranty cards. When vendors are willing to talk, they say they merely want to be compensated for their time and the cost of materials, or that the software they have copied is in the public domain.

Though most of these black market activities are clearly illegal, many consumers and small-time pirates are proud of their behaviour. They may even think themselves smart for figuring out a way to avoid the "unfair" prices charged by "big corporations." Few people see the pirating of a new software program or a first-run movie as a threat to the public good, as they would embezzling from a bank. Similarly, most businesspeople who "borrow" software from another department, even though they lack a site license, do not think they are doing anything wrong. No social stigma attaches to their illegal behaviour.

Deviance, then, is a complex concept. Sometimes it is trivial, sometimes profoundly harmful. Sometimes it is accepted by society and sometimes soundly rejected. What accounts for deviant behaviour and people's reaction to it? In the next section we will examine four theoretical explanations for deviance.

Explaining Deviance

Why do people violate social norms? We have seen that deviant acts are subject to both informal and formal sanctions of social control. The nonconforming or disobedient person may face disapproval, loss of friends, fines, or even imprisonment. Why, then, does deviance occur?

Early explanations for deviance identified supernatural causes or genetic factors (such as "bad blood" or evolutionary throwbacks to primitive ancestors). By the 1800s, there were substantial research efforts to identify biological factors that lead to deviance and especially to criminal activity. While such research was discredited in the 20th century, contemporary studies, primarily by biochemists, have sought to isolate genetic factors leading to a likelihood of certain personality traits. Although criminality (much less deviance) is hardly a personality characteristic, researchers have focused on traits that might lead to crime, such as aggression. Of course, aggression can also lead to success in the corporate world, professional sports, or other areas of life.

The contemporary study of possible biological roots of criminality is but one aspect of the larger sociobiology debate. In general, sociologists reject any emphasis on genetic roots of crime and deviance. The limitations of current knowledge, the possibility of reinforcing racist and sexist assumptions, and the disturbing implications for rehabilitation of criminals have led sociologists to largely draw on other approaches to explain deviance (Sagarin and Sanchez 1988).

p. 77

Functionalist Perspective

According to functionalists, deviance is a common part of human existence, with positive (as well as negative) consequences for social stability. Deviance helps to define the limits of proper behaviour. Children who see one parent scold the other for belching at the dinner table learn about approved conduct. The same is true of the driver who receives a speeding ticket, the department store cashier who is fired for yelling at a customer, and the university student who is penalized for handing in papers weeks overdue.

Durkheim's Legacy Émile Durkheim (1964, original edition 1895) focused his sociological investigations mainly on criminal acts, yet his conclusions have implications for all types of deviant behaviour. In Durkheim's view, the punishments established within a culture (including both formal and informal mechanisms of social control) help to define acceptable behaviour and thus contribute to stability. If improper acts were not committed and then sanctioned, people might stretch their standards of what constitutes appropriate conduct.

Kai Erikson (1966) illustrated this boundary-maintenance function of deviance in his study of the Puritans of 17th-century New England. By today's standards, the Puritans placed tremendous emphasis on conventional morals. Their persecution of Quakers and execution of women as witches represented continuing attempts to define and redefine the boundaries of their community. In effect, their changing social norms created "crime waves," as people whose behaviour was previously acceptable suddenly faced punishment for being deviant (Abrahamson 1978; N. Davis 1975).

Durkheim (1951, original edition 1897) also introduced the term *anomie* into sociological literature to describe a loss of direction felt in a society when social control of individual behaviour has become ineffective. Anomie is a state of normlessness that typically occurs during a period of profound social change and disorder, such as a time of economic collapse. People become more aggressive or depressed, and this results in higher rates of violent crime and suicide. Since there is much less agreement on what constitutes proper behaviour during times of revolution, sudden prosperity, or economic depression, conformity and obedience become less significant as social forces. It also becomes much more difficult to state exactly what constitutes deviance.

p. 10

Merton's Theory of Deviance What do a mugger and a teacher have in common? Each is "working" to obtain money that can then be exchanged for desired goods. As this example illustrates, behaviour that violates accepted norms (such as mugging) may be performed with the same basic objectives in mind as those of people who pursue more conventional lifestyles.

Using the above analysis, sociologist Robert Merton (1968) adapted Durkheim's notion of anomie to explain why people accept or reject the goals of a society, the socially approved means of fulfilling their aspirations, or both. Merton maintained that one important cultural goal in capitalist societies is success, measured largely in terms of money. In addition to providing this goal for people, our society offers specific instructions on how to pursue success—go to school, work hard, do not quit, take advantage of opportunities, and so forth.

What happens to individuals in a society with a heavy emphasis on wealth as a basic symbol of success? Merton reasoned that people adapt in certain ways, either by conforming to or by deviating from such cultural expectations. Consequently, he developed the ***anomie theory of deviance,*** which posits five basic forms of adaptation (see Table 7-3).

Conformity to social norms, the most common adaptation in Merton's typology, is the opposite of deviance. It involves acceptance of both the overall societal goal ("become affluent") and the approved means ("work hard"). In Merton's view, there must be some consensus regarding accepted cultural goals and legitimate means for attaining them. Without such consensus, societies could exist only as collectives of people—rather than as unified cultures—and might function in continual chaos.

Of course, in a society such as ours, conformity is not universal. For example, the means for realizing objectives are not equally distributed. People in the lower social classes often identify with the same goals as those of more powerful and affluent citizens yet lack equal access to high-quality education and training for skilled work. Even within a society, institutionalized means for realizing objectives vary. For example, a Statistics Canada report found that in 1997 access to legalized gambling varied from province to province. Lotteries were legal in all provinces, government casinos were legal in approximately half of the provinces, and VLTs (video lottery terminals) were legal in most provinces (Marshall 1999).

The other four types of behaviour represented in Table 7-3 all involve some departure from conformity. The "innovator" accepts the goals of a society but pursues them with means regarded as improper. For example, Harry King—a professional thief who specialized in safecracking for 40 years—gave a lecture to a sociology class and was asked if he had minded spending time in prison. King responded,

> I didn't exactly like it. But it was one of the necessary things about the life I had chosen. Do you like to come here and teach this class? I bet if the students had their wishes they'd be somewhere else, maybe out stealing, instead of sitting in this dumpy room. But they do it because it gets them something they want. The same with me. If I had to go to prison from time to time, well, that was the price you pay. (Chambliss 1972:x)

Harry King saw his criminal lifestyle as an adaptation to the goal of material success or "getting something you want." Denied the chance to achieve success through socially approved means, some individuals (like King) turn to illegitimate paths of upward mobility.

In Merton's typology, the "ritualist" has abandoned the goal of material success and become compulsively committed to the institutional means. Work becomes simply a way of life rather than a means to the goal of success, as in the case of bureaucratic officials who blindly apply rules and regulations without remembering the larger goals of an organization. Certainly this would be true of a welfare caseworker who refuses to assist a homeless family because their last apartment was in another district.

The "retreatist," as described by Merton, has basically withdrawn (or "retreated") from both the goals *and* the means of a society. In Canada, drug addicts and residents of skid row are typically portrayed as retreatists. There is also growing concern that adolescents addicted to alcohol will become retreatists at an early age.

The final adaptation identified by Merton reflects people's attempts to create a *new* social structure. The "rebel" feels alienated from dominant means and goals and may seek a dramatically different social order. Members of revolutionary political organizations, such as the

Table 7-3 Modes of Individual Adaptation

Mode	Institutionalized Means (Hard Work)	Societal Goal (Acquisition of Wealth)
NONDEVIANT		
Conformity	+	+
DEVIANT		
Innovation	−	+
Ritualism	+	−
Retreatism	−	−
Rebellion	±	±

Note: + indicates acceptance; − indicates rejection; ± indicates replacement with new means and goals.

Source: Merton 1968:1940.

Irish Republican Army (IRA) or right-wing militia groups, can be categorized as rebels according to Merton's model.

The graffiti of teenagers can be seen on walls in most urban settings. According to the interactionist Edwin Sutherland, teenagers are socialized into engaging in such deviant acts.

Merton has stressed that he was not attempting to describe five types of individuals. Rather, he offered a typology to explain the actions that people *usually* take. Thus, leaders of organized crime syndicates will be categorized as innovators, since they do not pursue success through socially approved means. Yet they may also attend church and send their children to medical school. Conversely, "respectable" people may occasionally cheat on their taxes or violate traffic laws. According to Merton, the same person will move back and forth from one mode of adaptation to another, depending on the demands of a particular situation.

Merton's theory, though popular, has had relatively few applications. Little effort has been made to determine to what extent all acts of deviance can be accounted for by his five modes. Moreover, while Merton's theory is useful in examining certain types of behaviour, such as illegal gambling by disadvantaged people functioning as innovators, his formulation fails to explain key differences in rates. Why, for example, do some disadvantaged groups have lower rates of reported crime than others? Why is criminal activity not viewed as a viable alternative by many people in adverse circumstances? Merton's theory of deviance does not answer such questions easily (Cloward 1959; Hartjen 1978).

Still, Merton has made a key contribution to the sociological understanding of deviance by pointing out that deviants (such as innovators and ritualists) share a great deal with conforming people. The convicted felon may hold many of the same aspirations that people with no criminal background have. Therefore, we can understand deviance as socially created behaviour, rather than as the result of momentary pathological impulses.

Interactionist Perspective

The functionalist approach to deviance explains why rule violation continues to exist in societies despite pressures to conform and obey. However, functionalists do not indicate how a given person comes to commit a deviant act or why on some occasions crimes do or do not occur. The emphasis on everyday behaviour that is the focus of the interactionist perspective is reflected in two explanations of crime—cultural transmission and routine activities theory.

Cultural Transmission White teenagers in suburban Los Angeles attempt to achieve fame within a subculture of "taggers." These young people "tag" (spray graffiti on) poles, utility boxes, bridges, and freeway signs in the San Fernando Valley. While law enforcement officials prefer to view them as "visual terrorists," the taggers gain respect from their peers by being "up the most" on prominent walls and billboards and by displaying the flashiest styles. Even parents may tolerate or endorse such deviant behaviour by declaring, "At least my kid's not shooting people. He's still alive" (Wooden 1995:124).

These teenagers demonstrate that humans *learn* how to behave in social situations—whether properly or improperly. There is no natural, innate manner in which people interact with one another. These simple ideas are not disputed today, but this was not the case when sociologist Edwin Sutherland (1883–1950) first advanced the argument that an individual undergoes the same basic socialization process whether learning conforming or deviant acts.

Sutherland's ideas have been the dominating force in criminology. He drew on the ***cultural transmission*** school, which emphasizes that one learns criminal behaviour through interactions with others. Such learning includes not only techniques of lawbreaking (for example, how to break into a car quickly and quietly) but also the motives, drives, and rationalizations of criminals. We can also use the cultural transmission approach to explain the behaviour of people who engage in habitual—and ultimately life-threatening—use of alcohol or drugs.

Sutherland maintained that through interactions with a primary group and significant others, people acquire definitions of proper and improper behaviour. He used the term ***differential association*** to describe the process through which exposure to attitudes *favourable* to criminal acts leads to violation of rules. Research suggests that this view of differential association also applies to such noncriminal deviant acts as sitting down during the singing of the national anthem or lying to a friend (E. Jackson et al. 1986).

To what extent will a given person engage in activity regarded as proper or improper? For each individual, it will depend on the frequency, duration, and importance of two types of social interaction experiences—those that endorse deviant behaviour and those that promote acceptance of social norms. People are more likely to engage in norm-defying behaviour if they are part of a group or subculture that stresses deviant values, such as a street gang.

Sutherland offers the example of a boy who is sociable, outgoing, and athletic and who lives in an area with a high rate of delinquency. The youth is very likely to come into contact with peers who commit acts of vandalism, fail to attend school, and so forth, and may come to adopt such behaviour. However, an introverted boy living in the same neighbourhood may stay away from his peers and avoid delinquency. In another community, an outgoing and athletic boy may join a Little League baseball team or a scout troup because of his interactions with peers. Thus, Sutherland views learning improper behaviour as the result of the types of groups to which one belongs and the kinds of friendships one has with others (Sutherland and Cressey 1978).

According to its critics, however, the cultural transmission approach may explain the deviant behaviour of juvenile delinquents or graffiti artists, but it fails to explain the conduct of the first-time impulsive shoplifter or the impoverished person who steals out of necessity. While not a precise statement of the process through which one becomes a criminal, differential association theory does direct our attention to the paramount role of social interaction in increasing a person's motivation to engage in deviant behaviour (Cressey 1960; E. Jackson et al. 1986; Sutherland and Cressey 1978).

Routine Activities Theory Another, more recent interactionist explanation considers the requisite conditions for a crime or deviant act to occur: there must be at the same time and in the same place a perpetrator, a victim, and/or an object of property. ***Routine activities theory*** contends that criminal victimization is increased when motivated offenders and suitable targets converge. It goes without saying that you cannot have car theft without automobiles, but the greater availability of more valuable automobiles to potential thieves *heightens* the likelihood that such a crime will occur. Campus and airport parking lots, where vehicles may be left in isolated locations for long periods of time, represent a new target for crime unknown just a generation ago. Routine activity of this nature can occur even in the home. For example, adults may save money by buying 24-packs of beer, but buying in bulk also allows juveniles to siphon off contents without attracting attention to their "crime." The theory derives its name of "routine" from the fact that the elements of a criminal or deviant act come together in normal, legal, and routine activities.

Advocates of this theory see it as a powerful explanation for the rise in crime during the last 50 years. Routine activity has changed to make crime more likely. Homes left vacant during the day or during long vacations are more accessible as targets of crime. The greater presence of consumer goods that are highly portable, such as video equipment and computers, also makes crime more likely (Cohen and Felson 1979; Felson 1998).

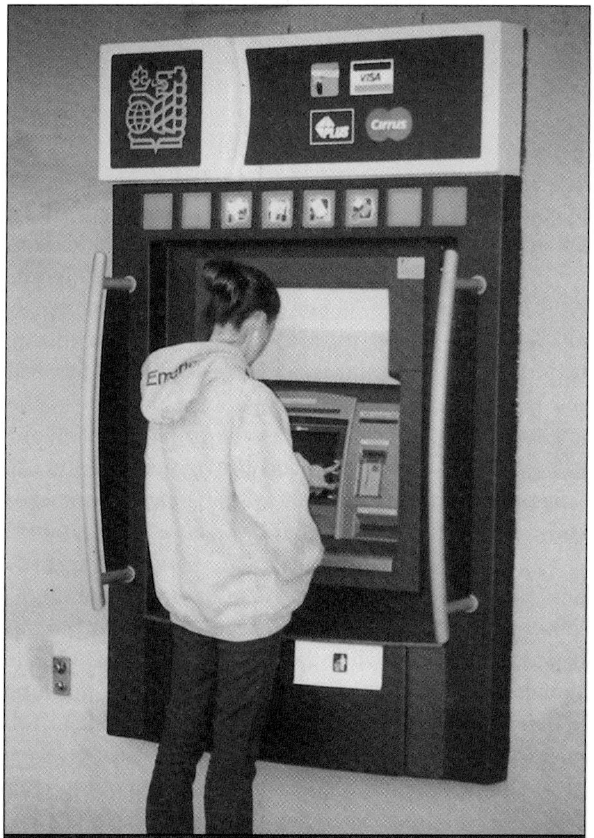

Outdoor ATMs invite trouble: they provide an ideal setting for the convergence of a perpetrator, a victim, and an article of property (cash). According to routine activities theory, crimes are more likely to occur wherever motivated offenders meet suitable targets.

Some significant research supports the routine activities explanation. Studies of urban crime have documented the existence of "hot spots" where people are more likely to be victimized because of their routine comings and goings (Cromwell et al. 1995; Sherman et al. 1989).

Perhaps what is most compelling about this theory is that it broadens our effort to understand crime and deviance. Rather than focus just on the criminal, routine activities theory also brings into the picture the behaviour of the victim. However, we need to resist the temptation to *expect* the higher victimization of some groups, such as racial and ethnic minorities, much less to consider it their own fault (Akers 1997).

Labelling Theory

The Saints and Roughnecks were two groups of high school males who were continually engaged in excessive drinking, reckless driving, truancy, petty theft, and vandalism. There the similarity ended. None of the Saints was ever arrested, but every Roughneck was frequently in trouble with police and townspeople. Why the disparity in their treatment? On the basis of his observation research in their high school, sociologist William Chambliss (1973) concluded that social class played an important role in the varying fortunes of the two groups.

The Saints effectively produced a facade of respectability. They came from "good families," were active in school organizations, expressed the intention of attending university, and received good grades. People generally viewed their delinquent acts as a few isolated cases of "sowing wild oats." By contrast, the Roughnecks had no such aura of respectability. They drove around town in beat-up cars, were generally unsuccessful in school, and were viewed with suspicion no matter what they did.

We can understand such discrepancies by using an approach to deviance known as ***labelling theory.*** Unlike Sutherland's work, labelling theory does not focus on why some individuals come to commit deviant acts. Instead, it attempts to explain why certain people (such as the Roughnecks) are *viewed* as deviants, delinquents, "bad kids," "losers," and criminals, while others whose behaviour is similar (such as the Saints) are not seen in such harsh terms. Reflecting the contribution of interactionist theorists, labelling theory emphasizes how a person comes to be labelled as deviant or to accept that label. Sociologist Howard Becker (1963:9; 1964), who popularized this approach, summed it up with this statement: "Deviant behavior is behavior that people so label."

Labelling theory is also called the ***societal-reaction approach,*** reminding us that it is the *response* to an act and not the behaviour itself that determines deviance. For example, studies have shown that some school personnel and therapists expand educational programs designed for learning-disabled students to include those with behavioural problems. Consequently, a "troublemaker" can be improperly labelled as learning-disabled, and vice versa.

A recent study by three British psychologists underscores the implications of using different labels to describe people with learning difficulties or disabilities. A total of 111 subjects completed a questionnaire designed to assess attitudes toward three labelled groups: "mentally subnormal adults," "mentally handicapped adults," and "people with learning difficulties." The researchers found that subjects reacted more positively to the label "people with learning difficulties" than to the other labels. Subjects view "people with learning difficulties" as more competent and as deserving of more rights than "mentally handicapped" or "mentally subnormal" individuals (Eayrs et al. 1993).

Traditionally, research on deviance has focused on people who violate social norms. In contrast, labelling theory focuses on police, probation officers, psychiatrists, judges, teachers, employers, school officials, and other regulators of social control. These agents, it is argued, play a significant role in creating the deviant identity by designating certain people (and not others) as "deviant." An important aspect of labelling theory is the recognition that some individuals or groups have the power to *define* labels and apply them to others. This view recalls the conflict perspective's emphasis on the social significance of power.

In recent years the practice of *racial profiling,* in which people are identified as criminal suspects purely on the basis of their race, has come under public scrutiny. American studies confirm the public's suspicions that in some jurisdictions, police officers are much more likely to stop black males than white males for routine traffic violations. In Canada as well as in the United States and many European countries, the events of September 11, 2001, have caused civil rights activists to raise concerns about the use of racial profiling in safety and security policies and practices.

The labelling approach does not fully explain why certain people accept a label and others are able to reject it. In fact, this perspective may exaggerate the ease with which societal judgments can alter our self-images. Labelling theorists do suggest, however, that how much power one has relative to others is important in determining a person's ability to resist an undesirable label. Competing approaches (including that of Sutherland) fail to explain why some deviants continue to be viewed as conformists rather than as violators of rules. According to Howard Becker (1973), labelling theory was not conceived as the *sole* explanation for deviance; its proponents merely hoped to focus more attention on the undeniably important actions of those people officially in charge of defining deviance (N. Davis 1975; compare with Cullen and Cullen 1978).

The popularity of labelling theory is reflected in the emergence of a related perspective, called social constructionism. According to the ***social constructionist perspective,*** deviance is the product of the culture we live in. Social constructionists focus specifically on the decision-making process that creates the deviant identity. They point out that "missing children," "deadbeat dads," "spree killers," and "date rapists" have always been with us, but at times have become *the* major social concern of the moment because of intensive media coverage (Liska and Messner 1999; Wright et al. 2000).

Conflict Theory

For many years a husband who forced his wife to have sexual intercourse—without her consent and against her will—was not legally considered to have committed rape. The laws defined rape as pertaining only to sexual relations between people not married to each other. These laws reflected the overwhelmingly male composition of government and legal decision makers. Conflict theorists would not be surprised by this. They point out that people with power protect their own interests and define deviance to suit their own needs.

Feminist legal scholar Catherine MacKinnon (1987) argues that male sexual behaviour represents "dominance eroticized," in that male sexuality is linked to dominance and power. Edwin Schur (1983: 148) expands on this view of male sexuality, stating that "forced sex is the ultimate indicator and preserver of male dominance." Canadian laws have historically sanctioned the abuse of women within marriage, based on the assumption of male control and ownership of his family (Johnson 1996). According to Status of Women Canada (2000), female victims of spousal abuse are more likely to be subjected to sexual assault and more severe forms of violence, such as beating and choking, than male victims.

Sociologist Richard Quinney (1974, 1979, 1980) is a leading exponent of the view that the criminal justice system serves the interests of the powerful. Crime, according to Quinney (1970), is a definition of conduct created by authorized agents of social control—such as legislators and law enforcement officers—in a politically organized society. He and other conflict theorists argue that lawmaking is often an attempt by the powerful to coerce others into their own morality (see also S. Spitzer 1975).

This helps to explain why our society has laws against gambling, drug usage, and prostitution, many of which are violated on a massive scale (we will examine these "victimless crimes" later in the chapter). According to the conflict school, criminal law does not represent a consistent application of societal values, but instead reflects competing values and interests. Thus, marijuana is outlawed in Canada because it is alleged to be harmful to users, yet cigarettes and alcohol are sold legally almost everywhere.

Conflict theorists contend that the entire criminal justice system of Canada treats suspects differently on the basis of their racial, ethnic, or social class background. The case of Donald Marshall, a First Nations man from Nova Scotia who was wrongfully convicted of murder, and who served years in prison for a crime he did not commit, is one of the most illustrative examples of the bias against First Nations persons in Canadian legal history.

Quinney (1974) argues that, through such differential applications of social control, the criminal justice system helps to keep the poor and oppressed in their deprived position. In his view, disadvantaged individuals and groups who represent a threat to those with power become the primary targets of criminal law. He maintains the real criminals in poor neighbourhoods are not the people arrested for vandalism and theft but rather absentee landlords and exploitative store owners. Even if we do not accept this challenging argument, we cannot ignore

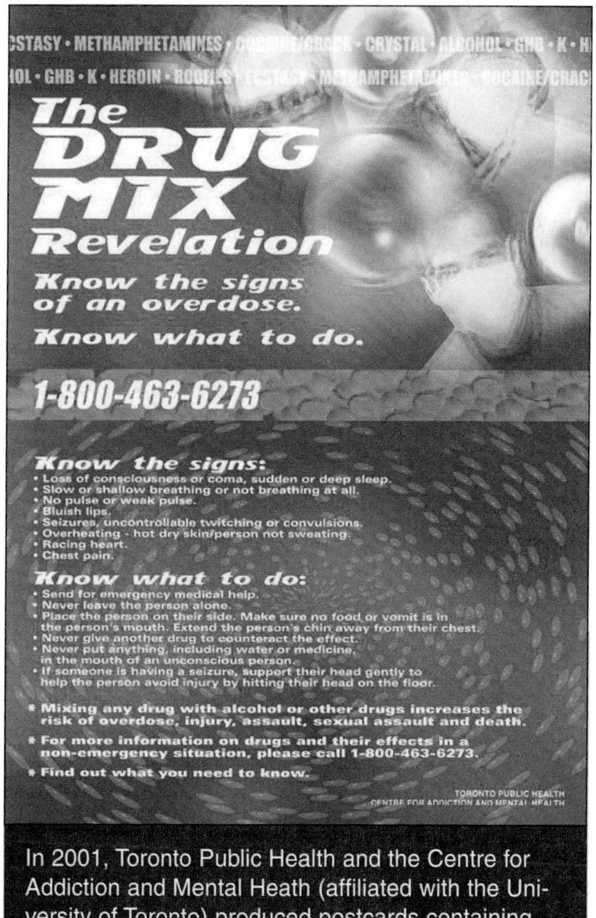

In 2001, Toronto Public Health and the Centre for Addiction and Mental Heath (affiliated with the University of Toronto) produced postcards containing practical information about an overdose. The postcards, part of a harm-reduction strategy, will be distributed to Toronto high schools, colleges, and areas of the city popular with young adults.

the role of the powerful in creating a social structure that perpetuates suffering.

The perspective advanced by labelling and conflict theorists forms quite a contrast to the functionalist approach to deviance. Functionalists view standards of deviant behaviour as merely reflecting cultural norms, whereas conflict and labelling theorists point out that the most powerful groups in a society can shape laws and standards and determine who is (or is not) prosecuted as a criminal. Thus, the label "deviant" is rarely applied to the corporate executive whose decisions lead to large-scale environmental pollution. In the opinion of conflict theorists, agents of social control and powerful groups can generally impose their own self-serving definitions of deviance on the general public.

Feminist Perspectives

Although feminist theories of deviance are varied and diverse, most tend to challenge other mainstream theories on the grounds that women's experiences have not been included and that gender-based perspectives have not been employed. Feminist theories of deviance are generally eager to understand the gendered nature of institutions such as the criminal justice system, and the inequities in the system that lead to differential treatment of men and women.

Many feminist perspectives contend that courts, prisons, law enforcement agencies, welfare agencies, and families alike are organized on the basis of gender as well as power, class, race, and sexuality (Elliot and Mandell 1998). Of concern are ways in which factors such as gender, sexuality, class, and race intersect to produce patterns of and responses to deviant behaviour. As well, these perspectives in general hold the view that since gender relations are not "natural," but rather produced by social, cultural, and historical conditions, gendered patterns of deviance will reflect these conditions. For example, the social acceptability of smoking for women (and the labelling of some women smokers as deviants) has been shaped by history, class, and sexuality. From the 1800s to the 1920s in North America, smoking by women was associated with prostitution and lesbianism. Women who smoked were labelled "sluts," "whores," and "sinners" and were considered "fallen women" (Greaves 1996:18).

As previously mentioned, feminist perspectives are diverse and varied. For example, liberal feminist perspectives tend to view women's rates of crime and deviance as a reflection of the degree to which they participate in all areas of social life—sports, politics, business, education, and so on. Because women are confronted with obstacles in their climb to top corporate positions, they are limited in their opportunities to engage in particular deviant acts such as corporate crime.

In contrast, radical feminist perspectives see patriarchy (the set of social relations that maintains male control) as the key to understanding female crime and deviance. Patriarchy, according to radical feminist analysis, puts men in control of women's bodies and minds and sets in place oppressive social institutions, such as the family and the law, in order to maintain control. Sexual offences for women, therefore, are more common, since men control the institutions that regulate activities such as prostitution. This imbalance of power results in a higher rate of arrest and conviction for the female prostitute than for the male customer.

Crime

Crime is a violation of criminal law for which some governmental authority applies formal penalties. It represents a deviation from formal social norms administered by the state. Laws divide crimes into various categories, depending on the severity of the offense, the age of the offender, the potential punishment that can be levied, and the court that holds jurisdiction over the case.

Crimes tend to impact some groups more than others; for example, their impact can be gender-specific and age-specific. In Canada, of all the victims of crimes against the person, women and girls make up the vast majority of victims of sexual assault (82 percent), criminal harassment (78 percent), kidnapping or abduction (62 percent), and common assault (52 percent) (Status of Women Canada 2000).

Types of Crime

Rather than relying solely on legal categories, sociologists classify crimes in terms of how they are committed and how society views the offenses. In this section, we will examine four types of crime as differentiated by sociologists: professional crime, organized crime, white-collar crime, and "victimless crimes."

Professional Crime

Although the adage "crime doesn't pay" is familiar, many people do make a career of illegal activities. A ***professional criminal*** is a person who pursues crime as a day-to-day occupation, developing skilled techniques and enjoying a certain degree of status among other criminals. Some professional criminals specialize in burglary, safecracking, hijacking of cargo, pickpocketing, and shoplifting. Such people have acquired skills that reduce the likelihood of arrest, conviction, and imprisonment. As a result, they may have long careers in their chosen "professions."

Edwin Sutherland (1937) offered pioneering insights into the behaviour of professional criminals by publishing an annotated account written by a professional thief. Unlike the person who engages in crime only once or twice, professional thieves make a business of stealing. They devote their entire working time to planning and executing crimes and sometimes travel across the nation to pursue their "professional duties." Like people in regular occupations, professional thieves consult with their colleagues concerning the demands of work, thus becoming part of a subculture of similarly occupied individuals. They exchange information on possible places to burglarize, on outlets for unloading stolen goods, and on ways of securing bail bonds if arrested.

Organized Crime

A 1978 United States government report uses three pages to define the term *organized crime.* For our purposes, we will consider ***organized crime*** to be the work of a group that regulates relations between various criminal enterprises involved in the smuggling and sale of drugs, prostitution, gambling, and other illegal activities. Organized crime dominates the world of illegal business just as large corporations dominate the conventional business world. It allocates territory, sets prices for goods and services, and acts as an arbitrator in internal disputes.

Organized crime is a secret, conspiratorial activity that generally evades law enforcement. Organized crime takes over legitimate businesses, gains influence over labour unions, corrupts public officials, intimidates witnesses in criminal trials, and even "taxes" merchants in exchange for "protection" (National Advisory Commission on Criminal Justice 1976). An example of the intimidation tactics used by organized crime is the gunning down of the Montreal crime reporter Michel Auger in 2000. Auger specialized in stories on organized crime and biker gangs in Quebec. Auger was shot five times, but recovered. Although it has not yet been proven inconclusively that biker gangs were responsible for the execution-style attack, the attack came a day after his paper, *Le Journal,* printed one of his articles on biker-related murders.

There has always been a global element in organized crime. But recently law enforcement officials and policy-makers have acknowledged the emergence of a new form of organized crime that takes advantage of advances in electronic communications. *Transnational* organized crime includes drug and arms smuggling, money laundering, and trafficking in illegal immigrants and stolen goods, such as automobiles (Office of Justice Programs 1999).

White-Collar and Technology-Based Crime

Income tax evasion, stock manipulation, consumer fraud, bribery and extraction of "kickbacks," embezzlement, and misrepresentation in advertising—these are all examples of ***white-collar crime,*** illegal acts committed in the course of business activities, often by affluent, "respectable" people. Edwin Sutherland (1949, 1983) likened these crimes to organized crime because they are often perpetrated through occupational roles (Friedrichs 1998).

A new type of white-collar crime has emerged in recent decades: computer crime. The use of such "high technology" allows one to carry out embezzlement or electronic fraud without leaving a trace, or to gain access to a company's inventory without leaving one's home. An adept programmer can gain access to a firm's computer by telephone and then copy valuable files. It is virtually impossible to track such people unless they are foolish enough to call from the same phone each time. According to a 2000 study by the FBI and the Computer Security Institute, 70 percent of companies in the United States relying on computer systems reported theft of electronic information for an estimated loss of US$265 million in 1999 alone (Zuckerman 2000).

Sutherland (1940) coined the term *white-collar crime* in 1939 to refer to acts by individuals, but the term has been broadened more recently to include offenses by businesses and corporations as well. *Corporate crime,* or any act by a corporation that is punishable by the government, takes many forms and includes individuals, organizations, and institutions among its victims. Corporations may engage in anticompetitive behaviour, acts that lead to environmental pollution, tax fraud, stock fraud and manipulation, the production of unsafe goods, bribery and corruption, and worker health and safety violations (Simpson 1993).

"BUT IF WE GO BACK TO SCHOOL AND GET A GOOD EDUCATION, THINK OF ALL THE DOORS IT'LL OPEN TO WHITE-COLLAR CRIME."

Given the economic and social costs of white-collar crime, one might expect the criminal justice system to take this problem quite seriously. Yet research done in the United States shows that white-collar offenders are more likely to receive fines than prison sentences. In federal courts—where most white-collar cases end up—probation is granted to 40 percent of those who have violated antitrust laws, 61 percent of those convicted of fraud, and 70 percent of convicted embezzlers (Gest 1985). Amitai Etzioni's study (1985, 1990) found that in 43 percent of the incidents, either no penalty was imposed or the company was required merely to cease engaging in the illegal practice and to return any funds gained through illegal means (for a different view, see Manson 1986).

Moreover, conviction for such illegal acts does not generally harm a person's reputation and career aspirations nearly so much as conviction for street crime would. Apparently, the label "white-collar criminal" does not carry the stigma of the label "felon convicted of a violent crime." Conflict theorists don't find such differential labelling and treatment surprising. They argue that the criminal justice system largely disregards the white-collar crimes of the affluent, while focusing on crimes often committed by the poor. If an offender holds a position of status and influence, his or her crime is treated as less serious, and the sanction is much more lenient (Maguire 1988).

Victimless Crimes

White-collar or street crimes endanger people's economic or personal well-being against their will (or without their direct knowledge). By contrast, sociologists use the term ***victimless crimes*** to describe the willing exchange among adults of widely desired, but illegal, goods and services (Schur 1965, 1985).

While the term *victimless crime* is widely used, many people object to the notion that there is no victim other than the offender in such crimes. Excessive drinking, compulsive gambling, and illegal drug use contribute to an enormous amount of personal and property damage. And feminist sociologists contend that the so-called victimless crime of prostitution, as well as the more disturbing aspects of pornography, reinforce the misconception that women are "toys" who can be treated as objects rather than people (J. Flavin 1998; A. Jolin 1994).

Nonetheless, some activists are working to decriminalize many of these illegal practices. Supporters of decriminalization are troubled by the attempt to legislate a moral code of behaviour for adults. In their view, it is impossible to prevent prostitution, gambling, and other victimless crimes. The already overburdened criminal justice system should instead devote its resources to "street crimes" and other offenses with obvious victims. However, opponents of decriminalization insist that such offenses do indeed have victims, in the sense that they can bring harm to innocent people. For example, a person with a drinking problem can become abusive to a spouse or children; a compulsive gambler or drug user may steal to pursue his obsession. According to critics of decriminalization, society must not give tacit approval to conduct that has such harmful consequences (National Advisory Commission on Criminal Justice 1976; Schur 1968, 1985).

The controversy over decriminalization reminds us of the important insights of labelling and conflict theories presented earlier. Underlying this debate are two interesting questions: Who has the power to define gambling, prostitution, and public drunkenness as "crimes"? And who has the power to label such behaviours as "victimless"? It is generally the government and, in some cases, the police and the courts.

Again, we can see that criminal law is not simply a universal standard of behaviour agreed on by all members of society. Rather, it reflects the struggle among competing individuals and groups to gain governmental support for their particular moral and social values. For example, such organizations as Mothers Against Drunk Driving (MADD) and Students Against Drunk Driving (SADD) have had success in recent years in modifying public attitudes toward drunkenness. Rather than being viewed as a victimless crime, drunkenness is increasingly being associated with the potential dangers of driving while under the influence of alcohol. As a result, the mass media are giving greater (and more critical) attention to people who are guilty of drunk driving, and many state and provincial governments have instituted more severe fines and jail terms for a wide variety of alcohol-related offenses.

Crime Statistics

Crime statistics are not as accurate as social scientists would like. However, since they deal with an issue of grave concern to people in many countries, they are frequently cited as if they were completely reliable. Such data do serve as an indicator of police activity, as well as an approximate indication of the level of certain crimes. Yet it would be a mistake to interpret these data as an exact representation of the incidence of crime.

Public opinion polls reveal that Canadians believe the rate of crime is increasing in this country, despite the release of statistics that indicate the national crime rate has been on a downward trend since 1991 (Statistics Canada 2003b). In 2002, the rate of violent crime in Canada dropped 2 percent; the rate of attempted murder fell 6 percent over the previous year, while homicides rose 4 percent after remaining stable the previous two years (Statistics Canada 2003b).

Within Canada, vast regional differences exist in rates of crime. As Figure 7-2 illustrates, in 2002, Saskatchewan's crime rates were the highest among the provinces, followed

FIGURE 7-2

Crime Rates by Province and Territory, 2002

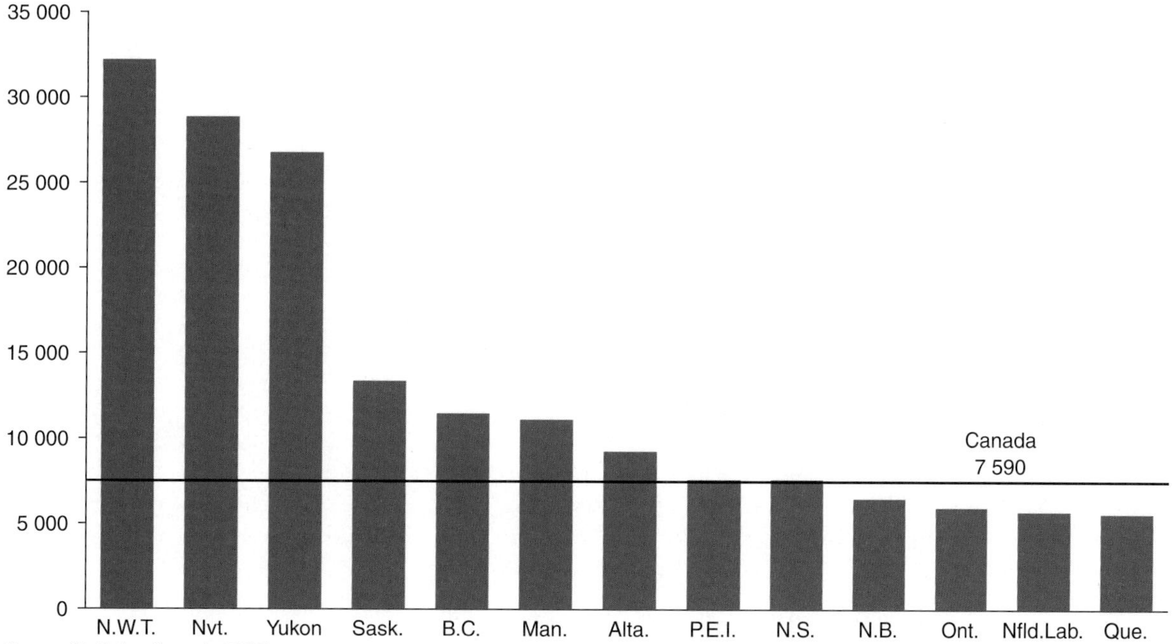

Source: Statistics Canada 2003b.

by those of British Columbia and Manitoba. Newfoundland and Labrador, Quebec, and Ontario had the lowest rates of crime in the country. In 2002, rates of violent crimes decreased, driven by a 3 percent decline in the rate of robberies and a 2 percent decline in the rate of assaults (Statistics Canada 2003b). Prior to 1993, the violent crime rate had increased each year since 1977. In 2000, the rates of violent crime were approximately the same as they were in 1990; however, they are 54 percent higher than 20 years before that (Statistics Canada 2001d).

Canada's crime rates are significantly lower than those of our American neighbours, particularly for violent crimes such as homicide, the American rate for which is more than three times greater than that in Canada (Nelson and Fleras 1995). Research has shown, however, that Canadian and American rates converge in the area of spousal assault, showing that "Canadian men are just as, if not more, likely to beat their spouses as American men" (DeKeseredy and Schwartz 1998:vii).

International comparisons aside, results from the Canadian National Survey on woman abuse on campus reveal that it is not only women in marital or cohabiting relationships who are in danger of abuse, but also those at post-secondary institutions who are in dating relationships (DeKeseredy and Schwartz 1998). Despite the fact that women attending post-secondary institutions in Canada are most likely to be sexually assaulted not only by men they know, but by men who might actually like them, and that the assault is most likely to take place in a private location, they fear "stranger danger" (DeKeseredy and Schwartz 1998). Table 7-4 illustrates the perception of safety of 1835 Canadian women students on campuses across the country.

Sociologists have several ways of measuring crime. Historically, they have relied on official statistics, but underreporting has always been a problem with such measures. Because members of racial and ethnic minority groups have not always trusted law enforcement agencies, they have often refrained from contacting the police. Feminist sociologists and others have noted that many women do not report sexual assault or spousal abuse out of fear that officials will regard the crime as their fault. Partly because of the deficiencies of official statistics, ***victimization surveys*** question ordinary people, not police officers, to learn how much crime occurs.

Unfortunately, like other crime data, victimization surveys have particular limitations. They require first that victims understand what has happened to them and also that victims disclose such information to interviewers. Fraud, income tax evasion, and blackmail are examples of crimes that are unlikely to be reported in victimization studies. Even though victimization surveys have their limitations, they can be helpful in augmenting police statistics. For example, both police statistics and victimization surveys report that, while the majority of offenders of violent crimes tend to be males, victims are equally likely to be male and female (Johnson 1996).

International Crime Rates

If it is difficult to develop reliable crime data in Canada, it is even more difficult to make useful cross-national

Taking Sociology to Work

HOLLY JOHNSON: Chief of Research, Canadian Centre for Justice Statistics Statistics Canada

Holly Johnson uses her background in criminology to improve conditions for women and children who are victims of violence. Johnson works as a senior researcher at the Canadian Centre for Justice Statistics, created in 1981 as a partnership between the federal, provincial, and territorial governments to collect and report information on crime and the administration of justice in Canada.

The primary focus of her work at Statistics Canada, her teaching at Queen's University (where she is a part-time sociology faculty member), and in her extensive writing and lecturing is domestic violence and other crimes of violence against women. Johnson is the author of *Dangerous Domains: Violence Against Women in Canada* published in 1996 and based on the first national survey on the topic for which she was the principal investigator.

Johnson is currently head of a unit designed to bridge the gap between statistics and their application to policy development in the justice community. "Our mandate is to pursue analytical projects that will help to more fully explore criminal justice data," she says. It is part of a larger initiative by Statistics Canada to expand its capacity to analyze data and to create links to researchers in the academic community. Her involvement extends to other countries such as Costa Rica, Paraguay, Australia, and the United States, and to international organizations through the auspices of the United Nations.

Initially, Johnson thought she would apply her background in criminology to a practitioner role. She did in fact spend a few years as a probation officer and then a correctional officer while completing her master's degree at the University of Ottawa. She quickly became fascinated with the research process and has maintained that focus throughout her 14-year career at Statistics Canada.

Since defending her PhD thesis at the University of Manchester, Johnson has undertaken innovative research that combines justice and non-justice statistics, using surveys such as the General Social Survey on Victimization and the National Longitudinal Survey on Children and Youth, as well as police statistics and statistical profiles of communities. "Our objective is to mine Statistics Canada data to enhance the policy process for criminal justice practitioners," says Johnson.

Let's Discuss

1. How might the research done by someone like Holly Johnson be of use in the day-to-day activities of those working as practitioners in the field of criminal justice?
2. If you were to study the subject of violence against women in Canada, what factors do you think would be key to the understanding of this social problem?

Table 7-4 Reported Feelings of Safety on Campus and Surrounding Areas of 1835 Canadian Women Post-Secondary Students

Activity	% reporting feeling unsafe	% reporting feeling very unsafe
Walking alone after dark	36.1	25.9
Riding a bus or streetcar alone after dark	35.7	12.9
Riding a subway alone after dark	34.8	38.7
Walking alone to a car in a parking lot after dark	42.5	25.7
Waiting for public transportation alone after dark	41.0	31.2
Walking past men they don't know while alone after dark	36.3	38.9

Source: DeKeseredy and Schwartz 1998:3; Kelly and DeKeseredy 1994.

comparisons. Nevertheless, with some care, we can offer preliminary conclusions about how crime rates differ around the world.

During the 1980s and 1990s, violent crimes were much more common in the United States than in Canada and western Europe. Murders, rapes, and robberies were reported to the police at much higher rates in the United States. Yet the incidence of certain other types of crime appears to be higher elsewhere. For example, England, Italy, Australia, and New Zealand all have higher rates of car theft than in the United States (Rotella 1999; Russell 1995).

Why are rates of violent crime so much higher in the United States? While there is no simple answer to this question, sociologist Elliot Currie (1985, 1998) has suggested that American society places greater emphasis on individual economic achievement than do other societies. At the same time, many observers have noted that the culture of the United States has long tolerated, if not condoned, many forms of violence. When coupled with sharp disparities between poor and affluent citizens, significant unemployment, and substantial alcohol and drug abuse, all these factors combine to produce a climate conducive to crime.

There are, however, disturbing increases in violent crime evident in other Western societies. For example, crime in Russia has skyrocketed since the overthrow of Communist party rule (with its strict controls on guns and criminals) in 1991. Whereas there were fewer than 260 homicides in Moscow in 1978 and again in 1988, there are now more than 1000 homicides per year. Organized crime has filled a power vacuum in Moscow since the end of communism; one result is that gangland shootouts and premeditated "contract hits" have become more common. Some prominent reformist politicians have been targeted as well. Russia is the only nation in the world that incarcerates a higher proportion of its citizens than the United States. Russia imprisons 580 per 100 000 of its adults on a typical day compared to 550 in the United States, 150 in Canada, fewer than 100 in Mexico or Britain, and only 16 in Greece (Currie 1998; Shinkai and Zvekic 1999).

SOCIAL POLICY AND SOCIAL CONTROL

Illicit Drug Use in Canada and Worldwide

The Issue

Vancouver spends more money per capita in dealing with illicit drugs than any other city in Canada (Bula 2000). The Mayor of Vancouver, Philip Owen, claims that although Vancouver's drug problem is so well-known, and has been highlighted in many media reports, this does not mean that other big cities are not struggling with the same concerns. Owen states: "Everyone has a drug problem, all the big-city mayors have talked about this. Every single one is looking for solutions. But nobody is prepared to stand up to the plate" (Bula 2000). In response to this problem, Vancouver authorities have devised a drug strategy and harm-reduction plan. According to the mayor, this is an "international crisis," and cities such as Yokohama, Japan, and Seattle, Washington, have asked for a copy of Vancouver's drug strategy (Bula 2000).

The Setting

National surveys have shown that in Canada, people living in British Columbia were most likely to report the personal use of illicit substances (Nelson and Fleras 1995). The drug "problem" is particularly apparent in Vancouver's Downtown Eastside, an area that is the poorest in all of Canada, and that houses some of the most severe social, economic, and health problems in the country. The death rate in the area is high due to the growing incidence of hepatitis C and HIV, acquired through intravenous-injection drug use. Activities such as youth prostitution and panhandling become the means through which addicts can sustain their addiction.

Sociological Insights

Functionalists view alienation and anomie to be the cause of many forms of addiction, including alcohol and drug addiction (Nelson and Fleras 1995). The activities of addicts, according to functionalist theorists, have functional consequences for society. For example, they demonstrate the boundaries of so-called "rule-breaking behaviour" and they create social agreement and cohesion regarding unacceptable behaviours.

Conflict theorists, in contrast, ask the questions "Who benefits?" and "Why is it that some drug users receive the label 'addict,' while other users do not?" Conflict thinkers argue that the state and its various agencies, such as prisons, police, and rehabilitation programs, serve to benefit from such labels because they create employment for correction officers, police officers, social workers, and counsellors. They also address the reasons why society does not label those addicted to prescription drugs and "legal" drugs such as tobacco, in the same manner as it labels and scapegoats those addicted to drugs such as cocaine and heroin.

Feminist approaches to addiction are as diverse as feminist theories themselves. Some argue that for women, addiction grows out of their overall status of subordination in society; that is, that women's powerlessness leads to various forms of self-destructive escapes such as drug use (Lundy 1991). Other feminist theories argue that the concept of gender and the various related roles and behaviours deny both men and women full expression of their own humanity; addiction becomes a metaphor for the gender stereotypes in our society (Nelson and Fleras 1995).

Interactionist approaches frame drug addiction in the context of continuous action on the part of the drug addict, and reaction on the part of those around her or him. They stress the process through which the person is identified as an "addict" and the impact that this label has on her or his sense of self. Goffman's dramaturgical approach is an example of this process of individual action and social reaction, in which the individual plays many roles, as would an actor. The drug addict, for example, may play one role in dealing with the police (for example, presenting himself or herself as someone trying to get "clean") while presenting a different image to peers.

Policy Initiatives

Vancouver's drug strategy and harm-reduction plan is the first of its kind in North America. It shifts the focus away from drug use as a criminal activity towards drug use as a health and safety issue; under the plan, users would receive treatment rather than jail terms and special treatment beds would be allocated to young users.

The drug strategy and harm-reduction plan, similar to those implemented in many European cities, is based on a four-pillar approach. The four pillars are:

1. Enforcement. This pillar includes a pilot drug-treatment court that would weigh various options of treatment, an increase in the police drug and organized-crime squads to target larger dealers, and the creation of a "drug action team" that would respond to neighbourhood drug issues.
2. Harm reduction. This notion encompasses the creation of an overdose-death prevention campaign, the provision of short-term shelter and housing for drug users on the street, and the establishment of street-drug testing.
3. Treatment. The treatment element of the plan would provide treatment beds for young people outside the downtown eastside; special treatment for women who are pregnant and/or have children; needle exchanges in primary health-care clinics, hospitals and pharmacies; pilot day centres for addicts; and different kinds of housing for users and those trying to go clean.
4. Prevention. This pillar of the plan would give communities and neighbourhoods more power to combat drug abuse and to develop a pilot citywide school curriculum on drugs and drug abuse.

Let's Discuss

1. Which do you think poses the greatest risk to society—illegal drugs, such as heroin and cocaine, or legal drugs such as alcohol and tobacco?
2. Why have certain drugs, and the individuals who use them, been treated so differently?
3. Should drug addiction be treated as a health issue or a criminal issue? Why or why not?

Chapter Resources

Summary

Conformity and deviance are two ways in which people respond to real or imagined pressures from others. In this chapter, we examine the relationship between conformity, deviance, and mechanisms of social control.

1. A society uses ***social control*** to bring about acceptance of basic norms.
2. Stanley Milgram defined ***conformity*** as going along with one's peers; ***obedience*** is defined as compliance with higher authorities in a hierarchical structure.
3. Some norms are so important to a society they are formalized into ***laws.*** Socialization is a primary source of conforming and obedient behaviour, including obedience to law.
4. Deviant behaviour violates social norms. Some forms of deviance carry a negative social ***stigma,*** while other forms are more or less accepted.
5. From a functionalist point of view, ***deviance*** and its consequences help to define the limits of proper behaviour.
6. Interactionists maintain that we *learn* criminal behaviour from interactions with others (***cultural transmission***). They also stress that for crime to occur, there has to be a convergence of motivated

offenders and suitable targets of crime (***routine activities theory***).

7. The theory of ***differential association*** holds that deviance results from exposure to attitudes favourable to criminal acts.
8. An important aspect of ***labelling theory*** is the recognition that some people are *viewed* as deviant while others engaged in the same behaviour are not.
9. The conflict perspective views laws and punishments as reflecting the interests of the powerful.
10. ***Crime*** represents a deviation from formal social norms administered by the state.
11. Sociologists differentiate among professional crime, organized crime, white-collar crime, and victimless crimes (such as drug use and prostitution).
12. Crime statistics are among the least reliable social data, partly because so many crimes are not reported to law enforcement agencies.
13. Harm-reduction plans shift the focus away from drug use as a criminal activity towards drug use as a health and safety issue.

Critical Thinking Questions

1. What mechanisms of formal and informal social control are evident in your university or college classes and in day-to-day life and social interactions at your school?
2. What approach to deviance do you find most persuasive: that of functionalists, conflict theorists, interactionists, labelling theorists, or feminist theorists? Why is this approach more convincing than the others? What are the main weaknesses of each approach?
3. Rates of violent crime in the United States are higher than in Canada, western Europe, Australia, or New Zealand. Draw on as many of the theories discussed in the chapter as possible to explain why the United States is such a comparably violent society.

Key Terms

Anomie theory of deviance Robert Merton's theory that explains deviance as an adaptation either of socially prescribed goals or of the norms governing their attainment, or both. (page 157)

Conformity Going along with one's peers, individuals of a person's own status who have no special right to direct that person's behaviour. (148)

Control theory A view of conformity and deviance that suggests that our connection to members of society leads us to systematically conform to society's norms. (152)

Crime A violation of criminal law for which some governmental authority applies formal penalties. (162)

Cultural transmission A school of criminology that argues that criminal behaviour is learned through social interactions. (158)

Deviance Behaviour that violates the standards of conduct or expectations of a group or society. (152)

Differential association A theory of deviance proposed by Edwin Sutherland that holds that violation of rules results from exposure to attitudes favourable to criminal acts. (159)

Formal social control Social control carried out by authorized agents, such as police officers, judges, school administrators, and employers. (150)

Informal social control Social control carried out casually by ordinary people through such means as laughter, smiles, and ridicule. (150)

Labelling theory An approach to deviance that attempts to explain why certain people are viewed as deviants while others engaging in the same behaviour are not. (160)

Obedience Compliance with higher authorities in a hierarchical structure. (148)

Organized crime The work of a group that regulates relations between various criminal enterprises involved in the smuggling and sale of drugs, prostitution, gambling, and other illegal activities. (163)

Professional criminal A person who pursues crime as a day-to-day occupation, developing skilled techniques and enjoying a certain degree of status among other criminals. (162)

Routine activities theory The notion that criminal victimization increases when there is a convergence of motivated offenders and suitable targets. (159)

Social constructionist perspective An approach to deviance that emphasizes the role of culture in the creation of the deviant identity. (161)

Social control The techniques and strategies for preventing deviant human behaviour in any society. (147)

Societal-reaction approach Another name for *labelling theory*. (160)

Stigma A label used to devalue members of deviant social groups. (154)

Victimization surveys Questionnaires or interviews used to determine whether people have been victims of crime. (165)

Victimless crime A term used by sociologists to describe the willing exchange among adults of widely desired, but illegal, goods and services. (164)

White-collar crime Crimes committed by affluent individuals or corporations in the course of their daily business activities. (163)

Additional Readings

Boritch, Helen. 1997. *Fallen Woman: Female Crime and Criminal Justice in Canada.* Toronto: ITP Nelson. A comprehensive account and interpretation of rates of female crime in Canada, and the treatment of female crime in the criminal justice system.

DeKeseredy, Walter S., and Martin D. Schwartz. 1998. *Women Abuse on Campus: Results from the Canadian National Survey.* Thousand Oaks: Sage Publications. This volume provides the results of a national survey on the abuse of women on Canadian post-secondary campuses. The authors expose a "hidden campus curriculum" that contributes to the perpetuation of gender inequality.

Finkenauer, James O., and Patricia W. Gavin. 1999. *Scared Straight: The Panacea Phenomenon Revisited.* Prospect Heights, IL: Waveland Press. A critical look at programs in which prisoners speak to juveniles in an effort to scare them away from crime. Drawing on data from both the United States and Norway, the authors find such programs have had little success, but remain immensely popular with the general public.

Gamson, Joshua. 1998. *Freaks Talk Back: Tabloid Talk Shows and Sexual Nonconformity.* Chicago: University of Chicago Press. A sociologist looks at the presentation of socially dysfunctional or stigmatized behaviours on television talk shows.

Internet Connection

www.mcgrawhill.ca/college/schaefer

For additional Internet exercises relating to the sociological study of deviance, visit the Schaefer Online Learning Centre at ***http://www.mcgrawhill.ca/college/schaefer****. Please note that while the URLs listed were current at the time of printing, these sites often change—check the Online Learning Centre for updates.*

This chapter introduces us to many different types of crimes and theories, all geared toward bringing about a greater understanding of deviant behaviour. Take a virtual field trip to Dark Horse Multimedia, Inc.'s The Crime Library™ (**http://www. crimelibrary. com**). Choose one criminal listed on the site and read the online biography and view any pictures provided.

(a) Which person did you choose? Why did you choose that person?

(b) What crimes did the person allegedly commit? Can this person's deviant behaviour serve as an example of any of the "Types of Crimes" found in your text? If so, how?

(c) What social and historical forces played a part in the person's behaviour or decisions?

(d) What fact that you learned about this person surprised you the most? Why?

(e) Which of the theories presented in the text do you think would be most useful for gaining an understanding of the person's behaviour? Why that theory?

(f) According to Merton's theory presented in your text, which "Mode(s) of Individual Adaptation" would the criminal you read about be considered an example of? Why?

(g) What informal and formal social controls were used with this person?

CHAPTER

8 STRATIFICATION IN CANADA AND WORLDWIDE

This poster advertising "Asian Week" at McDonald's in Germany attests to the global reach of multinational corporations today. But while the world is shrinking through aspects of globalization like this, there is still a huge gap between rich and poor nations and between rich and poor citizens within nations.

Income per person, averaged globally, currently rises by about 0.8 percent per year, but in more than one hundred countries in the last fifteen years income has actually dropped. Some 1.3 billion people—about 30 percent of the population of the developing world—remain in absolute poverty, living on less than a dollar a day. And the gulf between the poorest and the wealthiest people on the planet is widening very fast. In 1960, the income of the richest 20 percent of the world's population was thirty times that of the poorest 20 percent; in 1998, it was eighty-two times greater. The combined wealth of the world's richest 225 people (a total of $1 trillion) exceeds the annual income of the poorest 47 percent of the planet's population, about 2.5 billion people. Indeed, the assets of the world's three richest individuals or families—Microsoft's Bill Gates, the Walton family of Wal-Mart stores, and the renowned investor Warren Buffett—are now greater than the combined GDPs of the forty-eight poorest countries. Meanwhile, as the rich get richer in the developed countries, average household consumption in Africa has plummeted 20 percent over the last twenty-five years. In India, an estimated 60 percent of all newborns are in such poor condition from malnutrition, low birth weight, and other causes that they would be immediately placed in intensive care were they born in California. Never in human history have we seen such differentials between rich and poor.

. . . [A]bout half the people on the planet—some three billion, all told—rely on agriculture for their main income, and of that perhaps one billion of these agriculturalists are mainly subsistence farmers, which means they survive by eating what they grow. Over 40 percent of people on the planet—about 2.4 billion—use fuelwood, charcoal, straw, or cow dung as their main source of energy; 50 to 60 percent rely on these biomass fuels for at least some of their primary energy needs. Over 1.2 billion people lack access to clean drinking water; many are forced to walk kilometres to get what water they can find. And about a billion people depend directly on fishing for a large proportion of their animal protein.

These people live mainly in Asia, Africa, and Latin America. They depend on local natural resources for their day-to-day survival, and they have little access to the vast technical ingenuity so abundant in the rich countries of North America, Europe, and East Asia. Deforestation, polluted water, depleted fisheries and eroded cropland harshly affect their lives in countless immediate and intimate ways, and natural resources will remain critically important to their well-being for decades to come. Yet many of us manage to ignore the contradiction these people present to our rosy world-view, because we rarely see them or go to the places where they live. *(Homer-Dixon 2000:32–36)* ■

Students protesting sweatshop labour in developing countries mock Nike with its own slogan: "Just do it."

Thomas Homer-Dixon is Director of the Peace and Conflict Studies Program at the University of Toronto. In part, the focus of his recent book, *The Ingenuity Gap,* is on the technical disparities that implicitly segregate some parts of the planet from others. Specifically, Homer-Dixon points to the primitive mechanisms on which most of the world's population depends as evidence of the failure of modern systems to distribute the benefits of the technological revolution. However, even in those areas where the economics of the developed world have begun to make inroads, benefits to the local people are minimal. In their 1998 book, *Nike Culture,* sociologists Robert Goldman and Stephen Papson examine the global stratification that Nike, and companies like it, help to perpetuate. People can pay hundreds of dollars for a pair of celebrity-endorsed sports shoes, yet the workers who manufacture them are rewarded with pennies. Critics of Nike's practices have claimed that in 1996, the 45 Indonesian workers who participated in the making of a pair of Air Pegasus shoes shared a total of $2.56. This exploitation is not the only complaint raised by international human rights groups. Charges of physical harassment and dangerous conditions have also helped to fuel concern about human rights violations in these Third World production facilities.

Craig Kielburger, a teenager from Ontario, has been fighting the global battle against child labour since he was 12. In 1995, Craig, with the support of his family, flew to Asia, alone. There he visited factories and saw firsthand the frightening conditions in which children younger than he laboured on products for multinational corporations. When he returned home, Craig committed himself to the cause and helped to found Free the Children, an international movement against child labour. Meetings with leaders such as the Pope, Nelson Mandela, and Mother Theresa have given Craig a high profile that has caught many corporations' attention. In 1998, Nike announced that it would no longer buy products from suppliers who hired anyone under the age of 16.

Nike, however, is not their only target. Many apparel manufacturers contract out their production to take advantage of cheap labour and overhead costs. Other initiatives have also arisen to protest the exploitation of children in the Third World. A campus-based movement—ranging from sit-ins and "knit-ins" to demonstrations and building occupation—has been aimed at ridding campus stores of all products made in sweatshops, both at home and abroad. Pressed by their students, many colleges and universities have agreed to adopt anti-sweatshop codes governing the products they make and stock on campus. And Nike and Reebok, partly in response to student protests, have raised the wages of some 100 000 workers in their Indonesian factories (to about 20 cents an hour—still far below what is needed to raise a family) (Appelbaum and Dreier 1999; Bonacich and Appelbaum 2000).

The global corporate and technological culture focuses our attention on worldwide stratification, as seen in the enormous gap between those enjoying the advantages and those excluded from them and condemned to live in destitution. Ever since people first began to speculate about the nature of human society, their attention has been drawn to the differences between socioeconomic groups within any society. The term ***social inequality*** describes a condition in which members of a society have different amounts of wealth, prestige, or power. Some degree of social inequality characterizes every society.

When a system of social inequality is based on a hierarchy of groups, sociologists refer to it as ***stratification:*** a structured ranking of entire groups of people that perpetuates an unequal and stable distribution of economic rewards and power in a society. These unequal rewards are evident not only in the distribution of wealth and income, but even in the distressing mortality rates of impoverished communities. Stratification involves the ways in which society's systems perpetuate social inequalities, thereby producing groups of people arranged in rank order from low to high. By contrast, Canada's socioeconomic inequities are claimed to be a product of individual qualities and effort. The term ***meritocracy*** refers to a system in which individuals earn their place in society, based on their individual merit. There is some debate about whether capitalist countries such as Canada and the United States are true meritocracies. Evidence suggests that there are significant advantages to being born into a wealthy Canadian family.

Stratification is a crucial subject of sociological investigation because of its pervasive influence on human interactions and institutions. It inevitably results in social inequality because certain groups of people stand higher in social rankings, control scarce resources, wield power, and receive special treatment. As we will see, the consequences of stratification show up in the unequal distribution of wealth and income within and among societies. The term ***income*** refers to salaries, wages, and monies brought in by investments. By contrast, ***wealth*** is an inclusive term encompassing all of a person's material assets, including land, stocks, and other types of property. ***Net worth*** is the amount by which the value of someone's assets exceeds his or her debts.

In this chapter we will first examine three general systems of stratification. We will pay particular attention to Karl Marx's theories of class and to Max Weber's analysis of the components of stratification. The feminist perspective will provide a glimpse into gender-based stratification both in Canada and globally. We will also consider and compare functionalist and conflict theorists' explanations for the existence of stratification.

We will then look at how sociologists measure social class. We will examine the consequences of stratification in terms of wealth and income, health, and life chances. Next, we will take a look at social mobility, the movement of individuals up and down social hierarchies.

This chapter also focuses on who controls the world marketplace. The impact of colonialism and neocolonialism on social inequality will be studied, as will world systems analysis, the immense power of multinational corporations, and the consequences of modernization. After this macro-level examination of the disparity between rich and poor countries, we will focus on stratification *within* the nations of the world. Finally, in the social policy section, we will address the issue of welfare reform in North America and Europe. ■

Understanding Stratification

Systems of Stratification

Look at the three general systems of stratification examined here—slavery, castes, and social classes—as ideal types useful for purposes of analysis. Recall that an *ideal type*, as defined by Weber, is the pure form of a social concept, not necessarily one that has been experienced in the real world. Any stratification system may include elements of more than one type. For example, both before and after Upper Canada passed the Act Against Slavery of 1793, institutionalized discrimination could be found in Canada alongside the existing socioeconomic class divisions.

pp. 10, 130

To understand these systems better, it may be helpful to review the distinction between *achieved status* and *ascribed status*. *Ascribed status* is a social position "assigned" to a person without regard for that person's unique characteristics or talents. By contrast, *achieved status* is a social position attained by a person largely through his or her own effort. The two are closely linked. Canada's most affluent families generally inherit wealth and status, while many members of racial and ethnic minorities inherit disadvantaged status. Age and gender, as well, are ascribed statuses that influence a person's wealth and social position.

pp. 101–102

Slavery

The most extreme form of legalized social inequality for individuals or groups is ***slavery***. What distinguishes this oppressive system of stratification is that enslaved individuals are *owned* by other people who treat these human beings as property, just as if they were household pets or appliances.

Slavery, an ascribed status, has varied in the way it has been practised. In ancient Greece, the main source of

Jacob Lawrence's painting, *Harriet Tubman* Series No. 9, graphically illustrates the torment of slavery as once practised in the United States. Slavery is the most extreme form of legalized social inequality.

slaves consisted of captives of war and piracy. Although succeeding generations could inherit slave status, it was not necessarily permanent. A person's status might change depending on which city-state happened to triumph in a military conflict. In effect, all citizens had the potential to become slaves or to be granted freedom, depending on the circumstances of history.

By contrast, even the 1793 Upper Canada Act Against Slavery failed to liberate those Canadian blacks who were already owned by white masters. According to the act, freedom was afforded to slaves in the way that caused the least inconvenience possible for the existing owners. Those who were slaves at the time of the enactment remained the slaves—they were still the property of their masters. Children born to slaves after the act had passed would only become free once they reached the age of 25. On the more positive side, the act prohibited new slaves from being brought in to the province. In addition, slaves who reached the province on their own initiative after enactment in 1793 were to be considered free people.

Castes

Castes are hereditary systems of rank, usually religiously dictated, that tend to be fixed and immobile. The caste system is generally associated with Hinduism in India and other countries. In India there are four major castes, called *varnas.* A fifth category of outcastes, referred to as *untouchables,* is considered to be so lowly and unclean as to have no place within this system of stratification. There are also many minor castes. Caste membership is an ascribed status (at birth, children automatically assume the same position as their parents). Each caste is quite sharply defined, and members are expected to marry within that caste.

Caste membership generally determines one's occupation or role as a religious functionary. An example of a lower caste in India is the *Dons,* whose main work is the undesirable job of cremating bodies. The caste system promotes a remarkable degree of differentiation. Thus, the single caste of chauffeurs has been split into two separate subcastes: drivers of luxury cars have a higher status than drivers of economy cars.

In recent decades, industrialization, urbanization, and increased participation in the global community have led to changes in India's traditionally rigid caste system. Many villagers have moved to urban areas where their low-caste status is unknown. Schools, hospitals, factories, and public transportation facilitate contacts between different castes that were previously avoided at all costs. In addition, the government has tried to reform the caste system. India's constitution, adopted in 1950, includes a provision abolishing discrimination against untouchables. Even though the castes endure in some aspects of Indian life, change seems inevitable. This is perhaps most visible in the political arena, where various political parties compete for the support of frustrated untouchable voters, who constitute one third of India's electorate. For the first time India has someone from an untouchable background serving in the symbolic but high-status position of president. Meanwhile, however, dozens of low-caste people continue to be killed for overstepping their lowly status in life (C. Dugger 1999; U. Schmetzer 1999).

Social Classes

A ***class system*** is a social ranking based primarily on economic position in which achieved characteristics can influence social mobility. In contrast to slavery and caste systems, the boundaries between classes are imprecisely defined, and one can move from one stratum, or level, of society to another. Yet, class systems maintain stable stratification hierarchies and patterns of class divisions, and they too are marked by unequal distribution of wealth and power.

Income inequality is a basic characteristic of a class system. In 2000, the median family income in Canada was

$51 000. In other words, half of all households had incomes higher than this and half had lower. In the previous year, the average (mean) income of a Canadian family was $68 347. The discrepancy between these numbers is a function of the fact that some Canadians made significantly more than the median, thus pulling up the overall average. Figure 8-1 shows the salaries made by CEOs (chief executive officers) in Canada and around the world in 1998. The existence of social classes in this country is emphasised by the fact that these administrators made ten times the median income of the average Canadian worker. When we compare these CEO's salaries with the income of someone earning the country's highest minimum wage, the gap is staggering.

In Canada, social class is studied by comparing *income quintiles.* Earners are separated into five groups (quintiles), each representing 20 percent of the population. While there is no official recognition of these categories as classes, there is little doubt of the implications associated with them, particularly as they apply to the upper and lower quintiles. In 2000, for instance, the 20 percent of Canadians at the bottom of the income scale took home just 5.2 percent of all the income earned in the country. By comparison, the top 20 percent of earners claimed 43.6 percent of the total. In real dollars, those at the top took home on average more than six times more than those at the bottom (Statistics Canada, 2003d).

An important part of any claim of stratification is establishing the institutionalized nature of the social inequalities. While income is certainly a marker of inequality, in a meritocracy such as Canada, the argument can be made that everyone has equal access to opportunities and that differences in income and wealth reflect an individual's effort and talents, and are therefore justified. We have accepted, to some degree, that disparity of income is a predictable and acceptable cost associated with our free market economy. However, the differences found in market income are mirrored in another area where that argument is less convincing. This area is government transfers, the money that Ottawa or the provinces give back to Canadian taxpayers. During the same year when top Canadian earners were enjoying six times the income of those at the other

FIGURE 8-1

Around the World: What's a CEO Worth?

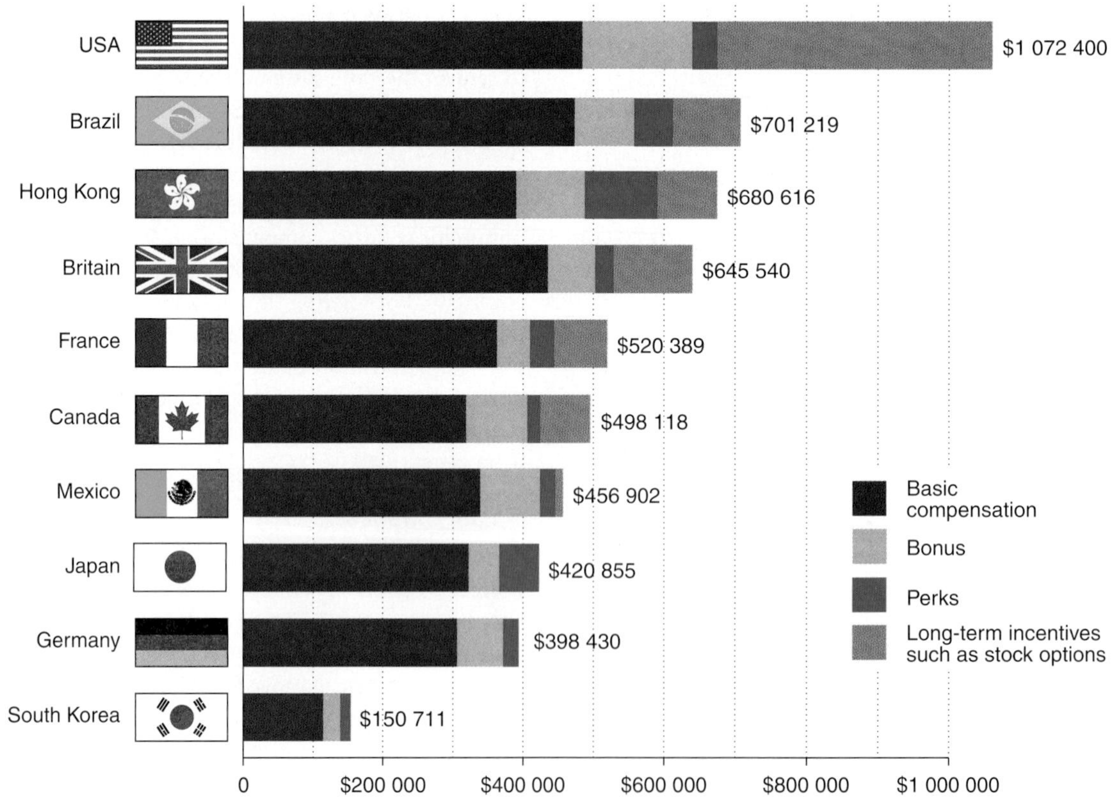

Note: The average annual pay package of the chief executive officer (CEO) of an industrial company with annual revenues of $250 million to $500 million in 10 countries. Figures are from April 1998 and are not weighted to compensate for different costs of living or levels of taxation.

Source: Towers Perrin in A. Bryant 1999:Section 4, p. 1.

end of the income scale, they were also receiving monies from government at the same disproportionate rate. The numbers indicate that the top group was given 39.2 percent of all government transfers, while the bottom quintile received just 6.2 percent of the pie. While not conclusive evidence that Canada is a stratified society, these numbers do suggest that the unequal distribution of income is not entirely linked to achievement.

Social class is one of the independent or explanatory variables most frequently used by social scientists to shed light on social issues. In later chapters, we will analyze the relationships between social class and divorce patterns (Chapter 11), religious behaviour (Chapter 12), and formal schooling (Chapter 12), as well as other relationships in which social class is a variable.

Perspectives on Stratification

Sociologists have engaged in heated debates and reached varying conclusions about stratification and social inequality. No theorist stressed the significance of class for society—and for social change—more strongly than Karl Marx. Marx viewed class differentiation as the crucial determinant of social, economic, and political inequality. By contrast, Max Weber questioned Marx's emphasis on the overriding importance of the economic sector and argued that stratification should be viewed as having many dimensions.

Karl Marx's View of Class Differentiation

Sociologist Leonard Beeghley (1978:1) aptly noted that "Karl Marx was both a revolutionary and a social scientist." Marx was concerned with stratification in all types of human societies, beginning with primitive agricultural tribes and continuing into feudalism. But his main focus was on the effects of economic inequality on all aspects of 19th-century Europe. The plight of the working class made him feel that it was imperative to strive for changes in the class structure of society.

In Marx's view, social relations during any period of history depend on who controls the primary mode of economic production, such as land or factories. Using this type of analysis, Marx examined social relations within ***capitalism***—an economic system in which the means of production are largely in private hands and the main incentive for economic activity is the accumulation of profits (Rosenberg 1991). Marx focused on two classes—the bourgeoisie and the proletariat. The ***bourgeoisie,*** or capitalist class, owns the means of production, such as factories and machinery, while the ***proletariat*** is the working class. In capitalist societies, the members of the bourgeoisie maximize profit in competition with other firms. In the process, they exploit workers, who must exchange their labour for subsistence wages.

According to Marx, exploitation of the proletariat will inevitably lead to the destruction of the capitalist system because the workers will revolt. But, first, the working class must develop ***class consciousness***—a subjective awareness of common vested interests and the need for collective political action to bring about social change. Workers must often overcome what Marx termed ***false consciousness,*** or an attitude held by members of a class that does not accurately reflect its objective position. A worker with false consciousness may adopt an individualistic viewpoint toward capitalist exploitation ("*I* am being exploited by *my* boss"). By contrast, the class-conscious worker realizes that *all* workers are being exploited by the bourgeoisie and have a common stake in revolution (Vanneman and Cannon 1987).

Ultimately, the proletariat will overthrow the rule of the bourgeoisie and the government (which Marx saw as representing the interests of capitalists) and will eliminate private ownership of the means of production. In his rather utopian view, classes and oppression will cease to exist in the postrevolutionary workers' state.

How accurate were Marx's predictions? He failed to anticipate the emergence of labour unions, whose power in collective bargaining weakens the stranglehold that capitalists maintain over workers. Moreover, as contemporary conflict theorists note, he did not foresee the extent to which political liberties and relative prosperity could contribute to "false consciousness." Still, the Marxist approach to the study of class is useful in stressing the importance of stratification as a determinant of social behaviour and the fundamental separation in many societies between two distinct groups, the rich and the poor.

Max Weber's View of Stratification

Unlike Karl Marx, Max Weber insisted that no single characteristic (such as class) totally defines a person's position within the stratification system. Instead, writing in 1916, he identified three analytically distinct components of stratification: class, status, and power (Gerth and Mills 1958).

Weber used the term ***class*** to refer to people who have a similar level of wealth and income, for example, Canadian workers who try to support their families through jobs that pay the minimum wage. According to Weber's definition, these wage earners constitute a class because they have the same economic position and fate. While Weber agreed with Marx on the importance of the economic dimension of stratification, he argued that the actions of individuals and groups could not be understood *solely* in economic terms.

Weber used the term ***status group*** to refer to people who rank the same in prestige or lifestyle. An individual gains status through membership in a desirable group, such as the medical profession. But status is not the same

How would it feel to be a member of the Supreme Court of Canada? Do you think that all Canadians have equal access to this building?

as economic class standing. In our culture, a successful pickpocket may be in the same income class as a university professor, yet the thief is widely regarded as a member of a low-status group, while the professor holds high status.

For Weber, the third major component of stratification reflects a political dimension. ***Power*** is the ability to exercise one's will over others. In Canada, power stems from membership in particularly influential groups, such as corporate boards of directors, government bodies, and advocacy groups. Conflict theorists generally agree that two major sources of power—big business and government—are closely interrelated (see Chapter 13).

In Weber's view, then, each of us has not one rank in society but three. Our position in a stratification system reflects some combination of class, status, and power. The notion of ***status consistency*** refers to the fact that when someone has a high ranking in one area, he or she tends to be similarly placed in the others.

Pierre Trudeau, one of Canada's most beloved prime ministers, came from a privileged background; his family was part of Montreal's monied elite. He was the son of a wealthy, French-Canadian businessman, a position in life that afforded him the best of opportunities, including an education at the esteemed London School of Economics. His class, status, and power, therefore, were all very high.

Of course, these ranks can be inconsistent, too. Wayne Gretsky belongs to an enviable class in terms of income, prestige, and occupation. However, Canada's most famous athlete has little educational status and comes from a working-class family. John Diefenbaker, Canada's prime minister from 1957 to 1963, achieved a high position of power, despite coming from modest roots and living most of his early life in the rural communities of Saskatchewan and the Northwest Territories.

A widely published poet may achieve high status while earning a relatively modest income. Successful professional athletes have little power but enjoy a relatively high position in terms of class and status. To understand the workings of a culture more fully, sociologists must carefully evaluate the ways in which it distributes its most valued rewards, including wealth and income, status, and power (Duberman 1976; Gerth and Mills 1958).

Feminist Views of Stratification

Some feminist perspectives incorporate the ideas of both Marx and Weber and add critical examinations of the impact of patriarchal structure when analyzing stratification. In general, as outlined in earlier chapters, feminist theory examines the place of women in a society, relative to men. Historically, Canadian women have been disadvantaged. Regardless of the indicator used—class, status, or power—women have endured an inferior position within our social structure.

When we look at income levels as the indicator of class, the figures reveal that even after more than 30 years of proactive feminism, Canadian women continue to struggle at wage levels below those earned by men. Almost three quarters of the female wage earners in Canada are concentrated in a few female-dominated sectors in which earnings continue to be low. In addition, the persistence of traditional distribution of household responsibilities has a detrimental effect on workforce participation. According to author Katherine Marshall, Canadian women in homes with two full-time workers are expected to carry the full load of daily housework. In 28 percent of those homes, women are the ones mainly responsibly for chores (Marshall 1999:26).

The status of women in Canada is a reflection of their struggle to gain equality in the workplace. Ghettoization in low-paying, female-dominated sectors and a continuing expectation that women will shoulder most of the non-paid work in the home have served to limit their ability to advance in their careers and along other status-enhancing paths.

The underrepresentation of women in positions of power remains a problem. While Canadians do have females in political and corporate positions of power, their numbers do not come close to matching women's 51 percent of the total population.

The issue for feminist theorists in each of these areas is the degree to which the current state of affairs is attributable to structural influences. In other words, given that women are inherently as capable as men, their second-class position in our society must be explained by external, or structural factors. If women's social position is defined by institutional and cultural influences, then the argument can be made that Canada is a stratified society—stratified by gender. As the statistics show, women of colour are at an even lower position in the Canadian hierarchy. This is evidence of stratification along another dimension.

Is Stratification Universal?

Must some members of society receive greater rewards than others? Do people need to feel socially and economically superior to others? Can social life be organized without structured inequality? These questions have been debated for centuries, especially among political activists. Utopian socialists, religious minorities, and members of recent countercultures have all attempted to establish communities that, to some extent or other, would abolish inequality in social relationships.

Social science research has found that inequality exists in all societies—even the simplest. For example, when anthropologist Gunnar Landtman (1968, original edition 1938) studied the Kiwai Papuans of New Guinea, he initially noticed little differentiation among them. Every man in the village did the same work and lived in similar housing. However, on closer inspection, Landtman observed that certain Papuans—the men who were warriors, harpooners, and sorcerers—were described as "a little more high" than others. By contrast, villagers who were female, unemployed, or unmarried were considered "down a little bit" and were barred from owning land.

Stratification is universal in that all societies maintain some form of differentiation among members. Depending on its values, a society may assign people to distinctive ranks based on their religious knowledge, skill in hunting, beauty, trading expertise, or ability to provide health care. But why has such inequality developed in human societies? And how much differentiation among people, if any, is actually essential?

Functionalist and conflict sociologists offer contrasting explanations for the existence and necessity of social stratification. Functionalists maintain that a differential system of rewards and punishments is necessary for the efficient operation of society. Conflict theorists argue that competition for scarce resources results in significant political, economic, and social inequality.

Functionalist View

Would people go to school for many years to become physicians if they could make as much money and gain as much respect working as street cleaners? Functionalists say no, which is partly why they believe that a stratified society is universal.

In the view of Kingsley Davis and Wilbert Moore (1945), society must distribute its members among a variety of social positions. It must not only make sure that these positions are filled but also see that they are staffed by people with the appropriate talents and abilities. Rewards, including money and prestige, are based on the importance of a position and the relative scarcity of qualified personnel. Yet this assessment often devalues work performed by certain segments of society, such as women's work as homemakers or occupations traditionally filled by women or low-status work in fast-food outlets.

Davis and Moore argue that stratification is universal and that social inequality is necessary so that people will be motivated to fill functionally important positions. But, critics say, unequal rewards are not the only means of encouraging people to fill critical positions and occupations. Personal pleasure, intrinsic satisfaction, and value orientations also motivate people to enter particular careers. Functionalists agree but note that society must use some type of reward to motivate people to enter unpleasant or dangerous jobs and jobs that require a long training period. This response does not justify stratification systems in which status is largely inherited, such as slave or caste societies. Similarly, it is difficult to explain the high salaries our society offers to professional athletes or entertainers on the basis of how critical these jobs are to the survival of society (R. Collins 1975; Kerbo 2000; Tumin 1953, 1985).

Even if stratification is inevitable, the functionalist explanation for differential rewards does not explain the wide disparity between the rich and the poor. Critics of the functionalist approach point out that the richest 10 percent of households account for 20 percent of the nation's income in Sweden, 25 percent in France, and 30.5 percent in Canada. In their view, the level of income inequality found in contemporary industrial societies cannot be defended—even though these societies have a legitimate need to fill certain key occupations (World Bank 2000a:238–239).

Conflict View

The writings of Karl Marx are at the heart of conflict theory (although the writings of feminist scholars have done much to advance it in recent years). p. 10
Marx viewed history as a continuous struggle between the oppressors and the oppressed that would ultimately culminate in an egalitarian, classless society. In terms of

stratification, he argued that the dominant class under capitalism—the bourgeoisie—manipulated the economic and political systems in order to maintain control over the exploited proletariat. Marx did not believe that stratification was inevitable, but he did see inequality and oppression as inherent in capitalism (E. Wright et al. 1982).

Like Marx, contemporary conflict theorists believe that human beings are prone to conflict over such scarce resources as wealth, status, and power. However, where Marx focused primarily on class conflict, more recent theorists have extended this analysis to include conflicts based on gender, race, age, and other dimensions. British sociologist Ralf Dahrendorf is one of the most influential contributors to the conflict approach.

Dahrendorf (1959) modified Marx's analysis of capitalist society to apply to *modern* capitalist societies. For Dahrendorf, social classes are groups of people who share common interests resulting from their authority relationships. In identifying the most powerful groups in society, he includes not only the bourgeoisie—the owners of the means of production—but also the managers of industry, legislators, the judiciary, heads of the government bureaucracy, and others. In that respect, Dahrendorf has merged Marx's emphasis on class conflict with Weber's recognition that power is an important element of stratification (Cuff et al. 1990).

Conflict theorists, including Dahrendorf, contend that the powerful of today, like the bourgeoisie of Marx's time, want society to run smoothly so that they can enjoy their privileged positions. Because the status quo suits those with wealth, status, and power, they have a clear interest in preventing, minimizing, or controlling societal conflict.

One way for the powerful to maintain the status quo is to define and disseminate the society's dominant ideology. The term *dominant ideology* describes a set of cultural beliefs and practices that helps to maintain powerful social, economic, and political interests. For Karl Marx, the dominant ideology in a capitalist society serves the interests of the ruling class. From a conflict perspective, the social significance of the dominant ideology is that a society's most powerful groups and institutions not only control wealth and property, but, even more importantly, they control the means of producing beliefs about reality primarily through education and the media (Abercrombie et al. 1980, 1990; Robertson 1988).

p. 62

The powerful, such as leaders of government, also use limited social reforms to buy off the oppressed and reduce the danger of challenges to their dominance. For example, minimum wage laws and unemployment compensation unquestionably give some valuable assistance to needy men and women. Yet these reforms also serve to pacify those who might otherwise rebel. Of course, in the view of conflict theorists, such manoeuvres can never entirely eliminate conflict, since workers will continue to demand equality, and the powerful will not give up their control of society.

Conflict theorists see stratification as a major source of societal tension and conflict. They do not agree with Davis and Moore that stratification is functional for a society or that it serves as a source of stability. Rather, conflict sociologists argue that stratification will inevitably lead to instability and to social change (R. Collins 1975; L. Coser 1977).

Lenski's Viewpoint

Let's return to the question posed earlier—"Is stratification universal?"—and consider the sociological response. Some form of differentiation is found in every culture, from the most primitive to the most advanced industrial societies of our time. Sociologist Gerhard Lenski, in his sociocultural evolution approach, described how economic systems change as their level of technology becomes more complex, beginning with hunting and gathering and culminating eventually with industrial society. In subsistence-based, hunting-and-gathering societies, people focus on survival. While some inequality and differentiation are evident, a stratification system based on social class does not emerge because there is no real wealth to be claimed.

p. 113

As a society advances in technology, it becomes capable of producing a considerable surplus of goods. The emergence of surplus resources greatly expands the possibilities for inequality in status, influence, and power and allows a well-defined rigid social class system to develop. In order to minimize strikes, slowdowns, and industrial sabotage, the elites may share a portion of the economic surplus with the lower classes, but not enough to reduce their power and privilege.

As Lenski argued, the allocation of surplus goods and services controlled by those with wealth, status, and power reinforces the social inequality that accompanies stratification systems. While this reward system may once have served the overall purposes of society, as functionalists contend, the same cannot be said for the large disparities separating the haves from the have-nots in current societies. In contemporary industrial society, the degree of social and economic inequality far exceeds the need to provide for goods and services (Lenski 1966; Nolan and Lenski 1999).

Stratification by Social Class

Measuring Social Class

We continually assess how wealthy people are by looking at the cars they drive, the houses they live in, the clothes they wear, and so on. Yet it is not so easy to locate an individual within our social hierarchies as it would be in slavery or caste systems of stratification. To determine someone's class position, sociologists generally rely on the objective method.

The ***objective method*** of measuring social class views class largely as a statistical category. Researchers assign individuals to social classes on the basis of criteria such as occupation, education, income, and residence. The key to the objective method is that the *researcher,* rather than the person being classified, identifies an individual's class position.

The first step in using this method is to decide which indicators or causal factors will be measured objectively, whether wealth, income, education, occupation or a combination of these. The prestige ranking of occupations has proved to be a useful indicator of a person's class position. For one thing, it is much easier to determine accurately than income or wealth. The term ***prestige*** refers to the respect and admiration that an occupation holds in a society. "My daughter, the physicist" connotes something very different from "my daughter, the waitress." Prestige is independent of the particular individual who occupies a job, a characteristic that distinguishes it from esteem. ***Esteem*** refers to the reputation that a specific person has earned within an occupation. Therefore, one can say that the position of prime minister of Canada has high prestige, even though it has been occupied by people with varying degrees of esteem. A hairdresser may have the esteem of his clients, but he lacks the prestige of a corporation president.

Table 8-1 ranks the prestige of a number of well-known occupations. In a series of surveys done in the United States, sociologists assigned prestige rankings to about 500 occupations, ranging from physician to newspaper vendor. The highest possible prestige score was 100, and the lowest was 0. Physician, lawyer, dentist, and professor were the most highly regarded occupations. Sociologists have used such data to assign prestige rankings to virtually all jobs and have found a stability in rankings from 1925 to 1991. Similar studies in other countries have also developed useful prestige rankings of occupations (Hodge and Rossi 1964; Lin and Xie 1988; Treiman 1977).

Studies of social class tend to neglect the occupations and incomes of *women* as determinants of social rank. In an exhaustive study of 589 occupations, sociologists Mary Powers and Joan Holmberg (1978) examined the impact of women's participation in the paid labour force on occupational status. Since women tend to dominate the relatively low-paying occupations, such as bookkeepers and child care workers, their participation in the workforce leads to a general upgrading of the status of most male-dominated occupations. More recent research conducted in North America and Europe has assessed the occupations of husbands *and* wives in determining the

Table 8-1 Prestige Rankings of Occupations

Occupation	Score	Occupation	Score
Physician	86	Secretary	46
Lawyer	75	Insurance agent	45
Dentist	74	Bank teller	43
Professor	74	Nurse's aide	42
Architect	73	Farmer	40
Clergy	69	Correctional officer	40
Pharmacist	68	Receptionist	39
Registered nurse	66	Barber	36
High school teacher	66	Child care worker	35
Accountant	65	Hotel clerk	32
Airline pilot	60	Bus driver	32
Police officer and detective	60	Truck driver	30
Preschool teacher	55	Retail clerk (shoes)	28
Librarian	54	Garbage collector	28
Firefighter	53	Waiter and waitress	28
Social worker	52	Bartender	25
Electrician	51	Farm worker	23
Funeral director	49	Janitor	22
Mail carrier	47	Newspaper vendor	19

Sources: J. Davis and Smith 1999:1242–1246; Nakao and Treas 1990, 1994; NORC 1994.

class positions of families (Sørensen 1994). With more than half of all married women now working outside the home (see Chapter 10), this approach seems long overdue, but it also raises some questions. For example, how is class or status to be judged in dual-career families—by the occupation regarded as having greater prestige, the average, or some other combination of the two occupations?

Sociologists—and, in particular, feminist sociologists in Great Britain—are drawing on new approaches in assessing women's social class standing. One approach is to focus on the individual (rather than the family or household) as the basis of categorizing a woman's class position. Thus, a woman would be classified based on her own occupational status rather than that of her spouse (O'Donnell 1992).

Another feminist effort to measure the contribution of women to the economy reflects a more clearly political agenda. International Women Count Network, a global grassroots feminist organization, has sought to give a monetary value to women's unpaid work. Besides providing symbolic recognition of women's role in labour, this value would also be used to calculate pension programs and benefits that are based on wages received. In 1995 the United Nations placed a US$11 trillion price tag on unpaid labour by women, largely in child care, housework, and agriculture. Whatever the figure today, the continued undercounting of many workers' contribution to a family and to an entire economy makes virtually all measures of stratification in need of reform (United Nations Development Programme 1995; Wages for Housework Campaign 1999).

Another complication in measuring social class is that advances in statistical methods and computer technology have multiplied the factors used to define class under the objective method. No longer are sociologists limited to annual income and education in evaluating a person's class position. Today, studies use as criteria the value of homes, sources of income, assets, years in present occupations, neighbourhoods, and considerations regarding dual careers. Adding these variables will not necessarily paint a different picture of class differentiation in Canada and elsewhere, but it does allow sociologists to measure class in a more complex and multidimensional way.

Whatever the technique used to measure class, the sociologist is interested in real and often dramatic differences in power, privilege, and opportunity in a society. The study of stratification is a study of inequality. Nowhere is this more evident than in the distribution of wealth and income.

Consequences of Social Class

Wealth and Income

Nobel prizewinning economist Paul Samuelson has described the uneven distribution of income in the United States in these terms: "If we made an income pyramid out of a child's blocks, with each layer portraying $500 of income, the peak would be far higher than Mount Everest, but most people would be within a few feet of the ground" (Samuelson and Nordhaus 1998:344). This analogy is equally applicable to Canada.

As we discussed earlier in this chapter, the group at the top of the income ladder in Canada takes home a much larger share of the national wage pool than do those lower down. This discrepancy has been an enduring part of the Canadian class structure. Starting in the 17th century, First Nations peoples and habitants lived in spartan conditions while the owners of the Hudson's Bay Company and later, the North West Company, lived lives of luxury. With the arrival of the Industrial Revolution and the labour movement early in the 20th century, southern Ontario and Quebec saw some of these historical inequities addressed. In recent years, however, evidence suggests that the trend has been reversed.

The middle class, historically considered the bellwether of social mobility in Canada, suffered significant permanent job losses in the 1990s, attributable to structural changes in the workplace. Particularly hard hit were those workers in middle management and skilled blue-collar jobs. Both of these sectors were impacted by technological change that either made their task redundant or reduced its complexity substantially. Those at the middle of the corporate structure watched as their organizational and information management functions were taken over by more affordable and accessible desktop computers. The blue-collar workers in processing and assembly facilities suffered a similar fate at the robotic hands of computer-controlled devices.

A study done by Clarence Lochhead and Vivian Shalla for the Canadian Council on Social Development concluded: ". . . the labour market today is producing greater inequality among families with children than it did a decade ago, with especially severe income losses among lower-middle-income earners and the poor" (Lochhead and Shillington 1996). In the years from 1984 to 1993, Canadian workers falling into the middle- and lower-income group saw their wages fall in real terms. By contrast, those at the top of the income ladder saw their income increase. Among families with children under the age of 18, for example, those households ranked in the second quintile (where five is the highest) experienced a drop of almost three thousand dollars ($2985). During the same time, those in the top group enjoyed an increase of $5059 in their income.

Lochhead and Shalla conclude that the increasing income inequality in Canada's wage distribution ". . . is producing a two-tiered society." That conclusion might be interpreted as suggesting that Canada is headed down a road where those two tiers will be comprised of the very rich on the one level, and the very poor on the other.

Poverty

Measuring Poverty in Canada Canada has demonstrated ambivalence towards poverty, providing a relatively generous social safety net that works to protect people from starving or dying from exposure on the one hand, while trying to emulate American-style individualism on the other. In the United States, for example, 60 percent of the population believes that the government has no place in working to alleviate the discrepancies of income and wealth that exist among Americans. Canadians do not appear to be as willing to abandon people to the ravages of the marketplace. We want the government to respond to poverty, we are just not sure how much. Unlike most of the developed world, our country does not have an official poverty line. Statistics Canada, the federal government's data-gathering and analysis arm, uses four different markers to determine poverty. These range from comparisons of income to comparisons of expenditures. For instance, the Low Income Measure (LIM) compares a household's income against the median income of equivalent Canadian families. Any unit whose income is less than half that median is defined as poor. On the other hand, the ***Low Income Cut-Off (LICO)*** uses the amount a household spends on the basics—food, shelter and clothing—to make the same determination. Not having a set measure of poverty presents policymakers and public program administrators with clear challenges.

In January, 2001, Statistics Canada began using a new measure of poverty, one designed to reflect more than the relationship between income and distribution. The ***Market Basket Measure (MBM)*** now takes into consideration more than just subsistence needs. It calculates the amounts needed by various households to live a life comparable to community standards. For example, someone living in a town where 90 percent of the residents have Internet access would have the cost of that access included as part of their essential needs list.

Studying Poverty The efforts of sociologists and other social scientists to better understand poverty are complicated by the difficulty of defining it. This problem is evident even in government programs that conceive of poverty in either absolute or relative terms. ***Absolute poverty*** in developed countries refers to a minimum level of subsistence that no family should be expected to live below. This standard theoretically remains unchanged from year to year. Policies concerning minimum wages, housing standards, or hot lunch programs for children in schools in low-income neighbourhoods imply a need to bring citizens up to some predetermined level of existence. Canada's provincial governments, which have set the minimum wage paid to workers within their borders since 1996, have all, with the exception of Ontario, increased the minimum wage since then (see Table 8-2 for the minimum wage rates across Canada). Some of the increases have been meagre, like Alberta's 25-cent raise over five years. Others have been greater but still modest, like the 85-cent increase legislated in Manitoba.

By contrast, ***relative poverty*** is a floating standard of deprivation by which people at the bottom of a society, whatever their lifestyles, are judged to be disadvantaged *in comparison with the rest of the community in which they live.* Policies and programs in the ***social safety net***, those initiatives designed to alleviate the harshest conditions associated with being at the bottom of the income scale, are the domain of the provinces. Most current social programs view poverty in relative terms. Therefore, even if the poor of the 1990s are better off in absolute terms than the poor of the 1930s or 1960s, they are still seen as deserving special assistance from government.

There has been an ongoing debate in Canada over the usefulness of any official measure of poverty. Critics from the right argue that the almost complete absence of absolute poverty means that low-income Canadians are not starving to death on the streets, and that their lot is

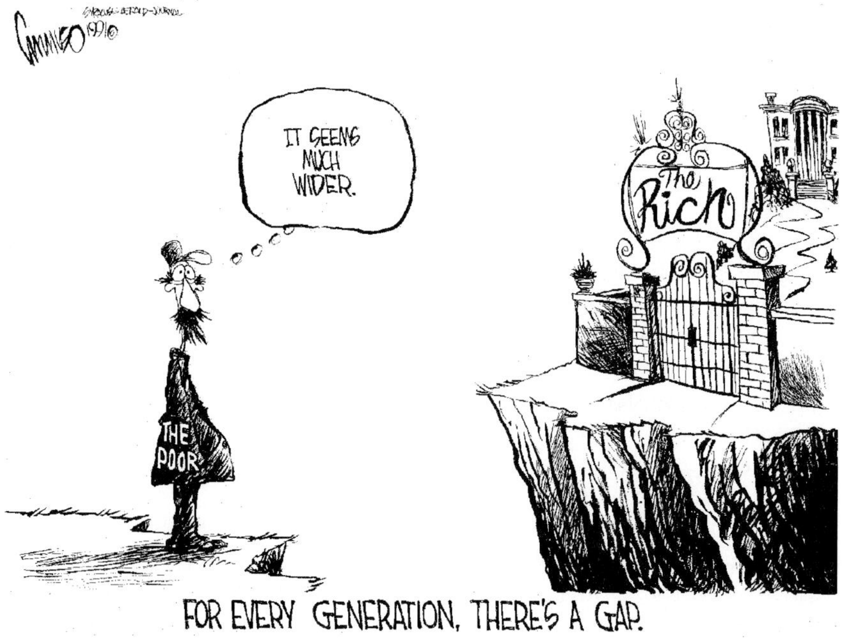

Table 8-2 Minimum Wages for Experienced Adult Workers, by Province, as of April 2001

Province/Territory	Wage
Alberta	$5.90
British Columbia	$8.00
Manitoba	$6.25
New Brunswick	$5.90
Newfoundland	$5.50
NWT	$6.50
Nova Scotia	$5.80
Nunavit	$6.50
Ontario	$6.85
PEI	$5.80
Quebec	$7.00
Saskatchewan	$6.00
Yukon Territory	$7.20

Source: Canadian Council on Social Development 2000.

more one of inconvenience than desperation. These proponents of meritocracy and individual responsibility take the functionalist position that poverty serves as a motivator. They also suggest that current measures of poverty are reflective of a socialist agenda, and classify far too many Canadians as poor. On the other side of the debate are the liberal thinkers, who take the position that poverty in a society as wealthy as Canada's is unconscionable. These proponents of social programs to prevent or at least reduce the incidence of poverty see the existing poverty lines as being too punitive in that they fail to acknowledge the plight of many Canadians who struggle with minimum wage and/or sporadic employment in an attempt to provide the basics of life for their families.

Over the past decade, changes to some of the cornerstones of Canada's safety net have pleased the former group and infuriated the latter. At the federal level, more stringent standards in determining who is eligible to receive employment insurance—known as *un*employment insurance in the days before public relations became a consideration in the naming of government programs—had a dramatic impact on seasonal workers in particular. The provincial jurisdiction over welfare has meant that there is no consistency in either access or standards across the country. With hardline conservative governments in Ontario and Alberta, standards covering accessibility to welfare have changed dramatically. The result is that the number of people in those provinces who are able to qualify for assistance has shrunk. In Ontario, the Progressive Conservative government of Mike Harris experimented with the idea of "workfare," a program that would require able welfare recipients to work for their cheques. The Social Policy section later in this chapter examines legislation associated with addressing poverty. It is quite clear that poverty, particularly when it is not absolute, is a subjective determination. With this in mind, we will consider just who it is that makes up the poor in Canada.

Who Are the Poor? Not only does the category of the poor defy any simple definition, it counters common stereotypes about "poor people." For example, many people in Canada believe that the vast majority of the poor are able to work but will not. Yet many poor adults *do* work outside the home. In fact, income statistics show that over 60 percent of Canadian households that could be classified as poor have at least one individual who works full-time, around the year. This figure suggests that the stereotype of the "lazy poor" is more one of convenience than fact.

A sizable number of the poor live in urban centres, but a majority live outside those neighbourhoods we might consider low-income. Poverty is no stranger in rural areas, ranging from Maritime fishing villages to hard-hit farming regions of Saskatchewan to First Nations communities. Included among the groups most affected by poverty in Canada are elderly people, particularly women, and children, particularly those living in single-parent families with their mothers. One surprising addition to this list comes from the revelation in recent years that some families of men and women who are part of the lower ranks of the Canadian armed forces have been forced to use food banks to supplement their wages. Table 8-3 provides additional statistical information regarding these low-income people in Canada. (The situation of the most destitute poor in Canada and worldwide, the homeless, will be examined in the social policy section of Chapter 15.) Box 8-1 gives further information on poverty in our country.

Women currently make up more than half the poor in this country. In 2001, Statistics Canada reported that 11.6 percent of women fell into this category, compared with 9.6 percent of men. What makes women's poverty more alarming than men's is the likelihood that a woman living below the poverty line is more than three times more likely than a man to have children who are wholly

Research in Action 8-1 Poverty in Canada

The Canadian Council on Social Development (CCSD) is a non-profit organization dedicated to "advancing economic and social security to all Canadians." The Council sees social issue research as a key to understanding the rationale and the potential impact of government and corporate policies. The organization has undertaken a broad range of data gathering and analysis that enable it to serve as a source of information and a respected advocate for Canadians.

Each year, the Council publishes a compendium of its findings on Canada's lower socioeconomic class in *The Canadian Fact Book on Poverty*. In the 2000 edition, it concluded that millions of Canadians lived in poverty, not because there were insufficient resources to provide adequate food, shelter, and clothing to all, but rather because of the skewed distribution of wealth in this country. Of particular concern was the number of Canadian children living in economically dysfunctional circumstances. The following are some of the conclusions from *The Canadian Fact Book on Poverty, 2000*:

- Children from homes with less than $20 000 annual income are 1.3 times more likely to live in substandard housing than are middle-class children.
- Poor children are 2.4 times more likely than children from wealthy homes to live in neighbourhoods with disproportionately high levels of crime.

Of particular concern was the number of Canadian children living in economically dysfunctional circumstances.

- Poor children are more likely to be aggressive.
- Poor children are more likely to be hyperactive.
- Poor children are more likely to suffer from serious health problems such as speech or hearing impairment.
- Poor children are more likely to become involved in delinquent behaviours.
- Poor children are less likely to participate in skill-building activities.

But the Council also found that children were not the only ones whose lives were negatively impacted by poverty. Adults living in households where the earnings were less than $30 000 had the following characteristics:

- Poor adults were more likely to be in poor-to-fair health.
- Poor adults were twice as likely to have serious health problems than those with high-incomes.
- Poor adults were more likely to suffer from chronic conditions such as asthma, high blood pressure, and ulcers.
- Poor adults had higher scores on the mental health distress index.
- Poor adults had a much lower sense of self-esteem.

Let's Discuss

1. What can be done to lessen the impact of poverty on Canadian children?
2. Who has the responsibility of ensuring that a nation's children do not live in poverty?

Source: Canadian Council on Social Development 2000.

Table 8-3 Percentage of Individuals and Census Families Living in Low Income[1], Canada, 1980, 1990, and 2000

Individuals and Selected Family Types[2]	Percentage in Low Income[1] 1980	1990	2001
Individuals	17.4	16.2	16.2
Couple families with no children	11.1	8.7	8.2
Couple families with at least one child under 18 years	11.7	10.5	11.2
Couple families whose children are all 18 years and over	5.5	5.2	5.8
Lone-parent families with at least one child under 18 years	55.3	53.5	45.8
Lone-parent families whose children are all 18 years and over	19.5	16.7	16.5

1. Those living below the low-income cut-offs.
2. Families living in single-family households with no aditional persons, e.g., grandparents, uncles, aunts, etc; all individuals except those living in the Yukon, Northwest Territories, Nunavut, or Indian reserves or institutions.

Source: Adapted by the authour, Statistics Canada 2003c.

or substantially dependant on her. During the last 20 years, female-headed families have become an increasing proportion of Canada's low-income population. In addition, the aging population has seen a rise in the numbers—but not the rate—of elderly women living in poverty. Even able-bodied, single women are overrepresented among the poor. In 1998, this type of woman was 25 percent more likely to be poor than a man of similar characteristics (Statistics Canada 1998d). The single greatest predictor of poverty among women in Canada is whether they are living without a spouse. Forty-three percent of women over 65 (compared with 31 percent of men) who lived alone in 2000 were low income (Statistics Canada, 2003d). This alarming trend, known as the *feminization of poverty,* is evident not just in Canada but around the world.

Conflict theorists and other observers trace the higher rates of poverty among women to three distinct factors: the difficulty in finding affordable child care, sexual harassment, and sex discrimination in the labour market (see Chapter 10) (Dalaker and Proctor 2000:vi).

p. 91
p. 138

Table 10-3 shows that 45.8 percent of single-parent families with children under 18 years live in low income. It is important to note, however, that within this number there is a significant overrepresentation of female-headed families. The same pattern is evident outside of Canada. In 1999, 11.8 percent of all people in the United States lived in poverty, compared to 27.8 percent of households headed by single mothers. This trend is also noticeable throughout Europe, in developing countries, and even in three widely differing nations whose legislation on behalf of women is the most advanced in the world: Israel, Sweden, and Russia. Similar to the situation in Canada, in these countries, national health care programs, housing subsidies, and other forms of government assistance cushion the impact of poverty somewhat, yet the feminization of poverty still advances (Abowitz 1986; Stanley 1995; Statistics Sweden 1999).

Sociologist William Julius Wilson (1980, 1987, 1989, 1996) and other social scientists have used the term ***underclass*** to describe the long-term poor who lack training and skills. While estimates vary depending on the definition, this group tends to consist disproportionately of women, visible minorities, and the elderly in Canadian society.

Poverty hits women particularly hard throughout the world, a situation known as the "feminization of poverty." Shown here are women and children in India.

Conflict theorists, among others, have expressed alarm at the portion of the population living on this lower rung of the stratification hierarchy and at society's reluctance to address the lack of economic opportunities for these people. Often, portraits of the underclass seem to "blame the victims" for their own plight while ignoring other factors that push people into poverty.

Poverty, of course, is not a new phenomenon. Yet the concept of the underclass describes a chilling development: individuals and families, whether employed or unemployed, who are beyond the reach of any safety net provided by existing social programs. Moreover, membership in the underclass is not an intermittent condition but a long-term attribute. The underclass is understandably alienated from the larger society and engages sporadically in illegal behaviour. These illegal acts do little to encourage society to address the long-term problems of the underclass.

Explaining Poverty Why is it that pervasive poverty continues within nations of vast wealth such as Canada and the United States? Sociologist Herbert Gans (1995) has applied functionalist analysis to the existence of poverty and argues that various segments of society actually *benefit* from the existence of the poor. Gans has identified a number of social, economic, and political functions that the poor perform for society, among them the following:

- The presence of poor people means that society's dirty work—physically dirty or dangerous, dead-end and underpaid, undignified and menial jobs—will be performed at low cost.

- Poverty creates jobs for occupations and professions that "service" the poor. It creates both legal employment (public health experts, welfare caseworkers) and illegal jobs (drug dealers, numbers "runners").
- The identification and punishment of the poor as deviants uphold the legitimacy of conventional social norms and "mainstream values" regarding hard work, thrift, and honesty.
- Within a relatively hierarchical society, the existence of poor people guarantees the higher status of the more affluent. As psychologist William Ryan (1976) has noted, affluent people may justify inequality (and gain a measure of satisfaction) by "blaming the victims" of poverty for their disadvantaged condition.
- Because of the lack of political power, the poor often absorb the costs of social change. Under the policy of deinstitutionalization, mental patients released from long-term hospitals have been "dumped" primarily into low-income communities and neighbourhoods. Similarly, halfway houses for rehabilitated drug abusers are often rejected by more affluent communities and end up in poorer neighbourhoods.

p. 156

In Gans's view, then, poverty and the poor actually satisfy positive functions for many nonpoor groups in Canada.

Stratification and Life Chances

Max Weber saw class as closely related to people's ***life chances***—that is, their opportunities to provide themselves with material goods, positive living conditions, and favourable life experiences (Gerth and Mills 1958). Life chances are reflected in such measures as housing, education, and health. Occupying a higher position in a society improves your life chances and brings greater access to social rewards. By contrast, people in the lower social classes are forced to devote a larger proportion of their limited resources to the necessities of life.

The affluent and powerful not only have more material possessions than others; they also benefit in many nonmaterial ways. This fact was brought home to us by the hit motion picture *Titanic,* which showed that one's "life" chances had literal consequences in determining who would survive the ship's sinking in 1912 (see Box 8-2). We can also see the effects of life chances in education. Canadian children from high-income families with low high school achievement are more likely to attend college than are children from less affluent families with the highest levels of achievement. This gap in educational opportunities has remained consistent for decades.

In Canada, there are clear financial consequences associated with level of education. A report by the Council of Ministers of Education, Canada (CMEC) indicated a clear association between the probability of being unemployed and educational attainment. For example, someone without a high school diploma is three times more likely than someone with a university degree to be unemployed as a young adult (CMEC 1995).

Class position also affects health in important ways. While Canadians have access to universal health care through the federally mandated system, wealthy Canadians have always been able to travel to the United States or elsewhere to gain faster, and in some cases, more advanced treatment. Reductions in federal transfer payments to the provinces during the 1990s combined with cost-cutting provincial budgets like those of Ontario, Alberta, and Saskatchewan have created what some analysts call "a creeping privatization of the health care system" (National Antipoverty Organization 1998). The evidence suggests that cuts in government spending meant that the share of health care

Functionalists point out that some people, such as the officials (standing) who deal with the homeless, actually benefit from the existence of poverty. Many occupations "service" the poor.

Eye on the Media

8-2 Social Class in the Movie *Titanic* and on the *SS Titanic*

The movie *Titanic* has been phenomenally successful. Millions of people in the United States, Japan, Canada, China, and elsewhere in the world have paid to see the film. By 2000, box office sales had surpassed US$1.8 billion internationally, making it the most successful motion picture ever. While the special effects depicting the ship's breakup on an iceberg were spectacular, film audiences were mainly drawn to the story of how aristocratic 17-year-old Rose, facing a loveless marriage to a society figure, became attracted to working-class Jack.

They were not traveling together on that ill-fated maiden voyage of the *Titanic.* Rose was ensconced in first-class luxury while Jack was traveling in third class, or steerage, thanks to a ticket he won in a poker game. Still, for purposes of the plot, they managed to meet on board. Jack had to borrow a suit and act "properly" in order to pass the class line and gain entrance to the stuffy first-class dining room. But Rose had no trouble leaving her rich friends for a bawdy evening among those in the lower decks.

The story of Rose and Jack was attractive because it was so romantic. After all, it typified a social class fantasy of the rich and poor falling in love and then struggling to survive. The theme of love between social class misfits is not new to motion pictures—consider Eliza Doolittle and Professor Henry Higgins in *My Fair Lady* and Vivian Ward and Edward Lewis in *Pretty Woman.* However, the fictional tale of Rose and Jack is particularly ironic because it uses as a backdrop a real tragedy that reinforces the fact that social inequality outweighs any iceberg.

The first attempt to alert steerage passengers to the need to head to the boat deck came at least 45 minutes after the other passengers were alerted.

When the *Titanic* sank in 1912, 1502 passengers and crew members perished and only 705 survived. The luxury liner was supposed to be "unsinkable," but there were still contingency plans for leading passengers to lifeboats in case of emergency. There was one glitch: These procedures were established only for first- and second-class passengers. Approximately 62 percent of the first-class passengers came away alive; even one third of the first-class male passengers survived, despite a rule of "women and children first." In third class, only 25 percent of the passengers survived.

Did the crew and the White Star Line purposely make the 381 steerage passengers expendable? There is no reason to think that, but, like all poorer people on land, they were given less thought and sometimes no thought at all. The first attempt to alert steerage passengers to the need to head to the boat deck came at least 45 minutes after the other passengers were alerted. Clogged passageways made it difficult for steerage passengers to find the lifeboats without being carefully guided. Jack's real-life counterparts had little chance to survive the calamity. Stratification does make a difference for a person's life chances.

Let's Discuss

1. If you were a passenger on the *Titanic,* how would you be able to distinguish the upper and lower classes? What features on board kept the classes separate?
2. Why did so many more first-class than lower-class passengers survive the ship's sinking?

Sources: Butler 1998; K. Crouse 1999; Riding 1998.

dollars going directly from Canadians' pockets to health care providers grew by 20 percent over the five-year period from 1991 to 1996. This shift toward services not covered by the government puts those Canadians with limited resources at a clear disadvantage.

In addition, class is increasingly being viewed as an important predictor of health. Children from impoverished backgrounds suffer more frequently from serious health problems such as sensory and/or cognitive dysfunctions (Canadian Council on Social Development 2000). These conditions continue on into adulthood, and become exacerbated by a disproportionate incidence of chronic problems such as asthma, high blood pressure, and alcoholism.

This combination of decreased access to health care and medical conditions that correlate highly with low incomes is, on its own, reason for concern. But if this trend is considered in light of the changes that have taken place in the distribution of income over the last 20 years, the implications are dramatic. Between 1990 and 2000, the poorest 10 percent of Canadians saw its share of the national income stay the same at less than 2 percent. During that same period, the top 10 percent of earners saw its share rise from 26 percent of the total to 28 percent (CCSD 2003). Both of these changes represent the movement of billions of dollars from the pockets of the have-nots to the bank accounts of the haves.

If health care is becoming increasingly privatized and the distribution of income is becoming increasingly skewed, as the data suggests, then the conclusion to be drawn is that in the future, fewer Canadians will be able to access the health care they need.

Like disease, crime can be particularly devastating when it attacks the poor. People in low-income families are more likely to be assaulted, raped, or robbed than are the most affluent people. Furthermore, if accused of a crime, a person with low income and status is likely to be represented by an overworked public defender. Whether innocent or guilty, the accused may sit in jail for months, unable to raise bail (Perkins and Klaus 1996).

Even the administration of lotteries underscores differences in life chances. A lottery participant is six times more likely to be struck by lightning than to win the jackpot, yet provincial lotteries such as Lotto 6/49 target low-income residents in their promotions. Video lottery terminals are more heavily concentrated in poor neighbourhoods than in wealthy communities. Lottery advertisements appear most frequently at the beginning of each month, when welfare cheques and other forms of government assistance tend to arrive. Based on studies of lottery purchases, lottery executives view the poor as more likely than the affluent to spend a high portion of their earnings for the very unlikely chance of winning the jackpot (Nibert 2000; Novak and Schmid 1999).

Some people have hoped that the Internet revolution would help level the playing field by making information and markets uniformly available. Unfortunately, however, not everyone is able to get onto the "infohighway," and so yet another aspect of social inequality has emerged—the *digital divide*. The poor, minorities, and those who live in rural communities are least likely to have access to a computer (National Telecommunications Information Administration 1999). Even in the workplace, those at the bottom of the socioeconomic ladder are disadvantaged. Only 41 percent of workers with a high school education worked at a computer, compared with 85 percent of those with a university degree. Only 36 percent of people with an annual income of less than $20 000 used a computer at work, compared with 80 percent of those with an income of $60 000 or more (Perspectives June 2001). At home the disparity was even more marked. A 1998 survey by Angus Reid found that of those with incomes in the highest quintile, 62.2 percent had computers in their homes. Only 15.4 percent of those falling into the lowest income group made the same claim.

Wealth, status, and power may not ensure happiness, but they certainly provide additional ways of coping with one's problems and disappointments. For this reason, the opportunity for advancement is of special significance to those who are at the bottom of society looking up. These people want the rewards and privileges that are granted to high-ranking members of a culture.

Social Mobility

Alexander Mackenzie began his working life as a stone mason, yet managed to move up the career ladder to become Canada's second prime minister. The rise of a person from a poor background to a position of great prestige, power, or financial reward is an example of social mobility. The term ***social mobility*** refers to movement of individuals or groups from one position of a society's stratification system to another. But how significant—how frequent, how dramatic—is mobility in a class society such as Canada?

Open versus Closed Class Systems

Sociologists use the terms *open class system* and *closed class system* to indicate the amount of social mobility in a society. An ***open system*** implies that the position of each individual is influenced by the person's *achieved* status. An open class system encourages competition among members of society. Canada and other developed nations are moving toward this ideal type by attempting to reduce barriers faced by women, racial and ethnic minorities, and people born with lower socioeconomic status.

At the other extreme of social mobility is the ***closed system,*** which allows little or no possibility of moving up. The slavery and caste systems of stratification are examples of closed systems. In such societies, social placement is based on *ascribed* statuses, such as race or family background, which cannot be changed.

Types of Social Mobility

An airline pilot who becomes a police officer moves from one social position to another of the same rank. Each occupation has the same prestige ranking: 60 on a scale ranging from a low of 0 to a high of 100 (see Table 8-1 on page 183). Sociologists call this kind of movement

horizontal mobility. However, if the pilot were to become a lawyer (prestige ranking of 75), he or she would experience ***vertical mobility,*** the movement from one social position to another of a different rank. Vertical mobility can also involve moving *downward* in a society's stratification system, as would be the case if the airline pilot becomes a bank teller (ranking of 43). Pitirim Sorokin (1959, original edition 1927) was the first sociologist to distinguish between horizontal and vertical mobility. Most sociological analysis, however, focuses on vertical rather than horizontal mobility.

One way of examining vertical social mobility is to contrast intergenerational and intragenerational mobility. ***Intergenerational mobility*** involves changes in the social position of children relative to their parents. Thus, a plumber whose father was a physician provides an example of downward intergenerational mobility. A film star whose parents were both factory workers illustrates upward intergenerational mobility.

Intragenerational mobility involves changes in social position within a person's adult life. A woman who enters the paid labour force as a teacher's aide and eventually becomes superintendent of the school district experiences upward intragenerational mobility. A professional athlete who fails to find work in the media after retirement will probably suffer downward intragenerational mobility.

Social Mobility in Canada

The belief in upward mobility is an important value in our society. Does this mean that Canada is a land of opportunity for all? Not unless such ascriptive characteristics as race, gender, and family background have ceased to be significant in determining one's future prospects. We can see the impact of these factors in the occupational structure.

Occupational Mobility

Similar research in Canada shows that occupational mobility is impacted by the opportunities available to one's generation. In Canada, even the chance to participate in the labour force, at any level, has been compromised during the last decade. Although the labour force grew by 9.5 percent from 1991 to 2001, almost half of this growth occured in highly skilled occupations that typically require advanced education (Statistics Canada 2003h). This increased competition for employment has been particularly hard on young people, who have found themselves victims of the "right-sizing" corporate agenda of the 1990s. This generation is faced with a depleted labour market, reduced by layoffs and a just-in-time mentality. The twenty-somethings of today have been cautioned that they are to be the first generation in over 100 years not expected to surpass the standard of living enjoyed by their parents. In other words, their chances of enjoying either inter- or intragenerational socioeconomic mobility is in question.

Two sociological studies conducted a decade apart offer insight into the degree of mobility in the occupational structure of the United States (Blau and Duncan 1967; Featherman and Hauser 1978). Taken together, these investigations lead to several noteworthy conclusions. First, occupational mobility (both intergenerational and intragenerational) has been common among males. Approximately 60 to 70 percent of sons are employed in higher-ranked occupations than their fathers.

Second, the mobility that does take place tends to be in small increments. Thus, the child of a labourer may become a craftsperson, but the odds against reaching the top are extremely high unless one begins from a relatively privileged position.

Third, as the later study by Featherman and Hauser (1978) documents, occupational mobility among black Americans remains sharply limited by racial discrimination. Featherman and Hauser offer evidence of a modest decline in the significance of race; yet, we must regard this conclusion with some caution, since they did not consider households with no adult male present or individuals who were not counted in the labour force.

Research suggests that for the poor, social mobility is becoming more and more difficult to achieve. Studies by sociologist Greg Duncan (1994; Duncan and Yeung 1995) and by economist Ann Huff Stevens (1994) report that in the late 1980s, the opportunity to advance out of poverty in the United States narrowed significantly for poor people in general and especially for young women and black children.

The Impact of Education

Another conclusion of both studies is that education plays a critical role in social mobility. The impact of formal schooling on adult status is even greater than that of family background, although the likelihood of a child acquiring a university degree increases with the family's socioeconomic status.

However, education's impact on mobility has diminished somewhat in the last decade. An undergraduate degree—a BA, a BSc, or a B.Eng.—serves less as a guarantee of upward mobility than it did in the past simply because more and more entrants into the job market now hold such a degree. It might be argued that the same does not hold true for B.Comm. graduates, but even that distinction may be short-lived. Moreover, intergenerational mobility is declining, since there is no longer such a stark difference between generations. In earlier decades many high school-educated parents successfully sent their children to university, but today's post-secondary students are increasingly likely to have at least one parent with a degree (Hout 1988).

The Impact of Gender

Studies of mobility, even more than those of class, have traditionally ignored the significance of gender, but some research findings are now available that explore the relationship between gender and mobility.

Women's employment opportunities are much more limited than men's (as Chapter 10 will show). Moreover, according to recent research, women whose skills far exceed the jobs offered them are more likely than men to withdraw entirely from the paid labour force. This withdrawal violates an assumption common to traditional mobility studies: that most people will aspire to upward mobility and seek to make the most of their opportunities.

Preet Heer is part of a young generation of visible minority women who have overcome traditional stratification of Canadian society. Ms. Heer is a graduate student at the School of Community and Regional Planning at the University of British Columbia.

A decade-long study revealed that the increased full-time, full-year participation of women in the Canadian labour force was largely responsibly for growth in the category of employees who earned more than $37 000. The gender-based wage gap narrowed modestly over the decade 1984 to 1994, but remained substantial. By 1995, women earned on average 65 cents for every dollar earned by men—up from 54 cents in 1981. For full-time, full-year workers, the wage gap narrowed slightly from 64 cents to 73 cents earned by women for every dollar earned by men (Scott and Ross 1996).

In contrast to men, women have a rather large range of clerical occupations open to them. But the modest salary ranges and limited prospects for advancement in many of these positions mean there is not much possibility of upward mobility. Moreover, self-employment as shopkeepers, entrepreneurs, independent professionals, and the like—an important road to upward mobility for men—is difficult for women, who find it hard to secure the necessary financing. Although sons commonly follow in the footsteps of their fathers, women are unlikely to move into their fathers' positions. Consequently, gender remains an important factor in shaping social mobility within Canada. Women are especially likely to be trapped in poverty and unable to rise out of their low-income status regardless of the society in which they live (P. Smith 1994).

In recent decades, many male workers in North America and elsewhere have experienced downward mobility, including unemployment. (As we will see in Chapter 13, this has resulted in part from corporate "downsizing," "restructuring," and, more recently, "rightsizing" as well as plant closings.) For the first time since World War II, university-educated men in their late 40s and 50s—who may have assumed they were in their prime earning years—are experiencing a significant decline in wages. Some have lost high-level jobs at major corporations and have shifted (after periods of unemployment) to lower-paying positions at small companies or to self-employment.

So far in the chapter we have focused on stratification and social mobility within Canada. In the next section we broaden our focus to consider stratification from a global perspective.

Stratification in the World System

Kwabena Afari is a pineapple exporter in Ghana. But for years his customers had to show a great deal of ingenuity to get in touch with him. First a call had to be placed to Accra, the capital city. Someone there would call the post office in Afari's hometown. Then the post office would send a messenger to his home. Afari has recently solved his problem by getting a cellular phone, but his longtime dilemma symbolizes the problems of the roughly 600 million people who live in sub-Saharan Africa and are being left behind by the trade and foreign investment transforming the global economy. One African entrepreneur notes, "It's not that we have been left behind. It's that we haven't even started" (Buckley 1997:8).

It is true that technology, the information highway, and innovations in telecommunications have all made the world a smaller and more unified place. Yet while the world marketplace is gradually shrinking in space and tastes, the profits of business are not being equally shared. There remains a substantial disparity between the world's "have" and "have-not" nations. For example, in 1995, the average value of goods and services produced per citizen (per capita gross national product) in the United States, Canada, Japan, Switzerland, and Norway was more than $25 000. By contrast, the figure was under $200 in six poorer countries. The 140 developing nations accounted for 78 percent of the world's population but possessed only about 16 percent of all wealth (Haub and Cornelius 1999). As Homer-Dixon points out at the beginning of this chapter, the gap between those nations at the top and those at the bottom of the ranking continues to increase dramatically. In 1960, those countries at the top had incomes 30 times that of those at the other end of the ranking. In 1995, that figure had risen to 82 times (United Nations 1998). These contrasts are illustrated in Figure 8-2. Three forces discussed below are particularly responsible for the domination of the world marketplace by a few nations: the legacy of colonialism, the advent of multinational corporations, and modernization.

Colonialism, Neocolonialism, and World Systems Analysis

Colonialism is the maintenance of political, social, economic, and cultural domination over a people by a foreign power for an extended period of time (W. Bell 1981b). In simple terms, it is rule by outsiders. The long reign of the British Empire over much of North America, parts of Africa, and India is an example of colonial domination. The same can be said of French rule over Algeria, Tunisia, and other parts of North Africa. Relations between the colonial nation and colonized people are similar to those between the dominant capitalist class and the proletariat as described by Karl Marx.

By the 1980s, this form of colonialism had largely disappeared. Most of the world's nations that were colonies before World War I had achieved political independence and established their own governments. However, for many of these countries, the transition to genuine self-rule was not yet complete. Colonial domination had established patterns of economic exploitation that continued even after nationhood was achieved—in part because former colonies were unable to develop their own industry and technology. Their dependence on more industrialized nations, including their former colonial masters, for managerial and technical expertise, investment capital, and manufactured goods kept former colonies in a subservient position. Such continuing dependence and foreign domination constitute ***neocolonialism.***

While Canada has been able to escape such dependence on its former colonial master, Britain, we have come under the influence of another global power. A provocative discussion over the years has revolved around Canadians' ability to define ourselves as an independent entity; to present a clear Canadian identity despite existing tenuously in the shadow of the United States. Former Prime Minister Pierre Elliott Trudeau made the famous remark that living next door to the Americans was like "sleeping with an elephant." This perception is particularly relevant when it comes to cultural and economic matters. Canada's economy thrives or shrivels substantially as a function of what happens in the market south of the border. And our culture, for all its quality and impact, often cannot be heard over the throbbing Dolby sound of American movies and television. The question of whether we are a colony of the United States, in the neocolonial sense of the term, is an ongoing debate.

The economic and political consequences of colonialism and neocolonialism are readily apparent. Drawing on the conflict perspective, sociologist Immanuel Wallerstein (1974, 1979, 2000) views the global economic system as divided between nations that control wealth and those from which wealth-creating resources are taken. Neocolonialism allows industrialized societies to accumulate even more capital. Canada's position as essentially a resource provider to the United States, while at the same time qualifying as a developed, postindustrial nation, is difficult to place in Wallerstein's model.

Wallerstein has advanced a ***world systems analysis*** to describe the unequal economic and political relationships in which certain industrialized nations (among them the United States, Japan, and Germany) and their global corporations dominate the *core* of the system. At the *semi-periphery* of the system are countries with marginal economic status, such as Israel, Ireland, and South Korea. Canada falls somewhere in between these two categories. We are included in the former group for recognition of our level of development and our standard of living. At the same time, we do not have the political or economic clout of the other nations at the top of the hierarchy. We are "guest" members of the powerful G8 economic coalition; invited to participate at the insistence of the United States, though with limited status. Wallerstein suggests that the poor developing countries of Asia, Africa, and Latin America are on the *periphery* of the world economic system. Core nations and their corporations control and exploit the developing nations' economies, much as the old colonial empires ruled their colonies (Chase-Dunn and Grimes 1995).

The division between core and periphery nations is significant and remarkably stable. A study by the International Monetary Fund (2000) found little change over the course of the *last 100 years* for the 42 economies that were studied. The only changes were upward movement into the core by Japan and to lower margins of the semi-periphery by China. However, few economists will deny

FIGURE 8-2

Gross National Product per Capita, 2000

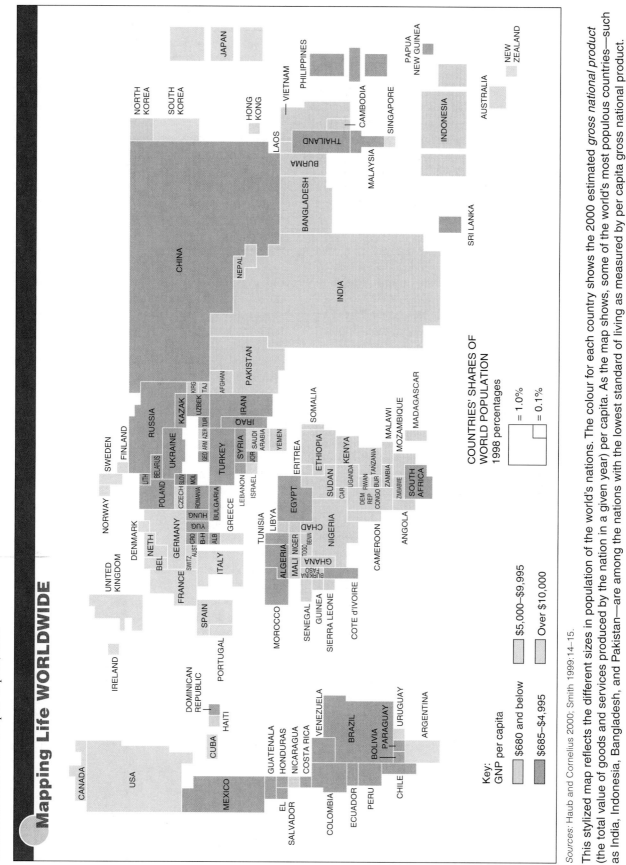

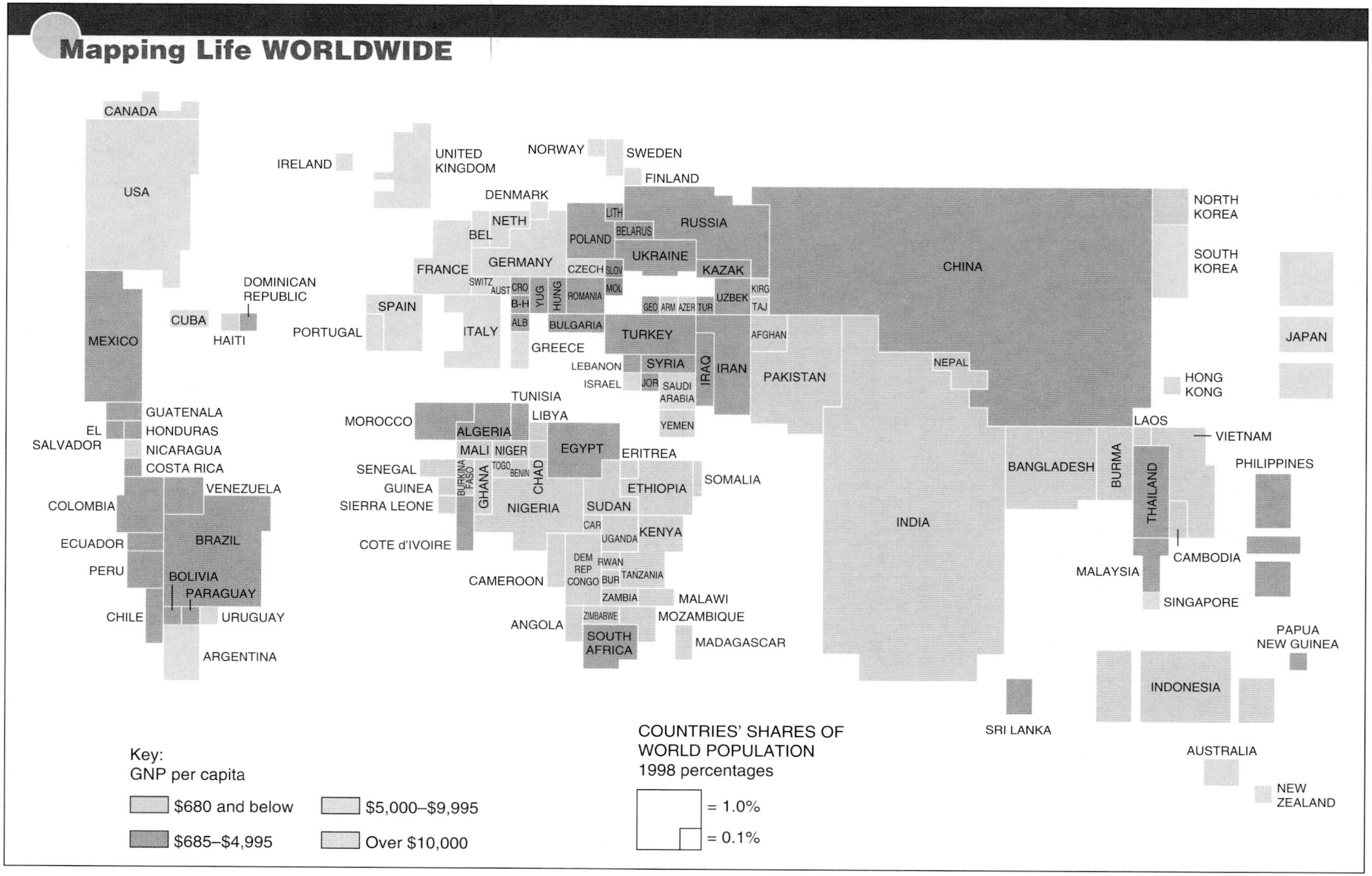

Sources: Haub and Cornelius 2000; Smith 1999:14–15.

This stylized map reflects the different sizes in population of the world's nations. The colour for each country shows the 2000 estimated *gross national product* (the total value of goods and services produced by the nation in a given year) per capita. As the map shows, some of the world's most populous countries—such as India, Indonesia, Bangladesh, and Pakistan—are among the nations with the lowest standard of living as measured by per capita gross national product.

that China's inclusion in or exclusion from the elite group is a matter of choice, and generally assume that within the next two decades China will assume a major role in the global economy.

Wallerstein's world systems analysis is the most widely used version of ***dependency theory.*** According to this theory, even as developing countries make economic advances, they remain weak and subservient to core nations and corporations within an increasingly intertwined global economy. This allows industrialized nations, with the United States at the forefront, to continue to exploit developing countries for their own gain. In a sense, dependency theory applies the conflict perspective on a global scale.

In addition to their political and economic impact, colonialism and neocolonialism have an important cultural component. The colonized people lose their native values and begin to identify with the culture of the colonial power. People may discard or neglect their native language as they attempt to emulate their colonizers. This process has been characterized by some of those opposed to contemporary neocolonialism as the "Americanization" of global culture. Every consumer product, book, film, or television program exported by a core nation is seen as an attack on the traditions and cultural autonomy p. 53 of the dependent people. Sembene Ousmane, one of Africa's most prominent writers and filmmakers, noted, "[Today] we are more familiar with European fairy tales than with our own traditional stories" (World Development Forum 1990:4).

Multinational Corporations

A key role in neocolonialism today is played by worldwide corporate giants. The term ***multinational corporations*** refers to commercial organizations that are headquartered in one country but do business throughout the world. Such private trade and lending relationships are not new; merchants have conducted business abroad for hundreds of years, trading gems, spices, garments, and other goods. However, today's multinational giants are not merely buying and selling overseas; they are also *producing* goods all over the world (Wallerstein 1974).

Moreover, today's "global factory" (the factories throughout the developing world run by multinational corporations) now has the "global office" alongside it. Multinationals based in core countries are beginning to establish reservations services, centres to process insurance claims, and data-processing centres in the periphery nations. As service industries become a more important part of the international marketplace, many companies have concluded that the low costs of overseas operations more than offset the expense of transmitting information around the world.

Do not underestimate the size of these global corporations. Table 8-4 shows that the total revenues of multinational businesses are on a par with the total value of goods and services exchanged in *entire nations.* Foreign sales represent an important source of profit for multinational corporations, a fact that encourages them to expand into other countries (in many cases, the developing nations). The economy of Canada is heavily dependent on foreign commerce, much of which is conducted by American multinationals.

Multinational corporations can actually help the developing nations of the world. They bring jobs and industry to areas where subsistence agriculture previously served as the only means of survival. Multinationals promote rapid development through diffusion of inventions and innovations from industrial nations. Viewed from a functionalist perspective, the combination of skilled technology and management provided by multinationals and the relatively cheap labour available in developing nations is ideal for a global enterprise. Multinationals can take maximum advantage of technology while reducing costs and boosting profits.

The international ties of multinational corporations also facilitate the exchange of ideas and technology around the world. They make the nations of the world more interdependent. And these ties may prevent certain disputes from reaching the point of serious conflict. A country cannot afford to sever diplomatic relations, or engage in warfare, with a nation that is the headquarters for its main business suppliers or is a key outlet for exports.

Conflict theorists challenge this favourable evaluation of the impact of multinational corporations. They emphasize that multinationals exploit local workers to maximize profits. Starbucks—the international coffee retailer based in Seattle—gets some of its coffee from farms in Guatemala. But to earn enough money to buy a pound of Starbucks' coffee, a Guatemalan farmworker would have to pick 500 pounds of beans, representing five days of work (Entine and Nichols 1996).

The pool of cheap labour in the developing world prompts multinationals to move factories out of core countries. An added bonus for the multinationals is that the developing world discourages strong trade unions. Organized labour in industrialized countries insists on decent wages and humane working conditions, but governments seeking to attract or keep multinationals may develop a "climate for investment" that includes repressive anti-labour laws restricting union activity and collective bargaining. If labour's demands in factories run by multinational corporations become threatening, the firm will simply move its plant elsewhere, leaving a trail of unemployment behind. Nike, for example, moved its factories from the United States to Korea to Indonesia to Vietnam, seeking the lowest labour costs. Conflict theorists conclude

Table 8-4 Comparing Multinational Corporations and Nations

Corporation	Revenues ($ millions)	Comparable Nations (or City)	Gross National Product ($ millions)
1. *General Motors (USA)*	$ 176 558	Denmark	$ 175 200
2. *Wal-Mart (USA)*	166 809	Norway plus Lebanon	167 000
3. *Exxon-Mobil (USA)*	163 881	Venezuela plus Malaysia	163 400
4. *Ford Motor (USA)*	162 558	Colombia plus Pakistan	162 200
5. *DaimlerChrysler (Germany)*	159 985	Hong Kong	158 200
11. *Royal Dutch/Shell (Brit./Neth.)*	105 366	Israel	96 500
16. *IBM (USA)*	87 548	Philippines plus Paraguay	88 100
29. *Philip Morris (USA)*	61 751	Pakistan	61 500
30. *Sony (Japan)*	60 052	Peru	60 500
41. *Nestlé (Switzerland)*	49 694	Algeria	46 400

Notes: Revenues are generally for 1999. GNP data are for 1998 and are based on local currencies converted to prevailing U.S. dollar equivalencies. Corporations are ranked by their placement on the *Fortune* 500 list of global corporations.

Sources: For corporate data: *Fortune* 2000. For GNP data: World Bank 2000b:9–11.

Protesters, like this one breaking the window of a Starbucks in Seattle, are demonstrating against what they see as the exploitative practices of large corporations, and the damaging effects they can have on developing nations.

that, on the whole, multinational corporations have a negative social impact on workers in both industrialized and developing nations.

Workers in Canada and other core countries are beginning to recognize that their own interests are served by helping to organize workers in developing nations. As long as multinationals can exploit cheap labour abroad, they will be in a strong position to reduce wages and benefits in industrialized countries. With this in mind, in the 1990s, labour unions, religious organizations, campus groups, and other activists mounted public campaigns to pressure companies such as Nike, Starbucks, Reebok, the Gap, and Wal-Mart to improve the wages and working conditions in their overseas operations (Cavanagh and Broad 1996).

Several sociologists confirm Homer-Dixon's assessment that the wealth created by globalization does not find its way into the pockets of workers in developing countries. This is true for both income and ownership of land. The upper and middle classes benefit most from economic expansion, while the lower classes are less likely to benefit. Multinationals invest in limited areas of an economy and in restricted regions of a nation. Although certain sectors of the host nation's economy expand, such as hotels and expensive restaurants, this very expansion appears to retard growth in agriculture and other economic sectors. Moreover, multinational corporations often buy out or force out local entrepreneurs and companies, thereby increasing economic and cultural dependence (Bornschier et al. 1978; Chase-Dunn and Grimes 1995; P. Evans 1979; Wallerstein 1979).

Feminist theory also sees the expansion of multinationals as potentially destructive. Women in developing countries, who are often powerless, are easier targets for exploitation through the devaluation of their labour by low wages and their lives by dangerous production practices.

Modernization

Millions of people around the world are witnessing a revolutionary transformation of their day-to-day life. Contemporary social scientists use the term ***modernization*** to describe the far-reaching process by which peripheral nations move from traditional or less developed institutions to those characteristic of more developed societies.

Wendell Bell (1981a), whose definition of modernization we are using, notes that modern societies tend to be urban, literate, and industrial. They have sophisticated transportation and media systems. Families tend to be organized within the nuclear family unit rather than the extended-family model (see Chapter 11). Members of societies that have undergone modernization shift allegiance from such traditional sources of authority as parents and priests to newer authorities such as government officials.

Many sociologists are quick to note that terms such as *modernization* and even *development* contain an ethnocentric bias. The unstated assumptions behind these terms are that "they" (people living in developing countries) are struggling to become more like "us" (in the core industrialized nations). Viewed from a conflict perspective, these terms perpetuate the dominant ideology of capitalist societies.

There is similar criticism of ***modernization theory***, a functionalist approach proposing that modernization and development will gradually improve the lives of people in developing nations. According to this theory, while countries develop at uneven rates, development in peripheral countries will be assisted by the innovations transferred from the industrialized world. Critics of modernization theory, including feminist and dependency theorists, counter that any such technology transfer only increases the dominance of core nations over developing countries and facilitates further exploitation. What concerns critics of modernization most is the pace of change that is now possible using the latest in data-gathering and data-processing technology. Change is taking place at such a rapid rate that its consequences—especially long term ones—cannot be adequately measured.

Current modernization studies generally take a convergence perspective. Using indicators such as degree of urbanization, energy use, literacy, and political democracy, researchers focus on how societies are moving closer together despite traditional differences. Initially, such modernization studies emphasized the convergence between countries such as Canada and the nations of Asia or between capitalist North America and the socialist democracies of western Europe. Now, however, this convergence perspective increasingly includes the developing countries of the Third World. Researchers recognize the interdependence of core industrialized nations and the developing world—as well as the continuing exploitation of the latter countries by the former. Conflict theorists view such a continuing dependence on foreign powers as an example of contemporary neocolonialism (Adelman 1993; C. Kerr 1960; O'Donnell 1992).

Stratification within Nations: A Comparative Perspective

At the same time that the gap between rich and poor nations is widening, so too is the gap between rich and poor citizens *within* nations. As discussed earlier, stratification in developing nations is closely related to their relatively weak and dependent position in the global economy. Local elites work hand in hand with multinational corporations and prosper from such alliances. At the same time, the economic system with its prevailing developmental values creates and perpetuates the exploitation of industrial and agricultural workers. That's why foreign investment in developing countries tends to increase economic inequality (Bornschier et al. 1978; Kerbo 2000). As Box 8-3 makes clear, inequality within a society is also evident in industrialized nations such as Japan.

In at least 15 nations around the world, the most affluent 10 percent of the population receives at least 40 percent of all income: Brazil (the leader at 48 percent), Chile, Colombia, Guatemala, Honduras, Lesotho, Mali, Mexico, Panama, Papua New Guinea, Portugal, Senegal, Sierra Leone, South Africa, and Zimbabwe (World Bank 2000a:238–239). Figure 8-3 (on page 200) compares the distribution of income in selected industrialized and developing nations.

Sociology in the Global Community

8-3 Inequality in Japan

A tourist visiting Japan may at first experience a bit of culture shock after noticing the degree to which everything in Japanese life is ranked: corporations, universities, even educational programs. These rankings are widely reported and accepted. Moreover, the ratings shape day-to-day social interactions: Japanese find it difficult to sit, talk, or eat together unless the relative rankings of those present have been established, often through the practice of meishi (the exchange of business cards).

The apparent preoccupation with ranking and formality suggests an exceptional degree of stratification, yet researchers have determined that Japan's level of income inequality is among the *lowest* of major industrial societies (see Figure 8-3 on page 200). Whereas the pay gap between Japan's top corporate executives and the nation's lowest-paid workers is about 8 to 1, the comparable figure for the United States would be 37 to 1. In addition, Japanese law prohibits the lucrative stock options that are a common perk in Canadian corporations.

This relative level of income equality in Japanese society dates back to post–World War II economic changes, including extensive land reform and the breakup of powerful holding companies. A lower level of inequality was helped along by an expanding economy combined with a labour shortage. However, during the 1990s the gap between rich and poor began to grow as a result of a severe economic recession and tax laws that let the rich hold on to more of their money.

Despite the relatively low level of *income* inequality in Japan, there are various other forms of inequality evident in Japanese society. For example, even though Japan is rather homogeneous—certainly when compared with Canada—in terms of race, ethnicity, nationality, and language, there is discrimination against the nation's Chinese and Korean minorities, and the *Burakumin* constitute a low-status subculture who encounter extensive prejudice.

Perhaps the most pervasive form of inequality in Japan today is gender discrimination. Japanese girls do not receive the same encouragement to achieve in education that boys do. It should be no surprise, then, that Japanese women occupy a subordinate position in higher education. Whereas 80 percent of the nation's male college students are in four-year universities, two thirds of female students are in women's junior colleges that promote traditional domestic roles for women. Even when Japanese women enter four-year universities, they often major in home economics, nutrition, or literature.

Even in developing countries, women are twice as likely to be managers as in Japan.

Overall, women earn only about 64 percent of men's wages. Fewer than 10 percent of Japanese managers are female—a ratio that is one of the lowest in the world. Even in developing countries, women are twice as likely to be managers as in Japan.

In 1985, Japan's parliament—at the time, 97 percent male—passed an Equal Employment bill that encourages employers to end sex discrimination in hiring, assignment, and promotion policies. However, feminist organizations were dissatisfied because the law lacked strong sanctions. In a landmark ruling issued in late 1996, a Japanese court for the first time held an employer liable for denying promotions due to sex discrimination. The court ordered a Japanese bank to pay 12 female employees a total of almost US$1 million and added that 11 of the women must immediately be promoted to management posts.

On the political front, Japanese women have made progress but remain underrepresented. In a study of women in government around the world, the Inter-Parliamentary Union found that, as of 1999, Japan ranked near the bottom of the countries studied, with less than 5 percent of its national legislators female.

Let's Discuss

1. What factors contribute to the relatively low level of income inequality in Japan?
2. Describe the types of gender discrimination found in Japan. Why do you think Japanese women occupy such a subordinate social position?

Sources: Abegglen and Stalk 1985; French 2000; Inter-Parliamentary Union 1999; Jordan 1996; Kerbo 1996; Kristof 1995; Magnier 1999; Nakane 1970; Sterngold 1992; Strom 2000b.

The decade of the 1980s was particularly cruel for many developing countries. Some nations—including Zambia, Bolivia, and Nigeria—saw per capita income plummet as dramatically as it did in Canada during the Great Depression of the 1930s. With these trends in mind, researcher Alan Durning (1990:26) observed that the term "developing nation" has become a cruel misnomer: Many of the world's less affluent nations are disintegrating rather than developing.

Feminist theories see life in developing countries as especially difficult for women. The example of women under the Taliban regime in Afghanistan is one extreme in this pattern. Karuna Chanana Ahmed, an anthropologist from India who has studied women in developing nations,

FIGURE 8-3

Distribution of Income in Nine Nations

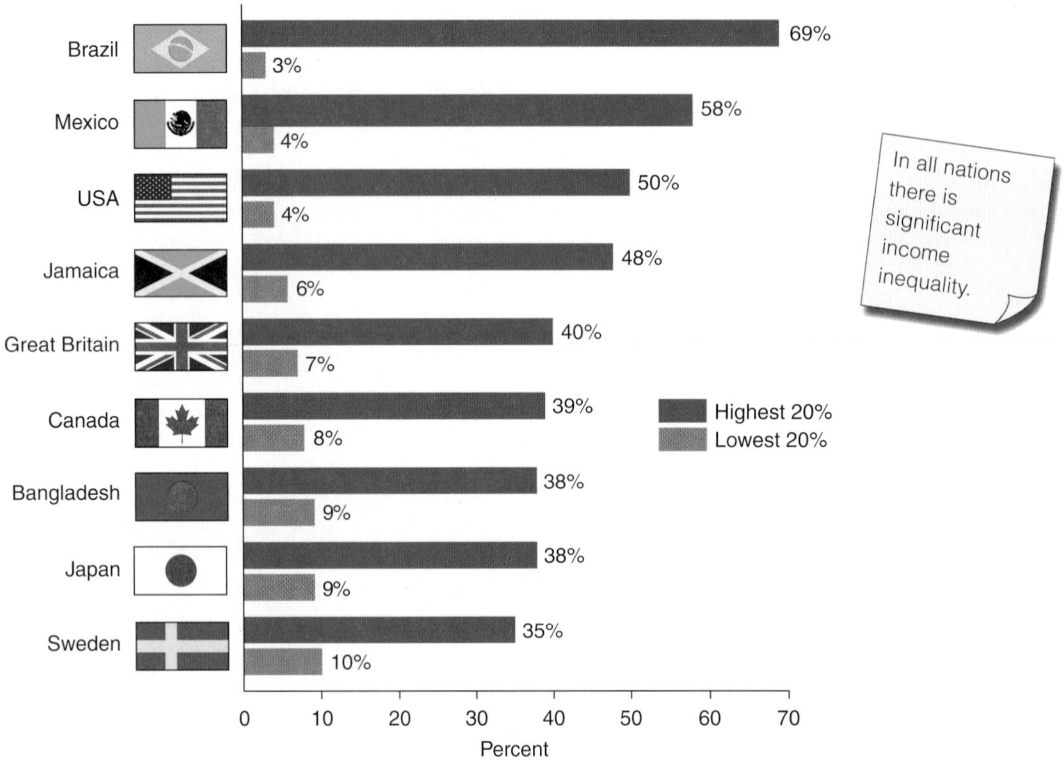

Note: Data are considered comparable although based on statistics covering 1986 to 1999.

Sources: World Bank 1997a:54–56; 2000a:238–239. U.S. data from the Congressional Budget Office cited in Shapiro and Greenstein 1999.

calls women the most exploited among oppressed people. Women face sex discrimination beginning at birth. They are commonly fed less than male children, are denied educational opportunities, and are often hospitalized only when critically ill. Whether inside or outside the home, women's work is devalued. When economies fail, as they did in Asian countries in the late 1990s and in Argentina in late 2001, women are the first to be laid off from work (J. Anderson and Moore 1993; Kristof 1998).

Surveys show a significant degree of *female infanticide* (the killing of baby girls) in China and rural areas of India. Only one third of Pakistan's sexually segregated schools are for women, and one third of these schools have no buildings. In Kenya and Tanzania, it is illegal for a woman to own a house. In Saudi Arabia, women are prohibited from driving, walking alone in public, and socializing with men outside their families (C. Murphy 1993). We will explore women's second-class status throughout the world more fully in Chapter 10.

What factors have contributed to the recent difficulties of developing nations? Certainly runaway population growth has hurt the standard of living of many Third World peoples. So, too, has the accelerating environmental decline evident in the quality of air, water, and other natural resources. (We will examine population growth and environmental decline in more detail in Chapters 14 and 15.) Still another factor has been the developing nations' collective debt of US$1.3 trillion. If we add to a nation's debt repayment the estimates of money being invested elsewhere by its wealthy citizens, the annual outflow of funds may reach US$100 billion (Durning 1990; Kerbo 2000).

Unfortunately, the massive exodus of money from poorer regions of the world only intensifies their destruction of natural resources. From a conflict view, less affluent nations are being forced to exploit their mineral deposits, forests, and fisheries to meet their debt obligations while offering only subsistence labour to local workers. The poor turn to the only means of survival available to them: marginal lands. They plough mountain slopes, burn plots in tropical forests, and overgraze grasslands—often knowing that their actions are destructive to the environment. But they see no alternative in their agonizing fight for simple survival (Durning 1990; Waring 1988).

Survival is at the heart of an important social policy issue: welfare—how to provide for the basic needs of the world's poorest, a topic we turn to now in the social policy section.

SOCIAL POLICY AND STRATIFICATION

Rethinking Welfare in North America and Europe

The Issue

- After five years on Ontario's welfare role, a single mother of two is a success story. The 28-year-old has landed a job at a storage company and moved up to a $9-an-hour customer service position. But at the same time, a worker in a nearby hotel earning just $6.85 per hour worries about being edged back into unemployment by the stiff competition for low-wage jobs.
- A single mother in Paris, France has waited for four months to obtain a place in government-subsidized day care for her daughter. Now she can seek a full-time job, but she is concerned about government threats to curtail such services to keep taxes down (Simons 1997).

These are the faces of people living on the edge—often women with children seeking to make a go of it amidst changing social policies. Governments in all parts of the world are searching for the right solution to welfare: How much subsidy should they provide? How much responsibility should fall on the shoulders of the poor?

The federal government has used the Team Canada approach to drum up international trade for Canada. This photo depicts Team Canada trade mission members at the conclusion of a mission in Hong Kong. Some social theorists argue that an increased dependence on foreign trade disproportionately benefits the wealthy.

The Setting

By the 1990s, there was intense debate in Canada and the other Western democracies over the issue of welfare. Welfare programs were costly, and there was widespread concern (however unfounded) that welfare payments discouraged recipients from seeking jobs. Those at both ends of the ideological spectrum vowed to "end welfare as we know it" (Pear 1996:20).

For the conservative element, like those in the governments of Ontario and Alberta, the goal was to make people who relied on the public purse accountable. "Workfare," a program to require able welfare recipients to work for their money, was proposed as a way of discouraging abuses of the system and providing some degree of dignity to those who had to rely on welfare. At the other end of the spectrum, social democrats like the former NDP government in British Columbia sought ways to improve the living conditions of those on welfare by revamping existing programs and increasing rates.

Countries vary widely in their commitment to social service programs. Because the Canadian system places some social assistance programs, such as employment insurance, under federal direction, and others, such as welfare, under provincial jurisdiction, the exact amount spent by the country on these initiatives is difficult to determine. However, most industrialized nations devote higher proportions of their expenditures to housing, social security, welfare, and unemployment compensation than the 54 percent allotted by the United States. By comparison, in Switzerland in 1997, 71 percent of central-government spending went to these social service areas and in Ireland, 60 percent. A study by sociologist Greg Duncan (1994) of welfare programs in the United States and seven European nations found that a higher proportion of the poor escape poverty in Europe.

Apparently, the greater benefits facilitate upward mobility (World Bank 2000a:256–257).

Sociological Insights

Many sociologists tend to view the debate over welfare throughout industrialized nations from a conflict perspective: the "haves" in positions of policymaking listen to the interests of other "haves," while the cries of the "have-nots" are drowned out. Critics of so-called welfare reform believe that Canada's economic problems are being unfairly blamed on welfare spending and the poor. From a conflict perspective, this backlash against welfare recipients reflects deep fears and hostility toward the country's visible minority underclass.

Those critical of the backlash note that "welfare scapegoating" conveniently ignores the lucrative federal handouts that go to *affluent* individuals and families. For example, while federal employment insurance benefits were being cut by 40 percent during the 1990s, millions of dollars were spent to finance trips by Team Canada, a trade delegation including the Prime Minister and executives from some of the country's most profitable companies. The group travelled the globe drumming up business opportunities for those enterprises.

Those who take a conflict perspective also urge policymakers and the general public to look closely at *corporate welfare,* the tax breaks, direct payments, and grants that the government makes to corporations, rather than focus on the comparatively small allowances being given to mothers on welfare and their children. These messages have received a mixed response. Overall, in Canada, despite the increase in poverty during the decade of the 1990s, the number of people on welfare has dropped. Between 1994 and 1995 for example, the drop was almost 1 percent, or close to 30 000 recipients. The numbers in Alberta dropped by 18.3 percent, while those in British Columbia rose by 5.9 percent, reflecting the priorities of the governments in those provinces (HRDC 1997).

Policy Initiatives

The direction of social policy in Canada over the past decade has been toward a leaner, more restrictive access to government subsidies for the poor. At the federal level, changes to qualifications for employment insurance resulted in a reduction of $6 billion in spending in this area between 1990 and1996. This was despite an announced cumulative surplus of $20 billion in the fund by 1998. In the provincially controlled area of social assistance, a number of provinces that have historically offered the highest benefits, including Ontario and Prince Edward Island, have cut benefits most dramatically (National Anti-poverty Organization 1998).

European governments have encountered many of the same demands by their citizens as those in North America: Keep our taxes low, even if it means reducing services to the poor. However, nations in eastern and central Europe have faced a special challenge since the end of communism. The governments in those nations had traditionally provided an impressive array of social services, but they differed from capitalist systems in several important respects. First, the communist system was premised on full employment, so there was no need to provide unemployment insurance; social services focused on the old and the disabled. Second, subsidies, such as for housing and even utilities, played an important role. With new competition from the West and tight budgets, some of these countries (as well as Sweden, despite its long history of social welfare programs) are beginning to realize that a system of universal coverage is no longer affordable and must be replaced by more targeted programs. Some of these countries' residents have sought refuge in western Europe, putting new demands on social service systems there just as people are calling for a moratorium on higher taxes (World Bank 1997a: 55–57; Kuptsch and Mazie 1999).

Both in North America and Europe, people are beginning to turn to private means to support themselves. For instance, they are investing money for their later years rather than depending on government social security programs. But that solution only works if you have a job and can save money. Increasing proportions of people are seeing the gap between themselves and the affluent widening with fewer government programs to assist them. Solutions are frequently left to the private sector, while government policy initiatives at the national level all but disappear.

Let's Discuss

1. How did the level of spending for social services in Canada change over the 1990s? What accounts for the differences?
2. Do you think welfare recipients should be required to work? What kind of support should they be given?
3. Have welfare reforms introduced by the various provincial governments been successful? Why or why not?

Chapter Resources

Summary

Stratification is the structured ranking of entire groups of people that perpetuates unequal economic rewards and power in a society. In this chapter, we examine three general systems of stratification, the explanations offered by functionalist, feminist, and conflict theorists for the existence of social inequality, the relationship between stratification and social mobility, and stratification within the world system as well as within nations.

1. Some degree of ***social inequality*** characterizes all cultures.
2. Systems of ***stratification*** include ***slavery***, ***castes***, and social ***class***.
3. Karl Marx saw that differences in access to the means of production created social, economic, and political inequality and distinct classes of owners and labourers.
4. Max Weber identified three analytically distinct components of stratification: ***class***, ***status***, and ***power***.
5. Functionalists argue that stratification is necessary so that people will be motivated to fill society's important positions; conflict theorists see stratification as a major source of societal tension and conflict.
6. According to feminist theories, one consequence of unequal distribution of ***wealth*** and ***income*** in Canada is the patriarchal nature of our society.
7. The category of the "poor" defies any simple definition and counters common stereotypes about "poor people." The long-term poor who lack training and skills form an ***underclass***.
8. One's ***life chances***—opportunities for obtaining material goods, positive living conditions, and favourable life experiences—are related to one's social class. Occupying a higher social position improves a person's life chances.
9. ***Social mobility*** is more likely to be found in an ***open system*** that emphasizes achieved status than in a ***closed system*** that focuses on ascribed characteristics. Race, gender, and family background are important factors in mobility.
10. Formerly colonized nations are kept in a subservient position, subject to foreign domination, through the process of ***neocolonialism***.
11. Drawing on the conflict perspective, the world systems analysis of sociologist Immanuel Wallerstein views the global economic system as divided between nations that control wealth *(core nations)* and those from which capital is taken *(periphery nations)*.
12. According to ***dependency theory***, even as developing countries make economic advances, they remain weak and subservient to core nations and corporations within an increasingly intertwined global economy.
13. ***Multinational corporations*** bring jobs and industry to developing nations, but they also tend to exploit the workers there in order to maximize profits.
14. According to ***modernization theory***, development in peripheral countries will be assisted by the innovations transferred from the industrialized world.
15. Social mobility is more limited in developing nations than in the core nations.
16. Many governments are struggling with how much of their tax revenues to spend on welfare programs. The sentiment that welfare recipients should be put to work is gaining favour in Canada.

Critical Thinking Questions

1. The Canadian Council on Social Development is a research organization devoted to "promoting better social and economic security for all Canadians. Among other things, the Council publishes annually *The Canadian Fact Book on Poverty* profiling the situation of Canada's economically disadvantaged.

   The Fraser Institute, a conservative alternative to the CCSD, is most known for its *Tax Freedom Day*, a calculation which informs Canadians of the calendar day each year when they stop working to pay their tax bill. Groups such as the CCSD exist to monitor the social health of the country. Do you think they serve a worthwhile purpose? How would you compare the value of the research done by the CCSD to that of the business-sponsored Fraser Institute? Does Canada benefit from having advocates for both ends of the ideological spectrum?
2. Sociological study of stratification generally is conducted at the macrolevel and draws most heavily on the functionalist and conflict perspectives. How might sociologists use the *interactionist*

perspective to examine social class inequalities within a college or university community?

3. Imagine that you have the opportunity to spend a year in a developing country studying inequality in that nation. How would you draw on the research designs of sociology (surveys, observation, experiments, existing sources) to better understand and document stratification in this developing country?

Key Terms

Absolute poverty In developed countries, a standard of poverty based on a minimum level of subsistence below which families should not be expected to live. (page 185)

Bourgeoisie Karl Marx's term for the capitalist class, comprising the owners of the means of production. (179)

Capitalism An economic system in which the means of production are largely in private hands and the main incentive for economic activity is the accumulation of profits. (179)

Castes Hereditary systems of rank, usually religiously dictated, that tend to be fixed and immobile. (177)

Class A group of people who have a similar level of wealth and income. (179)

Class consciousness In Karl Marx's view, a subjective awareness held by members of a class regarding their common vested interests and need for collective political action to bring about social change. (179)

Class system A social ranking based primarily on economic position in which achieved characteristics can influence social mobility. (177)

Closed system A social system in which there is little or no possibility of individual mobility. (191)

Colonialism The maintenance of political, social, economic, and cultural dominance over a people by a foreign power for an extended period of time. (194)

Dependency theory A theory that contends that industrialized nations continue to exploit developing countries for their own gain. (196)

Esteem The reputation that a particular individual has earned within an occupation. (183)

False consciousness A term used by Karl Marx to describe an attitude held by members of a class that does not accurately reflect their objective position. (179)

Horizontal mobility The movement of an individual from one social position to another of the same rank. (192)

Income Salaries, wages, and monies brought in by investments. (176)

Intergenerational mobility Changes in the social position of children relative to their parents. (192)

Intragenerational mobility Changes in a person's social position within his or her adult life. (192)

Life chances People's opportunities to provide themselves with material goods, positive living conditions, and favourable life experiences. (189)

Low Income Cut-Off (LICO) The Canadian equivalent of a poverty line, in place until January 2001, which stated the maximum proportion of a household's income that should be spent on the basics—food, shelter, and clothing. If a household spent a greater proportion on these basics, it would be considered poor. (185)

Market Basket Measure (MBM) A way of determining relative poverty that takes into consideration more than subsistence needs, and calculates the income needed by various households to live a life comparable to community standards. (185)

Meritocracy A social system in which individuals earn their place in society. (176)

Modernization The far-reaching process by which peripheral nations move from traditional or less developed institutions to those characteristic of more developed societies. (198)

Modernization theory A functionalist approach that proposes that modernization and development will gradually improve the lives of people in peripheral nations. (198)

Multinational corporations Commercial organizations that, while headquartered in one country, own or control other corporations and subsidiaries throughout the world. (196)

Neocolonialism Continuing dependence of former colonies on foreign countries. (194)

Net worth is the amount by which the value of someone's assets exceeds his or her debts. (176)

Objective method A technique for measuring social class that assigns individuals to classes on the basis of criteria such as occupation, education, income, and place of residence. (183)

Open system A social system in which the position of each individual is influenced by his or her achieved status. (191)

Power The ability to exercise one's will over others. (180)

Prestige The respect and admiration that an occupation holds in a society. (183)

Proletariat Karl Marx's term for the working class in a capitalist society. (179)

Relative poverty A floating standard of deprivation by which people at the bottom of a society, whatever their lifestyles, are judged to be disadvantaged in comparison with the rest of the community in which they live. (185)

Slavery A system of enforced servitude in which people are legally owned by others and in which enslaved status is transferred from parents to children. (176)

Social inequality A condition in which members of a society have different amounts of wealth, prestige, or power. (175)

Social mobility Movement of individuals or groups from one position of a society's stratification system to another. (191)

Social safety net A system of social programs, such as welfare, employment insurance, Canada Pension Plan, etc., designed to alleviate the harshest conditions associated with being at the bottom of the income chain. (185)

Status consistency The notion that someone with high status in one area—income, for instance—is likely to be similarly ranked in other areas. (180)

Status group People who have the same prestige or lifestyle, independent of their class positions. (179)

Stratification A structured ranking of entire groups of people that perpetuates an unequal and stable distribution of economic rewards and power in a society. (176)

Underclass Long-term poor people who lack training and skills. (188)

Vertical mobility The movement of a person from one social position to another of a different rank. (192)

Wealth An inclusive term encompassing all of a person's material assets, including land and other types of property. (176)

World systems analysis A view of the global economic system as divided between certain industrialized nations that control wealth and developing countries that are controlled and exploited. (194)

Additional Readings

Bluestone, Barry, and Bennett Harrison. 1999. *Growing Prosperity: The Battle for Growth with Equity in the 21st Century.* Boston: Harrison Century Foundation/ Houghton Mifflin. A critical look at the impact of the red-hot United States economy on the entire population.

Bonacich, Edna, and Richard Appelbaum. 2000. *Behind the Label: Inequality in the Los Angeles Apparel Industry.* Berkeley: University of California Press. Examines the new wave of sweatshops that has made Los Angeles the largest centre of clothing production in the United States.

McQuaig, Linda. 1998. *The Cult of Impotence: Selling the Myth of Powerlessness in the Global Economy.* Toronto: Penguin Books. A challenge to the perception that globalization is inevitable, and that average citizens of the world have little or no power to stop or influence the process.

The World Bank. *World Development Report.* New York: Oxford University Press. Published annually by the International Bank for Reconstruction and Development (the United Nations agency more commonly referred to as the World Bank), this volume provides a vast array of social and economic indicators regarding world development.

Internet Connection

www.mcgrawhill.ca/college/schaefer

For additional Internet exercises relating to publications and organizations trying to help end homelessness, and the connection between social class and the sinking of the Titanic, *visit the Schaefer Online Learning Centre at **http://www.mcgrawhill.ca/college/schaefer**. Please note that while the URLs listed were current at the time of printing, these sites often change—check the Online Learning Centre for updates.*

Marginalization and inequality are a central focus of this chapter. The Canadian Council on Social Development is an organization devoted to researching social issues in this country. Explore their web pages at **http://www.gdsourcing.com/works/CCSD.htm** to find the answers to the following questions:

(a) What are the factors limiting access to computers?
(b) Identify several consequences of childhood poverty.
(c) How does disability affect employment access?
(d) Do a comparison of urban and rural poverty in Canada.
(e) What is the Personal Security Index?
(f) What social trends are changing public education in Canada?

CHAPTER 9
RACIAL AND ETHNIC INEQUALITY

LOOK BEYOND COLOUR
E·R·A·C·I·S·M

Eracism is a community-based program aimed at eliminating racial and ethnic discrimination through education. One of Eracism's initiatives is to raise awareness of March 21 as the International Day for the Elimination of Racial Discrimination.

[Many Canadians] have shown themselves prepared to own up to sins of intolerance. In a short time, they have built a nation that is multicultural, generous and respected throughout the world. They have done so, in part, by manifesting a willingness to confront racism and hatred and stamp them out in whatever form they appear.

Stamping out white supremacy, anti-Semitism, homophobia and their variants unfortunately will not be easy. At this stage in Canada's history, a number of forces are conspiring to assist racist leaders. Memories, for one, are fading: the horrors of World War Two become increasingly remote with the death of each Holocaust survivor, and Holocaust deniers are attempting to promote a more benign view of past events. In addition, harsh economic realities are crushing the hopes and dreams of a generation—and pushing some of these young people towards the simplistic siren song of hate. Finally, with changing immigration patterns, Canadians are being forced to come to grips with the presence of growing numbers of visible minorities—and they are being asked to accommodate lifestyles and cultural differences that, at first blush, seem strange. The pollsters tell us that all of these things, rightly or wrongly, have left many Canadians feeling insecure, threatened and under siege. And onto the stage have stepped the Klansmen and the neo-Nazis, with their calls for a return to the so-called status quo—and to a time when things were supposedly better for "white" Canadians.

That is not all: racist leaders are aided ironically by advances in technology. With the investment of only a few hundred dollars, they can spread their hateful messages with impunity. They can do so across national and international borders, far from the eyes of police agencies, using computer bulletin boards, fax machines and the like. Increasingly, too, the Canadian ultra-rightists are co-operating with each other. At rallies, conferences and on telephone lines, they are coming together as never before to recruit, attack minorities and propagandize. A good example of the effectiveness of their networking is found in the case of schoolteacher Malcolm Ross. The Moncton resident claims to be a lone dissenting voice in the proverbial wilderness. In fact, he is beneficiary of the attentions of hundreds of neo-Nazis across Canada, the United States and Europe.

Who is susceptible to the recruitment techniques of these hate-mongers? Their numbers include the unemployed, the disenfranchised and, most significantly, the young people who have been marginalized by chronic unemployment and society's increasing selfishness. Among these newcomers to racism we see, for example, the skinheads, who bring a fondness for violence that defies comprehension.

Every citizen of this country must work—and work hard—at maintaining the multicultural society that is Canada. Using the law, using the eduction system, we must remain vigilant. Canadian racist leaders are better organized, better funded and better united than they have been at any time in our history. If we do not fight organized racism for ourselves, then we must do it for our children—because it is the hearts and minds of our children, after all, that the racist leaders are determined to keep. *(Kinsella 1994)* ■

Some people believe that Canada, with its multiculturalism and strong reputation as a haven for refugees, is immune from the kinds of hate-based activities usually associated with the anti-Semitism of the Nazis, the apartheid regimes of South Africa, and the pre–civil rights era in the United States. Author Warren Kinsella, a Toronto-based lawyer and political consultant, challenges that complacency in his analysis of the growth and persistence of far-right supremacist groups in this country. Kinsella makes it clear that while tolerance may be a defining feature of Canadian society, it is not embraced by all Canadians.

This chapter will focus on the Canadian experience, and the implications of a history dominated by a white, anglo majority. Canada has moved significantly in recent decades to embrace the principles outlined in the Bilingualism and Multiculturalism Act of 1972, with important implications for the so-called "charter groups"—French and English—as well as for the myriad of minorities. We begin by identifying the basic characteristics of a minority group and distinguishing between racial and ethnic groups. The next section of the chapter will examine the dynamics of prejudice and discrimination. After considering the functionalist, conflict, interactionist, and feminist perspectives on race and ethnicity, we'll take a look at patterns of intergroup relations, particularly in Canada. Finally, the social policy section will explore issues related to immigration worldwide. ■

Minority, Racial, and Ethnic Groups

Sociologists frequently distinguish between racial and ethnic groups. The term ***racial group*** is used to describe a group that is set apart from others because of visible physical differences. Whites, blacks, First Nations people, and Asians are all considered racial groups in Canada. While race does turn on physical differences, it is the culture of a particular society that constructs and attaches social significance to these differences, as we will see later. Unlike racial groups, an ***ethnic group*** is set apart from others primarily because of its national origin or distinctive cultural patterns. In Canada, Japanese Canadians, Jews, and Italian Canadians are all categorized as ethnic groups. As we will learn later in the chapter, ethnic distinctions sometimes reflect the dominant culture's construction of racial categories. For example, white Canadians may classify Chinese, Korean, Japanese, and Vietnamese Canadians as "Asian," thus obscuring the important differences among these groups.

However, Canada is a multicultural society in which members of these minority groups are encouraged to maintain their distinctness within the larger national mosaic. This contrasts with the melting pot model in the United States, where minorities are expected to assume the American identity while adding their particular cultural flavour to the pot.

Minority Groups

A numerical minority is any group that makes up less than half of some larger population. The population of Canada includes thousands of numerical minorities, including television actors, green-eyed people, tax lawyers, and descendants of United Empire loyalists. However, these numerical minorities are not considered to be minorities in the sociological sense; in fact, the number of people in a group does not necessarily determine its status as a social minority (or dominant group). When sociologists define a minority group, they are primarily concerned with the economic and political power, or powerlessness, of that group. A ***minority group*** is a subordinate group whose members have significantly less control or power over their own lives than the members of a dominant or majority group have over theirs.

Sociologists have identified five basic properties of a minority group—unequal treatment, physical or cultural traits, ascribed status, solidarity, and in-group marriage (Wagley and Harris 1958):

1. Members of a minority group experience unequal treatment as compared to members of a dominant group. For example, the management of an apartment complex may refuse to rent to Jamaican or Chinese Canadians. Social inequality may be created or maintained by prejudice, discrimination, segregation, or even extermination.
2. Members of a minority group share physical or cultural characteristics that distinguish them from the dominant group. Each society arbitrarily decides which characteristics are most important in defining the groups.
3. Membership in a minority (or dominant) group is not voluntary; people are born into the group. Thus, race and ethnicity are considered *ascribed* statuses. p. 101
4. Minority group members have a strong sense of group solidarity. William Graham Sumner, writing

in 1906, noted that people make distinctions between members of their own group (the *in-group*) and everyone else (the *out-group*). When a group is the object of long-term prejudice and discrimination, the feeling of "us versus them" can and often does become extremely intense.

p. 126

5. Members of a minority generally marry others from the same group. A member of a dominant group is often unwilling to marry into a supposedly inferior minority. In addition, the minority group's sense of solidarity encourages marriages within the group and discourages marriages to outsiders.

Race

The term *racial group* refers to those minorities (and the corresponding dominant groups) set apart from others by obvious physical differences. It is important to remember, however, that while the physical differences may be obvious, the concept of race has no basis in science. Studies of the human genome have confirmed that in fact all humans share the same set of biological ancestors. Nonetheless, the social consequences associated with how a culture depicts race are very real. Each society determines which differences are important while ignoring other characteristics that could serve as a basis for social differentiation. In Canada, we see differences in both skin colour and hair colour. Yet people learn informally that differences in skin colour have a dramatic social and political meaning, while differences in hair colour do not.

When observing skin colour, people in Canada tend to lump others rather casually into such categories as "black," "white," and "Asian." More subtle differences in skin colour often go unnoticed. However, this is not the case in other societies. Many nations of Central America and South America have colour gradients distinguishing people on a continuum from light to dark skin colour. Brazil has approximately 40 colour groupings, while in other countries people may be described as "Mestizo Hondurans," "Mulatto Colombians," or "African Panamanians." What we see as "obvious" differences, then, are subject to each society's social definitions.

Three groups make up the largest visible minorities in Canada: people of Chinese descent, blacks, and South Asians. There has been a threefold increase in the proportion of the visible minority population since 1981. By 2001, Canadians of Chinese ancestry made up 26 percent of the country's visible minority population (Statistics Canada 2003e). The Chinese, followed by South Asians and blacks, made up two-thirds of the visible minorities in Canada in 2001.

Biological Significance of Race

Viewed from a biological perspective, the term *race* would refer to a genetically isolated group with distinctive gene frequencies. But it is impossible to scientifically define or identify such a group. Contrary to popular belief, there are no "pure races." Nor are there physical traits—whether skin colour or baldness—that can be used to describe one group to the exclusion of all others. If scientists examine a smear of human blood under a microscope, they cannot tell whether it came from a person whose ancestors immigrated to Canada from Kenya or Sweden or Thailand.

Migration, exploration, and invasion have led to intermingling of races. In Canada, the most significant racial exogamy (marriage outside one's own racial or ethnic group), took place in the Red River Valley in what is now Manitoba. There, men of French-Canadian ancestry known as the voyageurs married First Nations women, and the **Metis** were born. While the first of these relationships, begun in the mid-1700s, were the product of economic interdependence, the Metis as a group emerged to take an important place in the exploration and political evolution of the country.

Some people would like to find biological explanations to help social scientists understand why certain peoples of the world have come to dominate others (see the discussion of sociobiology in Chapter 4). Given the absence of pure racial groups, there can be no satisfactory biological answers for such social and political questions.

p. 77

Social Construction of Race

Although the characteristics we interpret as race are genetically determined, culture plays an important role in their implications. In Canada, we have created many racial categories including First Nations, Asian, black, and white. One of the ironies of race as a category is that the majority group that establishes the designations—in the case of Canada, whites—often fails to recognize itself as a racial category. In other words, white Canadians do not have their social identities racialized. At the same time, despite the fact that there are significant differences among the various national and ethnic identities grouped under "First Nations," "Asian," and "black," they are used pervasively in Canadian society. On the eastern edge of the Pacific Rim, for example, Asian countries have populations as physically and culturally distinct from one group to another as Italians are from Swedes. Obscuring these differences to create a single category labelled "Asians" reflects a white bias.

The debate over the biological validity of race has raged for centuries. A number of different theories have emerged claiming distinct origins for peoples who share certain physical characteristics. Just recently, however, the

Human Genome Project finished mapping the human genetic profile, and scientists have gathered clear evidence that we all share a common set of ancestors. This confirms that race is indeed a social construction. However, the fact that the term *race* is socially constructed and has limitations does not diminish its social significance.

A dominant or majority group has the power not only to define itself legally but to define a society's values. Sociologist William I. Thomas (1923), an early critic of theories of racial and gender differences, saw that the "definition of the situation" could mould the personality of the individual. To put it another way, Thomas, writing from the interactionist perspective, observed that people respond not only to the objective features of a situation or person but also to the *meaning* that situation or person has for them. Thus, we can create false images or stereotypes that become real in their consequences. ***Stereotypes*** are unreliable generalizations about all members of a group that do not recognize individual differences within the group.

In the last 30 years, critics have pointed out the power of the mass media to perpetuate false racial and ethnic stereotypes. Television is a prime example: Almost all the leading dramatic roles are cast as whites, even in urban-based programs like *Friends*. Blacks tend to be featured mainly in crime-based dramas.

Ethnicity

Whereas race is attributed on the basis of physical features, ethnicity is a reflection of cultural affiliation. An ethnic group may share language, religion, and/or ancestry. As with race, ethnicity is subjectively assigned by one group to another, or assumed by a group as an identity. Canadian sociologist John Porter (1965) was one of the first to recognize the limiting potential when distinct ethnic identities compose a single society.

The distinction made between racial and ethnic minorities is not always clear. For example, citizens of Canada who are labelled as racially "black" do not share a common culture. Some come from the developing nations of Africa and the Caribbean, while others come from the more technologically advanced societies like the United States and England. The physical characteristics that have led them to be assigned to a racial group have no impact on their ethnic heritage, the cultural standards to which they were socialized. This is an ethnically diverse population. However, the consequences of being perceived as a member of a minority racial group are clear. Members of racial minorities have less access to both opportunity and status.

Another example in Canada relates to peoples from Asia, some of whom are referred to collectively as Indo-Canadians, while others are designated simply as coming from Asian cultural heritage. Both designations encompass a variety of religious, linguistic, and cultural standards. While these groupings are convenient classifications, they encourage stereotyping and obscure important differences, as well as the reality that many Canadians are of mixed ethnic ancestry. Table 9-1 profiles selected ethnic origins by single and multiple responses, according to the 2001 Canadian census.

In his 1965 classic, *The Vertical Mosaic*, Porter characterized the diversity of Canadian society as a mosaic resembling a tiled floor, in which each piece is distinct, but nonetheless forms part of a larger whole. Porter characterized the Canadian mosaic as "vertical," by which he implied that the ethnic distinctions that define Canadians make it easy to discriminate against minorities. In other words, encouraging immigrants to Canada to maintain their ethnic distinctiveness makes it easier to slot them

Caribana, which takes place each year in Toronto, is one of the largest celebrations of West Indies culture and arts in North America. The 18-day festival concludes with a massive tribute to the islands and their peoples on the first Monday in August.

Table 9-1 Population by Selected Ethnic Origins, Canada, 2001 Census

	Total Responses	Single Responses	Multiple Responses
Total Population	**29 639 035**	**18 307 545**	**11 331 490**
Ethnic Origin			
Canadian	11 682 680	6 748 135	4 934 545
English	5 978 875	1 479 525	4 499 355
French	4 668 410	1 060 760	3 607 655
Scottish	4 157 210	607 235	3 549 975
Irish	3 822 660	496 864	3 325 795
German	2 742 765	705 600	2 037 170
Italian	1 270 370	726 275	544 090
Chinese	1 094 700	936 210	158 490
Ukrainian	1 071 060	326 195	744 860
North American Indian	1 000 890	455 805	545 085
Dutch (Netherlands)	923 310	316 220	607 090
Polish	817 085	260 415	556 665
East Indian	713 330	581 665	131 665
Norwegian	363 760	47 230	316 530
Portuguese	357 690	252 835	104 855
Welsh	350 365	28 445	321 920
Jewish	348 605	186 475	162 130
Russian	337 960	70 895	267 070
Filipino	327 550	266 140	61 405
Métis	307 845	72 210	235 635
Swedish	282 760	30 440	252 325
Hungarian (Magyar)	267 255	91 800	175 455
American (USA)	250 005	25 205	224 805
Greek	215 105	143 785	71 325
Spanish	213 105	66 545	146 555
Jamaican	211 720	138 180	73 545
Danish	170 780	33 795	136 985
Vietnamese	151 410	119 120	32 290

Source: Statistics Canada 2003a.

into one of the lower levels of the mosaic. In the past, these characteristics of Canadian society may have led to the creation of ethnic stereotypes; they still may.

Characteristics of Ethnicity

Beyond the basic elements of shared customs, religion, language, and ancestry, ethnicity has four significant characteristics. First, ethnic affiliation is handed down from generation to generation. An ethnic group must have the capacity to pass on its standards of behaviour, its moral and ethical foundation, and its material culture. The stronger the ties within the group, the better the ability of its members to instill in their children the beliefs and expectations of their culture.

A second factor, linked to the first, is that ethnicity is an ascribed status. An ascribed status is one that is assigned to someone, as opposed to achieved status, which is earned. A child is born with a cultural identity defined by the ethnicity of his or her parents. And while it may be possible to change one's citizenship, it is not possible to change one's ethnicity. Even though it is possible to abandon one's cultural origins, as in the case of someone who renounces the religion practised by his or her parents, one's original ethnic linkage remains part of one's identity.

A third element of ethnicity is structure. The structures of an ethnic community—its institutions, roles, and distribution of power—evolve over many generations, the product of social interaction and interdependence. Particularly important to the survival of any ethnic group is its capacity to provide for its members. ***Institutional completeness*** refers to the degree to which an ethnic community provides for its own institutional needs, particularly in the key areas of religion, education, and social welfare. History has shown that those groups that have been able to remain institutionally independent have a better chance of maintaining the integrity of their community.

A good example of the importance of institutional completeness can be found on the Prairies, particularly in Saskatchewan and Manitoba. A century ago, when immigrant agriculturalists were recruited from eastern Europe, the Canadian government's settlement policy consisted of loading newcomers onto trains at Quebec City, then depositing them along the new Canadian Pacific line, somewhere beyond the Canadian Shield. Dozens of rural communities developed in the isolation of Prairie vastness and harsh climate. As a result, these settlements of German, Ukrainian, and Polish farm families had to fend for themselves. Today, that part of the country is still dotted with towns where the dominant language is German, Ukranian, or Polish, and the community institutions reflect the ethnic origins of the population.

The final component of ethnicity is identity. Ethnic identity can only be established if a group's institutions and standards are different enough from those of other groups to provide its members with a sense of distinctiveness. The concept of ***social distance*** refers to the degree of difference that exists between two cultures. There is very little social distance between the cultures of the United States and Canada. The more established the ethnicity, the clearer these lines of demarcation are likely to be, and, as a consequence, the easier it is to define membership. The fact that both the United States and Canada are relatively new cultures, and that they derive from the same source—the Anglo Saxon, Christian, British tradition—explains their similarities.

Social Construction of Ethnicity

We have already talked about how race is socially constructed. Ethnicity is effected by a similar process. The designation of a particular group as "ethnic" can be as much a function of that group's treatment within a given society as it is of any real or imagined cultural divide. A number of such groups have emerged in Canada, including the Doukhbors. While they are a Christian group from eastern Europe, not unlike many others who came to Canada in the late 1800s and early 1900s to settle the land in the West, these Russian immigrants have been singled out for harsh treatment by authorities because of their fervent adherence to religious doctrine. As with race, ethnicity is important within a society only when the dominant culture makes it so.

Despite categorization problems, sociologists continue to feel that the distinction between racial groups and ethnic groups is socially significant. That is because in most societies, including Canada, physical differences tend to be more visible than ethnic differences. Partly as a result of this fact, stratification along racial lines is more resistant to change than stratification along ethnic lines. Members of an ethnic minority sometimes can become, over time, indistinguishable from the majority—although this process may take generations and may never include all members of the group. By contrast, members of a racial minority find it much more difficult to blend in with the larger society and to gain acceptance from the majority.

Prejudice and Discrimination

As the full impact of the events of September 11, 2001, began to sink in, people in the Western world, and Americans in particular, responded with calls for retribution. To their credit, public figures warned against rash responses. President George W. Bush was among the first to remind his country that terrorist acts had been carried out by extremists who did not represent the majority of Muslims. Despite the President's caution, attacks on Muslims, or even people thought to be Muslims, occurred. In one instance, a man wearing a turban, mistaken by his attackers to be Muslim, was beaten to death. In Canada, concerns about similar acts of violence led Keith Norton, Chief Commissioner of the Ontario Human Rights Commission, to issue a statement reminding Ontarians that discrimination is against the law in that province. He urged people to guard against backlash, and to ". . . build bridges of goodwill and understanding." (Ontario Human Rights Commission 2001).

Prejudice is a negative attitude toward an entire category of people. The group may be race-based, ethnicity-based, or labelled as a social category defined by some other culturally relevant characteristic. A ***social category*** is a group defined by some culturally relevant characteristic; that is, one that has an impact on a person's status within a society. For example, your career puts you in a social category. If you are a doctor, you may be approached differently than if you are a labourer. Even seemingly trivial characteristics can have an effect. If you refuse to eat meat, you may be placed in a category that influences the way people perceive or treat you. Prejudice perpetuates inaccurate and often damaging characterizations, and is frequently the product of insufficient information.

When a prejudice involves the negative evaluation of someone based on an ethnic affiliation, it can be a product of ***ethnocentrism***—the tendency to assume that one's own culture is better than all others. From this perspective, an individual evaluates other cultures by comparing them negatively to his or her own. In effect, the holder of the prejudice is saying: The standards of my culture are the right ones, and my beliefs and my morality are superior. This prejudice becomes discrimination when it translates into action.

One important and widespread form of prejudice is ***racism***. Despite the obvious implications of the word, racism is not directed solely toward those with different skin colour or other physically distinguishing characteristics. It can also be based on ethnic indicators such as language and dress, informing an attitude that judges members as less deserving or less capable than those belonging to the dominant group (Stasiulis 1990).

As illustrated by the examples already provided in this chapter, Canada, despite its image as a safe haven for international refugees, is not without its hate groups that foment distrust and negative stereotypes of racial and ethnic minorities. The Ku Klux Klan has actively recruited new members in Canada for decades. In the 1920s, KKK membership in Saskatchewan was estimated at several thousand. Today, some of the leading figures of this organization have become visible in the media, including Jim Keegstra, the Alberta high school social studies teacher who taught Holocaust denial, and Wolfgang Droege, head of the ultra-right Heritage Front.

While the activity of hate groups in Canada seems limited, with some estimates indicating that membership in hate organizations is less than 1000 for the whole country (Barrett 1987), there is growing concern about the potential threat posed by an explosion of Internet sites devoted to spreading race- and ethnicity-based prejudice. Websites on the Internet advocating hatred numbered at least 2000 as of 1999. Among these are the *Zundelsite*, promoting hatred of Jews, and the *Heritage Front Resource Center*, which offers an array of material in support of white nationalism. Court challenges to these sites have had varied success. In January, 2002, the Canadian Human Rights Commission ordered the *Zundelsite* removed from the World Wide Web.

Particularly troubling are those sites disguised as video games for young people, or as "educational sites" about crusaders against prejudice, like Martin Luther King, Jr. The technology of the Internet has allowed race-hate groups to expand far beyond their traditional base in the southern United States (J. Sandberg 1999). It has also provided a platform for the worldwide distribution of material produced by anti-immigrant groups in Europe.

Discriminatory Behaviour

In 1997, Jason Lian and David Matthews published a study questioning whether John Porter's vertical mosaic still existed in Canada. The two researchers, from McMaster University and the University of British Columbia, respectively, came to the following conclusion:

> In sum, it is clear from these findings that educational achievement at any level fails to protect persons of visible minority background from being disadvantaged in terms of the income they receive (Lian and Matthews 1997:475)

The study found that there had been some improvement in return on educational attainment. For instance, French Canadians, who have suffered discrimination as a significant minority in Canada and even as a significant majority in their own province of Quebec for 200 years, had by the early 1990s reached a position of earning more than their counterparts of British extraction for the same level of education. The data also reveal a similar pattern for ethnic groups from Italy, Germany, and other parts of Europe.

However, Lian and Matthews found, such advances have not been enjoyed by all minority Canadians. Outcomes for those groups identified as "visible minorities with a racial identifier" were quite different. Asians and individuals from the Middle East gained less from having bachelor's, master's, or PhD degrees than did the non-visible minority population. Even further down the scale were First Nations peoples, who remained at the bottom of the Canadian income hierarchy.

Figure 9-1 shows the extent to which the population of Canada's largest city has been diversified by immigration.

FIGURE 9-1

Number of Immigrants per Country Who Landed in Toronto in 1999

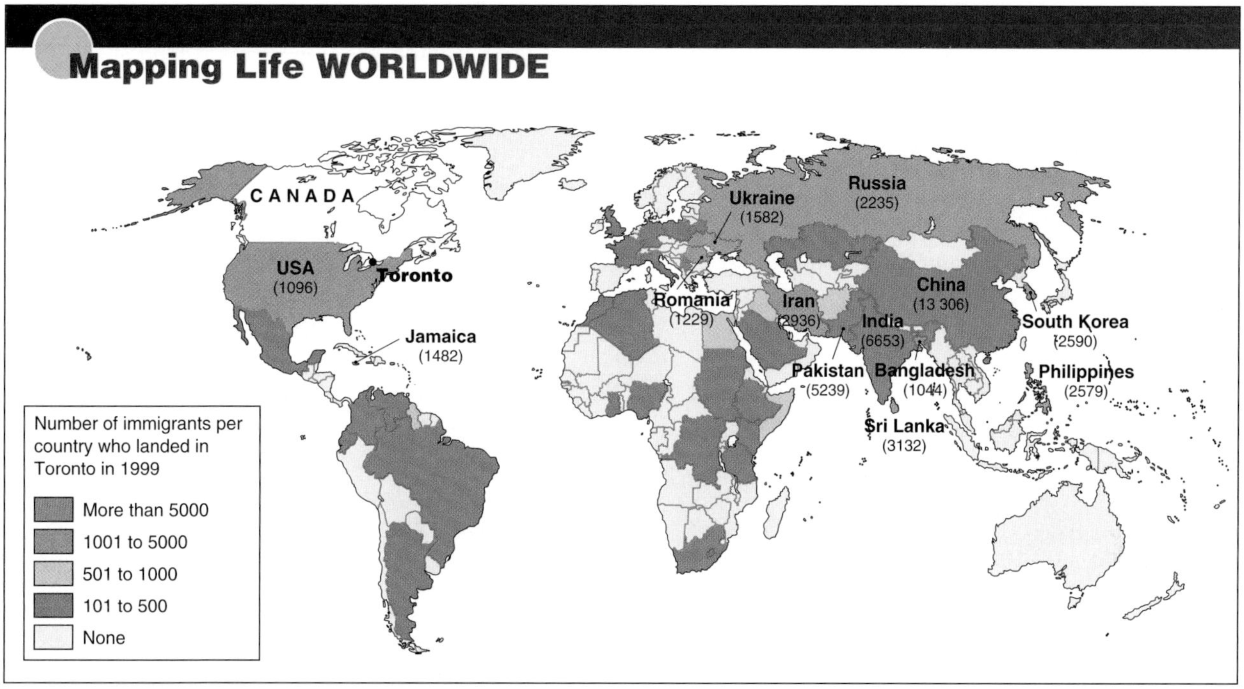

Source: Steven Fick, *Canadian Geographic* Magazine.

This map shows the sources of immigration to Canada's largest city. Like the rest of the country, Toronto has a diverse population that reflects its multicultural heritage.

However, the conclusions reached by Lian and Matthews cast some doubt on Canadians' claim that our multiculturalist society is without racism. The study suggests that while Canadians may be tolerant of difference, that tolerance is conditional. We are apparently willing to accept cultural variation from diverse European sources, but are less willing to accept difference if it is expressed as skin colour or as greater social distance. Beginning with the question "Does the vertical mosaic still exist?", the researchers ended with another, more troubling query: "Is Canada a racist society?"

Whereas prejudice can be seen as an attitude, discrimination can be characterized as behaviour. ***Discrimination*** is the denying of opportunities and equal rights to individuals and groups based on their membership in a particular social category. It is important to recognize that this process has an opposite effect on those who are not discriminated against. This is ***privilege***—access to opportunities provided to or denied people as a direct result of their membership in a particular societal group. White Anglo Saxon males in Canadian society have been the beneficiaries of such privilege since before Confederation.

There are two important expressions of discrimination that are of interest to sociologists: those that affect an individual's ability to participate in the economic opportunities available to most members of a particular society, and those that arbitrarily impose social segregation. Both of these types of discrimination are examples of ***marginalization***—the process by which an individual, as a result of her or his minority status, is provided only partial access to opportunities. The Lian and Matthews study demonstrated that visible minorities in Canada are indeed marginalized.

It is not surprising that prejudice often leads to discrimination. Suppose that you are a human resources manager for a large company, and you dislike people of a certain minority because of a *stereotype*—an unreliable generalization that all members of a group are the same and that, therefore, individual differences need not, or should not, be taken into consideration. This is a prejudice. However, if you refuse to offer a particular candidate a job because she belongs to a group about which you hold a stereotype, it is discrimination. As long as the stereotypes exist, it has the potential to influence behaviour, but that link is not inevitable.

Prejudiced attitude should not be equated with discriminatory behaviour. Although the two are generally related, they are not identical, and either condition can be

Research in Action 9-1 Minority Women and Federal Candidacy

There is a perception held by many women of colour, and supported by research, that they are members of a double minority, a situation that puts them at a distinct disadvantage in their efforts to participate in the mainstream of Canadian society. McGill University's Jerome Black examined the reality of this marginalization in his study *"Entering the Political Elite in Canada: The Case of Minority Women as Parliamentary Candidates and MPs."* In his findings, based on participation in the 1993 Canadian federal election, Black concludes that, despite efforts to compensate for the double set of obstacles faced by these women, "inequity continues to characterize the process of political elite access in Canada" (Black 2000).

Black suggests that Canadian women of colour are disadvantaged even in comparison with their counterparts in the United States. He argues that decades of visibility at the forefront of the American civil rights movement, as well as their positions of leadership in religious and other community organizations, have given black women a public status that has served them well in their efforts to assail the bastions of male political dominance.

In his contrasting of the experiences of minority women and females of English and/or French ancestry, Black found that minority women appeared to face more rigorous qualifying criteria in their attempts to enter federal politics. For instance, in a comparison of successful candidates for the 35th Canadian Parliament, minority women were found to have higher levels of accomplishment in both education and career attainments. One hundred percent of the visible minority women and 50 percent of women from southern European countries in the study had earned advanced degrees. This surpassed the 30 percent of women from English or French ancestry who achieved equivalent credentials. The same pattern held true for undergraduate degrees.

Canadian women of colour are disadvantaged even in comparison with their counterparts in the United States.

Besides the overachievement in credentials, the study revealed that this same group also appeared to have to work harder at establishing themselves within the party structure. It is customary for potential candidates to devote time to party activities as a volunteer. This practice intensifies as the election draws closer, particularly in the last month before nomination meetings. While all groups participate in this process, minority women, perhaps because of their awareness of the compounded disadvantage they face, contributed significantly more time to these activities than either male or female majority aspirants. Half the minority women candidates participated in this process, while only a third of other female candidates did.

The study also found there were factors that served to benefit minority women, although not always within the formal structure. Women in general were found on average to have better support from their personal and professional networks than did men. Minority women in all situations were found to have received more support for their political ambitions from family, friends, and their community. Within the formal partisan structure, minority women, more so than majority women or men, were encouraged by their parties to run for office. That encouragement carried over into the actual nomination process, in which three quarters of the minority MPs examined in the study had achieved their candidacy via acclamation.

Let's Discuss

1. Do you think enough has been done, or is being done, to encourage the participation of minority women at all levels of Canadian politics?
2. Is gender a factor when your family discusses political candidates? What about your circle of friends?

Source: Black 2000.

present without the other. A prejudiced person, perhaps because of social pressure or out of convenience, does not always act on his or her biases. As a human resources manager, you might feel pressure from your boss, company policy, or your fellow workers to provide an opportunity for our hypothetical minority applicant. Or, you might find her résumé so outstanding that you cannot let her go to the competition. In these cases, prejudice does not lead to discrimination. On the other hand, if the only reason you refused to hire this minority applicant was out of fear that your company's biggest client—a big-league bigot—would take his business elsewhere, that would be discrimination without prejudice.

Discrimination persists even for those minority group members who are well educated, highly qualified, and come from the most advantaged family backgrounds. Box 9-1 shows that even though more and more women of colour are entering the political arena, they must overcome greater obstacles than their white, male counterparts. In the past decade, more and more of these women have made it past traditional political party gatekeepers and through glass ceilings to become elected representatives in Parliament and the provincial legislatures. The term ***glass ceiling*** refers to an invisible barrier that blocks the promotion of a qualified individual in a work environment because of the individual's gender, race, or ethnicity (Schaefer 2002; H. Yamagata et. al. 1997).

The other side of discrimination is privilege, described earlier in this section. Feminist scholar Peggy McIntosh (1988) has come up with a list of advantages she enjoyed that come from white privilege. They include (1) not having to spend time with people she was trained to mistrust or who have learned to mistrust her kind; (2) being considered financially reliable when using cheques, credit cards, or cash; (3) never having to speak for all the people in her racial group; (4) taking a job without having coworkers suspect she got it because of race; and (5) being able to worry about racism without being regarded as self-serving.

Institutional Discrimination

Discrimination is practised not only by individuals in one-to-one encounters but also by institutions in their daily operations. Social scientists are particularly concerned with the ways in which structural factors such as employment, housing, health care, and government operations maintain the social significance of race and ethnicity. ***Institutional discrimination*** refers to the denial of opportunities and equal rights to individuals and groups that results from the normal operations of a society. This kind of discrimination consistently affects certain racial and ethnic groups more than others.

Changes to the Canadian Citizenship Act in 1967 introduced a new set of criteria for allowing immigrants into the country. While the previous standards had focused on race and ethnicity, the new act evaluated applicants on their ability to contribute to the Canadian economy. This method of evaluation became known as the "points system." While non-whites had been allowed in previously, the circumstances were narrowly defined and self-serving—blacks as slaves, Chinese as railway workers, minority women to be domestics or nannies. From the earliest days of immigration, Canada's policies restricted entrance on the basis of race and ethnicity, and that restrictive approach was further emphasized by the Immigration Act of 1952, which gave government the power to arbitrarily restrict the entry of individuals based solely on their ethnic or racial status (Pigler Christensen 2001). This policy reflected Ottawa's long-term strategy of institutional racism, in which exclusion was accomplished through proscriptive guidelines, avoiding formal policies that explicitly barred entry to ethnic and racial minorities. But perhaps the single most blatant act of institutional racism in Canadian history was the 60 years of residential schooling imposed on First Nations children and their families (Haig-Brown 1988).

In November 1999, *Lethal Weapon* star Danny Glover charged the city of New York with discrimination after several municipally licensed cabs passed him by. A former cabdriver himself, Glover declared that the Big Apple's cabbies needed diversity training.

The argument is often heard that since the Charter of Rights and Freedoms was entrenched in the repatriated Constitution Act of 1982, Canadian institutions have been unable to discriminate. The good intentions of those who wrote the Charter cannot be questioned, but the claim that discrimination has been eradicated certainly is open to debate.

Discrimination in educational institutions is seen as particularly punitive because of its potential for long-term impact on the life chances of the individuals against whom it is perpetrated. Henry et al. (1995) examined the implications of a "sacrosanct" curriculum in our universities, citing a Queen's University report that identified Eurocentric characteristics in that school's course offerings. The report identified:

- The need for course names that reflect their content (e.g., "The History of Political Thought" should be renamed "The History of Western Political Thought")

- The need for core courses (required for majors students) that include more than just the Eurocentric issues
- The need for anti-racist courses in the curriculum, and the need to make them mandatory in some curricula
- The need to hire faculty who can teach courses that do not have a Eurocentric focus
- The need to introduce more interdisciplinary studies, such as black studies and First Nations studies
- The need to develop supplementary programs for minority students that would help them meet academic standards.

These vestiges of European privilege are not unique. Across Canada, schools at all levels are working to identify and eliminate similar shortcomings.

In Canada, we often point south of the border when discrimination in the enforcement or judicial arms of the justice system is the topic. The overrepresentation of blacks in American jails is a repeated theme among those fighting for racial equality. However, as the case below illustrates, Canadian authorities have faced similar charges.

The *Canadian Human Rights Advocate* reported the case of the discriminatory treatment of a black man by Victoria police in the late 1980s. The man, a Canadian citizen with a graduate-level education, went to a local restaurant to eat. His order was taken by the server, but then as he waited for his meal, he was approached by another employee and told that he would have to move so that she could seat two people at the table he was occupying. As there were no other seats available at the time, he refused. The Victoria police were summoned, and on arriving, questioned the man pointedly about his citizenship, threatened him with deportation, and took him off to jail in handcuffs. He was held there for eight hours. The man subsequently complained to the provincial Human Rights Council, which concluded that he had been the victim of racial discrimination, and awarded damages (Kallen 1990). The argument could be made that this type of incident is more a reflection of the prejudices of the individual police officers; however, in their position as representatives of the state, it is the state that must be held accountable for their behaviour.

Institutional discrimination can also be found in the Canadian housing market. University of Calgary professor James Frideres points out that First Nations people in particular are subject to barriers when it comes to either buying or renting a home. Even though the Charter of Rights and Freedoms has discouraged landlords from overt racism in approving tenants, overt behaviour has been replaced by more subtle tactics. When they try to purchase a home, First Nations home buyers are often discouraged by realtors trying to protect the existing racial composition of a neighbourhood. Real estate companies worry that property values will drop if First Nations people move into a community, with an attendant loss in revenue and commissions (Bolaria 1995). As a result, First Nations people are discouraged from looking for a home in predominantly white neighbourhoods.

Since the enactment of the charter, Canadians have enacted other laws against institutional discrimination. The attempt to provide access to equal treatment across the social landscape has been effective for most Canadians most of the time, yet discriminatory practices continue to pervade nearly all areas of life in Canada today. In part, this is because various individuals and groups actually benefit from racial and ethnic discrimination in terms of money, status, and influence. Discrimination permits members of the dominant group to enhance their wealth, power, and prestige at the expense of others. Less qualified people may get jobs and promotions simply because they are members of the dominant group. Such individuals and groups will not surrender these advantages easily. We will now take a closer look at this functionalist analysis of discrimination, as well as the conflict, feminist, and interactionist perspectives.

Studying Race and Ethnicity

Relations among racial and ethnic groups lend themselves to analysis from the four major perspectives of sociology. Viewing race from the macrolevel, functionalists observe that racial prejudice and discrimination serve positive functions for dominant groups, whereas conflict theorists see the economic structure as a central factor in the exploitation of minorities. Some feminist perspectives, on the other hand, examine how gender, race, and class intersect to produce multiple degrees of inequality. The micro-level analysis of interactionist researchers stresses the manner in which everyday contact between people from different racial and ethnic backgrounds contributes to tolerance or leads to hostility.

Functionalist Perspective

What possible use could racial bigotry have for society? Functionalist theorists, while agreeing that racial hostility is hardly to be admired, point out that it indeed serves positive functions for those practising discrimination.

Anthropologist Manning Nash (1962) has identified three functions that racially prejudiced beliefs have for the dominant group:

1. Such views provide a moral justification for maintaining an unequal society that routinely deprives a minority of its rights and privileges. Before the

change in Canadian immigration policy allowing non-whites to apply for entrance, the discrimination against visible minorities was justified by claiming that there was only a limited number of menial jobs for which they were qualified (Satzewich 1991). It was reasonable to expect, therefore, that increasing the numbers of immigrants from those groups would only lead to unemployment and a drain on the welfare roles.
2. Racist beliefs discourage the subordinate minority from attempting to question its lowly status, which would be to question the very foundation of society. It is not difficult to imagine that an immigrant would hesitate to challenge the values of a society he or she has chosen as a new home.
3. Racial myths encourage support for the existing order by introducing the argument that any major societal change (such as the end of discrimination) would only bring greater poverty to the minority and lower the majority's standard of living. As a result, Nash suggests, racial prejudice grows when a society's value system is being threatened. A good example of this is the thriving Japanese fishing community on the West Coast prior to the Second World War, which was subsequently interned during the war.

Although racial prejudice and discrimination may serve the interests of the powerful, such unequal treatment can also be dysfunctional to a society and even to its dominant group. Sociologist Arnold Rose (1951) outlines four dysfunctions associated with racism:

1. A society that practises discrimination fails to use the resources of all individuals. Discrimination limits the search for talent and leadership to the dominant group.
2. Discrimination aggravates social problems such as poverty, delinquency, and crime and places the financial burden to alleviate these problems on the dominant group.
3. Society must invest a good deal of time and money to defend its barriers to full participation of all members.
4. Racial prejudice and discrimination often undercut goodwill and friendly diplomatic relations between nations.

Conflict Perspective

Conflict theorists would certainly agree with Arnold Rose that racial prejudice and discrimination have many harmful consequences for society. Sociologists such as Oliver Cox (1948), Robert Blauner (1972), and Herbert M. Hunter (2000) have used the ***exploitation theory*** (or *Marxist class theory*) to explain the basis of racial subordination in the United States and Canada. As we saw in Chapter 8, Karl Marx viewed the exploitation of the lower class as a basic part of the capitalist economic system. From a Marxist point of view, racism keeps minorities in low-paying jobs, thereby supplying the capitalist ruling class with a pool of cheap labour. Moreover, by forcing racial minorities to accept low wages, capitalists can restrict the wages of *all* members of the proletariat. Workers from the dominant group who demand higher wages can always be replaced by minorities who have no choice but to accept low-paying jobs.

As was pointed out earlier, Japanese Canadians were able to establish themselves and create a thriving community in and around Vancouver until the white population began to see them as an economic threat. Similarly, Canada recruited Chinese workers, first to work in the gold field of the 1850s, and subsequently to serve as labour on the construction of the Canadian Pacific Railway line. But, when the gold dried up and the rail construction was finished, the government imposed a head tax intended to stem the flow of immigrants from China.

However, the exploitation theory is too limited to explain prejudice in its many forms. Not all minority groups have been economically exploited to the same extent. In addition, many groups (such as the First Nations and the Mormons) have been victimized by prejudice for other than economic reasons. Still, as Gordon Allport (1979:210) concludes, the exploitation theory correctly "points a sure finger at one of the factors involved in prejudice, . . . rationalized self-interest of the upper classes."

Feminist Perspectives

Given the great diversity of feminist perspectives, it is, perhaps, not surprising to discover differences among these theories in their treatment of race. Some feminist perspectives have taken white, middle-class, heterosexual women's experiences to be the norm, while ignoring "the specificity of black, native, and other ethnic and cultural experiences" (Elliot and Mandell, 1998:14). While perspectives such as radical feminism treat women as a uniform, undifferentiated group, whose major source of oppression is sexism, other perspectives have strenuously challenged this point of view (Grant 1993; Brand 1993). Perspectives such as anti-racist feminism point out that gender is not the sole source of oppression as gender, race, and class intersect to produce multiple degrees of inequality. Unlike white, middle-class women, immigrant women, visible minority women, and First Nations women, for example, experience the compounded effects of inequality associated with their race and class as well as their gender.

Patricia Hill Collins (1998) uses the term "outsiders-within" to describe the condition of black women situated in academic, legal, business, and other communities. As "outsiders-within," Hill Collins argues, these women are members of a given community but at the same time are dually marginalized in that community as women and as blacks; they find themselves unable to access the knowledge and possess the full power granted to others in the community.

Interactionist Perspective

A Jamaican woman working in a southern Ontario automotive plant is transferred from a job on an assembly line to a similar position working next to a white man. At first, the white man is patronizing, assuming that she must be incompetent. She is cold and resentful; even when she needs assistance, she refuses to admit it. After a week, the growing tension between the two leads to a bitter quarrel. Yet, over time, each slowly comes to appreciate the other's strengths and talents. A year after they begin working together, these two workers become respectful friends. This is an example of what interactionists call the *contact hypothesis* in action.

The ***contact hypothesis*** states that interracial contact between people of equal status in cooperative circumstances will cause them to become less prejudiced and to abandon previous stereotypes. People begin to see one another as individuals and discard the broad generalizations characteristic of stereotyping. Note the factors of *equal status* and *cooperative circumstances.* In the example above, if the two workers had been competing for one vacancy as a supervisor, the racial hostility between them might have worsened (Allport 1979; Schaefer 2000b; Sigelman et al. 1996).

As blacks, Asians, and other minorities gain access to better paying and more responsible jobs, the contact hypothesis may take on even greater significance. The trend in our society is toward increasing contact between individuals from dominant and subordinate groups. This may be one way of eliminating—or at least reducing—racial and ethnic stereotyping and prejudice. Another may be the establishment of interracial coalitions, an idea suggested by sociologist William Julius Wilson (1999b). To work, such coalitions would obviously need to be organized so that all members have an equal role.

Contact between individuals occurs on the microlevel. We turn now to a consideration of intergroup relations on a macrolevel.

Patterns of Intergroup Relations

Racial and ethnic groups can relate to one another in a wide variety of ways, ranging from friendships and intermarriages to genocide, from behaviours that require mutual approval to behaviours imposed by the dominant group.

One devastating pattern of intergroup relations is ***genocide***—the deliberate, systematic killing of or blatant disregard for the well-being of an entire people or nation. This term describes the killing of 1 million Armenians by Turkey beginning in 1915 (Melson 1986). It is most commonly applied to Nazi Germany's extermination of 6 million European Jews, as well as gays, lesbians, and the Romani people ("Gypsies"), during World War II. The term *genocide* is also appropriate in describing the United States' policies toward aboriginal people's in the 19th century. In 1800, the aboriginal population of that country was about 600 000; by 1850, it had been reduced to 250 000 through warfare with the cavalry, disease, and forced relocation to inhospitable environments.

While the treatment of aboriginal groups within the territory that came to be known as Canada was not as extreme as that inflicted by American settlers, the disap-

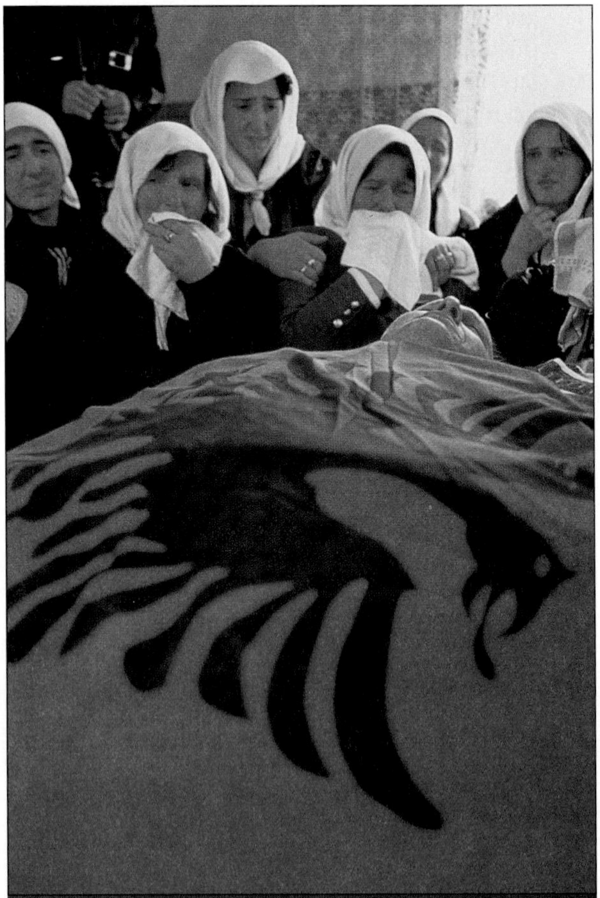

Ethnic Albanian women mourn the death of a man killed by Serbs in the province of Kosovo. Such "ethnic cleansings" have met with worldwide condemnation.

pearance of at least one aboriginal group can be directly attributed to policies of exclusion and genocide perpetrated by newcomers from Europe. The Beothuks of Newfoundland were decimated by new diseases, such as smallpox and typhus, that were carried by the settlers. As a result, the last member, a woman who lived in the white community for years after her family died, passed away in 1829 (Beaujot and McQuillan 1982).

The *expulsion* of a people is another extreme means of acting out racial or ethnic prejudice. In 1979, Vietnam expelled nearly 1 million ethnic Chinese, partly as a result of centuries of hostility between Vietnam and neighbouring China. In a more recent example of expulsion (which had aspects of genocide), Serbian forces began a program of "ethnic cleansing" in 1991 in the newly independent states of Bosnia and Herzegovina. Throughout the former nation of Yugoslavia, the Serbs drove more than 1 million Croats and Muslims from their homes. Some were tortured and killed, others abused and terrorized, in an attempt to "purify" the land for the remaining ethnic Serbs. In 1999, Serbs were again the focus of worldwide condemnation as they sought to "cleanse" the province of Kosovo of ethnic Albanians.

Genocide and expulsion are extreme behaviours. More typical intergroup relations as they occur in North America and throughout the world follow four identifiable patterns: (1) amalgamation, (2) assimilation, (3) segregation, and (4) multiculturalism. Each pattern defines the dominant group's actions. The minority groups' responses can be categorized as either acceptance or rejection responses. The acceptance response involves cooperation with assimilation and integration efforts. The rejection response can take the form of rebellion or avoidance designed to frustrate the goals of the dominant group.

Amalgamation

Amalgamation happens when a majority group and a minority group combine to form a new group. Through intermarriage over several generations, various groups in the society combine to form a new group. This can be expressed as $A + B + C \rightarrow D$, where A, B, and C represent different groups present in a society, and D signifies the end result, a unique cultural-racial group unlike any of the initial groups (Newman 1973).

The Metis represent the closest thing to ideal amalgamation that we can identify in Canadian society. The group was created when the voyageurs seeking furs and establishing posts for the Northwest Company moved into the Red River Valley in the 1700s. These traders established close relations with the local Cree and ultimately married into that group. The resultant families and their descendants have been recognized as a valid ethnic group since at least 1869, when Louis Riel, a seminary-educated member of the group, incited an uprising to prevent the transfer of their homeland from the Hudson's Bay Company to the new nation of Canada (Finlay et al. 1979). The Metis assumed aspects of both ancestral lines, continuing to live in the territory of their First Nations mothers, and adopting the knowledge and some of the skills traceable to their French roots.

Assimilation

Many Hindus in India complain about Indian citizens who copy the traditions and customs of the British. In Australia, Aborigines who have become part of the dominant society refuse to acknowledge their darker-skinned grandparents on the street. ***Assimilation*** is the process by which a person forsakes his or her own cultural tradition to become part of a different culture. Generally, it is practised by a minority group member who wants to conform to the standards of the dominant group. Assimilation can be described as an ideology in which $A + B + C \rightarrow A$. The

"Ho, ho, ho" apparently works in any language. As Japanese people assimilated the norms and values of mainstream North American culture, they created their own "Shogun Santa." This one can be found in the Little Tokyo neighbourhood of Los Angeles.

majority A dominates in such a way that members of minorities B and C imitate A and attempt to become indistinguishable from the dominant group (Newman 1973).

Assimilation can strike at the very roots of a person's identity as he or she seeks to blend in with the dominant group. Alphonso D'Abuzzo, for example, changed his name to Alan Alda, and the British actress Joyce Frankenberg changed her name to Jane Seymour. Name changes, switches in religious affiliation, and dropping of native languages can obscure one's roots and heritage. Moreover, assimilation does not necessarily bring acceptance for the minority group individual. A Chinese Canadian may speak flawless English, attend a Protestant church faithfully, and know the names of all members of the Hockey Hall of Fame. Yet he or she is still *seen* as different and may therefore be rejected as a business associate, a neighbour, or a marriage partner.

Segregation

Segregation refers to the physical separation of two groups of people in terms of residence, workplace, and social events. Generally, a dominant group imposes it on a minority group. Segregation is rarely complete, however. Intergroup contact inevitably occurs even in the most segregated societies.

In North America, the term *segregation* tends to bring to mind the rules against interracial commingling associated with the Southern United States prior to the 1970s. Images of "Black" or "White" water fountains and hooded Klansmen blockading schools against integration by black students are powerful reminders of segregation at its worst. In Canada, the kind of formal, legislated segregation associated with the American South has been uncommon, but not unheard of. Certainly, the internment of Japanese Canadians during the Second World War qualifies as segregation in its crudest form. However, minority groups have frequently chosen to establish their own enclaves, particularly in the large metropolitan areas. This is ***self-segregation***—the situation that arises when members of a minority deliberately develop residential, economic, and/or social network structures that are separate from those of the majority population. Jewish immigrants have been among the most active groups in establishing their own neighbourhoods in Canada, and unlike some others that have disappeared over time, these have endured. Most major Canadian cities also have a "Chinatown" area where the ancestors of many early Asian immigrants settled, and which flourish as economically vibrant areas today. Recent immigrant populations including those from southern Europe and Asia have indicated a preference for self-segregation (Kalbach 1990).

From 1948 (when it received its independence) to 1990, the Republic of South Africa severely restricted the movement of blacks and other non-whites by means of a wide-ranging system of segregation known as ***apartheid.*** Apartheid even included the creation of homelands where blacks were expected to live. However, decades of local resistance to apartheid, combined with international pressure, led to marked political changes in the 1990s. In 1994, a prominent black activist, Nelson Mandela, was elected as South Africa's president, the first election in which blacks (the majority of the nation's population) were allowed to vote. Mandela had spent almost 28 years in South African prisons for his anti-apartheid activities. His election was widely viewed as the final blow to South Africa's oppressive policy of apartheid.

Multiculturalism

In Canada, the ideal of pluralism was entrenched in law by the Multiculturalism Act of 1988. The act and its subsequent revisions have created a social environment in which minorities are not only permitted to engage in their distinct cultural expressions, but are encouraged to do so, through such initiatives as the federal government's funding of ethnic arts programs and the creation of cultural programming on community access television.

From the outset, the Canadian style of pluralism focused on two goals. First, the government wanted to quell the growing dissent in Quebec. The rise of the political wing of the separatist movement had been causing concern in Ottawa, and the government felt that unless the French language was given official status, and the French-Canadian culture given protection and support, the people of Quebec would follow their nationalist leaders out of Confederation (Li 1996). Second, the government wanted to bring the burgeoning minority population into the political fold. Since the major changes to Canadian immigration policy that introduced the "points system" in 1967, the proportion of new Canadians from non-traditional sources had increased dramatically (Keely et al. 1981). This group now represented a significant voting block, and the government was aware of its potential (Hawkins 1988).

Regardless of the motives behind the legislation, multiculturalism as a national policy has recognized the value of minority culture. In 1982, the government extended the scope of the policy by establishing a Race Relations Unit, designed to provide the sense of inclusion to visible minorities that had been afforded ethnic groups in the original act. The importance of race relations in Canadian society was further emphasized in 1997 with the federal government's creation of the Canadian Race Relations Foundation (Canadian Race Relations Foundation 1999), which strives to bring about racial harmony through the critical examination of both contemporary and historical racism.

Race and Ethnicity in Canada

Few societies have a more diverse population than Canada, a truly multiracial, multiethnic community. Of course this has not always been the case. The population of what is now Canada changed dramatically with the arrival of the first French settlers along the north shore of the St. Lawrence River in the early 1600s. Prior to that time, the continent had been peopled exclusively by First Nations groups for thousands of years, and while it was culturally diverse, it was racially monolithic. Since then, the Battle of the Plains of Abraham and the steady flow of immigration to this land have been the two critical forces in the formation of Canada's ethnic and racial landscape.

Canada's diversity is evident from the statistical profile presented in Table 9-1 on p. 212. That diversity, particularly with regard to race, has been increasing dramatically in recent years. Between the pre–points system days of the early 1960s and the last census of 2001, there was a gradual shift away from Europe and towards Asia as the source of the majority of immigrants to Canada (Statistics Canada 2003a).

That diversity, however, so obvious in statistics profiling the general population, is not evident in media representations, particularly on television. A study by Perigoe and Lazar (1992) monitored national evening news programs to determine the representations of people of colour. What they found was that news broadcasts seldom included visible minorities unless a story referred specifically to their community. In other types of programming, they made up less than 3 percent of the total participants.

Racial Groups

The 2001 Canadian census form specified ten categories of race, with an eleventh option for "Other." The rationale for the reintroduction of the race question, which was dropped in response to public fears about the potential for discrimination, is that data produced using other census information such as mother tongue has proven less accurate in determining race. Among the groups identified on the form are Chinese, South Asian (which includes East Indian, Pakistani, Punjabi, and Sri Lankan), Black (which includes African, Haitian, Jamaican, and Somali), Latin American, and Japanese. Interestingly, there is no "First Nations" category on the long form that is to be sent to one in five Canadian households.

First Nations People

"We have proved that we will not be assimilated. We have demonstrated that our culture has a viability that cannot be suppressed." So said Grand Chief John Kelly in 1970 (Kelly 1970). In his 1997 bestseller, *Reflections of a Siamese Twin: Canada at the End of the Twentieth Century,* John Ralston Saul suggests that Canada, rather than being a duality of French and English peoples, is in fact a "triangular reality" with the First Nations community as the third leg of the national foundation. He argues that for 300 years, until the middle of the 19th century, First Nations people were in fact in positions equal or superior to that of European settlers (Ralston Saul 1997:91).

Ralston Saul makes the point that Europeans were dependant upon First Nations peoples' knowledge and skills for their survival during this period. After a brief initial hostility, a period during which the doomed Beothuks found themselves attacked, the new immigrants realized the value of making alliances with First Nations people. Subsequent relations involved collaboration among the groups, which peaked during the boom years of the fur trade. Ultimately, First Nations people found themselves abandoning their traditional economy and material culture, as the demand for their furs provided greater access to European goods and ideas (Palmer Patterson 1972).

By the mid-1800s, the relationship between the British-based authority and First Nations people reflected

The ethnic mosaic of the Canadian community has marginalized First Nations peoples. In recent years, the Assembly of First Nations and local native groups have had great success in focusing attention on the ongoing discrimination to which they are subjected.

the dwindling autonomy of the latter. In 1857, the government gave up all pretence of recognizing First Nations peoples' right to self-determination, and passed the Gradual Civilization Act aimed at assimilation (Royal Commission on Aboriginal Peoples 1994). The most nefarious aspect of this legislation was its approval of government funding of the residential schools that appeared in the 1840s in Upper Canada (now Ontario). Attendance at these institutions became mandatory in 1920, and for the next 50 years served as brutal repositories of colonialism. Yet despite the reports of horrors that took place in these institutions, and that fact that they served the assimilation agenda poorly, residential schools remained a facet of First Nations childhood into the 1970s, when strong objections from the Indian Brotherhood forced Parliament to rescind the policy.

In 1876, 20 years after authorities had begun to move First Nations peoples onto reservations, the Indian Act placed them under the formal protection and administration of the federal government (Mawhiney 2001). This pivotal event relieved First Nations people of their status as self-governing, autonomous populations and transformed them into just another minority.

This status remained effectively unchanged until after the Second World War, when First Nations people adopted a more active political presence in Canadian society. They rebelled against their treatment, instigating a series of changes, including gaining the franchise in all Canadian provinces between 1949 and 1969, and the right to vote federally in 1960 (Satzewich 1990). In June, 1969, after a year of consultation with First Nations leaders, Ottawa published a White Paper entitled *Statement of the Government of Canada on Indian Policy.* The Paper was a sham, and demonstrated to First Nations people that they would have to be even more politically proactive in their pursuit of self-government and treaty rights. That effort was rewarded finally in December, 1997, when the Supreme Court of Canada handed down the Delgamuukw decision. That decision recognizes that First Nations people must be consulted whenever the integrity of their quality of life is threatened (Mawhiney 2001).

In 2001, Canada's First Nations population, those claiming to be aboriginal as either a single or multiple response to the census question on ancestry, totalled 1.3 million or 4.4 percent of the population (Statistics Canada 2003f). Between 1951 and 2001, the aboriginal population grew sevenfold while the overall Canadian population doubled. About half of the total aboriginal population lives in cities, with the largest concentration on the prairies. They are younger than the general aboriginal population by an average of 10 years, a phenomenon caused by the tendency of the young to leave rural reservations in favour of the big city. More than half of their number is poor, compared with 21.2 percent of other Canadians (Lee 1999). And, they are overrepresented in our penal institutions, making up 17 percent of all those in federal custody (Daily June 1/00).

After a century and a half of degradation, Canada's First Nations people are poised to regain their former status as independent, self-determining peoples. On December 13, 1999, ratification by the House of Commons officially marked the successful conclusion of treaty negotiations with the Nisga'a of Northern British Columbia, and established a precedent for First Nations claims for land and political autonomy (see Figure 9-2 for the sovereign indigenous nations' territorial boundaries within British Columbia). The Delgamuukw decision, giving First Nations persons authority over resources on traditional lands, is also evidence of this resurgence of Canada's aboriginal groups.

Asian Canadians

The 2001 census found that there were over 2 million Canadians whose origins could be traced to Asia. Over 1 million (1 029 400) of those people claimed Chinese heritage either as immigrants from or as descendants of immigrants from China, or as ethnic Chinese from such places as Vietnam. The Chinese are the largest visible minority group in Canada, making up 3.5 percent of the population (Statistics Canada 2003g).

A century and a half after their ancestors began arriving on the West Coast to take up jobs as labourers and small-business owners servicing the Fraser River gold rush of the 1850s, members of the Chinese Canadian community have attained middle-class status, many as professionals (Nguyen 1982; Reitz 1980). It has been a difficult and sometimes painful process.

Having established themselves as diligent and productive workers during the gold rush, Chinese people were actively recruited by the government of the day to provide the labour necessary to complete the last and most dangerous phase of the transcontinental Canadian Pacific Railway, through the Rocky and Selkirk mountains. In the early 1880s, 14 000 Chinese nationals were given five- to ten-year contracts, and put to work at a fraction of the wage white workers earned (Creese et al. 1991; Lampkin 1985).

In 1885, with the railway completed and white workers' group lobbying politicians to protect jobs, the federal government imposed the first of a series of head taxes designed to discourage Chinese immigrants. The initial tax was $50, but when it became clear that the amount was not a deterrent, Ottawa raised the amount to $100 in 1900, and then again to $500 in 1903, an amount equal to a year's wages (Finkel et al. 1993).

This was not the first time the federal government had discriminated against Chinese immigrants. In 1875, two decades after the gold rush, Canada disenfranchised

FIGURE 9-2

Sovereign Indigenous Nations Territorial Boundaries in British Columbia

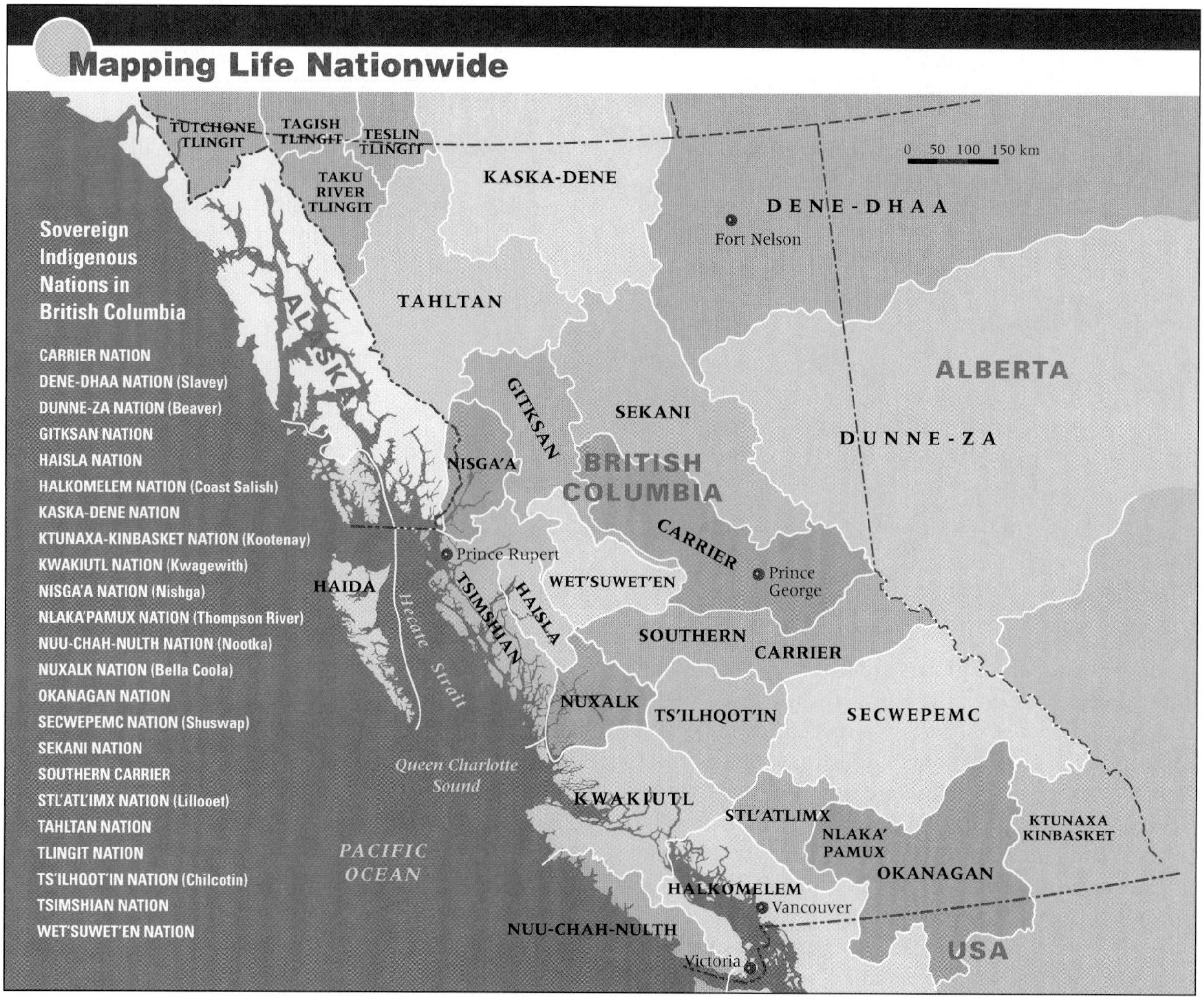

Source: Compiled by the Union of B.C. Indian Chiefs. Published by the Technical Support Section, Surveys and Resource Mapping Branch, Ministry of the Environment, Lands, and Parks. Victoria, 1991.

This map shows the traditional lands of the First Nations of British Columbia. The province has 65 independent nations, more than the rest of Canada combined.

them (Tarnopolsky 1991). In later periods, the institutional discrimination took other, sometimes more punitive forms such as the Chinese Immigration Act—also known as the Chinese Exclusion Act—of 1923, which completely barred them from entering Canada. The same piece of legislation denied those Chinese already in the country from holding public office or voting, and from sitting on juries (Naiman 1997). At the same time, in different parts of the country governments at both the provincial and municipal levels sought ways to further marginalize their visible minority populations. This was especially the case in British Columbia, where the majority of the Chinese immigrants had first found work and settled. Here, the legislature tried to keep Chinese children out of the public school system (Henry et al. 1995).

Gradually, through the latter part of the 20th century, Chinese Canadians have emerged from this imposed segregation. For the first time, in 1962, changes to the Immigration Act allowed them to apply for entry into Canada as independent rather than sponsored candidates. In 1976, the government finally replaced country of origin as the criterion for entry into Canada with family reunification and workforce eligibility. During the decades of the 1980s and 1990s, Chinese nationals and ethnics have been one of the minority groups that have benefited most from this new, less biased system.

Immigrants from China, initially denied membership in the communities within which they settled, ultimately established their own neighbourhoods. Chinatowns, like this one in Vancouver, have subsequently become cultural havens for their populations.

Other immigrant groups from Asia have endured similar injustices. Certainly for the Japanese, the struggle to become accepted members of this society has been exacerbated by racist actions and institutional discrimination. The most destructive race riot in British Columbia's history broke out when a ship carrying over 1000 Japanese and some Sikh immigrants arrived at the port of Vancouver in 1907 and was met by a mob organized by the Asiatic Exclusion League (Adachi 1976). The League had been established to incite working-class sentiment against immigration as a threat to job security.

Then, two decades later, those of Japanese origin were again the target of attack, only this time by the government itself. In 1941, against the advice of some of its most senior security officials, Parliament suspended the rights of all residents of Japanese descent, and ordered them rounded up and detained, and their property confiscated (Sunahara 1981). For the next four years, almost 14 000 people, many of whom were Canadian-born, were confined to camps constructed at sites such as British Columbia's Arrow Lakes.

For Indo-Canadians, no memory is more hurtful than that of the *Komagata Maru*. The story is similar to a number of other racist events in the country's history. The ship, carrying 400 passengers from Calcutta, India, arrived in Vancouver in the spring of 1914, on the eve of the First World War. Public protest and government ambivalence resulted in the ship remaining anchored in English Bay for three months, while debate raged, fuelled by racist rhetoric, and conditions onboard deteriorated. Finally, the captain was refused berth, and the ship was forced to return to India.

In 1939, the Supreme Court of Canada ruled that discrimination on the basis of race was legally enforceable (Henry et al. 1995). That ruling remained in place until the enactment of the multiculturalism policy part sought to end institutional discrimination. However, vestiges of prejudice remain within Canadian society even now, decades later.

Asian Canadians are, as we pointed out at the beginning of this chapter, a diverse group, and in recent decades have been the fastest-growing segment of Canada's immigrant population. Among the many groups included in this catch-all label are those from Japan, Hong Kong, and mainland China, as well as Taiwan, Korea, Thailand, and Vietnam.

Asian Canadians are often held up as a model or ideal immigrant minority, supposedly because, despite past suffering from prejudice and discrimination, they have succeeded economically, socially, and educationally without resorting to confrontations with the white, Anglo-Saxon majority. The existence of a model minority seems to reaffirm the notion that anyone can get ahead in Canada with talent and hard work, and implies that the failure of some minorities to match those successes has more to do with personal inadequacies than it does with any systemic discrimination (Hurh and Kim 1998).

Of course, the concept of a model minority ignores critical factors that can go a long way toward explaining discrepancies in outcomes for other minorities. It ignores, for example, the fact that immigrants from Hong Kong are more likely to speak English, at least as a second language, than are new arrivals from other Asian nations. They are also more familiar with the material and interpersonal aspects of Western culture. In addition, the stereotyping ignores the diversity within groups. There are rich, poor, and middle-class individuals in each of the nationalities that make up the "Asian" category of Canadian.

Ethnic Groups

Unlike racial minorities, members of subordinate ethnic groups are generally not hindered by physical differences from assimilating into the dominant culture of Canada. However, as pointed out earlier, Porter's image of the vertical mosaic is an accurate depiction of the stratification that continues—even 35 years after he coined the phrase—to exist within Canadian society.

French Canadians

John Porter coined the label "charter groups" for settlers who establish themselves in a territory and claim the right to screen subsequent arrivals. Canada has two charter groups: the French and the English. The relative status of the two groups, however, has been unequal since the British defeated the French in a farmer's field outside Quebec City in 1759. The dominance of the English-speaking elite began four years later with the Treaty of Paris, which awarded them dominion over all the former French colonial lands in North America, with the exception of St Pierre and Miquelon, and continued all but unchallenged until the 1960s. In the interim, Canada's francophone population lived an isolated, marginalized existence.

The Quebec Act of 1774 recognized the integrity of the community's Catholic roots and language, and the authority of French civil law (Russell 1993). This act was an effort by British governors to forestall rebellion. Aware of growing discontent to the south in the New England colonies, Britain understood the potential for French settlers, unhappy about the English victory, to join the looming American Revolution. The transfer of significant institutional authority to the Roman Catholic Church was made in exchange for a promise by Rome to control the population's aspiration to independence. While the transfer ensured the continued existence of a distinct French community, it did little to empower the people (Li 1996).

French rights were further entrenched in 1791 when the Constitution Act created Upper and Lower Canada, and recognized the special status of francophones. This status was confirmed again in the Confederation Act of 1867. However, recognition did not provide equality. Throughout the next century, francophones continued to lag behind their English compatriots in terms of education, income, and access to positions of influence in government and business. When voters finally threw out the Church-supported Union Nationale party in 1959, it was time for a change.

The following year, the new Liberal government began to institute a series of reforms intended to move the education of French-speaking Quebecers away from its parochial roots. The result was a sophisticated and university-trained generation of young people dissatisfied with their place in a province where they were part of a subservient majority (Milner 1978). The Quiet Revolution, a peaceful revolt by the Quebecois intelligencia between 1960 and 1966, protested the historical second class status of francophones in their own province. The Revolution spawned a period of social and economic reform, and a vigorous separatist movement that in turn produced the 40 years of political unrest that has followed.

The "quiet" aspect of the revolution was soon ended by the terrorist activities of the Front de Libération du Québec (FLQ) and other extremist groups, culminating in the 1970 October Crisis and the invocation of the War Measures Act by Prime Minister Pierre Elliott Trudeau. The momentum initiated by a generation of young, educated Québécois, however, was destined to change the place of their ethnic group within Canadian society.

In 1969, the Official Languages Act, a response to the findings of the Royal Commission of Bilingualism and Biculturalism, recognized French as one of the country's two official languages. The result was the creation of a national program to make French part of the daily lives of Canadians—all government communications were now available in both French and English, and all products carried bilingual labels. The French minority had at last become visible, not to mention audible, partners in Confederation.

After 200 years of subjugation to the dominant English majority, French Canadians rejected their second-class status during the Quiet Revolution of the 1960s, ultimately electing a separatist government to lead Quebec out of Confederation.

Francophones had managed to overcome 200 years of marginalization and reestablish their status as a legitimate force at the national level. As support grew steadily, the political arm of movement, the Parti Québécois (PQ), finally won the 1976 provincial election and formed a majority government in the National Assembly. A year later, with popular support surging, they launched Bill 101, the Charter of the French Language, to protect Quebec's linguistic heritage from further erosion. With this act, the French citizens of Canada reclaimed their influence on the national stage, and established that independence was more than empty rhetoric. Four years later in the first of two referenda on sovereignty, the PQ government asked the people of Quebec if they wanted to redefine their association with the rest of Canada. Quebec voters turned down the idea of sovereignty association by a substantial margin. Then, again in 1995, another Parti Québécois government posed a similar question in a second referendum. This time the count was much closer. The separatists lost by less than 1 percentage point in the final tally. Since that time, the electorate of Quebec has apparently permanently shelved *l'independence* as an option. However, while it seems unlikely that there will be another vote on separation, there are still those fighting to resurrect the movement for Quebec nationhood.

Europeans

The popular perception of the policy of multiculturalism is that it is intended to provide for the equal participation in Canadian society of non-European ethnic and racial groups. What is frequently ignored is that the status of Europeans in this country has never been homogeneous. There are the two charter groups—the French and the English—but beyond those there is a spectrum of national and ethnic minorities that have suffered discrimination, both interpersonal and institutional.

The majority of immigrants to Canada in the 17th and the first half of the 18th centuries were settlers from France. Then, following the defeat of the French on the Plains of Abraham, arrivals from France ceased and were replaced by newcomers from England, and then Scotland, and finally from Ireland. The Scots seem to have arrived early enough to receive a warm reception as Anglos needed to balance the French majority. The Irish were not so lucky. Arriving in huge numbers during the Irish Potato Famine of the 1840s in their home country, the Irish immigrants were seen as less than desirable, and were subject to both workplace and residential discrimination. As a result, many headed for the American border. In 1848, as many as two thirds of the Irish newcomers stepped off the boat and immediately headed to New England. Those who chose to remain in Canada found themselves relegated to poor neighbourhoods, such as the Pointe Charles area of Montreal.

The treatment of the Irish in Canada was a foretaste of the nation's future public attitudes and policy decisions about immigration. Immigration legislation passed by Parliament through the latter part of the 19th century and well into the 20th was utilitarian. As we can see from the experience of the Chinese, discussed earlier in this chapter, it served Canada's economic interests and ignored the needs of those who were recruited. The experience of the Chinese and Irish was repeated with other minority groups during the waves of immigration that followed over the next century.

Shortly after Confederation, politicians and the business community recognized that a declaration of Canadian nationhood was not likely to be respected by the American pioneers who were moving across the country by the tens of thousands. A simple geographic fact caused this concern: the Rocky Mountains. The pioneers had moved rapidly en masse across the flat prairie of the American mid-west, establishing farms and communities along the way. The problem was that once this mass of land-hungry humanity reached the mountains, they would have two choices: one, struggle to get their

This could be almost any urban street in Canada, despite the fact that it is populated almost exclusively by an ethnic minority. Can you guess from which country these people and their ancestors emigrated to settle in Canada?

wagons and animals over the craggy obstacle, or two, turn right and expand their settlement to the north. This was the problem facing the government of Canada.

The response was to send agents to recruit Europeans previously seen as undesirable. Government representatives were subsequently sent to middle and eastern parts of the continent to find "agriculturists"—or farmers (Henripin et al. 1974). During the 1880s and 1890s, therefore, thousands of Germans and Ukrainians and other non-traditional immigrants were brought to Canada, put on the newly completed railroad, and shipped off to the land beyond the Red River Valley to establish a Canadian presence. Conditions were harsh, the climate inhospitable, and the tools primitive, but most of these settlers survived, and the farming communities they established thrived. However, this imposed isolation physically segregated these new arrivals from the national mainstream. Their marginalization would impact of the ability of these minorities to integrate into the general society for generations to come.

Other, more infamous incidents of discrimination against these ethnic minorities occurred throughout the 20th century. One particularly distressing event took place in the summer of 1939 when, at the height of Hitler's "Final Solution," the *St. Louis*, a boat carrying Jewish refugees from Europe, was turned away at Halifax Harbour. Ultimately, the ship was forced to return to its port of departure, and its passengers handed back to the waiting German authorities.

In the case of the Doukhobors, a religious sect that fled to Canada to escape persecution in Russia, the colour of their skin failed to protect them from having their children apprehended by the state. Following a prolonged argument with British Columbia officials about their desire for religious education to be integrated into the curriculum, the RCMP raided the community and took all school-aged children into the custody of the province. The children were shipped off to camps that had been used for the Japanese internment during the Second World War, almost 100 miles away. The children were held there for several years with only limited and supervised access provided to their parents. See Box 9-2 for a description of how the media has portrayed the Doukhobors over the last 100 years.

During that same period following World War II, when the majority of immigrants were coming from the southern European countries of Italy, Greece, and Portugal, the attitude of the government remained exclusionary. These formerly restricted nationalities were given entry to the country as a gesture of good will acknowledging that they had suffered substantially during the war, and were under extreme fiscal pressures as a result of their disrupted economies. Nevertheless, Canadian officials were concerned about diluting the national culture (Beaujot and McQuillan 1982). As a consequence, the opportunities open to these new arrivals in both employment and housing were restricted. European immigrants accounted for 90 percent of pre-1961 immigration (Statistics Canada 2003g). By the end of the 20th century, Canadians of European ancestry were no longer considered the newcomers, and their status as a marginal population had all but disappeared.

SOCIAL POLICY AND RACE AND ETHNICITY

Global Immigration

The Issue

Worldwide immigration is at an all-time high. Each year, 2 to 4 million people move from one country to another. As of the mid-1990s, immigrants totalled about 125 million, representing 2 percent of the global population (Martin and Widgren 1996). In Canada, during the five-year period between 1991 and 1995, immigration accounted for more than half the country's population growth for the first time in our history. This trend to greater dependence on immigration has heightened the stakes in our ongoing debate as to whether immigrants represent a net benefit or a net cost to Canada: do they provide a benefit by bringing skills, education, and a solid work ethic, or do they represent a net cost because they use social services and displace Canadian workers from their jobs? These questions point to troubling issues, not just for Canada, but for many of the world's economic powers. Who should be allowed in? At what point should immigration be curtailed?

The Setting

The migration of people is not uniform across time or space. At certain times, wars or famines may precipitate large movements of people, either temporarily or permanently. Sometimes the reasons for a large migration cannot be clearly discerned, as in the period between 1931 and 1941, when more people emigrated from Canada than immigrated to the country, a phenomenon that has

Eye on the Media 9-2 The Doukhobors and the Canadian Media

The history of immigrants to Canada has, for the most part, been documented by a biased public press. Portrayals of the dangers presented by each successive wave of newcomers have been an integral part of the representations in the popular Canadian press. From the shiploads of poor Irish people who arrived during the famines of the 1840s to the Chinese miners and railways workers, the Japanese fishers, and the dispossessed Doukhobors, each group has had its reputation sullied by the perpetuation, and sometimes even the creation of, unfortunate stereotypes here in Canada. While most of these groups have gone on over time to establish a certain amount of power and influence, not to mention their own media in Canadian society, the small and isolated Doukhobor communities have not. In an article in the journal *Canadian Ethnic Studies*, researcher Larry Ewashen traces the treatment of the Doukhobors by the mainstream press, from their arrival in the late 1800s to the present.

This monument to the Doukhobor struggle acknowledges the multiculturalism of Canadian society. Functionalists would see the Doukhobor's protests as a necessary contribution to social stability in an ethnically diverse country.

The sensational acts of public resistance including nudity and arson appealed to the media's appetite for eye-catching headlines.

Ewashen tells how the Doukhobors arrived in Halifax in January, 1899, as religious refugees from Russia. Ironically, unlike many other immigrant groups, the Doukhobors were welcomed by Canadians and characterized in the local press as hardworking, Christian victims of tyranny. The new arrivals soon left the Maritimes, eventually settling along the shores of the Columbia River in the East Kootenay region of British Columbia. Despite the promising start, however, the over 2000 original settlers were soon to fall into disfavour. One of the major factors in their demonization was the behaviour of a tiny but very visible breakaway faction known as the Sons of Freedom. The sensational acts of public resistance including nudity and arson appealed to the media's appetite for eye-catching headlines, and thus it was on this group that the media focused for nearly a century. As recently as the summer of 2001, articles about the Doukhobors in the Canadian press continued to focus on the stereotype that the Sons of Freedom splinter group had created for the whole population.

The consequences of these negative portrayals have dogged the Doukhobor community for decades, overshadowing the peaceful and productive lives of the majority of the group's members. However, it appears that finally, a century after their arrival in Canada, the media image of the Doukhobor people may be changing. Considerable attention has been given in recent years by both print and broadcast journalists to the suffering endured by Doukhobor families in Castlegar, British Columbia, at the hands of authorities during the 1950s. When the Doukhobors' request that religious instruction be included in the curriculum was ignored, they protested by keeping their children home from school. In a series of incidents that seem more indicative of a police state than a developed democracy, the provincial government's Department of Child Welfare and the RCMP physically wrested the community's school-aged children from their homes and incarcerated them in internment camps. As might be expected, the actions were defended in the local press at the time—the incidents were not deemed important enough for national coverage—as a last resort against people who refused to send their children to school. Now, 40 years later, the horrific details of the seizures and the long-term consequences for both parents and children are being brought to the attention of Canadians.

Let's Discuss

1. Why do you think the media was so quick to adopt and sustain a negative stereotype of the Doukhobors?
2. Do you think that the Canadian media is free from prejudicial characterizations? Can you think of a minority group within your own community that has been subjected to negative portrayals in the media?

Source: Ewashen 1995.

FIGURE 9-3

Major Migration Patterns of the 1990s

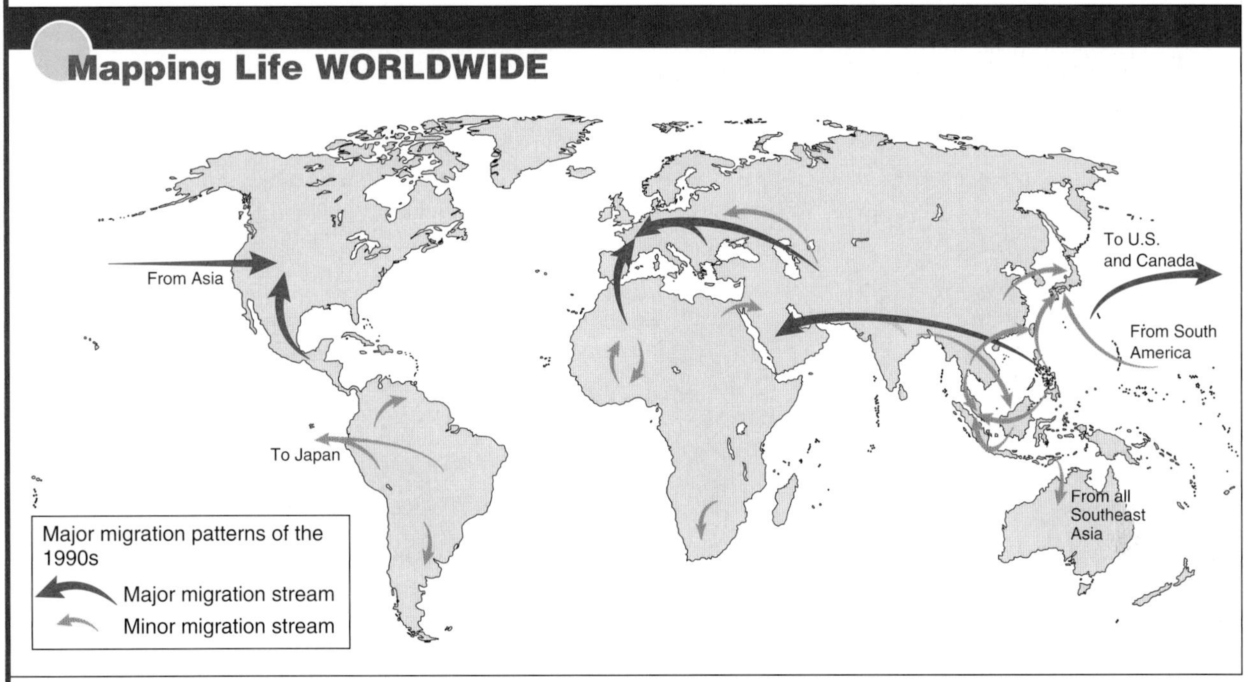

Source: Martin and Widgren 1996:21.

not been repeated since. Temporary dislocations occur when people leave and then wait until it is safe to return home. However, more and more migrants who cannot make an adequate living in their home nations are moving permanently to developed nations. Figure 9-3 shows the destinations of the major migration streams: into North America, the oil-rich areas of the Middle East, and the industrial economies of western Europe and Asia. Currently, seven of the world's wealthiest nations (including Canada, Germany, France, the United Kingdom, and the United States) shelter about one third of the world's migrant population, but less than one fifth of the total world population. As long as there are disparities in job opportunities among countries, there is little reason to expect this international migration trend to end.

Countries such as Canada that have long been a destination for immigrants have a history of policies to determine who is given preference to enter. Often, clear racial and ethnic biases are built into these policies. In the early 20th century, Canadian immigration policy excluded non-Europeans, and, while the law was directed mainly at restricting Asians from entering the country, it also was intended to discourage blacks emigrating from the United States and the Caribbean. During the late 1930s and early 1940s, the federal government refused to lift or loosen restrictive immigration quotas in order to allow Jewish refugees to escape the terror of the Nazi regime. In line with this policy, the SS *St. Louis,* mentioned earlier in this chapter, was denied permission to land in Halifax in 1939. This ship was forced to sail back to Europe, where it is estimated that at least a few hundred of the 900 Jewish refugees onboard later died at the hands of the Nazis (Morse 1967; G. Thomas and Witts 1974).

Since the 1960s, policies in Canada have encouraged the immigration of people with relatives here as well as people who have needed skills, or capital to invest. Changes to the Immigration Act in 1962 removed "nation of origin" as a condition of eligibility. This change has significantly altered the pattern of source nations. While European nations were previously the major source of immigration, in the last 20 years, immigrants have come primarily from Asia and some other countries (see Table 9-2). This means that an ever-growing proportion of Canada is of Chinese or Jamaican or Fijian heritage. To a large degree, fear and resentment of this growing racial and ethnic diversity is a key factor in opposition to immigration. In many nations, people are very concerned that the new arrivals do not reflect the cultural and racial heritage of the country.

Table 9-2 Top 10 Countries of Birth, Canada 2001

Immigrated Before 1961	Number	%
Total Immigrants	**894 465**	**100.0**
United Kingdom	217 175	24.3
Italy	147 320	16.5
Germany	96 770	10.8
Netherlands	79 170	8.9
Poland	44 340	5.0
United States	34 810	3.9
Hungary	27 425	3.1
Ukraine	21 240	2.4
Greece	20 755	2.3
China, People's Republic of	15 850	1.8

Immigrated 1991–2001(1)	Number	%
Total Immigrants	**1 830 680**	**100.0**
China, People's Republic of	197 360	10.8
India	156 120	8.5
Philippines	122 010	6.7
Hong Kong, Special Administrative Region	118 385	6.5
Sri Lanka	62 590	3.4
Pakistan	57 990	3.2
Taiwan	53 755	2.9
United States	51 440	2.8
Iran	47 080	2.6
Poland	43 370	2.4

(1) Includes data up to May 15, 2001.

Source: Statistics Canada, 2003g.

Sociological Insights

Despite people's fears about immigration, it provides many valuable functions. For the receiving society, it alleviates labour shortages, such as Canada is currently experiencing in the areas of health care and technology. Though Canada does not have a specific classification for skilled potential immigrants, The Immigration and Refugee Protection Act does provide special status for applicants who are deemed to have a demonstrable ability to become financially independent. For the sending nation, emigration can relieve economies unable to support large numbers of people. Another important consideration is the large amount of money that expatriates send *back* to their home nations. For example, worldwide immigrants from Portugal alone send more than $6 billion annually back to their home country (World Bank 1995).

There has been considerable research on the impact of immigration on a country's economy. Studies generally show that it has a positive impact on the economy, although areas experiencing high concentrations of immigrants may find it difficult to meet short-term social service needs. When migrants with skills or educational potential leave developing countries, it can be dysfunctional for those nations. No amount of money sent to relatives back at home can make up for the loss of valuable human resources from poor nations (Martin and Midgley 1999).

Conflict theorists note how much of the debate over immigration is phrased in economic terms. But this debate is intensified when the arrivals are of different racial and ethnic background from the host population. For example, Europeans often refer to "foreigners," but the term does not necessarily mean one of foreign birth. In Germany, "foreigners" refers to people of non-German ancestry, even if they were born in Germany; it does not refer to people of German ancestry born in another country who may choose to come to their "mother country." Fear and dislike of new ethnic groups divide countries throughout the world. In 1998, the One Nation Party of Australia sought office on a platform of removing all illegal immigrants and seizing their property to cover deportation costs (Martin and Widgren 1996; *Migration News* 1998b).

Policy Initiatives

During the summer of 1999, the long and rugged British Columbia coastline became the focus of Canada's fight against illegal immigration when four boatloads of Chinese nationals attempted to land in isolated areas. A year later, a report entitled *Refugee Protection and Border Security: Striking a Balance,* issued by the Department of Citizenship and Immigration, called for changes to the Immigration Act. The government responded with Bill C-11 in 2001. A set of core changes to the act involved alterations to the section on human smuggling. The new legislation increased the fines and the jail terms for those convicted under its provisions—up to $1 million and life in prison. The changes also created a new offence category to cover those who used force to coerce foreign nationals into coming to Canada, or attempted to disembark people at sea.

The events of September 11, 2001, have also resulted in changes to the way Canada views its borders. The Department of Foreign Affairs and International Trade has entered into an agreement with the United States to establish a "North American Zone of Confidence" with the creation of a "smart border" (Department of Foreign Affairs 2001). This new collaborative arrangement is intended to set up a continental security zone that would allow for the continued free flow of people and goods across the longest undefended border in the world, while at the same time addressing concerns about terrorist infiltration.

The entire world feels the overwhelming impact of economic globalization on immigration patterns. Europe is also wrestling with policy initiatives. The European Union agreement of 1997 gave the governing commission authority to propose Europe-wide legislation on immigration beginning in 2002. However, the policies must be accepted unanimously, which seems unlikely. An EU policy that would allow immigrants to live and work in one EU country would allow them to work anywhere. The immigration issue is expected to complicate efforts by the sending nations (such as Turkey) to become members of the EU (Light 1999; Sassen 1999).

The intense debate over immigration reflects deep value conflicts in the culture of many nations. One strand of our culture, for example, has traditionally emphasized egalitarian principles and a desire to help people in their time of need. At the same time, however, hostility to potential immigrants and refugees—whether Irish in the 1840s, Chinese in the 1880s, European Jews in the 1930s and 1940s, or Vietnamese and Jamaican immigrants today—reflects not only racial, ethnic, and religious prejudice, but also a desire to maintain the dominant culture of the in-group by keeping those viewed as outsiders out.

Let's Discuss

1. Did you or your parents or grandparents immigrate to Canada from another nation? If so, when and where did your family come from, and why? Did they face discrimination?
2. Do you live, work, or study with recent immigrants to Canada? If so, are they well accepted in your community, or do they face prejudice and discrimination?
3. Do you think that the concept of a "Zone of Confidence" is a positive step towards controlling access to North America by undesirable foreign nationals? What do you think the impact might be on legitimate refugees and immigrants?

Chapter Resources

Summary

The social dimensions of race and ethnicity are important factors in shaping people's lives in Canada and other countries. In this chapter, we examine the meaning of race and ethnicity and study the major racial and ethnic minorities of Canada.

1. A ***racial group*** is set apart from others by obvious physical differences, whereas an ***ethnic group*** is set apart primarily because of national origin or distinctive cultural patterns.
2. When sociologists define a ***minority group***, they are primarily concerned with the economic and political power, or powerlessness, of the group.
3. There is no biological basis for the concept of race, and there are no physical traits that can be used to describe one ***racial group*** to the exclusion of all others.
4. The meaning that people give to the physical differences between races gives social significance to race, leading to ***stereotypes***.
5. ***Prejudice*** often leads to ***discrimination***, but the two are not identical, and each can be present without the other.
6. ***Institutional discrimination*** results when the structural components of a society create and/or foster differential treatment of groups.

7. Functionalists point out that discrimination is both functional and dysfunctional in society. Conflict theorists explain racial subordination by ***exploitation theory***. Standpoint or anti-racist feminists point out that gender is not the sole source of oppression, and that gender, race, and class intersect to produce multiple degrees of inequality. Interactionists focus on the microlevel of race relations, posing ***contact hypotheses*** as a means of reducing prejudice and discrimination.
8. Four patterns describe typical intergroup relations in North America and elsewhere: ***amalgamation, assimilation, segregation***, and ***multiculturalism***.
9. In Canada, the ideal pattern of intergroup relations is ***multiculturalism***. In our country, there is an ongoing debate over whether the ideal is in fact the reality of life for most minority Canadians.
10. After a century and half of degradation, Canada's First Nations are poised to reclaim their status as an independent, self-determining people, as the legitimate third leg of John Ralston Saul's "triangular reality."
11. French Canadians were marginalized for most of the last 400 years, segregated in the rural countryside of Quebec. It was only after the Quiet Revolution of the 1960s, and the subsequent separatist movement, that Canada's first European settlers reclaimed their status as equal partners in Confederation.
12. Europeans who came neither from France nor England commonly found themselves stereotyped and marginalized by mainstream Canadian society. The Irish, the Ukrainians, and later the Italians all suffered discrimination in the early years of their particular wave of immigration.
13. Porter's "vertical mosaic" is as accurate a portrayal of Canadian multiculturalism today as it was in 1965. While significant progress has been made towards making Canada a truly pluralist society, stratification on the basis of race and ethnicity still exists.
14. The increase in immigration worldwide has raised questions in individual nations about how to control the process.

Critical Thinking Questions

1. How is institutional discrimination even more powerful than individual discrimination? How would functionalists, conflict theorists, feminists and interactionists examine institutional discrimination?
2. The text discusses that in Canada, multiculturalism might be more of an ideal than a reality. Can the community in which you grew up and the college or university you attend be viewed as genuine examples of multiculturalism? Examine the relations between dominant and subordinate racial and ethnic groups in your hometown and your college or university.
3. What place in our society do you see Canada's First Nations peoples occupying in the 21st century? Do you think they will become more integrated into the mainstream culture, or distance themselves from it by reestablishing their traditional communities?

Key Terms

Amalgamation The process by which a majority group and a minority group combine through intermarriage to form a new group. (page 221)

Apartheid The policy of the South African government designed to maintain the separation of blacks and other non-whites from the dominant whites. (222)

Assimilation The process by which a person forsakes his or her own cultural tradition to become part of a different culture. (221)

Contact hypothesis An interactionist perspective which states that interracial contact between people of equal status in cooperative circumstances will reduce prejudice. (220)

Discrimination The process of denying opportunities and equal rights to individuals and groups because of prejudice or for other arbitrary reasons. (215)

Ethnic group A group that is set apart from others because of its national origin or distinctive cultural patterns. (209)

Ethnocentrism The tendency to assume that one's own culture and way of life are superior to all others. (214)

Exploitation theory A Marxist theory that views racial subordination such as that in the United States and Canada as a manifestation of the class system inherent in capitalism. (219)

Genocide The deliberate, systematic killing of or blatant disregard for the well-being of an entire people or nation. (220)

Glass ceiling An invisible barrier that blocks the promotion of a qualified individual in a work environment because of the individual's gender, race, or ethnicity. (217)

Institutional completeness The degree to which an ethnic community provides for its own institutional needs, particularly in the key areas of religion, education, and social welfare. (213)

Institutional discrimination The denial of opportunities and equal rights to individuals and groups that results from the normal operations of a society. (217)

Marginalization The process by which an individual, as a result of her or his minority status, is provided only partial access to opportunities. This discrimination is often more intense in the case of women. (215)

Metis The group of people formed when French male fur traders married First Nations women in the Red River Valley area of Manitoba. (210)

Minority group A subordinate group whose members have significantly less control or power over their own lives than the members of a dominant or majority group have over theirs. (209)

Prejudice A negative attitude toward an entire category of people, such as a racial or ethnic minority. (214)

Privilege Access to opportunities provided to or denied people as a direct result of their membership in a particular societal group. (215)

Racial group A group that is set apart from others because of obvious physical differences. (209)

Racism The belief that one race is supreme and all others are innately inferior. (214)

Segregation The act of physically separating two groups; often imposed on a minority group by a dominant group. (222)

Self-segregation The situation that arises when members of a minority deliberately develop residential, economic, and/or social network structures that are separate from those of the majority population. (222)

Social category A group defined by some culturally relevant characteristic; that is, one that has an impact on a person's status within a society. (214)

Social distance The degree of difference between cultures, which can vary from slight (e.g., the Canadian and American cultures) to great (e.g., the Canadian culture and that of the Mongols of Northern China). (213)

Stereotypes Unreliable generalizations about all members of a group that do not recognize individual differences within the group. (211)

Additional Readings

Day, Richard J. F. 2000. *Multiculturalism and the History of Canadian Diversity.* Toronto: U of T Press. The author contends that formal legislation cannot resolve culture-based issues. Day criticizes the federal policy as fantasy, arguing that equality is a myth in a society as diverse as Canada's.

Kalbach, Madeline A., and Warren E. Kalbach, eds. 2000. *Perspectives on Ethnicity in Canada: A Reader.* Toronto: Harcourt Brace. Respected observers of Canada's experiment in pluralism analyze the effects of almost 30 years of multiculturalism.

O'Hearn, Claudine Chiawei, ed. 1998. *Half and Half: Writers on Growing Up Biracial and Bicultural.* New York: Parthenon Books. Eighteen essayists address the difficulties of fitting into, and the benefits of being part of, two worlds.

Schaefer, Richard T. 2002. *Racial and Ethnic Groups.* 9th ed. Upper Saddle River, NJ: Prentice Hall. Comprehensive in its coverage of race and ethnicity, this text also discusses women as a subordinate minority and examines dominant–subordinate relations in Canada, Northern Ireland, Israel and the Palestinian territory, Mexico, and South Africa.

Internet Connection

www.mcgrawhill.ca/college/schaefer

For additional Internet exercises relating to exclusionary policies and work by diverse Canadian artists, visit the Schaefer Online Learning Centre at ***http://www.mcgrawhill.ca/college/schaefer****. Please note that while the URLs listed were current at the time of printing, these sites often change—check the Online Learning Centre for updates.*

Sometimes referred to as "The Other" or "Forgotten" Holocaust, the conflicts in Nanking, China, which began in 1937 have recently become the subject of historical debate and interest. Masato Kajimoto offers an online documentary entitled *The Nanking Atrocities* (**http://web.missouri.edu/~jschool/nanking/index.htm**). On the site, visitors will find text, photographs, and videos to explore.

(a) What historical and social forces played a part in the "Nanking Atrocities"? Which groups and individuals were involved?

(b) What were some of the experiences of Chinese citizens living in Nanking at that time under Japanese military authority? What was the Chinese "scorched earth policy" and how did that affect citizens?

(c) How many people died during these times described on the site? Why is it hard for researchers to agree upon a precise figure?

(d) What role did members of the media play before and after these events, according to the site?

(e) What was the IMTFE? When and where did the postwar trials occur? What arguments were presented by the prosecution and the defense? Ultimately, who was found responsible and what were the punishments?

(f) Had you ever heard of these events before visiting the site? What impact did the stories and images have on you?

(g) How can the sociological theories in this chapter add to our understanding of the causes and consequences of this tragic form of intergroup relations?

CBC Video

Visit the Schaefer Online Learning Centre at **http://www.mcgrawhill.ca/college/schaefer** to view the CBC video segment "The Prairie Porter: The Treatment of Blacks in Western Canada" and answer related questions.

CHAPTER 10
GENDER RELATIONS

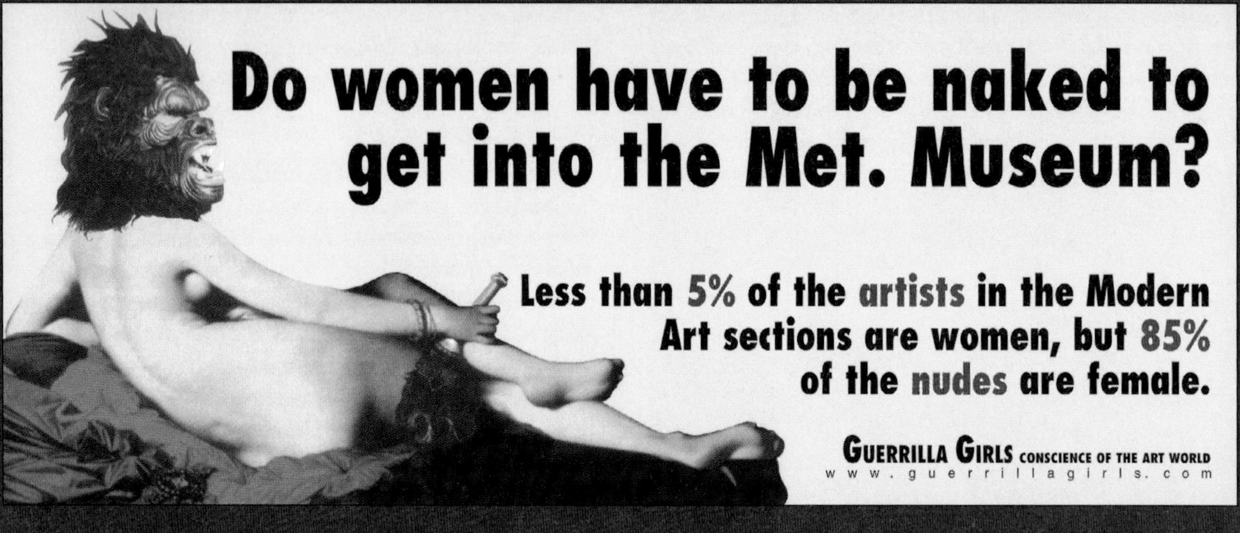
Do women have to be naked to get into the Met. Museum?
Less than 5% of the artists in the Modern Art sections are women, but 85% of the nudes are female.
GUERRILLA GIRLS CONSCIENCE OF THE ART WORLD
www.guerrillagirls.com

In 1989 a group called the Guerrilla Girls called attention to sexism in the art world with this poster, which protests the underrepresentation of female artists at the world-famous Metropolitan Museum of Art in New York City. This poster and others dealing with sexism in the arts can be viewed at www.guerrillagirls.com.

At last, after a long silence, women took to the streets. In the two decades of radical action that followed the rebirth of feminism in the early 1970s, Western women gained legal and reproductive rights, pursued higher education, entered the trades and the professions, and overturned ancient and revered beliefs about their social role. A generation on, do women feel free?

The affluent, educated, liberated women of the First World, who can enjoy freedoms unavailable to any women ever before, do not feel as free as they want to. And they can no longer restrict to the subconscious their sense that this lack of freedom has something to do with—with apparently frivolous issues, things that really should not matter. Many are ashamed to admit that such trivial concerns—to do with physical appearance, bodies, faces, hair, clothes—matter so much. But in spite of shame, guilt, and denial, more and more women are wondering if . . . something important is indeed at stake that has to do with the relationship between female liberation and female beauty.

The more legal and material hindrances women have broken through, the more strictly and heavily and cruelly images of female beauty have come to weigh upon us. . . .

During the past decade, women breached the power structure; meanwhile, eating disorders rose exponentially and cosmetic surgery became the fastest-growing medical specialty. During the past five years, consumer spending doubled, pornography became the main media category, ahead of legitimate films and records combined, and thirty-three thousand American women told researchers that they would rather lose ten to fifteen pounds than achieve any other goal. More women have more money and power and scope and legal recognition than we have ever had before; but in terms of how we feel about ourselves *physically,* we may actually be worse off than our unliberated grandmothers. Recent research consistently shows that inside the majority of the West's controlled, attractive, successful working women, there is a secret "underlife" poisoning our freedom; infused with notions of beauty, it is a dark vein of self-hatred, physical obsessions, terror of aging, and dread of lost control. *(Wolf 1992:9–10)* ■

In this excerpt from Naomi Wolf's book *The Beauty Myth,* a feminist confronts the power of a false ideal of womanhood. In recent decades, North American women have broken legal and institutional barriers that once limited their educational opportunities and career advancement. But, Wolf writes, psychologically they are still enslaved by unrealistic standards of appearance. The more freedom women have gained, in fact, the more obsessed they seem to have become with the ideal of the ultra-thin supermodel—an ideal that few women can ever hope to attain without jeopardizing their health or resorting to expensive cosmetic surgery.

Wolf implies that the Beauty Myth is a societal control mechanism that is meant to keep women in their place—as subordinates to men at home and on the job. But men too are captive to unrealistic expectations regarding their physical appearance. In hopes of attaining a brawny, muscular physique, more and more men are now taking steroids or electing to undergo cosmetic surgery.

The Beauty Myth is but one example of how cultural norms may lead to differentiation based on gender. Such differentiation is evident in virtually every human society about which we have information. We saw in Chapters 8 and 9 that most societies establish hierarchies based on social class, race, and ethnicity. This chapter will examine the ways in which societies stratify their members on the basis of gender.

We begin by looking at how various cultures, including our own, assign women and men to particular social roles. Then we will consider sociological explanations for gender stratification. Next, the chapter will focus on the diverse experiences of women as an oppressed majority, analyzing the social, economic, and political aspects of women's subordinate position. The chapter also examines the emergence of the feminist movement, its goals, and its contradictions. Finally, the social policy section will analyze links between abortion, new reproductive technology, and women's reproductive choices. ■

Social Construction of Gender

How many air passengers do you think feel a start when the captain's voice from the cockpit belongs to a female? Or what do we make of a father who announces that he will be late for work because his son has a routine medical checkup? Consciously or unconsciously, we are likely to assume that flying a commercial plane is a *man's* job and that most parental duties are, in fact, *maternal* duties. Gender is such a routine part of our everyday activities that we typically take it for granted and only take notice when someone deviates from conventional behaviour and expectations.

p. 241

Although a few people begin life with an unclear sexual identity, the overwhelming majority begin with a definite sex and quickly receive societal messages about how to behave. Many societies have established social distinctions between females and males that do not inevitably result from biological differences between the sexes (such as women's reproductive capabilities).

In studying gender, sociologists are interested in the gender-role socialization that leads females and males to behave differently. In Chapter 4, *gender roles* were defined as expectations regarding the proper behaviour, attitudes, and activities of males and females. The application of traditional gender roles leads to many forms of differentiation between women and men. Both sexes are physically capable of learning to cook and sew, yet most Western societies determine that women should perform these tasks. Both men and women are capable of learning to weld and fly airplanes, but these functions are generally assigned to men.

p. 86

Gender roles are evident not only in our work and behaviour but in how we react to others. We are constantly "doing gender" without realizing it. If the father discussed above sits in the doctor's office with his son in the middle of a workday, he will probably receive approving glances from the receptionist and from other patients. "Isn't he a wonderful father?" runs through their minds. But if the boy's mother leaves *her* job and sits with the son in the doctor's office, she will not receive such silent applause.

We socially construct our behaviour so that male–female differences are either created or exaggerated. For example, men and women come in a variety of heights, sizes, and ages. Yet traditional norms regarding marriage and even casual dating tell us that in heterosexual couples, the man should be older, taller, and wiser than the woman. As we will see throughout this chapter, such social norms help to reinforce and legitimize patterns of male dominance.

In recent decades, women have increasingly entered occupations and professions previously dominated by men. Yet our society still focuses on "masculine" and "feminine" qualities as if men and women must be evaluated in these terms. Clearly, we continue to "do gender," and this social construction of gender continues to define

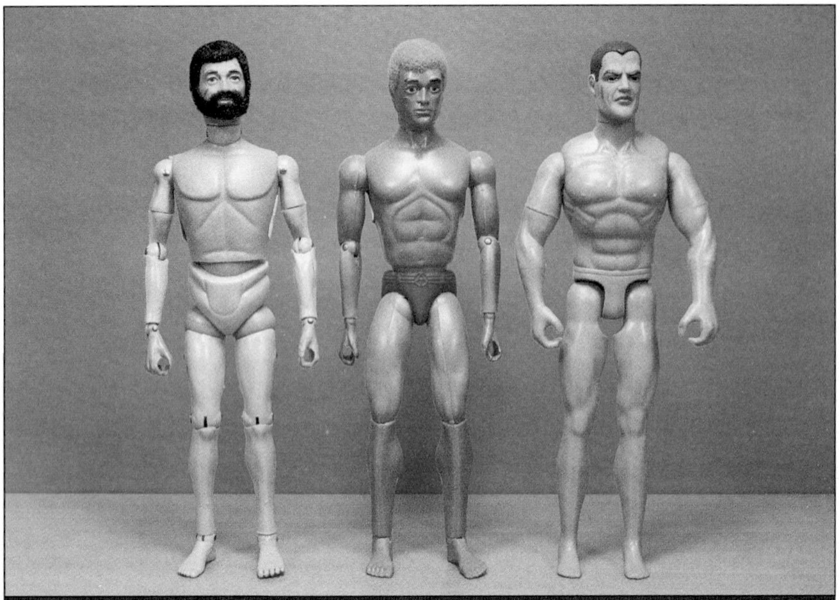

Society often exaggerates male–female differences in appearance and behaviour. In 1964, the G.I. Joe doll (left) had a realistic appearance, but by 1992 (middle) it had begun to acquire the exaggerated muscularity characteristic of professional wrestlers (right). The change intensified the contrast with ultra-thin female figures, like the Barbie doll (Angier 1998).

significantly different expectations for females and males in North America (Lorber 1994; L. Rosenbaum 1996; C. West and Zimmerman 1987).

Gender Roles in North America

Gender-Role Socialization

Male babies get blue blankets, while females get pink ones. Boys are expected to play with trucks, blocks, and toy soldiers; girls are given dolls and kitchen goods. Boys must be masculine—active, aggressive, tough, daring, and dominant—whereas girls must be feminine—soft, emotional, sweet, and submissive. These traditional gender-role patterns have been influential in the socialization of children in North America.

An important element in traditional views of proper "masculine" and "feminine" behaviour is fear of homosexuality. In Chapter 5, we defined *homophobia* as fear of and prejudice against homosexuality. p. 117 Homophobia contributes significantly to rigid gender-role socialization, since many people stereotypically associate male homosexuality with femininity and lesbianism with masculinity. Consequently, men and women who deviate from traditional expectations about gender roles are often presumed to be gay. Despite the advances made by the gay liberation movement, the continuing stigma attached to homosexuality in our culture places pressure on all males (whether gay or not) to exhibit only narrow "masculine" behaviour and on all females (whether lesbian or not) to exhibit only narrow "feminine" behaviour (Seidman 1994; see also Lehne 1995).

It is *adults,* of course, who play a critical role in guiding children into those gender roles deemed appropriate in a society. Parents are normally the first and most crucial agents of socialization. But other adults, older siblings, the mass media, and religious p. 84 and educational institutions also exert an important influence on gender-role socialization in Canada and elsewhere.

It is not hard to test how rigid gender-role socialization can be. Just try transgressing some gender norms—say, by smoking a cigar in public if you are female or carrying a purse if you are male. That was exactly the assignment given to a group of sociology students in the United States. Professors asked the students to behave in ways that they thought violated norms of how a man or woman should act. The students had no trouble coming up with gender norm "transgressions" (see Table 10-1), and they kept careful notes on how others reacted to their behaviour, ranging from amusement to disgust (Nielsen et al. 2000).

Gender-Role Socialization and Social Class

The 2000 movie *Billy Elliott* portrays the life of a young boy growing up in a British mining town, and the gender socialization he undergoes. His father and older brother, both striking coal miners, discover that Billy is secretly attending ballet classes rather than the boxing lessons he pretended to be taking. Billy's behaviour causes his father great concern and displeasure. He sees his son's dancing as a lack of conformity to gender-role expectations. Billy's father actively discourages him from pursuing his love of dance, until he comes to the realization that Billy possesses great talent. At that point, even though his son is defying cultural norms and community standards of appropriate male behaviour, the father begins to support and encourage Billy in his dream to become a professional dancer.

Research shows that patterns of gender socialization are not homogeneous, but rather vary, according to the social class to which one belongs. Working-class parents tend to be more concerned with their children's outward conformity to society's norms and roles (Kohn et al.

Table 10-1 An Experiment of Gender Norm Violations by University Students

Norm Violations by Women	Norm Violations by Men
Send men flowers	Wear fingernail polish
Spit in public	Needlepoint in public
Use men's bathroom	Throw Tupperware party
Buy jock strap	Cry in public
Buy/chew tobacco	Have pedicure
Talk knowledgeably about cars	Apply to babysit
Open doors for men	Shave body hair

Based on class projects, sociology students were asked to behave in ways that might be regarded as violating gender norms. This is a sample of their actual choices over a seven-year period. Do you agree that these actions test the boundaries of conventional gender behaviour?

Source: Nielsen et al. 2000:287.

1986). Middle-class parents, in contrast, tend to be more concerned with their children's motivation for certain behaviours and focus on developing qualities such as self-expression and self-control (Langman 1987). Moreover, upper-middle-class families are most likely to support more egalitarian gender relations and thus socialize their children accordingly (Langman 1987; Lips 1993). Children who are raised by middle-class, career-oriented mothers tend to hold more egalitarian attitudes relating to men and women's roles (Tuck et al. 1994).

Women's Gender Roles

How does a girl come to develop a feminine self-image whereas a boy develops one that is masculine? In part, they do so by identifying with females and males in their families and neighbourhoods and in the media. If a young girl regularly sees female characters on television working as defense attorneys and judges, she may believe that she herself can become a lawyer. And it will not hurt if women that she knows—her mother, sister, parents' friends, or neighbours—are lawyers. By contrast, if this young girl sees women portrayed in the media only as models, nurses, and secretaries, her identification and self-image will be quite different. Even if she does become a professional, she may secretly regret falling short of the media stereotype—a shapely, sexy young woman in a bathing suit (Wolf 1992).

Television is far from being alone in stereotyping women. Studies of children's books published in North America in the 1940s, 1950s, and 1960s found that females were significantly underrepresented in central roles and illustrations. Virtually all female characters were portrayed as helpless, passive, incompetent, and in need of a strong male caretaker. By the 1980s, there was somewhat less stereotyping in children's books, with some female characters shown to be active. Nevertheless, boys were still shown engaged in active play three times as often as girls (Kortenhaus and Demarest 1993).

Social research on gender roles reveals some persistent differences between men and women in North America and Europe. Women experience a mandate to both marry and be a mother. Often, marriage is viewed as the true entry into adulthood. And women are expected not only to become mothers but to *want* to be mothers. Obviously, men play a role in these events, but they do not appear to be as critical in identifying the life course for a man. Society defines men's roles by economic success. While women may achieve recognition in the labour force, it is not as important to their identity as it is for men (Doyle and Paludi 1998; Russo 1976).

Traditional gender roles have most severely restricted females. Throughout this chapter, we will see how women have been confined to subordinate roles within the political and economic institutions of Canada and elsewhere. Yet it is also true that gender roles have restricted males.

Men's Gender Roles

> During the game I always played the outfield. Right field. Far right field. And there I would stand in the hot sun wishing I was anyplace else in the world (Fager et al. 1971).

This is the childhood recollection of a man who, as a boy, disliked sports, dreaded gym classes, and had particular problems with baseball. Obviously, he did not conform to the socially constructed male gender role and no doubt paid the price for it.

Men's roles are socially constructed in much the same way as women's roles are. Family, peers, and the media all influence how a boy or a man comes to view his appropriate role in society. Robert Brannon (1976) and James Doyle (1995) have identified five aspects of the male gender role:

- Antifeminine element—show no "sissy stuff," including any expression of openness or vulnerability.

- Success element—prove one's masculinity at work and sports.
- Aggressive element—use force in dealing with others.
- Sexual element—initiate and control all sexual relations.
- Self-reliant element—keep cool and unflappable.

No systematic research has established all these elements as a common aspect among boys and men, but specific studies have confirmed individual elements.

Being antifeminine is basic to men's gender roles. Males who do not conform to the socially constructed gender role face constant criticism and even humiliation both from children when they are boys and from adults as men. It can be agonizing to be treated as a "chicken" or a "sissy"—particularly if such remarks come from one's father or brothers. At the same time, boys who successfully adapt to cultural standards of masculinity may grow up to be inexpressive men who cannot share their feelings with others. They remain forceful and tough—but as a result they are also closed and isolated (Faludi 1999; McCreary 1994; G. Sheehy 1999).

In the last 35 years, inspired in good part by the contemporary feminist movement (examined later in the chapter), increasing numbers of men in North America have criticized the restrictive aspects of the traditional male gender role. Some men have taken strong public positions in support of women's struggle for full equality and have even organized voluntary associations such as the White Ribbon Campaign (WRC), founded in Canada in 1991 to end men's violence against women. Nevertheless, the traditional male gender role remains well entrenched as an influential element of our culture (Messner 1997).

Cross-Cultural Perspective

To what extent do actual biological differences between the sexes contribute to the cultural differences associated with gender? This question brings us back to the debate over "nature versus nurture." In assessing the alleged and real differences between men and women, it is useful to examine cross-cultural data.

p. 75

The research of anthropologist Margaret Mead points to the importance of cultural conditioning—as opposed to biology—in defining the social roles of males and females. In *Sex and Temperament,* Mead (1963, original edition 1935; 1973) describes typical behaviours of each sex in three different cultures in New Guinea:

> In one [the Arapesh], both men and women act as we expect women to act—in a mild parental responsive way; in the second [the Mundugumor], both act as we expect men to act—in a fierce initiating fashion; and in the third [the Tchambuli], the men act according to our stereotypes for women—are catty, wear curls, and go shopping—while the women are energetic, managerial, unadorned partners. (Preface to 1950 ed.)

If biology determined all differences between the sexes, then cross-cultural differences, such as those described by Mead, would not exist. Her findings confirm the influential role of culture and socialization in gender-role differentiation. There appears to be no innate or biological reason to designate completely different gender roles for men and women.

In any society, gender stratification requires not only individual socialization into traditional gender roles within the family, but also the promotion and support of these traditional roles by other social institutions such as religion and education. Moreover, even with all major institutions socializing the young into conventional gender roles, every society has women and men who resist

Cultural conditioning is important in the development of gender role differences. This sister and brother from Sudest Island in Papua New Guinea expect women to be the honorary heads of the family.

and successfully oppose these stereotypes: strong women who become leaders or professionals, gentle men who care for children, and so forth. It seems clear that differences between the sexes are not dictated by biology. Indeed, the maintenance of traditional gender roles requires constant social controls—and these controls are not always effective.

Explaining Gender Relations

Cross-cultural studies indicate that societies dominated by men are much more common than those in which women play the decisive role. Sociologists have turned to all the major theoretical perspectives to understand how and why these social distinctions are established. Each approach focuses on culture, rather than biology, as the primary determinant of gender differences. Yet, in other respects, there are wide disagreements between advocates of these sociological perspectives.

The Functionalist View

Functionalists maintain that gender differentiation has contributed to overall social stability. Sociologists Talcott Parsons and Robert Bales (1955) argued that to function most effectively, the family requires adults who will specialize in particular roles. They viewed the traditional arrangement of gender roles as arising out of this need to establish a division of labour between marital partners.

Parsons and Bales contended that women take the expressive, emotionally supportive role and men the instrumental, practical role, with the two complementing each other. ***Instrumentality*** refers to emphasis on tasks, focus on more distant goals, and a concern for the external relationship between one's family and other social institutions. ***Expressiveness*** denotes concern for maintenance of harmony and the internal emotional affairs of the family. According to this theory, women's interest in expressive goals frees men for instrumental tasks, and vice versa. Women become "anchored" in the family as wives, mothers, and household managers; men are anchored in the occupational world outside the home. Of course, Parsons and Bales offered this framework in the 1950s, when many more women were full-time homemakers than is true today. These theorists did not explicitly endorse traditional gender roles, but they implied that dividing tasks between spouses was functional for the family unit.

Given the typical socialization of women and men in North America, the functionalist view is initially persuasive. However, it would lead us to expect girls and women with no interest in children to become baby-sitters and mothers. Similarly, males who love spending time with children might be "programmed" into careers in the business world. Such differentiation might harm the individual who does not fit into prescribed roles, while also depriving society of the contributions of many talented people who are confined by gender stereotyping. Moreover, the functionalist approach does not convincingly explain why men should be categorically assigned to the instrumental role and women to the expressive role.

The Conflict Response

Viewed from a conflict perspective, this functionalist approach masks underlying power relations between men and women. Parsons and Bales never explicitly presented the expressive and instrumental tasks as unequally valued by society, yet this inequality is quite evident. Although social institutions may pay lip service to women's expressive skills, it is men's instrumental skills that are most highly rewarded—whether in terms of money or prestige. Consequently, according to feminists and conflict theorists, any division of labour by gender into instrumental and expressive tasks is far from neutral in its impact on women.

Conflict theorists contend that the relationship between females and males has traditionally been one of unequal power, with men in a dominant position over women. Men may originally have become powerful in preindustrial times because their size, physical strength, and freedom from childbearing duties allowed them to dominate women physically. In contemporary societies, such considerations are not so important, yet cultural beliefs about the sexes are long established, as anthropologist Margaret Mead and feminist sociologist Helen Mayer Hacker (1951, 1974) both stressed. Such beliefs support a social structure that places males in controlling positions.

Thus, conflict theorists see gender differences as a reflection of the subjugation of one group (women) by another group (men). If we use an analogy to Marx's analysis of class conflict, we can say that males are like the bourgeoisie, or capitalists; they control most of the society's wealth, prestige, and power. Females are like the proletarians, or workers; they can acquire valuable resources only by following the dictates of their "bosses." Men's work is uniformly valued, while women's work (whether unpaid labour in the home or wage labour) is devalued.

pp. 10, 179

Feminist Perspectives

As we have noted in earlier chapters, feminist perspectives encompass a wide-ranging and diverse group of theories focusing on gender inequality, its causes, and its remedies. Feminist perspectives, however, despite their diversity, share the belief that women have been subordinated,

Conflict theorists emphasize that men's work is uniformly valued, while women's work (whether unpaid labour in the home or wage labour) is devalued. These women are making tents in a factory.

undervalued, underrepresented and excluded in male-dominated societies, which in practical terms means most of the world. As varied as political philosophies, feminist perspectives include liberal feminism, Marxist feminism, socialist feminism, standpoint feminism, cultural feminism, eco-feminism, and radical feminism, to name a few. Some of these streams will be discussed later on in this chapter. While some feminist perspectives can be categorized as outgrowths of conflict theory and interactionist approaches, others stand on their own as unique frameworks within which to study the conditions of women's lives.

While it might appear that there has been an explosion in the growth of feminist perspectives since the mid-1960s, the critique of women's position in society and culture goes back to some of the earliest works that have influenced sociology. Among the most important are Mary Wollstonecraft's *A Vindication of the Rights of Women* (originally published in 1792), John Stuart Mill's *The Subjection of Women* (originally published in 1869), and Friedrich Engels's *The Origin of Private Property, the Family, and the State* (originally published in 1884).

Engels, a close associate of Karl Marx, argued that women's subjugation coincided with the rise of private property during industrialization. Only when people moved beyond an agrarian economy could males "enjoy" the luxury of leisure and withhold rewards and privileges from women. Drawing on the work of Marx and Engels, contemporary feminist theorists often view women's subordination as part of the overall exploitation and injustice that they see as inherent in capitalist societies. Some radical feminist theorists, however, view the oppression of women as inevitable in *all* male-dominated societies, whether they be labelled "capitalist," "socialist," or "communist" (Feuer 1959; Tuchman 1992).

Feminist sociologists are more likely to embrace a political action agenda. Also, feminist perspectives argue that the very discussion of women and society has been distorted by the exclusion of women from academic thought, including sociology. Perhaps one of the best examples of this exclusion of women from academic sociology is that of the American sociologist Jane Addams (1860–1935). Although Addams made significant contributions to sociology through her work on women and the family, urban settlements, and working-class immigrants, she was viewed by mainstream sociology as an outsider and not as a legitimate member of academia. At the time, her efforts, while valued as humanitarian, were seen as unrelated to the research and conclusions being reached in academic circles, which, of course, were male academic circles (M. Andersen 1997; J. Howard 1999).

For most of the history of sociology, studies were conducted on male subjects or about male-led groups and organizations, and the findings were generalized to all people. For example, for many decades studies of urban life focused on street corners, neighbourhood taverns, and bowling alleys—places where men typically congregated. While the insights were valuable, they did not give a true impression of city life because they overlooked the areas where women were likely to gather (L. Lofland 1975).

Since men and women have had different life experiences, the issues they approach are different, and even when they have similar concerns, they approach them from different perspectives. For example, women who enter politics today typically do so for different reasons from men. Men often embark on a political career to make business contacts or build on them, a natural extension of their livelihood; women generally become involved because they want to help. This difference in interests is relevant to the likelihood of their future success. The areas in which women achieve political recognition revolve around such social issues as day care, the environment, education, and child protection—areas that do not attract a lot of big donors. Men focus on tax policies, business regulation, and trade agreements—issues that excite big donors. Sometimes women do become concerned with these issues but then they must constantly reassure voters they still are concerned about "family issues." Male politicians who occasionally focus on family issues, however, are seen as enlightened and ready to govern (G. Collins 1998).

Liberal Feminism

Liberal feminism advocates that women's equality can be obtained through the extension of the principles of equality of opportunity and freedom. Rather than advocating structural change to the capitalist economy or attempting to eliminate patriarchy, liberal feminist approaches assume that extending women's opportunities for education and employment, for example, will result in greater gender equality. The Royal Commission Report on the Status of Women in Canada, tabled in 1970 in the Canadian House of Commons, was grounded on the principles of liberal feminism.

Marxist Feminism

Marxist feminism places the system of capitalism at fault for the oppression of women. If the capitalist economy, with its private ownership of resources and its unequal class relations, were to be replaced with a socialist system, economic inequality between the sexes would also change. Marxist feminists believe that women are not oppressed by sexism or patriarchy, but rather by a system of economic production that is based upon unequal gender relations in the capitalist economy (Tong 1989).

Socialist Feminism

Gender relations, according to ***socialist feminism***, are shaped by both patriarchy and capitalism. Class and patriarchal gender relations are inextricably connected, thus equality for women implies that both the system of capitalism and the ideology of patriarchy must be challenged and eliminated. Socialist feminists, unlike Marxist feminists, who believe that the elimination of class distinctions will bring about gender equality, see patriarchy's grip in the home as well as in the public sphere (Luxton 1980).

Radical Feminism

Unlike Marxist feminist perspectives, radical feminism holds that the subordination of women will not be eradicated with the abolition of capitalism. Rather, radical feminist perspectives argue, the subordination of women occurs in all societies, regardless of whether or not they are capitalist, communist, or socialist. The root of all oppression, according to ***radical feminism***, is embedded in patriarchy (Code 1993). Some radical feminists (Firestone 1970) have based their view of women's oppression on reproduction, arguing that women's freedom from reproduction (i.e., through technological developments) will lead to their overall emancipation.

Standpoint Feminism

Standpoint feminist perspectives challenge other feminist perspectives such as the Marxist, socialist, and radical perspectives, which attempt to lay the blame for women's oppression in one cause or source, thus suppressing the wide range and diversity of women's experiences. ***Standpoint feminism*** takes into account women's diversity (e.g., class, race, ethnicity, sexuality, etc.) and maintains that their experiences cannot be easily expressed as a single account of "women's experiences." Given the diversity and difference in women's lives, standpoint feminism acknowledges that no *one* standpoint will represent *all* women's lives (Comack 1996).

Feminist theorists emphasize that male dominance in Canada and the world goes far beyond the economic sphere. In fact, while on the surface economic inequality may appear to be separate from gender inequality, it is actually inextricably related to spousal abuse, sexual harassment, and sexual assault—issues we have been discussing throughout this text. Violence towards women by men is a major component of many interrelated experiences that contribute to women's inequality in Canada and elsewhere.

Both functionalist and conflict theorists acknowledge that it is not possible to change gender roles drastically without dramatic revisions in a culture's social structure. Functionalists perceive potential for social disorder, or at least unknown social consequences, if all aspects of traditional gender stratification are disturbed. Yet, for conflict theorists, no social structure is ultimately desirable if it is maintained by oppressing a majority of its citizens. These theorists argue that gender stratification may be functional for men—who hold power and privilege—but it is hardly in the interests of women (R. Collins 1975; Schmid 1980).

The Interactionist Approach

While functionalists and conflict theorists studying gender stratification typically focus on macro-level social forces and institutions, interactionist researchers often examine gender stratification on the microlevel of everyday behaviour. As an example, studies show that men initiate up to 96 percent of all interruptions in cross-sex (male–female) conversations. Men are more likely than women to change topics of conversation, to ignore topics chosen by members of the opposite sex, to minimize the contributions and ideas of members of the opposite sex, and to validate their own contributions. These patterns reflect the conversational (and, in a sense, political) dominance of males. Moreover, even when women occupy a prestigious position, such as that of physician, they are more likely to be interrupted than their male

Studies show that as many as 96 percent of all interruptions in cross-sex (male–female) conversations are initiated by men.

counterparts are (A. Kohn 1988; Tannen 1990; C. West and Zimmerman 1983).

In certain studies, all participants are advised in advance of the overall finding that males are more likely than females to interrupt during a cross-sex conversation. After learning this information, men reduce the frequency of their interruptions, yet they continue to verbally dominate conversations with women. At the same time, women reduce their already low frequency of interruption and other conversationally dominant behaviours.

These findings regarding cross-sex conversations have been frequently replicated. They have striking implications when one considers the power dynamics underlying likely cross-sex interactions—employer and job seeker, college professor and student, husband and wife, to name only a few. From an interactionist perspective, these simple, day-to-day exchanges are one more battleground in the struggle for sexual equality—as women try to "get a word in edgewise" in the midst of men's interruptions and verbal dominance (Tannen 1994a, 1994b).

Women: The Oppressed Majority

Many people—both male and female—find it difficult to conceive of women as a subordinate and oppressed group. Yet take a look at the political structure of Canada: Women remain noticeably underrepresented. For example, in mid-2001, none of the provincial premiers in Canada was female. While the past decades have brought many firsts for women in Canadian public life—Beverly McLachlin as the first woman to serve as Chief Justice of the Supreme Court of Canada (2000), Catherine Callbeck of P.E.I. as the first female to be elected premier (1993), Kim Campbell as first woman to serve as Canada's prime minister (1993)—women remain underrepresented in both federal and provincial politics. As of 2000, women made up approximately 20 percent of those elected to the federal House of Commons, while women, as a group, made up approximately 51 percent of the Canadian population.

This lack of women in decision-making positions is evidence of women's powerlessness in Canada. In Chapter 9, we identified five basic properties that define a minority or subordinate group. If we apply this model to the situation of women in this country, we find that a numerical majority group fits our definition of a subordinate minority (Dworkin 1982; Hochschild 1973).

1. Women experience unequal treatment. In 2000, the mean income for male workers 15 years and over was $38 853; for comparable female workers, it was $24 912 (Statistics Canada 2003i).

   Visible minority women in Canada not only earned less than both visible and non–visible minority men, but also earned less than other women. In 2000, visible minority women workers 15 years and over earned an average of approximately $3000 less than non–visible minority women. As Table 10-2 illustrates, these women, in turn, earned less than both visible minority men and non–visible minority men (Statistics Canada 2003i).

Table 10-2 Average Employment Earnings for Visible Minority Women Compared with Non–Visible Minority Women, Visible Minority Men, and Non–visible Minority Men

Category	Earnings ($)
Visible Minority Women	22 621
Non–Visible Minority Women	25 247
Visible Minority Men	31 743
Non–Visible Minority Men	39 861

Note: Figures are for paid workers, 15 years and over, 2000.
Source: Statistics Canada 2003i.

The majority of women employed continue to work in occupations in which women have traditionally been concentrated—nursing and other health-related occupations; sales and service; clerical and administrative positions; and teaching (Statistics Canada 1999f).

Moreover, women are increasingly dominating the ranks of the impoverished, leading to what has been called the *feminization of poverty*.

p. 188

Globally, women and girls make up a disproportionate number of the world's poor. The United Nations Population Fund document "State of World Population Report 2000" stated that women and girls the world over are still being denied access to health care and education. In Canada, women make up a disproportionate number of those with low incomes. In 1997, 2.8 million women (19 percent of the total female population) were living with low incomes, compared with 16 percent of the male population (Statistics Canada 2000d).

2. Women, despite their diversity, share physical and cultural characteristics that distinguish them from the dominant group (men).
3. Membership in this subordinate group is involuntary.
4. Through the rise of contemporary feminism, women are developing a greater sense of group solidarity, as we will see later in the chapter.
5. Many women feel that their subordinate status is most irrevocably defined within the institution of marriage. Even when women are employed outside the home, they are still largely responsible for the care of their homes and families. As a result, they experience higher levels of time stress and have less time for leisure activities then do their male counterparts (Statistics Canada 2000d).

Nordic countries have the highest proportion of female political representatives in the world. In March 1996 Swedish Prime Minister Goran Persson posed with members of his new government, half of whom were women.

Sexism and Sex Discrimination

Just as visible minorities in Canada are victimized by racism, women suffer from the sexism of our society. ***Sexism*** is the ideology that one sex is superior to the other. The term is generally used to refer to male prejudice and discrimination against women. In Chapter 9, we noted that visible minorities can suffer from both individual acts of racism and institutional discrimination. *Institutional discrimination* was defined as the denial of opportunities and equal rights to individuals or groups that results from the normal operations of a society. In the same sense, women suffer both from individual acts of sexism (such as sexist remarks and acts of violence) and from institutional sexism.

p. 217

It is not simply that particular men in Canada and elsewhere are biased in their treatment of women. All the major institutions of our society—including the government, armed forces, large corporations, the media, the universities, and the medical establishment—are controlled by men. These institutions, in their "normal," day-to-day operations, often discriminate against women and perpetuate sexism. For example, if the central office of a nationwide bank sets a policy that single women are a bad risk for loans—regardless of their income and investments—the institution will discriminate against women as a group. It will do so even at bank branches in which loan officers hold no personal biases concerning women, but are merely "following orders." We will examine institutional discrimination against women within the educational system in Chapter 12.

Our society is run by male-dominated institutions, yet with the power that flows to men come responsibility and stress. Men have higher reported rates of certain types of mental illness, shorter life spans, and greater likelihood of death due to heart attack or strokes (see

Chapter 14). The pressure on men to succeed—and then to remain on top in a competitive world of work—can be especially intense. This is not to suggest that gender stratification is as damaging to men as it is to women. But it is clear that the power and privilege men enjoy are no guarantee of well-being.

The Status of Women Worldwide

The Hindu society of India makes life especially harsh for widows. When Hindu women marry, they join their husband's family. If the husband dies, the widow is the "property" of that family. In many cases, she ends up working as an unpaid servant; in others she is simply abandoned and left penniless. Ancient Hindu scriptures portray widows as "inauspicious" and advise that "a wise man should avoid her blessings like the poison of a snake" (J. Burns 1998:10). Such attitudes die slowly in the villages, where most Indians live.

It is estimated that women grow half the world's food, but they rarely own land. They constitute one-third of the world's paid labour force but are generally found in the lowest-paying jobs. Single-parent households headed by women—which appear to be on the increase in many nations—are typically found in the poorest sections of the population. The feminization of poverty has become a global phenomenon. As in Canada, women worldwide are underrepresented politically.

A detailed overview of the status of the world's women, issued by the United Nations in 1995, noted that "too often, women and men live in different worlds—worlds that differ in access to education and work opportunities, and in health, personal security, and leisure time." While acknowledging that much has been done in the last 20 years to sharpen people's awareness of gender inequities, the report identified a number of areas of continuing concern:

- Despite advances in higher education for women, women still face major barriers when they attempt to use their educational achievements to advance in the workplace. For example, women rarely hold more than 1 to 2 percent of top executive positions.
- Women almost always work in occupations with lower status and pay than men. In both developing and developed countries, many women work as unpaid family labourers. (Figure 10-1 shows the paid labour force participation of women in seven industrialized countries.)
- Despite social norms regarding support and protection, many widows around the world find that they have little concrete support from extended family networks.
- In many African and a few Asian nations, traditions mandate the cutting of female genitals, typically by practitioners who fail to use sterilized

FIGURE 10-1

Percentage of Adult Women in the Paid Labour Force by Country, 1960s and 1990s

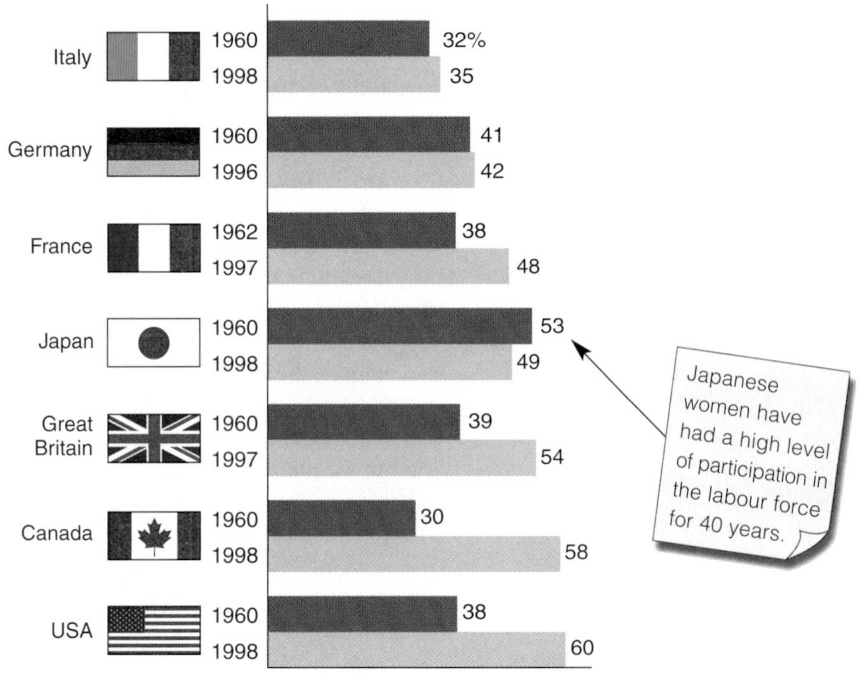

Source: Bureau of Labour Statistics 1999a.

instruments. This can lead to immediate and serious complications from infection or to long-term health problems.

- While males outnumber females as refugees, refugee women have unique needs, such as protection against physical and sexual abuse (United Nations 1995:xvi, xvii, xxii, 11, 46, 70).

Moreover, according to a *World Development Report* issued by the World Bank in 2000, there are twice as many illiterate women in developing countries as illiterate men. Some societies do not allow women to attend school. Of 1.2 billion people living on less than a dollar a day around the world, 70 percent are female (World Bank 2000c; 23, 277).

The recent United Nations report *State of World Population 2000* reiterated that, globally, women and girls bare a disproportionate brunt of the world's burdens. The report stated that discrimination, abuse, and violence remain "firmly rooted" in cultures around the world, where women and girls are denied access to education, health care, and safety. The report pointed out that governments around the world recently pledged to halve the 1990 rate of global illiteracy for women and girls by 2005 (United Nations Population Fund 2000).

What conclusions can we make about women's equality worldwide? First, as anthropologist Laura Nader (1986:383) has observed, even in the relatively more egalitarian nations of the West, women's subordination is "institutionally structured and culturally rationalized, exposing them to conditions of deference, dependency, powerlessness, and poverty." While the situation of women in Sweden and Canada is significantly better than in Saudi Arabia and Bangladesh, women nevertheless remain in a second-class position in the world's most affluent and developed countries.

Second, there is a link between the wealth of industrialized nations and the poverty of the developing countries. Viewed from a conflict perspective, the economies of developing nations are controlled and exploited by industrialized countries and multinational corporations based in those countries. Much of the exploited labour in developing nations, especially in the nonindustrial sector, is performed by women. Women workers typically toil long hours for low pay, but contribute significantly to their families' incomes. The affluence of Western industrialized nations has come, in part, at the expense of women in developing countries (Jacobson 1993).

p. 196

Women in the Paid Workforce in Canada

One of the most significant social changes witnessed in Canada over the last half-century has been the movement of women into the paid workforce. Even though the majority of Canadian women now work for pay outside the home, most continue to experience gendered patterns of inequality relating to pay, working conditions, and opportunities for advancement.

A Statistical Overview

No longer is the adult woman associated solely with the role of caregiver. Instead, millions of women—married and single, with and without children—are working in the labour force (see Figure 10-2). In 2002, 56 percent of all women in Canada aged 15 and over had jobs in the paid

FIGURE 10-2

Employment of Women with Children Under Age 16, by Family Status, 1976–2002

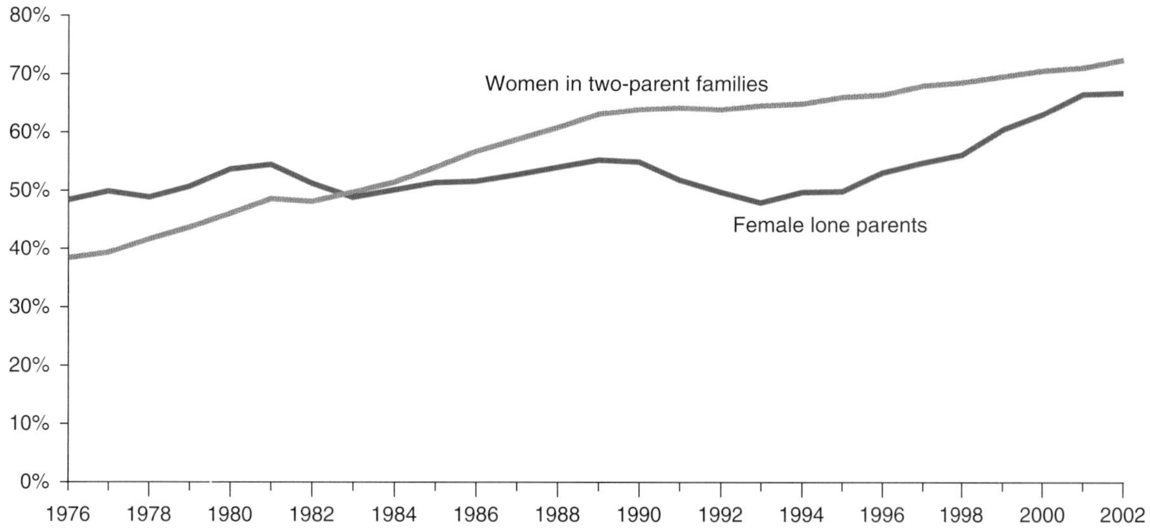

Source: Statistics Canada 2003j.

labour force, up from 42 percent in 1976. A majority of women are now members of the paid labour force, not full-time caregivers. The vast majority of employed women in Canada return to the paid labour force after childbirth. Of those who gave birth in 1993 or 1994, 21 percent returned to work one month after childbirth. Within one year of giving birth, 86 percent of Canadian mothers returned to paid work; within two years, 93 percent had returned (Statistics Canada 2000d).

Yet women entering the job market find their options restricted in important ways. Particularly damaging is occupational segregation, or confinement to sex-typed "women's jobs." For example, in 2002, women accounted for 87.3 percent of all nursing, therapy, and other health-related jobs; 75 percent of all clerical, administrative jobs; and 58.6 percent of all sales and service jobs. Entering such sex-typed occupations places women in "service" roles that parallel the traditional gender-role standard under which housewives "serve" their husbands.

Women are *underrepresented* in occupations historically defined as "men's jobs," which often carry much greater financial rewards and prestige than women's jobs. For example, in 2002, women accounted for approximately 46 percent of the paid labour force of Canada. Yet they constituted only 25.1 percent of senior managers; 21.3 percent of those employed in natural science, engineering, and mathematics fields; and 6.5 percent in trades, transport, and construction. Canadian women have, however, made gains in the areas of business and finance, medicine, and dentistry, where they now account for almost half of all professionals in these previously male-dominated fields (see Table 10-3). In Box 10-1, we consider unique situations that run *against* sex-typing: male nurses and female hockey players.

Women from all groups, particularly those from visible minorities or those from older age groups, are at increased risk of encountering attitudinal or organizational bias that prevents them from reaching their full potential. As we saw in Chapter 9, the term *glass ceiling* refers to an invisible barrier that blocks the promotion of a qualified individual in a work environment because of the individual's gender, race, or ethnicity. A recent study of Boards of Directors in Canada found that only 6.2 percent of the seats on these boards were held by women (Catalyst 1998).

p. 217

One response to the "glass ceiling" and other gender bias in the workplace is to start your own business and work for yourself. This route to success, traditionally taken by men from immigrant and racial minority groups, has become more common among women as they have increasingly sought paid employment outside the home. Women entrepreneurs constitute a rapidly growing employment category in Canada. As of 2002, women represented 35 percent of the self-employed, up from 31 percent in 1985. According to an international report on the status of women in 140 countries, Canadian women have started businesses at a rate three times the rate for men, while their success rate is twice the rate for men (Neft and Levine 1997).

Table 10-3 Canadian Women in Selected Occupations, 2002

Women as Percentage of Total Employed in Occupation	
Underrepresented	
Trades, transport, and construction	6.5%
Natural sciences, engineering, mathematics	21.3%
Senior management	25.1%
Overrepresented	
Nursing, therapy, other health-related	87.3%
Clerical and administrative	75.0%
Teaching	64.4%
Sales and service	58.6%
Roughly Equally Represented	
Business and finance	48.2%
Doctors, dentists, other health occupation	54.4%
Artistic, literary, recreational	53.5%

Source: Statistics Canada 2003j.

The workplace patterns described here have one crucial result: Women earn much less money than men in the paid labour force of Canada. In 2001, the average earnings of full-time female workers were about 72 percent of those for full-time male workers. Given these data, it is hardly surprising to learn that many women are living in poverty, particularly when they must function as heads of households. In the discussion of poverty in Chapter 8, we noted that female heads of households and their children accounted for most of the nation's poor people living in families. Yet not all women are in equal danger of experiencing poverty. First Nations women as well as women who are members of visible minorities suffer from "double jeopardy" or "multiple jeopardies." *Double jeopardy* refers to the discrimination that women experience as a result of the compounded effects of gender and race and ethnicity, while *multiple jeopardies* refers to the compounded effects of gender, race and ethnicity, class, age, and/or physical disability. First Nations women are more likely to live in poverty, to be unemployed, to experience poor health, be paid lower wages, to possess lower levels of education and even to live a shorter life than

Research in Action

10-1 Female Hockey Players and Male Nurses

When you sit down to watch ice hockey, you expect to watch men playing. When you are being assisted by a nurse, you expect it to be a woman. And in almost every case you would be correct, but not always.

In Canada, about 5 percent of all registered nurses are male (Canadian Institute for Health Information 1999). Sociologist E. Joel Heikes (1991) wondered what characteristics male nurses exhibit when entering a traditionally female occupation, so he conducted in-depth interviews with male registered nurses employed in hospital settings. Heikes reports that male nurses felt more visible than female nurses and typically responded by overachieving. Although they did not feel polarized from the female nurses, they did feel socially isolated as "tokens" in the workplace. Typically, they were excluded from traditionally female gatherings, such as female nurses' baby and bridal showers. Such social isolation did not reduce the male nurses' skills training, but it excluded them from informal interactions in which they could have "networked" with female nurses and learned more about the day-to-day workings of the hospital.

Stereotyping was also evident. Male nurses were commonly mistaken for physicians. Even though being mistaken for someone of higher status may appear to be advantageous, it can often have a negative impact on the male nurse. It is a constant reminder of his deviant position in a traditionally female occupation. The implicit message is that men should be doctors rather than nurses. When correctly identified as nurses, men face a much more serious form of stereotyping. Because of the persistence of traditional gender roles, it is assumed that all male nurses must be gay. Many male nurses told Heikes that they felt a need to deny this stigmatized identity.

Sociologist Christine Williams (1992, 1995) examined the underrepresentation of men in four predominantly female professions: nursing, elementary school teaching, librarianship, and social work. Drawing on in-depth interviews with 99 men and women in these professions, Williams found that the experience of tokenism is very different for women and men. While men in these traditionally female professions commonly experience negative stereotyping, they nevertheless benefit from hidden *advantages* stemming from their status as men, such as receiving early and disproportionate encouragement to become administrators. By contrast, women in traditionally male professions often find that their advancement is limited and their token status is hardly an asset.

Like male nurses, female hockey players are rare specimens, although they have actually been around almost as long as male players.

Like male nurses, female hockey players are rare specimens, although they have actually been around almost as long as male players. A photograph of the daughter of Lord Stanley, donor of the coveted Stanley Cup given to the champions in professional hockey, shows her playing the sport in 1890. A rivalry between the United States and Canadian women's teams goes back to 1916. But women were never taken very seriously as hockey players—until quite recently. In 1998, women made their first appearance on the rink in the Olympics.

While increasing numbers of women have come into their own in hockey, they still are put down for not being as "tough and strong" as male hockey players. Hockey rules do not allow women to body check, which calls for shoving an opponent hard into the boards on the side of the rink. Their game relies more on finesse than strength.

Using both observation and interviews, sociologist Nancy Theberge (1997) studied a female Canadian league. She found that while the players generally acknowledge that the game is more skill-oriented without body checking, they favour including body checking in women's hockey to make the sport more professional. They reason that if they can make a living at the sport, then they should accept the risk of injury that comes with "hard checks." Ironically, their willingness to accept a more intense level of the game comes at a time when many people feel that men's professional hockey has become too physical and too violent; hard body checking leads to the fights that accompany many games.

Theberge found that even without body checking, injury and pain were routine features of the lives of female hockey players. She notes, "For these athletes, overcoming injury and pain is a measure of both ability and commitment." Some observers, however, find it troubling that as women's involvement in hockey grows, the pressure increases to develop a system that normalizes injury and pain in the sport.

Let's Discuss

1. Have you ever played a sport or worked in a job that was stereotyped as being more appropriate for the opposite sex? If so, how comfortable were you with your role?
2. Do you think women's hockey rules should be amended to allow body checking? Why or why not? Should men's hockey rules be amended to discourage checking?

Sources: Canadian Institute for Health Information 1999; DeSimone 2000; Elliot 1997; Heikes 1991; Lillard 1998; Theberge 1997; Zimmer 1988.

non–First Nations women. As Nelson and Robinson (1999:261) explain:

> Women possessing multiple memberships in disadvantaged categories are in jeopardy of experiencing double, triple, or more forms of discrimination simultaneously. Since multiple jeopardies are difficult to disentangle, it is almost impossible to isolate which disadvantaged status has been accorded primary discrimination (Nelson and Robinson 1999).

Social Consequences of Women's Employment

"What a circus we women perform every day of our lives. It puts a trapeze artist to shame." These words by the writer Anne Morrow Lindbergh attest to the lives of women today who try to juggle their work and family lives.

The consequence of this "role complexity" for women is higher levels of severe time stress (Statistics Canada 2000d). In 1998, 38 percent of employed, married women between the ages of 25 and 44 who had children reported they were time-stressed, compared to 26 percent of employed, married men of the same age who had children. The variety of roles that married women with children must play, coupled with the greater responsibility for unpaid work in the home (e.g., cooking, laundry, caring for a sick child, grocery shopping, etc.) contributes to their time stress. Figure 10-3 shows the differences in severe time stress, according to gender and the presence of children. While married men's time stress was the same, regardless of whether or not they had children, married women with children experienced almost twice the time stress of their married counterparts without children.

This situation has many social consequences. For one thing, it puts pressure on child care facilities and on public financing of day care and even on the fast food industry, which provides many of the meals that women used to prepare during the day. For another, it raises questions about what responsibility male wage earners have in the household.

Who does do the housework when women become productive wage earners? Studies indicate that there continues to be a clear gender gap in the performance of housework, although the differences are narrowing. Still, the most recent study finds women doing more housework and spending more time on child care than men, whether it be on a workday or when off work. Taken together, then, a woman's workday on and off the job is much longer than a man's.

Canadian women in 1998 worked approximately 80 hours more per year than did Canadian men, calculating their total hours of paid and unpaid work (Statistics Canada 1999d). In addition, women are financially compensated for less of their work. Joanna Hemm, a 34-year-old banquet server from Ottawa, expressed the reality of women's unpaid labour as follows:

> Men have their jobs. . . . when they come home they feel the need to unwind. They don't regard housework or cooking or cleaning as something that needs to be stuck to (Freeze 2001).

According to Statistics Canada, 2.1 million Canadians looked after elderly or ill family members or friends in 1996 (Statistics Canada 1999b). Six out of every ten caregivers were women, who spent five hours, on average, per week (as opposed to three hours for men) providing care. Two thirds of these female caregivers were also in the paid labour force. See Figure 10-4 for an overview of the differences in men's and women's unpaid labour.

Sociologist Arlie Hochschild (1989, 1990) has used the phrase "second shift" to describe the double burden—work outside the home followed by child care and housework—that many women face and few men share equitably. On the basis of interviews with and observations of 52 couples over an eight-year period, Hochschild reports that the wives (and not their husbands) drive home from the office while planning domestic schedules and play dates for children—and then begin their second shift. Drawing on national studies, she concludes that women spend 15 fewer hours in leisure activities each week than their husbands do. In a year, these women work an extra month of 24-hour days because of the "second shift"; over a dozen years, they work an extra year of 24-hour days. Hochschild found that the married couples she studied were fraying at the edges, and so were their careers and their marriages. Juggling so many roles means that more things can go wrong for women, which contributes to stress. A study by a Harvard sociologist found that married women are 50 percent more likely

FIGURE 10-3

Percentage of People Aged 25–44 Employed Full-Time Who Are Severely Time Stressed, 1998

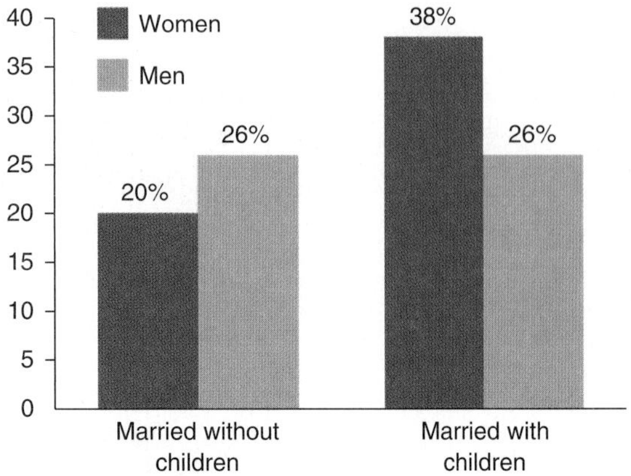

Source: Statistics Canada 2000d, p. 115.

FIGURE 10-4

Gender Differences in Daily Hours of Paid and Unpaid Labour, 1998

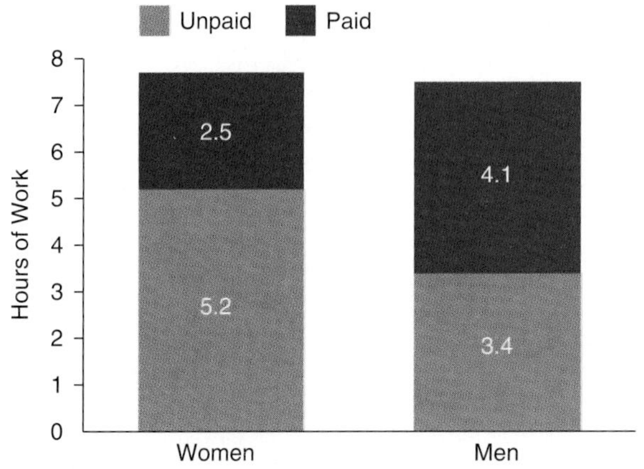

Source: Statistics Canada 1999d.

than married men to complain of being in a bad mood (Kessler 1998).

With such reports in mind, many feminists have advocated greater governmental and corporate support for child care, more flexible family leave policies, and other reforms designed to ease the burden on the nation's families.

p. 91

Most studies of gender, child care, and housework focus on the time actually spent by women and men performing these duties. However, sociologist Susan Walzer (1996) was interested in whether there are gender differences in the amount of time that parents spend *thinking* about the care of their children. Drawing on interviews with 25 couples, Walzer found that mothers are much more involved than fathers in the invisible, mental labour associated with taking care of a baby. For example, while involved in work outside the home, mothers are more likely to think about their babies and to feel guilty if they become so consumed with the demands of their jobs that they *fail* to think about their babies.

The very idea of what constitutes "work" in our society, whether it is done by men or women, at home or in the public sphere, is shaped by a "male work-role model" (Pleck and Corfman 1979). This model assumes that work will be full-time, continuous from graduation to retirement, that all other roles will be subordinate, and that one's self-actualization will be based on this role. Implicit to this model is the assumption of paid work and stereotypical masculinity (Nelson and Robinson 2002). Since Canadian women, on average, engage in greater amounts of mental and physical labour in the care of their families and households, they run a greater risk of not having their labour considered as "work."

Women: The Emergence of Feminism in Canada

Social movements involve the organized attempts of masses of people to bring about social change through their collective action. The women's movement, or feminist movement, is one such movement by which women and men have attempted to change their society not only for the betterment of women, but for the betterment of society as a whole. Often, however, those in the movement have been white, middle-class women who fought for their own vision of social or moral reform—a vision that might improve the welfare of some women (depending on their race, ethnicity, and class), but not necessarily all. From the mid-1800s to the mid-1900s women's movements emerged in 32 countries worldwide (Nelson and Robinson 1999).

In Canada, the "first-wave" of feminism beginning in the mid 1800s had three faces—moral reform (or maternal feminism), liberalism, and socialism (Banks 1981). It concentrated largely on female suffrage and efforts to expand educational and employment opportunities for girls and women. Nellie McClung, perhaps Canada's foremost "maternal feminist," believed women were the

Nellie McClung was one of a group of Canadian women's rights activists who later became known as the "Famous Five." Although the "Famous Five" were concerned about social injustice encountered by some Canadian women, their concerns excluded injustices due to ethnicity, race, and class.

Taking Sociology to Work

PRUDENCE HANNIS: Researcher and Community Activist, Quebec Native Women

Prudence Hannis is an Abenati First Nations woman who works with the organization Quebec Native Women, where she is responsible for the women's health portfolio. Her job entails the organizing and facilitating of various activities such as seminars on sexual abuse in local communities and producing a resource booklet on the subject for community members. Prudence is also working for the Centre of Excellence on Women's Health, Consortium Université de Montréal, where she focuses on First Nations women's health issues such as HIV and AIDS, prostitution, poverty, sexual discrimination, drug and alcohol abuse, and family violence. Prudence says that she has "great interest in the concept of empowerment and the potential of social economy and local development," and accordingly her master's thesis in sociology, which she is currently completing, will be on the topic of empowerment and First Nations communities. Prudence Hannis states: "Sociology is now, more than it has ever been, a part of my job . . . the purpose of my job is to defend First Nations women's concerns, to be their spokesperson when needed, to analyze critical situations for our sisters, and mostly, to determine ways in which women can empower themselves, their families, and their communities."

Let's Discuss

1. In your opinion, what role do class, race and gender play in the health of First Nations women?
2. Is there a health problem affecting First Nations women today that you think is the most crucial to address?

"guardians of the race" and that it was therefore their responsibility to "lift high the standard of morality" (Adamson et al. 1998:31). During the 1920s, McClung and four fellow suffragettes—Irene Parlby, Henrietta Muir Edwards, Louise McKinney, and Emily Murphy—petitioned the Supreme Court of Canada to declare that women could become members of the Senate. The "Famous Five," as they were later known, appealed the negative decision of the Supreme Court of Canada to the British Privy Council. In 1929, the British Privy Council declared that women were "persons" in the eyes of law, making them eligible for appointment to the Senate. The "Persons case" marked a significant achievement for Canadian women.

While the Famous Five were willing to fight for equality of some women, however, they were also willing to exclude others from their cause. Emily Murphy, Nellie McClung, and Louise McKinney were supporters of the eugenics movement, a movement that espoused the desirability of certain races, ethnic groups, and classes. Emily Murphy, for example, spoke out against "aliens of colour," targeting the "black and yellow" races and advocating "whites-only" immigration and citizenship policies. The progress of the women's movement has impacted Canadian women unevenly, depending on their race, ethnicity, and class.

Although women in Canada were granted the right to vote in federal elections in 1918 (Manitoba, Saskatchewan, Alberta, British Columbia, and Ontario had granted the provincial vote to women shortly before 1918), until 1960, First Nations women and men were entitled to vote only if they gave up their Indian status (Mossman 1994). It is worth noting that while Clare Brett Martin, in 1897, was the first woman to become a lawyer in the Commonwealth, "it was not until 1946 that the first Asian Canadian woman graduated from law school in Ontario" (Nelson and Robinson 1999: 493).

The "second wave" of feminism emerged in Canada in the 1960s, coinciding with the rise of feminist consciousness in the United States. The second wave of the movement in Canada focused on two areas of concern: (1) that women were treated differently and discriminated against (at home as well as in the paid workplace) and (2) that women's unique qualities were undervalued (arguing for the recognition of these qualities) (Black 1993). This wave saw the huge growth of feminist perspectives in the social sciences, where feminists scholars challenged mainstream or "malestream" sociology's treatment of gender as it relates to studying crime, deviance, morality, aging, politics, and so on.

During this period, feminism began to become entrenched in institutions. While essentially a grassroots movement, governments and international agencies around the world began to address some of the movement's concerns. In 1967, the Canadian government established the Royal Commission on the Status of Women and the United Nations declared 1975–1985 the decade for women. Today, there are movements on behalf of women in most countries of the world, however, the disparities of advantage and disadvantage remain great among the world's girls and women, not only between them and their male counterparts, but also between females in developing and developed countries.

SOCIAL POLICY AND GENDER RELATIONS

Abortion and Sex Selection: The "New Eugenics"

The Issue

Today in Canada, a woman's decision to have an abortion is usually made in consultation with her doctor based on factors related to her overall health and well-being. However, as new reproductive and genetic technologies, referred to collectively as "reprogenetics" (McTeer 1999), emerge in our society and around the world, the twinning of abortion and reprogenetics presents new ethical and moral considerations. The most controversial of these is what some sociologists are calling "the new eugenics"—a new movement to promote the reproduction of those with particular characteristics, while attempting to limit or control the reproduction of those with other, less desirable traits. Thus, with new reproductive and genetic technologies, abortion has the potential to become no longer a choice a woman makes simply on the basis of her health and well-being, but an instrument of social control as to what "type" (e.g., sex) of person is to be reproduced.

The Setting

Canada's first Criminal Code, established in 1892, made "procuring or performing an abortion a crime punishable by life imprisonment" (McTeer 1999:32). In 1968, amendments to the Criminal Code made abortion legal under certain conditions. The conditions included the approval of a special committee and that the abortion take place in an accredited hospital. However, hospitals and provincial governments were not required to establish the committee and many did not, thus making abortion inaccessible to many women in Canada, particularly those in non-urban areas. In 1988, the law on abortion was changed again; today, it is a decision "left to the pregnant woman alone, and usually made in consultation with her doctor" (McTeer 1999:33).

In 1993, approximately 105 000 abortions were performed in Canada—27 abortions for every 100 live births. Race, class, and age differences are apparent as they relate to the incidence of abortion in Canada (Calliste 2001). In 1995, over 42 percent of therapeutic abortions were performed on women between the ages of 18 and 24 (Statistics Canada 2000d). In the late 1980s, the Canadian government called for the establishment of a Royal Commission investigating new reproductive technologies. These technologies and/or procedures included assisted reproduction, for example, artificial insemination (AI), in vitro fertilization (IVF), and direct ovum and sperm transfer (DOST); surrogacy (one woman carrying a pregnancy to term for another); and prenatal diagnosis (PND), which can include identification of the sex of the fetus. With the emergence of those technologies, the question becomes "How can we as a society protect those who might be exploited or mistreated (e.g., surrogates, IVF-created human embryos, female fetuses) while still safeguarding women's reproductive rights relating to abortion and contraception?" (McTeer 1999).

In 1996, the Canadian government introduced Bill C-47, a legislative attempt to ban practices such as commercial surrogacy and sex selection for reasons other than those related to the health of the fetus (i.e., sex-linked hereditary diseases). Bill C-47, which set out to ban 13 different reproductive technological practices, died "on the order paper" when the 1997 federal election was called.

Sociological Insights

Sociologists see gender and social class as largely defining the issues surrounding abortion. The intense conflict over reproductive rights reflects broad differences over women's position in society. Sociologist Kristin Luker (1984) has offered a detailed study of activists in the pro-choice and pro-life movements. Luker interviewed 212 activists, overwhelmingly women, who spent at least five hours a week working for one of these movements. According to Luker, each group has a consistent, coherent view of the world. Feminists involved in defending abortion rights typically believe that men and women are essentially similar; they support women's full participation in work outside the home and oppose all forms of sex discrimination. By contrast, most pro-life activists believe that men and women are fundamentally different. In their view, men are best suited for the public world of work, whereas women are best suited for the demanding and crucial task of rearing children. These activists are troubled by women's growing participation in work outside the home, which they view as destructive to the family and ultimately to society as a whole. The pro-life, or antiabortion, activists see abortion as an act that denies

FIGURE 10-5

The Global Divide on Abortion

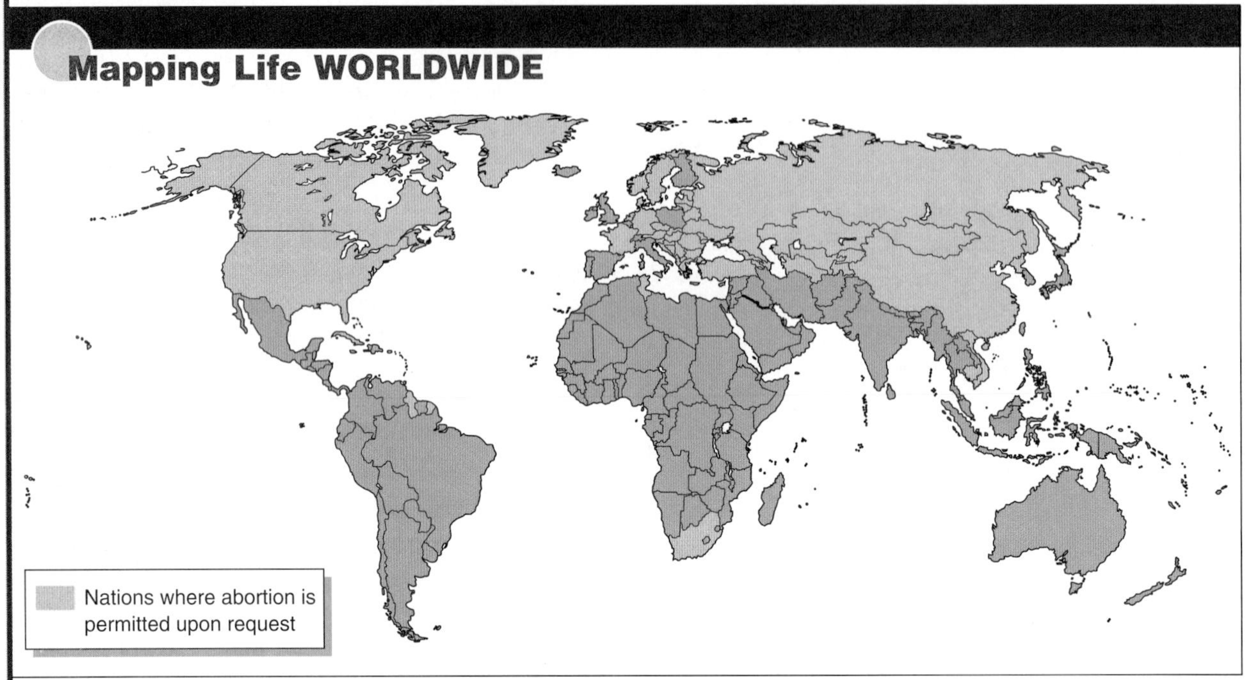

Note: Data current as of May 1998.

Source: United Nations Population Division, Department of Economy and Social Affairs 1998b.

nurturance and therefore diminishes the family since the family is viewed as the major source of nurturance in society. Thus, these activists hold a view similar to that of functionalism, which connects the family to particular functions (Collier et. al. 2001).

Feminist perspectives on abortion and reproductive technology have been led by the radical feminist vanguard, later to be joined by liberal and socialist perspectives (Nelson and Robinson 1999). The hope that technology offered women escape from the "tyranny of their reproduction biology" (Firestone 1970) is now being tempered by the possible negative impact that technology could have on women's lives. Thus, radical feminist perspectives are now joined by many other forms of feminism in defining abortion, reproductive rights, and reproductive technologies as feminist issues (Nelson and Robinson 1999).

Policy Initiatives

The policies of the United States and developing nations are intertwined. Throughout the 1980s, antiabortion members of Congress have often successfully blocked foreign aid to countries that might use the funds to encourage abortion. And yet these developing nations generally have the most restrictive abortion laws. As shown in Figure 10-5, it is primarily in Africa, Latin America, and parts of Asia that women are not able to terminate a pregnancy upon request. As might be expected, illegal abortions are most common in these nations. In general, the more restrictive a nation's legislation on abortion, the higher its rate of unsafe abortions, for pregnancies may typically be terminated by unskilled health providers or by the pregnant women themselves.

Globally, countries' responses to new reproductive and genetic technologies vary in terms of the guidelines and legislation set in place to regulate their use. For example, Australia, Austria, Brazil, Czech Republic, Denmark, Egypt, France, Germany, Hungary, Israel, Mexico, The Netherlands, Norway, Saudi Arabia, Singapore, South Africa, Spain, Sweden, Taiwan, Turkey, and the United Kingdom have some form of legislation to deal with how these technologies can be used. Other countries such as Argentina, Egypt, Finland, Italy, Poland, Japan, South Korea, Switzerland, and the United States have guidelines rather than legislation for the use of assisted reproductive technologies. Since the failure of Bill C-47 to become law, Canada has established a voluntary moratorium on certain reproductive and genetic practices.

Countries such as Greece, India, Jordan, and Portugal, however, have neither legislation nor guidelines. In countries such as India, where cultural preferences for male offspring remain strong, the coupling of prenatal diagnosis techniques such as ultrasound and amniocentesis, which identify the sex of the fetus, and the use of abortion can result in the birth of fewer female children. While prenatal diagnosis can be used to identify and abort fetuses with genetic abnormalities, they also open the door to sex selection for cultural or social reasons. Saraswati Raju, a professor of gender and demography at Jawaharlal Nehra University in New Delhi, states that the fate of the female infant in India has been getting worse in recent decades (Lakshimi 2001). The most recent Indian census showed that the percentage of girls under age 6 has dropped since the previous census. Although the government has banned the use of sex selection tests and doctors' associations have discouraged their use, the tests persist and the government is unable to stop the practice. Despite widespread societal efforts to improve the status of girls and women in Indian society, a baby girl is viewed as a liability and a strong cultural preference for male children persists.

Although it is rarer, sex selection can be used to produce female offspring as well. In 2000, a Scottish couple attempted to use a human rights bill in their country to force the British government to allow them to use sex selection technology to produce a daughter. The couple already had four boys and recently had lost their three-year old daughter in a tragic accident. While the case is ongoing, the couple plan to have the procedure done in the United States if they lose their court battle in Britain.

According to Maureen McTeer (1999), a former member of the Royal Commission on New Reproductive Technologies, sex selection violates our notions of equality as enshrined in the Canadian Charter of Rights and Freedoms and in our human rights laws. In addition, she argues, sex selection denies Canada's international commitment to eliminate discrimination against women.

Let's Discuss

1. Who is most vulnerable to exploitation through the use of new reproductive and genetic technologies?
2. How does the individual's right to reproduce conflict with society's need to regulate the use of these new technologies?
3. Do you know any one who has used some form of reproductive or genetic technology for the purpose of selecting the sex of their offspring? What was the basis for their decision to do so?

Chapter Resources

Summary

Gender is an ascribed status that provides a basis for social differentiation. This chapter examines the social construction of gender, theories of stratification by gender, and women as an oppressed majority group.

1. The social construction of gender continues to define significantly different expectations for females and males in Canada.
2. Gender roles show up in our work and behaviour and in how we react to others.
3. Females have been more severely restricted by traditional gender roles, but these roles have also restricted males.
4. The research of anthropologist Margaret Mead points to the importance of cultural conditioning in defining the social roles of males and females.
5. Functionalists maintain that sex differentiation contributes to overall social stability, whereas conflict theorists contend that the relationship between females and males has been one of unequal power, with men in a dominant position over women. This dominance also shows up in everyday interactions.
6. Feminist perspectives are diverse and vary in their explanation of the sources of women's inequality. Some, such as ***liberal feminism***, advocate that women's equality can be achieved through the extension of opportunities for women's education and employment. Other perspectives, such as ***standpoint feminism***, argue that women's experiences are diverse, thus the sources of their inequality are also diverse.

7. Although numerically a majority, in many respects women fit the definition of a subordinate minority group within Canada.
8. Women around the world experience ***sexism*** and institutional discrimination.
9. As women have taken on more and more hours of paid employment outside the home, they have been only partially successful in getting their husbands to take a greater role in homemaking duties, including child care.
10. The first wave of feminism in Canada began in the mid-1800s and concentrated largely on female suffrage and expanding educational and employment opportunities for women. The second wave emerged in the 1960s, and focused on differential and discriminatory treatment of women, and the need to recognize and value women's differences, while at the same time treat them equally.

Critical Thinking Questions

1. Sociologist Barbara Bovee Polk suggests that women are oppressed because they constitute an alternative subculture that deviates from the prevailing masculine value system. Does it seem valid to view women as an "alternative subculture"? In what ways do women support and deviate from the prevailing masculine value system evident in Canada?
2. In what ways is the social position of white women in Canada similar to that of Asian Canadian women, black women or First Nations women? In what ways is a woman's social position markedly different, given her racial and ethnic status?
3. In what ways do you think your behaviour, values, educational choices, or career plans have been influenced by gender socialization? Can you think of ways in which the social class of your family has influenced your gender socialization?

Key Terms

Expressiveness A term used to refer to concern for maintenance of harmony and the internal emotional affairs of the family. (page 245)

Instrumentality A term used to refer to emphasis on tasks, focus on more distant goals, and a concern for the external relationship between one's family and other social institutions. (245)

Liberal feminism The stream of feminism that asserts that women's equality can be obtained through the extension of the principles of equality of opportunity and freedom. (247)

Marxist feminism The stream of feminist sociological approaches that place the system of capitalism at fault for the oppression of women, and hold that women are not oppressed by sexism or patriarchy, but rather by a system of economic production that is based upon unequal gender relations in the capitalist economy. (247)

Radical feminism The stream of feminism that maintains that the root of all oppression of women is embedded in patriarchy. (247)

Sexism The ideology that one sex is superior to the other. (249)

Socialist feminism The stream of feminism that maintains gender relations are shaped by both patriarchy and capitalism, and thus equality for women implies that both the system of capitalism and the ideology of patriarchy must be challenged and eliminated. (247)

Standpoint feminism The stream of feminism that takes into account women's diversity and maintains that no *one* standpoint will represent *all* women's lives. (247)

Additional Readings

Epstein, Cynthia Fuchs, Carroll Seron, Bonnie Oglensky, and Robert Saute. 1999. *The Part-Time Paradox: Time Norms, Professional Life, Family and Gender.* New York: Routledge. The authors explore the conflict and tension between the time demands of career and family life; they also examine the choice of part-time work as a solution.

Mandell, Nancy, ed. 1998. *Feminist Issues: Race, Class, and Sexuality*. 2d ed. Scarborough: Prentice Hall Allyn and Bacon Canada. This book covers a broad and diverse range of topics, including beauty, status and aging, violence, men in feminism, women and religion, and lesbianism.

Nelson, Adie, and Barrie W. Robinson. 2000. *Gender in Canada*. 2d ed. Toronto: Prentice Hall. A comprehensive review of gender in Canada, covering such topics as intimate relations, gender and aging, marriage and parenting, work, and symbolic representations of gender.

Pollack, William. 1998. *Real Boys: Rescuing Our Sons from the Myths of Boyhood.* New York: Henry Holt. A researcher at Harvard Medical School explores why boys are confused by conventional expectations of masculinity.

Internet Connection

www.mcgrawhill.ca/college/schaefer

For additional Internet exercises relating to rural women in Canada and women's education and literacy, visit the Schaefer Online Learning Centre at ***http://www.mcgrawhill.ca/college/schaefer****. Please note that while the URLs listed were current at the time of printing, these sites often change —check the Online Learning Centre for updates.*

Political decisions made at the federal and provincial levels of government often have a gendered impact. Visit PAR-L's "The Policy Shop" at **http://www.unb.ca/par-l/policy1.htm** for resources on gender and policymaking in Canada.

(a) Identify some "hot issues" relating to gender at the federal level of government.
(b) Identify some "hot issues" relating to gender at the provincial level of government.
(c) Identify some "hot issues" relating to gender at the international level.
(d) Describe what a "gender-based" analysis of policymaking would involve.
(e) What kinds of efforts are being made at the federal level to ensure that Canada has a voice in international discussions on gender-related issues?
(f) What policy or policies do you think currently have the greatest differential impact on the genders?

CBC Video

Visit the Schaefer Online Learning Centre at **http://www.mcgrawhill.ca/college/schaefer** to view the CBC video segment "Military Women: Fighting for Fairness" and answer related questions.

CHAPTER 11

THE FAMILY AND INTIMATE RELATIONSHIPS

New technology has sparked a demand for testing services to determine who is and who is not the father of a child. When billboards advertising these services appeared in 1997, some people found them amusing while others perceived them as further evidence of the problems confronting the family.

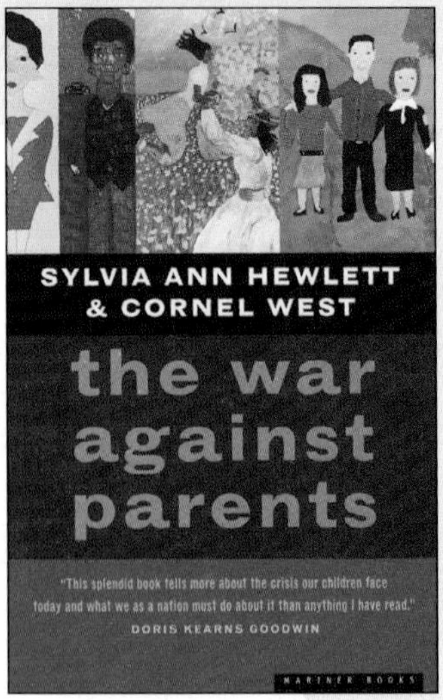

From the time of the breakdown of my marriage to Cliff's mother in 1979 to my marriage to Elleni in 1990, I was forced to deal with a difficult but nonetheless standard set of problems. My ex-wife was awarded custody of two-year-old Cliff and then decided to move to Atlanta. I had no recourse, legal or otherwise. And yet in my struggle to build a close relationship with my son, I now had to cope with an almost impossible set of barriers. Hundreds of miles separated me from Cliff, and I had limited visitation rights—a few specified weekends during the year plus three months in the summer. Besides which, what would I do with my son during our precious time together? My bachelor home did not provide a supportive context for a four-year-old or a nine-year-old—there were no kids on the block, no basketball hoop in the back yard. But I wrestled with these problems and over time developed a strategy that worked, albeit imperfectly.

I hit upon this great solution for the summers. I would take Cliff back to Sacramento, back to the loving, child-centred home that had been so good to me and my siblings a generation ago. It required a lot of stretching and bending of the rules, but I organized life so that I really could take two and a half months out of the year. It meant postponing book deadlines and taming an almost impossible travel schedule, but it was well worth it. Those summers in Sacramento stand out like jewels in my memory. My parents' home turned out to be a profoundly healing place in which Cliff and I could reach out to one another. It provided the deeply needed (and yet so hard to contrive) rhythms and routines of normal family life. Three meals a day; regular bedtimes; clean clothes; a bevy of cousins—Kahnie, Phillip and Phyllis, Cornel and Erika—just around the corner, on tap for casual play; bicycles and baseball gear in the garage all ready to be put to use whenever a grownup was available. And hovering in the backgrounds, loving, eagle-eyed grandparents. . . . The evening meal was particularly important, as all three generations gathered for a cookout in the back yard. Conversation and laughter flowed, advice was sought and help was freely offered, jokes and stories were traded, and the children, spellbound, hung on the edges, absorbing the spirit and the meaning of family life.

The rest of the year was a struggle. I maintained regular telephone contact with Cliff, calling him several times a week just to hear his voice and shoot the breeze. But in the rushed, tantalizing visits around Thanksgiving, Christmas, and Easter, it was always hard not to lapse into the role of being a "good-time dad," showering gifts on him in an attempt to make up for real time or a deeper agenda. *(Hewlett and West 1998:21–22)* ■

In this excerpt from *The War Against Parents* philosophy scholar Cornel West underscores how deeply family life has been altered by divorce, one of many social factors that have gradually but inevitably turned the traditional nuclear family on its head. The family of today is not what it was a century ago or even a generation ago. New roles, new gender distinctions, new child-rearing patterns have all combined to create new forms of family life. Today, for example, we are seeing more and more women take the breadwinner's role, whether married or as a single parent. Blended families—the result of divorces and remarriages—are almost the norm. And many people are seeking intimate relationships outside marriage, whether it be in gay partnerships or in cohabiting arrangements.

This chapter addresses family and intimate relationships in Canada as well as in other parts of the world. As we will see, family patterns differ from one culture to another and within the same culture. A ***family*** can be defined as a set of people related by blood, marriage (or some other agreed-upon relationship), or adoption who share the primary responsibility for reproduction and caring for members of society. A family, as defined by Statistics Canada, includes only heterosexual couples and excludes gays and lesbians. This definition, however, does not capture the diversity of families in Canada today.

In this chapter, we will see that the family is universal—found in every culture—however varied in its organization. We will look at the family and intimate relationships from the functionalist, conflict, interactionist and feminist points of view and at the variations in marital patterns and family life, including different family forms of child rearing. We'll pay particular attention to the increasing number of people in dual-income or single-parent families. We will examine divorce in Canada and consider such diverse lifestyles as cohabitation, remaining single, lesbian and gay relationships, and marriage without children. The social policy section will look at controversial issues surrounding the use of reproductive technology. ■

Global View of the Family

Among Tibetans, a woman may be simultaneously married to more than one man, usually brothers. This system allows sons to share the limited amount of good land. A Hopi woman may divorce her husband by placing her belongings outside the door. A Trobriand Island couple signals marriage by sitting in public on a porch eating yams provided by the bride's mother. She continues to provide cooked yams for a year while the groom's family offers in exchange such valuables as stone axes and clay pots (W. Haviland 1999).

As these examples illustrate, there are many variations in "the family" from culture to culture. Yet the family as a social institution is present in all cultures. Moreover, certain general principles concerning its composition, kinship patterns, and authority patterns are universal.

Composition: What Is the Family?

If we were to take our information on what a family is from what we see on television, we might come up with some very strange scenarios (see Box 11-1). The media don't always help us get a realistic view of the family. Moreover, many people still think of the family in very narrow terms—as a married couple and their unmarried children living together, like the family in the old *Cosby Show* or *Family Ties* or *Growing Pains.* However, this is but

In wedding ceremonies in Sumatra, Indonesia, the bride's headdress indicates her village and her social status—the more elaborate the headdress, the higher her status. After she is married, the bride and her husband live with her maternal family, and all property passes from mother to daughter.

Eye on the Media 11-1 The Family in TV Land

Put an alien creature from outer space in front of a television, and it would have no idea of what family life is like in North America. It would conclude that most adults are men, most adults are not married, almost no one is over age 50, very few adults have children, most mothers don't work for pay, and child care is simply not an issue. When parents are depicted, they are either not around for the most part or they are clueless. The baby boomers in *Everybody Loves Raymond* treat their parents like meddling invaders, which is also how the teenage generation treats their boomer parents in *Dawson's Creek*. Even the cartoon show *Rugrats*, aimed at young children, portrays talking babies as making their way in the world on their own.

These shows are beamed into the living rooms of Canadians each week. In fact, American programs, particularly dramas and comedies, are viewed substantially more often by Canadians than most Canadian programming. Many American television actors are household names in our country (Meisel 2001).

Whether the audience is Canadian or American, however, the fact is that *Friends, Third Rock from the Sun, Frasier, Will and Grace, Ally McBeal,* and similar programs present lives that most households find fascinating, but not exactly true to their own lives. Eight out of 10 adults in the United States think that almost no TV family is like their own; nearly half find no TV family like theirs.

These conclusions come out of a content analysis of prime-time TV programming conducted by Katharine Heintz-Knowles, a communications professor at the University of Washington and the mother of three children, who knows first-hand what a work–family conflict looks like. She has had to deal with finding sitters on short notice, taking children to work with her when a sitter was unavailable, and missing meetings to tend to a sick child. In fact, she acknowledges that her "life today is one big work–family conflict" (Gardner 1998:13). But when she watched television, she didn't see much of her life reflected on the screen.

Television Reality versus Social Reality

	Adult TV Characters	Adult Population
Women	38%	51%
Over age 50	14%	38%
Parents of minor children	15%	32%

Her study, called "Balancing Acts: Work/Family Issues on Prime-Time TV," carried out content analysis of 150 episodes of 92 different programs on commercial networks over a two-week period. She found that of the 820 TV characters studied, only 38 percent were women, only 15 percent could be identified as parents of minor children, and only 14 percent were over age 50 (see the table for how these percentages compare to the adult population of the United States). Only 3 percent of the TV characters faced recognizable conflicts between work and family, and no TV family made use of a child care centre. Canadians are presented with images of work–family roles that are strikingly similar to those of our American neighbours, since 80 percent of the characters on Canadian television, both in French and English shows, appear in American productions (Graydon 2001).

Eighty percent of the characters on Canadian television, both in French and English shows, appear in American productions.

Because television is the major storyteller in our lives today, its programs can shape our attitudes and beliefs. Unfortunately, television gives a distorted view of family life in North America, not only to our hypothetical alien, but also to viewers at home and in other societies on planet Earth. Canadian research has revealed that women with young families are critical of television's portrayal of poor role models; they expressed a desire to have their children exposed to positive portrayals of women successfully coping with a variety of situations and lifestyles (ComQuest Research Group 1993).

If very few shows depict real-life challenges in family life and possible solutions, then viewers may well go away thinking their own problems are unique and insoluble. By confronting these issues, television could call attention to what needs to be changed—both on an individual level and on a societal level—and offer hope for solutions. It appears, however, that most TV programmers offer up a fantasy world in order to satisfy people who seek entertainment and escape from their everyday lives.

Let's Discuss

1. How well does television portray the social reality of your family life?
2. Take the role of a television producer. What kind of show would you create to reflect family life today?

Sources: Blanco 1998; ComQuest Research Group 1993; Graydon 2001; National Partnership for Women and Families 1998.

one type of family, what sociologists refer to as a ***nuclear family.*** The term *nuclear family* is well chosen, since this type of family serves as the nucleus, or core, upon which larger family groups are built. Most people in Canada see the nuclear family as the preferred family arrangement. Yet, as Figure 11-1 shows, by 2001 only about 42 percent of the nation's family households fit this model.

The proportion of households in Canada composed of married couples with children at home has decreased steadily over the last 30 years, and this trend is expected to continue. At the same time, there have been increases in the number of single-parent households (see Figure 11-1). Similar trends are evident in other industrialized nations, including the United States, Great Britain, and Japan (see Figure 11-2).

A family in which relatives—such as grandparents, aunts, or uncles—live in the same home as parents and their children is known as an ***extended family.*** While not common, such living arrangements do exist in Canada. The structure of the extended family offers certain advantages over that of the nuclear family. Crises such as death, divorce, and illness put less strain on family members, since there are more people who can provide assistance and emotional support. In addition, the extended family constitutes a larger economic unit than the nuclear family. If the family is engaged in a common enterprise—a farm or a small business—the additional family members may represent the difference between prosperity and failure.

In considering these differing family types, we have limited ourselves to the form of marriage that is characteristic of Canada—monogamy. The term ***monogamy*** describes a form of marriage in which one woman and one man are married only to each other. Some observers, noting the rate of divorce in Canada, have suggested that "serial monogamy" is a more accurate description of the form that monogamy takes in Canada. Under ***serial monogamy,*** a person may have several spouses in his or her life but only one spouse at a time.

Some cultures allow an individual to have several husbands or wives simultaneously. This form of marriage is known as ***polygamy.*** In fact, most societies throughout the world, past and present, have preferred polygamy to monogamy. Anthropologist George Murdock (1949, 1957) sampled 565 societies and found that more than 80 percent had some type of polygamy as their preferred form. While polygamy steadily declined through most of the 20th century, in at least five countries in Africa 20 percent of men are still in polygamous marriages (Population Reference Bureau 1996).

There are two basic types of polygamy. According to Murdock, the most common—endorsed by the majority of cultures he sampled—was ***polygyny.*** Polygyny refers to the marriage of a man to more than one woman at the same time. The various wives are often sisters, who are expected to hold similar values and have already had experience sharing a household. In polygynous societies, relatively few men actually have multiple spouses. Most individuals live in typical monogamous families; having multiple wives is viewed as a mark of status.

The other principal variation of polygamy is ***polyandry,*** under which a woman can have more than one husband at the same time. This is the case in the culture of the Todas of southern India. Polyandry, however, tends to be exceedingly rare in the world today. It has been accepted by some extremely poor societies that practise female infanticide (the killing of baby girls) and thus have a relatively small number of women. Like many other societies, polyandrous cultures devalue the social worth of women.

Kinship Patterns: To Whom Are We Related?

Many of us can trace our roots by looking at a family tree or listening to elderly family members tell us about their lives—and about the lives of ancestors who died long before we were even born. Yet a person's lineage is more than simply a personal history; it also reflects societal patterns that govern descent. In every culture, children

FIGURE 11-1

Types of Family Households in Canada, 1981 and 2001

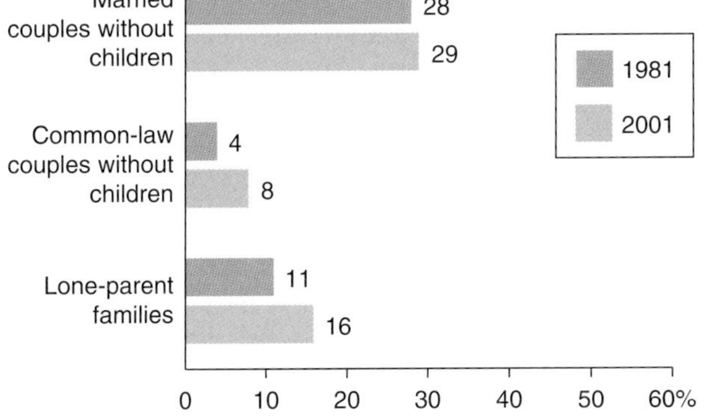

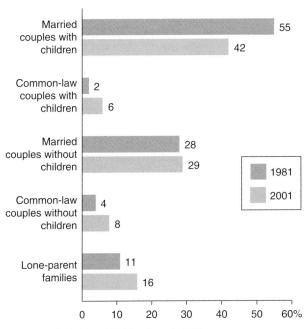

Source: Adapted from Statistics Canada 2002a.

FIGURE 11-2

The Nuclear Family in Industrialized Nations, 1960 and 1990

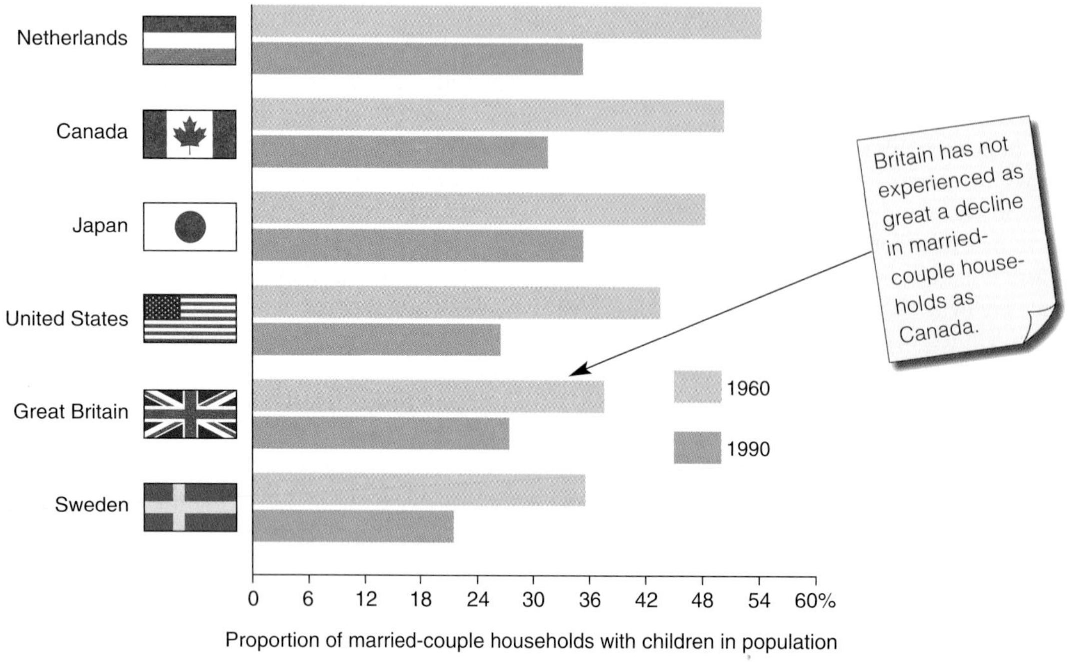

Source: Bureau of Labor Statistics data in Sorrentino 1990 and author's estimate.

encounter relatives to whom they are expected to show an emotional attachment. The state of being related to others is called ***kinship.*** Kinship is culturally learned and is not totally determined by biological or marital ties. For example, adoption creates a kinship tie that is legally acknowledged and socially accepted.

The family and the kin group are not necessarily the same. While the family is a household unit, kin do not always live together or function as a collective body on a daily basis. Kin groups include aunts, uncles, cousins, in-laws, and so forth. In a society such as Canada, the kinship group may come together only rarely, as for a wedding or funeral. However, kinship ties frequently create obligations and responsibilities. We may feel compelled to assist our kin and feel free to call upon relatives for many types of aid, including loans and baby-sitting.

How do we identify kinship groups? The principle of descent assigns people to kinship groups according to their relationship to an individual's mother or father. There are three primary ways of determining descent. Generally, Canada follows the system of ***bilateral descent,*** which means that both sides of a person's family are regarded as equally important. For example no higher value is given to the brothers of one's father than to the brothers of one's mother.

Most societies—according to George Murdock, 64 percent—give preference to one side of the family or the other in tracing descent. ***Patrilineal*** (from Latin *pater,* "father") ***descent*** indicates that only the father's relatives are important in terms of property, inheritance, and emotional ties. Conversely, in societies that favour ***matrilineal*** (from Latin *mater,* "mother") ***descent,*** only the mother's relatives are significant.

New forms of reproductive technology (discussed in the policy section) will force a new way of looking at kinship. Today a combination of biological and social processes can "create" a family member, requiring that more distinctions be made about who is related to whom (C. Cussins 1998).

Authority Patterns: Who Rules?

Imagine that you have recently married and must begin to make decisions about the future of your new family. You and your spouse face many questions. Where will you live? How will you furnish your home? Who will do the cooking, the shopping, the cleaning? Whose friends will be invited to dinner? Each time a decision must be made, an issue is raised: Who has the power to make the decision? In simple terms, who rules the family? The conflict perspective examines these questions in the context of traditional gender stratification, under which men have held a dominant position over women.

p. 245

Smile—it's family reunion time! The state of being related to others is called kinship. Kin groups include aunts, uncles, cousins, and so forth, as shown in this family from Slovakia.

More recently, conflict theorists have argued that the family contributes to societal injustice, denies opportunities to women that are extended to men, and limits freedom in sexual expression and selection of a mate. By contrast, the functionalist perspective focuses on the ways in which the family gratifies the needs of its members and contributes to the stability of society. The interactionist view considers more intimate, face-to-face relationships.

Functionalist View

There are six paramount functions performed by the family, first outlined more than 65 years ago by sociologist William F. Ogburn (Ogburn and Tibbits 1934):

1. **Reproduction.** For a society to maintain itself, it must replace dying members. In this sense, the family contributes to human survival through its function of reproduction.
2. **Protection.** Unlike the young of other animal species, human infants need constant care and economic security. The extremely long period of dependency for children places special demands on older family members. In all cultures, it is the family that assumes ultimate responsibility for the protection and upbringing of children.
3. **Socialization.** Parents and other kin monitor a child's behaviour and transmit the norms, values, and language of a culture to the child (see Chapters 3 and 4). pp. 84–86
4. **Regulation of sexual behaviour.** Sexual norms are subject to change over time (for instance, changes in customs for dating) and across cultures (Islamic Saudi Arabia compared with more permissive Denmark). However, whatever the time period or cultural values in a society, standards of sexual behaviour are most clearly defined within the family circle. The structure of society influences these standards. In male-dominated societies, for example, formal and informal norms generally permit men to express and enjoy their sexual desires more freely than women may.
5. **Affection and companionship.** Ideally, the family provides members with warm and intimate relationships and helps them feel satisfied and secure.

Societies vary in the way that power within the family is distributed. If a society expects males to dominate in all family decision making, it is termed a ***patriarchy***. Frequently, in patriarchal societies, such as Iran, the eldest male wields the greatest power, although wives are expected to be treated with respect and kindness. A woman's status in Iran is typically defined by her relationship to a male relative, usually as a wife or daughter. In many patriarchal societies women find it more difficult to obtain a divorce than a man does (G. Farr 1999). By contrast, in a ***matriarchy,*** women have greater authority than men. Matriarchies, which are very uncommon, emerged among Native American tribal societies and in nations in which men were absent for long periods of time for warfare or food gathering.

A third type of authority pattern, the ***egalitarian family,*** is one in which spouses are regarded as equals. This does not mean, however, that each decision is shared in such families. Wives may hold authority in some spheres, husbands in others. Many sociologists believe the egalitarian family has begun to replace the patriarchal family as the social norm in Canada.

Studying the Family

Do we really need the family? A century ago, Friedrich Engels (1884), a colleague of Karl Marx, described the family as the ultimate source of social inequality because of its role in the transfer of power, property, and privilege.

Of course, a family member may find such rewards outside the family—from peers, in school, at work—and may perceive the home as an unpleasant place. Nevertheless, unlike other institutions, the family is obligated to serve the emotional needs of its members. We *expect* our relatives to understand us, to care for us, and to be there for us when we need them.

6. **Providing of social status.** We inherit a social position because of the "family background" and reputation of our parents and siblings. The family unit presents the newborn child with an ascribed status of race and ethnicity that helps to determine his or her place within a society's stratification system. Moreover, family resources affect children's ability to pursue certain opportunities such as higher education and specialized lessons.

The family has traditionally fulfilled a number of other functions, such as providing religious training, education, and recreational outlets. Ogburn argued that other social institutions have gradually assumed many of these functions. Although the family once played a major role in religious life, this function has largely shifted to churches, synagogues, and other religious organizations. Similarly, education once took place at the family fireside; now it is the responsibility of professionals working in schools and colleges. Even the family's traditional recreational function has been transferred to outside groups such as Little Leagues, athletic clubs, and Internet chat rooms.

Conflict View

Conflict theorists view the family not as a contributor to social stability, but as a reflection of the inequality in wealth and power found within the larger society. Feminist theorists and conflict theorists note that the family has traditionally legitimized and perpetuated male dominance. Throughout most of human history—and in a very wide range of societies—husbands have exercised overwhelming power and authority within the family.

p. 14

Not until the "first wave" of contemporary feminism in North America in the mid-1800s was there a substantial challenge to the historic status of wives and children as the legal property of husbands.

While the egalitarian family has become a more common pattern in North America in recent decades—owing in good part to the activism of feminists beginning in the late 1960s and early 1970s—male dominance within the family has hardly disappeared. Sociologists have found that women are significantly more likely to leave their jobs when their husbands find better employment opportunities than men are when their wives receive desirable job offers (Bielby and Bielby 1992). And unfortunately, many husbands reinforce their power and control over wives and children through acts of domestic violence. (Box 11-2 considers cross-cultural findings about violence within the home.)

Conflict theorists also view the family as an economic unit that contributes to societal injustice. The family is the basis for transferring power, property, and privilege from one generation to the next. North America is widely viewed as a "land of opportunity," yet social mobility is restricted in important ways. Children "inherit" the privileged or less-than-privileged social and economic status of their parents (and, in some cases, of earlier generations as well). As conflict theorists point out, the social class of their parents significantly influences children's socialization experiences and the protection they receive. This means that the socioeconomic status of a child's family will have a marked influence on his or her nutrition, health care, housing, educational opportunities, and, in many respects, life chances as an adult. For that reason, conflict theorists argue that the family helps to maintain inequality.

p. 191

Interactionist View

Interactionists focus on the microlevel of family and other intimate relationships. They are interested in how individuals interact with one another, whether they are gay, lesbian, or heterosexual couples, etc. For example, interactionists have looked at the nature of family interactions and relationship quality (e.g., interparental conflict, parenting stress, love between parents and for their children), and found that those factors, rather than the parents' sexual orientation, strongly predict children's behavioural adjustment (Chan et al. 1998).

Another interactionist study might examine the role of the step-parent. The increased number of single parents who remarry has sparked an interest in those who are helping to raise other people's children. While children likely do not dream about one day becoming a stepmom or stepdad, this is hardly an unusual occurrence today. Studies have found that stepmothers are more likely to accept the blame for bad relations with their stepchildren, whereas stepfathers are less likely to accept responsibility. Interactionists theorize that stepfathers (like most fathers) may simply be unaccustomed to interacting directly with children when the mother isn't there (Bray and Kelly 1999; Furstenberg and Cherlin 1991).

Feminist Views

No single theory represents how feminist theories conceptualize the family. Feminist perspectives do, however, share certain assumptions in their study of family. Some of these assumptions include a rejection of the belief in

Sociology in the Global Community

11-2 Domestic Violence

"It's the same every Saturday night. The husband comes home drunk and beats her." This is how Tania Kucherenko describes her downstairs neighbours in Moscow after turning a deaf ear to the screams of terror and the sounds of furniture being overthrown and glass breaking. "There's nothing we can do. It's best not to interfere." Contempt for women runs deep in Russia, where women who dare to leave their husbands risk losing their legal status, a place to live, and the right to work (Bennett 1997:A1).

This billboard in Poland featuring the bruised face of a child reads, "Because he had to let off steam." It is a reminder to Poles that domestic violence is a serious problem in their country, affecting both wives and children.

Wife battering, child abuse, abuse of the elderly, and other forms of domestic violence are an ugly reality of family life across the world. In Japan, Tanzania, and Chile, more than half the women report physical abuse by a partner. While estimates are difficult to find on a topic so hidden from public view, one recent study concluded that around the world one third of all women have been beaten, or coerced into sex, or otherwise physically abused in their lifetime.

Drawing on studies conducted throughout the world, we can make the following generalizations:

- Women are most at risk of violence from the men they know.
- Violence against women is evident in all socioeconomic groups.
- Family violence is at least as dangerous as assaults committed by strangers.
- Though women sometimes exhibit violent behaviour toward men, most acts of violence that cause injury are perpetrated by men against women.
- Violence within intimate relationships tends to escalate over time.
- Emotional and psychological abuse can be at least as debilitating as physical abuse.
- Use of alcohol exacerbates family violence but does not cause it.

Using the conflict and feminist models, researchers have found that in relationships where the inequality is greater between men and women, the likelihood of assault on wives increases dramatically. This suggests that much of the violence between intimates, even when sexual in nature, is about power rather than sex.

The situation of battered women is so intolerable that it has been compared to that of prison inmates.

The situation of battered women is so intolerable that it has been compared to that of prison inmates. Criminologist Noga Avni (1991) interviewed battered women at a shelter in Israel and found that their day-to-day lives with their husbands or lovers shared many elements of life in an oppressive total institution, as described by Erving Goffman (1961). Physical barriers are imposed on these women; by threatening further violence, men are able to restrict women to their homes, damaging both their self-esteem and their ability to cope with repeated abuse. Moreover, as in a total institution, these battered women are cut off from external sources of physical p. 83 and emotional assistance and moral support. In Avni's view, society could more effectively aid victims of domestic violence if it better understood the essential imprisonment of these women. Women in these situations have few economic alternatives, and they fear that their children may also be victimized if they don't submit to the abuse.

The family can be a dangerous place not only for women but also for children and the elderly. Canada, for example, has established a child abuse telephone hotline called the Kids Help Phone Line (1-800-668-6868) for children needing help or support (DeKeseredy 2001). An Ontario study surveying 9953 residents in that province found that 31.2 percent of males aged 15 and older reported physical abuse while growing up; 21.1 percent of females of the same age reported experiencing abuse (MacMillan et al. 1997). An American national study in 1996 found approximately 450 000 elderly persons, or 1 in every 90, were abused or neglected.

Let's Discuss

1. How does the degree of equality in a relationship correlate to the likelihood of domestic violence? How might conflict theorists explain this?
2. Do you know of a family that experienced domestic violence? Did the victim(s) seek outside help, and was that help effective?

Sources: American Bar Association 1999; American Humane Association 1999; DeKeseredy 2001; Gelles and Cornell 1990; Heise et al. 1999; MacMillan et al. 1997; National Center on Elder Abuse 1998; Straus 1994.

the family's "naturalness" (Luxton 2001). Feminist theorists argue that the family is a socially constructed institution and, thus, varies according to time and place. Families are not seen as "monolithic" or the same, but rather as diverse, flexible, and changeable. While feminists' views on the family agree that women have a position of inequality and discrimination in the family, they argue that these too vary according to class, race, and ethnicity. The functional view of family is challenged by feminist theorists, who raise the question "For whom and for whose interests is the family functional?"

Canadian feminist theorist Margrit Eichler (2001) argues that the ways in which sociologists study the family often contain biases. These include a *monolithic bias*, which is a tendency to assume "the family" is uniform rather than diverse; a *conservative bias*, which treats recent changes in the family as fleeting and ignores or treats as rare some of the uglier aspects of family life (e.g., family violence); an *ageist bias*, which regards children and the aged only as passive members of families; a *sexist bias*, which is exhibited in patterns such as double standards and gender insensitivity; a *microstructural bias*, which overemphasizes micro-level variables and neglects macro-level variables; a *racist bias*, which explicitly or implicitly assumes the superiority of the family form of the dominant group and ignores race and racism when relevant; and a *heterosexist bias*, which either ignores same-sex families or treats them as problematic and deviant.

When fathers interact regularly with their children, it's a win/win situation. The fathers get close to their offspring, and studies show that the children end up with fewer behaviour problems.

Marriage and Family

Historically, the most consistent aspect of family life in this country has been the high rate of marriage. In fact, despite the increase in divorce rates in Canada in the 1970s and 1980s, Canada's rate of divorce is much lower than that of the United States. Of those who do divorce, most will go on to remarry (Baker 2001).

In this part of the chapter, we will examine various aspects of love, marriage, and parenthood in Canada and contrast them with cross-cultural examples. We're used to thinking of romance and mate selection as strictly a matter of individual preference. Yet, sociological analysis tells us that social institutions and distinctive cultural norms and values also play an important role.

Courtship and Mate Selection

"My rugby mates would roll over in their graves," says Tom Buckley of his online courtship and subsequent marriage to Terri Muir. But Tom and Terri are hardly alone these days in turning to the Internet for matchmaking services. By the end of 1999 more than 2500 websites were helping people find mates. You could choose from oneandonly.com or 2ofakind.com or cupidnet.com, among others. One service alone claimed 2 million subscribers. Tom and Terri carried on their romance via e-mail for a year before they met. According to Tom, "E-mail made it easier to communicate because neither one of us was the type to walk up to someone in the gym or a bar and say, 'You're the fuel to my fire' " (B. Morris 1999:D1).

Internet romance is only the latest courtship practice. In the central Asian nation of Uzbekistan and many other traditional cultures, courtship is defined largely through the interaction of two sets of parents. They arrange spouses for their children. Typically, a young Uzbekistani woman will be socialized to eagerly anticipate her marriage to a man whom she has met only once, when he is presented to her family at the time of the final inspection of her dowry. In Canada, by contrast, courtship is conducted primarily by individuals who may have a romantic interest in each other. In our culture, courtship often requires these individuals to rely heavily on intricate games, gestures, and signals. Despite such differences, courtship—whether in Canada, Uzbekistan, or elsewhere—is influenced by the norms and values of the larger society (C. J. Williams 1995).

Take our choice of a mate. Why are we drawn to a particular person in the first place? To what extent are these judgments shaped by the society around us?

Aspects of Mate Selection

Many societies have explicit or unstated rules that define potential mates as acceptable or unacceptable. These norms can be distinguished in terms of endogamy and exogamy. ***Endogamy*** (from the Greek *endon,* "within") specifies the groups within which a spouse must be found and prohibits marriage with others. For example, in Canada, many people are expected to marry within their own racial, ethnic, or religious group and are strongly discouraged or even prohibited from marrying outside the group. Endogamy is intended to reinforce the cohesiveness of the group by suggesting to the young that they should marry someone "of our own kind."

By contrast, ***exogamy*** (from the Greek *exo,* "outside") requires mate selection outside certain groups, usually one's own family or certain kinfolk. The ***incest taboo,*** a social norm common to virtually all societies, prohibits sexual relationships between certain culturally specified relatives. For people in Canada, this taboo means that we must marry outside the nuclear family. We cannot marry our siblings; however, we are able to marry our first cousins.

Endogamous restrictions may be seen as preferences for one group over another. In the United States, such preferences are most obvious in racial barriers. Until the 1960s, some states outlawed interracial marriages. This practice was challenged by Richard Loving (a white man) and Mildred Jeter Loving (a part-black, part–Native American woman), who married in 1958. Eventually, in 1967, the Supreme Court ruled that it was unconstitutional to prohibit marriage solely on the basis of race. The decision struck down statutes in Virginia and 16 other states.

In Canada, there is evidence to suggest that people are more likely to marry someone outside of their own ethnic group the longer they reside in Canada. Northern, western, and eastern European ethnic groups are the most likely to marry outside their own ethnic group, while Asians, Africans, and Latin Americans are the least likely. Despite the effort the Canadian government expends promoting the ideology and policies of multiculturalism, Canadian families are coming to resemble one another more and more through increased intermarriage between and among various ethnic groups. While 11 percent of immigrants to this country report more than one ethnic background, approximately one third of those born in Canada had a mixed ethnic background (Howell et al. 2001).

Increasing numbers of exogamous unions force a society to reconsider its definitions of race and ethnicity. In Chapter 9, we noted that race is socially constructed in Canada and around the world. As increasing proportions of children in Canada come from backgrounds of more than one race and/or ethnicity, single ethnic and racial identifiers become less relevant. The p. 210 Canadian census allows individuals to report two or more ethnic choices as well as to respond to an "Other" category for race, for those whose racial background does not fall neatly into one category (Howell et at. 2001).

The Love Relationship

Whatever else "love" is, most people would agree it is complicated. Listen to what a university student has to say on the subject:

> Love isn't in the air these days, at least not in New Haven . . . my peers and I find ourselves in a new world of romance, and we're feeling a little out of our league. We are children of the Age of Divorce, born into the AIDS crisis, reared on Madonna, *Friends,* and *Beverly Hills 90210.* No wonder we're confused. We know we want this thing called love. More than previous generations, though, we're unsure of what love is and how to get it—and we're not so sure that finding it will be worth the trouble (Rodberg 1999:1–2).

Interracial unions, which are becoming increasingly common and accepted, are blurring definitions of race. Would the children of this interracial couple be considered black or white?

Another student claims that "love, like everything else, must be pondered, and we have too many other things to ponder—no matter how much we profess to want love" (quoted in Rodberg 1999:4).

For a variety of reasons, hinted at in these quotations, this generation of post-secondary students seems more likely to "hook up" or cruise in large packs than engage in the romantic dating relationships of their parents and grandparents. Still, at some point in their adult lives the great majority of today's students will meet someone they "love" and enter into a long-term relationship that focuses on creating a family.

In North America, love is important in the courtship process. Living in their own home makes the affectional bond between husband and wife especially important. The couple is expected to develop its own emotional ties, free of the demands of other household members for affection. Sociologist William Goode (1959) observed that spouses in a nuclear family have to rely heavily on each other for the companionship and support that might be provided by other relatives in an extended-family situation.

Parents in North America tend to value love highly as a rationale for marriage, and they encourage their children to develop intimate relationships based on love and affection. In addition, songs, films, books, magazines, television shows, and even cartoons and comic books reinforce the theme of love. At the same time, our society expects parents and peers to help a person confine his or her search for a mate to "socially acceptable" members of the opposite sex.

Most North Americans take the importance of falling in love for granted, but love-and-marriage is by no means a cultural universal. In fact, in many cultures (both today and in the past) love and marriage are unconnected and are sometimes at odds with one another. For example, feelings of love are not a prerequisite for marriage among the Yaruros of inland Venezuela or in other cultures where there is little freedom for mate selection. The Yaruro male of marriageable age doesn't engage in the kind of dating behaviour so typical of young people in Canada. Rather, he knows that, under the traditions of his culture, he must marry one of his mother's brothers' daughters or one of his father's sisters' daughters. The young man's choice is further limited because one of his uncles selects the eligible cousin that he must marry (Freeman 1958; Lindholm 1999).

Many of the world's cultures give priority in mate selection to factors other than romantic feelings. In societies with *arranged marriages,* often engineered by parents or religious authorities, economic considerations play a significant role. The newly married couple is expected to develop a feeling of love *after* the legal union is formalized, if at all.

Within Canada, some subcultures carry on the arranged marriage practices of their native cultures (Nanda 1991). Young people among the Sikhs and Hindus who have immigrated from India and among Islamic Muslims and Hasidic Jews allow their parents or designated matchmakers to find spouses within their ethnic community. As one young Sikh declared, "I will definitely marry who my parents wish. They know me better than I know myself" (Segall 1998:48). This practice of arranged marriage may be gradually changing, however, due to the influence of the larger society's cultural practices. Young people who have emigrated without their families often turn to the Internet to find partners who share their background and goals. Matrimonial ads for the Indian community run on such websites as SuitableMatch.com and INDOLINK.com. One Hasidic Jewish woman noted that the system of arranged marriages "isn't perfect, and it doesn't work for everyone, but this is the system we know and trust, the way we couple, and the way we learn to love. So it works for most of us" (p. 53).

Variations in Family Life and Intimate Relationships

Within Canada, social class, race, ethnicity and sexual orientation create variations in family life. Understanding these variations will give us a more sophisticated understanding of contemporary family styles in our country.

Social Class Differences

Various studies have documented the differences in family organization among social classes in North America. The upper-class emphasis is on lineage and maintenance of family position. If you are in the upper class, you are not simply a member of a nuclear family but rather a member of a larger family tradition. As a result, upper-class families are quite concerned about what they see as "proper training" for children.

Lower-class families do not often have the luxury of worrying about the "family name"; they must first struggle to pay their bills and survive the crises often associated with life in poverty. Such families are more likely to have only one parent in the home, creating special challenges in child care and financial needs. Children in lower-class families typically assume adult responsibilities—including marriage and parenthood—at an earlier age than children of affluent homes. In part, this is because they may lack the money needed to remain in school.

Social class differences in family life are less striking than they once were. In the past, family specialists agreed that there were pronounced contrasts in child-rearing practices. Lower-class families were found to be more authoritarian in rearing children and more inclined to use physical punishment. Middle-class families were more permissive and more restrained in punishing their children. However, these differences may have narrowed as more and more families from all social classes have turned to the same books, magazines, and even television talk shows for advice on rearing children (M. Kohn 1970; Luster et al. 1989).

Among the poor, women often play a significant role in the economic support of the family. The National Council of Welfare (1999) reported that in 1997, 57.1 percent of lone-parent mothers in Canada were living below the poverty line, compared to 11.1 percent of couples with children.

Many racial and ethnic groups appear to have distinctive family characteristics. However, racial and class factors are often closely related. In examining family life among racial and ethnic minorities, keep in mind that certain patterns may result from class as well as cultural factors.

The ways in which race, ethnicity, gender, and class intersect contribute to the diversity of Canadian families. Above, Korean immigrant spouses work together in a family business.

Racial and Ethnic Differences

The ways in which race, ethnicity, gender, and class intersect contributes to the diversity of Canadian families. The subordinate status of racial and ethnic minorities and Canada's First Nations people has profound effects on the family life of these groups.

First Nations people are a heterogeneous group with different histories, geographies, languages, economies, and cultures. Their families, which often include those who are kin as well as those who come together in a common community purpose, have been fundamentally disrupted by hundreds of years of European domination. For example, the First Nations peoples of the Montagnais-Naskapi of the eastern Labrador Peninsula underwent major changes in family structure and gender relations as they moved to trapping, introduced by Europeans, and away from traditional hunting and fishing. The sexual division of labour became more specialized and families began to become smaller, approaching the size of a nuclear family (Leacock 2001).

First Nations families have been devalued and undermined by the Canadian government and religious institutions. In the past, children were sent away from their homes to residential schools, where they were punished for speaking their own language and expressing their own culture. There, they were often subjected to sexual and physical abuse by the hands of those who ran the schools—those who were assigned to be their guardians.

In the 1960s, First Nations children were put up for adoption and adopted by, most often, white families in Canada and the United States, rather than by those from within their own band (Eichler 1997). Today, after years of cultural oppression under government control, problems of domestic abuse, youth suicide, and substance abuse plague First Nations families.

Research carried out in Nova Scotia and Toronto on black families demonstrates the links between the effects of race, class, and gender and their impact on black families (Calliste 2001). Significantly more black families were headed by women than non-black families; these women-headed black families earn approximately half of the income of their married counterparts, who in turn earn less than non-black families headed by married couples. The study concludes that the high rate of teenage pregnancy and the feminization of poverty need to be addressed by black community groups and government in the form of education, employment equity, sex education, and parenting sessions (Calliste 2001: 417). Some similarities exist between Canadian black families and American black families, because the effects of race, class, and gender intersect to produce inequality for families in both countries.

Child-Rearing Patterns in Family Life

The Nayars of southern India acknowledge the biological role of fathers, but the mother's eldest brother is responsible for her children (Gough 1974). By contrast, uncles play only a peripheral role in child care in North America. Caring for children is a universal function of the

FIGURE 11-3

Distribution of Children Aged 0 to 14 by Family Structure, 2001

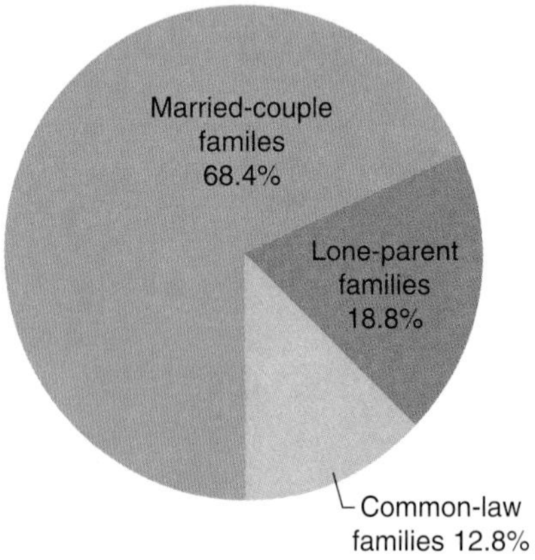

Source: Statistics Canada 2002a.

family, yet the ways in which different societies assign this function to family members can vary significantly. Within Canada, child-rearing patterns are varied. We'll take a look here at parenthood and grandparenthood, adoption, dual-income families, single-parent families, and stepfamilies. (See Figure 11-3 for an idea of the types of families in Canada in which children live today.)

Parenthood and Grandparenthood

The socialization of children is essential to the maintenance of any culture. Consequently, parenthood is one of the most important (and most demanding) social roles in North America. Sociologist Alice Rossi (1968, 1984) has identified four factors that complicate the transition to parenthood and the role of socialization. First, there is little anticipatory socialization for the social role of caregiver. The normal school curriculum gives scant attention to the subjects most relevant to successful family life—such as child care and home maintenance. Second, only limited learning occurs during the period of pregnancy itself. Third, the transition to parenthood is quite abrupt. Unlike adolescence, it is not prolonged; unlike socialization for work, you cannot gradually take on the duties of caregiving. Finally, in Rossi's view, our society lacks clear and helpful guidelines for successful parenthood. There is little consensus on how parents can produce happy and well adjusted offspring—or even on what it means to be "well adjusted." For these reasons, socialization for parenthood involves difficult challenges for most men and women in North America.

pp. 84–86

One recent development in family life in Canada has been the extension of parenthood, as adult children continue to (or return to) live at home. In 1990, more children over the age of 18 lived with their parents while completing post-secondary education than in the early 1980s (Boyd and Pryor 1990). In other instances, financial difficulties are at the heart of these living arrangements. While rents and real estate prices skyrocketed in the 1990s, salaries for younger workers did not keep pace, and many found themselves unable to afford their own homes. Moreover, with many marriages now ending in divorce—most commonly in the first seven years of marriage—divorced sons and daughters are returning to live with their parents, sometimes with their own children.

Is this living arrangement a positive development for family members? Social scientists have just begun to examine this phenomenon, sometimes called the "boomerang generation" or the "full-nest syndrome" in the popular press. One survey in the United States seemed to show that neither the parents nor their adult children were happy about continuing to live together. The children often felt resentful and isolated, but the parents also suffered: Learning to live without children in the home is an essential stage of adult life and may even be a significant turning point for a marriage (*Berkeley Wellness Letter* 1990; Mogelonsky 1996).

The love expressed by this mother and her two children testifies to successful parenting. Even though parenthood is a crucial social role, society generally provides few clear guidelines.

Taking Sociology to Work

KARLA JESSEN WILLIAMSON: Executive Director, The Arctic Institute of North America

Karla Jessen Williamson is a *kalaaleq*, a Greenland Inuk, born in Appamiut. She completed her bachelor's and master's degrees in education at the University of Saskatchewan and is in the process of getting her PhD in sociology from the University of Aberdeen in Scotland. Her master's thesis focused on child-raising practices in the community of Pangnirtung, Nunavut, and her PhD dissertation concentrates on Inuit gender relations in the post-colonial Greenland Inuit community. Presently, Williamson holds the position of Executive Director of the Arctic Institute of North America, a multidisciplinary research institute housed at the University of Calgary, mandated to study Canada's North. She oversees the functioning of the Institute, which includes research, teaching, and information dissemination related to the North. Her background in sociology provides grounding to her understanding of such issues as cultural preservation, cultural diversity, and socioeconomic development in Northern communities.

Prior to taking her latest post, she held teaching appointments at the University of Saskatchewan and was the editor of the *Journal of Indigenous Studies*. Williamson states that her own pursuit of science has been greatly shaped by her Inuit cultural background and in particular, her maternal grandmother, whose intellectual curiosity is based on Inuit *sitarsuaat*. According to Williamson, *sitarsuaat* is a concept that includes the capacity to understand the forces behind all intellects and how they "have been integrated, animating the environment, the universe and the spirit."

Let's Discuss

1. Why would a background in sociology be important in the running of an institute focusing on life in Northern communities?
2. What sociological issues might Northerners experience that would not be experienced by the majority of Canadians—those living in the south?

Sources: American Association for the Advancement of Science 2000; *University of Calgary Gazette* 2000.

As life expectancy increases in North America, more and more parents are becoming grandparents and even great-grandparents. After interviewing many grandparents, sociologists Andrew Cherlin and Frank Furstenberg, Jr. (1992) identified three principal styles of grandparenting:

1. More than half (55 percent) of grandparents surveyed functioned as "specialists in recreational care-giving." They enriched their grandchildren's lives through recreational outings and other special activities.
2. More than one fourth (29 percent) carried on a "ritualistic" (primarily symbolic) relationship with their grandchildren. In some instances, this was because the grandparents lived far away from their grandchildren and could see them only occasionally.
3. About one sixth (16 percent) of grandparents surveyed were actively involved in everyday routine care of their grandchildren and exercised substantial authority over them.

Adoption

In a legal sense, ***adoption*** is a "process that allows for the transfer of the legal rights, responsibilities, and privileges of parenthood" to a new legal parent or parents (E. Cole 1985:638). In many cases, these rights are transferred from a biological parent or parents (often called birth parents) to an adoptive parent or parents.

Viewed from a functionalist perspective, government has a strong interest in encouraging adoption. Policymakers, in fact, have both a humanitarian and a financial stake in the process. In theory, adoption offers a stable family environment for children who otherwise might not receive satisfactory care. Moreover, government data show that unwed mothers who keep their babies tend to be of lower socioeconomic status and often require public assistance to support their children. Government can lower its social welfare expenses if children are transferred to economically self-sufficient families. From a conflict perspective, however, such financial considerations raise the ugly spectre of adoption as a means whereby affluent (often infertile) couples "buy" the children of the poor (C. Bachrach 1986). For decades during the last century in Canada, many First Nations' children were adopted to white families in this country and the United States; this practice has since been identified as a form of cultural genocide (Johnson 1983).

With greater access to contraception and legal abortion, the rate of unplanned births to young women has declined since the 1950s, and the availability of Canadian infants has decreased. As well, more and more single mothers have been keeping their babies and supporting them through earnings or social assistance. In addition, the goals of family preservation in the Canadian child welfare system, and Canadians' current preference to adopt infants and younger children, will make the case for international adoption (most likely from developing countries) more compelling (Baker 2001). This supports the conflict view that the wealthier, more powerful countries have control over the poorer, less powerful countries. In this case, it involves the "purchase" of children.

Dual-Income Families

The idea of a family consisting of a wage-earning husband and a wife who stays at home has largely given way to the *dual-income household.* In Canadian two-parent families, 70 percent of women with children under 16 were employed in the paid labour force in 1999 (Statistics Canada 2001b). Why has there been such a rise in the number of dual-income couples? A major factor is economic need. The Vanier Institute of the Family (1999) estimated the costs of raising a child from birth to age 18 to be approximately $160 000. Raising children in urban centres, where the bulk of the Canadian population resides, is expensive. An Ontario study found two-child families in that province spent 18 percent of their gross income on child-related expenses (Douthitt and Fedyk 1990). Other factors contributing to the rise of the dual-income model include the nation's declining birthrate (see Chapter 14), the increase in the proportion of women with post-secondary education, the shift in the economy of North America from manufacturing to service industries, and the impact of the feminist movement in changing women's consciousness.

Single-Parent Families

In recent decades, the stigma attached to "unwed mothers" and other single parents has significantly diminished. ***Single-parent families,*** in which there is only one parent present to care for the children, can hardly be viewed as a rarity in Canada. In 2001, approximately 16 percent of families were headed by a lone parent (up from approximately 11 percent in 1981), the overwhelming majority of which were female-headed. Variation and diversity exists among lone-parent families. For example, in 1991, the percentage of female-headed black families was over three times the percentage of female-headed non-black families. The interaction of race, class, and gender is evident in patterns of black family structure (Calliste 2001).

While marital dissolution is the major cause of the increase in lone-parent families, never-married lone parents are growing in number. The children of these unions tend to divide their time between both parents (Marcil-Gratton 1999). This growing trend of non-legal relationships is evident in Canada as well as most industrialized countries. In Quebec, for example, 38 percent of all children and 48 percent of first births were categorized as "out-of-wedlock," but 90 percent of these children were born to parents living together in non-legal relationships (Le Bourdais and Marcil-Gratton 1994).

The lives of single parents and their children are not inevitably more difficult than life in a traditional nuclear family. It is as inaccurate to assume that a single-parent family is necessarily "deprived" as it is to assume that a two-parent family is always secure and happy. Nevertheless, life in a single-parent family can be extremely stressful, in both economic and emotional terms. Economic inequality and poverty are striking characteristics of lone-parent families. When compared to two-parent families, female-led, lone-parent families are the most vulnerable to poverty, a fact that contributes to the phenomenon known as the "feminization of poverty."

A family headed by a single mother faces especially difficult problems when the mother is a teenager. Draw-

In Canadian two-parent families, 70 percent of women with children under 16 were in the paid labour force in 1999. Above, a mother and father share the child care duties as the mother begins her day in the paid labour force.

Most households in Canada do not consist of two parents living with their unmarried children.

ing on two decades of social science research, sociologist Kristin Luker (1996:11) observes:

> The short answer to why teenagers get pregnant and especially to why they continue those pregnancies is that a fairly substantial number of them just don't believe what adults tell them, be it about sex, contraception, marriage, or babies. They don't believe in adult conventional wisdom.

Why might low-income teenage women wish to have children and face the obvious financial difficulties of motherhood? Viewed from an interactionist perspective, these women tend to have low self-esteem and limited options; a child may provide a sense of motivation and purpose for a teenager whose economic worth in our society is limited at best. Given the barriers that many young women face because of their gender, race, ethnicity, and class, many teenagers may believe that they have little to lose and much to gain by having a child.

Countries belonging to the Organization of Economic Co-operation and Development (OECD) (i.e., developed nations) have experienced an increase in lone-parent families since the early 1970s, with the greatest increase occurring in the United States (Baker 2001). However, poverty rates for these families vary among industrialized countries, depending on the availability of social welfare programs, the rates of male and female unemployment, government disincentives to work while receiving social assistance, the availability of social welfare programs, and the availability of special employment training programs and child care.

Despite the current concern over the increase in the number of lone-parent families, this family type has existed for over 100 years in Canada. In 1901, the ratio of lone-parent to two-parent families was only slightly lower than today's ratio. A major interdisciplinary study carried out at the University of Victoria, based on 1901 census data, concluded that the family has always been a variable and flexible institution. With unsanctioned or non-formalized divorce being more common in the past than is generally known, "there was much more volatility and shifting of marital status than anyone was prepared to admit at the state level" (Gram 2001).

Blended Families

Approximately 20 percent of Canadians have married, divorced, and remarried. The rising rates of divorce and remarriage have led to a noticeable increase in stepfamily relationships. In 1967, 12.3 percent of marriages involved one spouse who had been previously married, but by 1998 the rate had more than doubled to 33 percent (Dumas 1994; Ambert 2002).

Stepfamilies are an exceedingly complex form of family organization. Here is how one 13-year-old boy described his family.

> Tim and Janet are my stepbrother and sister. Josh is my stepdad. Carin and Don are my real parents, who are divorced. And Don married Anna and together they had Ethan and Ellen, my half-sister and brother. And Carin married Josh and had little Alice, my half-sister (Bernstein 1988).

The exact nature of these blended families has social significance for adults and children alike. Certainly resocialization is required when an adult becomes a step-parent or a child becomes a stepchild and stepsibling. Moreover, an important distinction must be made between first-time stepfamilies and households where there have been repeated divorces, breakups, or changes in custodial arrangements.

In evaluating the rise of stepfamilies, some observers have assumed that children would benefit from remarriage because they would be gaining a second custodial parent and potentially would enjoy greater economic security. However, after reviewing many studies on stepfamilies, sociologist Andrew Cherlin (1999:421) concluded that "the well-being of children in stepfamily households is no better, on average, than the well-being of children in divorced, single-parent households." Step-parents can play valuable and unique roles in their stepchildren's lives, but their involvement does not guarantee an improvement. In fact, standards may decline. Some studies conducted by an economist in the United States found that children raised in families with stepmothers are likely to have less health care, education, and money spent on their food than children raised by biological mothers. The measures are also negative for children raised by a stepfather but only half as negative as in the case of stepmothers. This doesn't mean that stepmothers are "evil"—it may be that the stepmother steps back out of concern of seeming too intrusive or relies mistakenly on the biological father to carry out these parental duties (Lewin 2000).

Family Violence in Canada

The family is often portrayed through the mass media and other institutions as a source of comfort, security, and safety; as a place to which its members retreat to escape the rough and tumble of the public world of work and school. This social construction of the family as a "haven in a heartless world"(Lasch 1977) often obscures the reality that many members of families face; that is, the family is a source of conflict and, possibly, danger. Sociologists Gelles and Straus (1988:18) point out that "You are more likely to be physically assaulted, beaten, and killed in your own home at the hands of a loved one than anyplace else, or by anyone else in society." There are various types of family violence, including violence against women, violence against children, sibling violence, and violence against elders (DeKeseredy 2001).

In 1999, Statistics Canada reported the rate of wife assault in Canada to be 3 percent, while the rate of those reporting wife assault over a five-year period was 8 percent, down from 12 percent in 1993 (Statistics Canada 2001f). Statistics Canada's definition of spousal "violence" or "assault" includes being beaten, slapped, choked, pushed, threatened with a gun, knife or other object, or being forced to have unwanted sexual activity. Between 1993 and 1999, the overall decline in spousal assault against women in Canada may have been due to factors such as increased availability of shelters for abused women, increased reporting to police by victims of abuse, mandatory arrest policies for men who assault their wives, growth in the number of treatment programs for violent men, changes in the economic and social status of women which allow them to more easily leave violent relationships, and changes in society's attitudes recognizing assault of female spouses as a crime (Statistics Canada 2001f).

Contrary to a commonly held assumption that spousal violence ends after the breakdown of a marriage, violence continues and often occurs for the first time after the couple separates. In 1999 in Canada, approximately 63 000 women and 35 000 men were assaulted for the first time after their marriages had broken down (Statistics Canada 2001f). Male "proprietariness" or male sexual jealousy has often been used to explain patterns of male violence towards female ex-partners, particularly in acts of killing (Gartner et al. 2001).

While spousal violence against women occurs in all cultures, First Nations women run a greater risk of being harmed in episodes of family violence. During the period 1993 to1999, 25 percent of First Nations women were assaulted by a current or former spouse, which was twice the rate of First Nations men and three times the rate of non-aboriginal women (Statistics Canada 2001f).

Canadian children and youth who die from homicide are most likely to be killed by family members (Statistics Canada 2001f). Family members were responsible for 63 percent of solved homicides of children and youth recorded by police in Canada between 1974 and 1999. In 1998, the majority of cases of violence towards children where abuse had been substantiated involved inappropriate punishment, while the most common form of child sexual abuse was touching and fondling of genitals. Children's exposure to family violence (e.g., hearing or seeing one parent assault the other) was the most common form of emotional maltreatment (Statistics Canada 2001f).

Divorce

"Do you promise to love, honour, and cherish . . . until death do you part?" Every year, people of all social classes and racial and ethnic groups make this legally binding agreement. Yet an increasing number of these promises shatter in divorce. While rates may vary among regions (Alberta and B.C. have rates higher than the national average, while the Atlantic provinces have rates that are lower), divorce is a nationwide phenomenon.

Statistical Trends in Divorce

Just how common is divorce? Surprisingly, this is not a simple question; divorce statistics are difficult to interpret.

The media frequently report that one out of every three marriages ends in divorce. But this figure is misleading, since many marriages last for decades. It is based on a comparison of all divorces that occur in a single year (regardless of when the couples were married) against the number of new marriages in the same year.

Divorce in Canada, and many other countries, began to increase in the late 1960s but then started to level off and even decline since the late 1980s (Bélanger 1999) (see Figure 11-4). This is partly due to the aging of the baby boomer population and the corresponding decline in the proportion of people of marriageable age.

Getting divorced obviously does not sour people on marriage. The majority of divorced people remarry, while lone parents have higher rates of remarriage than those without children (Baker 2001). Women are less likely than men to remarry because many retain custody of children after a divorce, which complicates establishing a new adult relationship (Bianchi and Spain 1996).

Some people regard the nation's high rate of remarriage as an endorsement of the institution of marriage, but it does lead to the new challenges of a remarriage kin network composed of current and prior marital relation-

FIGURE 11-4

Marriage and Divorce Rates in Canada, 1967–2000

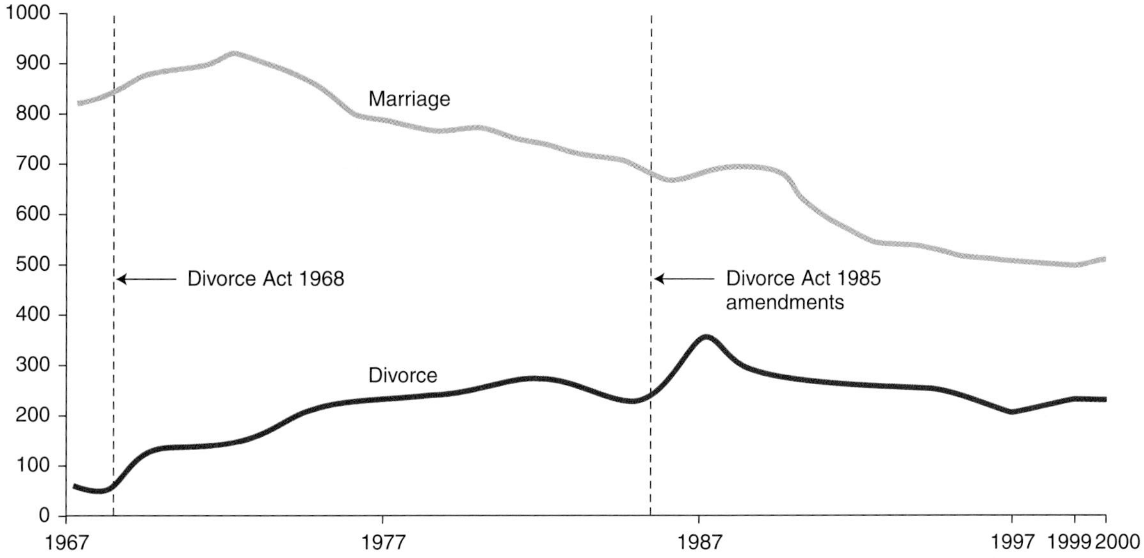

Source: Statistics Canada. Divorces (1987–1988, 1990, 1991, 1992, 1993, 1994, 1995, 1996–1997). In Baker 2001a:218; Statistics Canada, 2002b; Statisticts Canada, 2003k.

ships. This network can be particularly complex if children are involved or if an ex-spouse remarries.

Factors Associated with Divorce

Perhaps the most important factor in the increase in divorce throughout the 20th century has been the greater social *acceptance* of divorce. It's no longer considered necessary to endure an unhappy marriage. Most importantly, various religious denominations have relaxed negative attitudes toward divorce, and most religious leaders no longer treat it as a sin. The growing acceptance of divorce is a worldwide phenomenon. In 1998, a few months after a highly publicized divorce by pop superstar Seiko Matsuda, the prime minister of Japan released a survey showing that 54 percent of those polled supported uncontested divorce, compared to 20 percent in 1979 (Kyodo News International 1998a).

A few other factors deserve mention:

- No-fault divorce provisions, allowing a couple to end their marriage without fault on either side (such as specifying adultery), accounted for an initial surge in the divorce rate after they were introduced in 1985, although they appear to have had little effect beyond that.
- Divorce has become a more practical option in newly formed families, since they now tend to have fewer children than in the past.
- A general increase in family incomes, coupled with the availability of free legal aid for some poor people, has meant that more couples can afford costly divorce proceedings.
- As society provides greater opportunities for women, more and more wives are becoming less dependent on their husbands—both economically and emotionally. They may then feel more able to leave if the marriage seems hopeless.

Impact of Divorce on Children

Divorce is traumatic for all involved, as Cornel West made clear in the excerpt that opened this chapter. But it has special meaning for children involved in custody disputes. There were over 75 000 such children in Canada in 2000 (Statistics Canada 2002)). For some of these children, divorce signals the welcome end to being witness to a very dysfunctional relationship. An American study conducted by sociologists Paul Amato and Alan Booth (1997) found that in about a third of divorces, the children benefit from parental separation because it lessens their exposure to conflict. But in about 70 percent of all divorces, they found that the parents engaged in a low level of conflict; in these cases, the realities of divorce appear to be harder for the children to bear than living with the marital unhappiness. Other researchers, using differing definitions of conflict, have found greater unhappiness for children living in homes with marital differences. Still, it would be simplistic to assume that children are automatically better off following the breakup of their parents' marriage. The interests of the parents do not necessarily serve children well. A study based on a representative sample of Canadians showed that while men experience moderate increases in their level of economic well-being after divorce, women experience a dramatic economic decline (Finnie 1993). Since women's wages are lower than men's, and since they are more likely to be awarded child custody, children of divorce often encounter serious economic consequences.

Divorce can obviously be a painful experience for children, but we should avoid labelling young people as "children of divorce," as if this *parental* experience is the singular event defining the life of a girl or boy. Large-scale studies in the United States and Great Britain have shown that some of the alleged negative effects of divorce actually resulted from conditions (such as poverty) that existed *before* the parental separation. Moreover, if divorce does not lower children's access to resources and does not increase stress, its impact on children may be neutral or even positive. Divorce does not ruin the life of every child it touches, though its effect on a child is not always benign (Cherlin 1999; Wallerstein et al. 2000).

Family Diversity

Marriage is no longer the presumed route from adolescence to adulthood. In fact, it has lost much of its social significance as a rite of passage. The nation's marriage rate has dipped by 43 percent since 1960 because people are postponing marriage until later in life and more couples, including same-sex couples, are deciding to form partnerships without marriage (Popenoe and Whitehead 1999).

Cohabitation

Saint Paul once wrote, "It is better to marry than to burn." However, as journalist Tom Ferrell (1979) has suggested, more people than ever "prefer combustible to connubial bliss." One of the most dramatic trends of recent years has been the tremendous increase in male–female couples who choose to live together without marrying, thereby engaging in what is commonly called ***cohabitation.***

In 2001, one in seven Canadian couples were cohabiting. Younger Canadians are choosing cohabitation over marriage at increasing rates (Wilson 2001). According to the 2001 census, a total of 34 200 same-sex common-law couples were counted, representing 0.5 percent of all couples (Statistics Canada 2002c).

We can also find increases in cohabitation in the United States, France, Sweden, Denmark, and Australia.

This young couple in England are cohabiting, an increasingly popular alternative to marriage in many countries today.

Data released in Great Britain indicate that more than 12 percent of people ages 18 to 24 are cohabiting. One report notes that in Sweden it is almost universal for couples to live together before marriage. Demographers in Denmark call the practice of living together *marriage without papers.* In Australia, these couples are known as *de factos* (Blanc 1984; Levinson 1984; O'Donnell 1992; Thomson and Colella 1992).

Some countries have governmental policies that do not encourage marriage. For example, Sweden offers no married-couple allowance for tax purposes, no tax deduction for raising children, and no way for couples to jointly file their income taxes. Not surprisingly, many Swedish couples choose to cohabit rather than to marry. About half of the babies in Sweden are born to unmarried mothers—although there are proportionately many fewer unmarried *teenage* mothers in Sweden than in the United States (*The Economist* 1995).

In Canada, Quebec stands out from the rest of the country in its rates of marriage and cohabitation. It has the lowest marriage rate among the provinces and one of the lowest rates of marriage in the world (Wilson 2001). Quebec residents are increasingly turning away from traditional institutions such as church and state in the establishment of their families. More people in this province than any other live in common-law relationships; in 2001, the ratio was approximately one in every three couples. Moreover, Quebecers are more inclined than Canadians in other provinces to have children in common-law relationships. Cohabitation, then, is increasingly common for older Quebecers who have children and not just the younger, childless groups that represent the major trend in the rest of the country. Although common-law unions enjoy a longer duration in Quebec, nationally, cohabiting couples experience over twice the rate of breakdown than that of married couples (Beaujot et al. 1995). Research has shown that cohabiters generally have less commitment to their particular relationship and to the institution of marriage in general. As well, couples who choose cohabitation may share characteristics and values that have a negative impact on the stability of the relationship (Wu 1999).

Census figures have documented increases in cohabitation among older people in Canada (Wu 2000). Older couples may choose cohabitation rather than marriage for many reasons: because of religious differences, to preserve the full pension benefits they receive as single people, out of fear of commitment, to avoid upsetting children from previous marriages, because one partner or both are not legally divorced, or because one or both have lived through a spouse's illness and death and do not want to experience that again. But some older couples simply see no need for marriage and report being happy living together as they are.

Remaining Single

Looking at TV programs today, as Box 11-1 pointed out, you would be justified in thinking most households are composed of singles. While this is not the case, it is true that more and more people in Canada are *postponing* entry into first marriages. In 1996, 59 percent of all people between 25 and 29 years of age had never married, compared with 50 percent in 1991 (Statistics Canada 1997). As well as the postponement of marriage and the increase in common-law relationships, Canadians are experiencing a decline in any form of heterosexual union (Fox 2001).

The trend toward maintaining a single lifestyle for a longer period of time is related to the growing economic p. 251 independence of young people. This is especially significant for women. Freed from financial needs, women don't necessarily have to marry to enjoy a satisfying life.

There are many reasons why a person may choose not to marry. (Just ask *Ally McBeal's* Renee, Fish, Elaine, Cage, and, of course, Ally.) Singleness is an attractive option for those who do not want to limit their sexual intimacy to one lifetime partner. Also, some men and women do not want to become highly dependent on any one person—and do not want anyone depending heavily on them. In a society that values individuality and self-fulfillment, the single lifestyle can offer certain freedoms that married couples may not enjoy.

Remaining single represents a clear departure from societal expectations; indeed, it has been likened to "being single on Noah's Ark." A single adult must confront the inaccurate view that he or she is always lonely, is a workaholic, and is immature. These stereotypes help support the traditional assumption in North America and most other societies that to be truly happy and fulfilled, a person must get married and raise a family. To help counter these societal expectations, singles have formed numerous support groups, such as Alternative to Marriage Project (www.unmarried.org).

Lesbian and Gay Relationships

> We were both raised in middle-class families, where the expectation was we would go to college, we would become educated, we'd get a nice white-collar job, we'd move up and own a nice house in the suburbs. And that's exactly what we've done (*New York Times* 1998:B2).

Sound like an average family? The only break with traditional expectations in this case is that the "we" described here is a gay couple.

The lifestyles of lesbians and gay men vary greatly. Some live in long-term, monogamous relationships. Some couples live with children from former heterosexual marriages or adopted children. Some live alone, others with roommates. Others remain married and do not publicly acknowledge their homosexuality.

Recognition of same-sex partnerships is not uncommon in Europe, including Denmark, Holland, Switzerland, France, Belgium, and parts of Germany, Italy, and Spain. In 2001 the Netherlands converted their "registered same-sex partnerships" into full-fledged marriages, with divorce provisions (S. Daley 2000).

Gay activist organizations emphasize that despite the passage of laws protecting the civil rights of lesbians and gay men, lesbian couples and gay male couples are prohibited from marrying—and therefore from gaining traditional partnership benefits—some jurisdictions have passed legislation allowing for registration of domestic partnerships. A ***domestic partnership*** may be defined as two unrelated adults who reside together, agree to be jointly responsible for their dependents, basic living expenses, and other common necessities, and share a mutually caring relationship. Domestic partnership benefits can apply to such areas as inheritance, parenting, pensions, taxation, housing, immigration, workplace fringe benefits, and health care. While the most passionate support for domestic partnership legislation has come from lesbian and gay male activists, the majority of those eligible for such benefits would be cohabiting heterosexual couples.

Domestic partnership legislation, however, faces strong opposition from conservative religious and political groups. In the view of opponents, support for domestic partnership undermines the historic societal preference for the nuclear family. Advocates of domestic partnership counter that such relationships fulfill the same functions for the individuals involved and for society as the traditional family and should enjoy the same legal protections and benefits. The gay couple quoted at the beginning of this section consider themselves a family unit, just like the nuclear family that lives down the street in their suburb. They cannot understand why they have been denied a family membership at their municipal swimming pool and why they have to pay more than a married couple (*New York Times* 1998).

In 2001, after a decade of court challenges and demonstrations over the rights of same-sex couples, Nova Scotia became the first jurisdiction in Canada to register same-sex and common law relationships as legal domestic partnerships. This change will allow same-sex couples many of the same rights accorded married couples in that province—equal division of property and spousal support if the relationship dissolves, and full spousal benefits and pensions to partners. The registration of domestic partnerships, however, is not considered "marriage." In June 2003, the Ontario Court of Appeal decided that the existing definition of marriage violated the rights of same-sex couples under the Charter of Rights and Freedoms. This ruling immediately placed pressure on the federal government to consider legislation on same-sex unions.

Marriage is an emotionally charged issue among the gay and lesbian communities. Some believe that it represents a sign of legitimacy and normalization to their already established relationships. Others believe that marriage, given its history of patriarchy and oppression, is not an institution to be emulated by gay and lesbian couples. Nova Scotian Ross Boutilier, who, along with his partner, was among the first to register for domestic partnership, stated, "It does make a difference because it's a formalization of the understanding we have that we're in this together and this is an equal partnership" (Cox 2001).

In 2001, a lesbian couple in Halifax became the first same-sex couple in Canada to register their relationship as a "domestic partnership."

Marriage without Children

There has been a modest increase in childlessness in Canada. According to data from the General Social Survey, 12 percent of women between the ages of 20 and 39 state that they do not intend to have children (Dupuis 1998). Rates of childlessness began to increase for women born after 1941. These women entered young adulthood at a time when options were expanding for women in the form of advanced education and job opportunities. As well, this time in history witnessed the second wave of feminism, when ideas such as those expressed by Betty Friedan in *The Feminine Mystique* (1965) challenged conventional views about full-time motherhood and caregiving. Despite changing attitudes and the expansion of educational and employment options for women born after this date, women today continue to "pay a price in the labour market for marriage and motherhood, and shoulder more responsibility for housework and childcare at home than men" (Fox 2001:164). This reality contributes to the trend of women postponing marriage or never marrying, and postponing child bearing or remaining childless.

Childlessness within marriage has generally been viewed as a problem that can be solved through such means as adoption and artificial insemination. More and more couples today, however, choose not to have children and regard themselves as child-free, not childless. They do not believe that having children automatically follows from marriage, nor do they feel that reproduction is the duty of all married couples. Childless couples have formed support groups (with names like "No Kidding") and set up websites on the Internet (Terry 2000).

Economic considerations have contributed to this shift in attitudes; having children has become quite expensive. Aware of the financial pressures, some couples are having fewer children than they otherwise might, and others are weighing the advantages of a child-free marriage.

Meanwhile, some childless couples who desperately want children are willing to try any means necessary to get pregnant. The social policy section that follows explores the controversy surrounding recent advances in reproductive technology.

The ***family***, in its many varying forms, is present in all human cultures. This chapter examines the state of marriage, the family, and other intimate relationships in Canada and considers alternatives to the traditional nuclear family.

SOCIAL POLICY AND THE FAMILY

Reproductive Technology

The Issue

The 1997 feature film *Gattaca* told the story of a future in which genetic engineering enhanced people's genes. Those who were not "enhanced" in the womb—principally those whose parents could not afford the treatments—suffer discrimination and social hurdles throughout their lives. To borrow a line from the movie, "Your genes are your résumé."

Far-fetched? Perhaps, but today we are witnessing quite commonly aspects of reproductive technology that were regarded as so much science fiction just a generation ago. "Test tube" babies, frozen embryos, surrogate mothers, sperm and egg donation, and cloning of human cells are raising questions about the ethics of creating and shaping human life. How will these technologies change the nature of families and the definitions we have of motherhood and fatherhood? To what extent should social policy encourage or discourage innovative reproductive technology?

The Setting

In an effort to overcome infertility, many couples turn to a recent reproductive advance known as *in vitro fertilization* (IVF). In this technique, an egg and a sperm are combined in a laboratory dish. If the egg is fertilized, the resulting embryo (the so-called test tube baby) is transferred into a woman's uterus. The fertilized egg could be transferred into the uterus of the woman from whom it was harvested, or of a woman who has not donated the egg but who plays the role of surrogate (i.e., substitute). A surrogate mother carries the pregnancy to term and then transfers the child to the social mother. After this occurs, depending on the agreement between the social mother and the surrogate mother, the child may or may not be a part of the surrogate mother's life.

These possibilities, and many more, make the definition and attending responsibilities of motherhood complicated and somewhat murky. How should motherhood be defined—as providing gestation, as providing care for the child, as providing the egg, or all or some combination of these?

Sociological Insights

Replacing personnel is a functional prerequisite that the family as a social institution performs. Obviously, advances in reproductive technology allow childless couples to fulfill their personal and societal goals. The new technology also presents opportunities not previously considered. A small but growing number of same-sex couples are using donated sperm or eggs to have genetically related children and fulfill their desire to have children and a family (Bruni 1998).

p. 108

As mentioned earlier, sometimes it is difficult to define relationships. For example, in 1995, an American couple, John and Luanne Buzzanca, hired a married woman to carry a child to term for them—a child conceived of the sperm and egg of anonymous, unrelated donors. One month before birth, John filed for divorce and claimed he had no parental responsibilities, including child support. Eventually the court ruled that the baby girl had no legal parents; she is temporarily living with Luanne, who may seek to adopt the baby. While this is an unusual case, it suggests the type of functional confusion that can arise in trying to establish kinship ties (Weiss 1998).

Feminist sociologist Margrit Eichler has developed a typology of motherhood in this age of new reproductive technology. She states that there can be up to 25 types of mothers, considering that mothers can now be "partial biological mothers—genetic but not gestational, or gestational but not genetic" (Eichler 1997:80).

The possibility of cloning humans in the future, eerily foreshadowed in Andy Warhol's *The Twenty Marilyns*, poses major ethical dilemmas.

Her list of possible types of mothers include: (1) genetic and gestational but not social mothers (mothers who have given up their child); (2) genetic, non-gestational, and non-social mothers (those who provide an egg); (3) non-genetic, but gestational, social, exclusive, full mothers (those who receive an egg); (4) dead mother whose egg has been fertilized (mother #1), implanted in a carrier (mother #2), and transferred to a third woman (mother #3).

Eichler adds that new reproductive technologies have had a far less dramatic impact on fatherhood, the most noticeable change coming in the form of what she calls "post-mortem biological fathers" (Eichler 1997:72). This term refers to fatherhood that occurs after a man's death, when his sperm is harvested and used to impregnate a woman.

In the future depicted in *Gattaca,* the poor were at a disadvantage because they were not able to genetically control their lives. The conflict perspective would note that in the world today, the technologies available are often accessible only to the most affluent. In addition, a report by the Royal Commission on New Reproductive Technologies issued in 1993 warned these technologies could potentially be used for commercial purposes (e.g., surrogacy), making women of lower classes vulnerable to exploitation. Thus, today in Canada, there is a voluntary ban on the use of many technologies that could be used commercially and that would enable those with resources to "buy" a reproductive service and those with perhaps few resources to "sell" the services in demand.

Interactionists observe that the quest for information and social support connected with reproductive technology has created new social networks. Like other special-interest groups, couples with infertility problems band together to share information, offer support to one another, and demand better treatment. They develop social networks—sometimes through voluntary associations or Internet support groups—where they share information about new medical techniques, insurance plans, and the merits of particular physicians and hospitals. One Internet self-help group, Mothers of Supertwins, offers supportive services for mothers but also lobbies for improved counselling at infertility clinics to better prepare couples for the demands of many babies at one time (MOST 1999).

Policy Initiatives

In Japan, some infertile couples have caused a controversy by using eggs or sperm donated by siblings for in vitro fertilization. This violates an ethical (though not legal) ban on "extramarital fertilization," the use of genetic material from anyone other than a spouse for conception. While opinion is divided on this issue, most Japanese agree that there should be government guidelines on reproductive technology. Many nations, including England and Australia, bar payments to egg donors, resulting in very few donors in these countries. Even more countries limit how many times a man can donate sperm. Because the United States has no such restrictions, infertile foreigners who can afford the costs view that country as a land of opportunity (Efron 1998; Kolata 1998).

The legal and ethical issues connected with reproductive technology are immense. Many people feel we should be preparing for the possibility of a human clone. At this time, however, industrial societies are hard-pressed to deal with present advances in reproductive technology, much less future ones. Already, reputable hospitals are mixing donated sperm and eggs to create embryos that are frozen for future use. This raises the possibility of genetic screening as couples choose what they regard as the most "desirable" embryo—a "designer baby" in effect. Couples can select (some would say adopt) a frozen embryo that matches their requests in terms of race, sex, height, body type, eye colour, intelligence, ethnic and religious background, and even national origin (S. Begley 1999; Rifkin 1998).

Let's Discuss

1. What are some of the innovations in reproductive technology in recent years? What ethical and legal issues do they raise?
2. How do these technologies change the definition of motherhood and fatherhood?
3. If you were writing legislation to regulate reproductive technology, what guidelines (if any) would you include?

Chapter Resources

Summary

The ***family***, in its many varying forms, is present in all human cultures. This chapter examines the state of marriage, the family, and other intimate relationships in Canada and considers alternatives to the traditional nuclear family.

1. There are many variations in the family from culture to culture and even within the same culture.
2. The structure of the ***extended family*** can offer certain advantages over that of the ***nuclear family***.
3. We determine kinship by descent from both parents ***(bilateral descent)***, from the father ***(patrilineal)***, or from the mother ***(matrilineal)***.
4. Sociologists do not agree on whether the ***egalitarian family*** has replaced the ***patriarchal family*** as the social norm in Canada.
5. Sociologists have identified six basic functions of the family: reproduction, protection, socialization, regulation of sexual behaviour, companionship, and the providing of social status.
6. Conflict theorists argue that the family contributes to societal injustice and denies opportunities to women that are extended to men.
7. Interactionists focus on the microlevel—on how individuals interact in the family and other intimate relationships.
8. Feminist views on the family are diverse yet hold the common assumption that families are socially constructed.
9. Mates are selected in a variety of ways. Some marriages are arranged. Some people are able to choose their mates. Some societies require choosing a mate within a certain group ***(endogamy)*** or outside certain groups ***(exogamy)***.
10. In Canada, there is considerable variation in family life associated with social class, race, and ethnic differences.
11. Currently, the majority of all married couples in Canada have two partners active in the paid labour force.
12. Among the factors that contribute to the current divorce rate in Canada are the greater social acceptance of divorce and the liberalization of divorce laws.
13. More and more people are living together without marrying, thereby engaging in what is called ***cohabitation***. People are also staying single longer in general or deciding not to have children within marriage.
14. Nova Scotia has passed ***domestic partnership*** legislation. Such proposals continue to face strong opposition from conservative religious and political groups.
15. Reproductive technology has advanced to such an extent that ethical questions have arisen about the creation and shaping of human life.

Critical Thinking Questions

1. Recent political discussions have focused on the definition of "family." Should governments continue to promote the model of family that includes only opposite-sex couples? Are there ways in which "family" might be defined other than on the basis of sexual orientation? If so, name them. What groups in society would be most opposed to such a change? Why?
2. In an increasing proportion of couples in Canada, both partners work outside the home. What are the advantages and disadvantages of the dual-income model for women, for men, for children, and for society as a whole?
3. Given the current rate of divorce in Canada, is it more appropriate to view divorce as dysfunctional or as a normal part of our marriage system? What are the implications of viewing divorce as normal rather than as dysfunctional?

Key Terms

Adoption In a legal sense, a process that allows for the transfer of the legal rights, responsibilities, and privileges of parenthood to a new legal parent or parents. (page 277)

Bilateral descent A kinship system in which both sides of a person's family are regarded as equally important. (268)

Cohabitation The practice of living together as a male–female couple without marrying. (282)

Domestic partnership Two unrelated adults who have chosen to share one another's lives in a relationship of mutual caring, who reside together, and who agree to be jointly responsible for their dependents, basic living expenses, and other common necessities. (283)

Egalitarian family An authority pattern in which the adult members of the family are regarded as equals. (269)

Endogamy The restriction of mate selection to people within the same group. (273)

Exogamy The requirement that people select mates outside certain groups. (273)

Extended family A family in which relatives—such as grandparents, aunts, or uncles—live in the same home as parents and their children. (267)

Family A set of people related by blood, marriage (or some other agreed-upon relationship), or adoption who share the responsibility for reproducing and caring for members of society. (265)

Incest taboo The prohibition of sexual relationships between certain culturally specified relatives. (273)

Kinship The state of being related to others. (268)

Matriarchy A society in which women dominate in family decision making. (269)

Matrilineal descent A kinship system that favours the relatives of the mother. (268)

Monogamy A form of marriage in which one woman and one man are married only to each other. (267)

Nuclear family A married couple and their unmarried children living together. (267)

Patriarchy A society in which men dominate family decision making. (269)

Patrilineal descent A kinship system that favours the relatives of the father. (268)

Polyandry A form of polygamy in which a woman can have more than one husband at the same time. (267)

Polygamy A form of marriage in which an individual can have several husbands or wives simultaneously. (267)

Polygyny A form of polygamy in which a husband can have several wives at the same time. (267)

Serial monogamy A form of marriage in which a person can have several spouses in his or her lifetime but only one spouse at a time. (267)

Single-parent families Families in which there is only one parent present to care for children. (278)

Additional Readings

Baker, Maureen, ed. 2001. *Families: Changing Trends in Canada*. 4th ed. Toronto: McGraw-Hill Ryerson. An edited collection by sociologists examining such areas as family violence, ethnic families, biases in family literature, and divorce and remarriage.

Eichler, Margrit. 1997. *Family Shifts: Families, Policies, and Gender Equality*. Toronto: Oxford University Press. A sociologist outlines the ways in which our conception of family has not kept pace with recent developments in reproductive technologies.

Milan, Anne. 2000. "One Hundred Years of Families." *Canadian Social Trends*. Statistics Canada, Catalogue No. 11-008, (Spring):2–13. This article provides a demographic overview of the changing Canadian family.

Wallerstein, Judith S., Julia M. Lewis, and Sandra Blaeslee. 2000. *The Unexpected Legacy of Divorce*. New York: Hyperion. A study that tracks children for 25 years after their parents' divorce and examines the impact of this event on their lives.

Internet Connection

www.mcgrawhill.ca/college/schaefer

For additional Internet exercises relating to families in Canada, visit the Schaefer Online Learning Centre at ***http://www.mcgrawhill.ca/college/schaefer****. Please note that while the URLs listed were current at the time of printing, these sites often change—check the Online Learning Centre for updates.*

Sociologists who study families examine both the positive and negative aspects of family life. Domestic violence is an example of the dark side of relationships, an issue that, as this chapter demonstrates, is a worldwide problem. To learn more about this social problem, log onto the National Clearinghouse on Family Violence website on facts about family violence in Canada (**http://www.hc-sc.gc.ca/hppb/familyviolence/html/1facts.html**). Then, answer the following questions:

(a) Are there any myths about family violence that are dispelled by these statistics?

(b) What five statistics from the site reveal the most about the extent of the problem? Why did you choose these facts over the others? What general themes do your selections show about violence in the family?

(c) Based on the statistics presented on this website, develop a profile of an individual who would be at the greatest risk for family violence.

CHAPTER

12 RELIGION AND EDUCATION

In this billboard distributed by Volkswagen of France, the figure of Jesus at the Last Supper says to his apostles, "Rejoice, my friends, for a new Golf is born." While an image of Jesus is sacred for Christians, it is used here in a secular manner—to advertise cars.

I am the grandson of the late Joseph Michael Augustine.

My father was a devout Catholic. He was baptized Catholic, raised by strong Christian beliefs and ascended into heaven shortly after our parish priest stood over his bedside to read him his last rites.

I record this religious aspect of his life in the home of one of his daughter's—Aunt Madeline to me—where today I write from within a small, antiquated room in her basement. On each surrounding wall hang large, life-like portraits of religious figures with names like Pontifex Pius X and Leo XIII and His Holiness Pope John XXIII. As was my grandfather, my aunt is a member of the Catholic Church.

With such strong ties to the Catholic religion, should I not feel ashamed of the fact that I do not even understand why each of these figures looming above me is holding the same pose, with right hand raised in the air and two fingers pointing upwards, obviously communicating to the observer something of righteous significance?

Or should I be ashamed that I choose not to understand the righteous significance of these men with all their symbolic gestures, and how they seemingly stare right though me, from every direction of this room, as if God might strike me down for recording such thoughts on religion.

I do not wish to be disrespectful, for my grandfather did not raise us in this way. I respect the Catholic religion, and my family for practising its teachings. However, I was raised in the generation where aboriginal culture and spiritual traditions have since been reawakened, and despite being born into a strong Catholic family, I choose to honour our Great Spirit—God—through the practises and ceremonies originally given to the First Peoples of this land.

Rather than going to church, I attend a sweat lodge; rather than accepting bread and toast from the Holy Priest, I smoke a ceremonial pipe to come into Communion with the Great Spirit; and rather than kneeling with my hands placed together in prayer, I let sweetgrass be feathered over my entire being for spiritual cleansing and allow the smoke to carry my prayers into the heavens. I am a Mi'kmaq, and this is how we pray. *(Augustine 2000)* ■

This excerpt from Noah Augustine's article "Grandfather was a Knowing Christian," which appeared in the *Toronto Star*, contrasts the religious beliefs of his grandfather to those of his own. Augustine, a Mi'kmaq, came to practise aboriginal spiritual traditions—attending a sweat lodge and smoking a ceremonial pipe—even though he had been born into what he calls a "strong Catholic family." His grandfather, however, who was also a Mi'kmaq, practised Catholicism and was never "reawakened" by the spiritual traditions of his aboriginal heritage. Noah Augustine's reawakening represents part of a growing trend among First Nations people in Canada in which aboriginal spirituality is again being expressed after years of suppression by the dominant culture.

Religion plays a major role in people's lives, and religious practices of some sort are evident in every society. That makes religion a ***cultural universal***, along with other general practices found in every culture such as dancing, food preparation, the family, and personal names. At present, an estimated 4 billion people belong to the world's many religious faiths (see Figure 12-1).

p. 52

When religion's influence on other social institutions in a society diminishes, the process of ***secularization*** is said to be underway. During this process, religion will survive in the private sphere of individual and family life; it may even thrive on a personal level. But, at the same time, other social institutions—such as the economy, politics, and education—maintain their own sets of norms independent of religious guidance (Stark and Iannaccone 1992).

Education, like religion, is a *cultural universal.* As such it is an important aspect of socialization—the lifelong process of learning the attitudes, values, and behaviour considered appropriate to members of a particular culture, as we saw in Chapter 4. When learning is explicit and formalized—when some people consciously teach, while others adopt the role of learner—the process of socialization is called ***education.***

This chapter first looks at religion as it has emerged in modern industrial societies. It begins with a brief overview of the approaches that Émile Durkheim first introduced and those that later sociologists have used in studying religion. We will explore religion's role in societal integration, social support, social change, and social control. We'll examine three important dimensions of religious behaviour—belief, ritual, and experience—as well as the basic forms of religious organization. We will pay particular attention to the emergence of new religious movements.

The second part of this chapter focuses on the formal systems of education that characterize modern industrial societies, beginning with a discussion of four theoretical perspectives on education: functionalist, conflict, interactionist and feminist. As we will see, education can both perpetuate the status quo and foster social change. An examination of schools as formal organizations—as bureaucracies and subcultures of teachers and students—follows. Two types of education that are becoming more common in North America today, adult education and home schooling, merit special mention. The chapter closes with a social policy discussion of the controversy over religion in public schools. ■

Durkheim and the Sociological Approach to Religion

If a group believes that it is being directed by a "vision from God," sociologists will not attempt to prove or disprove this revelation. Instead, they will assess the effects of the religious experience on the group. What sociologists are interested in is the social impact of religion on individuals and institutions (M. McGuire 1981:12).

Émile Durkheim was perhaps the first sociologist to recognize the critical importance of religion in human societies. He saw its appeal for the individual, but—more importantly—he stressed the *social* impact of religion. In Durkheim's view, religion is a collective act and includes many forms of behaviour in which people interact with others. As in his work on suicide, Durkheim was not so interested in the personalities of religious believers as he was in understanding religious behaviour within a social context.

p. 8

Durkheim defined ***religion*** as a "unified system of beliefs and practices relative to sacred things." In his view, religion involves a set of beliefs and practices that are uniquely the property of religion—as opposed to other social institutions and ways of thinking. Durkheim (1947, original edition 1912) argued that religious faiths distinguish between certain events that transcend the ordinary and the everyday world. He referred to these realms as the *sacred* and the *profane.*

The ***sacred*** encompasses elements beyond everyday life that inspire awe, respect, and even fear. People become a part of the sacred realm only by completing some ritual, such as prayer or sacrifice. Believers have faith in the

FIGURE 12-1
Religions

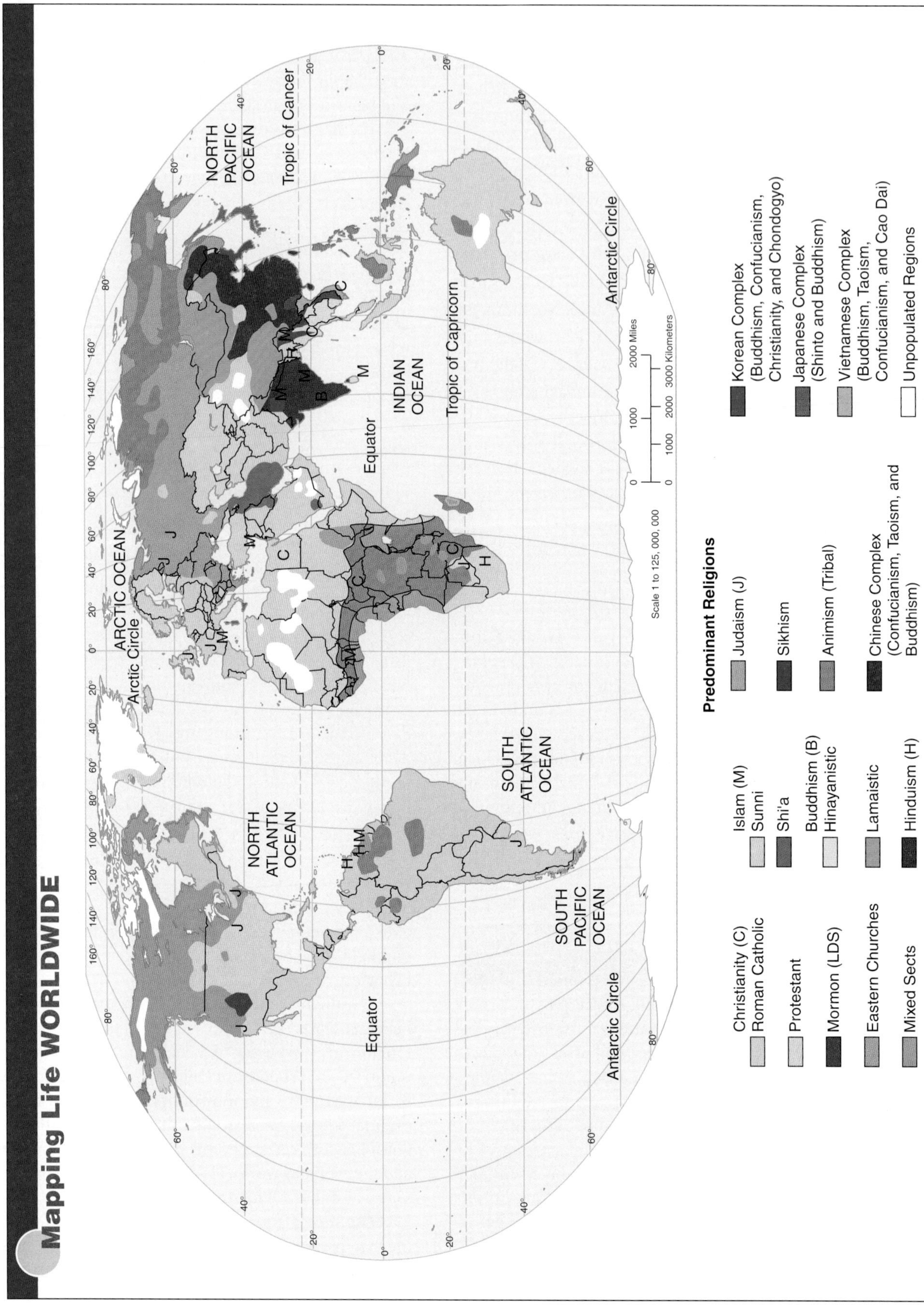
Mapping Life WORLDWIDE
ARCTIC OCEAN
Arctic Circle
NORTH PACIFIC OCEAN
Tropic of Cancer
NORTH ATLANTIC OCEAN
SOUTH ATLANTIC OCEAN
SOUTH PACIFIC OCEAN
INDIAN OCEAN
Equator
Tropic of Capricorn
Antarctic Circle
Scale 1 to 125, 000, 000
2000 Miles
3000 Kilometers
Predominant Religions
Christianity (C)
Roman Catholic
Protestant
Mormon (LDS)
Eastern Churches
Mixed Sects
Islam (M)
Sunni
Shi'a
Buddhism (B)
Hinayanistic
Lamaistic
Hinduism (H)
Judaism (J)
Sikhism
Animism (Tribal)
Chinese Complex (Confucianism, Taoism, and Buddhism)
Korean Complex (Buddhism, Confucianism, Christianity, and Chondogyo)
Japanese Complex (Shinto and Buddhism)
Vietnamese Complex (Buddhism, Taoism, Confucianism, and Cao Dai)
Unpopulated Regions

Source: Allen 1996:12–13.

sacred; this faith allows them to accept what they cannot understand. By contrast, the ***profane*** includes the ordinary and commonplace. It can get confusing, however, because the same object can be either sacred or profane depending on how it is viewed. A normal dining room table is profane, but it becomes sacred to Christians if it bears the elements of a communion. A candelabra becomes sacred for Jews when it is a menorah. For Confucians and Taoists, incense sticks are not mere decorative items; they are highly valued offerings to the gods in religious ceremonies marking new and full moons.

Following the direction established by Durkheim almost a century ago, contemporary sociologists view religions in two different ways. They study the norms and values of religious faiths through examination of their substantive religious beliefs. For example, it is possible to compare the degree to which Christian faiths literally interpret the Bible, or Muslim groups follow the Qur'an (or Koran), the sacred book of Islam. At the same time, sociologists examine religions in terms of the social functions they fulfill, such as providing social support or reinforcing the social norms. By exploring both the beliefs and the functions of religion, we can better understand its impact on the individual, on groups, and on society as a whole.

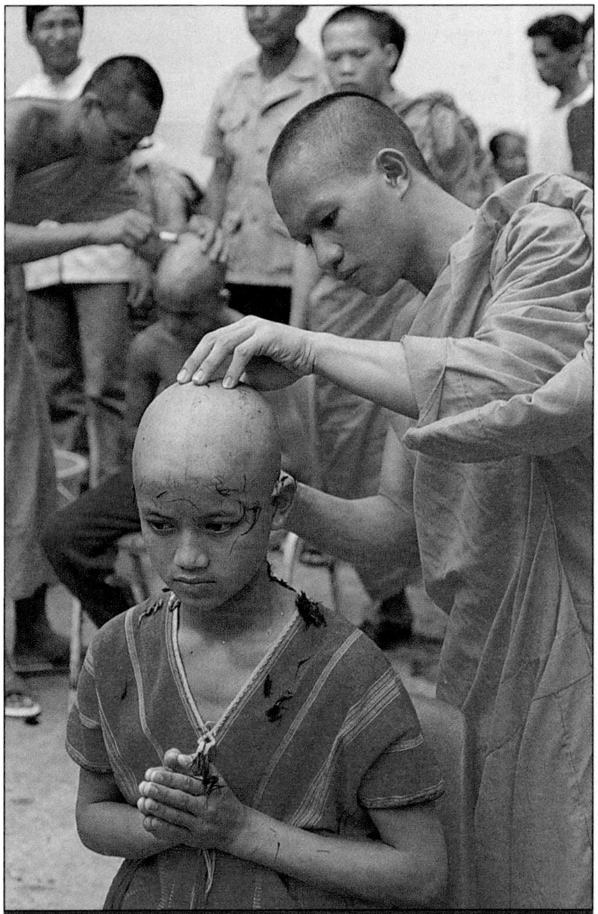

Young Buddhists in Thailand symbolically shave away the "earthly afflictions" represented by their hair.

The Role of Religion

Since religion is a cultural universal, it is not surprising that it plays a basic role in human societies. In sociological terms, these include both manifest and latent functions. Among its *manifest* (open and stated) functions, religion defines the spiritual world and gives meaning to the divine. Religion provides an explanation for events that seem difficult to understand, such as what lies beyond the grave.

p. 13

The *latent* functions of religion are unintended, covert, or hidden. Even though the manifest function of church services is to offer a forum for religious worship, they might at the same time fulfill a latent function as a meeting ground for unmarried members.

Functionalists and conflict theorists both evaluate religion's impact as a social institution on human societies. We'll consider a functionalist view of religion's role in integrating society, in social support, and in promoting social change, and then look at religion as a means of social control from the conflict perspective. Note that, for the most part, religion's impact is best understood from a macro-level viewpoint, oriented toward the larger society. The social support function is an exception: it is best viewed on the microlevel, directed toward the individual.

The Integrative Function of Religion

Émile Durkheim viewed religion as an integrative power in human society—a perspective reflected in functionalist thought today. Durkheim sought to answer a perplexing question: "How can human societies be held together when they are generally composed of individuals and social groups with diverse interests and aspirations?" In his view, religious bonds often transcend these personal and divisive forces. Durkheim acknowledged that religion is not the only integrative force—nationalism or patriotism may serve the same end.

How does religion provide this "societal glue"? Religion, whether it be Buddhism, Islam, Christianity, or Judaism, offers people meaning and purpose for their lives. It gives them certain ultimate values and ends to hold in common. Although subjective and not always fully accepted, these values and ends help a society to function as an integrated social system. For example, funerals, weddings, bar and bat mitzvahs, and confirmations serve to integrate people into larger communities by providing shared beliefs and values about the ultimate questions of life.

The integrative power of religion can be seen in the role that churches, synagogues, temples, and mosques have traditionally played and continue to play for immigrant groups in Canada. For example, Roman Catholic immigrants may settle near a parish church that offers services in their native language, such as Polish or Portuguese. Similarly, Korean immigrants may join a Presbyterian church with many Korean Canadian members and with religious practices like those of churches in Korea. Like other religious organizations, these Roman Catholic and Presbyterian churches help to integrate immigrants into their new homeland.

Yet another example of the integrative impact of religion is provided by the Universal Fellowship of Metropolitan Community Churches. It was established in the United States in 1968 to offer a welcoming place of worship for lesbians and gays. This spiritual community is especially important today, given the many organized religions openly hostile to homosexuality. The Metropolitan Community Church has 42 000 members in its local churches in 15 countries including Canada where there are three such churches in Toronto alone. As part of its effort to support lesbian and gay rights, the Metropolitan Community Church performs same-sex marriages, which it calls "holy union ceremonies" (L. Stammer 1999).

In some instances, religious loyalties are *dysfunctional;* they contribute to tension and even conflict between groups or nations. During the Second World War, the German Nazis attempted to exterminate the Jewish people; approximately 6 million European Jews were killed. In modern times, nations such as Lebanon (Muslims versus Christians), Israel (Jews versus Muslims as well as Orthodox versus secular Jews), Northern Ireland (Roman Catholics versus Protestants), and India (Hindus versus Muslims and, more recently, Sikhs) have been torn by clashes that are in large part based on religion.

Religious conflict (though on a less violent level) is evident in Canada as well. Christian fundamentalists in many communities battle against their liberal counterparts for control of the secular culture. p. 257 The battlefield is an array of familiar social issues, among them multiculturalism, abortion, sex education in schools, and gay and lesbian rights.

Religion and Social Support

Most of us find it difficult to accept the stressful events of life—death of a loved one, serious injury, bankruptcy, divorce, and so forth. This is especially true when something "senseless" happens. How can family and friends come to terms with the death of a talented university student, not even 20 years old, from a terminal disease?

Through its emphasis on the divine and the supernatural, religion allows us to "do something" about the calamities we face. In some faiths, adherents can offer sacrifices or pray to a deity in the belief that such acts will change their earthly condition. At a more basic level, religion encourages us to view our personal misfortunes as relatively unimportant in the broader perspective of human history—or even as part of an undisclosed divine purpose. Friends and relatives of the deceased university student may see this death as being "God's will" and as having some ultimate benefit that we cannot understand now. This perspective may be much more comforting than the terrifying feeling that any of us can die senselessly at any moment—and that there is no divine "answer" as to why one person lives a long and full life, while another dies tragically at a relatively early age.

Faith-based community organizations have taken on more and more responsibilities in the area of social assistance. In fact, as part of an effort to cut back on government-funded welfare programs, government leaders have advocated shifting

Although same-sex marriage is not legal in Canada, some churches, such as the Metropolitan Community Church in Toronto, perform "holy union" ceremonies joining same-sex couples.

the social "safety net" to private organizations in general and to churches and religious charities in particular. These organizations identify experienced leaders and assemble them into nonsectarian coalitions devoted to community development (K. Starr 1999).

Religion and Social Change

The Weberian Thesis

When someone seems driven to work and succeed we often attribute the "Protestant work ethic" to that person. The term comes from the writings of Max Weber, who carefully examined the connection between religious allegiance and capitalist development. His findings appeared in his pioneering work *The Protestant Ethic and the Spirit of Capitalism* (1958a, original edition 1904).

Weber noted that in European nations with both Protestant and Catholic citizens, an overwhelming number of business leaders, owners of capital, and skilled workers were Protestant. In his view, this was no mere coincidence. Weber pointed out that the followers of John Calvin (1509–1564), a leader of the Protestant Reformation, emphasized a disciplined work ethic, this-worldly concerns, and a rational orientation to life that have become known as the ***Protestant ethic.*** One by-product of the Protestant ethic was a drive to accumulate savings that could be used for future investment. This "spirit of capitalism," to use Weber's phrase, contrasted with the moderate work hours, leisurely work habits, and lack of ambition that he saw as typical of the times (Winter 1977; Yinger 1974).

Few books on the sociology of religion have aroused as much commentary and criticism as Weber's work. It has been hailed as one of the most important theoretical works in the field and as an excellent example of macro-level analysis. Like Durkheim, Weber demonstrated that religion is not solely a matter of intimate personal beliefs. He stressed that the collective nature of religion has social consequences for society as a whole.

Weber provides a convincing description of the origins of European capitalism. But this economic system has subsequently been adopted by non-Calvinists in many parts of the world. Apparently, the "spirit of capitalism" has become a generalized cultural trait rather than a specific religious tenet (Greeley 1989).

Conflict theorists caution that Weber's theory—even if it is accepted—should not be regarded as an analysis of mature capitalism as reflected in the rise of multinational corporations that cross national boundaries. Marxists would p. 196 disagree with Max Weber not on the origins of capitalism but on its future. Unlike Marx, Weber believed that capitalism could endure indefinitely as an economic system. He added, however, that the decline of religion as an overriding force in society opened the way for workers to express their discontent more vocally (R. Collins 1980).

Liberation Theology

Sometimes the clergy can be found in the forefront of social change. Many religious activists, especially in the Roman Catholic church in Latin America, support ***liberation theology***—the use of a church in a political effort to eliminate poverty, discrimination, and other forms of injustice evident in a secular society. Advocates of this religious movement sometimes sympathize with Marxism. Many believe that radical change, rather than economic development in itself, is the only acceptable solution to the desperation of the masses in impoverished developing countries. Activists associated with liberation theology believe that organized religion has a moral responsibility to take a strong public stand against the oppression of the poor, racial and ethnic minorities, and women (C. Smith 1991).

The term *liberation theology* dates back to the 1973 publication of the English translation of *A Theology of Liberation.* This book was written by a Peruvian priest, Gustavo Gutierrez, who lived in a slum area of Lima during the early 1960s. After years of exposure to the vast poverty around him, Gutierrez concluded that "in order to serve the poor, one had to move into political action" (R. M. Brown 1980:23; Gutierrez 1990).

Politically committed Latin American theologians came under the influence of social scientists who viewed the domination of capitalism and multinational corporations as central to the hemisphere's problems. One result was a new approach to theology that rejected the models developed in Europe and the United States and instead built on the cultural and religious traditions of Latin America.

While many worshippers support liberation theology, religious leaders in the Roman Catholic church are not happy with the radical movement. The official position of Pope John Paul II and others in the church hierarchy is that clergy should adhere to traditional pastoral duties and keep a distance from radical politics. The Pope specifically came out against church activists in his 1999 visit to Mexico City (S. Pagani 1999).

Liberation theology may possibly be dysfunctional, however. Some Roman Catholics have come to believe that by focusing on political and governmental injustice, the clergy are no longer addressing their personal and spiritual needs. Partly as a result of such disenchantment, some Catholics in Latin America are converting to mainstream Protestant faiths or to Mormonism.

Religion and Social Control: A Conflict View

Liberation theology is a relatively recent phenomenon and marks a break with the traditional role of churches. It was this traditional role that Karl Marx opposed. In his view, religion *impeded* social change by encouraging oppressed people to focus on other-worldly concerns rather than on their immediate poverty or exploitation. Marx described religion as an "opiate" particularly harmful to oppressed peoples. He felt that religion often drugged the masses into submission by offering a consolation for their harsh lives on earth: the hope of salvation in an ideal afterlife. For example, First Nations children, housed in residential schools in Canada, were forbidden to practise their own forms of spirituality and were forced to adopt the Christian religion. Christianity taught First Nations that obedience would lead to salvation and eternal happiness in the hereafter. Viewed from a conflict perspective, Christianity may have pacified certain oppressed groups and blunted the rage that often fuels rebellion (M. McGuire 1992; Yinger 1970).

Marx acknowledged that religion plays an important role in propping up the existing social structure. The values of religion, as already noted, reinforce other social institutions and the social order as a whole. From Marx's perspective, however, religion's promotion of stability within society only helps to perpetuate patterns of social inequality. According to Marx, the dominant religion reinforces the interests of those in power (Harap 1982).

Consider, for example, India's traditional caste system. It defined the social structure of that society, at least among the Hindu majority. The caste system was almost certainly the creation of the priesthood, but it also served the interests of India's political rulers by granting a certain religious legitimacy to social inequality.

p. 177

Contemporary Christianity, like the Hindu faith, reinforces traditional patterns of behaviour that call for the subordination of the less powerful. The role of women in the church is an example of uneven distribution of power. Assumptions about gender roles leave women in a subservient position both within many Christian churches and at home. In fact, women find it as difficult to achieve leadership positions in many churches as they do in large corporations. For example, 25 percent of ordained ministers in the United Church of Canada and approximately 10 percent of Anglican priests are female (Nason-Clark 1993). Among Canadian First Nations, however, women have traditionally been granted roles of spiritual leadership. Female clergy are more likely to serve in subsidiary pastoral roles and to wait longer for desirable assignments. While women play a significant role as volunteers in community churches, men continue to make the major theological and financial judgments for nationwide church organizations. Like Marx, conflict theorists argue that to whatever extent religion actually does influence social behaviour, it reinforces existing patterns of dominance and inequality.

From a Marxist perspective, religion functions as an "agent of de-politicization" (J. Wilson 1973). In simpler terms, religion keeps people from seeing their lives and societal conditions in political terms—for example, by obscuring the overriding significance of conflicting economic interests. Marxists suggest that by inducing a "false consciousness" among the disadvantaged, religion lessens the possibility of collective political action that can end capitalist oppression and transform society.

p. 179

Religious Behaviour

All religions have certain elements in common, yet these elements are expressed in the distinctive manner of each faith. The patterns of religious behaviour, like other patterns of social behaviour, are of great interest to sociologists, since they underscore the relationship between religion and society.

Religious beliefs, religious rituals, and religious experience all help to define what is sacred and to differentiate the sacred from the profane. Let us now examine these three dimensions of religious behaviour.

Belief

Some people believe in life after death, in supreme beings with unlimited powers, or in supernatural forces. ***Religious beliefs*** are statements to which members of a particular religion adhere. These views can vary dramatically from religion to religion.

The Adam and Eve account of creation found in Genesis, the first book of the Old Testament, is an example of a religious belief. Many people in Canada strongly adhere to this biblical explanation of creation. These people, known as *creationists,* are worried by the secularization of society and oppose teaching that directly or indirectly questions biblical scripture.

Ritual

Religious rituals are practices required or expected of members of a faith. Rituals usually honour the divine power (or powers) worshipped by believers; they also remind adherents of their religious duties and responsibilities. Rituals and beliefs can be interdependent; rituals generally involve the affirmation of beliefs, as in a public or private statement confessing a sin (Roberts 1995). Like any social institution, religion develops distinctive normative patterns to structure people's behaviour. Moreover, there are sanctions attached to religious rituals, whether rewards (bar mitzvah gifts) or penalties (expulsion from a religious institution for violation of norms).

In North America, rituals may be very simple, such as saying grace at a meal or observing a moment of silence to commemorate someone's death. Yet certain rituals, such as the process of canonizing a saint, are quite elaborate. Most religious rituals in our culture focus on services conducted at houses of worship. Attendance at a service, silent and spoken prayers, and singing of spiritual hymns and chants are common forms of ritual behaviour that generally take place in group settings. From an interactionist perspective, these rituals serve as important face-to-face encounters in which people reinforce their religious beliefs and their commitment to their faith.

The representation of religion can take many forms. This motorcycle club organizes itself as a strong Christian group, even though its attire and lifestyle may be objectionable to many Christians.

For Muslims, a very important ritual is the *hajj,* a pilgrimage to the Grand Mosque in Mecca, Saudi Arabia. Every Muslim who is physically and financially able is expected to make this trip at least once. Each year, 2 million pilgrims go to Mecca during the one-week period indicated by the Islamic lunar calendar. Muslims from all over the world make the *hajj,* including those in Canada, where many tours are arranged to facilitate this ritual.

Some rituals induce an almost trancelike state. The First Nations of the American Plains eat or drink peyote, a cactus containing the powerful hallucinogenic drug mescaline. Similarly, the ancient Greek followers of the god Pan chewed intoxicating leaves of ivy in order to become more ecstatic during their celebrations. Of course, artificial stimulants are not necessary to achieve a religious "high." Devout believers, such as those who practise the pentecostal Christian ritual of "speaking in tongues," can reach a state of ecstasy simply through spiritual passion.

Experience

In sociological study of religion, the term ***religious experience*** refers to the feeling or perception of being in direct contact with the ultimate reality, such as a divine being, or of being overcome with religious emotion. A religious experience may be rather slight, such as the feeling of exaltation a person receives from hearing a choir sing Handel's "Hallelujah Chorus." But many religious experiences are more profound, such as a Muslim's experience on a *hajj*. In his autobiography, the late American black activist Malcolm X (1964:338) wrote of his *hajj* and how deeply moved he was by the way that Muslims in Mecca came together across lines of race and colour. For Malcolm X, the colour blindness of the Muslim world "proved to me the power of the One God."

Still another profound religious experience is being "born again"—that is, at a turning point in one's life making a personal commitment to Jesus. According to a 1999 national survey, 46 percent of people in the United States claimed that they had a born-again Christian experience at some time in their lives. An earlier survey found that Baptists (61 percent) were the most likely to report such experiences; by contrast, only 18 percent of Catholics and 11 percent of Episcopalians stated that they had been born again. In Canada, 10 percent of Canadians have stated they are "born again" (CBC 2000). The collective nature of religion, as emphasized by Durkheim, is evident in these statistics. The beliefs and rituals of a particular faith can create an atmosphere either friendly or hostile to this type of religious experience. Thus, a Baptist would be encouraged to come forward and share such experiences with others, whereas an Episcopalian who claimed to have been born again would receive much less support (Princeton Religions Research Center 2000a).

Religious Organization

The collective nature of religion has led to many forms of religious association. In modern societies, religion has become increasingly formalized. Specific structures such as churches and synagogues are constructed for religious worship; individuals are trained for occupational roles within various fields. These developments make it possible to distinguish clearly between the sacred and secular parts of one's life—a distinction that could not be made in earlier societies in which religion was largely a family activity carried out in the home.

Sociologists find it useful to distinguish between four basic forms of organization: the ecclesia, the denomination, the sect, and the new religious movement or cult. We can see differences among these types of organizations in such factors as size, power, degree of commitment expected from members, and historical ties to other faiths.

Ecclesiae

An ***ecclesia*** (plural, *ecclesiae*) is a religious organization that claims to include most or all of the members of a society and is recognized as the national or official religion. Since virtually everyone belongs to the faith, membership is by birth rather than conscious decision. Examples of ecclesiae include the Lutheran church in Sweden, the Catholic church in Spain, Islam in Saudi Arabia, and Buddhism in Thailand. However, there can be significant differences even within the category of *ecclesia.* In Saudi Arabia's Islamic regime, leaders of the ecclesia hold vast power over actions of the state. By contrast, the Lutheran church in contemporary Sweden has no such power over the Riksdag (parliament) or the prime minister.

Generally, ecclesiae are conservative in that they do not challenge the leaders of a secular government. In a society with an ecclesia, the political and religious institutions often act in harmony and mutually reinforce each other's power over their relative spheres of influence. Within the modern world, ecclesiae tend to be declining in power.

Denominations

A ***denomination*** is a large, organized religion not officially linked with the state or government. Like an ecclesia, it tends to have an explicit set of beliefs, a defined system of authority, and a generally respected position in society. Denominations claim as members large segments of a population. Generally, children accept the denomination of their parents and give little thought to membership in other faiths. Denominations also resemble ecclesiae in that generally few demands are made on members. However, there is a critical difference between these two forms of religious organization. Although the denomination is considered respectable and is not viewed as a challenge to the secular government, it lacks the official recognition and power held by an ecclesia (Doress and Porter 1977).

Although approximately 46 percent of all Canadians were Roman Catholic in 1991, this country is marked by great religious diversity. With the exception of the First Nations, we are a country of immigrants and Canadian religious diversity reflects patterns of immigration and population change.

Protestantism follows Catholicism and is practised by 36.2 percent of the population in Canada; 11.5 percent of all people belonging to a Protestant denomination are members of the United Church. From 1981 to 1991, while the percentage of Hindus in Canada doubled, the percentage of Buddhists tripled. The percentage of Jews remained constant at 1.2 percent for both census periods. The percentage of people declaring no religious affiliation rose from 7.4 in 1981 to 12.5 in 1991; at the same time the percentage of those belonging to Protestant denominations dropped from 41.2 to 36.2. The only significant increase in affiliation to Protestant denominations was in the category "other Protestant" (see Table 12-1), which would include Christian fundamentalist denominations. That category rose 3 percent from 1981 to 1991.

These overall trends do not reveal the great diversity that exists regionally in relation to religious membership. In 1991, British Columbians were the Canadians most likely to declare no religious affiliation, with one in three reporting so. By contrast, in Newfoundland less than 2 percent declared no religious affiliation (Statistics Canada 1991).

Attendance at religious services tends to vary according to age, rural/urban setting, immigrant status, and family status. In 1998, married couples aged 25 to 44 with young children were more likely to worship regularly than those who were of the same age but childless (Statistics Canada 2000b). Seniors aged 75 and over had the highest rates of attendance. Those born in Canada were less likely to be regular attendees of religious services than were immigrants. Approximately 50 percent of Asian immigrants who entered Canada between 1994 and 1998 attended worship services regularly, compared to approximately one in five European immigrants who entered the country during the same period. According to the 2001 General Social Survey by Statistics Canada, Canadians' attendance at religious services has fallen dramatically over the last 15 years. In 2001, 20 percent of Canadians aged 15 and over attended religious services on a weekly basis, compared with 28 percent in 1986 (Statistics Canada 2003l).

In the last 20 years, some distinctions among denominations have started to blur. Certain faiths have even allowed members of other faiths to participate in some of their most sacred rituals, such as communion. Even more dramatic has been the appearance of ***megachurches***—large congregations that often lack direct ties to a worldwide denomination, as described in Box 12-1.

Sects

A ***sect*** can be defined as a relatively small religious group that has broken away from some other religious organi-

Table 12-1 Major Religious Denominations, Canada, 1991[1] and 2001

	2001 number	2001 %	1991 number	1991 %	Percentage Change 1991–2001
Roman Catholic	12 793 125	43.2	12 203 625	45.2	4.8
Protestant	8 654 854	29.2	9 427 675	34.9	-8.2
Christian Orthodox	479 620	1.6	387 395	1.4	23.8
Christian, not included elsewhere[2]	780 450	2.6	353 040	1.3	121.1
Muslim	579 640	2.0	253 265	0.9	128.9
Jewish	329 995	1.1	318 185	1.2	3.7
Buddhist	300 345	1.0	163 415	0.6	83.8
Hindu	297 200	1.0	157 015	0.6	89.3
Sikh	278 415	0.9	147 440	0.5	88.8
No religion	4 796 352	16.2	3 333 245	12.3	43.9

1. For comparability purposes, 1991 data are presented according to 2001 boundaries.
2. Includes persons who report "Christian," as well as those who report "Apostolic," "Born-again Christian," and "Evangelical."
Source: Statistics Canada 2003l.

zation to renew what it considers the original vision of the faith. Many sects, such as that led by Martin Luther during the Reformation, claim to be the "true church" because they seek to cleanse the established faith of what they regard as extraneous beliefs and rituals (Stark and Bainbridge 1985). Max Weber (1958b:114, original edition 1916) termed the sect a "believer's church," because affiliation is based on conscious acceptance of a specific religious dogma.

Sects are fundamentally at odds with society and do not seek to become established national religions. Unlike ecclesiae and denominations, sects require intensive commitments and demonstrations of belief by members. Partly owing to their "outsider" status in society, sects frequently exhibit a higher degree of religious fervour and loyalty than more established religious groups do. Recruitment focuses mainly on adults, and acceptance comes through conversion. One current-day sect is called the People of the Church, a movement within the Roman Catholic Church that began in Vienna, Austria. This sect has called for reforms of Catholicism, such as the ordination of women, local election of bishops, and optional celibacy for priests (*Religion Watch* 1995).

New Religious Movements or Cults

The Branch Davidians began as a sect of the Seventh-Day Adventists church, basing their beliefs largely on the biblical book of Revelation and its doomsday prophecies. In 1984, the Davidians' sect split, with one group emerging as a cult under the leadership of David Koresh. In 1993, violence erupted at their compound near Waco, Texas. After a 51-day standoff against federal authorities, Koresh and 85 of his followers died when the Federal Bureau of Investigation (FBI) attempted to seize control of the compound and its arsenal of weapons. In 1997, 38 members of the Heaven's Gate cult were found dead in Southern California after a mass suicide timed to occur with the appearance of the Hale-Bopp comet. They believed the comet hid a spaceship on which they could catch a ride once they had broken free of their "bodily containers." In Canada, news of the Order of the Solar Temple cult suicides in 1994 shocked the nation.

Partly as a result of the notoriety generated by such groups, the popular media have stigmatized the word *cult* by associating cults with the occult and the use of intense and forceful conversion techniques. The stereotyping of

Sociology in the Global Community

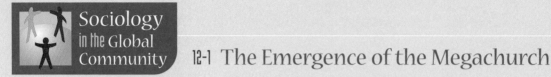

12-1 The Emergence of the Megachurch

The Yoido Full Gospel Church in Seoul, South Korea, has six daily services in a facility with 13 000 seats. Unable to serve all of its 700 000 members, the church reaches 30 000 other worshippers via closed-circuit television, and 50 000 tune in from 20 satellite congregations across the metropolitan area. Worshippers listen to the sermons of Pastor David Cho and join in with 11 choirs, accompanied by a pipe organ or a 24-piece orchestra.

This is just an example of the growing emergence worldwide of megachurches, large worship centres only loosely affiliated, if at all, with existing denominations.

Megachurches that begin with denominational ties frequently break them when they become financially self-sufficient. They often break away not so much on the basis of doctrinal issues as from a desire to be viewed as unique and to be free of church hierarchy.

Sociologists have observed the significant impact on religious organizations of these megachurches, whose growth is sometimes defined by the size of the parking lot. Their size often provokes hostility from more traditional churches that fear being overwhelmed or, in some cases, from the preexisting dominant faith (such as Buddhism in South Korea). Some people view the megachurch as the latest intrusion of European/North American culture into the local landscape, especially in Latin America and Africa.

Some people view the megachurch as the latest intrusion of European/North American culture into the local landscape.

Megachurches appeal particularly to younger people, who seem prepared to shop around for religious faith just as they would a post-secondary institution or an automobile. The very size of the megachurch facility may attract someone used to working in large bureaucracies or dealing with huge supermarkets or large medical clinics or shopping malls. People comfortable in these settings may find the anonymity of a huge religious place of worship preferable to the intimacy of a small church with 50 to 100 members genuinely interested in getting to know them as individuals. Perhaps most importantly, the megachurch is willing to use the latest marketing tools, multimedia presentations, and motivational techniques to reach out to those who feel disenchanted with traditional denominations.

Let's Discuss

1. What impact are the megachurches having on other religious organizations?
2. What advantages would megachurches have over more traditional churches with smaller congregations? What would be the disadvantages?

Sources: Carey and Mosemak 1999; M. Luo 1999; Ostling 1993; Schaller 1990.

the People of the Church, a movement within the Roman Catholic Church that began in Vienna, Austria. This sect has called for reforms of Catholicism, such as the ordination of women, local election of bishops, and optional celibacy for priests (*Religion Watch* 1995).

New Religious Movements or Cults

The Branch Davidians began as a sect of the Seventh-Day Adventists church, basing their beliefs largely on the biblical book of Revelation and its doomsday prophecies. In 1984, the Davidians' sect split, with one group emerging as a cult under the leadership of David Koresh. In 1993, violence erupted at their compound near Waco, Texas. After a 51-day standoff against federal authorities, Koresh and 85 of his followers died when the Federal Bureau of Investigation (FBI) attempted to seize control of the compound and its arsenal of weapons. In 1997, 38 members of the Heaven's Gate cult were found dead in Southern California after a mass suicide timed to occur with the appearance of the Hale-Bopp comet. They believed the comet hid a spaceship on which they could catch a ride once they had broken free of their "bodily containers." In Canada, news of the Order of the Solar Temple cult suicides in 1994 shocked the nation.

Partly as a result of the notoriety generated by such groups, the popular media have stigmatized the word *cult* by associating cults with the occult and the use of intense and forceful conversion techniques. The stereotyping of cults as uniformly bizarre and unethical has led sociologists to abandon the term and refer to a cult instead as a *new religious movement (NRM)*. While some NRMs, like the Branch Davidians, exhibit strange behaviour, many do not. They attract new members just like any other religion and often follow teachings similar to established Christian denominations, but with less ritual.

It is difficult to distinguish sects from cults. A ***new religious movement (NRM)*** or ***cult*** is a generally small, secretive religious group that represents either a new religion or a major innovation of an existing faith. NRMs are similar to sects in that they tend to be small and are often viewed as less respectable than more established faiths.

However, unlike sects, NRMs normally do not result from schisms or breaks with established ecclesiae or denominations. Some cults, such as those focused on UFO sightings, may be totally unrelated to the existing faiths in a culture. Even when a cult does accept certain fundamental tenets of a dominant faith—such as belief in Jesus as divine or Muhammad as a messenger of God—it will offer new revelations or new insights to justify its claim to be a more advanced religion (Stark and Bainbridge 1979, 1985).

Like sects, NRMs may undergo transformation over time into other types of religious organizations. An example is the Christian Science church, which began as a new religious movement under the leadership of Mary Baker Eddy. Today, this church exhibits the characteristics of a denomination. NRMs tend to be in the early stages of what may develop into a denomination, or they may just as easily fade away through loss of members or weak leadership (Richardson and van Driel 1997).

Comparing Forms of Religious Organization

How can we determine whether a particular religious group falls into the sociological category of ecclesia, denomination, sect, or NRM? As we have seen, these types of religious organizations have somewhat different relationships to society. Ecclesiae are recognized as national churches; denominations, although not officially approved by the state, are generally widely respected. By contrast, sects as well as NRMs are much more likely to be at odds with the larger culture.

Still, ecclesiae, denominations, and sects are best viewed as ideal types along a continuum rather than as mutually exclusive categories. Table 12-2 summarizes some of the primary characteristics of these ideal types. Since Canada has no ecclesia, sociologists studying this country's religions have naturally focused on the denomination and the sect. These religious forms have been pictured on either end of a continuum, with denominations accommodating to the secular world and sects making a protest against established religions. NRMs have also been included in Table 12-2 but are outside the continuum because they generally define themselves as a new view of life rather than in terms of existing religious faiths (Chalfant et al. 1994).

Advances in electronic communications have led to still another form of religious organization: the electronic church. Facilitated by cable television and satellite transmissions, *televangelists* (as they are called) direct their messages to more people—especially in the United States—than are served by all but the largest denominations.

Table 12-2 Characteristics of Ecclesiae, Denominations, Sects, and New Religious Movements

Characteristic	Ecclesia	Denomination	Sect	New Religious Movement (or Cult)
Size	Very large	Large	Small	Small
Wealth	Extensive	Extensive	Limited	Variable
Religious Services	Formal, little participation	Formal, little participation	Informal, emotional	Variable
Doctrines	Specific, but interpretation may be tolerated	Specific, but interpretation may be tolerated	Specific, purity of doctrine emphasized	Innovative, pathbreaking
Clergy	Well-trained, full-time	Well-trained, full-time	Trained to some degree	Unspecialized
Membership	By virtue of being a member of society	By acceptance of doctrine	By acceptance of doctrine	By an emotional commitment
Relationship to the State	Recognized, closely aligned	Tolerated	Not encouraged	Ignored or challenged

Source: Adapted from G. Vernon 1962; see also Chalfant et al. 1994.

The Internet, then, isn't suitable for some forms of religious and spiritual expression, but it certainly has added a new dimension to religious behaviour (G. Zelizer 1999).

We turn now to another major social institution in every society—education. It prepares citizens for the various roles demanded by other institutions, including religion. Education and religion sometimes get intertwined, as we will see in the social policy section about the role of religion in the schools.

Sociological Perspectives on Education

Education is a major industry in Canada. In the last few decades, an increasing proportion of people has obtained a high school diploma, and at least some post-secondary education (Figure 12-2 shows where Canada ranks among other developed nations). Seventeen percent of females and 18 percent of males over the age of 25 had not completed high school in 1998, compared with 26 percent and 27 percent, respectively, in 1990 (CESC 2000).

Globally, enrollments in educational institutions have been increasing; however, vast regional and national differences exist in this overall trend. For example, in less developed regions, while progress has been made, only 57 percent of boys and 48 percent of girls were enrolled in secondary education in the mid- to late 1990s (Population Reference Bureau 2000). These numbers mask the fact that most girls in less developed countries receive less education than boys, and in some of the world's poorest countries, fewer than half of young women receive the basic seven years of schooling (Population Reference Bureau 2000). According to the United Nations' *State of World Population Report 2000*, girls and women throughout the world are still routinely denied access to education.

The functionalist, conflict, interactionist, and feminist perspectives offer distinctive ways of examining education as a social institution.

Functionalist View

Like other social institutions, education has both manifest (open, stated) and latent (hidden) functions. The most basic *manifest* function of education is the transmission of knowledge. Schools teach students such things as how to read, speak foreign languages, and repair automobiles. Education has another important manifest function: bestowing status. Because many believe this function is performed inequitably, it will be considered later, in the section on the conflict view of education.

In addition to these manifest functions, schools perform a number of *latent* functions: transmitting culture, promoting social and political integration, maintaining social control, and serving as agents of change.

Transmitting Culture

As a social institution, education performs a conservative function—transmitting the dominant culture. Schooling exposes each generation of young people to the existing beliefs, norms, and values of their culture. In our society, we learn respect for social control and reverence for established institutions, such as religion, the family, and government. Of course, this is true in many other cultures as well.

In Great Britain, the transmission of the dominant culture in schools goes far beyond learning about monarchs and prime ministers. In 1996, the government's chief curriculum adviser—noting the need to fill a void left by the diminishing authority of the Church of England—proposed that British schools socialize students into a set of core values. These include honesty, respect for others, politeness, a sense of fair play, forgiveness, punctuality, nonviolent behaviour, patience, faithfulness, and self-discipline (Charter and Sherman 1996).

Sometimes nations need to reassess their ways of transmitting culture. When an economic crisis hit Asian countries in 1997 and 1998, many Asian students who had been studying abroad could no longer afford to do so. Now their home countries had to figure out how to accommodate thousands more students pursuing higher education at home. In South Korea, people also began to question the content of the curriculum. Their schools traditionally teach Confucian values with a focus on rote memorization. This leads to an emphasis on accumulating facts as opposed to using reasoning. Entrance to university turns on a highly competitive exam that tests knowledge of facts. Once in university, a student has virtually no opportunity to change his or her program, and the classes continue to rely on memorization. The combination of an economic crisis and growing complaints about the educational process has caused government officials to reevaluate the educational structure. Moreover, growth in juvenile crime, although low by our standards, has led the government to introduce a new civic education program emphasizing honesty and discipline (Institute of International Education 1998; Woodard 1998).

At all levels of the education system in Canada, controversy surrounds the exclusion from the curriculum of authors and historical figures who do not represent the dominant culture. Critics charge that standard academic curricula have failed to represent the important contributions of immigrants and First Nations, women and people of colour to history, literature, and other fields of study. The underlying questions raised by this debate, still to be resolved, are: Which ideas and values are essential for instruction? Which cultures should be transmitted by the schools and post-secondary institutions of Canada?

FIGURE 12-2

Percentage of Population Aged 25 to 54 Who Have Completed Post-Secondary Education, 2001

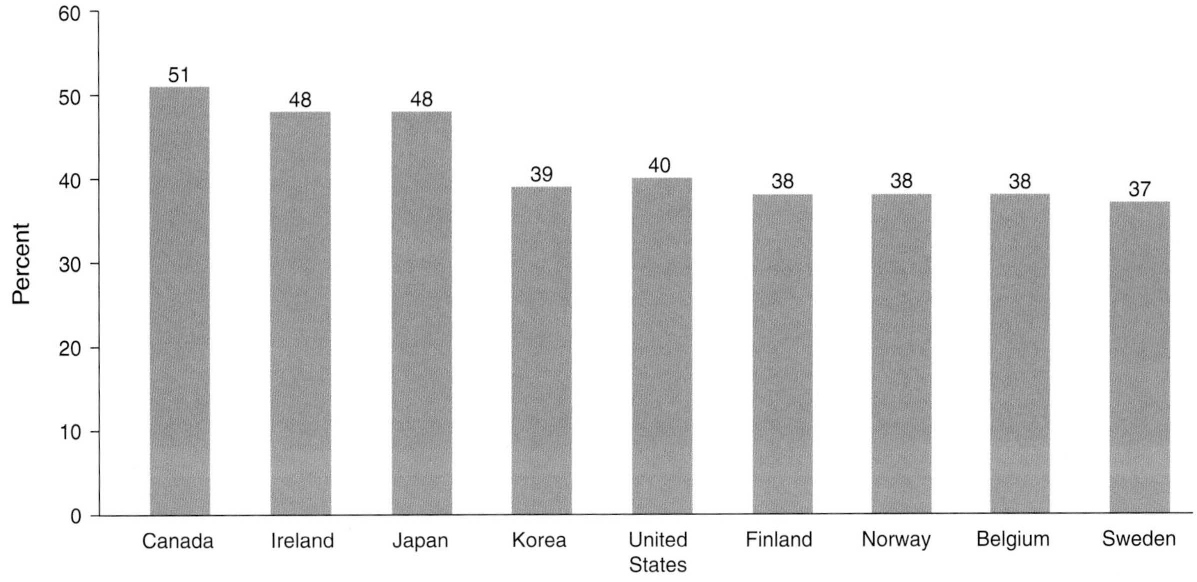

Source: Education at a Glance, OEDC Indicators, 2003, Table A2.3. Modified by author.

Promoting Social and Political Integration

Many prestigious American universities require their first- and second-year students to live together on campus in order to foster a sense of community among diverse groups. Education serves the latent function of promoting social and political integration by transforming a population composed of diverse racial, ethnic, and religious groups into a society whose members share—to some extent—a common identity. Schools have historically played an important role in socializing the children of immigrants into the norms, values, and beliefs of the dominant culture. From a functionalist perspective, the common identity and social integration fostered by education contribute to societal stability and consensus (Touraine 1974).

In Canada, perhaps the most egregious example of an attempt to promote social integration through education is that of residential schools. Residential schools were established by the Canadian government and operated by the Roman Catholic, Anglican, United, and Presbyterian churches for the purpose of assimilating First Nations children into the dominant culture. Operating up until the middle decades of the 20th century, these schools had as their express purpose the goal of cultural assimilation. First Nations children were taken from their homes and forced to speak languages other than their own. In residential schools, they learned the values and norms of the dominant European groups and at the same time learned that their own culture was inferior, and thus needed to be replaced. In this process of promoting conformity to the dominant culture, many aboriginal children were emotionally, physically, and sexually abused by those operating the residential schools. Today, many First Nations adults are enduring difficult lives due to their traumatizing experiences as children in these schools.

Maintaining Social Control

In performing the manifest function of transmitting knowledge, schools go far beyond teaching such skills as reading, writing, and mathematics. Like other social institutions, such as the family and religion, education prepares young people to lead productive and orderly lives as adults by introducing them to the norms, values, and sanctions of the larger society.

Through the exercise of social control, schools teach students various skills and values essential to their future positions within the labour force. They learn punctuality, discipline, scheduling, and responsible work habits, as well as how to negotiate their way through the complex-

Taking Sociology to Work

PAT DUFFY HUTCHEON: Secular Humanist

Pat Duffy Hutcheon is a secular humanist or, according to her own definition, "a non-believer in supernatural beings" (Todd 2001). Hutcheon is a retired University of British Columbia sociologist who, in 2000, won the Canadian Humanist of the Year Award. She is also a recipient of the American 2001 Humanist Distinguished Service Award (others who have received this award include Harvard paleontologist Stephen Jay Gould and zoologist Edward O. Wilson.) Growing up in the Prairies and attending churches there, she began to question how people could believe in religion. Hutcheon came to believe that people must rely on themselves to protect the world, not supernatural beings. She says, "My emphasis is on morality—and how human beings are the only ones responsible for it" (Todd 2001). In 1999, she published her book, *Building Character and Culture*, in which she outlines how to build ethical character based on virtues such as honesty, courage, non-violence, perseverance, responsibility, and respect for human dignity. Hutcheon's basic message is the belief that one does not have to be religious to be ethical.

Let's Discuss

1. How are those who do not believe in a supreme being viewed in our society?
2. What influences formed your religious beliefs? Do you hold the same views as you did five years ago?

Source: Hutcheon 1999; Todd 2001.

ities of a bureaucratic organization. As a social institution, education reflects the interests of the family and in turn prepares young people for their participation in yet another social institution—the economy. Students are being trained for what is ahead, whether it be the assembly line or a physician's office. In effect, then, schools serve as a transitional agent of social control—between parents and employers in the life cycle of most individuals (Bowles and Gintis 1976; M. Cole 1988).

Schools direct and even restrict students' aspirations in a manner that reflects societal values and prejudices. School administrators may allocate funds for athletic programs while giving much less support to music, art, and dance. p. 87 Teachers and guidance counsellors may encourage male students to pursue careers in the sciences but steer equally talented female students into careers as early childhood teachers. Such socialization into traditional gender roles can be viewed as a form of social control.

Serving as an Agent of Change

So far, we have focused on conservative functions of education—on its role in transmitting the existing culture, promoting social and political integration, and maintaining social control. Yet education can also stimulate or bring about desired social change. Sex education classes were introduced in public schools in response to higher rates of sexual activity among teens. Special "girls only" science and mathematics class were created in response to girls' low participation rates in fields such as science, technology, and engineering. Anti-racism programs in schools have responded to the prevalence of racism in schools themselves, and in society in general.

Education also promotes social change by serving as a meeting ground where distinctive beliefs and traditions can be shared. In 1998, there were approximately 36 000 international students in Canada, enrolled in undergraduate and graduate programs, either on a part-time or full-time basis. Students from France represented the largest group of international students, followed by those from the United States and China, respectively (Association of Universities and Colleges of Canada 2001). Cross-cultural exchanges between these visitors and citizens of Canada ultimately broaden the perspective of both the hosts and their guests. The same is certainly true when students from Canada attend schools in Europe, Latin America, Africa, or the Far East.

Numerous sociological studies have revealed that increased years of formal schooling are associated with openness to new ideas and more liberal social and political viewpoints. Sociologist Robin Williams points out that better educated people tend to have greater access to factual information, more diverse opinions, and the ability to make subtle distinctions in analysis. Formal education stresses both the importance of qualifying statements (in place of broad generalizations) and the need at least to question (rather than simply accept) established truths

In response to teen pregnancy rates, many schools have begun to offer sex education courses that promote abstinence. When schools attempt to remedy negative social trends, they are serving as agents of social change.

and practices. As we saw in Chapter 2, the scientific method relies on *testing* hypotheses and reflects the questioning spirit that characterizes modern education (R. Williams et al. 1964).

Conflict View

Sociologist Christopher Hurn (1985) has compared the functionalist and conflict views of schooling. According to Hurn, the functionalist perspective portrays contemporary education as basically benign. For example, it argues that schools rationally sort and select students for future high-status positions, thereby meeting society's need for talented and expert personnel. By contrast, the conflict perspective views education as an instrument of elite domination. Schools convince subordinate groups of their inferiority, reinforce existing social class inequality, and discourage alternative and more democratic visions of society.

Criticizing the functionalist view, conflict theorists argue that the educational system socializes students into values dictated by the powerful, that schools stifle individualism and creativity in the name of maintaining order, and that the level of change promoted by education is relatively insignificant. From a conflict perspective, the inhibiting effects of education are particularly apparent in the "hidden curriculum" as well as in the differential way in which status is bestowed.

The Hidden Curriculum

Schools are highly bureaucratic organizations (as we will see later). Many teachers rely on the rules and regulations of schools to maintain order. Unfortunately, the need for control and discipline can take precedence over the learning process. Teachers may focus on obedience to the rules as an end in itself. If this occurs, students and teachers alike become victims of what Philip Jackson (1968) has called the *hidden curriculum* (see also P. Freire 1970).

The term ***hidden curriculum*** refers to standards of behaviour that are deemed proper by society and are taught subtly in schools. According to this curriculum, children must not speak until the teacher calls on them and must regulate their activities according to the clock or bells. In addition, they are expected to concentrate on their own work rather than assist other students who learn more slowly.

A hidden curriculum is evident in schools around the world. For example, Japanese schools offer guidance sessions during lunch that seek to improve the classroom experience but also to develop healthy living skills. In effect, these sessions instill values and encourage behaviour useful for the Japanese business world, such as self-discipline and openness to group problem solving and decision making (Okano and Tsuchiya 1999).

In a classroom overly focused on obedience, value is placed on pleasing the teacher and remaining quiet—rather than on creative thought and academic learning (Leacock 1969). Habitual obedience to authority may result in the type of distressing behaviour documented by Stanley Milgram in his classic obedience studies. p. 149

Bestowal of Status

Both functionalist and conflict theorists agree that education performs the important function of bestowing status. As noted earlier, an increasing proportion of people in Canada are obtaining high school diplomas, post-secondary certificates, diplomas, degrees, and advanced professional degrees. From a functionalist perspective, this widening bestowal of status is beneficial not only to particular recipients but to society as a whole. p. 181 In the view of Kingsley Davis and Wilbert Moore (1945) society must distribute its members among a variety of social positions. Education can contribute to this process by sorting people into appropriate levels and courses of study that will prepare them for appropriate positions within the labour force.

In Tokyo's public schools, students learn adult responsibilities early on. In this classroom, classmates take turns serving the lunch.

Conflict sociologists are far more critical of the *differential* way education bestows status. They stress that schools sort pupils according to social class background. Although the educational system helps certain poor children to move into middle-class professional positions, it denies most disadvantaged children the same educational opportunities afforded children of the affluent. In this way, schools tend to preserve social class inequalities in each new generation (Giroux 1988; Labaree 1986; Mingle 1987).

Statistics Canada's Pan-Canadian Education Indicators Program reports on the many facets of education in Canada. One finding of the research has to do with educational attainment and family socioeconomic status, as measured by quartiles. When assessing the background of those who completed high school, the data indicate that 34 percent of those in the lowest quartile had not completed high school, compared with 23 percent of those in the upper quartile. At the same time, a gap exists in university participation rates between persons from the lowest to the highest quartile. Fewer than 20 percent of young people from the lowest quartile attend university, compared with 40 percent of those from the highest quartile (CESC 2000).

Even a single school can reinforce class differences by putting students in tracks. The term ***tracking*** refers to the practice of placing students in specific curriculum groups on the basis of test scores and other criteria. Tracking begins very early in the classroom, often in reading groups during the first grade. These tracks can reinforce the disadvantages that children from less affluent families may face if they haven't been exposed to reading materials and computers and other forms of educational stimulation in their homes during early childhood years.

Tracking and differential access to higher education are evident in many nations around the world. Japan's educational system mandates equality in school funding and insists that all schools use the same textbooks. Nevertheless, only the more affluent Japanese families can afford to send their children to *juku,* or cram schools. These afternoon schools prepare high school students for examinations that determine admission into prestigious colleges (Efron 1997).

According to a study of teachers' attitudes toward students in the "outback" in rural Australia—an area where sheep vastly outnumber people—students are being prepared to stay in the "bush." Only a small minority seek out electives geared toward preparation for college. However, beginning in the 1980s, parents questioned this agriculture-oriented curriculum in view of rural Australia's declining employment base (M. Henry 1989).

Conflict theorists hold that the educational inequalities resulting from tracking are designed to meet the needs of modern capitalist societies. Samuel Bowles and Herbert Gintis (1976) argue that capitalism requires a skilled, disciplined labour force and that the educational system of the United States is structured with this objective in mind. Citing numerous studies, they offer support for what they call the ***correspondence principle.***

According to this approach, schools with students from different social classes promote the values expected of individuals in each class and perpetuate social class divisions from one generation to the next. Thus, working-class children, assumed to be destined for subordinate positions, are more likely to be placed in high school vocational and general tracks, which emphasize close supervision and compliance with authority. By contrast, young people from more affluent families are largely directed to university preparatory tracks, which stress leadership and decision-making skills—corresponding to their likely futures. While the correspondence principle continues to be persuasive, researchers have noted that the impact of race and gender on students' educational experiences may even overshadow that of class (M. Cole 1988).

Conflict views of the development of the Canadian school system have included the idea that urban-based priorities were imposed upon rural schools, due to the power of the industrial and mercantile elites located nearby, in local towns (Johnson 1960).

Interactionist View

In George Bernard Shaw's play *Pygmalion,* later adapted into the hit Broadway musical *My Fair Lady,* flower girl Eliza Doolittle is transformed into a "lady" by Professor Henry Higgins. He changes her manner of speech and teaches her the etiquette of "high society." When she is introduced into society as an aristocrat, she is readily accepted. People treat her as a "lady" and she responds as one.

The labelling approach suggests that if we treat people in particular ways, they may fulfill our expectations. Children labelled as "troublemakers" come to view themselves as delinquents. A dominant group's stereotyping of racial minorities may limit their opportunities to break away from expected roles.

p. 160

Can this labelling process operate in the classroom? Because of their focus on micro-level classroom dynamics, interactionist researchers have been particularly interested in this question. Howard Becker (1952) studied public schools in low-income and more affluent areas of Chicago. He noticed that administrators expected less of students from poor neighbourhoods, and he wondered if teachers were accepting this view. Subsequently, in *Pygmalion in the Classroom,* psychologist Robert Rosenthal and school principal Lenore Jacobson (1968) documented what they referred to as a ***teacher-expectancy effect***—the impact that a teacher's expectations about a student's performance may have on the student's actual achievements. This appears to be especially true in lower grades (through grade three) (Brint 1998).

Between 1965 and 1966, children in a San Francisco elementary school were administered a verbal and reasoning pretest. Rosenthal and Jacobson then *randomly* selected 20 percent of the sample and designated them as "spurters"—children of whom teachers could expect superior performance. On a later verbal and reasoning test, the spurters were found to score significantly higher than before. Moreover, teachers evaluated them as more interesting, more curious, and better adjusted than their classmates. These results were striking. Apparently, teachers' perceptions that these students were exceptional led to noticeable improvements in performance.

Studies have revealed that teachers wait longer for an answer from a student believed to be a high achiever and are more likely to give such children a second chance. In one experiment, teachers' expectations were even shown to have an impact on students' athletic achievements. Teachers obtained better athletic performance—as measured in the number of sit-ups or push-ups performed—from those students of whom they *expected* higher numbers (R. Rosenthal and Babad 1985).

Despite these findings, some researchers continue to question the accuracy of this self-fulfilling prophecy because of the difficulties in defining and measuring teacher expectancy. Further studies are needed to clarify the relationship between teacher expectations and actual student performance. Nevertheless, interactionists emphasize that ability alone may be less predictive of academic success than one might think (Brint 1998).

Feminist Views

In 1928, in her book *A Room of One's Own*, Virginia Woolf advocated the value of educational reform so that the female student could "live and write her poetry"(Woolf 1997:123). She contended that even if one had to struggle in "poverty and obscurity" to bring about educational reform on behalf of girls and women, it was worthwhile. Although feminist perspectives on education are diverse, today many share the view that educational institutions must attempt to prevent gendered patterns of inequality found in the larger society from being perpetuated in the classroom.

Feminist perspectives on education raise a wide range of concerns stemming from the historical exclusion of girls and women in education and the persistent "chilly climate" that many females experience in educational institutions that treat them as outsiders. Some perspectives have articulated the need to understand how gender plays a role in the educational experiences of girls and women from elementary school to university, and how these experiences are connected to factors such as race, class, and age (Mandell 1998). The "hidden curriculum" of the school system contributes to gender socialization through classroom interaction patterns that give greater "air time" and praise to male students (Richardson and Robinson 1993). The hidden curriculum also uses language that is not gender-inclusive, curricula that are androcentric, and role models of male principals and female elementary school teachers that reinforce traditional patterns of male dominance and authority (Rees 1990).

Since the 1970s, Canadian universities and colleges have been developing women's studies programs that provide feminist frameworks for research, teaching, and educational reform.

Schools as Formal Organizations

In many respects, today's schools, when viewed as an example of a formal organization, are similar to factories, hospitals, and business firms. Like these organizations, schools do not operate autonomously; they are influenced by the market of potential students. This is especially true of private schools. Currently, approximately 5 percent of students in Canada attend private schools (Mackie 2001). The parallels between schools and other types of formal organizations will become more apparent as we examine the bureaucratic nature of schools, teaching as an occupational role, and the student subculture (Dougherty and Hammack 1992).

Bureaucratization of Schools

It is simply not possible for a single teacher to transmit culture and skills to children of varying ages who will enter many diverse occupations. The growing number of students being served by individual schools and school systems as well as the greater degree of specialization required within a technologically complex society have combined to bureaucratize schools.

Max Weber noted five basic characteristics of bureaucracy, all of which are evident in the vast majority of schools, whether at the elementary, secondary, or even post-secondary level.

1. **Division of labour.** Specialized experts teach particular age levels of students and specific subjects. Public elementary and secondary schools now employ instructors whose sole responsibility is to work with children with learning disabilities or physical impairments. In a college or university sociology department, one professor may specialize in sociology of religion, another in marriage and the family, and a third in industrial sociology.

p. 130

2. **Hierarchy of authority.** Each employee of a school system is responsible to a higher authority. Teachers must report to principals and assistant principals and may also be supervised by department heads. Principals are answerable to a superintendent of schools, and the superintendent is hired and fired by a board of education. Even the students are hierarchically organized by grade and within clubs and organizations.
3. **Written rules and regulations.** Teachers and administrators must conform to numerous rules and regulations in the performance of their duties. This bureaucratic trait can become dysfunctional; the time invested in completing required forms could instead be spent in preparing lessons or conferring with students.
4. **Impersonality.** As was noted in Chapter 6, the university has been portrayed as a giant, faceless bureaucracy that cares little for the uniqueness of the individual. As class sizes have swelled at schools, colleges, and universities, it has become more difficult for teachers to give personal attention to each student. In fact, bureaucratic norms may actually encourage teachers to treat all students in the same way despite the fact that students have distinctive personalities and learning needs.
5. **Employment based on technical qualifications.** At least in theory, the hiring of teachers and college and university professors is based on professional competence and expertise. Promotions are normally dictated by written personnel policies; people who excel may be granted lifelong job security through tenure. Teachers have achieved these protections partly because of the bargaining power of unions (Borman and Spring 1984; W. Tyler 1985).

Functionalists take a generally positive view of the bureaucratization of education. Teachers can master the skills needed to work with a specialized clientele, since they no longer are expected to cover a broad range of instruction. The chain of command within schools is clear. Students are presumably treated in an unbiased fashion because of uniformly applied rules. Finally, security of position protects teachers from unjustified dismissal. In general, then, functionalists observe that bureaucratization of education increases the likelihood that students, teachers, and administrators will be dealt with fairly—that is, on the basis of rational and equitable criteria.

A professor takes time to confer with a student. In large classes, it is difficult for instructors to give personal attention to individual students.

By contrast, conflict theorists argue that the trend toward more centralized education has harmful consequences for disadvantaged people. The standardization of educational curricula, including textbooks, will generally reflect the values, interests, and lifestyles of the most powerful groups in our society and may ignore those of racial and ethnic minorities. In addition, the disadvantaged, more so than the affluent, will find it difficult to sort through complex educational bureaucracies and to organize effective lobbying groups. Therefore, in the view of conflict theorists, low-income and minority parents will have even less influence over citywide and regional educational administrators than they have over local school officials (Bowles and Gintis 1976; Katz 1971).

Sometimes schools can seem overwhelmingly bureaucratic, with the effect of stifling rather than nourishing intellectual curiosity in students. This concern has led many parents and policymakers to push for school choice programs—allowing parents to choose the school that suits their children's needs and forcing schools to compete for their "customers."

Another significant countertrend to the bureaucratization of schools is the availability of education over the Internet. Increasingly, post-secondary institutions are reaching out via the Web, offering entire courses and even majors to students in the comfort of their homes. Online curricula provide flexibility for working students and others who may have difficulty attending conventional classes because of distance or disability. Research on this type of learning is just beginning, so the question of whether teacher–student contact can thrive online remains to be settled. Computer-mediated instruction may also have an impact on instructors' status as employees, which we will discuss next, as well as on alternative forms of education like adult education and home schooling.

Teachers: Employees and Instructors

Whether they serve as instructors of preschoolers or graduate students, teachers are employees of formal organizations with bureaucratic structures. There is an inherent conflict in serving as a professional within a bureaucracy. The organization follows the principles of hierarchy and expects adherence to its rules, but professionalism demands the individual responsibility of the practitioner. This conflict is very real for teachers, who experience all the positive and negative consequences of working in bureaucracies.

A teacher undergoes many perplexing stresses every day. While teachers' academic assignments have become more specialized, the demands on their time remain diverse and contradictory. There are conflicts inherent in serving as an instructor, a disciplinarian, and an employee of a school district at the same time. For university professors, different types of role strain arise. While formally employed as teachers, they are also expected to work on committees and are encouraged to conduct scholarly research. In many universities, security of position (tenure) is based primarily on the publication of original scholarship. As a result, instructors must fulfill goals that compete for time.

University professors rarely have to take on the role of disciplinarian, but this task has become a major focus of schoolteachers' work in countries such as the United States. Order is needed to establish an environment in which students can actually learn. Some observers sense that schools have been the scene of increasingly violent misbehaviour in recent years, although these concerns may be overblown (see Box 12-2).

Canada is becoming an increasingly "schooled society" (Guppy and Davies 1998), which will contribute to the employment prospects of students wishing to become teachers. The increasing proportion of our population between the ages of 5 and 19, the resultant increase in the number of schools, and overall increases in enrollments in post-secondary education contribute to this trend (McVey and Kalbach 1995). As well, the demographic composition of teachers is changing, reflecting the aging population; a greater number of retiring teachers will need to be replaced in the near future. This trend is also occurring in the United States where, due to teacher shortages in some regions, school boards are advertising for and recruiting teachers from Canada.

The status of any job reflects several factors, including the level of education required, financial compensation, and the respect given the occupation within society. The teaching profession (see Table 8-1, page 183) is feeling pressure in all three of these areas. First, the amount of formal schooling required for teaching remains high, and now the public has begun to call for new competency examinations for teachers. Second, statistics demonstrate that teachers' salaries are significantly lower than those of many professionals and skilled workers. Wages differ by field of study; graduates of education and social science, who are disproportionately female, earn less, for example, than graduates of commerce and engineering, who are disproportionately male (Statistics Canada 1999e). Finally, as we have seen, the overall prestige of the teaching profession has declined in the last decade. Many teachers have become disappointed and frustrated and have left the educational world for careers in other professions. Many are simply "burned out" by the severe demands, limited rewards, and general sense of alienation that they experience on the job.

The Student Subculture

An important latent function of education relates directly to student life: Schools provide for students' social and

Research in Action 12-2 Violence in the Schools

Littleton Colorado, and Taber, Alberta, were two relatively unexceptional locations before they became associated with school killings. Now, they resonate with the sound of gunshots, of kids killing kids on school grounds. In addition to killings like these, school-based violence can take the form of minor discipline problems (e.g., disobedience, taunting, and teasing), obscene gesturing, verbal and physical threats, aggression, bullying, assault (with or without a weapon), vandalism, extortion and gang-related activities (Day et al. 1995). As a result, people no longer perceive schools as safe havens. But how accurate is that impression?

In Canada, there is growing concern on the part of school officials surrounding the problem of violence in schools. Many researchers, however, disagree with school officials about its prevalence. There are those who suggest that violence in our schools is relatively low key and that we should not assume that what is happening in American schools is happening here (West 1993). Some studies actually suggest that school-based violence is decreasing (Fitzpatrick 1994; West 1993). On the other hand, some studies point to an increase in certain forms of school-based violence. One study surveying 881 schools, conducted by the Ontario Teachers' Federation, reported a 150 percent increase in incidents such as biting, kicking, punching, and the use of weapons over the period from 1987 to 1990 (Roher 1993). This study's findings, however, must be viewed with caution as the number of schools supplying data for the 1987–1990 period varied and a significant number of schools reported that there was no assault (Day et al. 1995).

A child has less than a one-in-a-million chance of being killed at school.

As well, research on the problem of school-based violence indicates great regional variation. For example, students in the Niagara region of Ontario and in Nova Scotia did not consider violence a particular problem (Robb 1993; Rodgers 1993). Though there are obviously many opinions on the prevalence of school-based violence in Canada, one observation does not seem to be disputed: there is a greater scope and severity of youth violence spilling over into the schools in the United States than in this country.

Even in the United States, however, studies of school violence put the recent spate of school killings in perspective:

- A child has less than a one-in-a-million chance of being killed at school.
- The number of people shot and killed in school in the 1997–1998 school year was 40 (including adults), about average over the last six years.
- According to the Center for Disease Control in Atlanta, 99 percent of violent deaths of school-aged children in 1992–1994 occurred *outside* school grounds.
- Fewer students are now being found with guns in school.

Sources: Bowles 1999; Chaddock 1998; Department of Education 1999; Day et al. 1995; Donohue, Schiraldi, and Ziedenberg 1998; D. Grossman et al. 1997; National Center for Education Statistics 1998; S. Schaefer 1996.

recreational needs. Education helps toddlers and young children develop interpersonal skills that are essential during adolescence and adulthood. During high school and the years of post-secondary education, students may meet future partners and may establish lifelong friendships.

When people observe high schools and post-secondary institutions from the outside, students appear to constitute a cohesive, uniform group. However, the student subculture is actually much more complex and diverse. High school cliques and social groups may crop up based on race, social class, physical attractiveness, placement in courses, athletic ability, and leadership roles in the school and community. In his classic community study of "Elmtown," August Hollingshead (1975) found some 259 distinct cliques in a single high school. These cliques, whose average size was five, were centred on the school itself, on recreational activities, and on religious and community groups.

We can find a similar diversity at the post-secondary level. Burton Clark and Martin Trow (1966) and, more recently, Helen Lefkowitz Horowitz (1987) have identified distinctive subcultures among post-secondary students. Here are four ideal types of subcultures that come out of their analyses:

1. The *collegiate* subculture focuses on having fun and socializing. These students define what constitutes a "reasonable" amount of academic work (and what amount of work is "excessive" and leads to being labelled as a "grind"). Members of the collegiate subculture have little commitment to academic pursuits.
2. By contrast, the *academic* subculture identifies with the intellectual concerns of the faculty and values knowledge for its own sake.

- Data from the National School Safety Center at Pepperdine University in the United States suggest there has been a 27 percent decline in school-associated violent deaths from 1992 through the 1997–1998 school year.
- Twenty-three times more children are killed in gun *accidents* than in school killings.

Schools, then, are safer than neighbourhoods, but people still are unnerved by the perception of an alarming rise in schoolyard violence that has been generated by heavy media coverage of the recent incidents. Some conflict theorists object to the huge outcry about recent violence in schools. After all, they note, violence in and around city schools has a long history. It seems that only when middle-class, white children are the victims does school violence become a plank on the national policy agenda. When violence hits the middle class, the problem is viewed not as an extension of delinquency, but as a structural issue in need of remedies.

Meanwhile, feminists observe that the offenders are male and, in some instances, the victims are disproportionately female. The precipitating factor for violence is often a broken-off dating relationship—yet another example of violence of men against women (or, in this case, boys against girls).

Increasingly, efforts to prevent school violence are focusing on the ways in which the socialization of young people contributes to violence. For example, the *Journal of the American Medical Association* published a study of Second Step, a violence prevention curriculum for elementary school students that teaches social skills related to anger management, impulse control, and empathy. The study evaluated the impact of the program on urban and suburban elementary school students and found that it appeared to lead to a moderate decrease in physically aggressive behaviour and an increase in neutral and prosocial behaviour in school.

A national study done in Canada, providing a "snap-shot" of violence prevention programs in Canadian schools (Day et. al. 1995), concluded that the school boards' response to school violence must be one in which students themselves are involved in the development of policies. School boards, the study concluded, must not take the view that certain youth are "out-of hand" and need to be controlled; rather, they must make a strong effort to promote a prosocial environment, develop comprehensive policies, establish developmentally appropriate consequences for certain behaviours, and institute a multifaceted violence-prevention program (on both the macro- and microlevels).

Let's Discuss

1. Has a violent episode ever occurred at your school? If so, how did students react? Do you feel safer at school than at home, as experts say you are?
2. What steps have administrators at your school taken to prevent violence? Have they been effective, or should other steps be taken?

3. The *vocational* subculture is primarily interested in career prospects and views college or university as means of obtaining degrees that are essential for advancement.
4. Finally, the *nonconformist* subculture is hostile to the university or college environment and seeks out ideas that may or may not relate to studies. It may find outlets through campus publications or issue-oriented groups.

Each student is eventually exposed to these competing subcultures and must determine which (if any) seems most in line with his or her feelings and interests.

The typology used by these researchers reminds us that school is a complex social organization—almost like a community with different neighbourhoods. Of course, these four subcultures are not the only ones evident on post-secondary campuses. For example, one might find subcultures of mature students and part-time students.

Sociologist Joe Feagin has studied a distinctive collegiate subculture: black students at predominantly white American universities. These students must function academically and socially within universities where there are few black faculty members or black administrators, where harassment of blacks by campus police is common, and where the curricula place little emphasis on black contributions. Feagin (1989:11) suggests that "for minority students life at a predominantly white college or university means long-term encounters with *pervasive whiteness.*" In Feagin's view, black students at such institutions experience both blatant and subtle racial discrimination, which has a cumulative impact that can seriously damage the students' confidence (see also Feagin et al. 1996).

Today, many classrooms in Canada integrate disabled students with those who are not, contributing to greater diversity of the student population.

Adult Education

Picture a college, university-college, or university student. Most likely, you will imagine someone under 25 years of age. This reflects the belief that education is something experienced and completed during the first two or three decades of life and rarely supplemented after that. However, many post-secondary institutions have witnessed a dramatic increase in the number of older students pursuing higher education. These older students are more likely to be female than is the typical 19- or 20-year-old post-secondary student. Viewed from a conflict perspective, it is not surprising that women are overrepresented among older students; they are the most likely to miss out on higher education the first time around (F. Best and Eberhard 1990).

The 1998 General Social Survey by Statistics Canada found that 15 percent of Canadians aged 25 and over reported that they had taken a course or training session in the last month. As well, in 2000–2001 approximately 29 percent of undergraduates were 25 years of age or older (Statistics Canada 2003m). Obviously, sociological models of the post-secondary subculture will have to be revised significantly in light of such changes. Moreover, as the age of the "typical" college student increases, there will be a growing need for on-campus child care.

p. 91

One explanation for the adult education boom is that society is changing rapidly in an age of technological innovation and a growing knowledge-based economy. Business firms have come to accept the view of education as lifelong and may encourage (or require) employees to learn job-related skills. Thus, secretaries are sent to special schools to be trained to use the latest computer software. Realtors attend classes to learn about alternative forms of financing for home buyers. In occupation after occupation, longtime workers and professionals are going back to school to adapt to the new demands of their jobs. Taking a conflict perspective, Canadian sociologist David Livingstone (1999) argues that despite Canadians' growing technological proficiency and growing levels of training and education, employers are failing to fully utilize their skills, thus contributing to "underemployment."

Not all adult education happens at the formal level. According to the 1998 General Social Survey, more than 6 million Canadians aged 25 and over reported that they engaged in "informal" learning during the previous month. This type of learning involves self-directed activity done at the learner's own time and pace and aimed to "enrich their ability to function within their communities and homes, to deal with family issues and enjoy their leisure time. Increasingly, people are also encouraged to view lifelong learning as a means of combating the mental deterioration associated with aging" (Silver et al. 2001: 19). Although gender had little effect on whether or not one was likely to study informally, gendered patterns of subject interest were found to exist. Women were more likely to study health and child care than men, while men were more likely to study trade-related subjects (Silver et al. 2001).

Home Schooling

When most people think of school, they think of bricks and mortar and the teachers, administrators, and other employees who staff school buildings. But for an increasing number of students in Canada and the United States, home is the classroom and the teacher is a parent. Estimates of the number of children being home schooled in Canada vary. The Home-School Legal Defense Association (HSLDA) estimates the number to be as high as 80 000, while Statistics Canada reported 19 114 registered home-schooled students in 1997 (Wake 2000). Statistics Canada warned, however, that those figures underestimate the total number, since many home schools are not registered.

As greater numbers of Canadian children are being home schooled with the aid of computers, parents must oversee their children's computer use.

In the past, families that taught their children at home lived in isolated environments or held strict religious views at odds with the secular environment of public schools. But today, home schooling is attracting a broader range of families not necessarily tied to organized religion. Poor academic quality, threat of school strikes, peer pressure, and school violence are motivating many parents to teach their children at home. In addition, the growing presence of computers in the home and the availability of educational resources online have motivated some parents to educate their children at home. Rates of home schooling in Canada have increased every year since 1980. The greatest increases have been in Western Canada, where the number of registered home-schoolers grew by 10 percent between 1995–96 and 1996–97 (Wake 2000).

While supporters of home schooling feel children can do just as well or better in home schools as in public schools, critics counter that because home-schooled children are isolated from the larger community, they lose an important chance to improve their socialization skills. But proponents of home schooling claim their children benefit from contact with others besides their own age group. They also see home schools as a good alternative for children who suffer from attention deficit disorder (ADD) and learning disorders (LDs). Such children often do better in smaller classes, which present fewer distractions to disturb their concentration (National Homeschool Association 1999).

Quality control is an issue in home schooling. While home schooling is legal in Canada, the provincial governments require that parents register their children. In Alberta, where home schooling is particularly popular, estimates point to a high number of unregistered children—children the government cannot monitor in terms of curricular and academic achievement. Many of these children are from families where the motivating factor to home school is religion; these families believe that the secular school system does not reflect their values, particularly those concerning abortion, homosexuality, and evolution. In 1988, Canada's Supreme Court ruled that the province of Alberta had a "compelling interest" in ensuring that the children of that province were properly educated (Mitchell 1999). This would mean making sure that home-schooled children followed a government-approved curriculum and were tested annually according to provincial standards. Despite the court ruling, many Christian parents continue to believe that the government should not be in the business of monitoring their children's education and that the values of secular education are not those to which they want their children exposed. Home schooling works, particularly for those who have made a commitment to it (Calhoun 2000; Matthews 1999; Paulson 2000).

Who are the people who are running home schools? In general, they tend to have higher-than-average incomes and educational levels. Most are two-parent families, and their children watch less television than average—both factors that are likely to support superior educational performance. The same students, with the same types of family and the same support from their parents, would probably do just as well in the public schools. As research has repeatedly shown, small classes are better than big classes, and strong parental and community involvement is key (Schnaiberg 1999).

Home schooling allows parents to integrate religion into their children's studies if they choose, but controversy brews when public schools do so, as the next section shows.

SOCIAL POLICY AND RELIGION

Religion in the Schools

The Issue

Should public schools be allowed to sponsor organized prayers in the classroom? Should the Lord's Prayer be part of the agenda at weekly school assemblies? How about reading Bible verses? Or just a collective moment of silence? Can public school athletes offer up a group prayer in a team huddle? Should students be able to initiate voluntary prayers at school events? Should a school be allowed to post the Ten Commandments in a hallway? Each of these situations has been an object of great dissension among those who see a role for prayer in public schools and those who want to maintain a strict separation of church and state.

Another area of controversy centres on the teaching of theories about the origin of humans and of the universe. Mainstream scientific thinking theorizes that humans evolved over billions of years from one-celled organisms, and that the universe came into being 15 billion years ago as a result of a "big bang." But these theories are challenged by people who hold to the biblical account of the creation of humans and the universe some 10 000 years ago—a viewpoint known as ***creationism.*** Creationists want their theory taught in the schools as the only one or, at the very least, as an alternative to the theory of evolution.

Who has the right to decide these issues? And what is considered the "right" decision? Religion in the public schools constitutes one of the thorniest issues in Canadian public policy today.

The Setting

In Canada, the Charter of Rights provides for freedom of religion. The Charter, along with the Canadian Constitution, protects the rights and privileges held by denominational schools at the time of Confederation in 1867. This has meant that in addition to the public school system, some provinces fund Catholic school education, while Quebec, where the majority of schools are Catholic, funds Protestant education. In 1999, a government-mandated task force in Quebec recommended that the Catholic and Protestant status for public schools be abolished and replaced with "secular" public schools. In the case of nondenominational or so-called "secular" schools, where explicit religious affiliation is not established, the issue of religious content in the form of prayers and Bible readings has become a contentious one.

Quebec is not the only province to experience these tensions in the secular schools. In 1999, Saskatchewan became the fourth province in Canada to oppose prayer in public schools. In 1993, a complaint by nine Saskatoon parents launched a challenge against the 100-year-old tradition of encouraging public school teachers to say the Lord's Prayer in classrooms and assemblies. The Saskatchewan Act, part of the provincial constitution, permitted prayer and Bible readings in the public schools. The group of nine Saskatoon parents, which included Muslims, Jews, Unitarians, and atheists, complained that this practice violated the Saskatchewan Human Rights Code. More specifically, they argued, it violated their children's (and other children's) right to freedom of conscience and that students were being denied the right to enjoy an education without discrimination because of creed or religion. As a result, in 1999, a board of inquiry ruled that it was discriminatory to require recitation of the Lord's Prayer in Saskatoon classrooms and assemblies.

Sociological Insights

Supporters of school prayer and of creationism feel that strict court rulings force too great a separation between what Émile Durkheim called the *sacred* and the *profane.* They insist that use of nondenominational prayer can in no way lead to the establishment of an ecclesia in Canada. Moreover, they believe that school prayer—and the teaching of creationism—can provide the spiritual guidance and socialization that many children today do not receive from parents or regular church attendance. Many communities also believe that schools should transmit the dominant culture of Canada by encouraging prayer.

According to a 1998 General Social Survey, 55 percent of adults in the United States disapprove of a Supreme Court ruling against the required reading of the Lord's Prayer or Bible verses in public schools. A national survey in 1999 showed that 68 percent of the public favours teaching creationism along with evolution in public schools, and 40 percent favours teaching *only* creationism. No other Western society has such a large body of opinion supporting views that depart so much from contemporary scientific understanding. Perhaps this is a reflection of a deep-rooted and enduring strain of religious fundamentalism in the United States, and the fact that religious belief in general is stronger in the United States than in Canada and other Western societies (Davis and Smith 1999; G. Johnson 1999; Lewis 1999).

Opponents of school prayer argue that a religious majority in a community might impose religious viewpoints specific to its faith, at the expense of religious minorities. Viewed from a conflict perspective, organized school prayer could reinforce the religious beliefs, rituals, and interests of the powerful; violate the rights of the powerless; increase religious dissension; and threaten the multiculturalism of Canada. These critics question whether school prayer can remain truly voluntary. Drawing on the interactionist perspective and small-group research, they suggest that children will face enormous social pressure to conform to the beliefs and practices of a religious majority.

Policy Initiatives

The latest case involving the Saskatoon Board of Education provides a good example of how in some communities policymakers are trying to find a compromise between those who want prayer in schools and those who do not. In 2001, two years after the Lord's Prayer was removed from the daily routine of public schools, the Saskatoon public school board is considering a Christian education program for children of religious parents. Modelled after the Logos Christian Education program already in place in Edmonton public schools, Christian students would receive instruction in a separate classroom with a religious environment. Opposition to the proposal has been raised by those who feel that the Logos program would divide students along religious lines and undermine the basis of the public school system.

The activism of religious fundamentalists in the nation's public school system raises a more general question: Whose ideas and values deserve a hearing in classrooms? Critics see this campaign as one step toward sectarian religious control of public education. They worry that, at some point in the future, teachers may not be able to use books, or make statements, that conflict with fundamentalist interpretations of the Bible. For advocates of a liberal education who are deeply committed to intellectual (and religious) diversity, this is a genuinely frightening prospect.

Let's Discuss

1. Was there any organized prayer in the school you attended? Do you think promoting religious observance is a legitimate function of the social institution of education?
2. How might a conflict theorist view the issue of organized school prayer?
3. In what ways have Christian fundamentalists and their allies attempted to reshape public education in Canada?

Chapter Resources

Summary

Religion and ***education*** are cultural universals, found throughout the world, although in varied forms. This chapter examines the dimensions and functions of religion, types of religious organizations, sociological views of education, and schools as examples of formal organizations.

1. Émile Durkheim stressed the social impact of religion and attempted to understand individual religious behaviour within the context of the larger society.
2. Religion serves the functions of integrating people in a diverse society and providing social support in time of need.
3. Max Weber saw a connection between religious allegiance and capitalistic behaviour through a religious orientation known as the ***Protestant ethic.***
4. ***Liberation theology*** uses the church in a political effort to alleviate poverty and social injustice.
5. From a Marxist point of view, religion serves to reinforce the social control of those in power. It lessens the possibility of collective political action that can end capitalist oppression and transform society.
6. Religious behaviour is expressed through ***beliefs, rituals,*** and ***religious experience.***

7. Sociologists have identified four basic types of religious organization: the ***ecclesia,*** the ***denomination,*** the ***sect,*** and the ***new religious movement (NRM)*** or ***cult.*** Advances in communication have led to a new type of church organization—the electronic church.
8. Transmission of knowledge and bestowal of status are manifest functions of education. Among its latent functions are transmitting culture, promoting social and political integration, maintaining social control, and serving as an agent of social change.
9. In the view of conflict theorists, education serves as an instrument of elite domination through the ***hidden curriculum*** and by bestowing status unequally.
10. Teacher expectations about a student's performance can sometimes have an impact on the student's actual achievements.
11. Today, most schools in Canada are organized in a bureaucratic fashion. Weber's five basic characteristics of bureaucracy are all evident in schools.
12. For over three decades, the proportion of older adults enrolled in Canadian post-secondary institutions has been rising steadily, in part because of sweeping changes in business, industry, and technology. For many Canadians, education has become a lifelong pursuit.
13. Home schooling has become a viable alternative to traditional public and private schools. More than 19 000 children in Canada are now educated at home.
14. How much religion—if any—should be permitted in the schools is a matter of debate in Canadian society today.

Critical Thinking Questions

1. From a conflict point of view, explain how religion could be used to bring about social change.
2. What role do new religious movements (or cults) play in the organization of religion? Why are they so often controversial?
3. What are the functions and dysfunctions of tracking in schools? Viewed from an interactionist perspective, how would tracking of high school students influence the interactions between students and teachers? In what ways might tracking have positive and negative impacts on the self-concepts of various students?

Key Terms

Correspondence principle The tendency of schools to promote the values expected of individuals in each social class and to prepare students for the types of jobs typically held by members of their class. (page 308)

Creationism A literal interpretation of the Bible regarding the creation of humanity and the universe used to argue that evolution should not be presented as established scientific fact. (316)

Cultural universals General practices found in every culture. (293)

Denomination A large, organized religion not officially linked with the state or government. (300)

Ecclesia A religious organization that claims to include most or all of the members of a society and is recognized as the national or official religion. (300)

Education A formal process of learning in which some people consciously teach while others adopt the social role of learner. (293)

Hidden curriculum Standards of behaviour that are deemed proper by society and are taught subtly in schools. (307)

Liberation theology Use of a church, primarily Roman Catholicism, in a political effort to eliminate poverty, discrimination, and other forms of injustice evident in a secular society. (297)

Megachurches Large worship centres affiliated only loosely, if at all, with existing denominations. (300)

New religious movement (NRM) or cult A generally small, secretive religious group that represents either a new religion or a major innovation of an existing faith. (302)

Profane The ordinary and commonplace elements of life, as distinguished from the sacred. (295)

Protestant ethic Max Weber's term for the disciplined work ethic, this-worldly concerns, and rational orientation to life emphasized by John Calvin and his followers. (297)

Religion A unified system of beliefs and practices relative to sacred things. (293)

Religious beliefs Statements to which members of a particular religion adhere. (298)

Religious experience The feeling or perception of being in direct contact with the ultimate reality, such as a divine being, or of being overcome with religious emotion. (299)

Religious rituals Practices required or expected of members of a faith. (298)

Sacred Elements beyond everyday life that inspire awe, respect, and even fear. (293)

Sect A relatively small religious group that has broken away from some other religious organization to renew what it views as the original vision of the faith. (300)

Secularization The process through which religion's influence on other social institutions diminishes. (293)

Teacher-expectancy effect The impact that a teacher's expectations about a student's performance may have on the student's actual achievements. (309)

Tracking The practice of placing students in specific curriculum groups on the basis of test scores and other criteria. (308)

Additional Readings

Ballantine, Jeanne H. 1997. *The Sociology of Education: A Systematic Analysis*. 4th ed. Englewood Cliffs, NJ: Prentice-Hall. A comprehensive approach to education that includes theoretical frameworks, current educational issues, and the process and structure of education systems.

Bibby, Reginald. 1996. *Fragmented Gods: The Poverty and Potential of Religion in Canada.* Toronto: Irwin. A comprehensive picture of religion in Canada and its potential in the future.

Guppy, Neil, and Scott Davies. 1998. *Education in Canada: Recent Trends and Future Challenges*. Ottawa: Statistics Canada. An in-depth statistical analysis of the state of education in Canada based on 1991 census data. Particular attention is paid to gender, race, ethnicity, and social class.

Internet Connection

www.mcgrawhill.ca/college/schaefer

For additional Internet exercises relating to belief systems and student subcultures, visit the Schaefer Online Learning Centre at ***http://www.mcgrawhill.ca/college/schaefer****. Please note that while the URLs listed were current at the time of printing, these sites often change—check the Online Learning Centre for updates.*

The Research in Action box in this chapter (see Box 12-2) details some of the social facts regarding violence in schools. In order to address this problem, organizations have begun to emerge and are utilizing the Internet as a tool for communication. Bully B'ware is an organization in British Columbia whose purpose is to raise awareness of bullying and to take action against it. Visit its website at **http://www.bullybeware.com/moreinfo.html** and then answer the following questions.

(a) What can schools do to eliminate bullying?
(b) What role can students play in an anti-bullying campaign?
(c) Do you think students might consider reporting acts of bullying as "ratting"?
(d) Why is reporting bullying considered to be a social taboo in many schools?

CBC Video

Visit the Schaefer Online Learning Centre at **http://www.mcgrawhill.ca/college/schaefer** to view the CBC video segments "Children Having Children: Teen Pregnancy and the Politics of Sex Education" and "Our Minds are Not for Sale: The Commercialization of Public Education" and answer related questions.

CHAPTER

13 GOVERNMENT AND THE ECONOMY

Voter turnout has been on the decline in Canada and other Western democracies. A clothing store in the United States offered this public service advertisement to encourage citizens to vote.

Now at the peak of what should be its key citizenship years, Nexus is confronting two challenges to the definition of what it means to be a citizen. First, the boundaries of the common good are becoming fuzzy. We've described how globalization is slowly eroding the foundations of the old, insular Canadian welfare state and replacing it with a more outward-looking "competition state." For Nexus, this process is having two polarizing effects.

On the one hand, the generation has reacted to sweeping global forces by turning inward, to embellish its own personal identity with something distinct from whatever fad seems to be sweeping the world. Often, as in the case of Nexus Québécois, the inward pull manifests itself in a return to cultural identity groups, where there is a strong sense of difference. Other times, it means the creation of new and smaller tribes, where members can find an authentic sense of community. Snowboarders and squeegee kids are obvious examples. These more local attachments help to combat the feeling of "rootlessness" that globalization can bring. In the words of Nexus journalist and political commentator Irshad Manji, "As institutional and geographic borders lose their legitimacy, our search for belonging intensifies."

On the other hand, Nexus is fearful of being left behind in a global economy and is therefore turning its gaze outward. Globalization is diverting Nexus loyalties to larger collectives —to North America, to the G7, or to the Western world—rather than keeping her eyes fixed on the traditional nation-state. Today, members of this generation are actively encouraged to study in the U.S. or abroad and often find themselves working in the foreign offices of global Canadian companies or for multinational corporations. Perhaps the most poignant example of shifting loyalties was the 1998 NHL All-Star Game. In what was once "Canada's game," Nexus saw *North America* pitted against the world. Another bastion of Canadianism sacrificed on the altar of global competition. *(Barnard, Cosgrave, and Welsh: 214–215)* ■

In *Chips and Pop: Decoding the Nexus Generation*, Barnard, Cosgrave, and Welsh look at the forces that were acting on young, post-adolescents in Canadian society at the end of the 20th century. It is not difficult to see their point that contemporary young adults are being pulled in different directions by the forces of a local and global culture that seems beyond their control. As governments struggle to maintain both their political and economic relevance in a world increasingly dominated by transnational corporations, their message is largely ignored by youth who are caught up in the pervasive consumerism of globalization. As they bounce from individualism to corporatism, these young people are left unsure of their own place in a new culture that offers no clear messages about expectations for their participation. The result for the Nexus generation is a sense of exclusion confirmed by their experience of minimum wage employment and governments with no apparent interest in addressing their concerns.

Within the framework of any political system, be it local, provincial, national, or international, there is a power elite made up almost exclusively of middle-aged men who reflect the standards of the dominant, contemporary culture. By ***political system,*** sociologists mean the structures and processes used for implementing and achieving society's goals, such as the allocation of valued resources. Like religion and the family, the political system is a cultural universal; it is found in every society. In Canada, the political system holds the ultimate responsibility for addressing the social policy issues examined in this textbook—poverty, child care, the AIDS crisis, sexual harassment, and so forth.

The term ***economic system*** refers to the structures and processes through which goods and services are produced, distributed, and consumed. As with social institutions such as the family, religion, and government, the economic system shapes other aspects of the social order and is, in turn, influenced by them. Throughout this textbook, you have been reminded of the economy's impact on social behaviour—for example, individual and group behaviour in factories and offices. You have studied the work of conflict and feminist theorists, who emphasized that the economic system of a society can promote social inequality. And you learned that foreign investment in developing countries can intensify inequality among residents.

pp. 10–11

p. 196

It is difficult to imagine two social institutions more intertwined than government and the economy. In addition to being a large employer in any nation, government at all levels regulates commerce and entry into many occupations. At the same time, the economy generates the revenue to support government services. While government and the economy are distinctive institutions, the interrelationship between the two makes it useful to consider them together while noting characteristics unique to each.

This chapter will present a sociological analysis of the impact of government and the economy on people's lives. We begin with macro-level analysis of capitalism and socialism as ideal types of economic systems. Next, we examine the sources of power in a political system and the three major types of authority. We will see how politics works in Canada, with particular attention to political socialization, citizens' participation in politics, the changing role of women in politics, and the influence of interest groups on political decision-making. We'll also look at two models of power in democracies: the elite and the pluralist models. Then we take a look at the changing nature of the Canadian and North American economies, as well as global economic process and structure as we open the 21st century. Finally, the social policy section explores the evolving role of women in Canadian public life. ■

Economic Systems

The sociocultural evolution approach developed by Gerhard Lenski categorizes preindustrial societies according to the way in which the economy is organized. The principal types of preindustrial societies, as you recall, are hunting-and-gathering societies, horticultural societies, and agrarian societies.

p. 182

As noted in Chapter 5, the *Industrial Revolution*—which began primarily in England during the period 1760 to 1830—brought about changes in the social organization of the workplace. People left their homesteads and began working in central locations such as factories. As the industrial revolution proceeded, a new form of social structure emerged: the *industrial society,* a society that depends on mechanization to produce its goods and services.

p. 114

Two basic types of economic systems distinguish contemporary industrial societies: capitalism and socialism. As described in the following sections, capitalism and socialism serve as ideal types of economic systems. No nation precisely fits either model. Instead, the economy of each individual country represents a mixture of capitalism and socialism, although one type or the other is generally useful in describing a society's economic structure. China's economy, for example, is primarily socialistic, while the United States economy reflects the capitalistic ideal. Canada's economic model, sometimes referred to as a social democracy, lies somewhere between the two, incorporating aspects of both capitalism and socialism.

Capitalism

In preindustrial societies, land functioned as the source of virtually all wealth. The Industrial Revolution changed all that. It required that certain individuals and institutions be willing to take substantial risks in order to finance new inventions, machinery, and business enterprises. Eventually, bankers, industrialists, and other holders of large sums of money—known as *capital*—replaced landowners as the most powerful economic force. These people invested their funds in the hope of realizing even greater profits and thereby became owners of the means of production.

The transition to private ownership of business was accompanied by the emergence of the capitalist economic system. *Capitalism* is an economic system in which capital, primarily in the form of currency, is used as a tool to create wealth. In this model, the means of production are largely in private hands and the main incentive for economic activity is the accumulation of profits. In practice, capitalist systems vary in the degree to which the government regulates private ownership and economic activity (Rosenberg 1991).

p. 179

Immediately following the Industrial Revolution, the prevailing form of capitalism was what is termed ***laissez-faire*** ("let it be"). Under the principle of laissez-faire, as expounded and endorsed by British economist Adam Smith (1723–1790), people could compete freely with minimal government intervention in the economy. Business retained the right to regulate itself and essentially operated without fear of excess government regulation (Smelser 1963). Even a staunch capitalist like Smith recognized the dangers of an unfettered marketplace.

Two centuries later, capitalism has taken on a somewhat different form. Private ownership and maximization of profits still remain the most significant characteristics of capitalist economic systems. However, in contrast to the era of laissez-faire, capitalism today features extensive government regulation of economic relations. Without restrictions, business firms could—as they have in the past—mislead consumers, endanger the safety of their workers, and even defraud the companies' investors—all in the pursuit of greater profits. That is why the government of a capitalist nation often monitors prices, sets safety standards for industries, protects the rights of consumers, and regulates collective bargaining between labour unions and management. Yet, under capitalism as an ideal type, government rarely takes over ownership of an entire industry.

Contemporary capitalism also differs from laissez-faire in another important respect: It tolerates monopolistic practices. A ***monopoly*** exists when a single business firm controls the market. In recent years, the United States government has charged Microsoft with being a monopoly within the computer industry. An ***oligopoly*** exists when a small group of companies controls the market. The Canadian government has repeatedly investigated the oil industry in this country over concerns that the prices at the gas pumps are deliberately manipulated by the few, huge, international players. Domination of an industry allows the firm or firms to effectively control a commodity by dictating pricing, standards of quality, and availability. Buyers have little choice but to yield to the firm's decisions; there is no other place to purchase the product or service. Both of these practices violate the ideal of free competition cherished by Adam Smith and other supporters of laissez-faire capitalism.

The "Cola Wars," the battle between Coke and Pepsi for domination of the soft drink market, have reached every corner of the planet. Here, Coca-Cola made its "biggest" statement on the steps of the Opera House in Hanoi, Vietnam.

Some capitalistic nations, such as Canada, outlaw monopolies through legislation. Such laws prevent any business from taking over so much of the competition in an industry that it gains control of the market. The federal government allows monopolies to exist only in certain exceptional cases, such as for some of the utility and transportation industries. Even then, regulatory agencies scrutinize these officially approved monopolies and protect the public. In Canada, many of the tolerated monopolies are in the form of government-owned *crown corporations.* A crown corporation is a company that is owned by the government, but operates as an independent financial entity. Some crown corporations, such an Hydro Quebec and the Saskatchewan Liquor and Gaming Authority, actually are self sustaining entities that turn a profit for the governments of those provinces. Others, such as the British Columbia Ferry Corporation and the Canadian Broadcasting Corporation, are able to function only because of the subsidies that the provincial and federal governments provide out of tax revenues.

Conflict theorists point out that while these types of enterprises may be rare examples of *pure* monopolies within a capitalist system, they are not the only monopolies in Canada. As the concern about government control within the oil industry indicates, competition is much more restricted than one might expect in what is called a *free enterprise system.* In numerous sectors—the banking and airline industries in particular—a few companies largely dominate the field and discourage the entry of new enterprises into the marketplace.

Socialism

Socialist theory was refined in the writings of Karl Marx and Friedrich Engels. These European social critics were disturbed by the exploitation of the working class as it emerged during the Industrial Revolution. In their view, capitalism forced large numbers of people to exchange their labour for low wages. The owners of an industry profit from the labour of their workers, primarily because they pay workers less than the value of the goods produced.

p. 11

p. 179

As an ideal type, a socialist economic system attempts to eliminate such economic exploitation by placing the ownership of the means of production and the distribution of resources into the hands of workers either directly, or indirectly through the government. Under ***socialism,*** the means of production and distribution in a society are collectively rather than privately owned. The basic objective of the economic system is to meet people's needs rather than to maximize profits. Socialists reject the laissez-faire philosophy that free competition benefits the general public. Instead, they believe that the central government, acting as the representative of the people, should make basic economic decisions. Therefore, public ownership of all major industries—including steel production, automobile manufacturing, and agriculture—is a major feature of socialism as an ideal type.

In practice, socialist economic systems vary in the extent to which they tolerate private ownership. For example, in a ***social democracy*** such as Sweden, or to a lesser degree, Canada, the economy is for the most part dominated by private businesses operating within a political framework that is responsible for the redistribution of wealth. Certain aspects of the Canadian economy are socialist, and certain aspects are capitalist. Air Canada, for example, was once a crown corporation, and it dominated passenger airline service in Canada to the point of monopoly. Then, the rules changed and private airlines were allowed to compete with it. Ironically, claims of monopolistic practices have reappeared since Air Canada, the private corporation, took over control of its rival, Canadian Airlines.

Socialist societies differ from capitalist nations in their commitment to the common good, the idea that a community is responsible for the well-being of its citizens. For example, in Canada, the various provincial governments, operating under the Canada Healthcare Act, provide subsidized health care to all Canadians. By contrast, the United States government provides health care and health insurance only for the elderly and poor through the Medicare and Medicaid programs. In socialist societies, the wealth of the people as a collectivity is used to provide health care, housing, education, and other key services for each individual and family.

Marx believed that each socialist state would eventually evolve into a *communist* society. As an ideal type, ***communism*** refers to an economic system under which all property is communally owned and no social distinctions are made on the basis of people's ability to contribute to the economy. In recent decades, the Soviet Union, the People's Republic of China, Vietnam, Cuba, and nations in eastern Europe have been considered examples of communist economic systems. However, this represents an incorrect usage of a term with sensitive political connotations. All nations known as communist in the 20th century have actually failed to live up to the standards of the ideal type.

By the early 1990s, Communist parties were no longer ruling the nations of eastern Europe. The first major challenge to Communist rule came in 1980 when Poland's Solidarity movement, led by Lech Walesa and backed by many workers, questioned the injustices of that society. While martial law initially forced Solidarity underground, it eventually negotiated the end of Communist party rule in 1989. Inspired by the reform instigated by Soviet President Mikhial Gorbachev, including his order to tear down the Berlin Wall, citizen protest forced dominant Communist parties throughout eastern Europe to relinquish their hold on power. The former Soviet Union, Czechoslovakia, and Yugoslavia were subdivided to accommodate the ethnic, linguistic, and religious differences within these areas. As of 1998, China, Cuba, and Vietnam remained socialist societies ruled by Communist parties. However, even in these countries capitalism was making inroads. For example, by 1995, 60 percent of Vietnam's economic output and 25 percent of China's came from the private sector (Steinfeld 1999; World Bank 1996:15).

Cuba, in particular, is adjusting to a dual economy. While the Communist government leader Fidel Castro remains firmly committed to Marxism, the centrally controlled economy has struggled following the end of Soviet aid in 1990. Despite this loss of $6 to 9 billion in annual subsidy and the continued trade embargo by the United States, Cuba's economy has gradually recovered since 1994, recording steady growth through the end of the decade. Reluctantly, President Castro has allowed small-scale, family-managed businesses, such as restaurants and craft shops, to operate and accept dollars rather than the heavily devalued Cuban peso. This leads to an ironic situation in which government-employed teachers and doctors earn less than the small business operators, taxi drivers, and hotel workers who have access to foreign currency. This situation underscores how difficult it is to understand any nation's economy without considering its position in the global context (J. McKinley 1999).

As we have seen, capitalism and socialism serve as ideal types of economic systems. To varying degrees, the economy of each industrial society—including Canada, the United States, and Japan—includes certain elements of both capitalism and socialism. Whatever the differences, whether they more closely fit the ideal type of capitalism or socialism, all industrial societies rely chiefly on mechanization in the production of goods and services.

Politics and Government

An economic system does not exist in a vacuum. Someone or some group makes important decisions about how to use resources and how to allocate goods, whether it be a tribal chief or a parliament or a dictator. A cultural universal common to all economic systems, then, is the exercise of power and authority. The struggle for power and authority inevitably involves ***politics,*** which political scientist Harold Lasswell (1936) tersely defined as "who gets what, when, and how." In their study of politics and government, sociologists are concerned with social interactions among individuals and groups and their impact on the larger political and economic order.

While power and influence are most commonly analyzed in terms of their economic and political applications, there is another area where they are just as critical. *Ideological power and authority* is the ability to change attitudes or agendas by controlling peoples' perceptions. We are able to make capitalism and democracy work because the populations that live under them are convinced that they are the best systems available to them.

Power

Power is at the heart of a political system. According to Max Weber, ***power*** is the ability to exercise one's will over others. To put it another way, whoever can control the outcomes of others is exercising power. Power relations can involve large organizations, small groups, or even people in an intimate association.

pp. 179–80

There are three basic sources of power within any political system—coercion, influence, and authority. ***Coercion*** is the actual or threatened use of force to impose one's will on others. When leaders imprison or even execute political dissidents, they are applying force; so, too, are terrorists when they seize or bomb an embassy or assassinate a political leader. ***Influence,*** on the other hand, refers to the exercise of power through a process of persuasion. A person may reconsider his or her choice of career because of comments by peers, the expert advice of a school guidance counsellor, or a passionate description of a profession by someone in the field looking to recruit talented youth. In each case, sociologists would view such efforts to persuade people as examples of influence. Now let's take a look at the third source of power: authority.

Types of Authority

The term ***authority*** refers to power that has been ***institutionalized***—formalized within a social institution—and is recognized by the people over whom it is exercised. Sociologists commonly use the term in connection with those whose power is *legitimized* through elected or publicly acknowledged positions. ***Legitimization*** is the process of having power authorized by those people who may be subject to its use. A person's authority is limited by the constraints of a particular social role. Perhaps most importantly, the power lies outside the individual. Thus, a soccer referee has the authority to award a penalty kick if she thinks there has been an infraction on the field. She does not, however, have the authority to give parking tickets to those spectators who have left the cars in a no-parking zone outside the stadium. Conversely, a police officer has no authority over players' actions within the context of the game.

Max Weber (1947, original edition 1913) developed a classification system regarding authority that has become one of the most useful and frequently cited contributions of early sociology. He identified three ideal types of authority: traditional, legal-rational, and charismatic. Weber did not insist that only one type applies to a given society or organization. All can be present, but their relative importance will vary. Sociologists have found Weber's typology valuable in understanding different manifestations of legitimate power within a society.

Traditional Authority

Until the middle of this century, Japan was ruled by a revered emperor, whose power was absolute and passed down from generation to generation. In a political system based on ***traditional authority***, legitimate power is *ascribed*, in other words, conferred by custom and accepted practice. A king or queen is accepted as ruler of a nation simply by virtue of inheriting the crown; a tribal chief rules because that is the accepted practice. The ruler may be loved or hated, competent or destructive; in terms of legitimacy, that does not matter. For the traditional leader, authority rests in custom, not in personal characteristics, technical competence, or perhaps not even written law, although constitutional monarchs such as the Queen of England are an exception. People accept this authority because "this is how things have always been done." Traditional authority is absolute when the ruler has the ability to determine laws and policies.

Legal-Rational Authority

The Confederation Act of 1867 gave the Canadian Parliament, and implicitly, its elected membership, the authority to make policies and enact laws to implement and enforce those policies. Power made legitimate by law is known as ***legal-rational authority.*** Leaders derive their legal-rational authority from the written rules and regulations of political systems. Generally, in societies based on legal-rational authority, leaders are allowed specific areas in which they may exercise their authority, but are not thought to be endowed with divine inspiration, as in certain societies with traditional forms of authority.

One of the most hotly contested points of globalization is the debate over the transfer of legal-rational authority from the explicit control of elected governments to the implicit control of corporations. Opponents of the North American Free Trade Agreement claimed that enactment of the accord would make the United States government a de facto authority in both Canada and Mexico. However, as globalization of the marketplace proceeds, it is the transnational power of corporations that presents the greatest challenge to state authority.

In recent years, a similar debate has taken place with regard to the federal–provincial division of powers within Canada. The government in Ottawa has reluctantly relinquished some of its traditional authority, thereby transforming it into new, legal-rational provincial authority.

Charismatic Authority

Joan of Arc was a simple peasant girl in medieval France, yet she was able to rally the French people and lead them in major battles against English invaders. Adolf Hitler was a poorly educated, failed artist with no political experience who managed to excite such nationalistic passion in the German people that they followed him into a destructive war. How was this possible? As Weber observed, power can be legitimized by the *charisma* of an individual. The term ***charismatic authority*** refers to power made legitimate by a leader's exceptional personal or emotional appeal to his or her followers. Charisma lets a person lead or inspire without relying on set rules or traditions. In fact, charismatic authority is derived more from the beliefs of followers than from the actual qualities of leaders. So long as people *perceive* a leader as having qualities setting him or her apart from ordinary citizens, that leader's authority will remain secure and often unquestioned.

Unlike traditional rulers, charismatic leaders often become well known by breaking with established

King Bhumibol Adulyadoj of Thailand reviews the Royal Honor Guard during a ceremony honouring his birthday. In a political system based on traditional authority, power is conferred according to accepted custom—in this case, on the basis of royal birth.

institutions and advocating dramatic changes in the social structure and the economic system. Their stronghold over their followers makes it easier to build protest movements that challenge the dominant norms and values of a society. Thus, charismatic leaders such as Jesus, Mohammed, Mahatma Gandhi, Winston Churchill, and Martin Luther King all used their power to press for changes in accepted social behaviour. But so did Adolf Hitler.

Observing from an interactionist perspective, sociologist Carl Couch (1996) points out that the growth of the electronic media has facilitated the development of charismatic authority. During the 1930s and 1940s, Canadian Prime Minister William Lyon Mackenzie King and the heads of other countries all used radio to issue direct appeals to citizens. In recent decades, television has allowed leaders to "visit" people's homes and communicate with them. Time and again, Saddam Hussein has rallied the Iraqi people through shrewd use of television appearances. In both Taiwan and South Korea in 1996, troubled political leaders facing reelection campaigns spoke frequently to national audiences and exaggerated military threats from neighbouring China and North Korea, respectively. Perhaps the most famous politician to use this medium was former United States president Ronald Regan, known as the "Great Communicator."

Weber identified traditional, legal-rational, and charismatic authority as ideal types. In reality, particular leaders and political systems combine elements of two or more of these forms. Pierre Elliott Trudeau, arguably Canada's most influential prime minister, wielded power largely through the legal-rational basis of his authority, while at the same time using his significant charisma to crystallize and sustain public support for his position.

Political Behaviour in Canada

Canadian citizens take for granted many aspects of their political system. They are accustomed to living in a nation with a Charter of Rights, several major political parties representing a broad ideological spectrum, voting by secret ballot, an elected prime minister and Parliament, and provincial and local governments distinct from the national government. Yet, of course, each society has its own ways of governing itself and making decisions. The Canadian political landscape has its own structure and processes. Residents of the People's Republic of China and Cuba are accustomed to one-party rule by the Communist party, and even United States citizens have traditionally had just two choices. But in Canada, our federal elections have seen a parade of alternatives. In recent elections, representatives of the Natural Law Party and the Green Party vied for seats with the more established groups. Even the Marijuana Party managed to garner enough votes in 2000 to gain official party status. In this section, we will examine a number of important aspects of political behaviour within Canada.

Political Socialization

Do your political views coincide with those of your parents? Did you vote in the last election? Have you registered to vote, or do you plan to do so? The process by which you acquire political attitudes and develop patterns of political behaviour is known as ***political socialization***. This involves not only becoming familiar with the prevailing political leanings of your society, but also coming to understand and accept the political system, whatever its limitations and problems.

Chapter 6 identified five functional prerequisites that a society must fulfill to survive. One of these was the need to teach recruits to accept the values and customs of the group. In a political sense, this function is crucial; each succeeding generation must be encouraged to understand its society's basic political values and particular methods of decision making. The principal institutions of political socialization are those that also socialize us to other cultural norms: the family, schools, and the media.

Many observers see the family as playing a particularly significant role in the process. Parents pass on their political attitudes and evaluations to their sons and daughters through discussions at the dinner table and also through the example of their political involvement or apathy. Early socialization does not always determine a person's political orientation; there are changes over time and between generations. Yet research on political socialization continues to show that parents' views have an important impact on their children's political choices (M. Jennings and Niemi 1981).

Schools provide young people with information and analysis of the political world. Much less flexible than the family or peer groups, schools are easily susceptible to centralized and uniform control. That is why totalitarian societies commonly use educational institutions to indoctrinate the students in certain political beliefs. Even in democracies, where local schools are not under the pervasive control of the national government, political education will generally reflect the norms and values of the prevailing political order.

In the view of conflict theorists, students in almost every country learn much more than factual information about their political and economic way of life. They are socialized to view capitalism and representative democracy as the "normal" and most desirable p. 62 ways of organizing a nation. As indicated earlier in this chapter, this is a form of power effected by influencing ideology. At the same time, schools often present com-

Children in Canada are socialized to see freedom of expression as an essential part of the democratic process. These students are using that freedom in an attempt to influence the policies of a government they feel is not serving their interests.

peting values and forms of government in a negative fashion or simply ignore them. From a conflict perspective, this type of political education serves the interests of those in positions of power while ignoring the significant social issues of the marginalized and powerless. Canada is not exempt from this claim.

Political socialization can take different forms in different types of societies. Using observation research, sociologist Benigno Aguirre (1984) concluded that the Cuban government encouraged certain types of crowd behaviour to reinforce its legitimacy. The Committees for the Defence of the Revolution—which functioned much as the Communist party did when it ruled the Soviet Union—mobilized Cubans for parades, celebrations, protests, and testimonials on behalf of deceased revolutionary leaders. Through these mobilizations, Cuba's rulers hoped to convey the political message that Fidel Castro's communist government had and deserved widespread popular support.

Participation and Apathy

In theory, a representative democracy will function most effectively and fairly if an informed and active electorate communicates its views to government leaders. Unfortunately, this is hardly the case in Canada or most of the other capitalist democracies. Virtually all citizens may be familiar with the basics of the political process, and most tend to identify to some extent with a political party or ideology, but only a small minority (often members of the higher social classes) actually participates in political organizations on a local or national level. Only a small minority of Canadians belongs to a political party.

The failure of most citizens to become involved in political parties diminishes the democratic process. Within the Canadian political system, the political party serves as an intermediary between people and government. Through competition in regularly scheduled elections, the parties provide for challenges to public policies and for an orderly transfer of power. An individual dissatisfied with the state of the nation or a local community can become involved in the political party process in many ways, such as by joining a political club supporting candidates for public office or working to change the party's position on controversial issues.

By the 1980s, it became clear that many people in Canada were beginning to be turned off by political parties, politicians, and big government. Traditionally, voter turnout has been the highest for elections at the federal level, with lower participation in provincial elections, and even lower yet for city council and school board elections. While participation at all levels has diminished steadily for the past decade, the drop between the 1997 and 2000 national elections was particularly dramatic. According to Elections Canada, 13 178 698 ballots were cast in 1997. This was slightly over 67 percent of the total eligible voters. Four years later, the number had dropped to 12 813 647, just 60.3 percent of all Canadians who might have voted.

The impact of this lack of participation in the process can be clearly seen by analyzing the support gained by the victorious Liberal government. The federal Liberals formed a majority government in those two elections. A ***majority government*** is one in which one party controls more than half the seats in a legislative house. In the Canadian Parliament there are 301 seats, meaning that a party must win 151 seats to capture a majority. In 1997, the Liberals gained a slim majority of 155 seats. In 2000, they won 172 seats. The importance of a majority is that it gives the dominant party the ability to control the outcomes of votes in the House of Commons.

In 1997, the Liberals gained a majority by capturing just over 38 percent of the popular vote. In 2000, that proportion rose to almost 41 percent. However, even in the 2000 election, the Liberals had the explicit support of less

Research in Action 13-1 Why Don't Young People Vote?

In 1971, there was great optimism. All through the 1960s, young people had actively participated in a range of political issues—from supporting the Quiet Revolution of the Quebec separatists, to demonstrating against the American involvement in Vietnam, to protesting the treatment of minorities. Canadian youth, particularly those in the country's universities, saw the Sixties as an opportunity for change, and in atypical Canadian fashion, they weren't necessarily peaceful in how they went about expressing their displeasure. At Sir George Williams University (now Concordia University) in Montreal, black students from developing countries stormed a building and ransacked computers to protest discrimination they felt they had suffered at the hands of the school's policies. In Vancouver, the Gastown riots were the result of street protests against the Vietnam War. But the most famous of the 1960s' protests in Canada was the violence of the Quebec separatist groups such as Rassemblement pour l'Independence Nationale, and the Front de Libération du Québec.

Now, 30 years later, we can consider the available research and see what happened. Frankly, what is remarkable is what did *not* happen. First, young voters (those between 18 and 21) have not, for the most part, followed in their parents' radical footsteps. In fact, throughout the 1980s and the first half of the 1990s they showed a marked disinterest in things political. In the past few years, however, that has changed. While youth turnout at the ballot box has remained at historically low levels, there has been a rekindling of the Sixties' political spirit in the form of protests against globalization. In streets from Seattle to Quebec City to Genoa, young people of diverse nationalities have stormed chain link barriers and braved tear gas to express their displeasure with the direction that world economic and political leaders have chosen.

But the vigorous political involvement that has characterized the resistance to globalization has not inspired young people to storm the nation's polling booths with the same enthusiasm.

But the vigorous political involvement that has characterized the resistance to globalization has not inspired young people to storm the nation's polling booths with the same enthusiasm. What is behind this voter apathy among the young? The popular explanation is that people, especially young people, are alienated from the political system, turned off by the shallowness and negativity of candidates and campaigns. True, studies document that young voters are susceptible to cynicism and distrust, but these are not necessarily associated with voter apathy. Numerous studies show the relationship between how people perceive the candidates and issues and their likelihood of voting is a very complex one. Communication scholars Erica Weintraub Austin and Bruce Pinkleton completed a survey of less experienced eligible voters and found that those who believe that they can see through the "lies" told by politicians via the media are *more* apt to think their participation can make a difference. In any event, young people do vote as they age. Any disaffection with the voting booth is certainly not permanent.

Other explanations for the lower turnout among the young seem more plausible. Besides Canada, the United States is the only other western democracy to require citizens to, in effect, vote

Sources: Austin and Pinkleton 1995; Bureau of the Census 1998f; Casper and Bass 1998; Clymer 2000; Cook 1991; Landers 1988; Leon 1996; Shogan 1998.

than a quarter of Canada's eligible voters (21 242 783 eligible voters divided by 5 230 222 votes for Liberals equals 24.6 percent) (Gidengil et al. 2001). This possibility of gaining control of Parliament with the support of a relatively small proportion of the population is a function of Canadians' disinterest in the democratic process.

While a few nations still command high voter turnout, it is increasingly common to hear national leaders of other countries complain of voter apathy. In the 1996 United States presidential election, voter turnout had fallen to less than 49 percent of all eligible voters. Japan typically enjoyed 70 percent turnout in its Upper House elections in the 1950s through mid-1980s, but by 1998 turnout was closer to 58 percent. In the 1998 British general elections, there was only a 34 percent turnout in London and 28 percent in the rest of England (A. King 1998; Masaki 1998).

Political participation makes government accountable to the voters. If participation declines, government can operate with less of a sense of accountability to society. This issue is most serious for the least powerful individuals and groups in Canada. An indication of the marginalization of the least powerful in Canadian society is the drop in voter turnout in the poorest areas of the country. Not surprisingly, the lowest participation rate in the 1997 federal election was in Newfoundland, one of the twice. They must first *register* to vote, often at a time when issues are not on the front burner and candidates haven't even declared. Then they must vote on election day. Young people, who tend to be mobile and to lead hectic lives, find it difficult to track voting requirements (which vary in provincial elections) and be present where they are legally eligible to vote. Lack of time is the single biggest reason that voters gave for not voting in recent elections. In the United States, an attempt was made to facilitate young voter registration by allowing people to register when they applied for or renewed driver's licences, but this attempt to simplify the registration process has done little to change voting apathy. A year after this program went in to effect, only 66 percent of the voting-age population reported they were registered, the lowest rate for an American presidential election since 1968.

While young people in Canada generally tend to be less active in politics on the federal level than their counterparts in other countries, they often participate in debates of issues that impact directly on their lives, such as taxes and financing for education. Many issues such as poverty and violent crime also seem very far removed from their immediate concerns. Sometimes issues such as landlord policies or student–police relations surface on campuses, mobilizing the youth vote, but this activism often declines as the issue fades from view.

Protestors demonstrate against globalization during an economic summit of world leaders in Quebec City in April, 2001.

The entry of young people into the electorate during the 1970s came at a time when the traditional, well organized multi-party system that actively sought out new voters, of whatever age, suffered a decline. No longer are potential new voters greeted by political party faithful all too ready to guide a recruit through the voting process.

These studies do not point to easy solutions for reversing the three-decade pattern of low turnout among the newest voters. Facilitating the registration and voting process, identifying local issues of interest, grass-roots campaigning, and more careful evaluation of media campaigning may all help. We also need to continue to research potential reasons why so many people between the ages of 18 and 21 fail to even register to vote and why many more who take that step fail to vote.

Let's Discuss

1. How often do you vote? If you do not vote, what accounts for your apathy? Are you too busy to register? Are community issues uninteresting to you?
2. Do you think voter apathy is a serious social problem? What might be done to increase voter participation in your age group and community?

poorest provinces, where only 55 percent of eligible voters went to the polls to elect a federal government. In 2000, that proportion increased to 57 percent, a number slightly higher than only two other jurisdictions, Nunavut and the Northwest Territories, neither of which is in danger of being considered a seat of power in Canada. The segment of the voting population that has shown the *most* voter apathy—the young—is highlighted in Box 13-1.

Women in Politics

Women continue to be dramatically underrepresented in the halls of government. As of 2001, the Parliament of Canada had 62 sitting female members of the 301 possible seats. This represents 20.5 percent of the total. Since Confederation, 154 women have sat in the House of Commons, a small fraction of the total number of elected representatives. The first woman to sit as a Member of Parliament was Agnes Campbell McPhail—not surprisingly, a candidate for the Progressive Party. McPhail was elected in 1921 and maintained her status as a legislator for 22 years.

Sexism has been the most serious barrier to women interested in holding office. Women first became eligible to vote in Canada when the Manitoba legislature passed a law to that effect in 1916. At the federal level, female relatives of members of the military were given the right to vote in 1917. However, the franchise was not extended to all Canadian women until the election of 1921. It was not until the fall of 1929 that women in Canada were acknowledged under the law to be "persons." Despite this fact, women often continued to encounter prejudice and discrimination within the political process, whether they were participating as candidates or simply attempting to exercise their democratic right independently. In spite of this resistance, Canadian women have steadily improved their numbers in and their influence over the political process in this country.

But while women politicians may be enjoying more electoral success now than in the past, there is evidence that the media cover them differently from men. A content analysis of newspaper coverage of recent races in the United States showed that reporters wrote more often about a female candidate's personal life, appearance, or personality than a male candidate's, and less often about her political positions and voting record. Furthermore, when political issues were raised in newspaper articles, reporters were more likely to illustrate them with statements made by male candidates than by female candidates (J. Devitt 1999).

Figure 13-1 shows the representation of women in national legislatures throughout the world. While the proportion of women has increased in Canada and many other nations, women still do not account for half the members of the national legislature in any country. Sweden ranks the highest, with 43 percent.

A new dimension of women and politics began to emerge in the 1980s. Surveys detected a growing "gender gap" in the political preferences and activities of males and females. Women were more likely to be left-leaning in their political choices, favouring parties such as the Liberals and the New Democrats, and criticizing right-wing parties such as the Conservatives and the Canadian Alliance (formerly the Reform Party). This was reflected in women's choices in the 2000 federal election. Outside of Quebec, which is excluded from these calculations because of the impact of the Bloc Quebecois on the numbers, 38 percent of male voters supported the Canadian Alliance as compared to 27 percent of women. On the left, support for the NDP reflected women's preferences. Sixteen percent of female voters and only 9 percent of males cast a ballot for that party in the federal election. According to political analysts, support for the right to choose a legal abortion, for a national day care program, and for parental leave from work have been major factors in determining the party affiliations of women voters. As one analyst put it, "Women have traditionally felt more vulnerable, and the safety net—whether it's for older women, women in poverty, or single heads of households—has been a more immediate experience in their lives." (Marks 1998:3).

Interest Groups

Common needs or common frustrations may lead people to band together in social movements to have an effect in the political arena. Examples include the civil rights movement of the 1960s and the anti–nuclear power movement of the 1980s. We will consider social movements in more detail in Chapter 16. People can also influence the political process through membership in interest groups (some of which, in fact, may be part of larger social movements).

An ***interest group*** is a voluntary association of citizens who attempt to influence public policy. The National Action Committee on the Status of Women is considered an interest group; so too are Egale Canada, a group lobbying for the protection of gays and lesbians in the courts, and the Cryonics Society of Canada, dedicated to creating a more favourable legislative environment for people who wish to have themselves frozen as a defence against death. Such groups are a vital part of the political process of Canada. Many interest groups (often known as *lobbies*) are national or international in scope and address a wide array of social, economic, and political issues. For example, there are two groups lobbying in Washington, DC, for softwood lumber mills. One group solicits support for trade and Canadian producers, while the other looks for help for the American counterparts. At the end of March 2002, the latter group won out when the United States government imposed a 29 percent countervailing duty on imports of softwood from Canada. The victory may, however, be short-lived, as Canadian producers prepare to challenge the ruling.

One way in which American interest groups influence the legislative process is through their political action committees. A ***political action committee*** (or ***PAC***) is a political committee established by an interest group—say, a national bank, corporation, trade association, or cooperative or membership association—to solicit contributions for particular candidates or political parties. Political action committees distribute substantial funds to candidates, raising concerns that they might have too much influence on those who win electoral contests and take office.

As new concerns arise, new lobby groups emerge. In 1999, NetCoalition was created to represent a variety of Internet-based companies, including America Online, Excite, and Amazon.com. This collective of the largest players in the Internet field spent millions of dollars lobbying legislative bodies in every part of the globe on such issues as immigration policy, privacy, and limiting restrictions on the Internet. For instance, NetCoalition opposed

FIGURE 13-1

Women in National Legislatures

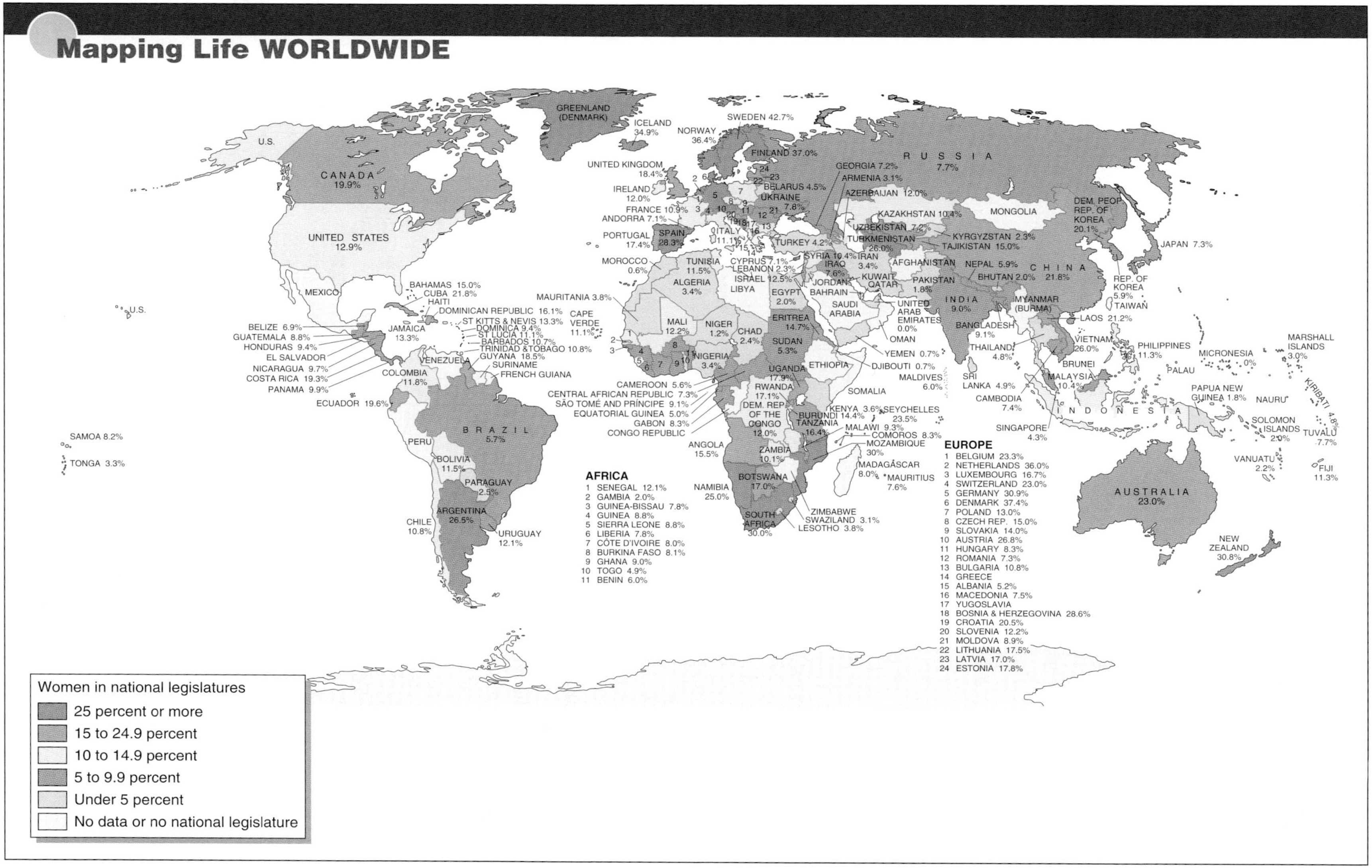

Source: Inter-Parliamentary Union 2000.

Each colour on the map indicates a certain percentage of women in the national legislatures (as of September 2000), as designated by the key.

government efforts to prevent Napster, an Ontario-based company that developed web-based software for downloading free music, from facilitating the downloading of music over the web (NetCoalition.com 2000; Shiver, Jr. 2000).

Models of Power Structure in Canada

Who really holds power in Canada? Is it true that voters genuinely run the country through elected representatives? Or is it true that, behind the scenes, a small elite controls both the government and the economic system? It is difficult to determine the location of power in a society as complex as ours. In exploring this critical question, social scientists have developed two basic views of our nation's power structure: the power elite and the pluralist models.

Power Elite Models

Karl Marx essentially believed that 19th-century representative democracy was a sham. He argued that industrial societies were dominated by relatively small numbers of people who owned factories and controlled natural resources. He called this group the *bourgeoisie*. In Marx's view, government officials and military leaders were essentially servants of this capitalist class and followed their wishes. Therefore, any key decisions made by politicians inevitably served the interests of the dominant bourgeoisie, and ignored the wishes of the working class, or *proletariat*. Like others who hold an ***elite model*** of power relations, Marx believed that society is controlled by a small group of individuals who share a common set of political and economic interests.

Mills's Model

Sociologist C. Wright Mills took this model a step further in his pioneering work *The Power Elite* (1956). Mills, an American, described a small ruling elite of military, industrial, and governmental leaders who, he argued, controlled the fate of the United States. Mills extended this analysis to other nations, arguing that while the influence of the military was disproportionate in American life, the influence of corporate leaders was mirrored in every other major capitalist country, including Canada. Power rested in the hands of a few, both inside and outside government—the ***power elite.***

A pyramid illustrates the power structure within Canada, and arguably, in every other developed, democratic nation in Mills's model (see Figure 13-2a). At the top are the corporate rich, leaders of the executive branch of government, and, primarily in the United States, heads of the military (whom Mills called the "warlords"). Directly below are local opinion leaders, members of the legislative branch of government, and leaders of special-interest groups. Mills contended that such individuals and groups would basically follow the wishes of the dominant power elite. At the bottom of the pyramid are the unorganized, exploited masses.

This power elite model is, in many respects, similar to the work of Karl Marx. The most striking difference is that Mills felt that the economically powerful coordinate their manoeuvres with other establishment groups to serve their common interests. Yet, reminiscent of Marx, Mills argued that the corporate rich were the most powerful element of the power elite (first among "equals"). And, of course, there is a further dramatic parallel between the work of these conflict theorists. The powerless masses at the bottom of Mills's power elite model certainly bring to mind Marx's portrait of the oppressed workers of the world, who have "nothing to lose but their chains."

A fundamental element in Mills's thesis is that the power elite not only includes relatively few members but also operates as a self-conscious, cohesive unit. Although not necessarily diabolical or ruthless, the elite comprises similar types of people who regularly interact with one another and have essentially the same political and economic interests. Mills's power elite is not a conspiracy but rather a community of interest and sentiment among a small number of influential people (A. Hacker 1964).

Admittedly, Mills failed to clarify when the elite opposes protests and when it tolerates them; he also failed to provide detailed case studies that would substantiate the interrelationship between members of the power elite. Nevertheless, his challenging theories forced scholars to look more critically at democratic political systems.

Domhoff's Model

More recently, sociologist G. William Domhoff (1998) has agreed with Mills that powerful elites run the industrial and postindustrial societies of the developed world. He finds that in North America it is still largely white, male, and upper class. But Domhoff stresses the role played both by elites of the corporate community and by the leaders of policy-formation organizations such as chambers of commerce and labour unions. Many of the people in both groups are also members of the social upper class.

While these groups overlap, as Figure 13-2b shows, they do not necessarily agree on specific policies. Domhoff notes that in the electoral arena two different coalitions have exercised influence. A *corporate-conservative coalition* has played a large role in generating support for candidates who support a business-focused agenda. But there is also a *liberal-labour coalition* based in unions, local environmental organizations, a segment of the minority group

FIGURE 13-2

Power Elite Models

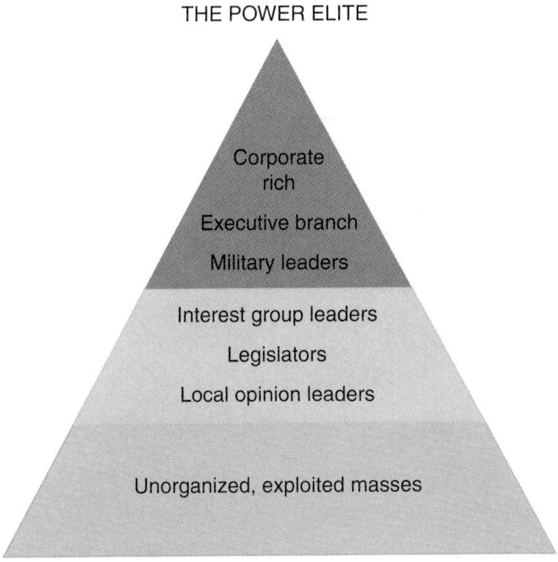

a. C. Wright Mills's model, 1956

Source: Domhoff 1998, p. 3.

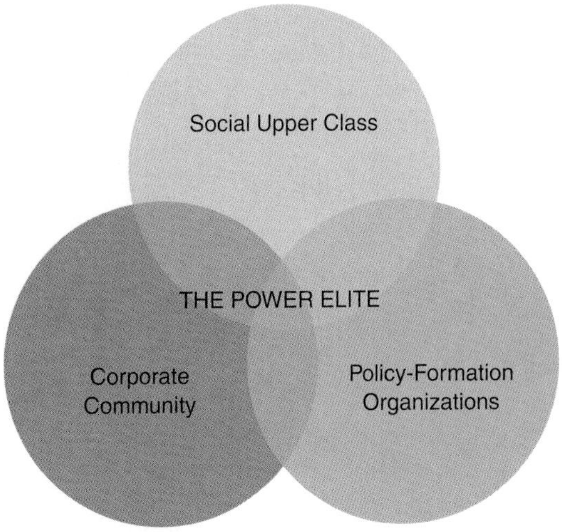

b. William Domhoff's model, 1998

community, liberal churches, and the university and arts communities (Zweigenhaft and Domhoff 1998).

Sociologists have come to accept the notion that a limited number of people exercise a vast amount of power. While the elite groups can be identified, their composition changes over time, as does the influence of particular groups. In the 1950s during the military build-up in the Cold War between Communist countries and Western democracies, the military was appropriately included in Mills's model as a major player. Since that time, the influence of the military has been in decline for several decades, reflecting Domhoff's model. However, the events of September 11, 2001, have rekindled the military's flame, and both the political influence and the economic power of the military industrial complex in the United States have been given new priority.

Pluralist Model

Several social scientists insist that power in Canada and other Western democracies is more widely shared than the elite models indicate. In their view, a pluralist model more accurately describes these political systems. According to the ***pluralist model,*** many conflicting groups within the community have access to government, so that no single group is dominant. Many argue that pluralism is the foundation of Canada's Multiculturalism Act of 1972, which requires Parliament to preserve and promote the distinct identity of Canadian ethnic minorities. In other words, it is the government's responsibility to see that members of minority groups have an equal place in Canadian society, including equal access to power.

Under the policy of multiculturalism, the government recognizes the right of each ethnic group to sustain the essential elements of its cultural heritage, and to protection from systemic discrimination based on that affiliation. However, the pluralist model suggests that these groups must also have the opportunity to play a significant role in making decisions. While the 1972 act entrenches that right for all Canadians, there are those who claim that the reality is quite different. Given that the membership of ethnic groups in Canada can range from several hundred to several million people, it is difficult to imagine a scenario in which all groups have equal influence. Nonetheless, the very diversity of the Canadian ethnic landscape means that minority voices can be heard.

Perhaps the best example of Canada's willingness to listen to minorities came when the government was studying the idea of legislating recognition of French Canadians to formally acknowledge their place in the larger society. Ottawa began the process in the mid-1960s by setting a royal commission to examine public attitudes toward the ideas of bilingualism and biculturalism. During that investigative process, first the Commission and then the politicians began to hear from other ethnic groups concerned about being ignored by the legislation. A delegation of community leaders from the Western provinces boarded a train and went to the national capital to make their case. History shows us that they were effective in influencing the government's agenda, and when the act was finally introduced, "biculturalism" had been replaced with "multiculturalism." The anecdote makes a substantial case for the efficacy of minority power in Canada, even in the era before we embraced multiculturalism in law.

However, while a balance of ethnic-based influence has arguably been achieved in Canada, there is little illusion about the overall imbalance in the distribution of power. The pluralist model has not escaped serious questioning. Domhoff (1978, 1998) reexamined studies of decision making and argued that the pluralists had failed to trace how local business and other elites prominent in decision making were part of a larger national ruling class. In addition, studies of community power can examine decision making only on issues that become part of the political agenda. This focus fails to address the possible power of elites to keep certain matters that threaten their dominance entirely *out* of the realm of government debate.

The face of the workplace is changing as more women and minorities make their appearance. Women are also showing up in the executive suites, as exemplified by Heather Reisman, President and CEO of Indigo.

Historically, pluralists have stressed ways in which large numbers of people could participate in or influence governmental decision making. As Box 13-2 suggests, new communications technologies like the Internet are increasing the opportunity to be heard, not just in advanced countries like Canada but in developing countries the world over. One common point of the elite and pluralist perspectives stands out, however: Power within the political system, even in the most ardent democracies, is unequally distributed. All citizens may be equal in theory, yet those high in the nation's power structure are "more equal." New communications technology may or may not change that distribution of power.

The Changing Economy

As advocates of the power elite model point out, the trend in capitalist societies has been toward concentration of ownership by giant corporations, especially *transnational* ones. p. 196 A transnational corporation is characterized by its lack of a specific nation-state anchor. For instance, while we may consider the Royal Bank as a quintessential Canadian company, its acquisitions in other parts of the world mean that it need not depend entirely on its Canadian operations. The potential influence of these huge conglomerates can be inferred from their size. A report by the Institute for Policy Studies based on 1999 data found that 51 of the planet's top economies belonged to corporations (Anderson and Cavanagh 2001). At the top of that group was the giant American retailer Wal-Mart, whose sales ranked it as the 14th-largest economic power in the world.

In the following sections, we will examine developments in the global economy that have interested sociologists: the changing face of the workforce, deindustrialization, the emergence of e-commerce, and the rise of a contingency (or temporary) workforce. As these trends show, any change in the economy inevitably has social and political implications and soon becomes a concern of policymakers.

The Face of the Workforce

The workforce in Canada is constantly changing. During the Second World War, when men were mobilized to fight abroad, women entered the workforce in large numbers. With significant changes to the Immigration Act in 1967, the face of Canadian immigration, and thus the workforce, changed dramatically. Then, with the implementation of multiculturalism in 1972 and the creation of the Charter of Rights ten years later, the opportunity for minorities to participate fully in the economic sector was firmly established. The active recruitment of women into the workplace is the subject of this chapter's social policy section.

While predictions are not always reliable, the predictions of women's increasing participation in the labour

Eye on the Media

13-2 Political Activism on the Internet

David Suzuki has for decades been the voice of Canadian environmental activism. Suzuki, through his television specials, lectures, and books, has brought the messages of ozone depletion and ocean degradation to millions. But in the 1990s, the foundation named after him concluded that these media were simply not keeping pace with the times, and the David Suzuki Foundation website (**www.davidsuzuki.org**) was established.

Not just in Canada, but in places like China, Mexico, Indonesia, Kosovo, and Malaysia, citizens are making themselves heard through *cyberactivism*—the use of the Internet for political purposes. In China, 10 000 members of the fast-growing Falun Gong religious sect surprised government officials with a mass rally organized on the web. (A similar incident took place in Canada in 2001 when thousands of protesters converged on a meeting of world leaders in Quebec City—the result of an e-mail campaign begun 11 months before the World Trade Organization meetings in Seattle in 1999.) In Kosovo, the staff of *Koha Ditore,* a dissident newspaper, took to the web after Serbian soldiers closed their office. And in Mexico, the revolutionary *Zapatista* movement gained support from an online campaign for self-rule in the state of Chiapas.

As these incidents illustrate, organizers find the web especially useful in circumventing the restrictive controls of authoritarian regimes. Websites can be established outside a country's borders, beyond the control of government officials yet still accessible to the country's citizens. What is more, government officials who would like to clamp down on such activities are constrained by their desire to reap the commercial benefits of the web. For example, Chinese officials have decided to advance information technology despite the challenges it poses to government control, according to Elizabeth Economy of the Council on Foreign Relations. The technology is simply too important to China's economic modernization for the government to suppress it. From a conflict theory perspective, then, the Internet seems to have the potential to level the playing field for opposition groups—or at least to minimize the ruling party's clout.

Not just in Canada, but in places like China, Mexico, Indonesia, Kosovo, and Malaysia, citizens are making themselves heard through cyberactivism.

Also growing in importance are borderless organizations that unite people of like mind from around the world. These are very tightly knit communities, notes Professor Juan Enriquez of Harvard University. Labour groups and environmental organizations like Greenpeace have become particularly adept at using e-mail to mobilize activists quickly, wherever they are needed. The result: a completely new kind of power structure, compared to the more familiar face-to-face approach of government lobbyists. "The new people with power are those with credibility and an e-mail list," says political consultant Jennifer Laszlo. "You have no idea who they are, where they are, what color they are" (Engardio 1999:145).

Let's Discuss

1. Have you ever used the Internet for protest purposes? Have you searched for sites that present an alternative view on such issues as the environment and globalization? What are the advantages and disadvantages of the Internet, from your point of view?
2. Are you familiar with some of the websites of dissident political organizations abroad? Describe what you have learned from them.

Sources: Crossette 1999; Engardio 1999; MacFarquhar 1999; Miller 1999; Owens and Palmer 2000; Van Slambrouck 1998, 1999b.

force have been borne out by historical trends. In 1929, only 4 percent of Canadian women worked outside the home. By the end of the century, that proportion had grown to 59.5 percent. In 1999, women made up 46 percent of the total labour force. It's possible that by 2015 the proportions of male and female workers may be the same. But women have not been the only historically marginalized group to make inroads into the paid labour force.

Two factors have had a significant impact on the participation of ethnic and racial minorities in the Canadian economy. The first, as already mentioned, was the changes to the immigration policies that provided non-white applicants equal access. The second has been the emergence of Canada's aboriginal peoples as independent players in the mainstream economy. An increasing demand for self-determination combined with initiatives such as the federal government's *Gathering Strength—Canada's Aboriginal Action Plan* in 1998 have resulted in more of the country's 800 000 First Nations people entering the workforce either as employees—often of band-owned enterprises—or as entrepreneurs.

The workforce more and more reflects the diversity of the population as ethnic minorities enter the labour force and immigrants and their children move from marginal jobs or employment in the informal economy to positions of greater visibility and responsibility. The impact of this changing labour force is not merely statistical. A more diverse workforce means that relationships between workers are more likely to cross gender, racial, and ethnic lines. Interactionists note that people will find themselves supervising and being supervised by people very different from themselves. In response to these changes, many businesses have instituted some type of cultural diversity training programs as of 2000 (Melia 2000).

pp. 191–92

Deindustrialization

What happens when a company decides it is more profitable to move its operations out of a long-established community to another part of the country or out of the country altogether? People lose jobs; stores lose customers; the local government's tax base declines and it cuts services. This devastating process has occurred again and again in the last decade or so.

The term ***deindustrialization*** refers to the systematic, widespread withdrawal of investment in basic aspects of productivity such as factories and plants. Giant corporations that deindustrialize are not necessarily refusing to invest in new economic opportunities. Rather, the targets and locations of investment change. Initially, deindustrialization in Canada began with a relocation of plants from the city cores to suburban industrial parks, during the 1950s and 1960s. The next step has been relocation from the suburban areas of Canada's industrial heartland in Southern Ontario to other parts of North America such as the southern United States or even Mexico. In extreme cases, some facilities have simply closed. In 1999, the small Ontario community of Hawkesbury lost its carpet factory after failing to compete in the global market. In British Columbia, resource-based towns like Tumbler Ridge have seen their primary employers shut down operations as a result of international competition. And in the Maritimes, major fish-processing facilities have shut their doors as stocks have diminished and costs climbed.

While deindustrialization often involves the relocation or closing of facilities, in some instances it takes the form of corporate restructuring, as companies seek to reduce costs in an effort to bolster shrinking profits. When such restructuring occurs, the impact on the bureaucratic hierarchy of formal organizations can be significant. A large corporation may choose to sell off or entirely abandon less productive divisions and eliminate layers of management viewed as unnecessary. Wages and salaries may be frozen and fringe benefits cut—all in the name of "restructuring." Increasing reliance on automation also spells the end of work as we have known it.

The term ***downsizing*** was introduced in 1987 to refer to reductions in the workforce. While the term tends to bring to mind images of corporate giants trimming their workforces to be more competitive in the global market, figures from Statistics Canada tell a different story. During the 1990s, 73 percent of jobs lost to the process alternatively known as "rationalization" and "right-sizing" have been in the public sector, most dramatically in the areas of health care, education, and consumer services (Statistics Canada 2000f).

Viewed from a conflict perspective, the unprecedented attention given to downsizing in the mid-1990s reflected sustained—some might even argue increasing—marginalization of the working class. Conflict theorists note that job loss, affecting factory workers in particular, has long been a feature of industrialization. But when large numbers of middle-class managers and other white-collar employees with substantial incomes began to be laid off, suddenly there was great concern in the media over downsizing. By mid-2000, the phenomenon of downsizing was even spreading to dot-com companies, the sector of the economy that flew high in the 1990s

When Canadian corporations deindustrialize at home, they often move their investments outside the country to take advantage of cheap labour, as in this telephone repair plant in Mexico.

(Richtel 2000; Safire 1996; R. Samuelson 1996a, 1996b). Not surprisingly, the impact of these layoffs has been, like the corporations that enforce them, transnational. As the growth and merger mania of the 1980s and 1990s created huge interconnected corporate entities, it also set the stage for their collapse to have massive consequences. The recent demise of the American energy giant Enron has had implications for employees and subcontractors and pensioners from Houston, where the company was based, to every corner of the free-market world, including Canada.

Trade unions are organizations that seek to improve the material status of their members, all of whom perform a similar job or work for a common employer. They constitute a significant part of the workforce in many industrial nations. In Canada, however, the majority of union members work for government. In 2000, 18.7 percent of those working for private industry were unionized, while 69.9 percent of those in the public sector belonged to a union. In the 1990s, labour unions and their members were somewhat reluctant to fight downsizing since they recognized that increased international competition caused plant closings. As a result, many union–management negotiations now deal less with preventing layoffs than with establishing retirement plans for existing workers, benefits for part-time workers, company commitment to retraining programs, and equitable severance arrangements (Clawson and Clawson 1999; S. Franklin 2000).

The social costs of deindustrialization and downsizing cannot be underestimated. Plant closings lead to substantial unemployment in a community, which can have a devastating impact on both the micro- and the macrolevel. On the microlevel, the unemployed person and his or her family must adjust to a loss of spending power. Both marital happiness and family cohesion may suffer as a result. Although many dismissed workers eventually reenter the paid labour force, they often must accept less desirable positions with lower salaries and fewer benefits. Unemployment and underemployment are tied into many of the social problems discussed throughout this textbook, among them the need for child care, the controversy over welfare, and the issue of protecting Canada's national health care program.

p. 192

pp. 91, 201

On the societal level, or macrolevel, the impact of a plant closing on a community can be as difficult as it is for an individual worker and his or her family. As noted earlier, the community will experience a significant loss of tax revenues, thereby straining its ability to support police and fire protection, schools, parks, and other public services. Moreover, rising unemployment in a community leads to a reduced demand for goods and services. Sales by retail firms and other businesses fall off, and this can lead to further layoffs.

The impact of deindustrialization is evident not only in Canada but also in Asia and western Europe. In an effort to remain competitive within a global economy, many European companies have laid off workers. French sociologist Loic Wacquant (1993) has studied urban rioting in the United States and Europe and suggests that most communities that are the scene of riots share a common sociological profile. They typically are former working-class communities that were sustained by factories that formed the heart of a manufacturing economy. As their countries' economies shifted to the service- and information-based economy of postindustrial society, the local factories closed, leaving these working-class communities behind. In Europe, right-wing politicians and political movements have exploited the difficulties of these communities by scapegoating immigrants (rather than deindustrialization) as the cause of a loss of jobs (Tagliabue 1996).

E-Commerce

Another development following close on the heels of deindustrialization is the emergence of e-commerce, as online businesses replace bricks-and-mortar establishments. ***E-commerce*** refers to the numerous ways that people with access to the Internet can do business from

their computer. Amazon.com, for example, began in 1995 as a supplier of book titles but soon became the prototype for online businesses, branching into selling a variety of merchandise, including toys and hardware equipment. By 2000 Amazon.com boasted 20 million customers in 160 countries. The growth of e-commerce means jobs in a new line of industry as well as growth for related industries, such as warehousing, packing, and shipping.

E-commerce has brought new social dynamics to the retail trade. Consider the impact on traditional retail outlets and on face-to-face interaction with local storeowners. Even established companies like Nike, The Bay, and Lee Valley Tools are establishing their own online "stores," bypassing the retail outlets that they have courted for years to reach customers in their homes or offices. Megamalls once replaced personal ties to stores for many shoppers; the growth of e-commerce with its "cybermalls" is just the latest change in the economy.

An accountant studies a ledger in an office. Increasing numbers of educated, white-collar professionals (such as accountants) have joined low-level "temp" workers in the contingency workforce.

Some observers note that e-commerce offers more opportunities to consumers in rural areas and to those with disabilities. To its critics, however, e-commerce signals more social isolation, more alienation, and greater disconnect for the poor and disadvantaged who are not a part of the new information technology (Amazon.com 2000; Drucker 1999; Hansell 1999; Stoughton and Walker 1999).

Internet consumerism, however, has not taken the marketplace by storm, as had been predicted in the late 1990s. Instead, many e-retailers have struggled to establish a demand for their service. Consumer concerns about security and value have prevented these and other companies from stimulating the anticipated demand. However, during the Christmas season of 2001, the e-marketplace was able to outperform its predictions as traditional malls faced fewer shoppers and traditional retailers faced shrinking profit margins.

The Contingency Workforce

In the past, the term "temp" typically conjured up images of a replacement receptionist or a worker covering for someone on vacation. However, in association with the deindustrialization and downsizing described above, a "contingency workforce," in which workers are hired only for as long as they are needed, has emerged in the countries with free-market capitalist economies, and we have witnessed the emergence of what has been referred to as the "just-in-time" workforce. The rationale behind this phenomenon is that workers, like inventory, should be brought on board only when and where they are needed. This practice has had a disproportionate impact on women, as reflected in figures that show they make up 70 percent of the part-time labour force but only 46 percent of the full-time group.

Unemployed workers and entrants to the paid labour force accept positions as temporary or part-time workers. Some do so for flexibility and control over their work time, but others accept these jobs because they are the only ones available. Young people are especially likely to fill temporary positions. Employers find it attractive and functional to shift toward a contingency workforce because it allows them to respond more quickly to workforce demands—as well as to hire employees without having to offer the fringe benefits that full-time employees enjoy. Across Canada, large and small companies have come to rely on part-time or temporary workers, most of whom work part-time involuntarily. Many of these workers feel the effects of deindustrialization and shifts in the global economy. They lost their full-time jobs when companies moved operations to developing nations (Cooper 1994; Francis 1999).

It is difficult to estimate the size of the contingency workforce in Canada. Heidi Hartmann of the American Institute for Women's Policy Research notes that there is no agreement among social scientists as to how to define a "contingent worker" or how many there are. However, in its tracking of Canadian employment patterns in 1999, Statistics Canada calculated that 18 percent of the workforce was employed something less than full-time, full-year. Of those, 73 percent said they worked part-time by choice (Statistics Canada 2000g).

During the 1970s and 1980s, temporary workers typically held low-skill positions at fast-food restaurants, telemarketing firms, and other service industries. Today, the contingent workforce is evident at virtually *all* skill levels and in *all* industries. Clerical "temps" handle word processing and filing duties, managers are hired on a short-term basis to reorganize departments, freelance writers prepare speeches for corporate executives, and blue-collar workers are employed for a few months when a factory receives an unusually high number of orders. A significant minority of temporary employees are contract workers who are being "rented" for specific periods of time by the companies that previously downsized them—and are now working at lower salary levels without benefits or job security (Kirk 1995; Uchitelle 1996).

Workers often blame forces outside their control—indeed, outside the country—for the problems they experience as a result of deindustrialization and the rise of a contingency workforce. The relocation of factories to other countries has unquestionably contributed to job loss in Canada. But there are growing indications that automation is substantially reducing the need for human labour in both manufacturing and service industries. By the year 2020, it is projected that less than 2 percent of the entire global labour force will be engaged in factory work. In Chapter 16, we will look at the role of technology in promoting social and economic change (Rifkin 1996).

In the struggles of part-time workers and the unemployed to make ends meet, we find government and the economy intertwined, as the government steps in with assistance, whether it be unemployment compensation, government-funded child care, or welfare. In the social policy section that follows, we examine the issue of gender equality, providing another example of the link between government and the economy.

SOCIAL POLICY AND THE ECONOMY

Gender Equality

The Issue

Prior to the emergence of the vocal and very visible contemporary women's movement of the 1960s, the rights of females in Canada were restricted by a set of laws and cultural perceptions that fostered the idea that women's contributions to the family and the broader society were less valuable than those of men. The following anecdote demonstrates just how extreme and entrenched that attitude was. In Saskatchewan, in the late 1950s, a husband and wife divorced after many years of marriage. The court assigned all of the couple's assets to the husband, reflecting the legal position that it was his income that paid for the property, vehicles, furniture, and other possessions. The court further ordered that a savings account, which the wife had accumulated over decades by carefully managing her housekeeping money, was also to be turned over to the husband. The wife, like other divorced women of her time, was left destitute.

In 1995, in the preamble to the Canadian government's policy initiative *Setting the Stage for the Next Century: The Federal Plan for Gender Equality*, Shiela Finestone, then the Secretary of State for the Status of Women, said:

> There is no question that women—and men—are living in a better Canada because of advances in gender equality. These advances have created change in the workplace, in public policy and public attitudes, and in our individual lives (Status of Women Canada 1995).

Finestone's introduction to the new federal policy reaffirmed Canada's commitment to changing the status of women within our society, first established in law in the Charter of Rights and Freedoms ten years earlier. ***Affirmative action*** refers to positive efforts to recruit minority group members or women for jobs, promotions, and educational opportunities. While government programs do not make specific references to affirmative action either in the 1995 Plan or in the Charter, the objectives of both these documents make it clear that there is a commitment to advancing women's full participation in Canadian society. In Canada, unlike the United States, programs designed to assist women in overcoming historical disadvantages focus on removing barriers rather than mandating how those barriers should be removed. Many people feel that affirmative action programs constitute reverse discrimination against qualified whites and males. Does government have a responsibility to make up for past discrimination? If so, how far should it take it?

The Setting

The struggle for gender equality in Canada did not spring fully formed from the protest movements of the 1960s, but rather was the product of an ongoing effort by thousands of women over many decades. Table 13-1 traces the advancement of women's rights in this country, and illustrates the long and frustrating road this process has followed.

Sociological Insights

Sociologists, depending on their theoretical perspective, have different views of the roles of various institutions in creating a gender-neutral society. As might be expected, feminist theorists question whether the pace and scope of the movement towards equality for women in Canada have been adequate. But even amongst this group, there is disagreement about which area of society should be the focus of our efforts.

Radical feminists see patriarchy as being at the core of women's oppression. They argue that in order for women to achieve full participation, society needs fundamental restructuring to eliminate patriarchal tradition. This requires much more than legislation. While Canadian law has gone a long way towards recognizing women's rights to property and self-determination, obstacles perpetuated by the culture remain in place in both the public and private spheres. Radical feminists point to underpaid wage work, sexual harassment and unpaid housework and child care as evidence that patriarchal oppression persists.

Marxist feminists, who align themselves with the conflict theory camp, view the capitalist system as the primary obstacle to women's rightful place as equal partners in society. These analysts provide evidence of the continuing wage disparity between men and women in Canada as proof that ours remains a gender-stratified society. Phenomena such as the glass ceiling discussed in Chapter 9 apparently still exist in the Canadian workplace, arbitrarily limiting advancement for women.

Of course, not all social theorists believe that gender inequality should be addressed through proactive measures such as affirmative action. Functionalists suggest that these types of interventions may have a negative effect on society by unsettling the natural balance created by tradition and precedent. For these sociologists, the slow and self-generating process of social evolution can be relied on, over time, to make changes that will be beneficial to the community as a whole.

Most sociologists though—and especially conflict theorists—view affirmative action as an attempt to reduce inequality embedded in the social structure by increasing opportunities of groups, such as women and visible minorities, that have been deprived of access in the past.

Policy Initiatives

Canada's commitment to gender equality extends to encompass its partnerships with other countries, particularly those to whom significant amounts of aid are provided. The Canadian International Development Agency has established a clear policy outlining its expectations with regards to the treatment of girls and women. Wielding economic influence, the agency has had some success, within the limitations imposed by recognizing cultural diversity and national autonomy, in convincing developing countries that progress in the 21st century must include full participation by women.

The agency's policy is intended to establish a gender-neutral political and economic environment that reflects equal status for men and women. It has done this by convincing participating states that the well-being of the country is tied inextricably to the well-being of all citizens.

The agency's policy is based on the following principles:

- Gender equality must be considered as an integral part of all CIDA policies, programs and projects.
- Achieving gender equality requires the recognition that every policy, program, and project affects women and men differently.
- Achieving gender equality does not mean that women become the same as men.
- Women's empowerment is central to achieving gender equality.
- Promoting the equal participation of women as agents of change in economic, social, and political processes is essential to achieving gender equality (Simpson 1999).

Given its positive profile on the global stage, Canada represents a model to be imitated by many underdeveloped nations. Using the leverage provided by its international relief and development arms, this country has a unique

Table 13-1 Progress of Women's Rights in Canada

1916	First provinces give women right to vote—Alberta, Saskatchewan, and Manitoba
1918	Women are given full federal right to vote
1920	Women are given right to be elected to Parliament
1921	First woman elected to the House of Commons
1928	Supreme Court of Canada decides that women are not "persons" and cannot be appointed to the Senate of Canada
1929	British Privy Council overturns Supreme Court decision
1930	First woman Senator
1952	First province enacts equal pay legislation—Ontario
1955	Restrictions on the employment of married women in the federal public service are removed
1956	Legislation is enacted guaranteeing equal pay for equal work within federal jurisdiction
1957	First woman Cabinet Minister
1961	Canadian Bill of Rights is passed
1977	Canadian Human Rights Act forbids discrimination on the basis of sex and ensures equal pay for work of equal value for women; Canadian Labour Code is similarly amended and provides for 17 weeks of maternity leave
1978	Canadian Labour Code is amended, eliminating pregnancy as a basis for lay-off or dismissal
1982	Canadian Charter of Rights and Freedoms, Section 28, is enacted—Charter guarantees apply equally to men and women
1983	Canadian Human Rights Act is amended to prohibit sexual harassment and to ban discrimination on the basis of pregnancy and family or marital status
1984	First woman Governor General
1984	Canadian Constitution is amended to affirm that Aboriginal and treaty rights are guaranteed equally to both men and women
1985	Section 15 of the Canadian Charter of Rights and Freedoms comes into effect, guaranteeing equality for all Canadians before and under law and equal protection and benefit of law
1985	Court Challenges Program expanded to address equality rights cases
1985	Indian Act is amended, restoring status and right to band membership to Indian women who had lost such status through marriage to a non-Indian
1986	Employment Equity Act is introduced, applicable to Crown corporations and federally regulated business, aimed at redressing historic and systemic discrimination of "larger group" populations
1993	Guidelines on women refugee claimants are instituted for the Immigration and Refugee Board
1994	Funding for equality test cases is reinstated as Charter Law Development Program
1995	Gender-based analysis of legislation and policies is adopted by the federal government

Source: Status of Women Canada 1995.

and important role to play in advocating the increased inclusion of women in those countries still striving to achieve economic and political stability.

Let's Discuss

1. Do you think it is more important for women to gain equality within the home or in the workplace? Why?
2. Do you think claims of reverse discrimination have any validity? What should be done about them?
3. If you could draft a law that would provide equality for women in Canadian society, what provisions would it include?

Chapter Resources

Summary

The ***economic system*** of a society has an important influence on social behaviour and on other social institutions. Each society must have a ***political system*** to establish procedures for the allocation of valued resources.

1. As the Industrial Revolution proceeded, a new form of social structure emerged: the ***industrial society.***
2. Economic systems of ***capitalism*** vary in the degree to which the government regulates private ownership and economic activity, but all emphasize the profit motive.
3. The basic objective of a ***socialist*** economic system is to eliminate economic exploitation and meet people's needs.
4. Marx believed that ***communism*** would naturally evolve out of the socialism stage.
5. There are three basic sources of ***power*** within any political system : ***coercion, influence,*** and ***authority.***
6. Max Weber identified three ideal types of authority: ***traditional, legal-rational,*** and ***charismatic.***
7. The principal institutions of ***political socialization*** in Canada are the family, schools, and the media.
8. Political participation makes government accountable to its citizens, but there is a great deal of apathy in both Canada and other countries.
9. Women are still underrepresented in office but are becoming more successful at winning elections to public office.
10. Sometimes people band together in ***interest groups*** to influence public policy.
11. Advocates of the ***elite model*** of the power structure of Canada see the country as being ruled by a small group of individuals who share common political and economic interests (a ***power elite***), whereas advocates of a ***pluralist model*** believe that power is more widely shared among conflicting groups.
12. The nature of the Canadian economy is changing. Sociologists are interested in the changing face of the workforce, the effects of ***deindustrialization,*** increased use of a contingency workforce, and the emergence of e-commerce.
13. The struggle for women's equality in Canada has been ongoing over the last century. Over the past 40 years there have been significant improvements in women's access to political and economic opportunities, partly due to ***affirmative action*** efforts, but the goal of a gender-neutral environment has not yet been achieved. Through its foreign aid and international relations policies and programs, Canada has begun to work for women's equality in other parts of the world.

Critical Thinking Questions

1. The plight of the Nexus generation outlined at the beginning of the chapter suggests that people the age of most university students are marginalized by the economic and political mainstream in Canada. Do you agree or disagree with this portrayal? Base your answer on the information and ideas contained in this chapter.
2. Who really holds power in the college or university you attend? Describe the distribution of power at your school, drawing on the elite and pluralist models where they are relevant.
3. Imagine that you have a summer job working for your local Member of the Legislative Assembly (MLA) or Member of the National Assembly (MNA). She has assigned you to work on a project to find solutions to the problem of youth participation in the democratic process in your province. How could you use what you have learned about sociology to conceptualize the problem? What type of research would you suggest to the project team?

Key Terms

Affirmative action Positive efforts to recruit minority group members or women for jobs, promotions, and educational opportunities. (page 341)

Authority Power that has been institutionalized and is recognized by the people over whom it is exercised. (326)

Charismatic authority Power made legitimate by a leader's exceptional personal or emotional appeal to his or her followers. (327)

Coercion The actual or threatened use of force to impose one's will on others. (326)

Communism As an ideal type, an economic system under which all property is communally owned and no social distinctions are made on the basis of people's ability to contribute to the economy. (325)

Deindustrialization The systematic, widespread withdrawal of investment in basic aspects of productivity such as factories and plants. (338)

Downsizing Reductions taken in a company's workforce as part of deindustrialization. (338)

E-commerce Numerous ways that people with access to the Internet can do business from their computer. (339)

Economic system The structures and processes through which goods and services are produced, distributed, and consumed. (323)

Elite model A view of society as controlled by a small group of individuals who share a common set of political and economic interests. (334)

Influence The exercise of power through a process of persuasion. (326)

Institutionalize To formalize within a social institution. (326)

Interest group A voluntary association of citizens who attempt to influence public policy. (332)

Laissez-faire A form of capitalism under which people compete freely, with minimal government intervention in the economy. (324)

Legal-rational authority Power made legitimate by law. (327)

Legitimization The process by which power is authorized by those people who may be subject to its use. (326)

Majority government A government in which one party controls more than half of the seats in a legislative house. (329)

Monopoly Control of a market by a single business firm. (324)

Oligopoly Control of the market by a small group of companies. (324)

Pluralist model A view of society in which many competing groups within the community have access to government so that no single group is dominant. (335)

Political action committee (PAC) A political committee established by an interest group—say, a national bank, corporation, trade association, or cooperative or membership association—to solicit contributions for candidates or political parties. (332)

Political socialization The process by which individuals acquire political attitudes and develop patterns of political behaviour. (328)

Political system The structures and processes used for implementing and achieving society's goals. (323)

Politics In Harold D. Lasswell's words, "who gets what, when, and how." (326)

Power The ability to exercise one's will over others. (326)

Power elite A small group of military, industrial, and government leaders who control the fate of the United States and every other major capitalistic country. (334)

Social democracy An economy that is for the most part dominated by private business operating within a political framework that is responsible for the redistribution of wealth. (325)

Socialism An economic system under which the means of production and distribution are collectively owned. (325)

Trade unions Organizations that seek to improve the material status of their members, all of whom perform a similar job or work for a common employer. (339)

Traditional authority Legitimate power conferred by custom and accepted practice. (327)

Additional Readings

Enloe, Cynthia. 1990. *Bananas, Beaches, and Bases: Making Feminist Sense of International Politics.* Berkeley: University of California Press. Enloe studied the lives of women on military bases and of diplomatic wives as part of her examination of the male-dominated agenda of international politics.

Gleick, James. 1999 *Faster: The Acceleration of Just About Everything.* New York: Pantheon Books. A journalistic look at the ever-increasing pace of life in the workplace and throughout the lives of people in industrial nations.

Molot, Maureen Appel, and Fen Osler Hampson, eds. 2000. *Canada among Nations, 2000: Vanishing Borders.* Toronto: Oxford University Press. The authors analyze the impact of the North American Free Trade Agreement as it has effectively removed the national barriers between Canada, the United States, and Mexico.

Norrie, Kenneth Harold, and Douglas Owram. 1996. *A History of the Canadian Economy.* 2d ed. Toronto: Harcourt Brace. A classic look at the emergence of the Canadian economic model, and how our continued dependence on staples—raw materials such as wood, ore, and grain—has left us in a peculiar position among developed countries.

Rogers, Jackie Krasas. 2000. *Temps: The Many Faces of the Changing Workplace.* Ithaca, NY: Cornell University Press. An examination of the growing use of temporary workers in both low- and high-skill jobs.

Internet Connection

www.mcgrawhill.ca/college/schaefer

For additional Internet exercises relating to voting and telecommuting, visit the Schaefer Online Learning Centre at ***http://www.mcgrawhill.ca/college/schaefer****. Please note that while the URLs listed were current at the time of printing, these sites often change—check the Online Learning Centre for updates.*

Max Weber's writings have been crucial in expanding sociologists' understanding of the workings of political institutions, government, and bureaucracies. In particular, his work on types of authority helps to frame the relationship of those in power to the people they lead. First, direct your web browser to an Internet search engine such as Lycos® (**http://www.lycos.com**) or Alta Vista (**http://www.altavista.com**). Second, think of a leader from politics, religion, or history that you always wanted to learn more about. If you need an idea, just flip through your textbook and you will find pictures and names of many such leaders. Search for that person's name and visit links dedicated to her or his life.

(a) Which person did you choose? Why did you select her or him?
(b) When did this person live? What group or nation did this person lead? What role has this person played in history?
(c) What type of authority did he or she have over followers? Was it traditional, legal-rational, or charismatic authority, or some combination? What reasons/examples can you give to support your choice?
(d) Did the person you studied ever use force to exert or maintain power over others? Did the person ever use influence? How so?
(e) What is your opinion of this leader in light of all you have learned?

CHAPTER

14 POPULATION, AGING, AND HEALTH

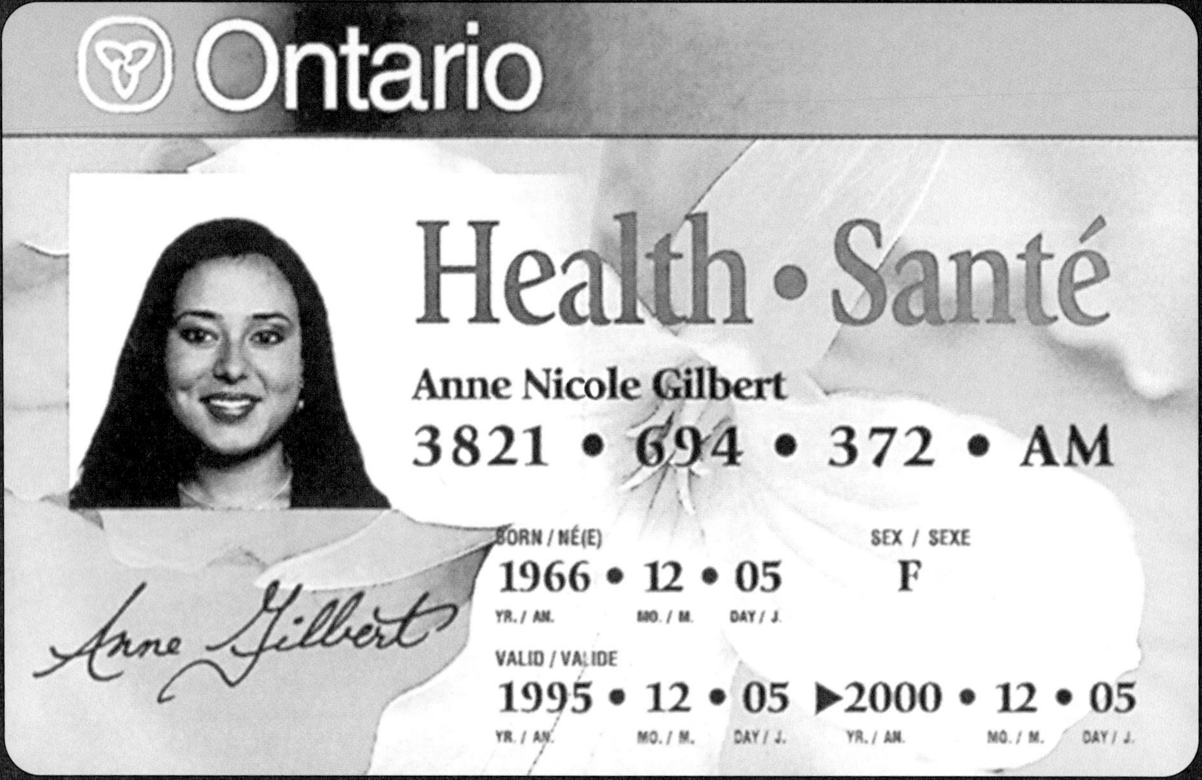

The condition of medicare has become a major concern for Canadians, with public debates and private discussions focusing on whether the present system requires restructuring or dismantling. The Ontario health card, necessary for health care in that province, can also be used in other provinces, illustrating the Canada Health Act's principle of portability.

Yet still I smoked. My teeth were yellow and my fingers brown. My clothes stank and so, I'm sure, did my breath. There were holes in my sweaters and scars on my furniture. My computer keyboard was regularly choked with ashes. My car looked and smelled as if there'd been an all-night poker game in the front seat. Once, sheltering a cigarette in my pocket (shades of Ridley), I set fire to a favourite windbreaker, and more than once, holding a phone to my ear, I caught the acrid smell of burning hair. In 1996, now in my sixties, I went into hospital for surgery to fix an abdominal aortic aneurysm. About four days into my recovery, a night nurse, the one who used to prowl the halls on in-line skates, asked if I'd like to get out of bed and go downstairs with her for a cigarette, joining that sorry gaggle of people outside every hospital who lean on their IVs, bare bums exposed to the winds, as they suck on the toxin that put them there in the first place. "Are you *kidding*?" I snorted. But my first day home, with the physical craving presumably under control, I pawed through my cupboards until I found a half-full package of stale Rothmans and lit up in the living room.

Why? I still can't answer. If anyone asked, and they did, all the time, I'd say I hated my habit. It's hard to duck the fact that I probably hated myself for being such a slave to it. *(Gzowski 2001:63–64)* ■

In this excerpt from his essay "How to Quit Smoking in Fifty Years or Less," Peter Gzowski describes how his addiction to tobacco dominated his life despite the fact he hated his cigarette-smoking habit. In 2002, Gzowski, the much-loved, Canadian, former radio-show host writer and literacy advocate, died from lung disease caused from years of smoking. Each year approximately 45 000 Canadians like Gzowski die from smoking-related diseases; tobacco causes one in six deaths worldwide. Sociologists take great interest in the topics of health and illness, examining patterns related to social class, race and ethnicity, gender, and sexual orientation.

The population explosion in all parts of the world is another social issue of great concern today. Sociologists who study population and fertility patterns have a key role in policymaking on these issues.

This chapter takes a sociological overview of certain aspects of population as well as the population-related issues of health, illness, and medicine as a social institution. We will begin with Thomas Robert Malthus's controversial analysis of population trends and Karl Marx's critical response to it. A brief overview of world population history follows. We'll pay particular attention to the current problem of overpopulation, and the prospects for and potential consequences of stable population growth in Canada and the United States.

In the second half of the chapter we will examine how functionalists, conflict theorists, interactionists, feminist, and labelling theorists look at health-related issues. Then we will study the distribution of diseases in a society by gender, social class, race and ethnicity, and age. We'll also look at the evolution of the health care system of Canada. Sociologists are interested in the roles that people play within the health care system and the organizations that deal with issues of health and sickness. Therefore, we will analyze the interactions among doctors, nurses, and patients; the role of government in providing health services; and alternatives to traditional health care. Finally, the social policy section will explore the issue of how to finance health care worldwide. ■

Demography: The Study of Population

The study of population issues engages the attention of both natural and social scientists. The biologist explores the nature of reproduction and casts light on factors that affect ***fertility***, the level of reproduction among women of childbearing age. The medical pathologist examines and analyzes trends in the causes of death. Geographers, historians, and psychologists also have distinctive contributions to make to our understanding of population. Sociologists, more than these other researchers, focus on the *social* factors that influence population rates and trends.

In their study of population issues, sociologists are keenly aware that various elements of population—such as fertility and *mortality* (the amount of death)—are profoundly affected by the norms, values, and social patterns of a society. Fertility is influenced by people's age of entry into sexual unions and by their use of contraception—both of which, in turn, reflect the social and religious values that guide a particular culture. Mortality is shaped by a nation's level of nutrition, acceptance of immunization, and provisions for sanitation, as well as its general commitment to health care and health education. Migration from one country to another can depend on marital and kinship ties, the relative degree of racial and religious tolerance in various societies, and people's evaluations of employment opportunities.

Demography is the scientific study of population. It draws on several components of population, including size, composition, and territorial distribution, to understand the social consequences of population (see Figure 14-1). Demographers study geographical variations and historical trends in their effort to develop population forecasts. They also analyze the structure of a population—the age, gender, race, and ethnicity of its members. A key figure in this type of analysis was Thomas Malthus.

Malthus's Thesis and Marx's Response

The Reverend Thomas Robert Malthus (1766–1834) was educated at Cambridge University and spent his life teaching history and political economy. He strongly criticized two major institutions of his time—the church and slavery—yet his most significant legacy for contemporary scholars is his still-controversial *Essays on the Principle of Population,* published in 1798.

Essentially, Malthus held that the world's population was growing more rapidly than the available food supply. Malthus argued that food supply increases in an arithmetic progression (1, 2, 3, 4, and so on), whereas population expands by a geometric progression (1, 2, 4, 8, and so on). According to his analysis, the gap between food

FIGURE 14-1

World Population, 2000

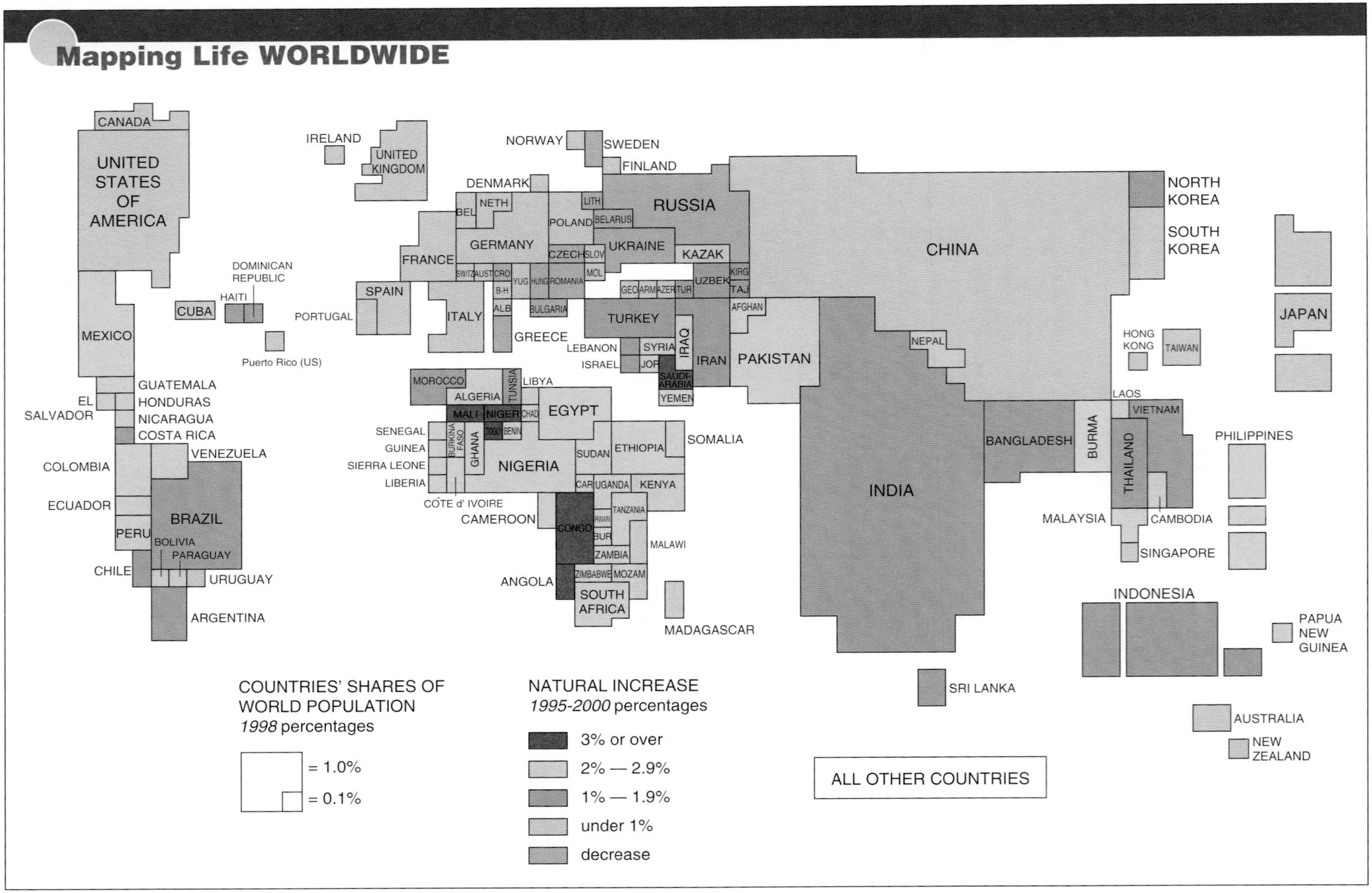

Sources: Smith 1999:14–15; population data from Haub and Cornelius 2000.

Based on an estimate of population data for 2000, this map of the world has been redrawn so that the size of each country is shown as proportional to its population rather than its geographic area. For example, note how India and China are represented on this map.

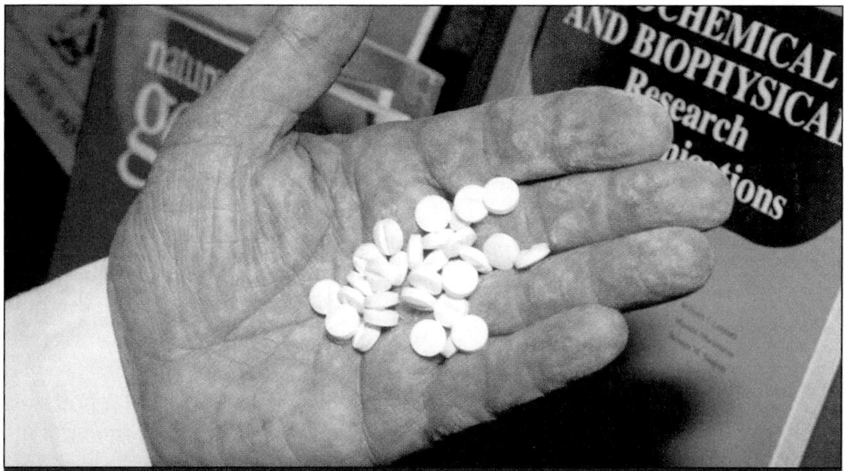

Fertility is influenced by the use of contraceptives, which is in turn affected by a population's social and religious values. In some provinces in Canada, the morning-after pill is available at pharmacies without a prescription.

supply and population will continue to grow over time. Even though the food supply will increase, it will not increase nearly enough to meet the needs of an expanding world population.

Malthus advocated population control to close the gap between rising population and food supply, yet he explicitly denounced artificial means of birth control because they were not sanctioned by religion. For Malthus, the appropriate way to control population was to postpone marriage. He argued that couples must take responsibility for the number of children they choose to bear; without such restraint, the world would face widespread hunger, poverty, and misery (Malthus et al. 1960, original edition 1824; Petersen 1979).

Karl Marx strongly criticized Malthus's views on population. Marx pointed to the nature of economic relations in Europe's industrial societies as the central problem. He could not accept the Malthusian notion that rising world population, rather than capitalism, was the cause of social ills. In Marx's opinion, there was no special relationship between world population figures and the supply of resources (including food). If society were well ordered, increases in population should lead to greater wealth, not to hunger and misery.

Of course, Marx did not believe that capitalism operated under these ideal conditions. He maintained that capitalism devoted its resources to the financing of buildings and tools rather than to more equitable distribution of food, housing, and other necessities of life. Marx's work is important to the study of population because he linked overpopulation to the unequal distribution of resources—a topic that will be taken up again later in this chapter. His concern with the writings of Malthus also testifies to the importance of population in political and economic affairs.

The insights of Malthus and Marx regarding population issues have come together in what is termed the *neo-Malthusian view.* Best exemplified by the work of Paul Ehrlich (1968; Ehrlich and Ehrlich 1990), author of *The Population Bomb,* neo-Malthusians agree with Malthus that world population growth is outstretching natural resources. However, in contrast to the British theorist, they insist that birth control measures are needed to regulate population increases. Neo-Malthusians have a Marxist flavour in their condemnation of developed nations that, despite their low birthrates, consume a disproportionately large share of world resources. While rather pessimistic about the future, these theorists stress that birth control and sensible use of resources are essential responses to rising world population (Tierney 1990; Weeks 1999; for a critique, see Commoner 1971).

The Reverend Thomas Robert Malthus suggested that the world's population was growing more rapidly than the available food supply.

Studying Population Today

The relative balance of births and deaths is no less important today than it was during the lifetime of Malthus and Marx. The suffering that Malthus spoke of is certainly a reality for many people of the world who are hungry and poor. Malnutrition remains the largest contributing factor to illness and death among children in the developing countries. Almost 18 percent of these children will die before age five—a rate over 11 times higher than in developed nations. Warfare and large-scale migration intensify problems of population and food supply. For example, strife in Bosnia, Iraq, and Sudan caused very uneven distribution of food supplies, leading to regional concerns about malnutrition and even starvation. Combatting world hunger may require reducing human births, dramatically increasing the world's food supply, or perhaps both at the same time. The study of population-related issues seems to be essential today (World Bank 2000C:277).

In Canada and most other countries, the census is the primary mechanism for collecting population information. A ***census*** is an enumeration or counting of a population. The Constitution Act of Canada requires that a census be held every ten years to determine representation in the House of Commons. The five-year census, which is mandated by Statistics Canada, provides the basis for government policies and decision making for social programs such as housing, health care, day care, and federal–provincial transfer payments (Flanders 2001). The questions asked on the census reflect changing social and political patterns that reveal the dynamic nature of Canadian society. Table 14-1 shows some of the milestones of the Canadian census that reflect changing values and attitudes on such matters as unpaid work, common-law and same-sex partnerships, and fertility of those labelled mentally ill. As well, the study of our population is supplemented by vital statistics; these records of births, deaths, marriages, and divorces are gathered through a registration system maintained by governments. In addition, Statistics Canada provides up-to-date information based on surveys of such topics as educational trends, the status of women, children, racial and ethnic minorities, agricultural crops, medical care, and time spent on leisure and recreational activities, to name only a few.

In administering a nationwide census and conducting other types of research, demographers employ many of the skills and techniques described in Chapter 2, including questionnaires, interviews, and sampling. The precision of population projections depends on the accuracy of a series of estimates that demographers must make. First, they must determine past population trends and establish a base population as of the date for which the forecast began. Next, birthrates and death rates must be established, along with estimates of future fluctuations. In making projections for a nation's population trends, demographers must consider migration as well, since a significant number of individuals may enter and leave a country.

Elements of Demography

Demographers communicate population facts with a language derived from the basic elements of human life—

Table 14-1 Selected Milestones in the History of the Census in Canada

1921:	The population questions no longer include those on "insanity and idiocy" and fertility.
1931:	Questions are added to gauge the extent and severity of unemployment, and to analyze its causes.
1956:	The first five-year national census is conducted. It is introduced to monitor the rapid economic growth and urbanization that took place during the postwar years.
1971:	The majority of respondents now complete the census questionnaire themselves, a process called *self-enumeration*. Under the new Statistics Act, it becomes a statutory requirement to hold censuses of population and of agriculture every five years.
1986:	The Census of Population contains a question on disability, which is also used to establish a sample of respondents for the first post-censal survey on activity limitation. Also for the first time, the Census of Agriculture asks a question on computer use for farm management.
1991:	For the first time, the census asks a question on common-law relationships.
1996:	A question on unpaid work is included in the census.
2001:	The definition of "common-law" is expanded to include both opposite-sex and same-sex partners. Also, the Census of Agriculture asks about production of certified organic products.

Source: Adapted from Flanders 2001:4.

birth and death. The ***birthrate*** (or, more specifically, the *crude birthrate*) is the number of live births per 1000 population in a given year. In 2000, for example, there were an estimated 11.4 live births per 1000 people in Canada. The birthrate provides information on the actual reproductive patterns of a society.

One way demography can project future growth in a society is to make use of the ***total fertility rate (TFR)***. The TFR is the average number of children born alive to any woman, assuming that she conforms to current fertility rates. The TFR estimated for Canada in 2000 was 1.6 live births per woman, as compared with over 3.66 births per woman in a developing country such as Kenya.

Mortality, like fertility, is measured in several different ways. The ***death rate*** (also known as the *crude death rate*) is the number of deaths per 1000 population in a given year. In 2000, Canada had an estimated death rate of 7.39 per 1000 population. The ***infant mortality rate*** is the number of deaths of infants under one year of age per 1000 live births in a given year. This particular measure serves as an important indicator of a society's level of health care; it reflects prenatal nutrition, delivery procedures, and infant screening measures. The infant mortality rate also functions as a useful indicator of future population growth, since those infants who survive to adulthood will contribute to further population increases.

Nations vary widely in the rate of death of newborn children. In 2000, the estimated infant mortality rate for Canada was 5 deaths per 1000 live births, whereas for the world as a whole it was an estimated 57 deaths per 1000 live births. At the same time, some nations have lower rates of infant mortality than Canada, including Switzerland, Japan, and Sweden (see Figure 14-4 on page 369).

A general measure of health used by demographers is ***life expectancy***, the median number of years a person can be expected to live under current mortality conditions. Usually the figure is reported as life expectancy *at birth*. At present, Japan reports a life expectancy at birth of 81 years, slightly higher than Canada's figure of 79 years. By contrast, life expectancy at birth is less than 45 in several developing nations, including Gambia.

The ***growth rate*** of a society is the difference between births and deaths, plus the difference between *immigrants* (those who enter a country to establish permanent residence) and *emigrants* (those who leave a country permanently) per 1000 population. For the world as a whole, the growth rate is simply the difference between births and deaths per 1000 population, since worldwide immigration and emigration must of necessity be equal. In 2000, Canada had an estimated growth rate of 1 percent, compared with an estimated 1.4 percent for the entire world (Haub and Cornelius 2000).

World Population Patterns

One important aspect of demographic work involves study of the history of population. But how is this possible? After all, official national censuses were relatively rare before 1850. Researchers interested in early population must turn to archeological remains of settlements, burial sites, baptismal and tax records, and oral history sources.

On October 13, 1999, in a maternity clinic in Sarajevo, Bosnia-Herzegovina, Helac Fatina gave birth to a son, who has been designated as the six billionth person on this planet. Yet until modern times, there were relatively few humans living in the world. One estimate placed the world population of a million years ago at only 125 000 people. As Table 14-2 indicates, the population has exploded in the last 200 years, and continues to accelerate rapidly (WHO 2000:3).

Demographic Transition

The phenomenal growth of world population in recent times can be accounted for by changing patterns of births

Table 14-2 Estimated Time for Each Successive Increase of 1 Billion People in World Population

Population Level	Time Taken to Reach New Population Level	Year of Attainment
First billion	Human history before 1800	1804
Second billion	123 years	1927
Third billion	33 years	1960
Fourth billion	14 years	1974
Fifth billion	13 years	1987
Sixth billion	12 years	1999
Seventh billion	14 years	2013
Eighth billion	15 years	2028
Ninth billion	16 years	2054

Note: Data for 2013 through 2054 are projections.
Source: United Nations Population Division 1999.

and deaths. Beginning in the late 1700s—and continuing until the middle 1900s—there was a gradual reduction in death rates in northern and western Europe. People were able to live longer because of advances in food production, sanitation, nutrition, and public health care. While death rates fell, birthrates remained high; as a result, there was unprecedented population growth during this period of European history. However, by the late 1800s, the birthrates of many European countries began to decline, and the rate of population growth also decreased (Bender and Smith 1997).

The changes in birthrates and death rates in 19th-century Europe serve as an example of demographic transition. Demographers use this term to describe an observed pattern in changing vital statistics. Specifically, ***demographic transition*** is the change from high birthrates and death rates to relatively low birthrates and death rates. This concept, which was introduced in the 1920s, is now widely used in the study of population trends.

As illustrated in Figure 14-2, demographic transition is typically viewed as a three-stage process:

1. *Pretransition stage:* high birthrates and death rates with little population growth.
2. *Transition stage:* declining death rates, primarily the result of reductions in infant deaths, along with high to medium fertility—resulting in significant population growth.
3. *Posttransition stage:* low birthrates and death rates with little population growth.

FIGURE 14-2

Demographic Transition

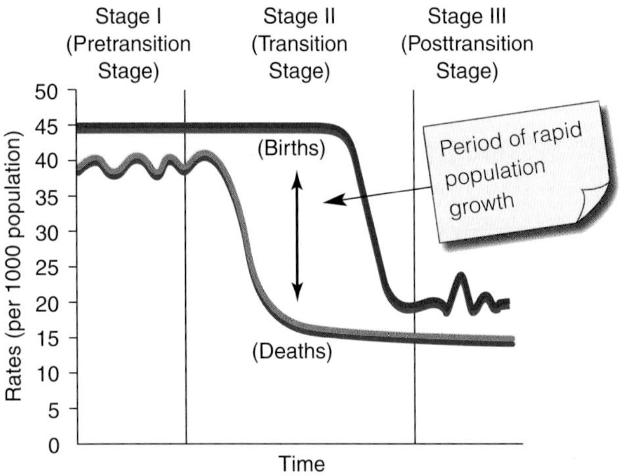

Demographers use the concept of *demographic transition* to describe changes in birthrates and death rates during stages of a nation's development. This graph shows the pattern that took place in presently developed nations. In the first stage, both birthrates and death rates were high, so that there was little population growth. In the second stage, the birthrate remained high while the death rate declined sharply, which led to rapid population growth. By the last stage, which many developing countries have yet to enter, the birthrate also declined, and there was again little population growth.

Demographic transition should be regarded not as a "law of population growth" but rather as a generalization of the population history of industrial nations. This concept helps us understand the growth problems faced by the world in the 1990s. About two thirds of the world's nations have yet to pass fully through the second stage of demographic transition. Even if such nations make dramatic advances in fertility control, their populations will nevertheless increase greatly because of the large base of people already at prime childbearing age.

The pattern of demographic transition varies from nation to nation. One particularly useful distinction is the contrast between the transition now occurring in developing nations—which include about two thirds of the world's population—and that which occurred over almost a century in more industrialized countries. Demographic transition in developing nations has involved a rapid decline in death rates without adjustments in birthrates.

Specifically, in the post–World War II period, the death rates of developing nations began a sharp decline. This revolution in "death control" was triggered by antibiotics, immunization, insecticides (such as DDT, used to strike at malaria-bearing mosquitoes), and largely successful campaigns against such fatal diseases as smallpox. Substantial medical and public health technology was imported almost overnight from more developed nations. As a result, the drop in death rates that had taken a century in Europe was telescoped into two decades in many developing countries.

Birthrates scarcely had time to adjust. Cultural beliefs about the proper size of families could not possibly change as quickly as the falling death rates. For centuries, couples had given birth to as many as eight or more children, knowing that perhaps only two or three would survive to adulthood. Consequently, whereas Europeans had had several generations to restrict their birthrates, peoples of developing nations needed to do the same in less than a lifetime. Many did not, as is evident from the astronomical "population explosion" that was already under way by the middle 1900s. Families were more willing to accept technological advances that prolonged life than to abandon fertility patterns that reflected centuries of tradition and religious training (Crenshaw et al. 2000; McFalls 1998).

The Population Explosion

Apart from war, rapid population growth has been perhaps the dominant international social problem of the

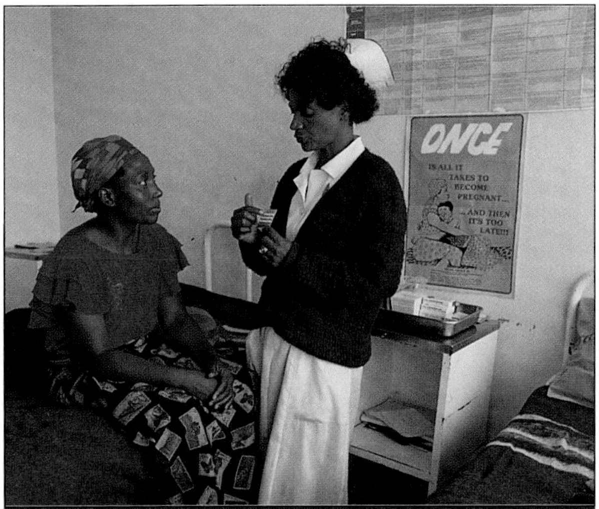

A nurse in Zambia, Africa, instructs a client in how to use birth control pills. Family planning clinics have helped to slow the population growth rate in developing countries.

past 30 years. Often this issue is referred to in emotional terms as the "population bomb" or the "population explosion." Such striking language is not surprising, given the staggering increases in world population during the last two centuries (refer to Table 14-2). The population of our planet rose from 1 billion around the year 1800 to 6.1 billion by 2000 (Haub and Cornelius 2000).

By the middle 1970s, demographers had observed a slight decline in the growth rate of many developing nations. These countries were still experiencing population increases, yet their *rates* of increase had declined as death rates could not go much lower and birthrates began to fall. It appears that family planning efforts have been instrumental in this demographic change. Beginning in the 1960s, governments in certain developing nations sponsored or supported campaigns to encourage family planning. For example, in good part as the result of government-sponsored birth control campaigns, Thailand's total fertility rate fell from 6.1 births per woman in 1970 to only 2.0 in 1998. And China's strict one-child policy resulted in a *negative* growth rate in some urban areas: see Box 14-1.

Through the efforts of many governments (among them Canada's) and private agencies (among them Planned Parenthood), the fertility rates of many developing countries have declined. However, some critics, reflecting a conflict orientation, have questioned why Canada and other industrialized nations are so enthusiastic about population control in the developing world. In line with Marx's response to Malthus, they argue that large families and even population growth are not the causes of hunger and misery. Rather, the unjust economic domination by the developed states of the world results in an unequal distribution of world resources and in widespread poverty in exploited developing nations (Fornos 1997).

Even if family planning efforts are successful in reducing fertility rates, the momentum toward growing world population is well established. The developing nations face the prospect of continued population growth, since a substantial proportion of their population is approaching childbearing years. This is evident in Figure 14-3 (on page 360), comparing the population pyramids of Kenya and Canada.

A ***population pyramid*** is a special type of bar chart that distributes the population by gender and age; it is generally used to illustrate the population structure of a society. As Figure 14-3 shows, a substantial portion of the population of Kenya consists of children under the age of 15, whose childbearing years are still to come. Thus, the built-in momentum for population growth is much greater in Kenya (and in many developing countries in other parts of the world) than in western Europe or Canada.

Consider, also, population data for India, which in 2000 surpassed 1 billion in population. Sometime between the years 2040 and 2050 India's population will surpass China's. The substantial momentum for growth built into India's age structure means that the nation will face a staggering increase in population in the coming decades—even if its birthrate declines sharply (J. Mann 2000).

Population growth is not a problem in all nations. A handful of countries are even adopting policies that *encourage* growth. One of them is Japan, where the total fertility rate has fallen sharply. Nevertheless, a global perspective underscores the serious consequences that could result from overall continued population growth.

A tragic new factor has emerged in the last 15 years that will restrict worldwide population growth: the spread of AIDS. Presently, about 31 million people around the world are infected with the HIV virus. According to the United Nations, there are at least 28 developing countries (with at least 1 million population) where the number of HIV-infected adults is very high. Of the 28 countries under study, 24 are in Africa; the others are India, Thailand, Brazil, and Haiti. AIDS has lowered the aggregate life expectancy of the 24 African countries by six years. The epidemic has its greatest mortality impact in otherwise relatively robust years of life. It is estimated that in the five most affected countries, mortality during 1985–2005 will increase by 160 percent in the age group 35–49 years (compared with 33 percent for the population in general). These are exactly the ages that can contribute most to a society's economic development (United Nations Population Division 1998a).

pp. 116–19

Sociology in the Global Community

14-1 Population Policy in China

In a residential district in Shanghai, a member of the local family planning committee knocks on the door of a childless couple. Why, she inquires, have they not started a family?

Such a question would have been unthinkable a generation earlier, when family planning officials, in an attempt to avoid a looming population explosion, sometimes resorted to sterilization to enforce the government rule of one child per family. Since then, Shanghai's birthrate has fallen so far it is now lower than the death rate—a situation that has left the city short of workers.

To remedy the shortage, the government has quietly begun to grant exceptions to the one-child policy to adults who are only children themselves. But the new leniency hasn't reversed the decline in the birthrate, as officials were hoping, for government propaganda stressing the economic benefits of fewer children seems to have changed the public's attitude toward childbearing. Stopping Chinese couples from having babies may be difficult, muses Jin Zuegong, a member of the Municipal Planning Commission in Shanghai, but persuading them to have babies may be even more difficult.

Not just Shanghai, but all of China is grappling with the unintended consequences of the draconian population control measures instituted in 1979. Nationwide, China's negative birthrate is straining its productive potential.

Not just Shanghai, but all of China is grappling with the unintended consequences of the draconian population control measures instituted in 1979.

Though employers hire rural workers to fill jobs left vacant in the shrinking cities, the relocation of rural workers only strains the economy of the farming areas they desert. And the negative birthrate is compromising the ability of the younger generation to provide for the old—a crucial function in a country that has no old-age pension system.

One of the most challenging results of the one-child policy is the so-called one-two-four household, in which a single child supports both parents and all four grandparents. That is, if a Chinese woman has only one child, that child may someday have to take care of as many as six old people, explains Dr. Li Liang. And if that child marries another only child, together they may need to support as many as 12 elderly.

Chinese families are beset, too, by the unforeseen results of their attempts to circumvent the one-child policy. In the past, in an effort to ensure that their one child would be a male capable of perpetuating the family line, many couples chose to abort female fetuses, or quietly allowed female infants to die of neglect. As a result, China's sex ratio at birth (the ratio of male newborns to female newborns) is now about 114 to 100—well above the normal rate of 105 or 106 to 100. This difference in birthrates translates into 1.7 million fewer female births per year than normal—and down the line, to many fewer childbearers than normal.

Sources: Cardarelli 1996; Chow and Zhao 1995; Farley 1997; Longman 1999; Reuters 1995; Riley 1996; Rosenthal 1999a; Wiseman 2000.

Fertility Patterns in Canada

During the last four decades, Canada and other industrial nations have passed through two different patterns of population growth—the first marked by high fertility and rapid growth (stage II in the theory of demographic transition), the second marked by declining fertility and little growth (stage III). Sociologists are keenly aware of the social impact of these fertility patterns.

The Baby Boom

The most recent period of high fertility in Canada has often been referred to as the *baby boom.* During World War II, large numbers of military personnel were separated from their spouses, but when they returned, the annual number of births began to rise dramatically. Still, the baby boom was not a return to the large families common in the 1800s.

It would be a mistake to attribute the baby boom solely to the return home of large numbers of soldiers. High wages and general prosperity during the postwar period encouraged many married couples to have children and purchase homes. In addition, several sociologists—as well as feminist author Betty Friedan (1963)—have noted that there were pervasive pressures on women during the 1950s to marry and become mothers and homemakers (Bouvier 1980).

The dramatic increase in births between 1946 and 1966 produced an age cohort in Canada that would make up approximately one third of the population. By the end of the boom in 1966, the age structure reflected a young, dependent population with a high percentage of Canadians under 15 years of age. As the baby boomers have

This Chinese billboard advocates the one-child family. Note that the single, happy child is a daughter—an attempt to counter the traditional preference for male children.

In 1995 the Chinese government, alarmed by the long-term implications of sex-selected abortion and infanticide, outlawed gender screening of unborn children except when medically necessary. The government also included measures aimed at improving the status of women in its new five-year plan. But those measures alone may not be enough to remedy the problem. Incentives, like improved educational opportunities for girls, may be needed to overcome the traditional preference for boys, and the resulting negative effect on the birthrate. Still, research suggests that parental attitudes toward female children may be changing. In one study, researchers found that China's one-child policy not only increased the value Chinese parents place on their children, but that the gender of the child made no difference in parents' estimation of that value.

Chinese women have a long way to go before they equal men in status, however. Like women everywhere, they have borne the brunt of the economic dislocation caused by recent market reforms and the redistribution of rural farmland. In privatized government factories, their need for maternity benefits and child care now limits their employment opportunities; on rural farms, they struggle to cope in their husbands' absence. The female suicide rate in rural China is now the highest in the world, surpassing the rate for males. Experts think this alarming statistic reflects a fundamental lack of self-esteem among rural Chinese women. The social patterns of centuries, unlike birthrates, cannot be changed in a generation.

Let's Discuss

1. Try to imagine life in a society that is so heavily populated, basic resources like food, water, and living space are running short. Does the government of such a society have a right to sterilize people who do not voluntarily limit the size of their families? Why or why not?
2. The Chinese government's one-child policy seems to have backfired. What other policies might have worked better? Explain why.

aged, society has responded to their needs in education, recreation, consumer preferences, housing, and so on. Now, a significant challenge to society is to meet the needs of aging baby boomers as they begin to require greater medical attention at a time when health care resources are severely strained.

Stable Population Growth

Although the total fertility rate of Canada has remained low in the last two decades, the nation continues to grow in size because of two factors: the momentum built into our age structure by the postwar population boom, and immigration. The 2001 census revealed that Canada's fertility rate was 1.5 children, below the 2.1 children needed to sustain the population (Armstrong 2002). Despite low levels of fertility, Canada's population grew 4 percent between 1996 and 2001. Because of the upsurge of births beginning in the late 1940s—in 1956 the fertility rate in Canada was 4 children per woman—there were more people in their childbearing years than in older age groups (where most deaths occur). This growth of population represented a demographic "echo" of the baby boom generation, many of whom are now parents. Based on the 2001 rate of population growth, beginning as soon as 2011 Canada will stop growing (Armstrong 2002). This prediction is based upon current fertility rates and assumes that immigration rates will remain stable.

Despite these trends, in the 1980s and early 1990s, some analysts projected that there would be relatively low fertility levels and moderate net migration over the coming decades. As a result, it seemed possible that Canada might reach ***zero population growth (ZPG).*** ZPG is the state of a population in which the number of births

FIGURE 14-3

Population Structures of Kenya and Canada, 2000

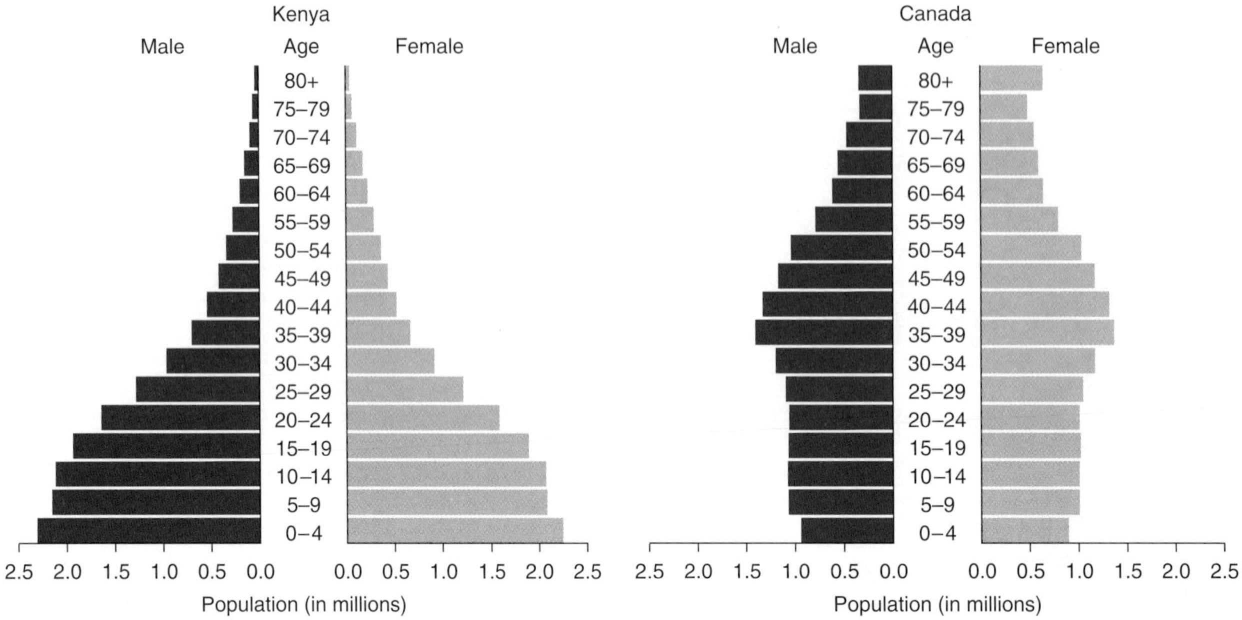

Source: Bureau of the Census 2002.

plus immigrants equals the number of deaths plus emigrants. Thirty countries, most of them in Europe, are now at or approaching ZPG. In the recent past, although some nations have achieved ZPG, it has been relatively short-lived. However, given the current international concern over world population, more nations may attempt to maintain ZPG in the early 21st century (Kent 1999; McFalls 1998; McFalls et al. 1984; Population Reference Bureau 1978).

What would a society with stable population growth be like? In demographic terms, it would be quite different from the Canada of the 1990s. There would be relatively equal numbers of people in each age group, and the median age of the population would be higher. Based on 2001 census data, by 2035 the percentage of Canadians 65 and older will double to 25 percent from the current 12 percent (Armstrong 2002). As a result, the population pyramid of Canada would look more like a rectangle.

There would also be a much larger proportion of older people, especially age 75 and over. They would place a greater demand on the nation's social service programs and health care institutions. On a more positive note, the economy would be less volatile under ZPG, since the number of entrants into the paid labour force would remain stable. ZPG would also lead to changes in family life. With fertility rates declining, women would devote fewer years to child rearing and to the social roles of motherhood; the proportion of married women entering the labour force would continue to rise (Spengler 1978; Weeks 1999).

According to the latest United States Census Bureau projections, however, that country is *not* moving toward ZPG. Instead, the nation's population is growing faster than was expected. Previous projections indicated that the American population would stabilize between 290 and 300 million by the middle of the next century, but demographers now believe that by 2050, the population of the United States will reach 391 million.

In contrast, for the first time in 100 years Canada is growing more slowly than the United States, whose growth rate was 5.4 percent between 1995 and 2000 (Armstrong 2002). Canada's rate of growth remains ahead of countries such as Japan and Germany and behind countries such as Mexico, whose population grew 8.5 percent between 1995 and 2000.

In Canada over the next five to fifteen years, it is expected that, due to low or non-existent rates of growth and an older population, labour shortages will occur. Occupations that are likely to be in demand include skilled and technical trades workers, teachers, health care workers, information technology experts, and academics (Armstrong 2002). As you can see, population growth owes much to the age structure of a given region or country. In the next part of this chapter, we will look at aging from a sociological perspective.

Aging and Society

The meanings of youth and old age are socially constructed by the society in which we live. Older Sherpas, living in Nepal, value their independence and prefer not to live with their children. Among the Fulani of Africa, however, older men and women move to the edge of the family homestead. Since this is where people are buried, the elderly sleep over their own graves, for they are already viewed as socially dead. Like gender stratification, age stratification varies from culture to culture. One society may treat older people with great reverence, while another sees them as unproductive and "difficult" (M. C. Goldstein and Beall 1981; Stenning 1958; Tonkinson 1978).

It is understandable that all societies have some system of age stratification and associate certain social roles with distinct periods in one's life (see Box 14-2). Some of this age differentiation seems inevitable; it would make little sense to send young children off to war or to expect most older citizens to handle physically demanding tasks such as loading goods at shipyards. However, as is the case of the social construction of gender, age stratification in North America goes far beyond the physical constraints of human beings at different ages.

This elderly woman in the central region of China is honoured among her people for her age. Older people in many other cultures in which youth is prized are not granted the same honour.

"Being old" is a master status that commonly overshadows all others in our society. The insights of labelling theory help us analyze the consequences of aging. Once people are labelled "old," this designation has a major impact on how others perceive them and even on how they view themselves. Negative stereotypes of the elderly contribute to their position as a minority group subject to discrimination, as we'll see later in the chapter.

p. 160

The model of five basic properties of a minority or subordinate group (introduced in Chapter 9) can be applied to older people in Canada to clarify their subordinate status:

pp. 209–10

1. The elderly experience unequal treatment in employment and may face prejudice and discrimination.
2. The elderly share physical characteristics that distinguish them from younger people. In addition, their cultural preferences and leisure-time activities often differ from those of the rest of society.
3. Membership in this disadvantaged group is involuntary.
4. Older people have a strong sense of group solidarity, as is reflected in the growth of senior citizens' centres, retirement communities, and advocacy organizations.
5. Older people generally are married to others of comparable age.

There is one crucial difference between older people and other subordinate groups, such as racial and ethnic minorities or women: *All* of us who live long enough will eventually assume the ascribed status of being an older person (M. Barron 1953; J. Levin and Levin 1980; Wagley and Harris 1958).

Explaining the Aging Process

Aging is one important aspect of socialization—the lifelong process through which an individual learns the cultural norms and values of a particular society. There are no clear-cut definitions for different periods of the aging cycle in Canada. *Old age* has typically been regarded as beginning at 65, which corresponds to the retirement age for many workers, but not everyone in our society accepts this definition. With life expectancy being extended, writers are beginning to refer to people in their 60s as the "young old" to distinguish them from those in their 80s and beyond (the "old old").

The particular problems of the elderly have become the focus for a specialized area of research and inquiry known as gerontology. ***Gerontology*** is the scientific study of the sociological and psychological aspects of aging and the problems of the aged. It originally developed in the 1930s, as an increasing number of social scientists became aware of the plight of the elderly.

Sociology in the Global Community

14-2 Aging Worldwide: Issues and Consequences

An electric water kettle is wired so that people in another location can determine if it has been used in the previous 24 hours. This may seem a zany bit of modern technology, but it symbolizes a change taking place around the globe—the growing needs of an aging population. Welfare Network Ikebukuro Honcho has installed these wired hot pots in Japan so that volunteers can monitor if the elderly have used the devices to prepare their morning tea. An unused pot initiates contacts to see if the older person needs help. This technological monitoring system is an indication of the tremendous growth of Japan's elderly population and, of particular social significance, the increasing numbers who live *alone*.

Around the world, there are more than 419 million people aged 65 or over; they represent about 7 percent of the world's population. In an important sense, the aging of the world's population represents a major success story that has unfolded during the later stages of the 20th century. Through the efforts of both national governments and international agencies, many societies have drastically reduced the incidence of diseases and their rates of death. Consequently, these nations—especially the industrialized countries of Europe and North America—have increasingly higher proportions of older members.

The overall population of Europe is older than that of any other continent. As the proportion of older people in Europe continues to rise, many governments that have long prided themselves on their social welfare programs are examining ways to shift a larger share of the costs of caring for the elderly to the private sector and charities.

An unused pot initiates contacts to see if the older person needs help.

Germany and France have instituted or are weighing plans to raise the age at which retirees will qualify for pensions.

In most developing countries, people over 60 are likely to be in poorer health than their counterparts in industrialized nations. Yet few of these nations are in a position to offer extensive financial support to the elderly. Ironically, modernization in the developing world, while bringing with it many social and economic advances, has undercut the traditionally high status of the elderly. In many cultures, the earning power of younger adults now exceeds that of older family members.

In 1996, the United Nations co-sponsored an international conference that examined social and economic policies dealing with the "Oldest Old"—those people age 80 and over. This rapidly increasing group deserves special attention. First, the oldest old in both industrialized and developing countries will probably have to depend for their security on a declining proportion of the population that is of working age. Second, in their search for support systems from either family or government, the oldest old may be forced to migrate, which will affect the immigration policies of many nations. Finally, the needs of the oldest old may intensify the pressures on their children (older workers) to postpone retirement for 5 or 10 additional years.

Let's Discuss

1. For an older person, how might life in Pakistan differ from life in France?
2. Do you know an aged person who lives alone? What arrangements have been made (or should be made) for care in case of emergency?

Sources: Crossette 1996a; Hani 1998; Haub and Cornelius 1999; Longworth 1996; M. Specter 1998a; Strom 2000a.

Gerontologists rely heavily on sociological principles and theories to explain the impact of aging on the individual and society. They also draw on the disciplines of psychology, anthropology, physical education, counselling, and medicine in their study of the aging process. Two influential views of aging—disengagement theory and activity theory—can be best understood in terms of the sociological perspectives of functionalism and interactionism, respectively. The conflict and feminist perspectives also contribute to our sociological understanding of aging.

Functionalist Approach: Disengagement Theory

Elaine Cumming and William Henry (1961) introduced ***disengagement theory*** to explain the impact of aging during one's life course. This theory, based on a study of elderly people in good health and relatively comfortable economic circumstances, contends that society and the aging individual mutually sever many of their relationships. In keeping with the functionalist perspective, disengagement theory emphasizes that passing social roles on from one generation to another ensures social stability.

According to this theory, the approach of death forces people to drop most of their social roles—including those of worker, volunteer, spouse, hobby enthusiast, and even reader. Younger members of society then take on these functions. The aging person, it is held, withdraws into an increasing state of inactivity while preparing for death. At the same time, society withdraws from the elderly by segregating them residentially (retirement homes and communities), educationally (programs designed solely for senior citizens), and recreationally (senior citizens' social centres). Implicit in disengagement theory is the view that society should *help* older people to withdraw from their accustomed social roles.

Since it was first outlined more than three decades ago, disengagement theory has generated considerable controversy. Some gerontologists have objected to the implication that older people want to be ignored and "put away"—and even more to the idea that they should be encouraged to withdraw from meaningful social roles. Critics of disengagement theory insist that society *forces* the elderly into an involuntary and painful withdrawal from the paid labour force and from meaningful social relationships. Rather than voluntarily seeking to disengage, older employees find themselves pushed out of their jobs—in many instances, even before they are entitled to maximum retirement benefits (Boaz 1987).

Although functionalist in its approach, disengagement theory ignores the fact that postretirement employment has been *increasing* in recent decades. Some employees move into a "bridge job"—employment that bridges the period between the end of a person's career and his or her retirement. Unfortunately, the elderly can easily be victimized in such "bridge jobs." Psychologist Kathleen Christensen (1990), warning of "bridges over troubled water," emphasizes that older employees do not want to end their working days as minimum-wage jobholders engaged in activities unrelated to their career jobs (Doeringer 1990; Hayward et al. 1987).

Interactionist Approach: Activity Theory

Often seen as an opposing approach to disengagement theory, ***activity theory*** argues that the elderly person who remains active and socially involved will be best adjusted. Proponents of this perspective acknowledge that a 70-year-old person may not have the ability or desire to perform various social roles that he or she had at age 40. Yet they contend that old people have essentially the same need for social interaction as any other group.

The improved health of older people—sometimes overlooked by social scientists—has strengthened the arguments of activity theorists. Illness and chronic disease are no longer quite the scourge of the elderly that they once were. The recent emphasis on fitness, the availability of better medical care, greater control of infectious diseases, and the reduction of fatal strokes and heart attacks have combined to mitigate the traumas of growing old. Accumulating medical research also points to the importance of remaining socially involved. Among those who decline in their mental capacities later in life, deterioration is most rapid in old people who withdraw from social relationships and activities (Liao et al. 2000; National Institute on Aging 1999b).

The Days Inn motel chain hires many retirees to work full- or part-time as reservationists. *Activity theory* argues that the elderly person who remains active will be best adjusted.

Admittedly, many activities open to the elderly involve unpaid labour, for which younger adults may receive salaries. Such unpaid workers include hospital volunteers (versus aides and orderlies), drivers for charitable organizations (versus chauffeurs), tutors (as opposed to teachers), and craftspeople for charity bazaars (as opposed to carpenters and dressmakers). However, some companies have recently initiated programs to hire retirees for full-time or part-time work. For example, about 130 of the 600 reservationists at the Days Inn motel chain are over 60 years of age.

Disengagement theory suggests that older people find satisfaction in withdrawal from society. Functionally speaking, they conveniently recede into the background and allow the next generation to take over. Proponents of activity theory view such withdrawal as harmful for both the elderly and society and focus on the potential contributions of older people to the maintenance of society. In their opinion, aging citizens will feel satisfied only when they can be useful and productive in society's terms—primarily by working for wages (Civic Ventures 1999; Dowd 1980; Quadagno 1999).

The Conflict Approach

Conflict theorists have criticized both disengagement theory and activity theory for failing to consider the impact of social structure on patterns of aging. Neither approach, they say, attempts to question why social interaction "must" change or decrease in old age. In addition, these perspectives, in contrast to the conflict perspective, often ignore the impact of social class on the lives of the elderly.

The privileged position of the upper class generally leads to better health and vigour and to a lower likelihood of dependency in old age. Affluence cannot forestall aging indefinitely, but it can soften the economic hardships faced in later years. Although pension plans, retirement packages, and insurance benefits may be developed to assist older people, those whose wealth allows them access to investment funds can generate the greatest income for their later years.

By contrast, working-class jobs often carry greater hazards to health and a greater risk of disability; aging will be particularly difficult for those who suffer job-related injuries or illnesses. Working-class people also depend more heavily on government and private pension programs. During inflationary times, their relatively fixed incomes from these sources barely keep pace with escalating costs of food, housing, utilities, and other necessities (Atchley 1985).

Conflict theorists have noted that the transition from agricultural economies to industrialization and capitalism has not always been beneficial for the elderly. As a society's production methods change, the traditionally valued role of older people within the economy tends to erode. Their wisdom is no longer relevant.

According to the conflict approach, the treatment of older people in Canada reflects the many divisions in our society. The low status of older people is seen in prejudice and discrimination against them, age segregation, and unfair job practices—none of which is directly addressed by either disengagement or activity theory.

Feminist Approaches

Feminist frameworks view aging in women from a variety of perspectives. However, feminist researchers have frequently challenged two biases in the study of women's aging. They are 1) an androcentricity in the discussion of the life course (assuming that generalizations on the male life course can be applied to women) and 2) a lack of diversity in identifying the stages and central issues that mark women's lives (Jones et al. 1990). In sociological research in previous decades, women's aging was seen almost exclusively in the context of marriage and family development (Nelson and Robinson 1999). This perspective, to a large degree, implies women's biological determinism; that is, that their life course is largely shaped by reproduction and nurturing of children. Moreover, studies on family life often contain an *ageist* bias; they adopt the perspective of middle-aged adults while regarding the aged as passive members of families (Eichler 2001). This bias also results in a failure to recognize that aging family members, particularly women, not only receive care but also give care to the younger members. Thus, they are not solely dependent, but are interdependent members of the family (Connidis 1989).

Perhaps most importantly, feminist perspectives have drawn attention to how aging impacts women of diverse backgrounds and characteristics. Aging does not manifest itself in all women in a universal, uniform manner, but rather intersects with class, race and ethnicity, and sexual orientation to produce diverse patterns and conditions.

The four perspectives considered here take different views of the elderly. Functionalists portray them as socially isolated with reduced social roles; interactionists see older people as involved in new networks of people in a change of social roles; conflict theorists regard older people as victimized by social structure, with their social roles relatively unchanged but devalued; and feminist perspectives have challenged the androcentricity and biological determinism implicit in many explanations of women's aging. Feminist perspectives also draw attention to how aging intersects with class, race and ethnicity, and sexual orientation. Table 14-3 summarizes these perspectives.

An Aging Canadian Population

As an index of aging, the United Nations uses the proportion of individuals 65 years of age and older to classify a population as "young," "mature," or "aged" (McVey and Kalbach 1995). A population is "young" if its proportion of older adults is under 4 percent; it is considered "mature" if its proportion of those 65 years of age and older is between 4 and 8 percent; and it is considered "aged" if this age group makes up 8 percent or more (McVey and Kalbach 1995). Canada became an "aged" population according to census data by 1971, when 8.1 percent of Canadians were 65 years of age and older. By 2001, 13 percent of the population was 65 years of age and older, following a steady increase of the proportion of this group in the total population (Statistics Canada 2002c). According to Health Canada (2000), by 2016, approximately 20 percent of our population will be in this age group.

National averages of aging, however, mask great diversity within Canada as it relates to such factors as

Table 14-3 Theories of Aging

Sociological Perspective	View of Aging	Social Roles	Portrayal of Elderly
Functionalist	Disengagement	Reduced	Socially isolated
Interactionist	Activity	Changed	Involved in new networks
Conflict	Competition	Relatively unchanged	Victimized, organized to confront victimization
Feminist	Challenges androcentric bias and assumptions of homogeneity	Socially constructed, diverse according to class, race and ethnicity, sexual orientation	Caught in a double-standard, men gain status and women lose status

region, gender, and race and ethnicity. There is a vast variation among regions in the percentage of the older age group, resulting in some regions being classified as "aged" populations while others are considered "young." Saskatchewan, for example, has the oldest population, with 14.1 percent of its population 65 years of age or older, while Yukon Territory and the Northwest Territories have the youngest population, with only 3.2 percent of their residents 65 years of age or older. Although the overall trend in Canada is towards the aging of the population, regional responses in the form of specialized housing, health care, caregiving services, and other social services may vary.

Gender differences sharply punctuate overall rates of aging in Canadian society. The proportion of older women in Canada has been increasing steadily since 1961. Given women's greater life expectancy, they constitute a disproportionate number of the aged. Due to women's lower average incomes and overall financial security, they are more likely to experience poverty than their male counterparts. The feminization of poverty, then, is accentuated by an aging population of which women make up a disproportionately high number. While some may view their greater life expectancy as a positive gain, for many women, particularly immigrants, women of colour, First Nations women, and those of lower social class, living longer means an even greater chance of living in poverty. First Nations men and women, as will be discussed in the next section on health, are more likely to suffer from poor health and have lower life expectancies due to the prevailing conditions of poverty in their lives.

Ageism

It "knows no one century, nor culture, and is not likely to go away any time soon." This is how physician Robert Butler (1990:178) described prejudice and discrimination against the elderly, which he called ***ageism.*** Ageism reflects a deep uneasiness among young and middle-aged people about growing old. For many, old age symbolizes disease, disability, and death; seeing the elderly serves as a reminder that *they* may someday become old and infirm. The notion of ageism was popularized by Maggie Kuhn, a senior citizen who took up the cause of elderly rights after

This First Nations woman carries a triple burden: she is female in a society that favours male, elderly in a society that values youth, and a minority member in a society that favours the dominant cultures.

she was forced to retire from her position at the United Presbyterian Church. Kuhn formed the Gray Panthers in 1971, a national organization dedicated to the fight against age discrimination (R. Thomas 1995).

With ageism all too common in North America, it is hardly surprising that older people are barely visible on television. A content analysis of 1446 American fictional television characters in the early 1990s revealed that only 2 percent were age 65 and over—even though this age group accounted for about 13 percent of the nation's population. A second study found older women particularly underrepresented on television (Robinson and Skill 1993; Vernon et al. 1990).

Feminist perspectives have drawn attention to the social construction of gender as it relates to ageism in North American society. While men's aging is seen as a sign of wisdom and experience, women's aging is seen as a sign of decline and diminishing status. Standards of beauty in our society are based on women's youth and sexual attractiveness and are often narrowly defined and frequently impossible to achieve (Abu-Laban and McDaniel 1995). Aging women are therefore seen as a departure from our culture's norms of physical beauty and sexual attractiveness. The culture, through messages transmitted by mass media, encourages us to "steal beauty back from the ravages of time" (Nelson and Robinson 1999:464). Thus, a multibillion-dollar beauty industry of cosmetics, fashion, fitness, and cosmetic surgery is flourishing (Wolf 1991) among an aging population in the midst of an anti-aging culture.

A young woman checks her weight on the bathroom scale. In North America, an intense fear of becoming obese causes some young women to develop a culture-bound syndrome known as *anorexia nervosa.*

Sociological Perspectives on Health and Illness

From a sociological point of view, social factors contribute to the evaluation of a person as "healthy" or "sick." How, then, can we define health? We can imagine a continuum with health on one end and death on the other. In the preamble to its 1946 constitution, the World Health Organization defined ***health*** as a "state of complete physical, mental, and social well-being, and not merely the absence of disease and infirmity" (Leavell and Clark 1965:14). With this definition in mind, the "healthy" end of our continuum represents an ideal rather than a precise condition. Along the continuum, people define themselves as "healthy" or "sick" on the basis of criteria established by each individual, relatives, friends, coworkers, and medical practitioners. Because health is relative, we can view it in a social context and consider how it varies in different situations or cultures (Twaddle 1974; Wolinsky 1980).

Why is it that you may consider yourself sick or well when others do not agree? Who controls definitions of health and illness in our society, and for what ends? What are the consequences of viewing yourself (or being viewed) as ill or disabled? Drawing on five sociological perspectives—functionalism, conflict theory, interactionism, labelling theory, and feminist theories—we can gain greater insight into the social context shaping definitions of health and treatment of illness.

Functionalist Approach

Illness entails at least a temporary disruption in a person's social interactions both at work and at home. Consequently, from a functionalist perspective, "being sick" must be controlled so that not too many people are released from their societal responsibilities at any one time. Functionalists contend that an overly broad definition of illness would disrupt the workings of a society.

"Sickness" requires that one take on a social role, even if temporarily. The ***sick role*** refers to societal expec-

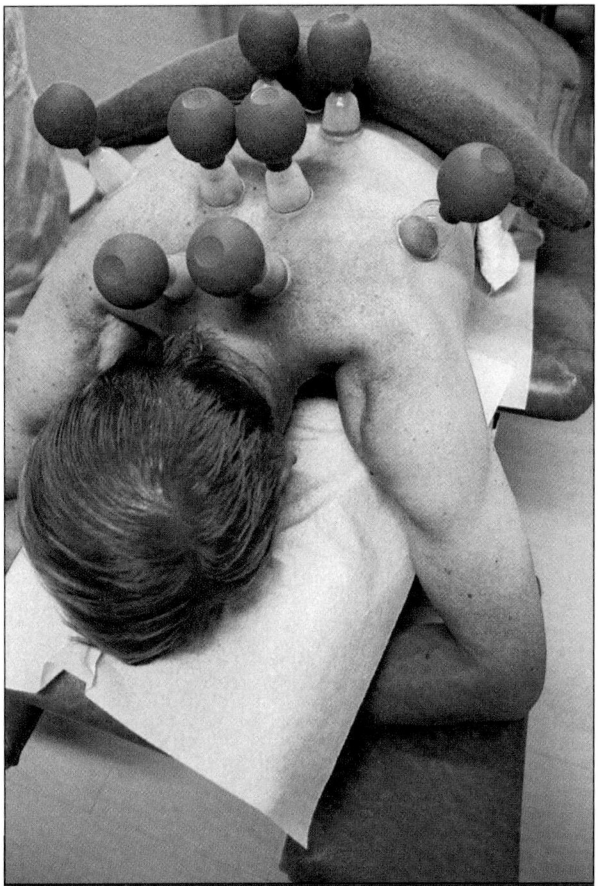

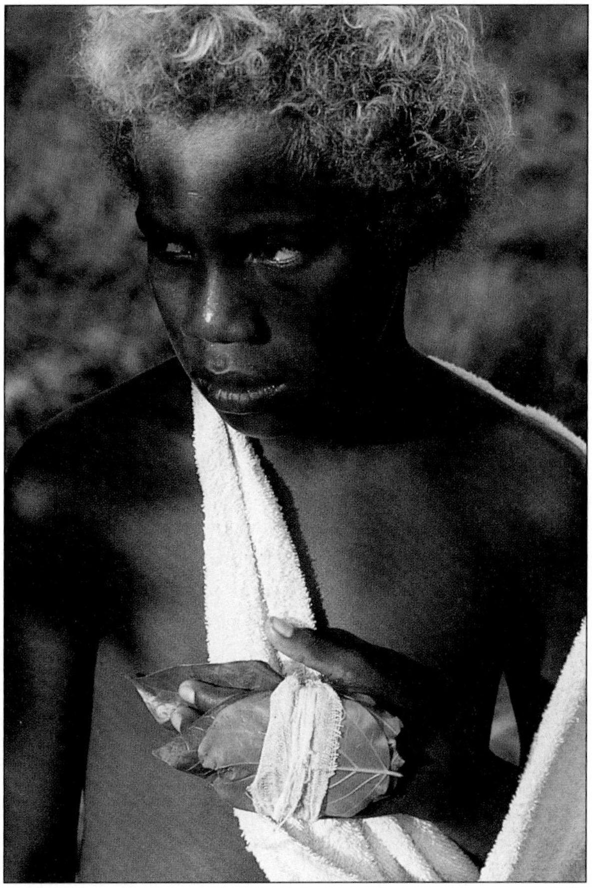

Health care takes many forms around the world. Cupping—a traditional practice used in ancient China, India, Egypt, and Greece—survives in modern Finland (left). Physiotherapists there use suction cups to draw out blood in order to lower patients' blood pressure, improve their circulation, and relieve muscular pain. In the western Pacific (right), the Malaitan people of Laulasi Island, one of the Solomon Islands, believe that a leaf called *raralu* has medicinal properties that reduce swelling. This boy has squeezed a *raralu* leaf to release its juices and used it to bandage his broken finger.

tations about the attitudes and behaviour of a person viewed as being ill. Sociologist Talcott Parsons (1951, 1972, 1975), well known for his contributions to functionalist theory (see Chapter 1), has outlined the behaviour required of people considered "sick." They are exempted from their normal, day-to-day responsibilities and generally are not blamed for their condition. Yet they are obligated to try to get well, and this may include seeking competent professional care. Attempting to get well is particularly important in the world's developing countries. In modern automated industrial societies, we can absorb a greater degree of illness or disability, but in horticultural or agrarian societies, the availability of workers is far more critical (Conrad 1997).

According to Parsons's theory, physicians function as "gatekeepers" for the sick role, either verifying a patient's condition as "illness" or designating the patient as "recovered." The ill person becomes dependent on the doctor because the latter can control valued rewards (not only treatment of illness but also excused absences from work and school). Parsons suggests that the doctor–patient relationship is somewhat like that between parent and child. Like a parent, the physician helps the patient to return to society as a full and functioning adult (Segall 1976).

There have been a number of criticisms of the concept of the sick role. First, patients' judgments regarding their own state of health may be related to their gender, age, social class, and ethnic group. For example, younger people may fail to detect warning signs of a dangerous illness while the elderly may focus too much on the slightest physical malady. Second, the sick role may be more applicable to people experiencing short-term illnesses than to those with recurring, long-term illnesses. Finally, even simple factors, such as whether a person is employed or not, seem to affect willingness to assume the sick role—as does the impact of socialization into a particular occupation or activity. For example, beginning in childhood, athletes learn to define certain ailments as "sports injuries" and therefore do not regard themselves as "sick" (Curry 1993). Nonetheless, sociologists continue to rely on Parsons's model for functionalist analysis of the relationship between illness and societal expectations for the sick.

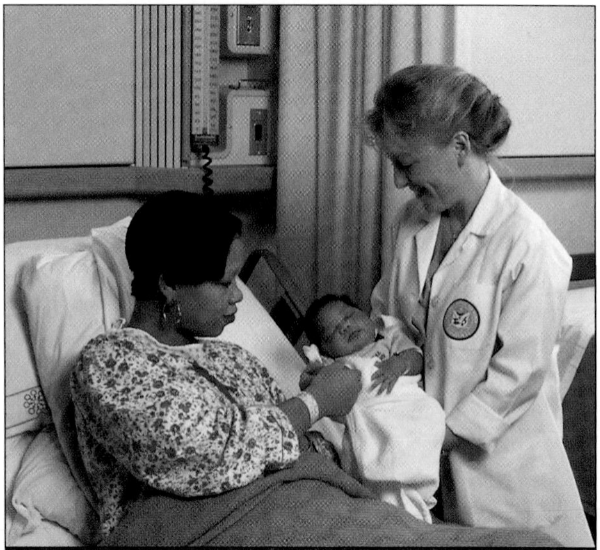

A midwife hands a newborn baby to its mother. Despite the fact that midwives first brought professionalism to child delivery, physicians insist on treating midwifery as a subordinate occupation.

Conflict Approach

Functionalists seek to explain how health care systems meet the needs of society as well as those of individual patients and medical practitioners, but conflict theorists take issue with this view. They express concern that the profession of medicine has assumed a preeminence that extends well beyond whether to excuse a student from school or an employee from work. Sociologist Eliot Freidson (1970:5) has likened the position of medicine today to that of state religions yesterday—it has an officially approved monopoly of the right to define health and illness and to treat illness. Conflict theorists use the term *medicalization of society* to refer to the growing role of medicine as a major institution of social control (Conrad and Schneider 1992; McKinlay and McKinlay 1977; Zola 1972, 1983).

Social control involves techniques and strategies for regulating behaviour in order to enforce the distinctive p. 147 norms and values of a culture. Typically, we think of informal social control as occurring within families and peer groups, and formal social control as carried out by authorized agents such as police officers, judges, school administrators, and employers. However, viewed from a conflict perspective, medicine is not simply a "healing profession"; it is a regulating mechanism as well.

How does it manifest its social control? First, medicine has greatly expanded its domain of expertise in recent decades. Physicians have become much more involved in examining a wide range of issues, among them sexuality (including homosexuality), old age, anxiety, obesity, child development, alcoholism, and drug addiction. Society tolerates such expansion of the boundaries of medicine because we hope that these experts can bring new "miracle cures" to complex human problems as they have to the control of certain infectious diseases. The social significance of medicalization is that once a problem is viewed using a *medical model*—once medical experts become influential in proposing and assessing relevant public policies—it becomes more difficult for "common people" to join the discussion and exert influence on decision making. It also becomes more difficult to view these issues as being shaped by social, cultural, or psychological factors, rather than simply by physical or medical factors (R. Caplan 1989; Conrad and Schneider 1992; Starr 1982).

Second, medicine serves as an agent of social control by retaining absolute jurisdiction over many health care procedures. It has even attempted to guard its jurisdiction by placing health care professionals such as chiropractors and nurse-midwives outside the realm of acceptable medicine. Despite the fact that midwives first brought professionalism to child delivery, they have been portrayed as having invaded the "legitimate" field of obstetrics in North America. Nurse-midwives have sought licensing as a way to achieve professional respectability, but physicians continue to exert power to ensure that midwifery remains a subordinate occupation (Friedland 2000).

The medicalization of society is but one concern of conflict theorists as they assess the workings of health care institutions. As we have seen throughout this textbook, when analyzing any issue, conflict theorists seek to determine who benefits, who suffers, and who dominates at the expense of others. Viewed from a conflict perspective, there are glaring inequities in health care delivery within Canada. For example, northern and rural areas tend to be underserved because medical services concentrate where people are numerous and/or wealthy.

Similarly, from a global perspective, there are obvious inequities in health care delivery. Today, the United States has about 25 physicians per 1000 people, while African nations have fewer than 1 per 1000. This situation is only worsened by the "brain drain"—the immigration to industrialized nations of skilled workers, professionals, and technicians who are desperately needed by their home countries. As part of this brain drain, physicians and other health care professionals have come to developed countries from developing countries such as India, Pakistan, and various African states. Conflict theorists view such emigration out of the developing world as yet another way in which the world's core industrialized nations enhance their quality of life at the expense of developing countries (World Bank 2000b:190–91).

In another example of global inequities in health care, multinational corporations based in industrialized countries have reaped significant profits by "dumping" unapproved drugs on unsuspecting consumers in the developing world. In some cases, fraudulent capsules and tablets are manufactured and marketed as established products in developing countries. These "medications" contain useless ingredients or perhaps one tenth of the needed dosage of a genuine medication. Even when the drugs dumped on developing countries are legitimate, the information available to physicians and patients is less likely to include warnings of health hazards and more likely to include undocumented testimonials than in industrialized nations (Silverman et al. 1992).

Conflict theorists emphasize that inequities in health care resources have clear life-and-death consequences. For example, in 2000, the infant mortality rate in Sierra Leone ranged as high as 157 infant deaths per 1000 live births. By contrast, Japan's infant mortality rate was only 3.5 deaths per 1000 live births and Iceland's was only 2.6. From a conflict perspective, the dramatic differences in infant mortality rates around the world (see Figure 14-4) reflect, at least in part, unequal distribution of health care resources based on the wealth or poverty of various communities and nations.

In 2000, the United States had a rate of 7 infant deaths per 1000 live births (although it is estimated that the rate in some poor, inner-city neighbourhoods in this country exceeds 30 deaths per 1000 live births). Yet, despite the wealth of the United States, at least 22 nations have lower infant mortality rates, among them Canada, Great Britain, and Japan. Conflict theorists point out that, unlike the United States, Canada and these other countries offer some form of government-supported health care for all citizens, which typically leads to greater availability and greater use of prenatal care than is the case in the United States. (We will examine government's role in health care in greater detail in the social policy section of this chapter.)

Interactionist Approach

In examining health, illness, and medicine as a social institution, interactionists generally focus on micro-level study of the roles played by health care professionals and patients. They emphasize that the patient should not always be viewed as passive, but instead as an actor who often shows a powerful intent to see the physician (Alonzo 1989; Zola 1983).

Sometimes patients play an active role in health care by *failing* to follow a physician's advice. For example, some patients stop taking medications long before they should, some take an incorrect dosage on purpose, and others never even fill their prescriptions. Such noncompliance results in part from the prevalence of self-medication in our society; many people are accustomed to self-diagnosis and self-treatment. On the other hand, patients' active involvement in their health care can sometimes have very *positive* consequences. Some patients read books about preventive health care techniques, attempt to

FIGURE 14-4

Infant Mortality Rates, 2000

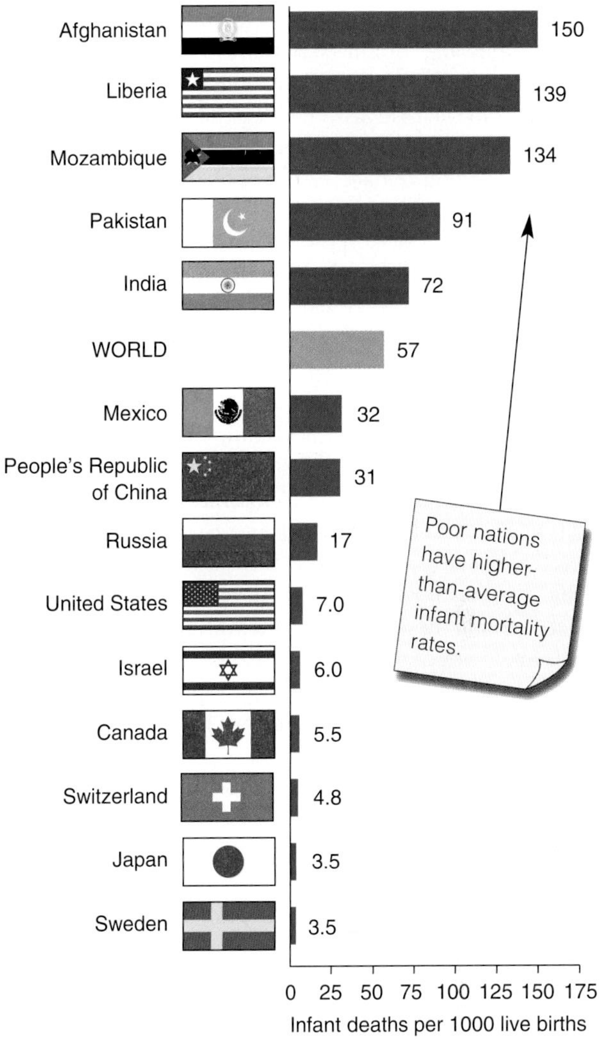

Source: Haub and Cornelius 2000.

maintain healthful and nutritious diets, carefully monitor any side effects of medication, and adjust dosage based on such perceived side effects.

Interactionist perspectives attempt to illuminate the "social meaning" of illness, as well as how these meanings affect one's self-concept and relationships with others. For example, in the case of someone suffering from a mental illness such as depression, interactionist approaches might shed light upon the social stigma of the illness. In addition, these approaches might focus on how the stigma of the illness impacts upon the individual's interpersonal relationships with family, friends, and coworkers. The interactionist perspective has been especially helpful in unravelling cultural differences that affect health care in a multicultural society such as that of Canada. For example, regular exercise is not part of the culture of some ethnic groups; attitudes on diet, smoking, drinking, and body image and fatalistic views of illness may be culturally specific (Levy and Hawks 1996). Cultural sensitivity is necessary at all levels of health care delivery in order to effectively treat a diverse patient population where many face language barriers, racism, social isolation, and inequality. Determining the different cultural meanings that individuals might attach to a doctor's report, referral to a medical specialist, or a health survey are examples of how interactionists might approach the study of health and illness.

Labelling Approach

Labelling theory helps us to understand why certain people are *viewed* as deviants, "bad kids," or criminals whereas others whose behaviour is similar are not. p. 160 Labelling theorists also suggest that the designation "healthy" or "ill" generally involves social definition by others. Just as police officers, judges, and other regulators of social control have the power to define certain people as criminals, health care professionals (especially physicians) have the power to define certain people as "sick."

An example from history illustrates the labelling of women by the medical profession as fragile and possessing a limited source of energy. During the early years of the last century, women who expended energy pursuing intellectual activities (such as advanced education) were perceived to be endangering their womanhood. The medical establishment viewed the female body as a closed system of energy in which use of the brain would leave less energy to be used in other parts, such as the reproductive system. Women's brains and ovaries, according to doctors of the time, competed for the same supply of energy. Women who spent too much energy in intellectual pursuits were labelled "unhealthy" and unwomanly:

> A young woman . . . who consumed her vital force in intellectual activities was necessarily diverting these energies from the achievement of true womanhood. She would become weak and nervous, perhaps sterile . . . capable of bearing only sickly and neurotic children . . . The brain and ovary could not develop at the same time (Smith-Rosenberg and Rosenberg 1974:340).

Patriarchical views of women's health during this period even went so far as to suggest that male semen had a therapeutic and soothing effect on the female reproductive organs (Smith-Rosenberg and Rosenberg 1986).

By the late 1980s, the power of a label—"person with AIDS"—had become quite evident. This label often functions as a master status that overshadows all other aspects of a person's life. pp. 102–04 Once someone is told that he or she has tested positive for HIV, the virus associated with AIDS, that person is forced to confront immediate and difficult questions: Should I tell my family members, my sexual partner(s), my friends, my coworkers, my employer? How will these people respond?

Former basketball star Magic Johnson carries the label "person with AIDS." This label often functions as a master status, overshadowing all other aspects of a person's life. Above, Johnson carries the Olympic flame during the torch relay in January 2002.

People's intense fear of this disease has led to prejudice and discrimination—even social ostracism—against those who have (or are suspected of having) AIDS. Consequently, a person who has AIDS must deal with not only the serious medical consequences of the disease, but also the distressing social consequences associated with the label.

p. 116

According to labelling theorists, we can view a variety of life experiences as illnesses or not. Recently, premenstrual syndrome, posttraumatic disorders, and hyperactivity have been "labelled" medically recognized disorders. Disagreements continue in the medical community over whether chronic fatigue syndrome constitutes a medical illness. Following the 1991 Gulf War against Iraq, more than 21 000 American soldiers and other personnel reported a variety of symptoms ranging from fatigue and rashes to respiratory disorders. These symptoms have come to be called the Gulf War Syndrome (or Illness), although the government has yet to officially recognize a clear link between the combat situation and subsequent symptoms.

Probably the most noteworthy recent medical example of labelling is the case of homosexuality. For years, psychiatrists classified being gay or lesbian not as a lifestyle but as a mental disorder subject to treatment. This official sanction by the psychiatry profession became an early target of the growing gay and lesbian rights movement in North America. In 1974, members of the American Psychiatric Association voted to drop homosexuality from the standard manual on mental disorders (Adam 1995; Charmaz and Paterniti 1999; Monteiro 1998).

Feminist Approaches

Many feminist approaches to health and illness have pointed to a historical pattern of concentrating on women's reproductive potential, overshadowing a diversity of concerns related to health and illness. Early research on women focused on their roles as mothers and wives as they related to women's mental health, while comparable studies on men focused more on their physical health and job conditions. This bias still can be found in the research literature, even though most women now work in the paid labour force (Janzen 1998).

Other feminist perspectives point out the need to recognize that patterns of women's health and illness are as diverse as Canadian women themselves and that this diversity (e.g., poor women, immigrants, refugees, women of colour, lesbians, disabled women) must not be masked by talking about "women" as a universal category. As one feminist sociologist argues:

> Women are often discussed as a single group defined chiefly by their biological sex, members of an abstract universal (and implicitly white) category. In reality, we are a mixed lot, our gender roles and options shaped by history, culture and deep divisions across class and colour lines . . . Traditionally women as a group are defined by this reproductive potential. Usually ignored are the many ways that gender as a social reality gets into the body and transforms our biology (Krieger 1994:18).

Sociological investigations of women's health must, many feminist theories argue, shift the focus from reproduction potential and roles as mothers and wives to women's health and illness, which reflect the diversity of Canadian women.

An Overview

As you know by now, many of the sociological approaches described above should not be regarded as mutually exclusive. In the study of health-related issues, they share certain common themes. First, any person's health or illness is more than an organic condition, since it is subject to the interpretation of others. Owing to the impact of culture, family and friends, and the medical profession, health and illness are not purely biological occurrences

These United States Marines wore gas masks while in combat situations in the Gulf War in 1991. Many soldiers who were not protected complained later of a number of symptoms, ranging from fatigue to rashes to respiratory disorders. These symptoms came to be labelled the Gulf War Syndrome.

but are sociological occurrences as well. Second, since members of a society (especially industrial societies) share the same health delivery system, health is a group and societal concern. Although health may be defined as the complete well-being of an individual, it is also the result of his or her social environment. As we shall see in the next section, such factors as a person's social class, race and ethnicity, gender, and age can influence the likelihood of contracting a particular disease (Cockerham 1998).

Social Epidemiology and Health

Social epidemiology is the study of the distribution of disease, impairment, and general health status across a population. Epidemiology initially concentrated on the scientific study of epidemics, focusing on how they started and spread. Contemporary social epidemiology is much broader in scope, concerned not only with epidemics but also with nonepidemic diseases, injuries, drug addiction and alcoholism, suicide, and mental illness. Epidemiology draws on the work of a wide variety of scientists and researchers, among them physicians, sociologists, public health officials, biologists, veterinarians, demographers, anthropologists, psychologists, and meteorologists.

Researchers in social epidemiology commonly use two concepts: incidence and prevalence. ***Incidence*** refers to the number of *new* cases of a specific disorder occurring within a given population during a stated period of time, usually a year. For example, the incidence of AIDS in Canada in 2002 was 174 cases. By contrast, ***prevalence*** refers to the total number of cases of a specific disorder that exist at a given time. The prevalence of AIDS in Canada in 2002 was about 18 000 cases (Health Canada 2003).

When incidence figures are presented as rates, or as the number of reports per 100 000 people, they are called ***morbidity rates***. (The term ***mortality rate***, you will recall, refers to the incidence of *death* in a given population.) Sociologists find morbidity rates useful because they reveal that a specific disease occurs more frequently among one segment of a population than another. As we shall see, social class, race, ethnicity, gender, and age can all affect a population's morbidity rates.

Social Class

Social class is clearly associated with differences in morbidity and mortality rates. Studies in Canada and other countries have consistently shown that people in the lower classes have higher rates of mortality and disability. Health Canada has identified 12 determinants of health, which include income and social status, employment, education, gender, and culture (see Table 14-4).

Table 14-4 12 Determinants of Health Identified by Health Canada

- Income and social status
- Employment
- Education and social environments
- Physical environments
- Healthy child development
- Personal health practices and coping skills
- Health services
- Social support networks
- Biology and genetic endowment
- Gender
- Culture

Source: Health Canada 2002.

While available data do suggest the relationship between health and social class, they mask the vast diversity within Canada. For example, because social class, race, and gender intersect, First Nations women are affected by poor health to a much greater degree than non–First Nations women. First Nations women who, on average, have lower incomes, were almost three times as likely to report a heart problem in 1997 than were all Canadian women in general. As well, First Nations women between 25 and 34 have rates of suicide over four times those of non–First Nations women (Statistics Canada 2000d).

Numerous studies document the impact of social class on health. An examination of data from 11 countries in North America and Europe found strong associations between household income and health, and between household income and life expectancy, when comparing families of similar size. Researchers from the Harvard School of Public Health found that higher overall mortality rates—as well as higher incidence of infant mortality and deaths from coronary heart disease, cancer, and homicide—were associated with lower incomes.

Why is class linked to health? Crowded living conditions, substandard housing, poor diet, and stress all contribute to the ill health of many low-income people in Canada. In certain instances, limited education and literacy may lead to a lack of awareness of measures necessary to maintain good health.

Another factor in the link between class and health is evident at the workplace: the occupations of people in the working and lower classes of Canada tend to be more dangerous than those of more affluent citizens. Miners, for example, must face the possibility of injury or death due to explosions and cave-ins; they are also likely to develop respiratory diseases such as black lung. Workers in textile mills may contract a variety of illnesses caused by exposure to toxic substances, including one disease commonly known as *brown lung disease* (R. Hall 1982). In recent years, the nation has learned of the perils of asbestos poisoning, a particular worry for construction workers.

In the view of Karl Marx and contemporary conflict theorists, capitalist societies such as Canada care more about maximizing profits than they do about the health and safety of industrial workers. As a result, government agencies do not take forceful action to regulate conditions in the workplace, and workers suffer many preventable, job-related injuries and illnesses.

Research also shows that the lower classes are more vulnerable to environmental pollution than the affluent; this is the case not only where the lower classes work but also where they live (Moffatt 1995).

Sociologists Link and Phelan maintain that socioeconomic status is "a fundamental cause of disease" since it is linked to access to resources "that can be used to avoid risks or minimize the consequences of disease once it occurs . . . resources that include money, knowledge, power, prestige and kinds of interpersonal resources embodied in the concepts of social support and social network" (Link and Phelan 1995:87).

An Innu youth openly sniffs gas in the community of Davis Inlet, Newfoundland, where in 2001 alcohol and substance abuse were at crisis levels.

Race and Ethnicity

Health profiles of many racial and ethnic minorities reflect the social inequality evident in Canada. The most glaring examples of the relationship between race and ethnicity and health can be found within Canada's First Nations communities. The health of First Nations people reflects patterns of exclusion, past and present, that have limited and continue to limit their access to many of the social determinants of health—determinants such as income, employment, education, and literacy. First Nations people not only experience a lack of material resources but also face limited opportunities, isolation, discrimination, and racism.

A 1996 study prepared at the request of the Canadian Task Force on the Periodic Health Examination concluded that First Nations people "sustain a disproportionate share of the burden of physical disease and mental illness" (MacMillan et al. 1996:1569). Many First Nations populations have an increased risk of death from alcoholism, homicide, suicide, and pneumonia; overall death rates for both men and women are higher among the First Nations population than their counterparts in the overall Canadian population (MacMillan et al. 1996). Rates of tuberculosis (TB) between 1984 and 1989 among registered First Nations and Inuit were approximately nine times the Canadian average (MacMillan et al. 1996). First Nations communities have identified problems such as substance abuse, unemployment, suicide, and family violence as concerns affecting their members' health. A study in Ontario found that 80 percent of the First Nations women in its sample had been victims of family violence (Stout 1996). The health of First Nations people as well as that of other disadvantaged ethnic and racial minorities is interwoven with the conditions of poverty. In the case of First Nations people, this interrelationship is one that few studies have assessed (MacMillan et al. 1996).

Gender

A large body of research indicates that, in comparison with men, women experience a higher prevalence of many illnesses, though they tend to live longer. Females born in 2000 have a life expectancy of approximately 82 years; males born at the same time were expected to live for about 77 years. The difference in life expectancy between Canadian men and women has been attributed to such factors as risk-taking behaviour such as drinking and dangerous driving on the part of males; levels of danger associated with male-dominated occupations, such as mining and construction; and women's tendency to use health care services more often and at earlier stages of their illness. The difference in life expectancy between men and women has decreased to a gap of 5.2 years in 2000 from a gap of 7.4 years in 1976 (Statistics Canada 2003n). This has been attributed to a reduction of deaths due to cardiovascular disease in men, contributed to by a decrease in smoking. Smoking rates for women, however, have been increasing steadily for about three decades, contributing to higher rates of lung cancer and heart disease (Lem 2000). The narrowing of the gender gap in life expectancy is predicted to continue in this century due to women's changing roles and their exposure to stress, and the general aging of the population (McVey and Kalbach 1995).

Recent studies suggest that the genuine differences in morbidity between women and men may be less pronounced than previously assumed (Macintyre et al. 1996). Using the 1994 National Population Health Survey (NPHS) data, Canadian sociologists found no "clear excess of ill-health among women" (McDonough and Walters 2000:3). The researchers concluded that there is a need to further examine gender differences rather than to operate on the widely held assumption that women experience greater ill-health even though they live longer. The authors also concluded that while existing gender differences should not be minimized, for many age groups the health of women and men is more similar than previously assumed. Other researchers argue that women are much more likely than men to seek treatment, to be diagnosed as having diseases, and thus to have their illnesses reflected in data examined by epidemiologists.

From a conflict perspective, women have been particularly vulnerable to the medicalization of society, with everything from birth to beauty treated in an increasingly medical context. Such medicalization may contribute to women's higher morbidity rates as compared with those of men. Ironically, while women have been especially affected by medicalization, medical researchers have often excluded women from clinical studies. Female physicians and researchers charge that sexism is at the heart of such research practices and insist that there is a desperate need for studies with female subjects.

Moreover, many feminist researchers state the need for greater investigation into the health effects of discrimination as a function of one's gender, race, sexual orientation and/or disability, as well as how these variables interact to produce varying levels of health and disease. They argue that since gender is not a uniform category, research approaches are needed that will lead to a better understanding of the "dynamics of diversity" among and within the various groups of Canadian women (Vissandjee 2001:3).

Research on the relationship between culture and gender as they relate to health reveals that immigrant women's experiences differ from those that are depicted to be the Canadian "norm" (Repper et al. 1996). Certain immigrant women, for example, are less likely to participate in cancer screening programs (e.g., mammograms and pap smears), while others with concerns arising from female genital mutilation are reluctant to consult health care providers (Vissandjee 2001).

Despite renewed attention to women's health, recent studies confirm that women still are sometimes neglected by the medical establishment. In the United States, for example, even federally funded clinical research ignores the requirement since 1993 that their data be analyzed to see if women and men respond differently. Similarly, a content analysis of medical journals in the 1990s found that even the most recent published research focuses primarily on men: no studies excluded men, 20 percent excluded women, and another 30 percent failed to report the findings from female participants (General Accounting Office 2000; Vidaver et al. 2000).

Age

Health is the overriding concern of the elderly. Most older people in Canada report having at least one chronic illness, but only some of these conditions are potentially life threatening or require medical care. At the same time, health problems can affect the quality of life of older people in important ways. Arthritis and visual or hearing impairments can interfere with the performance of everyday tasks.

As the Canadian population ages, led by the baby boom generation, to which roughly one third of all Canadians belong, our society will experience a greater prevalence of particular types of diseases. The Vancouver Brain Research Centre predicts that in 20 years, brain diseases such as Alzheimer's and Parkinson's diseases, to which older people are more prone, will be the leading cause of death and disability among Canadians (Fong 2001). In Canada today, approximately 300 000 people have Alzheimer's disease, while another 100 000 are afflicted with Parkinson's disease. Since the likelihood of contracting these diseases increases with age, it is predicted that 750 000 Canadians will be afflicted with Alzheimer's disease and 300 000 will have Parkinson's disease by 2020 (Fung 2001). The incidence of brain diseases related to vision (e.g., glaucoma and macular degeneration) as well as stroke is currently on the increase and will continue to rise as the baby boomers make their way into the senior years. Overall, these brain diseases will surpass heart disease and cancer, which currently are the leading causes of death and disability. Gender is of particular importance in the study of health and aging, since women on average

As people age and become more susceptible to chronic diseases, some of them lose the ability to care for themselves. This Alzheimer's patient is being fed by his spouse.

live longer lives. Living longer means older women are at increased risk of disease, and thus greater life expectancy can actually be viewed as a threat to women's health (Rodin and Ickovics 1990). Despite the fact that women make up a greater proportion of the elderly and therefore have greater health care needs, they receive little research attention (Weber 1998).

Social support is a key factor related to the health of both older men and women. In older women, research reveals that depression is more strongly related to social support than to physical health (Albarracin et al. 1997). Older people tend to visit doctors more frequently and require hospitalization more often than do their younger counterparts (Canadian Institute for Health Information 2000). Given the demographic shift towards an older population accentuated by baby boomers, it is obvious that the disproportionate use of the health care system in Canada by older people is a critical factor in all discussions about the cost of health care and possible reforms of the health care system (Bureau of the Census 1999a:134, 138).

Sexual Orientation

Since heterosexuality is assumed to be the norm in Canadian society, there is a lack of attention paid to gay and lesbians in health research (Weber 1998). There does, however, tend to be more research carried out on gays than lesbians (Lynch and Ferri 1997). Lesbians, then, face the combined effects of sexism and sexual orientation as they relate to health research and provision of health care. Research on health is conducted using mainly white, middle-class women, which results in a lack of knowledge about the health of bisexual women, older lesbians, lesbians of colour, and lesbians from rural areas (Hart 1995). Health care services often assume a woman's heterosexuality by asking her to respond to a questionnaire with options of "single," "married," "divorced," or "widowed" (O'Hanlan 2002).

The assumption of diversity is, however, being integrated into some health care systems such as the Vancouver/Richmond Health Board, which represents the needs of lesbian, gay, bisexual, and transgender patients as well as other groups who traditionally have not been well served by the health care system. As well, there have been concerns expressed over the curricula of Canadian medical schools regarding gay, lesbian, and bisexual issues. Medical schools are being prompted to ensure that the doctors they graduate are competently trained to care for *all* Canadians (Robinson and Cohen 1996).

In sum, to achieve the goal of 100 percent access and zero health disparities, public health officials must overcome inequities that are rooted not just in age, but in social class, race and ethnicity, gender, and sexual orientation. If that were not enough, they must also deal with a geographical disparity in health care resources. Dramatic differences in the availability of physicians, hospitals, and nursing homes also exist between urban and rural areas within the same province. In the next section we will look more closely at issues surrounding the delivery of health care in Canada.

Health Care in Canada

In 1947 Swift Current, Saskatchewan, became the first region in North America to embrace a public hospital insurance program, in which all of its citizens were provided access to hospital services without direct payment. The following year, Saskatchewan Premier Tommy Douglas introduced a program for the entire province, based largely on the Swift Current model. Ten years later, the federal government followed suit by introducing the first national hospital insurance plan in North America. In 1962, Saskatchewan was again at the forefront of public health care when it introduced North America's first medicare program, which would cover doctor's fees incurred outside of hospitals. The program sparked the highly profiled Saskatchewan doctors' strike, which saw many doctors threatening to leave the province if this perceived threat to "free enterprise" in medical care went through. Critics of the medicare plan accused the government of "communist" and "socialist" tendencies, and of attempting to destroy the private relationship between physicians and patients.

The doctors' strike, which lasted three weeks, became the focus of media attention not only in Canada, but also in the United States. The American Medical Association supported the dissenting Saskatchewan doctors in their attempt to resist the public administration of medical care and to preserve "free enterprise."

In 1968, the public administration of medical care became national policy, after the provinces and territories moved to implement their own insurance plans for in-hospital care. Justice Emmett Hall, after carrying out a review of the Canadian health care system in 1979, reported it to be among the best in the world. He did, however, warn that the system was being weakened by extra-billing by doctors and user fees creating a "two-tiered" system. These unresolved issues still pose a threat to the principles of accessibility, universality, and public administration, which, as discussed in a later section, are cornerstones of Canadian medicare.

Physicians, Nurses, and Patients

The preeminence of physicians within the health care system of Canada, whose fees made up approximately 13 percent of total health care spending in 2001 (Canadian Institute for Health Information 2001), has traditionally given them a position of dominance in their dealings with governments, patients, nurses, and other health professionals. The functionalist and interactionist perspectives combine to offer a framework for understanding the professional socialization of physicians as it relates to patient care. Functionalists suggest that established physicians and medical school professors serve as mentors or role models who transmit knowledge, skills, and values to the passive learner—the medical student. Interactionists emphasize that students are moulded by the medical school environment as they interact with their classmates.

Both approaches argue that the typical training of physicians in Canada leads to rather dehumanizing physician–patient encounters. As Dr. Lori Arviso Alvord writes in *The Scalpel and the Silver Bear,* "I had been trained by a group of physicians who placed much more emphasis on their technical abilities and clinical skills than on their abilities to be caring and sensitive" (Alvord and Van Pelt 1999:13). Despite many efforts to formally introduce a humanistic dimension of patient care into the medical school curriculum, patient overload and underfunding of hospitals tend to undercut positive relations.

Interactionists have closely examined how compliance and negotiation occur between physician and patient. They concur with Talcott Parsons's view that the relationship is generally asymmetrical, with doctors holding a position of dominance and control of rewards. Just as physicians have maintained dominance in their interactions with patients, doctors have similarly controlled interactions with nurses. Despite p. 253 their training and professional status, nurses commonly take orders from physicians. Traditionally, the relationship between doctors and nurses has paralleled the male dominance of North America: Most physicians have been male, whereas virtually all nurses have been female.

Like other women in subordinate roles, nurses have been expected to perform their duties without challenging the authority of men. Psychiatrist Leonard Stein (1967) refers to this process as the *doctor–nurse game.* According to the rules of this "game," the nurse must never disagree openly with the physician. When she has recommendations concerning a patient's care, she must communicate them indirectly in a deferential tone. For example, if asked by a hospital's medical resident, "What sleeping medication has been helpful to Mrs. Brown in the past?" (an indirect request for a recommendation), the nurse will respond with a disguised recommendation statement, such as "Pentobarbital mg 100 was quite effective night before last." Her careful response allows the physician to authoritatively restate the same prescription as if it were *his* idea.

Like nurses, female physicians have traditionally found themselves in a subordinate position because of gender. Although enrollments in medical schools across Canada are approaching or have approached gender equity, faculty in medical schools are still predominantly male.

A study of male and female medical residents suggests that the increasing number of women physicians may alter the traditional doctor–patient relationship. Male residents were found to be more focused on the intellectual challenges of medicine and the prestige associated with certain medical specialties. By contrast, female residents were more likely to express a commitment to caring for patients and devoting time to them. p. 245 In terms of the functionalist analysis of gender stratification offered by sociologists Talcott Parsons and Robert Bales, male residents took the *instrumental,* achievement-oriented role, while female residents took the *expressive,* interpersonal-oriented role. As women continue to enter and move higher in the hierarchies of the medical profession, there will surely be sociological studies to see if these apparent gender differences persist (Geckler 1995).

Patients have traditionally relied on medical personnel to inform them of health care issues, but increasingly they are now turning to the media for health care information. Recognizing this change, pharmaceutical firms are advertising their prescription drugs directly to potential customers through television and magazine advertisements. The Internet is also a growing source for patient information.

Medical professionals are understandably suspicious of these new sources of information. The American Academy of Pediatrics published a study in 1998 that investigated websites with information on treating childhood diarrhea. They found that only 20 percent of the sources of information conformed to current recommended medical practices. The study noted that even if the source of information was a major medical centre, it did not improve the likelihood of compliance. Reflecting its professional stake in the issue, the Academy concluded that patients need to be "warned" not to use Internet medical information. However, there is little doubt that web research is transforming an increasing proportion of patient–physician encounters, as patients arrive for their doctor's appointments armed with the latest printout from the Internet (Kolata 2000; McClung et al. 1998).

Health Care Alternatives

Canada, along with most Western, industrialized countries, follows a medical model of illness. This model, dominated by doctors who are graduates of Western medical schools, is based on the assumption that when specific body parts break down, they can be treated according to a neutral scientific process (Weitz 1996). The cause of illness, then, is viewed to be largely biological. The medical model considers illness to be a deviation from the norm and advocates "treatment" of the specific body part considered to be the cause of illness.

Polls suggest that 60 to 70 percent of Canadians have used some form of alternative therapy in the last six months (Canadian Institute for Health Information 2001). In recent decades, there has been growing interest in *holistic* (this term is also spelled *wholistic*) medical principles first developed in China. ***Holistic medicine***, also referred to as integrative, alternative, or complementary medicine, refers to therapies in which the health care practitioner considers the person's physical, mental, emotional, and spiritual characteristics. The individual is regarded as a totality, rather than as a collection of interrelated organ systems. Treatment methodologies include massage, chiropractic medicine, acupuncture (which involves the insertion of fine needles into surface points), respiratory exercises, and the use of herbs as remedies. Nutrition, exercise, and visualization may also be used to treat ailments generally treated through medication or hospitalization (Sharma and Bodeker 1998).

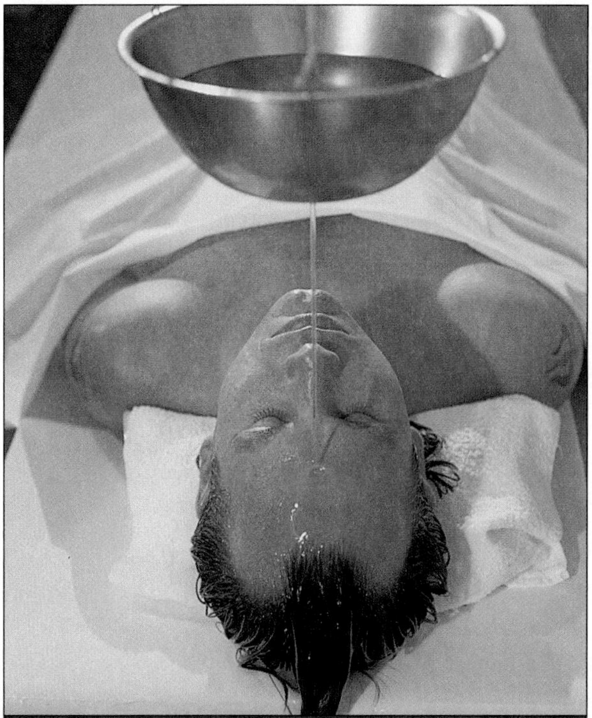

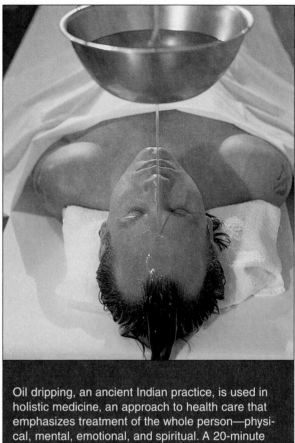

Oil dripping, an ancient Indian practice, is used in holistic medicine, an approach to health care that emphasizes treatment of the whole person—physical, mental, emotional, and spiritual. A 20-minute drip of warm, herb-infused oil is often prescribed for those who suffer from insomnia, hypertension, and digestive problems.

Canada's ethnic and racial diversity and recent waves of immigration have provided Canadians greater exposure to alternative forms of medical treatment. Because of the monopoly of the Western medical model, these forms of treatment have remained outside of the boundaries of government-sponsored health care. However, in 1996, the Vancouver Hospital and Health Science Centre in British Columbia opened the Tzu Chi Institute for Complementary and Alternative Medicine, whose mandate was to integrate traditional Asian therapies and Western medicare. As well, various post-secondary institutions across Canada now offer credit courses in alternative therapies such as acupuncture. The recent resurgence of holistic medicine comes amidst a widespread recognition of the value of nutrition and the dangers of overreliance on prescription drugs (especially those used to reduce stress, such as Valium).

The medical establishment—professional organizations, research hospitals, and medical schools—has generally served as a stern protector of traditionally accepted health care techniques. However, a major break-

Taking Sociology to Work

KELSIE LENOR WILSON-DORSETT: Deputy Director, Department of Statistics, Government of Bahamas

Kelsie Wilson-Dorsett was born in the Bahamas, where she received her primary and secondary education. She graduated from McMaster University in Hamilton, Ontario, with a combined Honours degree in sociology and political science. Her master's degree in sociology, completed at the University of Western Ontario in London, specialized in demography.

Currently, Wilson-Dorsett holds the positions of Deputy Director, Department of Statistics and Head of the Social Statistics Division, Government of Bahamas, where she oversees the country's census, vital statistics, and other surveys. In this position, she is responsible for the execution of the Bahamas' first Living Conditions Survey (BLCS) which, when completed, will enable the government to establish a poverty line and to measure the incidence and extent of poverty in that country.

Wilson-Dorsett's study of sociology, specializing in demography, is directly related to her current job. She states "the study of sociology has enabled me to put meaning to the figures which come into my office and has provided me with avenues to interpret these figures and determine the direction of future data collection. The analysis of census data, for instance, allows me to see where my country was several years ago, where it is now, and where it is likely to be in the years ahead."

Let's Discuss

1. What challenges do you think might be part of Wilson-Dorsett's job as she oversees a national census in a country like the Bahamas?
2. What other areas of specialization besides demography within the discipline of sociology would be helpful for someone interpreting the results of a project such as the Living Conditions Survey (BLCS)?

through occurred in 1992 when the American government's National Institutes of Health—that nation's major funding source for biomedical research—opened an Office of Alternative Medicine, empowered to accept grant requests. Possible areas of study include herbal medicine, mind–body control techniques, and the use of electromagnetism to heal bones. A national study published in *The Journal of the American Medical Association* indicates that 46 percent of the general public uses alternative medicine. Most of it is not covered by insurance. In fact, out-of-pocket expenses for alternative medicine match all out-of-pocket expenses for traditional physician services (Eisenberg et al. 1998; Stolberg 2000).

While many observers applaud the use of alternative medical procedures, conflict theorists note the difference between those who can afford to use alternatives *in addition to* conventional medicine and those who have no choice. For example, Cubans have recently begun to rely more on traditional cures, such as sitting on cobalt blocks to ease circulatory problems, in response to a shortage of government resources. Likewise, in low-income neighbourhoods in the United States, people often rely on alternative care techniques out of necessity, not choice (Kovaleski 1999).

In some cases, movements for political change have generated health care alternatives. For example, as part of the larger feminist movement beginning in the 1960s, women became more vocal in their dissatisfaction with the North American health care system. The appearance of the book *Our Bodies, Ourselves* (Boston Women's Health Book Collective 1969, 1992) marked the emergence of the contemporary women's health movement. Women realized that they are by far the most frequent users of health services for themselves, their children, and other dependent family members. Activists agree that women should assume more responsibility for decisions concerning their health. The movement therefore has taken many forms, including organizations working for changes in the health care system, women's clinics, and "self-help" groups.

The goals of the women's health movement are ambitious, but the health care system has proved to be fairly resistant to change. Conflict theorists point out that physicians, medical schools, hospitals, and drug companies all have a vested interest in keeping women in a rather dependent and uninformed position as health care consumers. Despite an increase in female doctors, women remain underrepresented in all key decision-making positions in the health care system of Canada.

The Role of Government

In 1984, the federal government's Canada Health Act became the basis for the administration of our health care system, known as *medicare*. The act set out to ensure (in theory) that all Canadians receive access to hospital and doctors' services on the basis of need, not on the ability to pay. It also sets the conditions and criteria under which the provinces and territories receive transfer payments—payments that are then used to finance health care services in their respective jurisdictions. The principles of the Canada Health Act are:

1. *Public administration*: health care of a province or territory must be carried out by public institutions on a non-profit basis.
2. *Comprehensiveness*: all services carried out by hospitals and doctors and deemed to be medically necessary must be insured.
3. *Universality*: all residents of a province or territory are entitled to uniform health coverage.
4. *Portability*: health coverage must be maintained when a person moves or travels from province to province or outside Canada.
5. *Accessibility*: reasonable access to necessary medical services should be available to all Canadians (Health Canada 2001).

In many respects the principles of public administration, comprehensiveness, universality, portability, and accessibility represent Max Weber's idea of "ideal types"; that is, they act as abstract measuring rods against which we are able to compare our perceptions of reality. For example, most Canadians would be able to give an example of how our health care system today may not measure up to at least one of these principles. Whether the concern is waiting lists for surgery, access to specialists in remote locations, the growth of private, fee-for-service clinics, long waits in hospital emergency wards, waiting lists for specialized tests such as MRIs, the closing of rural hospitals, the reduction of beds in urban hospitals, or the shortage of nurses nation-wide, Canadians consider the delivery of health care services a concern of top priority (Canadian Institute for Health Information 2001). Canadians living in northern or rural areas, or outside major metropolitan areas, immigrants, those with low incomes, First Nations persons, and disabled persons represent some of the groups vulnerable to the so-called "crisis" in the Canadian health care system. We will look further into government's role in health care in the social policy section of this chapter.

SOCIAL POLICY AND HEALTH

Financing Health Care Worldwide

The Issue

In many developing nations of the world, health care issues centre on very basic needs of primary care. The goals established at the UN's World Health Assembly in 1981 were modest by North American standards: safe water in the home or within 15 minutes' walking distance; immunization against major infectious diseases; availability of essential drugs within an hour's walk or travel; and the presence of trained personnel for pregnancy and childbirth. While significant progress has been made in some areas, many developing countries have seen little improvement; in some places, health care has deteriorated (World Bank 1997b). The focus of this social policy section, however, is on those industrialized (or developed) nations where the availability of health care is really not an issue. The question is more one of accessibility and affordability. What steps are being taken to make the available services reachable and affordable?

The Setting

The Canadian health care system, despite its flaws, is the envy of other countries. Many Americans, in particular, praise the Canadian system for its universality and accessibility. At a Canadian Medical Association conference in 1995, Dr. Theodore Marmor of the Yale School of Management praised medicare as "Canada's postwar miracle," arguing that claims of it being a "fundamentally troubled and gravely threatened system" are distorted (Canadian Medical Association Journal 1995; 152: 1505).

Contrast what you have learned about the Canadian health care system thus far in this chapter with the situation in the United States and elsewhere in the developed world.

The United States is now the only Western industrial democracy that does not treat health care as a basic right. According to the United States Bureau of the Census in 2000, some 44 million people in the United States had no health insurance the entire year. The uninsured typically include self-employed people with limited incomes, illegal immigrants, and single mothers who are the sole providers for their families. Black Americans, Asian Americans, and Hispanics are less likely than whites to carry private health insurance. Although people with lower incomes are least likely to be covered, substantial numbers of households at all income levels go without coverage for some or most of any given year (Mills 2000).

National health insurance is a general term for legislative proposals that focus on ways to provide the entire population with health care services. First discussed by government officials in the United States in the 1930s, it has come to mean many different things, ranging from narrow health insurance coverage with minimal public subsidies to broad coverage with large-scale public funding.

Opponents of national health insurance insist that it would be extremely costly and would lead to significant tax increases. Defenders counter, however, that Canada and other countries have maintained broad governmental health coverage for decades:

- Great Britain's National Health Service is almost totally tax-supported, and health care services are free to all citizens.
- Under Sweden's national health system, medical care is delivered primarily by publicly funded hospitals and clinics, while a national health insurance system sets fees for health care services and reimburses providers of health care.
- Although Canadians rely on private physicians and hospitals for day-to-day treatment, health care is guaranteed as a right for all citizens. Income taxes finance public medical insurance and medical fees are set by the government.

Ironically, while these countries offer extensive health coverage for all citizens, the United States has higher health care costs than any other nation: an average annual cost of US$3701 per person, compared with US$1665 in Canada and only US$1246 in Great Britain. As Figure 14-5 shows, most industrial nations finance a substantially larger share of health care costs through public expenditures than does the United States (Bureau of the Census 1997a:835; Lassey et al. 1997).

Sociological Insights

As conflict theorists suggest, the United States health care system, like other social institutions, resists basic change. In general, those who receive substantial wealth and power through the workings of an existing institution will have a strong incentive to keep things as they are. In this case, private insurance companies are benefiting financially from the current system and have a clear interest in opposing certain forms of national health insurance. In addition, the American Medical Association (AMA), one of Washington's most powerful lobbying groups, has been successfully fighting national health insurance since the 1930s. Overall, there are more than 200 political action committees (PACs) that represent the medical, pharmaceutical, and insurance industries. These PACs contribute millions of dollars each year to members of Congress and use their influence to block any legislation that would threaten their interests (Dolbeare 1982; Kemper and Novak 1991).

FIGURE 14-5

Government Expenditure for Health Care

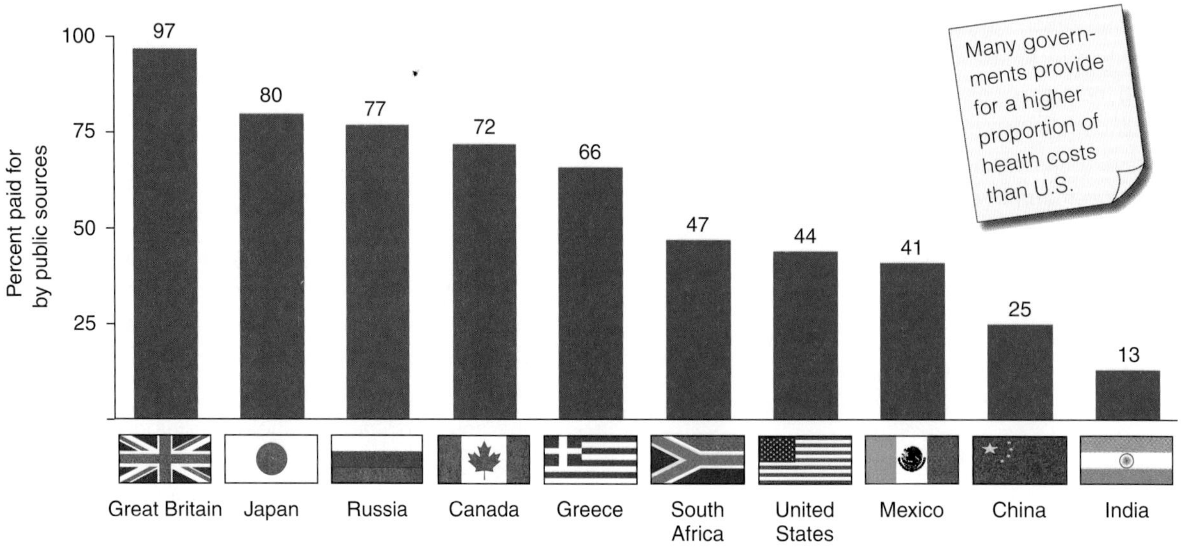

Source: WHO 2000:192–195.

Those who look at the system from the conflict perspective are disturbed by the possibility that illness may be exploited for profit. Moreover, in Canada, defenders of publicly funded health care argue that the growth of private, for-profit hospitals and fee-for-service clinics will create a two-tiered system. Such hospitals and clinics, critics argue, would accentuate the have–have not status of Canadians, making some medical services more accessible to those who can afford them. Obviously, conflict thinkers would argue that a postal clerk, for example, should have the same access to an MRI as a highly paid, professional hockey player. With private clinics, the hockey player may be able to afford the fee for the diagnostic test, while the postal clerk, who may not be able to afford the cost of the test, may be forced to wait until time is available in the publicly funded system. The increasing costs of Canadian medicare have led many to question the sustainability of its present structure (see Figure 14-6). Critics of the corporatization of health care worry that the growing pressures on physicians and other health care providers to make cost-effective decisions may lead to inadequate and even life-threatening patient care (Sherrill 1995).

Shirley Douglas, whose father Tommy Douglas is considered to be the founder of Canadian medicare, is seen here in Ottawa protesting the privatization of public health care.

Policy Initiatives

With the increasing cost of health care accelerated by the cost of technology and the demographic pressures of an aging population, it is doubtful, given current levels of funding, whether our present system of health care can be sustained over the long term. The strain in the current system

FIGURE 14-6

Total Health Expenditure, Canada, 1975 to 2001

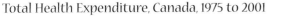

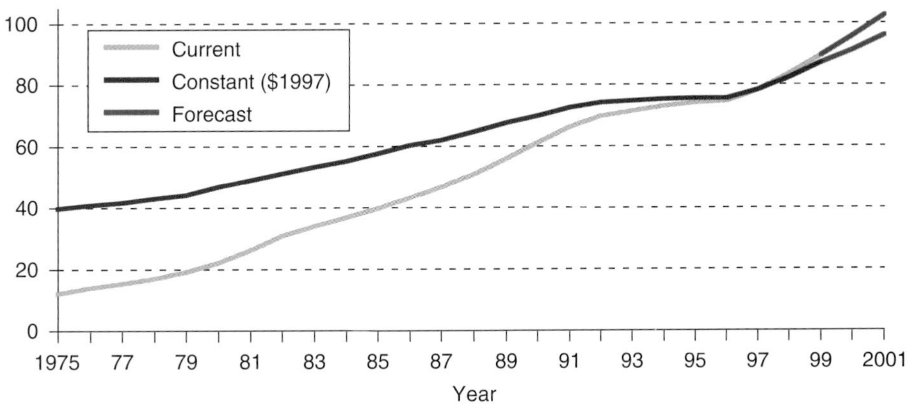

Source: Copyright © CIHI 2001.

FIGURE 14-7

Public and Private Shares of Total Health Expenditure, by Use of Funds, Canada, 1999

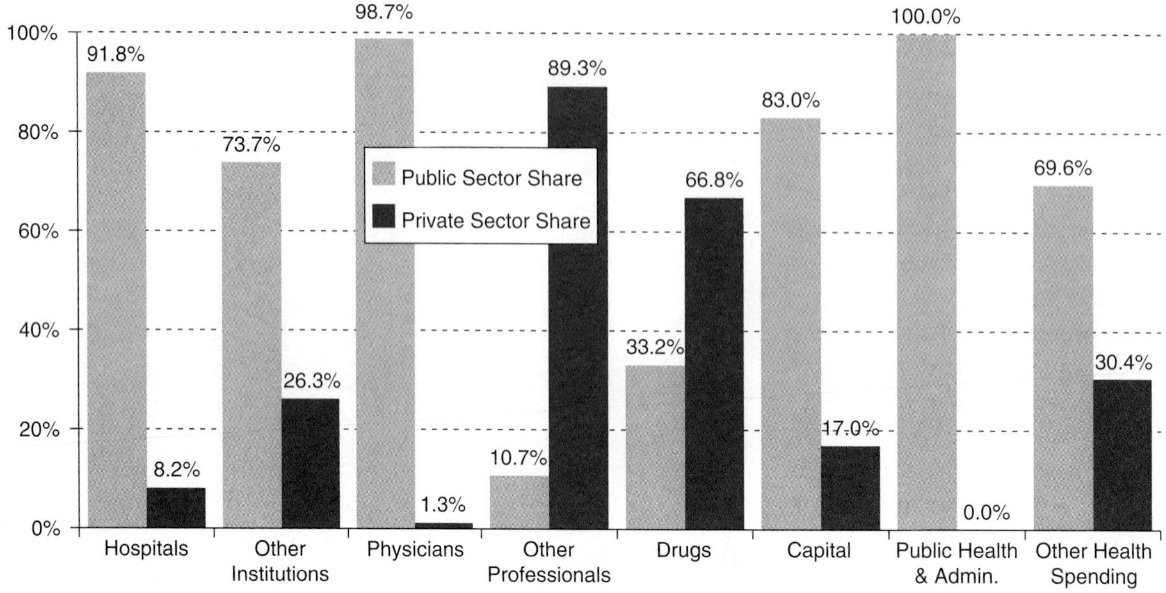

While hospitals and physicians are almost totally publicly funded, "other" health care professionals such as chiropractors are not.

Source: Copyright © CIHI 2001.

has manifested itself in hospital overcrowding and long waiting lists for specialists, surgery, and specialized diagnostic tests. In 2000, in response to some of these pressures in publicly funded health care, the province of Alberta introduced the controversial Bill 11—a bill that would provide for the regulation of contracting surgical services to private, for-profit facilities. The Canadian Nurses Association was one of many professional organizations to oppose the bill, claiming that privatized health care is not what is needed to alleviate the current strain in the system. Rather, the Association argued, adequate funding for the public health care system is the solution. In 2000, the Prime Minister established a royal commission on the future of Canada's health care system, asking Roy Romanow, the former premier of Saskatchewan, to be its head. Mr. Romanow has been investigating all aspects of the system, considering various options for the delivery of health care in this country, including private, for-profit facilities. Some social scientists argue that the way in which health care is delivered—publicly or privately—may affect a society's social cohesion. A two-tiered system that provides unequal access to and unequal quality of health care (based on people's ability to pay) may lead to a diminished sense of trust in the community (Drache and Sullivan 1999). See Figure 14-7 for public and private health spending in Canada in 1998.

Many industrial countries are paying greater attention to unequal health care delivery. Addressing this problem, however, often creates difficulties. Great Britain, for example, in attempting to meet the needs of previously underserved rural areas, has closed facilities in London and other metropolitan areas and tried to reassign medical staff to rural areas. In addition to concerns about quality and availability of medical care, the National Health Service remains underfunded (R. Moseley 2000).

As governments throughout the world take greater responsibility for health care and as care becomes increasingly expensive, governments can be expected to give more and more attention to controlling expenditures.

Let's Discuss

1. What changes would you make to improve the way health care in Canada is delivered?
2. Do you believe that the principles of the Canada Health Act (i.e., public administration, comprehensiveness, universality, portability, and accessibility) should be maintained? At what cost?
3. Should health care be a basic right of all people?

Chapter Resources

Summary

Sociologists focus on the social factors that influence population rates and trends. The meanings of ***health,*** sickness, and disease are also shaped by social definitions of behaviour. This chapter considers sociological perspectives on various aspects of population, the current problems of overpopulation, health and illness, the distribution of diseases in a society, and the evolution of the health care system as a social institution.

1. Thomas Robert Malthus suggested that the world's population was growing more rapidly than the available food supply and that this gap would increase over time. However, Karl Marx saw capitalism, rather than rising world population, as the cause of social ills.
2. The primary mechanism for obtaining population information in Canada and most other countries is the ***census.***
3. Roughly two thirds of the world's nations have yet to pass fully through the second stage of ***demographic transition***, and thus they continue to experience significant population growth.
4. The developing nations face the prospect of continued population growth, since a substantial portion of their population is approaching the childbearing years. Some of the developed nations, however, have begun to stabilize population growth.
5. According to Talcott Parsons's functionalist perspective, physicians function as "gatekeepers" for the ***sick role***, either verifying a person's condition as "ill" or designating the person as "recovered."
6. Conflict theorists use the term *medicalization of society* to refer to medicine's growing role as a major institution of social control.
7. Like other forms of stratification, age stratification varies from culture to culture.
8. "Being old" is a master status that seems to overshadow all others in North America.
9. The particular problems of the aged have become the focus for a specialized area of research and inquiry known as ***gerontology***.
10. ***Disengagement theory*** implicitly suggests that society should help older people withdraw from their accustomed social roles, whereas ***activity theory*** argues that the elderly person who remains active and socially involved will be best adjusted.
11. From a conflict perspective, the low status of older people is reflected in prejudice and discrimination against them and in unfair job practices.
12. An increasing proportion of the population of Canada is composed of older people.
13. ***Ageism*** reflects a deep uneasiness on the part of younger people about growing old.
14. Labelling theorists suggest that the designation of a person as "healthy" or "ill" generally involves social definition by others. These definitions affect how others see us and how we view ourselves.
15. Contemporary ***social epidemiology*** is concerned not only with epidemics but also with nonepidemic diseases, injuries, drug addiction and alcoholism, suicide, and mental illness.
16. Studies have consistently shown that people in the lower classes have higher rates of mortality and disability.
17. Racial and ethnic minorities have higher rates of morbidity and mortality than do the dominant groups. Older people are especially vulnerable to mental health problems, like Alzheimer's disease.
18. The preeminent role of physicians within Canada's health care system has given them a position of dominance in their dealings with nurses and patients.
19. Many people seek alternative health care techniques, such as ***holistic medicine*** and self-help groups.
20. In the developed world, an aging population and technological breakthroughs have made health care both more extensive and more costly. At the same time, developing nations struggle to provide primary care for a burgeoning population. Throughout the world, an important issue is who is to pay for this care.

Critical Thinking Questions

1. Some European nations are now experiencing population declines. Their death rates are low and their birthrates are even lower than in stage III of the demographic transition model. Does this pattern suggest that there is now a fourth stage in the demographic transition? Even more important, what are the implications of negative population growth for an industrialized nation in the 21st century?
2. Sociologist Talcott Parsons has argued that the doctor–patient relationship is somewhat like that between parent and child. Does this view seem accurate? Should the doctor–patient relationship become more egalitarian? How might functionalist and conflict theorists differ in their views of the power of physicians within Canada's health care system?
3. Relate what you have learned about ageism to the ways in which our society socially constructs "old age." How is ageism evident in the mass media in Canada? How is gender related to ageism?

Key Terms

Activity theory An interactionist theory of aging that argues that elderly people who remain active and socially involved will be best adjusted. (page 363)

Ageism Prejudice and discrimination against the elderly. (365)

Birthrate The number of live births per 1000 population in a given year. Also known as the *crude birthrate.* (355)

Census An enumeration, or counting, of a population. (354)

Death rate The number of deaths per 1000 population in a given year. Also known as the *crude death rate.* (355)

Demographic transition A term used to describe the change from high birthrates and death rates to relatively low birthrates and death rates. (356)

Demography The scientific study of population. (351)

Disengagement theory A functionalist theory of aging that contends that society and the aging individual mutually sever many of their relationships. (362)

Fertility The amount of reproduction among women of childbearing age. (351)

Gerontology The scientific study of the sociological and psychological aspects of aging and the problems of the aged. (361)

Growth rate The difference between births and deaths, plus the differences between immigrants and emigrants, per 1000 population. (355)

Health As defined by the World Health Organization, a state of complete physical, mental, and social well-being, and not merely the absence of disease and infirmity. (366)

Holistic medicine A means of health maintenance using therapies in which the health care practitioner considers the person's physical, mental, emotional, and spiritual characteristics. (377)

Incidence The number of *new* cases of a specific disorder occurring within a given population during a stated period of time. (372)

Infant mortality rate The number of deaths of infants under one year of age per 1000 live births in a given year. (355)

Life expectancy The median number of years a person can be expected to live under current mortality conditions. (355)

Morbidity rates The incidence of diseases in a given population. (372)

Mortality rate The incidence of death in a given population. (372)

Population pyramid A special type of bar chart that shows the distribution of population by gender and age. (357)

Prevalence The total number of cases of a specific disorder that exist at a given time. (372)

Sick role Societal expectations about the attitudes and behaviour of a person viewed as being ill. (366)

Social epidemiology The study of the distribution of disease, impairment, and general health status across a population. (372)

Total fertility rate (TFR) The average number of children born alive to a woman, assuming that she conforms to current fertility rates. (355)

Zero population growth (ZPG) The state of a population with a growth rate of zero, achieved when the number of births plus immigrants is equal to the number of deaths plus emigrants. (359)

Additional Readings

Albert, Terry, and Gregory Williams. 1998. *The Economic Burden of AIDS in Canada.* Ottawa: Canadian Policy Research Networks. The authors suggest that HIV/AIDS is now affecting "young marginalized populations" of Aboriginal people, injection drug users, young gay men, and vulnerable women. They provide estimates of the direct and indirect costs of care and treatment for a person with HIV/AIDS throughout a lifetime.

Cockerham, William C. 1999. *Health and Social Change in Russia and Eastern Europe.* New York: Routledge. An examination of the sociological causes of the decline in life expectancy—unusual in an industrialized society—that began in the 1960s in the countries of the former Soviet Union.

McTeer, Maureen A. 1999. *Tough Choices: Living and Dying in the 21st Century.* Toronto: Irwin Law. The author examines the ways in which science and technology are influencing medical practice and our society's choices about life and death.

McVey, Wayne W., Jr., and Warren Kalbach. 1995. *Canadian Population.* Scarborough: Nelson Canada. This book introduces current demographic trends in Canadian society and provides a foundation for the understanding of Canada's population dynamics.

Internet Connection

www.mcgrawhill.ca/college/schaefer

For additional Internet exercises relating to zero population growth and political cartoons about health care issues, visit the Schaefer Online Learning Centre at ***http://www.mcgrawhill.ca/college/schaefer****. Please note that while the URLs listed were current at the time of printing, these sites often change—check the Online Learning Centre for updates.*

Formal socialization into the medical profession begins at medical school. Pretend that you are a future doctor and that you are choosing which medical school to attend. Visit the Association of American Medical Colleges at **http://www.aamc.org/meded/medschls/start.htm** for an alphabetical listing of medical schools in the United States and Canada. Select two schools and answer the following questions for each where appropriate:

(a) What are the admission requirements of the school?

(b) How much does it cost to attend the school? How might the cost of medical school affect a future doctor's career decisions?

(c) If offered, what is the demographic make-up of the faculty and the students? Does this make-up reflect patterns found in the wider society?

(d) What values drive the school's philosophy or mission?

(e) What values and ethical considerations does the school stress to students?

(f) What areas of specialization does the school offer?

(g) How large a part does technology play in the educational process?

(h) Does the school appear to embrace alternative medicine techniques, such as holistic or herbal medicines?

(i) After your "visits," which school would you choose if you wanted to be a doctor? Why?

CBC Video

Visit the Schaefer Online Learning Centre at **http://www.mcgrawhill.ca/college/schaefer** to view the CBC video segment "How Old is 'Old'?: Re-Thinking our Views on Mandatory Retirement" and answer related questions.

CHAPTER

15 COMMUNITIES AND THE ENVIRONMENT

In India, pollution is becoming a controversial political issue. This billboard graphically suggests the harmful effect of pollution on public health.

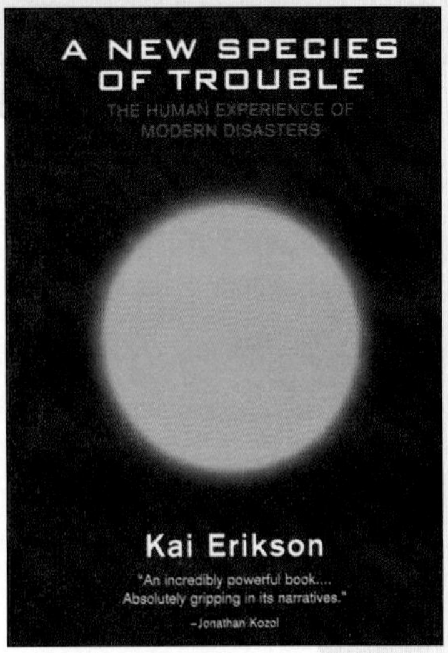
A NEW SPECIES
OF TROUBLE
THE HUMAN EXPERIENCE OF
MODERN DISASTERS
Kai Erikson
"An incredibly powerful book....
Absolutely gripping in its narratives."
–Jonathan Kozol

Over the past twenty years, research errands of one kind or another have taken me to a number of communities still stunned by the effects of a recent disaster. These include a valley in West Virginia known as Buffalo Creek, devastated by a fearsome flood; an Ojibwa Indian reserve in Canada called Grassy Narrows, plagued by contamination of the waterways along which members of the band had lived for centuries; a town in South Florida named Immokalee, where three hundred migrant farm workers were robbed of the only money most of them had ever saved; a group of houses in Colorado known as East Swallow, threatened by vapors from silent pools of gasoline that had gathered in the ground below; and the neighbourhoods surrounding Three Mile Island.

In one respect, at least, these events were altogether different. A flood. An act of larceny. A toxic poisoning. A gasoline spill. A nuclear accident. My assignment in each of those cases was to learn enough about the people who thought they had been damaged by the blow to appear on their behalf in a court of law, so each was a separate research effort, and each resulted in a separate research report.

In another respect, though, it was clear from the beginning that those scenes of trouble had much in common. I was asked to visit them in the first place, obviously, because the persons who issued the invitations thought they could see resemblances there. And just as obviously, I was drawn to them because they touched a corresponding set of curiosities and preoccupations in me. Moreover, common themes seemed to come into focus as I moved from one place to another, so that those separate happenings (and the separate stories told of them) began to fuse into a more inclusive whole. One of the excitements of sociological work in general is to watch general patterns—dim and shapeless at first—emerge from a wash of seemingly unconnected details. . . . *(Erikson 1994:11–12)* ■

In this passage from *A New Species of Trouble,* Kai Erikson explains how he brought his sociological imagination to bear on five seemingly unrelated disasters in five different communities. Each disaster, he realized, had been caused not by natural forces, but by human disregard for the natural world or for other human beings. But while ignorance or negligence is often thought to be at the bottom of such catastrophes, Erikson saw a larger, more sweeping process at work—a "new species of trouble." Consumerism and rapid increases in population, he thought, lay at the bottom of these calamities. The ever-increasing wants and needs of ever-growing numbers of people had begun to outstrip the capacity of the environment to tolerate their encroachments.

As this excerpt shows, communities and their environments are intimately connected. Environmental issues, in fact, can make or break a community because they determine how safe, healthy, and satisfying our living conditions are. This chapter explores the important role that communities of all sorts, from rural towns to suburbs and big-city neighbourhoods, play in people's lives. Communities give people the feeling that they are a part of something larger than themselves. In sociological terms, a ***community*** may be formally defined as a spatial or political unit of social organization that gives people a sense of belonging. That sense of belonging can be based either on shared residence in a particular city or neighbourhood or on a common identity, like that of gays and lesbians (Dotson 1991; see also Hillery 1955).

Anthropologist George Murdock (1949) has observed that there are only two truly universal units of human social organization: the family and the community. This chapter looks at the importance of communities from a sociological perspective. We will begin with the successive development of early communities, preindustrial cities, and industrial and postindustrial cities. We will examine the dramatic urbanization evident around the world in the 20th century, and contrast two different views of urban growth. Then we'll look at the three types of communities found in Canada—central cities, suburbs, and rural areas. We will also consider a new type of community brought about by technological change: the online community. Later in the chapter, we will examine the environmental problems facing the world as we enter the 21st century and will draw on the functionalist and conflict perspectives to better understand environmental issues. Finally, in the social policy section, we will analyze the distressing phenomenon of homelessness in Canada and elsewhere. ■

How Did Communities Originate?

Early Communities

For most of human history, people used very basic tools and knowledge to survive. They satisfied their need for an adequate food supply through hunting, foraging for fruits or vegetables, fishing, and herding. In comparison with later industrial societies, early civilizations were much more dependent on the physical environment and much less able to alter that environment to their advantage. The emergence of horticultural societies, in which people actually cultivated food rather than merely gathering fruits and vegetables, led to many dramatic changes in human social organization.

pp. 113–14

It was no longer necessary to move from place to place in search of food. Because people had to remain in specific locations to cultivate crops, more stable and enduring communities began to develop. As agricultural techniques became more and more sophisticated, a cooperative division of labour involving both family members and others developed. It gradually became possible for people to produce more food than they actually needed for themselves. They could give food, perhaps as part of an exchange, to others who might be involved in nonagricultural labour. This transition from subsistence to surplus represented a critical step in the emergence of cities.

Eventually, people produced enough goods to cover both their own needs and those of people not engaged in agricultural tasks. Initially, the surplus was limited to agricultural products, but it gradually evolved to include all types of goods and services. Residents of a city came to rely on community members who provided craft products and means of transportation, gathered information, and so forth (Lenski et al. 1995).

With these social changes came an even more elaborate division of labour, as well as a greater opportunity for differential rewards and privileges. So long as everyone was engaged in the same tasks, stratification was limited to such factors as gender, age, and perhaps the ability to perform the task (a skillful hunter could win unusual respect from the community). However, the surplus allowed for expansion of goods and services, leading to greater differentiation, a hierarchy of occupations, and social inequality. Therefore, surplus was a precondition not only for the establishment of cities but also for the

This painting shows 12th-century traders in a port city on the Mediterranean Sea. Such early settlements represented one type of preindustrial city.

division of members of a community into social classes (see Chapter 8). The ability to produce goods for other communities marked a fundamental shift in human social organization.

Preindustrial Cities

It is estimated that, beginning about 10 000 B.C., permanent settlements free from dependence on crop cultivation emerged. Yet, by today's standards of population, these early communities would barely qualify as cities. The ***preindustrial city***, as it is termed, generally had only a few thousand people living within its borders and was characterized by a relatively closed class system and limited mobility. Status in these early cities was usually based on ascribed characteristics such as family background, and education was limited to members of the elite. All the residents relied on perhaps 100 000 farmers and their own part-time farming to provide them with the needed agricultural surplus. The Mesopotamian city of Ur had a population of about 10 000 and was limited to roughly 220 acres of land, including the canals, the temple, and the harbour.

Why were these early cities so small and relatively few in number? A number of key factors restricted urbanization:

- *Reliance on animal power (both humans and beasts of burden) as a source of energy for economic production.* This limited the ability of humans to make use of and alter the physical environment.
- *Modest levels of surplus produced by the agricultural sector.* Between 50 and 90 farmers may have been required to support one city resident (Davis 1995, originally published in 1949).
- *Problems in transportation and storage of food and other goods.* Even an excellent crop could easily be lost as a result of such difficulties.
- *Hardships of migration to the city.* For many peasants, migration was both physically and economically impossible. A few weeks of travel was out of the question without more sophisticated techniques of food storage.
- *Dangers of city life.* Concentrating a society's population in a small area left it open to attack from outsiders, as well as more susceptible to extreme damages from plagues and fires.

Gideon Sjoberg (1960) examined the available information on early urban settlements of medieval Europe, India, and China. He identified three preconditions of city life: advanced technology in both agricultural and nonagricultural areas, a favourable physical environment, and a well-developed social organization.

For Sjoberg, the criteria for defining a "favourable" physical environment are variable. Proximity to coal and iron helps only if a society knows how to *use* these natural resources. Similarly, proximity to a river is particularly beneficial only if a culture has the means to transport water efficiently to the fields for irrigation and to the cities for consumption.

A sophisticated social organization is also an essential precondition for urban existence. Specialized social roles bring people together in new ways through the exchange of goods and services. A well-developed social organization ensures that these relationships are clearly defined and generally acceptable to all parties. Admittedly, Sjoberg's view of city life is an ideal type, since inequality did not vanish with the emergence of urban communities.

Industrial and Postindustrial Cities

Imagine how life could change by harnessing the energy of air, water, and other natural resources to power society's tasks. Advances in agricultural technology led to dramatic changes in community life, but so did the process of industrialization. The *Industrial Revolution,* which began in the middle of the 18th century, focused on the application of nonanimal sources of power to labour tasks. Industrialization had a wide range of effects on people's lifestyles as well as on the structure of communities. Emerging urban settlements

p. 114

Table 15-1 **Comparing Types of Cities**

Preindustrial Cities (through 18th century)	Industrial Cities (18th through mid-20th century)	Postindustrial Cities (beginning late 20th century)
Closed class system—pervasive influence of social class at birth	Open class system—mobility based on achieved characteristics	Wealth based on ability to obtain and use information
Economic realm controlled by guilds and a few families	Relatively open competition	Corporate power dominates
Beginnings of division of labour in creation of goods	Elaborate specialization in manufacturing of goods	Sense of place fades, transitional networks emerge
Pervasive influence of religion on social norms	Influence of religion limited to certain areas as society becomes more secularized	Religion becomes more fragmented; greater openness to new religious faiths
Little standardization of prices, weights, and measures	Standardization enforced by custom and law	Conflicting views of prevailing standards
Population largely illiterate, communication by word of mouth	Emergence of communication through posters, bulletins, and newspapers	Emergence of extended electronic networks
Schools limited to elites and designed to perpetuate their privileged status	Formal schooling open to the masses and viewed as a means of advancing the social order	Professional, scientific, and technical personnel are increasingly important

Sources: Based on Sjoberg 1960:323–328; E. Phillips 1996:132–135.

became centres not only of industry but also of banking, finance, and industrial management.

The factory system that developed during the Industrial Revolution led to a much more refined division of labour than was evident in early preindustrial cities. The many new occupations that were created produced a complex set of relationships among workers. Thus, the ***industrial city*** was not merely more populous than its preindustrial predecessors; it was also based on very different principles of social organization. Sjoberg outlined the contrasts between preindustrial and industrial cities, as summarized in Table 15-1.

In comparison with preindustrial cities, industrial cities have a more open class system and more mobility. After initiatives in industrial cities by women's rights groups, labour unions, and other political activists, formal education gradually became available to many children from poor and working-class families. While ascribed characteristics such as gender, race, and ethnicity remained important, a talented or skilled individual had a greater opportunity to better his or her social position. In these and other respects, the industrial city is genuinely a "different world" from the preindustrial urban community.

In the latter part of the 20th century, a new type of urban community emerged. The ***postindustrial city*** is a city in which global finance and the electronic flow of information dominate the economy. Production is decentralized and often takes place outside of urban centres, but control is centralized in multinational corporations whose influence transcends urban and even national boundaries. Social change is a constant feature of the postindustrial city. Economic and spatial restructuring seems to occur each decade if not more frequently. In the postindustrial world, cities are forced into increasing competition for economic opportunities, which deepens the plight of the urban poor (E. Phillips 1996; D. Smith and Timberlake 1993).

pp. 114–15

Sociologist Louis Wirth (1928, 1938) argued that a relatively large and permanent settlement leads to distinctive patterns of behaviour, which he called ***urbanism.*** He identified three critical factors contributing to urbanism: the size of the population, population density, and the heterogeneity (variety) of the population. A frequent result of urbanism, according to Wirth, is that we become insensitive to events around us and restrict our attention to primary groups to which we are emotionally attached. Today, people living in postindustrial cities are developing new types of attachments through the use of electronic communication: see the case study of the Blacksburg Electronic Village, pages 403–404.

Urbanization

Urbanization is a fact of life in Canada. In the 100 years between 1871 and 1971, the urban–rural distribution of the Canadian population went from being predominantly rural (80 percent) in 1871 to predominantly urban (65 percent) in 1971 (Statistics Canada 1983).

Urbanization shows up throughout the world. In 1920, only 14 percent of the world's people lived in urban areas, but by 2000 that proportion had risen to 45 percent, and by the year 2025 it is expected to be as high as 61 percent (Haub and Cornelius 2000; World Resources Institute et al. 1996).

During the 19th and early 20th centuries, rapid urbanization occurred primarily in European and North American cities. Since World War II, however, there has been an urban "explosion" in the world's developing countries (see Figure 15-1). Such rapid growth is evident in the rising number of "squatter settlements," areas occupied by the very poor on the fringe of cities, described in Box 15-1.

Some metropolitan areas have spread so far that they have connected with other urban centres. Such a densely populated area, containing two or more cities and their suburbs, has become known as a ***megalopolis.*** An example of this is the huge urban area stretching along the north shore of the St. Lawrence River and the lower Great Lakes from eastern Ontario to Windsor. In excess of 6 million people, more than 20 percent of the country's population, live between Toronto and Windsor alone. Even when it is divided into autonomous political jurisdictions, the megalopolis can be viewed as a single economic entity. The megalopolis is also evident in Great Britain, Germany, Italy, Egypt, India, Japan, and China.

Functionalist View: Urban Ecology

Human ecology is concerned with the interrelationships between people and their spatial setting and physical environment. Human ecologists have long been interested in how the physical environment shapes people's lives (for example, rivers can serve as a barrier to residential expansion) and also how people influence the surrounding environment (central heating has facilitated settlement in the Arctic). ***Urban ecology*** focuses on such relationships as they emerge in urban areas. Although the urban ecological approach examines social change in cities, it is nevertheless functionalist in its orientation because it emphasizes that different elements in urban areas contribute to stability.

Early urban ecologists such as Robert Park (1916, 1936) and Ernest Burgess (1925) concentrated on city life but drew on the approaches used by ecologists in studying plant and animal communities. With few exceptions, urban ecologists trace their work back to the ***concentric-zone theory*** devised in the 1920s by Burgess (see Figure 15-2a on page 395). Burgess proposed a theory for describing land use in industrial cities. At the centre, or nucleus, of such a city is the central business district. Large department stores, hotels, theatres, and financial institutions occupy this highly valued land. Surrounding this urban centre are succeeding zones with other types of land use and that illustrate the growth of the urban area over time.

Note that the creation of zones is a *social* process, not the result of nature alone. Families and business firms compete for the most valuable land; those possessing the most wealth and power are generally the winners. The concentric-zone theory proposed by Burgess also represented a dynamic model of urban growth. As urban growth proceeded, each zone would move even farther from the central business district.

Because of its functionalist orientation and its emphasis on stability, the concentric-zone theory tended to understate or ignore certain tensions apparent in metropolitan areas. For example, the growing use by the affluent of land in a city's peripheral areas has been uncritically approved despite the displacement of poor and minority families who have, for decades, occupied these historically less expensive neighbourhoods. Moreover, the urban ecological

FIGURE 15-1

Urbanization around the World, 2000.

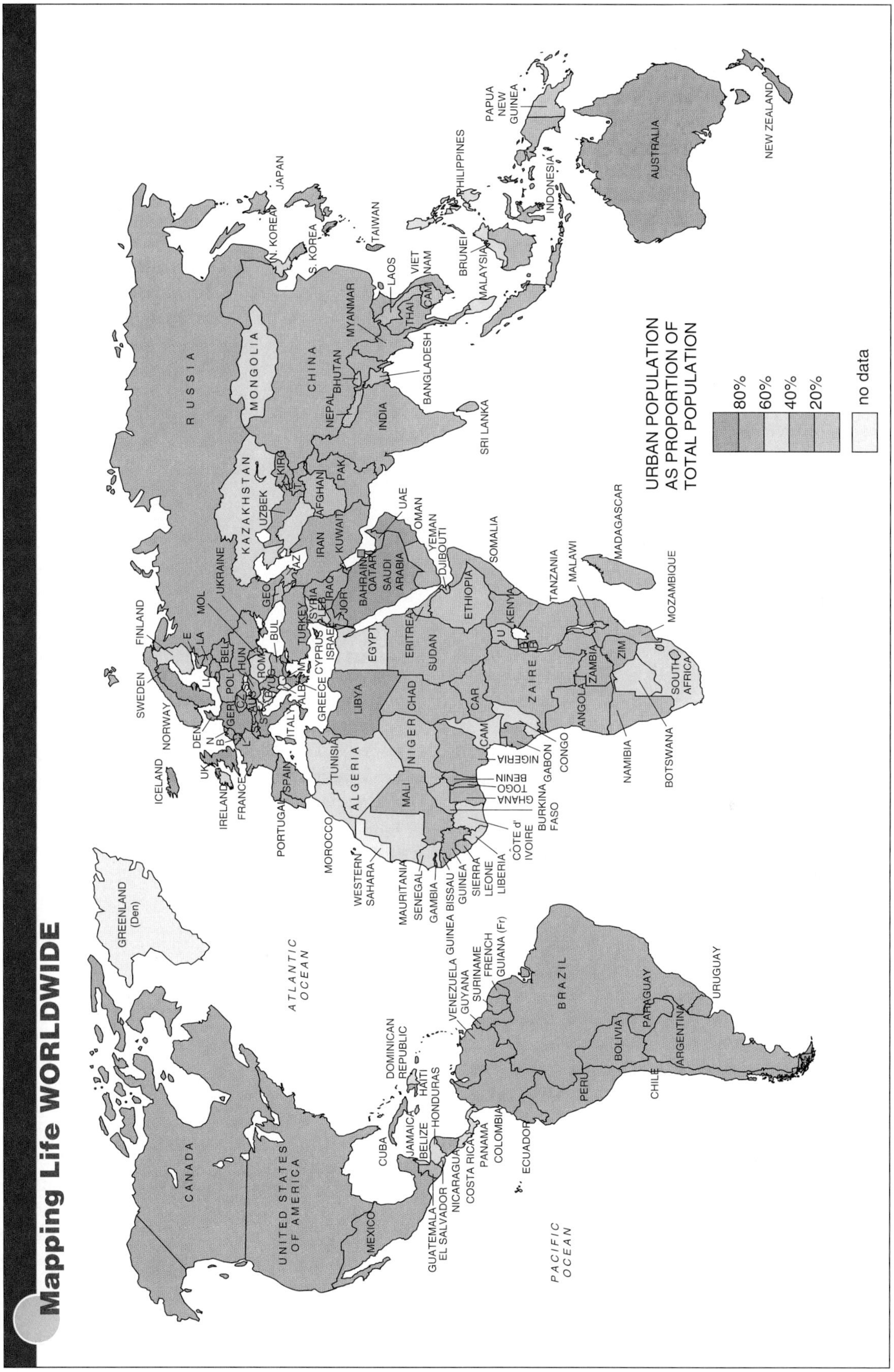

Source: Based on data in Haub and Cornelius 2000

Sociology in the Global Community

15-1 Squatter Settlements

Bariadas, favelas, bustees, kampungs, and *bidonvilles:* The terms vary depending on the nation and language, but the meaning is the same—"squatter settlements." In ***squatter settlements***, areas occupied by the very poor on the fringe of cities, housing is constructed by the settlers themselves from discarded material, including crates from loading docks and loose lumber from building projects. While the term "squatter settlement" has wide use, many observers prefer to use a less pejorative term, such as "autonomous settlements."

This type of settlement is very typical of cities in the world's developing nations. In such countries, new housing has not kept pace with the combined urban population growth resulting from births and migration from rural areas. In addition, squatter settlements swell when city dwellers are forced out of housing by astronomical jumps in rent. By definition, squatters living on vacant land are trespassers and can be legally evicted. However, given the large number of poor people who live in such settlements (by UN estimates, 40 or 50 percent of inhabitants of cities in many developing nations), governments generally look the other way.

Obviously squatters live in substandard housing, yet this is only one of the many problems they face. Residents do not receive most public services, since their presence cannot be legally recognized. Police and fire protection, paved streets, and sanitary sewers are virtually nonexistent. In some countries, squatters may have trouble voting or enrolling their children in public schools.

Despite such conditions, squatter settlements are not always as bleak as they may appear from the outside. You can often find a well developed social organization rather than disorganized collections of people. A thriving "informal economy" typically develops: residents establish small, home-based businesses such as grocery stores, jewellery shops, and the like. Rarely, however, can any but the most ambitious entrepreneurs climb out of poverty through success in this underground economy.

Squatter settlements are not always as bleak as they may appear from the outside.

Local churches, men's clubs, and women's clubs are often established in specific neighbourhoods within the settlements. In addition, certain areas may form governing councils or membership associations. These governing bodies may face the usual problems of municipal governments, including charges of corruption and factional splits. Yet, in many cases, they seem to serve their constituents effectively. In Peru, squatters hold annual elections, whereas the rest of the nation has not held local elections for more than 70 years.

Squatter settlements remind us that respected theoretical models of social science in Canada may not directly apply to other cultures. The various ecological models of urban growth, for example, would not explain metropolitan expansion that locates the poorest people on the urban fringes. Furthermore, solutions that are logical for a highly industrialized nation may not be relevant in the developing nations. Planners in developing nations, rather than focusing on large-scale solutions to urban problems, must think in terms of basic amenities, such as providing water taps or electrical power lines to the ever-expanding squatter settlements.

Let's Discuss

1. Do you know of any "squatters" in your own community? If so, describe them and the place where they live.
2. Given the number of homeless people in Canada, why aren't there more squatters?

Sources: Castells 1983; Patton 1988; Yap 1998.

perspective gave little thought to gender inequities, such as the establishment of men's softball and golf leagues in city parks without any programs for women's sports. Consequently, the urban ecological approach has been criticized for its failure to address issues of gender, race, and class.

By the middle of the 20th century, urban populations had spilled beyond the traditional city limits. No longer could urban ecologists focus exclusively on *growth* in the central city, for large numbers of urban residents were abandoning the cities to live in suburban areas. As a response to the emergence of more than one focal point in some metropolitan areas, C. D. Harris and Edward Ullman (1945) presented the ***multiple-nuclei theory*** (see Figure 15-2b). In their view, all urban growth does not radiate outward from a central business district. Instead, a metropolitan area may have many centres of development, each of which reflects a particular urban need or activity. Thus, a city may have a financial district, a manufacturing zone, a waterfront area, an entertainment centre, and so forth. Certain types of business firms and certain types of housing will naturally cluster around each distinctive nucleus (Schwab 1993).

The rise of suburban shopping malls is a vivid example of the phenomenon of multiple nuclei within metro-

FIGURE 15-2

Comparison of Ecological Theories of Urban Growth

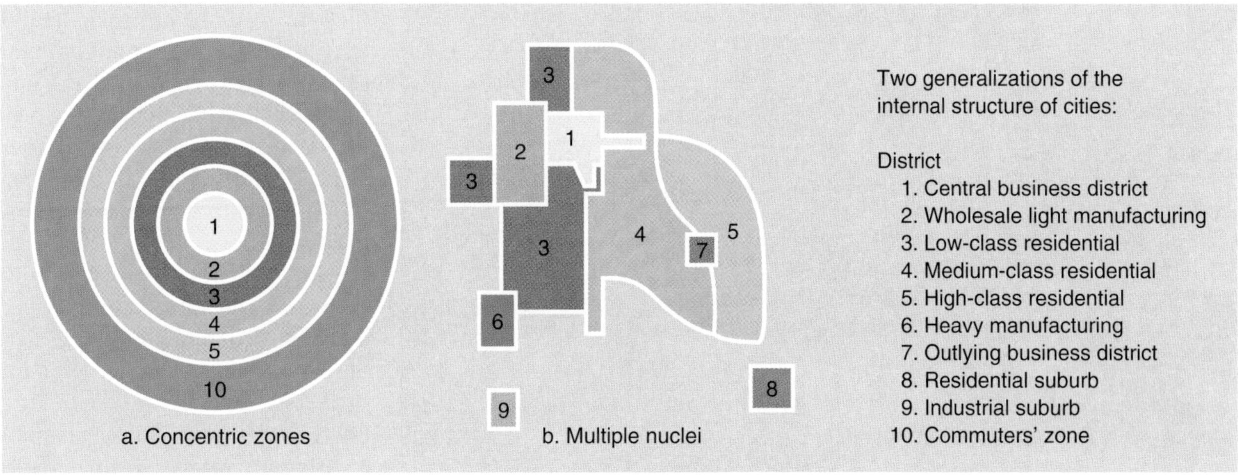

Source: C. Harris and Ullmann 1945:13.

politan areas. Initially, all major retailing in cities was located in the central business district. Each residential neighbourhood had its own grocers, bakers, and butchers, but people travelled to the centre of the city to make major purchases at department stores. However, as major metropolitan areas expanded and the suburbs became more populous, an increasing number of people began to shop nearer their homes. Today, the suburban mall is a significant retailing and social centre for communities across Canada.

In a refinement of multiple-nuclei theory, contemporary urban ecologists have begun to study what journalist Joel Garreau (1991) has called "edge cities." These communities, which have grown up on the outskirts of major metropolitan areas, are economic and social centres with identities of their own. By any standard of measurement—height of buildings, amount of office space, presence of medical facilities, presence of leisure-time facilities, or, of course, population—edge cities qualify as independent cities rather than large suburbs.

Conflict View: New Urban Sociology

Contemporary sociologists point out that metropolitan growth is not governed by waterways and rail lines, as a purely ecological interpretation might suggest. From a conflict perspective, communities are human creations that reflect people's needs, choices, and decisions—but some people have more influence over these decisions than others. Drawing on conflict theory, an approach that has come to be called the ***new urban sociology*** considers the interplay of local, national, and worldwide forces and their effect on local space, with special emphasis on the impact of global economic activity (Gottdiener and Hutchison 2000).

New urban sociologists note that ecological approaches typically have avoided examining the social forces, largely economic in nature, that have guided urban growth. For example, central business districts may be upgraded or abandoned, depending on whether urban policymakers grant substantial tax exemptions to developers. The suburban boom in the post–World War II era was fuelled by federal housing policies that channelled investment capital into the construction of single-family homes rather than to affordable rental housing in the cities. Similarly, while some observers suggest that the growth of sun-belt cities in the American South is due to a "good business climate," new urban sociologists counter that this term is actually a euphemism for hefty state and local government subsidies and antilabour policies intended to draw manufacturers (Gottdiener and Feagin 1988; M. Smith 1988).

The new urban sociology draws generally on the conflict perspective and more specifically on sociologist Immanuel Wallerstein's *world systems analysis.* Wallerstein argues that certain industrialized nations (among them, the United States, Japan, and Germany) hold a dominant position at the *core* of the global economic system. Countries such as Canada and Sweden, while technologically and economically advanced to the same level as core countries, do not have the same level of global influence. These countries are referred to as *semi-peripheral,* indicating their proximity to but marginalization from the core of power. At the same time, the poor developing countries of Asia, Africa, and Latin America are on the *periphery* of the global

pp. 194, 196

Though the African country of Kenya is mostly rural, Nairobi, a city with almost a million residents, is a modern urban area with international business connections. According to world systems analysis, the cities of developing nations exist on the periphery of the global economy, controlled and exploited by the more powerful industrialized nations.

economy, where they are controlled and exploited by core industrialized nations. Through use of world systems analysis, new urban sociologists consider urbanization from a global perspective. They view cities not as independent and autonomous entities but rather as the outcome of decision-making processes directed or influenced by a society's dominant classes and by core industrialized nations. New urban sociologists note that the rapidly growing cities of the world's developing countries have been shaped first by colonialism and then by a global economy controlled by core nations and multinational corporations (Gottdiener and Feagin 1988; D. Smith 1995).

The urban ecologists of the 1920s and 1930s were not ignorant of the role that the larger economy played in urbanization, but their theories emphasized the impact of local rather than national or global forces. By contrast, through a broad, global emphasis on social inequality and conflict, new urban sociologists are interested in such topics as the existence of an underclass, the power of multinational corporations, and deindustrialization, as well as issues to be examined later in this chapter, such as urban fiscal crises, residential segregation, and homelessness.

pp. 188, 196, 338

Developers, builders, and investment bankers are not especially interested in urban growth when it means providing housing for middle- or low-income people. This lack of interest contributes to the problem of homelessness, which will be discussed in the social policy section at the end of the chapter. These urban elites counter that the nation's housing shortage and the plight of the homeless are not their fault—and insist that they do not have the capital needed to construct and support such housing. But affluent people *are* interested in growth and *can* somehow find capital to build new shopping centres, office towers, and ballparks.

Why, then, can't they provide the capital for affordable housing, ask new urban sociologists? Part of the answer is that developers, bankers, and other powerful real estate interests view housing in quite a different manner from tenants and most homeowners. For a tenant, an apartment is shelter, housing, a home. But for developers and investors—many of them large (and sometimes multinational) corporations—an apartment is simply a housing investment. These financiers and owners are primarily concerned with maximizing profit, not with solving social problems (Feagin 1983; Gottdiener and Hutchison 2000).

As we have seen throughout this textbook—in studying such varied issues as deviance, race and ethnicity, and aging—no single theoretical approach necessarily offers sociologists the only valuable perspective. As is shown in Table 15-2, urban ecology and new urban sociology offer significantly different ways of viewing urbanization that enrich our understanding of this complex phenomenon.

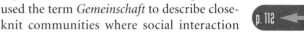

Types of Communities

Communities vary substantially in the degree to which their members feel connected and share a common identity. Ferdinand Tönnies (1988, original edition 1887) used the term *Gemeinschaft* to describe close-knit communities where social interaction among people is intimate and familiar. It is the kind of place where people in a coffee shop will stop talking when anyone enters, because they are sure to know whoever walks through the door. A shopper at the small grocery store in this town would expect to know every employee, and probably every other customer as well. By contrast, the ideal type of *Gesellschaft* describes modern urban life, in which people feel little in common with others and often form social relationships as a result of interactions focused on immediate tasks, such as purchasing a prod-

p. 112

Table 15-2 Comparing Approaches to Urbanization

	Urban Ecology	New Urban Sociology
Theoretical Perspective	Functionalist	Conflict
Primary Focus	Relationship of urban areas to their spatial setting and physical environment	Relationship of urban areas to global, national, and local forces
Key Source of Change	Technological innovations such as new methods of transportation	Economic competition and monopolization of power
Initiator of Actions	Individuals, neighbourhoods, communities	Real estate developers, banks and other financial institutions, multinational corporations
Allied Disciplines	Geography, architecture	Political science, economics

uct. Contemporary city life in Canada generally resembles a *Gesellschaft.*

The following sections will examine different types of communities found in Canada, focusing on the distinctive characteristics and problems of central cities, suburbs, and rural communities.

Central Cities

Numbers released in February, 2000, indicated that 78 percent of the country's population lived in Metropolitan Influence Zones (MIZs), which, as we will see later, are areas outside of large metropolitan population centres, but still influenced by them. These territories account for just 4 percent of Canada's landmass and are contained within a narrow strip less than 150 kilometres wide along the American border. Even those who live outside central cities, such as residents of suburban and rural communities, find that urban centres heavily influence their lifestyles.

Urban Dwellers

Many urban residents are the descendants of European immigrants—Irish, Italians, Jews, Poles, and others—who came to Canada in the 19th and early 20th centuries. The cities socialized these newcomers to the norms, values, and language of their new homeland and gave them an opportunity, though limited, to work their way up the economic ladder. In addition, a substantial number of Canadians who had been born and raised on farms came to the cities from rural areas in the period following World War II.

Even today, cities in Canada are the destinations of immigrants from around the world—including Vietnam, Jamaica, India, and China. Yet, unlike those who came to this country 100 years ago, current immigrants are arriving at a time of growing urban decay. This makes it more difficult for them to find employment and decent housing.

pp. 229, 231–33

Urban life is noteworthy for its diversity, so it would be a serious mistake to see all city residents as being alike. Sociologist Herbert J. Gans (1991) has distinguished between five types of people found in our cities:

1. *Cosmopolites.* These residents remain in cities to take advantage of unique cultural and intellectual benefits. Writers, artists, and scholars fall into this category.
2. *Unmarried and childless people.* Such people choose to live in cities because of the active nightlife and varied recreational opportunities.
3. *Ethnic villagers.* These urban residents prefer to live in their own tight-knit communities. Typically, immigrant groups isolate themselves in such neighbourhoods to avoid resentment from well-established urban dwellers.
4. *The deprived.* Very poor people and families have little choice but to live in low-rent, and often run-down, urban neighbourhoods.
5. *The trapped.* Some city residents wish to leave urban centres but cannot because of their limited economic resources and prospects. Gans includes the "downward mobiles" in this category—people who once held higher social positions but who are forced to live in less prestigious neighbourhoods owing to loss of a job, death of a wage earner, or old age. Both elderly individuals living alone and

Many racial and ethnic minorities, like the Indo-Canadian community, live in close-knit, urban neighbourhoods.

> families may feel "trapped" in part because they resent changes in their communities. Their desire to live elsewhere may reflect their uneasiness with unfamiliar immigrant groups who have become their neighbours.

These categories remind us that the city represents a choice (even a dream) for certain people and a nightmare for others. Gans's work underscores the importance of neighbourhoods in contemporary urban life. Ernest Burgess, in his study of life in Chicago in the 1920s, had given special attention to the ethnic neighbourhoods of that city. Many decades later, residents in such districts as Chinatowns or Greektowns continue to feel attached to their own ethnic communities rather than to the larger unit of a city. Even outside ethnic enclaves, a special sense of belonging can take hold in a neighbourhood.

In a more recent study in Chicago, Gerald Suttles (1972) coined the term ***defended neighbourhood*** to refer to people's definitions of their community boundaries. Neighbourhoods acquire unique identities because residents view them as geographically separate—and socially different—from adjacent areas. The defended neighbourhood, in effect, becomes a sentimental union of similar people. Neighbourhood phone directories, community newspapers, school and parish boundaries, and business advertisements all serve to define an area and distinguish it from nearby communities.

In some cases, a neighbourhood must literally defend itself. Plans for urban renewal or a superhighway may threaten to destroy an area's unique character and sense of attachment. In resisting such changes, a neighbourhood may use the strategies and tactics of community organization developed by pioneering organizer Saul Alinsky (1909–1972). Like many conflict sociologists, Alinsky was concerned with the ways in which society's most powerful institutions protect the privileges of certain groups (such as real estate developers) while keeping other groups (such as slum dwellers) in a subservient position. Alinsky (1946) emphasized the need for community residents to fight for power in their localities. In his view, it was only through the achievement and constructive use of power that people could better themselves (Horwitt 1989).

The Canadian courts have repeatedly upheld the right of communities to restrict the freedoms of individuals living within them. Age restrictions, prohibitions against pets, limitations on the size and design of exterior decoration are all restrictions that have been applied to dwelling places for many years. While each of these is defensible as necessary to maintain the look or feel of a particular neighbourhood, there is a fine line distinguishing discrimination based on these criteria from that based on less socially acceptable ones such as race, gender, or ethnicity.

Issues Facing Cities

People and neighbourhoods vary greatly within any large city, yet they all face common problems associated with crowded conditions in limited space. High incidence of crime, air pollution, overcrowded transportation arteries, noise—these unpleasant realities and many more are an increasing feature of contemporary urban life.

Yet, for all the shared experience, there are competing interests among the various populations that inhabit downtown cores. Beginning with the farm-to-factory boom of the early 20th century, there was a prolonged period of urban growth during which downtown neighbourhoods flourished. The reversal of this process began with the advent of the suburb, following the boom in automobile sales after the Second World War. During this period, core areas of major cities were rapidly abandoned by middle-class Canadians looking for detached, single family homes. In an ever-widening circle, peripheral neighbourhoods emerged. As this demographic moved out of the city centres, it was replaced by other members of society eager to take advantage of lower rents created by the exodus. This group was, for the most part, transient and often without full-time employment. Gradually, these neighbourhoods deteriorated, becoming infamous for their association with crime.

Then, during the early years of the 1990s, an odd reversal took place. Those wealthier individuals who had left the cities, now tired of commuting, began to return to the core along with their children. ***Gentrification*** refers to the process of transforming a community from a home for those at the bottom of the socioeconomic ladder to an upscale collection of condominiums and boutiques. According to *the Impact of Urban Growth on Affordable Housing*, a study funded by a grant from the Alberta Real Estate Foundation, housing affordability decreases as the density and numbers of city dwellers increases. The pace of urban growth, combined with the downloading of housing responsibilities from federal to provincial to municipal governments, has created a situation in which a housing crisis is seen as imminent.

Gentrification devalues these buildings that once provided affordable housing for low-income families and individuals. As the land becomes more valuable, these buildings are demolished or upgraded for a new class of resident. Rising in their place are upscale, exclusive condominiums and apartments well beyond the reach of existing area residents.

A similar process has taken place in American cities where the separation of people on the basis of race, ethnicity, or socioeconomic status has become a serious problem. The segregation has resulted from the policies of financial institutions, the business practices of real estate agents, the actions of home sellers, and even urban planning initiatives (for example, in decisions about where to locate public housing). Sociologists Douglas Massey and Nancy Denton (1993) have used the term "American apartheid" to refer to the residential patterns of the nation. In their view, we no longer perceive segregation as a problem but rather accept it as a feature of the urban landscape. For subordinate minority groups, segregation means not only limited housing opportunities but also less access to employment, retail outlets, and medical services.

Another critical problem for the cities has been mass transportation. Since 1950, the number of cars in Canada has multiplied twice as fast as the number of people. Growing traffic congestion in metropolitan areas has led many cities to recognize a need for safe, efficient, and inexpensive mass transit systems. However, the federal government has traditionally given much more assistance to highway programs than to public transportation. Conflict theorists note that such a bias favours the relatively affluent (automobile owners) as well as corporations such as auto manufacturers, tire makers, and oil companies. Meanwhile, low-income residents of metropolitan areas, who are much less likely to own cars than members of the middle and upper classes, face higher fares on public transit along with deteriorating service (Mason 1998).

In 1997, Transport Canada's annual report demonstrated changing federal priorities. "Over the last few years, government's role in transportation has been redefined and the economic regulatory framework has been lessened, paving the way for a significantly greater role for market forces." Of particular interest is the choice of the word "paving," which reflects an apparent preference for an infrastructure designed to facilitate the use of the private automobile over public transit.

The increased emphasis on building roads and highways is reflected in spending reports, which indicate that subsidies for highways and associated facilities rose by almost $100 million in the five-year period between 1993 and 1998, from $232 million to $321 million (Transport Canada 1997). The same skewed spending patterns are also found in the budgets of the provinces. For example, provincial governments spent 78 percent of their transportation dollars on highways, and less than 10 percent on transit in 1996 (Transport Canada 1997).

Some developers and investors are less interested in providing affordable housing than in building new sports stadiums, preferably with government subsidies. However, subsidized facilities rarely yield the employment or broad economic benefit they promise.

What these figures reveal is a bias in favour of an emerging elite within Canadian society—those able to afford a private automobile at a time when vehicle purchase prices and fuel costs have climbed dramatically in recent years. Those Canadians using public transportation systems are disproportionately from the lower-income group. Because of economic circumstances, they have no choice but to rely on transit.

Despite irrefutable evidence linking the private automobile with increased levels of air pollution in metropolitan areas, governments at all levels seem determined to facilitate its use.

Ironically, while many communities are insisting that they cannot afford to maintain public services and are shifting them to the private sector, some nevertheless find substantial funds to attract and keep professional sports franchises. The most prominent example of this in Canada is Toronto's Skydome, a stadium built specifically to maintain the economic viability of professional American baseball in Toronto. While Montreal's "Big O" stadium cost millions more, the fact that it was originally built as a facility for amateur sport puts it in a different category. Local politicians and business leaders claim that winning a sports franchise boosts the local economy and enhances community spirit. But critics counter that professional sports teams build profits for a wealthy few—and offer tax write-offs to corporations that maintain lavish luxury boxes—without genuinely revitalizing neighbourhoods, much less an entire city. These critics refer to the use of significant public funds to attract professional sports franchises as "stadium welfare." They counter the pro-stadium lobby's estimates of generated revenue by suggesting that those dollars, had they not gone to pay for hockey or baseball tickets, would have been spent elsewhere in the community.

Suburbs

The term *suburb* derives from the Latin *sub urbe,* meaning "under the city." Until recent times, most suburbs were just that—tiny communities totally dependent on urban centres for jobs, recreation, and even water.

Today the term *suburb* defies any simple definition. Generally, it refers to any community near a large city; however, the term is not used by Statistics Canada, the federal government's data-gathering arm. Instead, Statistics Canada has traditionally made the distinction between urban and rural populations. The latest census in 2001 identified populations in one of four categories:

1. *Census Metropolitan Areas* (CMAs) Urban, suburban, and rural areas of more than 100 000 people, which are socially and economically integrated
2. *Census Areas* (CAs) The same as CMAs, but with a population threshold of only 10 000
3. *Metropolitan Influence Zones* (MIZs) The areas outside CMAs, classified into one of four categories reflecting the degree of influence the CMAs have on them
4. *Census Area Influence Zones* (also called MIZs) Those areas outside of CAs, classified into one of four categories reflecting the degree of influence the CAs have on them.

Three social factors differentiate suburbs from cities. First, suburbs are generally less dense than cities; in the newest suburbs, there is often no more than one dwelling on a hectare of land. Second, the suburbs consist almost exclusively of private space. Private ornamental lawns replace common park areas for the most part. Third, suburbs have more exacting building design codes than cities, and these codes have become increasingly precise in the last decade. While the suburbs may be diverse in population, such design standards give the impression of uniformity.

It can also be difficult to distinguish between suburbs and rural areas. Certain criteria generally define suburbs: Most people work at urban (as opposed to rural) jobs, and local governments provide services such as water supply, sewage disposal, and fire protection. In rural areas, these services are less common, and a greater proportion of residents is employed in farming and related activities (Baldassare 1992).

Suburban Expansion

Whatever the precise definition of a suburb, it is clear that suburbs have expanded. In fact, suburbanization has been the most dramatic population trend in Canada throughout the 20th century. Suburban areas grew at first along railroad lines, then at the termini of streetcar tracks, and by the 1950s along the nation's growing systems of freeways and expressways. The suburban boom has been especially evident since World War II.

Suburbanization is not necessarily prompted by expansion of transportation services to the fringe of a city. The 1923 earthquake that devastated Tokyo encouraged decentralization of the city. Until the 1970s, dwellings were limited to a height of approximately 31 metres. Initially, the poor were relegated to areas outside municipal boundaries in their search for housing; many chose to live in squatter-type settlements. With the advent of a rail network and rising land costs in the central city, middle-class Japanese began moving to the suburbs after World War II (P. Hall 1977).

Proponents of the new urban sociology contend that factories were initially moved from central cities to suburbs as a means of reducing the power of labour unions.

Neighbourhoods like this one began springing up around Canadian cities during the 1950s and 1960s. Today, the suburbs still provide less expensive land for developers marketing homes to families.

Subsequently, many suburban communities induced businesses to relocate there by offering them subsidies and tax incentives. As sociologist William Julius Wilson (1996) has observed, federal housing policies contributed to the suburban boom by withholding mortgage capital from inner-city neighbourhoods, by offering favourable mortgages to new home buyers to assist in the rapid development of massive amounts of affordable tract housing in the suburbs. Moreover, federal funding for provincial construction of new roads provided a substantial boost for freeway systems (which made commuting to the cities much easier), while undermining urban communities by building freeway networks through the heart of cities.

All of these factors contributed to the movement of Canadians out of the city cores and into the suburbs. In the United States, the process was the same, but the motivation was different, with whites fleeing the to the suburbs, leaving behind segregated black and Hispanic neighbourhoods. The Canadian model tended to be based on class. In Canada, suburbanization was fuelled by the availability of affordable housing more than it was by a desire to flee the city.

Diversity in the Suburbs

In the United States, as whites moved to suburban tracts, they left behind a black population which grew to dominate the vacated space. In Canada, that same process saw the predominantly white, working class playing "musical neighbourhoods," with the members of each stratum of society upgrading their living arrangements as the socioeconomic group ahead of them moved up. Visible minority populations like the Chinese tended to remain isolated in their traditional urban pockets.

Suburbs in Canada remained relatively homogeneous for many years, in part because of immigration laws restricting access for non-white applicants. Those people of colour allowed entry to Canada were almost exclusively from the "sponsored" category, which meant they were required to live with family members or friends who sponsored them, most of whom lived in the segregated, urban neighbourhoods. As the immigration laws changed and individuals were able to qualify for landed immigrant status on their own, the option of choosing to live in suburban areas became more feasible. As a result, the population profile of these communities changed. Even in the United States, where the large non-white population was deliberately discouraged from expanding beyond its core by racist mortgage policies and real estate agents conscious of devaluing properties, urban neighbourhood integration has occurred.

Suburban diversification has taken place in Canada over the past 20 years in particular. While exact comparison of numbers with the United States is difficult because of Statistics Canada's urban–rural designation, it is a safe assumption that there are some parallels between the Canadian and American experience. Data from the United States indicates that the segregation that occurred in cities is not being mirrored in the suburbs. This is not to say that the suburbs are completely integrated, but that the separation that does exist is based more on socioeconomic factors than on race or ethnicity. Studies in both countries have demonstrated that the composition of neighbourhoods, while essentially reflecting the presence of visible minorities within the population as a whole, shows no signs of class integration. In fact, it appears that white, Asian, Indo-Canadian, and other groups share neighbourhoods that are defined on the basis of family income.

Not all suburban residents appreciate the diversity of the suburbs—especially if it means that less affluent families or members of minority groups will be moving into their communities. ***Zoning laws*** are enacted, in theory, to ensure that certain standards of housing construction are satisfied; these laws generally stipulate land use and architectural design of housing. Zoning laws can also separate industrial and commercial enterprises from residential areas. Thus, a suburb might wish to prevent a factory from moving to a quiet residential neighbourhood. However, some zoning laws serve as thinly veiled efforts to keep low-income people out of a suburb and have been attacked as "snob statutes." By requiring that a person own a certain number of square feet of land before he or she can build a home—or by prohibiting prefabricated or modular housing—a community can effectively prevent the construction of any homes that lower-class families might be able to afford. The courts have generally let such exclusionary zoning laws stand, even when charges have been made that their enactment was designed to keep out racial minorities and new immigrants with large families (Salins 1996).

Some urban and suburban residents are moving to communities even more remote from the central city or to rural areas altogether. Initial evidence suggests that this move to rural areas is only furthering the racial disparities in metropolitan areas (Bureau of the Census 1997b; Holmes 1997).

Rural Communities

As we have seen, the people of Canada live mainly in urban areas. Yet millions of Canadians live in towns of 2500 people or less that are not adjacent to a city. As is true of the suburbs, it would be a mistake to view rural communities as fitting into one set image. Turkey farms, coal mining towns, cattle ranches, and gas stations along isolated stretches of the TransCanada Highway are all part of the rural landscape in Canada.

The urbanization that swept Europe during the early stages of the Industrial Revolution took somewhat longer to affect population distributions in North America, simply because of the easy availability of land. However, the transition from a rural-based Canadian population to an urban one is all but complete. At the beginning of the 20th century, the majority of Canadians lived in what would be classified as a rural setting. During the 100 years since then, that proportion (62.5 percent in 1901) has dropped dramatically, down to 24.3 percent in 1981, and then to 20.4 percent in 2001 (Statistics Canada 2002d). The changes that have occurred in the urban–rural distribution of Canada's population have had a greater impact in some parts of the country than in others.

While Canada's economic foundations are solidly set in our history as hewers of wood, miners, and grain growers, all of these activities have been declining in importance to the national bottom line. At the same time that farming has been in decline, so have mining and logging—the two nonagricultural staples of the rural economy. When these jobs disappear, the rural populations who want to remain economically self-sufficient face special problems. Jobs are never overabundant in rural areas, and those that remain tend to pay low wages, a sharp contrast from the substantial union wages that once characterized the staples sector.

The abrupt drop in rural numbers has also had an impact on the social fabric of those communities substantially dependent on farming. Over ninety-eight percent of Canadian farms are family-owned (Canada Agriculture Museum 2003). This means that the economic disruption will, in most cases, also lead to an upheaval in the home. Under these circumstances, changing jobs becomes much more than simply moving from one employer to another, or changing career paths. It means that the family's day-to-day existence will be dramatically altered.

Rural business activities have accounted for just 29 percent of the economy of Canada in recent years (Beshiri 2001). But even that apparently low figure does not reflect the true decline in traditionally rural enterprises. Like the cities, small-town Canada has seen most of the job growth in the last decade in the service and wholesale sector.

Two other factors play a particularly important role in the struggle for survival being experienced by many communities in rural Canada. Outside of the relatively stable farm regions of the Prairies, where a vulnerable but nonetheless sustained economic structure has been alive for the past century, Canada's small towns and the surrounding districts are almost exclusively dependant on single employer enterprises. Mines and large sawmills have become the economic backbone of these places. As world markets become more competitive and the resources these industries rely on become more expensive to extract or run out altogether, these towns and villages are watching their job pool evaporate.

The coal mining community of Tumbler Ridge in northeastern British Columbia is an example of just such a process. The town, built in the 1980s by a provincial government keen to take advantage of the growing global demand for coal, has seen that demand dry up and its employer leave. While some success has been achieved at recasting the remote community as an ideal retirement site—inexpensive housing and a year-round natural playground at your door—it is doubtful that it can regain its former level of activity.

Ironically, while one set of problems is being created for rural communities by businesses leaving, another set, perhaps just as threatening, is being created by businesses arriving. The names Wal-Mart and Canadian Tire strike terror in the hearts of small-town merchants. Many residents welcome the new employment opportunities and the convenience and savings associated with these discount stores. However, for the long-time owners of the town's hardware or clothing stores, the prospect of a formidable 20 000-square-metre competitor with a national reputation is intimidating. Even when such discount stores provide a boost to a town's economy—and this is

Abandoned buildings are a common feature of small, single-industry towns where market dynamics or a depleted resource resulted in the employer leaving. Once thriving rural communities are on the decline throughout Canada and the United States.

not always the case—they can undermine the community's sense of identity and shared destiny (Curtius 1999).

Compounding the challenges faced by the residents of rural Canada are inadequacies associated with access to services. Those amenities taken for granted in large cities, such as affordable day care, are seldom found outside municipalities. Even services considered essential have been impacted. Health care provision is a perfect example. As the nation as a whole struggles with the economic realities of a public medical care system, some provinces, most notably Saskatchewan and Ontario, have trimmed the number of facilities situated in rural locations. The argument that the service is still available half an hour or an hour's drive away provides little solace to families with an emergency, or with someone in acute care whom they wish to visit.

Government fiscal policies, aimed primarily at balancing budgets, have found the sparsely populated countryside an easy target for program restraint. As rural communities decline from a loss of residents and economic base, policymakers have been confronted with an unpleasant task: deciding which ailing towns and counties to support with funds for economic development and which rural communities will, in effect, be allowed to die. New schools, health care clinics and roads can help salvage a declining area, but budgetary realities will not allow governments to invest in every region. This is not a new problem. The provincial legislature in Newfoundland faced an identical dilemma four decades ago when it came to the conclusion that many of that province's out port villages were simply too remote to sustain.

In a similar vein, Canadians living outside urban centres have historically been poor cousins when it comes to housing. A study done for Canadian Mortgage and Housing, released in February 2001, concluded that almost one third of all the homes in rural Canada failed to meet minimum standards for amenities and quality of construction.

On a more positive note, advances in electronic communication, particularly those involving satellite service, have provided rural residents with a level of connectedness that few could have imagined even a decade ago. Use of computers in the home and at work has lagged behind; however, the proportion of farms and small-town homes with a computer has started to catch up with that of the larger cities. Critical to this improvement was the federal government's commitment to getting rural Canada online. On March 30, 1999, Canada became the first of the Organization of Economic Co-operation and Development (OCED) countries to complete its goal to have every school in the country connected to the Internet.

No matter where people make their homes—whether in the city, suburb, or country village—economic and technological change will have an impact on their quality of life.

Community and Technological Change: A Case Study

Blacksburg, Virginia, a small American college town whose population swells each year with the influx of students returning from summer break, lies in the Appalachian Mountain range. This rural community, at first glance no different from any other small town, has acquired an international reputation as an electronic village, one of the first of its kind. Foreigners visiting Washington, D.C., frequently seek out the town, which they expect will look something like Las Vegas. Andrew Cohill, a professor at Virginia Polytechnic Institute and State University, says he frequently hears from visitors eager to see the electronic village. He tells them there's nothing to see (Yaukey 1997).

Blacksburg Electronic Village (BEV) is an online community that connects 85 percent of Blacksburg's residents and 75 percent of its businesses (www.bev.net). The network began in 1987, when Virginia Tech invested US$16 million in a high-speed voice and data network for use throughout the university. By the early 1990s university administrators were talking with Blacksburg officials and representatives of Bell Atlantic about providing affordable high-speed Internet access to everyone in town. In 1993 universal Internet access became a reality. The majority of residents have modems in their homes; schools, libraries, and the senior centre offer public access to those who don't. Citizens of Blacksburg can now communicate with city hall, schools, and businesses via e-mail. Soon they will be able to pay their bills, register their cars, and license their dogs online.

Like many other aspects of modern society, the concept of community is evolving in response to technological change. Many people now speak of communities or neighbourhoods on the Internet. As we saw earlier, several of the changes communities and urban areas have undergone in recent years can be traced to the growth of electronic information networks.

BEV has had a positive effect on the town, users in Blacksburg agree. An enhanced sense of community is the most pervasive outcome. Seniors have greeted the new service enthusiastically: The senior centre houses ten computers, and a special service tailored to the needs of elders has 180 subscribers. The strengthening of local bonds has surprised some, perhaps because it runs counter to the conventional wisdom that the Internet will unite people from around the world in a global online community. One retired physicist didn't think BEV would catch on, but was pleasantly surprised by the speed with which residents adopted it.

BEV has also brought some noticeable economic benefits to the town. Some residents, like the proprietor of Green Dreams, an online retailer of homemade vinegars, have seized the opportunity to become online entrepreneurs. And a corporate research centre at the edge of town has been attracting more and more startup ventures, bringing new jobs and income to the college town. CEOs of the innovative new companies like the fresh air, low crime rate, and cutting-edge intellectual climate of Blacksburg. One, the head of Blue Ridge Interactive, an online purveyor of magazines, raves about the supportive atmosphere in the town (Clark 1999; Yaukey 1997; Zajac 1999).

The wider implications of the electronic village are only beginning to become clear. If the installation of universal high-speed access to the Internet can draw new companies away from more heavily populated areas like northern Virginia, it may contribute to the decay of older urban areas, worsening the plight of inner-city residents. And BEV users are concerned about the fact that not all families in rural Montgomery County can afford to tap into the network, which requires an in-home computer and a small monthly connection fee. Roger Ehrich, a professor of computer science at Virginia Tech, believes the best way to level the playing field is to provide Internet access to children at school, wherever they live (Zajac 1999).

Finally, the advent of the electronic community has the potential to revolutionize not just communities, but the way sociological research on communities is done. Automatic electronic monitoring of online response rates may someday replace telephone surveys and the distribution, collection, and coding of paper questionnaires. In the future, scholars may be able to visit far-flung electronic communities without leaving the comfort of their offices, and to travel safely through otherwise dangerous villages.

Within all communities, environmental issues play a part in determining the quality of life people enjoy or must endure. We'll turn now to a closer look at these important concerns.

The Environment

In September, 2000, a group of protestors from Kirkland Lake, Ontario, filled a life-sized metal moose with garbage, and delivered it to the grounds of Toronto's Nathan Phillips Square. The moose, nicknamed Smelly Nelly, was created by students from Timiskaming District Secondary School in nearby New Liskeard. Nelly was residents' way of expressing their concern over Toronto's plan to ship 900 000 tonnes of trash to the abandoned Adams Mine outside the northern town. Participants were unwilling to accept assurances of the plan's safety, citing the potential dangers to the community's water supply (Canadian Press 2000).

While some people would consider this protest an extreme one, it demonstrated the lengths to which activists must go to reverse the wave of destruction humans have unleashed on the environment in recent centuries. With each passing year, we are learning more about the environmental damage caused by burgeoning population levels and consumption patterns. Though disasters like the ones sociologist Kai Erikson investigated (see chapter opening) are still comparatively rare, we can see the superficial signs of despoliation almost everywhere. Our air, our water, and our land are being polluted, whether we live in Kirkland Lake, Mexico City, or Lagos, Nigeria.

Environmental Problems: An Overview

In recent decades, the planet has witnessed a series of environmental catastrophes. Some, like the Chernobyl nuclear disaster in the former Soviet Union, and the sinking of the oil tanker *Exxon Valdez* in Prince William

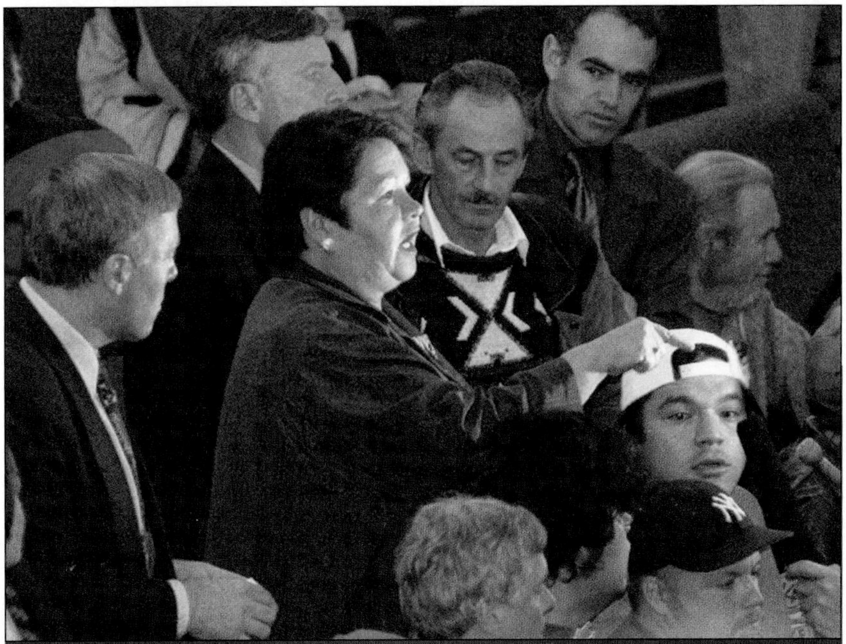

While the Internet has provided a new venue for social protest, face-to-face confrontation at public meetings remains a critical element of the environmental movement. Here, Kirkland Lake, Ontario, residents protest a plan to ship garbage from Toronto to an open pit mine in their town.

Sound off the coast of Alaska, have captured the attention of both the public and the media.

In 1986, a series of explosions set off a catastrophic nuclear reactor accident at Chernobyl, a part of Ukraine (in what was then the Soviet Union). This accident killed at least 32 000 people. Some 300 000 residents had to be evacuated, and the area became uninhabitable for 30 kilometres in any direction. High levels of radiation were found as far as 50 kilometres from the reactor site, and radioactivity levels were well above normal as far away as Sweden and Japan. According to one estimate, the Chernobyl accident and the resulting nuclear fallout may ultimately result in 100 000 excess cases of cancer worldwide (Shcherbak 1996).

For every major story, though, there are hundreds of smaller incidents of environmental degradation. From the denuded sugar maple stands of Quebec and New York to the air quality warnings that have become a fact of life in the Fraser Valley outside Vancouver, the air, water, and soil of North America is under assault. It is not only humans who are at risk; Box 15-2 describes some of the actions that have been taken to protect Canada's endangered species.

Our image of Canada as a vast, unspoiled wilderness with two or three big cities and a dozen or so smaller ones tends to downplay the impact we have on the environment. With 300 million Americans consuming the planet's resources at levels that have created blackouts in California and elsewhere, and a government in Washington fuelling an appetite for gasoline by mining protected wilderness areas, Canadians often adopt an attitude of righteousness about environmental issues. However, a 2000 report by the Commission for Environmental Cooperation, a body established as part of the North American Free Trade Agreement (NAFTA) to monitor and compare pollution levels in Canada, the United States and Mexico, ranked Ontario as the third worst jurisdiction in the three countries. With levels of pollutants surpassed only by Texas and Pennsylvania, Ontario's toxic discharges are a reflection of a national environmental policy that covers just four substances. This compares poorly to the American Clean Air Act of 1990, which has both an extensive list of standards and an enforcement policy with teeth.

Air Pollution

More than 1 billion people on the planet are exposed to potentially health-damaging levels of air pollution (World Resources Institute 1998). Unfortunately, in cities around the world, residents have come to accept smog and polluted air as "normal." Air pollution in urban areas is caused primarily by emissions from automobiles and secondarily by emissions from electric power plants and heavy industries. Urban smog not only limits visibility; it can lead to health problems as uncomfortable as eye irritation and as deadly as lung cancer. Such problems are especially severe in developing countries. The World Health Organization estimates that up to 700 000 premature deaths *per year* could be prevented if pollutants were brought down to safer levels (Carty 1999).

For all the bad news, however, there has been progress. Precipitated by the alarm over toxic rain in the 1970s, government and industry have worked to reduce the levels of air-borne pollutants from a variety of standards. Controls on emissions from coal-fired power plants and heavy industry in Central Canada have reversed a decades-long slide in air quality. In other, less industrialized parts of the country the focus has been on carbon dioxide as the number of cars in every driveway increases, and people continue to commute long distances in single occupant vehicles. Both Ontario's Drive Clean program

Research in Action 15-2 Protecting Canada's Endangered Species

Canada covers 13 million square kilometres of land and water containing a significant proportion of the planet's species—20 percent of all wildlife, 24 percent of the globe's wetlands, 20 percent of all the fresh water, and almost 10 percent all forests. Scientists have identified over 71 000 plant and animal species, from 5000 types of algae at one end of the food chain to 193 types of mammals at the other. This impressive scope of biodiversity presents Canada with a critical role in the protection of the planet. In their 2000 report, *Protecting Wild Species at Risk in Canada*, authors Jean-Luc Bourdages and Christine Labelle have documented the historical and contemporary context of this issue.

Canada's recognition of the importance of protecting the natural environment against human incursion began with the enactment of the National Parks Act in the 1880s. This important piece of legislation demonstrated the commitment and the foresight of the nation's lawmakers to protecting the environment, long before the proliferation of such damaging phenomena as automobiles and highways, urban sprawl, and the technological advances that would lead to massive over-harvesting of oceans and forests. In June, 2000, the act was further strengthened by Bill C-27, an initiative specifically intended to protect all flora and fauna existing within the national park system.

The insight demonstrated before the turn of the 20th century gave birth to another important undertaking in the early part of the last century, when Canada joined with the United States to create the Migratory Bird Convention to control hunting and deter commercial trade. Since that time, Canada has enacted several pieces of legislation designed to enhance the protection of wild species. These include the Canada Wildlife Act of 1973, and the adoption of several international agreements during the 1990s, including the International Convention on Biodiversity. In addition to Ottawa's efforts, several provinces—Ontario in 1973, New Brunswick in 1974, Quebec in 1989, Manitoba in 1990, and Nova Scotia in 1998—have created legal protection for species at risk of extinction.

The impact of humans on the environment continues to be a threat to species nearing extinction.

Aside from the obvious impact of the human footprint in densely populated areas such as the contiguous urban corridor running from Quebec City to Windsor, other specific activities present a challenge to those interested in maintaining the natural environment. It is perhaps ironic that one of the reasons given by activists for protecting species—the undiscovered potential of seemingly valueless plants and animals—in itself represents a threat. For instance, recent pharmacological research has identified the bark of the Pacific Yew tree as an important source of taxol, a substance effective in fighting cancer. The consequence of this discovery is perhaps predictable. Biologists are now concerned about the over-harvesting of this slow-growing, uncommon tree. Of course, they have faced similar challenges in the past. At one time, poachers preyed on bears for their gall bladders, believed to be a booster of sexual potency in some cultures.

While all its efforts to protect the environment have earned Canada international recognition, this country has yet to specifically legislate federal protection for endangered species. This means that in many jurisdictions, the impact of humans on the environment continues to be a threat to species nearing extinction. However, it is encouraging to note that the Liberal government has indicated its desire to address this situation. In April, 2000, Bill C-33 was tabled "for the specific purpose of protecting species at risk." Unfortunately, the bill died with the dissolution of Parliament for a federal election. Nonetheless, the precedent is positive, and Canadians can expect similar legislation during the government's current term.

Let's Discuss

1. Why do you think the natural environment is important to sociologists? What role can sociology play in protecting the environment?
2. What by-laws exist within your community that specifically address the issue of endangered species? Is it possible for cities and towns to play an important part in protecting endangered species?

Source: Bourdages and Labelle 2000.

and British Columbia's Aircare program require vehicles to pass a rigorous emissions test to qualify to have its insurance renewed or for the driver to be able to renew his or her licence.

People are capable of changing their behaviour, but they are also unwilling to make such changes permanent. For example, during the 1984 Olympics in Los Angeles, residents were asked to carpool and stagger work hours to relieve traffic congestion and improve the quality of air the athletes would breathe. These changes resulted in a remarkable 12 percent drop in ozone levels. However, when the Olympians left, people reverted to their normal behaviour and the ozone levels climbed back up (Nussbaum 1998).

Water Pollution

Through the first two thirds of the 20th century, Canadian government and industry, including the agriculture industry of the corporate farm, participated in the unregulated dumping of waste and ignored the potentially devastating effects it could have on the environment. Government estimates indicate that perhaps as many as 1.5 million Canadians live in municipalities where wastewater is returned to the environment without undergoing any treatment process. The consequences of those practices are now catching up with us.

In April 2000, a chlorinator in the town of Walkerton, Ontario, broke down, allowing untreated water to enter the municipal system. The result was an *E.coli* bacteria contamination of the town's water system. Within a week, two people in the community fell deathly ill, but no connection was made to the tainted water supply. Over the next several weeks, analyses of the town's water by an independent testing laboratory provided conflicting results—first testing positive for *E. coli* and coliform bacteria, then negative. During this period of uncertainty, the Walkerton Public Utilities Commission continued to pump water from the untreated well. Then, in the second week of May, a major storm hit the region, and torrents of water covered farm fields and washed away huge amounts of cattle manure. The overflow inundated the untreated well, filling it with deadly runoff. For more than a week, the town's water system continued to deliver the deadly liquid to homes, even after residents began turning up in local hospitals in large numbers, complaining of cramps, vomiting, and fever. In the end, seven people died and over 2300 suffered serious symptoms.

The events at Walkerton took place despite the fact that there was a Public Utilities Commission charged with maintaining the safety of Walkerton's water supply; despite the fact that a government-approved testing facility had repeatedly warned officials of the dangerous state of the community's water; despite having a regional health authority with an interest in monitoring the health of area residents; and despite a provincial Ministry of the Environment responsible for monitoring water contamination issues.

In the end, an inquiry found that the town's utility manager, Stan Koebel, bore primary responsibility for the outbreak and the lack of initial response to the unsafe water. The regional health board and the Province of Ontario were not found directly responsible for the deaths; however, the coroner did point to the provincial government's cost-cutting measures as a contributing factor. Just a few short months later, a very similar set of circumstances began to emerge in rural Saskatchewan.

Water has been touted as "the gold of the 21st century," and with incidents of contamination and shortage becoming increasingly common, it's easy to see why. As our cities continue to grow, draining their once adequate reservoirs and placing larger demands for agricultural products on rural areas, the availability and quality of water, even in a country as rich in this resource as Canada, will continue to deteriorate.

Fish poisoned by a deadly cyanide spill lie on the bank of the Tisa River in Yugoslavia. Throughout the world, industrial pollutants have rendered many water bodies unsafe for fishing, drinking, or swimming.

Contamination of Land

In the spring of 2001, the *Ottawa Citizen* reported that the State of Michigan had appealed directly to the Canadian government to stop a plan by the City of Toronto to have its garbage transported across the border and dumped in a massive landfill (Blackwell 2001). Ironically, Michigan's Department of the Environment had been counselled by the Kirkland Lake Chamber of Commerce to appeal against the proposed dumping. The northern Ontario mining town had earlier been successful in stopping a plan to transport Toronto's garbage by train to a nearby abandoned mine.

A significant part of land contamination comes from the tremendous demand for landfills to handle the nation's waste. Recycling programs aimed at reducing the need for landfills are perhaps the most visible aspect of environmentalism. Plus, a new way to be green has developed: the Internet. For example, over-the-Net commercial transactions allow the downloading of new software, reducing the need for wasteful packaging and shipping materials, including fuel for delivery trucks. And the availability of e-mail and electronic networking encourages people to work at home rather than contribute to the pollution caused by commuting (Belsie 2000; Booth 2000).

What are the basic causes of our growing environmental problems? Neo-Malthusians such as Paul Ehrlich and Anne Erhlich (P. Ehrlich 1968; P. Ehrlich and Ehrlich 1990) see world population growth as the central factor in environmental deterioration. They argue that population control is essential in preventing widespread starvation and environmental decay. Barry Commoner (1971, 1990), a biologist, counters that the primary cause of environmental ills is the increasing use of technological innovations that are destructive to the world's environment—among them plastics, detergents, synthetic fibres, pesticides, herbicides, and chemical fertilizers. In the following sections, we will contrast the functionalist and conflict approaches to the study of environmental issues.

Functionalism and Human Ecology

Earlier, we noted that human ecology is concerned with interrelationships between people and their environment. Environmentalist Barry Commoner (1971:39) has stated that "everything is connected to everything else." Human ecologists, as we've seen, focus on how the physical environment shapes people's lives and also on how people influence the surrounding environment.

In an application of the human ecological perspective, sociologist Riley Dunlap suggests that the natural environment serves three basic functions for humans, as it does for the many animal species (Dunlap 1993; Dunlap and Catton 1983):

1. *The environment provides the resources essential for life.* These include air, water, and materials used to create shelter, transportation, and needed products. If human societies exhaust these resources—for example, by polluting the water supply or cutting down rain forests—the consequences can be dire.
2. *The environment serves as a waste repository.* More so than other living species, humans produce a huge quantity and variety of waste products—bottles, boxes, papers, sewage, garbage, to name just a few. Various types of pollution have become more common because human societies are generating more wastes than the environment can safely absorb.
3. *The environment "houses" our species.* It is our home, our living space, the place where we reside, work, and play. At times we take this for granted, but not when day-to-day living conditions become unpleasant and difficult. If our air is "heavy," if our tap water turns brown, if toxic chemicals seep into our neighbourhood, we remember why it is vital to live in a healthful environment.

Dunlap (1993) points out that these three functions of the environment actually compete with one another. Human use of the environment for one of these functions will often strain its ability to fulfill the other two. For example, with world population continuing to rise, we have an increasing need to raze forests or farmland and build housing developments. But each time we do so, we are reducing the amount of land providing food, lumber, or habitat for wildlife.

The tension between the three essential functions of the environment brings us back to the human ecologists' view that "everything is connected to everything else." In facing the environmental challenges of the 21st century, government policymakers and environmentalists must determine how they can fulfill human societies' pressing needs (for example, for food, clothing, and shelter) while at the same time preserving the environment as a source of resources, a waste repository, and our home.

Conventional wisdom holds that concern for environmental quality is limited to the world's wealthy industrialized nations. However, the results of the 1992 Health of the Planet survey conducted in 24 countries by the Gallup International Institute show that there is *widespread* environmental concern around the planet.

Conflict View of Environmental Issues

In Chapter 8, we drew on world systems analysis to show how a growing share of the human and natural resources of the developing countries is being redistributed to the core industrialized nations. This process only intensifies the destruction of natural resources in poorer regions of the world. From a conflict perspective, less affluent nations are being forced to exploit their mineral deposits, forests, and fisheries in order to meet their debt obligations. The poor turn to the only means of survival available to them: They plough mountain slopes, burn plots in tropical forests, and overgraze grasslands (Livernash and Rodenburg 1998).

Brazil exemplifies the interplay between economic troubles and environmental destruction. Each year more than 28 500 square kilometres of the Amazon rain forest are cleared for crops and livestock through burning. This elimination of the rain forest affects worldwide weather patterns and heightens the gradual warming of the earth in a process known as the *greenhouse effect.* More than 160 nations gathered in Kyoto, Japan, in December 1997 for the Conference of the Parties on Climate Change. The preconference goal was to develop a strategy to reduce production of "greenhouse gases" by the year 2010 to pre-1900 levels. The treaty, known as the Kyoto Protocol, does call for industrial nations to reduce their emissions. However, it set no similar goals for developing countries, which, like Brazil, are struggling to move ahead economically.

These socioeconomic patterns, with harmful environmental consequences, are evident not only in Latin America but also in many regions of Africa and Asia. Conflict theorists are well aware of the environmental implications of land use policies in the Third World, but they contend that such a focus on the developing countries can contain an element of ethnocentrism. Who, they ask, is more to blame for environmental deterioration: the poverty-stricken and "food-hungry" populations of the world or the "energy-hungry" industrialized nations (G. Miller 1972:117)?

Conflict theorists point out that Western industrialized nations account for only 25 percent of the world's population but are responsible for 85 percent of worldwide consumption. A mere 6 percent of the world's people consume more than half the world's nonrenewable resources and more than one third of all the raw materials produced. Such data lead conflict theorists to charge that the most serious threat to the environment comes from "affluent megaconsumers and megapolluters" (Bharadwaj 1992; G. Miller 1972).

Allan Schnaiberg (1994) further refines this analysis by criticizing the focus on affluent consumers as the cause of environmental troubles. In his view, a capitalist system has a "treadmill of production" because of its inherent need to build ever-expanding profits. This treadmill necessitates creating an increasing demand for products, obtaining natural resources at minimal cost, and manufacturing products as quickly and cheaply as possible—no matter what the long-term environmental consequences of this approach.

Environmental Justice

In 1987, the California utility Pacific Gas and Electric (PG&E) announced that it had discovered levels of hexavalent chromium, a chemical linked to cancer since the 1920s, in the groundwater around its gas compressor station near the town of Hinkley. After reporting levels ten times the legal limit, the company made an offer to purchase surrounding properties, which might have been contaminated by leaching from its waste ponds. The story might have ended there if it were not for the keen eye of a neophyte legal assistant, Erin Brockovich.

The story of the town and its fight to have PG&E held accountable for the illness and death attributed to the toxic discharge was made famous in the Academy Award winning film of the same name. By linking medical records to the real estate transactions associated with the company's buyout offer, Brockovich was able to win a multimillion dollar settlement for the residents of the community.

While this story has become the best known example of recent environmental justice, it is by no means the only one. Nor does it demonstrate the whole picture. The law, in its inexorable and even-handed way, has also provided access to justice for those wishing to defend their rights to access markets. In a suit filed against the State of California in 1999, a Canadian company, Methanex, announced its intention to fight a ban on one of its products. The product, a gasoline additive called MTBE, had been found in the groundwater of the community of South Tahoe. The company, citing poor handling methods as the cause of the contamination, sued for almost US$1 billion, claiming lost business. The outcome of the case has yet to be decided, but its potential impact is clear. The threat of being taken to court and forced to pay millions or hundreds of millions of dollars in damages can only serve as a deterrent to future environmental restrictions. How many governments can afford to fight such battles?

SOCIAL POLICY AND COMMUNITIES

Seeking Shelter Worldwide

The Issue

A chance meeting brought two old classmates together. In late 1997, Prince Charles encountered Clive Harold during a tour of the offices of a magazine sold by the homeless in London. But while Prince Charles can call several palaces home, Harold is homeless. This modern-day version of the "The Prince and the Pauper" intrigued many people with its message that "it can happen to anyone." Harold had been a successful author and journalist until his marriage fell apart and alcohol turned his life inside out (*Chicago Tribune* 1997b).

The issue of inadequate shelter manifests itself in many ways, for all housing problems can be considered relative. For a middle-class family in Canada, it may mean a somewhat smaller house than they need because that is all they can afford. For a single working adult in Tokyo, it may mean having to commute two hours to a full-time job. For many people worldwide, however, the housing problem consists of merely finding shelter of any kind that they can afford, in a place where anyone would reasonably wish to live. Prince Charles of Buckingham Palace and Clive Harold, homeless person, are extreme examples of a continuum present in all communities in all societies. What can be done to ensure adequate shelter for those who can't afford it?

In a story the press dubbed "The Prince and the Pauper," Prince Charles was surprised to run into an old classmate while visiting the office of a magazine sold by the homeless—and was even more surprised to learn that the fellow was himself homeless.

The Setting

Homelessness is evident in both industrialized and developing countries. According to experts at the Centre for Applied Research at the University of Toronto, there have been only a handful of attempts to count Canada's homeless population, and none of those have been any more successful than the efforts in the United States. Estimates may range from 25 000 to more than 300 000 for the number of people who do not have homes in Canada, but compiling an accurate list is both difficult and expensive.

In Great Britain, some 175 000 people are accepted as homeless by the government and are given housing. An even larger number, perhaps 1 million people, are turned away from government assistance or are sharing a household with relatives or acquaintances but want separate accommodations. While an accurate figure is not available, it is estimated that 1 percent of Western Europeans are homeless; they sleep in the streets, depend on night shelters and hostels, or live in precarious accommodations (B. Lee 1992; Platt 1993; Stearn 1993).

In Japan, the problem of homelessness is just as serious. A single protest drew roughly 6000 homeless people to Tokyo in 1998. The Japanese usually hide such misfortune, thinking it shameful, but a severe economic downturn had victimized many formerly prosperous citizens, swelling the numbers of the homeless. A chronic space shortage in the heavily populated island nation, together with opposition to the establishment of homeless shelters in residential neighbourhoods, compounds the problem (Hara 2000).

In developing countries, rapid population growth has outpaced the expansion of housing by a wide margin, leading to a rise in homelessness. For example, estimates of homelessness in Mexico City range from 10 000 to 100 000, and these estimates do not include the many people living in caves or squatter settlements (see Box 15-1). By 1998, in urban areas alone, 600 million people around the world were either homeless or inadequately housed (G. Goldstein 1998; Ross 1996).

Sociological Insights

Both in Canada and around the world, being homeless functions as a master status that largely defines a person's position within society. In this case, homelessness tends to mean that in many important respects, the individual is *outside* society. Without a home address and telephone, it is difficult to look for work or even apply for public assistance.

pp. 102–03, 154

Moreover, the master status of being homeless carries a serious stigma and can lead to prejudice and discrimination. Poor treatment of people suspected of being homeless is common in stores and restaurants, and many communities have reported acts of random violence against homeless people.

The profile of homelessness has changed significantly during the last 20 years. In the past, homeless people were primarily older white males living as alcoholics in skid-row areas. However, best estimates suggest that today's homeless are comparatively younger. As with counting the overall number of homeless Canadians, calculating their age in any precise way is impossible.

Changing economic and residential patterns account for much of this increase in homelessness. In recent decades, the process of urban renewal has included a noticeable boom in gentrification. In some instances, city governments have promoted gentrification by granting lucrative tax breaks to developers who convert low-cost rental units into luxury apartments and condominiums. Conflict theorists note that although the affluent may derive both financial and emotional benefits from gentrification and redevelopment, the poor often end up being thrown out on the street.

There is an undeniable connection between the nation's growing shortage of affordable housing and the rise in homelessness (Elliot and Krivo 1991). Yet sociologist Peter Rossi (1989, 1990) cautions against focusing too narrowly on housing shortage while ignoring structural factors, such as the decline in the demand for manual labour in cities and the increasing prevalence of chronically unemployed young men among the homeless. Rossi contends that structural changes have put everyone in extreme poverty at higher risk of becoming homeless—especially poor people with an accumulation of disabilities (such as drug abuse, bad health, unemployment, and criminal records). Being disabled in this manner forces the individual to rely on family and friends for support, often for a prolonged period. If the strain on this support network is so great that it collapses, homelessness may result. While many researchers accept Rossi's theory, the general public often prefers to "blame the victim" for becoming homeless (B. Lee 1992).

Homeless women often have additional problems that distinguish them from homeless men. Homeless women report more recent injuries or acute illnesses, as well as more chronic health problems, than homeless men. Moreover, these women have experienced more disruption in their families and social networks than homeless men (Liebow 1993).

Sociologists attribute homelessness in developing nations not only to income inequality but also to population growth and an influx of people from rural areas and areas experiencing natural disaster, famine, or warfare. A major barrier to constructing decent, legal, and affordable housing in the urban areas of these developing nations is the political power of large-scale landowners and small-scale land speculators—anyone buying a few lots as investment. In the view of conflict theorists, these groups conspire to enhance their own financial investment by making the supply of legally buildable land scarce. (This problem is not unknown in the cities of North America, but a World Bank survey shows that the increase in the cost of land is twice as great in developing nations as in industrial countries.) In many cases, residents who can afford building materials have no choice but to become squatters. Those who can't are likely to become homeless.

Policy Initiatives

Thus far, policymakers have often been content to steer the homeless toward large, overcrowded, unhealthy shelters. Many neighbourhoods and communities have resisted plans to open large shelters or even smaller residences for the homeless, often raising the familiar cry of "Not in my backyard!"

The Government of Canada's Homeless Initiative was announced in 1999, and funded with $753 million over the next three years. The goal of the program was to create partnerships with local governments in the ten Canadian cities with a "documented" and "significant absolute homeless problem," to develop affordable, stable housing alternatives. Those ten urban centres contain 80 percent of the nation's homeless population. The main program associated with the initiative has as its goals (1) to ensure that no one is forced to live on the street, (2) to reduce the number of Canadians dependent on shelters, transition, and supportive housing, and (3) to help the homeless achieve self-sufficiency.

Even though media portrayals of the homeless person seldom get beyond the life-weary male with an addiction, the actual population is much more diverse. For instance, Aboriginals are more at risk of falling victim to this condition than members of other groups, resulting in homelessness becoming endemic both on and off reserves and in both urban and rural settings. At particular risk are young First Nations females in Western Canada, who outnumber males on the streets of our large Prairie cities.

The stereotype that overlooks the impact of homelessness on Aboriginals also fails to recognize the degree

In Japan in 1998, as many as 6000 homeless people marched on the Tokyo Metropolitan Office to protest the lack of shelter facilities. This biting cartoon from the *Japan Times* acknowledges their plight.

to which women in Canada are affected by this condition. One of the difficulties faced by service providers seeking to assist this population is their relative invisibility. Research done in both Canada and the United States indicates that women's homelessness is often disguised in an attempt to limit others' perceptions of their vulnerability. Women on the street are, for obvious reasons, more susceptible to violence. Another significant factor contributing to this phenomenon is the fact that homeless females are often involved in prostitution. This finding correlates with information that identifies these women as generally younger than their male counterparts. Finally, homeless women have a profile that distinguishes them in many ways from men. Proportionately, they are more likely to be dealing with a mental illness, less likely to be alcoholics, more likely to have dependent children, and more likely to have maintained some social network.

Canadians' attitudes toward and opinions of homelessness show some recognition that the problem is not going away. Longitudinal surveys tell us that Canadians believe that the number of people living without stable accommodation is increasing, and that this number includes more women and families than historically was the case. We also understand that "make-do" responses such as temporary shelters and food banks are not capable of dealing with the challenges facing this population. In addition, Canadians now think it is possible for someone to have an income, whether it be from work or social assistance, and still live on the street.

Despite occasional media spotlights on the homeless and the booming economy, affordable housing has become harder to find. Two out of three low-income renters receive no housing allowance, and most spend a disproportionately large share of their income to maintain their shelter. Research shows that this worsening of affordable housing stems from a substantial drop in the number of unsubsidized, low-cost rental housing units in the private market and a growing number of low-income renter households.

Developing nations have special problems. They have understandably given highest priority to economic productivity as measured by jobs with living wages. Unfortunately, even the most ambitious economic and social programs may be overwhelmed by minor currency fluctuations, a drop in the value of a nation's major export, or an influx of refugees from a neighbouring country. Some of the reforms implemented have included promoting private (as opposed to government-controlled) housing markets, allowing dwellings to be places of business as well, and loosening restrictions on building materials.

All three of these short-term solutions have shortcomings. Private housing markets invite exploitation; mixed residential/commercial use may only cause good housing to deteriorate faster; and the use of marginal building materials leaves low-income residential areas more vulnerable to calamities such as floods, fires, and earthquakes. Large-scale rental housing under government supervision, the typical solution in North America and Europe, has been successful only in economically advanced city-states like Hong Kong and Singapore (Strassman 1998).

In sum, homeless people both in Canada and abroad are not getting the shelter they need, and they lack the political clout to corral the attention of policymakers.

Let's Discuss

1. Have you ever worked as a volunteer in a shelter or soup kitchen? If so, were you surprised by the type of people who lived or ate there? Has anyone you know ever had to move into a shelter?
2. Is gentrification of low-income housing a problem where you live? Have you ever had difficulty finding an affordable place to live?
3. What kind of assistance is available to homeless people in the community where you live? Does the help come from the government, from private charities, or both? What about housing assistance for people with low incomes, such as rent subsidies—is it available?

Chapter Resources

Summary

A ***community*** is a spatial or political unit of social organization that gives people a sense of belonging. This chapter explains how communities originated and analyzes the process of urbanization from both the functionalist and conflict perspectives. It describes various types of communities, including the central cities, the suburbs, and rural communities, and it introduces the new concept of an electronic community. The functionalist and conflict perspectives are also used to explore environmental issues.

1. Stable communities began to develop when people stayed in one place to cultivate crops; surplus production enabled cities to emerge.
2. Gideon Sjoberg identified three preconditions of city life: advanced technology in both agricultural and nonagricultural areas, a favourable physical environment, and a well-developed social organization.
3. There are important differences between the ***preindustrial city***, the ***industrial city***, and the ***postindustrial city***.
4. Urbanization is evident not only in Canada but throughout the world; by 2000, 45 percent of the world's population lived in urban areas.
5. The ***urban ecological*** approach is functionalist because it emphasizes that different elements in urban areas contribute to stability.
6. Drawing on conflict theory, ***new urban sociology*** considers the interplay of a community's political and economic interests as well as the impact of the global economy on communities in Canada and other countries.
7. Many urban residents are immigrants from other nations and tend to live in ethnic neighbourhoods.
8. In the last three decades, cities have confronted an overwhelming array of economic and social problems, including crime, unemployment, and the deterioration of schools and public transit systems.
9. Suburbanization was the most dramatic population trend in Canada throughout the 20th century. In recent decades, suburbs have witnessed increasing diversity in race and ethnicity.
10. Farming, mining, and logging have all been in decline in the rural communities of Canada.
11. Technological advances like electronic information networks are changing the economy, the distribution of population, and even the concept of community.
12. Three broad areas of environmental concern are air pollution, water pollution, and contamination of land.
13. Using the human ecological perspective, sociologist Riley Dunlap suggests that the natural environment serves three basic functions: It provides essential resources, it serves as a waste repository, and it "houses" our species.
14. Conflict theorists charge that the most serious threat to the environment comes from Western industrialized nations.
15. ***Environmental justice*** is concerned with the disproportionate subjection of minorities to environmental hazards.
16. Soaring housing costs, unemployment, cutbacks in public assistance, and rapid population growth have all contributed to rising homelessness around the world. Most social policy is directed toward sending the homeless to large shelters.

Critical Thinking Questions

1. How can the functionalist and conflict perspectives be used in examining the growing interest among policymakers in privatizing public services presently offered by cities and other communities?
2. How has your home community (your city, town, or neighbourhood) changed over the years you have lived there? Have there been significant changes in the community's economic base and in its racial and ethnic profile? Have the community's social problems intensified or lessened over time? Is unemployment currently a major problem? What are the community's future prospects as it approaches the 21st century?
3. Imagine that you have been asked to study the issue of air pollution in the largest city in your province. How might you draw on surveys, observation research, experiments, and existing sources to help you study this issue?

Key Terms

Community A spatial or political unit of social organization that gives people a sense of belonging, based either on shared residence in a particular place or on a common identity. (page 389)

Concentric-zone theory A theory of urban growth that sees growth in terms of a series of rings radiating from the central business district. (392)

Defended neighbourhood A neighbourhood that residents identify through defined community borders and a perception that adjacent areas are geographically separate and socially different. (398)

Gentrification The process of transforming a community from a home for those at the bottom of the socioeconomic ladder to an upscale collection of condominiums and boutiques. (399)

Human ecology An area of study concerned with the interrelationships between people and their spatial setting and physical environment. (392)

Industrial city A city characterized by relatively large size, open competition, an open class system, and elaborate specialization in the manufacturing of goods. (391)

Megalopolis A densely populated area containing two or more cities and their surrounding suburbs. (392)

Multiple-nuclei theory A theory of urban growth that views growth as emerging from many centres of development, each of which may reflect a particular urban need or activity. (394)

New urban sociology An approach to urbanization that considers the interplay of local, national, and worldwide forces and their effect on local space, with special emphasis on the impact of global economic activity. (395)

Postindustrial city A city in which global finance and the electronic flow of information dominate the economy. (391)

Preindustrial city A city with only a few thousand people living within its borders and characterized by a relatively closed class system and limited mobility. (390)

Squatter settlements Areas occupied by the very poor on the fringes of cities, in which housing is often constructed by the settlers themselves from discarded material. (394)

Urban ecology An area of study that focuses on the interrelationships between people and their environment in urban areas. (392)

Urbanism Distinctive patterns of social behaviour evident among city residents. (391)

Zoning laws Legal provisions stipulating land use and architectural design of housing, sometimes used as a means of keeping racial minorities and low-income people out of suburban areas. (401)

Additional Readings

Duany, Andres, Elizabeth Plater-Zybert, and Jeff Speck. 2000. *Suburban Nation: The Rise of Sprawl and the Decline of the American Dream*. New York: North Point Press. A critical look at most post–World War II suburban development, both residential and commercial.

Fitzpatrick, Kevin, and Mark LaGory. 2000. *Unhealthy Places: The Ecology of Risk in the Urban Landscape*. New York: Routledge. Two sociologists take a spatial view of urban ecology and raise the concept of the "urban health penalty"—the effect of place on an individual's access to health resources.

Mitchell, William J. 1999. *E-topia*. Cambridge: MIT Press. A futuristic view of what the world's cities might look like in an age of cybernetics. Written by a dean of architecture, the book predicts a variety of cityscapes based on different cultural traditions, all unified by a global digital network. Visit the author's website at (**http://mitpress.mit.edu/e-books/City_of_Bits/**) for his companion book *City of Bits* (Cambridge: MIT Press, 1996).

Internet Connection

www.mcgrawhill.ca/college/schaefer

For additional Internet exercises relating to the Canadian International Development Association and Greenpeace, visit the Schaefer Online Learning Centre at ***http://www.mcgrawhill.ca/college/schaefer****. Please note that while the URLs listed were current at the time of printing, these sites often change—check the Online Learning Centre for updates.*

The Centre for Indigenous Environmental Resources (CIER) is "dedicated to the protection, preservation and renewal of Mother Earth." The organization was established in 1994 to help First Nations communities deal with environmental issues arising either from their desire to engage in traditional practices, or from economic affiliations. Visit the site at **http://www.cier.mb.ca/** and consider the value of such an initiative by answering the following questions:

(a) CIER has three primary goals. Do you think any or all of these are attainable? Which goal do you think is most important? Why?

(b) The organization is developing a database that will integrate the environmental wisdom of First Nations culture with the latest scientific information. What is the value of such a process?

(c) The National Environmental Education and Training Program is offered in conjunction with the University of Manitoba. The program is team-taught by an Aboriginal scholar, a Western scientific scholar and an elder. What advantages might this approach have over more traditional Canadian university formats?

(d) Do you think this organization is making an important and unique contribution to fighting environmental degradation in Canada? If so, how?

CHAPTER 16

SOCIAL MOVEMENTS, SOCIAL CHANGE, AND TECHNOLOGY

Social change often reflects accessibility to new technology. A recent music innovation is IDM (intelligent dance music), experimental techno music made totally from electronic sources. This pixel painting appears as the cover art of the techno music compilation of England's Warp Records.

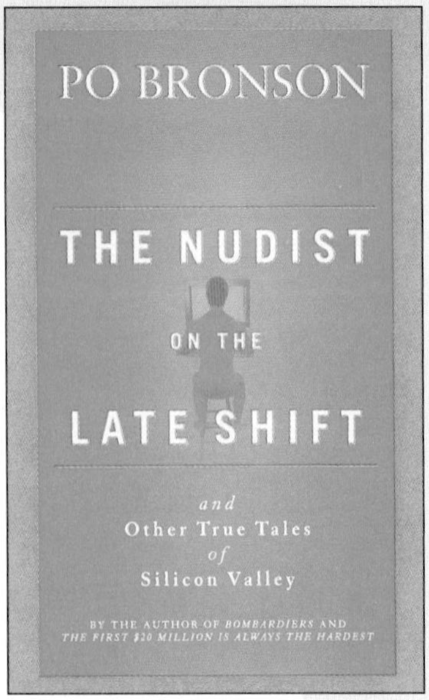

From the moment I met him, Sabeer Bhatia has given credit to the power of the idea. The idea was so powerful that when his friend and coworker Jack Smith, who was driving home to Livermore across the Dunbarton Bridge, called Sabeer on his car phone to brainstorm the pregnant thought that had just occurred to him, Sabeer heard one sentence of it and said, "Oh, my! Hang up that cellular and call me back on a secure line when you get to your house! We don't want anyone to overhear!"

It was so powerful an idea that when Jack did call Sabeer back fifteen minutes later, their minds melded as they talked, completely in sync, leaping from one ramification to the next as simultaneously as the steps of two soldiers marching side by side. It was so powerful that sleep that night was impossible for Sabeer, with the idea now in his head, exploding, autocatalytic, a bonfire of the mind. He stayed up all night, sitting at the glass-topped dining table in his small Bayside Village apartment, writing the business plan, which he took to his day job the next morning, looking so haggard that his boss stopped him and said, "You've got to cut out the partying, Sabeer." . . .

The idea came about this way: Sabeer and Jack had wanted to start a company, and they had been brainstorming possible business ideas for a few months. They wanted to e-mail each other notes, but they had been afraid that their bosses might glean their e-mail and accuse them of spending their working hours on personal projects (an accurate accusation). The budding entrepreneurs had personal America Online accounts, but these couldn't be accessed through the office network. On the evening he was driving home across the Dunbarton Bridge, Jack Smith had been frustrated all day by this problem. Then it occurred to him:

Free e-mail accounts that can be accessed anonymously, over the Web.

In getting over their own obstacle to coming up with a business idea, they came up with just that idea. . . .

It was the kind of idea that inspires legions of entrepreneurs. It was the kind of idea that spurs thousands of young people to give up their lives elsewhere and crash the Valley party. It sent the message and cc'd the entire world: to make it in Silicon Valley, you just have to come up with the right idea. . . .

Nowadays, meet Sabeer at a party and ask what he does, and he will tell you only that he works in high tech, just like hundreds of thousands of other young people in the valley. . . . Push him for more detail about his job, and he'll say he works at Hotmail. Ask if he's an engineer and he'll say no, he's the president. He's not being reclusive or coy, it just hasn't sunk in that he might be special.

What is Hotmail but e-mail on the Web? *(Bronson 1999:78–79, 80)* ■

Po Bronson specializes in writing about that hotbed of technology known as Silicon Valley. In this excerpt from his book *The Nudist on the Late Shift,* Bronson profiles the inventor of Hotmail and highlights the importance of a good idea—even so simple an idea as accessing e-mail on the Internet. Combining the convenience of e-mail with the global reach of the web, Hotmail allows anyone in the world to communicate instantly with anyone else, as long as both have access to the web. To appreciate the impact of this idea, drop into any cyber café—whether it be in Bangkok, Bali, or Bismarck—and observe the flurry of e-mail being sent and received by backpackers, tourists, students, and businesspeople alike.

The development of the computer as an integral part of day-to-day life in Canada and other countries is an example of social change. ***Social change*** has been defined as significant alteration over time in behaviour patterns and culture (Moore 1967). Social changes that have had long-term and important consequences include the emergence of slavery as a system of stratification (see Chapter 8), the Industrial Revolution (Chapter 5), the increased participation of women in the paid labour forces of Canada, the United States, and Europe (Chapter 10), and the worldwide population explosion (Chapter 14). As we will see, social movements have played an important role in promoting social change.

This chapter examines social movements and the process of social change, with special emphasis on the impact of technological advances. Efforts to explain long-term social changes have led to the development of theories of change; we will consider the evolutionary, functionalist, conflict, and feminist approaches to change. We will see how vested interests can block changes that they see as threatening.

We'll also look at various aspects of our technological future through discussion of telecommuting, the Internet, biotechnology, and technological accidents. We will examine the effects of technological advances on culture and social interaction, social control, and stratification and inequality. Taken together, the impact of these technological changes may be approaching a level of magnitude comparable to that of the Industrial Revolution. Finally, the social policy section will discuss the ways in which technological advances have intensified concerns over privacy and censorship. ■

Social Movements

Although such factors as physical environment, population, technology, and social inequality serve as sources of change, it is the *collective* effort of individuals organized in social movements that ultimately leads to change. Sociologists use the term ***social movements*** to refer to organized collective activities to bring about or resist fundamental change in an existing group or society (Benford 1992). Herbert Blumer (1955:19) recognized the special importance of social movements when he defined them as "collective enterprises to establish a new order of life."

In many nations, including Canada, social movements have had a dramatic impact on the course of history and the evolution of social structure. Consider the actions of Quebec separatists, abolitionists, suffragists, and the Metis of 1837. Members of each social movement stepped outside traditional channels for bringing about social change and yet had a noticeable influence on public policy. Equally dramatic collective efforts in Eastern Europe helped to topple Communist regimes in a largely peaceful manner, in nations that many observers had felt were "immune" to such social change (Ramet 1991).

Social movements imply the existence of conflict, but we can also analyze their activities from a functionalist perspective. Even when unsuccessful, social movements contribute to the formation of public opinion. Initially, the ideas of Margaret Sanger and other early advocates of birth control were viewed as "radical," yet contraceptives are now widely available in the United States and Canada. Moreover, functionalists view social movements as training grounds for leaders of the political establishment. Such heads of state as Cuba's Fidel Castro and South Africa's Nelson Mandela came to power after serving as leaders of revolutionary movements. More recently, Poland's Lech Walesa, Russia's Boris Yeltsin, and Czech playwright Vaclav Havel led protest movements against Communist rule and subsequently became leaders of their countries' governments.

How and why do social movements emerge? Obviously, people are often discontented with the way things are. But what causes them to organize at a particular moment in a collective effort to work for change? Sociologists rely on two explanations for why people mobilize: the relative-deprivation and resource-mobilization approaches.

Relative Deprivation

Those members of a society who feel most frustrated and disgruntled by the social and economic conditions of

Two views on abortion among social movements in France: In the top photo, members of the pro-choice movement take to the streets. One sign states, "A child if I want it, when I want it." In the bottom photo, a member of the pro-life movement wears a T-shirt that states. "To abort is to kill."

their lives are not necessarily "worst off" in an objective sense. Social scientists have long recognized that what is most significant is how people *perceive* their situation. Karl Marx pointed out that although the misery of the workers was important in reflecting their oppressed state, so was their position *relative* to the capitalist ruling class (Marx and Engels 1955, original edition 1847).

The term ***relative deprivation*** is defined as the conscious feeling of a negative discrepancy between legitimate expectations and present actualities (J. Wilson 1973). In other words, things aren't as good as you hoped they would be. Such a state may be characterized by scarcity rather than complete lack of necessities (as we saw in the distinction between absolute and relative poverty in Chapter 8). A relatively deprived person is dissatisfied because he or she feels downtrodden relative to some appropriate reference group. Thus, blue-collar workers who live in cramped apartments —though hardly at the bottom of the economic ladder—may nevertheless feel deprived in comparison with corporate managers and professionals who live in lavish and exclusive suburbs.

p. 185

In addition to the feeling of relative deprivation, two other elements must be present before discontent will be channelled into a social movement. People must feel that they have a *right* to their goals, that they deserve better than what they have. For example, the struggle against European colonialism in Africa intensified when growing numbers of Africans decided that it was legitimate for them to have political and economic independence. At the same time, the disadvantaged group must perceive that it cannot attain its goals through conventional means. This belief may or may not be correct. Whichever is the case, the group will not mobilize into a social movement unless there is a shared perception that it can end its relative deprivation only through collective action (Morrison 1971).

p. 194

Critics of this approach have noted that an increase in feelings of deprivation is not always necessary before people are moved to act. In addition, this approach fails to explain why certain feelings of deprivation are transformed into social movements, whereas in other similar situations, there is no collective effort to reshape society. Consequently, in recent years, sociologists have given increasing attention to the forces needed to bring about the emergence of social movements (Alain 1985; Finkel and Rule 1987; Orum 1989).

Resource Mobilization

It takes more than desire to start a social movement. It helps to have money, political influence, access to the media, and volunteers. The term ***resource mobilization*** refers to the ways in which a social movement utilizes such resources. The success of a movement for change will depend in good part on what resources it has and how effectively it mobilizes them (see also Gamson 1989; Staggenborg 1989a, 1989b).

Sociologist Anthony Oberschall (1973:199) has argued that to sustain social protest or resistance, there must be an "organizational base and continuity of leadership." As people become part of a social movement, norms develop to guide their behaviour. Members of the movement may be expected to attend regular meetings of organizations, pay dues, recruit new adherents, and boycott "enemy" products or speakers. An emerging social movement may give rise to special language or new words for familiar terms. In recent years, social movements have been responsible for such new terms of self-reference as *senior citizens* (used to replace *old folks*), *gays* (used to replace *homosexuals*), and *people with disabilities* (used to replace *the handicapped*).

Leadership is a central factor in the mobilization of the discontented into social movements. Often, a movement will be led by a charismatic figure, such as René Lévesque. As Max Weber described it in 1904, *charisma* is that quality of an individual that sets him or her apart from ordinary people. Of course, charisma can fade abruptly; this helps account for the fragility of certain social movements (Morris 2000).

p. 327

Yet many social movements do persist over long periods of time because their leadership is frequently well organized and ongoing. Ironically, as Robert Michels (1915) noted, political movements fighting for social change eventually take on bureaucratic forms of organization. Leaders tend to dominate the decision-making process without directly consulting followers.

pp. 134–35

Why do certain individuals join a social movement whereas others who are in similar situations do not? Some of them are recruited to join. Karl Marx recognized the importance of recruitment when he called on workers to become *aware* of their oppressed status and develop a class consciousness. In agreement with the contemporary resource-mobilization approach, Marx held that a social movement (specifically, the revolt of the proletariat) would require leaders to sharpen the awareness of the oppressed. They must help workers to overcome feelings of *false consciousness,* or attitudes that do not reflect workers' objective position, in order to organize a revolutionary movement. Similarly, one of the challenges faced by women's liberation activists of the late 1960s and early 1970s was to convince women that they were being deprived of their rights and of socially valued resources.

p. 179

Unlike the relative-deprivation approach, the resource-mobilization perspective focuses on strategic difficulties facing social movements. Any movement for fundamental change will almost certainly arouse opposition; effective mobilization will depend in part on how the movement deals with resistance to its activities.

Gender and Social Movements

Sociologists point out that gender is an important element in understanding social movement development. In our male-dominated society, women have traditionally found it more difficult to assume leadership positions in social movement organizations and have often disproportionately served as volunteers in these movements. In these positions, their work was not always recognized, nor were their voices as easily heard as men's. In the past 300 years, the position of women within social movements has changed so that women now assume much more of a leadership role. However, gender bias still causes the real extent of women's influence to be overlooked. Traditional examination of the sociopolitical system tends to focus on such male-dominated corridors of power as legislatures and corporate boardrooms to the neglect of more female-dominated domains, such as households, community-based groups, or faith-based networks. But efforts to influence family values, child rearing, relationships between parents and schools, and spiritual values are clearly significant to a culture and society (Ferree and Merrill 2000; Noonan 1995).

Scholars of social movements now realize that gender can affect even the way we view organized efforts to bring about or resist change. For example, an emphasis on using rationality and an adversarial approach to achieve goals helps to obscure the importance of passion and cooperation in successful social movements. Calls for a more serious study of the role of passion and cooperation are frequently seen as applying only to the women's movement, because these qualities are traditionally thought of as feminine. Yet it would be difficult to find any movement, from labour battles to voting rights to animal rights, in which passion was not part of the consensus-building force (Ferree and Merrill 2000; Taylor 1995).

New Social Movements

Beginning in the late 1960s, European social scientists observed that there was a change in both the composition and the targets of emerging social movements. Previously, traditional social movements had focused on economic issues, often led by people sharing the same occupation or by labour unions. However, many social movements that have become active in recent decades—including the contemporary women's movement, the gay rights movement, and the environmental movement—did not have the social class roots typical of the labour protests in Canada, the United States, and Europe over the preceding 100 years (Tilly 1993).

The term ***new social movements*** was introduced to refer to organized collective activities that promote autonomy and self-determination as well as improvements in the quality of life. These movements may be involved in developing collective identities, have complex agendas that go beyond a single issue, and often cross national boundaries. Educated, middle-class people are significantly represented in some of these new social movements, such as the women's movement and the movement for Quebec independence. However, marginalized people are also involved in new social movements; as one example, some homeless people create communities of squatters who take over abandoned buildings and fight efforts to evict them (Buechler 1995).

New social movements generally do not view government as their ally in the struggle for a better society. While they typically do not seek to overthrow the government, they may criticize, protest, or harass public officials. Researchers have found that members of new social movements show little inclination to accept established authority, even scientific or technical authority. This is especially evident in the environmental and anti–nuclear power movements, where movement activists present their own experts to counter those of government or big business (Garner 1996; A. Scott 1990).

The environmental social movement is one of many new movements that have adopted a worldwide focus. In their efforts to reduce air and water pollution, curtail global warming, and protect endangered animal species, environmental activists have realized that strong regulatory measures within a single country are not sufficient. Similarly, labour union leaders and human rights advocates cannot adequately address exploitative sweatshop conditions in a developing country if a multinational corporation can simply move the factory to another country where it pays workers even less. Whereas traditional views of social movements tended to emphasize resource mobilization on a local level, new social movement theory offers a broader, global perspective on social and political activism. Moreover, today's technology provides new ways to unite groups of people across distances and publicize their concerns. A social movement can even be "virtual," as Box 16-1 on pages 424–425 shows.

Theories of Social Change

A new millennium provides the occasion to offer explanations of social change, but this is clearly a challenge in the diverse and complex world we inhabit today. Nevertheless, theorists from several disciplines have sought to analyze social change. In some instances, they have examined historical events to arrive at a better understanding of contemporary changes. We will review four theoretical approaches to change—evolutionary, functionalist, conflict, and feminist theories—and then take a look at global change today.

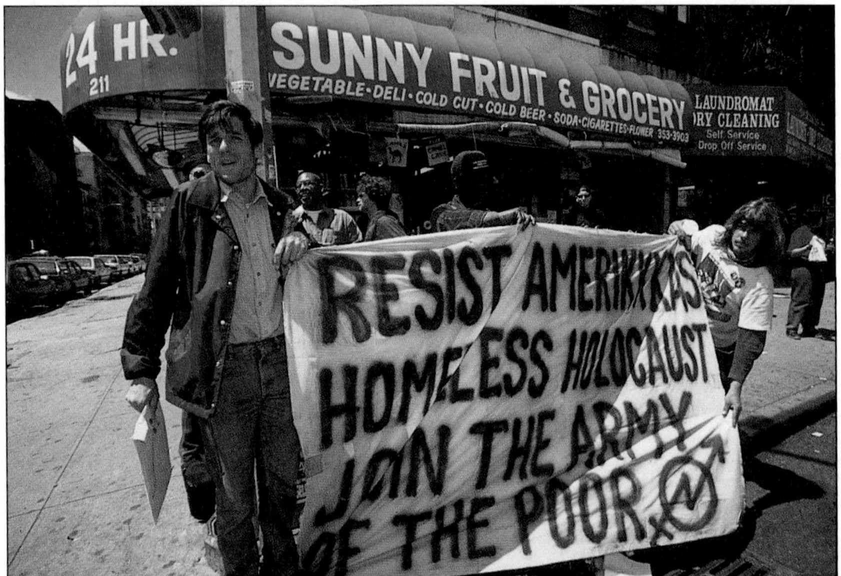

These homeless people, who had taken over abandoned buildings, resisted efforts to evict them from their squats. They are an example of marginalized people who are now involved in *new social movements*.

Evolutionary Theory

Charles Darwin's (1809–1882) pioneering work in biological evolution contributed to 19th-century theories of social change. According to his approach, there has been a continuing progression of successive life forms. For example, since human beings came at a later stage of evolution than reptiles, we represent a "higher" form of life. Social theorists sought an analogy to this biological model and originated ***evolutionary theory***, which views society as moving in a definite direction. Early evolutionary theorists generally agreed that society was inevitably progressing to a higher state. As might be expected, they concluded in ethnocentric fashion that their own behaviour and culture were more advanced than those of earlier civilizations.

August Comte (1798–1857), a founder of sociology, was an evolutionary theorist of change. He saw human societies as moving forward in their thinking from mythology to the scientific method. Similarly, Émile Durkheim (1933, original edition 1893) maintained that society progressed from simple to more complex forms of social organization.

pp. 8–9

The writings of Comte and Durkheim are examples of ***unilinear evolutionary theory***. This approach contends that all societies pass through the same successive stages of evolution and inevitably reach the same end. English sociologist Herbert Spencer (1820–1903) used a similar approach: Spencer likened society to a living body with interrelated parts that were moving toward a common destiny. However, contemporary evolutionary theorists such as Gerhard Lenski are more likely to picture social change as multilinear than to rely on the more limited unilinear perspective. ***Multilinear evolutionary theory*** holds that change can occur in several ways and that it does not inevitably lead in the same direction (Haines 1988; J. Turner 1985).

p. 9

Multilinear theorists recognize that human culture has evolved along a number of lines. For example, the theory of demographic transition graphically demonstrates that population change in developing nations has not necessarily followed the model evident in industrialized nations. Sociologists today hold that events do not necessarily follow in a single or several straight lines but instead are subject to disruptions—a topic we will consider later in the discussion of global social change.

p. 356

Functionalist Theory

Functionalist sociologists focus on what *maintains* a system, not on what changes it. This might seem to suggest that functionalists can offer little of value to the study of social change. Yet, as the work of sociologist Talcott Parsons demonstrates, functionalists have made a distinctive contribution to this area of sociological investigation.

Parsons (1902–1979), a leading proponent of functionalist theory, viewed society as naturally being in a state of equilibrium. By "equilibrium," he meant that society tends toward a state of stability or balance. Parsons would view even prolonged labour strikes or civilian riots as temporary disruptions in the status quo rather than as significant alterations in social structure. Therefore, according to his ***equilibrium model***, as changes occur in one part of society, there must be adjustments in other parts. If this does not take place, the society's equilibrium will be threatened and strains will occur.

p. 13

Reflecting an evolutionary approach, Parsons (1966) maintained that four processes of social change are inevitable. The first, *differentiation,* refers to the increasing complexity of social organization. A change from "medicine man" to physician, nurse, and pharmacist is an illustration of differentiation in the field of health. This process is accompanied by *adaptive upgrading,* whereby social institutions become more specialized in their purposes. The division of labour among physicians into obstetricians, internists, surgeons, and so forth is an example of adaptive upgrading.

The third process identified by Parsons is the *inclusion* of groups into society that were previously excluded because of such factors as gender, race, and social class background. Medical schools have practised inclusion by admitting increasing numbers of women and visible minorities. Finally, Parsons contends that societies experience *value generalization,* the development of new values that tolerate and legitimate a greater range of activities. The acceptance of preventive and alternative medicine is an example of value generalization; our

Visible minorities are now accepted in many exclusive golf clubs that were previously restricted, illustrating the process of *inclusion* described by Talcott Parsons. The phenomenal success of pro golfer Tiger Woods has helped the process along.

Eye on the Media 16-1 Virtual Social Movements

We are accustomed to think of social movements in terms of protest marches and door-to-door petition drives. But the World Wide Web allows for alternative ways of trying to organize people and either bring about fundamental change or resist change. The Internet itself has often been referred to as a "virtual community," and as in any community there are people who seek to persuade others to their point of view. Furthermore, the Internet serves to "bring people together"—say, by transforming the cause of the Mexican Zapatista into an international lobbying effort or linking environmentalists on every continent through Greenpeace International or e-mailing information and news from abroad to dissidents in China.

Being like-minded and in face-to-face contact, critical to conventional social movements, is not necessary on the Internet. Moreover, people can engage in their own virtual community with little impact on their everyday lives. On the Internet, for example, one can mount a petition drive to free a death row inmate without taking days and weekends away from one's job and family. Dissidents can communicate with one another using computers in Internet cafés, with little concern for being traced or monitored by the government.

Two new studies by Matthew Zook and research by sociologist Roberta Garner examined how many websites express ideological points of view that are contentious or hostile to existing institutions. Garner looked at 542 websites that could be regarded as "ideological postings"; some reflect the interests of a particular group or organization and some are only the opinions of isolated individuals. Among the sites were postings that reflected extreme patriotic views, white racism, attachment to cults, regional separatism and new forms of nationalism, and militant environmentalism.

The Internet itself has often been referred to as a "virtual community," and as in any community there are people who seek to persuade others to their point of view.

While the Garner sample was not random and therefore may not be representative of all ideological postings, the hundreds of sites did show some consistencies, many of them also noted by Zook:

- Like conventional social movements, these sites serve as an alternative source of information, bypassing mainstream sources of opinions found in newspaper editorials.
- These nonmainstream movements enjoy legitimacy because no gate-keeper keeps them off the web. By virtue of being on a website, even an unsophisticated one, the information has the appearance of being just as legitimate as that found on a website for a TSE 300 corporation or CTV news. And because the information appears on *individual* sites, it seems to be more real and even sincere than messages that come from the mass media of television or radio.
- The sites make little reference to time or specific events, except to historic moments. There is not much sense of movement along an agenda.
- The sites rely heavily on written documents, either in the form of

Sources: Calhoun 1998; Castells 2000; Garner 1999; Rosenthal 2000; Van Slambrouck 1996b; Zook 1996.

society has broadened its view of health care. All four processes identified by Parsons stress consensus—societal agreement on the nature of social organization and values (B. Johnson 1975; R. Wallace and Wolf 1980).

Parsons's approach explicitly incorporates the evolutionary notion of continuing progress. However, the dominant theme in his model is balance and stability. Society may change, but it remains stable through new forms of integration. For example, in place of the kinship ties that provided social cohesion in the past, there are laws, judicial processes, and new values and belief systems.

Functionalists assume that social institutions will not persist unless they continue to contribute to the overall society. This leads functionalists to conclude that deliberately altering institutions will threaten societal equilibrium. Critics note that the functionalist approach virtually disregards the use of coercion by the powerful to maintain the illusion of a stable, well-integrated society (Gouldner 1960). Feminist theorists are among the most outspoken detractors of functionalist theory, arguing that it provides a convenient defence of the patriarchal status quo.

Conflict Theory

The functionalist perspective minimizes change. It emphasizes the persistence of social life and sees change as a means of maintaining the equilibrium (or balance) of a society. By contrast, conflict theorists contend that social institutions and practices persist because powerful

- manifestos or established documents such as the Constitution or the Bible. Written testimonials (such as "How I Became a Conservative") also proliferate on these websites.
- The presentations are still fairly unsophisticated. While there are glossy animated websites, most sites look like a printed page.
- Unlike conventional social movements, these virtual sites are generally not geared for action. Despite expressions of concern or foreboding (such as the site "Are You Ready for Catastrophic Natural Disasters?"), there were few calls to do anything. Sites like "Glory to the Cuban Revolution" seek to inform visitors, serve as a resource, and, perhaps, bring people around to their point of view.

Zook as well as Garner and her student researchers found that these sites often seem to define themselves by their choice of links on the web. In other words, with whom do they wish to be associated? This is particularly true of well-established social movements that have expanded to use the Internet. For example, both the leading abortion rights groups and anti-abortion organizations feature links to other groups, but only to those that are like-minded.

The entire process of "links" is very important in the Internet network. How one defines one's ideology determines how a site may be located and who makes links. For example, the website of a female national socialist from Sweden boldly encourages visitors to establish a link from their website to hers as long as they are a part of the "white aryan movement on the Net." Using the term "militia" as opposed to "patriotic" would bring different people to one's site. The terms one uses are important since webpages act as recruiting tools to attract new members to a movement and may, in fact, be the only realistic way that some groups will attract followers.

People in conventional social movements commonly try to infiltrate other groups holding opposing views to learn their strategy or even disrupt their ability to function. There is a parallel to that emerging on the Internet. The term *hactivists* (a merging of "hackers" with "*activists*") refers to people who invade computer systems electronically, placing embarrassing information on their enemies' webpages or, at the very least, defacing them. During the height of the 1999 NATO attacks on Yugoslavia, movements opposed to the military action bombarded the official NATO website with requests meant to overload it and paralyze its operation.

Research into virtual social movements is still exploratory. Social movement researchers such as Garner and Zook are interested in establishing the relationship between ideological websites and "real" organizations. Do these sites merely reflect a single posting? Or are they the visible manifestation of a broader consensus? And sociologists will be interested in examining a more representative sample of such sites to determine how often they explicitly call for social change.

Let's Discuss

1. What are some of the advantages of having a virtual social movement on the Internet? What might be some disadvantages?
2. If you were to create a webpage designed to attract followers to a social movement, what would it be like?

groups have the ability to maintain them. Change has crucial significance, because it is needed to correct social injustices and inequalities.

Karl Marx accepted the evolutionary argument that societies develop along a particular path. However, unlike Comte and Spencer, he did not view each successive stage as an inevitable improvement over the previous one. History, according to Marx, proceeds through a series of stages, each of which exploits a class of people. Ancient society exploited slaves; the estate system of feudalism exploited serfs; modern capitalist society exploits the working class. Ultimately, through a socialist revolution led by the proletariat, human society will move toward the final stage of development: a classless communist society, or "community of free individuals" as Marx described it in *Das Kapital* in 1867 (see Bottomore and Rubel 1956:250).

As we have seen, Karl Marx had an important influence on the development of sociology. His thinking offered insights into such institutions as the economy, the family, religion, and government. pp. 10–11 The Marxist view of social change is appealing because it does not restrict people to a passive role in responding to inevitable cycles or changes in material culture. Rather, Marxist theory offers a tool for those who wish to seize control of the historical process and gain their freedom from injustice. In contrast to functionalists' emphasis on stability, Marx argues that conflict is a normal and desirable aspect of social change. In fact, change must be encouraged as a means of eliminating social inequality (Lauer 1982).

One conflict sociologist, Ralf Dahrendorf (1959), has noted that the contrast between the functionalist perspective's emphasis on stability and the conflict perspective's focus on change reflects the contradictory nature of society. Human societies are stable and long-lasting, yet they also experience serious conflict. Dahrendorf found that the functionalist approach and the conflict approach were ultimately compatible despite their many areas of disagreement. Indeed, Parsons spoke of new functions that result from social change, and Marx recognized the need for change so that societies could function more equitably.

Feminist Theories

Unlike other sociological perspectives such as functionalism, discussed above, social change is the hallmark of feminist perspectives. Feminist sociologists, diverse as they are, share a desire to deepen their understanding of society in order to change the world; it is their desire to make it more just and humane (Lengermann and Niebrugge-Brantley 1998). Confronting social injustice in order to promote change for those groups in society who are disadvantaged by their "social location"—their class, race, ethnicity, sexual preference, age, or global location—is a key feature of feminist perspectives. As feminist sociologist Patricia Hill Collins (1998:xiv) explains, change is sought for "people differently placed in specific political, social, and historic contexts characterized by injustice."

Increasingly, feminist perspectives advance the view that acknowledging women's differences must be paramount in guiding the direction of social change. The interests of white, middle-class women, for example, must not be assumed to represent the interests of all women. Social change must be inclusive of the interests of women of diverse backgrounds. As feminist theorists Rosemary Hennessy and Chrys Ingraham ask, "What are the consequences of this way of thinking for transforming the inequities in women's lives?" and "How is this way of explaining the world going to improve life for all women?" (Lengermann and Niebrugge-Brantley 1998:445)

Global Social Change

We are at a truly dramatic time in history to consider global social change. Sociologists point to recent political events as evidence of this trend: the collapse of communism; the presence of terrorism in various parts of the world, including the United States and Canada; the dismantling of the welfare system in some developed nations; revolution and famine in Africa and Eastern Europe; the spread of AIDS; the computer revolution; and the cloning of a complex animal, Dolly the sheep.

In this era of massive social, political, and economic change on a global scale, is it possible to predict change? Some technological changes seem obvious, but the collapse of communist governments in the former Soviet Union and Eastern Europe took people by surprise in its speed and its unexpectedness. However, prior to the Soviet collapse, sociologist Randall Collins (1986, 1995), a conflict theorist, had observed a crucial sequence of changes that most observers had missed.

In seminars as far back as 1980—and in a book published in 1986—Collins argued that Soviet expansionism in the 20th century had resulted in an overextension of resources, including disproportionate spending on military forces—although there are few who would be willing to take up Collins's position after the events of September 11, 2001. Nonetheless, such overextension strains a regime's stability. Moreover, geopolitical theory suggests that nations in the middle of a geographic region (like the Soviet Union) tend to fragment over time into smaller units.

Collins predicted that the coincidence of social crises on several frontiers would precipitate the collapse of the Soviet Union. The success of the Iranian revolution in 1979 led to an upsurge of Islamic fundamentalism in nearby Afghanistan and in Soviet republics with substantial Muslim populations. At the same time, there was growing resistance to communist rule throughout Eastern Europe and within the Soviet Union itself. Collins predicted that the rise of a dissident form of communism within the Soviet Union might facilitate the breakdown of the regime. Beginning in the late 1980s, Soviet leader Mikhail Gorbachev chose not to use military power and other types of repression to crush dissidents in Eastern Europe, offered plans for democratization and social reform of Soviet society, and seemed willing to reshape the Soviet Union into a loose federation of somewhat autonomous states. But, in 1991, six republics on the western periphery declared their independence, and within months the entire Soviet Union had formally disintegrated into Russia and a number of independent nations.

Sociologist Maureen Hallinan (1997) cautions that we need to move beyond the restrictive models of social change—the linear view of evolutionary theory and the assumptions about equilibrium within functionalist theory. She and other sociologists have looked to "chaos theory" advanced by mathematicians to consider erratic events as a part of change. Hallinan noted that upheavals and major chaotic shifts do occur and that sociologists must learn to predict their occurrence, as Collins did with the Soviet Union. Imagine the dramatic nonlinear social change that will result from major innovations in the areas of communication and biotechnology, a topic we will discuss later in the chapter.

Resistance to Social Change

Efforts to promote social change are likely to meet with resistance. In the midst of rapid scientific and technological innovations, many people are frightened by the demands of an ever-changing society. Moreover, certain individuals and groups have a stake in maintaining the existing state of affairs.

Social economist Thorstein Veblen (1857–1929) coined the term ***vested interests*** to refer to those people or groups who will suffer in the event of social change. For example, for many years, the Canadian Medical Association (CMA) took a strong stand against the professionalization of midwifery. While the doctors' public objections were based on claims of health risks, there cannot be any doubt that the potential for loss of income and authority over a medical procedure played a major role in determining their resistance. In general, those with a disproportionate share of society's wealth, status, and power, such as members of the Canadian Medical Association, have a vested interest in preserving the status quo (Starr 1982; Veblen 1919).

Economic and Cultural Factors

Economic factors play an important role in resistance to social change. For example, it can increase initial costs for manufacturers to meet high standards for the safety of products and workers. Conflict theorists argue that, in a capitalist economic system, many firms are not willing to pay the price of meeting necessary safety standards. They may resist social change by cutting corners within their plants or by pressuring the government to ease regulations.

Communities, too, protect their vested interests, often in the name of "protecting property values." The abbreviation "NIMBY" stands for "not in my backyard," a cry often heard when people, such as those in Kirkland Lake (Chapter 15), protest landfills, prisons, nuclear power facilities, and even bike trails and group homes for people with developmental disabilities. The targeted community may not challenge the need for the facility but may simply insist that it be located elsewhere. The "not in my backyard" attitude has become so common that it is almost impossible for policymakers to find acceptable locations for such facilities as dump sites for hazardous wastes (J. Jasper 1997).

Like economic factors, cultural factors frequently shape resistance to change. William F. Ogburn (1922) distinguished between material and nonmaterial aspects of culture. *Material culture* includes inventions, artifacts, and technology; *nonmaterial culture* encompasses ideas, norms, communication, and social organization. Ogburn pointed out that one cannot devise methods for controlling and utilizing new technology before the introduction of a technique. Thus, nonmaterial culture typically must respond to changes in material culture. Ogburn introduced the term ***culture lag*** to refer to the period of maladjustment during which the nonmaterial culture is still adapting to new material conditions. One example is the Internet. Its rapid uncontrolled growth raises questions about whether to regulate it and, if so, how much (see the social policy section in this chapter).

pp. 53–54

In certain cases, changes in material culture can add strain to the relationships between social institutions. For example, new means of birth control have been developed in recent decades. Large families are no longer economically necessary, nor are they commonly endorsed by social norms. But certain religious faiths, among them Roman Catholicism, continue to extol large families and to disapprove methods of limiting family size such as contraception and abortion. This represents a lag between aspects of material culture (technology) and nonmaterial culture (religious beliefs). Conflicts may emerge

"Not in my backyard!" say these demonstrators, objecting to the placement of a new incinerator in their neighbourhood. The phenomenon of NIMBY has become so common that it is almost impossible for policymakers to find acceptable locations for incinerators, landfills, and dump sites for hazardous wastes.

between religion and other social institutions, such as government and the educational system, over the dissemination of birth control and family-planning information (M. Riley et al. 1994a, 1994b).

Resistance to Technology

Technological innovations are examples of changes in material culture that have often provoked resistance. The *Industrial Revolution*, which began primarily in England during the period 1760 to 1830, was a scientific revolution focused on the application of nonanimal sources of power to labour tasks. As this revolution proceeded, societies relied on new inventions that facilitated agricultural and industrial production and on new sources of energy such as steam. In some industries, the introduction of power-driven machinery reduced the need for factory workers and made it easier to cut wages.

pp. 390–91

Strong resistance to the Industrial Revolution emerged in some countries. In England, beginning in 1811, masked craft workers took extreme measures: They conducted nighttime raids on factories and destroyed some of the new machinery. The government hunted these rebels, known as ***Luddites***, and ultimately banished some while hanging others. In a similar effort in France, some angry workers threw their wooden shoes (*sabots*) into factory machinery to destroy it, thereby giving rise to the term *sabotage.* While the resistance of the Luddites and the French workers was short-lived and unsuccessful, they have come to symbolize resistance to technology over the last two centuries.

Are we now in the midst of a second technological revolution, with a contemporary group of Luddites engaged in resistance? Many sociologists believe that we are now living in a *postindustrial society.* It is difficult to pinpoint exactly when this era began. Generally, it is viewed as having begun in the 1950s, when for the first time the majority of workers in industrial societies became involved in services rather than in the actual manufacturing of goods (D. Bell 1999; Fiala 1992). Similarly, there are those who say we are in a period of postmodernism, in which progress is directed by a combination of physical and social environmental considerations rather than by science alone.

pp. 114–15

Just as the Luddites resisted the Industrial Revolution, people in many countries have resisted postindustrial technological changes. The term *neo-Luddites* refers to those who are wary of technological innovations and who question the incessant expansion of industrialization, the increasing destruction of the natural and agrarian world, and the "throw it away" mentality of contemporary capitalism with its resulting pollution of the environment. Neo-Luddites insist that whatever the presumed benefits of industrial and postindustrial technology, such technology has distinctive social costs and may represent a danger to the future of the human species and our planet (Bauerlein 1996; Rifkin 1995b; Sale 1996; Snyder 1996).

Today's version of Luddites are protesting technological innovations that they regard as destructive. This Greenpeace demonstrator in Montreal scales a giant corn "monster" in protest of genetically engineered food (see the discussion later in this chapter).

Such concerns are worth remembering as we turn now to examine aspects of our technological future and their possible impact on social change.

Technology and the Future

Technology is information about how to use the material resources of the environment to satisfy human needs and desires. Technological advances—the wheel, the plough, the airplane, the automobile, the television, the atomic bomb, and, more recently, the computer, the fax machine, and the cellular phone—have brought striking changes in our cultures, our patterns of

p. 53

socialization, our social institutions, and our day-to-day social interactions. Technological innovations are, in fact, emerging and being accepted with remarkable speed. For example, scientists at Monsanto, a multinational food biotechnology company, estimated in 1998 that the amount of genetic information used in practical applications will double every year. Part of the reason for this explosion in using new technology is that it is becoming cheaper. In 1974, it cost $3.9 million to determine the chemical structure of a single gene; less than 25 years later that cost was $240 (Belsie 1998). It is important, however, to keep in mind the concept of cultural lag when considering our "acceptance" of technological innovation. The long-term implications of much of the knowledge being discovered by science today are not well understood. The recent debate over the consequences of eating genetically modified organisms (GMOs) has brought this issue to the public's attention.

The technological knowledge with which we work today represents only a tiny portion of the knowledge that will be available in the year 2050. We are witnessing an information explosion as well: The number of volumes in major libraries is increasing rapidly, and beyond those walls, the volume of information available on the Internet has increased geometrically in just a few short years. Individuals, institutions, and societies will face unprecedented challenges in adjusting to the technological advances still to come (Cetron and Davies 1991; Wurman 1989).

In the following sections, we will examine various aspects of our technological future and consider their overall impact on social change, including the strains they will bring. We will focus in particular on recent developments in computer technology and biotechnology.

Computer Technology

The last decade has witnessed an explosion of computer technology in Canada and around the world. We will now examine two aspects of the technological and social changes related to computers: telecommuting and the Internet.

Telecommuting

As the Industrial Revolution proceeded, the factory and the office replaced the home as the typical workplace. But the postindustrial revolution has brought people home again. *Telecommuters*, as you will recall from Chapter 6, are employees who work full-time or part-time at home rather than in an outside office. They are linked to their supervisors and colleagues through computer terminals, phone lines, and fax machines. As part of a shift toward postindustrial societies linked within a global economy, telecommuting crosses international boundaries, oceans, and continents (Hall 1999).

p. 137

Telecommuting clearly facilitates communication between a company's employees who work in different locations, including those who work at home. Telecommuting also reduces time spent on transportation and can be helpful in a family's child care arrangements. At the same time, working at home can be isolating and stressful—and even more stressful if a parent must attempt to combine working at home and caring for children. Moreover, companies still need to encourage face-to-face communication in staff meetings and social settings. Overall, while telecommuting unquestionably offers distinct advantages for many employees and companies, it also presents new challenges (Marklein 1996).

The rise of telecommuting is especially beneficial for one subordinate group in Canada: people with disabilities. Computer terminals lend themselves to ancillary devices that make them adaptable to most types of physical impairments. For example, people who are blind can work at home using word processors that read messages in a computer voice or translate them into Braille (Nelson 1995).

p. 103

Each year, more Canadians perform their jobs either partially or fully at home through use of computer systems. The dramatic increase in use of computer networks such as the Internet has unquestionably contributed to the rise in telecommuting (Halal 1992; Rifkin 1995b).

The Internet

The Internet is the world's largest computer network. In 2002, an estimated 7.5 million Canadian households had

In our postindustrial society, computers are in use almost everywhere imaginable.

at least one member who used the Internet regularly (Statistics Canada 2003o).

The Internet actually evolved from a computer system built in 1962 by the United States military to enable scholars and military researchers to continue to do government work even if part of the nation's communications system was destroyed by a nuclear attack. Until recently, it was difficult to gain access to the Internet without holding a position at a university or a government research laboratory. Today, however, virtually anyone can reach the Internet with a phone or cable line, a computer, and a modem. And it is possible to buy and sell cars, trade stocks, auction off items, research new medical remedies, vote, track down long-lost friends—to mention just a few of the thousands of online possibilities (Reddick and King 2000).

While the rise of the Internet facilitates telecommuting and the spread of a home-based economy, much of the focus of the Internet has been on new forms of communication and social interaction. Early users established a subculture with specific norms and values. These pioneers generally resent formal rules for Internet communication, believe that access to information should be free and unlimited, and distrust efforts to centralize control of the Internet. The subculture of early Internet users also developed argot terms, such as "flaming" (hurling abuse online) and "chat rooms" (bulletin boards for people with common interests), and, much to the dismay of those trying to control the system, "hacking."

The expansion of the Internet has led to a proliferation of chat rooms and webpages where people can gather and exchange information on such diverse topics as artificial intelligence, baseball, erotica, the Hubble space telescope, Japanese animation, and women's history in Tudor England. At the same time, the spectacular growth of the Internet has posed challenges. It is no longer possible for the Internet pioneers to enforce the informal norms that they developed. For example, in 1994 "spam" was introduced by an attorney who challenged these norms by placing an advertisement for his legal services on every one of a computer network's more than 5000 discussion groups. This episode illustrates the danger that chat rooms could be swamped with advertising that will drown out noncommercial speech (Wiener 1994).

Other troubling issues have been raised about day-to-day "life" on the Internet. What, if anything, should be done about use of the Internet by neo-Nazis and other extremist groups who exchange messages of hatred and even bomb-making recipes? What, if anything, should be done about the issue of sexual expression on the Internet? Should there be censorship of "hot chat" and X-rated film clips? Or should there be *complete* freedom of expression? As evidenced by the recent court order to remove the "Zundelsite" associated with white supremacist Ernst Zundel (discussed in Chapter 9), governments at all levels seem to have come down on the side of censorship. The impact of technological change on issues of privacy and censorship will be examined in the social policy section at the end of this chapter.

While many people in Canada embrace the Internet, we should note that information is not evenly distributed throughout the population. The same people, by and large, who experience poor health and have few job opportunities also have been left stranded on the information highway. Moreover, this pattern of inequality is global. The core nations that Immanual Wallerstein describes in his *world system analysis* have a virtual monopoly on information technology while the developing nations of Asia, Africa, and Latin America are on the periphery, depending on the industrial giants for both the technology and the information it provides. In Box 16-2 on pp. 432–433 we explore this "global disconnect" in knowledge.

pp. 194–96

Biotechnology

Sex selection of fetuses, genetically engineered organisms, cloning of sheep and cows—these have been among the significant and yet controversial scientific advances in the field of biotechnology in recent years. George Ritzer's concept of McDonaldization applies to the entire area of biotechnology. Just as the fast-food concept has permeated society, it seems there is now no phase of life exempt from therapeutic or medical intervention. Biotechnology holds itself out as totally beneficial to human beings, but ultimately it reveals itself as in constant need of monitoring and adjustment. As we will see in the following sections, biotechnological advances have raised many difficult ethical and political decisions (Weinstein and Weinstein 1999).

p. 54

Sex Selection

Advances in reproductive and screening technology have brought us closer to effective techniques for sex selection, as discussed in the social policy section of Chapter 10. In Canada, the prenatal test of amniocentesis has been used for more than 25 years to ascertain the presence of certain defects that require medical procedures prior to birth. However, such tests also identify the sex of the fetus, as can ultrasound scans. This outcome has had profound social implications.

In many societies, young couples planning to have only one child will want to ensure that this child is a boy because their culture places a premium on a male heir. In such instances, advances in fetal testing may lead to abortion if the fetus is found to be female. Kuckreja Sohoni, a social scientist from India, notes that many parents in India are "mortally afraid" of having baby girls. Well aware of the pressure on Indian women to produce sons, Sohoni (1994:96), the mother of three teenage girls, admits, "had ultrasound been available when I was having children, I shudder to think how easily I would have been persuaded to plan a sex-selected family."

In July 1995, the Canadian federal minister of health announced a moratorium on nine reproductive technologies and practices, including sex-selection for non-medical purposes, commercial surrogacy arrangements, the sale of embryos, and the creation of animal-human hybrids. Bill C-47, designed to allow the federal government to use its criminal power to ban sex-selection for non-medical purposes as well as other reproductive technologies and practices, was introduced in 1996. The bill died on the Order Paper when the government called a general election in 1997.

From a functionalist perspective, we can view sex selection as an adaptation of the basic family function of regulating reproduction. However, conflict and feminist theorists emphasize that sex selection may intensify the male dominance of our society and undermine the principle of equality.

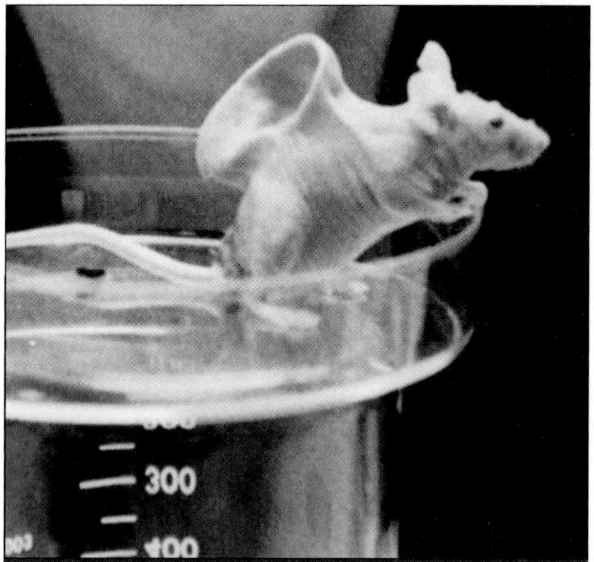

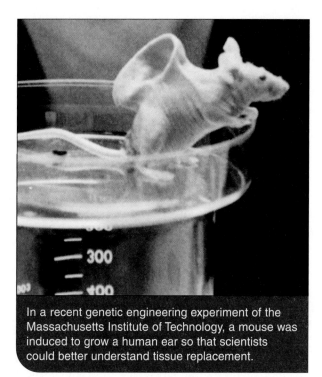

In a recent genetic engineering experiment of the Massachusetts Institute of Technology, a mouse was induced to grow a human ear so that scientists could better understand tissue replacement.

Genetic Engineering

Even more grandiose than sex selection—but not necessarily improbable—is altering human behaviour through genetic engineering. Fish and plant genes have already been mixed to create frost-resistant potato and tomato crops; more recently, human genes have been implanted in pigs to provide humanlike kidneys for organ transplants.

One of the latest developments in genetic engineering is gene therapy. Geneticists in Japan have managed to disable genes in a mouse fetus that carry an undesirable trait and replace them with genes carrying a desirable trait. Such advances raise staggering possibilities for altering animal and human life forms, but gene therapy remains highly experimental and must be assessed as a long, long shot (Kolata 1999).

A new era in genetic research was ushered in in 1980, when the United States Supreme Court ruled, by a five-to-four vote, that a genetically engineered organism that cleans up oil spills constituted a new invention and could be patented. This legitimization of people owning biological material has resulted in a stampede of research and patent filings by corporations in that country. From 1981 to early 1995, the United States Patent and Trademark Office approved 11 815 patents for genetically engineered substances. Some corporations believe that genetic engineering is a high-stakes gamble worth taking: In 1995, one company paid $31 million for an exclusive licence to develop products derived from a gene that seems to play a role in obesity.

The debate on genetic engineering escalated in 1997 when scientists in Scotland announced that they had cloned a sheep. After many unsuccessful attempts, scientists finally were able to replace the genetic material of a sheep's egg with DNA from an adult sheep and thereby create a lamb that was a clone of the adult. The very next year, Japanese researchers successfully cloned cows. There is now good scientific evidence that we have the technological capacity to reproduce human beings artificially. Not surprisingly, the debate over the prudence of putting this technology to use has lagged behind the science.

The Canadian government has banned any federal support for human cloning and urged private laboratories to abide by a voluntary moratorium until the ethical issues can be carefully considered. William F. Ogburn probably could not have anticipated such scientific developments when he wrote of culture lag 70 years earlier; however, the successful cloning of sheep illustrates again how quickly material culture can change and how non-material culture moves more slowly in absorbing such changes (J. Morrow 1997; Sale 1997; Wilmut et al. 1997).

While cloning grabs the headlines, there is a growing controversy concerning food that has been genetically modified (the GMOs mentioned earlier in this chapter). This controversy began in Europe but has since spread to other parts of the world, including Canada. The idea behind the technology is to increase food production and make agriculture more economical. Critics use the term "Frankenfood" (as in "Frankenstein") to refer to everything from breakfast cereals using genetically engineered grains to "fresh" tomatoes in the produce department. They object to tampering with nature and are concerned

Research in Action 16-2 Global Disconnect

Students in colleges and universities in North America expect to be able to use the Internet or leave messages through voice mail. They complain when the computer is "slow" or the electronic mailbox is "full." Despite their complaints, they take these services for granted and generally do not even pay directly for them. But in much of the world, it is very different.

The United Nations has tried for years to assist the nation of Madagascar to upgrade its telephone system to be able to handle a 300 baud communication device—the slowest speed available. At this glacial rate, it would take about two minutes to transmit this page without the colour and without the graphics. By comparison, in Canada, most people are *discarding* systems 50 times faster and turning to devices that transmit information 180 times faster. The irony is that it costs more per minute to use a telephone in Madagascar and much of Africa than in Canada, so we have a continent paying more per minute to transmit information much more slowly.

This is but one example of the haves and have-nots in the information age. As shown on the map on page 433, the Internet is virtually monopolized by North America and Europe and a few other industrial nations. They have the most *Internet hosts,* computers directly connected to the worldwide network of interconnected computer systems.

In Madagascar, there are 3 telephone lines per 1000 people, and for all low-income nations the average is 16.

This inequality is not new. We also find dramatic differences in the presence of newspapers, telephones, televisions, and even radios throughout the world. For example, in Madagascar, there are 3 telephone lines per 1000 people, and for all low-income nations the average is 16. Often in developing nations, and especially their rural areas, radio and television transmission is sporadic, and the programming may be dominated by recycled information from the United States.

The consequences of the global disconnect for developing nations are far more serious than not being able to "surf the Net." Today we have the true emergence of what sociologist Manuel Castells refers to as a "global economy" because the world has the capacity to work as a single unit in real time. However, if large numbers of people and, indeed, entire nations are disconnected from the informational economy, their slow economic growth will continue, with all the negative consequences it has for people. The educated and skilled will immigrate to labour markets that are a part of this global economy, deepening the impoverishment of the nations on the periphery.

Let's Discuss

1. What factors might make it difficult to remedy the global disconnect in developing nations?
2. What are some of the social and economic consequences for nations that are not "connected"?

Sources: Castells 1996, 2000; World Bank 2000a; Wresch 1996.

about the possible health effects of genetically modified food. Supporters of the food include not just the biotech companies but also those who see the technology as a way to help feed burgeoning populations in Africa and Asia (Golden 1999).

Technological Accidents

A carpenter who single-handedly makes a ladder has quite a different investment in the quality of the product than does a technician who develops a small part for a space shuttle. Our increasing reliance on technology has led to a growing separation between people and the outcomes of their actions.

Sociologist Charles Perrow (1999) introduced the term ***normal accidents*** to refer to failures that are inevitable given the manner in which human and technological systems are detached. Whether in a hospital or an aerospace program, catastrophes are often caused not by massive errors but rather by what appear to be (when considered in isolation) almost incidental human misjudgments and minor technical flaws. In studying normal accidents, engineers focus on the system design, the physical environment, and the possibility of mechanical failure; social scientists evaluate possible *human* error. Evidence suggests that 60 to 80 percent of normal accidents are attributed to human factors (Erikson 1994). However, normal accidents can also be caused by inadvertent or unanticipated consequences of technology. For example, recent research seems to indicate a link between the fertility drugs that have been used for several decades to help couples have children, and certain forms of cancer.

As technology continues to advance at a rapid pace, there are always new possibilities for accidents. For example, the disastrous 1986 launch of the United States space shuttle *Challenger* ended in the deaths of seven

THE GLOBAL DISCONNECT

Mapping Life WORLDWIDE

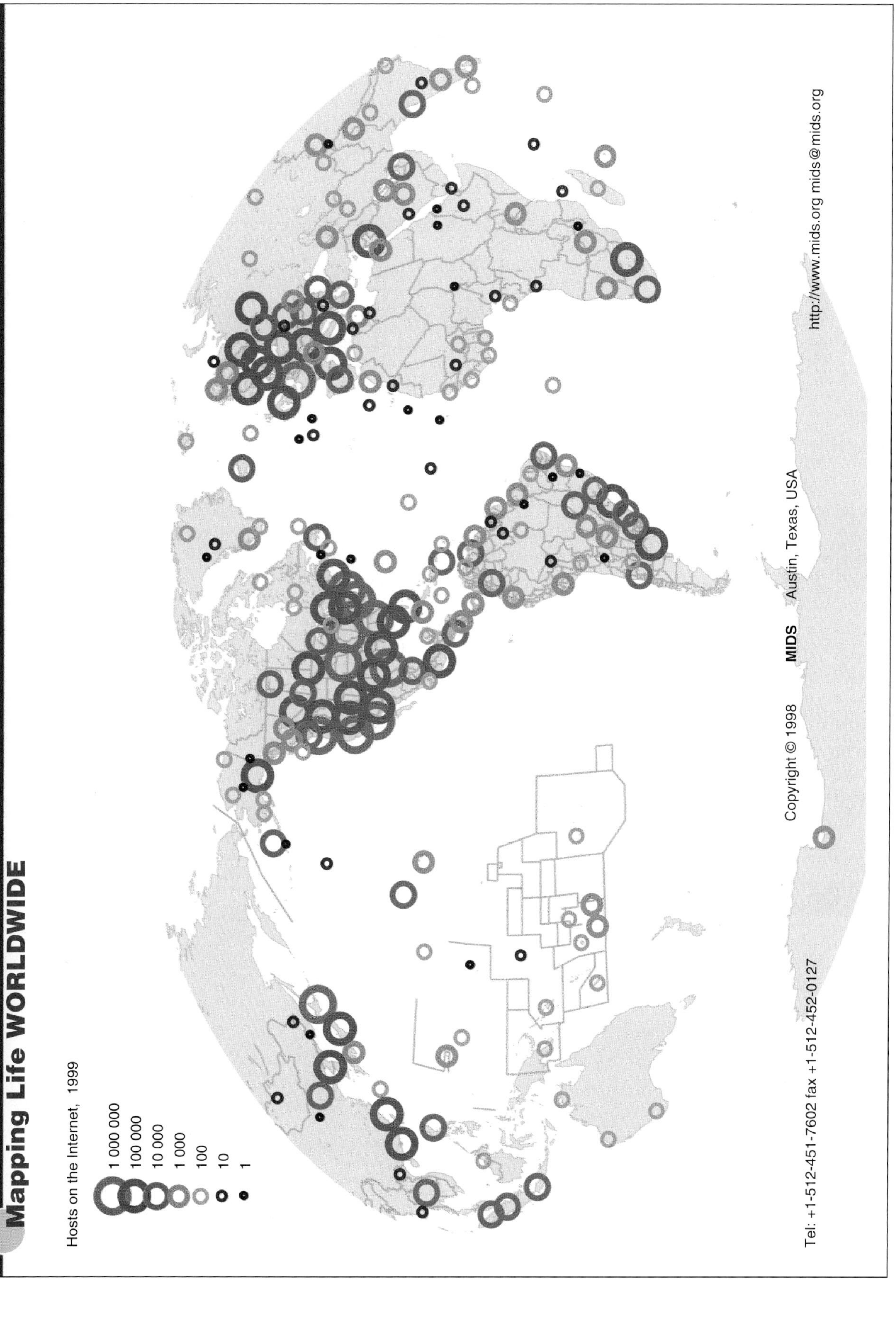

Source: Matrix Information and Directory Services 1999.

astronauts. More recently, it became apparent that electronic communication devices are vulnerable to failure. In 1998 the Galaxy IV communications satellite malfunctioned, knocking out its paging systems. Some hospitals could not page their doctors, so old-fashioned "phone trees" were established during the week of no service. The malfunction also took several broadcasters off the air. While the foul-up was ultimately corrected, this incident does underscore the possibilities for chaos in an ever-expanding electronic system (Swanson and Kirk 1998; Vaughan 1996).

System accidents are uncommon, even rare. But, like the death of any individual, which occurs only once, this infrequency is not all that reassuring. As the technology we use in our daily lives gets ever more complex, it is inevitable that the potential for failure increases. Given the serious consequences of a systems failure, we can anticipate that social scientists will work even more closely with engineers to explore how better equipment, training, and organization can reduce the likelihood of normal accidents (Perrow 1999; see also L. Clarke 1999; D. Miller 2000).

These are but a few vignettes of technological change, viewed from the vantage point of the turn of the century, that raise questions about the future. Sociologists are not fortune-tellers; the focus of the discipline is to examine the society around us, rather than to project decades ahead. But sociologists have no problem in asserting that social change (and technological change) is a given in our world. And so, they remind us, is resistance to change. We cannot know what is ahead. But the sociological imagination—with its probing and theorizing, with its careful empirical studies—can assist us in understanding the past and present and anticipating and adjusting to the future.

Technology and Society

A bank machine that identifies a person by his or her facial structure, a small device that sorts through hundreds of odours to ensure the safety of a chemical plant, a cell phone that recognizes its owner's voice—these are real-life examples of technology that were so much science fiction a few short decades ago. Today's computer chip cannot only think but can see, smell, and hear, too (Salkever 1999).

Technological advances can dramatically transform the material culture. Word processing on computers, the pocket calculator, the photocopying machine, and the compact disc player have largely eliminated use of the typewriter, the adding machine, the mimeograph machine, and the turntable—all of which were themselves technological advances.

Technological change also can reshape *nonmaterial* culture. In the following sections, we will examine the effects of technological advances on culture and social interaction, social control, and stratification and inequality.

Culture and Social Interaction

In Chapter 3, we emphasized that language is the foundation of every culture. From a functionalist perspective, language can bring together members of a society and promote cultural integration. However, from a conflict perspective, the use of language can intensify divisions between groups and societies—just look at the battles over the use of English in Quebec.

The Internet has often been lauded as a democratizing force that will make huge quantities of information available to great numbers of people around the world. However, while the Internet and its World Wide Web open up access to most societies, 35 percent of the material is transmitted in English (see Figure 16-1). Without special computer programs, documents in languages such as Chinese and Japanese cannot be transmitted in readable fashion (Colker 1996; P. Schaefer 1995).

The domination of the Internet by the English language is not surprising. English has largely become the international language of commerce and communication, and for decades has been the language used for com-

FIGURE 16-1

Language Use on the Internet Worldwide, 2003 (projection)

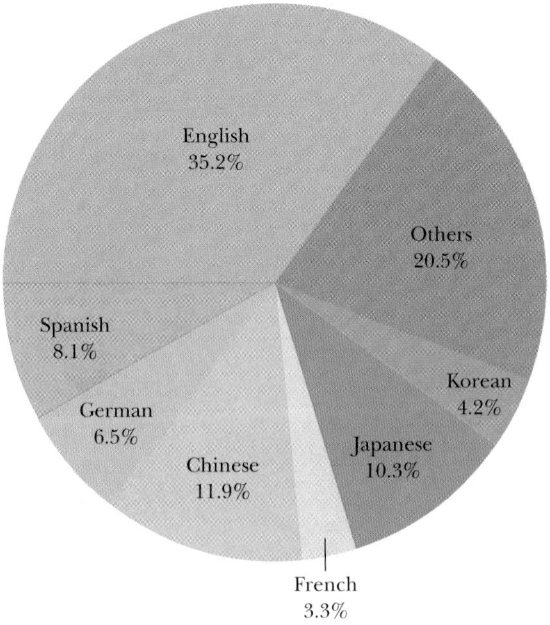

Source: Global Reach 2003.

munications between pilots and air traffic controllers worldwide. Nevertheless, members of other cultures resent the way in which English is the accepted standard on the Internet. In Russia, for example, it is easier for someone to download the works of Tolstoy translated into English than it is to get Tolstoy's work as originally written in Russian (Specter 1996a).

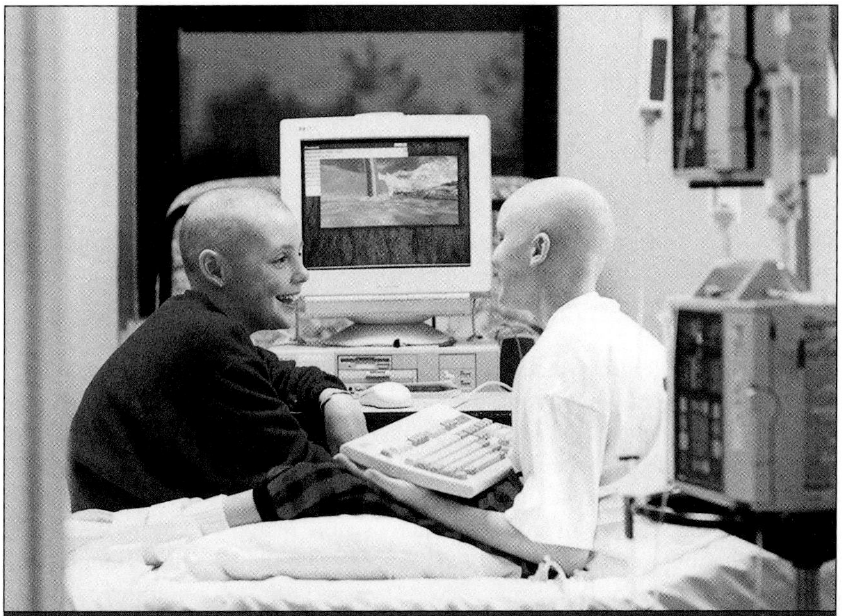

Two young patients at a New York City hospital communicate electronically with peers at a hospital in California. Electronic communication has proved useful in promoting social interaction among children who are seriously ill. The new technology, known as Starbright World, was developed with the assistance of director Steven Spielberg.

How will social interaction *within* a culture be transformed by the growing availability of electronic forms of communication? Will people turn to e-mail, websites, and faxes rather than telephone conversations and face-to-face meetings? Certainly, the technological shift to telephones reduced the use of letter writing as a means of maintaining kinship and friendship ties. But, while it is sometimes assumed that computers and other forms of electronic communication will be socially isolating, there are indications that computers actually put users in touch with large numbers of people on an interactive basis (L. Miller 1995). And in late 1998, the Internet was the means of putting two people together—a father and a daughter who had not seen each other in 50 years. The daughter had spent 14 years searching for her father through American state and federal agencies. But after only three hours on the Internet searching the white pages (telephone directories which list numbers for the whole country), she found her father's number in Detroit, Michigan. An emotional family reunion soon followed at the daughter's home in California.

Computer-mediated communication also takes place in chat rooms as well as in the more unconventional multi-user domains (MUDs), which allow people to assume new identities in role-playing games. Sociologist Sherry Turkle (1995, 1999) studied this interaction by anonymously visiting MUDs and other electronic chat rooms over a ten-year period and by conducting face-to-face interviews with more than 1000 people who communicate by electronic mail and actively participate in MUDs. The interviews were especially important because Turkle wanted to be able to distinguish between the users' on-screen personae and their real identities. Turkle concluded that many MUD users' lives were enhanced by the opportunity to engage in role playing and "become someone else." A new sense of self emerges that is "decentred and multiple," expanding on George Herbert Mead's notion of self. At the same time, she warns that some individuals may become so gratified by their online lives that they lose touch with their families, friends, and work responsibilities. Indeed, psychologists and therapists are giving increasing attention to what is being called "Internet addiction" (Belluck 1996).

pp. 79–80

pp. 106–07

If electronic communication can facilitate social interaction within a community—if it can create ties among people in different communities or even countries who "meet" in chat rooms or MUDs—then is there genuinely a new interactive world known as "cyberspace"? The term *cyberspace* was introduced in 1984 by William Gibson, a Canadian science fiction writer. He came up with this term after he walked by a video arcade and noticed the intensity of the players hunched over their screens. Gibson felt that these video game enthusiasts "develop a belief that there's some kind of actual space behind the screen. Some place that you can't see but you know is there" (Elmer-DeWitt 1995:4; see also Shields 1996; Wellman et al. 1996).

The emergence of cyberspace can be viewed as yet another step away from Ferdinand Tönnies's concept of the familiar, intimate *Gemeinschaft* to the comparatively impersonal *Gesellschaft* and as yet another way in which social cohesion is being eroded in contemporary society. Critics of electronic communication question whether nonverbal communication, voice

p. 112

inflections, and other forms of interpersonal interaction will be lost as people turn to e-mail and chat rooms (P. Schaefer 1995; Schellenberg 1996). A 1998 study that used survey analysis found that people who spend even a few hours a week online experience higher levels of depression and loneliness than if they had used the computer network less frequently (R. Kraut et al. 1998).

But while some conclude that by opening up the world to interaction, we may have reduced face-to-face interaction, others have reached different conclusions. One study surveyed more than 2000 American households to assess the impact of the Internet on the everyday lives of its users. It found that parents report that they often surf the web together with their children, and that the Internet has had little effect on their children's interactions with friends. This study concludes that about two thirds of the population in the United States are using the Internet more than ever and without sacrificing their social lives (Cha 2000).

Social Control

A data entry employee pauses to say hello to a colleague. A checker at the supermarket takes a moment to banter with a customer. A customer service telephone representative takes too much time helping callers. Each of these situations is subject to computer surveillance. Given the absence of strong protective legislation, employees in Canada are subject to increasing and pervasive supervision by computers. Supervisors have always scrutinized the performance of their workers, but with so much work now being handled electronically, the possibilities for surveillance have risen dramatically. It is not uncommon to phone a large corporation and have a recorded message inform you that your conversation may be monitored "for customer service quality."

With Big Brother watching and listening in more and more places, computer and video technology has facilitated supervision, control, and even domination by employers or government. There is a danger that electronic monitoring of employees can become a substitute for effective management and can lead to perceptions of unfairness and intrusiveness. An American study found that 35 percent of firms keep track of their workers by recording their phone calls and voice mail, looking through their computer files, or videotaping. About a quarter of these firms said they do not inform their employees of these surveillance practices (Grimsley 1997). In Canada, companies, educational institutions, government departments, and other organizations have implemented policies that permit them to monitor employee Internet use and e-mail.

In recent years, a new type of corporate surveillance has emerged. A number of Internet sites are highly critical of the operations of various corporations. On McSpotlight, one could find attacks on nutritional practices at McDonald's; on Up Against the Wal, one could study advice on how to fight plans to open new Wal-Mart stores in a community. The Internet sites of such "anti-corporate vigilantes" are generally protected by the Charter of Rights and Freedoms, but powerful corporations are carefully monitoring the sites in an attempt to counteract the activities of their critics (Neuborne 1996).

Technological advances have also created the possibility for a new type of white-collar crime: computer crime. It is now possible to gain access to a computer's inventory without leaving home and to carry out embezzlement or electronic fraud without leaving a trace. Typically, discussions of computer crime focus on computer theft and on problems caused by computer "hackers," but widespread use of computers has facilitated many new ways of participating in deviant behaviour. Consequently, greatly expanded police resources may be needed to deal with online child molesters, prostitution rings, software pirates, con artists, and other types of computer criminals. There is now a computer crime division within the RCMP and most of the major municipal and provincial police forces across the country. The consensus of the heads of these sections is that cases

p. 163

"Keystroke! . . . Keystroke! . . . Keystroke!"

are increasing and becoming more difficult to solve (Computer Security Institute 1999; Piller 2000).

Not all the technological advances relevant to social control have been electronic in nature. DNA data banks have given police a powerful weapon in solving crimes; they have also opened the way to free wrongfully convicted citizens. In 1969, 17-year-old David Milgaard was convicted of murdering a young woman and sent to prison. Twenty-eight years later, at the age of 46, Milgaard was granted his freedom by the Canadian justice system after DNA testing proved conclusively that he was not the person responsible. Efforts are under way to make such testing and other forms of DNA evidence as easily available as fingerprinting. While appropriate safeguards must be devised, the expansion of such DNA data banks has the potential to revolutionize law enforcement in Canada, and, as international police collaboration increases, globally—especially in the area of sex crimes, where biological evidence is telling (Butterfield 1996; DPIC 2000c).

Another connection between technology and social control is the use of computer databases and electronic verification of documents to reduce illegal immigration into Canada, particularly after the terrorist acts against the World Trade Center and the Pentagon in the United States. While concerned about the issue of illegal entry, many members of Canada's visible minority communities nevertheless believe that *their* privacy, rather than that of the majority white population, is most likely to be infringed upon by government authorities. The next section of the chapter looks more fully at how technological changes can intensify stratification and inequality based on race, ethnicity, and other factors.

Stratification and Inequality

An important continuing theme in sociology is stratification among people. Thus far, there is little evidence to suggest that technology will reduce inequality; in fact, it may only intensify it. Technology is costly, and it is generally impossible to introduce advances to everyone simultaneously. So who gets this access first? Conflict theorists contend that as we travel further and further along the electronic frontier through advances such as telecommuting and the Internet, the disenfranchised poor will be isolated from mainstream society in an "information ghetto," just as racial and ethnic minorities have traditionally been subjected to residential segregation (Ouellette 1993).

Available data show clear differences in use of computers based on income, level of education, and age. There is a significant relationship between the income of a household in Canada and the probability of computer use. Among those families in the highest income quartile, 53.7 percent had computers. This is more than four times the rate of families at the bottom of the income scale (12.4 percent). Figures also reveal that computer use rises dramatically with the level of education of the adults in a household. Perhaps not surprisingly, computer use is lowest among seniors, traditionally one of the poorest cohorts in the Canadian population (Statistics Canada 2000a).

This issue goes beyond individual interest or lack of interest in computers. Accessibility is a major concern. Given that phone and cable companies are for-profit enterprises, it is not unreasonable to suggest that access to computer technology and in particular, the Internet, may bypass poor neighbourhoods and minority populations. Researchers in the United States concluded that regional telephone companies' plans for these advanced communications networks target affluent areas and may lead to an exclusionary "electronic redlining" similar to discrimination in fields such as banking, real estate, and insurance. Industry executives counter that they have repeatedly stated their intention to deploy the information superhighway to *all* areas. The United States Congress has proposed regulatory legislation to ensure equal access to the information superhighway by mandating the wiring of schools, libraries, and hospitals. Several communities, such as Manchester, New Hampshire, and Oakland, California, have recently arranged for computer hookups in publicly built low-income housing (Lohr 1994; Lieberman 1999).

Technological advances of the present and future may not be equally beneficial to men and women. Feminist sociologists point out that technology is not necessarily gender-neutral. For example, many studies have shown the differential use of computers by boys and girls. Computer games, which often serve as a means of early socialization to computers, typically involve sports or skills associated with traditional male gender roles. As a result, computer camps and video arcades have become predominantly male settings.

The existence of a gender gap associated with the use of computer technology in Canada is perhaps best demonstrated by a recent Statistics Canada analysis of computer game playing amongst adolescent boys and girls. While 11 percent of the male respondents reported playing 10 or more hours a week of computer games, just 1 percent of females reported the same usage. Even more dramatic is the comparison of proportions of adolescents who said they never played the electronic games—54 percent of the girls compared with just 15 percent of the boys (Statistics Canada 1999a).

The issue of technology and inequality is especially sensitive when viewed in a cross-cultural perspective. Although industrialization has dramatically improved the standard of living of many workers, it has allowed elites to amass untold wealth. Moreover, the activities of multinational corporations have increased the inequality between industrialized core nations (such as Canada, the United States, Germany, and Japan) and the periphery of developing countries.

SOCIAL POLICY AND TECHNOLOGY

Privacy and Censorship in a Global Village

The Issue

An envelope is slipped through your mail slot, larger and brighter than the bills and other pieces of personal correspondence. Behind the plastic window of the envelope is your full name and address; it has obviously been sent by someone who knows where you live. On the front, in colourful letters, it exclaims: "GET MAJOR AIR! TIPS ON NEW TECHNIQUES FOR THE SNOWBOARDING EXPERT."

As it happens, you just bought a new, enhanced-performance snowboard last month—the person who sent this to you obviously knows what your interests are. So, you open the envelope, and inside is a marketing package from a magazine subscription company that you have never dealt with or even heard of. "What is this?" you wonder. "Where did they get this information about me?" Then it dawns on you that you have been added to someone's database as a snowboarder. Someone, probably the store where you made your purchase, has sold that information and your contact address to a direct marketing company. For a moment, you consider phoning the store and complaining, but then conclude that it would be a waste of time. After all, in the 21st century, this happens all the time.

Canadians have become accustomed to this type of experience. The pervasiveness of computers in the marketplace, in every store, restaurant, and service centre Canadians deal with has made the gathering and sorting of consumer data easy and inexpensive. This data is valuable because it can be sold to information-hungry retail corporations for large sums money. Information has become such an important commodity that companies have been created just for the purpose of gathering and selling it. Most of us have at least one plastic card in our wallets whose main purpose is to record our purchases, whether it is a discount card from a grocery chain or music store or a more generic card such as AIR MILES®. These cards offer consumers discounts, seemingly for free: you make a purchase, the cashier slides the card through a capture device, and your savings and/or point total is recorded. However, the apparent "free" nature of this transaction belies the fact that you have just handed over a bit of information about yourself that can be sold—because you have already given permission for this to take place by signing the original agreement with the card company—to the highest bidder in the marketplace. Your name has been added to one or more lists of people with whom you have something in common. You might, as in the example above, all be snowboarders, or you might be fond of buying a particular brand of soap, or of renting movies of a certain genre.

The Setting

These lists may at first seem innocent enough. Does it really matter if companies can buy lists for marketing with our names, addresses, and telephone numbers? Part of the problem is that computer technology has made it increasingly easy for any individual, business firm, or government agency to retrieve more and more information about any of us. For decades, information from motor vehicle offices, voter registration lists, and credit bureaus has been electronically stored, yet the incompatibility of different computer systems prevented access from one system to another. Today, having some information about a person has made it much easier to get other and perhaps more sensitive information (Stoll 1995).

The question of how much free expression should be permitted on the Internet relates to the issue of censorship. Some of the X-rated material is perfectly legal, if inappropriate for children who use the Net. Some of the sites are clearly illegal, such as those that serve the needs of pedophiles and prey on young children. Some are morally and legally elusive, such as the "upskirt" sites that post images taken by video cameras aimed under the skirts of unsuspecting women in public places. This example illustrates a culture lag in which the material culture (the technology) is changing faster than the nonmaterial culture (the values defining right from wrong, and good from bad).

Sociological Insights

Functionalists can point to the manifest function of the Internet in its ability to facilitate communications. They also can identify the latent function of providing a forum for groups with few resources to communicate with literally tens of millions of people. Poorly financed groups can range from hate organizations to special interest groups vying against powerful wealthy interests. Thus, the

functionalist perspective would see many aspects of technology fostering communication; the issue of censorship depends on how one views the content of the message, and the issue of privacy hinges on how information is used.

Even if computers and other forms of modern technology are peering deeper and deeper into our daily lives, some observers insist that we *benefit* from such innovations and can exist quite well with a bit less privacy. Sociologist Amitai Etzioni (1996:14A) bluntly states, "The genie is out of the bottle. We must either return to the Stone Age (pay cash, use carrier pigeons, and forget insurance) or learn to live with shrunken privacy." Etzioni adds that there are many instances in which preservation of the common good requires giving up some part of our privacy. Amnesty International, the global human rights advocacy group, has applauded the expansion of the Internet. This group sees it as a means to reach a wider audience and, in the case of specific cases of torture or repression, to speedily disseminate information worldwide so that appropriate steps can be taken to end unjust situations (S. Perry 1998a).

Viewed from a conflict perspective, however, there is the ever-present danger that a society's most powerful groups will use technological advances to invade the privacy of the less powerful and thereby maintain or intensify various forms of inequality and injustice. For example, in 1989, the People's Republic of China used various types of technology to identify protestors who had participated in pro-democracy demonstrations at Tiananmen Square and elsewhere. Some protestors identified in this manner received long prison terms because of their activism. During the same period, the Chinese government intercepted the news reports, telephone calls, and facsimile messages of foreign journalists covering the demonstrations. While encouraging e-commerce, the government began in 2000 to undertake a "security certification" of all Internet content and service providers in China. Conflict theorists argue that control of technology in almost any form remains in the hands of those who already wield the most power, usually at the expense of the powerless and poor (Pomfret 2000).

Interactionists view the privacy and censorship debate as one that parallels concerns people have in any social interaction. Just as we may disapprove of some associations that relatives or friends have with other people, we also express concern over controversial websites and attempt to monitor people's social interaction. Obviously, the Internet facilitates interactions with a broad range of people, with minimal likelihood of detection compared to face-to-face interaction. Moreover, one can easily move a website from one country to another, avoiding not only detection but also prosecution.

Policy Initiatives

Canadians gained protection from invasive information gathering in legislation enacted on January 1, 2001. The Personal Information Protection and Electronic Documents Act came into force on that day with the intent of forestalling exploitation of Canadians through the unauthorized use or sale of information about them. The act makes it mandatory for each company to have specific approval from each individual for the use of their personal information. The act covers federally controlled sectors such as banks, telephone companies, broadcast media, and airlines, as well as all business activities within the Yukon, Northwest Territories, and Nunavut. As of 2002, it also applied to any information concerning someone's health, and in 2004 it will cover all commercial activities.

In a statement accompanying the announcement of the legislation, Canada's Privacy Commissioner, George Radwanski, said: "It is important that Canadians realize they have fundamental rights when it comes to privacy, and that they are not obliged to give information about themselves to everybody who asks."

In the United States, the 1996 Communications Decency Act made it a federal crime to transmit "indecent" or "patently offensive" material over the Internet without maintaining safeguards to ensure that children cannot see it. Private e-mail and online chat room communications with anyone under the age of 18 were subjected to the same standard. Violations of the law could lead to up to two years in prison and a US$250 000 fine (Fernandez 1996; Lappin 1996).

Civil liberties advocates in the United States insisted that such governmental action infringed on private communications between consenting adults and inevitably limited freedom of speech. They noted that at one point America Online even banned use of the term *breast,* thereby preventing any meaningful discussion of breast cancer or breast examinations. Lawsuits challenging the constitutionality of the Communications Decency Act were supported by such organizations as the American Civil Liberties Union (ACLU), the American Library Association, the American Society of Newspaper Editors, and the National Writers Union. In 1997, the United States Supreme Court declared that major parts of the act were unconstitutional. The Court called government attempts to regulate content on the Internet an attack on the First Amendment guarantee of freedom of speech (Fernandez 1996; A. Harmon 1998).

Censorship and privacy are also issues globally. In Myanmar (or Burma), the government has ruled that fax machines and computer modems are illegal. In Saudi Arabia, access to the Internet was banned until 1999. Now all Internet connections are routed through a government hub where computers block access to thousands of sites catalogued on a rapidly expanding censorship list—for example, all gambling sites, all free-wheeling chat rooms, and all sites critical of the ruling Saudi family. By contrast, the openness of the Internet in other parts of the Middle East allows scattered Palestinian refugees to communicate with one another and establish websites that provide a history of Palestinian settlements. While China encourages expansion of the Internet, it has been wary of facilitating communication that it regards as disruptive. The government has blocked all websites related to the Falun Gong spiritual group, and in 2000 it announced that "state secrets" (very vaguely defined) were banned from the Internet. Meanwhile, the British government is constructing an Internet spy centre that is geared to watch all online activity in Great Britain. It will be able to track every website a person visits (Africa News Service 1998; Jehl 1999; MacLeod 2000; Rosenthal 1999b, 2000; T. Wilkinson 1999).

While some people chastise government efforts to curb technology, others decry their *failure* to limit certain aspects of technology. The United States is developing an international reputation of being opposed to efforts to protect people's privacy. The United States has been vocal in opposing efforts by the 15 European Union countries to implement a tough law designed to protect citizens from computer-age invasions of privacy. The American technology industry does not want to have access to information blocked, since information is vital to global commerce. While a compromise is likely, this case illustrates the fine line between safeguarding privacy and stifling the electronic flow of information (Center for Public Integrity 1998; S. Perry 1998b; Shenon 1998).

The conflict over privacy and censorship is far from over. As technology continues to advance in the 21st century, there are sure to be new battlegrounds.

Let's Discuss

1. What are some of the ways that people can obtain information about us? Are you aware of any databases that contain information about your personal life?
2. Do you think corporations and employers have a right to monitor employees' e-mail and phone calls? Why or why not?

Chapter Resources

Summary

Social movements are organized collective activities to promote or resist charge. ***Social change*** is significant alteration over time in behaviour patterns and culture, including norms and values. ***Technology*** is information about how to use the material resources of the environment to satisfy human needs and desires. This chapter examines social movements and their role in social change, sociological theories of social change, resistance to change, and the impact of technology on society and on social change.

1. A group mobilizes into a social movement when there is a shared perception that its ***relative deprivation*** can be ended only through collective action.
2. The success of a social movement will depend in good part on how effectively it mobilizes its resources.
3. ***New social movements*** tend to focus on more than just economic issues and often cross national boundaries.
4. Early advocates of the evolutionary theory of social change believed that society was inevitably progressing to a higher state.
5. Talcott Parsons, a leading advocate of functionalist theory, viewed society as naturally being in a state of equilibrium or balance.
6. Conflict theorists see change as having crucial significance, since it is needed to correct social injustices and inequalities.
7. Feminist theories seek to confront social injustice in order to promote change for those groups in society that are disadvantaged by their class, race, ethnicity, sexual preference, age, and/or global location.
8. In general, those with a disproportionate share of society's wealth, status, and power have a vested interest in preserving the status quo and will resist change.
9. The period of maladjustment when the nonmaterial culture is still adapting to new material conditions is known as ***culture lag.***
10. In the computer age, *telecommuters* are linked to their supervisors and colleagues through computer terminals, phone lines, and fax machines.
11. Early users of the Internet, the world's largest computer network, established a subculture with specific norms and values and with distinctive argot terms.
12. Advances in biotechnology have raised difficult ethical questions about sex selection of fetuses and genetic engineering.
13. Social scientists focus on human error in the ***normal accidents*** associated with increasing reliance on technology.
14. The domination of the Internet by the English language is not surprising, since English has largely become the international language of commerce and communication.
15. Computer and video technology has facilitated supervision, control, and even domination by employers or government.
16. Conflict theorists fear that the disenfranchised poor may be isolated from mainstream society in an "information ghetto," just as racial and ethnic minorities have been subjected to residential segregation.
17. Computer technology has made it increasingly easy for any individual, business firm, or government agency to retrieve more and more information about any of us and thereby infringe on our privacy; it is also easy to disseminate pornographic material to millions of people at a time. How much government should restrict access to electronic information is an important policy issue today.

Critical Thinking Questions

1. Select one social movement that is currently working for change in Canada. Analyze that movement, drawing on the concepts of relative deprivation and resource mobilization.
2. In the last few years we have witnessed phenomenal growth in the use of cellular phones in all parts of the world. Analyze this example of material culture from the point of view of culture lag. Consider how usage, government regulation, and privacy issues are being worked out to keep up with the new technology.
3. In what ways has social interaction in your college or university community been affected by the kinds of technological advances examined in this chapter? Are there particular subcultures that are more likely or less likely to use new forms of electronic communication?

Key Terms

Culture lag A period of maladjustment during which the nonmaterial culture is still adapting to new material conditions. (page 427)

Equilibrium model A functionalist view of society as tending toward a state of stability or balance. (423)

Evolutionary theory A theory of social change that holds that society is moving in a definite direction. (422)

Luddites Rebellious craft workers in 19th-century England who destroyed new factory machinery as part of their resistance to the Industrial Revolution. (428)

Multilinear evolutionary theory A theory of social change that holds that change can occur in several ways and does not inevitably lead in the same direction. (423)

New social movements Organized collective activities that promote autonomy and self-determination as well as improvements in the quality of life. (422)

Normal accidents Failures that are inevitable given the manner in which human and technological systems are detached. (432)

Relative deprivation The conscious feeling of a negative discrepancy between legitimate expectations and present actualities. (420)

Resource mobilization The ways in which a social movement utilizes such resources as money, political influence, access to the media, and personnel. (421)

Social change Significant alteration over time in behaviour patterns and culture, including norms and values. (419)

Social movements Organized collective activities to promote or resist change in an existing group or society. (419)

Unilinear evolutionary theory A theory of social change that holds that all societies pass through the same successive stages of evolution and inevitably reach the same end. (423)

Vested interests Those people or groups who will suffer in the event of social change and who have a stake in maintaining the status quo. (427)

Additional Readings

Goyder, John. 1997. *Technology and Society: a Canadian perspective.* Peterborough: Broadview Press. This book by a University of Waterloo professor asks the difficult questions about the relationship between technological advance and social evolution.

Ignatieff, Michael. 2000. *The Rights Revolution.* Toronto: House of Anansi Press. With this number-one national bestseller, Ignatieff looks at the use of "rights" as a bargaining chip in the national dialogue. The result, as the title indicates, is a revolutionary approach to human rights that is being monitored globally.

Simard, Rene. 2000. *Reaching Out: Canada, International Science and Technology, and the Knowledge-based Economy.* Ottawa: Industry Canada. Simard examines the attempt by Canada to create a new place for itself in the new global economy. How well can Canada compete in the 'knowledge-based" marketplace of the 21st century?

Internet Connection

www.mcgrawhill.ca/college/schaefer

For additional Internet exercises relating to online courses and the "digital divide," visit the Schaefer Online Learning Centre at ***http://www.mcgrawhill.ca/college/schaefer****. Please note that while the URLs listed were current at the time of printing, these sites often change—check the Online Learning Centre for updates.*

The Network for Creative Social Change was founded in Nova Scotia as a means to identify opportunities for systemic change. Go to the site at **http://www.chebucto.ns.ca/CommunitySupport/** and find answers to the following questions:

(a) Do you think the Network for Creative Social Change would have been possible 20 years ago? Why or why not?

(b) What is meant by "systemic change"? Why is this type of social change important?

(c) How does the organization perceive the role of science in creating and/or helping to resolve some of the most critical issues facing contemporary Canadian society?

(d) How does the Multilateral Agreement of Investment represent a threat to Canadian society?

(e) What is the Genuine Progress Index? Why do its proponents argue that it is a more accurate measure of the improvement of citizens' lives than are the measures currently in use by most governments and international organizations?

Glossary

Numbers following the definitions indicate pages where the terms were identified. Consult the index for further page references.

A

Absolute poverty In developed countries, a standard of poverty based on a minimum level of subsistence below which families should not be expected to exist. (185)

Achieved status A social position attained by a person largely through his or her own efforts. (102)

Activity theory An interactionist theory of aging that argues that elderly people who remain active will be best adjusted. (363)

Adoption In a legal sense, a process that allows for the transfer of the legal rights, responsibilities, and privileges of parenthood to a new legal parent or parents. (277)

Affirmative action Positive efforts to recruit minority group members or women for jobs, promotions, and educational opportunities. (341)

Ageism A term coined by Robert N. Butler to refer to prejudice and discrimination against the elderly. (365)

Agrarian society The most technologically advanced form of preindustrial society. Members are primarily engaged in the production of food but increase their crop yield through such innovations as the plow. (114)

Alienation The condition of being estranged or disassociated from the surrounding society. (131)

Amalgamation The process by which a majority group and a minority group combine through intermarriage to form a new group. (221)

Androcentrism A worldview that favours the male perspective. (40)

Anomie Durkheim's term for the loss of direction felt in a society when social control of individual behaviour has become ineffective. (10)

Anomie theory of deviance A theory developed by Robert Merton that explains deviance as an adaptation either of socially prescribed goals or of the norms governing their attainment, or both. (157)

Anticipatory socialization Processes of socialization in which a person "rehearses" for future positions, occupations, and social relationships. (83)

Apartheid The former policy of the South African government designed to maintain the separation of blacks and other non-whites from the dominant whites. (222)

Argot Specialized language used by members of a group or subculture. (63)

Ascribed status A social position "assigned" to a person by society without regard for the person's unique talents or characteristics. (101)

Assimilation The process by which a person forsakes his or her own cultural tradition to become part of a different culture. (221)

Authority Power that has been institutionalized and is recognized by the people over whom it is exercised. (326)

B

Bilateral descent A kinship system in which both sides of a person's family are regarded as equally important. (268)

Birthrate The number of live births per 1000 population in a given year. Also known as the *crude birthrate.* (355)

Bourgeoisie Karl Marx's term for the capitalist class, comprising the owners of the means of production. (179)

Bureaucracy A component of formal organization in which rules and hierarchical ranking are used to achieve efficiency. (130)

Bureaucratization The process by which a group, organization, or social movement becomes increasingly bureaucratic. (133)

C

Capitalism An economic system in which capital, primarily in the form of currency, is used as a tool to create wealth, the means of production are largely in private hands, and the main incentive for economic activity is the accumulation of profits. (179)

Castes Hereditary systems of rank, usually religiously dictated, that tend to be fixed and immobile. (177)

Causal logic The relationship between a condition or variable and a particular consequence, with one event leading to the other. (30)

Census An enumeration, or counting, of a population. (354)

Charismatic authority Max Weber's term for power made legitimate by a leader's exceptional personal or emotional appeal to his or her followers. (327)

Class A term used by Max Weber to refer to a group of people who have a similar level of wealth and income. (179)

Class consciousness In Karl Marx's view, a subjective awareness held by members of a class regarding their common vested interests and need for collective political action to bring about social change. (179)

Classical theory An approach to the study of formal organizations that views workers as being motivated almost entirely by economic rewards. (136)

Class system A social ranking based primarily on economic position in which achieved characteristics can influence mobility. (177)

Closed system A social system in which there is little or no possibility of individual mobility. (191)

Coalition A temporary or permanent alliance geared toward a common goal. (129)

Code of ethics The standards of acceptable behaviour developed by and for members of a profession. (38)

Coercion The actual or threatened use of force to impose one's will on others. (326)

Cognitive theory of development Jean Piaget's theory explaining how children's thought progresses through four stages. (82)

Cohabitation The practice of living together as a male–female couple without marrying. (282)

Colonialism The maintenance of political, social, economic, and cultural dominance over a people by a foreign power for an extended period of time. (194)

Communism As an ideal type, an economic system under which all property is communally owned and no social distinctions are made on the basis of people's ability to contribute to the economy. (325)

Community A spatial or political unit of social organization that gives people a sense of belonging, based either on shared residence in a particular place or on a common identity. (389)

Concentric-zone theory A theory of urban growth that sees growth in terms of a series of rings radiating from the central business district. (392)

Conflict perspective A sociological approach that assumes that social behaviour is best understood in terms of conflict or tension between competing groups. (14)

Conformity Going along with one's peers, individuals of a person's own status, who have no special right to direct that person's behaviour. (148)

Contact hypothesis An interactionist perspective that states that interracial contact between people of equal status in cooperative circumstances will reduce prejudice. (220)

Content analysis The systematic coding and objective recording of data, guided by some rationale. (37)

Control group Subjects in an experiment who are not introduced to the independent variable by the researcher. (36)

Control theory A view of conformity and deviance that suggests that our connection to members of society leads us to systematically conform to society's norms. (152)

Control variable A factor held constant to test the relative impact of an independent variable. (33)

Correlation A relationship between two variables whereby a change in one coincides with a change in the other. (30)

Correspondence principle A term used by Bowles and Gintis to refer to the tendency of schools to promote the values expected of individuals in each social class and to prepare students for the types of jobs typically held by members of their class. (308)

Counterculture A subculture that deliberately opposes certain aspects of the larger culture. (64)

Creationism A literal interpretation of the Bible regarding the creation of man and the universe used to argue that evolution should not be presented as established scientific fact. (316)

Crime A violation of criminal law for which formal penalties are applied by some governmental authority. (162)

Cult Due to the stereotyping, this term has been abandoned by sociologists in favour of *new religious movements.* (302)

Cultural relativism The viewing of people's behaviour from the perspective of their own culture. (66)

Cultural transmission A school of criminology that argues that criminal behaviour is learned through social interactions. (158)

Cultural universals General practices found in every culture. (52, 293)

Culture The totality of learned, socially transmitted behaviour. (51)

Culture lag Ogburn's term for a period of maladjustment during which the nonmaterial culture is still adapting to new material conditions. (54, 427)

Culture shock The feeling of surprise and disorientation that is experienced when people witness cultural practices different from their own. (64)

D

Death rate The number of deaths per 1000 population in a given year. Also known as the *crude death rate.* (355)

Defended neighbourhood A neighbourhood that residents identify through defined community borders and through a perception that adjacent areas are geographically separate and socially different. (398)

Degradation ceremony An aspect of the socialization process within total institutions, in which people are subjected to humiliating rituals. (83)

Deindustrialization The systematic, widespread withdrawal of investment in basic aspects of productivity such as factories and plants. (338)

Demographic transition A term used to describe the change from high birthrates and death rates to relatively low birthrates and death rates. (356)

Demography The scientific study of population. (351)

Denomination A large, organized religion not officially linked with the state or government. (300)

Dependency theory An approach that contends that industrialized nations continue to exploit developing countries for their own gain. (196)

Dependent variable The variable in a causal relationship that is subject to the influence of another variable. (30)

Deviance Behaviour that violates the standards of conduct or expectations of a group or society. (152)

Differential association A theory of deviance proposed by Edwin Sutherland that holds that violation of rules results from exposure to attitudes favourable to criminal acts. (159)

Diffusion The process by which a cultural item is spread from group to group or society to society. (53)

Discovery The process of making known or sharing the existence of an aspect of reality. (53)

Discrimination The process of denying opportunities and equal rights to individuals and groups because of prejudice or other arbitrary reasons. (215)

Disengagement theory A functionalist theory of aging introduced by Cumming and Henry that contends that society and the aging individual mutually sever many of their relationships. (362)

Domestic partnership Two unrelated adults who have chosen to share one another's lives in a relationship of mutual caring, who reside together, and who agree to be jointly responsible for their dependents, basic living expenses, and other common necessities. (283)

Dominant ideology A set of cultural beliefs and practices that helps to maintain powerful social, economic, and political interests. (62)

Downsizing Reductions taken in a company's workforce as part of deindustrialization. (338)

Dramaturgical approach A view of social interaction, popularized by Erving Goffman, under which people are examined as if they were theatrical performers. (15, 80)

Dyad A two-member group. (128)

Dysfunction An element or a process of society that may disrupt a social system or lead to a decrease in stability. (13)

E

Ecclesia A religious organization that claims to include most or all of the members of a society and is recognized as the national or official religion. (300)

E-commerce Numerous ways that people with access to the Internet can do business from their computers. (339)

Economic system The structures and processes through which goods and services are produced, distributed, and consumed. (323)

Education A formal process of learning in which some people consciously teach while others adopt the social role of learner. (293)

Egalitarian family An authority pattern in which the adult members of the family are regarded as equals. (269)

Elite model A view of society as controlled by a small group of individuals who share a common set of political and economic interests. (334)

Endogamy The restriction of mate selection to people within the same group. (273)

Equilibrium model Talcott Parsons's functionalist view of society as tending toward a state of stability or balance. (423)

Esteem The reputation that a particular individual has earned within an occupation. (183)

Ethnic group A group that is set apart from others because of its national origin or distinctive cultural patterns. (209)

Ethnocentrism The tendency to assume that one's culture and way of life are superior to all others. (66, 214)

Ethnography The study of an entire social setting through extended systematic observation. (35)

Eurocentrism A worldview that assumes European values are the desired standard. (40)

Evolutionary theory A theory of social change that holds that society is moving in a definite direction. (422)

Exogamy The requirement that people select mates outside certain groups. (273)

Experiment An artificially created situation that allows the researcher to manipulate variables. (36)

Experimental group Subjects in an experiment who are exposed to an independent variable introduced by a researcher. (36)

Exploitation theory A Marxist theory that views racial subordination such as that in the United States and Canada as a manifestation of the class system inherent in capitalism. (219)

Expressiveness A term used by Parsons and Bales to refer to concern for maintenance of harmony and the internal emotional affairs of the family. (245)

Extended family A family in which relatives—such as grandparents, aunts, or uncles—live in the same home as parents and their children. (267)

F

Face-work A term used by Erving Goffman to refer to the efforts of people to maintain the proper image and avoid embarrassment in public. (80)

False consciousness A term used by Karl Marx to describe an attitude held by members of a class that does not accurately reflect its objective position. (179)

Family A set of people related by blood, marriage (or some other agreed-upon relationship), or adoption who share the primary responsibility for reproduction and caring for members of society. (265)

Feminist perspectives Various diverse streams of sociological analysis having in common the attempt to explain, understand, and change the ways in which gender socially organizes our public and private lives in such a way as to produce inequality between men and women. (14)

Fertility The amount of reproduction among women of childbearing age. (351)

Folkways Norms governing everyday social behaviour whose violation raises comparatively little concern. (58)

Formal norms Norms that generally have been written down and that specify strict rules for punishment of violators. (57)

Formal organization A special-purpose group designed and structured for maximum efficiency. (130)

Formal social control Social control carried out by authorized agents, such as police officers, judges, school administrators, and employers. (150)

Functionalist perspective A sociological approach that emphasizes the way that parts of a society are structured to maintain its stability. (13)

G

Gemeinschaft A term used by Ferdinand Tönnies to describe close-knit communities, often found in rural areas, in which strong personal bonds unite members. (112)

Gender roles Expectations regarding the proper behaviour, attitudes, and activities of males and females. (86)

Gender socialization An aspect of socialization through which we learn the attitudes, behaviours, and practices associated with being male and female according to our society and social groups within it. (86)

Generalized others A term used by George Herbert Mead to refer to the child's awareness of the attitudes, viewpoints, and expectations of society as a whole that a child takes into account in his or her behaviour. (79)

Genocide The deliberate, systematic killing of or blatant disregard for an entire people or nation. (220)

Gentrification The process of transforming a community from a home for those at the bottom of the socioeconomic ladder to an upscale collection of condominiums and boutiques. (399)

Gerontology The scientific study of the sociological and psychological aspects of aging and the problems of the aged. (361)

Gesellschaft A term used by Ferdinand Tönnies to describe communities, often urban, that are large and impersonal with little commitment to the group or consensus on values. (112)

Glass ceiling An invisible barrier that blocks the promotion of a qualified individual in a work environment because of the individual's gender, race, or ethnicity. (217)

Goal displacement Overzealous conformity to official regulations within a bureaucracy. (133)

Group Any number of people with similar norms, values, and expectations who interact meaningfully with one another on a regular basis. (106)

Growth rate The difference between births and deaths, plus the difference between immigrants and emigrants, per 1000 population. (355)

H

Hawthorne effect The unintended influence that observers or experiments can have on their subjects. (37)

Health As defined by the World Health Organization, a state of complete physical, mental, and social well-being, and not merely the absence of disease and infirmity. (366)

Hidden curriculum Standards of behaviour that are deemed proper by society and are taught subtly in schools. (307)

Holistic medicine A means of health maintenance using therapies in which the health care practitioner considers the person's physical, mental, emotional, and spiritual characteristics. (377)

Homophobia Fear of and prejudice against homosexuality. (117)

Horizontal mobility The movement of an individual from one social position to another of the same rank. (192)

Horticultural societies Preindustrial societies in which people plant seeds and crops rather than subsist merely on available foods. (114)

Human ecology An area of study concerned with the interrelationships between people and their spatial setting and physical environment. (392)

Human relations approach An approach to the study of formal organizations that emphasizes the role of people, communication, and participation within a bureaucracy and tends to focus on the informal structure of the organization. (136)

Hunting-and-gathering society A preindustrial society in which people rely on whatever foods and fibre are readily available in order to live. (113)

Hypothesis A speculative statement about the relationship between two or more variables. (30)

I

Ideal type A construct or model that serves as a measuring rod against which specific cases can be evaluated. (10)

Impression management A term used by Erving Goffman to refer to the altering of the presentation of the self in order to create distinctive appearances and satisfy particular audiences. (80)

Incest taboo The prohibition of sexual relationships between certain culturally specified relatives. (273)

Incidence The number of *new* cases of a specific disorder occurring within a given population during a stated period of time. (372)

Income Salaries and wages and monies brought in by investments. (176)

Independent variable The variable in a causal relationship that, when altered, causes or influences a change in a second variable. (30)

Industrial city A city characterized by relatively large size, open competition, an open class system, and elaborate specialization in the manufacturing of goods. (391)

Industrial society A society that depends on mechanization to produce its economic goods and services. (114)

Infant mortality rate The number of deaths of infants under one year of age per 1000 live births in a given year. (355)

Influence The exercise of power through a process of persuasion. (326)

Informal norms Norms that generally are understood but are not precisely recorded. (57)

Informal social control Social control carried out by people casually through such means as laughter, smiles, and ridicule. (150)

In-group Any group or category to which people feel they belong. (126)

Innovation The process of introducing new elements into a culture through either discovery or invention. (53)

Institutional completeness The degree to which an ethnic community provides for its own institutional needs, particularly in the key areas of religion, education, and social welfare. (213)
Institutional discrimination The denial of opportunities and equal rights to individuals and groups that results from the normal operations of a society. (217)
Institutionalize To formalize within a social institution. (326)
Instrumentality A term used by Parsons and Bales to refer to emphasis on tasks, focus on more distant goals, and a concern for the external relationship between one's family and other social institutions. (245)
Interactionist perspective A sociological approach that generalizes about fundamental or everyday forms of social interaction. (15)
Interest group A voluntary association of citizens who attempt to influence public policy. (332)
Intergenerational mobility Changes in the social position of children relative to their parents. (192)
Interview A face-to-face or telephone questioning of a respondent to obtain desired information. (34)
Intragenerational mobility Changes in a person's social position within his or her adult life. (192)
Invention The combination of existing cultural items into a form that did not previously exist. (53)
Iron law of oligarchy A principle of organizational life developed by Robert Michels under which even democratic organizations will become bureaucracies ruled by a few individuals. (135)

K

Kinship The state of being related to others. (268)

L

Labelling theory An approach to deviance that attempts to explain why certain people are viewed as deviants while others engaging in the same behaviour are not. (160)
Laissez-faire A form of capitalism under which people compete freely, with minimal government intervention in the economy. (324)
Language An abstract system of word meanings and symbols for all aspects of culture. It also includes gestures and other nonverbal communication. (55)
Latent functions Unconscious or unintended functions; hidden purposes. (13)
Law Governmental social control. (57)
Legal-rational authority Max Weber's term for power made legitimate by law. (327)
Legitimization The process by which power is authorized by those people who may be subject to its use. (326)
Liberal feminism The stream of feminism that asserts that women's equality can be obtained through the extension of the principles of equality of opportunity and freedom. (247)
Liberation theology Use of a church, primarily Roman Catholicism, in a political effort to eliminate poverty, discrimination, and other forms of injustice evident in a secular society. (297)
Life chances Max Weber's term for people's opportunities to provide themselves with material goods, positive living conditions, and favourable life experiences. (189)
Life expectancy The median number of years a person can be expected to live under current mortality conditions. (355)
Looking-glass self A concept used by Charles Horton Cooley that emphasizes the self as the product of our social interactions with others. (78)
Low Income Cut-Off (LICO) The Canadian equivalent of a poverty line, in place until January 2001, which stated the maximum proportion of a household's income that should be spent on the basics—food, shelter, and clothing. If a household spent a greater proportion on these basics, it would be considered poor. (185)
Luddites Rebellious craft workers in 19th-century England who destroyed new factory machinery as part of their resistance to the Industrial Revolution. (428)

M

Macrosociology Sociological investigation that concentrates on large-scale phenomena or entire civilizations. (12)
Majority government A government in which one party controls more than half of the seats in a legislative house. (329)
Manifest functions Open, stated, and conscious functions. (13)
Marginalization The process by which an individual, as a result of her or his minority status, is provided only partial access to opportunities. This discrimination is often more intense in the case of women. (215)
Market Basket Measure (MBM) A way of determining relative poverty that takes into consideration more than subsistence needs, and calculates the income needed by various households to live a life comparable to community standards. (185)
Marxist feminism The stream of feminist sociological approaches that place the system of capitalism at fault for the oppression of women, and hold that women are not oppressed by sexism or patriarchy, but rather by a system of economic production that is based upon unequal gender relations in the capitalist economy. (247)
Master status A status that dominates other statuses and thereby determines a person's general position within society. (102)
Material culture The physical or technological aspects of our daily lives. (53)
Matriarchy A society in which women dominate in family decision making. (269)
Matrilineal descent A kinship system that favours the relatives of the mother. (268)
McDonaldization The process by which the principles of the fast-food restaurant have come to dominate certain sectors of society, both in Canada and throughout the world. (125)
Megachurches Large worship centres affiliated only loosely, if at all, with existing denominations. (300)
Megalopolis A densely populated area containing two or more cities and their surrounding suburbs. (392)
Meritocracy A social system in which individuals earn their place in society. (176)
Metis The group of people formed when French male fur traders married First Nations women in the Red River Valley area of Manitoba. (210)
Microsociology Sociological investigation that stresses study of small groups and often uses laboratory experimental studies. (12)
Minority group A subordinate group whose members have significantly less control or power over their own lives than the members of a dominant or majority group have over theirs. (209)
Modernization The far-reaching process by which a society moves from traditional or less developed institutions to those characteristic of more developed societies. (198)
Modernization theory A functionalist approach that proposes that modernization and development will gradually improve the lives of people in peripheral nations. (198)
Monogamy A form of marriage in which one woman and one man are married only to each other. (267)
Monopoly Control of a market by a single business firm. (324)
Morbidity rates The incidence of diseases in a given population. (372)
Mores Norms deemed highly necessary to the welfare of a society. (58)
Mortality rate The incidence of death in a given population. (372)
Multiculturalism A policy that promotes cultural and racial diversity and full and equal participation of individuals and communities of all origins as a fundamental characteristic of Canadian identity. (65)
Multilinear evolutionary theory A theory of social change that holds that change can occur in several ways and does not inevitably lead in the same direction. (423)

Multinational corporations Commercial organizations that are headquartered in one country but do business throughout the world. (196)

Multiple-nuclei theory A theory of urban growth that views growth as emerging from many centres of development, each of which may reflect a particular urban need or activity. (394)

N

Natural science The study of the physical features of nature and the ways in which they interact and change. (6)

Negotiated order A social structure that derives its existence from the social interactions through which people define and redefine its character. (101)

Negotiation The attempt to reach agreement with others concerning some objective. (100)

Neocolonialism Continuing dependence of former colonies on foreign countries. (194)

Net worth is the amount by which the value of someone's assets exceeds his or her debts. (176)

New religious movement (NRM) or **cult** A generally small, secretive religious group that represents either a new religion or a major innovation of an existing faith. (302)

New social movements Organized collective activities that promote autonomy and self-determination as well as improvements in the quality of life. (422)

New urban sociology An approach to urbanization that considers the interplay of local, national, and worldwide forces and their effect on local space, with special emphasis on the impact of global economic activity. (395)

Nonmaterial culture Cultural adjustments to material conditions, such as customs, beliefs, patterns of communication, and ways of using material objects. (54)

Nonverbal communication The sending of messages through the use of posture, facial expressions, and gestures. (15)

Normal accidents Failures that are inevitable, given the manner in which human and technological systems are detached. (432)

Norms Established standards of behaviour maintained by a society. (57)

Nuclear family A married couple and their unmarried children living together. (267)

O

Obedience Compliance with higher authorities in a hierarchical structure. (148)

Objective method A technique for measuring social class that assigns individuals to classes on the basis of criteria such as occupation, education, income, and place of residence. (183)

Observation A research technique in which an investigator collects information through direct participation in and/or observation of a group, tribe, or community. (35)

Oligopoly Control of the market by a small group of companies. (324)

Open system A social system in which the position of each individual is influenced by his or her achieved status. (191)

Operational definition An explanation of an abstract concept that is specific enough to allow a researcher to measure the concept. (29)

Organized crime The work of a group that regulates relations between various criminal enterprises involved in the smuggling and sale of drugs, prostitution, gambling, and other activities. (163)

Out-group A group or category to which people feel they do not belong. (126)

P

Patriarchy A society in which men dominate family decision making. (269)

Patrilineal descent A kinship system that favours the relatives of the father. (268)

Personality In everyday speech, a person's typical patterns of attitudes, needs, characteristics, and behaviour. (75)

Peter Principle A principle of organizational life, originated by Laurence J. Peter, according to which each individual within a hierarchy tends to rise to his or her level of incompetence. (133)

Pluralist model A view of society in which many competing groups within the community have access to governmental officials so that no single group is dominant. (335)

Political action committee (PAC) A political committee established by an interest group—say, a national bank, corporation, trade association, or cooperative or membership association—to solicit contributions for candidates or political parties. (332)

Political socialization The process by which individuals acquire political attitudes and develop patterns of political behaviour. (328)

Political System The structures and processes used for implementing and achieving society's goals. (323)

Politics In Harold D. Lasswell's words, "who gets what, when, and how." (326)

Polyandry A form of polygamy in which a woman can have several husbands at the same time. (267)

Polygamy A form of marriage in which an individual can have several husbands or wives simultaneously. (267)

Polygyny A form of polygamy in which a husband can have several wives at the same time. (267)

Population pyramid A special type of bar chart that shows the distribution of the population by gender and age. (357)

Postindustrial city A city in which global finance and the electronic flow of information dominate the economy. (391)

Postindustrial society A society whose economic system is primarily engaged in the processing and control of information. (114)

Postmodern society A technologically sophisticated society that is preoccupied with consumer goods and media images. (115)

Power The ability to exercise one's will over others. (180, 326)

Power elite A term used by C. Wright Mills for a small group of military, industrial, and government leaders who control the fate of the United States and every other major capitalist country. (334)

Preindustrial city A city with only a few thousand people living within its borders and characterized by a relatively closed class system and limited mobility. (390)

Prejudice A negative attitude toward an entire category of people, such as a racial or ethnic minority. (214)

Prestige The respect and admiration that an occupation holds in a society. (183)

Prevalence The total number of cases of a specific disorder that exist at a given time. (372)

Primary group A small group characterized by intimate, face-to-face association and cooperation. (125)

Privilege Access to opportunities provided to or denied people as a direct result of their membership in a particular societal group. (215)

Profane The ordinary and commonplace elements of life, as distinguished from the sacred. (295)

Professional criminal A person who pursues crime as a day-to-day occupation, developing skilled techniques and enjoying a certain degree of status among other criminals. (162)

Proletariat Karl Marx's term for the working class in a capitalist society. (179)

Protestant ethic Max Weber's term for the disciplined work ethic, this-worldly concerns, and rational orientation to life emphasized by John Calvin and his followers. (297)

Q

Qualitative research Research that relies on what is seen in the field or naturalistic settings more than on statistical data. (27)

Quantitative research Research that collects and reports data primarily in numerical form. (27)

Questionnaire A printed research instrument employed to obtain desired information from a respondent. (34)

R

Racial group A group that is set apart from others because of obvious physical differences. (209)

Racism The belief that one race is supreme and all others are innately inferior. (214)

Radical feminism The stream of feminism that maintains that the root of all oppression of women is embedded in patriarchy. (247)

Random sample A sample for which every member of the entire population has the same chance of being selected. (31)

Reference group Any group that individuals use as a standard in evaluating themselves and their own behaviour. (127)

Relative deprivation The conscious feeling of a negative discrepancy between legitimate expectations and present actualities. (420)

Relative poverty A floating standard of deprivation by which people at the bottom of a society, whatever their lifestyles, are judged to be disadvantaged in comparison with the nation as a whole. (185)

Reliability The extent to which a measure provides consistent results. (32)

Religion According to Émile Durkheim, a unified system of beliefs and practices relative to sacred things. (293)

Religious beliefs Statements to which members of a particular religion adhere. (298)

Religious experience The feeling or perception of being in direct contact with the ultimate reality, such as a divine being, or of being overcome with religious emotion. (299)

Religious rituals Practices required or expected of members of a faith. (298)

Representative sample A selection from a larger population that is statistically found to be typical of that population. (31)

Resocialization The process of discarding former behaviour patterns and accepting new ones as part of a transition in one's life. (83)

Resource mobilization The ways in which a social movement utilizes such resources as money, political influence, access to the media, and personnel. (421)

Rites of passage Rituals marking the symbolic transition from one social position to another. (82)

Role conflict Difficulties that occur when incompatible expectations arise from two or more social positions held by the same person. (104)

Role exit The process of disengagement from a role that is central to one's self-identity and reestablishment of an identity in a new role. (105)

Role strain Difficulties that result from the differing demands and expectations associated with the same social position. (105)

Role taking The process of mentally assuming the perspective of another, thereby enabling one to respond from that imagined viewpoint. (79)

Routine activities theory The notion that criminal victimization increases when there is a convergence of motivated offenders and suitable targets. (159)

S

Sacred Elements beyond everyday life that inspire awe, respect, and even fear. (293)

Sanctions Penalties and rewards for conduct concerning a social norm. (59)

Sapir-Whorf hypothesis A hypothesis concerning the role of language in shaping cultures. It holds that language is culturally determined and serves to influence our mode of thought. (55)

Science The body of knowledge obtained by methods based upon systematic observation. (6)

Scientific management approach Another name for the *classical theory* of formal organizations. (136)

Scientific method A systematic, organized series of steps that ensures maximum objectivity and consistency in researching a problem. (27)

Secondary analysis A variety of research techniques that make use of publicly accessible information and data. (37)

Secondary group A formal, impersonal group in which there is little social intimacy or mutual understanding. (126)

Sect A relatively small religious group that has broken away from some other religious organization to renew what it views as the original vision of the faith. (300)

Secularization The process through which religion's influence on other social institutions diminishes. (293)

Segregation The act of physically separating two groups; often imposed on a minority group by a dominant group. (222)

Self According to George Herbert Mead, the sum total of people's conscious perceptions of their own identity as distinct from others. (78)

Self-segregation The situation that arises when members of a minority deliberately develop residential, economic, and/or social network structures that are separate from those of the majority population. (222)

Serial monogamy A form of marriage in which a person can have several spouses in his or her lifetime but only one spouse at a time. (267)

Sexism The ideology that one sex is superior to the other. (249)

Sexual harassment Any conduct, comment, gesture or contact of a sexual nature that is likely to cause offense or humiliation to any employee or that might, on reasonable grounds, be perceived by that employee as placing a condition of a sexual nature on employment or on any opportunity for training or promotion. (138)

Sick role Societal expectations about the attitudes and behaviour of a person viewed as being ill. (366)

Significant others A term used by George Herbert Mead to refer to those individuals who are most important in the development of the self, such as parents, friends, and teachers. (80)

Single-parent families Families in which there is only one parent present to care for children. (278)

Slavery A system of enforced servitude in which people are legally owned by others and in which enslaved status is transferred from parents to children. (176)

Small group A group small enough for all members to interact simultaneously, that is, to talk with one another or at least be acquainted. (127)

Social category A group defined by some culturally relevant characteristic; that is, one that has an impact on a person's status within a society. (214)

Social change Significant alteration over time in behaviour patterns and culture, including norms and values. (419)

Social constructionist perspective An approach to deviance that emphasizes the role of culture in the creation of the deviant identity. (161)

Social control The techniques and strategies for preventing deviant human behaviour in any society. (147)

Social democracy An economy that is for the most part dominated by private business operating within a political framework that is responsible for the redistribution of wealth. (325)

Social distance The degree of difference between cultures, which can vary from slight (e.g., the Canadian and American cultures) to great (e.g., the Canadian culture and that of the Mongols of Northern China). (213)

Social epidemiology The study of the distribution of disease, impairment, and general health status across a population. (372)

Social inequality A condition in which members of a society have different amounts of wealth, prestige, or power. (175)

Social institutions Organized patterns of beliefs and behaviour centred on basic social needs. (107)

Social interaction The ways in which people respond to one another. (99)

Socialism An economic system under which the means of production and distribution are collectively owned. (325)

Socialist feminism The stream of feminism that maintains gender relations are shaped by both patriarchy and capitalism, and thus equality for women implies that both the system of capitalism and the ideology of patriarchy must be challenged and eliminated. (247)

Socialization The process whereby people learn the attitudes, values, and actions appropriate for individuals as members of a particular culture. (75)

Social mobility Movement of individuals or groups from one position of a society's stratification system to another. (191)

Social movements Organized collective activities to bring about or resist fundamental change in an existing group or society. (419)

Social network A series of social relationships that links a person directly to others and therefore indirectly to still more people. (106)

Social role A set of expectations of people who occupy a given social position or status. (104)

Social safety net A system of social programs, such as welfare, employment insurance, Canada Pension Plan, etc., designed to alleviate the harshest conditions associated with being at the bottom of the income chain. (185)

Social science The study of various aspects of human society. (6)

Social structure The way in which a society is organized into predictable relationships. (99)

Societal-reaction approach Another name for *labelling theory.* (160)

Society A fairly large number of people who live in the same territory, are relatively independent of people outside it, and participate in a common culture. (51)

Sociobiology The systematic study of the biological bases of social behaviour. (77)

Sociocultural evolution The process of change and development in human societies that results from cumulative growth in their stores of cultural information. (113)

Sociological imagination An awareness of the relationship between an individual and the wider society. (5)

Sociology The systematic study of social behaviour and human groups. (5)

Squatter settlements Areas occupied by the very poor on the fringes of cities, in which housing is often constructed by the settlers themselves from discarded material. (394)

Standpoint feminism The stream of feminism that takes into account women's diversity and maintains that no *one* standpoint will represent *all* women's lives. (247)

Status A term used by sociologists to refer to any of the full range of socially defined positions within a large group or society. (101)

Status consistency The notion that someone with high status in one area—income, for instance—is likely to be similarly ranked in other areas. (180)

Status group A term used by Max Weber to refer to people who have the same prestige or lifestyle, independent of their class positions. (179)

Stereotypes Unreliable generalizations about all members of a group that do not recognize individual differences within the group. (211)

Stigma A label used to devalue members of deviant social groups. (154)

Stratification A structured ranking of entire groups of people that perpetuates unequal economic rewards and power in a society. (176)

Subculture A segment of society that shares a distinctive pattern of mores, folkways, and values that differs from the pattern of the larger society. (63)

Survey A study, generally in the form of interviews or questionnaires, that provides sociologists and other researchers with information concerning how people think and act. (33)

Symbols The gestures, objects, and language that form the basis of human communication. (79)

T

Teacher-expectancy effect The impact that a teacher's expectations about a student's performance may have on the student's actual achievements. (309)

Technology Information about how to use the material resources of the environment to satisfy human needs and desires. (53, 113)

Telecommuters Employees who work full-time or part-time at home rather than in an outside office and who are linked to their supervisors and colleagues through computer terminals, phone lines, and fax machines. (137)

Theory In sociology, a set of statements that seeks to explain problems, actions, or behaviour. (8)

Total fertility rate (TFR) The average number of children born alive to a woman, assuming that she conforms to current fertility rates. (355)

Total institutions A term coined by Erving Goffman to refer to institutions that regulate all aspects of a person's life under a single authority, such as prisons, the military, mental hospitals, and convents. (83)

Tracking The practice of placing students in specific curriculum groups on the basis of test scores and other criteria. (308)

Trade unions Organizations that seek to improve the material status of their members, all of whom perform a similar job or work for a common employer. (339)

Traditional authority Legitimate power conferred by custom and accepted practice. (327)

Trained incapacity The tendency of workers in a bureaucracy to become so specialized that they develop blind spots and fail to notice obvious problems. (132)

Triad A three-member group. (128)

U

Underclass Long-term poor people who lack training and skills. (188)

Unilinear evolutionary theory A theory of social change that holds that all societies pass through the same successive stages of evolution and inevitably reach the same end. (423)

Urban ecology An area of study that focuses on the interrelationships between people and their environment. (392)

Urbanism Distinctive patterns of social behaviour evident among city residents. (391)

V

Validity The degree to which a scale or measure truly reflects the phenomenon under study. (32)

Value neutrality Max Weber's term for objectivity of sociologists in the interpretation of data. (40)

Values Collective conceptions of what is considered good, desirable, and proper—or bad, undesirable, and improper—in a culture. (60)

Variable A measurable trait or characteristic that is subject to change under different conditions. (30)

Verstehen The German word for "understanding" or "insight"; used by Max Weber to stress the need for sociologists to take into account people's emotions, thoughts, beliefs, and attitudes. (10)

Vertical mobility The movement of a person from one social position to another of a different rank. (192)

Vested interests Veblen's term for those people or groups who will suffer in the event of social change and who have a stake in maintaining the status quo. (427)

Victimization surveys Questionnaires or interviews used to determine whether people have been victims of crime. (165)

Victimless crime A term used by sociologists to describe the willing exchange among adults of widely desired, but illegal, goods and services. (164)

W

Wealth An inclusive term encompassing all of a person's material assets, including land and other types of property. (176)

White-collar crime Crimes committed by affluent individuals or corporations in the course of their daily business activities. (163)

World systems analysis Immanuel Wallerstein's view of the global economic system as divided between certain industrialized nations that control wealth and developing countries that are controlled and exploited. (194)

X

Xenocentrism The belief that the products, styles, or ideas of one's society are inferior to those that originate elsewhere. (66)

Z

Zero population growth (ZPG) The state of a population with a growth rate of zero, achieved when the number of births plus immigrants is equal to the number of deaths plus emigrants. (359)

Zoning laws Legal provisions stipulating land use and architectural design of housing sometimes used as a means of keeping racial minorities and low-income people out of suburban areas. (401)

References

A

ABC News. 1992. *Primetime Live: True Colors.* Transcript of November 26 episode.

Abegglen, James C., and George Stalk, Jr. 1985. *Kassha: The Japanese Corporation.* New York: Basic Books.

Abelson, Reed. 1997. "When Waaa Turns to Why." *New York Times,* November 1, pp. C1, C6.

Abercrombie, Nicholas, Bryan S. Turner, and Stephen Hill, eds. 1990. *Dominant Ideologies.* Cambridge, MA: Unwin Hyman.

Abercrombie, Nicholas, Stephen Hill, and Bryan S. Turner. 1980. *The Dominant Ideology Thesis.* London: George Allen and Unwin.

Aberle, David F., A. K. Cohen, A. K. Davis, M. J. Leng, Jr., and F. N. Sutton. 1950. "The Functional Prerequisites of a Society." *Ethics* 60(January):100–111.

Abowitz, Deborah A. 1986. "Data Indicate the Feminization of Poverty in Canada, Too." *Sociology and Social Research* 70(April):209–213.

Abrahams, Ray G. 1968. "Reaching an Agreement over Bridewealth in Labwor, Northern Uganda: A Case Study." Pp. 202–215 in *Councils in Action,* edited by Audrey Richards and Adam Kuer. Cambridge: Cambridge University Press.

Abrahamson, Mark. 1978. *Functionalism.* Englewood Cliffs, NJ: Prentice-Hall.

Abu-Laban, Sharon M., and Susan A. McDaniel. 1995. "Ageing Women and Standards of Beauty." Pp. 97–122 in *Feminist Issues: Race, Class and Sexuality,* edited by Nancy Mandell. Scarborough: Prentice Hall Canada.

Abu-Laban, Yasmeen, and Daiva Stasiulis. 2000. "Constructing Ethnic Canadians: The Implications for Public Policy and Inclusive Citizenship." *Canadian Public Policy* vol. XXVI (4).

Adachi, Ken. 1976. *The Enemy that Never Was: A History of Japanese Canadians.* Toronto: McClelland and Stewart.

Adam, Barry D. 1992. "Sociology and People Living with AIDS." Pp. 3–18 in *The Social Context of AIDS,* edited by Joan Huber and Beth E. Schneider. Newbury Park, CA: Sage.

———. 1995. *The Rise of a Gay and Lesbian Movement.* Rev. ed. New York: Twayne.

Adamson, Nancy, Linda Briskin, and Margaret McPhail. 1998. *Feminist Organizing for Change: The Contemporary Women's Movement in Canada.* Toronto: Oxford University Press.

Addams, Jane. 1910. *Twenty Years at Hull-House.* New York: Macmillan.

———. 1930. *The Second Twenty Years at Hull-House.* New York: Macmillan.

Adelman, Melvin L. 1993. "Modernization Theory and Its Critics." Pp. 347–358 in *Encyclopedia of American Social History,* edited by Mary Kupiec Coyton, Elliot J. Gorn, and Peter W. Williams. New York: Charles Sculines.

Adler, Patricia A., and Peter Adler. 1998. *Peer Power: Preadolescent Culture and Identity.* New Brunswick, NJ: Rutgers University Press.

———, and John M. Johnson. 1992. "Street Corner Society Revisited." *Journal of Contemporary Ethnography* 21(April):3–10.

———, Steven J. Kless, and Peter Adler. 1992. "Socialization to Gender Roles: Popularity among Elementary School Boys and Girls." *Sociology of Education* 65(July):169–187.

Africa News Service. 1998. "CPJ's 10 Enemies of the Press." Accessed October 8 (www. elibrary.com/getdoc. cgi?id=113_ rydocid= 435731@ library_F+type=O~&dinst=).

Aguirre, Benigno E. 1984. "The Conventionalization of Collective Behavior in Cuba." *American Journal of Sociology* 90(3):541–566.

AIDS Alert. 1999. "AIDS Complacency Leads Back to Risk Behavior." November 14, pp. 127–128.

Akers, Ronald L. 1997. *Criminological Theories: Introduction and Evaluation.* 2d ed. Los Angeles, CA: Roxbury Publishing Co.

Alain, Michel. 1985. "An Empirical Validation of Relative Deprivation." *Human Relations* 38(8):739–749.

Alba, Richard D., and Gwen Moore. 1982. "Ethnicity in the American Elite."*American Sociological Review* 47(June):373–383.

Albarracin, Dolores, Martin Fishbein, and Eva Goldstein de Muchinik. 1997. "Seeking Social Support in Old Age as a Reasoned Action: Structural and Volitional Determinants in a Middle-Aged Sample of Argentinean Women." *Journal of Applied Social Psychology* 27:463–476.

Albas, Daniel, and Cheryl Albas. 1988. "Aces and Bombers: The Post-Exam Impression Management Strategies of Students." *Symbolic Interaction* 11(Fall): 289–302.

Albert, Terry, and Gregory Williams. 1998. *The Economic Burden of AIDS in Canada.* Ottawa: Canadian Policy Research Networks.

Albrecht, Gary L., Katherine D. Seelman, and Michael Bury (Eds.) 2000 Handbook of Disability Studies. Thousand Oaks, CA: Sage.

Alfino, Mark, John S. Carpeto, and Robin Wyngard. 1998. *McDonaldization Revisited: Critical Essays on Consumer Culture.* Westport, CT: Praeger.

Alinsky, Saul. 1946. *Reveille for Radicals.* Chicago: University of Chicago Press.

Allen, Bem P. 1978. *Social Behavior: Fact and Falsehood.* Chicago: Nelson-Hall.

Allen, John L. 1996. *Student Atlas of World Politics.* 2d ed. Madison, WI: Brown and Benchmark.

Allport, Gordon W. 1979. *The Nature of Prejudice.* 25th anniversary ed. Reading, MA: Addison-Wesley.

Alter, Jonathon. 2000. "The Death Penalty on Trial." *Newsweek,* June 12, pp. 24–32, 34.

Altman, Lawrence K. 1998. "Parts of Africa Showing H.I.V. in 1 in 4 Adults." *New York Times,* June 24, pp. A1, A6.

Alvord, Lori Arviso, and Elizabeth Cohen Van Pelt. 1999. *The Scalpel and the Silver Bear.* New York: Bantam.

Alzheimer's Association. 1999. "Statistics/ Prevalence." Accessed January 10, 2000 (http://www.alz.org/facts/stats.htm).

Amato, Paul, and Alan Booth. 1997. *A Generation at Risk.* Cambridge, MA: Harvard University Press.

Amazon.com. 2000a. *About Amazon.com.* Accessed September 30, 2000 (http://www.amazon.com/exec).

American Association for the Advancement of Science. 2000. *Author abstracts, Conference Proceedings from Arctic Science 2000.* Whitehorse, Yukon: American Association for the Advancement of Science.

American Association of Health Plans. 1998a. "Number of People in HMOs, 1976–96." Accessed August 11, 1998 (http://www.aahp.org/menus/index. cfm?cfid=64953%cftoken=32374).

———. 1998b. "Demographic Characteristics of Health Plan Enrollees." Accessed August 11, 1998 (http://www. aahp.org/menus/index.cfm?cfid= 64953%cftoken=32374).

American Association of University Women. 1992. *How Schools Shortchange Girls.* Washington, DC: American Association of University Women.

American Bar Association. 1997. *Section of Individual Rights and Responsibilities. Section of Litigation (Capital Punishment).* (February). Chicago: Division for Policy Administration, ABA.

———. 1999. "Commission on Domestic Violence." Accessed July 20, 1999 (http://www.abanet.org/domviol/stats.html).

American Civil Liberties Union. 2000. "State and Local Laws Protecting Lesbians and Gay Men Against Workplace Discrimination." Accessed January 19 (http://www.aclu.org/issues/gay/gaylaws.html).

———. 1999a. "Domestic Partnerships: List of Cities, States and Counties." Accessed September 2, 1999 (http: www.aclu.org/issues/gay/dpstate.html).

———. 1999b. "School Prayer Amendment Returns." Accessed November 8, 1999 (http://www.aclu.org/action/prayer106.html).

American Humane Association. 1999. "Child Abuse and Neglect Data." Accessed July 20, 1999 (http://www.Americanhumane.org/cpfactdata.htm).

American Medical Association Council on Scientific Affairs. 1992. "Assault Weapons as a Public Health Hazard in the United States." *Journal of the American Medical Association* 267:3067–3070.

American Society of Plastic Surgeons. 2002. *National Clearinghouse of Plastic Surgery Statistics.* Accessed February 1, 2002 (http://www.plasticsurgery.org/mediactr/stats_ncs.htm).

American Sociological Association. 1993. The Sociology Major as Preparation for Careers in Business and Organizations. Washington, DC: American Sociological Association.

———. 1995a. *Careers in Sociology.* 2d ed. Washington, DC: American Sociological Association.

———. 1995b. *The Sociological Advantage.* Washington, DC: American Sociological Association.

———. 1997. *Code of Ethics.* Washington, DC: American Sociological Association. Accessible at http://www.asanet.org/members/ecoderev.html.

———. 1999. *Careers in Sociology.* 5th ed. Washington, DC: American Sociological Association.

———. 2000a. 2000 *Medical School Graduation Questionnaire All Schools Report.* Washington, DC: AAMC.

———. 2000b. *U.S. Medical School Faculty: Annual Data.* Accessed October 1, 2000 (http://www.aamc.org/findinfo/infores/datarsc/facros/frspubs/usmsf.htm).

———. 2001. *Guide to Graduate Departments of Sociology.* Washington, DC: ASA.

Amnesty International. 1999. "Facts and Figures on the Death Penalty." Accessed August 4 (http://www.amnesty.excite.com/abolish/act500299.html).

Amnesty International. 2000. "The Death Penalty: List of Abolitionist and Retentionist Countries." April. Accessed August 7, 2000 (http://www.amnesty.org/ailib/aipub/2000/ACT/A5000500.htm).

Amselle, Jorge, and Amy C. Allison. 2000. "Two Years of Success: An Analysis of California Test Scores After Proposition 227." Washington, DC: READ Institute, Center for Equal Opportunity. Accessed at http://www.ceousa.org/.

Andersen, Margaret. 1997. *Thinking About Women: Sociological Perspectives on Sex and Gender.* 4th ed. Boston: Allyn and Bacon.

Anderson, Elijah. 1978. *A Place on the Corner.* Chicago: University of Chicago Press.

———. 1990. *Streetwise: Race, Class, and Change in an Urban Community.* Chicago: University of Chicago Press.

———. 1999. *Code of the Streets.* New York: Norton.

———, and Molly Moore. 1993. "The Burden of Womanhood." *Washington Post National Weekly Edition* 10(March 22–28):6–7.

Anderson, Sarah, and John Cavanagh. 2001. "Top 200: The Rise of Corporate Global Power." *The Institute for Policy Studies.* Accessed April 18 (http://www.ips-dc.org/reports/top200text.htm).

Andersson-Brolin, Lillemor. 1988. "Ethnic Residential Segregation: The Case of Sweden." *Scandinavian Journal of Development Alternatives* 7(March):33–45.

Angier, Natalie. 1998. "Drugs, Sports, Body Image and G.I. Joe." *New York Times,* December 22, pp. D1, D3.

Anti-Defamation League. 1998. *Audit of Anti-Semitic Incidents, 1997.* New York: Anti-Defamation League.

Appelbaum, Richard, and Peter Dreier. 1999. "The Campus Anti-Sweatshops Movement." *The American Prospect* (September–October), pp. 71–78.

Appleby, Julie. 1999. "Rethinking Managed Care." *USA Today,* October 7, pp. A1–A2.

Arber, Sara, and Jay Ginn. 1991. *Gender and Later Life: A Sociological Analysis of Resources and Constraints.* London: Sage.

Archer, Margaret. 1988. *Culture and Agency: The Place of Culture in Social Theory.* Cambridge: Cambridge University Press.

Armer, J. Michael, and John Katsillis. 1992. "Modernization Theory." Pp. 1299–1304 in *Encyclopedia of Sociology,* vol. 4, edited by Edgar F. Borgatta and Marie L. Borgatta. New York: Macmillan.

Armstrong, Jane. 2002. "Canada is 30 million, but will that last?" *The Globe and Mail,* March 13, pp. A1, A7.

Arnold, Wayne. 2000. "Manila's Talk of the Town Isn't Talk at All." *New York Times,* July 5, p. C1.

Aronson, Elliot. 1999. *The Social Animal.* 8th ed. New York: Worth.

Associated Press. 1998. "Environmental Test Case Averted." *Christian Science Monitor,* September 21, p. 18.

———. 2000. "Opinions on Gay Relationships." *Los Angeles Times,* June 1, p. A31.

Association of American Medical Colleges. 2000a. *2000 Medical School Graduate Report: All Schools Report.* Washington, DC: AAMC.

———. 2000b. *United States Medical School Faculty: Annual Data.* Washington, DC: AAMC.

Association of Universities and Colleges of Canada. 2001. "About Canada's Universities." Accessed July 28, 2001 (http://www.aucc.ca/en/acuindex.html).

Astin, Alexander, Sarah A. Parrott, William S. Korn, and Linda J. Sax. 1994. *The American Freshman: Thirty Year Trends.* Los Angeles: Higher Education Research Institute.

Atchley, Robert C. 1985. *The Social Forces in Later Life: An Introduction to Social Gerontology.* 4th ed. Belmont, CA: Wadsworth.

Atkinson, Anthony Barnes, and John Micklewright. 1992. *Economic Transformation in Eastern Europe and the Distribution of Income.* Cambridge: Cambridge University Press.

Augustine, Noah. 2000. "Grandfather was a Knowing Christian." *The Toronto Star,* August 9, p. A17.

Austin, Erica Weintraub, and Bruce E. Pinkleton. 1995. "Positive and Negative Effects of Political Disaffection on the Less Experienced Voter." *Journal of Broadcasting and Electronic Media* 39(Spring):215–235.

Axtell, Roger E. 1990. *Do's and Taboos around the World.* 2d ed. New York: John Wiley and Sons.

Azumi, Koya, and Jerald Hage. 1972. *Organizational Systems.* Lexington, MA: Heath.

B

Bachrach, Christine A. 1986. "Adoption Plans, Adopted Children, and Adoptive Mothers." *Journal of Marriage and the Family* 48(May):243–253.

Bachu, Amara. 1999. "Is Childlessness Among American Women on the Rise?" Working Paper No. 37, Population Division, U.S. Bureau of Census, Washington, DC.

Bailey, Susan McGee, and Patricia B. Campbell. 2000. "The Gender Wars in

Education." *Wellesley Centers for Women Research Report* 20(Fall/Winter):20.
Bainbridge, William Sims. 1999. "Cyberspace: Sociology's Natural Domain." *Contemporary Sociology* 28(November):664–667.
Baker, Linda. 1994. "Day-Care Disgrace." *The Progressive* 58(June):26–27.
Baker, Maureen. 2001a. "Paid and Unpaid Work: How do Families Divide Their Labour?" Pp. 96–115 in *Families: Changing Trends in Canada,* 4th ed., edited by Maureen Baker. Toronto: McGraw-Hill Ryerson.
——— 2001b. "The Future of Family Life." Pp. 285–302 in *Families: Changing Trends in Canada,* 4th ed., edited by Maureen Baker. Toronto: McGraw-Hill Ryerson.
Baldassare, Mark. 1992. "Suburban Communities." Pp. 475–494 in *Annual Review of Sociology,* edited by Judith Blake and John Hagan. Palo Alto, CA: Annual Reviews.
Ballantine, Jeanne H. 1997. *The Sociology of Education: A Systematic Analysis.* 4th ed. Englewood Cliffs, NJ: Prentice-Hall.
Banks, Olive. 1981. *Three Faces of Feminism.* New York: St. Martin's Press.
Barkey, Karen. 1991. "The Use of Court Records in the Reconstruction of Village Networks: A Corporative Perspective." *International Journal of Comparative Sociology* 32(January–April):195–216.
Barnard, Robert, Dave Cosgrave, and Jennifer Welsh. 1998. *Chips and Pop: Decoding the Nexus Generation.* Toronto: Malcolm Lester Books.
Bartlett, Donald L., and James B. Steele. 1998. "Corporate Welfare." *Time* 152(November 9):36–39.
Barna Research Group. 1998. "The Cyberchurch Is Coming." April 20, 1998. Accessed November 10, 1999 (http://www.barna.org/cgi-bin/PagePressRelease.asp?/Press Release ID=9).
Barret, Stanley R. 1987. *Is God a Racist? The Right Wing in Canada.* Toronto: U of T Press.
Barron, Milton L. 1953. "Minority Group Characteristics of the Aged in American Society." *Journal of Gerontology* 8: 477–482.
Basso, Keith H. 1972. "Ice and Travel among the Fort Norman Slave: Folk Taxonomies and Cultural Rules." *Language in Society* 1(March):31–49.
Bates, Colleen Dunn. 1999. "Medicine's Gender Gap." *Shape,* October.
Bauerlein, Monika. 1996. "The Luddites Are Back." *Utne Reader* (March–April):24, 26.
Baugher, Eleanor, and Leatha Lamison-White. 1996. "Poverty in the United States: 1995." *Current Population Reports,* ser. P60, no.194. Washington, DC: U.S. Government Printing Office.
Bauman, Kurt J. 1999. "Extended Measures of Well-Being: Meeting Basic Needs." *Current Population Reports,* ser. P70, no. 67. Washington, DC: U.S. Government Printing Office.
Beaujot, Roderic, Ellen M. Gee, Fernando Rajulton, and Zenaida R. Ravanera. 1995. *Family over the Life Course.* Ottawa: Minister of Industry.
Beaujot, Roderic, and Kevin McQuillan. 1982. *Growth and Dualism: The Demographic Development of Canadian Society.* Toronto: Gage Publishing Limited.
Becerra, Rosina M. 1999. "The Mexican-American Family." Pp. 153–171 in *Ethnic Families in America: Patterns and Variations,* 4th ed., edited by Charles H. Mindel, Robert W. Habenstein, and Roosevelt Wright, Jr. Upper Saddle River, NJ: Prentice-Hall.
Becker, Anne E. 1995. *Body, Self, and Society: The View from Fiji.* Philadelphia: University of Pennsylvania Press.
——— and R. A. Burwell. 1999, *Acculturation and Disordered Eating in Fiji.* Presented at the annual meeting of the American Psychiatric Association.
Becker, Howard S. 1952. "Social Class Variations in the Teacher–Pupil Relationship." *Journal of Educational Sociology* 25(April):451–465.
———. 1963. *The Outsiders: Studies in the Sociology of Deviance.* New York: Free Press.
———, ed. 1964. *The Other Side: Perspectives on Deviance.* New York: Free Press.
———. 1973. *The Outsiders: Studies in the Sociology of Deviance.* Rev. ed. New York: Free Press.
———, Blanche Greer, Everett C. Hughes, and Anselm Strauss. 1961. *Boys in White: Student Culture in Medical School.* Chicago: University of Chicago Press.
Beeghley, Leonard. 1978. *Social Stratification in America: A Critical Analysis of Theory and Research.* Santa Monica, CA: Goodyear Publishing.
Begley, Sharon. 1998. "Why Wilson's Wrong." *Newsweek* 131(June 22):61–62.
———. 1999. "Designer Babies." *Newsweek* 132(November 9):61–62.
Bélanger, Alain, and Jean Dumas. 1998. *Report of the Demographic Situation in Canada 1997.* Ottawa: Ministry of Industry.
Belkin, Lisa. 1999. "Getting the Girl." *New York Times Magazine,* July 25, pp. 26–31, 38, 54–55.
Bell, Daniel. 1953. "Crime as an American Way of Life." *Antioch Review* 13(Summer):131–154.
———. 1999. *The Coming of Post-Industrial Society: A Venture in Social Forecasting.* With new foreword. New York: Basic Books.
Bell, Wendell. 1981a. "Modernization." Pp. 186–187 in *Encyclopedia of Sociology.* Guilford, CT: DPG Publishing.
———. 1981b. "Neocolonialism." P. 193 in *Encyclopedia of Sociology.* Guilford, CT: DPG Publishing.
Bellafante, Ginia. 1998. "Feminism: It's All About Me!" *Time* 151(June 20):54–62.
Belluck, Pam. 1996. "The Symptoms of Internet Addiction." *New York Times,* December 1, p. E5.
———. 1999. "On Assisted Suicide, Kevorkian Is Seen as 'Distraction.' " *New York Times,* March 30, p. A17.
Belsie, Laurent. 2000. "Strange Webfellows." *Christian Science Monitor,* March 2, pp. 15–16.
———. 1998. "Genetic Research Data Will Double Annually." *Christian Science Monitor,* July 30, p. B4.
Bendavid, Naftali. 1998. "Surge in Executions Just the Beginning." *Chicago Tribune,* January 4, pp. 1, 14.
Bender, William, and Margaret Smith. 1997. "Population, Food, and Nutrition." *Population Bulletin* 51(February).
Bendick, Marc, Jr., Charles W. Jackson, and J. Horacio Romero. 1993. *Employment Discrimination against Older Workers: An Experimental Study of Hiring Practices.* Washington, DC: Fair Employment Council of Greater Washington.
Bendix, B. Reinhard. 1968. "Max Weber." Pp. 493–502 in *International Encyclopedia of the Social Sciences,* edited by David L. Sills. New York: Macmillan.
Benedetto, Richard. 1998. "Turncoats in Key Groups Lead Democratic Rebound." *USA Today,* November 5, p. 4A.
Benford, Robert D. 1992. "Social Movements." Pp. 1880–1887 in *Encyclopedia of Sociology,* vol. 4, edited by Edgar F. Borgatta and Marie L. Borgatta. New York: Macmillan.
Benner, Richard S. and Susan Tyler Hitchcock. 1986. *Life after Liberal Arts.* Charlottesville: Office of Career Planning and Placement, University of Virginia.
Bennet, James. 1996. "The Delegates: Where Image Meets Reality." *New York Times,* August 12, pp. A1, A11.
Berger, Peter, and Thomas Luckmann. 1966. *The Social Construction of Reality.* New York: Doubleday.
Berke, Richard L. 1994. "Defections among Men to G.O.P. Helped Insure Rout of Democrats." *New York Times,* November 11, pp. A1, A27.
Berkeley Wellness Letter. 1990. "The Nest Refilled." 6(February):1–2.
Berlin, Brent, and Paul Kay. 1991. *Basic Color Terms: Their Universality and Evolution.* Berkeley, CA: University of California Press.
Bernstein, Jared, Elizabeth C. McNichol, Lawrence Mishel, and Robert Zahradnik. 2000. *Pulling Apart: A State-by-State Analysis of Income Trends.* Washington, DC: Center on Budget and Policy Priorities.
Bernstein, Anne C. 1988. "Unraveling the Tangles: Children's Understanding of Stepfamily Kinship." Pp. 83–111 in *Relative Strangers: Studies of Step-Family*

Press, edited by W. R. Beer, Totowa, NJ: Rowan and Liten Field.
Best, Amy L. 2000. *Prom Night: Youth, Schools and Popular Culture.* New York: Routledge.
Best, Fred, and Ray Eberhard. 1990. "Education for the 'Era of the Adult.' " *The Futurist* 21(May–June): 23–28.
Bettelheim, Bruno, and Morris Janowitz. 1964. *Social Change and Prejudice.* New York: Free Press.
Bharadwaj, Lakshmik. 1992. "Human Ecology." Pp. 848–867 in *Encyclopedia of Sociology,* vol. 2, edited by Edgar F. Borgatta and Marie L. Borgatta. New York: Macmillan.
Bianchi, Suzanne M., and Daphne Spain. 1996. "Women, Work, and Family in America." *Population Bulletin* 51(December).
Bibby, Reginald W. 1990. *Mosaic Madness.* Toronto: Stoddart.
———. 1995. *The Bibby Report: Social Trends Canadian Style.* Toronto: Stoddart.
———. 1996. *Fragmented Gods: The Poverty and Potential of Religion in Canada.* Toronto: Irwin.
———, and Donald C. Posterski. 1992. *Teen Trends.* Toronto: Stoddart.
Bielby, William T., and Denise D. Bielby. 1992. "I Will Follow Him: Family Ties, Gender-Role Beliefs, and Reluctance to Relocate for a Better Job." *American Journal of Sociology* 97(March): 1241–1267.
Billson, Janet Mancini. 1994. "What Are Employers Looking for in BA, MA, and PhD Sociology Graduates?" *Student Sociologist* (Spring):1–3.
———, and Bettina J. Huber. 1993. *Embarking upon a Career with an Undergraduate Degree in Sociology.* 2d ed. Washington, DC: American Sociological Association.
Black, Donald. 1995. "The Epistemology of Pure Sociology." *Law and Social Inquiry* 20(Summer):829–870.
Black, Jerome H. 2000. "Entering the Political Elite in Canada: The Case of Minority Women as Parliamentary Candidates and MPs." *Canadian Review of Sociology and Anthropology* 37(2).
Black, Naomi. 1993. "The Canadian Women's Movement: The Second Wave." Pp. 151–176 in *Changing Patterns: Women in Canada,* 2d ed., edited by Sandra Burt, Lorraine Code, and Lindsay Dorney. Toronto: McClelland and Stewart.
Blackwell, Tom. 2001. "Michigan Seeks to Stop Delivery of Toronto's Trash." *Ottawa Citizen* March 6, final ed., p. A6.
Blair, Jayson. 1999. "Wrongful Arrest of Actor Is Blamed on Bias." *New York Times,* July 18, p. 30.
Blakely, Earl J., and Mary Gail Snyder. 1997. *Fortress America: Gated Communities in the United States.* Washington, DC: Brookings Institution Press/ Lincoln Institute.
Blanc, Ann Klimas. 1984. "Nonmarital Cohabitation and Fertility in the United States and Western Europe." *Population Research and Policy Review* 3:181–193.
Blanchard, Fletcher A., Teri Lilly, and Leigh Ann Vaughan. 1991. "Reducing the Expression of Racial Prejudice." *Psychological Science* 2(March): 101–105.
Blanco, Robert. 1998. "The Disappearance of Mom and Dad." *USA Today,* December 17, p. D1.
Blau, Peter M., and Otis Dudley Duncan. 1967. *The American Occupational Structure.* New York: Wiley.
———, and Marshall W. Meyer. 1987. *Bureaucracy in Modern Society.* 3d ed. New York: Random House.
———. 1972. *Racial Oppression in America.* New York: Harper and Row.
Blendon, Robert J. 1986. "The Problem of Cost, Access and Distribution of Medical Care." *Daedalus* 115(Spring): 119–135.
Bloom, Stephen G. 2000. *Postville: A Clash of Cultures in Heartland America.* San Diego, CA: Harcourt Brace.
Bluestone, Barry, and Bennett Harrison. 1999. *Growing Prosperity: The Battle for Growth with Equity in the 21st Century.* Boston, MA: Harrison Century Foundation/Houghton Mifflin.
———, and ———. 1982. *The Deindustrialization of America.* New York: Basic Books.
Blumer, Herbert. 1969. *Symbolic Interactionism: Perspective and Method.* Englewood Cliffs, NJ: Prentice-Hall.
———. 1955. "Collective Behavior." Pp. 165–198 in *Principles of Sociology,* 2d ed., edited by Alfred McClung Lee. New York: Barnes and Noble.
Boaz, Rachel Floersheim. 1987. "Early Withdrawal from the Labor Force." *Research on Aging* 9(December):530–547.
Bobo, Lawrence. 1991. "Social Responsibility, Individualism, and Redistribution Policies." *Sociological Forum* 6:71–92.
Bolaria, B. Singh. 1995. *Social Issues and Contradictions in Canadian Society.* 2d ed. Toronto: Harcourt Brace.
Bonacich, Edna, and Richard Appelbaum. 2000. *Behind the Label: Inequality in the Los Angeles Apparel Industry.* Berkeley, CA: University of California Press.
Bond, James T., Ellen Galinsky, and Jennifer E. Swanberg. 1998. The 1997 National Study of the Changing Work Force. New York: Families and Work Institute.
Booth, William. 2000. "Has Our Can-Do Attitude Peaked?" *Washington Post National Weekly Edition* 17 (February 7):29.
Boritch, Helen. 1997. *Fallen Woman: Female Crime and Criminal Justice in Canada.* Toronto: ITP Nelson.
Borman, Kathryn M., and Joel H. Spring. 1984. *Schools in Central Cities: Structure and Process.* New York: Longman.
Bornschier, Volker, Christopher Chase-Dunn, and Richard Rubinson. 1978. "Cross-National Evidence of the Effects of Foreign Investment and Aid on Economic Growth and Inequality: A Survey of Findings and a Reanalysis." *American Journal of Sociology* 84 (November):651–683.
Boston Women's Health Book Collective. 1969. *Our Bodies, Ourselves.* Boston: New England Free Press.
———. 1992. *The New Our Bodies, Ourselves.* New York: Touchstone.
Bottomore, Tom, and Maximilien Rubel, eds. 1956. *Karl Marx: Selected Writings in Sociology and Social Philosophy.* New York: McGraw-Hill.
Bourdages, Jean-Luc, and Christine Labelle. 2000. *Protecting Wild Species at Risk in Canada.* Ottawa: Parliamentary Research Branch. PRB 00-19E.
Bouvier, Leon F. 1980. "America's Baby Boom Generation: The Fateful Bulge." *Population Bulletin* 35(April).
Bowles, Samuel, and Herbert Gintis. 1976. *Schooling in Capitalist America: Educational Reforms and the Contradictions of Economic Life.* New York: Basic Books.
Bowles, Scott. 1999. "Fewer Violent Fatalities in Schools." *USA Today,* April 28, p. 4A.
Boyd, Monica. 1998. "Canadian, Eh? Ethnic Origin Shifts in the Canadian Census." *Canadian Ethnic Studies* 31(3):1–19.
———, and Edward Prior. 1990. "Young Adults Living in Their Parents' Home." Pp. 188–191 in *Canadian Social Trends,* edited by C. McKie and K. Thompson. Toronto: Thompson Educational Press.
Bradley, Martin B. et al. [5 authors]. 1992. *Churches and Church Membership in the United States 1990.* Atlanta, GA: Glenmary Research Center.
Bragg, Rick. 1999. "Fearing Isolation in Old Age, Gay Generation Seeks Haven." *New York Times,* October 21, pp. A1, A16.
Brand, Dionne. 1993. "A Working Paper on Black Women In Toronto: Gender, Race, and Class." Pp. 220–241in *Returning the Gaze: Essays on Racism, Feminism and Politics,* edited by Himani Bannerji. Toronto: Sister Vision Press.
Brandon, Karen. 1995. "Computer Scrutiny Adds to Furor over Immigrants." *Chicago Tribune,* December 5, pp. 1, 16.
Brannigan, Augustine. 1992. "Postmodernism." Pp. 1522–1525 in *Encyclopedia of Sociology,* vol. 3, edited by Edgar F. Borgatta and Marie L. Borgatta. New York: Macmillan.

Brannon, Robert. 1976. "Ideology, Myth, and Reality: Sex Equality in Israel." *Sex Roles* 6:403–419.

Braxton, Greg. 1999. "A Mad Dash for Diversity." *Los Angeles Times,* August 9, pp. F1, F10.

Bray, James H., and John Kelly. 1999. *Stepfamilies: Love, Marriage, and Parenting in the First Decade.* New York: Broadway Books.

Brewer, Rose M. 1989. "Black Women and Feminist Sociology: The Emerging Perspective." *American Sociologist* 20(Spring):57–70.

Brint, Steven. 1998. *Schools and Societies.* Thousand Oaks, CA: Pine Forge Press.

Bronson, P. 1999. *The Nudist in the Late Shift and Other True Tales of Silicon Valley.* New York: Random House.

Brown, Amanda, and Jim Stanford. *Flying without a Net: The 'Economic Freedom' of Working Canadians in 2000.* Canadian Centre for Policy Alternatives. Accessed April 18, 2002 (http://www.ccsd.ca/efru2000.pdf).

Brown, Robert McAfee. 1980. *Gustavo Gutierrez.* Atlanta: John Knox.

Bruni, Frank. 1998. "A Small-But-Growing Sorority Is Giving Birth to Children for Gay Men." *New York Times,* June 25, p. A12.

Bryant, Adam. 1999. "American Pay Rattles Foreign Partners." *New York Times,* January 17, sec. 6, pp. 1, 4.

Buckley, Stephen. 1997. "Left Behind Prosperity's Door." *Washington Post National Weekly Edition,* March 24, pp. 8–9.

Buechler, Steven M. 1995. "New Social Movement Theories." *Sociological Quarterly* 36(3):441–464.

Bula, Francis. 2000. "This is An International Crisis." *The Vancouver Sun,* November 21, pp. A1, A6.

Bulle, Wolfgang F. 1987. *Crossing Cultures? Southeast Asian Mainland.* Atlanta: Centers for Disease Control.

Bunzel, John H. 1992. *Race Relations on Campus: Stanford Students Speak.* Stanford, CA: Portable Stanford.

Bureau of the Census. 1970. *Statistical Abstract of the United States, 1970.* Washington, DC: U.S. Government Printing Office.

———. 1975. *Historical Statistics of the United States, Colonial Times to 1970.* Washington, DC: U.S. Government Printing Office.

———. 1981. *Statistical Abstract of the United States, 1981.* Washington, DC: U.S. Government Printing Office.

———. 1991a. "Marital Status and Living Arrangements: March 1990." *Current Population Reports,* ser. P-20, no. 450. Washington, DC: U.S. Government Printing Office.

———. 1991b. "Half of the Nation's Population Lives in Large Metropolitan Areas." Press release, February 21.

———. 1994. *Statistical Abstract of the United States, 1994.* Washington, DC: U.S. Government Printing Office.

———. 1995. *Statistical Abstract of the United States, 1995.* Washington, DC: U.S. Government Printing Office.

———. 1996a. *1992 Women-Owned Businesses.* Washington, DC: U.S. Government Printing Office.

———. 1996b. *Statistical Abstract of the United States, 1996.* Washington DC: U.S. Government Printing Office.

———. 1997a. *Statistical Abstract of the United States, 1997.* Washington, DC: U.S. Government Printing Office.

———. 1997b. "Geographical Mobility: March 1995 to March 1996." *Current Population Reports,* ser. P-20, no. 497. Washington, DC: U.S. Government Printing Office.

———. 1998a. "Race of Wife by Race of Husband." Internet release of June 10.

———. 1998c. *Statistical Abstract of the United States, 1998.* Washington, DC: U.S. Government Printing Office.

———. 1998d,e. Unpub.Tables—Marital Status and Living Arrangements: March 1998 (Update). Accessed July 26, 1999 (http://www.census.gov/prod/99pubs/p20-514u.pdf).

———. 1998f. Voting and Registration: November 1996. Internet release of October 17, 1997. Accessed July 17, 1998 (http://www.census.gov/population/socdemo/voting/history/vot01.txt).

———. 1999a. *Statistical Abstract of the United States, 1996.* Washington, DC: U.S. Government Printing Office.

———. 1999b. "The Asian and Pacific Islander Population in the United States: March 1998 (Update) (PP1-113). Table 9." *Total Money Income in 1997 of Families.* Accessed August 3, 1999 (http://www.census.gov/population/sucdemo/race/api98/table09.txt).

———. 1999i. "Money Income in the United States." *Current Population Reports,* ser. P-60, no. 206. Washington, DC: U.S. Government Printing Office.

———. 2000a. *Statistical Abstract of the United States, 2000.* Washington, DC: U.S. Government Printing Office.

———. 2000b. "The Hispanic Population in the United States." *Current Population Reports,* ser. P20–527. Washington, DC: U.S. Government Printing Office.

———. 2000c. "National Population Projections." Internet release of January 13. Accessed May 11, 2000 (http://www.census.gov/population/www/projection/natsum-T3html).

———. 2000d. "Money Income in the United States 1999." *Current Population Reports,* ser. P60, no. 209. Washington, DC: U.S. Government Printing Office.

Bureau of the Census. 2002e. "Population Pyramid Summary for Canada." *International Data Base.* Accessed April 4, 2002 (http://www.census.gov/cgi-bin/ipc/idbpyrs.pl?cty=cA&out-s&ymax=200).

Bureau of Labor Statistics. 1999a. "Comparative Civilian Labor Force Statistics for Ten Countries 1959–1990." Posted April 13, 1999. Accessed October 9, 1999 (ftp://ftp.bls.gov/pub/special.requests/ForeignLabor/flslforc.txt).

———. 1999b. "What Women Earned in 1998." *Issues in Labor Statistics.* Washington, DC: U.S. Government Printing Office.

———. 2000. "Employment Status of the Civilian Population by Race, Sex, Age, and Hispanic Origin." Accessed at http://www.bls.gen/news.release.

Bureau of Primary Health Care. 1999. Home Page. Accessed January 18, 2000 (http://www.bphc.hrsa.gov/bphcfactsheet.htm).

Burgess, Ernest W. 1925. "The Growth of the City." Pp. 47–62 in *The City,* edited by Robert E. Park, Ernest W. Burgess, and Roderick D. McKenzie. Chicago: University of Chicago Press.

Burkett, Elinor. 2000. *The Baby Boom: How Family Friendly America Cheats the Childless.* New York: Free Press.

Burns, John R. 1998. "Once Widowed in India, Twice Scorned." *New York Times,* March 29, p. A1.

Burt, Martha R. et al. 1999. *Homeless: Programs and the People They Save.* Washington, DC: Urban Institute.

Bush, Melanie. 1993. "The Doctor Is Out," *Village Voice* 38, June 22,p. 18.

Butler, Daniel Allen. 1998. *"Unsinkable:" The Full Story.* Mechanicsburg, PA: Stackpole Books.

Butler, Robert N. 1990. "A Disease Called Ageism." *Journal of American Geriatrics Society* 38(February): 178–180.

Butterfield, Fox. 1996. "U.S. Has Plan to Broaden Availability of DNA Testing." *New York Times,* June 14, p. A8.

C

Calhoun, Craig. 1998. "Community Without Propinquity Revisited." *Sociological Inquiry* 68(Summer):373–397.

Calhoun, David B. 2000. "Learning at Home." P. 193 in *Yearbook of the Encyclopedia Britannica 2000.* Chicago: Encyclopedia Britannica.

Calliste, Agnes. 2001. "Black Families in Canada. Exploring the Interconnections of Race, Class and Gender." Pp. 401–419 in *Family Patterns, Gender Relations,* edited by Bonnie J. Fox. Toronto: Oxford University Press.

Campbell, Bruce, Carlos Salas, and Robert Scott. 2000. "NAFTA at Seven." Washington, DC: Economic Policy Institute. Accessed April 18, 2002 (http://www.epinet.org/briefingpapers/nafta01/).

Camus, Albert. 1948. *The Plague.* New York: Random House.

Canada Mortgage and Housing Corporation. *No Room of Her Own: A Literature Review on Women and Homelessness.* Accessed April 18, 2002 (http://www.cmhc-schl.gc.ca/en/imquaf/ho/ho_015.cfm).

Canadian Broadcasting Corporation. 2000. *Stockwell Day's New Alliance.* Accessed April 5, 2002 (http://www.cbc.ca/insidecbc/newsinreview/Sep2000/stockwell/separation.htm).

Canadian Centre for Policy Alternatives. 2001. *New Report Shows NAFTA Has Harmed Workers in All Three Countries.* Accessed August 22, 2001 (http://www.policyalternatives.ca/whatsnew/naftaatsevenpr.html).

Canadian Council on Social Development. 2000. *The Canadian Fact Book on Poverty, 2000.* Ottawa: Canadian Council on Social Development.

———. 2001. *Minimum Wages Rates for Experienced Adult Workers in Canada and the Provinces.* Accessed May 4, 2001 (http://www.ccsd.ca/fs_minw.htm).

Canadian Environmental Defence Fund. "Justice at Walkerton." Accessed April 29, 2002 (http://www.edcanada.org/walkerton).

Canadian Institute for Health Information. 1999. *Supply and Distribution of Registered Nurses in Canada.* Ottawa: Canadian Institute for Health Information.

———. 2001. *Health Care in Canada.* Accessed January 27, 2002 (http://www.cihi.ca/HealthReport2001).

Canadian Press. 2000. "Garbage-filled Moose Carries Message." *St. John's Telegram*, September 26, final ed., p. 8.

Canadian Press Newswire. 2000. "Angus Reid Group changes name to reflect ties with Paris-based Ipsos." Canadian Business and Current Affairs (CBCA), on-line data base. October 2. Accessed April 8, 2002 (http://delos.lib.sfu.ca:8366/cgi-bin/slri/z3950.CGI/134.87.144.15.917141763/?cbca.db)

Canadian Society of Environmental Biologists. 2000. "Toronto City's Plans to Ship Garbage to Adam's Mine." Sept. 13. Accessed February 1, 2002 (http://www.cgocable.net/~exworld/cseb/news/adamsmine.html).

Canadian Sociology and Anthropology Association. *Statement of Professional Ethics.* Accessed April 17, 2002 (http://alcor.concordia.ca/~csaa1/csaa.html).

Caplan, Ronald L. 1989. "The Commodification of American Health Care." *Social Science and Medicine* 28(11): 1139–1148.

Cardarelli, Luise. 1996. "The Lost Girls: China May Come to Regret Its Preference for Boys." *Utne Reader,* May–June, pp. 13–14.

Carey, Anne R., and Elys A. McLean. 1997. "Heard It Through the Grapevine?" *USA Today,* September 15, p. B1.

———, and Grant Jerding. 1999. "What Workers Want." *USA Today*, August 17, p. B1.

———, and Jerry Mosemak. 1999. "Big on Religion." *USA Today,* April 1, p. D1.

Carty, Win. 1999. "Greater Dependence on Cars Leads to More Pollution in World's Cities." *Population Today* 27(December):1–2.

Casper, Lynne M., and Loretta E. Bass. 1998. "Voting and Registration in the Election of November 1996." *Current Population Reports,* ser. P-20, no. 504. Washington, DC: U.S. Government Printing Office.

Castelli, Jim. 1996. "How to Handle Personal Information." *American Demographics* 18(March):50–52, 57.

Castells, Manuel. 1983. *The City and the Grass Roots.* Berkeley: University of California Press.

———. 1996. *The Information Age: Economy, Society and Culture.* Vol. 1 of *The Rise of the Network Society.* London: Blackwell.

———. 1997. *The Power of Identity.* Vol. 1 of *The Information Age: Economy, Society and Culture.* London: Blackwell.

———. 1998. *End of Millennium.* Vol. 3 of *The Information Age: Economy, Society and Culture.* London: Blackwell.

———. 2000. *The Information Age: Economy, Society and Culture* (3 vols.). 2d. ed. Oxford and Malden, MA: Blackwell.

Catalyst. 1998. *The Catalyst Census of Women Board Directors in Canada.* Toronto: Catalyst.

Cavanagh, John, and Robin Broad. 1996. "Global Reach: Workers Fight the Multinationals." *The Nation* 262(March 18):21–24.

CBS News. 1979. Transcript of *Sixty Minutes* segment, "I Was Only Following Orders." March 31, pp. 2–8.

———. 1998. "Experimental Prison." *Sixty Minutes.* June 30.

Center for the American Woman and Politics. 1999. *Women in Elective Office 1998.* New Brunswick, NJ: CAWP, Rutgers University.

Centers for Disease Control and Prevention. 2000a. "Abortion Surveillance: Preliminary Analysis—United States, 1997." *Morbidity and Mortality Weekly Reports,* January 7, p. 2.

———. 2000b. "Commentary." *HIV/AIDS Surveillance Supplemental Report 5,* January 18, p. 1.

Center for Public Integrity. 1998. *Nothing Sacred: The Politics of Privacy.* Washington, DC: CPI.

Cetron, Marvin J., and Owen Davies. 1991. "Trends Shaping the World." *Futurist* 20(September–October):11–21.

Cha, Ariena Eunjung. 2000. "Painting a Portrait of Dot-Camaraderie." *The Washington Post,* October 26, pp. E1, E10.

Chaddock, Gail Russell. 1998. "The Challenge for Schools: Connecting Adults with Kids." *Christian Science Monitor,* August 4, p. B7.

Chalfant, H. Paul, Robert E. Beckley, and C. Eddie Palmer. 1994. *Religion in Contemporary Society.* 3d ed. Itasca, IL: F. E. Peacock.

Chambliss, William. 1972. "Introduction." Pp. ix–xi in Harry King, *Box Man.* New York: Harper and Row.

———. 1973. "The Saints and the Roughnecks." *Society* 11(November–December):24–31.

Chan, R.W., B. Rayboy and C.J. Patterson. 1998. "Psychological Adjustment Among Children Conceived via Donor Insemination by Lesbian and Heterosexual Mothers." *Child Development* 69:443–457.

Charmaz, Kathy, and Debora A. Paterniti, eds. 1999. *Health, Illness, and Healing: Society, Social Context, and Self.* Los Angeles, CA: Roxbury.

Charter, David, and Jill Sherman. 1996. "Schools Must Teach New Code of Values." *London Times,* January 15, p. 1.

Chase-Dunn, Christopher, and Peter Grimes. 1995. "World-Systems Analysis." Pp. 387–417 in *Annual Review of Sociology, 1995,* edited by John Hagan. Palo Alto, CA: Annual Reviews.

Cheng, Wei-yuan, and Lung-li Liao. 1994. "Women Managers in Taiwan." Pp. 143– 159 in *Competitive Frontiers: Women Managers in a Global Economy,* edited by Nancy J. Adler and Dafna N. Izraeli. Cambridge, MA: Blackwell Business.

Cherlin, Andrew J. 1999. *Public and Private Families: An Introduction.* 2d ed. New York: McGraw-Hill.

———, and Frank Furstenberg. 1992. *The New American Grandparent: A Place in the Family, A Life Apart.* Cambridge, MA: Harvard University Press.

———, and ———. 1994. "Stepfamilies in the United States: A Reconsideration." Pp. 359–381 in *Annual Review of Sociology, 1994,* edited by John Hagan. Palo Alto, CA: Annual Reviews.

Chesney-Lind, Meda, and Noelie Rodriguez. 1993. "Women under Lock and Key." *Prison Journal* 63:47–65.

Chicago Tribune. 1997a. "China Aborting Female Fetuses." October 17, p. 13.

———. 1997b. "In London, Prince Meets a Pauper, an Ex-Classmate." December 5, p. 19.

Child & Family Canada. 1994. *The Distribution of Income in Canada.* Accessed May 12, 2001 (http://www.cfc-efc.ca/docs/000000327.htm).

Childcare Resource and Research Unit. 2000. *Early Childhood Care and Education in Canada, Provinces and Territories*

1998. Centre for Urban and Community Studies: University of Toronto.

Chin, Ko-lin. 1996. *Chinatown Gangs: Extortion, Enterprise, and Ethnicity.* New York: Oxford University Press.

Chow, Esther Ngan-Ling, and S. Michael Zhao. 1995. "The Impact of the One-Child Policy on Parent-Child Relationships in the People's Republic of China." Presented at the annual meeting of the American Sociological Association, August, Washington, DC.

Christiansen, Kathleen. 1990. "Bridges over Troubled Water: How Older Workers View the Labor Market." Pp. 175–207 in *Bridges to Retirement,* edited by Peter B. Doeringer. Ithaca, NY: IRL Press.

Citizens' Forum on Canada's Future. 1991. *Report to the People and Government of Canada.* Ottawa: Privy Council Office.

Citizenship and Immigration Canada. 2001. *Pursuing Canada's Commitment to Immigration: The Immigration Plan for 2002.* Cat. no. Ci51-105/2001. October. Ottawa: Minister of Works and Government Services.

Civic Ventures. 1999. *The New Face of Retirement: Older Americans, Civic Engagement, and the Longevity Revolution.* Washington, DC: Peter D. Hart Research Associates.

Clark, Brian L. 1999. "Internet Life: Our Town. Online." *Money* 28(September):36.

Clark, Burton, and Martin Trow. 1966. "The Organizational Context." Pp. 17–70 in *The Study of College Peer Groups,* edited by Theodore M. Newcomb and Everett K. Wilson. Chicago: Aldine.

Clark, Candace. 1983. "Sickness and Social Control." Pp. 346–365 in *Social Interaction: Readings in Sociology,* 2d. ed., edited by Howard Robboy and Candace Clark. New York: St. Martin's.

Clark, Charles, and Jason M. Fields. 1999. "First Glance: Preliminary Analysis of Relationship, Marital Status, and Grandparents Items on the Census 2000 Dress Rehearsal." Presented at the annual meeting of the American Sociological Association, August, Chicago.

Clark, Thomas. 1994. "Culture and Objectivity." *The Humanist* 54(August):38–39.

Clarke, Lee. 1999. *Mission Improbable: Using Fantasy Documents to Tame Disaster.* Chicago: University of Chicago Press.

Clawson, Dan, and Mary Ann Clawson. 1999. "What Has Happened to the U.S. Labor Movement? Union Decline and Renewal." Pp. 95–119 in *Annual Review of Sociology,* edited by Karen S. Hook and John Hagan. Palo Alto, CA: Annual Reviews.

Cloud, John. 1998. "Sex and the Law." *Time* 151(March 23):48–54.

Cloward, Richard A. 1959. "Illegitimate Means, Anomie, and Deviant Behavior." *American Sociological Review* 24(April):164–176.

Clymer, Adam. 2000. "College Students Not Drawn to Voting or Politics, Poll Shows." *New York Times,* January 2, p. A14.

Coatney, Caryn. 1998. "Arrest of Abortion Doctors Puts Australia Laws on Spot." *Christian Science Monitor,* March 25, p. 6.

Cockerham, William C. 1998. *Medical Sociology.* 7th ed. Upper Saddle River, NJ: Prentice-Hall.

Code, Lorraine. 1993. "Feminist Theory." Pp. 19–57 in *Changing Patterns: Women in Canada,* 2d. ed., edited by Sandra Burt, Lorraine Code, and Lindsay Dorney. Toronto: McClelland and Stewart.

Coeyman, Marjorie. 1999. "Schools Question the Benefits of Tracking." *Christian Science Monitor,* September 21, p. 20.

Cohen, David, ed. 1991. *The Circle of Life: Ritual from the Human Family Album.* San Francisco: Harper.

Cohen, Lawrence E., and Marcus Felson. 1979. "Social Change and Crime Rate Trends: A Routine Activities Approach." *American Sociological Review* 44:588–608.

Cohen, Patricia. 1998. "Daddy Dearest: Do You Really Matter?" *New York Times,* July 11, p. B7.

Cole, David. 1999. *No Equal Justice: Race and Class in the American Criminal Justice System.* New York: The New Press.

Cole, Elizabeth S. 1985. "Adoption, History, Policy, and Program." Pp. 638–666 in *A Handbook of Child Welfare,* edited by John Laird and Ann Hartman. New York: Free Press.

Cole, Mike. 1988. *Bowles and Gintis Revisited: Correspondence and Contradiction in Educational Theory.* Philadelphia: Falmer.

Colker, David. 1996. "Putting the Accent on World Wide Access." *Los Angeles Times* (May 21), p. E3.

Collier, Jane, Michelle Rosaldo, and Sylvia Yanagisako. 2001. "Is There A Family? New Anthropological Views." Pp. 11–21 in *Family Patterns, Gender Relations,* 2d ed., edited by Bonnie J. Fox. Toronto: Oxford University Press.

Collins, Gail. 1998. "Why the Women Are Fading Away." *New York Times,* October 25, pp. 54–55.

Collins, Patricia Hill. 1991. *Black Feminist Thought: Knowledge, Consciousness, and the Politics of Empowerment.* New York: Routledge.

———. 1998. *Fighting Words: Black Women and the Search for Justice.* Minneapolis: University of Minnesota.

Collins, Randall. 1975. *Conflict Sociology: Toward an Explanatory Sociology.* New York: Academic.

———. 1980. "Weber's Last Theory of Capitalism: A Systematization." *American Sociological Review* 45(December):925–942.

———. 1986. *Weberian Sociological Theory.* New York: Cambridge University Press.

———. 1995. "Prediction in Macrosociology: The Case of the Soviet Collapse." *American Journal of Sociology* 100(May):1552–1593.

Comack, Elizabeth. 1996. *Women in Trouble.* Halifax: Fernwood Publishing.

Commission on Behavioral and Social Sciences Education. 1998. *Protecting Youth at Work.* Washington, DC: National Academy Press.

Commission on Civil Rights. 1976. *A Guide to Federal Laws and Regulations Prohibiting Sex Discrimination.* Washington, DC: U.S. Government Printing Office.

———. 1981. *Affirmative Action in the 1980s: Dismantling the Process of Discrimination.* Washington, DC: U.S. Government Printing Office.

Commoner, Barry. 1971. *The Closing Circle.* New York: Knopf.

———. 1990. *Making Peace with the Planet.* New York: Pantheon.

Communications Canada. 2001. "Facts on Canada." Accessed April 11, 2001 (http://www.infocan.gc.ca/facts/multi_e.html).

CompuSearch/InfoGroup Inc. 1993. *Quantitative Research Study Produced for Lifestyles TV Inc.,* pp. 24–27.

Computer Security Institute. 1999. "1999 CSI/FBI Computer Crime and Security Survey." *Computer Security Issues and Trends* 5(Winter):1–15.

ComQuest Research Group. 1993. *Lifestyles Television Focus Group Report.* Vancouver: Bureau of Broadcast Measurement.

Connidis, Ingrid A. 1989. *Family Ties and Ageing.* Toronto: Butterworths.

Conrad, Peter, ed. 1997. *The Sociology of Health and Illness: Critical Perspectives.* 5th ed. New York: St. Martin's.

———, and Joseph W. Schneider. 1992. *Deviance and Medicalization: From Badness to Sickness.* Expanded ed. Philadelphia: Temple University Press.

Cook, P. J., and J. A. Leitzel. 1996. *Perversity, Futility, Jeopardy: An Economic Analysis of the Attack on Gun Control.* Durham, NC: Sanford Institute of Public Policy, Duke University.

Cook, Rhodes. 1991. "The Crosscurrents of the Youth Vote." *Congressional Quarterly Weekly Report* 49(June 29):1802.

Cooley, Charles H. 1902. *Human Nature and the Social Order.* New York: Scribner.

Cooper, Kenneth J. 1994. "Wrong Turns on the Map?" *Washington Post National Weekly Edition* 12(January 31):14.

Cooper, Richard T. 1998. "Jobs Outside High School Can Be Costly, Report

Finds." *Los Angeles Times*, November 6, p. A1.
Coser, Lewis A. 1956. *The Functions of Social Conflict.* New York: Free Press.
———. 1977. *Masters of Sociological Thought: Ideas in Historical and Social Context.* 2d ed. New York: Harcourt, Brace and Jovanovich.
Coser, Rose Laub. 1984. "American Medicine's Ambiguous Progress." *Contemporary Sociology* 13(January):9–13.
Côté, James E., and Anton L. Allahar. 1994. *Generation on Hold: Coming of Age in the Late Twentieth Century.* Toronto: Stoddart.
Couch, Carl. 1996. *Information Technologies and Social Orders.* Edited with an introduction by David R. Maines and Shing-Ling Chien. New York: Aldine de Gruyter.
Council of Ministers of Education, Canada. 1995. *A Report on Education in Canada, 1995.* Toronto: Council of Ministers of Education, Canada.
Cox, Craig. 1999. "Prime-Time Activism." *Utne Reader* (September–October), pp. 20–22.
Cox, Kevin. 2001. "Nova Scotia Gay Couple Given Legal Recognition." *The Globe and Mail,* June 5, p. A5.
Cox, Oliver C. 1948. *Caste, Class and Race: A Study in Social Dynamics.* Detroit: Wayne State University Press.
Craig, Maxine. 1997. "The Decline and Fall of the Conk; or How to Read a Process." *Fashion Theory* 1(4): 399–420.
Creese, Gillian, Neil Guppy, and Martin Meissner. 1991. *Ups and Downs on the Ladder of Success: Social Mobility in Canada.* Ottawa: Statistics Canada.
Crenshaw, Edward M., Matthew Christenson, and Doyle Ray Oakey. 2000. "Demographic Transition in Ecological Focus." *American Sociological Review* 65(June):371–391.
Cressey, Donald R. 1960. "Epidemiology and Individual Contact: A Case from Criminology." *Pacific Sociological Review* 3(Fall):47–58.
Cromwell, Paul F., James N. Olson, and D'Aunn Wester Avarey. 1995. *Breaking and Entering: An Ethnographic Analysis of Burglary.* Newbury Park, CA: Sage.
Crossette, Barbara. 1996a. "'Oldest Old,' 80 and Over, Increasing Globally." *New York Times,* December 22, p. 7.
———. 1996b. "Snubbing Human Rights," *New York Times,* April 28, p. E3.
———. 1999. "The Internet Changes Dictatorship's Rules." *New York Times,* August 1, sec. 4, p. 1.
Crouse, Kelly. 1999. "Sociology of the Titanic." *Teaching Sociology Listserv.* May 24.
Cuff, E. C., W. W. Sharrock, and D. W. Francis, eds. 1990. *Perspectives in Sociology.* 3d ed. Boston: Unwin Hyman.
Cullen, Francis T., Jr., and John B. Cullen. 1978. *Toward a Paradigm of Labeling Theory,* ser. 58. Lincoln: University of Nebraska Studies.
Cumming, Elaine, and William E. Henry. 1961. *Growing Old: The Process of Disengagement.* New York: Basic Books.
Currie, Elliot. 1985. *Confronting Crime: An American Challenge.* New York: Pantheon.
———. 1998. *Crime and Punishment in America.* New York: Metropolitan Books.
Curry, Timothy Jon. 1993. "A Little Pain Never Hurt Anyone: Athletic Career Socialization and the Normalization of Sports Injury." *Symbolic Interaction* 26(Fall):273–290.
Curtius, Mary. 1999. "Struggling Town Split Over Wal-Mart Plan." *Los Angeles Times,* July 5, pp. A1, A16–18.
Cushman, John H., Jr. 1998a. "Pollution Policy Is Unfair Burden, States Tell E. P. A." *New York Times,* May 10, pp. 1, 20.
———. 1998b. "Nike Pledges to End Child Labor and Apply U.S. Rules Abroad." *New York Times,* May 13, p. C1.
Cussins, Choris M. 1998. In *Cyborg Babies: From Techno-Sex to Techno-Tots,* edited by Robbie Davis-Floyd and Joseph Dumit. New York: Routledge.

D

Dahl, Robert A. 1961. *Who Governs?* New Haven, CT: Yale University Press.
Dahrendorf, Ralf. 1958. "Toward a Theory of Social Conflict." *Journal of Conflict Resolution* 2(June):170–183.
———. 1959. *Class and Class Conflict in Industrial Sociology.* Stanford, CA: Stanford University Press.
Dalaker, Joseph, and Bernadette D. Proctor. 2000. "Poverty in the United States." *Current Population Reports,* ser. P60, no. 210. Washington, DC: U.S. Government Printing Office.
Daley, Suzanne. 1997. "Reversing Roles in a South African Dilemma." *New York Times,* October 26, sec. WE, p. 5.
———. 2000. "French Couples Take Plunge that Falls Short of Marriage." *New York Times,* April 18, pp. A1, A4.
Dalfen, Ariel K. 2000. "Cyberaddicts in Cyberspace? Internet Addiction Disorder." *Wellness Options.* (Winter): 38–39.
Dao, James. 1995. "New York's Highest Court Rules Unmarried Couples Can Adopt." *New York Times,* November 3, pp. A1, B2.
Dart, John. 1997. "Lutheran Women Wait Longer for Pastor Jobs, Survey Finds." *Los Angeles Times,* May 3, pp. B1, B5.
Daskal, Jennifer. 1998. *In Search of Shelter: The Growing Shortage of Affordable Rental Housing.* Washington, DC: Center on Budget and Policy Priorities.
Davies, Christie. 1989. "Goffman's Concept of the Total Institution: Criticisms and Revisions." *Human Studies* 12(June):77–95.
Davies, Scott, and Margaret Denton. 1996. "The Employment of Masters and PhD Graduates from Eleven Sociology Departments." Accessed January 24, 2002 (http://www.mcmaster.ca/socscidocs/survey.htm).
Davis, Darren W. 1997. "The Direction of Race of Interviewer Effects Among African-Americans: Donning the Black Mask." *American Journal of Political Science* 41(January):309–322.
Davis, James. 1982. "Up and Down Opportunity's Ladder." *Public Opinion* 5(June–July):11–15, 48–51.
Davis, James Allan, and Tom W. Smith. 1999. *General Social Surveys, 1972–1998.* Storrs, CT: The Roper Center.
———, and ———. 1999. *General Social Surveys, 1972–1998* [MRDF]. Storrs, CT: The Roper Center for Public Opinion Research.
Davis, Kingsley. 1937. "The Sociology of Prostitution." *American Sociological Review* 2(October):744–755.
———. 1940. "Extreme Social Isolation of a Child." *American Journal of Sociology* 45(January):554–565.
———. 1947. "A Final Note on a Case of Extreme Isolation." *American Journal of Sociology* 52(March):432–437.
———. [1949] 1995. *Human Society.* Reprint, New York: Macmillan.
———, and Wilbert E. Moore. 1945. "Some Principles of Stratification." *American Sociological Review* 10(April): 242–249.
Davis, Nanette J. 1975. *Sociological Constructions of Deviance: Perspectives and Issues in the Field.* Dubuque, IA: Wm. C. Brown.
Day, David M., Carol A. Golench, Jyl MacDougall, and Cheryl A. Beals-Gonzaléz. 1995. *School-based Violence Prevention in Canada: Results of A National Survey of Policies and Programs.* Ministry of the Solicitor General: Supply and Services Canada. Accessed December 16, 2001 (http://www.eurowrc.org/os/education/education_en/os.edu_en.html).
Day, Jennifer Cheeseman. 1993. "Population Projections of the United States by Age, Sex, Race, and Hispanic Origin: 1993–2050," *Current Population Reports,* ser. P-25, no. 1104. Washington, DC: U.S. Government Printing Office.
Daycare Action Council. 2000. Interview, January 5. Chicago: Daycare Action Council of Illinois.
Death Penalty Information Center. 2000a. "The Death Penalty in 1999: Year End Report." Accessed February 13, 2000 (http://www.essential.org/dpic/yrendrpt99.html).

———. 2000b. "History of the Death Penalty. Part II." Accessed February 13, 2000 (http://www.essential.org/dpic/history3.html#Innocence).

———. 2000c. "Innocence: Freed From Death Row." Accessed March 20, 2000 (http://www.essential.org/dpic/Innocent/ist.html.)

Deegan, Mary Jo, ed. 1991. *Women in Sociology: A Bio-Biographical Sourcebook.* Westport, CT: Greenwood.

DeKeseredy, Walter S. 2001. "Patterns of Family Violence." Pp. 238–266 in *Families: Changing Trends in Canada,* 4th ed., edited by Maureen Baker. Toronto: McGraw-Hill Ryerson.

———, and Martin D. Schwartz. 1998. *Woman Abuse on Campus: Results from the Canadian National Survey.* Thousand Oaks, CA: Sage Publications.

Deloria, Jr., Vine. 1999. *For This Land: Writings on Religion in America.* New York: Routledge.

Denzin, Norman K., and Yvonna S. Lincoln, eds. 2000. *Handbook of Qualitative Research.* 2d ed. Thousand Oaks, CA: Sage.

DePalma, Anthony. 1999. "Rules to Protect a Culture Make for Confusion." *New York Times,* July 14, pp. B1, B2.

DeParle, Jason. 1998. "Shrinking Welfare Rolls Leave Record High Share of Minorities." *New York Times,* July 27, pp. A1, A12.

Department of Education. 1999. *Report on State Implementation of the Gun-Free Schools Act. School Year 1997–98.* Rockville, MD: Westat.

Department of Foreign Affairs. 2001. *The Canada-U.S. Smart Border Declaration.* Accessed May 6, 2002 (http://www.dfait-maeci.gc.ca/anti-terrorism/declaration-e.asp).

Department of Health and Human Services. 2000. "Change in TANF Caseloads (January 1993–September 1999)." Accessed August 8, 2000 (http://www.acf.dhhs.gov/news/stats/caseload.htm).

Department of Health and Welfare, Canada. 1973. *Working Paper on Social Security in Canada.* Ottawa: Ministry of Supply and Services.

Department of Justice. 1999a. *Uniform Crime Reports, 1998.* Washington, DC: U.S. Government Printing Office.

———. 1999b. *Correctional Populations in the United States, 1996.* Washington, DC: Bureau of Justice Statistics.

Department of Labor. 1995a. *Good for Business: Making Full Use of the Nation's Capital.* Washington, DC: U.S. Government Printing Office.

———. 1995b. *A Solid Investment: Making Full Use of the Nation's Human Capital.* Washington, DC: U.S. Government Printing Office.

———. 1998. "Work and Elder Care: Facts for Caregivers and Their Employers." Accessed November 20 (http://www.dol.gov/dol/wb/public/wb_pubs/elderc.htm).

DeSimone, Bonnie. 2000. "Gold Tendency." *Chicago Tribune Magazine,* February 20, pp. 9–19.

Devine, Don. 1972. *Political Culture of the United States: The Influence of Member Values on Regime Maintenance.* Boston: Little, Brown.

Devitt, James. 1999. *Framing Gender on the Campaign Trail: Women's Executive Leadership and the Press.* New York: Women's Leadership Conference.

Dickerson, Marla. 1998. "Belief in Ideas Inspires Women to Start Businesses." *Los Angeles Times,* February 24, pp. D1, D13.

Dionne, Annette, Cecile, and Yvonne. 1997. "Letter." *Time,* December 1, p. 39.

Doeringer, Peter B., ed. 1990. *Bridges to Retirement: Older Workers in a Changing Labor Market.* Ithaca, NY: ILR Press.

Doig, Stephen, Reynolds Farley, William Frey, and Dan Gillman. 1993. *Blacks on the Block—New Patterns of Residential Segregation in a Multi-Ethnic Country.* Cambridge, MA: Harvard University Press.

Dolbeare, Kenneth M. 1982. *American Public Policy: A Citizen's Guide.* New York: McGraw-Hill.

Domhoff, G. William. 1978. *Who Really Rules? New Haven and Community Power Reexamined.* New Brunswick, NJ: Transaction.

———. 1998. *Who Rules America?* 3d ed. Mountain View, CA: Mayfield.

Domino, John C. 1995. *Sexual Harassment and the Courts.* New York: HarperCollins.

Donohue, Elizabeth, Vincent Schiraldi, and Jason Ziedenberg. 1998. *School House Hype: School Shootings and Real Risks Kids Face in America.* New York: Justice Policy Institute.

Doob, Christopher Bates. 1999. *Racism: An American Cauldron.* 3d ed. New York: Longman.

Dorai, Frances. 1998. *Insight Guide: Singapore.* Singapore: Insight Media, APA Publications.

Doress, Irwin, and Jack Nusan Porter. 1977. *Kids in Cults: Why They Join, Why They Stay, Why They Leave.* Brookline, MA: Reconciliation Associates.

Dornbusch, Sanford M. "The Sociology of Adolescence." Pp. 233–259 in *Annual Review of Sociology, 1989,* edited by W. Richard Scott and Judith Blake. Palo Alto, CA: Annual Reviews.

Dotson, Floyd. 1991. "Community." P. 55 in *Encyclopedic Dictionary of Sociology,* 4th ed. Guilford, CT: Dushkin.

Dougherty, Kevin, and Floyd M. Hammack. 1992. "Education Organization." Pp. 535–541 in *Encyclopedia of Sociology,* vol. 2, edited by Edgar F. Borgatta and Marie L. Borgatta. New York: Macmillan.

Douglas, Jack D. 1967. *The Social Meanings of Swank.* Princeton, NJ: Princeton University Press.

Douthitt, Robin A., and Joanne Fedyk. 1990. *The Cost of Raising Children in Canada.* Toronto: Butterworths.

Dowd, James J. 1980. *Stratification among the Aged.* Monterey, CA: Brooks/Cole.

Downie, Andrew. 2000. "Brazilian Girls Turn to a Doll More Like Them." *Christian Science Monitor.* January 20. Accessed January 20, 2000 (http://www.csmonitor.com/durable/2000/01/20/fpls3-csm.shtml).

Doyle, James A. 1995. *The Male Experience.* 3d ed. Dubuque, IA: Brown & Benchmark.

———, and Michele A. Paludi. 1998. *Sex and Gender: The Human Experience.* 4th ed. New York: McGraw-Hill.

Doyle Driedger, Sharon. 1998. "After Divorce." *Maclean's Magazine,* April 20, pp. 38–44.

DPIC 2000c. (See Death Penalty Information Center. 2000c).

Drache, Daniel, and Terrence J. Sullivan, eds. 1999. "Health, Health Care and Social Cohesion." *Public Success, Private Failures: Market Limits in Health Reform.* Toronto: Routledge. Accessed August 1, 2001 (http://www.founders.ner/fn/papers).

Drucker, Peter F. 1999. "Beyond the Information Revolution." *Atlantic Monthly* 284(October):42–57.

Du Bois, W. E. B. 1909. *The Negro American Family.* Atlanta University. Reprinted 1970, Cambridge, MA: M.I.T. Press.

———. 1911. "The Girl Nobody Loved," *Social News* 2(November):3.

Duberman, Lucille. 1976. *Social Inequality: Class and Caste in America.* Philadelphia: Lippincott.

Dugger, Celia W. 1999. "Massacres of Low-Born Touch Off a Crisis in India." *New York Times,* March 15, p. A3.

Dumas, Jean. 1994. *Report on the Demographic Situation in Canada 1993.* Cat. no. 91-209E. Ottawa: Statistics Canada.

Duncan, Greg J. 1994. "Welfare Can Fuel Upward Mobility." *Profiles* 18(May):6.

———, and Ken R. Smith. 1989. "The Rising Affluence of the Elderly: How Far, How Fair, and How Frail." Pp. 261–289 in *Annual Review of Sociology, 1989,* edited by W. Richard Scott and Judith Blake. Palo Alto, CA: Annual Reviews.

———, and Wei-Jun J. Yeung. 1995. "Extent and Consequences of Welfare Dependence among America's Children." *Children and Youth Service Review* 17(1–3):157–182.

Duneier, Mitchell. 1994a. "On the Job, but Behind the Scenes." *Chicago Tribune,* December 26, pp. 1, 24.

———. 1994b. "Battling for Control." *Chicago Tribune,* December 28, pp. 1, 8.

Dunlap, Riley E. 1993. "From Environmental to Ecological Problems." Pp. 707–738 in *Introduction to Social Problems,* edited by Craig Calhoun and George Ritzer. New York: McGraw-Hill.

———, and William R. Catton, Jr. 1983. "What Environmental Sociologists Have in Common." *Sociological Inquiry* 53(Spring):113–135.

Durkheim, Émile. [1893] 1933. *Division of Labor in Society.* Translated by George Simpson. Reprint, New York: Free Press.

———. [1912] 1947. *The Elementary Forms of the Religious Life.* Reprint, Glencoe, IL: Free Press.

———. [1897] 1951. *Suicide.* Translated by John A. Spaulding and George Simpson. Reprint, New York: Free Press.

———. [1845] 1964. *The Rules of Sociological Method.* Translated by Sarah A. Solovay and John H. Mueller. Reprint, New York: Free Press.

Durning, Alan B. 1990. "Life on the Brink." *World Watch* 3(March–April):22–30.

Durrant, Joan E., and Linda Rose-Krasnor. 1995. *Corporal Punishment Research Review and Policy Development.* Ottawa: Ontario Health Canada and Department of Justice Canada.

Dvany, Andres, Elizabeth Plater-Zyberk, and Jeff Speck. 2000. *Surburban Nation: The Rise of Sprawl and the Decline of the American Dream.* New York: Farrar, Straus & Giroux.

Dworkin, Rosalind J. 1982. "A Woman's Report: Numbers Are Not Enough." Pp. 375–400 in *The Minority Report,* edited by Anthony Dworkin and Rosalind Dworkin. New York: Holt.

E

Eayrs, Caroline B., Nick Ellis, and Robert S. P. Jones. 1993. "Which Label? An Investigation into the Effects of Terminology on Public Perceptions of and Attitudes toward People with Learning Difficulties." *Disability, Handicap, and Society* 8(2):111–127.

Ebaugh, Helen Rose Fuchs. 1988. *Becoming an Ex: The Process of Role Exit.* Chicago: University of Chicago Press.

Eckenwiler, Mark. 1995. "In the Eyes of the Law." *Internet World* (August):74, 76–77.

Eckholm, Erik. 1994. "While Congress Remains Silent, Health Care Transforms Itself." *New York Times,* December 18, pp. 1, 34.

The Economist. 1995. "Home Sweet Home." 336(September 9):25–26, 29, 32.

———. 1998. "Cruel and Ever More Unusual." 346(February 14).

Edmonston, Barry, and Jeff Passel. 1999. "How Immigration and Intermarriage Affect the Racial and Ethnic Composition of the U.S. Population" in *Immigration and Opportunity, Race, Ethnicity, and Employment in the United States,* edited by Frank D. Bean and Stephanie Bell-Rose. New York: Russell Sage Foundation.

Edwards, Harry. 1984. "The Black 'Dumb Jock,'" *College Board Review* 131(Spring):8–13.

Efron, Sonni. 1997. "In Japan, Even Tots Must Make the Grade." *Los Angeles Times,* February 16, pp. A1, A17.

———. 1998. "Japanese in Quandary on Fertility." *Los Angeles Times,* July 27, pp. A1, A6.

Egan, Timothy. 1995. "Many Seek Security in Private Communities." *New York Times,* September 3, pp. 1, 22.

———. 1998. "New Prosperity Brings New Conflict to Indian Country." *New York Times,* March 8, pp. 1, 24.

———. 1999. "What Price the Most Expensive Diamond of All?" *New York Times,* July 17, p. A7.

Ehrenreich, Barbara, and Deidre English. 1973. *Witches, Midwives, and Nurses: A History of Women Healers.* Old Westbury, NY: Feminist Press.

Ehrlich, Paul R. 1968. *The Population Bomb.* New York: Ballantine.

———, and Anne H. Ehrlich. 1990. *The Population Explosion.* New York: Simon and Schuster.

Eichler, Margrit. 1997. *Family Shifts: Families, Policies, and Gender Equality.* Toronto: Oxford University Press.

———. 2001. "Biases in Family Literature." Pp. 51–66 in *Families: Changing Trends in Canada.* 4th ed., edited by Maureen Baker. Toronto: McGraw-Hill Ryerson.

Eisenberg, David M. et al. 1998. "Trends in Alternative Medicine Use in the United States, 1990–1997." *Journal of the American Medical Association* 280(November 11):1569–1636.

Ekman, Paul, Wallace V. Friesen, and John Bear. 1984. "The International Language of Gestures." *Psychology Today* 18(May):64–69.

Ekos Research. 1998. *Canadians and Telework: The Information Highway and Canadian Communications.* Press Release. Nov. 4, Ottawa-Hull.

El-Badry, Samira. 1994. "The Arab-American Market." *American Demographics* 16(January):21–27, 30.

Elias, Marilyn. 1996. "Researchers Fight Child Consent Bill." *USA Today,* January 2, p. A1.

Elliot, Patricia, and Nancy Mandell. 1998. "Feminist Theories." Pp. 2–25 in *Feminist Issues: Race, Class, and Sexuality,* 2d ed., edited by Nancy Mandell, Scarborough: Prentice Hall Allyn and Bacon Canada.

Elliott, Helene. 1997. "Having an Olympic Team Is Their Miracle on Ice." *Los Angeles Times,* March 25, Sports section, p. 5.

Elliott, Marta, and Lauren J. Krivo. 1991. "Structural Determinants of Homelessness in the United States." *Social Problems* 38(February):113–131.

Elliott, Michael. 1994. "Crime and Punishment." *Newsweek* 123(April 18):18–22.

Ellis, Virginia, and Ken Ellingwood. 1998. "Welfare to Work: Are There Enough Jobs?" *Los Angeles Times,* February 8, pp. A1, A30.

Ellison, Ralph. 1952. *Invisible Man.* New York: Random House.

Elmer-DeWitt, Philip. 1995. "Welcome to Cyberspace." *Time* 145(Special Issue, Spring):4–11.

El Nasser, Haya. 1999. "Soaring Housing Costs Are Culprit in Suburban Poverty." *USA Today,* April 28, pp. A1, A2.

Ely, Robin J. 1995. "The Power of Demography: Women's Social Construction of Gender Identity at Work." *Academy of Management Journal* 38(3):589–634.

Engardio, Pete. 1999. "Activists Without Borders." *Business Week,* October 4, pp. 144–145, 148, 150.

Engels, Friedrich. 1884. "The Origin of the Family, Private Property and the State." Pp. 392–394, excerpted in *Marx and Engels: Basic Writings on Politics and Philosophy,* edited by Lewis Feuer. Garden City, NY: Anchor, 1959.

England, Paula. 1999. "The Impact of Feminist Thought on Sociology." *Contemporary Sociology* 28(May): 263–268.

Entine, Jon, and Martha Nichols. 1996. "Blowing the Whistle on Meaningless 'Good Intentions.'" *Chicago Tribune,* June 20, sec. 1, p. 21.

Epstein, Steven. 1997. *Impure Science: AIDS, Activism, and the Politics of Knowledge.* Berkeley: University of California Press.

Erikson, Kai. 1966. *Wayward Puritans: A Study in the Sociology of Deviance.* New York: Wiley.

———. 1994. *A New Species of Trouble: The Human Experience of Modern Disasters.* New York: Norton.

Espenshade, Edward B., Jr. 1990. *Rand McNally Goode's World Atlas.* 18th ed. Chicago: Rand McNally.

Etzioni, Amitai. 1964. *Modern Organization.* Englewood Cliffs, NJ: Prentice-Hall.

———. 1985. "Shady Corporate Practices." *New York Times,* November 15, p. A35.

———. 1990. "Going Soft on Corporate Crime." *Washington Post,* April 1, p. C3.

———. 1996. "Why Fear Date Rape?" *USA Today,* May 20, p. 14A.

Evans, Peter. 1979. *Dependent Development.* Princeton, NJ: Princeton University Press.

Evans, Sara. 1980. *Personal Politics: The Roots of Women's Liberation in the Civil Rights Movement and the New Left.* New York: Vintage.

Everitt, Joanna. "The Gender Gap in Canada: Now You See It, Now You Don't." *The Canadian Review of Sociology and Anthropology* 35(2).

Ewashen, Larry A. 1995. "Doukhobors and the Media." *Canadian Ethnic Studies* 27(3).

F

Fager, Marty, Mike Bradley, Lonnie Danchik, and Tom Wodetski. 1971. *Unbecoming Men.* Washington, NJ: Times Change.

Fahs, Ivan J., Dan A. Lewis, C. James Carr, and Mark W. Field. 1997. "Homelessness in an Affluent Suburb: The Story of Wheaton, Illinois." Paper presented at the annual meeting of the Illinois Sociological Association, October, Rockford, IL.

Faludi, Susan. 1999. *Stiffed: The Betrayal of the American Man.* New York: William Morrow.

Farhi, Paul, and Megan Rosenfeld. 1998. "Exporting America." *Washington Post National Weekly Edition* 16(November 30):6–7.

Farley, Maggie. 1997. "Loophole Lets More Chinese Have 2 Children." *Los Angeles Times,* October 20, pp. A1, A14–A15.

———. 1998. "Indonesia's Chinese Fearful of Backlash." *Los Angeles Times,* January 31, pp. A1, A8–A9.

Farr, Grant M. 1999. *Modern Iran.* New York: McGraw-Hill.

Feagin, Joe R. 1983. *The Urban Real Estate Game: Playing Monopoly with Real Money.* Englewood Cliffs, NJ: Prentice-Hall.

———. 1989. *Minority Group Issues in Higher Education: Learning from Qualitative Research.* Norman, OK: Center for Research on Minority Education, University of Oklahoma.

———, Harnán Vera, and Nikitah Imani. 1996. *The Agony of Education: Black Students at White Colleges and Universities.* New York: Routledge.

Featherman, David L., and Robert M. Hauser. 1978. *Opportunity and Change.* New York: Aeodus.

Federman, Joel. 1998. *1998 National Television Violence Study: Executive Summary.* Santa Barbara: University of California, Santa Barbara.

Federman, Maya et al. [8 authors]. 1996. "What Does It Mean to Be Poor in America?" *Monthly Labor Review* 119(May):3–17.

Feinglass, Joe. 1987. "Next, the McDRG." *The Progressive* 51(January):28.

Feldman, Linda. 1999. "Control of Congress in Seniors' Hands." *Christian Science Monitor,* June 21, pp. 1–4.

Felson, Marcus. 1998. *Crime and Everyday Life: Insights and Implications for Society.* 2d ed. Thousand Oaks, CA: Pine Forge Press.

Fernandez, John R. 1999. *Race, Gender and Rhetoric.* New York: McGraw-Hill.

Fernández, Sandy. 1996. "The Cyber Cops." *Ms.* 6(May–June):22–23.

Ferree, Myra Marx, and David A. Merrill. 2000. "Hot Movements, Cold Cognition: Thinking about Social Movements in Gendered Frames." *Contemporary Society* 29(May):454–462.

Ferrell, Tom. 1979. "More Choose to Live outside Marriage." *New York Times,* July 1, p. E7.

Feuer, Lewis S., ed. 1959. *Karl Marx and Friedrich Engels: Basic Writings on Politics and Philosophy.* Garden City, NY: Doubleday.

Fiala, Robert. 1992. "Postindustrial Society." Pp. 1512–1522 in *Encyclopedia of Sociology,* vol. 3, edited by Edgar F. Borgatta and Marie L. Borgatta. New York: Macmillan.

Fields, Jason M., and Charles L. Clark. 1999. "Unbinding the Ties: Edit Effects of Marital Status on Same Gender Groups." Paper presented at the annual meeting of the American Sociological Assocation, August, Chicago.

Finder, Alan. 1995. "Despite Tough Laws, Sweatshops Flourish." *New York Times,* January 6, pp. A1, B4.

Findlay, Steven. 1998. "85% of American Workers Using HMOs." *USA Today,* January 20, p. 3A.

Fine, Gary Alan. 1984. "Negotiated Orders and Organizational Cultures." Pp. 239–262 in *Annual Review of Sociology, 1984,* edited by Ralph Turner. Palo Alto, CA: Annual Reviews.

Finkel, Alvin, and Margaret Conrad with Veronica Stong-Boag. 1993. *History of the Canadian Peoples: 1867 to Present.* Toronto: Copp Clark Putnam.

Finkel, Steven E., and James B. Rule. 1987. "Relative Deprivation and Related Psychological Theories of Civil Violence: A Critical Review." *Research in Social Movements* 9:47–69.

Finnie, Ross. 1993. "Women, Men and the Economic Consequences of Divorce: Evidence from Canadian Longitudinal Data." *Canadian Review of Sociology and Anthropology* 30(2):205–241.

Fiore, Faye. 1997. "Full-Time Moms a Minority Now, Census Bureau Finds." *Los Angeles Times,* November 26, pp. A1, A20.

Firestone, David. 1999. "School Prayer Is Revived As an Issue In Alabama." *New York Times,* July 15, p. A14.

Firestone, Shulamith. 1970. *The Dialectic of Sex: The Case for Feminist Revolution.* New York: Bantam.

Firmat, Gustavo Perez. 1994. *Life on Hyphen: The Cuban-American Way.* Austin: University of Texas Press.

Fitzpatrick, Eleanor. 1994. *Violence Prevention: A Working Paper and Proposal for Action.* St. John's: Avalon Consolidated School Board.

Fitzpatrick, Kevin, and Mark LaGray. 2000. *Unhealthy Places: The Ecology of Risk in the Urban Landscape.* New York: Routledge.

Flacks, Richard. 1971. *Youth and Social Change.* Chicago: Markham.

Flanders, John. 2001. "Getting Ready for the 2001 Census." *Canadian Social Trends.* (Spring) Statistics Canada. Catalogue No. 11-008. Ottawa: Minister of Industry.

Flavin, Jeanne. 1998. "Razing the Wall: A Feminist Critique of Sentencing Theory, Research, and Policy." Pp. 145–164 in *Cutting the Edge,* edited by Jeffrey Ross. Westport, CT: Praeger.

Fleras, Augie, and Jean Leonard Elliott. 1992. *The Nations Within. Aboriginal-State Relations in Canada, the United States, and New Zealand.* Toronto: Oxford University Press.

———, and ———. 1999. *Unequal Relations: An Introduction to Race, Ethnic and Aboriginal Dynamics.* Scarborough: Prentice-Hall.

Fleras, Augie, and Jean Lock Kunz. 2001. *Media and Minorities: Representing Diversity in Multicultural Canada.* Toronto: Thompson Educational Publishing.

Fletcher, Connie. 1995. "On the Line: Women Cops Speak Out." *Chicago Tribune Magazine,* February 19, pp. 14–19.

Fick, Steven. 2001. In "Toronto: A Global Village," by Gwyn Dyer. *Canadian Geographic* (January/February):54.

Floyd, Richard, and Stephen Dooley. 1998. *The Target Inclusion Model: Including Members of the Subject Population on the Research Team.* Paper presented to the Canadian Learneds Society, Lenoxville.

Fong, Petti. 2001. "Brain Diseases 'Loom as Next Big Health Threat.'" *The Vancouver Sun,* March 20, p. A3.

Fornos, Werner. 1997. *1997 World Population Overview.* Washington, DC: The Population Institute.

Fortune. 2000. "The Fortune Global 200." 142(July 24):F1–F24.

Fox, Bonnie. 2001. "As Times Change: A Review of Trends in Personal and Family Life." Pp. 153–175 in *Family Patterns, Gender Relations,* 2d ed., edited by Bonnie J. Fox. Toronto: Oxford University Press.

Francis, David R. 1999. "Part-time Workers Face Full-time Problems." *Christian Science Monitor,* July 1, p. 11.

Franklin, John Hope, and Alfred A. Moss. 2000. *From Slavery to Freedom: A History of African Americans.* 8th ed. Upper Saddle River, NJ: Prentice-Hall.

Franklin, Stephen. 2000. "Hard Times at End?" *Chicago Tribune,* January 29, section 2, pp. 1–2.

Frazee, Valerie. 1997. "Establishing Relations in Germany." *Workforce* 76(No. 4):516.

Freeman, Jo. 1973. "The Origins of the Women's Liberation Movement." *American Journal of Sociology* 78 (January): 792–811.

———. 1975. *The Politics of Women's Liberation.* New York: McKay.

Freeman, Linton C. 1958. "Marriage without Love: Mate Selection in Non-Western Countries." Pp. 20–30 in *Mate Selection,* edited by Robert F. Winch. New York: Harper and Row.

Freeze, Colin. 2001. "Women Outwork Men By Two Weeks Every Year." *The Globe and Mail,* March 13, p. A1.

Freidson, Eliot. 1970. *Profession of Medicine.* New York: Dodd, Mead.

Freire, Paulo. 1970. *Pedagogy of the Oppressed.* New York: Herder and Herder.

French, Howard W. 2000. "Women Win a Battle, But Job Bias Still Rules Japan." *New York Times,* February 26, p. A3.

Freudenheim, Milt. 1990. "Employers Balk at High Cost of High-Tech Medical Care." *New York Times,* April 29, pp. 1, 16.

Fridlund, Alan. J., Paul Erkman, and Harriet Oster. 1987. "Facial Expressions of Emotion: Review of Literature 1970–1983." Pp. 143–224 in *Nonverbal Behavior and Communication,* 2d ed., edited by Aron W. Seigman and Stanley Feldstein. Hillsdale, NJ: Lawrence Erlbaum Associates.

Friedan, Betty. 1963. *The Feminine Mystique.* New York: Dell.

Friedland, Jonathon. 2000. "An American in Mexico Champions Midwifery as a Worthy Profession." *Wall Street Monitor,* February 15, pp. A1, A12.

Friedrichs, David O. 1998. "New Directions in Critical Criminology and White Collar Crime." Pp. 77–91 in *Cutting the Edge,* edited by Jeffrey Ross. Westport, CT: Praeger.

Fuller, Bruce, and Xiaoyan Liang. 1993. *The Unfair Search for Child Care.* Cambridge, MA: Preschool and Family Choice Project, Harvard University.

———, and Sharon Lynn Kagan. 2000. *Remember the Children: Mothers Balance Work and Child Care Under Welfare Reform.* Berkeley: Graduate School of Education, University of California.

Fullerton, Howard N., Jr., 1997. "Labor Force 2006: Slowing Down and Changing Composition." *Monthly Labor Review* (November):23–38.

———. 1999. "Labor Force Projections to 2008: Steady Growth and Changing Composition." *Monthly Labor Review* (November):19–32.

Furstenberg, Frank, and Andrew Cherlin. 1991. *Divided Families: What Happens to Children When Parents Part.* Cambridge, MA: Harvard University Press.

G

Gable, Donna. 1993a. "On TV, Lifestyles of the Slim and Entertaining." *USA Today,* July 27, p. 3D.

———. 1993b. "Series Shortchange Working-Class and Minority Americans." *USA Today,* August 30, p. 3D.

Gabor, Andrea. 1995. "Crashing the 'Old Boy' Party." *New York Times,* January 8, sec. 3, pp. 1, 6.

Galant, Debra. 2000. "Finding a Substitute for Office Chitchat." *New York Times,* February 16, sec. Retirement, p. 20.

Gale, Elaine. 1999. "A New Point of View." *Los Angeles Times,* January 11, pp. B1, B3.

Galt, Virginia. 1998. "Where the Boys Aren't: At the Top of the Class." *The Globe and Mail,* February 26, p. A6.

Gamson, Josh. 1989. "Silence, Death, and the Invisible Enemy: AIDS Activism and Social Movement 'Newness.' " *Social Problems* 36(October): 351–367.

Gans, Herbert J. 1991. *People, Plans, and Policies: Essays on Poverty, Racism, and Other National Urban Problems.* New York: Columbia University Press and Russell Sage Foundation.

———. 1995. *The War against the Poor: The Underclass and Antipoverty Policy.* New York: Basic Books.

Gardner, Carol Brooks. 1989. "Analyzing Gender in Public Places: Rethinking Goffman's Vision of Everyday Life." *American Sociologist* 20(Spring):42–56.

———. 1990. "Safe Conduct: Women, Crime, and Self in Public Places." *Social Problems* 37(August):311–328.

———. 1995. *Passing By: Gender and Public Harassment.* Berkeley: University of California Press.

Garfinkel, Harold. 1956. "Conditions of Successful Degradation Ceremonies." *American Journal of Sociology* 61(March):420–424.

Garner, Roberta. 1996. *Contemporary Movements and Ideologies.* New York: McGraw-Hill.

———. 1999. "Virtual Social Movements." Presented at Zaldfest: A conference in honor of Mayer Zald. September 17, Ann Arbor, MI.

Garreau, Joel. 1991. *Edge City: Life on the New Frontier.* New York: Doubleday.

Gartner, Rosemary, Myrna Dawson, and Maria Crawford. 2001. "Confronting Violence in Women's Lives." Pp.473–490 in *Family Patterns, Gender Relations,* edited by Bonnie J. Fox. Toronto: Oxford University Press.

Garza, Melita Marie. 1993. "The Cordi-Marian Annual Cotillion." *Chicago Tribune,* May 7, sec. C, pp. 1, 5.

Gaskell, Jane, Arlene McLaren, and Myra Novogrodsky. 1995. "What Is Worth Knowing?" Pp. 100–118 in *Gender in the 1990s: Images, Realities and Issues,* edited by Edna D. Nelson and Barry W. Robinson. Scarborough: Nelson Canada.

Gates, Henry Louis, Jr. 1991. "Delusions of Grandeur." *Sports Illustrated* 75(August 19):78.

———. 1999. "One Internet, Two Nations." *New York Times,* October 31, p. A15.

Gauette, Nicole. 1998. "Rules for Raising Japanese Kids." *Christian Science Monitor,* October 14, pp. B1, B6.

Gay Men's Health Crisis. 2000. "Facts and Statistics." Accessed February 1, 2000 (http://www.gmhc.org/basics/statmain.html).

Gearty, Robert. 1996. "Beware of Pickpockets." *Chicago Daily News,* November 19, p. 5.

Gecas, Viktor. 1982. "The Self-Concept." Pp. 1–33 in *Annual Review of Sociology, 1982,* edited by Ralph H. Turner and James F. Short, Jr. Palo Alto, CA: Annual Reviews.

———. 1992. "Socialization." Pp. 1863–1872 in *Encyclopedia of Sociology,* vol. 4, edited by Edgar F. Borgatta and Marie L. Borgatta. New York: Macmillan.

Geckler, Cheri. 1995. *Practice Perspectives and Medical Decision-Making in Medical Residents: Gender Differences—A Preliminary Report.* Wellesley, MA: Center for Research on Women.

Gee, Ellen M., Barbara A. Mitchell, and Andrew V. Wister. 1995. "Returning to the Parental 'Nest': Exploring a Changing Canadian Life Course." *Canadian Studies in Population* 22 (2):121–144.

Gelles, Richard J., and Claire Pedrick Cornell. 1990. *Intimate Violence in Families.* 2d ed. Newbury Park, CA: Sage.

Gelles, Richard J., and Murray A. Straus. 1998. *Intimate Violence: The Causes and Consequences of Abuse in the American Family.* New York: Simon and Schuster.

General Accounting Office. 2000. *Women's Health: NIH Has Increased Its Efforts to Include Women in Research.* Washington, DC: U.S. Government Printing Office.

Gerth, H. H., and C. Wright Mills. 1958. *From Max Weber: Essays in Sociology.* New York: Galaxy.

Geyh, Paul. 1998. "Feminism Fatale?" *Chicago Tribune,* July 26, sec. 13, pp. 1, 6.

Gidengil, Elisabeth, Andre Blais, Richard Nadeau, and Neil Nevitte. 2001. "Women to the Left? Gender Differences in Political Beliefs and Policy Differences." Unpublished paper. Accessed April 18, 2002 (http://www.fas.umontreal.ca/POL/Ces-eec/documents/GenderDifferences.pdf).

Gillespie, Mark. 1999. "Poll Releases, April 6, 1999: U.S. Gun Ownership Continues Broad Decline." Accessed July 2, 2000 (http://www.gallup.com/poll/releases/pr990406.asp).

Giordano, Peggy C., Stephen A. Cernkovich, and Alfred DeMaris.

1993. "The Family and Peer Relations of Black Adolescents." *Journal of Marriage and Family* 55(May):277–287.
Giroux, Henry A. 1988. *Schooling and the Struggle for Public Life: Critical Pedagogy in the Modern Age.* Minneapolis: University of Minnesota Press.
Given, Lisa. 2000. "The Promise of 'Life-long Learning' and the Canadian Census: The Marginalization of Mature Students' Information Behaviours." *Canadian Association for the Information Science 2000: Dimensions of A Global Information Science.* Accessed July 23, 2001 (http://slis.ualberta.ca/cais2000/given/htm).
Glauber, Bill. 1998. "Youth Binge Drinking Varies Around World." *St. Louis Post-Dispatch,* February 9, p. E4.
Global Reach. 2000. *Global Internet Statistics* (by language). September 30, 2000. Accessed November 7, 2000 (http://www.glreach.com/globstats/index.php3).
Goffman, Erving. 1959. *The Presentation of Self in Everyday Life.* New York: Doubleday.
———. 1961. *Asylums: Essays on the Social Situation of Mental Patients and Other Inmates.* Garden City, NY: Doubleday.
———. 1963a. *Stigma: Notes on Management of Spoiled Identity.* Englewood Cliffs, NJ: Prentice-Hall.
———. 1963b. *Behavior in Public Places.* New York: Free Press.
———. 1971. *Relations in Public.* New York: Basic Books.
———. 1979. *Gender Advertisements.* New York: Harper and Row.
Goldberg, Carey. 1998. "Little Drop in College Binge Drinking." *New York Times,* August 11, p. A14.
Golden, Frederic. 1999. "Who's Afraid of Frankenfood?" *Time,* November 29, pp. 49–50.
Goldman, Benjamin A., and Laura Fitton. 1994. *Toxic Wastes and Race Revisited: An Update of the 1987 Report on the Racial and Social Economic Characteristics of Communities with Hazardous Waste.* Washington, DC: Center for Policy Alternatives, United Church of Christ Commission for Racial Justice, and NAACP.
Goldman, Robert, and Stephen Papson. 1998. *Nike Culture: The Sign of the Swoosh.* London: Sage Publications.
Goldstein, Greg. 1998. "World Health Organization and Housing." Pp. 636–637 in *The Encyclopedia of Housing,* edited by Willem van Vliet. Thousand Oaks, CA: Sage Publications.
Goldstein, Melvyn C., and Cynthia M. Beall. 1981. "Modernization and Aging in the Third and Fourth World: Views from the Rural Hinterland in Nepal." *Human Organization* 40(Spring): 48–55.
Goleman, Daniel, 1991. "New Ways to Battle Bias: Fight Acts, Not Feelings." *New York Times,* July 16, pp. C1, C8.
Goliber, Thomas J. 1997. "Population and Reproductive Health in Sub-Saharan Africa." *Population Bulletin* 52(December).
Goode, Erica. 1999. "For Good Health, It Helps to Be Rich and Important." *New York Times,* June 1, pp. 1, 9.
Goode, William J. 1959. "The Theoretical Importance of Love." *American Sociological Review* 24(February):38–47.
Goodgame, Dan. 1993. "Welfare for the Well-Off." *Time* 141(February 22):36–38.
Gottdiener, Mark, and Joe R. Feagin. 1988. "The Paradigm Shift in Urban Sociology." *Urban Affairs Quarterly* 24(December):163–187.
———, and Ray Hutchison. 2000. *The New Urban Sociology*. 2d ed. New York: McGraw-Hill.
Gottfredson, Michael, and Travis Hirschi. 1990. *A General Theory of Crime.* Palo Alto, CA: Stanford University Press.
Gottschalk, Peter, Sara McLanahan, and Gary Sandefur. 1994. "The Dynamics and Intergenerational Transmission of Poverty and Welfare Participation." Pp. 85–108 in *Confronting Poverty: Prescriptions for Change,* edited by Sheldon H. Danziger, Gary D. Sandefur, and Daniel H. Weinburg. Cambridge, MA: Harvard University Press.
Gough, E. Kathleen. 1974. "Nayar: Central Kerala." Pp. 298–384 in *Matrilineal Kinship,* edited by David Schneider and E. Kathleen Gough. Berkeley: University of California Press.
Gouldner, Alvin. 1960. "The Norm of Reciprocity." *American Sociological Review* 25(April):161–177.
———. 1970. *The Coming Crisis of Western Sociology.* New York: Basic Books.
Gove, Walter R., ed. 1980. *The Labelling of Deviance.* 2d ed. Beverly Hills, CA: Sage.
———. 1987. "Sociobiology Misses the Mark: An Essay on Why Biology but Not Sociobiology Is Very Relevant to Sociology." *American Sociologist* 18(Fall):258–277.
Goyder, John. 1997. *Technology and Society: a Canadian perspective.* Peterborough: Broadview Press.
Gram, Karen. 2001. "Hard Times in the Good Ol' Days." *The Vancouver Sun,* May 5, p. A 21.
Gramsci, Antonio. 1929. "Selections from the Prison Notebooks." In Quintin Hoare and Geoffrey Nowell Smith, eds. London: Lawrence and Wishort.
Grant, Judith. 1993. *Fundamental Feminism: Contesting the Core Concepts of Feminist Theory.* New York and London: Routledge.
Graydon, Shari. 2001. "The Portrayal of Women in Media: The Good, the Bad, and the Beautiful." Pp. 179–195 in *Communications in Canadian Society,* 5th ed., edited by Craig McKie and Benjamin D. Singer. Toronto: Thompson Educational Publishing.
Greaves, Lorraine. (1996). *Smoke Screen: Women's Smoking and Social Control.* Halifax: Fernwood Publishing.
Greeley, Andrew M. 1989. "Protestant and Catholic: Is the Analogical Imagination Extinct?" *American Sociological Review* 54(August):485–502.
Green, Dan S., and Edwin D. Driver. 1978. "Introduction." Pp. 1–60 in *W. E. B. DuBois on Sociology and the Black Community,* edited by Dan S. Green and Edwin D. Driver. Chicago: University of Chicago Press.
Greenburg, Jan Crawford. 1999. "Sampling for Census Restricted." *Chicago Tribune,* January 26, pp. 1, 10.
Greene, Jay P. 1998. "A Meta-Analysis of the Effectiveness of Bilingual Education." Sponsored by the Toms River Policy Initiative. Accessed July 1, 1998 (http://data.Fas.harvard.edu/pepg/biling.htm).
Greenhouse, Linda. 1998a. "High Court Ruling Says Harassment Includes Same Sex." *New York Times,* March 5, pp. A1, A17.
———. 1998b. "Overturning of Late-Term Abortion Ban Is Let Stand." *New York Times,* March 24, p. A13.
Greenhouse, Steven. 1998. "Equal Work, Less-Equal Perks." *New York Times,* March 30, p. C1.
Grimsley, Kirstin Downey. 1997. "Big Boss May Be Watching—and Listening." *Washington Post National Weekly Edition,* June 2, p. 20.
Grossman, David C. et al. 1997. "Effectiveness of a Violence Prevention Curriculum among Children in Elementary School." *Journal of the American Medical Association* 277(May 28):1605–1617.
Groves, Martha. 1999. "New Adoptions Open Up the Family Circle." *Los Angeles Times,* August 8, p. A3.
Groza, Victor, Daniela F. Ileana, and Ivor Irwin. 1999. *A Peacock or a Crow: Stories, Interviews, and Commentaries on Romanian Adoptions.* Euclid, OH: Williams Custom Publishing.
Guppy, Neil, and Scott Davies. 1998. *Education in Canada: Recent Trends and Future Challenges.* Ottawa: Statistics Canada.
Guralnik, Jack M. et al. [5 authors]. 1993. "Educational Status and Active Life Expectancy among Older Blacks and Whites." *New England Journal of Medicine* 329(July 8):110–116.
Guterman, Lila. 2000. "Why the 25-Year-Old Battle over Sociology Is More than Just 'An Academic Sideshow.'" *Chronicle of Higher Education,* July 7, pp. A17–A18.
Gutiérrez, Gustavo. 1990. "Theology and the Social Sciences," in Paul E. Sigmund,

Liberation Theology at the Crossroads: Democracy or Revolution? New York: Oxford University Press, pp. 214–225.

Gwynne, S. C., and John F. Dickerson. 1997. "Lost in the E-Mail." *Time* 149(April 21):88–90.

Gzowski, Peter. 2001. "How to Quit Smoking in Fifty Years or Less." Pp. 63–64 in *Addicted: Notes from the Belly of the Beast*, edited by Lorna Crozier and Patrick Land. Vancouver: Greystone Books.

H

Haas, Michael, ed. 1999. *The Singapore Puzzle.* Westport, CT: Praeger.

Hacker, Andrew. 1964. "Power to Do What?" Pp. 134–146 in *The New Sociology,* edited by Irving Louis Horowitz. New York: Oxford University Press.

Hacker, Helen Mayer. 1951. "Women as a Minority Group." *Social Forces* 30(October):60–69.

———. 1974. "Women as a Minority Group, Twenty Years Later." Pp. 124–134 in *Who Discriminates against Women?,* edited by Florence Denmark. Beverly Hills, CA: Sage.

Hafner, Katie. 2000. "For the Well Connected, All the World's an Office." *New York Times,* March 30, pp. D1, D7.

Hahn, Harlan. 1993. "The Political Implications of Disability Definitions and Data." *Journal of Disability Policy Studies* 4(2):41–52.

Haig-Brown, Celia. 1988. *Resistance and Renewal: Surviving the Indian Residential School.* Vancouver: Arsenal Pulp Press.

Haines, Valerie A. 1988. "Is Spencer's Theory an Evolutionary Theory?" *American Journal of Sociology* 93(March):1200–1223.

Halal, William E. 1992. "The Information Technology Revolution." *Futurist* 26(July–August):10–15.

Halbfinger, David M. 1998. "As Surveillance Cameras Peer, Some Wonder if They Also Pry." *New York Times,* February 22, p. A1.

Hall, Kay. 1999. "Work From Here." *Computer User* 18(November):32.

Hall, Mimi. 1993. "Genetic-Sex-Testing a Medical Mine Field." *USA Today,* December 20, p. 6A.

Hall, Peter. 1977. *The World Cities.* London: Weidenfeld and Nicolson.

Hall, Robert H. 1982. "The Truth about Brown Lung." *Business and Society Review* 40(Winter 1981–82):15–20.

Hallinan, Maureen T. 1997. "The Sociological Study of Social Change." *American Sociological Review* 62(February):1–11.

Hani, Yoko. 1998. "Hot Pots Wired to Help the Elderly." *Japan Times Weekly International Edition,* April 13, p. 16.

Hansell, Saul. 1999. "Amazon's Risky Christmas." *New York Times,* November 3, sec. 3, pp. 1, 15.

Hara, Hiroko. 2000. "Homeless Desperately Want Shelter, Jobs." *Japan Times International* 40(January 16), p. 14.

Harap, Louis. 1982. "Marxism and Religion: Social Functions of Religious Belief." *Jewish Currents* 36(January): 12–17, 32–35.

Harlow, Harry F. 1971. *Learning to Love.* New York: Ballantine.

Harmon, Amy. 1998. "The Law Where There Is No Land." *New York Times,* March 16, pp. C1, C9.

Harrah's Entertainment. 1996. *Harrah Survey of Casino Entertainment.* Memphis, TN: Harrah's Entertainment.

Harrington, Michael. 1980. "The New Class and the Left." Pp. 123–138 in *The New Class,* edited by B. Bruce-Briggs. Brunswick, NJ: Transaction.

Harris, Chauncy D., and Edward Ullman. 1945. "The Nature of Cities." *Annals of the American Academy of Political and Social Science* 242(November):7–17.

Harris, David. 1999. *Driving While Black: Racial Profiling on Our Nation's Highways.* New York: American Civil Liberties Union.

Harris, Judith Rich. 1998. *The Nurture Assumption: Why Children Turn Out the Way They Do.* New York: Free Press.

Harris, Marvin. 1997. *Culture, People, Nature: An Introduction to General Anthropology.* 7th ed. New York: Longman.

Hart, Stacey. 1995. *(Re)searching Lesbian Health Care: Methodological Considerations for Future Directions.* Accessed April 18, 2002 (http://www.usc.edu/isd/archives/queerfrontiers/queer/papers/hart.html).

Hartjen, Clayton A. 1978. *Crime and Criminalization.* 2d ed. New York: Praeger.

Haub, Carl, and Deana Cornelius. 1999. *1999 World Population Data Sheet.* Washington, DC: Population Reference Bureau.

———, and ———. 2000. *2000 World Population Data Sheet.* Washington, DC: Population Reference Bureau.

Haviland, William A. 1999. *Cultural Anthropology (Case Studies in Cultural Anthropology).* 9th ed. Ft. Worth: Harcourt Brace.

Hayward, Mark D., William R. Grady, and Steven D. McLaughlin. 1987. "Changes in the Retirement Process." *Demography* 25(August):371–386.

Health Canada. 2000. "The Changing Face of Heart Disease and Stroke in Canada 2000." Accessed January 30, 2002 (http://www.hc-sc.gc.ca/hpb/lcdc/bcrdd/hdsc2000/index.html/).

———. 2001. *Canada Health Act Annual Report 1999–2000.* Ottawa: Queen's Printers.

———. 2002. "Women's Health Strategy." Ottawa: Health Canada, Women's Health Bureau. Accessed April 4, 2002 (http://www.hc-sc.gc.ca/english/women/womenstrat.htm).

Health Care Financing Administration. 2000. *National Health Expenditures Projections: 1998–2008.* Accessed October 1, 2000. (http://www.hcfa.gov/stats/NHE-Proj/proj1998/default.htm).

Heckert, Druann, and Amy Best. 1997. "Ugly Duckling to Swan: Labeling Theory and the Stigmatization of Red Hair." *Symbolic Interaction* 20(No. 4):365–384.

Hedley, R. Alan. 1992. "Industrialization in Less Developed Countries." Pp. 914–920 in *Encyclopedia of Sociology,* vol. 2, edited by Edgar F. Borgatta and Marie L. Borgatta. New York: Macmillan.

Heikes, E. Joel. 1991. "When Men Are the Minority: The Case of Men in Nursing." *Sociological Quarterly* 32(3):389–401.

Heise, Lori, M. Ellseberg, and M. Gottemuelle. 1999. "Ending Violence Against Women." *Population Reports,* ser. L, no. 11. Baltimore: Johns Hopkins University School of Public Health.

Henley, Nancy, Mykol Hamilton, and Barrie Thorne. 1985. "Womanspeak and Manspeak: Sex Differences and Sexism in Communication, Verbal and Nonverbal." Pp. 168–185 in *Beyond Sex Roles,* 2d ed., edited by Alice G. Sargent. St. Paul, MN: West.

Henly, Julia R. 1999. "Challenges to Finding and Keeping Jobs in the Low-Skilled Labor Market." *Poverty Research News* 3(No. 1):3–5.

Henneberger, Melinda. 1995. "Muslims Continue to Feel Apprehensive." *New York Times,* April 14, p. B10.

Hennessy, Rosemary. 1993. *Maternalist Feminism and the Politics of Discourse.* New York: Routledge.

Henry, Francis, C. Tator, W. Mattis, and T. Reese. 1995. *The Colour of Democracy: Racism in Canadian Society.* Toronto: Harcourt Brace.

Henry, Mary E. 1989. "The Function of Schooling: Perspectives from Rural Australia." *Discourse* 9(April):1–21.

Herrmann, Andrew. 1994. "Survey Shows Increase in Hispanic Catholics." *Chicago Sun-Times,* March 10, p. 4.

Hersch, Patricia. 1998. *A Tribe Apart: A Journey into the Heart of the American Adolescence.* New York: Fawcett Books.

Herskovits, Melville J. 1930. *The Anthropometry of the American Negro.* New York: Columbia University Press.

———. 1941. *The Myth of the Negro Past.* New York: Harper.

———. 1943. "The Negro in Bahia, Brazil: A Problem in Method." *American Sociological Review* 8(August):394–402.

Hess, John L. 1990. "Confessions of a Greedy Geezer." *The Nation* 250(April 2):451–455.

Hewlett, Sylvia Ann, and Cornel West. 1998. *The War Against Parents*. Boston: Houghton Mifflin.
Hillery, George A. 1955. "Definitions of Community: Areas of Agreement." *Rural Sociology* (2):111–123.
Hirschi, Travis. 1969. *Causes of Delinquency*. Berkeley: University of California Press.
Hochschild, Arlie Russell. 1973. "A Review of Sex Role Research." *American Journal of Sociology* 78(January):1011–1029.
———. 1990. "The Second Shift: Employed Women Are Putting in Another Day of Work at Home." *Utne Reader* 38(March–April):66–73.
———, with Anne Machung. 1989. *The Second Shift: Working Parents and the Revolution at Home*. New York: Viking Penguin.
Hodge, Robert W., and Peter H. Rossi. 1964. "Occupational Prestige in the United States, 1925–1963." *American Journal of Sociology* 70(November):286–302.
Hoebel, E. Adamson. 1949. *Man in the Primitive World: An Introduction to Anthropology*. New York: McGraw-Hill.
Hoffman, Adonis. 1997. "Through an Accurate Prism." *Los Angeles Times*, August 8, p. M1.
Hoffman, Donald L., and Thomas P. Novak. 1998. "Bridging the Racial Divide on the Internet." *Science* 200(April 17):390–391.
Hoffman, Lois Wladis. 1985. "The Changing Genetics/Socialization Balance." *Journal of Social Issues* 41(Spring):127–148.
Hofstede, Geert. 1997. *Cultures and Organizations: Software of the Mind*. Rev. ed. New York: McGraw-Hill.
Holden, Constance. 1980. "Identical Twins Reared Apart." *Science* 207(March 21):1323–1328.
———. 1987. "The Genetics of Personality." *Science* 257(August 7):598–601.
Hollingshead, August B. 1975. *Elmtown's Youth and Elmtown Revisited*. New York: Wiley.
Holmes, Steven A. 1997. "Leaving the Suburbs for Rural Areas." *New York Times*, October 19, p. 34.
Holmes, Tracy. 2000. "Performance Anxiety." *Peace Arch News*, February 2, p. 11.
Homans, George C. 1979. "Nature versus Nurture: A False Dichotomy." *Contemporary Sociology* 8(May):345–348.
Homer-Dixon, Thomas. 2000. *The Ingenuity Gap: Can We Solve the Problems of the Future?* Toronto: Vintage Canada.
Hondagneu-Sotelo, Pierrette. 1994. "Regulating the Unregulated? Domestic Workers' Social Networks." *Social Problems* 41(February):50–64.
Horgan, John. 1993. "Eugenics Revisited." *Scientific American* 268(June): 122–128, 130–133.
Horn, Jack C., and Jeff Meer. 1987. "The Vintage Years." *Psychology Today* 21(May):76–77, 80–84, 88–90.
Horovitz, Bruce. 1995. "Marketers Tap Data We Once Called Our Own." *USA Today*, December 19, pp. A1, A2.
Horowitz, Helen Lefkowitz. 1987. *Campus Life*. Chicago: University of Chicago Press.
Horowitz, Irving Louis. 1983. *C. Wright Mills: An American Utopia*. New York: Free Press.
Horwitt, Sanford D. 1989. *Let Them Call Me Rebel: Saul Alinsky—His Life and Legacy*. New York: Knopf.
Hosokawa, William K. 1969. *Nisei: The Quiet Americans*. New York: Morrow.
Housing and Urban Development. 1999. *Stuart B. McKinney Homeless Programs*. Washington, DC: U.S. Government Printing Office.
Hout, Michael. 1988. "More Universalism, Less Structural Mobility: The American Occupational Structure in the 1980s." *American Journal of Sociology* 91(May):1358–1400.
Howard, Judith A. 1999. "Border Crossings between Women's Studies and Sociology." *Contemporary Sociology* 28(September):525–528.
Howard, Michael C. 1989. *Contemporary Cultural Anthropology*. 3d ed. Glenview, IL: Scott, Foresman.
Howell, Nancy, Patricia Albanese, and Kwaku Obusu-Mensah. 2001. "Ethnic Families." Pp. 116–142 in *Families: Changing Trends in Canada*, 4th ed., edited by Maureen Baker. Toronto: McGraw-Hill Ryerson.
Huang, Gary. 1988. "Daily Addressing Ritual: A Cross-Cultural Study." Presented at the annual meeting of the American Sociological Association, Atlanta.
Huber, Bettina J. 1985. *Employment Patterns in Sociology: Recent Trends and Future Prospects*. Washington, DC: American Sociological Association.
Huddy, Leonie, Joshua Billig, John Bracciodieta, Lois Hoeffler, Patrick J. Moynihan, and Patricia Pugliani. 1997. "The Effect of Interviewer Gender on the Survey Response." *Political Behavior* 19(September):197–220.
Huffstutter, P. J., Tini Tran, and David Reyes. 1999. "Pirates of the High-Tech Age." *Los Angeles Times*, July 25, pp. A1, A28–A29.
Hughes, Everett. 1945. "Dilemmas and Contradictions of Status." *American Journal of Sociology* 50 (March):353–359.
Human Resources Development Canada. 2000. *Job Futures 2000*. Accessed May 3, 2002 (http://www.jobfutures.ca/job futures/fos/U880.html#Occupations).
Human Rights Campaign. 2000. "Hate Crime Laws that Include 'Sexual Orientation.'" Accessed August 6, 2000 (http://www.hrc.org/mindset_ issues.asp).
Hunt, Geoffrey et al. 1993. "Changes in Prison Culture: Prison Gangs and the Case of the 'Pepsi Generation.'" *Social Problems* 40(August):398–409.
Hunter, Herbert, ed. 2000. *The Sociology of Oliver C. Cox: New Perspectives: Research in Race and Ethnic Relations*, vol. II. Stanford, CT: JAI Press.
Hunter, James Davison. 1991. *Culture Wars: The Struggle to Define America*. New York: Basic Books.
Hurh, Won Moo. 1994. *Korean Immigrants in America: A Structural Analysis of Ethnic Confinement and Adhesive Adaptation*. Rutherford, NJ: Fairleigh Dickinson University Press.
———. 1998. *The Korean Americans*. Westport, CT: Greenwood Press.
Hurn, Christopher J. 1985. *The Limits and Possibilities of Schooling*. 2d ed. Boston: Allyn and Bacon.
———, and Kwang Chung Kim. 1998. "The 'Success' Image of Asian Americans: Its Validity, and Its Practical and Theoretical Implications." *Ethnic and Racial Studies* 12(October):512–538.
Hurst, Erik, Ming Ching Luoh, and Frank P. Stafford. 1996. "Wealth Dynamics of American Families, 1984–1994." Institute for Social Research, University of Michigan, Ann Arbor, MI. Unpublished paper.
Hutcheon, Pat Duffy. 1999. *Building Character and Culture*. Westport, CT: Praeger.

I

Ibarra, Herminia. 1995. "Race, Opportunity, and Diversity of Social Circles in Managerial Networks." *Academy of Management Journal* 38(3):673–703.
Ignatieff, Michael. 2000. *The Rights Revolution*. Toronto: House of Anansi Press.
Illinois Coalition Against the Death Penalty. 2000. "Basic Facts on the Death Penalty in Illinois." Accessed February 17, 2000 (http://www. keynet/nicadp/).
Immigration and Naturalization Service. 1999a. *Legal Immigration, Fiscal Year 1998*. Washington, DC: U.S. Government Printing Office.
——— 1999b. *1997 Statistical Yearbook of the Immigration and Naturalization Service*. Washington, DC: U.S. Government Printing Office.
Inglehart, Ronald, and Wayne E. Baker. 2000. "Modernization, Cultural Change, and the Persistence of Traditional Values." *American Sociological Review* 65(February):19–51.
Institute for Social Research. 1994. *World Values Survey, 1990-1993*. Ann Arbor: The Regents of the University of Michigan.
Institute of International Education. 1998. "Foreign Students in U.S. Institutions 1997–98." *Chronicle of Higher Education* 45(December 11):A67.

Instituto del Tercer Mundo. 1999. *The World Guide 1999/2000.* Oxford, England: New International Publications.

Inter-Parliamentary Union. 1999. "Women in National Parliaments. Situation as of 30 September 1999." Accessed October 3, 1999 (http://www.ipu.org/wmn-e/classif.htm). Geneva, Switzerland: Inter-Parliamentary Union.

———. 2000. "Women in Parliaments: Situations as of 15 September 2000." Accessed August 27, 2000 (http://www.ipu.org/wmn-e/classif.htm).

International Monetary Fund. 2000. *World Economic Outlook: Asset Prices and the Business Cycle.* Washington, DC: International Monetary Fund.

Irwin, Katherine. 1998. "Getting a Tattoo: Self Transformation and Defining Deviance Down." Presented at the annual meeting of the American Sociological Association, San Francisco.

———. 1999a. "Getting a First Tattoo: Techniques of Legitimation and Social Change." University of Colorado, Boulder, CO. Unpublished paper.

———. 1999b. "Body Deviant's Subculture." University of Colorado, Boulder, CO. Unpublished paper.

———. 2000. "Becoming a Body Deviant: The Process of Collecting Tattoos." Presented at the annual meeting of the American Sociological Association, Washington.

J

Jackson, Andrew. 2001. *Low Income Trends in the 1990s.* Paper presented at the Saskatoon Public Library, January 18.

Jackson, Andrew, and Sylvain Schetagne. 2001. *Still Struggling: An Update on Teenagers at Work.* Ottawa: Canadian Council on Social Development.

Jackson, Elton F., Charles R. Tittle, and Mary Jean Burke. 1986. "Offense-Specific Models of the Differential Association Process." *Social Problems* 33(April):335–356.

Jackson, Philip W. 1968. *Life in Classrooms.* New York: Holt.

Jacobson, Jodi. 1993. "Closing the Gender Gap in Development." Pp. 61–79 in *State of the World,* edited by Lester R. Brown. New York: Norton.

Jagger, Alison M., and Paula S. Rothenberg. 1984. *Feminist Frameworks.* 2d ed. New York: McGraw-Hill.

Janofsky, Michael. 1999. "New Mexico Bans Creationism from State Curriculum." *New York Times,* October 9, p. A7.

Japan Times Staff. 1999. "80% Back Capital Punishment." *Japan Times International Edition* 14(December 7):8.

Jasper, James M. 1997. *The Art of Moral Protest: Culture, Biography, and Creativity in Social Movements.* Chicago: University of Chicago Press.

Jehl, Douglas. 1999. "The Internet's 'Open Sesame' Is Answered Warily." *New York Times,* March 18, p. A4.

Jencks, Christopher. 1994. *The Homeless.* Cambridge, MA: Harvard University Press.

Jenkins, Richard. 1991. "Disability and Social Stratification." *British Journal of Sociology* 42(December):557–580.

Jennings, M. Kent, and Richard G. Niemi. 1981. *Generations and Politics.* Princeton, NJ: Princeton University Press.

Jobtrak.com. 2000a. "Jobtrak.com's Poll Finds that Students and Recent Grads Only Plan to Stay with Their First Employer No Longer than Three Years." Press release January 6. Accessed June 29, 2000 (http://static.jobtrak.com/mediacenter/press_polls/poll_010600.html).

———. 2000b. "79% of College Students Find the Quality of an Employer's Website Important in Deciding Whether or Not to Apply for a Job." Accessed on June 29, 2000 (http://static.jobtrak.com/mediacenter/press_polls/polls_061200.html).

Johnson, Anne M., Jane Wadsworth, Kaye Wellings, and Julie Field. 1994. *Sexual Attitudes and Lifestyles.* Oxford: Blackwell Scientific.

Johnson, Benton. 1975. *Functionalism in Modern Sociology: Understanding Talcott Parsons.* Morristown, NJ: General Learning.

Johnson, Dirk. 1993. "More and More, the Single Parent Is Dad." *New York Times,* August 31, pp. A1, A15.

———. 1996b. "Rural Life Gains New Appeal, Turning Back a Long Decline." *New York Times,* September 23, pp. A1, B6.

Johnson, George. 1999. "It's a Fact: Faith and Theory Collide Over Evolution." *New York Times,* August 15, sec. 4, pp. 1, 12.

Johnson, Harry M. 1960. *Sociology: A Systematic Introduction.* New York: Harcourt, Brace and World.

Johnson, Holly. 1996. *Dangerous Domains: Violence Against Women in Canada.* Scarborough: Nelson Canada.

Johnson, Patrick. 1983. *Native Children and the Child Welfare System.* Toronto: Canadian Council on Social Development in association with James Lorimer Publishing.

Johnston, David Cay. 1996. "The Divine Write-Off." *New York Times,* January 12, pp. D1, D6.

Jolin, Annette. 1994. "On the Backs of Working Prostitutes: Feminist Theory and Prostitution Policy." *Crime and Delinquency* 40(No. 2):69–83.

Jones, Arthur F., Jr., and Daniel H. Weinberg. 2000. "The Changing Shape of the Nation's Income Distribution." *Current Population Reports,* ser. P60, no. 204. Washington, DC: US Government Printing Office.

Jones, Charisse. 1999. "Minority Farmers Say They've Been Cheated." *USA Today,* January 5, p. 9A.

Jones, Charles, Lorna Marsden, and Lorne Tepperman. 1990. *Lives of Their Own.* Toronto: Oxford University Press.

Jones, James T., IV. 1988. "Harassment Is Too Often Part of the Job." *USA Today,* August 8, p. 5D.

Jones, Stephen R. G. 1992. "Was There a Hawthorne Effect?" *American Journal of Sociology* 98(November):451–568.

Jordan, Mary. 1996. "Out of the Kitchen, Onto the Ballot." *Washington Post National Weekly Edition,* October 21, P. 16.

Juhasz, Anne McCreary. 1989. "Black Adolescents' Significant Others." *Social Behavior and Personality* 17(2):211–214.

Juteau, Danielle. 2000. "Patterns of Social Differentiation in Canada." *Canadian Public Policy,* vol. XXVI Special Supplement, 2.

K

Kaiser Family Foundation. 2000. *The State of the HIV/AIDS Epidemic in America.* Menlo Park, CA: Kaiser Family Foundation.

Kalb, Claudia. 1999. "Our Quest to Be Perfect." *Newsweek* 134(August 9): 52–59.

Kanagae, Haruhiko. 1993. "Sexual Harassment in Japan: Findings from Survey Research." Presented at the annual meeting of the Pacific Sociological Association, Portland, OR.

Kanellos, Nicholás. 1994. *The Hispanic Almanac: From Columbus to Corporate America.* Detroit: Visible Ink Press.

Kang, Mee-Eun. 1997. "The Portrayal of Women's Images in Magazine Advertisements: Goffman's Gender Analysis Revisited." In *Sex Roles* 37(December): 979–996.

Kantrowitz, Barbara, and Pat Wingert. 1999. "Beyond Littleton: How Well Do You Know Your Kids?" *Newsweek,* May 10, pp. 36–40.

Katovich, Michael A. 1987. Correspondence. June 1.

Katz, Michael. 1971. *Class, Bureaucracy, and the Schools: The Illusion of Educational Change in America.* New York: Praeger.

Keating, Noah and Brenda Munro. 1988. "Farm Women/Farm Work." *Sex Roles* 19(August):155–168.

Kelley, Robin D. G. 1996. "Freedom Riders (the Sequel)." *The Nation* 262(February 5):18–21.

Kelly, John. 1995. "We are all in the Ojibway Circle." In *Ink Lake,* edited by Michael Ondaatje. Toronto: Vintage Canada.

Kelly, Katy, and Doug Levy. 1995. "HMOs Dogged by Issue of Cost vs. Care." *USA Today,* October 17, pp. D1, D2.

Kelsoe, John R. et al. [12 authors]. 1989. "Re-evaluation of the Linkage Relationship between Chromosome LTP Loci and the Gene for Bipolar Affective Disorder in the Old Order Amish." *Nature* 342(November 16): 238–243.

Kemper, Vicki, and Viveca Novak. 1991. "Health Care Reform: Don't Hold Your Breath." *Washington Post National Weekly Edition* 8(October 28):28.

Kennedy, Bruce P., Ichiro Kawachi, and Deborah Prothrow-Stith. 1996. "Income Distribution and Mortality: Cross Sectional Ecological Study of the Robin Hood Index in the United States." *British Medical Journal* 312(April 20):1004–1007.

Kennickell, Arthur B., Martha Starr-McCluer, and Brian J. Surette. 2000. "Recent Changes in U.S. Family Finances: Results from the 1998 Survey of Consumer Finances." *Federal Reserve Bulletin* (January):1–29.

Kent, Mary Mederios. 1999. "Shrinking Societies Favor Procreation." *Population Today* 27(December):4–5.

Kephart, William M., and William M. Zellner. 1998. *Extraordinary Groups: An Examination of Unconventional Life-Styles.* 6th ed. New York: St. Martin's.

Kerbo, Harold R. 1996. *Social Stratification and Inequality: Class Conflict in Historical and Comparative Perspective.* 3d ed. New York: McGraw-Hill.

———. 2000. *Social Stratification and Inequality: Class Conflict in Historical, Comparative, and Global Perspective.* New York: McGraw-Hill.

Kerr, Clark. 1960. *Industrialization and Industrial Man: The Problems of Labor and Management in Economic Growth.* Cambridge, MA: Harvard University Press.

Kilborn, Peter T. 1999. "Gimme Shelter: Same Song, New Time." *New York Times,* December 5, p. 5.

———. 2000. "Learning at Home, Students Take the Lead." *New York Times,* May 24, pp. A1, A17.

Kim, Kwang Chung. 1999. *Koreans in the Hood: Conflict with African Americans.* Baltimore: Johns Hopkins University Press.

King, Anthony. 1998. "London Mayor Is Casualty of Voters' Apathy." *The Daily Telegraph* (London), May 19, p. 12.

King, Leslie. 1998. "'France Needs Children': Pronatalism, Nationalism, and Women's Equity." *Sociological Quarterly* 39(Winter):33–52.

———, and Madonna Harrington Meyer. 1997. "The Politics of Reproductive Benefits: U.S. Insurance Coverage of Contraceptive and Infertility Treatments." *Gender and Society* 11(February):8–30.

Kinsella, Warren. 1994. *Web of Hate: Inside Canada's Far Right Network.* Toronto: Harper Collins.

Kinsey, Alfred C., Wardell B. Pomeroy, and Clyde E. Martin. 1948. *Sexual Behavior in the Human Male.* Philadelphia: Saunders.

———, ———, and Paul H. Gebhard. 1953. *Sexual Behavior in the Human Female.* Philadelphia: Saunders.

Kinzer, Stephen. 1993. "German Court Restricts Abortion, Angering Feminists and the East." *New York Times,* May 29, pp. 1, 3.

Kirk, Margaret O. 1995. "The Temps in the Gray Flannel Suits." *New York Times,* December 17, p. F13.

Kitchener, Richard F. 1991. "Jean Piaget: The Unknown Sociologist." *British Journal of Sociology* 42(September): 421–442.

Kleinknecht, William. 1996. *The New Ethnic Mobs: The Changing Face of Organized Crime in America.* New York: Free Press.

Kohn, Alfie. 1988. "Girltalk, Guytalk." *Psychology Today* 22(February):65–66.

Kohn, Melvin L. 1970. "The Effects of Social Class on Parental Values and Practices." Pp. 45–68 in *The American Family: Dying or Developing,* edited by David Reiss and H. A. Hoffman. New York: Plenum.

Kohn, Melvin L., Kazimierz M. Slomeznsky, and Carrie Schoenbach. 1986. "Social Stratification and the Transmission of Values in the Family: A Cross-National Assessment." *Sociological Forum* 1, 1:73–102.

Kolata, Gina. 1998. "Infertile Foreigners See Opportunity in U.S." *New York Times,* January 4, pp. 1, 12.

———. 2000. *Clone. The Road to Dolly, and the Path Ahead.* New York: William Morrow.

———. 2000b. "Web Research Transforms Visit to the Doctor." *New York Times.* (March 6): A1, A18.

Komarovsky, Mirra. 1991. "Some Reflections on the Feminist Scholarship in Sociology." Pp. 1–25 in *Annual Review of Sociology, 1991,* edited by W. Richard Scott and Judith Blake. Palo Alto, CA: Annual Reviews.

Kortenhaus, Carole M., and Jack Demarest. 1993. "Gender Role Stereotyping in Children's Literature: An Update." *Sex Roles* 28(3–4):219–232.

Kourvetaris, George. 1999. "The Greek-American Family: A Generational Approach." Pp. 68–101 in *Ethnic Families in America: Patterns and Variations,* 4th ed., edited by Charles H. Mindel, Robert W. Habenstein, and Roosevelt Wright, Jr. Upper Saddle River, NJ: Prentice-Hall.

Kovaleski, Serge F. 1999. "Choosing Alternative Medicine by Necessity." *Washington Post National Weekly Edition* 16(April 5):16.

Krach, Constance A., and Victoria A. Velkoff. 1999. "Centenarians in the United States 1990." *Current Population Reports,* ser. P-23, no. 199RV. Washington, DC: U.S. Government Printing Office.

Krahn, Harvey J., and Graham S. Lowe. "Women's Employment." *Work, Industry and Canadian Society.* 3d ed. Toronto: ITP Nelson.

Kraut, Robert et al. 1998. "Internet Paradox: A Social Technology That Reduces Social Involvement and Psychological Well-Being." *American Psychologist* 55(September):1017–1031.

Krieger, Nancy, and Elizabeth Fee. 1994. "Man-made Medicine and Women's Health." Pp. 11–29 in *Women's Health Politics and Power: Essays on Sex/Gender, Medicine and Public Health,* edited by Elizabeth Fee and Nancy Krieger. Amityville, NY: Baywood Publications.

Kristof, Nicholas D. 1995. "Japan's Invisible Minority: Better Off Than in Past, but Still Outcasts," *New York Times,* November 30, p. A18.

———. 1998. "As Asian Economies Shrink, Women Are Squeezed Out." *New York Times,* June 11, pp. A1, A12.

Kunkel, Dale et al. 1999. *Sex on TV: A Biennial Report to Kaiser Family Foundation.* Santa Barbara, CA: University of California, Santa Barbara.

Kuptsch, Christine, and David M. Mazie. 1999. "Social Protection." Pp. 316–318 in *Enyclopedia Britannica Yearbook 1999.* Chicago: Encyclopedia Britannica.

Kwong, Peter, and JoAnn Lum. 1988. "Chinese-American Politics: A Silent Minority Tests Its Clout." *The Nation* 246(January 16):49–50, 52.

Kyodo News International. 1998a. "More Japanese Believe Divorce Is Acceptable." *Japan Times* 38(January 12), p. B4.

L

Labaree, David F. 1986. "Curriculum, Credentials, and the Middle Class: A Case Study of a Nineteenth Century High School." *Sociology of Education* 59(January):42–57.

Ladner, Joyce. 1973. *The Death of White Sociology.* New York: Random Books.

La Ganga, Maria L. 2000. "The Age of the Aging Electorate." *Los Angeles Times,* January 13, pp. A1, A17.

Lakoff, Robin Tolmach. 2000. *The Language War.* Berkeley: University of California Press.

Lakshimi, Rama. 2001. "Gender Prejudice in India Still Against Daughters." *The Globe and Mail,* April 4, p. A10.

Lampkin, Lorna. 1985 *Visible Minorities in Canada.* Research paper for the Abella Royal Commission on Equality in Employment. Ottawa: Ministry of Supply and Services.

Landers, Robert K. 1988. "Why America Doesn't Vote." *Editorial Research Reports (Congressional Quarterly)* 8 pt. 1, pp. 82–95.

Landtman, Gunnar. 1968. *The Origin of Inequality of the Social Class.* New York: Greenwood (original edition 1938, Chicago: University of Chicago Press).

Lang, Eric. 1992. "Hawthorne Effect." Pp. 793–794 in *Encyclopedia of Sociology,* vol. 2, edited by Edgar F. Borgatta and Marie L. Borgatta. New York: Macmillan.

Langman, L. 1987. "Social Stratification." Pp. 211–249 in *Handbook of Marriage and the Family,* edited by Marvin B. Sussman and Suzanne K. Steinmetz. New York: Plenum.

Lappé, Anthony. 1999 "There Is No Average Day When You Live in a Tree." *New York Times Magazine,* December 12, p. 29.

Lappin, Todd. 1996. "Aux Armes, Netizens!" *The Nation* 262(February 26):6–7.

Larson, Jan. 1996. "Temps Are Here to Stay." *American Demographics* 18(February):26–31.

Lasch, Christopher. 1977. *Haven in a Heartless World: The Family Besieged.* New York: Basic Books.

Lassey, Marie L., William R. Lassey, and Martin J. Jinks. 1997. *Health Care Systems around the World: Characteristics, Issues, Reforms.* Upper Saddle River, NJ: Prentice-Hall.

Lasswell, Harold D. 1936. *Politics: Who Gets What, When, How.* New York: McGraw-Hill.

L.A. Times Poll. 2000. "Abortion Poll." *Los Angeles Times,* June 18, p. A14.

Lauer, Robert H. 1982. *Perspectives on Social Change.* 3d ed. Boston: Allyn and Bacon.

Laumann, Edward O., John H. Gagnon, and Robert T. Michael. 1994a. "A Political History of the National Sex Survey of Adults." *Family Planning Perspectives* 26(February):34–38.

———, ———, ———, and Stuart Michaels. 1994b. *The Social Organization of Sexuality: Sexual Practices in the United States.* Chicago: University of Chicago Press.

Leacock, Eleanor. 2001. "Women in an Egalitarian Society: The Montagnais-Naskapi of Canada." Pp. 55–66 in *Family Patterns, Gender Relations,* 2d ed., edited by Bonnie J. Fox. Toronto: Oxford University Press.

Leacock, Eleanor Burke. 1969. *Teaching and Learning in City Schools.* New York: Basic Books.

Leavell, Hugh R., and E. Gurney Clark. 1965. *Preventive Medicine for the Doctor in His Community: An Epidemiologic Approach.* 3d ed. New York: McGraw-Hill.

Le Bourdais, Celine, and Nicole Marcil-Gratton. 1994. "Quebec's Pro-Active Approach to Family Policy: 'Thinking and Acting Family.'" *Canada's Changing Families: Challenges to Public Policy,* edited by Maureen Baker. Ottawa: Vanier Institute of the Family.

Lee, Barrett A. 1992. "Homelessness." Pp. 843–847 in *Encyclopedia of Sociology,* vol. 2, edited by Edgar F. Borgatta and Marie L. Borgatta. New York: Macmillan.

Lee, Heon Cheol. 1999. "Conflict Between Korean Merchants and Black Customers: A Structural Analysis." Pp. 113–130 in *Koreans in the Hood: Conflict with African Americans,* edited by Kwang Chung Kim. Baltimore: Johns Hopkins University Press.

Lee, Kevin. 1999. "Measuring Poverty among Canada's Aboriginal People." *Perception* 23(2):9–12. Accessed April 18, 2002 (http://www.ccsd.ca/perception/e0999.pdf).

Lehne, Gregory K. 1995. "Homophobia among Men: Supporting and Defining the Male Role." Pp. 325–336 in *Men's Lives,* edited by Michael S. Kimmel and Michael S. Messner. Boston: Allyn and Bacon.

Leinward, Donna. 2000. "20% Say They Used Drugs with Their Mom and Dad." *USA Today,* August 24, pp. 1A, 2A.

Lemann, Nicholas. 1991. "The Other Underclass." *Atlantic Monthly* 268(December):96–102, 104, 107–108, 110.

Lem, Sharon. 2000. "Life Expectancy Gender Gap Narrowing." *The Toronto Sun,* June 7. Accessed July 30, 2001 (http://www.canoe.ca/Health0003-6/07_men.html).

Lengermann, Patricia Madoo, and Jill Niebrugge-Brantley. 1996. "Contemporary Feminist Theory." Pp. 436–486 in *Sociological Theory,* 4th ed., edited by George Ritzer. New York: McGraw-Hill.

———, and ———. 1998. *The Women Founders: Sociology and Social Theory, 1830–1930.* Boston: McGraw-Hill.

Lenski, Gerhard. 1966. *Power and Privilege: A Theory of Social Stratification.* New York: McGraw-Hill.

———, Jean Lenski, and Patrick Nolan. 1995. *Human Societies: An Introduction to Macrosociology.* 7th ed. New York: McGraw-Hill.

Leo, John. 1987. "Exploring the Traits of Twins." *Time* 129(January 12):63.

Leon, Sy. 1996. *None of the Above: Why Non-Voters Are America's Political Majority.* San Francisco: Fox and Wilkes.

Levin, Jack, and William C. Levin. 1980. *Ageism.* Belmont, CA: Wadsworth.

Levinson, Arlene. 1984. "Laws for Live-In Lovers." *Ms.* 12(June):101.

Levy, R., and J. Hawks. 1996. "Multicultural Medicine and Pharmacy Management: Part One: New Opportunities for Managed Care." *Drug Benefit Trends* 7(3):27–30.

Lewin, Tamar. 1992. "Hurdles Increase for Many Women Seeking Abortions." *New York Times,* March 15, pp. 1, 18.

———. 1997. "Abortion Rate Declined Again in '95, U.S. Says, but Began Rising Last Year." *New York Times,* December 5, p. A10.

———. 1998. "Report Finds Girls Lagging Behind Boys in Technology." *New York Times,* October 14, p. B8.

———. 1998a. "Debate Centers on Definition of Harassment." *New York Times,* March 22, pp. A1, A20.

———. 2000. "Differences Found in Care with Stepmothers." *New York Times,* August 17, p. A16.

Lewis, Anthony. 1999. "Abroad at Home: Something Rich and Strange," *New York Times* (October 12): accessed at *The New York Times on the Web.*

Li, Peter S. 2000. "Earning Disparities between Immigrants and Native-born Canadians." *Canadian Review of Sociology and Anthropology/Revue canadiene de sociologie anthropologie* 37(3).

Lian, Jason Z., and David Ralph Matthews. 1998. "Does the Vertical Mosaic Still Exist? Ethnicity and Income in Canada, 1991." *Canadian Review of Sociology and Anthropology/Revue canadiene de sociologie anthropologie* 35(4).

Liao, Youlian, Daniel L. McGee, Guichan Cao, and Richard S. Cooper. 2000. "Quality of the Last Year of Life of Older Adults: 1986–1993." *Journal of American Medical Association* 283(January 26):512–518.

Lieberman, David. 1999. "On the Wrong Side of the Wires." *USA Today,* October 11, pp. B1, B2.

Liebow, Elliot. 1993. *Tell Them Who I Am: The Lives of Homeless Women.* New York: Free Press.

Light, Ivan. 1999. "Comparing Incomes of Immigrants." *Contemporary Sociology* 28(July):382–384.

Liker, Jeffrey K., Carol J. Hoddard, and Jennifer Karlin. 1999. "Perspectives on Technology and Work Organization." Pp. 575–596 in *Annual Review of Sociology 1999,* edited by Karen S. Cook and John Hagen. Palo Alto, CA: Annual Reviews.

Lillard, Margaret. 1998. "Olympics Put Spotlight on Women's Hockey." *Rocky Mountain News,* February 1, p. 8C.

Lilliston, Ben. 1994. "Corporate Welfare Costs More Than Welfare to the Poor, Group Reports." *The Daily Citizen,* January 18, p. 8.

Lin, Na, and Wen Xie. 1988. "Occupational Prestige in Urban China." *American Journal of Sociology* 93(January):793–832.

Lin, Nan. 1999. "Social Networks and Status Attainment." Pp. 467–487 in *Annual Review of Sociology 1999,* edited by Karen S. Cook and John Hagen. Palo Alto, CA: Annual Reviews.

Lindholm, Charles. 1999. "Isn't it Romantic?" *Culture Front Online* Spring:1–5.

Lindner, Eileen, ed. 1998. *Yearbook of American and Canadian Churches, 1998.* Nashville: Abingdon Press.

———, ed. 2000. *Yearbook of American and Canadian Churches.* Nashville: Abingdon Press.

Link, Bruce G., and Jo Phelan. 1995. "Social Conditions as Fundamental Causes of Disease." *Journal of Health and Social Behaviour* (Extra Issue), 80–94.

Linn, Susan, and Alvin F. Poussaint. 1999. "Watching Television: What Are Children Learning About Race and Ethnicity?" *Child Care Information Exchange* 128(July):50–52.

Linton, Ralph. 1936. *The Study of Man: An Introduction.* New York: Appleton-Century.

Lips, Hilary M. 1993. *Sex and Gender: An Introduction.* 2d ed. Mountain View, CA: Mayfield.

Lipset, Seymour Martin.1996. *American Exceptionalism: A Double-Edged Sword.* New York: Norton.

Lipson, Karen. 1994. "'Nell' Not Alone in the Wilds." *Los Angeles Times*, December 19, pp. F1, F6.

Liska, Allen E., and Steven F. Messner. 1999. *Perspectives on Crime and Deviance.* 3d ed. Upper Saddle River, NJ: Prentice-Hall.

Livernash, Robert, and Eric Rodenburg. 1998. "Population Change, Resources, and the Environment." *Population Bulletin* 53(March).

Livingstone, David. 1999. *The Education-Jobs Gap: Underemployment or Economic Democracy?* Toronto: Garamond Press.

Llanes, José. 1982. *Cuban Americans: Masters of Survival.* Cambridge, MA: Abt Books.

Lochhead, Clarence, and Richard Shillington. 1996. *A Statistical Profile of Urban Poverty.* Accessed June 28, 2001 (http://www.ccsd.ca/urbhi.html).

Lockhart, Hugh. 2000. "Sweet Sacrifice." *The National Post,* February 9, pp. 23, 24, 26.

Lofflin, John. 1988. "A Burst of Rural Enterprise." *New York Times*, January 3, sec. 3, pp. 1, 23.

Lofland, Lyn H. 1975. "The 'Thereness' of Women: A Selective Review of Urban Sociology." Pp. 144–170 in *Another Voice,* edited by M. Millman and R. M. Kanter. New York: Anchor/Doubleday.

Logan, John R., and Richard D. Alba. 1995. "Who Lives in Affluent Suburbs? Racial Differences in Eleven Metropolitan Regions." *Sociological Focus* 28(October):353–364.

Lohr, Steve. 1994. "Data Highway Ignoring Poor, Study Charges." *New York Times*, May 24, pp. A1, D3.

Longman, Phillip. 1999. "The World Turns Gray." *U.S. News & World Report* 126(March 1):30–35.

Longworth, R. C. 1993. "UN's Relief Agendas Put Paperwork before People." *Chicago Tribune*, September 14, pp. 1, 9.

———. 1996. "Future Shock: The Graying of the Industrial World." *Chicago Tribune*, September 4, pp. 1, 20.

Lorber, Judith. 1994. *Paradoxes of Gender.* New Haven, CT: Yale University Press.

Los Angeles Times. 1995. "Multicultural Medicine." October 21, p. B7.

Lott, John R., Jr. 1998. *More Guns, Less Crime: Understanding Crime and Gun Control Laws.* Chicago: University of Chicago Press.

Lowman, John, and Ted Palys. 2000. "Ethics and Institutional Conflict of Interest: The Research Confidentiality Controversy at Simon Fraser University." *Sociological Practice: A Journal of Clinical and Applied Sociology* 2 (4) (Dec.): 245–264.

Lowry, Brian, Elizabeth Jensen, and Greg Braxton. 1999. "Networks Decide Diversity Doesn't Pay." *Los Angeles Times*, July 20, p. A1.

Lukacs, Georg. 1923. *History and Class Consciousness.* London: Merlin.

Luker, Kristin. 1984. *Abortion and the Politics of Motherhood.* Berkeley: University of California Press.

———. 1996. *Dubious Conceptions: The Politics of Teenage Pregnancy.* Cambridge, MA: Harvard University Press.

———. 1999. "Is Academic Sociology Politically Obsolete?" *Contemporary Sociology* 28(January):5–10.

Lum, Joann, and Peter Kwong. 1989. "Surviving in America: The Trials of a Chinese Immigrant Woman." *Village Voice* 34(October 31):39–41.

Lundy, Colleen. 1991. "Women and Alcohol: Moving Beyond Disease Theory." Pp. 57–73 in *Health Futures: Alcohol and Drugs*, edited by Douglas J. McCready. Waterloo: Interdisciplinary Research Committee, Wilfred Laurier University.

Luo, Michael. 1999. "Megachurches Search for Ideas to Grow Again." *Los Angeles Times*, June 7, pp. B1, B3.

Luster, Tom, Kelly Rhoades, and Bruce Haas. 1989. "The Relation between Parental Values and Parenting Behavior: A Test of the Kohn Hypothesis." *Journal of Marriage and the Family* 51(February):139–147.

Lustig, Myron W., and Jolene Koester. 1999. *Intercultural Competence.* 3d ed. New York: Longman.

Luxton, Meg. 1980. *More Than a Labour of Love: Three Generations of Women's Work in the Home.* Toronto: Women's Press.

———. 2001. "Husbands and Wives." Pp. 176–198 in *Family Patterns, Gender Relations*, 2d ed., edited by Bonnie J. Fox. Toronto: Oxford University Press.

Lynch, Margaret, and Richard Ferri. 1997. "Health Needs of Lesbian Women and Gay Men." *Clinicians Reviews. 7(1):85-88, 91-92, 95, 98-102, 105-107, 108-115, 117-118.*

Lyotard, Jean François. 1993. *The Postmodern Explained: Correspondence, 1982–1985.* Minneapolis: University of Minnesota Press.

M

MacFarquhar, Neil. 1999. "For First Time in War, E-Mail Plays a Vital Role." *New York Times*, March 29, p. A12.

Macintyre, Sally, Kate Hunt, and Helen Sweeting. 1996. "Gender Differences in Health: Are Things Really As Simple As They Seem?" *Social Science and Medicine* 42, 617–24.

Mack, Raymond W., and Calvin P. Bradford. 1979. *Transforming America: Patterns of Social Change.* 2d ed. New York: Random House.

Mackie, Richard. 2001. "Ontario Opposed School Subsidies Before Courts, UN." *The Globe and Mail,* June 13. Accessed June 15, 2001 (http://www.globeandmail.com).

MacKinnon, Catharine A. 1987. *Feminism Unmodified: Discourses on Life and Law.* Cambridge, MA: Harvard University Press.

MacLeod, Alexander. 2000. "UK Moving to Open All (E-) Mail." *The Christian Science Monitor,* May 5, pp. 1, 9.

MacMillan, Angus B., David R. Offord and Jennifer L. Dingle. 1996. "Aboriginal Health." *Canadian Medical Association Journal* 155(11):1569–78.

MacMillan, H. L. et al. [8 authors]. 1997. "Prevalence of Child Physical and Sexual Abuse in the Community: Results from the Ontario Health Supplement." *Journal of the American Medical Association* 278:131–135.

Magnier, Mark. 1999. "Equality Evolving in Japan." *Los Angeles Times*, August 30, pp. A1, A12.

Maguire, Brendan. 1988. "The Applied Dimension of Radical Criminology: A Survey of Prominent Radical Criminologists." *Sociological Spectrum* 8(2): 133–151.

Maines, David R. 1977. "Social Organization and Social Structure in Symbolic Interactionist Thought." Pp. 235–259 in *Annual Review of Sociology, 1977,* edited by Alex Inkles. Palo Alto, CA: Annual Reviews.

———. 1982. "In Search of Mesostructure: Studies in the Negotiated Order." *Urban Life* 11(July):267–279.

Malcolm X, with Alex Haley. 1964. *The Autobiography of Malcolm X.* New York: Grove.

Malthus, Thomas Robert. 1798. *Essays on the Principle of Population.* New York: Augustus Kelly, Bookseller; reprinted in 1965.

———, Julian Huxley, and Frederick Osborn. [1824] 1960. *Three Essays on Population.* Reprint, New York: New American Library.

Mandell, Nancy, ed. 1998. *Feminist Issues.* 2d ed. Scarborough: Prentice Hall Allyn and Bacon.

Mann, Jim. 2000. "India: Growing Implications for U.S." *Los Angeles Times,* May 17, p. A5.

Manson, Donald A. 1986. *Tracking Offenders: White-Collar Crime.* Bureau of Justice Statistics Special Report. Washington, DC: U.S. Government Printing Office.

Marcil-Gratton, Nicole. 1999. "Growing up with Mom and Dad? Canadian Children Experience Shifting Family Structures." *Transition* 29 (1), September: 4–7.

Marklein, Mary Beth. 1996. "Telecommuters Gain Momentum." *USA Today,* June 18, p. 6E.

Marks, Alexandra. 1998. "Key Swing Vote in 1998: Women," *Christian Science Monitor,* July 14, p. 3.

Marmor, Theodore. 1995. P. 1505 in "Medicare Canada's Postwar Miracle, US Management Expert Tells CMA Conference" by J. Rafuse. *CMA Journal* 152 (9).

Marshall, Kathleen. 1999. *The Gambling Industry: Raising the Stakes.* Statistics Canada. Ottawa: Minister of Industry.

Martin, Philip, and Elizabeth Midgley. 1999. "Immigrants to the United States." *Population Bulletin* 54(June):1–42.

Martin, Philip, and Jonas Widgren. 1996. "International Migration: A Global Challenge." *Population Bulletin* 51(April).

Martin, Susan E. 1994. "Outsider Within the Station House: The Impact of Race and Gender on Black Women Politics." *Social Problems* 41(August):383–400.

Martineau, Harriet. 1896. "Introduc-tion" to the translation of *Positive Philosophy* by Auguste Comte. London: Bell.

———. [1837] 1962. *Society in America.* Edited, abridged, with an introductory essay by Seymour Martin Lipset. Reprint, Garden City, NY: Doubleday.

Martyna, Wendy. 1983. "Beyond the He/Man Approach: The Case for Nonsexist Language." Pp. 25–37 in *Language, Gender and Society,* edited by Barrie Thorne, Cheris Kramorae, and Nancy Henley. Rowley, MA: Newly House.

Marx, Karl, and Friedrich Engels. [1847] 1955. *Selected Work in Two Volumes.* Reprint, Moscow: Foreign Languages Publishing House.

Masaki, Hisane. 1998. "Hashimoto Steps Down." *The Japan Times* 38 (July 20):1–5.

Mascia-Lees, Frances E., and Patricia Sharp, eds. 1992. *Tattoo, Torture, Mutilation, and Adornment: The Denaturalization of the Body in Culture and Text.* Albany: State University of New York Press.

Mason, J. W. 1998. "The Buses Don't Stop Here Anymore." *American Prospect* 37(March):56–62.

Massey, Douglas S., and Nancy A. Denton. 1993. *American Apartheid: Segregation and the Making of the Underclass.* Cambridge, MA: Harvard University Press.

Matloff, Norman. 1998. "Now Hiring! If You're Young." *New York Times,* January 26, p. A21.

Matrix Information and Directory Services. 1999. "Current World Map of the Internet." Austin, TX: MIDS. Also accessible online (http://www.mids.org/mapsale/world/index.html).

Matsushita, Yoshiko. 1999. "Japanese Kids Call for a Sympathetic Ear." *Christian Science Monitor,* January 20, p. 15.

Matthews, Jay. 1999. "A Home Run for Home Schooling." *Washington Post National Weekly Edition* 16(March 29):34.

Mauro, Tony. 1999. "Will Every Childish Taunt Turn Into a Federal Case?" *USA Today,* May 25, pp. A1, A2.

Mawhiney, Anne-Marie. 2001. "First Nations in Canada." Pp. 153–166 in *Canadian Social Welfare,* 4th ed., edited by Joanne C. Turner and Francis J. Turner. Toronto: Pearson Education.

Maxwell, Joe. 1992. "African Megachurch Challenged over Teaching." *Christianity Today* 36(October 5):58.

Mayer, Karl Ulrich, and Urs Schoepflin. 1989. "The State and the Life Course." Pp. 187–209 in *Annual Review of Sociology, 1989,* edited by W. Richard Scott and Judith Blake. Palo Alto, CA: Annual Reviews.

Mayor's Task Force on Homelessness. 1997. *Report to Wheaton City Council on the Mayor's Task Force on Homelessness.* Wheaton, IL: Mayor's Task Force on Homelessness.

McClung, H. Juhling, Robert D. Murray, and Leo A. Heitlinger. 1998. "The Internet as a Source for Current Patient Information." *Pediatrics* 10(June 6): electronic edition.

McCormick, John, and Claudia Kalb. 1998. "Dying for a Drink." *Newsweek,* June 15, pp. 30–31, 33–34.

McCreary Centre Society. 2001. *No Place to Call Home.* Burnaby, B.C: McCreary Centre Society.

McCreary, D. 1994. "The Male Role and Avoiding Femininity." *Sex Roles* 31: 517–531.

McDonald, Kim A. 1999. "Studies of Women's Health Produce a Wealth of Knowledge on the Biology of Gender Differences." *Chronicle of Higher Education* 45(June 25):A19, A22.

McDonough, Peggy, and Vivienne Walters. 2000. "Gender, Work and Health: An Analysis of the 1994 National Population Health Survey." *Centres of Excellence for Women's Health Research Bulletin* 1(1):3–4.

McFalls, Joseph A., Jr. 1998. "Population: A Lively Introduction." *Population Bulletin* 53(September).

———, Brian Jones, and Bernard J. Gallegher III. 1984. "U.S. Population Growth: Prospects and Policy." *USA Today,* January, pp. 30–34.

McGue, Matt, and Thomas J. Bouchard Jr. 1998. "Genetic and Environmental Influence on Human Behavioral Differences." Pp. 1–24 in *Annual Review of Neurosciences.* Palo Alto, CA: Annual Reviews.

McGuire, Meredith B. 1981. *Religion: The Social Context.* Belmont, CA: Wadsworth.

———. 1992. *Religion: The Social Context.* 3d ed. Belmont, CA: Wadsworth.

McIntosh, Peggy. 1988. "White Privilege and Male Privilege: A Personal Account of Coming to See Correspondence Through Work and Women's Studies." Working Paper No. 189, Wellesley College Center for Research on Women, Wellesley, MA.

McKenzie, Evan. 1994. *Privatopia: Homeowner Associations and the Rise of Residential Private Government.* New Haven, CT: Yale University Press.

McKinlay, John B., and Sonja M. McKinlay. 1977. "The Questionable Contribution of Medical Measures to the Decline of Mortality in the United States in the Twentieth Century." *Milbank Memorial Fund Quarterly* 55(Summer):405–428.

McKinley, James C., Jr. 1999. "In Cuba's New Dual Economy, Have-Nots Far Exceed Haves." *New York Times,* February 11, pp. A1, A6.

McKinnon, Jesse and Karen Humes. 2000. "The Black Population in the United States." *Current Population Reports.* Ser. P20 No. 530. Washington, DC: US Government Printing Office.

McLane, Daisann. 1995. "The Cuban-American Princess." *New York Times Magazine,* February 26, pp. 42–43.

McLaughlin, Abraham. 1998. "Tales of Journey from Death Row to Freedom." *Christian Science Monitor,* November 16, p. 2.

McNamara, Robert S. 1992. "The Population Explosion." *The Futurist* 26 (November–December):9–13.

McQuaig, Linda. 1998. *The Cult of Impotence: Selling the Myth of Powerlessness in the Global Economy.* Toronto: Penguin Canada.

McTeer, Maureen A. 1999. *Tough Choices: Living and Dying in the 21st Century.* Toronto: Irwin Law.

McVey, Wayne W., Jr., and Warren Kalbach. 1995. *Canadian Population.* Scarborough: Nelson Canada.

Mead, George H. 1934. In *Mind, Self and Society,* edited by Charles W. Morris. Chicago: University of Chicago Press.

———. 1964a. In *On Social Psychology,* edited by Anselm Strauss. Chicago: University of Chicago Press.

———. 1964b. "The Genesis of the Self and Social Control." Pp. 267–293 in *Selected Writings: George Herbert Mead,* edited by Andrew J. Reck. Indianapolis: Bobbs-Merrill.

Mead, Margaret. [1935] 1963. *Sex and Temperament in Three Primitive Societies.* Reprint, New York: Morrow.

———. 1973. "Does the World Belong to Men—Or to Women?" *Redbook* 141(October):46–52.

Mechanic, David, and David Rochefort. 1996. "Comparative Medical Systems." Pp. 475–494 in *Annual Review of Sociology, 1996,* edited by John Hagan. Palo Alto, CA: Annual Reviews.

Mehren, Elizabeth. 1999. "Working 9 to 5 at Age 95." *USA Today*, May 5, pp. A1, A21–A22.

Meisel, John. 2001. "Stroking the Airwaves: The Regulation of Broadcasting by the CRTC." Pp. 217–232 in *Communications in Canada*, 5th ed., edited by Craig McKie and Benjamin D. Singer. Toronto: Thompson Educational Publishing.

Melia, Marilyn Kennedy. 2000. "Changing Times." *Chicago Tribune*, January 2, sec. 17, pp. 12–15.

Melson, Robert. 1986. "Provocation or Nationalism: A Critical Inquiry into the Armenian Genocide of 1915." Pp. 61–84 in *The Armenian Genocide in Perspective,* edited by Richard G. Hovannisian. Brunswick, NJ: Transaction.

Mendez, Jennifer Brikham. 1998. "Of Mops and Maids: Contradictions and Continuities in Bureaucratized Domestic Work." *Social Problems* 45(February):114–135.

Merton, Robert K. 1968. *Social Theory and Social Structure.* New York: Free Press.

———, and Alice S. Kitt. 1950. "Contributions to the Theory of Reference Group Behavior." Pp. 40–105 in *Continuities in Social Research: Studies in the Scope and Method of the American Soldier,* edited by Robert K. Merton and Paul L. Lazarsfeld. New York: Free Press.

———, G. C. Reader, and P. L. Kendall. 1957. *The Student Physician.* Cambridge, MA: Harvard University Press.

Messner, Michael A. 1997. *Politics of Masculinities: Men in Movements.* Thousand Oaks, CA: Sage.

Meyers, Thomas J. 1992. "Factors Affecting the Decision to Leave the Old Order Amish." Presented at the annual meeting of the American Sociological Association, Pittsburgh.

Michels, Robert. 1915. *Political Parties.* Glencoe, IL: Free Press (reprinted 1949).

Mifflin, Lawrie. 1999. "Many Researchers Say Link Is Already Clear on Media and Youth Violence." *New York Times*, May 9, p. 23.

Migration News. 1998a. "Canada: Immigration, Diversity Up." 5(January). Accessed May 22, 1998 (http://migration.ucdavis.edu).

———. 1998b. "Immigration in EU, France: New Law, Australia: Immigration Unchanged." 5(May). Accessed May 6, 1998 (http://migration.ucdavis.edu).

Milan, Anne. 2000. "One Hundred Years of Families." *Canadian Social Trends.* Statistics Canada, Cat. no. 11-008 (Spring):2–13.

Milgram, Stanley. 1963. "Behavioral Study of Obedience." *Journal of Abnormal and Social Psychology* 67(October):371–378.

———. 1975. *Obedience to Authority: An Experimental View.* New York: Harper and Row.

Miller, David L., and Richard T. Schaefer. 1993. "Feeding the Hungry: The National Food Bank System as a Non-Insurgent Social Movement." Presented at the annual meeting of the Midwest Sociological Society, Chicago.

Miller, D. W. 2000. "Sociology, Not Engineering May Explain Our Vulnerability to Technological Disaster." *Chronicle of Higher Education* (October 15):A19–A20.

Miller, Greg. 1999. "Internet Fueled Global Interest in Disruptions." *Chicago Tribune*, December 2, p. A24.

Miller, G. Tyler, Jr. 1972. *Replenish the Earth: A Primer in Human Ecology.* Belmont, CA: Wadsworth.

Miller, Michael. 1998. "Abortion by the Numbers." *The Village Voice* 43, January 27, p. 58.

Mills, C. Wright. 1956. *The Power Elite.* New York: Oxford University Press.

———. 1959. *The Sociological Imagination.* London: Oxford University Press.

Mills, Robert J. 2000. "Health Insurance Coverage." *Current Population Reports,* ser. P60, no. 211. Washington, DC: U.S. Government Printing Office.

Milton S. Eisenhower Foundation. 1999. *To Establish Justice, To Insure Domestic Tranquility: A Thirty Year Update of the National Commission on the Causes and Prevention of Violence.* Washington, DC: Milton S. Eisenhower Foundation.

Miner, Horace. 1956. "Body Ritual Among the Nacirema." *American Anthropologist* 58(June):503–507.

Mingle, James R. 1987. *Focus on Minorities.* Denver: Education Commission of the States and the State Higher Education Executive Officers.

Mitchell, Alanna. 1999. "Home Schooling Goes AWOL." *The Globe and Mail,* February 2, p. A1, A6.

Mitchell, Barbara A. 1998. "Too Close for Comfort? Parental Assessments of 'Boomerang Kid' Living Arrangements." *Canadian Journal of Sociology* 23(1).

Mizrahi, Terry. 1986. *Getting Rid of Patients.* New Brunswick, NJ: Rutgers University Press.

Moffatt, Susan. 1995. "Minorities Found More Likely to Live Near Toxic Sites." *Los Angeles Times*, August 30, pp. B1, B3.

Mogelonsky, Marcia. 1996. "The Rocky Road to Adulthood." *American Demographics* 18(May):26–29, 32–35, 56.

Molot, Maureen Appel, and Fen Osler Hampson, eds. 2000. *Canada among Nations, 2000: Vanishing Borders.* Toronto: Oxford University Press.

Monaghan, Peter. 1993. "Sociologist Jailed Because He 'Wouldn't Snitch' Ponders the Way Research Ought to Be Done." *Chronicle of Higher Education* 40(September 1):A8, A9.

Monteiro, Lois A. 1998. "Ill-Defined Illnesses and Medically Unexplained Symptoms Syndrome." *Footnotes* 26(February):3, 6.

Moore, Wilbert E. 1968. "Occupational Socialization." Pp. 861–883 in *Handbook of Socialization Theory and Research,* edited by David A. Goslin. Chicago: Rand McNally.

Morehouse Medical Treatment and Effectiveness Center. 1999. *A Synthesis of the Literature: Racial and Ethnic Differences in Acccess to Medical Care.* Menlo Park, CA: Henry J. Kaiser Family Foundation.

Morehouse Research Institute and Institute for American Values. 1999. *Turning the Corner on Father Absence in Black America.* Atlanta: Morehouse Research Institute and Institute for American Values.

Morin, Richard. 1999. "Not a Clue." *Washington Post National Weekly Edition* 16(June 14):34.

———. 2000. "Will Traditional Polls Go the Way of the Dinosaur?" *Washington Post National Weekly Edition* 17(May 15):34.

Morland, John, Jr. 1996. "The Individual, the Society, or Both? A Comparison of Black, Latino, and White Beliefs about the Causes of Poverty." *Social Forces* 75(December):403–422.

Morris, Aldon. 2000. "Reflections on Social Movement Theory: Criticisms and Proposals." *Contemporary Sociology* 29(May):445–454.

Morris, Bonnie Rothman. 1999. "You've Got Romance! Seeking Love on Line." *New York Times*, August 26, p. D1.

Morrison, Denton E. 1971. "Some Notes toward Theory on Relative Deprivation, Social Movements, and Social Change." *American Behavioral Scientist* 14(May–June):675–690.

Morrow, John K. 1997. "Of Sheep Cloning and Cold Fusion." *Chicago Tribune*, March 7, p. 23.

Morse, Arthur D. 1967. *While Six Million Died: A Chronicle of American Apathy.* New York: Ace.

Morse, Jodie. 1999. "Cracking Down on the Homeless." *Time,* December 2000, pp. 69–70.

Moseley, Ray. 2000. "Britons Watch Health Service Fall to Its Knees." *Chicago Tribune,* January 22, pp. 1, 2.

Moskos, Charles C., Jr. 1991. "How Do They Do It?" *New Republic* 205 (August 5):20.

Mosley, J., and E. Thomson. 1995. Pp. 148–165 in *Fatherhood: Contemporary Theory, Research and Social Policy*, edited by W. Marsiglo. Thousand Oaks, CA: Sage.

Mossman, M.J. 1994. "Running Hard to Stand Still: The Paradox of Family Law Reform." *Dalhousie Law Journal* 17(5).

MOST. 1999. MOST Quarterly. Internet vol. 1. Accessed July 19, 1999 (http://www.mostonline.org/qtrly/qtrly-index.htm).

Murdock, George P. 1945. "The Common Denominator of Cultures." Pp. 123–142 in *The Science of Man in the World Crisis*, edited by Ralph Linton. New York: Columbia University Press.

———. 1949. *Social Structure*. New York: Macmillan.

———. 1957. "World Ethnographic Sample." *American Anthropologist* 59(August): 664–687.

Murphy, Caryle. 1993. "Putting Aside the Veil." *Washington Post National Weekly Edition* 10 (April 12–18): pp. 10–11.

Murphy, Dean E. 1997. "A Victim of Sweden's Pursuit of Perfection." *Los Angeles Times*, September 2, pp. A1, A8.

N

Nader, Laura. 1986. "The Subordination of Women in Comparative Perspective." *Urban Anthropology* 15(Fall–Winter):377–397.

Naifeh, Mary. 1998. "Trap Door? Revolving Door? Or Both? Dynamics of Economic Well-Being, Poverty 1993–94." *Current Population Reports*, ser. P-70, no. 63. Washington, DC: U.S. Government Printing Office.

Naiman, Joanne. 1997. *How Societies Work: Class, Power and Change in Canadian Society*. Concord: Irwin Publishing.

Nakane, Chie. 1970. *Japanese Society*. Berkeley: University of California Press.

Nakao, Keiko, and Judith Treas. 1990. *Computing 1989 Occupational Prestige Scores*. Chicago: NORC.

———, and ———. 1994. "Updating Occupational Prestige and Socio-economic Scores: How the New Measures Measure Up." Pp. 1–72 in *Sociological Methodology, 1994*, edited by Peter V. Marsden. Oxford: Basil Blackwell.

Nakhaie, M. Reza. 2001. "Ethnic and Gender Distribution of Sociologists and Anthropologists, 1971–96: Canada." *Journal of Sociology* 26(2).

Nanda, Serena. 1991. *Cultural Anthropology*. Belmont, CA: Wadsworth Publishing Company.

Nash, Manning. 1962. "Race and the Ideology of Race." *Current Anthropology* 3(June):285–288.

Nason-Clark, Nancy. 1993. "Gender Relations in Contemporary Christian Organizations." Pp. 215–234 in *The Sociology of Religion: A Canadian Focus*, edited by W.E. Hewitt. Toronto: Butterworths.

National Abortion and Reproductive Rights Action League. 1999b. "NARAL Factsheets: Public Funding for Abortion." Accessed October 9, 1999 (http://www.naral.org/publications/facts/1999/public_funding.html).

National Advisory Commission on Criminal Justice. 1976. *Organized Crime*. Washington, DC: U.S. Government Printing Office.

National Anti-poverty Organization. 1998. *Government Expenditure Cuts to Health Care and Post Secondary Education: Impacts on Low Income Canadians*. Ottawa: National Anti-poverty Organization.

National Archives of Canada. 1993. *Nunavut Territory, 1993*. Ref. no. NMC161029. Ottawa: Department of Indian and Northern Affairs.

National Center for Educational Statistics. 1997. "Digest of Education Statistics 1997." Washington, DC: U.S. Government Printing Office. Accessed September 29, 1999 (http://nces.ed.gov/pubs).

———. 1998. *Students' Report of School Crime: 1989 and 1995*. Washington, DC: U.S. Government Printing Office.

———. 1999. *Digest of Education Statistics, 1998*. Washington, DC: U.S. Government Printing Office.

National Center for Health Statistics. 1974. *Summary Report: Final Divorce Statistics, 1974*. Washington, DC: U.S. Government Printing Office.

———. 1990. *Annual Survey of Births, Marriages, Divorces, and Deaths: United States, 1989*. Washington, DC: U.S. Government Printing Office.

———. 1997a. *U.S. Deceased Life Tables for 1989–91*. Washington, DC: U.S. Government Printing Office.

———. 1997b. "Births and Deaths: United States, 1996." *Monthly Vital Statistics Report* 46(September 11).

———. 1999. "Infant, Neonatal, and Postnatal Mortality Rates by Race and Sex." *National Vital Statistics Report* 47(June 30):86–87.

———. 2000. "Births, Marriages, Divorces, and Deaths: Provisional Data for January 1999." *Monthly Vital Statistics Reports* 48(January 25):1–2.

National Center on Elder Abuse. 1998. *The National Elder Abuse Incidence Study*. Washington, DC: American Public Human Services Association.

National Center on Women and Family Law. 1996. *Status of Marital Rape Exemption Statutes in the United States*. New York: National Center on Women and Family Law.

National Council of Welfare. 1999. *Poverty Profile 1997*. Ottawa: National Council of Welfare.

National Homeschool Association. 1999. *Homeschooling Families: Ready for the Next Decade*. Accessed November 19, 2000 (http://www.n-h-a.org/decade.htm).

National Institute on Aging. 1999a. *Early Retirement in the United States*. Washington, DC: U.S. Government Printing Office.

———. 1999b. *The Declining Disability of Older Americans*. Washington, DC: U.S. Government Printing Office.

National Law Center on Homelessness and Poverty. 1996. *Mean Sweeps: A Report on Anti-Homeless Laws, Litigation, and Alternatives in 50 United States Cities*. Washington, DC: National Law Center on Homelessness and Poverty.

National Marriage Project. 2000. *The State of Our Unions*. New Brunswick, NJ: The National Marriage Project.

National Organization of Men Against Sexism (NOMAS). 1999. "Statement of Principles." Accessed October 11, 1999 (http://www.nomas.org/statemt_of_principles.htm).

National Partnership for Women and Families. 1998. *Balancing Acts: Work/Family Issues on Prime-Time TV. Executive Summary*. Washington, DC: The National Partnership for Women and Families.

National Telecommunications and Information Administration. 2000. *Falling Through the Net: Toward Digital Inclusion*. Washington, DC: U.S. Government Printing Office.

National Vital Statistics Reports. 2000. "Births, Marriages, Divorces and Deaths: Provisional Data for October 1999." *National Vital Statistics Reports* 48(September 6).

Navarro, Vicente. 1984. "Medical History as Justification Rather Than Explanation: A Critique of Starr's *The Social Transformation of American Medicine*." *International Journal of Health Services* 14(4):511–528.

Neft, Naomi, and Ann D. Levine. 1997. *Where Women Stand: An International Report on the Status of Women in 140 Countries*. New York: Random House.

Nelson, Adie, and Augie Fleras. 1998. *Social Problems in Canada: Conditions and Consequences*. 2d ed. Scarborough: Prentice-Hall.

Nelson, Adie, and Barrie W. Robinson. 1999. *Gender in Canada*. Scarborough, Prentice Hall.

Nelson, Adie, and Barrie Robinson. 2002. *Gender in Canada*. Toronto: Pearson Education Canada Inc.

Nelson, Jack. 1995. "The Internet, the Virtual Community, and Those with

Disabilities." *Disability Studies Quarterly* 15(Spring):15–20.
NetCoalition.com. 2000. "NetCoalition Joins Friend of the Court Brief in Napster Case." Press release, August 30. Washington, DC: NetCoalition.com.
Neuborne, Ellen. 1996. "Vigilantes Stir Firms' Ire with Cyber-antics." *USA Today,* February 28, pp. A1, A2.
Newman, William M. 1973. *American Pluralism: A Study of Minority Groups and Social Theory.* New York: Harper and Row.
Newsday. 1997. "Japan Sterilized 16,000 Women." September 18, p. A19.
New York Times. 1993a. "Child Care in Europe: Admirable but Not Perfect, Experts Say." February 15, p. A13.
———. 1995. "Reverse Discrimination of Whites Is Rare, Labor Study Reports." March 31, p. A23.
———. 1998. "2 Gay Men Fight Town Hall for a Family Pool Pass Discount." July 14, p. B2.
———. 1999a. "Woman Strikes Deal to Quit Redwood Home." December 19, p. 33.
———. 2000. "Technology's Gender Gap." September 5, p. A26.
Nguyen, S. D. 1982. "The Psycho-social Adjustment and Mental Health Needs of Southeast Asian Refugees." *Psychiatric Journal of the University of Ottawa* 7(1) 6–34.
Nibert, David. 2000. *Hitting the Lottery Jackpot: Government and the Taxing of Dreams.* New York: Monthly Review Press.
NICHD. 1999a. "Higher Quality Care Related to Less Problem Behavior." Accessed July 28, 1999 (http://www.nih.gov/nichd/docs/news/DAYCAR99.htm).
———. 1999b. "Child Outcomes When Child Care Center Classes Meet Recommended Standards for Quality." *American Journal of Public Health* 89(July):1072–1077.
Nie, Norman H. 1999. "Tracking Our Techno-Future." *American Demographics* (July):50–52.
———, and Lutz Erbring. 2000. "Study of the Social Consequences of the Internet." Accessible online (http://www.stanford.edu/group/sigss/). Palo Alto, CA: Stanford Institute for the Quantitative Study of Society.
Nielsen, Joyce McCarl, Glenda Walden, and Charlotte A. Kunkel. 2000. "Gendered Heteronormativity: Empirical Illustrations in Everyday Life." *Sociological Quarterly* 41(No. 2):283–296.
Nixon, Howard L., II. 1979. *The Small Group.* Englewood Cliffs, NJ: Prentice-Hall.
Nock, Steven L., James D. Wright, and Laura Sanchez. 1999. "America's Divorce Problem." *Society* 36(May/June):43–52.
Nolan, Patrick, and Gerhad Lenski. 1999. *Human Societies: An Introduction to Macrosociology.* New York: McGraw-Hill.
Noll, Roger G., and Andrew Zimbalist. 1997. *Sports, Jobs and Taxes: The Economic Impact of Sports Teams and Stadiums.* Washington, DC: The Brookings Institution.
Noonan, Rita K. 1995. "Women against the State: Political Opportunities and Collective Action Frames in Chile's Transition to Democracy." *Sociological Forum* 10:81–111.
NORC (National Opinion Research Center). 1994. *General Social Surveys 1972–1994.* Chicago: National Opinion Research Center.
Norrie, Kenneth Harold, and Douglas Owram. 1996. *A History of the Canadian Economy.* 2d ed. Toronto: Harcourt Brace.
North Carolina Abecedarian Project. 2000. *Early Learning, Later Success: The Abecedarian Study.* Chapel Hill, NC: Frank Porter Graham Child Development Center.
Novak, Tim, and Jon Schmid. 1999. "Lottery Picks Split by Race, Income." *Chicago Sun-Times,* June 22, pp. 1, 24, 25.
Nussbaum, Daniel. 1998. "Bad Air Days." *Los Angeles Times Magazine,* July 19, pp. 20–21.

O

Oberschall, Anthony. 1973. *Social Conflict and Social Movements.* Englewood Cliffs, NJ: Prentice-Hall.
O'Donnell, Mike. 1992. *A New Introduction to Sociology.* Walton-on-Thames, United Kingdom: Thomas Nelson and Sons.
O'Donnell, Rosie. 1998. Statement at the National Partnership for Women and Families Annual Luncheon, June 10.
Office of Justice Programs. 1999. "Transnational Organized Crime." *NCJRS Catalog* 49(November/December):21.
Ogburn, William F. 1922. *Social Change with Respect to Culture and Original Nature.* New York: Huebsch (reprinted 1966, New York: Dell).
———, and Clark Tibbits. 1934. "The Family and Its Functions." Pp. 661–708 in *Recent Social Trends in the United States,* edited by Research Committee on Social Trends. New York: McGraw-Hill.
O'Hanlan, Kate. 2002. "Lesbian Health and Homophobia: Perspectives for Treating Obstetrician/Gynecologist." Accessed April 4, 2002 (http://www.ohanlan.com/lhr.htm).
O'Hare, William P., and Brenda Curry-White. 1992. "Is There a Rural Underclass?" *Population Today* 20(March): 6–8.
Okano, Kaori, and Motonori Tsuchiya. 1999. *Education in Contemporary Japan: Inequality and Diversity.* Cambridge: Cambridge University Press.
Oliver, Melvin L., and Thomas M. Shapiro. 1995. *Black Wealth/White Wealth: New Perspectives on Racial Inequality.* New York: Routledge.
Ontario Human Rights Commission. 2001. Toronto: Queen's Printer for Ontario.
Orum, Anthony M. 1989. *Introduction to Political Sociology: The Social Anatomy of the Body Politic.* 3d ed. Englewood Cliffs, NJ: Prentice-Hall.
———. 2001. *Introduction to Political Sociology.* 4th ed. Upper Saddle River, NJ: Prentice-Hall.
Orwell, George. 1949. *1984.* New York: Harcourt Brace Jovanovich.
Ostling, Richard N. 1993. "Religion." *Time International,* July 12, p. 38.
Ouellette, Laurie. 1993. "The Information Lockout." *Utne Reader,* September–October, pp. 25–26.
Owens, Lynn, and L. Kendall Palmer. 2000. *Public Betrayals and Private Portrayals: Activist Intention in Tension on the WWW.* Presented at the annual meeting of the American Sociological Association, Washington, DC.

P

Pagani, Steve. 1999. "End the 'Culture of Death,' Pope Tells America." Reuters Wire Service, January 23.
Page, Charles H. 1946. "Bureaucracy's Other Face." *Social Forces* 25 (October):89–94.
Palen, J. John. 1995. "The Suburban Revolution: An Introduction." *Sociological Focus* 28(October):347–351.
Palmer Patterson, E. 1972. *The Canadian Indian: A History Since 1500.* New York: Collier-Macmillan of Canada Ltd.
Pappas, Gregory et al. [4 authors]. 1993. "The Increasing Disparity in Mortality between Socioeconomic Groups in the United States, 1960 and 1986." *New England Journal of Medicine* 329(July 8):103–109.
Park, Robert E. 1916. "The City: Suggestions for the Investigation of Human Behavior in the Urban Environment." *American Journal of Sociology* 20(March):577–612.
———. 1936. "Succession, an Ecological Concept." *American Sociological Review* 1(April):171–179.
Parker, Suzi. 1998. "Wedding Boom: More Rings, Tuxes, Bells, and Brides." *Christian Science Monitor,* July 20, pp. 1, 14.
Parsons, Talcott. 1951. *The Social System.* New York: Free Press.
———. 1966. *Societies: Evolutionary and Comparative Perspectives.* Englewood Cliffs, NJ: Prentice-Hall.
———. 1972. "Definitions of Health and Illness in the Light of American Values and Social Structure." Pp. 166–187 in *Patients, Physicians and Illness,* edited by Gartley Jaco. New York: Free Press.

———. 1975. "The Sick Role and the Role of the Physician Reconsidered." *Milbank Medical Fund Quarterly, Health and Society* 53(Summer):257–278.

———, and Robert Bales. 1955. *Family, Socialization, and Interaction Process.* Glencoe, IL: Free Press.

Pasternak, Judy. 1998. "'Edge City' Is Attempting to Build a Center." *Los Angeles Times*, January 1, p. A5.

Pate, Antony M., and Edwin E. Hamilton. 1992. "Formal and Informal Deterrents to Domestic Violence: The Dade County Spouse Assault Experiment." *American Sociological Reviews* 57(October):691–697.

Patterson, Orlando. 1998. "Affirmative Action." *Brookings Review* 16(Spring): 17–23.

Patton, Carl V., ed. 1988. *Spontaneous Shelter: International Perspectives and Prospects.* Philadelphia: Temple University Press.

Paulson, Amanda. 2000. "Where the School Is Home." *Christian Science Monitor*, October 10, pp. 18–21.

Pear, Robert. 1983. "$1.5 Billion Urged for U.S. Japanese Held in War." *New York Times*, June 17, pp. A1, D16.

———. 1996. "Clinton Endorses the Most Radical of Welfare Trials." *New York Times*, May 19, pp. 1, 20.

———. 1997a. "New Estimate Doubles Rate of H.I.V. Spread." *New York Times*, November 26, p. A6.

———. 1997b. "Now, the Archenemies Need Each Other." *New York Times*, June 22, sec. 4, pp. 1, 4.

Pelton, Tom. 1994. "Hawthorne Works' Glory Now Just So Much Rubble." *Chicago Tribune*, April 18, pp. 1, 6.

Peressini, T., L. McDonald, and D. Hulchanski. 1995. "Estimating Homelessness: Towards A Methodology for Counting The Homeless in Canada." Toronto: Centre for Applied Social Research, University of Toronto. Accessed April 18, 2002 (http://www.cmhc-schl.gc.ca/en/imquaf/ho/ho_005.cfm).

Perkins, Craig, and Patsy Klaus. 1996. *Criminal Victimization 1994.* Washington, DC: U.S. Government Printing Office.

Perlez, Jane. 1996. "Central Europe Learns about Sex Harassment." *New York Times*, October 3, p. A3.

Perrow, Charles. 1999. *Normal Accidents: Living with High Risk Technologies.* Updated edition. New Brunswick, NJ: Rutgers University Press.

———. 1986. *Complex Organizations.* 3d ed. New York: Random House.

Perry, Suzanne. 1998a. "Human Rights Abuses Get Internet Spotlight." Reuters, February 4.

———. 1998b. "U.S. Data Companies Oppose Primary Laws." Reuters, March 19.

Pescovitz, David. 1999. "Sons and Daughters of HAL Go on Line." *New York Times*, March 18, pp. D1, D8.

Peter, Laurence J., and Raymond Hull. 1969. *The Peter Principle.* New York: Morrow.

Petersen, William. 1979. *Malthus.* Cambridge, MA: Harvard University Press.

Phelan, Michael P., and Scott A. Hunt. 1998. "Prison Gang Members' Tattoos as Identity Work: The Visual Comments of Moral Careers." *Symbolic Interaction* 21(No. 3):277–298.

Philip, Margaret. 2001. "Teens' Dilemma: Cash or Class." *The Globe and Mail*, March 27, p. A7.

Phillips, E. Barbara. 1996. *City Lights: Urban–Suburban Life in the Global Society.* New York: Oxford University Press.

Piaget, Jean. 1954. *The Construction of Reality in the Child.* Translated by Margaret Cook. New York: Basic Books.

Pigler Christensen, Carole. 2001. "Immigrant Minorities in Canada." Pp. 180–209 in *Canadian Social Welfare*, 4th ed., edited by Joanne C. Turner and Francis J. Turner. Toronto: Pearson Education.

Piller, Charles. 2000. "Cyber-Crime Loss at Firms Doubles to $10 Billion." *Los Angeles Times*, May 22, pp. C1, C4.

Pinderhughes, Dianne. 1987. *Race and Ethnicity in Chicago Politics: A Reexamination of Pluralist Theory.* Urbana: University of Illinois Press.

Platt, Steve. 1993. "Without Walls." *Statesman and Society* 6(April 2):5–7.

Pleck, J. H., and E. Corfman. 1979. "Married Men: Work and Family." *Families Today: A Research Sampler on Families and Children* vol. 1, pp. 387–411.

Plomin, Robert. 1989. "Determinants of Behavior." *American Psychologist* 44(February):105–111.

Pollack, Andrew. 1996. "It's See No Evil, Have No Harassment in Japan." *New York Times*, May 7, pp. D1, D6.

Pollard, Kelvin M. 1994. "Population Stabilization No Longer in Sight for U.S." *Population Today* 22(May):1–2.

Pomfret, John. 2000. "A New Chinese Revolution." *Washington Post National Weekly Edition*, February 21, pp. 17–19.

Ponczek, Ed. 1998. "Are Hiring Practices Sensitive to Persons with Disabilities?" *Footnotes* 26(No. 3):5.

Popenoe, David, and Barbara Dafoe Whitehead. 1999. *Should We Live Together? What Young Adults Need to Know About Cohabitation Before Marriage.* Rutgers, NJ: The National Marriage Project.

Population Reference Bureau. 1978. "World Population: Growth on the Decline." *Interchange* 7(May):1–3.

———. 1996. "Speaking Graphically." *Population Today* 24(June/July):b.

———. 2000a. "More Youths Take Alternative Route to Finish High School." *Population Today* 28(January):7.

Population Reference Bureau. 2000b. *The World Youth 2000.* Washington, DC: Population Reference Bureau. Accessed April 18, 2002 (http://www.prb.org/Content/NavigationMenu/Other_reports/2000-2002/The_Worlds_Youth_2000_Data_Sheet.htm).

Porter, John. 1965. *The Vertical Mosaic: An Analysis of Social Class and Power in Canada.* Toronto: University of Toronto Press.

Porter, Rosalie Pedalino. 1997. "The Politics of Bilingual Education." *Society* 34(No. 6):31–40.

Power, Carla. 1998. "The New Islam." *Newsweek* 131(March 16):34–37.

Powers, Mary G., and Joan J. Holmberg. 1978. "Occupational Status Scores: Changes Introduced by the Inclusion of Women." *Demography* 15(May):183–204.

Princeton Religion Research Center. 2000a. "Nearly Half of Americans Describe Themselves as Evangelicals." *Emerging Trends* 22(April):5.

———. 2000b. "Latest Religious Preferences for U.S." *Emerging Trends* 22(March):2.

Privacy Commissioner of Canada. 2000. *The Personal Information Protection and Electronic Documents Act.* Accessed April 18, 2002 (http://www.privcom.gc.ca/legislation/02_06_01_e.asp).

Public Legal and Education Service of New Brunswick. 2001. *Sexual Harassment in Schools* (March). Saint John: Public Legal and Education Service of New Brunswick.

Pula, James S. 1995. *Polish Americans: An Ethnic Community.* New York: Twayne.

Purnick, Joyce. 1996. "G.O.P. Quest to Narrow Gender Gap." *New York Times*, November 14, p. B1.

Putnam, Robert D. 2000. *Bowling Alone: The Collapse and Revival of American Community.* New York: Simon and Schuster.

Pyle, Amy. 1998. "Opinions Vary on Studies That Back Bilingual Classes." *Los Angeles Times*, March 2, pp. B1, B3.

Q

Quadagno, Jill. 1999. *Aging and the Life Course: An Introduction to Social Gerontology.* New York: McGraw-Hill.

Quinney, Richard. 1970. *The Social Reality of Crime.* Boston: Little, Brown.

———. 1974. *Criminal Justice in America.* Boston: Little, Brown.

———. 1979. *Criminology.* 2d ed. Boston: Little, Brown.

———. 1980. *Class, State and Crime.* 2d ed. New York: Longman.

R

Ramet, Sabrina. 1991. *Social Currents in Eastern Europe: The Source and Meaning of the Great Transformation.* Durham, NC: Duke University Press.

Ralston Saul, John. 1993. *Voltaire's Bastards: The Dictatorship of Reason in the West.* Toronto: Penguin Canada.
———. 1997. *Reflections of a Siamese Twin: Canada at the End of the 20th Century.* Toronto: Viking.
Ravitch, Diane. 2000. *Left Back: A Century of Failed School Reforms.* New York: Simon and Schuster.
Reddick, Randy, and Elliot King. 2000. *The Online Student: Making the Grade on the Internet.* Fort Worth: Harcourt Brace.
Rees, Ruth. 1990. *Women and Men in Education: A national survey of gender distribution in school systems.* Toronto: Canadian Education Association.
Reese, William A., II, and Michael A. Katovich. 1989. "Untimely Acts: Extending the Interactionist Conception of Deviance." *Sociological Quarterly* 30(2):159–184.
Reinharz, Shulamit. 1992. *Feminist Methods in Social Research.* New York: Oxford University Press.
Reitz, Jeffrey. 1980. *The Survival of Ethnic Groups.* Toronto: McClelland and Stewart.
Religion Watch. 1991. "Current Research: New Findings in Religious Attitudes and Behavior." 6(September):5.
———. 1995. "European Dissenting Movement Grows among Laity Theologians." 10(October):6–7.
Remnick, David. 1998. "Bad Seeds." *New Yorker* 74(July 20):28–33.
———. 1998. *King of the World.* New York: Random House.
Rennison, Callie Marie. 1999. "Criminal Victimization 1998. Changes 1997–98 with Trends 1993–98." *Bureau of Justice Statistics National Crime Victimization Survey* (July).
Repper, J., R. Perkins, S. Owen, D. Deighton, and J. Robinson. 1996. "Evaluating Services for Women with Serious and Ongoing Mental Health Problems: Developing an Appropriate Research Method." *Journal of Psychiatric and Mental Health Nursing* 3, 39–46.
Reskin, Barbara, and Irene Padavic. 1994. *Women and Men at Work.* Thousand Oaks, CA: Pine Forge Press.
Reuters. 1995. "New Chinese Law Prohibits Sex-Screening of Fetuses." *New York Times*, November 15.
Rheingold, Harriet L. 1969. "The Social and Socializing Infant." Pp. 779–790 in *Handbook of Socialization Theory and Research,* edited by David A. Goslin. Chicago: Rand McNally.
Richardson, Diane, and Victoria Robinson. 1993. *Thinking Feminist: Key Concepts in Women's Studies.* New York: The Guildford Press.
Richardson, James T., and Barend van Driel. 1997. "Journalists' Attitudes Toward New Religious Movements." *Review of Religious Research* 39(December):116–136.
Richburg, Keith B. 1985. "Learning What Japan Has to Teach." *Washington Post National Weekly Edition* 3, November 4, p. 9.
Richtel, Matt. 2000. "www.layoffs.com." *New York Times,* June 22, pp. C1, C12.
Rideout, Victoria J., Ulla G. Foehr, Donald F. Roberts, and Mollyann Brodie. 1999. *Kids & Media @ the New Millennium.* New York: Kaiser Family Foundation.
Riding, Alan. 1998. "Why 'Titanic' Conquered the World." *New York Times*, April 26, sec. 2, pp. 1, 28, 29.
Rifkin, Jeremy. 1995a. *The End of Work: The Decline of the Global Labor Force and the Dawn of the Post-Market Era.* New York: Tarcher/Putnam.
———. 1995b. "Afterwork." *Utne Reader* (May–June):52–62.
———. 1996. "Civil Society in the Information Age." *The Nation* 262(February 26):11–12, 14–16.
———. 1998. *The Biotech Century: Harnessing the Gene and Remaking the World.* New York: Tarcher/Putnam.
Riley, Matilda White, Robert L. Kahn, and Anne Foner. 1994a. *Age and Structural Lag.* New York: Wiley Inter-Science.
———, and ———, in association with Karin A. Mock. 1994b. "Introduction: The Mismatch between People and Structures." Pp. 1–36 in *Age and Structural Lag,* edited by Matilda White Riley, Robert L. Kahn, and Ann Foner. New York: Wiley Inter-Science.
Riley, Nancy E. 1996. "China's 'Missing Girls:' Prospects and Policy." *Population Today* (February):pp. 4–5.
Rimer, Sara. 1998. "As Centenarians Thrive, 'Old' Is Redefined." *New York Times*, June 22, pp. A1, A14.
Ringel, Cheryl. 1997. *Criminal Victimization 1996.* Washington, DC: U.S. Government Printing Office.
Ritzer, George. 1995a. *Modern Sociological Theory.* 4th ed. New York: McGraw-Hill.
———. 1995b. *The McDonaldization of Society.* Rev. ed. Thousand Oaks, CA: Pine Forge Books.
———. 2000. *The McDonaldization of Society.* New Century Edition. Thousand Oaks, CA: Pine Forge Press.
Robb, N. 1993. "School of Fear." *OH&S Canada*:43–48.
Robbins, Catherine C. 1999. "A Zoo in Peril Stirs a Debate About Navajo Tradition." *New York Times*, March 28, p. 63.
Roberts, D. F. 1975. "The Dynamics of Racial Intermixture in the American Negro—Some Anthropological Considerations." *American Journal of Human Genetics* 7(December): 361–367.
———, Lisa Henriksen, Peter G. Christenson, and Marcy Kelly. 1999. "Substance Abuse in Popular Movies and Music." Accessible online (http://www.whitehousedrugpolicy.gov/news/press/042899.html). Washington, DC: Office of Juvenile Justice.
Roberts, Keith A. 1995. *Religion in Sociological Perspective.* 3d ed. Belmont, CA: Wadsworth.
Roberts, Sam. 1994. "Hispanic Population Now Outnumbers Blacks in Four Major Cities as Demographics Shift." *New York Times,* October 9, p. 34.
———. 1974. "Private Opinions on Public Opinion: Question Is, What Is the Question?" *New York Times,* August 21, p. E7.
Robertson, Roland. 1988. "The Sociological Significance of Culture: Some General Considerations." *Theory, Culture, and Society* 5(February):3–23.
Robinson, Gregory, and May Cohen. 1996. "Gay, Lesbian and Bisexual Health Care Issues and Medical Curricula. *Canadian Medical Association Journal* 155, 709–711. Accessed April 4, 2002 (http://www.cma.ca/cmaj/vol-155/issue-06/0709.htm).
Robinson, James D., and Thomas Skill. 1993. "The Invisible Generation: Portrayals of the Elderly on Television." University of Dayton. Unpublished paper.
Rocks, David. 1999. "Burger Giant Does as Europeans Do." *Chicago Tribune,* January 6, sec. 3, pp. 1, 4.
Rodberg, Simon. 1999. "Woman and Man at Yale." *Culturefront Online.* Accessed September 9, 1999 (http://www. culturefront.org/culturefront/magazine/99/spring/article.5.html).
Rodger, M. 1993. "Helping Students, Families and Schools in the Niagara Region Resolve Conflict." *Brock Education* 3(1):12–14.
Rodin, Judith, and Jeanette R. Ickovics. 1990. "Women's Health: Review and Research Agenda as We Approach the 21st Century." *American Psychologist* 45, 1018–1034.
Roethlisberger, Fritz J., and W. J. Dickson. 1939. *Management and the Worker.* Cambridge, MA: Harvard University Press.
Rogers, Jackie Krasas. 2000. *Temps: The Many Faces of the Changing Workplace.* Ithaca, NY: Cornell University Press.
Roher, Eric M. 1993. "Violence in a School Setting." *Brock Education* 3(1), 1–4.
Romero, Mary. 1988. "Chicanas Modernize Domestic Service." *Qualitative Sociology* 11:319–334.
Rose, Arnold. 1951. *The Roots of Prejudice.* Paris: UNESCO.
Rose, Peter I., Myron Glazer, and Penina Migdal Glazer. 1979. "In Controlled Environments: Four Cases of Intense Resocialization." Pp. 320–338 in *Socialization and the Life Cycle,* edited by Peter I. Rose. New York: St. Martin's.
Rosenbaum, Lynn. 1996. "Gynocentric Feminism: An Affirmation of Women's

Values and Experiences Leading Us toward Radical Social Change." *SSSP Newsletter* 27(1):4–7.

Rosenberg, Douglas H. 1991. "Capitalism." Pp. 33–34 in *Encyclopedic Dictionary of Sociology,* 4th ed., edited by Dushkin Publishing Group. Guilford, CT: Dushkin.

Rosenblatt, Robert A. 2000. "AARP Struggles to Bridge Boomer Generation Gap." *Los Angeles Times,* May 16, pp. A1, A10.

Rosenthal, Elizabeth. 1999a. "Women's Suicides Reveal Rural China's Bitter Roots." *New York Times,* January 24, pp. A1, A8.

———. 1999b. "Web Sites Bloom in China, and Are Waded." *New York Times,* December 23, pp. A1, A10.

———. 2000. "China Lists Controls to Restrict the Use of E-Mail and Web." *New York Times,* January 27, pp. A1, A10.

Rosenthal, Robert, and Elisha Y. Babad. 1985. "Pygmalion in the Gymnasium." *Educational Leadership* 45(September):36–39.

———, and Lenore Jacobson. 1968. *Pygmalion in the Classroom.* New York: Holt.

Rosman, Abraham, and Paula G. Rubel. 1994. *The Tapestry of Culture: An Introduction to Cultural Anthropology.* 5th ed. Chapter 1, Map. P. 35. New York: McGraw-Hill.

Ross, David P., and Paul Roberts. 1999. "Rethinking Child Poverty." *Perception* 23(1) June.

Ross, John. 1996. "To Die in the Street: Mexico City's Homeless Population Booms as Economic Crisis Shakes Social Protections." *SSSP Newsletter* 27(Summer):14–15.

Rossi, Alice S. 1968. "Transition to Parenthood." *Journal of Marriage and the Family* 30(February):26–39.

———. 1984. "Gender and Parenthood." *American Sociological Review* 49(February):1–19.

Rossi, Peter H. 1987. "No Good Applied Social Research Goes Unpunished." *Society* 25(November–December): 73–79.

———. 1989. *Down and Out in America: The Origins of Homelessness.* Chicago: University of Chicago Press.

———. 1990. "The Politics of Homelessness." Presented at the annual meeting of the American Sociological Association, Washington, DC.

Rossides, Daniel W. 1997. *Social Stratification: The Interplay of Class, Race, and Gender.* 2d ed. Upper Saddle River, NJ: Prentice-Hall.

Roszak, Theodore. 1969. *The Making of a Counterculture.* Garden City, NY: Doubleday.

Rotella, Sebastin. 1999. "A Latin View of American-Style Violence." *Los Angeles Times,* November 25, p. A1.

Roth, Jeffrey A., and Christopher S. Koper. 1999a. "Impacts of the 1994 Assault-Weapons Ban: 1994–96." *National Institute of Justice Research in Brief* (March).

———, and ———. 1999b. *Impact Evaluation of the Public Safety and Recreational Firearms Use Protection Act of 1994.* Washington, DC: Urban Institute.

Roxane Laboratories. 2000. *Daily Dosing of Available Antiretroviral Agents.*

Royal Commission on Aboriginal Peoples. 1997. *People to People, Nation to Nation: Looking Forward, Looking Back.* Ottawa: Canada Communications Group Publishing.

Royal Commission on New Reproductive Technologies. 1993. *Proceed with Care.* Ottawa: Minister of Government Services.

Royal Commission on the Status of Women in Canada. 1970. *Report.* Ottawa: Information Canada.

Rubin, Alissa J. 1998. "Where Are We Now?" *Los Angeles Times,* January 22, pp. E1, E4.

Russell, Cheryl. 1995. "Murder is All-American." *American Demographics* 17(September):15–17.

Russo, Nancy Felipe. 1976. "The Motherhood Mandate." *Journal of Social Issues* 32:143–153.

Ryan, William. 1976. *Blaming the Victim.* Rev. ed. New York: Random House.

S

Sadker, Myra Pollack, and David Sadker. 1985. "Sexism in the Schoolroom of the '80s." *Psychology Today* 19(March): 54–57.

Sadker, Myra, and David Sadker. 1994. *Failing at Fairness: How America's Schools Cheat Girls.* New York: Scribner.

———. 1995. *Failing at Fairness: How America's Schools Cheat Girls.* New York: Touchstone.

Safire, William. 1996. "Downsized." *New York Times Magazine,* May 26, pp. 12, 14.

Sagarin, Edward, and Jose Sanchez. 1988. "Ideology and Deviance: The Case of the Debate over the Biological Factor." *Deviant Behavior* 9(1):87–99.

Sale, Kirkpatrick. 1996. *Rebels against the Future: The Luddites and Their War on the Industrial Revolution* (with a new preface by the author). Reading, MA: Addison-Wesley.

———. 1997. "Ban Cloning? Not a Chance." *New York Times,* March 7, p. A17.

Salem, Richard, and Stanislaus Grabarek. 1986. "Sociology B.A.s in a Corporate Setting: How Can They Get There and of What Value Are They?" *Teaching Sociology* 14(October):273–275.

Salholz, Eloise. 1990. "Teenagers and Abortion." *Newsweek* 115(January 8): 32–33, 36.

Salins, Peter D. 1996. "How to Create a Real Housing Crisis." *New York Times,* October 26, p. 19.

Salkever, Alex. 1999. "Making Machines More Like Us." *Christian Science Monitor,* December 20, electronic edition.

Samuelson, Paul A., and William D. Nordhaus. 1998. *Economics.* 16th ed. New York: McGraw-Hill.

Samuelson, Robert J. 1996a. "Are Workers Disposable?" *Newsweek* 127, February 12, p. 47.

———. 1996b. "Fashionable Statements," *Washington Post National Weekly Edition* 13, March 18, p. 5.

Sandberg, Jared. 1999. "Spinning a Web of Hate." *Newsweek* 134(July 19):28–29.

Sassen, Saskia. 1999. *Guests and Aliens.* New York: The New Press.

Satzewich, Victor. 1990. "The Political Economy of Race and Ethnicity." Pp. 251–268 in *Race and Ethnic Relations in Canada,* edited by Peter S. Li. Toronto: Oxford University Press.

———. 1991. "Social Stratification: Class and Racial Inequality." Pp. 98–121 in *Social Issues and Contradictions in Canadian Society,* edited by B. Singh Bolaria. Toronto: Harcourt Brace.

Saukko, Paula. 1999. "Fat Boys and Goody Girls." In *Weighty Issues: Fatness and Thinness as Social Problems,* edited by Jeffrey Sobal and Donna Maurer. New York: Aldine de Gruyter.

Saunders, Doug. 2001. "Mullets for the Multitudes." *The Globe and Mail,* February 3. Accessed February 3, 2001 (http://www.globeandmail.com).

Savisbinksy, Joel S. 2000. *Breaking the Watch: The Meanings of Retirement in America.* Ithaca, NY: Cornell University Press.

Sawyer, Tom. 2000. "Antiretroviral Drug Costs." Correspondence to author from Roxane Laboratories, Cincinnati, OH, January 19.

Sax, Linda J., A. W. Astin, W. S. Korn, and K. M. Mahoney. 1999. *The American Freshman: National Norms for Fall 1999.* Los Angeles: Higher Education Research Institute.

Scarce, Rik. 1994. "(No) Trial (But) Tribulations: When Courts and Ethnography Conflict." *Journal of Contemporary Ethnography* 23(July):123–149.

———. 1995. "Scholarly Ethics and Courtroom Antics: Where Researchers Stand in the Eyes of the Law." *American Sociologist* 26(Spring):87–112.

Schaefer, Peter. 1995. "Destroy Your Future." *Daily Northwestern,* November 3, p. 8.

Schaefer, Richard T. 1998a. "Differential Racial Mortality and the 1995 Chicago Heat Wave." Presentation at the annual meeting of the American Sociological Association, August, San Francisco.

———. 1998b. *Alumni Survey.* Chicago, IL: Department of Sociology, DePaul University.
———. 2002. *Racial and Ethnic Groups.* 9th ed. Upper Saddle River, NJ: Prentice-Hall.
Schaefer, Sandy. 1996. "Peaceful Play." Presentation at the annual meeting of the Chicago Association for the Education of Young Children, Chicago.
Schaller, Lyle E. 1990. "Megachurch!" *Christianity Today* 34(March 5):10, 20–24.
Schellenberg, Kathryn, ed. 1996. *Computers in Society.* 6th ed. Guilford, CT: Dushkin.
Schlenker, Barry R., ed. 1985. *The Self and Social Life.* New York: McGraw-Hill.
Schmetzer, Uli. 1999. "Modern India Remains Shackled to Caste System." *Chicago Tribune,* December 25, p. 23.
Schmid, Carol. 1980. "Sexual Antagonism: Roots of the Sex-Ordered Division of Labor." *Humanity and Society* 4(November):243–261.
Schmitt, Eric. 1998. "Day-Care Quandary: A Nation at War with Itself." *New York Times,* January 11, sec. 4, pp. 1, 4.
Schnaiberg, Allan. 1994. *Environment and Society: The Enduring Conflict.* New York: St. Martin's.
Schnaiberg, Lynn. 1999. "Study Finds Home Schoolers Are Top Achievers on Tests." *Education Week* 18(March 31):5.
Schneider, Barbara, and David Stevens. 1999. *The Ambitious Generation: America's Teenagers Motivated but Directionless.* New Haven, CT: Yale University Press.
Schulman, Kevin A. et al. 1999. "The Effect of Race and Sex on Physicians' Recommendations for Cardiac Catheterization." *New England Journal of Medicine* (February 25):618–626.
Schur, Edwin M. 1965. *Crimes without Victims: Deviant Behavior and Public Policy.* Englewood Cliffs, NJ: Prentice-Hall.
———. 1968. *Law and Society: A Sociological View.* New York: Random House.
———. 1983. *Labelling Women Deviant: Gender, Stigma and Social Control.* Philadelphia: Temple University Press.
———. 1985. "'Crimes without Victims': A 20 Year Reassessment." Paper presented at the annual meeting of the Society for the Study of Social Problems.
Schwab, William A. 1993. "Recent Empirical and Theoretical Developments in Sociological Human Ecology." Pp. 29–57 in *Urban Sociology in Transition,* edited by Ray Hutchison. Greenwich, CT: JAI Press.
Schwartz, Howard D., ed. 1987. *Dominant Issues in Medical Sociology.* 2d ed. New York: Random House.
Scott, Alan. 1990. *Ideology and the New Social Movements.* London: Unwin Hyman.
Scott, Ellen Kaye. 1993. "How to Stop the Rapists? A Question of Strategy in Two Rape Crisis Centers." *Social Problems* 40 (August):343–361.
Scott, Katherine, and David Ross. 1996. *The Progress of Children.* Ottawa: Canadian Council on Social Development.
Second Harvest. 1997. *1997 Annual Report.* Chicago, IL: Second Harvest.
Segall, Alexander. 1976. "The Sick Role Concept: Understanding Illness Behavior." *Journal of Health and Social Behavior* 17(June):163–170.
Segall, Rebecca. 1998. "Sikh and Ye Shall Find." *Village Voice* 43(December 15): 46–48, 53.
Segerstrale, Ullica. 2000. *Defense of the Truth: The Battle for Science in the Sociobiology Debate and Beyond.* New York: Oxford University Press.
Seidman, Steven. 1994. "Heterosexism in America: Prejudice against Gay Men and Lesbians." Pp. 578–593 in *Introduction to Social Problems,* edited by Craig Calhoun and George Ritzer. New York: McGraw-Hill.
Senior Action in a Gay Environment (SAGE). 1999. *One Family All Ages.* New York: SAGE.
Serrano, Richard A. 1996. "Militias: Ranks Are Swelling." *Los Angeles Times,* April 18, pp. A1, A6.
Sexton, J. Bryan, and Robert L. Helmreich. 2000. "Analyzing Cockpit Communications: The Links Between Language, Performance, Error and Workload." *Human Performance in Extreme Environments* 5(1):63–68.
Shaheen, Jack G. 1999. "Image and Identity: Screen Arabs and Muslims." In *Cultural Diversity: Curriculum, Classrooms, and Climate Issues,* edited by J. Q. Adams and Janice R. Welsch. Macomb, IL: Illinois Staff and Curriculum Development Association.
Shapiro, Isaac, and Robert Greenstein. 1999. *The Widening Income Gulf.* Washington, DC: Center on Budget and Policy Priorities.
Shapiro, Joseph P. 1993. *No Pity: People with Disabilities Forging a New Civil Rights Movement.* New York: Times Books.
Sharma, Hari M., and Gerard C. Bodeker. 1998. "Alternative Medicine." In *Britannica Book of the Year 1998.* Chicago: Encyclopaedia Britannica, pp. 228–229.
Shcherbak, Yuri M. 1996. "Ten Years of the Chernobyl Era." *Scientific American* 274(April):44–49.
Sheehy, Gail. 1999. *Understanding Men's Passages: Discovering the New Map of Men's Lives.* New York: Ballantine Books.
Shenon, Philip. 1995. "New Zealand Seeks Causes of Suicides by Young." *New York Times,* July 15, p. 3.
———. 1998. "Sailor Victorious in Gay Case on Internet Privacy." *New York Times,* June 12, pp. A1, A14.
Sherman, Lawrence W., Patrick R. Gartin, and Michael D. Buerger. 1989. "Hot Spots of Predatory Crime: Routine Activities and the Criminology of Place." *Criminology* 27:27–56.
Sherrill, Robert. 1995. "The Madness of the Market." *The Nation* 260(January 9–16):45–72.
Shields, Rob, ed. 1996. *Cultures of Internet: Virtual Spaces, Real Histories, Living Bodies.* London: Sage.
Shilts, Randy. 1987. *And the Band Played On: Politics, People, and the AIDS Epidemic.* New York: St. Martin's.
Shinkai, Hiroguki, and Uglješa Zvekic. 1999. "Punishment." Pp. 89–120 in *Global Report on Crime and Justice,* edited by Graeme Newman. New York: Oxford University Press.
Shiver, Jube Jr., 2000. "International Firms Gain Foothold in Washington." *Los Angeles Times,* March 12, pp. A1, A21.
Shogan, Robert. 1998. "Politicians Embrace Status Quo as Nonvoter Numbers Grow." *Los Angeles Times,* May 4, p. A5.
Short, Kathleen, Thesia Garner, David Johnson, and Patricia Doyle. 1999. "Experimental Poverty Measures: 1990 to 1997." *Current Population Reports,* ser. P-60, no. 205. Washington, DC: U.S. Government Printing Office.
Shupe, Anson D., and David G. Bromley. 1980. "Walking a Tightrope." *Qualitative Sociology* 2:8–21.
Sigelman, Lee, Timothy Bledsoe, Susan Welch, and Michael W. Combs. 1996. "Making Contact? Black–White Social Interaction in an Urban Setting." *American Journal of Sociology* 5(March):1306–1332.
Silicon Valley Cultures Project. 1999. The Silicon Valley Cultures Project Website. Accessed July 30, 1990 (www.sjsu.edu/depts/anthrology/svcp).
Silver, Cynthia, Cara Williams, and Trish McOrmond. 2001. "Learning On Your Own." *Canadian Social Trends.* Statistics Canada. Catalogue No. 11-008. Spring. Ottawa: Minister of Industry.
Silver, Ira. 1996. "Role Transitions, Objects, and Identity." *Symbolic Interaction* 19(1):1–20.
Silverman, Milton, Mia Lydecker, and Philip R. Lee. 1990. "The Drug Swindlers." *International Journal of Health Services* 20:561–572.
Simard, Rene. 2000. *Reaching Out: Canada, International Science and Technology, and the Knowledge-based Economy.* Ottawa: Industry Canada.
Simmel, Georg. 1950. *Sociology of Georg Simmel.* Translated by K. Wolff. Glencoe, IL: Free Press (originally written in 1902–1917).

Simmons, Ann M. 1998. "Where Fat Is a Mark of Beauty." *Los Angeles Times*, September 30, pp. A1, A12.

Simons, Marlise. 1989. "Abortion Fight Has New Front in Western Europe." *New York Times*, June 28, pp. A1, A9.

———. 1997. "Child Care Sacred as France Cuts Back the Welfare State." *New York Times*, December 31, pp. A1, A6.

Simpson, Ann. 1999. *Public Deliberation Guide. A World in Common: Talking about What Matters in a Borderless World.* Ottawa: Canadian Council for International Cooperation.

Simpson, Sally. 1993. "Corporate Crime." Pp. 236–256 in *Introduction to Social Problems*, edited by Craig Calhoun and George Ritzer. New York: McGraw-Hill.

Sjoberg, Gideon. 1960. *The Preindustrial City: Past and Present.* Glencoe, IL: Free Press.

Smart, Barry. 1990. "Modernity, Postmodernity, and the Present." Pp. 14–30 in *Theories of Modernity and Postmodernity*, edited by Bryan S. Turner. Newbury Park, CA: Sage.

Smelser, Neil. 1963. *The Sociology of Economic Life.* Englewood Cliffs, NJ: Prentice-Hall.

Smith, Christian. 1991. *The Emergence of Liberation Theology: Radical Religion and Social Movement Theory.* Chicago: University of Chicago Press.

Smith, Dan. 1999. *The State of the World Atlas.* 6th ed. London: Penguin Books.

Smith, David A. 1995. "The New Urban Sociology Meets the Old: Rereading Some Classical Human Ecology." *Urban Affairs Review* 20(January):432–457.

———, and Michael Timberlake. 1993. "World Cities: A Political Economy/Global Network Approach." Pp. 181–207 in *Urban Sociology in Transition*, edited by Ray Hutchison. Greenwich, CT: JAI Press.

Smith, Michael Peter. 1988. *City, State, and Market.* New York: Basil Blackwell.

Smith, Patricia K. 1994. "Downward Mobility: Is It a Growing Problem?" *American Journal of Economics and Sociology* 53(January):57–72.

Smith, Tom W. 1996. *A Survey of the Religious Right: Views on Politics, Societies, Jews and Other Minorities.* New York: American Jewish Committee.

———. 2001. "Measuring Inter-Racial Friendships: Experimental Comparisons." *Public Opinion Quarterly*, forthcoming.

Smith-Rosenberg, Carroll, and Charles Rosenberg. 1974. "The Female Animal: Medical and Biological Views of Woman and Her Role in Nineteenth-Century America," *The Journal of American History* 60 (March):332–356.

Snell, Tracy L. 1997. *Capital Punishment 1996.* Washington, DC: U.S. Government Printing Office.

Snow, David A., and Leon Anderson. 1993. *Down on Their Luck: A Study of Homeless Street People.* Berkeley, CA: University of California Press.

———, Theren Quist, and Daniel Cress. 1996. "The Homeless as Bricoleurs: Material Survival Strategies on the Streets." Pp. 86–96 in *Homelessness in America: A Reference Book*, edited by Jim Baumohl. Phoenix: Oryx Press.

Snyder, Thomas D. 1996. *Digest of Education Statistics 1996.* Washington, DC: U.S. Government Printing Office.

Sohoni, Neera Kuckreja. 1994. "Where Are the Girls?" *Ms.* 5(July–August):96.

Son, In Soo, Suzanne W. Model, and Gene A. Fisher. 1989. "Polarization and Progress in the Black Community: Earnings and Status Gains for Young Black Males in the Era of Affirmative Action." *Sociological Forum* 4(September):309–327.

Sørensen, Annemette. 1994. "Women, Family and Class." Pp. 27–47 in *Annual Review of Sociology, 1994*, edited by Annemette Sørensen. Palo Alto, CA: Annual Reviews.

Sorokin, Pitirim A. 1959. *Social and Cultural Mobility.* New York: Free Press (original edition 1927, New York: Harper).

Sorrentino, Constance. 1990. "The Changing Family in International Perspective." *Monthly Labor Review* 113(March):41–56.

Spain, Daphene. 1992. *Gendered Spaces.* Chapel Hill, NC: The University of North Carolina Press.

Specter, Michael. 1998a. "Population Implosion Worries a Graying Europe." *New York Times*, July 10, pp. A1, A6.

———. 1998b. "Doctors Powerless as AIDS Rakes Africa." *New York Times*, August 6, pp. A1, A7.

Spengler, Joseph J. 1978. *Facing Zero Population Growth: Reactions and Interpretations, Past and Present.* Durham, NC: Duke University Press.

Spitzer, Steven. 1975. "Toward a Marxian Theory of Deviance." *Social Problems* 22(June):641–651.

Spradley, James P., and David W. McCurdy. 1980. *Anthropology: The Cultural Perspective.* 2d ed. New York: Wiley.

Sproull, Lee, and Sara Kiesler. 1991. *Connections: New Ways of Working in the Networked Organization.* Cambridge, MA: M.I.T. Press.

St. John, Eric. 1997. "A Prescription for Participation." *Black Issues in Higher Education* 14(December 11):18–23.

Staggenborg, Suzanne. 1988. "Consequences of Professionalization and Formalization." *American Sociological Review* 53(August):585–606.

———. 1989a. "Stability and Innovation in the Women's Movement: A Comparison of Two Movement Organizations." *Social Problems* 36(February): 75–92.

———. 1989b. "Organizational and Environmental Influences on the Development of the Pro-Choice Movement." *Social Forces* 68(September):204–240.

Stammer, Larry B. 1999. "Former Baptists Leader Seeks a Dialogue with Gay Church." *Los Angeles Times*, July 27, pp. B1, B5.

Stanley, Alessandra. 1995. "Rich or Poor, Russian Mothers Go It Alone." *New York Times*, October 22, pp. 1, 5.

Stark, Rodney, and William Sims Bainbridge. 1979. "Of Churches, Sects, and Cults: Preliminary Concepts for a Theory of Religious Movements." *Journal for the Scientific Study of Religion* 18(June):117–131.

———. 1985. *The Future of Religion.* Berkeley: University of California Press.

———, and Laurence R. Iannaccone. 1992. "Sociology of Religion." Pp. 2029–2037 in *Encyclopedia of Sociology*, vol. 4, edited by Edgar F. Borgatta and Marie L. Borgatta. New York: Macmillan.

Starr, Kevin. 1999. "Building from Within." *Los Angeles Times*, March 7, p. 1.

Starr, Paul. 1982. *The Social Transformation of American Medicine.* New York: Basic Books.

Stasiulis, Daivak. 1990. "Theorizing Connections: Gender, Race, Ethnicity and Class." Pp. 269–305 in *Race and Ethnic Relations in Canada*, edited by Peter S. Li. Toronto: Oxford University Press.

Statistics Canada. 1983. "Historical Statistics of Canada". *Statistics Canada Population Series.* A1-A247 (A67–69). Cat. no. 11-516-XIE. Accessed June 20, 2001 (http://www.statcan.ca/english/IPS/Data/11-516-XIE.htm).

———. 1991. *Census Population by Religion.* Catalogue No. 93-319-XPB. Accessed June 15, 2001 (http://www.statcan.ca/english/Pgdb/People/Population/demo33.htm).

———. 1993. *Religions in Canada.* Catalogue No. 93-319-XPB. Accessed January 15, 2001 (http:// www.statcan.ca/english/Pgdb./People/Population demo32.htm).

———. 1996a. *1996 Census of Canada.* Ottawa: Ministry of Supply and Services.

———. 1996b. *Population by Ethnic Origin.* Accessed March 28, 2002 (http://www.statcan.ca/english/Pgdb/People/Population/demo28c.htm).

———. 1996c. *Visible Minority Population.* Accessed March 28, 2002 (http://www.statcan.ca/english/Pgdb/People/Population/demo40a.htm).

———. 1996d. "1996: Immigration and Citizenship." *The Daily*. November 4. Accessed on January 26, 2002 (http://www.statcan.ca/Daily/English/971104/d971104.htm).

———. 1997a. "1996 Census: Marital status, common-law unions and families." *The Daily*. October 14. Accessed April 23, 2002 (http://www.statcan.ca/Daily/English/971014/d971014.htm).
———. 1997b. "Canadian Families: Diversity and Change." Cat. no. 12F0061XFE.
———. 1998a. "1996 Census: Education, Mobility and Migration." *The Daily*. April 14. Accessed April 23, 2002 (http://www.statcan.ca/Daily/English/980414/d980414.htm).
———. 1998b. *Juristat*. July 22. No. 85-002-XIE. Accessed May 6, 2002 (http://www.statcan.ca/english/data/85-002-XIE).
———. 1998c. *Total Population by Visible Minority Population (14) and Age Groups (13), Showing Sex (3), for Canada, Provinces, Territories and Forward Sortation Areas, 1996 Census*. Catalogue No. 95FO222XDB96005. Ottawa: Minister of Industry.
———. 1998d. *Census Families in Private Households by Family Structure (2) and 1995 Family Income (3), for Canada, Provinces and Territories and Forward Sortation Areas, 1996 Census*. Cat. no. 95F0249XDB9605. Ottawa: Minister of Industry.
———. 1999a. *Hours per Week Playing Computer Games*. E-stat. H523929, H523918, H523923, H523924 H523929.
———. 1999b. "Eldercare in Canada: Content, Context, and Consequences, 1996." Cat. No. 89-570-XPE.
———. 1999c. *Income in Canada*, Cat. no. 75-202-XPE. Accessed April 4, 2001 (http://www.statcan.ca/english/IPS/Data/75-202-XPE.htm).
———. 1999d. *Overview of the Time Use of Canadians in 1998*. Catalogue No. 12F0080XIE. Ottawa: Minister of Industry.
———. 1999e. "Survey of Labour and Income Dynamics: The wage gap between men and women." *The Daily*. December 20. Accessed April 21, 2002 (http://www.statcan.ca/Daily/English/991220/d991220a.htm).
———. 1999f. *Earnings of Men and Women*. Catalogue No. 13-217-XIB. Ottawa: Minister of Industry.
———. 1999g. "Computer Use and Internet Use by Members of Rural Households." *Rural and Small Town Canada Analysis Bulletin* 1(7).
———. 1999h. "Canadian Crime Statistics, 1998." *Juristat: Canadian Centre for Justice Statistics*, 19(9).
———. 2000a. "Plugging in: The Increase in Household Internet Use continues in 1999." *The Daily*. December 4. No. 56F0004MIE.
———. 2000b. "Attending Religious Services." *The Daily*. December 12. Accessed April 21, 2002 (http://www.statcan.ca/Daily/English/001212/d001212b.htm).
———. 2000c. "University Education: Recent Trends in Participation, Accessibility and Returns." Catalogue No. 81-003-XPB. *Education Quarterly Review* 6(4). Ottawa: Minister of Industry.
———. 2000d. *Women in Canada: 2000. A Gender-Based Statistical Report*. Catalogue No. 89-503-XPE. Ottawa: Ministry of Industry.
———. 2000e. *Canadian Social Trends*. Catalogue No. 11-008, Spring, p. 16.
———. 2000f. "The Labour Market in the 1990s." *The Daily*. January 20. Accessed May 23, 2002 (http://www.statcan.ca/Daily/English/000120/d000120c.htm).
———. 2000g. "Part-time by Choice." *The Daily*. November 24. Accessed May 23, 2002 (http://www.statcan.ca/Daily/English/001124/d001124b.htm).
———. 2001a. "Population Structure and Change in Predominantly Rural Regions." *The Daily*. January 16. No. 21-006XIE.
———. 2001b. "Family Income, 1999." *The Daily*. November 6. Accessed May 5, 2002, (http://www.statcan.ca/Daily/English/011106/d011106b.htm).
———. 2001c. "Survey of Approaches to Education Planning." *The Daily*. April 10. Accessed April 22, 2002 (http://www.statcan.ca/Daily/English/010410/d010410a.htm).
———. 2001d. "Crime Statistics." *The Daily*. July 19. Accessed August 15, 2001 (http://www.statcan.ca/Daily/English/010719/d010719b.htm).
———. 2001e. "Social Participation and Inclusion." July. Accessed April 22, 2002 (http://www.statcan.ca/english/freepub/89F0123XIE/32.htm).
———. 2001f. *Family Violence in Canada: A Statistical Profile*. Ministry of Industry. Accessed January 19, 2002 (http://www.statcan.ca/english/freepub/85-224-XIE/0100085-224-XIE.pdf).
Statistics Sweden. 1999. *Social Report 1997: National Report on Social Conditions in Sweden: February 18, 1999 (Update)*. Accessed July 14, 2000 (http://www.sos.se/sos.publ/refereng/9700-72e.htm).
Status of Women Canada. 1995 *Setting the Stage for the Next Century: The Federal Plan for Gender Equality*. Ottawa: Status of Women Canada.
———. 2000. *National Day of Remembrance and Action on Violence Against Women*. News Release. December 5. Accessed April 22, 2002 (http://www.swc-cfc.gc.ca/news2000/1205-e.html).
Stearn, J. 1993. "What Crisis?" *Statesmen and Society* 6(April 2):7–9.
Stedman, Nancy. 1998. "Learning to Put the Best Shoe Forward." *New York Times*, October 27.
Steffenhagen, Janet. 2001. "City Streets Draw Non-B.C. Youths." *The Vancouver Sun*, March 26, p. A3.
Stein, Leonard. 1967. "The Doctor–Nurse Game." *Archives of General Psychiatry* 16:699–703.
Steinfeld, Edward S. 1999. "Beyond the Transition: China's Economy at Century's End." *Current History* 98(September):271–275.
Stenning, Derrick J. 1958. "Household Viability among the Pastoral Fulani." Pp. 92–119 in *The Developmental Cycle in Domestic Groups*, edited by John R. Goody. Cambridge, Eng.: Cambridge University Press.
Stephen, Elizabeth Hervey. 1999. "Assisted Reproductive Technologies: Is the Price Too High?" *Population Today* (May):1–2.
Stephenson, Marylee. 2000. "Corporate Profile." Accessed April 4, 2002 (http://www.csresors.com/stephenson.html).
Sternberg, Steve. 1999. "Virus Makes Families Pay Twice." *USA Today*, May 24, p. 6D.
Sterngold, James. 1992. "Japan Ends Fingerprinting of Many Non-Japanese," *New York Times* May 21, p. A11.
Stevens, Ann Huff. 1994. "The Dynamics of Poverty Spells: Updating Bane and Ellwood." *American Economic Review* 84 (May):34–37.
Stevenson, David, and Barbara L. Schneider. 1999. *The Ambitious Generation: America's Teenagers, Motivated but Directionless*. New Haven: Yale University Press.
Stevenson, Robert J. 1998. *The Boiler Room and Other Telephone Sales Scams*. Urbana, IL: University of Illinois Press.
Stolberg, Sheryl. 1995. "Affirmative Action Gains Often Come at a High Cost." *Los Angeles Times*, March 29, pp. A1, A13–A16.
Stolberg, Sheryl Gay. 2000. "Alternative Care Gains a Foothold." *New York Times*, January 31, pp. A1, A16.
Stoll, Clifford. 1995. *Silicon Snake Oil: Second Thoughts on the Information Superhighway*. New York: Anchor/Doubleday.
Stoughton, Stephanie, and Leslie Walker. 1999. "The Merchants of Cyberspace." *Washington Post National Weekly Edition* 16(February 15):18.
Stout, Madeline Dion. 1996. *Aboriginal Canada: Women and Health: A Canadian Perspective*. Paper prepared for the Canada–USA Forum on Women's Health. Ottawa: Health Canada.
Strassman, W. Paul. 1998. "Third World Housing." Pp. 589–592 in *The Encyclopedia of Housing*, edited by Willem van Vliet. Thousand Oaks, CA: Sage.
Straus, Murray A. 1994. "State-to-State Differences in Social Inequality and

Social Bonds in Relation to Assaults on Wives in the United States." *Journal of Comparative Family Studies* 25(Spring):7–24.
Strauss, Anselm. 1977. *Negotiations: Varieties, Contexts, Processes, and Social Order.* San Francisco: Jossey Bass.
Strom, Stephanie. 2000a. "In Japan, the Golden Years Have Lost Their Glow." *New York Times,* February 16, 7.
———. 2000b. "Tradition of Equality Fading in New Japan." *New York Times,* January 4, pp. A1, A6.
Strum, Charles. 1993. "Schools' Tracks and Democracy." *New York Times,* April 1, pp. B1, B7.
Sugimoto, Yoshio. 1997. *An Introduction to Japanese Society.* Cambridge, Eng.: Cambridge University Press.
Sumner, William G. 1906. *Folkways.* New York: Ginn.
Sunhara, Ann Gomer. 1981. "Deportation: The Final Solution to Canada's "Japanese Problem." Pp. 246–261 in *Ethnicity Power and Politics in Canada,* edited by Jorgen Dahlie and Tissa Fernando. Toronto: Methuen.
Sutherland, Edwin H. 1937. *The Professional Thief.* Chicago: University of Chicago Press.
———. 1940. "White-Collar Criminality." *American Sociological Review* 5 (February):1–11.
———. 1949. *White Collar Crime.* New York: Dryden.
———. 1983. *White Collar Crime: The Uncut Version.* New Haven, CT: Yale University Press.
———, and Donald R. Cressey. 1978. *Principles of Criminology.* 10th ed. Philadelphia: Lippincott.
Suttles, Gerald D. 1972. *The Social Construction of Communities.* Chicago: University of Chicago Press.
Swanson, Stevenson. 1999. "Shaker Ranks Down to the Faithful Few." *Chicago Tribune,* April 4, p. 6.
——— and Jim Kirk. 1998. "Satellite Outage Felt by Millions." *Chicago Tribune,* May 21, pp. 1, 26.
Synott, Anthony. 1987. "Shame and Glory: A Sociology of Hair." *The British Journal of Sociology* 38: 381–413.
Szasz, Thomas S. 1971. "The Same Slave: An Historical Note on the Use of Medical Diagnosis as Justificatory Rhetoric." *American Journal of Psychotherapy* 25(April):228–239.

T

Taeuber, Cynthia M. 1992. "Sixty-Five Plus in America." *Current Population Reports,* ser. P-23, no. 178. Washington, DC: U.S. Government Printing Office.
Tagliabue, John. 1996. "In Europe, a Wave of Layoffs Stuns White-Collar Workers." *New York Times,* June 20, pp. A1, D8.
Takezawa, Yasuko I. 1995. *Breaking the Silence: Redress and Japanese American Ethnicity.* Ithaca, NY: Cornell University Press.
Talbot, Margaret. 1998. "Attachment Theory: The Ultimate Experiment." *New York Times Magazine,* May 24, pp. 4–30, 38, 46, 50, 54.
Tarnopolsky, Walter Surma. 1991. *Discrimination and the Law in Canada: Race, Ethnic and Cultural Equality.* Vancouver: Western Judicial Centre.
Tannen, Deborah. 1990. *You Just Don't Understand: Women and Men in Conversation.* New York: Ballantine.
———. 1994a. *Talking from 9 to 5.* New York: William Morris.
———. 1994b. *Gender and Discourse.* New York: Oxford University Press.
Taylor, Verta. 1995. "Watching for Vibes: Bringing Emotions into the Study of Feminist Organizations." Pp. 223–233 in *Feminist Organizations: Harvest of the New Women's Movement,* edited by Myra Marx Ferree and Patricia Yancy Martin. Philadelphia: Temple University Press.
Telsch, Kathleen. 1991. "New Study of Older Workers Finds They Can Become Good Investments." *New York Times,* May 21, p. A16.
Terry, Sara. 2000. "Whose Family? The Revolt of the Child-Free." *Christian Science Monitor,* August 29, pp. 1, 4.
Theberge, Nancy. 1997. "'It's Part of the Game'—Physicality and the Production of Gender in Women's Hockey." *Gender and Society* 11(February):69–87.
Third International Mathematics and Science Study. 1998. *Mathematics and Science Achievement in the Final Year of Secondary School.* Boston, MA: TIMSS International Study Center.
Thomas, Gordon, and Max Morgan Witts. 1974. *Voyage of the Damned.* Greenwich, CT: Fawcett Crest.
Thomas, Jim. 1984. "Some Aspects of Negotiating Order: Loose Coupling and Mesostructure in Maximum Security Prisons." *Symbolic Interaction* 7(Fall): 213–231.
Thomas, Pattie and Erica A. Ownes. 2000 "Age Cure!: The Business of Passing." Present at the annual meeting of the American Sociological Association, Washington, DC.
Thomas, Robert McG., Jr. 1995. "Maggie Kuhn, 89, the Founder of the Gray Panthers, Is Dead." *New York Times,* April 23, p. 47.
Thomas, William I. 1923. *The Unadjusted Girl.* Boston: Little, Brown.
Thomson, Elizabeth, and Ugo Colella. 1992. "Cohabitation and Marital Stability: Quality or Commitment?" *Journal of Marriage and the Family* 54(May):259–267.
Thornton, Russell. 1987. *American Indians Holocaust and Survival: A Population History Since 1492.* Norman: University of Oklahoma Press.
Tidmarsh, Lee. 2000. "If I Shouldn't Spank, What Should I Do? Behaviour Techniques for Disciplining Children." *Canadian Family Physician* 46:1119–1123.
Tierney, John. 1990. "Betting the Planet." *New York Times Magazine,* December 2, pp. 52–53, 71, 74, 76, 78, 80–81.
Tilly, Charles. 1993. *Popular Contention in Great Britain 1758–1834.* Cambridge, MA: Harvard University Press.
Todd, Douglas. 2001. "Emphasis on Morality." *The Vancouver Sun,* February 26, p. A:15.
Tolbert, Kathryn. 2000. "In Japan, Traveling Alone Begins at Age 6." *Washington Post National Weekly Edition* 17(May 15):17.
Tong, Rosemary. 1989. *Feminist Theory: A Comprehensive Introduction.* Boulder, CO: Westview.
Tonkinson, Robert. 1978. *The Mardudjara Aborigines.* New York: Holt.
Tönnies, Ferdinand. [1887] 1988. *Community and Society.* Rutgers, NJ: Transaction.
Topolnicki, Denise M. 1993. "The World's 5 Best Ideas." *Money* 22(June):74–83, 87, 89, 91.
Touraine, Alain. 1974. *The Academic System in American Society.* New York: McGraw-Hill.
Transport Canada. 1998. *Transportation in Canada: 1997 Annual Report.* Cat. No. T1-10/1997E. Ottawa: Minster of Public Works and Government Services.
Treas, Judith. 1995. "Older Americans in the 1990s and Beyond." *Population Bulletin* 50(May).
Treiman, Donald J. 1977. *Occupational Prestige in Comparative Perspective.* New York: Academic.
Tuchman, Gaye. 1992. "Feminist Theory." Pp. 695–704 in *Encyclopedia of Sociology,* vol. 2, edited by Edgar F. Borgatta and Marie L. Borgatta. New York: Macmillan.
Tuck, Bryan, Jan Rolfe, and Vivienne Adair. 1994. "Adolescents' Attitudes Toward Gender Roles within Work and its Relationship to Gender, Personality Type and Parental Occupations." *Sex Roles* 31, 9–10: 547–558.
Tucker, James. 1993. "Everyday Forms of Employee Resistance." *Sociological Forum* 8(March):25–45.
Tumin, Melvin M. 1953. "Some Principles of Stratification: A Critical Analysis." *American Sociological Review* 18(August):387–394.
———. 1985. *Social Stratification.* 2d ed. Englewood Cliffs, NJ: Prentice-Hall.
Ture, Kwame, and Charles Hamilton. 1992. *Black Power: The Politics of Liberation.* Rev. ed. New York: Vintage Books.
Turkle, Sherry. 1995. *Life on the Screen: Identity in the Age of the Internet.* New York: Simon and Schuster.

———. 1999. "Looking Toward Cyberspace: Beyond Grounded Sociology," *Contemporary Sociology* 28(November):643–654.
Turner, Bryan S., ed. 1990. *Theories of Modernity and Postmodernity.* Newbury Park, CA: Sage.
Turner, Craig. 1998. "U.N. Study Assails U.S. Executions as Biased." *Los Angeles Times*, March 4, p. A1.
Turner, J. H. 1985. *Herbert Spencer: A Renewed Application.* Beverly Hills, CA: Sage.
Turner, Margery Austin, and Felicity Skidmore, eds. 1999. *Mortgage Lending Discrimination: A Review of Existing Evidence.* Washington, DC: Urban Institute.
Twaddle, Andrew. 1974. "The Concept of Health Status." *Social Science and Medicine* 8(January):29–38.
Tyler, William B. 1985. "The Organizational Structure of the School." Pp. 49–73 in *Annual Review of Sociology, 1985,* edited by Ralph H. Turner. Palo Alto, CA: Annual Reviews.

U

Uchitelle, Louis. 1996. "More Downsized Workers Are Returning as Rentals." *New York Times*, December 8, pp. 1, 34.
———. 1999. "Divising New Math to Define Poverty." *New York Times*, October 18, pp. A1, A14.
UNAIDS. 2000. *Report on the Global HIV/AIDS Epidemic, June 2000.* Geneva, Switzerland: Joint United Nations' Programme on HIV/AIDS (UNAIDS).
United Nations. 1995. *The World's Women, 1995: Trends and Statistics.* New York: United Nations.
United Nations Development Programme. 1995. *Human Development Report 1995.* New York: Oxford University Press.
United Nations Human Rights Commission. 1997. "U.N. Human Rights Commission Acts on Texts." M2 PressWire. 4/9.
United Nations Population Division. 1998a. "Demographic Input of HIV/AIDS." Accessed (http://www.undp.org/popin/wdtrends/demoimp.htm).
———. 1998b. *World Abortion Policies.* New York: Department of Economic and Social Affairs, UNPD.
———. 1999. *The World at Six Billion.* New York: UNPD.
United Nations Population Fund. 2000. *State of World Population 2000: Lives Together, Worlds Apart: Men and Women in a Time of Change.* New York: United Nations Population Fund.
U.S. Conference of Mayors. 1999. *A Status Report on Hunger and Homelessness in America's Cities.* Washington: U.S. Conference of Mayors.
U.S. English. 1999. "States with Official English Laws." Accessed July 27, 1999 (http://www.us-english.org/states.htm).
University of Calgary Gazette. 2000. "Quid Novi." *Gazette*, May 29, 30(5). Accessed July 2, 2001 (http://www.ucalgary.ca/unicomm/Gazette/Archives/index.html).
Uttley, Alison. 1993. "Who's Looking at You, Kid?" *Times Higher Education Supplement* 30(April 30):48.

V

Vallas, Steven P. 1999. "Rethinking Post-Fordism: The Meaning of Workplace Flexibility." *Sociological Theory* 17(March):68–101.
Vancouver Sun. 2000. "Youth Violence in Canada." December 2, p. B4.
van den Berghe, Pierre. 1978. *Race and Racism: A Comparative Perspective.* 2d ed. New York: Wiley.
Vanderpool, Tim. 1995. "Secession of the Successful." *Utne Reader* (November–December):32, 34.
Vanier Institute of the Family. 1999. *Profiling Canadian Families.* Ottawa: Vanier Institute of the Family.
Vanneman, Reeve, and Lynn Weber Cannon. 1987. *The American Perception of Class.* Philadelphia: Temple University Press.
Van Slambrouck, Paul. 1998. "In California, Taking the Initiative—Online." *Christian Science Monitor*, November 13, pp. 1, 11.
———. 1999a. "Netting a New Sense of Connection." *Christian Science Monitor*, May 4, pp. 1, 4.
———. 1999b. "Newest Tool for Social Protest: The Internet." *Christian Science Monitor*, June 18, p. 3.
van Vucht Tijssen, Lieteke. 1990. "Women between Modernity and Postmodernity." Pp. 147–163 in *Theories of Modernity and Postmodernity,* edited by Bryan S. Turner. London: Sage.
Vaughan, Diane. 1996. *The* Challenger *Launch Decision: Risky Technology, Culture, and Deviance at NASA.* Chicago: University of Chicago Press.
———. 1999. "The Dark Side of Organizations: Mistake, Misconduct, and Disaster." Pp. 271–305 in *Annual Review of Sociology*, edited by Karen J. Cook and John Hagan. Palo Alto: Annual Reviews.
Veblen, Thorstein. 1919. *The Vested Interests and the State of the Industrial Arts.* New York: Huebsch.
Vega, William A. 1995. "The Study of Latino Families: A Point of Departure." Pp. 3–17 in *Understanding Latino Families: Scholarship, Policy, and Practice,* edited by Ruth E. Zambrana. Thousand Oaks, CA: Sage.
Venkatesh, Sudhir Alladi. 1997. "The Social Organization of Street Gang Activity in an Urban Ghetto." *American Journal of Sociology* 103(July):82–111.
Ventura, Stephanie J., and Christine A. Bachrach. 2000. "Nonmarital Childbearing in the United States, 1990–91." *National Vital Statistics Reports* 48 (October 18).
———, Joyce A. Martin, Sally C. Curtin, T. J. Mathews, and Melissa M. Park. 2000a. "Births: Final Data for 1998." *National Vital Statistics Reports* 48(March 28).
Verhovek, Sam Howe. 1997. "Racial Tensions in Suit Slowing Drive for 'Environmental Justice,'" *New York Times*, September 7, pp. 1, 16.
Vernon, Glenn. 1962. *Sociology and Religion.* New York: McGraw-Hill.
Vernon, Jo Etta A. et al. [4 authors]. 1990. "Media Stereotyping: A Comparison of the Way Elderly Women and Men Are Portrayed on Prime-Time Television." *Journal of Women and Aging* 2(4):55–68.
Vidaver, R. M. et al. 2000. "Women Subjects in NIH-funded Clinical Research Literature: Lack of Progress in Both Representation and Analysis by Sex. *Journal of Women's Health Gender Based Medicine* 9(June):495–504.
Vissandjee, Bilkis. 2001. "The Consequences of Cultural Diversity." *The Canadian Women's Health Network* 4(2): 3–4.
Vladimiroff, Christine. 1998. "Food for Thought." *Second Harvest Update* (Summer):2.
Vobejda, Barbara, and Judith Havenmann. 1997. "Experts Say Side Income Could Hamper Reforms." *Washington Post,* November 3, p. A1.

W

Wacquant, Loïc J. D. 1993. "When Cities Run Riot." *UNESCO Courier* (February), pp. 8–15.
Wages for Housework Campaign. 1999. *Wages for Housework Campaign.* Circular. Los Angeles.
Wagley, Charles and Marvin Harris. 1958. *Minorities in the New World: Six Case Studies.* New York: Columbia University Press.
Waitzkin, Howard, and John D. Stoeckle. 1976. "Information Control and the Micropolitics of Health Care." *Journal of Social Issues* 10(6):263–76.
Wake, Bev. 2000. "Home Schooling Gets Top Marks: More Parents are Home Schooling their Children because of Better Internet Access and the Availability of Educational Material." *Ottawa Citizen.* September 7, p. C3.
Wallace, Ruth A., and Alison Wolf. 1980. *Contemporary Sociological Theory.* Englewood Cliffs, NJ: Prentice-Hall.
Wallerstein, Immanuel. 1974. *The Modern World System.* New York: Academic Press.
———. 1979. *Capitalist World Economy.* Cambridge, Eng.: Cambridge University Press.

———. 2000. *The Essential Wallerstein.* New York: The New Press.
Wallerstein, Judith S., Judith M. Lewis, and Sandra Blakeslee. 2000. *The Unexpected Legacy of Deviance.* New York: Hyperion.
Wallis, Claudia. 1987. "Is Mental Illness Inherited?" *Time* 129(March 9):67.
Walzer, Susan. 1996. "Thinking about the Baby: Gender and Divisions of Infant Care." *Social Problems* 43(May):219–234.
Waring, Marilyn. 1988. *If Women Counted: A New Feminist Economics.* San Francisco: Harper and Row.
Warner, Judith. 1996. "France's Anti-abortion Movement Gains Momentum." *Ms.* 7(September–October):20–21.
Watts, Jerry G. 1990. "Pluralism Reconsidered." *Urban Affairs Quarterly* 25(June):697–704.
Weber, Bruce, Greg Duncan, and Leslie Whitener. 2000. "Rural Dimensions of Welfare Reform." *Poverty Research News* 4(September–October):3–4.
Weber, Martha L. 1998. "She Stands Alone: A Review of the Recent Literature on Women and Social Support." *Prairie Women's Health Centre of Excellence.* Winnipeg: Prairie Women's Health Centre of Excellence.
Weber, Max. [1913–1922] 1947. *The Theory of Social and Economic Organization.* Translated by A. Henderson and T. Parsons. New York: Free Press.
———. [1904] 1949. *Methodology of the Social Sciences.* Translated by Edward A. Shils and Henry A. Finch. Glencoe, IL: Free Press.
———. [1904] 1958a. *The Protestant Ethic and the Spirit of Capitalism.* Translated by Talcott Parsons. New York: Scribner.
———. [1916] 1958b. *The Religion of India: The Sociology of Hinduism and Buddhism.* New York: Free Press.
Wechsler, Henry. 2000. "Binge Drinking: Should We Attack the Name or the Problem?" *Chronicle of Higher Education* 47(October 20):B12–13.
Wechsler, Henry et al. 2000. "College Binge Drinking in the 1990s: A Continuing Program." *Journal of American College Health* 48(March):199–210.
Weeks, John R. 1999. *Population: An Introduction to Concepts and Issues.* 7th ed. Belmont, CA: Wadsworth.
Weinfeld, M. 1994. "Ethnic Assimilation and the Retention of Ethnic Cultures." Pp. 238–266 in *Ethnicity and Culture in Canada: The Research Landscape,* edited by J.W. Berry and J.A. Laponce. Toronto: University of Toronto Press.
Weinstein, Deena. 1999. *Knockin' The Rock: Defining Rock Music as a Social Problem.* New York: McGraw-Hill/Primis.
———. 2000. *Heavy Metal: The Music and Its Culture.* Cambridge, MA: Da Capo.
———, and Michael A. Weinstein. 1999. "McDonaldization Enframed." Pp. 57–69 in *Resisting McDonaldization,* edited by Barry Smart. London: Sage.
Weisman, Steven R. 1992. "Landmark Harassment Case in Japan." *New York Times,* April 17, p. A3.
Weiss, Rick. 1998. "Beyond Test-Tube Babies." *Washington Post National Weekly Edition* 15(February 16):6–7.
Weitz, Rose. 1996. *The Sociology of Health, Illness and Health Care: A Critical Approach.* Belmont Cal.: Wadsworth.
Welfare to Work Partnership. 2000. "Business Partners Find Success but Call for Renewed Community Action." *Trends in Executive Opinions* (2000 Series No. 1), p.1.
Wellman, Barry et al. [6 authors]. 1996. "Computer Networks as Social Networks: Collaborative Work, Telework, and Virtual Community." Pp. 213–238 in *Annual Review of Sociology, 1996,* edited by John Hagan. Palo Alto, CA: Annual Reviews.
Welsh, Sandy. 1999. "Gender and Sexual Harassment." Pp. 169–190 in *Annual Review of Sociology, 1999,* edited by Karen S. Cook and John Hagan. Palo Alto, CA: Annual Reviews.
West, Candace, and Don H. Zimmerman. 1983. "Small Insults: A Study of Interruptions in Cross Sex Conversations between Unacquainted Persons." Pp. 86–111 in *Language, Gender, and Society,* edited by Barrie Thorne, Cheris Kramarae, and Nancy Henley. Rowley, MA: Newbury House.
———, and ———. 1987. "Doing Gender." *Gender and Society* 1(June):125–151.
West, William G. 1993. "Violence in the Schools/Schooling in Violence: Escalating Problem or Moral Panic? A Critical Perspective." *Orbit.* 24 (1), 6–7.
Whyte, William Foote. 1981. *Street Corner Society: Social Structure of an Italian Slum.* 3d ed. Chicago: University of Chicago Press.
———. 1989. "Advancing Scientific Knowledge through Participatory Action Research." *Sociological Forum* 4(September):367–385.
Wickham, DeWayne. 1998. "Affirmative Action not in Real Jeopardy." *USA Today,* April 7, p. 13A.
Wickman, Peter M. 1991. "Deviance." Pp. 85–87 in *Encyclopedic Dictionary of Sociology,* 4th ed., by Dushkin Publishing Group. Guilford, CT: Dushkin.
Wiener, Jon. 1994. "Free Speech on the Internet." *The Nation* 258(June 13): 825–828.
Wilford, John Noble. 1997. "New Clues Show Where People Made the Great Leap to Agriculture." *New York Times,* November 18, pp. B9, B12.
Wilhelm, Anthony. 1998. *Buying into the Computer Age: A Look at Hispanic Families.* Claremont, CA: The Thom Rivera Policy Institute.
Wilkinson, Tracy. 1999 "Refugees Forming Bonds on Web." *Los Angeles Times,* July 31, p. A2.
Willet, Jeffrey G., and Mary Jo Deegan. 2000. "Liminality? and Disability: The Symbolic Rite of Passage of Individuals with Disabilities." Presented at the annual meeting of the American Sociological Association, Washington, DC.
Williams, Carol J. 1995. "Taking an Eager Step Back." *Los Angeles Times,* June 3, pp. A1, A14.
Williams, David R., and Chiquita Collins. 1995. "U.S. Socioeconomic and Racial Differences in Health: Patterns and Explanations." Pp. 349–386 in *Annual Review of Sociology, 1995,* edited by John Hagan. Palo Alto, CA: Annual Reviews.
Williams, Lena. 1995. "Not Just a White Man's Game: Blacks in Business Master the Art of Networking." *New York Times,* November 9, pp. D1, D10.
Williams, Patricia J. 1997. "Of Race and Risk." *The Nation.* Digital Edition. Accessed December 12, 1999 (http://www.thenation.com).
Williams, Robin M., Jr. 1970. *American Society.* 3d ed. New York: Knopf.
———, in collaboration with John P. Dean and Edward A. Suchman. 1964. *Strangers Next Door: Ethnic Relations in American Communities.* Englewood Cliffs, NJ: Prentice-Hall.
Williams, Simon Johnson. 1986. "Appraising Goffman." *British Journal of Sociology* 37(September):348–369.
Williams, Wendy M. 1998. "Do Parents Matter? Scholars Need to Explain What Research Really Shows." *Chronicle of Higher Education* 45(December 11):B6–B7.
Wilmut, Ian et al. [5 authors]. 1997. "Viable Offering Derived from Fetal and Adult Mammalian Cells." *Nature* 385(February 27):810–813.
Wilson, Edward O. 1975. *Sociobiology: The New Synthesis.* Cambridge, MA: Harvard University Press.
———. 1978. *On Human Nature.* Cambridge, MA: Harvard University Press.
Wilson, John. 1973. *Introduction to Social Movements.* New York: Basic Books.
Wilson, Susannah. 2001. "Intimacy and Commitment in Family Formation." Pp. 144–63 in *Families: Changing Trends in Canada,* 4th ed., edited by Maureen Baker. Toronto: McGraw-Hill Ryerson.
Wilson, Warner, Larry Dennis, and Allen P. Wadsworth, Jr. 1976. "Authoritarianism Left and Right." *Bulletin of the Psychonomic Society* 7(March): 271–274.
Wilson, William Julius. 1980. *The Declining Significance of Race: Blacks and Changing American Institutions.* 2d ed. Chicago: University of Chicago Press.
———. 1987. *The Truly Disadvantaged: The Inner City, the Underclass and Public Policy.* Chicago: University of Chicago Press.

———, ed. 1989. *The Ghetto Underclass: Social Science Perspectives.* Newbury Park, CA: Sage.
———. 1996. *When Work Disappears: The World of the New Urban Poor.* New York: Knopf.
———. 1999a. "Towards a Just and Livable City: The Issues of Race and Class." Address at the Social Science Centennial Conference, April 23, 1999. Chicago, IL: DePaul University.
———. 1999b. *The Bridge Over the Racial Divide: Rising Inequality and Coalition Politics.* Berkeley: University of California Press.
Winsberg, Morton. 1994. "Specific Hispanics." *American Demographics* 16(February):44–53.
Winter, J. Alan. 1977. *Continuities in the Sociology of Religion.* New York: Harper and Row.
Wirth, Louis. 1928. *The Ghetto.* Chicago: University of Chicago Press.
———. 1938. "Urbanism as a Way of Life." *American Journal of Sociology* 44(July):1–24.
Wiseman, Paul. 2000. "China's Little Emperors: The Offspring of Policy." *USA Today*, February 23, p. 10D.
Withers, Edward J., and Robert S. Brown. 2001. "The Broadcast Audience: A Sociological Perspective." Pp. 121–150 in *Communications in Canadian Society,* 5th ed., edited by Craig McKie and Benjamin D. Singer. Toronto: Thompson Educational Publishing.
Wolf, Naomi. 1990. *The Beauty Myth: How Images of Beauty Are Used Against Women.* New York: Morrow.
Wolf, Naomi. 1991. *The Beauty Myth.* New York: Anchor Books.
———. 1992. *The Beauty Myth: How Images of Beauty Are Used against Women.* New York: Anchor.
Wolf, Richard. 1996. "States Can Expect Challenges after Taking over Welfare." *USA Today*, October 1, p. 8A.
Wolff, Edward N. 1999. "Recent Trends the Distribution of Household Wealth Ownership." In *Back to Shared Prosperity: The Growing Inequality of Wealth and Income in America,* edited by Ray Marshall. New York: M.E. Sharpe.
Wolinsky, Fredric P. 1980. *The Sociology of Health.* Boston: Little, Brown.
Wolraich et al. 1998. "Guidance for Effective Discipline." *Pediatrics* 101(April):723–728.
Women's International Network. 1995. "Working Women: 4 Country Comparison." *WIN News* 21(September 9): 82.
Wood, Daniel B. 2000. "Minorities Hope TV Deals Don't Just Lead to 'Tokenism.'" *Christian Science Monitor*, January 19.
Woodard, Colin. 1998. "When Rate Learning Fails against the Test of Global Economy." *Christian Science Monitor*, April 15, p. 7.
Wooden, Wayne. 1995. *Renegade Kids, Suburban Outlaws: From Youth Culture to Delinquency.* Belmont, CA: Wadsworth.
Woolf, Virigina. 1977. *A Room of One's Own.* San Diego, CA: Harvest/HBJ.
World Bank. 1995. *World Development Report 1994: Workers in an Integrating World.* New York: Oxford University Press.
———. 1996. *World Development Report 1996: From Plan to Market.* New York: Oxford University Press.
———. 1997a. *World Development Indicators 1997.* Washington, DC: International Bank for Reconstruction and Development/The World Bank.
———. 1997b. *World Development Report 1997: The State in a Changing World.* New York: Oxford University Press.
———. 2000a. *World Development Report 1999/2000: Entering the 21st Century.* New York: Oxford University Press.
———. 2000b. *World Development Indicators 2000.* Washington, DC: World Bank.
———. 2000c. *World Development Report 2000/2001.* New York: Oxford University Press.
World Development Forum. 1990. "The Danger of Television." 8(July 15):4.
World Health Organization. 1998. *Unsafe Abortion: Global and Regional Estimates of Incidence of and Mortality Due to Unsafe Abortion.* Geneva, Switzerland: WHO.
———. 2000. *The World Health Report 2000. Health Systems: Improving Performance.* Geneva, Switzerland: WHO.
World Resources Institute. 1998. *1998–99 World Resources: A Guide to the Global Environment.* New York: Oxford University Press.
———. The United Nations Environment Programme, United Nations Development Program, The World Bank. 1996. *World Resources, 1996–1997.* New York: Oxford University Press.
Wresch, William. 1996. *Disconnected: Haves and Have-Nots in the Information Age.* New Brunswick, NJ: Rutgers University Press.
Wright, Eric R., William P. Gronfein, and Timothy J. Owens. 2000. "Deinstitutionalization, Social Rejection, and the Self-Esteem of Former Mental Patients." *Journal of Health and Social Behavior* (March).
Wright, Erik Olin, David Hachen, Cynthia Costello, and Joy Sprague. 1982. "The American Class Structure." *American Sociological Review* 47(December):709–726.
Wright, James D. 1995. "Ten Essential Observations on Guns in America." *Society* 32(March/April):63–68.
Wu, Zheng. 1990. "Premaritial Cohabitation and the Timing of First Marriage." *Canadian Review of Sociology and Anthropology* 36(1):109–127.
Wurman, Richard Saul. 1989. *Information Anxiety.* New York: Doubleday.
Wuthnow, Robert, and Marsha Witten. 1988. "New Directions in the Study of Culture." Pp. 49–67 in *Annual Review of Sociology, 1988,* edited by W. Richard Scott and Judith Blake. Palo Alto, CA: Annual Reviews.

Y

Yamagata, Hisashi, Kuang S. Yeh, Shelby Stewman, and Hiroko Dodge. 1997. "Sex Segregation and Glass Ceilings: A Comparative Statistics Model of Women's Career Opportunities in the Federal Government over a Quarter Century." *American Journal of Sociology* 103(November):566–632.
Yap, Kioe Sheng. 1998. "Squatter Settlements." Pp. 554–556 in *The Encyclopedia of Housing,* edited by Willem van Vliet. Thousand Oaks, CA: Sage.
Yaukey, John. 1997. "Blacksburg, VA: A Town That's Really Wired." *Gannett News Service*, April 8, pp. 1–3.
Yax, Laura K. 1999. "National Population Projections." Accessed October 30, 1999 (http://www.census.gov/population/www/projections/natproj.html).
Yinger, J. Milton. 1970. *The Scientific Study of Religion.* New York: Macmillan.
———. 1974. "Religion, Sociology of." In *Encyclopaedia Britannica*, vol. 15. Chicago: Encyclopedia Britannica, pp. 604–613.
Young, Margaret, and Jay Sinha. *Bill D-11: The Immigration and Refugee Protection Act.* Ottawa: Parliamentary Research Branch. LS-397E.

Z

Zajac, Andrew. 1999. "Notes from a Wired Community." *Chicago Tribune*, April 5, pp. C3–C4.
Zelizer, Gerald L. 1999. "Internet Offers Only Fuzzy Cyberfaith, Not True Religious Experiences." *USA Today*, August 19, p. 13A.
Zellner, William M. 1978. "Vehicular Suicide: In Search of Incidence." Western Illinois University, Macomb. Unpublished M.A. thesis.
———. 1995. *Counter Cultures: A Sociological Analysis.* New York: St. Martin's Press.
———. 2001. *Extraordinary Groups: An Examination of Unconventional Lifestyles.* 7th ed. New York: Worth.
Zhao, John Z., Fernando Rajulton, and Z. R. Ravanera. 1995. "Leaving the Parental Home: Effects of Family Structure, Gender, and Culture." *Canadian Journal of Sociology* 20(1):31–50.
Zhou, Xueguang, and Liren Hou. 1999. "Children of the Cultural Revolution: The State and the Life Course in the People's Republic of China." *American Sociological Review* 64(February):32–36.

Zimbardo, Philip G. 1972. "Pathology of Imprisonment." *Society* 9(April):4, 6, 8.

———. 1992. *Psychology and Life.* 13th ed. New York: HarperCollins.

———, Craig Haney, W. Curtis Banks, and David Jaffe. 1974. "The Psychology of Imprisonments: Privation, Power, and Pathology." In *Doing Unto Others: Joining, Molding, Conforming, Helping, and Loving*, edited by Zick Rubin. Englewood Cliffs, NJ: Prentice-Hall.

Zimmer, Lynn. 1988. "Tokenism and Women in the Workplace." *Social Problems* 35(February):64–77.

Zola, Irving K. 1972. "Medicine as an Institution of Social Control." *Sociological Review* 20(November):487–504.

———. 1983. *Socio-Medical Inquiries.* Philadelphia: Temple University Press.

Zook, Matthew A. 1996. "The Unorganized Militia Network: Conspiracies, Computers, and Community." *Berkeley Planning Journal* 11:1–15.

Zuckerman, M. J. 2000. "Criminals Hot on Money Trail to Cyberspace." *USA Today,* March 21, p. 8A.

Zweigenhaft, Richard L., and G. William Domhoff. 1998. *Diversity in the Power Elite: Have Women and Minorities Reached the Top?* New Haven: Yale University Press.

Census Update References

Ambert, Anne-Marie. 2002. "Divorce: Facts, Causes, and Consequences." The Vanier Institute of the Family. Accessed October 1, 2003. (http:// www.vifamily. ca/cft/divorce/html#Remarriage)

Canada Agriculture Museum. 2000. "Agriculture in Canada." Accessed September 24, 2003. (http://www.agriculture.technomuses.ca/english/tour/agriculture.cfm).

Canadian Council on Social Development. 2003. "Census Shows Growing Polarization of Income in Canada." Accessed September 10, 2003. (http://www.ccsd. ca/pr2003/census income.htm).

Canadian Education Statistics Council (CESC). 2000. *Education Indicators in Canada: Report of the Pan-Canadian Education Indicators Program 1999.* Toronto: Canadian Education Statistics Council with Statistics Canada and Council of Ministers of Education, Canada.

Dupuis, D. 1998. "What influences people's plans to have children?" in *Canadian Social Trends*, Spring, 2-5.

Ekos Research Associates. 2001. "Rethinking the Information Highway." Ottawa: Ekos Research Associates.

Galt, Virginia. 2003. "Drive is on for telework." *The Globe and Mail.* September 24, p. C7.

Global Reach. 2003. *Global Internet Statistics* (by language). Accessed September 30, 2003. (http://www.global-reach.biz/globalstats).

Health Canada. 2003. "HIV and AIDS in Canada: Surveillance Report to December 31, 2002." Ottawa: Minister of Public Works and Government Services Canada.

OECD. 2003. "Education at a Glance: OECD Indicators." Paris: OECD.

Statistics Canada. 1997. "1996 Census: Marital status, common-law unions and families." *The Daily*, October 14.

Statistics Canada. 2002a. "Profile of Canadian families and households: Diversification continues." 2001 Census (Analysis series). Accessed September 25, 2003. (http://www12.statcan.ca/english/census01/Products/Analytic/companion/fam/contents.cfm).

———. 2002b. "Divorces." *The Daily*, December 2. Accessed September 25, 2003. (http://www.statcan.ca/daily/english/021202/d021202f.htm)

———. 2002c. "Profile of Canadian population by age and sex: Canada ages." 2001 Census (Analysis series). No. 96F0030XIE2001002.

———. 2002d. "A national overview—population and dwelling counts, 2001 Census." Accessed September 24, 2003. (http://www.statcan.ca/english/ips/data/93-360-XPB.htm). No. 93-360-XPB.

———. 2003a. "Population by Selected Ethnic Origins, Canada." Census of the Population, 2001. Accessed July 22, 2003 (http://www.statcan.ca/english/Pgdb/demo28a.htm).

———. 2003b. "Crime Statistics." *The Daily*, July 24. Accessed September 24, 2003. (http://www.statcan.ca/daily/english//030724/d030724.htm).

———. 2003c. "Income of Canadian Families." No. 96F0030XIE2001014.

———. 2003d. "Family Income." *The Daily*, June 25. Accessed September 24, 2003. (http://www.statcan.ca/daily/english/030625/d030625b.htm)

———. 2003e. "Census of population: Immigration, birthplace and birthplace of parents, citizenship, ethnic origin, visible minorities, and Aboriginal peoples." *The Daily*, January 21 (http://www.statcan.ca/Daily/English/030121/d030121a.htm).

———. 2003f. "Aboriginal Peoples of Canada." 2001 Census (Analysis series). Accessed September 15, 2003. (http://www12.statcan.ca/english/census01/products/analytic companion/abor/contents.cfm). No. 96F0030XIE2001007.

———. 2003g. "Canada's ethnocultural portrait: The changing mosaic." 2001 Census (Analysis series). Accessed September 24, 2003. (http://www12.statcan.ca/english/census01/products/analytic/ companion/etoimm/contents.cfm). No. 96F0030XIE2001008.

———. 2003h. "Census of population: Labour force activity, occupation, industry, class of worker, place of work, mode of transportation, language of work and unpaid work." The Daily, February 11. Accessed September 15, 2003. (http://www.statcan.ca/daily/english/030211/d030211a.htm).

———. 2003i. "Earnings of Canadians." 2001 Census. No. 97F0019XCB01057.

———. 2003j. "Women in Canada: Work Chapter Updates." No. 89F0133XIE.

———. 2003k. "Marriages." *The Daily*, June 2. Accessed September 24, 2003. (http://www.statcan.ca/daily/english/030602/d030602a.htm)

———. 2003l. "Religions in Canada." 2001 Census (Analysis series). No. 96F0030XIE2001015.

———. 2003m. "University enrolment by age groups." *The Daily*, April 17. Accessed September 24, 2003. (http://www.statcan.ca/daily/english/030417/d030417b.htm).

———. 2003n. "Deaths." *The Daily*, April 2. Accessed September 24, 2003. (http://www.statcan.ca/daily/english/030402/d030402b.htm).

———. 2003o. "Household Internet Use Survey." The Daily, September 18. Accessed September 24, 2003. (http://www.statcan.ca/daily/english/030918/d030918b.htm).

Wu, Zheng. 2000. *Cohabitation: An Alternative Form of Living.* Don Mills, Ontario: Oxford University Press.

Acknowledgments

CHAPTER 1

P. 4: Quotation from Doug Saunders. 2001. "Mullets for the Multitudes." *The Globe and Mail*, February 3. Reprinted with permission from The Globe and Mail.

P. 18: Quotation in Box 1–2 from Carol Brooks Gardner. 1989. "Analyzing Gender in Public Places: Rethinking Goffman's Vision of Everyday Life," *The American Sociologist*, **20** (Spring): 45, 49, 56. © 1989. Reprinted by permission of Transaction Publishers, Rutgers University. All rights reserved.

CHAPTER 2

P. 26: Quotation from James E. Côté and Anton L. Allahar. 1994. *Generation on Hold: Coming of Age in the Late Twentieth Century*: xiv–xvii. Copyright © 1995 J.E. Côté and Anton L. Allahar. Reproduced by permission of Stoddart Publishing Co. Limited.

P. 31: Cartoon by Mike Keefe, Denver Post. © Mike Keefe, dePIXon Studios, Inc.

P. 44: Figure 2-3 "Women whose first conjugal union was common-law were nearly twice as likely to separate." From Statistics Canada. 2000. *Canadian Social Trends*, Cat. no. 11-008, Spring.

CHAPTER 3

P. 50: Quotation from Horace Miner. 1956. "Body Ritual among the Nacirema," *American Anthropologist*, Vol. 58 No. 3. Reprinted by permission of the American Anthropological Association.

P. 56: Figure 3–2 from Edward B. Espenshade, Jr. 1990. *Rand McNally Goode's World Atlas*, 18/e: 25. Map © by Rand McNally, R. L. #00-S-22.

P. 60: Figure 3-3 "Valued Means of Teenagers and Adults." From Bibby and Posterski. 1992. *Teen Trends*:19. Copyright © 1992 Reginald W. Bibby and Donald C. Posterski. Reproduced with permission of Stoddart Publishing Co., Limited.

P. 63: Figure 3–4 illustration by Jim Willis. 1996. "The Argot of Pickpockets," *New York Daily News* (November 19): 5. © New York Daily News, LP. Reprinted by permission.

P. 64 Cartoon © 2000 Sidney Harris

P. 66: Figure 3-5 "Applicability of Traits to Canadians and Americans." From Bibby. 1995. *The Bibby Report: Social Trends Canadian Style*:14. Copyright © 1995 Reginald W. Bibby. Reproduced with permission of Stoddart Publishing Co., Limited.

CHAPTER 4

P. 74: Quotation from Patricia A. Adler and Peter Adler. 1998. *Peer Power: Preadolescent Culture and Identity*: 2–3. Copyright © 1998 by Patricia Adler and Peter Adler. Reprinted by permission of Rutgers University Press.

CHAPTER 5

P. 98: Quotations from Philip G. Zimbardo. 1972. "Pathology of Imprisonment," *Society*, 9 (April): 4. Reprinted by permission of Copyright Clearance Center. And from Philip G. Zimbardo, C. Haney, W. C. Banks, & D. Jaffe. 1974. "The Psychology of Imprisonment: Privation, Power, and Pathology." In Z. Rubin (Ed.), *Doing Unto Others: Explorations in Social Behavior*: 61–73. Published by Prentice-Hall. Reprinted by permission of Philip G. Zimbardo, Stanford University.

P. 107: Cartoon TOLES © The Buffalo News. Reprinted with permission of UNIVERSAL PRESS SYNDICATE. All rights reserved.

P. 112: Cartoon © The New Yorker Collection 1986 Dean Victor from cartoonbank.com. All rights reserved.

P. 117: Figure 5-2 from L. K. Altman. 1998. "The Geography of AIDS," *New York Times* (June 24): A1. Copyright © 1998 by The New York Times Co. Reprinted by permission.

P. 118: Figure 5-3 based on data from Roxane Laboratories. Reprinted by permission of Roxane Laboratories, Columbus, OH.

CHAPTER 6

P. 124: Quotation from John Ralston Saul. 1992. *Voltaire's Bastards*:482–83. Copyright © 1992 by John Ralston Saul. Reprinted by permission of Penguin Books Canada Limited.

P. 126: Cartoon © The New Yorker Collection 1979 Robert Weber from cartoonbank.com. All rights reserved.

P. 131: Cartoon © 2000 Sidney Harris

P. 140: Table 6-3 from Public and Legal Education Service of New Brunswick. 2001. Reproduced with permission from Public and Legal Education and Information Service of New Brunswick, <www.legal-info-legale.nb.ca>.

CHAPTER 7

P. 153: Table 7-1 © 1989 by JAI Press. Reprinted by permission of University of California Press. Reprinted from *The Sociological Quarterly* Vol. 30 No. 2 Issue: Summer 1989, pp 159–184 by permission.

P. 155: Figure 7-1 Copyright, 1999, Los Angeles Times. Reprinted with permission

P. 157: Table 7-3 Adapted with the permission of The Free Press; copyright renewed 1985 by Robert K. Merton.

P. 163: Cartoon © 2000 by Sidney Harris.

P. 165: Figure 7-2: "Crime rates by province and territory, 2002," adapted from the Statistics Canada Web site (http://www.statcan.ca/Daily/english/030724/d030724a.htm).

CHAPTER 8

P. 174: Quotation from Thomas Homer-Dixon. 2000. *The Ingenuity Gap*: 32–36. Copyright © 2000 by Resource & Conflict Analysis Inc. Reprinted by permission of Knopf Canada, a division of Random House of Canada Limited.

P. 178: Figure 8-1 Copyright © 1999 by The New York Times Co. Reprinted by permission

P. 185: Cartoon Reprinted by permission of The Syracuse Newspapers and editorial cartoonist, Frank Cammuso.

P. 187: Table 8-3: "Percentage of Individuals and Census Families Living in Low Income, Canada, 1980, 1990, and 2000," adapted from the Statistics Canada Web site (http://www12. statcan.ca/english/census01/Products/Analytic/companion/inc/canada.cfm#4).

P. 195: Figure 8-2 Carl Haub and Diana Cornelius, 2000 World Population Data Sheet. Washington, D.C.: Population Reference Bureau, 2000. Reprinted by permission.

CHAPTER 9

P:208: Quotation from Warren Kinsella. 1997. *Web of Hate*. Copyright © 1994, 2001 by Warren Kinsella. Reprinted by permission of HarperCollins Publishing Ltd.

P. 212: Table 9-1: "Population by selected origins, Canada, 2001 Census," adapted from the Statistics Canada Web site (http://www.statcan.ca/english/Pgdb/demo28a.htm).

P. 215: Figure 9-1 from Steven Fick. 2001. *Canadian Geographic Magazine* (January/February):54.

P. 225: Figure 9-2 from The Union of BC Indian Chiefs.

P. 232: Table 9-2: "Top 10 Countries of Birth, Canada, 2001," adapted from the Statistics Canada Web site (http://www12.statcan.ca/english/census01/products/analytic/companion/etoimm/canada.cfm).

CHAPTER 10

P. 240: Quotation from Naomi Wolf. 1991. *The Beauty Myth*: 9, 10. Reprinted by permission of Chatto & Windus, a division of Random House U.K., and the author, represented by Abner Stein Literary Agency.

P. 243: Table 10-1 Joyce McCarl Nielsen, Glenda Walden, and Charlotte A. Kunkel, "Gendered Heteronormalinity: Empirical Illustrations in Everyday Life," *Sociological Quarterly* Vol. 41 (No. 2): 283-296. © 2000 by The Midwest Sociological Society. Reprinted by permission.

P. 248: Cartoon © 2000 Sidney Harris

P. 248: Table 10-2: "Average Employment Earnings for Visible Minority Women Compared with Non-Visible Minority Women, Visible Minority Men, and Non-Visible Minority Men," adapted from the Statistics Canada publication "Wage and Salary Groups (22) in Constant (2000) Dollars, Sex (3), Visible Minority Groups (14) and Immigrant Status (3) for Paid Workers 15 Years and Over, for Canada, Provinces and Territories, 1995 and 2000-20% Sample Data (Earnings of Canadians)," Catalogue 96F0030, July 24, 2003 available at: http://www.statcan.ca/english/IPS/Data/97F0019XIE2001057.htm).

P. 251: Figure 10-2: "Employment of Women with Children under Age 16, by Family Status, 1976-2002," adapted from the Statistics Canada publication "Women in Canada: Work Chapter Updates," Catalogue 89F0133, May 2003.

P. 252: Table 10-3: "Canadian Women in Selected Occupations, 2002," adapted from the Statistics Canada publication "Women in Canada: Work Chapter Updates," Catalogue 89F0133, May 2003.

P. 254: Figure 10-3 "Percentage of people aged 25–44 employed full-time who are severely time-stressed, 1998" from Statistics Canada. 2000d. *Women in Canada 2000: a gender based statistical report.* Cat. no. 89-503, September.

P. 255: Figure 10-4 adapted from Statistics Canada. 1999d. *Overview of the time use of Canadians in 1998.*" Cat. no. 12F0080, November.

CHAPTER 11

P. 267: Figure 11-1: "Types of Family Households in Canada, 1981 and 2001," adapted from the Statistics Canada publication "Profile of Canadian families and households: Diversification continues, 2001 Census (Analysis series)," Catalogue 96F0030, May 13, 2003, available at (http://www12.statcan.ca/english/census01/Products/Analytic/companion/fam/canada.cfm).

P. 276: Figure 11-3: "Distribution of Children Aged 0 to 14 by Family Structure, 2001," adapted from the Statistics Canada publication "Profile of Canadian families and households: Diversification continues, 2001 Census (Analysis series)," Catalogue 96F0030, May 13, 2003, available at (http://www12.statcan.ca/english/census01/Products/Analytic/companion/fam/canada.cfm).

P. 279: Cartoon Signe Wilkinson, Cartoonists & Writers Syndicate/cartoonweb.com.

P. 281: Figure 11-4: "Marriage and Divorce Rates in Canada, 1967-2000," adapted from the Statistics Canada publication "Divorces," 1995, Catalogue 84-213, January 1997, and from the Statistics Canada Web site (http://www.statcan.ca/Daily/english/021202/d021202f.htm) and (http://www.statcan.ca/Daily/english/030602/d030602a.htm).

CHAPTER 12

P. 292: Quotation from Augustine. 2000. "Grandfather was a Knowing Christian." *Toronto Star*, August 9:A17. Reprinted with permission of Noah Augustine.

P. 301: Table 12-1: "Major Religious Denominations, Canada, 1991 and 2001," adapted from the Statistics Canada publication "Religions in Canada, 2001 Census (Analysis series)," Catalogue 96F0030, May 13, 2003, available at: (http://www12.statcan.ca/english/census01/Products/Analytic/companion/rel/canada.cfm).

P. 315: Cartoon. Reprinted with permission of Graham Harrop.

CHAPTER 13

P. 322: Quotation from Robert Barnard, Dave Cosgrave, and Jennifer Welsh. 1998. *Chips and Pop: Decoding the Nexus Generation.* Reprinted with permission of Raincoast Publishers <http://raincoast.com>.

P. 333: Figure 13-1 from Inter-Parliamentary Union. 2000. "Women in National Parliaments." Accessed January, 2000, at http://www.pu.org/wmn-e/world.htm. Reprinted by permission of Inter-Parliamentary Union, Geneva.

P. 335: Figure 13-2 Richard L. Zweigenhaft and G. William Domhoff, Diversity in the Power Elite. Copyright © 1998. Reprinted by permission of Yale University Press.

P. 339: Cartoon by Tony Auth. © 1999 The Philadelphia Inquirer. Reprinted by permission of Universal Press Syndicate. All rights reserved.

P. 343: Table 13-1 from Status of Women Canada. 1995. *Setting the Stage for the Next Century: The Federal Plan for Gender Equality.* Reproduced with the permission of the Minister of Public Works and Government Services Canada, 2001. <http://www.swc-cfc-gc.ca>.

CHAPTER 14

P. 350: Quotation from Peter Gzowski. 2001. "How to Quit Smoking in Fifty Years or Less" in *Addicted: Notes from the Belly of the Beast*, Lorna Crozier and Patrick Lane, eds. Copyright ©2001 Greystone Books (Douglas & McIntyre Publishing Group). Reprinted with permission of the publisher.

P. 352: Figure 14-1 from Carl Haub and Diana Cornelius. 1999. *World Population Data Sheet 1999.* Reprinted by permission of Population Reference Bureau.

P. 354: Table 14-1 Adapted from Statistics Canada 2001e. *Canadian Social Trends.* Cat. no. 11-008, Spring.

P. 369: Figure 14-4 Carl Haub and Deana Cornelius. 1999 World Population Data Sheet. Copyright 1999. Reprinted by permission of The Population Reference Bureau.

P. 381: Figure 14-6 copyright ©2001, CIHI. *National Health Expenditure Trends, 1975–2001*, copied with permission. Published by the Canadian Institute for Health Information, Ottawa, Canada.

P. 382: Figure 14-7 copyright ©2001, CIHI. *National Health Expenditure Trends, 1975–2001*, copied with permission. Published by the Canadian Institute for Health Information, Ottawa, Canada.

CHAPTER 15

P. 388: Quotation from Kai Erikson. 1994. *A New Species of Trouble: The Human Experience of Modern Disasters*: 11–12. Copyright © 1994 by Kai Erikson. Used by permission of W. W. Norton Company, Inc.

P. 392: Cartoon by Henry Martin. © Tribune Media Services, Inc. All rights reserved. Reprinted by permission.

P. 412: Cartoon © Roger Dahl. Reprinted by permission.

CHAPTER 16

P. 418: Quotation from Po Bronson. 1999. *The Nudist on the Late Shift*: 78–79, 80. Copyright © 1999 by Po Bronson. Reprinted by permission of Random House and Curtis Brown Ltd.

P. 433: Map from Matrix Information and Directory Service. 2000. Reprinted by permission of Matrix Information and Directory Service, <www.mids.org>.

P. 436: Cartoon © 1985 Carol*Simpson. Reprinted by permission of Carol*Simpson Productions

P. 439: Cartoon © Mike Keefe, dePIXon Studios, Inc.

Photo Credits

CHAPTER 1

Chapter Opener: Courtesy of Art Director & Designer Yoshimaru Takahasi for the Osaka 1st Century Association Bid for the 2008 Olympics.
p. 4. Angela Wyant/ Stone/ Getty Images
p. 6. Index Stock
p. 7. CP Picture Archive. Photograph by Tom Hanson.
p. 9. Corbis-Betterman
p. 12. Richard Floyd
p. 13. CP Picture Archive. Photograph by Andre Forget.
p. 14. Richard Floyd
p. 11. Figure 1-1: Bibliotheque Nationale, Paris; Culver Pictures

CHAPTER 2

Chapter Opener: Source: Statistics Canada
p. 26. CP Picture Archive. Photograph by Andre Forget.
p. 28. CP Picture Archive. Photograph by Paul Chiasson.
p. 31. Cartoon by Mike Keefe, Denver Post. ©Mike Keefe, dePIXon Studios, Inc.
p. 34. Betty Press/Woodfin Camp
p. 35. Richard Floyd
p. 36. Courtesy of AT&T
p. 39. Mark Reinstein/Image Works
p. 40. CP Picture Archive. Photograph by Dick Loek.
p. 41. Bob Daemmrich/Image Works
p. 42. Courtesy of Marylee Stephenson
p. 43. Esbin & Anderson/Image Works

CHAPTER 3

Chapter Opener: Barry Dawson, *Street Graphics India* (New York: Thames & Hudson, 1999), pp. 24-25
p. 50. Robert Burke/Liason
p. 52. Fujifotos/Image Works
p. 57. Richard Floyd
p. 58. Richard Floyd
p. 63. Mario Corvetto/Image Works
p. 64. Cartoon ©2000 Sidney Harris
p. 65. Jerry Alexander/Tony Stone
p. 67. Richard Floyd

CHAPTER 4

Chapter Opener: Setagaya Volunteer Association, Tokyo, Japan
p. 76. Anthony Suau/Liaison
p. 79. Elizabeth Crews/Image Works
p. 80. Jim Cummins / FPG International/ Getty Images
p. 82. Thomas S. England/Photo Researchers
p. 84. Keystone/Sygma
p. 87. Tom Wagner/Saba
p. 90. Mary Kate Denny/Photo Edit
p. 92. Svenne Nordlov/Tio Foto

CHAPTER 5

Chapter Opener: Courtesy of interTREND Communications, Inc., Torrence, California
p. 98. ©Philip G. Zimbardo, Stanford University
p. 100. Michael Probst/AP Photo
p. 101. Richard Floyd
p. 102. Richard Floyd
p. 104. ©1985 Sarah Leen
p. 105. Anna Clopet/Liaison
p. 107. Cartoon TOLES © The Buffalo News. Reprinted with permission of UNIVERSAL PRESS SYNDICATE. All rights reserved.
p. 110. Richard Floyd
p. 111. Richard Floyd
p. 112. John Brooks/Liaison
p. 112. Richard Floyd

CHAPTER 6

Chapter Opener: Photo by M. Rutledge, courtesy of the Canadian Museum of Flight.
p. 124. Jon Berkeley /Artville/ Getty Images.
p. 126. Cartoon © The New Yorker Collection 1979 Robert Weber from cartoonbank.com. All rights reserved.
p. 127. Courtesy of János John Maté
p. 128. Theo Westenberger
p. 129. CBS Photo Archive
p. 131. Cartoon © 2000 Sidney Harris
p. 132. Archive Photos
p. 133. CP Picture Archive. Photograph by Janet Durrans.
p. 137. Rolb Crandall/Stock Boston
p. 139. Bob Daemmrich/Image Works

CHAPTER 7

Chapter Opener: Source: Health Canada
p. 149. ©1965 by Stanley Milgram from the film, "Obedience," distributed by Pennsylvania State University, PCR.
p. 152. Carolina Kroon/ Impact Visuals
p. 153. Reed Saxon/ AP Photo
p. 158. Stephen Frisch/ Stock Boston
p. 159. Richard Floyd
p. 161. Courtesy of the Centre for Addiction and Mental Health
p. 163. Cartoon ©2000 by Sidney Harris
p. 166. Courtesy of Holly Johnson

CHAPTER 8

Chapter Opener: Courtesy of Heye & Partners, Germany
p. 174. Associated Press AP. Photograph by Vincent Yu.
p. 175. Hampton University
p. 177. L.D. Gordon/Image Bank
p. 180. Richard Floyd
p. 185. Cartoon reprinted by permission of The Syracuse Newspapers and editorial cartoonist, Frank Cammuso.
p. 188. Julius Wilson
p. 189. Porter Gifford/ Liaison
p. 190. 20th Century Fox, Japan/ AP Photo
p. 193. Richard Floyd
p. 197. CP Picture Archive. Photograph by Stephan Savoia.
p. 201. CP Picture Archive. Photograph by Fred Chartrand.

CHAPTER 9

Chapter Opener: Courtesy of the Surrey Delta Multicultural Coordinating Society
p. 208. CP Picture Archive. Photograph by Tim Fraser.
p. 211. Canadian Press TRSTR. Photograph by Rick Eglington.
p. 217. Mike Albans/ Daily News
p. 220. Art Zamur/ Gamma Liaison
p. 221. Alon Reininger/Contact Press Images
p. 223. Canadian Press CP. Photograph by Joe Bryksa.
p. 226. Richard Floyd
p. 227. Canadian Press CP. Photograph by STF Staff.
p. 228. CP Picture Archive. Photograph by Christine Vanzella.
p. 230. Richard Floyd

CHAPTER 10

Chapter Opener: Courtesy Guerilla Girls

p. 246. B. Mahoney/ Image Works
p. 248. Cartoon © 2000 Sidney Harris
p. 249. Eric Roxfelt/ AP Photo
p. 255. National Archives of Canada/PA30212
p. 256. Courtesy of Prudence Hannis

CHAPTER 11

Chapter Opener: Genetica DNA Laboratories, Inc.
p. 265. Saloa/ Liaison
p. 269. Eastcott/ Woodfin Group
p. 271. Michael Dean
p. 272. Michael Newman/ Photo Edit
p. 273. Bill Truslow/ Liaison
p. 275. Blair Seitz/ Photo Reserachers
p. 276. Cliff Moore/ Princeton Stock Photos
p. 277. Courtesy of Karla Jessen Williamson
p. 278. Richard Floyd
p. 279. Cartoon Signe Wilkinson, Cartoonists & Writers Syndicate/cartoonweb.com
p. 282. Jon Bradley/ Tony Stone
p. 284. CP Picture Archive. Photograph by Andrew Vaughan.
p. 286. © Andy Warhol Foundation, Inc./ Art Resource

CHAPTER 12

Chapter Opener: Thomas Coex/ Agence France Press
p. 292. CP Picture Archive. Photograph by Andrew Vaughan.
p. 295. Richard Vogel/ Liaison
p. 296. CP Picture Archive. Photograph by Kevin Frayer.
p. 299. Steve McCurry/ Magnum
p. 306. Glenn Baglo / *The Vancouver Sun*
p. 307. Mary Kate Denny/ Photo Edit
p. 308. Joe McNally/ Sygma
p. 310. Richard Floyd
p. 314. Bob Daemmrich/ Stock Boston
p. 315. Reprinted with permission of Graham Harrap.

CHAPTER 13

Chapter Opener: Milton Glaser
p. 322. CP Picture Archive. Photograph by Fred Thornhill.
p. 324. Reuters/ Claro Cortes/ Archive Photos
p. 327. AP Photo
p. 329. CP Picture Archive. Photograph by Chuck Stoody.
p. 331. CP Picture Archive. Photograph by Roberto Candia.
p. 336. CP Picture Archive. Photograph by Tannis Toohey.
p. 338. Bob Daemmrich/ Stock Boston
p. 339. Cartoon by Tony Auth. © 1999 The Philadelphia Inquirer. Reprinted by permission of UNIVERSAL PRESS SYNDICATE. All rights reserved.
p. 340. Stacy Pick/ Stock Boston

CHAPTER 14

Chapter Opener: © Queen's Printer for Ontario, 2002. Reproduced with permission.
p. 350. CP Picture Archive. Photograph by Andrew Stawicki.
p. 353. Remy De LaMauviniere/ AP Photo
p. 353. Corbis Bettmann
p. 357. A. Ramey/ Woodfin Camp
p. 359. Wally McNamee/ Woodfin Camp
p. 361. Bonnie Haaland
p. 363. Patrick Murphy Racey
p. 365. Lionel Delevigne/ Stock Boston
p. 366. Jonathan Nouro/ Photo Edit
p. 367. Stephanie Maze/Woodfin Camp
p. 367. David Austen/ Stock Boston
p. 368. Stephen Agricola/ Stock Boston
p. 370. CP Picture Archive. Photograph by Todd Warshaw Pool.
p. 371. Eric Bouvet/ Gamma Liaison
p. 373. CP Picture Archive. Photograph by Ryan Remiorz.
p. 375. Bill Aron/ Photo Edit
p. 377. A. Ramey/ Woodfin Camp
p. 378. Courtesy of Kelsie Lenor Wilson-Dorsett
p. 381. CP Picture Archive. Photograph by Fred Chartrand.

CHAPTER 15

Chapter Opener: Barry Dawson, *Street Graphics India* (New York: Thames & Hudson, 1999), p. 110.
p. 390. Image Works Archive
p. 392. Cartoon by Henry Martin. © Tribune Media Services, Inc. All rights reserved. Reprinted by permission.
p. 396. M.J. Griffith/ Photo Researchers
p. 398. Jean Marc Gibous/ Gamma Liaison
p. 399. Jim Pickerall/ Stock Boston
p. 401. Richard Floyd
p. 403. Joe Sohm/ Image Works
p. 405. CP Picture Archive. Photograph by Jim Rankin.
p. 407. AP Photo
p. 410. AP Photo
p. 412. Cartoon © Roger Dahl. Reprinted by permission.

CHAPTER 16

Chapter Opener: Image courtesy of Warp Records
p. 420. Frederique Jouval/ Sygma
p. 422. Lisa Terry/ Gamma Liaison
p. 423. Chris O'Meara/ AP Photo
p. 427. Jim West/ Impact Visuals
p. 428. Reuters/ Shaun Best/ Archive Photos
p. 429. Joe Sohm/ Image Works
p. 431. AP Photo
p. 435. Stan Godlewski
p. 436. Cartoon © 1985 Carol*Simpson. Reprinted by permission of Carol*Simpson Productions
p. 439. Cartoon © Mike Keefe, dePIXon Studios, Inc.

TABLE OF CONTENTS

Chapter 1 James Lemass/Picture Cube
Chapter 2 PhotoDisc
Chapter 3 PhotoDisc
Chapter 4 Corbis Digital
Chapter 5 PhotoDisc
Chapter 6 PhotoDisc
Chapter 7 PhotoDisc
Chapter 8 20th Century Fox, Japan/AP Photo
Chapter 9 Patrick Ward/Stock Boston
Chapter 10 PhotoDisc
Chapter 11 Karen Su/Tony Stone
Chapter 12 Glen Allison/Tony Stone
Chapter 13 CP Picture Archive. Photograph by Chuck Stoody
Chapter 14 Charles Gupton/Tony Stone
Chapter 15 Chad Ehlers/Tony Stone
Chapter 16 Watzmann/Actikon Press/ Saba Press

Name Index

A

B

C

D

H

I

J

K

L

M

S

Y

Z

Subject Index

A

B

C

Q

R

S